Fodor's

CHINA

7th Edition

Fodor's Travel Publications   New York, Toronto, London, Sydney, Auckland
www.fodors.com

Eugene Fodor:
The Spy Who Loved Travel

As Fodor's celebrates our 75th anniversary, we are honoring the colorful and adventurous life of Eugene Fodor, who revolutionized guidebook publishing in 1936 with his first book, *On the Continent, The Entertaining Travel Annual.*

Eugene Fodor's life seemed to leap off the pages of a great spy novel. Born in Hungary, he spoke six languages and graduated from the Sorbonne and the London School of Economics. During World War II he joined the Office of Strategic Services, the budding spy agency for the United States. He commanded the team that went behind enemy lines to liberate Prague, and recommended to Generals Eisenhower, Bradley, and Patton that Allied troops move to the capital city. After the war, Fodor worked as a spy in Austria, posing as a U.S. diplomat.

In 1949 Eugene Fodor—with the help of the CIA—established Fodor's Modern Guides. He was passionate about travel and wanted to bring his insider's knowledge of Europe to a new generation of sophisticated Americans who wanted to explore and seek out experiences beyond their borders. Among his innovations were annual updates, consulting local experts, and including cultural and historical perspectives and an emphasis on people—not just sites. As Fodor described it, "The main interest and enjoyment of foreign travel lies not only in 'the sites,' . . . but in contact with people whose customs, habits, and general outlook are different from your own."

Eugene Fodor died in 1991, but his legacy, Fodor's Travel, continues. It is now one of the world's largest and most trusted brands in travel information, covering more than 600 destinations worldwide in guidebooks, on Fodors.com, and in ebooks and iPhone apps. Technology and the accessibility of travel may be changing, but Eugene Fodor's unique storytelling skills and reporting style are behind every word of today's Fodor's guides.

Our editors and writers continue to embrace Eugene Fodor's vision of building personal relationships through travel. We invite you to join the Fodor's community at fodors.com/community and share your experiences with like-minded travelers. Tell us when we're right. Tell us when we're wrong. And share fantastic travel secrets that aren't yet in Fodor's. Together, we will continue to deepen our understanding of our world.

Happy 75th Anniversary, Fodor's! Here's to many more.

Tim Jarrell, Publisher

FODOR'S CHINA
Editor: Margaret Kelly

Editorial Contributors: Stephanie Butler, Kelly Kealy

Writers: Jo Baker, Cherise Fong, Sophie Friedman, Daniel Garber, Chris Horton, Helena Iveson, Dana Kaufman, Samantha Leese, Doretta Lau, Eileen Wen Mooney, Paul Mooney, Patrick Scally, Dan Siekman, Dorothy So, Michael Standaert

Production Editor: Jennifer DePrima
Maps & Illustrations: David Lindroth and Mark Stroud, *cartographers;* Bob Blake, Rebecca Baer, *map editors;* William Wu, *information graphics*
Design: Fabrizio La Rocca, *creative director;* Guido Caroti, Siobhan O'Hare, *art directors;* Tina Malaney, Nora Rosansky, Chie Ushio, Jessica Walsh, Ann McBride, *designers;* Melanie Marin, *senior picture editor*
Cover Photo: (Jinshangling Great Wall) Best View Stock/photolibrary.com
Production Manager: Steve Slawsky

7th Edition

ISBN 978-0-307-48053-8

ISSN 1070-6895

SPECIAL SALES
This book is available at special discounts for bulk purchases for sales promotions or premiums. Special editions, including personalized covers, excerpts of existing books, and corporate imprints, can be created in large quantities for special needs. For more information, write to Special Markets/Premium Sales, 1745 Broadway, New York, NY 10019, or e-mail specialmarkets@randomhouse.com.

AN IMPORTANT TIP & AN INVITATION
Although all prices, opening times, and other details in this book are based on information supplied to us at press time, changes occur all the time in the travel world, and Fodor's cannot accept responsibility for facts that become outdated or for inadvertent errors or omissions. So **always confirm information when it matters,** especially if you're making a detour to visit a specific place. Your experiences—positive and negative—matter to us. If we have missed or misstated something, **please write to us.** Share your opinion instantly through our online feedback center at fodors.com/contact-us.

PRINTED IN SINGAPORE

10 9 8 7 6 5 4 3 2 1

CONTENTS

ABOUT
THIS BOOK

Our Ratings

Sometimes you find terrific travel experiences and sometimes they just find you. But usually the burden is on you to select the right combination of experiences. That's where our ratings come in.

As travelers we've all discovered a place so wonderful that its worthiness is obvious. And sometimes that place is so experiential that superlatives don't do it justice: you just have to be there to know. These sights, properties, and experiences get our highest rating, **Fodor's Choice,** indicated by orange stars throughout this book.

Black stars highlight sights and properties we deem **Highly Recommended,** places that our writers, editors, and readers praise again and again for consistency and excellence.

By default, there's another category: any place we include in this book is by definition worth your time, unless we say otherwise. And we will.

Disagree with any of our choices? Care to nominate a place or suggest that we rate one more highly? Visit our feedback center at www.fodors.com/feedback.

Budget Well

Hotel and restaurant price categories from ¢ to $$$$ are defined in the opening pages of each chapter. For attractions, we always give standard adult admission fees; reductions are usually available for children, students, and senior citizens. Want to pay with plastic? **AE, D, DC, MC, V** following restaurant and hotel listings indicate whether American Express, Discover, Diners Club, MasterCard, and Visa are accepted.

Restaurants

Unless we state otherwise, restaurants are open for lunch and dinner daily. We mention dress only when there's a specific requirement and reservations only when they're essential or not accepted—it's always best to book ahead.

Hotels

Hotels have private bath, phone, TV, and air-conditioning and operate on the European Plan (aka EP, meaning without meals), unless we specify that they use the Continental Plan (CP, with a Continental breakfast), Breakfast Plan (BP, with a full breakfast), or Modified American Plan (MAP, with breakfast and dinner) or are all-inclusive (including all meals

and most activities). We always list facilities but not whether you'll be charged an extra fee to use them, so when pricing accommodations, find out what's included.

Listings	
★	Fodor's Choice
★	Highly recommended
✉	Physical address
✛	Directions or Map coordinates
🏠	Mailing address
☎	Telephone
🖨	Fax
🌐	On the Web
✉	E-mail
💲	Admission fee
⊙	Open/closed times
Ⓜ	Metro stations
💳	Credit cards
Hotels & Restaurants	
🏨	Hotel
🛏	Number of rooms
🛎	Facilities
❍	Meal plans
✕	Restaurant
🛎	Reservations
👔	Dress code
🚭	Smoking
🍷	BYOB
Outdoors	
🏌	Golf
⛺	Camping
Other	
⏱	Family-friendly
⇒	See also
✉	Branch address
☞	Take note

Experience
China

WHAT'S WHERE

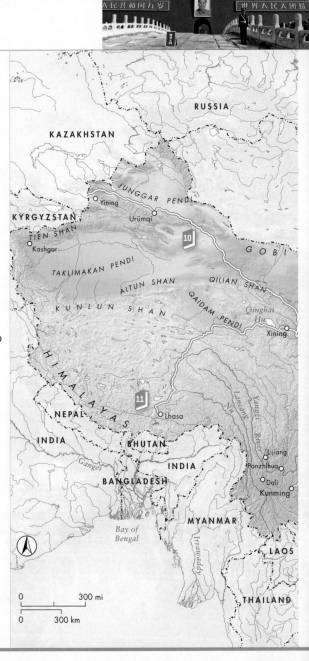

Numbers refer to chapters.

2 Beijing. Beijing is in massive flux, and the construction never stops. Feel the ancient pulse beneath the current clamor.

3 Beijing to Shanghai: Hebei, Shandong, Anhui, Jiangsu. Discover a cultural and natural treasure trove— Huang Shan peaks are islands in a sea of clouds, and canal-laced Suzhou is the Venice of the Orient.

4 Shanghai. In the 1920s Shanghai was known as the Whore of the Orient, but we like to think of her as a classy lady who knows how to have a good time. The party stopped for a few decades after the revolution, but now Shanghai is back in swing.

5 East Coast: Zhejiang, Fujian. Fujian's Xiamen is an undiscovered pearl, with all the history, culture, and infrastructure of more popular tourist magnets. Zhejiang's Hangzhou is the famous southernmost city of the Grand Canal.

6 Hong Kong. A city of contrasts—east and west, old and new, work hard and play harder. Long nights of bar-hopping are offset by tai chi sessions at dawn.

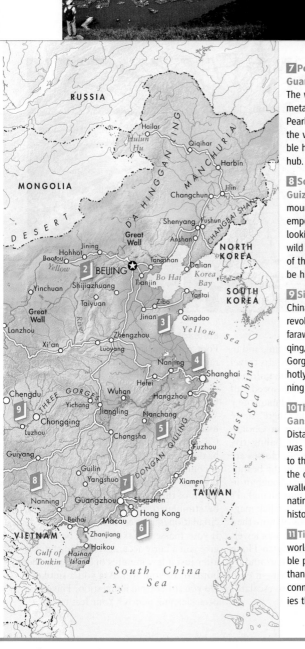

7 Pearl River Delta: Guangzhou and Shenzhen. The word "engine" is used metaphorically to describe the Pearl River Delta region, but the vibrations are still palpable here in China's industrial hub.

8 Southwest: Guangxi, Guizhou, Yunnan. The mountains are high and the emperor is far away. If you're looking to take a walk on the wild tribal side, then any or all of these three regions should be high on your to-visit list.

9 Sichuan, Chongqing. China's latest industrial revolution is happening in faraway Sichuan and Chongqing, where the nearby Three Gorges Dam (in Hubei), while hotly debated, remains a stunning sight.

10 The Silk Road: Shaanxi, Gansu, Qinghai, Xinjiang. Distant and mysterious, this was ancient China's lifeline to the outside world. Visit the country's last remaining walled cities—Xi'an is fascinating for its cultural and its historical importance.

11 Tibet. The roof of the world is not the most accessible place, but that's changing thanks to the new train line connecting Lhasa to major cities throughout China.

QUINTESSENTIAL CHINA

Be Moved

Getting there is often half the fun, and in China there are limitless ways to travel from point A to point B. China already has the world's longest high-speed rail network, and has plans to add many new lines in the coming years. But there's more than just trains. Sightseeing in Chongqing? Cross the Yangtze or Jialing rivers in an old-school cable car. Horses are the best way to get around in the beautiful countryside surrounding Songpan in Sichuan. If you're flying into Shanghai's Pudong Airport, take the superslick maglev train into town at speeds of more than 260 miles per hour. China's crown jewels of passenger transport belong to Hong Kong, where it's normal to get around by light rail, bus, taxi, trolley, boat—it even has the longest covered outdoor escalator system in the world.

Reflexology

Foot-massage spas are becoming all the rage in China, but if you thought this was a new trend brought on by an upwardly mobile (and naturally more footsore) Chinese populace, think again. While Western medicine sees the foot as mere locomotion, practitioners of traditional Chinese reflexology think that bodily health is reflected in the sole. Each organ is connected to a specific reflex point on the foot. With precise and skillful manipulation of these points, vital functions can be stimulated, toxins eliminated, blood circulation improved, and nerves soothed. If your masseur is skilled, he'll be able to give you a fairly accurate health diagnosis after just a few minutes of looking at the bottoms of your feet. Are you a smoker? Do you suffer from indigestion? Have you been sleeping poorly? Your feet tell all.

Chinese culture is rich, diverse, and will hit you like a ton of bricks. Keep an open mind while you're traveling, because this will be an experience of a lifetime.

China Beyond the Han

The Han are far and away the dominant ethnic group in China, but there is surprising ethnic diversity, from Uighurs with almost European features in Xinjiang to nomadic Mongols, to the Dai and Hani of Xishuangbanna. Officially there are 56 ethnic groups that make up the great Chinese nation. Though small in number relative to the Han, the minorities have historically been a force to be reckoned with. Rulers of the last dynasty (the Qing) were Manchus. Though Chinese history is rife with examples of inter-tribal war and Han incursion into non-Han territory (Tibet being the latest and most famous example), the revolution, in theory, leveled the playing field. Traveling through areas less dominated by the Han Chinese offers views of the country far different from the usual Beijing-Shanghai-Three Gorges tour.

All the Tea in China

For a vast majority of the Chinese people the day begins and ends with tea. Whether it's being savored in a delicate ceremonial porcelain cup or slurped out of a glass mason jar, you can bet that the imbiber takes tea consumption seriously. Ask a Chinese person about the best tea and the answer will very likely depend on where they're from. The highly prized Pu'er tea has a dark color and heavy, almost earthy flavor. It gets its name from the region of southern Yunnan Province where it's grown. Fujian produces the best oolong teas, thanks to the high mountains and favorable climate. Oolong is usually served with much ceremony. Perhaps the most expensive tea in China is a variant of green tea from the Longjing ("Dragon Well") region of Hangzhou. Longjing tea is served in clear glasses, so one can watch the delicate dance of the long, thin leaves as they float to the top.

IF YOU LIKE

Contemporary Art

China has one of the most vibrant, eclectic, and often downright avant-garde art scenes this side of Paris. Beijing is arguably the center of China's contemporary art scene, and it's in China's capital that well-known artists like sculptor Wang Guangyi (who blends propaganda and icons from the cultural revolution for what some consider cynical effect) and painter Feng Mengbo (whose hallmarks include mixing oil painting and computer graphics) ply their trades.

Dashanzi 798 Art District, Beijing. This former military electronics complex in Beijing's Chaoyang district houses dozens of galleries and the workshops of many of the city's up-and-coming artists.

Suzhou Creek Art District, Shanghai. In a renovated factory area on Suzhou Creek, more than 100 of Shanghai's top artists have their studios. Galleries including EastLink, Shanghart and Art Scene Warehouse have also moved in since 2000.

Guangdong Museum of Art, Guangzhou. Denizens of the Pearl River Delta, though normally thought of as caring more about making money than art, have a number of museums and galleries worth visiting. This museum is well respected throughout China.

He Xiangning Museum, Shenzhen. This beautiful new museum in the Overseas Chinese Town district hosts an annual exhibit each autumn featuring the best works of art students from all over China.

Bicycling

In the not-too-distant past, China was known as "The Bicycle Kingdom," but as cars become more popular, the iconic sea of bicycles that once filled the avenues of Beijing and Shanghai has dried to a trickle.

But this doesn't mean that bicycling enthusiasts should lose heart. While the two-wheeled herd has thinned out considerably, you'll hardly be riding alone. Most hotels will be able to help you out with bicycle rentals, or a brand new Flying Pigeon (the bike of China) should only set you back a few hundred yuan.

Beijing. Though notorious for its bad air and automobile gridlock, the capital is still our favorite urban bicycling ground. Its wide avenues and impossible-to-maneuver-by-car back alleyways make it an ideal city to tour by bicycle.

Xi'an. The city center is small enough to make it perfect for exploring by bike. For a unique experience, take a tour on top of the city wall, the only one left fully intact in all of China.

Shanghai. The Pearl of the Orient is also two-wheel friendly, though you'll be asked to dismount and walk along the Nanjing pedestrian area.

Chengdu. The spiciest city in China is also as flat as a Ping-Pong table, which makes it one of our favorites for exploring by bike.

Taking It to the Extreme

An increasing number of Middle Kingdom visitors are coming not merely to see the Great Wall but to engage in more adrenaline-intensive activities (jumping over the Great Wall on a skateboard, for example). This new breed of China travelers will be happy to hear that adventure sports are alive and well in the People's Republic.

The Great Wall, Huang Hua. This crumbling section of the wall, just a few hours outside of Beijing, is far more rugged than the more tourist-popular Badaling section, and offers amazing views and seriously challenging climbs.

Rock Climbing, Yangshuo. Yangshuo has become *the* spot for aficionados of rock climbing, and the area has hundreds of routes for climbers of all levels. Possibly one of the most challenging routes is the inside track of Moon Hill, which draws some of the world's best climbers each year.

Long-Distance Bicycling. Rural touring is exploding in China, and an increasing number of Western visitors are choosing to see the country not by train or tour bus but by bicycle. Bike Asia runs tours for all levels of experience and endurance, from the rolling hills of Guangxi and Guizhou to the serious-riders-only mountains of Tibet.

Windsurfing, Qingdao. It's no accident that this seaside city in Northeast China was chosen to host the Olympic sailing events of 2008. The shape of the beaches combined with average wind speeds makes Qingdao an ideal place for those who get their kicks sailing.

Adventurous Dining

Much has been written about the cuisine of China, and for a very good reason—it's some of the best (and most varied) on the planet. Most visitors will be happy to stick with well-known dishes such as Peking duck or kung pao chicken, but for those who want a culinary walk on the wild side, might we suggest a few less well-known regional favorites?

Stinky Tofu, Fujian. Though it's hotly contested whether this highly odiferous dish originated first in Fujian or later in Taiwan, the overpowering snack is readily available on both sides of the Taiwan Strait. Its cubes of tofu fermented and deep fried to a crispy brown smell like extremely ripe cheese. Best enjoyed by those who prefer their food on the pungent side.

Yak-Butter Tea, Yunnan, Tibet. This beverage is ubiquitous throughout both Tibet and the higher mountain regions of Yunnan Province. Thick and tangy, the main ingredients of yak butter tea are yak butter, tea, and salt. Though its adherents drink it by the gallon, considering it delicious and healthy, unsuspecting imbibers have likened its flavor to melted blue cheese, or even wood polish.

Stewed Chicken Feet, Guangzhou. To a Cantonese chef, nothing should ever go to waste, and the claws of the humble chicken, stewed until the fat and skin are nearly dripping from its tiny bones, is considered a crucial part of any dim sum feast.

CHINA'S WORLD HERITAGE SITES

China was awarded two more World Heritage sites in 2010, bringing its total to 40. Given China's huge tourism numbers, sites can be overrun at peak travel times, but it doesn't take much to get away from the crowds.

Forbidden City

(A) Sitting at the heart of Beijing across from Tiananmen Square, the nearly 500-year-old Forbidden City is one of the world's most impressive imperial compounds. For the emperors and their courts, this moat-encircled compound was literally their city within a city, featuring 1,000 buildings covering more than 7.8 million square feet. Today the Forbidden City is home to the Palace Museum and its world-class collection of priceless paintings, bronzes, pottery, and documents that once belonged to the Qing imperial collection.

Temple of Heaven

(B) The Temple of Heaven—known in Chinese as the Altar of Heaven—was once the altar where Ming and Qing emperors made sacrifices to heaven. The emperor and his court visited the Temple of Heaven twice each year to perform ceremonies with the hope of ensuring a good harvest—even a minor mistake could spell disaster for China. The complex was built in the early 15th century by the Yongle Emperor, who was also behind the construction of the Forbidden City.

Great Wall

(C) The Great Wall of China is one of country's most iconic structures, as well as one of the world's most ambitious engineering projects. Originally intended to prevent invasion by nomadic tribes north of China, the wall was an imperial obsession for more than 1,000 years, beginning in the 5th century BC. Built primarily of stone and rammed earth, the

wall stretches 5,500 miles (8,850 kilometers) from its easternmost point on the Bohai Sea to its western terminus at Lop Nur in Xinjiang.

Old Town of Lijiang

(D) The Old Town of Lijiang is renowned for its winding cobblestone streets, charming wooden homes, and clear, fish-filled mountain streams. The area has been home to the Naxi people (with their unique culture and architecture) for eight centuries. One of China's most popular destinations for domestic or international travelers, Lijiang is visited by millions each year. UNESCO has raised concerns that overcommercialization is affecting the site's heritage value, but it is still a must-visit destination for many tourists.

Yunnan Three Parallel Rivers Protected Areas

(E) Northwest Yunnan is one of the world's biodiversity hot spots, primarily owing to the steep river valleys through which the upper reaches of the Yangtze, Mekong, and Salween rivers flow. These protected areas contain unforgettable scenery, including the awe-inspiring Tiger Leaping Gorge and hundreds of varieties of rhododendrons, and rare animals such as the red panda and snow leopard.

South China Karst

(F) Spread across the southwestern regions of Yunnan, Guizhou, and Guangxi, the South China Karst area is recognized for the diversity of its limestone scenery. The Stone Forest, outside of Yunnan's capital Kunming, is the best-known site in this group, featuring stone spires and strangely shaped monoliths that boggle the mind. A stony paradise for shutterbugs, Stone Forest and the other South China Karst sites are very popular, but still large enough to allow you to find your own quiet corner to take photos or just marvel at these improbable wonders.

CHINA'S WORLD HERITAGE SITES

Emei Shan

(G) Mist-shrouded Emei Shan is located in lush southern Sichuan Province. Emei Shan is one of China's four sacred Buddhist mountains. Emei's seemingly endless stone paths are usually hiked over one or two days. Hikers on Emei go there for the luxuriant and diverse foliage, the charming, run-down monasteries, the occasional waterfall, and the gangs of Tibetan macaques roaming its slopes. Emei's peak is famous for its sunrises, in which the sun rises from a sea of clouds.

Mogao Caves

(H) The northwestern city of Dunhuang in Gansu Province was once an important stopover on the Silk Road that connected China with Europe via Central Asia. Along with bringing traders and goods in from the West, the Silk Road also brought Buddhism. The Mogao Caves near Dunhuang were first established more than 2,300 years ago as places for Buddhists to practice their faith. Over time, the caves grew into a complex of nearly 500 temples featuring astonishingly well-preserved Buddhist painting and architecture collected during a 1,000-year period.

Terracotta Warriors

(I) The Terracotta Army at the mausoleum of the first Qin Emperor is one of the biggest archeological discoveries in the last half century. In 1974 farmers discovered pits with thousands of life-sized statues of soldiers, horses, chariots, musicians and acrobats—their find instantly captured China's, and the world's—imagination. The army was commissioned by Qin Shihuang, China's first emperor, and buried with him in the early 3rd century with the hope that the warriors would protect him in the afterlife. Each 6-foot-tall statue is believed to have been modeled after a living human from the emperor's time.

Potala Palace

(J) The Potala Palace is one of the world's most impressive buildings. Looking out over the valley below, its 13 stories house more than 1,000 rooms with countless shrines and statues throughout. Prior to serving as the residence of Dalai Lamas, the Potala was originally used by the historic Tibetan king Songtsen Gampo as a retreat for meditation. Its first palace was begun in the 7th century, with construction finishing in 1645. The Potala suffered during the 1959 Tibetan uprising that led to the current Dalai Lama's fleeing Tibet, and also was at risk during the Cultural Revolution, but this great building still stands tall today, a monument to the greatness of Tibet's past.

Summer Palace

(K) In Beijing's northern suburbs, the Summer Palace is where many an emperor went to escape his virtual imprisonment within the city center's Forbidden City. A peaceful retreat with a tranquil lake, a hill with scenic views of the city below, and a fantastic collection of gardens, statues, and pagodas, the Summer Palace is a great place to escape Beijing without actually leaving the city.

Chengde Mountain Resort

(L) Beijing summers can be unbearably hot, even if you're the emperor of China. The Qing emperors, who were accustomed to the cooler climes of Manchuria, decided it was better to relocate their courts during the sweltering summer heat to higher, cooler ground, choosing a mountain in Chengde, Hebei Province, to serve as their summer capital. Legendary emperors, including Kangxi, Yongzheng, and Qianlong, escaped the heat while continuing to perform their imperial duties. The compound is loosely modeled on the Forbidden City, but its gardens, pagoda, and outlying temples give it a character all its own.

CHINA TODAY

Government

Mao Zedong's announcement of the establishment of the People's Republic of China on October 1, 1949, finished one turbulent chapter in Chinese history and began another. The fall of the Qing, growing incursion by foreign countries, and the devastation of World War II sandwiched between two periods of bloody civil war gave way to purges of the country's artists and intellectuals, increasing isolationism, the colossal failure of the Great Leap Forward, and the tragic chaos of the Cultural Revolution.

The last quarter century has been characterized by relative stability and growth. Since the late 1970s the sole power holder in the People's Republic of China, the Chinese Communist Party, has brought hundreds of millions out of poverty and significantly relaxed its iron grip on personal freedoms. Diplomatically, Beijing has also become an increasingly savvy power broker on the global stage, while Western powers have been distracted by war and economic woes.

The party has no shortage of challenges that threaten its mandate to rule, including widespread corruption, an increasingly vociferous and media-savvy populace, environmental disasters, and a widening wealth gap.

Economy

China is undergoing the greatest economic expansion the world has ever seen, with the country now the world's most important producer and consumer of just about everything. Since the launch of Paramount Leader Deng Xiaoping's reform and open policy in 1978, the Middle Kingdom has experienced roughly 10 percent annual GDP growth and has become the world's second-largest economy, trailing only that of the United States (for now).

China's coastal region was the early beneficiary of economic reforms, with cities such as Shanghai, Beijing, Shenzhen, and Guangzhou powering an export-focused economic model. Today the story is the awakening of markets in second- and third-tier cities as the country moves toward a consumption-driven economy.

Media

The media in China has primarily served as a government mouthpiece since 1949. Since 1999 the Internet has not only provided Chinese people with greater access to information, it has also given rise to "Netizens," Chinese who use the Internet to voice their concerns and displeasures with modern society.

Beijing's attempts to manage the Internet have drawn much criticism beyond China's borders, but that hasn't stopped the Internet from becoming a part of daily life for more and more Chinese. With more than 400 million people regularly going online, China is the world's largest Internet market.

Government attempts to control it have caused some of the world's biggest Internet companies to pull out of the country or be blocked. Google made headlines in 2010, when it shut down its Beijing operations and redirected traffic to its Hong Kong site. Sites including Facebook and Twitter were blocked in 2009, presumably owing to government concerns about the potential for social media to be used in organizing anti-government activities.

Religion

Officially an atheist country for the last 60+ years, China is home to large numbers of Buddhists, Muslims, Christians, and Taoists. Until recently, practicing

any religion could lead to detention or worse, but now the country's temples, mosques, and churches are active once more—although the watchful eye of the government is never far away.

Despite its general increasing tolerance toward religion, the Chinese government has taken strong measures against groups that it considers a threat to its rule, most notably the Falun Gong, which it considered a cult and banned in 2000. Buddhists in Tibet and Uighur Muslims in Xinjiang have also clashed with police and soldiers in recent years, leading to heightened tension in those regions.

Sports

Despite its Olympic success, China has not been able to develop popular home-grown sports leagues. Men's soccer is seen as one of the country's biggest disappointments—China's national team has only qualified for the World Cup once. The national soccer league is riddled with corruption and empty seats, with most Chinese preferring to watch European matches.

Basketball is also extremely popular in China—even remote mountaintop villages have a court or two. In the late 1990s NBA games began to be broadcast on the mainland to the delight of sports fans. Everyone from kids to grandparents seemed to have a Chicago Bulls cap, and Michael Jordan was as recognizable as Bill Clinton. Today Kobe Bryant and a new generation of stars are being emulated by Chinese streetballers, and many former NBA players are finding second careers in the Chinese Basketball Association.

Sexual Mores

China is often thought of as a sexually conservative country, but you don't get to be the world's most populous country by being a bunch of prudes. Over the centuries Chinese society has seen it all, from polygamy to prostitutes, from eunuchs to transvestite actors.

Premarital sex in China may be discouraged, but young Chinese all over the country are engaging in sex, whether it be with a steady boyfriend or girlfriend or a drunken one-night stand. Public displays of affection in broad daylight aren't commonplace, but also not unheard-of.

Part and parcel with China's economic development has been the return of prostitution. More often than not, Chinese hotels will have on-site prostitution, and the odd international five-star occasionally gets busted for offering "special services" to guests. Officially discouraged by the government, it is generally understood that prostitution is a major contributor to China's "gray GDP."

Homosexuality was officially considered a mental illness in China until 2001—since then the country has become considerably more accepting of gays, lesbians, and transgendered individuals. These days nearly every major city has a few gay bars, and even straight Chinese take fashion cues from their homosexual "comrades"—a handful of the country's biggest celebrities are effeminate men or boyish women.

Sexual relations between Chinese and foreigners are generally accepted, but there is occasional friction or unpleasantness. On the short end of China's gender-imbalance stick, some Chinese men resent socially active foreign men and the Chinese women who date them. On the flip side of that coin, a Chinese man who is dating a foreign woman is often hailed as a stud.

FLAVORS OF CHINA

Chinese cuisine spans the entire spectrum of flavors, ingredients, and cooking styles. Almost every city or town is known for at least one or two specialty dishes. Wheat is the staple of choice in China's dry north, but in the wet south rice is favored. Most large Chinese cities offer a bit of everything from around the country, plus lots of local specialties. There's plenty of delicious street food out there too, but caution is suggested, as hygiene levels can vary.

Vegetables and Tofu

Vegetables are usually a part of any Chinese meal, with most varieties common to Western countries available—plus many that aren't, such as bitter melon or morning glory. Cold dishes such as pickled radishes or cucumber chunks in garlic and vinegar are a common way to start off a meal. Hot vegetable dishes can take on all forms. Many, especially leafy greens, are often simply chopped and stir-fried with just a bit of seasoning. Where you are in China often affects the cooking method of your favorite veggie. If you're hungry for potatoes in Harbin, they may be cooked with green pepper and eggplant in a red sauce, whereas in Yunnan, spicy mashed potatoes, crispy hash browns, and even potato and pumpkin soup are more common. Tofu, known in China as *doufu*, is available in a wide variety of shapes, sizes, and colors. Firm white tofu is commonly eaten in the Sichuanese style—bathed in a spicy and numbing sauce—but it is also served in soups with spinach or other greens. The more adventurous might try tofu with preserved eggs. Tofu skin (*doufu pi*) is a byproduct of normal tofu production, and contains fewer impurities. It can be stir-fried with peppers or mushrooms, and is a popular ingredient for cooking in hot pot. Vegetarians traveling in China

should keep in mind that many restaurants will add small amounts of pork, ham, oyster sauce, or other non-veggie items to seemingly vegetarian dishes, including tofu. Make sure you emphasize no meat whatsoever when ordering to maximize the chance of getting what you want.

Meat

Chinese cuisine features nearly every type of meat imaginable—nothing is too strange to consume, and there are no prohibitions on consumption of certain animals. Dog, bullfrog, rabbit, and snake are perfectly ordinary ingredients, as are all varieties of organs, including kidneys, liver, ears, and even penises. Pork and chicken are the most popular meats. Beef is also commonly consumed, but lamb tends to be found mainly only in Muslim dishes. It's difficult to find Western-style large chunks of meat—shredded, sliced, or cubed, it all comes small and chopstick-ready. Chicken is often cooked on the bone. In Beijing, Peking duck is a specialty that can't be missed—wrap it in pancakes with scallions and dip it in tangy sauce. Dishes from the predominantly Muslim northwest feature hearty stews, usually with lamb or chicken. Sichuan cuisine, while too spicy for some, features some great meat dishes, including the accessible kung pao chicken. In Yunnan, the local ham is famous, and works great adding flavor to fried vegetable dishes. Iron plate beef (*tiebanniurou*) is a popular fajita-style dish that can be found countrywide, and features strips of beef cooked with onion and green pepper in gravy, served on an iron hotplate. If you're into street snacks, slender kebabs of barbecued meat can be found for sale across the country, usually flavored with chili and cumin. Yunnan takes this a step further—the

province is known for its night stalls selling all manner of skewered treats.

Seafood

Fish holds a special place in Chinese cuisine—it's both a status dish and an auspicious symbol. Any banquet celebrating a festival or a special occasion will feature a fish. The fish is usually cooked and served whole, swimming in soy sauce with a dressing of scallions. In the seafaring south, superstitious eaters never turn the fish over, but eat "through" it. The quality and variety of seafood is much better on China's coast, but it is consumed countrywide, with farmed fish keeping inland diners happy. Most river or lake fish should be avoided, owing to pollution issues.

Seafood is kept alive as long as possible to preserve freshness, so don't be surprised to find yourself choosing your ingredients from tanks at the front of the restaurant or watching your fish being killed in front of you. Given this extra difficulty when ordering, Hong Kong is a great place to eat seafood. All manner of shellfish are on the menu, from expensive abalone to simple clams. Generally cooking styles are simple, and focus on the flavor of the ingredients. Some diners may find shellfish less well cooked than they are used to. Shrimp is usually served with the shells on.

Shark-fin soup is one of the most expensive delicacies to be found in China, and is often served to esteemed guests or at important business banquets. Many Chinese are unaware of the massive negative impact the harvesting of shark fins is having on the oceanic ecosystem. Prior to an expensive banquet, you may want to tell your host that you do not eat shark-fin soup for environmental reasons—this can save you the social awkwardness of refusing it when it is placed before you.

Staple foods

As noted earlier, China's staple foods are split along a north-south divide, but that doesn't mean that people in the north don't eat rice and southerners don't enjoy a bowl of wheat noodles.

Wheat is the primary grain grown in China's north, and wheat flour is used in making a wide variety of noodles as well as dumplings, breads, and pancakes. *Lamian*—wheat noodles made fresh by an entertaining process of stretching, swinging, and smacking wheat dough—are one of the most popular noodles in China. Lanzhou-style lamian are available almost anywhere in China, and are typically served in a mutton broth with green onions and sprigs of cilantro. Stir-fried noodles (*chaomian*) are also popular, and can be made with virtually any ingredient. Xinjiang cuisine features some of the most delicious noodles found in China, ranging from chunks of diced noodles to long, flat, wide noodles and everything in between. Dumplings are a popular wheat-based staple, and can be a meal on their own. They can be prepared by boiling, steaming, or boiling and then pan-frying. Steamed buns with filling (*baozi*) or without (*mantou*) are often eaten for breakfast. Steamed rice is most commonly eaten white, with other dishes piled on top of it, but many people enjoy it stir-fried with any imaginable combination of vegetables, egg, meats or seafood. Rice noodles can be found throughout southern China, from fat spaghetti-like *mixian* to fettucine-style *fen*, to *fensi*, a transparent noodle that resembles vermicelli.

FAQ

Will I need a visa?

Yes! Most foreign nationals traveling to China must have an entry visa. These visas are not issued upon arrival. Americans are currently charged a flat rate of $140 per visa, regardless of duration. Tourist visas vary in length from 30 days to six months, and allow for one or multiple entries over the course of their validity. The number of entries and length of stay are up to you when you fill out the application. Applications can be completed in person if you live in a city with a Chinese consulate. If not, there are many visa service centers available on the Web that will process your application through the mail. Fees may vary, so shop around and check the Better Business Bureau if you have any questions regarding legitimacy.

What's the best way to get around?

Domestic airline services connecting cities in China have increased greatly in the past decade, and even smaller out-of-the-way cities have small airports. If you have more time, train travel is also an option. The country is crisscrossed by one of the world's most extensive railway systems, and train travel is one way to get a feel for the vastness of China. Often it is also cheaper than flying, and is very dependable. China is also converting several lines between major metropolises into high-speed (or bullet) train routes. Bus routes between cities are also well established, and in rural areas are often the only way to travel between small towns. Car rental is becoming more popular, but drivers must first obtain a Chinese driver's license, which is a time-consuming and convoluted process.

Should I take a package tour?

If you are traveling to China to see only the major tourist attractions, or are very concerned about the language differences, a package tour is the answer. However, if your travel plans allow for improvisation or you want to stray a bit off the beaten path, skip the tours. Part of the adventure of traveling is exploring the unknown, and with most packages you will be with other tourists and have little say in where you stay or eat, or how long you have to view a specific site. Also, once in China you can find any number of small tours that last from an afternoon to a few days and will help tailor your trip so it is uniquely your own.

How big is the language barrier?

For the uninitiated, Chinese can be very intimidating. The language is tonal, has no alphabet, and regional dialects vary widely. Learning a few phrases in Mandarin Chinese before you go helps tremendously. Nonetheless, interest in learning English is a national phenomenon in China, and schoolchildren are all taught English from the first grade. Tourist destinations and other places catering to foreigners will usually have at least one designated English speaker. You may even be assisted by random locals who want to practice their language skills.

Are any subjects off-limits?

As anywhere, be respectful. The Chinese are gregarious and curious, and you may be surprised at what they think about the rest of the world. There is no one subject that is strictly forbidden or generally considered offensive, but you may want to speak cautiously when discussing touchy subjects like religious tolerance or Tibet.

Will my bankcard work at Chinese ATMs?

Banks in China are ubiquitous, and most ATMs accept cards with the Cirrus or Plus logos. Those with Visa or MasterCard logos are also widely accepted. This is true even in rural areas, especially if they are accustomed to foreign travelers passing through. That said, in more remote places the Bank of China is more reliable than smaller local banks. ATMs usually have an option for directions in English. If you encounter a machine with no English or that won't accept your card, chances are the bank around the corner will be more helpful.

Can I use my credit cards?

Resorts and major hotels tend to accept credit cards, but for daily purchases like food and drink or souvenir shopping, it is best to use cash. Credit-card use is growing in China, but is by no means widespread.

Can I drink the water?

No. Tap water in China can contain any number of chemicals and/or parasites that can quickly ruin your vacation. In major cities some hotels have begun to install water-filtration systems, but even these are questionable. Although it can be cumbersome to carry with you, bottled water is sold cheaply everywhere and remains the most reliable option. The boiled water or hot tea that is served in restaurants is also considered safe.

Are the toilets as bad as I've heard?

They can be. Bathrooms in hotels generally should be clean and well maintained, and many have Western-style toilets instead of the typical Asian "squat" toilet. Restaurant, train-station, and other public restrooms range from clean to abysmal, so be prepared. In rural areas you can often expect the worst. When going out for the day, it is always a good idea to take some toilet paper and perhaps baby wipes or hand sanitizer. Public toilets on the street charge a small admission fee, so keep some small change with you.

Should I bring any medications?

The Centers for Disease Control recommend updating your usual vaccinations and visiting a doctor or clinic that specializes in travel medicine four to six weeks before traveling to China. Of course, if you have a daily medication regime, plan accordingly. An anti-diarrhea medication may be a life-saver, especially on long bus rides or train journeys. Also, if you suffer from motion sickness you may want to bring the proper medicine from home.

Can I trust Chinese hospitals?

For minor injuries, bumps or bruises, and general maladies like colds or flu, Chinese hospitals are perfectly reliable. Major cities usually have both Western and traditional Chinese-style hospitals, but rural areas generally have fewer medical options. Travel insurance providing medical evacuation services is highly recommended in case of serious injury or illness, and is both inexpensive and readily available.

Should I be concerned about crime?

Violent crime against foreigners is almost unheard of in China. However, petty theft can be a worry when traveling on long-distance buses and trains or when staying at small guesthouses. Always keep your money, passport, and anything else you consider vital on your person when traveling, and be vigilant in crowded places.

GREAT ITINERARIES

BEIJING AND THE SILK ROAD

Day 1: Welcome to Beijing

Beijing is the cultural heart of China and the nation's top travel destination. Try to catch the daily flag-raising ceremony in Tiananmen Square. Most first-time visitors to China are drawn here as soon as they recover from jet lag. As you watch goose-stepping People's Liberation Army soldiers march from the Forbidden City into the world's largest public square under the watchful eye of Mao Zedong, you'll know you're not in Kansas anymore. After the flag raising, take a stroll around the square and soak in the atmosphere. And of course, a tour of the Forbidden City is an essential Beijing experience.

Logistics: Avoid unlicensed taxi touts who approach you in Beijing's airport. Proceed to the taxi stand outside, where a ride to your hotel should cost in the range of Y100. Tiananmen Square is best approached on foot or by subway, as taxis aren't allowed to let you off anywhere nearby.

Day 2: The Great Wall

If you're really pressed for time, you could visit the Badaling section of the Great Wall in an afternoon, but we recommend a day trip out to the more impressive sections at Mutianyu, Simatai, or Jinshanling.

Logistics: The most economical way to reach any section of the Great Wall is by group tour bus. If you don't want to be rushed, however, you're better off hiring private transportation for the day.

Day 3: Jewels of the Empire

Beijing is dotted with numerous imperial palaces and pleasure gardens. The lovely Summer Palace in the city's northwest has come to symbolize the decadence that brought about the fall of the Qing Dynasty. The Temple of Heaven is considered to be the perfect example of Ming Dynasty architecture, and is a great place to take a break from the frenetic pace of the capital.

Logistics: Each of these imperial sites will take about three or four hours to tour properly, and are all best reached by taxi. There's no need to ask the driver to wait, though, as plenty of taxis are constantly coming and going.

Day 4: Capital Entertainment

Beijing is teeming with cultural performances, fabulous restaurants, and sprawling outdoor markets. If you're looking to do some souvenir shopping, plan on spending a few hours at Beijing Curio City or the Silk Alley Market in the Chaoyang district. In the evening, music enthusiasts will want to take in a glass-shattering performance of Beijing Opera. If that's not your thing, experience the city's more modern nightlife around Qianhai Lake, where fashionable bars and shops stay open late.

Logistics: Unless you're willing to try your luck on one of Beijing's public buses, these destinations are best reached by taxi.

Days 5–8: Xi'an, China's Ancient Capital

For most of China's history, Xi'an was the nation's capital. As the eastern terminus of the Silk Road, the area is packed with historically significant destinations, most of which can be covered in just a few days. One entire day should be devoted to visiting the Terracotta Warriors Museum and surrounding sites east of the city. The famous warriors, built to protect China's first emperor in the afterlife, are only part of a huge tomb complex that stretches for

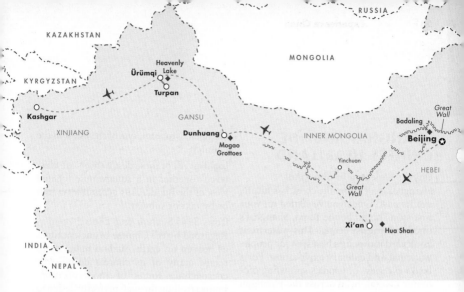

miles. If you have the time, we also recommend a day trip to the spectacular peaks of Hua Shan.

Logistics: Flights from Beijing to Xi'an take about two hours, with very frequent departures. Trains depart from Beijing's West Rail Station and take 12 hours. Most sites within Xi'an can be reached on foot. The Terracotta Warriors and Hua Shan are east of Xi'an, so you'll want to book a tour or catch one of the cheap public buses.

Travel Note:

If you're not interested in continuing farther west along the Silk Road, Xi'an is the perfect transportation hub from which to catch a flight or train to Lhasa, Chengdu, Shanghai, or any other destination of your choice.

Days 9–10: Dunhuang

Once the border between China and the unknown barbarian lands to the west, Dunhuang was also a major stop for merchants and religious pilgrims traveling the Silk Road. Filled with more than 1,000 years of Buddhist carvings, the Mogao Grottoes are widely considered to be the best surviving example of early religious art in China.

Logistics: Flights from Xi'an to Dunhuang take three hours and depart regularly during the busy summer months, less often in the off-season.

Days 11–14: Ürümqi and Turpan

Xinjiang is China's vast western frontier, where the pagodas and temples of the East melt into the bazaars and minarets of Central Asia. The capital, Ürümqi, is certainly interesting as far as large cities in China go, but for a real taste of the region you'll want to head out to the countryside. Heavenly Lake is perhaps the most beautiful body of water in the whole country. The small city of Turpan provides a fascinating look into the Silk Road history that once defined the area and the Uighur minority way of life that dominates today. If you've an extra couple of days, head even farther west to Kashgar, closer to Baghdad than Beijing in both distance and culture.

Logistics: During the busy summer season, flights regularly connect Dunhuang with Ürümqi. Other times of the year you'll need to make the long journey by train or make a connecting flight in Lanzhou or Xi'an. There are multiple daily flights between Ürümqi and Kashgar, as well as between Ürümqi and Beijing.

SHANGHAI AND THE CHINESE HEARTLAND

Day 1: Welcome to Shanghai

Shanghai is all about the country's future, not its past. Once you've settled in, your first stop should be the Bund, Shanghai's unofficial tourist center. This waterfront boulevard is the city's best spot for people-watching and culinary exploration. For a bird's-eye view of China's sprawling economic capital, head across the Huangpu River to Pudong, where you can mount the Oriental Pearl Tower, the Jinmao Tower, or the Shanghai World Financial Center, aka the 'Bottle Opener.' There's also the Yu Garden, where you can relax amid carefully designed landscaping and traditional architecture evoking the China of yore.

Logistics: Unless you fear cutting-edge technology, you'll want to take the ultra-fast maglev train from the airport into the city center. Shanghai is surprisingly easy to navigate on foot, although taxis are ubiquitous if your feet get tired. To get between the Bund and Pudong, the Y2 ferry across the Huangpu River departs every 10 minutes.

Day 2: Paris of the East

Shanghai's colonial history adds immeasurably to the city's charm. Be sure to visit the French Concession. Whether you're a fan of colonial architecture or enjoy sipping cappuccino in quiet cafés, this is a pleasant area to spend time in. Walk through Xintiandi, where restored traditional houses mix with bars, boutiques, and small museums. Spend some time searching for the perfect souvenir on Nanjing Road. Alternatively, you could brush up on your Chinese history at the Shanghai Museum, one of the finest in the country.

Logistics: All of these destinations are clustered together in a square mile located west of the Bund, easily accessible on foot or by taxi or subway.

Days 3–4: Suzhou and Zhouzhuang

Regarded by the Chinese in ancient times as heaven on earth, Suzhou manages to retain many of its charms despite the encroaching forces of modernization. Enjoy strolling through perfectly designed gardens and temples along the gently flowing branches of the Grand Canal. Luckily, Suzhou is close enough to work well as a day trip. Riding on a gondola past Zhouzhuang's signature tile-roof wooden houses, you'll understand why it was called the "Venice of the East." If you have only one day to get out of Shanghai, the area's water villages should be your destination.

Logistics: Transportation between Shanghai and Suzhou is most conveniently available by bus, of either the intercity or tourist variety; seats on a tourist coach to Zhouzhuang are also easily booked. If you're planning to visit both destinations, you'll probably want to spend the night at a hotel in Suzhou.

Days 5–8: Huang Shan

China's top natural scenic attraction, Huang Shan (Yellow Mountain) is an impossibly beautiful collection of 72 jagged peaks famous for grotesquely twisted pine trees and unusual rock formations. This area has provided the inspiration for generations of Chinese poets and artists, which is why its vistas and valleys may seem familiar to you. There are numerous ways to the top, either on foot or by cable car. To take part in Huang Shan's essential experience, spend a night at one of the

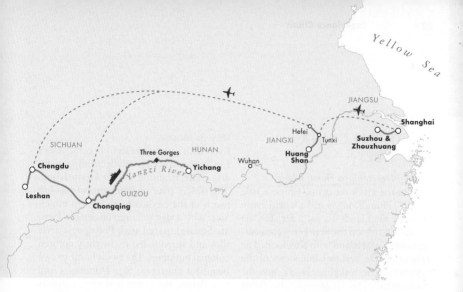

mountaintop guesthouses before waking at dawn to watch the sun rise over an eerie sea of fog.

Logistics: Unless you're willing to spend 10 or more hours on a bus from Shanghai, your best bet is to fly into Huang Shan's airport in the nearby town of Tunxi. There's no need to book a tour of the mountain, as paths and scenic viewpoints are all well marked in English.

Day 9–10: Chengdu

As the capital of Sichuan Province, Chengdu has long been one of China's great cultural centers. Famous for its fiery local cuisine, the city has also managed to partially maintain a pleasant atmosphere of yesteryear. Essential sites include the Buddhist Wenshu Monastery and for animal lovers, the Giant Panda Breeding Research Base. No matter how little time you have available to spend here, make the day trip south to Leshan to see the world's largest stone-carved Buddha. With toes the size of a small bus, the seated Grand Buddha is impressive, to say the least.

Logistics: Like most tourist hubs, the airport near Huang Shan offers fairly frequent flights to major cities such as Chengdu only during the busy warmer months. You may find it easier to connect through Hefei or Shanghai. All hotels and travel agencies in Chengdu can book tours to Leshan, or you can travel on your own by public bus.

Travel note: If you're pressed for time and are set on cruising the Yangtze River, skip Chengdu and fly directly to Chongqing.

Days 11–14: The Three Gorges

Despite higher water levels caused by construction of the Three Gorges Dam, a cruise along the Yangtze River through the Three Gorges is impressive. Along the way, you'll pass over abandoned metropolises that were humming with life only a few years ago as well as their modern counterparts built on higher ground. Be sure to book yourself on a luxury boat catering to foreigners, or you'll end up spending three days on a damp, rat-infested ship. Don't miss a visit to the Little Three Gorges, where monkeys play near the water's edge.

Logistics: Boats depart from Chongqing, a two-hour bullet train ride away from Chengdu. If you book your tour in Chengdu, transportation to Chongqing is almost always included. Most cruises disembark at Yichang in Hubei Province, where you can get a flight back to most travel hubs.

SOUTHERN CHINA AND TIBET

Day 1: Welcome to Hong Kong

Despite the city's return to Chinese rule in 1997, Hong Kong is still a world away from the mainland. To get a feel for the city, take a ride on the Star Ferry connecting Hong Kong Island with Kowloon. The ferry offers the best possible views of the business district's skyline. Don't miss the smoke-filled Man Mo Temple and Hong Kong's famous assortment of antiques shops and art galleries. Ride the very steep tram to the summit of Victoria Peak, with views of the entire harbor.

Logistics: The new airport is connected to Kowloon and Hong Kong Island by express train, taking about 30 minutes. Taxis are available everywhere, although much of the city can be explored on foot. The tram to Victoria Peak is open until midnight.

Day 2: Getting out of the City

While the business districts clustered around the harbor feature some of the world's densest urban jungle, Hong Kong also has a relaxed natural side. The express ferry to Lantau can whisk you away from the city in about 40 minutes. Arriving at the town of Mui Wo, you can catch a bus to the island's top two attractions: Po Lin Monastery, featuring the world's tallest outdoor bronze statue of Buddha, and Tai O, an old fishing village dotted with terrific seafood restaurants. For even greater solitude, take the ferry to one of the smaller Outer Islands.

Logistics: Ferries for Lantau leave from the Outlying Islands Ferry Pier on Hong Kong Island. On the island, private buses travel between all of the main attractions.

Day 3: Macau

Even with a recent push to become Asia's Las Vegas, Macau is still decidedly quieter and more traditional than Hong Kong. The slower pace of development has left much of the city's colonial charm intact. Start with a visit to Largo do Senado (Senate Square), paved with Portuguese-style tiles and surrounded by brightly colored colonial buildings. The city is home to two beautiful churches, São Domingos and São Paulo, the latter featuring exhibits on the early history of Asian Christianity.

Logistics: TurboJets from Hong Kong to Macau depart frequently and at all times of the day, making the trip in about an hour. If you're not comfortable traveling around the city by taxi, book a tour before you leave Hong Kong.

Days 4–8: Yangshuo and Longsheng

The scenery in northern Guangxi is some of the most beautiful in all of China. Enchanted by dramatic groupings of sheer limestone karst mountains, visitors often find themselves loath to leave. You'll see more of the countryside by taking the four-hour Li River Cruise down to Yangshuo. Yangshuo is a laid-back town popular with backpackers, and an excellent base from which to explore natural sites like Green Lotus Peak and Moon Hill. If you've more time, head back through Guilin to the town of Longsheng, home to the famously photogenic Dragon's Backbone Rice Terraces.

Logistics: Direct flights to Guilin depart from Hong Kong airport, or nearby Shenzhen, just across the border.

Days 9–14: Northwest Yunnan

Sandwiched between the Tibetan Plateau and Myanmar, this area has long attracted foreigners with its mix of minority cultures and stunning natural beauty. Dali,

beside the waters of Erhai Lake, is home to the Bai people, who settled here 4,000 years ago; the elegant Three Pagodas north of town is one of China's most iconic images. Farther north lies Lijiang, home of the Naxi people and the only place in the country where traditional Chinese music is said to survive in its original form. The highlight of the region is Tiger Leaping Gorge, one of the deepest river gorges in the world and a popular two-day hike.

Logistics: Most flights from Guilin to either Dali or Lijiang connect through Kunming. Travel between these destinations is by public bus or tour coach.

Days 15–18: Lhasa

Lhasa is the capital of a nation within a nation, with only tenuous ties to the rest of China. These ties have increased considerably with the opening of the train line to Tibet, yet the city is still unique. Start your tour of the city with a walk around the Barkhor, followed by a visit to Jokhang Temple, respectively Tibetan Buddhism's holiest pilgrimage circuit and holiest religious site. Don't miss the Sera Monastery, where monks hold animated theological debates every afternoon. Climb the long steps to the Potala Palace, followed by a visit to what was once the world's largest monastic complex, Drepung Monastery. If you spend only one day outside of Lhasa, make the two-hour trip to the mountaintop Ganden Monastery, with awe-inspiring views of the surrounding Lhasa River Valley. The five-day round-trip between Lhasa and Everest Base Camp with a number of stops along the way is the essential Tibet experience.

Logistics: Multiple daily flights connect Chengdu with Lhasa. Sites within Lhasa are accessible on foot or by taxi. Travel to sites outside Lhasa, like Everest Base Camp, must be arranged through an official tour operator.

Travel Note: Those wishing to visit Tibet can book flight or train tickets from many major transportation hubs.

THE PEOPLE OF CHINA

People often think of China as an ancient, monolithic culture comprised of a single, massive group of genetically similar people. In actuality, China contains a rich mosaic of different cultures and ethnicities, and officially recognizes 56 distinct ethnic groups. Ranging from populations of a few thousand to 1.2 billion, each group has made a unique contribution to China's cultural diversity with its language, costume, cuisine, philosophies, and traditions.

The largest of these groups is the Han people, who make up more than 90 percent of China's total population and around one-fifth of all humanity. They trace their origins to the Yellow River region, and take their name from the Han Dynasty, which was established in 206 BC. The Han have had the biggest impact on China's history, and every major dynasty but two—the Yuan and the Qing—has been Han.

Most of Eastern and Central China is dominated by the Han, with the outlying regions a fascinating stir-fry of people and cultures. Mountainous Yunnan Province in the country's southwest is home to the largest variety of ethnic groups, with some like the Jinuo and Pumi found nowhere else. Tibetans, Naxi, Bai, Yi, and Lisu are major ethnic groups found in the highlands of northwest Yunnan. In southern Yunnan, near the borders with Laos and Vietnam, there are ethnic Dai, Hani, and Miao, who have more in common with Southeast Asia than northern China.

The Mongols and Manchus are the two Chinese ethnic groups that can claim to have ruled the Han. Kublai Khan founded the Yuan Dynasty in 1271, but keeping control over China and other territories proved too much for the Mongols, and the dynasty was finished just under a century later. Today Mongols in China are primarily found in Inner Mongolia in the country's north, where many still live nomadic lives on the grasslands.

The Qing Dynasty of the Manchus had more staying power, running from 1644 to 1912 and producing several notable emperors. Under Qing rule Han Chinese adopted some Manchu customs including the long braids worn by men and the disfigurement and binding of women's feet. Most Manchus in China live in the northeastern provinces of Jilin, Liaoning, and Heilongjiang.

Tibetans—known for their unique brand of Buddhism—are the best-known ethnic group inhabiting China's more rugged geography, but there are plenty of others. The Muslim Uighurs of Xinjiang in northwest China are more numerous than Tibetans, and are related to modern-day Turks—some Uighurs have blonde hair and green eyes.

Outside of China, few people know of the Zhuang people, but they are China's second-largest ethnic group. The Zhuang speak a language related to Thai, and are primarily found in Guangxi, which is officially an "autonomous region" and ruled by the Zhuang, at least in theory.

The Hui are China's largest Muslim group, and are known for being skilled businesspeople—not a big surprise, considering that they are descended from Silk Road traders. Of China's minorities, the Hui are the most widely dispersed—Hui-run Muslim restaurants can be found in virtually every city or large town. The Miao people are spread across Southern China, and are typically found in mountain villages.

Terracotta soldiers

THE AGE OF EMPIRES

When asked his opinion on the historical impact of the French Revolution, Chairman Mao quipped, "It's too early to tell." Though a bit tongue in cheek, China does measure its history in millennia, and in its grand timeline, interactions with the West have been mere blips.

According to historical records, Chinese civilization stretches back to the 15th century BC—markings found on turtle shells carbon dated to around 1500BC bear some similarity to modern Chinese script. China then resembled city-states rather than a unified nation. Iconic figures such as Lao Tzu (the father of Taoism), Sun Tzu (author of the Art of War), and Confucius lived during this period. Generally, 221BC is accepted as the beginning of Imperial China, when the city-states united under various banners.

Over the next 2,200 years (give or take a few), China alternated between periods of harmony and political upheaval. Its armies conquered new territory and were in turn conquered by external invaders (most of whom wound up themselves being assimilated).

By the early 18th century, the long, slow decline of the Qing—the last of China's Imperial dynasties—was already in progress, making the ancient nation ripe for exploitation by rising European powers. The Imperial era ended with the forced abdication of child Emperor Puyi (whose life is chronicled in Bernardo Bertolucci's The Last Emperor), and it's here that the history of modern China, first with the founding of the republic under Sun Yat-sen and then with the establishment of the People's Republic under Mao Zedong, truly begins.

Writing Appears

1500BC   1200BC   900BC

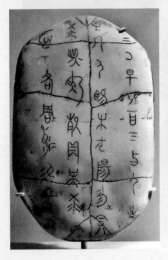

(left) Oracle shell with early Chinese characters. (top, right) The Great Wall stretches 4,163 miles from east to west. (bottom, right) Confucius, Lao-tzu, and a Buddhist Arhat.

circa 1500 BC — Writing Appears

The earliest accounts of Chinese history are still shrouded in myth and legend, and it wasn't until 1959 that stories were verified by archaeological findings. For millennia, people formed communities in the fertile lands of what is now central China. The first recorded Chinese characters are said to have been developed 3,500 years ago. Though sometimes referred to as the Shang Dynasty, this period was more of a precursor to modern Chinese dynasties than a truly unified kingdom.

722-475 BC — The Warring States Period

China was so far from unified that these centuries are collectively remembered as the Warring States Period. As befitting such a contentious time, military science progressed, iron replaced bronze, and weapons material improved. Some of China's greatest luminaries lived during this period, including the father of Taoism, Lao-tzu, Confucius, and Sun-Tzu, one of the greatest military tacticians and the author of the infamous *Art of War*, which is still studied in military academies around the world.

221-207 BC — The First Dynasty

The Qin Dynasty eventually defeated all of the other warring factions thanks to their cutting-edge military technology, namely the cavalry. The Qin were also called Ch'in, which may be where the word China first originated. The first Emperor, Qin Shi Huang, unified much of the lands and established a legal code and vast bureaucracy to hold it together. The Qin dynasty also standardized the written and spoken language and introduced a common currency.

(left) Terracotta warrior.
(top right) Temple of Xichan in Fuzhou

In order to protect his newly unified country, Qin Shi Huang ordered the creation of the massive Great Wall of China, which was built and rebuilt over the next 1,000 years. He was also a sculpture enthusiast and commissioned a massive army of stone soldiers to follow him into the afterlife. Buried with him, these terracotta warriors would remain hidden from the eyes of the world for two thousand years, until they were found by a farmer digging in a field just outside of Xian. These warriors are among the most important archaeological finds of the 20th century.

265-220 BC Buddhism Arrives

Emperor Qin's dreams of a unified China fell apart, and eventually the kingdom split into three warring factions. But what was bad for stability turned out to be good for literature. The Three Kingdoms Period is still remembered in song and story. *The Romance of the Three Kingdoms* is as popular among Asian book worms as the *Legend of King Arthur* is among Western readers. It's still widely read and has been translated into almost every language. Variations of the story have been adapted for manga, television series, and video games.

The Three Kingdoms period was filled with court intrigue, murder, and massive battles that, while exciting to read about centuries later, weren't much fun at the time. Armies ravaged the countryside, and most people lived and died in misery. Perhaps it was the carnage and disunity of the time that turned the country into a magnet for forces of harmony; it was during this period that Buddhism was first introduced into China, traveling over the Himalayas from India, via the Silk Road.

(left) Statue of Genghis Khan. (top right) Donguan Mosque in Xining, Qinghai. (bottom right) Empress Shengshen

Religion Diversifies

618-845

Chinese spiritual life continued to diversify. Nestorian Monks from Asia Minor arrived bearing news of Christianity, and Saad ibn Abi Waqqas (a companion of the Prophet Muhammad) supposedly visited the Middle Kingdom to spread the word of Islam. During this era, Wu Zetian, onetime concubine, seized power from the Tang Dynasty and became the first (and only) woman to assume the title of emperor. She ruled for 25 years through puppet emperors and finally, for 15 years as Emperor Shengshen.

Ghengis Invades

1271-1368

In Xanadu did Kublai Khan a stately pleasure dome decree . . .

Or so goes the famed Coleridge poem. But Kublai's grandfather Temujin (better known as Ghengis Khan) had bigger things in mind. One of the greatest war tacticians in history, he united the restive nomads of Mongolia's grassy plains and eventually sacked, looted, and pillaged much of the known west and most of the Chinese landmass. By the time Ghengis died in 1227, his grandson was well-tutored and ready to take on the rest of China.

By 1271, Kublai had established a capital in a land-locked city that would only much later become known as Beijing. This marks the beginning of the first (but not last) non-Han dynasty. Kublai Khan kept fighting southward and by 1279, Guangzhou fell to the Mongols, and Khan became the ultimate monarch of China. Though barbarians at heart, the Mongols must be credited for encouraging the arts and a number of early public works projects, including extending the highways and grand canals.

(left) Emperor Chengzu of the Ming Dynasty. (top right) Forbidden City in Beijing (bottom right) Child emperor Puyi.

Ming Dynasty

1368-1644

Many scholars believe that the Mongols' inability to relate with the Han is what ultimately pushed the Han to rise up and overthrow them. The reign of the Ming Dynasty was the last ethnically Han Dynasty to rule over a unified China. At its apex, the Bright Empire encompassed a landmass easily recognized as China, even by today's mapmakers. The Ming Emperors built a huge army and navy, refurbished the agricultural system, and printed many books using movable type long before Gutenberg. In the 13th century, Emperor Yongle began construction of the famous Forbidden City in Beijing, a veritable icon of China.

Also during the Ming Dynasty, China's best known explorer, Zheng He, plied the seven seas in massive treasure fleets that dwarfed in size and range the ships of Christopher Columbus. A giant both in stature and persona, Admiral Zheng (who was also a eunuch) spent two decades expanding China's knowledge of the world outside of its already impressive borders. He traveled as far as India, Africa, and (some say) even the coast of the New World.

Qing Dynasty

1644-1911

The final dynasty represented a serious case of minority rule. They were Manchus from the northeast. The early Qing dynasty was a brutal period as forces loyal to the new emperor crushed those loyal to the old. The Qing Dynasty peaked in the mid-to-late 18th century but soon after, its military powers began to wane. In the 19th century, Qing control weakened and prosperity diminished. By 1910 China was fractured, a baby sat on the Imperial throne, and the Qing Dynasty was on its deathbed.

(top left) A depiction of the Second Opium War. (bottom left) Chiang Kai-shek (top, right) Mao Zedong on December 6, 1944. (bottom, right) Sun Yat Sen.

The Opium Wars

1834-1860

European powers were hungry to open new territories up for trade, but the Qing weren't buying. The British East India Company, strapped for cash, realized they could sell opium in China at huge profits. The Chinese government quickly banned the nefarious trade and in response, a technologically superior Britain declared war. After a humiliating defeat in the first Opium War, China was forced to cede Hong Kong. Other foreign powers soon followed with territorial demands of their own.

Republican Era

1912-1949

China's Republican period was chaotic and unstable. The revolutionary Dr. Sun Yat-sen —revered by most Chinese as the father of modern China—was unable to build a cohesive government without the aid of regional warlords and urban gangsters. When he died of cancer in 1925, power passed to Chiang Kai-shek, who set about unifying China under the Kuomintang. What began as a unified group of both left- and right-wingers quickly deteriorated, and by the mid-1920s, civil war between the Communists and Nationalists was brewing.

The '30s and '40s were bleak decades for the Chinese people, caught between a vicious war with Japan and periodic clashes between Kuomintang and Communist forces. After Japan's defeat in 1945, China's civil war kicked into high gear. Though the Kuomintang were armed with superior weapons and backed by American money, the majority of Chinese people rallied behind the Communists. Within four years, the Kuomintang were driven off the mainland to Taiwan, where the Republic of China exists to the present day,

(top left) 1950s Chinese stamp with Mao and Stalin. (top right) Shenzhen (bottom left) Poster of Mao's slogans.

1949-Present

The People's Republic

On October 1, 1949, Mao Zedong declared from atop Beijing's Gate of Heavenly Peace that "The Chinese People have stood up." And so the People's Republic of China was born. The Communist party set out to overhaul China's ancient feudal system, emphasizing class struggle, redistribution of wealth, and elimination of foreign dominance. The next three decades would see a massive, often painful transformation of Chinese society from feudalism into the modern age.

The Great Leap Forward was a disaster—Chinese peasants were encouraged to cram 100 years of industrial development into as many weeks. Untenable decisions led to industrial and agricultural ruin, widespread famine, and an estimated 30 million deaths. The trauma of this period, however, pales in comparison to The Great Proletarian Cultural Revolution. From 1966–1976, fear and zealotry gripped the nation as young revolutionaries heeded Chairman Mao's call to root out class enemies. During this decade, millions died, millions were imprisoned, and much of China's accumulated religious,

historical, and cultural heritage literally went up in smoke.

Like a phoenix rising from its own ashes, China rose from its own self-inflicted destruction. In the early 1980s, Deng Xiao-ping took the first steps in reforming China's stagnant economy. With the maxim "To Get Rich is Glorious," Deng loosened central control on the economy and declared Special Economic Zones where the seeds of capitalism could be incubated. Three decades later, the nation is one of the world's most vibrant economic engines. Though China's history is measured in millennia, her brightest years may well have only just begun.

DID YOU KNOW?

Beijing's Lama Temple (Yonghe Temple) is one of the largest and most important Tibetan Buddhist monasteries in the world. The temple houses a 55-feet-high golden statue of Maitreya Buddha.

Beijing

WORD OF MOUTH

"If you want to see Mao's body at Chairman Mao's Mausoleum, go first thing in the morning. We made the mistake of coming out of the subway at Gate of Heavenly Peace, and by the time we saw that and walked over to the Mausoleum, the line was huge!"
—luv2globetrot

WELCOME TO BEIJING

TOP REASONS TO GO

★ **The Forbidden City.**
Built by more than 200,000 workers, it's the largest palace in the world and has the best-preserved and most complete collection of imperial architecture in China.

★ **Tiananmen Square.**
The political heart of modern China, the square covers 100 acres, making it the largest public square in the world.

★ **Temple of Heaven.**
One of the best examples of religious architecture in China, the sprawling, tree-filled complex is a pleasant place for wandering: watch locals practice martial arts, play traditional instruments, and enjoy ballroom dancing on the grass.

★ **Magnificent Markets.**
So much to bargain for, so little time! Visit outdoor Panjiayuan (aka the Dirt Market), the Silk Alley Market, or the Yashow Market.

★ **Summer Palace.** This garden complex dates back eight centuries, to when the first emperor of the Jin Dynasty built the Gold Mountain Palace on Longevity Hill.

1 Dongcheng District.
Dongcheng (East District) encompasses the Forbidden City, Tiananmen Square, Wangfujing (a major shopping street), the Lama Temple, and many other historical sights dating back to imperial times.

2 Xicheng District.
Xicheng (West District), west of Dongcheng, includes Beihai Park, former playground of the imperial family, and a series of connected lakes bordered by willow trees, courtyard-lined *hutongs*, and lively bars.

2

GETTING ORIENTED

Laid out like a target with ring roads revolving around a bull's-eye, with **Chang'an Jie** (Eternal Peace Street) cutting across the middle, Beijing sprawls outward from the central point of the **Forbidden City.** The ring roads are its main arteries, and, along with Chang'an Jie, you will find yourself traveling them just about anytime you go from one place to another aboveground. As you explore Beijing, you'll find that taxis are often the best way to get around. However, if the recently expanded subway system goes where you're headed, it's often a faster option than dealing with traffic. The city is divided into 18 municipal and suburban districts (*qu*). Only six of these districts are the central stomping grounds for most visitors.

3 Southern Districts: Chongwen and Xuanwu. These areas have some of the city's oldest neighborhoods and a long history of folk arts, with opera theaters and acrobatic shows still staged here. Chongwen also has some famous restaurants.

4 Chaoyang District. Chaoyang is the biggest and busiest district, occupying the areas north, east, and south of the eastern Second Ring Road. It's home to foreign embassies, multinational companies, the Central Business District, and the Olympic Park.

5 Haidian District. Haidian is the technology and university district. It's northwest of the Third Ring Road and packed with shops selling electronics and students cramming for the next exam.

Updated by
Paul Mooney

Beijing is a vibrant jumble of neighborhoods and districts. It's a city that was transformed almost overnight in preparation for the 2008 Olympics, often leveling lively old *hutongs* (alleyway neighborhoods) to make way for the glittering towers that are fast dwarfing their surroundings. Still, day-to-day life seems to pulse the lifeblood of a Beijing that once was.

Hidden behind Beijing's pressing search for modernity is an intriguing historic core. Many of the city's ancient sites were built under the Mongols during the Yuan Dynasty (1271–1368). A number of the capital's imperial palaces, halls of power, mansions, and temples were rebuilt and refurbished during the Ming and Qing dynasties. Despite the ravages of time and the Cultural Revolution, most sites are in good shape, from the Niujie Mosque, with Koranic verse curled around its arches, to Tiananmen Square, the bold brainchild of Mao Zedong.

The city is divided into 18 municipal and suburban districts (*qu*). Only six of these districts are the central stomping grounds for most visitors; this chapter focuses on those districts. **Dongcheng** (East District) encompasses the Forbidden City, Tiananmen Square, Wangfujing (a major shopping street), the Lama Temple, and many other historical sites dating back to imperial times. **Xicheng** (West District), directly west of Dongcheng, is a lovely lake district that includes Beihai Park, former playground of the imperial family, and a series of connected lakes bordered by willow trees, courtyard-lined hutongs, and lively bars. The southern districts include **Chongwen** in the southeast and **Xuanwu** in the southwest. These areas have some of the oldest neighborhoods in the city, and a long history of traditional folk arts, with opera theaters and acrobatic shows still staged here. The Chongwen District is also home to some of the city's most famous restaurants, some more than 100 years old. **Chaoyang** is the biggest and busiest district, occupying the areas north, east, and south of the eastern Second Ring Road. As it lies outside the Second Ring Road, which marked the eastern demarcation of the old city wall, there is little of historical interest here. The district is home to foreign embassies, multinational companies, the Central

Business District, and the Olympic Park. **Haidian,** the technology and university district, is northwest of the Third Ring Road; it's packed with shops selling electronics and students cramming for the next exam.

STREET VOCABULARY

Here are some terms you'll see over and over again. These words will appear on maps and street signs, and they are part of the name of just about every place you go:

Dong is east, **xi** is west, **nan** is south, **bei** is north, and **zhong** means middle. **Jie** and **lu** mean street and road respectively, and **da** means big.

Gongyuan means park. Jingshan Park is also called Jingshan Gongyuan.

Nei means inside and **wai** means outside. You will often come across these terms on streets that used to pass through a gate of the old city wall. Andingmen Nei Dajie, for example, is the section of the street located inside the Second Ring Road (where the gate used to be), whereas Andingmen Wai Dajie is the section outside the gate.

Qiao, or bridge, is part of the place name at just about every entrance and exit on the ring roads.

Men, meaning door or gate, indicates a street that once passed through an entrance in the old wall that surrounded the city until it was mostly torn down in the 1960s. The entrances to parks and some other places are also referred to as *men.*

PLANNING

WHEN TO GO

The best time to visit Beijing is spring or early fall, when the weather is pleasant and crowds are a bit smaller. Book at least one month in advance for travel during these two times of year. In winter Beijing's Forbidden City and Summer Palace can look fantastical and majestic, when the traditional tiled roofs are covered with a light dusting of snow and the venues are devoid of tourists.

Avoid the two long national holidays: Chinese New Year, which ranges from mid-January to mid-February; and National Day holiday, the first week of October, when Chinese normally get a lengthy holiday. Millions of Chinese travel during these weeks, making it difficult to book hotels, tours, and transportation.

The weather in Beijing is at its best in September and October, with a good chance of sunny days and mild temperatures. Winters are cold, but it seldom snows. Although hotels are usually well heated, some restaurants may be poorly heated, so be prepared with a warm sweater when dining out. Late April through June is lovely, but come July the days are hot and excruciatingly humid with a greater chance of rain. Spring is also the time of year for Beijing's famous dust storms.

GETTING AROUND

On Foot: Though traffic and modernization have put a bit of a cramp in Beijing's walking style, meandering remains one of the best ways to experience the capital—especially the old hutongs that are rich with culture and sights.

Bike Travel: The proliferation of cars (some 1,000 new automobiles take to the streets of the capital every day, bringing the total to more than 4 million vehicles) has made biking less pleasant and more dangerous here. Fortunately, most streets have wide, well-defined bike lanes often separated from other traffic by an island. If a flat tire or sudden brake failure strikes, seek out the nearest street-side mechanic, easily identified by the bike parts and pumps. Bikes can be rented at many hotels and next to some subway stations.

Subway Travel: The subway is the best way to avoid Beijing's frequent traffic jams. With the opening of new lines, Beijing's subway service is becoming increasingly convenient. Beijing now has eight lines, and an express line to the airport. Most tourist spots are located close to Line 1, which runs east–west through Tiananmen Square, and Line 2, which runs in a loop tracing Beijing's ancient city walls (and the Second Ring Road). Transfers between these lines can be made at the Fuxingmen and Jianguomen stations. The subway runs from about 5 am to midnight daily, depending on the station. Fares are Y2 per ride for any distance, and transfers are free. Stations are marked in both Chinese and English, and stops are announced in both languages, also.

Taxi Travel: The taxi experience in Beijing has improved significantly as the city's taxi companies gradually shift to cleaner, more comfortable new cars. In the daytime, flag-fall for taxis is Y10 for the first 3 km (2 mi) and Y2 per km thereafter. The rate rises to Y3 per km on trips over 15 km and after 11 pm, when the flag-fall also increases to Y11. At present, there is also a Y1 gas surcharge for any rides exceeding 3 km. ■TIP→ Be sure to check that the meter has been engaged to avoid fare negotiations at your destination. Taxis are easy to hail during the day but can be difficult during evening rush hour, especially when it's raining. If you're having difficulty, go to the closest hotel and wait in line there. Few taxi drivers speak English, so ask your hotel concierge to write down your destination in Chinese. ■TIP→ You can also use the translations throughout this book; simply point at the Chinese character and your cabbie will know where to go. Be sure to take a hotel card with you for the return trip.

GOOD TOURS

Taking a tour will make it easier to sightsee without the hassle. However, if you're adventurous, you can easily explore the city on your own, even if you don't speak Chinese. You can't rely on taxi drivers to know the English names of the major tourist sites, but armed with the names in Chinese in this guide, you should have few or no problems getting around. If you do opt for an organized tour, keep in mind that a little research pays off.

Shoppers enjoy a sunny day in the Xidan neighborhood.

GENERAL TOURS

China Culture Center. With a reputation for well-informed English-speaking guides, CCC is popular with both visitors and expats looking for more than just the standard tour highlights. ⊠ *Kent Center, 29 Anjialou, Liangmaqiao Road, Chaoyang District* ☎ *010/6432–9341; 010/6432–1041 weekends* ⊕ *www.chinaculturecenter.org.*

China International Travel Service. CITS is China's official travel agency, dating to 1954. In Beijing the company offers everything from customized tours to group tours and business trips. ⊠ *28 Jianguomenwai Dajie, Chaoyang District* ✛ *Across from the Friendship Store* ☎ *010/6515–8565* ⊕ *www.cits.net.*

WildChina. This foreign-managed travel company is probably the best in China. WildChina has excellent guides who know the city well and who don't waste your time taking you to souvenir shops. The company offers a three-day tour of Beijing that includes major historic sites, a hike on a wild part of the Great Wall, a visit to the hutongs, and an introduction to the cuisines of the capital city. It's pricey but worth it. ⊠ *Room 801, Oriental Place, 9 East Dongfang Lu, North Dongsanhuan Lu, Chaoyang District* ☎ *010/6465–6602* ⊕ *www.wildchina.com.*

BIKE TOURS

Many of Beijing's pleasures are best sampled off the subway and out of taxis. In other words, pedal! Rent bikes (available at many hotels and near some subway exits) and take an impromptu sightseeing tour. Beijing is flat, and there are bike lanes on most main roads. Pedaling among the city's cyclists isn't as challenging as it looks: copy the locals—keep it slow and ring your bell often. And, of course, be very careful.

Punctured tire? Not to worry: curbside repairmen line most streets. Remember to park your bike (and lock it to something stationary, as bike theft is common) only in designated areas. There are designated bike-parking lots throughout the city with attendants charging a nominal fee, usually about 3 mao.

CycleChina. If a guided three-hour afternoon bicycle tour of a hutong, or a trip through Beijing sitting in a motorbike sidecar sounds like fun, call CycleChina. They also offer bike tours of the Great Wall. ✉ *12 Jingshan East Street, Dongcheng District ✛ Across from the east gate of Jingshan Park* ☎ *010/6402–5653 or 139/1188–6524* ⊕ *www.cyclechina.com.*

Bicycle Kingdom. Offering bicycle rentals and suggested itineraries covering some of Beijing's lesser known historical sites, Kingdom is a great resource. A variety of bikes are available for rent here from Y100 for the first day and Y50 for each additional day (or Y300 per week). Helmets are available for Y20 per day or Y100 a week. ✉ *34 Dong Huangchenggen Nanjie, Wangfujing, Dongcheng District* ☎ *133/8140–0738 (English); 010/6526–5857* ⊕ *www.bicyclekingdom.com.*

PEDICAB TOURS

Pedicabs (basically large tricycles with room for passengers behind a pedaling driver) were once the vehicles of choice for Beijingers laden with a week's worth of groceries or tourists eager for a street's-eye city tour. Today many residents are wealthy enough to bundle their purchases into taxis or their own cars, and the tourist trade has moved on to the tight schedules of air-conditioned buses. But pedicabs have made a big comeback in Beijing in recent years and can now be hired near major tourist sites. A ride through the hutongs near Houhai is the most popular pedicab journey. ■TIP➜ Be absolutely sure to negotiate the fare in advance, clarifying which currency will be used (yuan or dollars), whether the fare is considered a one-way or round-trip (some drivers will demand payment for a round-trip whether or not you use the pedicab for the return journey), and whether it is for one person or two. Beginning in 2008, government-approved pedicab tours were supposed to be fixed at Y35 per hour, though the actual price is often higher. Feel free to tip your driver for good service on longer tours. Independent pedicabs for hutong tours can be found in the small plaza between the Drum Tower and the Bell Tower.

Beijing Hutong Tourist Agency. This agency was one of the first to offer guided pedicab tours of Beijing's back alleys, with glimpses of old courtyard houses and daily Beijing life. This half-day trip winds its way through what was once Beijing's most prestigious neighborhood (Houhai), stops at the Drum and Bell towers, and finishes with tea at Prince Gong's Palace. It's also possible to arrange to visit the home of a local family. Advance reservations are recommended. Tours, which begin at the entrance to Qianhai (Lotus Lane) directly opposite the north entrance of Beihai Park, start at 9 and 2 daily, and cost Y180 per person, or Y360 if you're riding solo. ✉ *26 Di'anmen Xidajie, Dongcheng District* ☎ *010/6615–9097.*

BEIJING'S SUBWAY

The subway in Beijing is faster and cheaper than a taxi, and the city plans to expand the system by 2015. Although Beijing's subway system has been expanded to eight lines, most first-time visitors to Beijing stick to the original two lines, which provide access to the most popular areas of the capital, and the airport extension. **Line 1** runs east and west along Chang'an Jie past the China World Trade Center, Jianguomen (one of the embassy districts), the Wangfujing shopping area, Tiananmen Square and the Forbidden City, Xidan (another major shopping location), and the Military Museum, before heading out to the far western suburbs. **Line 2** (the loop line) runs along a sort of circular route around the center of the city shadowing the Second Ring Road. Important destinations include the Drum and Bell towers, Lama Temple, Dongzhimen (with a connection to the airport express), Dongsishitiao (near Sanlitun and the Worker's Stadium), Beijing Train Station, and Qianmen (Front Gate) south of Tiananmen Square. Free transfers between Line 1 and 2 can be made at either Fuxingmen or Jianguomen stations. ■TIP→ Need a visual? Flip to the inside back cover of this book for a helpful subway map.

If both you and your final destination are near the Second Ring Road or on Chang'an Jie, the best way to get there is probably by subway. It stops just about every half mile, and you'll easily spot the entrances (with blue subway logos) dotting the streets. Each stop is announced in both English and Chinese, and there are clearly marked signs in English or pinyin at each station. Transferring between lines is easy and free,

with the standard Y2 ticket including travel between any two destinations. ■TIP→ When planning a trip on Line 13, make sure you are transferring from the correct station. If your destination is on the west side of the line, leave from Xizhimen; if it's on the east side of the line, leave from Dongzhimen.

Subway tickets can be purchased from electronic kiosks and ticket windows in every station. Start off by finding the button that says "English," insert your money, and press another button to print. Single-ride tickets cost Y2, and unless you want a pocketful of coins you'll need to pay with exact change; the machines don't accept Y1 bills, only Y1 coins. It's also possible to buy a stored value subway card with a Y20 deposit and a purchase of Y10–Y100.

In the middle of each subway platform, you'll find a map of the Beijing subway system along with a local map showing the position of exits. Subway cars also have a simplified diagram of the line you're riding above the doors.

Trains can be very crowded, especially during rush hour, and it's not uncommon for people to push onto the train before exiting passengers can get off. Prepare to get off by making your way to the door before you arrive at your station. Be especially wary of pickpockets.

⚠ Unfortunately, the subway system is not convenient for disabled people. In some stations there are no escalators, and sometimes the only entrance or exit is via steep steps.

HIKING TOURS

Beijing Hikers. This outfitter offers guided group and private hiking trips aimed at expat hikers and tourists. The trips are rated from one to five in terms of difficulty, and they take you into the hills around Beijing. You might visit a rural village, historic temple, or the Great Wall. Group tours depart from the Starbucks in the Lido Hotel and start at Y250 per person. Book in advance. ⊠ *26 Xinhualian, Ligang Building No. 2, Suite 601, Chaoyang District* ☎ *010/6432–2786 or 139/1002–5516* ⊕ *www.beijinghikers.com.*

VISITOR CENTERS

Beijing Travel Hotline (☎ *12301* ⊕ *www.bjta.gov.cn*)

Beijing International Travel and Tours Company (⊠ *28 Jianguomenwai Dajie, Chaoyang District* ✛ *Behind Gloria Plaza Hotel* ☎ *010/6515–8565* ⊕ *www.btgtravel.com.cn.*

EXPLORING BEIJING

Laid out like a target with ring roads revolving around a bull's-eye, with **Chang'an Jie** (Eternal Peace Avenue) cutting across the middle, Beijing is a bustling metropolis sprawling outward from the central point of the **Forbidden City.** The ring roads are its main arteries and, along with Chang'an Jie, you will find yourself traveling them just about anytime you go from one place to another aboveground. As you explore Beijing, you'll find that taxis are often the best way to get around. However, if the recently expanded subway system goes where you're headed, it's often a faster option than dealing with traffic, which has become increasingly congested in recent years with the rise of private automobiles.

DONGCHENG DISTRICT

Dongcheng District, with its idyllic hutongs and plethora of historical sites, is one of Beijing's most pleasant areas. It's also one of the smaller districts in the city, which makes it easy to get around. A day exploring Dongcheng will leave you feeling as if you've been introduced to the character of the capital. From the old men playing chess in the hutongs to the sleek, chauffeured Audis driving down Chang'an Jie, to the colorful shopping on Wangfujing, Dongcheng offers visitors a thousand little tastes of what makes Beijing a fascinating city. ■ TIP➔ Note that indoor photography in many temples and sites like the Forbidden City is not permitted.

GETTING HERE AND AROUND

Dongcheng is easily accessible by subway, with stops along most of its perimeter: Tiananmen East station to Jianguomen on Line 1 forms the south side of this district; Jianguomen to Gulou Dajie on Line 2 forms the district's north and east sides. Line 2 stops at the Lama Temple, the Ancient Observatory, Wangfujing, and Tiananmen Square. Taxi travel during peak hours (7 to 9 am and 5 to 8 pm) is difficult. At other times traveling by taxi is affordable, convenient, and the fastest option (especially at noon, when much of the city is at lunch, and after 10 pm). Renting a bike to see the sites is also a good option. ⚠ If you do rent a

2

bike, be extremely cautious of traffic. Think about renting a helmet as well. Bus travel within the city, especially during rush hours, is laborious and should be avoided unless you speak or read Chinese.

MAKING THE MOST OF YOUR TIME

Most of Dongcheng can be seen in a day, but it's best to set aside two, because the **Forbidden City** and **Tiananmen Square** will likely take the better part of one day. The climb up Coal Hill (also called Prospect Hill) in **Jingshan Park** will take about 30 minutes for an average walker. From there, hop a taxi to the **Lama Temple,** which is worth a good two hours, then visit the nearby **Confucius Temple.**

TOP ATTRACTIONS

Fodor's Choice
★

Confucius Temple. This tranquil temple to China's great sage has endured close to eight centuries of additions and restorations. The Hall of Great Accomplishment in the temple houses Confucius's funeral tablet and shrine, flanked by copper-colored statues depicting China's wisest Confucian scholars. As in Buddhist and Taoist temples, worshippers can offer sacrifices (in this case to a mortal, not a deity). The 198 tablets lining the courtyard outside the Hall of Great Accomplishment contain 51,624 names belonging to advanced Confucian scholars from the Yuan, Ming, and Qing dynasties. Flanking the Gate of Great Accomplishment are two carved stone drums dating to the Qianlong period (1735–96). In the Hall of Great Perfection you'll find the central shrine to Confucius. Check out the huge collection of ancient musical instruments.

In the front and main courtyards of the Temple, you'll find a cemetery of stone tablets. These tablets, or stelae, stand like rows of creepy crypts. On the front stelae you can barely make out the names of thousands of scholars who passed imperial exams. Another batch of stelae, carved in the mid-1700s to record the *Thirteen Classics,* philosophical works attributed to Confucius, line the west side of the grounds.

■ TIP➜ We recommend combining a tour of the Confucius Temple with the nearby Lama Temple. Access to both is convenient from the Yonghegong subway stop at the intersection of Line 2 and Line 5. You can also easily get to the Temple of Heaven by taking Line 5 south to Tiantandongmen.

The complex is now combined with the Imperial Academy next door, once the highest educational institution in the country. Established in 1306 as a rigorous training ground for high-level government officials, the academy was notorious, especially during the early Ming Dynasty era, for the harsh discipline imposed on scholars perfecting their knowledge of the Confucian classics. ⊠ *Guozijian Lu off Yonghegong Lu near Lama Temple, Dongcheng District* ☎ *010/8401–1977* ⚏ *Y30* ☉ *Daily 8:30–5* Ⓜ *Yonghegong.*

★ **Drum Tower.** Until the late 1920s, the 24 drums once housed in this tower were Beijing's timepiece. Sadly, all but one of these huge drums have been destroyed. Kublai Khan built the first drum tower on this site in 1272. You can climb to the top of the present tower, which dates from the Ming Dynasty. The nearby **Bell Tower,** renovated after a fire in 1747, offers fabulous views of the hutongs. ⊠ *North end of Dianmen*

Continued on page 58

THE FORBIDDEN CITY

Undeniably sumptuous, the Forbidden City, once home to a long line of emperors, is Beijing's most enduring emblem. Magnificent halls, winding lanes, and stately courtyards await you—welcome to the world's largest palace complex.

As you gaze up at roofs of glazed-yellow tiles—a symbol of royalty—try to imagine a time when only the emperor ("the son of God") was permitted to enter this palace, accompanied by select family members, concubines, and eunuch-servants. Now, with its doors flung open, the Forbidden City's mysteries beckon.

The sheer grandeur of the site—with 800 buildings and more than 8,000 rooms—conveys the pomp and circumstance of Imperial China. The shady palaces, musty with age, recall life at court, where corrupt eunuchs and palace officials schemed and bored concubines gossiped.

BUILDING TO GLORY
Under the third Ming emperor, Yongle, 200,000 laborers built this complex over the course of 14 years, finishing in 1420. Yongle relocated the Ming capital to Beijing (from Nanjing in the south) to strengthen China's northern frontier. After Yongle, the palace was home to 23 Ming and Qing emperors, until the dynastic system crumbled in 1911.

In imperial times, no buildings were allowed to exceed the height of the palace. Moats and massive timber doors protected the emperor. Gleaming yellow roof tiles marked the vast complex as the royal court's exclusive dominion. Ornate interiors displayed China's most exquisite artisanship, including ceilings covered with turquoise-and-blue dragons, walls draped with priceless scrolls, intricate cloisonné screens, sandalwood thrones padded in delicate silks, and floors of golden-hued bricks. Miraculously, the palace survived fire, war, and imperial China's collapse.

MORE THAN FENG SHUI
The Forbidden City embodies Feng Shui, architectural principles used for thousands of years throughout China. Each main hall faces south, opening to a courtyard flanked by lesser buildings. This symmetry repeats itself along a north–south axis that bisects the imperial palace, with a broad walkway paved in marble. This path was reserved exclusively for the emperor's sedan chair.

The entire complex follows the principles of Feng Shui.

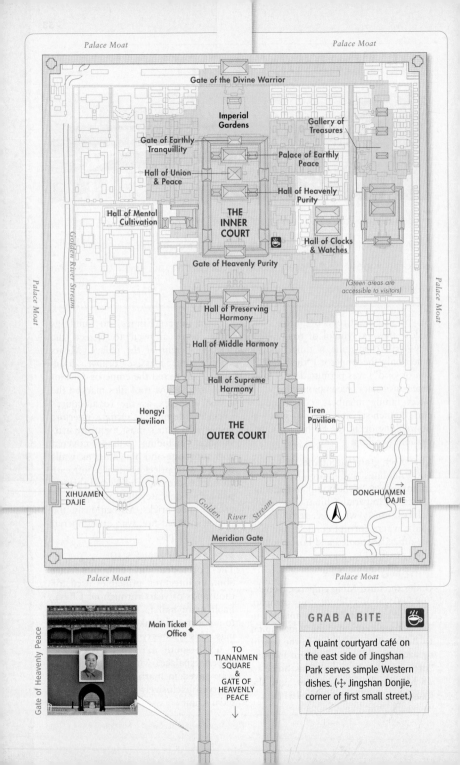

Palace Moat

Palace Moat

Gate of the Divine Warrior

Imperial Gardens

Gallery of Treasures

Gate of Earthly Tranquillity

Palace of Earthly Peace

Hall of Union & Peace

Hall of Heavenly Purity

Hall of Mental Cultivation

THE INNER COURT

Hall of Clocks & Watches

Gate of Heavenly Purity

(Green areas are accessible to visitors)

Golden River Stream

Palace Moat

Hall of Preserving Harmony

Hall of Middle Harmony

Hall of Supreme Harmony

Palace Moat

Hongyi Pavilion

Tiren Pavilion

THE OUTER COURT

← XIHUAMEN DAJIE

DONGHUAMEN DAJIE →

Golden River Stream

Meridian Gate

Palace Moat

Palace Moat

Gate of Heavenly Peace

Main Ticket Office ◆

TO TIANANMEN SQUARE & GATE OF HEAVENLY PEACE ↓

GRAB A BITE

A quaint courtyard café on the east side of Jingshan Park serves simple Western dishes. (⚑ Jingshan Donjie, corner of first small street.)

WHAT TO SEE

The most impressive way to reach the Forbidden City is through the **Gate of Heavenly Peace** (Tiananmen), connected to Tiananmen Square. The Great Helmsman himself stood here to establish the People's Republic of China on October 1, 1949.

The **Meridian Gate** (Wumen), sometimes called Five Phoenix Tower, is the main southern entrance to the palace. Here, the emperor announced yearly planting schedules according to the lunar calendar; it's also where errant officials were flogged. The main ticket office and audio-guide rentals are just west of this gate.

The central entrance of the Meridian was reserved for the emperor. The one day the empress was allowed to walk through it was her wedding day.

THE OUTER COURT

The **Hall of Supreme Harmony** (Taihedian) was used for coronations, royal birthdays, and weddings. Bronze vats, once kept brimming with water to fight fires, ring this vast expanse. The hall sits atop three stone tiers with an elaborate drainage system with 1,000 carved dragons. On the top tier, bronze cranes symbolize longevity. Inside, cloisonné cranes flank the imperial throne, above which hangs a heavy bronze ball— placed there to crush any pretender to the throne.

Take a close look at the bronze vats and you'll see the telltale scratch marks of greedy foreign soldiers who scraped the gold with their bayonets.

Emperors greeted audiences in the **Hall of Middle Harmony** (Zhonghedian). It also housed the royal plow, with which the emperor would turn a furrow to commence spring planting.

The highest civil service examinations, which were personally conducted by the emperor, were once administered in the **Hall of Preserving Harmony** (Baohedian). Behind the hall, a 200-ton marble relief of dragons, the palace's most treasured stone carving, adorns the staircase.

The Hall of Supreme Harmony was the site of many imperial weddings.

A short jaunt to the right is **Hall of Clocks and Watches** (Zhongbiaoguan), where you'll find a collection of early timepieces. It's pure opulence: there's a plethora of jeweled, enameled, and lacquered timepieces (some astride elephants, others implanted in ceramic trees). Our favorites? Those crafted from red sandalwood. *(Admission: Y10)*

You'll see that lions in the palace live in pairs. A female lion playing with a cub symbolizes imperial fertility. A male lion, sitting majestically with a sphere beneath his paw, represents power.

Marble dragons will greet you behind the Hall of Preserving Harmony.

Emperors Throne in the Palace of Heavenly Purity

THE INNER COURT

Now you're approaching the very core of the palace. Several emperors chose to live in the Inner Palace with their families. The **Hall of Heavenly Purity** (Qianqinggong) holds another imperial throne; the **Hall of Union and Peace** (Jiaotaidian) was the venue for the empress's annual birthday party; and the **Palace of Earthly Peace** (Kunninggong) was where royal couples consummated their marriages. The banner above the throne bizarrely reads DOING NOTHING.

On either side of the Inner Palace are six western and six eastern palaces—the former living quarters of concubines, eunuchs, and servants. The last building on the western side, the **Hall of Mental Cultivation** (Yangxindian), is the most important of these; starting with Emperor Yongzheng, all Qing Dynasty emperors attended to daily state business in this hall.

AN EMPEROR CHEAT SHEET

JIAJING (1507–1567)

Ming Emperor Jiajing was obsessed with Taoism, which he hoped would give him longevity, but which also led him to ignore state affairs for 25 years. His other fixation was the pursuit of girls: his 18 concubines conspired to strangle him in his sleep, but their plot was uncovered. Nearly all of the girls, and their families, were killed.

YONGZHENG (1678–1735)

The third emperor of the Qing Dynasty, Yongzheng was tyrannical but efficient. He became emperor amid rumors that he had forged his father's will. He appeased his brothers by promoting them, but then proceeded to murder and imprison anyone who posed a challenge, including his own brothers, two of whom died in prison.

Pagoda in the Imperial Garden

The Gallery of Treasures (Zhenbaoguan), actually a series of halls, has breathtaking examples of imperial ornamentation. The first room displays candleholders, wine vessels, tea sets, and a golden pagoda commissioned by Qing emperor Qian Long in honor of his mother. A cabinet on one wall contains the 25 imperial seals. Jade bracelets, golden hair pins, and coral fill the second hall; carved jade landscapes a third. *(Admission: Y10)*

HEAD FOR THE GREEN

North of the Forbidden City's private palaces, beyond the **Gate of Earthly Tranquillity,** lie the most pleasant parts of the Forbidden City: the **Imperial Gardens** (Yuhuayuan), composed of ancient cypress trees and stone mosaic pathways. During festivals, palace inhabitants climbed the Hill of Accumulated Elegance. You can exit the palace at the back of the gardens through the park's **Gate of the Divine Warrior** (Shenwumen).

FAST FACTS

Address: The main entrance is just north of the Gate of Heavenly Peace, which faces Tiananmen Square on Chang'an Jie.

Phone: 010/8513-2255

Web site: www.dpm.org.cn

Admission: Y60

Hours: Oct. 16–Apr. 15, daily 8:30–4:30; Apr. 16–Oct. 15, daily 8:30–5

UNESCO Status: Declared a World Heritage Site in 1987. You must check your bags prior to entry and also pass through a metal detector.

■ The palace is always packed with visitors, but it's impossibly crowded on national holidays.

■ Allow 2–4 hours to explore the palace. There are souvenir shops and restaurants inside.

■ You can hire automated audio guides at the Meridian Gate for Y40 and a Y100 returnable deposit.

CIXI (1835–1908)

The Empress Dowager served as de facto ruler of China from 1861 until 1908. She was a concubine at 16 and soon became Emperor Xianfeng's favorite. She gave birth to his only son to survive: the heir apparent. Ruthless and ambitious, she learned the workings of the imperial court and used every means to gain power.

PUYI (1906–1967)

Puyi, whose life was depicted in Bertolucci's classic *The Last Emperor,* took the throne at age two. The Qing dynasty's last emperor, he was forced to abdicate after the dynasty fell. During an attempted restoration in 1917, he held the throne for 12 days. Puyi was forced out of the Imperial City in 1924 by a warlord.

Dajie, Dongcheng District ☎ *010/6404–1710* 🎫 *Y20 for Drum Tower,
Y15 for Bell Tower* 🕙 *Daily 9–5:15* Ⓜ *Guloudajie.*

Forbidden City. ⇨ *See the feature earlier in this chapter.*

Jingshan Park (Coal Hill Park). This park was built around a small peak
formed from earth excavated for the Forbidden City's moats. Ming rulers ordered the hill's construction to improve the feng shui of their new
palace to the south. Climb a winding stone staircase past peach and
apple trees to Wanchun Pavilion, the park's highest point. ✉ *Jingshanqian Dajie, opposite the north gate of the Forbidden City, Xicheng and
Dongcheng districts* ☎ *010/6404–4071* 🎫 *Y2* 🕙 *Daily 6 am–10 pm.*

★ **Lama Temple.** Beijing's most visited religious site and one of the most
important functioning Buddhist temples in Beijing, this Tibetan Buddhist masterpiece has five main halls and numerous galleries hung with
finely detailed *thangkhas* (Tibetan religious scroll paintings). The entire
temple is decorated with Buddha images—all guarded by somber lamas
dressed in brown robes. Originally a palace for Prince Yongzheng, it
was transformed into a temple once he became the Qing's third emperor
in 1723. The temple flourished under Emperor Qianlong, housing some
500 resident monks. This was once the official "embassy" of Tibetan
Buddhism in Beijing, but today only about two dozen monks live in
this complex.

**DID YOU
KNOW?**

Unlike most "feudal" sites in Beijing, the Lama Temple survived the
1966–1976 Cultural Revolution unscathed on the direct orders of Premier
Zhou Enlai.

Don't miss the **The Hall of Heavenly Kings**; with statues of Maitreya,
the future Buddha, and Weitou, China's guardian of Buddhism, this hall
is worth a slow stroll. In the courtyard beyond, a pond with a bronze
mandala represents paradise. The Statues of Buddhas of the Past, Present, and Future hold court in **The Hall of Harmony**. Look on the west
wall where an exquisite silk thangkha of White Tara—the embodiment
of compassion—hangs. Images of the Medicine and Longevity Buddhas
line **The Hall of Eternal Blessing**. In **The Pavilion of Ten Thousand
Fortunes** you see the breathtaking 26-meter (85-foot) Maitreya Buddha
carved from a single sandalwood block. ■TIP➜ Combine a visit to the
Lama Temple with the Confucius Temple and the Imperial Academy, which
are a five-minute walk away, within the hutong neighborhood opposite the
main entrance. ✉ *12 Yonghegong Dajie, Beixingqiao, Dongcheng District* ☎ *010/6404–4499* 🎫 *Y25* 🕙 *Daily 9–4:30* Ⓜ *Yonghegong, Line 2.*

Fodor's Choice
★ **Tiananmen Square.** The world's largest public square, and the very heart
of modern China, Tiananmen Square owes little to grand imperial
designs and everything to Mao Zedong. At the height of the Cultural
Revolution, hundreds of thousands of Red Guards crowded the square;
in June 1989 the square was the scene of tragedy when student demonstrators were killed.

Today the square is packed with sightseers, families, and undercover
policemen. Although formidable, the square is a little bleak, with no
shade, benches, or trees. Come here at night for an eerie experience—it's
a little like being on a film set. Beijing's ancient central axis runs right

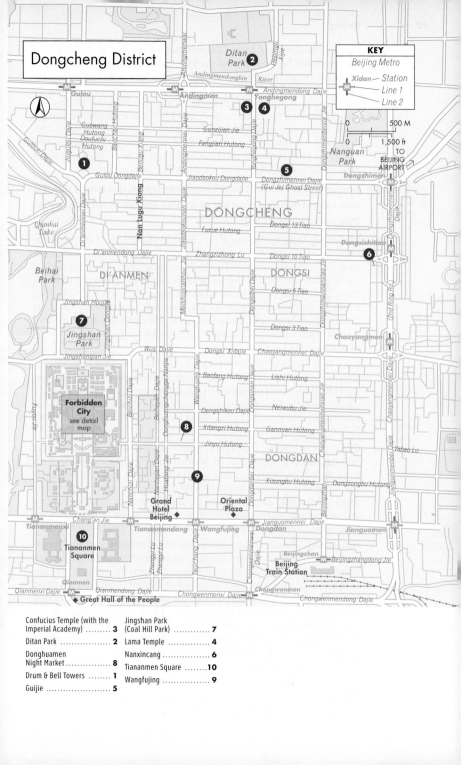

Dongcheng District

TO
BEIJING
AIRPORT

Ditan
Park ❷

Andingmendongbin

River

Andingmendong Dajie

Gulou Ⓜ
Andingmen Ⓜ
Yonghegong Ⓜ
❸
❹

Guowang
Hutong
Doufuchi
Hutong

Guozijian Jie

Fangjian Hutong

Nanguan
Park

❶

Gulou Dongdajie

Jiaodaokou Dongdajie

Dongzhimennei Dajie
(Gui Jie) Ghost Street

❺

Dongzhimen Ⓜ

DONGCHENG

Fuxue Hutong

Dongsi 13 Tiao

Qianhai
Lake

Zhangzizhong Lu

Dongsi 10 Tiao

Dongsishitiao Ⓜ
❻

Beihai
Park

DI'ANMEN

Di'anmendong Dajie

DONGSI

Dongsi 6 Tiao

Jingshan Houjie

Dongsi 3 Tiao

Chaoyangmen Ⓜ

❼

Jingshan
Park

Jingshanqian Jie

Wusi Dajie

Dongsi Xidajie

Chaoyangmennei Dajie

Baofang Hutong

Lishi Hutong

Forbidden
City
see detail
map

Dengshikou Dajie

Neiwubu Jie

❽

Xitangzi Hutong

Ganmian Hutong

Jinyu Hutong

DONGDAN

Yabao Lu

❾

Xizongbu Hutong

Dongzongbu Hutong

Grand
Hotel
Beijing ◆

Oriental
Plaza ◆

Jianguomennei Dajie

Chang'an Jie

Tiananmenxi Ⓜ
Tiananmendong Ⓜ
Wangfujing Ⓜ
Dongdan Ⓜ
Jianguomen Ⓜ

❿

Tiananmen
Square

Beijingzhan

Beijing
Train Station

Beijingzhandong Jie Ⓜ

Qianmen

Qianmenxi Dajie

Qianmendong Dajie

Chongwenmenxi Dajie

Chongwenmen Ⓜ

Chongwenmendong Dajie

◆ Great Hall of the People

through the center of Mao Zedong's mausoleum, the Forbidden City, the Drum and Bell towers, and the Olympic Green. The square is sandwiched between two grand gates: the Gate of Heavenly Peace (Tiananmen) to the north and the Front Gate (Qianmen) in the south. Along the western edge is the Great Hall of the People. The National Museum of China lies along the eastern side. The 125-foot granite obelisk you see is the Monument to the People's Heroes; it commemorates those who died for the revolutionary cause of the Chinese people. ⊠ *Bounded by Chang'an Jie to the north and Qianmen Dajie to the south, Dongcheng District* 🖾 *Free* ⊙ *24-hrs year-round* Ⓜ *Tiananmen East.*

DID YOU KNOW?

A network of tunnels lies beneath Tiananmen Square. Mao Zedong is said to have ordered them dug in the late 1960s after Sino-Soviet relations soured. They extend across Beijing.

Wangfujing. Wangfujing, one of the city's oldest and busiest shopping districts, is still lined with a handful of *laozihao*, or old brand name shops, some dating back a century. This short walking street is a pleasant place for window-shopping. Also on Wangfujing is the gleaming Oriental Plaza, with its expensive high-end shops (think Tiffany's, KENZO, Paul Smith, Burberry, Ermenegildo Zegna, and Audi), interspersed with Levi Jeans, Esprit, Starbucks, Pizza Hut, KFC, Häagen-Dazs and a modern cinema multicomplex. ⊠ *Wangfujing, Dongcheng District.*

IF YOU HAVE TIME

Ditan Park *(Temple of Earth Park).* In this 16th-century park are the square altar where emperors once made sacrifices to the earth god and the Hall of Deities. This is a lovely place for a stroll, especially if you're already near the Drum Tower or Lama Temple. ⊠ *Yonghegong Jie, just north of Second Ring Rd., Dongcheng District* ☎ *010/6421–4657* 🖾 *Y2* ⊙ *Daily 6 am–9 pm.*

Guijie *(Ghost Street).* This 1,442-meter stretch is lined with more than 100 restaurants, many open 24 hours a day, so it attracts the spill off from nightclubs. Although the restaurants here are generally just average, at night the street is crawling with diners, more likely attracted by shiny red lanterns and lights than the food. The wide range of cuisines and restaurants serve a diversity of dishes, including Sichuan, Beijing, Cantonese, Xinjiang, and much more. ⊠ *Guijie, Dongcheng District.*

Nanxincang. China's oldest existing granary, dating back to the Yongle period (1403–24), is now Beijing's newest entertainment venue. It's home to three art galleries, a teahouse, and several bars and restaurants. The structures at Nanxincang—just 10 years younger than those of the Forbidden City—were among the more than 300 granaries that existed in this area during imperial days. Have a glass of wine on the second floor of Yuefu, an audio and book shop, where you can admire the old interior, then have dinner at one of the excellent restaurants in the compound. ⊠ *Dongsishitiao, one block west of the Second Ring Road, Dongcheng District.*

A portrait of the Great Helmsman gazes down on Tiananmen Square.

| NEED A BREAK? | Crunchy deep-fried scorpions and other critters are sold at the **Donghua-men Night Market**, at the northern end of Wangfujing's wide walking boulevard. |

XICHENG DISTRICT

Xicheng District is home to an eclectic mix of a few of Beijing's favorite things: delicious food, venerable hutongs and old courtyard houses, charming lakes, and engaging nightlife. The lakes at Shichahai are fun for all ages, both day and night. Take a boat ride on the lake in the warmer months, or ice-skate here in the cold winter months when the lakes are crowded with parents taking their children out for a day of fun.

Our top experience? Taking a walk or bicycle tour of the surrounding hutongs: there is no better way to scratch the surface of this sprawling city (before it disappears!) than by exploring the hutongs lined by courtyard houses. Wander in and out of historic sites in the area, such as Prince Gong's palace, the courtyard house of famed opera legend Mei Lanfang, and the Drum and Bell towers (which fall right between Dongcheng and Xicheng). In the evening, find a restaurant or bar with a view of the lake.

GETTING HERE AND AROUND

The Line 1 subway stops include Tiananmen West, Xidan, and Fuxingmen, while Line 2 makes stops from Fuxingmen to the Drum Tower (Gulou), following Xicheng's perimeter. Xizhimen is a major terminus with access to the northwest via subway. ■ TIP→ Houhai and Beihai Park are more conveniently reached by taxi.

MAKING THE MOST OF YOUR TIME

Xicheng's must-see sites are few in number but all special. Walk around **Beihai Park** in the early afternoon. When you get tired, either retire to one of Houhai's many cafés or take a pedicab hutong tour. If you come to Beijing in the winter, **Qianhai** will be frozen and you can rent skates, runner-equipped bicycles to pedal across the ice, or, the local favorite, a chair with runners welded to the bottom and a pair of metal sticks with which to propel yourself—quite a tiring sport. Dinner along the shores of **Houhai** is a great option—stick around into the evening to enjoy the booming bar scene. Plan to spend a few hours shopping at **Xidan** on your last day in Beijing; this is great place to pick up funky, cheap gifts.

TOP ATTRACTIONS

★ **Beihai Park.** A white stupa (dome-shaped Buddhist shrine) is perched on a small island just north of the south gate. Also at the south entrance is the **Round City,** which contains a white-jade Buddha and an enormous jade bowl given to Kublai Khan. Nearby, the well-restored **Temple of Eternal Peace** houses a variety of Buddhas. Climb to the stupa from Yongan Temple. Once there, you can pay an extra Y1 to ascend the Buddha-bedecked **Shanyin Hall.**

The lake is Beijing's largest and most beautiful public waterway. On summer weekends the lake teems with paddleboats. The **Five Dragon Pavilion,** on Beihai's northwest shore, was built in 1602 by a Ming Dynasty emperor who liked to fish under the moon. ⊠ *Beihai Nan Men, Weijin Lu, Xicheng District* ☎ *010/6404–0610* 🕙 *Y10; extra fees for some sites* ⊙ *Daily 6 am–8:30 pm.*

Qianhai and Houhai. Most people come to these lakes, along with Xihai to the northwest, to stroll and enjoy the shoreside bars and restaurants. In summer you can boat or fish. In winter, sections of the frozen lakes are fenced off for skating. You can easily combine this with a trip to Beihai Park or the Bell and Drum towers. ⊠ *North of Beihai Lake, Xicheng District.*

WORTH NOTING

Museum of Antique Currency. This museum in a tiny courtyard house within the Deshengmen tower complex showcases a small but impressive selection of rare Chinese coins. Explanations are in Chinese only. Also in the courtyard are coin and curio dealers. ⊠ *Deshengmen Jianlou, Bei'erhuan Zhonglu, Xicheng District* ☎ *010/6201–8073* 🕙 *Y20* ⊙ *Tues.–Sun. 9–4.*

Prince Gong's Palace. This grand compound sits in a neighborhood once reserved for imperial relatives. Built in 1777 during the Qing Dynasty, it fell to Prince Gong—brother of Qing emperor Xianfeng and later an adviser to Empress Dowager Cixi—after the original inhabitant was executed for corruption. With nine courtyards joined by covered walkways, it was once one of Beijing's most lavish residences. The largest hall offers summertime Beijing opera and afternoon tea to guests on guided hutong tours. Some literary scholars believe this was the setting for *Dream of the Red Chamber,* one of China's best-known classical novels. ⊠ *17 Qianhai Xijie, Xicheng District* ☎ *010/8328–8149* 🕙 *Y40* ⊙ *Daily 7:30–4:30.*

Xicheng District

Ande Lu
Ande Lu

❶

Andingmenxibin River

Deshengmendong Dajie (2nd Ring Rd.)

Xihai

Deshengmenxi Dajie

Xizhimenbei Dajie

Xizhimen
Train Station

Xizhimennei Dajie

XINJIEKOU

Xinjiekoubei Dajie

❷

Houhai

Houhai Beiyan

Gulou Dajie

Guowang
Hutong
Doufuchi
Hutong

❹

Silver Ingot
Bridge

Houhai Nanyan

Tangfang Hutong

Guanyuan
Park

Xizhimennan Dajie

Naodachang Jie

Ping'antixi Dajie

Xinjiekounan Dajie

Huguosi
Hutong

Deshengmennei Dajie

Dingfu
Hutong

Liuyin Jie

❸

Qianhaibeiyan

Qianhai

Han Cang

Di'anmennei Dajie

Di'anmenxi Dajie
Di'anmendong Dajie

Fuchengmenbei Dajie

Baitasi Lu

Xisibei Dajie

Xishiku Dajie

Beihai
◆

Jingshan Houjie

Fuchengmenwai Dajie

XISI

Fangshan
Restaurant
❺

Jingshan Xijie

Jingshan
Park

Fuchengmennan Dajie

Taipingqiao Dajie

Xi'anmen Dajie

Wenjin Jie

Jingshanqian Jie

XICHENG

Wuding Hutong

Fengsheng Hutong

Xisinan Dajie

Xithuangchenggen Nanjie

Fuyou Jie

Shichahai
◆

Zhonghai

Forbidden
City

Picai Hutong

Naoshikoubei Jie

Xidanbei Dajie

Fuyou Jie

Lingjing Hutong

XIDAN

Fuxingmennei Dajie

Nanhai

KEY
Beijing Metro
Ⓜ — Station
Ⓜ — Line 1
Ⓜ — Line 2

Xinwenhua Jie

Xirongxian Hutong

Dongrongxian Hutong

Xichangan Jie

Tiananmen
Square
◆

0   500 M
0   1,500 ft

Soong Ching-ling's Former Residence. Soong Ching-ling (1893–1981) was the youngest daughter of the wealthy, American-educated bible publisher, Charles Soong. At the age of 18, disregarding her family's strong opposition, she eloped to marry the much older Sun Yat-sen. When her husband founded the Republic of China in 1911, Soong Ching-ling became a significant political figure. In 1924 she headed the Women's Department of the Nationalist Party. Then in 1949 she became the vice president of the People's Republic of China. Throughout her career she campaigned tirelessly for the emancipation of women, and she helped lay the foundations for many of the rights that modern-day Chinese women enjoy today. This former palace was her residence and workplace and now houses a small museum, which documents her life and work. ⊠ *46 Houhai Beiyan, Xicheng District* ☎ *010/6407–3653* 🚉 *Y20* ⊙ *Daily 9–5.*

SOUTHERN DISTRICTS: CHONGWEN AND XUANWU

Life in the southern part of Beijing has a completely different rhythm. The sites in this part of town are ancient reminders of the Beijing that once was—a more religious and artistically inspired Beijing, a Beijing as rich in culture and history as it was in resources and political power. This area is crowded with small shops, European architecture, opera and acrobatic theaters, and street performers and magicians. A lazy stroll through Source of Law Temple or Antiques Street (Liulichang) on a quiet afternoon is sure to remind you of the city's past.

GETTING HERE AND AROUND
The southern portion of the Line 2 subway runs across the northern fringe of these districts, making stops at Beijing Train Station, Chongwenmen, Qianmen, Hepingmen, Xuanwumen, and Changchun Jie. Line 5 stops at the Temple of Heaven and runs north–south with transfers to Line 1 at Dongdan, and transfers to Line 2 at Chongwenmen and the Lama Temple.

For destinations in the south of Chongwen and Xuanwu, it's advisable to take a taxi, as things are a bit more spread out, and it may be hard to find your way on foot.

MAKING THE MOST OF YOUR TIME
The southern districts of Beijing have some great attractions beyond the major players, like the **Temple of Heaven.**

Liulichang is renowned for paintings and Chinese art supplies; it's worth spending a few hours browsing here. The **Source of Law Temple** and the **Niujie Mosque** are laid-back, interesting temples; a trip to one makes visiting the other quite easy, as they are very close together. Visiting the reconstructed **Ming Dynasty City Wall Ruins** makes for a pleasant stroll before dinner.

The **Ruifuxiang Silk Shop** (⊠ *5 Dazhalan Dajie* ☎ *010/6303–5313*), established in 1893, has thick bolts of silk, cotton, cashmere, and wool piled high, in more colors than you'll find in a box of crayons: chartreuse, candy-pink, chocolate-brown, fresh-cut-grass-green—you name it. Clerks deftly cut yards of cloth while tailors take measurements for

Playing with ribbons in Beihai Park.

colorful *qipaos* (traditional gowns). In this corner of Beijing, life seems to continue much as it did a century ago.

TOP ATTRACTIONS

★ **Liulichang** *(Antiques Street).* This quaint old street is best known for its antiques, books, and paintings. The street has been completely restored, and a multitude of small shops, many privately owned, make it a fun place to explore, even if you're just window-shopping. Liulichang was built more than 500 years ago during the Ming Dynasty. It was the site of a large factory that made glazed tiles for the Imperial Palace. Gradually other smaller tradesmen began to cluster around and at the beginning of the Qing Dynasty, many booksellers moved there. The area became a meeting place for intellectuals and a prime shopping district for art objects, books, handicrafts, and antiques. In 1949, Liulichang still had more than 170 shops, but many were taken over by the state; the street was badly ransacked during the Cultural Revolution. Following large-scale renovation of the traditional architecture, the street reopened in 1984 under the policy that shops could only sell arts, crafts, and cultural objects. Today the street is a mixture of state-run and privately owned stores. ✉ *Liulichang, Xuanwu District.*

Ming Dynasty City Wall Ruins Park. The new Ming Dynasty City Wall Ruins Park is a renovated section of Beijing's old inner-city wall. The structure was rebuilt using original bricks that had been snatched decades earlier after the city wall had been torn down. This rebuilt section of the wall is a nicely landscaped area with paths full of Chinese walking their dogs, flying kites, practicing martial arts, and playing with their children. At the eastern end of the park is the grand Dongbianmen Watch Tower,

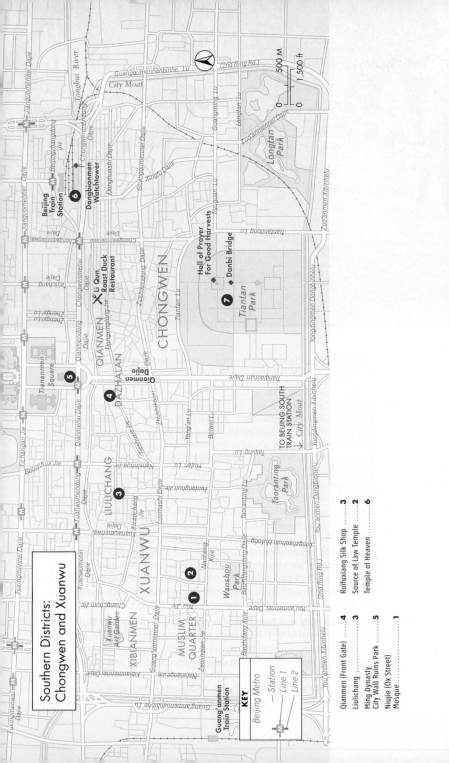

Southern Districts:
Chongwen and Xuanwu

Guangqumenhanbinhe Lu (2nd Ring Rd.)

City Moat

Tonghui River

Longtan Park

Beijing Train Station

Dongbianmen Watchtower

CHONGWEN

CHONGWEN

Li Qun Roast Duck Restaurant

QIANMEN

DAZHALAN

Tiantan Park

Hall of Prayer For Good Harvests

Danbi Bridge

7

Tiananmen Square

5

4

LIULICHANG

3

XUANWU

Taoranting Park

TO BEIJING SOUTH TRAIN STATION

City Moat

MUSLIM QUARTER

XIBIANMEN

Wanshou Park

XIBIANMEN

QIANMEN

Xuanwu Art Garden

Niu Jie

2

1

Guang'anmen Train Station

KEY

Beijing Metro

— Station
—— Line 1
—— Line 2

Qianmen (Front Gate) **4**	Ruifuxiang Silk Shop **3**
Liulichang **3**	Source of Law Temple **2**
Ming Dynasty City Wall Ruins Park **5**	Temple of Heaven **6**
Niujie (Ox Street) Mosque **1**	

0   500 M

0   1,500 ft

home to the popular Red Gate Gallery. ⊠ *Dongbianmen, Dongdajie Street Chongwen District* ▨ *Free* ⊙ *Daily 8–5:30.*

★ **Niujie (Ox Street) Mosque.** Originally built during the Liao Dynasty in 996, Nuijie is Beijing's oldest and largest mosque. It sits at the center of the Muslim quarter and mimics a Chinese temple from the outside, with its hexagonal wooden structure. When the mosque was built, only traditional Chinese architecture was allowed in the capital. An exception was made for the Arabic calligraphy that decorates many of the mosque's walls and inner sanctums. The interior arches and posts are inscribed with Koranic verse, and a special moon tower helps with determining the lunar calendar. The Spirit Wall stands opposite the main entrance and prevents ghosts from entering the mosque, this wall covered with carved murals works on the premise that ghosts can't turn sharp corners. Two dark tombs with Chinese and Arabic inscriptions are kept in one of the small courtyards. They belong to two Persian imams who came to preach at the mosque in the 13th and 14th centuries. Because Muslims must pray in the direction of Mecca, which is westward, the main prayer hall opens onto the east. At the rear of the complex is a minaret from which a muezzin calls the faithful to prayer. From this very tower, imams (the prayer leaders of a mosque) measure the beginning and end of Ramadan, Islam's month of fasting and prayer. Ramadan begins when the imam sights the new moon, which appears as a slight crescent.

The hall is open only to Muslims and can fit up to 1,000 worshippers. All visitors must wear long trousers or skirts and keep their shoulders covered. Women are not permitted to enter some areas. It's most convenient to get to the mosque by taxi. If you want to take the subway, it's a 20-minute walk from Line 2's Changchunjie station, though Line 4 will get you closer when it opens. ⊠ *88 Niu Jie, Xuanwu District* ▨ *Y10* ⊙ *Daily 6 am–8 pm.*

Fodor's Choice **Temple of Heaven.** A prime example of Chinese religious architecture, ★ this is where emperors once performed important rites. It was a site for imperial sacrifices, meant to please the gods so they would generate bumper harvests. Set in a huge, serene, mushroom-shaped park southeast of the Forbidden City, the Temple of Heaven is surrounded by splendid examples of Ming Dynasty architecture, including curved cobalt blue roofs layered with yellow and green tiles. Construction began in the early 15th century under Yongle, whom many call the "architect of Beijing." Shaped like a semicircle on the northern rim to represent heaven and square on the south for the earth, the grounds were once believed to be the meeting point of the two. The area is double the size of the Forbidden City and is still laid out to divine rule: buildings and paths are positioned to represent the right directions for heaven and earth. This means, for example, that the northern part is higher than the south.

The temple's hallmark structure is a magnificent **blue-roofed wooden tower** built in 1420. It burned to the ground in 1889 and was immediately rebuilt using Ming architectural methods (and timber imported from Oregon). The building's design is based on the calendar: four

center pillars represent the seasons, the next 12 pillars represent months, and 12 outer pillars signify the parts of a day. Together these 28 poles, which also correspond to the 28 constellations of heaven, support the structure without nails. A carved dragon swirling down from the ceiling represents the emperor.

Across the Danbi Bridge, you'll find the **Hall of Prayer for Good Harvests.** The middle section was once reserved for the Emperor of Heaven, who was the only one allowed to set foot on the eastern side, while aristocrats and high-ranking officials walked on the western strip. ■TIP➔ If you're coming by taxi, enter the park through the southern entrance (Tiantan Nanmen). This way you approach the beautiful Hall of Prayer for Good Harvests via the Danbi Bridge—the same route the emperor favored.

Directly east of this hall is a long, twisting platform, which once enclosed the animal-killing pavilion. The Long Corridor was traditionally hung with lanterns on the eve of sacrifices. Today it plays host to scores of Beijingers singing opera, playing cards and chess, and fan dancing.

Be sure to whisper into the echo wall encircling the **Imperial Vault of Heaven.** This structure allows anyone to eavesdrop. It takes a minute to get the hang of it, but with a friend on one side and you on the other it's possible to hold a conversation by speaking into the wall. Tilt your head in the direction you want your voice to travel for best results. Just inside the south gate is the **Round Altar,** a three-tiered, white-marble structure where the emperor worshipped the winter solstice; it is based around the divine number nine. Nine was regarded as a symbol of the power of the emperor, as it is the biggest single-digit odd number, and odd numbers are considered masculine and therefore more powerful.

The Hall of Abstinence, on the western edge of the grounds, this is where the emperor would retreat three days before the ritual sacrifice. To understand the significance of the harvest sacrifice at the Temple of Heaven, it is important to keep in mind that the legitimacy of a Chinese emperor's rule depended on what is known as the *tian ming*, or the mandate of heaven, essentially the emperor's relationship with the gods.

A succession of bad harvests, for example, could be interpreted as the emperor losing the favor of heaven and could be used to justify a change in emperor or even in dynasty. When the emperor came to the Temple of Heaven to pray for good harvests and to pay homage to his ancestors, there may have been a good measure of self-interest to his fervor.

The sacrifices consisted mainly of animals and fruit placed on altars surrounded by candles. Many Chinese still offer sacrifices of fruit and incense on special occasions, such as births, deaths, and weddings.

■TIP➔ We recommend buying an all-inclusive ticket. If you buy only a ticket into the park, you will need to pay an additional Y20 to get into each building.

Beijing's new subway Line 5 (purple line) makes getting to the Temple of Heaven easier than ever. Get off at the Tiantan Dongmen (Temple of Heaven East Gate) stop. The line also runs to the Lama Temple (Yonghegong), so combining the two sites in a day makes perfect sense.

MAO ZEDONG (1893–1976)

Some three decades after his passing, Mao Zedong continues to evoke radically different feelings. Was he the romantic poet-hero who helped the Chinese stand up against foreign aggression? Or was he a monster whose policies caused the deaths of tens of millions of people? Born into a relatively affluent farming family in Hunan, Mao became active in politics at a young age; he was one of the founding members of the Chinese Communist Party in 1921. When the People's Republic of China was established in 1949, Mao served as chairman. After a good start in improving the economy, he launched radical programs in the mid-1950s. The party's official assessment is that Mao was 70% correct and 30% incorrect. His critics reverse this ratio.

Automatic audio guides (Y40) are available at stalls inside all four entrances. ⊠ *Yongdingmen Dajie (South Gate), Xuanwu District* ☎ *010/6702–8866* 🎫 *All-inclusive ticket Y35; entrance to park only Y15* ⊙ *Daily 6 am–10 pm; ticket booth closes 4:30.*

WORTH NOTING

Qianmen (Front Gate). From its top looking south, you can see that the Qianmen is actually two gates: Sun-Facing Gate (Zhengyangmen) and Arrow Tower (Jian Lou), which was, until 1915, connected to Zhengyangmen by a defensive half-moon wall. The central gates of both structures opened only for the emperor's biannual ceremonial trips to the Temple of Heaven. The gate now defines the southern edge of Tiananmen Square. ⊠ *Xuanwumen Jie, Xuanwu District* Ⓜ *Qianmen.*

Source of Law Temple. This temple is also a school for monks—the Chinese Buddhist Theoretical Institute houses and trains them here. Of course, the temple functions within the boundaries of current regime policy. You can observe both elderly practitioners chanting mantras in the main prayer halls, as well as robed students kicking soccer balls in a side courtyard. Before lunch the smells of a vegetarian stir-fry tease the nose. The dining hall has simple wooden tables set with cloth-wrapped bowls and chopsticks. Dating from the 7th century but last rebuilt in 1442, the temple holds a fine collection of Ming and Qing statues, including a sleeping Buddha and an unusual grouping of copper-cast Buddhas seated on a 1,000-petal lotus. ⊠ *7 Fayuan Si Qianjie, Xuanwu District* ☎ *010/6353–4171* 🎫 *Y5* ⊙ *Daily 8:30–3:30.*

▌MUSLIM QUARTER

Recent urban renewal has wiped out much of Beijing's old Muslim Quarter, one of the oldest areas in the city dating back to the 10th century. The main survivor is the **Niujie (Ox Street) Mosque**, which was built in 996; it is often crowded with members of Beijing's Muslim community. Like other mosques in China, the Niujie Mosque looks like a traditional Buddhist temple with the addition of inscriptions in Arabic. The Tower for Observing the Moon and the main hall have restricted entry, and women can visit only certain areas. A few Muslim shops—mainly halal restaurants and butchers—remain in the neighborhood, which is now dominated by high-rise apartment buildings.

CHAOYANG DISTRICT

Chaoyang is where you'll find a lot of the action in Beijing: the nightlife in this district is positively sizzling. The bars and clubs are vibrant and full of Chinese office workers, university students, and foreigners including expats, English teachers, and embassy staff. During the day, all these people work in this area, as it's home to the CBD (Central Business District), as well as the embassies and the residences of the people who run Beijing's portion of the global economy.

GETTING HERE AND AROUND

The heart of Chaoyang District is accessible via Lines 1 and 2 on the subway, but the district is huge and the sites are broadly distributed. Taking taxis between sites is usually the easiest way to get around. The 798 Art District is especially far away from central Beijing, and so a taxi is also the best bet (about Y30 from the center of town). Buses go everywhere, but they are slow and amazingly crowded.

MAKING THE MOST OF YOUR TIME

You can spend years lost in the Chaoyang District and never get bored. There's plenty to do, but very few historical sights. Spend a morning shopping at the **Silk Alley Market** or **Panjiayuan Antiques Market** and the afternoon cooling off at **Ritan Park** or **Chaoyang Park,** the latter a large and pleasant park with a lot of activities for kids. Next, head to one of the numerous bar streets for refreshment. If you like contemporary art, browse the galleries at **798 Art District.** There are a number of nice cafés here as well. **Vincent Café & Creperie** (☎ *010/8456–4823*) serves a variety of crepes and fondues. **Café Pause** has great coffee, a modest but good wine selection, and great atmosphere.

TOP ATTRACTIONS

★ **798 Art District.** The Art District, to the northeast of Beijing, is the site of several state-owned factories, including Factory 798, which originally produced electronics. Beginning in 2002, artists and cultural organizations began to move into the area, gradually developing the old buildings into galleries, art centers, artists' studios, design companies, restaurants, and bars. There are regularly scheduled art exhibits. ✉ *Chaoyang District.*

Ancient Observatory. This squat tower of primitive stargazing equipment peeks out next to the elevated highways of the Second Ring Road. It dates to the time of Genghis Khan, who believed that his fortunes could be read in the stars. Many of the bronze devices on display were gifts from Jesuit missionaries who arrived in Beijing and shortly thereafter ensconced themselves as the Ming court's resident stargazers. To China's imperial rulers, interpreting the heavens was key to holding on to power; a ruler knew when, say, an eclipse would occur, or he could predict the best time to plant crops. Celestial phenomena like eclipses and comets were believed to portend change; if left unheeded they might cost an emperor his legitimacy—or mandate of heaven. Records of celestial

Chaoyang District

TO
BEIJING
AIRPORT

Dongzhimenwai Jie

DONGZHIMEN

Xindong Lu

Xinyunnan Lu

Liangma

River

TO DASHANZI

Nongzhaguan Beitu

National
Agriculture
Exhibition Center

Dongzhimennei Dajie

Dongzhimen

Dongzhimenwai Dajie

Dongzhimenwai Dajie

Dongsanhuanbei Lu

Dongsishitiao

Sanlitun Lu

Xindong Lu

Yaxiu (Yashow)
Market

Gongrentiyuchangbei Lu

Gongrentiyuchangbei Lu

Workers'
Gymnasium

Workers'
Stadium ❶

Dongzhimennan Dajie

Dongzhimenbei Dajie (2nd Ring Rd.)

Baijiazhuang Lu

KEY

Beijing Metro

Xidan — Station
Line 1
Line 2

Chaoyangmen

Gongren Tiyuchang
Nanlu

Nansanlitun Lu

Tuanjiehu
Park

Tuanjiehu Lu

Chaoyangmenwai Dajie

Chaoyangmennei Dajie

Chaowaishichang Jie

Fangcaodi Lu

Shenlu Jie

Guandongdianbei Jie

Chaoyang Beilu

Chaoyangmenwai Dajie

Hujialoube Jie

3rd Ring Rd.

CHAOYANG

Chaoyang Lu

Jintai Xilu

Ritan Beilu

Dongdaqiao Lu

Guandongdian Nanjie

Temple
of the Sun

Yabao Lu

Ritan
Park

Ritan Donglu

Guanghua Lu

Guanghua Lu

The Stone
Boat

Guanghua Lu

Xiushui Beijie

CENTRAL
BUSINESS
DISTRICT

Beijing
Friendship
Store

Xiushui Nanjie

Silk Alley
Market

Guomao

Jianguomenbei Dajie

Jianguomenwai Dajie

Jianguo Lu

Guomao

❸ Jianguomen

Yonganli

Guomao

Dongsanhuanzhong Lu

Panjiayuan
Antique
Market

0   500 M

0   1,500 ft

Tonghui   River

observations at or near this site go back more than 500 years, making this the longest documented astronomical viewing site in the world.

The main astronomical devices are arranged on the roof. Writhing bronze dragon sculptures adorn some of the astronomy pieces at Jianguo Tower, the main building that houses the observatory. Among the sculptures are an armillary sphere to pinpoint the position of heavenly bodies and a sextant to measure angular distances between stars, along with a celestial globe. Inside, the dusty exhibition rooms shelter ancient star maps with information dating back to the Tang Dynasty. A Ming Dynasty star map and ancient charts are also on display. Most of the ancient instruments were looted by the Allied Forces in 1900, only to be returned to China at the end of World War I. ⊠ *2 Dongbiaobei Hutong, Jianguomenwai Dajie, Chaoyang District* ☎ *010/6524–2202* 🎟 *Y10* ⊗ *Daily 9–4* Ⓜ *Jianguomen.*

WORTH NOTING

Workers' Stadium. North of Ritan Park is the Workers' Stadium complex, where many of the biggest visiting acts (including Britney Spears and Celine Dion) perform. The famous Sanlitun Bar Street is several blocks east of Workers' Stadium and runs north–south; this is the area that's known for great bars catering to foreigners, expats, and young Chinese. ⊠ *Gongti Rd, Chaoyang District* 🎟 *Varies according to event* ⊗ *Varies according to event* Ⓜ *Dongsishitiao.*

HAIDIAN DISTRICT

In the last decade or so, with the Chinese Internet and tech booms, the rise of the middle class, and, with it, university education, Haidian has become an educational and techno mecca. The major IT players are all located here (including offices of Microsoft, Siemens, NEC, and Sun).

GETTING HERE AND AROUND

Subway Line 13 stops at Wudaokou, the heart of Haidian. Line 4 stops at both the Beijing Zoo and the Old Summer Palace. Otherwise, the Summer Palace, Old Summer Palace, Fragrant Hills Park, and the Beijing Botanical Garden are all rather far away in the northwest of the city and are best reached by taxi. To save money, take the train to the Xizhimen (or Wudaokou) subway station and take a taxi from there.

MAKING THE MOST OF YOUR TIME

Because the **Summer Palace** is so large, with its lovely lakes and ancient pavilions, it makes for an entire morning of great exploring. The **Old Summer Palace** is close by, so visiting the two sites together is ideal if you've got the energy.

Fragrant Hills Park is a charming outing, but keep in mind that it takes at least an hour and a half to get there from the city center. The **Botanical Garden,** with some 2,000 types of orchids, bonsai, and peach and pear blossoms, along with the **Temple of the Reclining Buddha,** is also fun, especially for green thumbs. Plan to spend most of a day if you go to either of these sites.

If you want to shop for electronics, spend an afternoon wandering the five floors of the **Hailong Shopping Mall** (⊠ *1 Zhongguancun Dajie*).

Evenings in Wudaokou are a pleasure. After dinner, take advantage of the hopping beer gardens. A mug of Tsingtao is a great way to start a summer night off right.

A GOOD TOUR

Haidian may be Beijing's technology and university district, but there's a lot of Old Beijing left here. Before you leave your hotel, ask for a boxed lunch (or grab some food at a nearby supermarket). Jump in a cab and head for the **Summer Palace.** Saunter around the lakes and ancient pavilions, and finally settle down somewhere secluded to enjoy a picnic.

When you're done with lunch and sightseeing, hop a cab to **Hailong Shopping Mall.** Go in and explore—the five-story shopping mall has every kind of computer or electronic device you could possibly want, often at deep discounts. ■TIP→ Be careful when buying software, though, as most of it is pirated and illegal to bring back to the United States.

After you've shopped and you're ready to drop, head over to the **Wudaokou Binguan** for a selection of wonderful "snacks" that usually add up to a great dinner, and don't miss the *zhapi,* or mugs of fresh-from-the-tap beer. Taxi it on home in the wee hours.

TOP ATTRACTIONS

★ **Big Bell Temple.** This 18th-century temple shields China's biggest bell and more than 400 smaller bells and gongs from the Ming, Song, and Yuan dynasties. The Buddhist temple—originally used for rain prayers—has been restored after major damage inflicted during the Cultural Revolution. Before it opened as a museum in 1985, the buildings were used as Beijing No. 2 Food Factory. The bells here range from a giant 7 meters (23 feet) high to hand-sized chimes, many of them corroded to a pale green by time.

The giant, two-story bell, cast with the texts of more than 100 Buddhist scriptures (230,000 Chinese characters), is also said to be China's loudest. Believed to have been cast during Emperor Yongle's reign, the 46-ton relic can carry more than 15 km (10 mi) when struck forcibly. The bell rings 108 times on special occasions like Spring Festival, one strike for each of the 108 personal worries defined in Buddhism. People used to throw coins into a hole in the top of the bell for luck. The money was swept up by the monks and used to buy food. Enough money was collected in a month to buy provisions that would last for a year. ■TIP→ You can ride the subway to the temple: transfer from Dongzhimen on Line 2 to the aboveground Line 13, and go one stop north to Dazhong Si station. ⊠ *1A Beisanhuanxi Lu, Haidian District* ☎ *010/6255–0843* 🖭 *Y10* ☉ *Daily 8:30–4:30* Ⓜ *Dazhong Si.*

Fodor'sChoice **Old Summer Palace.** About the size of New York's Central Park, this
★ ruin was once a grand collection of palaces—the emperor's summer retreat from the 15th century to 1860, when it was looted and blown up by British and French soldiers. More than 90% of the original structures were Chinese-style wooden buildings, but only the European-style stone architecture (designed after Versailles by Jesuits and added during the Qing Dynasty) survived the fires. Many of the priceless relics that were looted are still on display in European museums, and China's efforts to recover them have been mostly unsuccessful. Beijing has chosen to

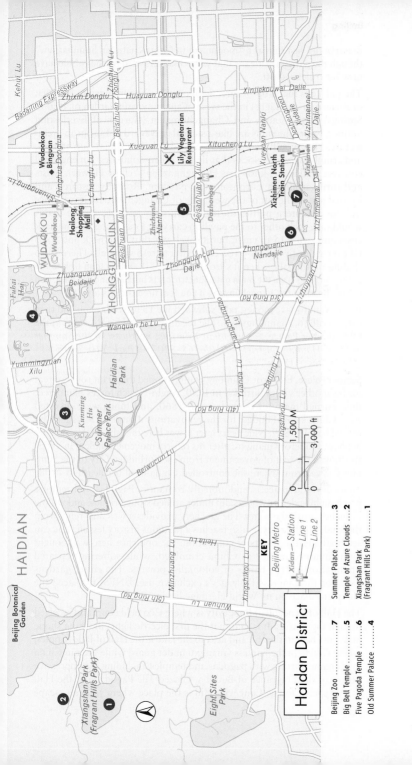

Haidan District

HAIDIAN

Beijing Botanical
Garden

Xiangshan Park
(Fragrant Hills Park)

Eight Sites
Park

Yuanmingyuan
Xilu

Fuhai
Hai

Zhuangguancun
Beidajie

ZHONGGUANCUN

WUDAOKOU

Wudaokou
Binguan

Hailong
Shopping
Mall

Lily Vegetarian
Restaurant

Xizhimen North
Train Station

Kehui Lu

Badaling Expressway

Zhixin Donglu

Huayuan Donglu

Xinjiekouwai Dajie

Shuangqing Lu

Qinghua Dongdua

Xueyuan Lu

Xitucheng Lu

Chengfu Lu

Zhichunlu

Zhichun Lu

Beisihuan Zhonglu

Beisihuan Xilu

Haidian Nanlu

Zhongguancun
Dajie

Zhongguancun
Nandajie

Dazhongsi

Beisanhuan Xilu

Deshengmen
Xidajie

Xizhimennei
Dajie

Xueyuan Nanlu

Xizhimen

Xizhimenwai Dajie

Zhichun Lu

Wanquan he Lu

(3rd Ring Rd)

Haidian
Park

Kunming
Hu

Summer
Palace Park

Belwucun Lu

Changchunqiao Lu

Yuanda Lu

Baqing Lu

(4th Ring Rd)

Xingshikou Lu

1,500 M

3,000 ft

0

0

Minzhuang Lu

Heita Lu

(5th Ring Rd)

Xingshikou Lu

Wuhuan Lu

Xiangshan Park
(Fragrant Hills Park)

KEY

Beijing Metro

Xidan — Station

Line 1

Line 2

Beijing Zoo **7**

Big Bell Temple **5**

Five Pagoda Temple **6**

Old Summer Palace **4**

Summer Palace **3**

Temple of Azure Clouds ... **2**

Xiangshan Park
(Fragrant Hills Park) **1**

preserve the vast ruin as a "monument to China's national humiliation," though the patriotic slogans that were once scrawled on the rubble have now been cleaned off.

The palace is made up of three idyllic parks: Yuanmingyuan (Garden of Perfection and Light) in the west, Wanchunyuan (Garden of 10,000 Springs) in the south, and Changchunyuan (Garden of Everlasting Spring), where the ruins are like a surreal graveyard to European architecture. Here you'll find ornately carved columns, squat lion statues, and crumbling stone blocks that lie like fallen dominoes. An engraved concrete wall maze, known as Huanghuazhen (Yellow Flower), twists and turns around a European-style pavilion. Recently restored and located just to the left of the west gate of Changchunyuan, it was once the site of lantern parties during midautumn festivals. Palace maids would race each other to the pavilion carrying lotus lanterns. The park costs an extra Y15 to enter, but it's well worth it. The park and ruins take on a ghostly beauty if you come after a fresh snowfall. There's also skating on the lake when it's frozen over. ■TIP➔ **It's a long trek to the European ruins from the main gate. Electric carts buzz around the park; hop on one heading to Changchunyuan if you feel tired. Tickets are Y5.**

If you want to save money, take subway Line 13 to Wudaokou and then catch a cab to Yuanmingyuan. The recently opened Line 4 stops at the Old Summer Palace. ✉ *Qinghuan Xilu (just northeast of the Summer Palace), Haidian District* ☎ *010/6265–8207* 🎫 *Park Y10; extra Y15 fee for sites* ☉ *Daily 7–7.*

*Fodor's*Choice **Summer Palace.** Emperor Qianlong commissioned this giant royal retreat
★ for his mother's 60th birthday in 1750. Anglo-French forces plundered, then burned many of the palaces in 1860, and funds were diverted from China's naval budget for the renovations. Empress Dowager Cixi retired here in 1889. Nine years later it was here that she imprisoned her nephew, Emperor Guangxu, after his reform movement failed. In 1903, she moved the seat of government from the Forbidden City to the Summer Palace, from where she controlled China until her death in 1908.

Nowadays the place is undoubtedly romantic. Pagodas and temples perch on hillsides; rowboats dip under arched stone bridges; and willow branches brush the water. The greenery provides a welcome relief from the loud, bustling city. It also teaches a fabulous history lesson. You can see firsthand the results of corruption: the opulence here was bought with siphoned money as China crumbled, while suffering repeated humiliations at the hands of colonialist powers. The entire gardens were for the Empress Dowager's exclusive use. UNESCO placed the Summer Palace on its World Heritage list in 1998.

The **Hall of Benevolent Longevity** is where Cixi held court and received foreign dignitaries. It is said that the first electric lights in China shone here. Just behind the hall and next to the lake is the **Hall of Jade Ripples**, where Cixi kept the hapless Guangxu under guard while she ran China in his name. Strung with pagodas and temples, including the impressive Tower of the Fragrance of Buddha, Glazed Tile Pagoda, and the Hall that Dispels Clouds, **Longevity Hill** is the place where you can escape

The marble ruins of the Old Summer Palace can be found in Changchunyuan (Garden of Everlasting Spring).

the hordes of visitors—take your time exploring the lovely northern side of the hill.

Most of this 700-acre park is underwater. **Kunming Lake** makes up around three-fourths of the complex, and is largely man-made. The excavated dirt was used to build Longevity Hill. This giant body of water extends southward for 3 km (2 mi); it's ringed by tree-lined dikes, arched stone bridges, and numerous gazebos. In winter, you can skate on the ice. The less traveled southern shore near Humpbacked Bridge is an ideal picnic spot. ■ **TIP→ Arrive like Cixi did: come to the park by boat. In summer, craft leave every hour from near the Millennium Monument in Xizhimen (on Fuxing Lu), or from near Beijing Zoo. The journey takes about an hour, and Y158 gets you onto the boat and into the Summer Palace.**

At the west end of the lake you'll find the **Marble Boat**, which doesn't actually float and was built by the Dowager Empress Cixi with money meant for the Navy. The **Long Corridor** is a wooden walkway that skirts the northern shoreline of Kunming Lake for about half a mile until it reaches the marble boat. The ceiling and wooden rafters of the Long Corridor are richly painted with thousands of scenes from legends and nature—be on the lookout for Sun Wukong (the Monkey King). Cixi's home, in the Hall of Joyful Longevity, is near the beginning of the Long Corridor. The residence is furnished and decorated as Cixi left it. Her private theater, called the Grand Theater Building, just east of the hall, was constructed for her 60th birthday and cost 700,000 taels of silver.

Subway Line 10 will get you pretty close if you take it all the way to Bagou, and then catch a taxi for Y10. Line 4 may be open by the time

Overlooking one of the three lakes at the Summer Palace.

you read this and will have a Summer Palace stop. Otherwise, you'll have to take a taxi. It's best to come early in the morning to get a head start before the busloads of visitors arrive. You'll need the better part of a day to explore the grounds. Automatic audio guides can be rented for Y40 at stalls near the ticket booth. ⊠ *Yiheyuan Lu and Kunminghu Lu, 12 km (7½ mi) northwest of downtown Beijing, Haidian District* 🕾 *010/6288–1144; for information on arrival by boat: 010/6858–9215* 📷 *Y60 summer all-inclusive, Y50 winter* ♥ *Daily 6:30–8 (ticket office closes at 6 pm).*

Xiangshan Park *(Fragrant Hills Park).* This hillside park northwest of Beijing was once an imperial retreat. From the eastern gate you can hike to the summit on a trail dotted with small temples. If you're short on time, ride a cable car to the top. ⊠ *Haidian District* 🕾 *010/6259–1155* 📷 *Y10; one-way cable car, Y60* ♥ *Daily 6–6.*

WORTH NOTING

Beijing Zoo. Though visitors usually go straight to see the giant pandas, don't miss the other interesting animals, like tigers from the northeast, yaks from Tibet, enormous sea turtles from China's seas, and red pandas from Sichuan. The zoo started out as a garden belonging to one of the sons of Shunzhi, the first emperor of the Qing Dynasty. In 1747, the Qianlong emperor had it refurbished (along with other imperial properties, including the summer palaces) and turned it into a park in honor of his mother's 60th birthday. In 1901, the Empress Dowager gave it another extensive face-lift and used it to house a collection of animals given to her as a gift by a Chinese minister who had bought them during a trip to Germany. By the 1930s, most of the animals had died and were stuffed and put on display in a museum on the grounds. ⊠ *137 Xiwai Dajie, Haidian District* ☎ *Apr.–Oct., Y15; Nov.–Mar., Y10 plus Y5 for the panda site* ⊙ *Apr.–Oct., 7:30–6; Nov.–Mar., 7:30–5.*

Five-Pagoda Temple. Hidden among trees just behind the zoo and set amid carved stones, the temple's five pagodas reveal obvious Indian influences. It was built during the Yongle years of the Ming Dynasty (1403–1424), in honor of an Indian Buddhist who came to China and presented a temple blueprint to the emperor. Elaborate carvings of curvaceous figures, floral patterns, birds, and hundreds of Buddhas decorate the pagodas. Also on the grounds is the **Beijing Art Museum of Stone Carvings**, with its collection of some 1,000 stelae and stone figures. ⊠ *24 Wuta Si, Baishiqiao, Haidian District* ☎ *010/6217–3836* ☎ *Y15* ⊙ *Daily 9–4:30.*

Temple of Azure Clouds. Once the home of a Yuan Dynasty official, the site was converted into a Buddhist temple in 1366 and enlarged during the 16th and 17th centuries by imperial eunuchs who hoped to be buried here. The temple's five main courtyards ascend a slope in **Fragrant Hills Park.** Although severely damaged during the Cultural Revolution, the complex has been beautifully restored.

The main attraction is the Indian-influenced **Vajra Throne Pagoda**. Lining its walls and five pagodas are gracefully carved stone-relief Buddhas and bodhisattvas. The pagoda once housed the remains of Nationalist China's founding father, Dr. Sun Yat-sen, who lay in state here between March and May 1925, while his mausoleum was being constructed in Nanjing. A hall in one of the temple's western courtyards houses about 500 life-size wood and gilt arhats (Buddhists who have reached Enlightenment)—each displayed in a glass case. ⊠ *Xiangshan Park, Haidian District* ☎ *010/6259–1155* ☎ *Park Y10; temple Y10* ⊙ *Daily 8–4:30, park closes at 6.*

WHERE TO EAT

Updated by
Eileen Wen
Mooney

China's economic boom has fueled a culinary revolution in Beijing, with just about every kind of food now available in the capital. Today you can eat a wide variety of regional cuisines, including unusual specialties from Yunnan, earthy Hakka cooking from southern China, Tibetan yak and *tsampa* (barley flour), numbingly spicy Sichuan cuisine, and chewy noodles from Shaanxi.

The capital also offers plenty of international cuisines, including French, German, Thai, Japanese, Brazilian, Malaysian, and Italian, among others.

You can spend as little as $5 per person for a decent meal or $100 and up on a lavish banquet. The venues are part of the fun, ranging from swanky restaurants to holes-in-the-wall and refurbished courtyard houses. Reservations are always a good idea, so book as far ahead as you can and reconfirm as soon as you arrive.

People tend to eat around 6 pm and even though the last order is usually taken around 9 pm, some places remain open until the wee morning hours. Tipping can be tricky. Though it isn't required, some of the larger, fancier restaurants will add a 15% service charge to the bill. Be aware before you go out that small and medium venues take only cash payment; more established restaurants usually accept credit cards.

Great local beers and some international brands are available everywhere in Beijing, and many Chinese restaurants now have extensive wine menus.

Use the coordinate (✣ A1) at the end of each listing to locate a site on the corresponding map.

WHAT IT COSTS IN YUAN					
	¢	$	$$	$$$	$$$$
Restaurants	under Y40	Y40–Y80	Y81–Y120	Y121–Y180	over Y180

Prices are for a main course. Note: the term "main course" may not be appropriate for some restaurants, as Chinese dishes are normally shared.

DONGCHENG DISTRICT

$$
FRENCH
✕ **Café de la Poste.** In almost every French village, town, or city there is a Café de la Poste, where people go for a cup of coffee, a beer, or a simple family meal. This haunt lives up to its name: It's a steak-lover's paradise, with such favorites as finely sliced marinated beefsteak served with lemon-herb vinaigrette and steak tartare. If the next table orders banana flambé, we promise the warm scent of its rum will soon have you smitten enough to order it yourself. ✉ *58 Yonghegong Dajie, Dongcheng District* ☎ *010/6402–7047* ▭ *No credit cards* Ⓜ *Yonghegong* ✣ *E1.*

$$$$
CANTONESE
Fodor's Choice
★
✕ **Huang Ting.** Beijing's traditional courtyard houses, facing extinction as entire neighborhoods are demolished to make way for highrises, provide the theme here. The walls are constructed from original hutong bricks taken from centuries-old courtyard houses that have been destroyed. This is arguably one of Beijing's best Cantonese restaurants, serving southern favorites such as braised shark fin with crab meat, seared abalone with seafood, and steamed scallop and bean curd in black-bean sauce. The dim sum is delicate and refined, and the deep-fried taro spring rolls and steamed pork buns are not to be missed. ✉ *The Peninsula, 8 Jinyu Hutong, Wangfujing, Dongcheng District* ☎ *010/6512–8899 Ext. 6707* ▭ *AE, DC, MC, V* Ⓜ *Dongdan* ✣ *E4.*

$$$$
INTERNATIONAL
★
✕ **Jing.** Consistently rated among the city's best, Jing serves up East–West fusion cuisine in an ultramodern setting replete with polished red wooden floors, cream-colored chairs, and gauzy curtain dividers. Signature appetizers include outstanding duck rolls, tiger prawns, and fragrant coconut soup. The fillet of barramundi and risotto with seared langoustines are standout main courses. For dessert, don't miss the warm chocolate cake with almond ice cream. There's also an excellent selection of international wines. ✉ *The Peninsula Beijing, 8 Jinyu Hutong, Wangfujing, Dongcheng District* ☎ *010/6523–0175 Ext. 6714* ▭ *AE, DC, MC, V* Ⓜ *Dongdan* ✣ *E4.*

$$
BEIJING
✕ **Lai Jin Yu Xuan.** A gem tucked inside Zhongshan Park on the west side of the Forbidden City, Lai Jin is known for its Red Mansion banquet, based on dishes from Cao Xueqin's classic 18th-century novel, *The*

CHINESE CUISINE

To help you navigate China's cuisines, we have used the following terms in our restaurant reviews.

Beijing: As the seat of government for several dynasties, Beijing cuisine has melded the culinary traditions of many cultures. Specialties include Peking duck, *ma doufu* (spicy tofu), zhajiang noodles, flash-boiled tripe, and a wide variety of snack food.

Cantonese: A diverse cuisine that roasts and fries, braises and steams. Spices are used in moderation. Dishes include steamed fish, sweet-and-sour pork, and roasted goose.

Chinese: Catchall term used for restaurants that serve cuisine from multiple regions of China.

Chinese fusion: Any Chinese cuisine with international influences.

Chiu chow: Known for its vegetarian and seafood dishes, which are mostly poached, steamed, or braised. Specialties include *popiah* (non-fried spring rolls) and fish-ball noodle soup.

Hunan: Flavors are spicy, with chili peppers, ginger, garlic, and dried salted black beans and preserved vegetables. Signature dishes are Mao's braised pork, steamed fish head with coarse chopped salted chilies, and cured pork with smoked bean curd.

Guizhou: The two most important cooking condiments that are used to prepare Guizhou's fiery hot cuisine are *zao lajiao* (pounded dried peppers brined in salt) and fermented tomatoes. The latter are used to make sour fish soup, the region's hallmark dish.

Northern Chinese (Dongbei): Staples are lamb and mutton, preserved vegetables, noodles, steamed breads, pancakes, stuffed buns, and dumplings.

Sichuan (central province): Famed for bold flavors and spiciness from chilies and numbing Sichuan peppercorns. Dishes include kong pao chicken, mapo bean curd, "dan dan" spicy noodles, twice-cooked pork, and tea-smoked duck.

Shanghainese and Jiangzhe: Cuisine characterized by rich flavors produced by braising and stewing, and the use of rice wine in cooking. Signature dishes are steamed hairy crabs and "drunken chicken."

Taiwanese: Diverse cuisine centers on seafood. Specialties include "three cups chicken" with a sauce made of soya, rice wine, and sugar; oyster omelets; cuttlefish soup; and dried tofu.

Tibetan: Cuisine reliant on foodstuffs grown at high altitudes including barley flour, yak meat, milk, butter, and cheese.

Tan Family Cuisine: Tan family cuisine originated in the home of Tan Zongjun (1846–1888), a native of Guangdong, who secured a high position in the Qing inner court in Beijing. He added other regional influences into his cooking, which resulted in this new cuisine.

Yunnan (southern province): This region's cuisine is noted for its use of vegetables, bamboo shoots, and flowers in its spicy preparations. Dishes include rice-noodle soup with chicken, pork, and fish; steamed chicken with ginseng and herbs; and cured Yunnan ham.

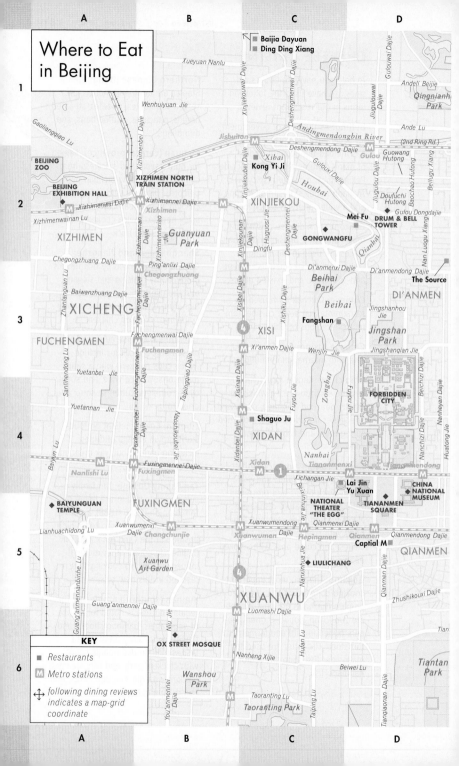

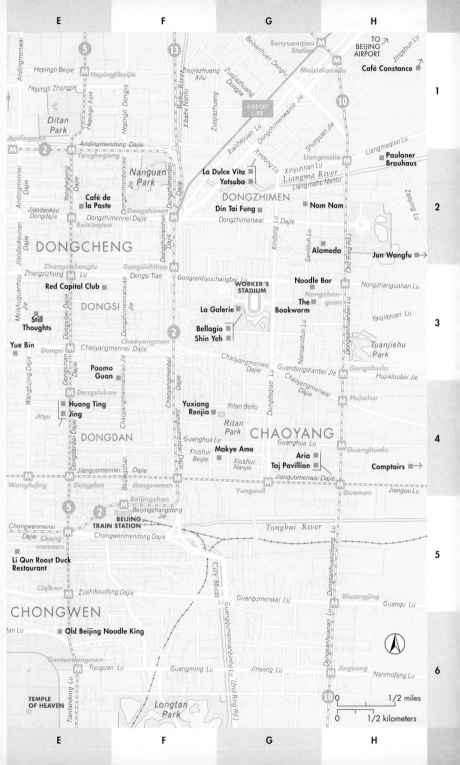

Dream of the Red Chamber. The two-level restaurant sits beside a small pond amid willow and peach trees. The two daily dishes are *qie xiang* (eggplant with nuts) and *jisi haozigan* (shredded chicken with crown-daisy chrysanthemum). After your meal, take a lazy stroll across the park to the nearby teahouse with the same name, where you can enjoy a cup of tea in the courtyard surrounded by ancient cypress and scholar trees. ⊠ *Inside Zhongshan Park, on the west side of the Forbidden City, Dongcheng District* ☎ *010/6605–6676* ▭ *No credit cards* ✛ *C4.*

¢　✕ **Paomo Guan.** The bright red-and-blue bamboo shading on the front
NORTHERN　porch of this adorable spot will immediately catch your eye. Paomo
CHINESE　Guan focuses on *paomo*—a Shaanxi trademark dish. Guests break a large piece of unleavened flat bread into little pieces and then put them in their bowl. After adding condiments, the waiter takes your bowl to the kitchen where broth—simmered with spices, including star anise, cloves, cardamom, cinnamon sticks, and bay leaves—is poured over the bread bits. ⊠ *59 Chaoyangmennei Nanxiaojie, Dongcheng District* ☎ *010/6525–4639* ▭ *No credit cards* ✛ *F3.*

$$$$　✕ **Red Capital Club.** Occupying a meticulously restored courtyard home
CHINESE　in one of Beijing's few remaining traditional neighborhoods, the Red
Fodor's Choice　Capital Club oozes nostalgia. Cultural Revolution memorabilia and
★　books dating from the Great Leap Forward era adorn every nook of the small bar, while the theme of the dining room is imperial. The fancifully written menu reads like a fairy tale, with dreamily named dishes. South of Clouds is a Yunnan dish of fish baked over bamboo—it's said to be a favorite of a former Communist marshal. Dream of the Red Chamber is a fantastic eggplant dish cooked according to a recipe in the classic novel by the same name. ⊠ *66 Dongsi Jiutiao, Dongcheng District* ☎ *010/6402–7150* ⌂ *Reservations essential* ▭ *AE, DC, MC, V* ☾ *No lunch* ✛ *E3.*

$$$$　✕ **The Source.** The Source serves a set menu of Sichuan specialties, which
SICHUAN　completely changes every two weeks. The menu includes several appe-
Fodor's Choice　tizers, both hot and mild dishes, and a few surprise concoctions from the
★　chef. On request, the kitchen will tone down the spiciness. The Source's location was once the backyard of a Qing Dynasty general regarded by the Qing court as "The Great Wall of China" for his military exploits. The grounds have been painstakingly restored; an upper level overlooks a small garden filled with pomegranate and date trees. The central yard's dining is serene and acoustically protected from the hustle and bustle outside. ⊠ *14 Banchang Hutong, Kuanjie, Dongcheng District* ☎ *010/6400–3736* ⌂ *Reservations essential* ▭ *AE, DC, MC, V* ✛ *D2.*

$　✕ **Still Thoughts.** Soft Buddhist chants hum in this clean, cheerful restau-
VEGETARIAN　rant. Even though there is no meat on the menu, carnivores may still be
★　happy here as much of the food is prepared to look and taste like meat. Try the crispy Peking "duck," or a "fish" (made of tofu skin) that even has scales carved into it. *Zaisu jinshen,* another favorite, has a filling that looks and tastes like pork. It is wrapped in tofu skin, deep-fried, and coated with a light sauce. ⊠ *18A Dafosi Dongjie, Dongcheng District* ☎ *010/6400–8941* ▭ *No credit cards* ✛ *E3.*

¢　✕ **Yue Bin.** Located on a narrow alley opposite the National Museum
BEIJING　of Art, Yue Bin's home-style cooking attracts neighborhood residents

Street food is ubiquitous in Beijing; kebabs, from China's northwest, are local favorites.

as well as hungry museumgoers. In business since 1949, it has managed to maintain its popularity throughout decades. The no-frills dining room is just big enough for half a dozen spotless tables. Don't leave without trying *suanni zhouzi*, pork elbow in a marinade of raw garlic and vinegar; the *guota doufuhe*, bite-size tofu stuffed with minced pork; or the *wusitong*, a roll of duck and vegetables. ⊠ *43 Cuihua Hutong, Dongcheng District* ☎ *010/6524–5322* ▭ *No credit cards* ✣ *E3*.

XICHENG DISTRICT

$$$$
BEIJING
★

✕ **Fangshan.** In a traditional courtyard villa on the shore of Beihai, you can get a taste of China's imperial cuisine. Established in 1925 by three royal chefs, Fangshan serves dishes once prepared for the imperial family, based on recipes gathered across China. The place is best known for its filled pastries and steamed breads—traditional snack foods developed to satisfy Empress Dowager Cixi's sweet tooth. To experience Fangshan's exquisite imperial fare, order one of the banquet-style set meals at Y500 per person. Be sure to make reservations two or three days in advance. ⊠ *Beihai Park, northwest of the Forbidden City, Xicheng District* ☎ *010/6401–1879* ♙ *Reservations essential* ▭ *AE, DC, MC, V* Ⓜ *Tiananmen West* ✣ *C3*.

$
SHANGHAINESE
AND JIANGZHE

✕ **Kong Yi Ji.** Named for the down-and-out protagonist of a short story by Lu Xun (one of China's most famous writers), this restaurant is set behind a small bamboo forest. Upon entering, the first thing you'll see is a bust of Lu Xun. The old-fashioned menu, which is bound with thread in a traditional fashion, features some of the dishes made famous in the story, such as *huixiang dou*, or aniseed-flavored broad beans. A wide selection of *huangjiu,* sweet rice wine, is served in heated silver pots; it's sipped from a special ceramic cup. ⊠ *South shore of Shichahai, Deshengmennei Dajie, Xicheng District* ☎ 010/6618–4915 ☰ *AE, MC, V* ⊹ *C2.*

$$$$
CHINESE
Fodor'sChoice
★

✕ **Mei Fu.** In a plush, restored courtyard on Houhai's south bank, Mei Fu oozes intimate elegance. The interior is filled with antique furniture and velvet curtains punctuated by pebbled hallways and waterfalls. Black-and-white photos of Mei Lanfang, China's famous opera star, who performed female roles, hang on the walls. Diners choose from set menus, starting from Y300 per person, which feature typical Jiangsu and Zhejiang cuisine, such as fried shrimp, pineapple salad, and tender leafy vegetables. A Y200 (per person) lunch is also available. ⊠ *24 Daxiangfeng Hutong, south bank of Houhai Lake, Xicheng District* ☎ *010/6612–6845* ⌲ *Reservations essential* ☰ *MC, V* ⊹ *D2.*

$
BEIJING

✕ **Shaguo Ju.** Established in 1741, Shaguo Ju serves a simple Manchu favorite—*bairou,* or white-meat pork, which first became popular 300 years ago. The first menu pages list all the dishes cooked in the *shaguo* (the Chinese term for a casserole pot). The classic *shaguo bairou* consists of strips of pork neatly lined up, concealing bok choy and glass noodles below. Shaguo Ju emerged as a result of ceremonies held by imperial officials and wealthy Manchus in the Qing Dynasty, which included sacrificial offerings of whole pigs. The meat offerings were later given away to the nightwatch guards, who shared the "gifts" with friends and relatives. Such gatherings gradually turned into a small business, and white meat became very popular. ⊠ *60 Xisi Nan Dajie, Xicheng District* ☎ *010/6602–1126* ☰ *No credit cards* Ⓜ *Xidan* ⊹ *C4.*

SOUTHERN DISTRICTS: CHONGWEN AND XUANWU

$
ECLECTIC
Fodor'sChoice
★

✕ **Capital M.** One of the few restaurants in the capital with both stunning views and a chef with versatile culinary skills. The Aussie-bred-and-trained chef, Robert Cunningham, prepares a menu that is contemporarily innovative and unique in taste. Try his subtle and complex Kashgar-inspired chicken, served with chickpeas, currants, pistachios, and infused with a mix of spices. The hearty weekend brunch should not be missed. The backdrop to this culinary experience is a bold and colorful muraled wall sandwiched between the ornate ceiling and the starkly contrasting black-and-white-tiled floors, which when combined create a vibrant and cheerful atmosphere. The imposing Arrow and Zhengyang towers at the southern end of Tiananmen Square provide romantic views. ⊠ *2 Qianmen Pedestrian Street, Chongwen District* ☎ *010/6702–2727* ⌲ *Reservations essential* ☰ *AE, DC, MC, V* ⊹ *D5.*

$$
BEIJING
Fodor'sChoice
★

✕ **Li Qun Roast Duck Restaurant.** Juicy, whole ducks roasting in a traditional oven greet you upon entering this simple courtyard house. This family-run affair, far from the crowds and commercialism of Quanjude, is Beijing's most famous Peking duck eatery. Li Qun is a choice option for those who enjoy a good treasure hunt: the restaurant is hidden deep in a hutong neighborhood. It should take about 10 minutes to walk there from Chongwenmen Xi Dajie, though you may have to stop several times and ask for directions. It's so well known by locals, however, that when they see foreigners coming down the street, they automatically point in the restaurant's direction. Sure, the restrooms and dining room are a bit shabby, but the place is charming. Ask for an English menu and feast to your heart's content! ⌧ *11 Beixiangfeng Hutong, Zhengyi Lu, Chongwen District* ☏ *010/6705–5578* ⌖ *Reservations essential* ▤ *No credit cards* Ⓜ *Chongwen* ✛ *E5.*

¢ ✕**Old Beijing Noodle King.** Close to the Temple of Heaven, this noodle

NORTHERN house serves hand-pulled noodles and traditional local dishes in a lively

CHINESE old-time atmosphere. Waiters shout across the room to announce customers arriving. Try the tasty *zhajiang* noodle accompanied by meat sauce and celery, bean sprouts, green beans, soybeans, slivers of cucumber, and red radish. ⌧ *29 Chongwenmen Dajie, Hongqiao Market, Chongwen District* ☏ *010/6705–6705* ▤ *No credit cards* ✛ *E6.*

CHAOYANG DISTRICT

$$$ ✕**Alameda.** Specializing in Brazilian fare, Alameda serves simple but

BRAZILIAN delicious dishes. The weekday Y60 lunch specials are one of the best

Fodor'sChoice deals in town. Their menu is light yet satisfying, with plenty of Latin

★ influences. Crowds seek out the *feijoada*—Brazil's national dish—a hearty black-bean stew with pork and rice, served only on Saturdays. The glass walls and ceiling make it a bright, pleasant place to dine but magnify the din of the crowded room. ⌧ *Sanlitun Beijie, by the Nali shopping complex, Chaoyang District* ☏ *010/6417–8084* ▤ *AE, MC, V* ✛ *H2.*

$ ✕**Argana.** Beijing's only Moroccan restaurant offers up authentic and

MOROCCAN mouthwatering dishes such as a slow-cooked chicken *tagine*—the heavy clay pot and cone-shaped lid keep the spices and flavor intact. The couscous is delicious after it soaks up sauces from the chicken. Open your appetite with a fresh salad and close your meal with sweet mint tea. It's a small size restaurant with a limited number of seats, so it would be wise to call ahead of time and book your table. Argana also has a decent range of affordable Spanish wines. ⌧ *55 Xingfu Cun Zhonglu G/F, Jiezuo Daxia, Chaoyang District* ☏ *010/8448–8250* ▤ *AE, MC, V* ✛ *G3.*

$$$$ ✕**Aria.** Aria's outdoor dining is secluded within neatly manicured

INTERNATIONAL bushes and roses, providing a perfectly quiet lunch spot amid Beijing's

★ frenetic downtown. Sample the fish fillet topped with crispy pork skin. The best deal at this elegant restaurant is the weekday business lunch: for just Y198 you can enjoy a soup or salad, main course, dessert, and coffee or tea. Renaissance-style paintings decorate the walls. There is a posh dining area and bar on the first floor, and more intimate dining at the top of the spiral staircase. Live jazz enlivens the evenings. ⌧ *2/F China World Hotel, 1 Jianguomenwai Dajie, Chaoyang District* ☏ *010/6505–2266 Ext. 38* ▤ *AE, MC, V* Ⓜ *Guomao* ✛ *H4.*

$ ✕**Bellagio.** Chic Bellagio is a bright, trendy-but-comfortable restaurant

TAIWANESE serving up typical Sichuan dishes with a Taiwanese twist. A delicious

★ choice is their *migao* (glutinous rice with dried mushrooms and dried shrimp, stir-fried rice noodles, and meatball soup). You can finish your meal with a Taiwan-style crushed ice and toppings of red bean, green bean, mango, strawberry, or peanut. Bellagio is open until 4 am, making it a favorite with Beijing's chic clubbing set. The smartly dressed all-female staff—clad in black and white—have identical short haircuts.

✉ *6 Gongti Xilu, Chaoyang District* ☎ *010/6551–3533* ⌕ *Reservations essential* ▭ *AE, MC, V* ✢ *G3.*

$ ✕ **The Bookworm.** We love this Beijing hotspot when we're craving a double-dose of intellectual stimulation and good food. Thousands of English-language books fill the shelves and may be borrowed for a fee or read inside. New books and magazines are also for sale. This is a popular venue for guest speakers, poetry readings, and live-music performances. The French chef offers a set three-course lunch and dinner. For a nibble rather than a full meal, sandwiches, salads, and a cheese platter are also available. ✉ *Building 4, Nan Sanlitun Lu, Chaoyang District* ☎ *010/6586–9507* ▭ *No credit cards* ✢ *G3.*

CAFÉ
★

WORD OF MOUTH

"We liked the Li Qun Roast Duck Restaurant, which is in a hutong area south of Tiananmen Square. It's busy, so get your hotel to book you a table—it's a well-known place. At Li Qun, which appeared to be popular with expats and locals, we were able to order in English. Beijing Duck is roasted, but the crispy skin is served separately, along with pancakes, sliced green onions, and a dipping sauce. By the way, I found that rice wasn't always provided as a matter of course, so you may have to ask for it—the word is *mifan*, pronounced mee-FAHN." —Neil_Oz

$$ ✕ **Café Constance.** The opening of Café Constance, a German bakery, brought excellent rye, pumpernickel, and whole-wheat breads to Beijing. The hearty "small" breakfast begins with coffee, fresh fruit, muesli, unsweetened yogurt, eggs, and bacon; the big breakfast adds several cold cuts and breads and rolls. This is a true winner if you're looking for a good breakfast, simple meal, or a good cup of java and dessert. ✉ *Lucky St. No. 27, 29 Zaoying Lu, Chaoyang District* ☎ *010/5867–0201* ▭ *AE, MC, V* ✢ *H1.*

GERMAN

$ ✕ **Comptoirs de France Bakery.** This contemporary French-managed café serves a variety of sandwiches, excellent desserts, coffees, and hot chocolates. Besides the standard Americano, cappuccino, and latte, Comptoirs has a choice of unusual hot-chocolates flavors, including banana and Rhum Vieux and orange Cointreau. In the Sichuan peppercorn–infused hot chocolate, the peppercorns float in the brew, giving it a pleasant peppery aroma. ✉ *China Central Place, Building 15, N 102, 89 Jianguo Rd. (just northeast of Xiandai Soho), Chaoyang District* ☎ *010/6530–5480* ▭ *No credit cards* ✢ *H4.*

FRENCH

$$$ ✕ **Din Tai Fung.** The arrival of Din Tai Fung—one of Taipei's most famous restaurants—was warmly welcomed by Beijing's food fanatics. The restaurant's specialty is *xiaolong bao* (juicy fillings wrapped in a light unleavened-dough skin and cooked in a bamboo steamer), which are served with slivers of tender ginger in a light black vinegar. Xiaolong bao have three different fillings: ground pork, seafood, or crabmeat. If you can, leave some room for the scrumptious tiny dumplings packed with red-bean paste. This restaurant is frequented by both Beijing's up-and-coming middle class and old Taiwan hands, who are fervently loyal to its delicate morsels. ✉ *24 Xinyuan Xili Zhongjie, Chaoyang District* ☎ *010/6462–4502* ▭ *AE, MC, V* ✢ *G2.*

SHANGHAINESE
AND JIANGZHE
Fodor's Choice
★

2

¢   ✗ **Hai Wan Ju.** Haiwan means "a bowl as deep as the sea," fitting for this
NORTHERN   eatery that specializes in crockery filled with hand-pulled noodles. The
CHINESE   interior is simple, with traditional wooden tables and benches. A *xiao er* (a
"young brother" in a white mandarin-collar shirt and black pants) greets
you with a shout, which is then echoed in a thundering chorus by the
rest of the staff. The clanking dishes and constant greetings re-create the
busy atmosphere of an old teahouse. There are two types of noodles here:
guoshui, noodles that have been rinsed and cooled; and *guotiao*, meaning "straight out of the pot," which is ideal for winter days. Vegetables,
including diced celery, radish, green beans, bean sprouts, cucumber, and
scallions, are placed on individual small dishes. Nothing tastes as good as
a hand-pulled noodle: it's doughy and chewy, a texture that can only be
achieved by strong hands repeatedly stretching the dough. ⊠ *36 Songyu
Nanlu, Chaoyang District* ☎ *010/8731–3518* ▭ *AE, MC, V* ✛ *G4*.

$ ✗ **Jun Wangfu.** Tucked inside Chaoyang Park, Jun Wangfu excels in clas-
CANTONESE   sic Cantonese fare; it's frequented by Hong Kong expats. The comprehensive menu includes steamed tofu with scallops, spinach with taro
and egg, crispy goose, roast chicken, and steamed fish with ginger and
scallion. The fresh-baked pastry filled with *durian* (a spiny tropical fruit
with a smell so notoriously strong it is often banned from being brought
aboard airplanes) is actually a mouthwatering rarity—don't be scared
off by its overpowering odor. ⊠ *19 Chaoyang Gongyuan Nanlu, east of
Chaoyang Park south gate, Chaoyang District* ☎ *010/6507–7888* ✛ *H2*.

$$ ✗ **La Dolce Vita.** The food here lives up to the restaurant's name, "the
ITALIAN   good life." A basket of warm bread is served immediately upon being
★   seated—a nice treat in a city where good bread is hard to come by.
You'll have trouble deciding between ravioli, tortellini, and oven-fired
pizza, all of which are excellent. The rice-ball appetizer, with cheese and
bits of ham inside, is also fantastic. ⊠ *8 Xindong Lu North, Chaoyang
District* ☎ *010/6468–2894* ▭ *AE, MC, V* ✛ *G2*.

$$ ✗ **La Galerie.** Choose between two outdoor dining areas: one a wooden
CANTONESE   platform facing the bustling Guanghua Road; the other well hidden in
the back, overlooking the greenery of Ritan Park. Inspired Cantonese
food and dim sum fill the menu: *changfen* (steamed rice noodles) are
rolled and cut into small pieces, then stir-fried with crunchy shrimp,
strips of lotus root, and baby bok choy, accompanied by sweet soybean,
peanut, and sesame pastes. The *xiajiao* (steamed shrimp dumplings)
envelop juicy shrimp and water chestnuts. ⊠ *South gate of Ritan Park,
Guanghua Rd., Chaoyang District* ☎ *010/8563–8698* ▭ *AE, MC, V*
Ⓜ *Jianguomen* ✛ *G3*.

$ ✗ **Makye Ame.** Prayer flags lead you to the second floor entrance of this
TIBETAN   Tibetan restaurant, where a pile of mani stones and a large prayer wheel
greet you. Long Tibetan Buddhist trumpets, lanterns, and handicrafts
decorate the walls, and the kitchen serves a range of hearty dishes that
run well beyond the staples of yak-butter tea and *tsampa* (roasted barley
flour). Try the vegetable *pakoda* (a deep-fried dough pocket filled with
vegetables), curry potatoes, or roasted lamb spareribs. Heavy wooden
tables with brass corners, soft lighting, and Tibetan textiles make this an
especially soothing choice. ⊠ *11 Xiushui Nanjie, 2nd floor, Chaoyang
District* ☎ *010/6506–9616* ▭ *MC, V* Ⓜ *Jianguomen* ✛ *G4*.

$ ✕**Nam Nam.** A sweeping staircase to the second floor, a tiny indoor
VIETNAMESE fish pond, wooden floors, and posters from old Vietnam set the scene
in this atmospheric restaurant. The light, delicious cuisine is paired
with speedy service. Try the chicken salad, beef noodle soup, or the
raw or deep-fried vegetable or meat spring rolls. The portions are on
the small side, though, so order plenty. Finish off your meal with a real
Vietnamese coffee prepared with a slow-dripping filter and accompanied by condensed milk. ⊠ *7 Sanlitun Jie, Sanlitun, Chaoyang District*
☏ *010/6468–6053* ▭ *AE, MC, V* ✛ *G2.*

$ ✕**Noodle Bar.** With a dozen seats surrounding the open kitchen, this
CANTONESE petite dining room is a giant when it comes to flavor. The stark menu
lists little more than beef brisket, tendon, and tripe, which are stewed
to chewy perfection and complemented with noodles hand-pulled right
before your eyes. For those seeking a moment of respite in Beijing's busy
Sanlitun district, this is the place for a light lunch and a quick noodle-
making show. The service is efficient and friendly. ⊠ *Courtyard 4, Gongti
Beilu, Chaoyang District* ☏ *010/6501–8882* ▭ *AE, MC, V* ✛ *G3.*

$$ ✕**Paulaner Brauhaus.** Traditional German food is dished up in heaping
GERMAN portions at this spacious, bright restaurant in the Kempinski Hotel.
Wash it all down with delicious Bavarian beer made right in the restau-
rant: try the Maibock served in genuine German steins. In summer, you
can enjoy your meal outdoors in the beer garden. ⊠ *Kempinski Hotel,
50 Liangmaqiao Lu, Chaoyang District* ☏ *010/6465–3388* ▭ *AE, MC,
V* ✛ *H2.*

$$$ ✕**Shin Yeh.** The focus here is on Taiwanese flavors and freshness. *Caipu-
TAIWANESE dan* is a scrumptious turnip omelet and *fotiaoqiang* ("Buddha jumping
Fodor's Choice over the wall") is a delicate soup with medicinal herbs and seafood. Last
★ but definitely not least, try the *mashu*, a glutinous rice cake rolled in
ground peanuts. Service is friendly and very attentive. ⊠ *6 Gongti Xilu,
Chaoyang District* ☏ *010/6552–5066* ▭ *AE, MC, V* ✛ *G3.*

$ ✕**Taj Pavilion.** Beijing's best Indian restaurant, Taj Pavilion serves up all
INDIAN the classics, including chicken tikka masala, *palak panir* (creamy spinach with cheese), and *rogan josh* (tender lamb in curry sauce). Consistently good service and an informal atmosphere make this a well-loved
neighborhood haunt. ⊠ *China World Trade Center, L-1 28 West Wing,
1 Jianguomenwai Dajie, Chaoyang District* ☏ *010/6505–5866* ▭ *AE,
MC, V* Ⓜ *Guomao* ✛ *H4.*

$ ✕**Three Guizhou Men.** The popularity of this ethnic cuisine prompted
GUIZHOU three Guizhou friends to set up shop in Beijing. There are many dishes
here to recommend, but among the best are "beef on fire" (pieces of
beef placed on a bed of chives over burning charcoal) accompanied
by ground chilies; spicy lamb with mint leaves; and *mi doufu*, a rice-
flour cake in spicy sauce. ⊠ *Jianwai SOHO, Bldg. 7, 39 Dong Sanhuan Zhonglu, Chaoyang District* ☏ *010/5869–0598* ▭ *AE, MC, V*
Ⓜ *Guomao* ✛ *G5.*

$$$$ ✕**Yotsuba.** This tiny, unassuming restaurant is arguably the best Japa-
JAPANESE nese restaurant in town. It consists of a sushi counter—manned by a
Fodor's Choice Japanese master working continuously and silently—and two small
★ tatami-style dining areas, evoking an old-time Tokyo restaurant. The
seafood is flown in from Tokyo's Tsukiji fish market. Reservations are

a must for this dinner-only Chaoyang gem. ⊠ *2 Xinyuan Xili Zhongjie, Chaoyang District* ☎ *010/6467–1837* ⌂ *Reservations essential* ▤ *AE, MC, V* ⊙ *No lunch* ⊹ *G2.*

$　✕ **Yuxiang Renjia.** There are many Sichuan restaurants in Beijing, but if

SICHUAN　you ask native Sichuan residents, Yuxiang Renjia is their top choice.

Fodor's Choice　Huge earthen vats filled with pickled vegetables, hanging bunches of

★　dried peppers and garlic, and simply dressed servers evoke the Sichuan countryside. The restaurant does an excellent job of preparing provincial classics such as *gongbao jiding* (diced chicken stir-fried with peanuts and dried peppers) and *ganbian sijidou* (green beans stir-fried with olive leaves and minced pork). Thirty different Sichuan snacks are served for lunch on weekends, all at very reasonable prices. ⊠ *5/F, Lianhe Daxia, 101 Chaowai Dajie, Chaoyang District* ☎ *010/6588–3841* ▤ *AE, MC, V* Ⓜ *Chaoyangmen* ⊹ *F4.*

HAIDIAN DISTRICT

$$$$　✕ **Baijia Dayuan.** Staff dressed in rich-hued, traditional outfits welcome

BEIJING　you at this grand courtyard house. Bowing slightly, they'll say *"Nin jixiang"* ("May you have good fortune"). The mansion's spectacular setting was once the garden of Prince Li, son of the first Qing emperor. Cao Xueqin, the author of the Chinese classic *Dream of the Red Chamber*, is said to have lived here as a boy. Featured delicacies include bird's-nest soup, braised sea cucumber, abalone, and authentic imperial snacks. On weekends, diners are treated to short, live performances of Beijing opera. ⊠ *15 Suzhou St., Haidian District* ☎ *010/6265–4186* ⌂ *Reservations essential* ▤ *MC, V* ⊹ *C1.*

$$　✕ **Ding Ding Xiang.** Hotpot restaurants are plentiful in northern China,

NORTHERN　but few do it better than Ding Ding Xiang. A variety of meats, sea-

CHINESE　food, and vegetables can be cooked in a wide selection of broths (the wild mushroom broth is a must for mycophiles). Should you be visiting Beijing in the bitter winter months, look forward to paper-thin lamb slices dipped in a bubbling pot of broth. Despite the surly service and gaudy decor, this place is perennially crowded. ⊠ *Bldg 7, Guoxing Jiayuan, Shouti Nanlu, Haidian District* ☎ *010/8835–7775* ▤ *No credit cards* ⊠ *14 Dongzhong Jie, Dongzhimenwai, Dongcheng District* ☎ *010/6417–2546* ▤ *AE, MC, V* ⊹ *C1.*

WHERE TO STAY

Updated by
Eileen Wen
Mooney

The hotel scene in Beijing today is defined by a multitude of polished palaces. You can look forward to attentive service, improved amenities—such as conference centers, health clubs, and nightclubs—and, of course, rising prices. "Western-style" comfort, rather than history and character, is the main selling point for Beijing's hotels. Gone forever is the lack of high-quality hotels that distinguished Beijing in the '70s.

If you're looking for something more intimate and historical, check out the traditional courtyard houses that have been converted into small hotels—they offer a quiet alternative to the fancier establishments.

2

There are a few things you should know before you book. Beijing's busiest seasons are spring and fall, with summer following closely behind. Special rates can be had during the low season, so make sure to ask about deals involving weekends or longer stays. If you are staying more than one night, you can often get some free perks—ask about free laundry service or free airport transfers.

The local rating system does not correspond to those of any other country. What is called a five-star hotel here might only warrant three or four elsewhere. This is especially true of the state-run hotels, which often seem to be rated higher than they deserve. And lastly, children 16 and under can normally share a room with their parents at no extra charge—although there may be a modest fee for adding an extra bed. Ask about this when making your reservation.

Use the coordinate (✛ A1) at the end of each listing to locate a site on the corresponding map.

WHAT IT COSTS IN YUAN					
	¢	$	$$	$$$	$$$$
For two people	under Y700	Y700–Y1,100	Y1,101–Y1,400	Y1,401–Y1,800	over Y1,800

Prices are for two people in a standard double room in high season, excluding the 10% to 15% service charge.

DONGCHENG DISTRICT

¢–$
Fodor's Choice
★

🏠 **Banqiao No. 4.** It may seem impossible, but Banqiao No. 4 is a well-preserved courtyard house with an unbeatable central location. You might expect this stylish lodging to be expensive, but the rates are quite reasonable. Set in an old neighborhood with many intertwined alleyways, this hotel is only a few minutes' walk from the subway station and a 20-minute bike ride from the Lama Temple, Confucian Temple, and Beihai Park. In addition to tastefully furnished rooms, Banqiao 4 offers thoughtful extras like Wi-Fi access. The hotel has two suites that are perfect for families, with a large bed and a sofa bed. There is no restaurant, but the hotel is a 10-minute walk from Gui Jie and its dozens of eateries. **Pros:** reasonable prices; large rooftop terrace. **Cons:** some bathrooms are small. ⌂ *4 Banqiao Hutong, Beixinqiao, Dongcheng District* ☎ *010/8403–0968* ⌁ *16 rooms, 2 suites* ⌂ *In-room: Wi-Fi* ⊟ *AE, DC, MC, V* ⫿⊙⫿ *BP* Ⓜ *Beixinqiao* ✛ *E3.*

$–$$
Fodor's Choice
★

🏠 **Beijing Sihe Courtyard Hotel.** This lovely courtyard hotel is tucked inside one of the city's quaint hutongs. This old house, with a centuries-old date tree, was once the home of Mei Lanfang, the legendary male opera star known for playing female roles. Even though the hotel does not have its own kitchen, food service is provided by several restaurants in the neighborhood. The VIP room is the largest and best room and is worth reserving in advance. If that is not available, ask for one of the executive rooms. All rooms are furnished with rosewood beds, antique bureaus, and modern gadgets like satellite TV. Bicycles are available for free. **Pros:** lots of privacy; homey atmosphere. **Cons:** not many rooms

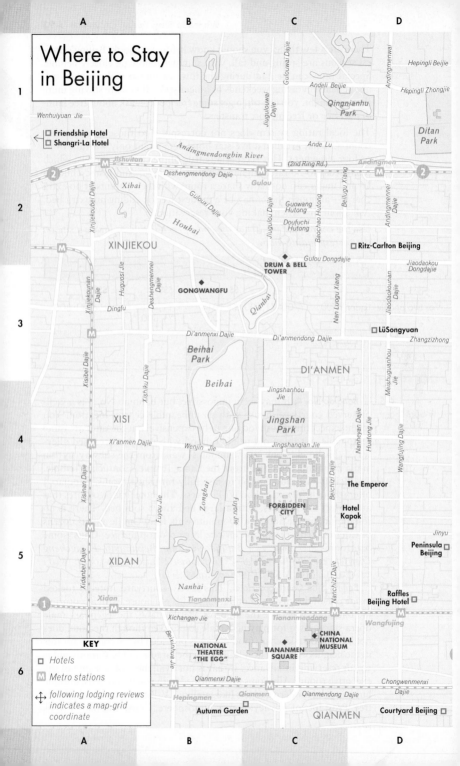

Where to Stay in Beijing

have courtyard views; no restaurant. ✉ *5 Dengcao Hutong, Dongcheng District* ☎ *010/5169–3555* ⇆ *12 rooms* ♨ *In-room: Internet* ▭ *AE, DC, MC, V* ⅩⅪ *BP* Ⓜ *Dongsi (Exit C)* ✛ *E4.*

$$$–$$$$
Fodor'sChoice
★

🎟 **The Emperor.** Located on a tree-lined avenue, The Emperor is a short walk from the Forbidden City, Tiananmen Square, and the famous shopping area, Wangfujing. It's nestled among traditional temples and houses, making it a tranquil oasis in the midst of a fast-evolving metropolis. Though fronted by a classical bIacade, the hotel features a cutting-edge interior created by a team of internationally renowned designers. Its rooms boast a modern aesthetic, and have wall-mounted flat-screen TVs, wireless Internet connections, and butler service. On the roof, the chic restaurant Shi serves fusion cuisine creatively prepared by Chinese chef John Hao, who puts a modern spin on traditional local dishes. Both the Yin bar and Shi offer breathtaking views over the Forbidden City. Also on the roof is the hotel's spa, an all-glass structure with amazing city views. **Pros:** best rooftop terrace in the city; views of the Forbidden City; unique design of rooms. **Cons:** restaurant on the expensive side. ✉ *33 Qihelou Jie, Dongcheng District* ☎ *010/6526–5566* ⊕ *www.theemperor.com.cn* ⇆ *46 rooms, 9 suites* ♨ *In-room: safe, Wi-Fi. In-hotel: restaurant, bar, spa, Wi-Fi hotspot* ▭ *AE, D, DC, MC, V* ⅩⅪ *EP* Ⓜ *Tiananmen Dong* ✛ *D4.*

$$$$
★

🎟 **Grand Hyatt Beijing.** This mammoth complex includes an upscale shopping mall, a cinema screening films in English, and a wide range of inexpensive eateries. Rooms and suites, many with floor-to-ceiling windows, are decorated with comfortable cherry-wood furnishings. The hotel's Olympic-size swimming pool is surrounded by lush vegetation, waterfalls, statues, and comfortable teak chairs and tables. Over the pool a "virtual sky" ceiling imitates different weather patterns. The gym is equipped with state-of-the-art exercise equipment. The Red Moon on the lobby level is one of the city's chicest bars and has live music every night. The hotel is within walking distance of Tiananmen Square and the Forbidden City. **Pros:** efficient service; plenty of shopping; impressive pool. **Cons:** small rooms; hard mattresses; pricey Internet. ✉ *1 Dongchang'an Jie, corner of Wangfujing, Dongcheng District* ☎ *010/8518–1234* ⊕ *www.beijing.grand.hyatt.com* ⇆ *825 rooms, 155 suites* ♨ *In-room: safe, refrigerator, Wi-Fi. In-hotel: 3 restaurants, bar, pool, gym, spa, Wi-Fi hotspot* ▭ *AE, DC, MC, V* ⅩⅪ *EP* Ⓜ *Wangfujing* ✛ *D5.*

$
Fodor'sChoice
★

🎟 **Hotel Kapok.** Just a few blocks from the east gate of the Forbidden City, this hotel is quite a find. One of a growing number of boutique hotels in Beijing, it's the work of local architect Pei Zhu, who came up with the minimalist design. Rooms are large and nicely designed, and have all the modern amenities of more expensive hotels. The entrances to some rooms face small bamboo and pebble gardens. **Pros:** cozy and comfortable rooms; near top tourist sites; close to shopping. **Cons:** no pool. ✉ *16 Donghuamen, Dongcheng District* ☎ *010/6525–9988* ⊕ *www.kapokhotelbeijing.com* ⇆ *89 rooms* ♨ *In-room: Wi-Fi. In-hotel: restaurant, Wi-Fi hotspot* ▭ *AE, D, DC, MC, V* ⅩⅪ *EP* Ⓜ *Tiananmen East* ✛ *D5.*

2

$$$$ ⊡ **Legendale.** Those fond of a classic ambience will be drawn to the
Fodor'sChoice   Legendale, surrounded by some of the city's best-preserved hutongs.
★   The hotel's palatial architecture is done up in rich blues, golds, and
burgundies, exuding an old-world elegance. The breathtaking gilded
staircase winds upward, creating a theaterlike ambience with balconies at each level and a domelike atrium drawing in an abundance
of natural light. Sparkling and ornate crystal chandeliers dangle from
the high ceilings; an antique Parisian fireplace is the centerpiece in the
opulent lobby. Camoes, with its hand-painted white and blue mural
depicting a seafaring scene from old Portugal, offers Macanese and
Portuguese cuisine. Petrus, a French restaurant, has a large wine collection, and Macao focuses on Chinese fare. **Pros:** plenty of pampering;
in a great neighborhood. **Cons:** stratopheric prices. ⊠ *90–92 Jinbao
Street, Dongcheng District* ☎ *010/8511–3388* ⊕ *www.legendalehotel.
com* ⟿ *390 rooms, 81 suites* ⚬ *In-room: safe, refrigerator, Internet. In-
hotel: 3 restaurants, pool, laundry service, Wi-Fi hotspot* ▤ *AE, DC,
MC, V* ⧦*EP* Ⓜ *Dengshikou* ✛ *E5.*

¢–$ ⊡ **LüSongyuan.** In 1980, the China Youth Travel Service set up this
delightful courtyard hotel on the site of an old Mandarin's residence.
The traditional wooden entrance is guarded by two *menshi* (stone
lions). Inside are five courtyards decorated with pavilions, rockeries,
and greenery. Rooms are basic, with large windows. There are no self-
service cooking facilities, but it has a reasonable Chinese restaurant.
It's all about location here: you're in the middle of an ancient neighborhood, within walking distance of Houhai, and just a block away from
many restaurants on Nan Luogu Xiang. **Pros:** convenient location; near
restaurants. **Cons:** cluttered courtyard; unenthusiastic service. ⊠ *22
Banchang Hutong, Kuanjie, Dongcheng District* ☎ *010/6401–1116*
⟿ *55 rooms* ⚬ *In-hotel: restaurant, bar, Internet terminal, Wi-Fi hotspot* ▤ *AE, DC, MC, V* ⧦*EP* ✛ *D3.*

$$$–$$$$ ⊡ **Peninsula Beijing.** Guests at the Peninsula Beijing enjoy an impressive
★   combination of modern facilities and traditional luxury. A waterfall cas-
cades through the spacious lobby, which is decorated with well-chosen
antiques. Rooms have teak and rosewood flooring, colorful rugs, and
gorgeous wood furnishings. There are high-tech touches like custom
bedside control panels that let you adjust lighting, temperature, and the
flat-screen TVs. Food fanatics, take note: one on-site restaurant, Jing,
serves delicious East-meets-West fusion food. Huang Ting, a second res-
taurant, provides a rustic setting for some of Beijing's tastiest dim sum.
Work off the meals in the fully equipped gym or swimming pool—or
take the 10-minute walk to the Forbidden City. If you're less ambitious,
relax in the hotel's spa. The Peninsula's arcade has designer stores,
including Chanel, Jean Paul Gaultier, and Tiffany & Co. **Pros:** near the
Forbidden City; close to sightseeing, restaurants, and shopping; rooms
are impeccable. **Cons:** lobby is too dark; hectic atmosphere. ⊠ *8 Jinyu
Hutong (Goldfish La.), Wangfujing, Dongcheng District* ☎ *010/8516–
2888* ⊕ *www.peninsula.com* ⟿ *525 rooms, 59 suites* ⚬ *In-room: safe,
refrigerator, Wi-Fi. In-hotel: 2 restaurants, room service, bar, tennis
court, pool, gym, spa, laundry service, Wi-Fi hotspot* ▤ *AE, DC, MC,
V* ⧦*EP* Ⓜ *Dongdan* ✛ *D5.*

FodorśChoice ★

Red Capital Residence

Hotel G

Hotel Kapok

2

$$$$ **Raffles Beijing Hotel.** Singaporean designer Grace Soh and her team transformed this hotel into a vivid, modern space while retaining its history. Crystal chandeliers illuminate the lobby, and the grand white staircase is enveloped in a royal-blue carpet. The atrium is adorned with 13 large cloth lanterns in olive green, plum, purple, and yellow—a welcome change from the ubiquitous red. The presidential suite is

WORD OF MOUTH

"I stayed at the Peninsula and it's in a great area—walkable to Tiananmen Square and the Forbidden City. St. Regis, Raffles and the Grand Hyatt were also nearby. However, this Peninsula was not as impressive as the Bangkok hotel." —moremiles

one of the largest, most luxurious accommodations in Beijing. For dining, choose between French and Italian restaurants. The Writer's Bar is replete with large leather armchairs and dark, polished floors. This is a great location for visitors who plan to do some sightseeing: Tiananmen Square, the Forbidden City, and Wangfujing are all nearby. **Pros:** near the Forbidden City; close to night market; wonderful French cuisine. **Cons:** restaurants very pricey; poor service. ⊠ *33 Dongchang'an Jie, off Wangfujing Dajie, Dongcheng District* ☎ *010/6526–3388* ⊕ *www. beijing.raffles.com* ⇥ *171 rooms, 24 suites* △ *In-room: refrigerator, Wi-Fi. In-hotel: 2 restaurants, room service, bar, pool, Wi-Fi hotspot* ▤ *AE, DC, MC, V* Ⓜ *Wangfujing* ⊕ *D5.*

$–$$ **Red Capital Residence.** Beijing's first boutique courtyard hotel is located
Fodor'sChoice in a carefully restored home in Dongsi Hutong. Each of the five rooms
★ is decorated with antiques and according to different themes, including the Chairman's Suite, the two Concubine's Private Courtyards, and the two Author's Suites (one inspired by Edgar Snow, an American journalist who lived in Beijing in the 1930s and 1940s, and the other by Han Suyin, a famous Japanese novelist). There is a cigar lounge where you can sit on original furnishings used by China's early revolutionary leaders, as well as a wine bar in a Cultural Revolution–era bomb shelter. Special arrangements can also be made for guests to tour Beijing at night in Madame Mao's Red Flag limousine. **Pros:** intimate feel; friendly service; plenty of atmosphere. **Cons:** small rooms; limited facilities. ⊠ *9 Dongsi Liutiao, Dongcheng District* ☎ *010/6402–7150* ⊕ *www.redcapitalclub.com.cn* ⇥ *5 rooms* △ *In-hotel: bar, laundry service* ▤ *AE, DC, MC, V* ⏏ Ⓒ*CP* ⊕ *E4.*

$$$–$$$$ **The Regent.** The Regent has an excellent location a block from the
★ Wangfujing shopping district and a short walk from the Forbidden City. The hotel has an imposing lobby decorated with beautiful carved furniture and a huge window overlooking the lobby lounge. The impressive rooms have plenty of natural light and king-size beds. Traveling executives will appreciate the large desks and wireless Internet connections. The hotel has good restaurants, including Li Jing Xuan, which offers excellent Cantonese dishes; Daccapo, which serves contemporary Italian; and Grill Bar, known for its thick and juicy steaks. **Pros:** convenient location; close to the metro. **Cons:** stained carpets; mediocre service. ⊠ *99 Jinbao Street, Dongcheng District* ☎ *010/8522–1888* ⊕ *www. regenthotels.com* ⇥ *500 rooms* △ *In-room: safe, Wi-Fi. In-hotel: 3*

restaurants, laundry service, Wi-Fi hotspot ☰ *AE, D, DC, MC, V* ⭐ *EP* Ⓜ *Dengshikou* ✛ *E5.*

$ 📷 **Zhuyuan Hotel** *(Bamboo Garden Hotel).* This charming hotel was once the residence of Kang Sheng, a sinister character responsible for "public security" during the Cultural Revolution. Kang neverthe-

less had fine taste in art and antiques, some of which are on display. The Bamboo Garden cannot compete with the high-rise crowd when it comes to amenities, but its bamboo-filled gardens make it a treasure for those looking for a true Chinese experience. It's within walking distance of the colorful Houhai, or Rear Lakes, area. The neighborhood is perfect if you want to experience the lifestyles of ordinary Beijingers. **Pros:** traditional feel; interesting neighborhood. **Cons:** courtyard is underused; pricey for what you get. ☒ *24 Xiaoshiqiao Hutong, Jiugulou Dajie, Dongcheng District* ☎ *010/5852–0088* 🛏 *40 rooms, 4 suites* ⚘ *In-hotel: restaurant, bar, bicycles (Y50/day), laundry service* ☰ *AE, DC, MC, V* Ⓜ *Gulou* ✛ *H3.*

XICHENG DISTRICT

$$$–$$$$ 📷 **Ritz-Carlton Beijing, Financial Street.** With an inspired East-I-West decor,
★   the Ritz-Carlton is ideal for travelers looking for a little extra. With ample amounts of glass and chrome, the Ritz-Carlton could be mistaken for many of the city's sleek financial buildings. The interior is stylish and contemporary, with crystal mythological animals to provide good luck. Greenfish Café offers a great contemporary buffet that offers low-calorie fare, and the chef at Cepe produces homemade pasta with phenomenal sauces and other Italian fare. The enormous health club has an indoor pool and a spa with six treatment rooms. The hotel is located in the western part of the city on the up-and-coming Financial Street, which is being touted as the city's Wall Street. **Pros:** impeccable service; luxurious atmosphere; spacious rooms. **Cons:** far from the city's attractions. ☒ *18 Beijing Financial St., Xicheng District* ☎ *010/6601–6666* ⊕ *www.ritzcarlton.com* 🛏 *253 rooms, 33 suites* ⚘ *In-room: safe, Wi-Fi. In-hotel: 3 restaurants, room service, bar, pool, gym, spa, Wi-Fi hotspot* ☰ *AE, DC, MC, V* ⭐ *EP* Ⓜ *Fuchengmen* ✛ *D2.*

CHONGWEN AND XUANWU

$ 📷 **Autumn Garden.** The Autumn Garden is a family-oriented courtyard
★   guesthouse hidden in one of the alleyways of Qianmen, an old business district. The hotel is difficult to find, but the staff will send a tricycle out to pick you up at a nearby landmark. The three wells in front of the building are the sign that you've reached your destination. The 300-year-old courtyard is well preserved, with persimmon and date trees providing shade. The location is excellent, as Tiananmen Square is only a couple of hundred steps to the east. There are many things to recommend this hotel, including the free cell phones loaned

to every guest, tea and coffee set out every evening, and free classes in cooking, mahjong, and calligraphy. If it's booked up, there's a sister hotel called Spring Garden. **Pros:** great location; plenty of atmosphere. **Cons:** neighborhood is confusing for newcomers; difficult to find. ✉ *23 Sanjing Hutong, Xuanwu District* ☎ *010/6303–4232* ⊕ *www. springgardenhotel.com* ↩ *8 rooms* ♿ *In-room: Wi-Fi. In-hotel: laundry service* ▤ *AE, DC, MC, V* ¶◯¶ *BP* Ⓜ *Qianmen* ✛ *C6.*

$ 🏨 **Courtyard Beijing.** Blending Eastern and Western styles, the Courtyard is situated in the Chongwen District. One problem is that this is a super-congested part of the city. However, there's a subway station just one block away, making quick escapes to quieter areas quite easy. You have a direct connection to the huge New World Shopping Center, one of the busiest malls in the city. **Pros:** convenient location; close to shopping and historic sites. **Cons:** in a traffic-clogged area; drab lobby. ✉ *3C Chongwenmenwai Dajie, Chongwen District* ☎ *010/6708–1188* ⊕ *www.courtyard.com/bjscy* ↩ *283 rooms, 16 suites* ♿ *In-room: safe, refrigerator, Wi-Fi. In-hotel: restaurant, pool, gym, laundry service, Wi-Fi hotspot* ▤ *AE, DC, MC, V* ¶◯¶ *EP* Ⓜ *Chongwenmen* ✛ *D6.*

CHAOYANG DISTRICT

$–$$ 🏨 **Courtyard by Northeast Beijing.** Located between the Lido Commercial
★ District and Wangjing High Tech Park, this hotel has a good location for business travelers. The spacious and stylish rooms are equipped with high-tech touches like LCD TVs and high-speed Internet access. The 24-hour fitness center features an indoor swimming pool and whirlpool bathed in natural light. Upgrade to the executive level and you can get free Continental breakfast and evening cocktails. The open-kitchen MoMo Café serves a variety of international dishes, while MoMo 2 Go offers sandwiches and salads. **Pros:** good value; ideal location for people doing business in the city's northeast. **Cons:** far from the tourist sights. ✉ *101 Jingshun Road, Chaoyang District* ☎ *010/5907–6666* ⊕ *courtyardbeijingnortheast.com* ↩ *258 rooms, 43 suites* ♿ *In-room: refrigerator, Wi-Fi. In-hotel: restaurant, bar, pool, gym* ▤ *AE, DC, MC, V* ¶◯¶ *EP* Ⓜ *None* ✛ *H1.*

$$$ 🏨 **Hotel G.** This vibrant and stylishly designed hotel is just minutes
Fodor's Choice from the major commercial district. The midcentury modern design uses
★ subtle Chinese accents to add an understated glamour. Its 110 rooms have designations that are easy to remember when booking: Good (studio), Great (deluxe studio), Greater (suite), and Greatest (deluxe suite). Rooms have a colorful and almost funky atmosphere. There's a split-level rooftop Mediterranean restaurant with a Tibetan-style tent and open fireplace, a sleek Japanese restaurant, and a glamorous lobby bar for cocktails. Hotel G claims to make the best hamburgers in town, using Argentinian premium beef with a choice of more than a dozen cheeses and sauce toppings. **Pros:** adjacent to one of the hottest nightlife areas; chic design. **Cons:** too colorful for some; can be noisy. ✉ *7 Gongti Xilu, Chaoyang District* ☎ *010/6552–3600* ⊕ *www.hotel-g.com* ↩ *110 rooms* ♿ *In-room: safe, refrigerator, Wi-Fi. In-hotel: 3 restaurants, gym* ▤ *AE, D, MC, V* ¶◯¶ *EP* Ⓜ *None* ✛ *F3.*

$$ ⊞ **Jianguo Hotel.** The Jianguo Hotel has maintained its friendly feel for years and continues to attract many diplomats, journalists, and business executives. Nearly half the rooms have balconies overlooking busy Jianguomenwai Dajie. The sunny atrium lobby is furnished with comfortable cushioned rattan sofas and chairs. Charlie's Bar, a longtime favorite, has a good lunch buffet, and Flo Justine's is one of the city's best French restaurants. The gym and pool facilities, however, are very basic. The hotel is a reasonably priced alternative for those attending conferences at the more expensive China World Hotel, just one block away. **Pros:** central location; reasonable rates. **Cons:** limited amenities; rooms are small. ⊠ *5 Jianguomenwai Dajie, Chaoyang District* ☎ *010/6500–2233* ⊕ *www.hoteljianguo.com* ⤳ *462 rooms, 54 suites* ⌂ *In-room: safe, refrigerator. In-hotel: 4 restaurants, bar, pool, laundry service, Wi-Fi hotspot* ⊟ *AE, DC, MC, V* ⫟⊙⫞ *EP* Ⓜ *Yonganli* ✛ *G5.*

$$ ⊞ **Jinglun Hotel.** The rooms of the elegantly refurbished Jinglun Hotel are decorated in a minimalist style. Just a 10-minute drive from Tiananmen Square and a few minutes from the China World Trade Center, the Jinglun is a well-appointed business and leisure hotel with competitive prices. The tiny, crowded lobby gives way to simple rooms with white-linen beds accented by dark purple, olive green, and yellow cushions. **Pros:** sleek design; unimpeded city views; great location. **Cons:** small rooms. ⊠ *3 Jianguomenwai Dajie, Chaoyang District* ☎ *010/6500–2266* ⊕ *www.jinglunhotel.com* ⤳ *642 rooms, 126 suites* ⌂ *In-room: safe, refrigerator, Wi-Fi. In-hotel: restaurant, bar, pool, gym, Wi-Fi hotspot* ⊟ *AE, DC, MC, V* ⫟⊙⫞ *BP* Ⓜ *Yonganli* ✛ *G5.*

$$ ⊞ **Kempinski Hotel.** This fashionable hotel is part of the Lufthansa Center, so you're close to shopping. It's also within walking distance of the Sanlitun neighborhood, with its dozens of bars and restaurants. There is an excellent German restaurant here, the Paulaner Brauhaus, which has its own microbrewery. A deli, with an outstanding bakery frequented by expats, is also on-site. We love Kranzler's Coffee Shop, which has an excellent Sunday brunch. A gym and swimming pool are on the 18th floor. **Pros:** excellent service; easy access to the airport. **Cons:** far from attractions. ⊠ *50 Liangmaqiao Lu, Chaoyang District* ☎ *010/6465–3388* ⊕ *www.kempinski.com* ⤳ *526 rooms, 114 suites* ⌂ *In-room: safe, Internet. In-hotel: 6 restaurants, room service, bars, pool, gym, bicycles, laundry service* ⊟ *AE, DC, MC, V* ⫟⊙⫞ *EP* Ⓜ *Liangmaqiao* ✛ *H2.*

$$
★
☾
⊞ **Kerry Centre Hotel.** This hotel is close to the city's embassy and business districts, making it an excellent choice for business travelers. It's also well situated for anyone who wants to be near ample shopping. What really distinguishes the Kerry from the rest of the pack is the amazing health club. With a full-service fitness center, a jogging track, squash and tennis courts, a spa, and, of course, a pool, it's *the* health club of choice for expats living in Beijing. Centro, the lobby bar, is arguably the most popular hotel bar in the city. The free wireless Internet throughout the lobby, including in the bar and restaurants, is an added plus. **Pros:** reasonably priced luxury; great location; first-class swimming pool and sports facilities. **Cons:** small rooms; poor food; congested area. ⊠ *1 Guang Hua Lu, Chaoyang District* ☎ *010/6561–8833*

Park Hyatt Beijing

St. Regis

⊕ *www.shangri-la.com* ↴ *487 rooms, 23 suites* ⌂ *In-room: safe, refrigerator, Internet. In-hotel: 2 restaurants, bar, tennis courts, pool, gym, Wi-Fi hotspot* ⊟ *AE, DC, MC, V* ⊺◉∣ *EP* Ⓜ *Guomao* ✛ *H5.*

$$-$$$ ⬚ **Kunlun Hotel.** Topped by a revolving restaurant, this 28-story tower is a bit over the top. The hotel was named for the Kunlun Mountains, a range between northwestern China and northern Tibet that features prominently in Chinese mythology. The lovely rooms are spacious, with nice touches like slippers and robes. The superior suites, with hardwood floors, marble baths, and chic furnishings, are the most attractive. The hotel restaurant serves great Shanghai-style food as well as reliable Thai and Japanese fare in very nicely designed venues. The Kunlun, close to Beijing's rising new diplomatic area, is popular with Chinese business travelers. This shouldn't be your top choice if sightseeing is your priority. **Pros:** imposing lobby; restful rooms. **Cons:** far from the sights. ✉ *2 Xinyuan Nanlu, Sanlitun, Chaoyang District* ☎ *010/6590–3388* ⊕ *www.hotelkunlun.com* ↴ *701 rooms, 50 suites* ⌂ *In-room: Internet. In-hotel: 6 restaurants, bar, pool, gym, Wi-Fi hotspot* ⊟ *AE, DC, MC, V* ⊺◉∣ *EP* ✛ *H2.*

$$$$ ⬚ **The Opposite House.** This boutique hotel has loftlike studios and a
★ two-level penthouse with a private rooftop terrace. The contemporary and uncluttered style and the casually dressed staff make you feel right at home. The sunny atrium lobby has two large ponds and is decorated with contemporary artworks, such as an emperor's robe made from transparent plastic. The rooms are designed to convey a sense of space and warmth by using a lot of natural wood. Everything is operated with a touch panel. **Pros:** bright common areas; spacious rooms. **Cons:** one of the city's most expensive hotels. ✉ *Bldg. 1, 11 Sanlitun Lu, Chaoyang District* ☎ *010/6417–6688* ↴ *98 studios, 1 penthouse* ⊕ *www.theoppositehouse.com* ⌂ *In-room: refrigerator, Wi-Fi. In-hotel: 3 restaurants, bars, pool* ⊟ *AE, D, DC, MC, V* ⊺◉∣ *CP* Ⓜ *None* ✛ *H3.*

$$$$ ⬚ **Park Hyatt Beijing.** This 63-story tower hotel offers plenty of pampering.
Fodor'sChoice Imagine your own spa-inspired bathroom with an oversize rain
★ showerhead, deep-soaking tub, and heated floors. The rooms themselves are large and functional, with expansive desks fitted with international power outlets and wireless access. The rooftop bar, designed to resemble a Chinese lantern, has dramatic views of the city. The restaurant features international cuisine and 360-degree views of Beijing. **Pros:** spectacular views of the city; centrally located. **Cons:** pricey. ✉ *2 Jianguomenwai Dajie, Chaoyang District* ☎ *010/8567–1234* ↴ *237 rooms, 18 suites.* ⊕ *beijing.park.hyatt.com* ⌂ *In-room: safe, refrigerator, Wi-Fi. In-hotel: restaurant, bar, pool, laundry service, Wi-Fi hotspot* ⊟ *AE, D, DC, MC, V* ⊺◉∣ *EP* Ⓜ *Guomao* ✛ *H6.*

$$$$ ⬚ **St. Regis.** Considered by many to be the best hotel in Beijing, the St.
Fodor'sChoice Regis is a favorite of business travelers and visiting dignitaries. This is
★ where Uma Thurman and Quentin Tarantino relaxed during the filming of *Kill Bill.* You won't be disappointed: the luxurious interiors combine classic Chinese elegance and modern furnishings. The Press Club Bar, with its wood paneling, overflowing bookcases, and grand piano, feels like a private club. The Japanese restaurant has tasty, moderately priced lunch specials. The Astor Grill is known for its steak and seafood dishes,

and Danielli's serves authentic Italian food. Don't miss the waffles with fresh blueberries at the incredible breakfast buffet. The St. Regis health club is arguably the most unique in Beijing: the equipment is state-of-the-art; the Jacuzzi is supplied with natural hot spring water pumped up from deep beneath the hotel; and the glass-atrium swimming pool, with plenty of natural light, is a lovely place for a relaxing swim. An added plus is that it's just a 10-minute taxi ride to the Forbidden City. If you can afford it, this is the place to stay. **Pros:** ideal location; near public transportation; lots of restaurants nearby. **Cons:** the little extras really add up here. ✉ *21 Jianguomenwai Dajie, Chaoyang District* ☎ *010/6460–6688* ⊕ *www.stregis.com/beijing* ⤳ *156 rooms, 102 suites* ♨ *In-room: refrigerator, Wi-Fi. In-hotel: 5 restaurants, bar, tennis court, pool, gym, spa, bicycles, laundry service, Wi-Fi hotspot, parking (paid)* ⊟ *AE, DC, MC, V* Ⓜ *Jianguomen* ✛ *F5.*

$$$–$$$$ 🏨 **Swissôtel.** In the large, impressive marble lobby you can enjoy jazz every Friday and Saturday evening. Rooms have high-quality, European-style furnishings in cream and light gray, plus temperature controls and coffeemakers. The hotel health club has an atrium-style swimming pool and an outdoor tennis court. The Western coffee shop has one of the best hotel buffets in Beijing. It's a short walk to the bustling Sanlitun bar area and the Nanxincang complex of restaurants, which are housed in a former Ming Dynasty granary. A subway entrance is just outside the hotel's front door. **Pros:** lovely lobby; great amenities. **Cons:** far from most sites; mediocre food. ✉ *2 Chaoyangmennei Dajie, Dongsishiqiao Flyover Junction (Second Ring Rd.), Chaoyang District* ☎ *010/6553–2288* 🖷 *010/6501–2501* ⊕ *www.swissotel-beijing.com* ⤳ *430 rooms, 50 suites* ♨ *In-room: safe, refrigerator, Internet. In-hotel: 2 restaurants, room service, bar, tennis court, pool, gym, laundry service* ⊟ *AE, DC, MC, V* Ⓜ *Dongsi Shitiao* ✛ *F3.*

$$ 🏨 **Traders Hotel.** Inside the China World Trade Center complex, this hotel is connected to a shopping mall. The hotel is a favorite of international business travelers who appreciate its central location, good service, and top-notch amenities. On top of all that, it's an excellent value. Rooms are done up in muted colors and have queen- or king-size beds. Guests have access to an excellent health club. **Pros:** moderately priced for a business hotel; near plenty of shopping. **Cons:** small lobby. ✉ *1 Jianguomenwai Dajie, Chaoyang District* ☎ *010/6505–2277* ⊕ *www.shangri-la.com* ⤳ *570 rooms, 27 suites* ♨ *In-room: safe, refrigerator, Internet. In-hotel: 2 restaurants, bar* ⊟ *AE, DC, MC, V* ⦿*EP* Ⓜ *Guomao* ✛ *H5.*

¢ 🏨 **Zhaolong International Youth Hostel.** If partaking in Beijing's lively nightlife scene is on your itinerary, consider this comfortable youth hostel in Sanlitun for your stay. The hostel offers spic-and-span rooms with two to six beds each, a reading room, a kitchen, and bicycle rentals. **Pros:** as cheap as it gets; clean and comfortable. **Cons:** just the basics. ✉ *2 Gongti Beilu, Sanlitun, Chaoyang District* ☎ *010/6597–2299 Ext. 6111* ⊕ *www.zhaolonghotel.com.cn* ⤳ *30 rooms* ♨ *In-room: no phone, no TV. In-hotel: bar, laundry facilities* ⊟ *AE, MC, V* ⦿*CP* Ⓜ *Tuanjiehu/ Nongzhanguan* ✛ *H3.*

HAIDIAN DISTRICT

$$$$ ⊞ **Eagle's Rest.** This hotel was designed by Jim Spear, a longtime resident
★   of Mutianyu Village. Take your time wandering through the peace-
ful village of Yingbeigou and exploring the surrounding lush hills.
It's here that you'll find Eagle's Rest retreat (be sure to spend time
on the patio overlooking the village and the Mutianyu Great Wall).
Even though the hotel melds perfectly with the village, it still provides
modern comforts. Enjoy the luxury of solitude and an aerie retreat
above the fray. **Pros:** rustic setting; near the Great Wall. **Cons:** need a
car to get around. ⊠ *12 Mutianyu Village, Beijing* ☎ *010/6162–6282*
⊕ *www.chinacountrysidehotels.com* ➴ *2 rooms* ⚲ *In-hotel: Wi-Fi hot-*
spot ⊟ *AE, MC, V* ⦿| *CP.*

$ ⊞ **Friendship Hotel.** The name is telling, as the hotel was built in 1954
to house foreigners, mostly Soviets, who had come to help rebuild
the nation. This is one of the largest garden-style hotels in Asia. The
architecture is traditional Chinese, and the public spaces are classic and
elegant. Rooms are large, but they are filled with somewhat outdated
furnishings. With 14 restaurants, an Olympic-size pool, and a driving
range, the hotel aims to be a one-stop destination. Its location far from
the main tourist trail means that it's better situated for people who need
to be close to the university area. **Pros:** a bit of history; good location
in northwest Beijing. **Cons:** away from the city center. ⊠ *3 Baishiqiao*
Lu, Haidian District ☎ *010/6849–8888* ⊕ *www.bjfriendshiphotel.com*
➴ *1,700 rooms, 200 suites* ⚲ *In-room: refrigerator, Internet. In-hotel:*
14 restaurants, bar, tennis courts, pool, gym ⊟ *AE, DC, MC, V* ⦿| *EP*
⊹ *A1.*

$$$ ⊞ **Shangri-La Hotel.** Set in delightful landscaped gardens, the Shangri-La
is a wonderful retreat for business travelers and those who don't mind
being far from the city center. A new tower, called the Valley Wing, was
completed in 2007. Each room is designed to have a garden or city view.
The hotel's Blu Lobster is headed by chef de cuisine Brian McKenna,
and offers exciting molecular gastronomy and innovative cuisine. **Pros:**
lovely gardens; excellent amenities. **Cons:** far from the city center. ⊠ *29*
Zizhuyuan Lu, Haidian District ☎ *010/6841–2211* ⊕ *www.shangri-la.*
com ➴ *670 rooms, 32 suites* ⚲ *In-room: safe, refrigerator, Wi-Fi. In-*
hotel: 7 restaurants, room service, pool, gym, laundry service, Wi-Fi
hotspot, parking (free) ⊟ *AE, DC, MC, V* ⦿| *EP* ⊹ *A1.*

BEIJING AIRPORT AREA

$$ ⊞ **Sino-Swiss Hotel.** This contemporary hotel overlooks a gorgeous out-
☾   door pool surrounded by trees, shrubs, and colorful umbrellas. All the
rooms and public areas are completely up to date. The restaurant Mongolian Gher offers barbecue and live entertainment inside a traditional
yurt (a tentlike structure), whereas the Swiss Chalet serves familiar Continental food on the outdoor terrace. Just five minutes from the airport,
the Sino-Swiss Hotel is convenient if you have an early-morning flight
or get stuck at the airport. **Pros:** good dining options; near the airport.
Cons: far from the downtown attractions. ⊠ *9 Xiao Tianzhu Nanlu,*
Beijing Capital Airport, Shunyi County ☎ *010/6456–5588* ⊕ *www.*

sino-swisshotel.com 🔄 *408 rooms, 35 suites* ⚙ *In-room: safe, refrigerator, Internet. In-hotel: 4 restaurants, bars, tennis courts, pool, gym, laundry service* 🖃 *AE, DC, MC, V* 🍽❘ *BP* ✢ *H1.*

ARTS AND NIGHTLIFE

Updated by
Helena Iveson

No longer Shanghai's staid sister, Beijing is reinventing herself as a party town with just a smattering of the pretensions of her southern sibling. There's now a venue for every breed of boozer, from beer-stained pub to designer cocktail lounge and everything in between. There are also more dance clubs than you can count. An emerging middle class means that you'll find most bars have a mixed crowd and aren't just swamps of expatriates, but there will be spots where one or the other set will dominate.

Bars aside, Beijing has an active, if not international-standard, stage scene. There's not much to see in English, although the opening of the Egg, properly known as the National Center for the Performing Arts, has changed that somewhat. Music and dance transcend language boundaries, and Beijing attracts some fine international composers and ballet troupes for the crowds. For a fun night on the town that you can enjoy in no other place in the world, Beijing opera, acrobatics, and kung fu performances remain the best bets.

THE ARTS

The arts in China took a long time to recover from the Cultural Revolution (1966–76), and political works are still generally avoided. Film and theater reflect an interesting mix of modern and avant-garde Chinese and Western influences. On any given night in Beijing, you can see a drama by the revered playwright Lao She, a satire by a contemporary Taiwanese playwright, or a stage version of *Animal Farm*.

As most of the stage is inaccessible to non-Chinese speakers, visitors to Beijing are more likely to hunt out the big visual spectacles, such as Beijing opera or kung fu displays. These long-running shows are tailored for travelers: your hotel will be able to recommend performances and venues and will likely be able to help you book tickets.

ACROBATICS AND KUNG FU

Chaoyang Theater. This space is the queen bee of acrobatics venues, especially designed to unleash oohs and ahhs. Spectacular individual and team acrobatic displays involving bicycles, seesaws, catapults, swings, and barrels are performed here nightly. It's touristy but fun. ✉ *36 Dongsanhuan Beilu, Chaoyang District* ☎ *010/6507–2421* Ⓜ *Hujialou.*

Fodor'sChoice
★

The Red Theatre. If it's Vegas-style stage antics you're after, the *Legend of Kung Fu* show is what you want. Extravagant martial arts—performed by dancers, not martial artists—are complemented by neon, fog, and heavy-handed sound effects. Shows are garish but also sometimes glorious. ✉ *44 Xingfu Dajie, Chongwen District* ☎ *010/6710–3671* ⊕ *www.redtheatre.cn* Ⓜ *Tiantan Dong Men.*

Tianqiao Acrobatic Theater. The Beijing Acrobatics Troupe of China is famous for weird, wonderful shows. Content includes a flashy show of offbeat contortions and tricks, with a lot of high-wire action. Shows are at 7:15 every night. ⊠ *30 Beiwei Lu, Xuanwu District* ☏ *010/8315–6300.*

ART GALLERIES

Artist Village Gallery. If you'd like a real change of pace from the city art scene, hire a driver or join a tour to visit the Artist Village in the eastern suburbs of Beijing. More than 500 artists live and work in studio spaces, peasant homes, and old buildings in and around the central village of Songzhuang. Though a trip out to the Artist Village can take a chunk out of your day, it's worth it. The countryside is a stark contrast to the city, and the art is of excellent quality. The gallery itself displays local works in a modern, well-appointed building. Visits are by appointment only, so talk with your hotel concierge before booking a car, or book online. ⊠ *1 Chunbei, Ren Zhuang, Tongxian Songzhuang* ☏ *139/0124–4283 or 010/6959–8343* ⊕ *www.artistvillagegallery.com.*

The CourtYard Gallery Lounge. Although the space here is minuscule—it's in the basement of the CourtYard Restaurant—this gallery still manages to attract some of the most sought-after names in contemporary Chinese art, such as Wang Qingsong, Zhang Dali, and the Gao Brothers. Plus you can have a well-made drink as you peruse the work. ⊠ *95 Donghuamen Dajie, Dongcheng District* ☏ *010/6526–8882* ⊕ *www. courtyard-gallery.com* Ⓜ *Tiananmen East.*

Red Gate Gallery. This gallery, one of the first to open in Beijing, displays and sells contemporary Chinese paintings and sculpture in the extraordinary space of the old Dongbianmen Watchtower, a centuries-old landmark. The venue is worth a visit even if you're not interested in the art. Be aware that the subway stop listed here is about a 25-minute walk from the gallery. ⊠ *Dongbianmen Watchtower, Chongwenmen Dongjie, Chongwen District* ☏ *010/6525–1005* ⊕ *www.redgategallery. com* Ⓜ *Jianguomen.*

BEIJING OPERA

★ **Chang'an Grand Theater** *(Chang'an Da Xiyuan).* At this contemporary theater, as at a cabaret, you sit at tables and can eat and drink while watching lively, colorful performances of Beijing opera. There's also a small museum where you can see costumes and masks from the past. ■TIP➔ **A great perk. English subtitles appear above the stage.** ⊠ *7 Jianguomennei Dajie, Dongcheng District* ☏ *010/6510–1309.*

Huguang Guildhall *(Huguang Huiguan).* The city's oldest Beijing opera theater, the Guildhall, has staged performances since 1807. The hall has been restored to display its original architecture and appearance, and it's one of the most atmospheric places to take in an opera. Even if you don't want to see a whole performance, the museum and gift shop are worth a browse. ⊠ *3 Hufangqiao, Xuanwu District* ☏ *010/6351–8284* ⊕ *www.beijinghuguang.com.*

Lao She Teahouse *(Lao She Chaguan).* This wooden teahouse is named after Lao She, a playwright and novelist who was terribly mistreated during the Cultural Revolution and, according to official records, killed

Fringe Art: The Dashanzi 798 Art District

If you are keen to see what the city's art scene has to offer beyond calligraphy, check out the **Dashanzi 798 Art District**. Just as the city is coming of age in the international, political, and economic arenas, so too are Chinese artists. Exploration of social taboos, the use of digital media, and clever installations are juxtaposed against more orthodox forms of canvas paintings and photography. Some efforts may seem like trite knockoffs of American pop art, and Mao references run rampant, but keep in mind this level of expression is still evolving for the public arena. Complete freedom of expression is not tolerated, and governmental closings, though rare, are not unheard of.

Built in the 1950s, the factory was a major industrial project designed by East German architects backed by Soviet aid. The factory's decline started in the 1980s, just as Beijing's contemporary art scene began to emerge. The massive relocation of pollutant factories outside the city in preparation for the 2008 Summer Olympic Games further accelerated the decline of the area's manufacturing roots and allowed for the incubation of modern art. The recent government declaration of Dashanzi as a protected arts district has paved the way for a resurgence of inventive local galleries, as well as design studios, restaurants, cafés, and bars. Many of the original artists have

moved on to cheaper studios in places such as Caochangdi, a small area outside the Fifth Ring Road that the *New York Times* dubbed "a new frontier for Chinese art." To get here, ask your hotel concierge to explain to a taxi driver, as it can be difficult to find.

The Dashanzi compound is more accessible, however, and is immensely walkable; keep in mind this is solely a pedestrian affair unless you arrive by private car. Cabs are not allowed to enter the compound so you'll be required to disembark at any of the entrance gates. Though it's open on weekdays (except Monday), most people visit on weekends, when throngs of locals and foreigners congregate to see what's on display.

To get a feel for what sells abroad, drop by internationally owned galleries such as 798 Photo Gallery or the Ullens Center for Contemporary Art. These established galleries are perennially popular. Also, check out Time-Zone 8 Book Shop, an avant-garde bookshop in the heart of Dashanzi.

UCCA (☎ *010/ 6438–6675* ⊕ *www. ucca.org.cn*). **Time-Zone 8 Book Shop** (☎ *010/8456–0336*). **798 Photo Gallery** (☎ *010/6438–1784* ⊕ *www.798photogallery.cn*). ✉ *4 Jiuxianqiao Rd., Dashanzi, Chaoyang District* ☎ *010/6438–4862 or 010/6437–6248* ⊕ *www.798space. com*.

himself in 1966. Now officially rehabilitated, his works are staged here every night. You can order a wide range of traditional snacks to munch on during the performance. ✉ *3 Qianmenxi Dajie, 3rd floor, Xuanwu District* ☎ *010/6303–6830* ⊕ *www.laosheteahouse.com*.

Fodor'sChoice
★ **Liyuan Theater** *(Liyuan Juchang)*. Though it's unashamedly touristy, it's our top pick. You can watch performers put on makeup before the show (come early) and then graze on snacks and sip tea while watching

English-subtitled shows. Glossy brochures complement the crooning. ⊠ *Qianmen Hotel, 175 Yongan Lu, Xuanwu District* ☎ *010/6301–6688 Ext. 8860* ⊕ *www.qianmenhotel.com.*

Tianqiao Happy Teahouse *(Tianqiao Le Chaguan).* The spirit of old Beijing lingers in this traditional theater that hosts Beijing operas as well as acrobatics, jugglers, illusionists, and contortionists. ⊠ *113 Tianqiao Shichang, Xuanwu District* ☎ *010/6303–9013.*

MUSIC

Beijing Concert Hall. Beijing's main venue for Chinese and Western classical-music concerts also hosts folk dancing and singing, and many celebratory events throughout the year. The 1,000-seat venue is the home of the China National Symphony Orchestra. ⊠ *1 Bei Xinhua Jie, Xicheng District* ☎ *010/6605–7006.*

Fodor'sChoice ★ **Forbidden City Concert Hall.** With a seating capacity of 1,400, this is one of Beijing's largest concert halls. It is also one of the most well appointed, with plush seating and top-notch acoustics. Despite the modern building, you'll walk through ancient courtyards to get to the hall—highly romantic. ⊠ *In Zhongshan Park, Xichangan Jie, on the west side of Tiananmen Square, Xicheng District* ☎ *010/6559–8285* Ⓜ *Tiananmen West.*

MAO Live House. This is the place to come for a glimpse into Beijing's cutting-edge music scene. The seedy little space is managed by a Japanese music label that prides itself on seeking out interesting new bands. The sound system is excellent and so are the prices of drinks. ⊠ *111 Gulou Dongdajie, Dongcheng District* ☎ *010/6402–5080* ⊕ *www.maolive.com* Ⓜ *Beixin Qiao.*

THEATER

Beijing Exhibition Theater. Chinese plays, Western and Chinese operas, and ballet performances are staged in this Soviet-style building that's part of the exhibition center complex. Talk about a wide range of shows: in 2010 the Michael Jackson musical *Thriller* was staged, followed closely by some traditional folk art performances. ⊠ *135 Xizhimenwai Dajie, Xicheng District* ☎ *010/6835–4455.*

ᗱ **China National Puppet Theater.** Shadow and hand-puppet shows convey traditional stories—it's lively entertainment for children and adults alike. This venue also attracts overseas performers, including the Moscow Puppet Theater. ⊠ *1 Anhuaxili, Chaoyang District* ☎ *010/6425–4847.*

Fodor'sChoice ★ **National Centre for Performing Arts.** Architecturally, the giant silver dome of this performing-arts complex is stunning, and its interior holds a state-of-the-art opera house, a music hall, and a theater. The "Egg" offers a world-class stage for national and international performers. If you don't wish to see a show, you can tour the inside of the building by paying for an entrance ticket. ⊠ *2 Xi Chang'an Jie, Xicheng District* ☎ *010/6655–0000* ⊕ *www.chncpa.org* Ⓜ *Tiananmen West.*

NIGHTLIFE

Beijing has spent the last decade shaking off its grim Communist image and putting the neon into its nightlife. There is a plethora of cocktail lounges, sports pubs, dance spots, beer halls, and strip bars. The city is changing at a fever pitch, which means that many bars and even bar streets are short-lived, as construction companies aggressively bulldoze the old to make way for swanky new developments. Many establishments are knocked together, seemingly overnight, and are of dubious quality.

Sanlitun—the heart of Beijing's nightlife—has spread its party presence around Gongti. Sanlitun Jiuba Jie, or "Bar Street," offers mainly crass live-music pubs; it's quite popular with locals. On Gongti West Gate, a stream of pumping dance clubs have attracted some big-name DJs—Tiesto, Felix Da Housecat, and Paul Oakenfold, among others. The city's main gay club, Destination, is also here.

Houhai, once a quiet lakeside neighborhood home to Beijing's *laobaixing* (ordinary folk), has exploded into a bumping bar scene. This is a great place to come for a drink at dusk: park yourself on an outdoor seat and enjoy. There are a few hidden gems here, but most of the bars are bland and expensive, with disappointingly weak drinks. Stick to the bottled beer to get your money's worth. The hutong, or mazelike neighborhoods, around the lake also hide some cute courtyard bars.

OFF THE BEATEN PATH

There are a couple of smaller pockets with notable watering holes, such as Chaoyang West Gate, which has a predominately expat feel; Dashanzi 798, an artsy warehouse area with wine bars; and Wudaokou, a student district in Haidian with cheap drinks aplenty.

BARS

DONGCHENG AND XICHENG DISTRICTS (INCLUDING HOUHAI)

Fodor'sChoice
★ **Amilal.** If you have the patience to track this cozy courtyard bar down a tiny alley, you'll be rewarded with one of the city's hidden gems. Grab a seat at one of the rough wooden tables, listen to the low-key live music that's often playing, and enjoy the laid-back hutong vibe that's so unique to Beijing. ✉ *48 Shoubi Hutong, off Gulou Dongdajie, Dongcheng District* ☎ *No phone.*

★ **Drum & Bell.** This bar has a perfect location—right between the Drum and Bell towers. The terrace is a comfy perch for a summer afternoon drink, where you scan the surrounding hutong rooftops. Don't get too plastered, though, because the staircase down is very steep. On the ground floor there are jumbles of scruffy sofas tossed with Cultural Revolution memorabilia. ✉ *41 Zhonglouwan Hutong, Dongcheng District* ☎ *010/8403–3600* Ⓜ *Gulou.*

★ **East Shore Live Jazz Café.** The closest thing Beijing has to New Orleans is this bar. Expect cigar smoke, velvet drapes, sepia photographs of jazz greats, and plenty of vintage instruments on display. The owner, local jazz legend Liu Yuan, says he wants to use the bar to promote home-grown jazz talents. On top of the live swing and jazz, the bar boasts the best views of Houhai, either through the floor-to-ceiling windows (complete with telescope) in the bar, or from the small, sparsely furnished rooftop. ■ TIP→ There are no guardrails on the roof, so drink and step with extreme care. ⊠ *Qianhai Nanyan Lu, 2nd fl., next to the Post Office, Xicheng District* ☏ *010/8403–2131.*

Fodor's Choice
★ **No Name Bar.** The first bar to open in Houhai is still around, even though its neighbors have already been torn down. It's very relaxed: many expats still list No Name as their favorite bar in the city. The service is refreshingly low-key—a nice change from the sycophantic staff at neighboring venues—and it's all tumbledown elegance with rattan and potted plants. Locals refer to it by the owner's name: Bai Feng. Anyone from tourists to old China hands can be found here. ⊠ *3 Qianhai East Bank, Xicheng District* ☏ *010/6401–8541.*

★ **Yugong Yishan.** This Beijing institution, in its second location, is a chilled-out bar run by two local music fans. It plays host to a range of live bands playing everything from blues to jazz to Afro-Caribbean beats, and attracts an equally diverse crowd. It occasionally charges an entrance fee, depending on the entertainment. Don't bother with the cocktails—instead, nod your head along to the music while sipping a good old Tsingtao beer. ⊠ *3–2 Zhangzizhong Lu, Dongcheng District* ☏ *010/8402–8477* ⊕ *www.yugongyishan.com* Ⓜ *Zhang Zizhong Lu.*

CHAOYANG DISTRICT

The Den. This old-school dive's attraction is sports on wide-screen TVs. The owner runs the city's amateur rugby club, so you'll find players and their supporters drinking rowdily. Open 24 hours a day, it's guaranteed to be buzzing every night, especially during happy hour, when you can grab half-price drinks and pizza until 10 pm. ⊠ *4 Gongti Donglu, next to the City Hotel, Chaoyang District* ☏ *010/6592–6290* Ⓜ *Tuanjie Hu.*

Fodor's Choice
★ **D.Lounge.** Raising the bar for bars in Beijing, this New York–style lounge is swank, spacious, and has an innovative drink list. At the moment, it's the place to rub elbows with the city's *it* crowd, and occasionally the doormen restrict entry to the more dapperly dressed. It's a bit tricky to find: walk behind Salsa Caribe and head south. ⊠ *Sanlitun Nanlu, Chaoyang District* ☏ *010/6593–7710.*

Face. Stylish without being pretentious, Face is justifiably popular, especially with the mature, well-heeled crowd. The complex has a multitude of restaurants, but the real gem is the bar. Grab a lounge bed surrounded by silky drapes, take advantage of the happy-hour drink specials, and enjoy some premier people-watching. ⊠ *26 Dongcaoyuan, Gongti Nanlu, Chaoyang District* ☏ *010/6551–6788.*

Fodor's Choice
★ **Q Bar.** Echo's cocktails—strong, authentic, and not super expensive—are a small legend here in Beijing. This tucked-away lounge off the main Sanlitun drag is an unpretentious option for an evening out. Don't be put off by the fact that it's in a bland, 1980s-style motel; in the summer the terrace more than makes up for that. ⊠ *Top floor of Eastern Inn Hotel, Sanlitun Nanlu, Chaoyang District* ☏ *010/6595–9239.*

Saddle Cantina. For a touch of Mexico, head to this terra-cotta-colored venue in downtown Beijing. It's packed on summer evenings thanks to its large terrace, perfect for downing one of the brilliant margaritas. The service is friendly, and the house band will have you tapping your feet. Sports fans will appreciate the games on the big screen, and everyone loves the half-priced cocktails between 4 and 8. ⊠ *81 Sanlitun Beilu, Chaoyang District* ☎ *010/6400–4330* Ⓜ *Tuanjie Hu.*

★ **Stone Boat.** This watering hole is a pavilion-style hut on the edge of a pretty lake in Ritan Park. There are dainty ducks, feisty fishermen, and park joggers to observe while you sip chilled white wine. This is one of Beijing's nicest outdoor bars, as long as you don't mind having to use the public toilets opposite the building. ⊠ *Lakeside, southwest corner of Ritan Park, Chaoyang District* ☎ *010/6501–9986* Ⓜ *Jianguomen.*

The Tree. For years now, expats have crowded this bar for its Belgian beer, wood-fired pizza, and quiet murmurs of conversation. It does, however, get a bit smoky; if you're sensitive you may want to give this venue a pass. For pasta instead of pizza, its sister restaurant Nearby the Tree is, well, nearby, at 100 meters to the southeast. ⊠ *43 Sanlitun Beijie, Chaoyang District* ☎ *010/6415–1954* Ⓜ *Tuanjie Hu.*

CHAOYANG WEST GATE
The World of Suzie Wong. It's no coincidence that this bar is named after a 1957 novel about a Hong Kong prostitute. Come here late at night and you'll find a healthy supply of modern Suzie Wongs and a crowd of expat clients. The sleaze factor is enhanced by its 1930s opium-den design, with China-chic beds overrun with cushions. Suzie Wong's, however, has a reputation for mixing a more-than-decent cocktail and good music. ⊠ *1A South Nongzhanguan Lu, Chaoyang West Gate, Chaoyang District* ☎ *010/6593–6049.*

SHOPPING

Updated by
Helena Iveson

Large markets and malls in Beijing are generally open from 9 am to 9 pm, though some shops close as early as 7 pm or as late as 10 pm. Weekdays are always less crowded. During rush hour, avoid taking taxis. If a shop looks closed (the lights are out or the owner is resting), don't give up. Many merchants conserve electricity or take catnaps if the store is free of customers. Just knock or offer the greeting "*ni hao.*" More likely than not, the lights will flip on and you'll be invited to come in and take a look. Shops in malls have regular hours and will only be closed on a few occasions throughout the year, like Chinese New Year.

Major credit cards are accepted in pricier venues. Cash is the driving force here, and ATMs abound. Before accepting those Mao-faced Y100 notes, most vendors will hold them up to the light, tug at the corners, and rub their fingers along the surface. Counterfeiting is becoming increasingly more difficult, but no one, including you, wants to be cheated. In some department stores, you must settle your bill at a central payment counter.

WHEN TO HAGGLE

Bargaining is acceptable, and expected, in markets and mom-and-pop shops, though not in department stores and malls. Also, an increasing number of higher-end local boutiques follow the lead of their Western peers in not allowing bargaining. The bottom line is to pay what you think is fair.

2

Shops frequented by foreigners sometimes have an employee with some fluency in English. But money remains the international language. In many cases, whether or not there is a common language—the shop assistant will still whip out a calculator, look at you to see what they think you'll cough up, then type in a starting price. You're expected to counter with your offer. Punch in your dream price. The clerk will come down Y10 or Y20 and so on and so on. Remember that the terms *yuan*, *kuai*, and *RMB* are often used interchangeably.

DONGCHENG DISTRICT

MALLS AND DEPARTMENT STORES

Malls at Oriental Plaza. This enormous shopping complex, which may have newer competition but a location that keeps the crowds coming, originates at the southern end of Wangfujing where it meets Chang'an Jie and stretches a city block east to Dongdan Dajie. A true city within a city, it's conveniently organized by "street" names, such as Gourmet Street (aka the Food Court) and Sky Avenue. Upscale shops include Kenzo and Armani Exchange, which have some of the best men's accessories between Tokyo and Naples. ⊠ *1 Dongchang'an Jie, Dongcheng District* ☎ *010/8518–6363* Ⓜ *Wangfujing.*

SILK AND FABRICS

Daxin Textiles Co. For a wide selection of all types of fabrics, from worsted wools to sensuous silks, head to this shop. It's best to buy the material here and find a tailor elsewhere, as sewing standards can be shoddy. ⊠ *Northeast corner of Dongsi, Dongcheng District* ☎ *010/6403–2378* Ⓜ *Dongsi.*

XICHENG DISTRICT

MALLS AND DEPARTMENT STORES

Seasons Place. This ritzy mall is further west in Beijing's Financial Street area. If you're staying at one of the business hotels nearby, Seasons Place will fulfill your shopping needs—as long as you're not on a budget. Designer labels like Louis Vuitton, Gucci, and Versace are here, as well as the Beijing branch of Hong Kong's fab department store, Lane Crawford. ⊠ *2 Jinrong Jie, Xicheng District* ☎ *010/6622–0088* ⊕ *www.seasonsplace.com* Ⓜ *Fuxingmen.*

TOYS

Three Stones Kite Store. For something more traditional, go fly a kite. But not the run-of-the-mill type you see anywhere. Here, for three generations, the same family has hand-painted butterflies and birds onto bamboo frames to delight adults and children alike. ⊠ *25 Di'anmen Xidajie, Xicheng District* ☎ *010/8404–4505* ⊕ *www.cnkites.com* Ⓜ *Zhangzizhonglu.*

SOUTHERN DISTRICTS: CHONGWEN AND XUANWU

CHINESE MEDICINE

★ **Tongrentang.** A first-time consultation with a Chinese doctor can feel a bit like a reading with a fortune-teller. With one test of the pulse, many traditional Chinese doctors can describe the patient's medical history and diagnose current maladies. China's most famous traditional Chinese medicine shop, Tongrentang, is one of the oldest establishments on Dashilan. Hushed and dimly illuminated, this 300-year-old old shop even smells healthy. Browse the glassed displays of deer antlers and pickled snakes, dried seahorses and frogs, and delicate tangles of roots with precious price tags of Y48,000. If you don't speak Chinese and wish to have a consultation with a doctor, consider bringing along a translator. ⊠ *24 Dashilan, Qianmen, Exit C, Chongwen District* ☎ *010/6701–5895* Ⓜ *Qianmen.*

⚠ Chinese medicine is wonderful, but not when practiced by lab-coated "doctors" sitting behind a card table on the street corner. If you're seeking Chinese medical treatment, visit a local hospital, Tongrentang medicine shop, or ask your hotel concierge for a legitimate recommendation.

MARKETS

☼ **Hongqiao Market** *(Pearl Market).* Hongqiao is full of tourist goods, ★ knockoff handbags, and cheap watches, but it's best known for its three stories of pearls, hence its nickname. Freshwater, seawater, black, pink, white: the quantity is overwhelming and quality varies by stall. Prices range wildly, though the cheapest items are often fakes. Fanghua Pearls (No. 4318), on the fourth floor, displays quality necklaces and earrings, with photos of Hillary Clinton and Margaret Thatcher shopping there to prove it. Fanghua has a second store devoted to fine jade and precious stones. Stallholders here can be pushy, but accept their haggling in the gamelike spirit it's intended. Or wear headphones to drown them out. ⊠ *Tiantan Lu, between Chongemenwai Lu and Tiyuguan Dajie, east of the northern entrance to Temple of Heaven, Chongwen District* ☎ *010/6711–7630* Ⓜ *Tiantan Dongmen.*

SILK AND FABRICS

Beijing Silk Shop. Since 1830 the Beijing Silk Shop has been supplying the city with quality bolts of silks and fabrics. There are tailors on-site to whip up something special, and the second floor has ready-to-wear clothing. To reach the shop, walk all the way down Dashilan then head directly onto Dashilan West Street. ■TIP→ Two larger stores on Dashilan specialize in silk. Ruifuxiang, at No. 5, is housed in a beautiful two-story building, as is Century Silk Store at No. 33. ⊠ *50 Dashilan Xi Jie, Xuanwu District* ☎ *010/6301–6658* Ⓜ *Qianmen.*

CHAOYANG DISTRICT

BOOKS

★ **The Bookworm.** Book lovers, hipsters, and aspiring poets take note: this lending library and bookstore offers a spacious second-story reading room with a full café and bar. All are welcome to browse: the magazine and new-books section are a stupendous sight for English-starved

EXPLORING TEA STREET

Tea Street. Maliandao hosts the ultimate tea party every day of the week. Literally a thousand tea shops perfume the air of this prime tea-shopping district, west of the city center. Midway down this near-mile-long strip looms the **Teajoy Market**, the Silk Alley of teas. Unless you're an absolute fanatic, it's best to visit a handful of individual shops, crashing tea parties wherever you go. Vendors will invite you to sit down in heavy wooden chairs to nibble on pumpkin seeds and sample their large selections of black, white, oolong, jasmine, and chrysanthemum teas. Prices range from a few kuai for a decorative container of loose green tea to thousands of yuan for an elaborate gift set. Tea Street is also the place to stock up on clay and porcelain teapots and service sets. Green and flower teas are sold loose; black teas are sold pressed into disks and wrapped in natural-colored paper. Despite the huge selection of drinking vessels available, you'll find that most locals prefer to drink their tea from a recycled glass jar. ⊠ *Located near Guanganmen Wai Dajie, Xuanwu District* Ⓜ *Xuanwumen.*

travelers. The store frequently hosts poetry readings and lectures. ⊠ *4 Sanlitun Nan lu, set back slightly in an alley 50 m south of the Gongti Beilu junction Chaoyang District* ☎ *010/6586–9507* ⊕ *www.beijingbookworm.com* Ⓜ *Tuanjiehu.*

COMPUTERS AND ELECTRONICS

Bainaohui Computer Shopping Mall. Next door to the Wonderful Electronic Shopping Mall is Bainao, which means "one hundred computers." (The Chinese word for computer translates literally as "electric brain.") Home to hundreds of laptops and PCs, this retail mall is crammed with vendors selling real and knockoff supplies and accessories. ⊠ *10 Chaoyangmenwai Dajie, Chaoyang District* ☎ *010/6599–5912* Ⓜ *Hujialou.*

Wonderful Electronic Shopping Mall. Cameras, tripods, flash disks, phones, and MP3 players (called MP-San in Chinese) abound. If you forgot the USB cable for your digital recorder or need extra camera batteries, this is the place. Bargain hard and you'll be rewarded. ⊠ *12 Chaoyangmenwai Dajie, Chaoyang District* ☎ *010/8561–4335* Ⓜ *Hujialou.*

FASHION DESIGNERS AND BOUTIQUES

Heyan'er. He Yan's design philosophy is stated in her label: "Bu Yan Bu Yu, or "No Talking." Her linen and cotton tunics and collarless jackets speak for themselves. From earth tones to aubergine hues and peacock patterns, He Yan's designs echo traditional Tibetan styles. ⊠ *15–2 Gongti Beilu* ☎ *010/6415–9442* Ⓜ *Dongsishitiao* ⊠ *Holiday Inn Lido, 6 Fangyuan Xilu* ☎ *010/6437–6854.*

The Red Phoenix. In this cramped-but-charming Sanlitun showroom, fashion diva Gu Lin designs embroidered satin qipaos, cropped jackets, and men's clothing for stylish foreigners and China's *xin xin ren lei* (literally the "new, new human being," referring to the country's latest flock of successful young professionals). ⊠ *30 Sanlitun Bei Jie, Chaoyang District* ☎ *010/6416–4423* Ⓜ *Nongzhanguan.*

JEWELRY

Shard Box Store. The signature collection here includes small to midsize jewelry boxes fashioned from the broken shards of antique porcelain. Supposedly the shards were collected during the Cultural Revolution, when scores of antique porcelain pieces were smashed in accordance with the law. Birds, trees, pining lovers, and dragons decorate these affordable ceramic-

and-metal containers, which range from Y20 to Y200. ☒ *1 Ritan Beilu, Chaoyang District* ☎ *010/8561–3712* ☒ *2 Jiangtai Lu, near the Holiday Inn Lido* ☎ *010/5135–7638.*

Treasure House. In the Sanlitun embassy district, Treasure House has a modest but slick collection, including silver cuff links and charms inscribed with the Chinese symbols for happiness and longevity. ☒ *1 Sanlitun Beixiaojie* ☎ *010/8451–6096 or 139/1055–5372* Ⓜ *Nongzhanguan.*

MARKETS

Beijing Curio City. This complex has four stories of kitsch and curio shops and a few furniture vendors, some of whom may be selling authentic antiques. Prices are high (driven up by free-spending tour groups), so don't be afraid to lowball your offer. Ignore the overpriced Duty Free shop at the entrance. ☒ *Dongsanhuan Nan lu, Exit Third Ring Rd. at Panjiayuan Bridge, Chaoyang District* ☎ *010/6774–7711* Ⓜ *Jinsong.*

Fodor's Choice
★

Panjiayuan Antiques Market. Every day the sun rises over thousands of pilgrims rummaging in search of antiques and the most curious of curios, though the biggest numbers of buyers and sellers is at the weekends. With more than 3,000 vendors crowding an area of 48,500 square meters, not every jade bracelet, oracle bone, porcelain vase, and ancient screen is authentic, but most people are here for the reproductions anyway. Behold the bounty: watercolors, scrolls, calligraphy, Buddhist statues, opera costumes, old Russian SLR cameras, curio cabinets, Tibetan jewelry, tiny satin lotus-flower shoes, rotary telephones, jade dragons, antique mirrors, infinite displays of "Maomorabilia." If you're buying jade, first observe the Chinese customers, how they hold a flashlight to the milky-green stone to test its authenticity. As with all Chinese markets, bargain with a vengeance, as many vendors inflate their prices astronomically for *waiguoren* ("outside country people"). A strip of enclosed stores forms a perimeter around the surprisingly orderly rows of open-air stalls. The friendly owner of the eponymous **Li Shu Lan** decorates her shop (No. 24-D) with antiques from her *laojia*, or countryside hometown. Stop by the **Bei Zhong Bao Pearl Shop** (No. 7-A) for medium-quality freshwater pearls cultivated by the Hu family. Also here are a sculpture zoo, a book bazaar, reproduction-furniture shops, and a two-story market stashing propaganda posters and Communist literature. Show the taxi driver the Chinese characters for Panjiayuan Shichang. ☒ *Third Ring Rd. at Panjiayuan Bridge, Chaoyang District* Ⓜ *Jinsong.*

Ritan Office Building Market. Don't let the gray-brick and red-trim exterior fool you: the offices inside the Ritan Building are strung with racks of brand-name dresses and funky-fab accessories. Unlike the tacky variations made on knockoff labels and sold in less expensive markets, the collections here, for the most part, retain their integrity—perhaps because many of these dresses are actually designer labels. They're also more expensive, and bargaining is discouraged. The **Ruby Cashmere Shop** (No. 1009) sells genuine cashmere sweaters and scarves at reduced prices. Upstairs, the burning incense and bright red walls of **You Gi** (No. 2006) provide a welcome atmosphere for perusing an overpriced but eccentric collection of Nepalese and Indian clothing and jewelry. ⊠ *15A Guanghua Lu, just east of the south entrance to Ritan Park, opposite the Vietnam Embassy, Chaoyang District* ☎ *010/6502–1528* Ⓜ *Yonganli.*

Fodor'sChoice ★ **Silk Alley Market.** Once a delightfully chaotic sprawl of hundreds of outdoor stalls, the Silk Alley Market is now corralled inside a huge shopping center. The government has been cracking down on an increasing number of certain copycat items, so if you don't see that knockoff Louis Vuitton purse or Chanel jacket, just ask; it might magically appear from a stack of plastic storage bins. You will face no dearth, however, of knockoff Pumas and Nikes or Paul Smith polos. Chinese handicrafts and children's clothes are on the top floors. Bargain relentlessly, check carefully the quality of each intended purchase, and guard your wallet against pickpockets. ⊠ *8 Xiushui Dong Jie, Chaoyang District* ☎ *010/5169–9003* ⊕ *www.xiushui.com.cn* Ⓜ *Yonganli.*

★ **Yaxiu Market** *(Yashow Market)*. Especially popular among younger Western shoppers, Yaxiu is yet another indoor arena stuffed to the gills with low-quality knockoff clothing and shoes. Prices are slightly cheaper than Silk Alley, but the haggling no less cruel. Don't be alarmed if you see someone sniffing sneakers or suede jackets: they're simply testing if the leather is real. The giant sign outside this bustling clothes market near Sanlitun reads "Yashow," but it's written "yaxiu" in pinyin. ■ **TIP**➔ The beauty salons on the 4th floor offer inexpensive manicures and foot rubs if you need a break. ⊠ *58 Gongti Beilu, Chaoyang District* ☎ *010/6416–8699* Ⓜ *Tuanjiehu.*

Zhaojia Chaowai Market. Beijing's best-known venue for affordable antiques and reproduction furniture houses scores of independent vendors who sell everything from authentic Qing Dynasty–era chests to traditional baskets, ceramics, carpets, and curios. Be sure to bargain; vendors routinely sell items for less than half their starting price. ⊠ *43 Huawei Bei Li, Chaoyang District* ☎ *010/6770–6402* Ⓜ *Jinsong.*

HAIDIAN DISTRICT

Travelers usually frequent the northwestern quadrant of Beijing to visit the Summer Palace or the Beijing Zoo, though because Haidian has several universities, cheap and cheerful boutiques aimed at students are commonplace. For something more refined, collectors of antiques can spend hours perusing the quiet halls of **Ai Jia Gu Dong Market** (⊠ *Chengshousi Lu, Beisanhuan Xilu, Haidian District* ☎ *010/6765–7187*

Inspecting the goods at the Panjiayuan Antiques Market.

Ⓜ *Zhichunlu*), a large antiques and jade market, hidden just under the South Fourth Ring Road beside the Big Bell Museum. It's open daily, but shops close early on weekdays.

SIDE TRIPS FROM BEIJING

Updated by
Paul Mooney

Not only is Beijing a fascinating city to visit, but its outskirts are packed with history- and culture-laden sites for the admirer of early empires and their antiquities. First and foremost, a trip to the Great Wall is a must—you simply can't miss it!

After the Great Wall, there are a variety of wonderful things to do and see: you can go horseback riding at Yesanpo, or take a dip at the beach and gorge yourself with fresh seafood in Beidaihe.

Buddhist temples and ancient tombs, as well as historical bridges and anthropological digs, are all located within a few hours of Beijing. For all these sites, getting there is half the fun—traveling through rural China, even for a day trip, is always something of an adventure.

THIRTEEN MING TOMBS

48 km (30 mi) north of Beijing.

A narrow valley just north of Changping is the final resting place for 13 of the Ming Dynasty's 16 emperors (the first Ming emperor was buried in Nanjing; the burial site of the second one is unknown; and the seventh Ming emperor was dethroned and buried in an ordinary tomb in northwestern Beijing). Ming monarchs once journeyed here

The site of the Ming Tombs was carefully chosen according to Feng Shui principles.

each year to kowtow before their clan forefathers and make offerings to their memory. The area's vast scale and imperial grandeur convey the importance attached to ancestor worship in ancient China.

The road to the Thirteen Ming Tombs begins beneath an imposing stone portico that stands at the valley entrance. Beyond the entrance, the **Shendao** (✉ Y30 [Y20 Nov.–Mar.] ⊗ Apr.–Oct., daily 8–5:30; Nov.–Mar., daily 8–5), or Sacred Way, once reserved for imperial travel, passes through an outer pavilion and between rows of stone sculptures—imperial advisers and huge elephants, camels, lions, and horses—on its 7-km (4½-mi) journey to the burial sites. The **spirit way** leads to **Changling** (☎ 010/6076–1888 ✉ Y45 ⊗ Apr.–Oct., daily 8–5:30; Nov.–Mar., daily 8–5:00), the head tomb built for Emperor Yongle in 1427. The designs of Yongle's great masterpiece, the Forbidden City, are echoed in this structure. Changling and a second tomb, **Dingling** (☎ 010/6076–1423 ✉ Y70 [Y50 Nov.–Mar.] ⊗ Apr.–Oct., daily 8:30–6; Nov.–Mar., daily 8:30–5:30), were rebuilt in the 1980s and opened to the public. Both complexes suffer from overrestoration and overcrowding, but they're worth visiting if only for the tomb relics on display in the small museums at each site. Dingling is particularly worth seeing because this tomb of Emperor Wanli is the only Ming Dynasty tomb that has been excavated. Unfortunately, this was done in 1956 when China's archaeological skills were sadly lacking, resulting in irrecoverable losses. Nonetheless, it is interesting to compare this underground vault with the tomb of Emperor Qianlong at Qingdongling. Allow ample time for a hike or drive northwest from Changling to the six fenced-off **unrestored tombs,** a short distance farther up the valley. Here crumbling walls conceal vast courtyards shaded by pine trees. At each tomb, a stone altar rests beneath a stela tower and burial mound. In some cases the wall that circles the burial chamber is accessible on steep stone stairways that ascend from either side of the altar. At the valley's terminus (about 5 km [3 mi] northwest of Changling), the **Zhaoling Tomb** rests beside a traditional walled village. This thriving hamlet is well worth exploring.

Picnics amid the ruins have been a favorite weekend activity among Beijingers for nearly a century; if you picnic here, be sure to carry out all trash. ⊠ *Changping County* ☎ *Y30 for Zhaoling tomb.*

FAHAI TEMPLE

20 km (12 mi) west of Beijing.

The stunning works of Buddhist mural art at Fahai Temple, which underwent extensive renovation and reopened in 2008, are among the most underappreciated sights in Beijing. Li Tong, a favored eunuch in the court of Emperor Zhengtong (1436–49), donated funds to construct Fahai Temple in 1443. The project was highly ambitious: Li Tong invited only celebrated imperial and court painters to decorate the temple. As a result, the murals in the only surviving chamber of that period, Daxiongbaodian (the Mahavira Hall), are considered the finest examples of Buddhist mural art from the Ming Dynasty. Sadly, statues of various Buddhas and one of Li Tong himself were destroyed during China's Cultural Revolution.

The most famous of the nine murals in Mahavira Hall is a large-scale triptych featuring Guanyin (the Bodhisattva of Compassion) and Wenshu (the Bodhisattva of Marvelous Virtue and Gentle Majesty) in the center, and Poxian (the Buddha of Universal Virtue) on either side. The depiction of Guanyin follows the theme of "moon in water," which compares the Buddhist belief in the illusoriness of the material world to the reflection of the moon in the water. Typically painted with Guanyin are her legendary mount Jin Sun and her assistant Shancai Tongzi. Wenshu is often presented with a lion, symbolic of the bodhisattva's wisdom and strength of will, while Poxian is shown near a six-tusked elephant, each tusk representing one of the qualities that leads to enlightenment. On the opposite wall is the *Sovereign Sakra and Brahma* mural, with a panoply of characters from the Buddhist canon.

The murals were painted during the time of the European Renaissance, and though the subject matter is traditional, there are comparable experiments in perspective taking place in the depiction of the figures, as compared with examples from earlier dynasties. Also of note is a highly unusual decorative technique; many contours in the hall's murals, particularly on jewelry, armor, and weapons, have been set in bold relief by the application of fine gold threads.

The temple grounds are also beautiful, but of overriding interest are the murals themselves. Visitors stumble through the dark temple with rented flashlights (free with your ticket). Viewing the murals in this way, it's easy to imagine oneself as a sort of modern-day Indiana Jones unraveling a story of the Buddha as depicted in ancient murals of

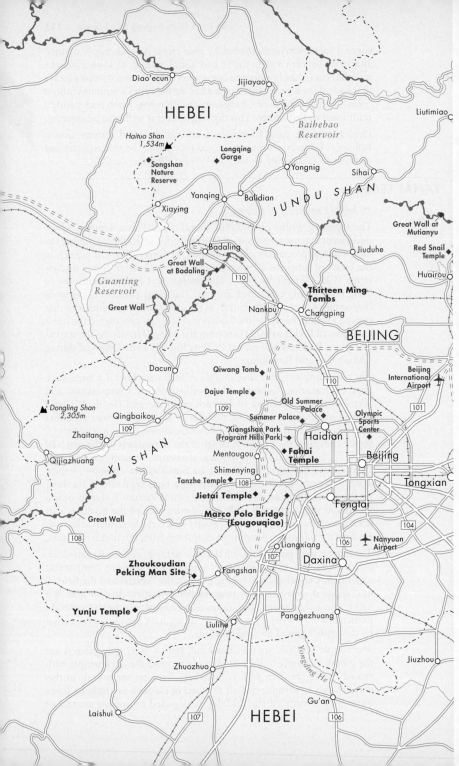

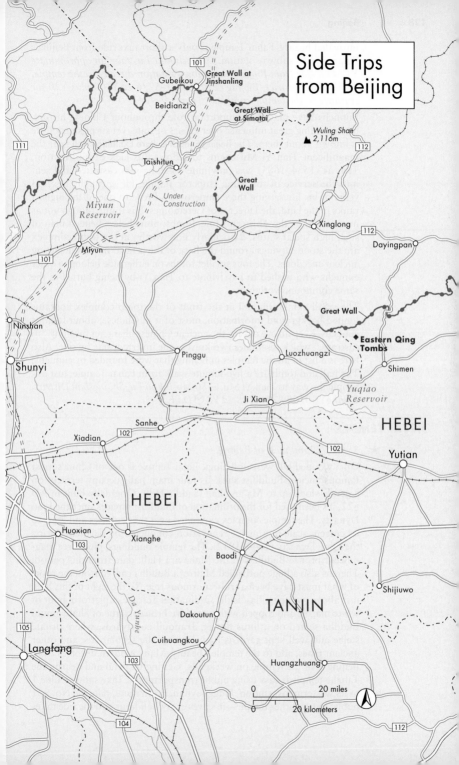

unrivaled beauty. Fahai Temple is only a short taxi ride from Beijing's Pingguoyuan subway station. ✉ *Moshikou Lu, take an approximate Y12 taxi ride from Pinguoyuan subway station directly to the temple, Shijingshan District, Beijing* ☎ *010/8871–5776* 🎫 *Y100 plus Y20 for entrance to the temple complex* ⊘ *Daily 9–4.*

Eunuchs have played an important role throughout Chinese history, often holding great influence over affairs of state, yet surprisingly little is known about them. The **Beijing Eunuch Culture Exhibition Hall** near the magnificent **Tian Yi Mu** begins to redress this lack of information. Tian Yi (1534–1605) was only nine when he was castrated and sent into the service of the Ming emperor Jiajing. He spent the next 63 years of his life serving three emperors and rose to one of the highest ranks in the land, the Director of Ceremonies. His tomb, though not as magnificent as the Thirteen Ming Tombs, nonetheless befits a man of such high social status. Particularly noteworthy in the tomb complex are the stone carvings around the base of the central mound depicting ancient anecdotes. The four smaller tombs on either side belong to other eunuchs who wished to pay tribute to Tian Yi by being buried in the same compound with him.

The small exhibition hall at the front of the tomb complex contains limited background information, most of it in Chinese, about famous eunuchs. Keep an eye out for the ancient Chinese character meaning "to castrate," which resembles two knives, one inverted, side by side. Also here is a list of all the temples in Beijing that were founded by eunuchs. The hall and tomb are a five-minute walk from Fahai Temple; just ask people the way to Tian Yi Mu. ✉ *80 Moshikou Lu, Shijingshan District, Beijing* ☎ *010/8872–4148* 🎫 *Y8* ⊘ *Daily 9–5.*

JIETAI TEMPLE

★ *35 km (22 mi) west of Beijing.*

On a wooded hill west of Beijing, Jietai Temple is one of China's most famous ancient Buddhist sites. Its four main halls occupy terraces on a gentle slope up to Ma'an Shan (Saddle Hill). Originally built in AD 622, it's been used for the ordination of Buddhist novices since the Liao Dynasty. The temple complex expanded over the centuries and grew to its current scale in a major renovation conducted by devotees during the Qing Dynasty (1644–1912). The temple buildings, plus three magnificent bronze Buddhas in the Mahavira Hall, date from this period. There is also a huge potbellied Maitreya Buddha carved from the roots of what must have been a truly enormous tree. To the right of this hall, just above twin pagodas, is the Ordination Terrace, a platform built of white marble and topped with a massive bronze statue of Shakyamuni Buddha seated on a lotus flower. Tranquil courtyards, where ornate stelae and well-kept gardens bask beneath the scholar tree and other ancient pines, add to the temple's beauty. Many modern devotees from Beijing visit the temple on weekends. Getting to Jietai and nearby the Tanzhe temple is easy using public transportation. Take subway Line 1 to its westernmost station, Pingguoyuan. From there, take the No. 931 public bus to either temple—it leaves every half hour and the ride takes

YESANPO AND BEIDAIHE

Yesanpo (150 km [90 mi] northeast of Beijing) is a sleepy village between Beijing and neighboring Hebei Province. Go here if you're craving a slower-paced scene and some outdoor fun. The accommodations aren't first class, but there are plenty of great things to do. Leave Beijing from Beijing West Station for the two-hour ride. Traditionally, locals have houses with extra rooms for guests, and owners will strive to make your stay as comfortable as possible. A clean room with two beds and an air conditioner should run you no more than Y150. There are also a few hotels on the main street by the train station with rooms running approximately Y200. This scenic town is nestled in a valley.

The area is best toured on horseback, and horses are available for rent for Y300 per day (with a guide), or Y100 for an hour or so. Yesanpo is also known for its whole barbecued lamb. Train No. 6437 leaves Beijing West Station at 5:44 pm and arrives at 8:29 pm. Return train 6438 leaves at 9:34 am daily.

Chairman Mao and the party's favorite spot for sand, sun, and seafood, **Beidaihe**, (250 km [170 mi] northeast of Beijing) is one of China's few beach resorts (though it's definitely no Bali). This crowded spot is just 2½ hours by train from Beijing Station. Nearly every building in town has been converted to a hotel, and every restaurant has tanks of pick-your-own seafood lining the street.

about 70 minutes. A taxi from Pingguoyuan to Jietai Temple should be Y50 to Y60; the bus fare is Y6. ⊠ *Mentougou County* ☎ *010/6980–6611* ⊒ *Y45* ⊙ *Daily 8–5.*

NEARBY

Farther along the road past Jietai Temple, **Tanzhe Temple** is a Buddhist complex nestled in a grove of *zhe* (cudrania) trees. Established around AD 400 and once home to more than 500 monks, Tanzhe was heavily damaged during the Cultural Revolution. It has since been restored, but if you look closely at some of the huge stone tablets, or *bei*, littered around the site you'll see that many of the inscriptions have been destroyed. The complex makes an ideal side trip from Jietai Temple or Marco Polo Bridge. ⊠ *10 km (6 mi) northeast of Jietai Temple, 45 km (28 mi) west of Beijing, Mentougou County* ☎ *010/6086–2500* ⊒ *Y55* ⊙ *Daily 7:30–5:30.*

MARCO POLO BRIDGE

16 km (10 mi) southwest of Beijing's Guanganmen Gate.

Built in 1192 and reconstructed after severe flooding during the Qing Dynasty, this impressive span—known as Marco Polo Bridge because it was allegedly praised by the Italian wayfarer—is Beijing's oldest bridge. Its 11 segmented-stone arches cross the Yongding River on what was once the Imperial Highway that linked Beijing with central China. The bridge's marble balustrades support nearly 485 carved-stone lions that decorate elaborate handrails. Note the giant stone slabs that comprise

Continued on page 140

THE GREAT WALL

For some people, the Great Wall is the main reason for a trip to China; for any visitor to Beijing, it's a must-see. Originally intended to keep foreigners out, the world's most famous wall has become the icon of an increasingly open nation. One of the country's most accessible attractions, the Great Wall promises both breathtaking scenery and cultural illumination.

Built by successive dynasties over two millennia, the Great Wall isn't one structure built at one time, but a series of defensive installations that shrank and grew. Especially vulnerable spots were more heavily fortified, while some mountainous regions were left un-walled altogether. The actual length of the wall remains a topic of considerable debate: at its longest, some estimates say the protective cordon spans 6,437 km (4,000 mi)—a distance wider than the United States. Although attacks, age, and pillaging (not to mention today's tourist invasion) have caused the crumbling of up to two-thirds of its length, new sections are being uncovered even today.

As kingdoms scrambled to protect themselves from marauding nomads, portions of wall cropped up, leading to a motley collection of northern borders. It was the first emperor of a unified China, Qin Shi-huang (circa 259–210 BC), founder of the Qin Dynasty, who linked these fortifications into a single network. By some accounts, Qin mustered nearly a million people, or one-fifth of China's workforce, to build this massive barricade, a mobilization that claimed countless lives and gave rise to many tragic folktales.

The Ming Dynasty fortified the wall like never before: for an estimated 5,000 km (3,107 mi), it stood 26 feet tall and 30 feet wide at its base. However, the wall failed to prevent the Manchu invasion that toppled the Ming in 1644. That historical failure hasn't tarnished the Great Wall's image, however. Although China once viewed it as a model of feudal oppression, the Great Wall is now touted as the national symbol. "Love China, Restore the Great Wall," declared Deng Xiaoping in 1984. Since then large sections have been repaired and opened to visitors, turning it also into a symbol of the tension between preservation and restoration in China.

AN ETERNAL WAIT

One legend concerns Lady Meng, whose husband was kidnapped on their wedding night and forced to work on the Great Wall. She traveled to the work site to await his return, believing her determination would bring him back. She waited so long that, in the end, she turned into a rock, which to this day stands at the head of the Great Wall in the beautiful seaside town of Qinhuangdao.

Boston Public Library

Circulation system messages:
Patron status is ok.

Title: Fodor's China.
ID: 39999069670196
Due: 12/23/2016 23:59:59
Circulation system messages:
Item checkout ok.

Total items: 1
12/2/2016 2:27 PM
Checked out: 8
Overdue: 0
Hold requests: 0
Ready for pickup: 0

Circulation system messages:
The End Patron Message is OK

Thank you for using the
3M SelfCheck™ System.

MATERIALS & TECHNIQUES

■ During the 2nd century BC, the wall was largely composed of packed earth and piled stone.

■ Some sections, like those in the Taklimakan Desert, were fortified with twigs, sand, and even rice (the jury's still out on whether workers' remains were used as well).

■ The more substantial brick-and-mortar ruins that wind across the mountains north of Beijing date from the Ming Dynasty (14th–17th centuries). Some Ming mortar kilns still exist in valleys around Beijing.

YOUR GUIDE TO THE GREAT WALL

As a visitor to Beijing, you simply must set aside a day to visit one of the glorious Great Wall sites just outside the capital. The closest, Badaling, is just an hour from the city's center—in general, the farther you go, the more rugged the terrain. So choose your adventure wisely!

BADALING, the most accessible section of the Great Wall, is where most tours go. This location is rife with Disneylike commercialism, though: from the cable car you'll see both the heavily reconstructed portions of wall and crowds of souvenir stalls.

If you seek the wall less traveled, book a trip to fantastic **MUTIANYU**, which is about the same distance as Badaling from Beijing. You can enjoy much more solitude here, as well as amazing views from the towers and walls.

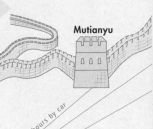

Mutianyu

Badaling

70 km; 1 hour by car

90 km; 1.25 hours by car

✪ BEIJING

TRANSPORTATION

CARS: The easiest and most comfortable way to visit the wall is by private car. Though taxis are occasionally willing to make the trip to more accessible sections like Badaling and Mutianyu, most hotels can arrange a four-passenger car and an English-speaking driver for 8 hours at around Y400–Y600. Settle details in advance, and remember that it's polite to invite your driver to eat meals with you. To ensure your driver doesn't return to Beijing without you, pay after the trip is over.

TOURS: In addition to the tour buses that gather around Tiananmen Square, most hotels and tour companies offer trips (in comfortable, air-conditioned buses or vans) to Badaling, Mutianyu, Simatai, and Jinshanling. ■TIP→ Smaller, private tours are generally more rewarding than large bus trips. Trips will run between Y100 and Y500 per person, but costs vary depending on the group size, and can sometimes be negotiated. Wherever you're headed, book in advance.

TOUR OPERATORS

OUR TOP PICKS

■ **CITS (China International Tour Service)** runs bus tours to Badaling and private tours to Badaling, Mutianyu, and Simatai. (Y400, Y500, Y600 per person) ✉ 1 Dongdan Bei DAJIE, Dongcheng District ☎ 010/6522–2991 ⊕ www.cits.net

■ **Beijing Service** leads private guided tours by car to Badaling, Mutianyu, and Simatai (Y420–Y560 per person for small groups of 3-4 people). ☎ 010/5166–7026 ✍ travel@beijingservice.com ⊕ www.beijingservice.com

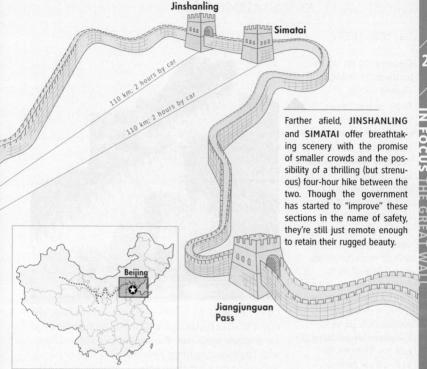

Jinshanling

Simatai

110 km; 2 hours by car

110 km; 2 hours by car

Beijing

Jiangjunguan
Pass

Farther afield, **JINSHANLING** and **SIMATAI** offer breathtaking scenery with the promise of smaller crowds and the possibility of a thrilling (but strenuous) four-hour hike between the two. Though the government has started to "improve" these sections in the name of safety, they're still just remote enough to retain their rugged beauty.

■ **Great Wall Adventure Club** organizes private bus and car trips to Jinshanling–Simatai (Y380–Y650) and Mutianyu (Y160–Y350). ☎ 138/1154–5162 ✎ greatwall@greatwalladventure.com ⊕ www.greatwalladventure.com

ADDITIONAL TOURS

■ **Abercrombie & Kent** also offers pricey personalized group tours to the wall. Call for prices. ☎ 010/6507–7125 ⊕ www.abercrombiekent.com

■ **Cycle China** runs good guided hiking tours of the unrestored Wall at Jiankou, as well as personalized tours to Simatai and Mutianyu. (Y550–Y750 for minimum of 5 people). ☎ 010/6402–5653, ⊕ www.cyclechina.com

■ **David Spindler**, a Great Wall expert, runs private tours to various sites. Contact him for prices, schedules, and details through Wild China ☎ 010/6465–6602 Ext. 314 ✎ info@wildchina.com ⊕ www.wildchina.com

■ **Dragon Bus Tours**, which picks up at major hotels, has tours to Badaling (with Ming Tombs), Mutianyu, and a bus to Simatai—with an occasional stop at a souvenir factory. (Y280–350; Y350-Y500 for Simatai) ☎ 010/6515–8565 ✎ service@beijinghighlights. com

■ **Gray Line/Panda Tours**, with branches in a dozen high-end hotels in Beijing, runs bus tours to Badaling (and Ming Tombs), Mutianyu, and Simatai—but beware of stops at souvenir factories. (Y280 per person) ✉ 4 fl., Shuang'an Dashi, 421 Beisanhuan, haidian ☎ 010/6525–8372 ⊕ www.pandatourchina.cn

GREAT WALL AT BADALING

GETTING THERE

Distance: 70 km (43 mi) northwest of Beijing, in Yanqing County

Tours: Beijing Service, CITS, Dragon Bus Tours, Gray Line/Panda Tours

By Car: A car for four people to Badaling should run no more than Y600 for five hours, sometimes including a stop at the Thirteen Ming Tombs.

By Bus: It's hard to wander south of Tiananmen Square without encountering the many buses going to Badaling. Choose wisely: look for the 1 or 5 bus at Qianmen, across from the southeastern corner of Tiananmen Square (departs 6:30 am–11:30 am for Y12–Y18 per person).

FAST FACTS

Phone: 010/6912–1383

Hours: Daily 6:30 am–7 pm

Admission: Y40 Apr.–Nov.; cable car is an additional Y35 one-way, Y50 round-trip

Web Site: www.badaling. gov.cn

Only one hour by car from downtown Beijing, the Great Wall at Badaling is where visiting dignitaries go for a quick photo-op. Postcard views abound here, with large sections of the restored Ming Dynasty brick wall rising majestically to either side of the fort. In the distance, portions of the early-16th-century Great Wall disintegrate into more romantic but inaccessible ruins.

Badaling is convenient to the Thirteen Ming Tombs and outfitted with tourist-friendly facilities, so it's popular with tour groups and is thus often crowded, especially on weekends. ■TIP→ People with disabilities find access to the wall at Badaling better than elsewhere in the Beijing area. You can either take the cable car to the top, or you can walk up the gently sloping steps, relying on handrails if necessary. On a clear day you can see for miles across leafy, undulating terrain from atop the battlements. The admission price also includes access to the China Great Wall Museum and the Great Wall Circle Vision Theater.

■TIP→ Most tours to Badaling will take you to the Thirteen Ming Tombs, as well. If you don't want a stop at the tombs—or at a tourist-trapping jade factory or herbal medicine center along the way—be sure to confirm the itinerary before booking.

GREAT WALL AT MUTIANYU

GETTING THERE

Distance: 90 km (56 mi) northeast of Beijing, in Huairou County

Tours: CITS, Gray Line/Panda Tours, Great Wall Adventure Tour

By Car: A car to Mutianyu should cost no more than Y600 for the day—it takes about an hour to get there.

By Bus: Take Bus 916/936 from Dongzhimen to Huairou (Y5). From there take a minibus to Mutianyu (Y25–Y30) or hire a taxi to take you there and back to the bus station (about Y50 each way, Y100–Y150 round-trip after bargaining). On weekends and national holidays, the tourist Bus 6 from outside the South Cathedral at Xuanwumen goes directly to Mutianyu (Y50, leaves 6:30–8:30 am).

FAST FACTS

Phone: 010/6162–6873 or 010/6162–6022

Hours: Daily 7:30 am–5:30 pm

Admission: Y45 (students half-price); chairlift, Y35; cable car, Y45 one-way, Y65 round trip with toboggan descent

★ **Fodor's Choice** Slightly farther from downtown Beijing than Badaling, the Great Wall at Mutianyu is more spectacular and, despite the occasional annoyances of souvenir stands, significantly less crowded. This long section of wall, first built during the Northern Qi Dynasty (6th century) and restored and rebuilt throughout history, can offer a solitary Great Wall experience, with unforgettable views of towers winding across mountains and woodlands. On a clear day, you'll swear you can see the deserts of Mongolia in the distance.

The lowest point on the wall is a strenuous one-hour climb above the parking lot. As an alternative, you can take a cable car on a breathtaking ride to the highest restored section (this is how President Bill Clinton ascended in 1998), from which several hiking trails descend. Take a gorgeous 1½-hour walk east to reach another cable car that returns to the same parking lot. Mutianyu is also known for its toboggan run.

■ **TIP→** For those taking a car, the road from Huairou, a suburb of Beijing, to Mutianyu follows a river upstream and is lined with restaurants selling fresh trout. In addition, Hongluo Temple is a short drive from the bottom of the mountain.

GREAT WALL AT SIMATAI

GETTING THERE

Distance: At around 110 km (68 mi) northeast of Beijing, Simatai is farther than Badaling and Mutianyu, but is well worth the trip—the road runs through lovely farmland, and few visitors make the trek.

Tours: Most hotels offer tours here, as do CITS, Gray Line/Panda Tours, and Great Wall Adventure Tour.

By Car: A car to Simatai should be no more than Y800 for the day. If you plan to hike from Jinshanling to Simatai, or vice versa, have your car drop you off at one and pick you up at the other.

By Bus: Take the early-morning Bus 916 from the bus station at Dongzhimen (Y20), starting at 6 am. On weekends and holidays, a luxury bus leaves Qianmen at 8:30 am (Y85 round-trip) and leaves Simatai at 3 pm.

FAST FACTS

Phone: 010/6903–5025 or 010/6903–1051

Hours: Daily 8 am–5 pm

Admission: Y40; cable car, Y30 one-way, Y50 round-trip. If you hike to Jinshanling, you will have to buy another Y5 ticket at the border.

★ Remote and largely unrestored, the Great Wall at Simatai is ideal if you're seeking adventure. Near the frontier garrison at Gubeikou, the wall traverses towering peaks and hangs precariously above cliffs. Be prepared for no-handrails hiking, tough climbs, and unparalleled vistas. Several trails lead to the wall from the parking lot.

In summer, a cable car takes you two-thirds of the way up; from there it's a steep 40-minute climb to the summit. Heading east from the Miyun reservoir at a moderate pace will take you to Wangjing Ta, the 12th watchtower, after about 3 hours. For a longer hike, head west over the bridge toward the restored Jinshanling section.

The hike to Jinshanling is a strenuous 9 km (5.6 mi), usually taking around 4 hours up and down sublime sections of the wall. Be aware that crossing to Jinshanling costs Y5. People who wish to hike from one to the other often ask their driver to wait for them at their destination. (Note that hikers usually go from Jinshanling to Simatai, where buses back to Beijing are easier to find.)

GREAT WALL AT JINSHANLING

GETTING THERE

Distance: 110 km (68 mi) northeast from Beijing

Tours: CITS, Cycle China, Gray Line/Panda Tours, Great Wall Adventure Tour

By Car: A car should be no more than Y800; the ride is about two hours. If you plan to hike from Jinshanling to Simatai, as many do, it makes sense to be dropped off at Jinshanling and have your car pick you up at Simatai.

By Train: Take train L671, which departs at 7:25 am from Beijing North Railway Station, to Gubeikou; there switch to a local minibus or taxi to Jinshanling.

By Bus: Take a minibus from Dongzhimen long-distance bus station to Miyun (Y8) and then change to a local bus or taxi. Or take a Chengde-bound bus from Dongzhimen and get off at Jinshanling; a cab can bring you to the entrance for Y10.

★ Though it lacks the rugged adventure of Simatai, Jinshanling is perhaps the least restored of the major Great Wall sections near Beijing, as well as the least visited. Besides being the starting point for a fantastic four-hour hike to Simatai, Jinshanling also serves as one of the few sections of the Great Wall on which you can camp overnight.

A starry night here is gorgeous and unforgettable—go with a tour group such as Cycle China. Don't forget to pack a piece of charcoal and paper to make rubbings of bricks that still bear the stamp of the date they were made.

FAST FACTS

Phone: 031/4883–0222 or 138/3144–8986

Hours: Daily 8 am–5 pm

Admission: Y50; Y398, Y498, Y598 for overnight stays. If you hike to Simatai, you will have to buy another Y5 ticket at the border

GREAT WALL MARATHON

Not for the faint of heart, the Great Wall Marathon (and half marathon) takes place each May. The marathon covers approximately 6.5 km (4 mi) of the Great Wall, with the rest of the course running through lovely valleys in rural Tianjin.

⊕ www.great-wall-marathon.com

the bridge's original roadbed. Carved imperial stelae at either end of the span commemorate the bridge and surrounding scenery.

The Marco Polo Bridge is best remembered in modern times as the spot where invading Japanese armies clashed with Chinese soldiers on June 7, 1937. The assault began Japan's brutal eight-year occupation of eastern China, which ended with Tokyo's surrender at the end of World War II. The bridge has become a popular field-trip destination for Beijing students. On the Beijing side of the span is the **Memorial Hall of the War of Resistance Against Japan.** Below the bridge on the opposite shore, local entrepreneurs rent horses (the asking price is Y120 per hour, but you should bargain) and lead tours of the often-dry, grassy riverbed. ⊠ *Near Xidaokou, Fengtai District, Beijing* ☎ *010/8389–4614* 🎟 *Y20* ☉ *Daily 7 am–8 pm.*

ZHOUKOUDIAN PEKING MAN SITE

48 km (30 mi) southwest of Beijing.

This area of lime mines and craggy foothills ranks among the world's great paleontological sites (and served as the setting for Amy Tan's *The Bonesetter's Daughter*). In 1929 anthropologists, drawn to Zhoukoudian by apparently human "dragon bones" found in a Beijing apothecary, unearthed a complete cranium and other fossils dubbed *Homo erectus pekinensis*, or Peking Man. These early remains, believed to be nearly 700,000 years old, suggest (as do similar *Homo erectus* discoveries in Indonesia) that humankind's most recent ancestor originated in Asia, not Europe (though today some scientists posit that humans evolved in Africa first and migrated to Asia). A large-scale excavation in the early 1930s further unearthed six skullcaps and other hominid remains, stone tools, evidence of fire, plus a multitude of animal bones, many at the bottom of a large sinkhole believed to be a trap for woolly rhinos and other large game. Sadly, the Peking Man fossils disappeared under mysterious circumstances during World War II, leaving researchers only plaster casts to contemplate. Subsequent digs at Zhoukoudian have yielded nothing equivalent to Peking Man, although archaeologists haven't yet abandoned the search. Trails lead to several hillside excavation sites. A small museum showcases a few (dusty) Peking Man statues, a collection of Paleolithic artifacts, two mummies, and some fine animal fossils, including a bear skeleton and a saber-toothed tiger skull. Because of the importance of Peking Man and the potential for other finds in the area, Zhoukoudian is a UNESCO World Heritage Site, but it may not be of much interest to those without a particular inclination for the subject. If you should find yourself here with little to do after your museum visit and the few dig locations, consider a little hike into the surrounding hills, which are named the Dragon Bone Mountains. ⊠ *Zhoukoudian* ☎ *010/6930–1278* 🎟 *Y30* ☉ *Daily 8:30–4:30.*

YUNJU TEMPLE

75 km (47 mi) southwest of Beijing.

Yunju Temple is best known for its mind-boggling collection of 14,278 minutely carved Buddhist tablets. To protect the Buddhist canon from destruction by Taoist emperors, the devout Tang-era monk Jing Wan carved Buddhist scriptures into stone slabs that he hid in sealed caves in the cliffs of a mountain. Jing Wan spent 30 years creating these tablets until his death in AD 637; his disciples continued his work for the next millennium into the 17th century, thereby compiling one of the most extensive Buddhist libraries in the world. A small pagoda at the center of the temple complex commemorates the remarkable monk. Although the tablets were originally stored inside Shijing Mountain behind the temple, they are now housed in rooms built along the temple's southern perimeter.

Four central prayer halls, arranged along the hillside above the main gate, contain impressive Ming-era bronze Buddhas. The last in this row, the Dabei Hall, displays the spectacular *Thousand-Armed Avalokitesh-vara*. This 13-foot-tall bronze sculpture—which actually has 24 arms and five heads and stands in a giant lotus flower—is believed to embody boundless compassion. A group of pagodas, led by the 98-foot-tall Northern Pagoda, is all that remains of the original Tang complex. These pagodas are remarkable for their Buddhist reliefs and ornamental patterns. Heavily damaged during the Japanese occupation and again by Maoist radicals in the 1960s, the temple complex remains under renovation. ⊠ *Off Fangshan Lu, Nanshangle Xiang, Fangshan County* ☎ *010/6138–9612* ☜ *Y40* ☉ *Daily 8:30–5 summer, 8:30–4:30 winter.*

EASTERN QING TOMBS

Fodor's Choice
★

125 km (78 mi) east of Beijing.

Modeled on the Thirteen Ming Tombs, the Eastern Qing Tombs replicate the Ming spirit ways, walled tomb complexes, and subterranean burial chambers. But they're even more extravagant in their scale and grandeur, and far less touristy. The ruins contain the remains of five emperors, 14 empresses, and 136 imperial concubines, all laid to rest in a broad valley chosen by Emperor Shunzhi (1638–61) while on a hunting expedition. By the Qing's collapse in 1911, the tomb complex covered some 18 square mi (46 square km) of farmland and forested hillside, making it the most expansive burial ground in all China.

The Eastern Qing Tombs are in much better repair than their older Ming counterparts. Although several of the tomb complexes have undergone extensive renovation, none is overdone. Peeling paint, grassy courtyards, and numerous stone bridges and pathways convey a sense of the area's original grandeur. Often visitors are so few that you may feel as if you've stumbled upon an ancient ruin unknown beyond the valley's farming villages.

Of the nine tombs open to the public, two are not to be missed. The first is **Yuling,** the resting place of the Qing Dynasty's most powerful sovereign, Emperor Qianlong (1711–99), who ruled China for 59 years. Beyond the outer courtyards, Qianlong's burial chamber is accessible from inside Stela Hall, where an entry tunnel descends some 65 feet

The Eastern Qing Tombs are the most expansive burial grounds in China.

(20 m) into the ground and ends at the first of three elaborately carved marble gates. Beyond, exquisite carvings of Buddhist images and sutras rendered in Tibetan adorn the tomb's walls and ceiling. Qianlong was laid to rest, along with his empress and two concubines, in the third and final marble vault, amid priceless offerings looted by warlords early in the 20th century.

Dingdongling was built for the infamous Empress Dowager Cixi (1835–1908). Known for her failure to halt Western-imperialist encroachment, Cixi once spent funds allotted to strengthen China's Navy on a traditional stone boat for the lake at the Summer Palace. Her burial compound, reputed to have cost 72 tons of silver, is the most elaborate (if not the largest) at the Eastern Qing Tombs. Many of its stone carvings are considered significant because the phoenix, which symbolized the female, is level with, or even above, the imperial (male) dragon—a feature, ordered, no doubt, by the empress herself. A peripheral hall paneled in gold leaf displays some of the luxuries amassed by Cixi and her entourage, including embroidered gowns, jewelry, imported cigarettes, and even a coat for one of her dogs. In a bow to tourist kitsch, the compound's main hall contains a wax statue of Cixi sitting Buddha-like on a lotus petal flanked by a chambermaid and a eunuch.

The Eastern Qing Tombs are a two- to three-hour drive from the capital. The rural scenery is dramatic, and the trip is one of the best full-day excursions outside Beijing. Consider bringing a bed sheet, a bottle of wine, and boxed lunches, as the grounds are ideal for a picnic. ⊠ *Near Malanguan, Hebei Province, Zunhua County* ☎ *0315/694–4467* ▨ *Y120* ⊙ *Daily 8:30–5*

ENGLISH	PINYIN	CHINESE
EXPLORING		
798 Art District	Qījiǔbā yìshù qū	798艺术区
Ancient Observatory	Běijīng gǔguānxiàng tái	北京古观象台
Beihai Park (North Lake)	Běihǎi	北海
Beijing Zoo	Běijīng dòngwù yuán	北京动物园
Big Bell Temple	Dàzhōngsì	大钟寺
Chaoyang District	Cháoyáng qū	朝阳区
Chongwen District	Chóngwén qū	崇文区
Confucius Temple	Kǒngmiào	孔庙
Ditan Park (Temple of the Earth)	Dìtán gōngyuán	地坛公园
Dongcheng District	Dōngchéng qū	东城区
Drum Tower	Gǔlóu	鼓楼
Five-Pagoda Temple	Wǔ Tǎ Sì	五塔寺
Forbidden City	Gùgōng	故宫
Guijie (Ghost Street)	Guǐjiē	簋街
Haidian District	Hǎidiàn qū	海淀区
Houhai (Back Lake)	Hòuhǎi	后海
Jingshan Park (Coal Hill)	Jǐngshān gōngyuán	景山公园
Lama Temple	Yōnghégōng	雍和宫
Liulichang	Liúlíchǎng	琉璃厂
Ming Dynasty City Wall Ruins Park	Míng chéngqiáng yízhǐ gōngyuán	明城墙遗址公园
Museum of Antique Currency	Běijīng gǔdài qiánbì bówùguǎn	北京古代钱币博物馆
Nanxincang	Nánxīncāng	南新仓
Niujie (Ox Street) Mosque	Niújiē qīngzhēnsì	牛街清真寺
Old Summer Palace	uánmíngyuán	圆明园
Prince Gong's Palace	Gōngwángfǔ	恭王府
Qianhai (Front Lake)	Qiánhǎi	前海
Qianmen Dajie	Qiánmén dàjiē	前门大街
Ruifuxiang Silk Shop	ruìfúxiáng chóubù diàn	瑞蚨祥绸布店
Soong Ching-ling's Former Residence	Sòng Qìnglíng gùjū	宋庆龄故居
Source of Law Temple	Fǎyuánsì	法源寺
Summer Palace	Yíhéyuán	颐和园
Temple of Azure Clouds	Bìyún sì	碧云寺

2

ENGLISH	PINYIN	CHINESE
Temple of Heaven	Tiāntán gōngyuán	天坛公园
Tiananmen Square	Tiānānmén guǎngchǎng	天安门广场
Wangfujing	Wángfǔjǐng	王府井
Workers' Stadium	Gōngrén tǐyùcháng	工人体育场
Xicheng District	Xīchéng qū	西城区
Xuanwu District	Xuānwǔ qū	宣武区
WHERE TO EAT		
Alameda	n/a	n/a
Argana	n/a	n/a
Aria	Ālìyǎ	阿郦雅
Baijia Dayuan	Báijiā dà zháimén	白家大宅门
Bellagio	Lùgǎng xiǎo zhèn	鹿港小镇
The Bookworm	Shūchóng	书虫
Café Constance	n/a	n/a
Café de la Poste	Yúnyóu yì	云游驿
Capital M	n/a	n/a
Comptoirs de France Bakery	Fǎpài	法派
Din Tai Fung	Dǐngtàifēng	鼎泰丰
Ding Ding Xiang	Dǐngdǐngxiāng	鼎鼎香
Fangshan	Fǎngshàn	仿膳
Hai Wan Ju	Hǎiwǎnjū	海碗居
Huang Ting	Huángtíng	凰庭
Jing	Jīng	京
Jun Wangfu	Jūnwángfǔ	君王府
Kong Yi Ji	Kǒngyǐjǐ	孔乙己
La Dolce Vita	Tiánmìshēnghuó	甜蜜生活
La Galerie	Zhōngguó yìyuàn	中国艺苑
Lai Jin Yu Xuan	Láijīn yùxuān	来今雨轩
Li Qun Roast Duck Restaurant	Lìqún kǎoyādiàn	利群烤鸭店
Makye Ame	Mǎjíāmǐ	玛吉阿米
Mei Fu	Méi fǔ	梅府
Nam Nam	Nàmenàme	那么那么
Noodle Bar	Miàn bā	面吧
Old Beijing Noodle King	Lǎo Běijīng zhájiàngmiàn dàwáng	老北京炸酱面大王
Paomo Guan	Pào mó guǎn	泡馍馆

ENGLISH	PINYIN	CHINESE
Paulaner Brauhaus	Pǔlānà píjiǔ fāng cāntīng	普拉那啤酒坊餐厅
Red Capital Club	Xīnhóngzī jùlèbù	新红资俱乐部
Shaguo Ju	Shāguō jū	沙锅居
Shin Yeh	Xīnyè	欣叶
The Source	Dōujiāngyuán	都江源
Still Thoughts	Jìngsī sùshí fāng	静思素食坊
Taj Pavilion	Tàijī lóu	泰姬楼
Three Guizhou Men	Sāngeguìzhōurén	三个贵州人
Yotsuba	Sìyè	四叶
Yue Bin	Yuèbīn fànguǎn	悦宾饭馆
Yuxiang Renjia	Yúxiāngrénjiā	渝乡人家

WHERE TO STAY

Autumn Garden	Chūnqiūyuán bīnguǎn nányuán	春秋园宾馆南园
Banqiao No. 4	Bǎnqiáo sì hào	板桥4号
Courtyard by Northeast Beijing	běijīng rénjì wànyí jiǔdiàn	北京人济万怡酒店
Courtyard Beijing	Běijīng Wànyí jiǔdiàn	北京万怡酒店
Eagle's Rest	Yīngzhī cháo	鹰之巢
The Emperor	Huángjiā yìzhàn	皇家驿栈
Friendship Hotel	Yǒuyì bīnguǎn	友谊宾馆
Grand Hyatt Beijing	Běijīng Dōngfāngjūnyuè jiǔdiàn	北京东方君悦酒店
Hotel G	Běijīng jí zhàn	北京极栈
Hotel Kapok	Mùmiánhuā jiǔdiàn	木棉花酒店
Jianguo Hotel	Jiànguó fàndiàn	建国饭店
Jinglun Hotel	Jīnglún fàndiàn	京伦饭店
Kempinski Hotel	Kǎibīnsījī fàndiàn	凯宾斯基饭店
Kerry Centre Hotel	Běijīng Jiālǐ zhōngxīn fàndiàn	北京嘉里中心饭店
Kunlun Hotel	Běijīng Kūnlún fàndiàn	北京昆仑饭店
Legendale	Lìjùn jiǔdiàn	励骏酒店
LüSongyuan	Lǚsōngyuán bīnguǎn	侣松园宾馆
The Opposite House	Yúshè	瑜舍
Park Hyatt Beijing	Běijīng Bòyuè jiǔdiàn	北京柏悦酒店
Peninsula Beijing	Wángfǔ Bàndǎo jiǔdiàn	王府半岛酒店
Raffles Beijing Hotel	Běijīng fàndiàn Láifóshì	北京饭店莱佛士
Red Capital Residence	Xīnhóngzī kèzhàn	新红资客栈
The Regent	Běijīng Lìjīng jiǔdiàn	北京丽晶酒店

ENGLISH	PINYIN	CHINESE
Ritz-Carlton Beijing, Financial Street	Běijīng Jīnróng jiē Lìsīkǎ'ěrdùn jiǔdiàn	北京金融街丽思卡尔顿酒店
Shangri-La Hotel	Běijīng Xiānggélīlā fàndiàn	北京香格里拉饭店
Sino-Swiss Hotel	Běijīng Guódū dàfàndiàn	北京国都大饭店
St. Regis	Běijīng guójì jùlèbù fàndiàn	北京国际俱乐部饭店
Swissôtel	gǎngao zhōngxīn Ruìshì jiǔdiàn	港澳中心瑞士酒店
Traders Hotel	Guómào fàndiàn	国贸饭店
Zhaolong International Youth Hostel	Zhàolóng qīngnián lǚshè	兆龙青年旅

ARTS AND NIGHTLIFE

Amilal	àn yī lā'ěr	按一拉尔
Beijing Concert Hall	Běijīng yīnyuètīng	北京音乐厅
Beijing Exhibition Theater	Běijīng zhǎnlǎnguǎn jùchǎng	北京展览馆剧场
Chang'an Grand Theater	Cháng'ān dàxìyuàn	长安大戏院
Chaoyang Theater	Cháoyáng jùchǎng	朝阳剧场
China National Puppet Theater	Zhōngguó guójiā mùǒujùyuà	中国国家木偶剧院
The Den	n/a	n/a
D.Lounge	n/a	n/a
Drum and Bell	Gǔzhōng kāfēiguǎn	鼓钟咖啡馆
East Shore Live Jazz Café	Dōng'àn kāfēi	东岸咖啡
Face	Fēi sè	飞色
Forbidden City Concert Hall	Zhōngshān gōngyuán yīnyuètáng	中山公园音乐堂
Huguang Guildhall	Húguǎng huìguǎn	湖广会馆
Lao She Teahouse	Lǎoshě cháguǎn	老舍茶馆
Liyuan Theater	Líyuán jùcháng	梨园剧场
MAO Live House	n/a	n/a
National Centre for Performing Arts	Guójiā dàjùyuàn	国家大剧院
No Name Bar (Bai Feng's)	Wúmíng jiǔbā	无名酒吧
Q Bar	n/a	n/a
The Red Theatre	Hóng jùchǎng	红剧场
Saddle Cantina	Mòxīgē cāntīng	n/a
Stone Boat	Shífǎng	石舫
Tango	Tángguǒ	糖果
Tianqiao Acrobatic Theater	n/a	天桥乐茶馆
Tianqiao Happy Teahouse	Tiānqiáolè cháguǎn	天桥乐茶馆

ENGLISH	PINYIN	CHINESE
The Tree	n/a	n/a
The World of Suzie Wong	Sūxīhuáng jùlèbù	苏西黄俱乐部
Yugong Yishan	Yúgōngyíshān	愚公移山
SHOPPING		
Ai Jia Gu Dong Market	Àijiā hóngmù dàgúanlóu	爱家红木大楼
Bainaohui Computer Shopping Mall	Bàinǎohuìdiànnǎo guǎngchǎng	百脑会电脑广场
Beijing Curio City	Běijīng gǔwán chéng	北京古玩城
Beijing Silk Shop	Běijīng qiānxiángyì sīchóu shāngdiàn	北京谦祥益丝绸商店
The Bookworm	Shūchóng	书虫
Daxin Textiles Co.	Dàxīn fǎngzhī	大新纺织
Heyan'er	Héyàn fúzhuāng diàn	何燕服装店
Hongqiao Market	Hóngqiáo shìchǎng	红桥市场
Malls at Oriental Plaza	Dōngfāng guǎngchǎng	东方广场购物中心
Panjiayuan Antique Market	Pānjiāyuán shìchǎng	潘家园市场
The Red Phoenix	Hóngfènghuáng fúzhuāng	红凤凰服装工作室
Ritan Office Building Market	Rìtán shāngwù lóu	日坛商务楼
Seasons Place	Jīnróngjiē gòuwùzhōngxīn	金融街购物中心
Shard Box Store	Shèndégé	慎 德阁
Silk Alley Market	Xiùshuǐ shìchǎng	秀水市场
Tea Street	Mǎliándǎo cháyè chéng	马连道茶叶批发市场
Tongrentang	Tóngréntáng	同仁堂
Treasure House	Bǎoyuèzāi	宝月斋
Wonderful Electronic Shopping Mall	Lándǎo dàshà	蓝岛大厦
Yaxiu Market	Yǎxiù shìchǎng	雅秀市场
Zhaojia Chaowai Antique Market	Zhàojiā Cháowài gǔdiǎnjiājù shìchǎng	n/a
SIDE TRIPS		
Beidaihe	Bǐidàihé	北戴河
Beijing Eunuch Culture Exhibition Hall	Běijīng huànguān wénhuà chénlièguǎn	北京宦官文化陈列馆
Changling	Chánglíng	长陵
Dingling	Dìnglíng	定陵
Eastern Qing Tombs	Qīngdōnglíng	清东陵
Fahai Temple	Fǎhǎi sì	法海寺

2

ENGLISH	PINYIN	CHINESE
The Great Wall	Chángchéng	长城
Huanghua Cheng	Huanghua cheng	黄花城
Jietai Temple	Jiètái sì	戒台寺
Marco Polo Bridge	Lúgōu qiáo	卢沟桥
The Spirit Way	Shén lù	神路
Tanzhe Temple	Tánzhè sì	潭哲寺
Thirteen Ming Tombs	Míng Shísānlíng	明十三陵
Tianjin	Tiānjīn	天津
Tian Yi Mu	Tiányì mù	田义幕
Yesanpo	Yěsān pō	野三坡
Yunju Temple	Yúnjū sì	云居寺
Zhaoling Tomb	Zhāo líng	n/a
Zhoukoudian Peking Man Site	Zhōukǒudiàn Běijīngrén xiànchǎng	周口店北京人现场

Beijing to Shanghai

HEBEI, SHANDONG, JIANGSU, AND ANHUI

WORD OF MOUTH

"Last weekend we flew to the yellow mountains to discover why people say that once you climb Mt. Huangshan, you never want to climb another mountain again. It turns out that Mt. Huangshan is the single largest stairmaster in the world, if not the universe."

—Summer_in_Shanghai

FROM BEIJING TO SHANGHAI

TOP RE TO GO

★ **Qingdao:** Life's a beach in China's premier seaside city. Enjoy some of the country's best seafood and wash it down with Tsingtao beer, the local brew. Stroll around the well-preserved architecture from the days when the Germans were in charge.

★ **Huangshan:** Yellow Mountain's towering granite peaks overlooking rice paddies and green fields have been a place of pilgrimage for centuries.

★ **Chengde:** Originally a summer retreat for an emperor, this town's magnificent temples, parks, and palaces now attract weekenders hunting for culture.

★ **Suzhou:** Classical gardens and a network of crisscrossing canals run throughout the moated city.

★ **Tongli:** A fine example of a town built on water, Tongli is a wonderful place to wander around. Quaint side streets and alleyways open onto canals and bridges.

1 Anhui. It may be one of China's poorest provinces, but it's rich in sublime mountain scenery at Huangshan. The peaks are a sacred site in China; ascend the photogenic summit to understand why.

2 Hebei. Wrapped around the nation's capital, Hebei's attractions are definitely worth a side trip. Chengde is home to an impressive display of imperial architecture, and in warm weather the seaside resorts of Beidaihe and Shanhaiguan become playgrounds for middle-class Chinese.

3 Jiangsu. Brimming with history, Jiangsu's attractions include stately monuments, memorials to horrific massacres, ancient peaks, and elegant gardens. Nanjing was the country's capital for six dynastic periods. Nearby Suzhou is renowned for its splendid gardens.

4 Shandong. Take a pilgrimage to Taishan, the most revered of all China's sacred mountains, or Qufu, the birthplace of Confucius. For the more earthly pleasures of sun, beer, and Bavarian architecture, don't miss the oceanside city of Qingdao, China's windsurfing (and drinking) capital.

GETTING ORIENTED

3

Stretching from Hebei, which is culturally and geographically Northern China, to the more refined province of Jiangsu, Eastern China is accessible thanks to a well-developed tourist infrastructure. All four provinces have air and rail links to the major transport hubs of Beijing and Shanghai. As you travel from north to south, you'll have a chance to judge for yourself whether Chinese stereotypes are accurate: Northerners are viewed as typically taller with light skin, and are thought to be very fond of wheat-based foods like noodles and bread. Southerners, on the other hand, are thought of as shorter and darker, and rice is their staple. This vague cultural border lies somewhere between Beijing and Shanghai.

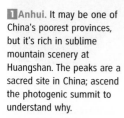

Updated by
Dana Kaufman
and Daniel
Garber

Tombs, monuments, elegant gardens, and ancient temples are just the beginning of what this brilliant region has to offer. This is where Confucius was born, where the Great Wall meets the sea, and where some of China's most celebrated landscapes have inspired painters and poets for millennia.

Hangzhou wows visitors with its legendary West Lake, and a bike ride through the city's stunning tea fields is an absolute must. This area, including Suzhou, with its well-preserved gardens and enchanting canals, even made a seasoned traveler like Marco Polo take notice. Huangshan's mysterious, misty peaks rise into the clouds in Anhui Province and have inspired whole schools of Chinese painting. Seven of China's 33 UNESCO World Heritage Sites dot this region, with Anhui's Xidi and Hongcun Villages and Shandong's Qufu (Confucius's ancestral birthplace) managing to retain their historic and artistic character. Buy Suzhou's famous silk direct from the silk-spinning worms, Tsingtao beer straight from the distillery in Qingdao, and Hangzhou's (as well as China's) most famous green tea picked fresh from the surrounding fields.

China's rise is changing the world, and by doing so creating a new world order as the balance of power gradually shifts eastward. This dramatic transformation is no secret, as media outlets the world over cover in detail every successful deal closed, every mine collapsed, every stunning achievement, and every glaring inequality. As the buildings grow taller, transportation becomes faster and people get richer, millions more are left behind. This has all come at a huge price, as the pollution becomes more threatening, the people more materialistic, and the corruption as endemic as ever.

Despite these obstacles, no region offers more contrasts. Take advantage of China's bullet trains, avoid the tour-group circuit (which envolves racing from one attraction to the next), and take advantage of China's safety (violent crime is rare compared to the rest of the world) and comfortable lodgings. Always look both ways when crossing the crowded streets, remember that the pedestrian in no way has the right of way in

China, and take a business card with your hotel's address in Chinese to show a taxi when you've had enough noise, smells, excitement, and pandemonium for one day's sanity to handle.

PLANNING

WHEN TO GO

No matter the month, there's great weather in some part of this region. In spring and summer, head to the coast at Qingdao and, farther north, Beidaihe and Shanǎhaiguan. Save the arduous ascents up Huangshan and Taishan for autumn, when the crowds and temperatures have died down.

Traveling a country of 1.3 billion is difficult when the 1.3 billion are also on vacation. The eastern region of China is heavily populated, and during the two weeklong public holiday periods, it seems like everyone takes to the road (or train, or plane).

Avoid traveling during the Chinese New Year, which is based on the lunar calendar and usually falls at the end of January. The weeklong National Day holiday at the start of October can easily be avoided with a bit of planning.

GETTING HERE AND AROUND

Cities that are connected by the CHR (China Highspeed Rail), such as Qingdao-Jinan and Nanjing-Suzhou, will be fairly easy and comfortable to reach. Buses are very efficient, and tickets can usually be bought the same day. Airline tickets can be purchased close to the departure date and usually stay consistent, assuming you avoid traveling during a Chinese holiday, when prices skyrocket. ⊕ *www.elong.com* is a great way to book hassle-free e-tickets using a foreign-issued credit card for a small surcharge.

AIR TRAVEL

Besides the major international airports in Beijing and Shanghai, other domestic air hubs include Nanjing, Qingdao, and Shijiazhuang (the capital of Hebei Province). Unlike other areas of the country, distances between sights in this region aren't great. The main operator is China Eastern Airlines, though there are a lot of smaller, regional carriers like Shandong Airlines, Hebei Airlines, and so forth.

BUS TRAVEL

With even more destinations and departures than the rail system, buses can be essential for trips of less than four or five hours. The actual vehicles vary wildly in terms of quality and comfort, but sometimes there's just no other option. In big cities, buses are usually in reasonable condition and have air-conditioning, assigned seating, and reliably punctual service. Remember to bring a pair of headphones, as drivers love to blast Chinese pop music to help stay awake. Never go with the army of touts who work at the main bus stations and offer cheaper, faster alternatives. The vast majority of these will be small, unsafe old vehicles soliciting every hitchhiker along the way and turning a 50-mile trip into an all day stop-and-go.

CAR TRAVEL

Hiring a driver is possible but can be very costly. Expect prices of at least $150 a day without an English-speaking guide, and substantially more with an English speaker. Five-star international hotels are your best places to inquire and make arrangements. There are many well-written English Web sites offering car service with English-speaking drivers, but once you inquire, an English speaker is often not possible.

TRAIN TRAVEL

China's excellent rail system is probably your best bet for getting around this region. The distances aren't quite long enough for air travel, and trains offer a greater variety of departure times and destinations. Tickets can be purchased either through your hotel, which is strongly recommended, or at the station, although the lines are long and vendors can be curt with non-Chinese speakers.

HEALTH AND SAFETY

Practice normal hygiene behavior. Non-squat toilets, found mainly in Western chain restaurants and international hotels, should not be difficult to find. Carry waterless hand sanitizer and toilet paper. Safe bottled water is widely available. Take all prescription medicine with you. For minor ailments, such as headaches and stomachaches, Chinese pharmacies are widespread and stocked with both Chinese and Western medicine. Antibiotics can be purchased easily and cheaply over the counter. Use your best judgment.

RESTAURANTS

Every locality has its own specialties—wild game in Chengde, fish and crustaceans in Jiangsu Province, or Qufu's Confucius family-style cuisine, a drawn-out banquet of dishes that have been refined over 2,000 years. The entire region is heavy on shallots, garlic, and a liberal use of oil. In the coastal haven of Qingdao, seafood is the catch of the day. Jiangsu cuisine, also called Huaiyang cuisine, is light, fresh, and sweet (though not as sweet as in Shanghai). Try Qingdao's famous fried clams or Suzhou's sweet-scented osmanthus chicken. As you travel inland to Anhui, the food is famously salty, relying heavily on preserved ham and soy sauce to enhance flavors. Anhui chefs make good use of local, mountain-grown mushrooms and bamboo shoots. Vegetarian options, available in or near any Buddhist temple, showcase chefs who manipulate tofu, wheat gluten, and vegetables to create interpretations of meat that even a voracious carnivore will appreciate.

HOTELS

Hotels in this region vary greatly, from very inexpensive, simple rooms with hard mattresses to exquisite, five-star properties on a par with major cities across the world., though you shouldn't expect to find much luxury in smaller cities such as Chengde and Tunxi (Huangshan). Limited English will be spoken at cheaper hotels, but clean and comfortable rooms can be found at very low rates. Most places accept credit cards, though several offer discounts if you pay in cash. Chinese hotels can be booked easily, without prepaying most of the time, through Chinese Web sites (in English): ⊕ *www.sinohotels.com* or ⊕ *www.elong.com*.

DINING AND LODGING PRICE CATEGORIES IN YUAN				
¢	$	$$	$$$	$$$$
Restaurants	under Y25	Y25–Y49	Y50–Y99	Y100–Y165	over Y165
Hotels	under Y700	Y700–Y1,099	Y1,100–Y1,399	Y1,400–Y1,800	over Y1,800

Restaurant prices are for a main course, excluding tips (there is no sales/retail tax in China). Hotel prices are for a standard double room, including taxes.

3

VISITOR INFORMATION

In the bigger cities you'll find storefronts and small street kiosks with clearly marked "Tourist Information" signage. However, finding someone who speaks enough English to be helpful might still be difficult, as these booths cater to domestic tourists. Your best bets for in-depth assistance are at the five-star international hotels' business centers. Be polite and persistent. The Chinese are notorious for pretending to understand, when in reality they do not. Write dates clearly when inquiring about tickets, speak slowly, and inspect any tickets given to you thoroughly before leaving. Look for copies of the English-language *Redstar* (Qingdao), *Map Magazine* (Nanjing) and *More Suzhou* in international hotels, foreign restaurants, and at Starbucks.

TOURS

Tour groups are always an option, but often full of scams and headaches. This is not to say there are not good ones out there, but do research, ask questions, and if the package price seems too high or low, be skeptical. The best source of information is on Fodor's forums (⊕ *www.fodors.com*), where many travelers share the good, the bad, and the ugly, like pressured tipping, frequent shopping stops, and low-quality food.

Beijing Discovery Tours (☎ *800/306–1264 www.beijingdiscoverytours. com*), an American-Chinese company, can arrange everything from your most basic travel needs to the most imperial desires. Despite the name, they can arrange private-only tours countrywide. Familiarize yourself with the Web site, send a detailed e–mail indicating what you want included (air travel, train, luxury hotels, etc.), and they will promptly respond with proposed costs. They are not cheap, but extremely reliable and thorough.

HEBEI

Many visitors travel through Hebei without a backward glance on the way to and from the capital, but the province has several sites worth a detour. Chengde is a must for history buffs and fans of the outdoors. The town's glory days were during the 18th century, when the Emperor Kangxi made the town his summer retreat and hunting ground, filling the place with a palace and temples. The emperors may be long gone, but the town still serves as a holiday destination, now for busloads of Beijing residents. Farther south, at the seaside resorts of Beidaihe and

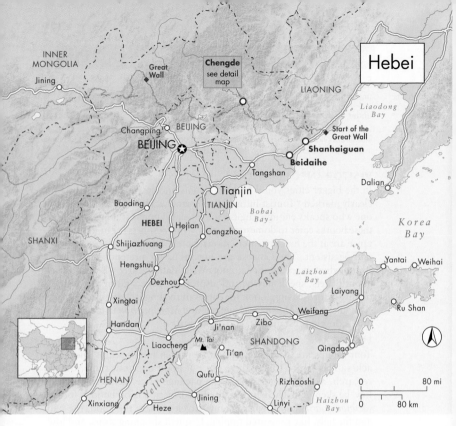

Shanhaiguan, where the Great Wall meets the sea, foreign visitors have the opportunity to mingle with Chinese vacationers.

CHENGDE

4 hrs (230 km [140 mi]) by train northeast of Beijing; 7 hrs (470 km [291 mi]) by train southwest of Shenyang.

An increasingly common stop on the China tour circuit, some visitors regard Chengde as one of the highlights of their trip. With the Wulie River running through the town and the Yanshan Mountains serving as an impressive backdrop, Chengde is filled with magnificent examples of imperial architecture.

Chengde had been just another village until the Qing Dynasty emperor Kangxi stumbled upon it during a hunting trip. Now it is a UNESCO World Heritage Site, home to one of the largest intact imperial gardens in China, the magnificent Mountain Resort, and the Eight Outer Monasteries. Although children enjoy romping through the imperial gardens, there's little else to entertain younger visitors. It's best to visit in summer or early autumn, as some tourist facilities close in the off-season.

GETTING HERE AND AROUND

TRAIN TRAVEL   Most travelers arrive on the K7711 direct train from Beijing, which departs from Beijing Main Rail Station at 8:07 am, arriving in Chengde at 12:29 pm. The city is on a northern rail line between Beijing and Shenyang. The journey takes 4½ hours from the capital. No trains run between Chengde and Beidaihe or Shanhaiguan.

BUS TRAVEL   Long-distance buses are uncomfortable and slow, but they're the only transport linking Chengde with Beidaihe and Shanhaiguan via Qinhuangdao. Several daily buses make this trip, all departing from Chengde's long-distance bus station near the Shenghua Hotel. Buses to Beijing also depart from this station.

TAXI TRAVEL   Chengde is a small city, so you shouldn't have to pay more than Y15 to get from the city center out to the temples.

SAFETY AND PRECAUTIONS

Chengde, like most Chinese cities, is a very safe place to explore. Violent crime is extremely rare, but petty theft can be a problem. Keep a close eye on your personal belongings in crowded places. Your biggest danger will probably involve navigating the streets. ■TIP➔ **Always look both ways when crossing the street. Pedestrians do not have the right of way, and Chinese drivers view basic rules of the road as a mere suggestions.**

TIMING

Chengde is a small city, and most of the main attractions are bunched northeast of the Mountain Resort, so one or two full days should be enough time to see the sights. That said, the Mountain Resort is huge, and could easily take up a full day. If you want to do any hiking in the surrounding countryside, plan on three full days.

TOURS

All hotels in Chengde run tours covering the main sights, at least during the high season. An English-speaking guide costs around Y100.

ESSENTIALS

Air Contact Qinhuangdao Airport Ticket Office (⊠ *169 Yingbin Lu, Qinhuangdao* ☎ *0335/306–2579*).

Bus Contact Chengde Long-Distance Station (⊠ *Wulie Lu at Xinhua Lu* ☎ *0314/212–3588*).

Medical Assistance Chengde Chinese-Western Hospital (⊠ *12 Xi Da Jie* ☎ *0314/202–2222*).

Train Contact Chengde Train Station (⊠ *Chezhan Lu* ☎ *0314/762–2602*).

Visitor and Tour Info Chengde CITS (⊠ *11 Zhonghua Lu* ☎ *0314/202–7483*).

EXPLORING

It isn't worth spending much time wandering around the city, but the massive size of the Mountain Resort, twice as large as Beijing's Summer Palace, means you will be doing plenty of walking. The other monasteries are close to the city.

TOP ATTRACTIONS

At the **Mountain Resort** *(Bishu Shanzhuang)*, Emperor Kangxi ordered construction of the first palaces in 1703. Within a decade dozens of ornate temples, pagodas, and spectacular gardens were spread over 1,500 acres. By the end of the 18th century nearly 100 imperial structures filled the town.

Besides luxurious quarters for the emperor and his court, great palaces and temples were completed to house visiting dignitaries and to impress them with the grandeur of the Chinese empire. Its interconnected palaces, in different architectural styles, reflect China's diversity. Replicas of famous temples representing China's religions stand on hillsides surrounding the palace, as though paying homage to the court.

Numerous buildings remain; some have been restored, but many have grass coming up through the cracks. Only eight of the temples are open to visitors (two of the originals were demolished, and another two are dilapidated). A number of rooms have been lovingly restored and display period furniture, ornaments, and costumed mannequins frozen in time. The surrounding landscape of lakes, grassy meadows, and cool forests is lovely for a stroll. Mountains in the northern half of the park and a giant pagoda in the center afford panoramas of the city of Chengde to the south and the temples to the north and east. The Mountain Resort and the temples are so massive that even with the influx of summer tourists they don't feel crowded. ⊠ *Center of town* ☎ *0314/2029771* ⌨ *Apr. 1–Oct. 31, Y120; Nov. 1–Mar. 31 Y90* ⊙ *Daily 7 am–6 pm.*

Viewing Chengde's **Eight Outer Monasteries** from above, it looks as though Emperor Kangxi built a Disneyland for China's religions. Originally there were a dozen temples, and each was built to reflect the architectural styles of a different minority group. The Eight Outer Monasteries are grouped on the eastern and northern slopes of the Mountain Resort in two different sections near the Wulie River. The eastern temples of Anyuan, Pule, and Puren can be reached by Bus 10 from the Mountain Resort, and the northern temples of Putuozongcheng, Xumifushou, Puning Si, Puyou, and Shuxiang can be reached by taking Bus 6 from the same place. Only Puning Si is still in use by monks. ⊠ *North of the Imperial Summer Villa* ⌨ *Y20–Y50* ⊙ *Daily 8–6.*

On the western bank of the Wulie River, the **Temple of Universal Peace** *(Puning Si* ⊠ *Puning Si Lu* ⌨ *Summer, Y80; winter, Y60* ⊙ *Daily 8–5)* is an interesting blend of traditional Chinese temple and Buddhist monastery. The fascinating compound is well worth a visit, particularly to see the awe-inspiring 72-foot-tall statue of Guanyin, a Buddhist deity of compassion. The temple was built in 1755 during the reign of Emperor Qianlong and modeled on the Samye Temple, the earliest Buddhist monastery in Tibet.

The **Temple of the Potaraka Doctrine** *(Putuozongcheng Miao* ⊠ *Shizhigou Lu* ⌨ *Summer, Y80; winter, Y60* ⊙ *Daily 8–6)* is modeled on the Potala Monastery in Lhasa, which is why it is known as the Little Potala. The temple, started in 1767, is the largest of the eight surviving temples in Chengde. Inside the imposing gate is a pavilion housing three

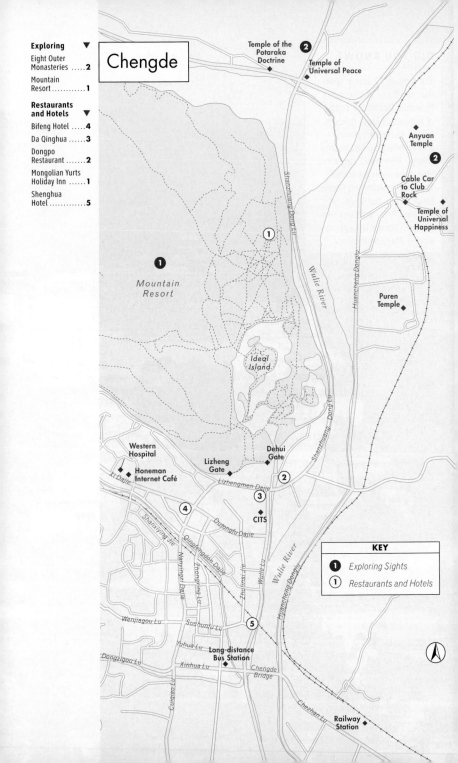

Chengde

Temple of the
Potaraka
Doctrine **2**

Temple of
Universal Peace

Anyuan
Temple

2

Cable Car
to Club
Rock

Temple of
Universal
Happiness

Puren
Temple

Shanzhuang Dong Lu

Wulie River

Huancheng Donglu

1

*Mountain
Resort*

*Ideal
Island*

Western
Hospital

Honeman
Internet Café

Xi Dajie

Shanxiying Jie

Lizheng
Gate

Dehui
Gate

2

Lizhengmen Dajie

3

4

Duanfu Dajie

CITS

Qianlongdian Dajie

Nanyingzi Dajie

Zhongxing Lu

Zhulinsi Jie

Wulie Lu

Shanzhuang Dong Lu

Wulie River

Huancheng Donglu

KEY

1 *Exploring Sights*

(1) *Restaurants and Hotels*

Wenjiagou Lu

Sushuntu Lu

Yuhua Lu

Cuigiao Lu

Dongzigou Lu

Xinhua Lu

Long-distance
Bus Station

5

*Chengde
Bridge*

Chezhan Lu

Railway
Station

stelae, the largest one inscribed in Han, Manchu, Mongolian, and Tibetan languages.

The **Temple of Universal Happiness** (*Pule Si*⊠ *East of Mountain Resort* 🎫 *Y50* ⊙ *Daily 8–6*) was built in 1766, when the imagery of Tibetan and Mongol Buddhism played an important role in the political and cultural arenas, especially in court circles. The architecture of the main building, the Pavilion of the Brilliance of the Rising Sun (Xuguangge) is similar to Beijing's Temple of Heaven. Look for the high, square, boxlike ceilings with a wooden Tibetan-style mandala motif. On top of the building's outer walls were eight brilliantly painted pagodas supported by lotus flower stands, only one of which remains. The lotus traditionally represents purity, and is a common motif in Buddhist temples.

3

WORTH NOTING

A cable car and a hiking trail lead up to Club Rock (Bangchui Feng), a phallic protrusion that spawned a local legend: if the rock should fall, so will the virility of local men. 🎫 *Y50* ⊙ *Daily 8–6.*

WHERE TO EAT

Given Chengde's role as a royal hunting ground, it's no surprise that the local specialty is wild game. Spiced deer meat sold in clusters for Y5 and pheasant and mushroom stuffed dumplings can be sampled at the visitor-friendly shops on the street south of the Summer Resort.

¢–$ ✕ **Da Qinghua.** Overlooking Lizheng Gate, this cheerful place with a
CHINESE   rustic wooden exterior is a good choice if you want to sample local dishes. Try the specialty: homemade dumplings filled with pheasant and local mushrooms. The picture menu helps—the staff do not speak English. To find it, look for the dragons on the building's exterior. ⊠ *19 Lizhengmen Da Jie* ☎ *0314/2036–2222* ▭ *No credit cards.*

$–$$ ✕ **Dongpo Restaurant.** With one branch near Dehui Gate (east of Lizheng
SICHUAN   Gate) and two others around town, Dongpo serves hearty Sichuan fare. There's no English menu, but classics like *gongbao jiding* (chicken with peanuts) and *niurou chao tudou* (beef and potatoes) are available. ⊠ *Shanzhuang Dong Lu* ☎ *0314/505–7766* ▭ *No credit cards.*

WHERE TO STAY

¢   🏨 **Bifeng Hotel.** Although not fit for an emperor, this is as good as it gets in Chengde. Not much to look at from the outside, inside it is clean and comfortable. The carpet needs replacing, so sleep on the bed. Be sure to exhaust yourself at the nearby Mountain Resort, making it easy to sleep anywhere! **Pros:** location, best in town. **Cons:** needs renovation, Chinese only breakfast. ⊠ *9 Huoshenmiao, Tower B Dehui Building, Chengde* ☎ *0314/ 205–0668* ⤵ *71 rooms In-hotel: restaurant, laundry service.* ▭ *MC, V.*

¢   🏨 **Mongolian Yurts Holiday Inn.** This hotel (no relation to the chain) is made up of 30 yurts. They may not be the type used by Genghis

Khan—they are made of concrete—but they can sleep two or three people and have modern touches like television sets. Located inside the Mountain Resort, this makes for a peaceful and unusual stay. The restaurant continues the Mongolian theme, so expect plenty of mutton on the menu. **Pros:** great location, quiet, it's a yurt. **Cons:** it's a yurt. ✉ *Inside the Mountain Resort* ☎ *0314/216–3094* ⤶ *30 yurts* ♿ *In-room: no a/c. In-hotel: restaurant* ➥ *No credit cards* ⊙ *Closed Nov.–Mar.*

¢–$ 🏨 **Shenghua Hotel.** At 14 stories tall, this silver tower of glass and steel soars above the city. Opposite of the rather dark reception areas, the rooms have plenty of windows and natural light. An excellent restaurant serves local specialties such as lightly battered stir-fried venison. The bilingual tour operator on staff can help you plan tours of the region. **Pros:** reliable services, near bus and train stations. **Cons:** a bit far from Mountain Resort and monasteries. ✉ *22 Wulie Lu* ☎ *0314/227–1000* ⊕ *www.shenghuahotel.com* ⤶ *111 rooms* ♿ *In-room: safe, refrigerator, Internet. In-hotel: 3 restaurants, bar, gym, laundry service* ➥ *MC, V.*

NIGHTLIFE AND THE ARTS

The main shopping street, Nanyingzi Dajie (parallel to Wuli River), is a good place to walk in the evening, when a night market stretches all the way down the street. Many of the vendors sell antiques and fun knickknacks.

Puning Song and Dance (✉ *Temple of Universal Peace, Puning Si Lu* ☎ *0314/216–2007*) has infrequent performances that are a bit touristy, but a great way to see the Temple of Universal Peace lighted up at night. The Y150 admission includes transport to and from your hotel. Have your hotel call ahead.

BEIDAIHE

4 hrs (260 km [160 mi]) by express train east of Beijing; 5 hrs (395 km [245 mi]) by train southwest of Shenyang; 1 hr (35 km [22 mi]) by minibus southwest of Shanhaiguan.

English railway engineers came across this small fishing village in the 1890s. Not long after, wealthy Chinese and foreign diplomats were visiting in droves. After Mao Zedong came to power, the new rulers developed a taste for sea air. Today the seaside retreat has an interesting mix of beach kitsch and political posturing (watch out for the rousing propaganda posters along the beachfront). Beidaihe is terrifyingly crowded during the summer and practically empty the rest of the year.

GETTING HERE AND AROUND

Most visitors come directly from Beijing, and the train is the most convenient option. There are nine double-decker tourist trains each day, and the journey takes about three hours. The train station in Beidaihe is not in the center of town. If you arrive late at night, taxi drivers may try to charge exorbitant rates.

AIR TRAVEL   The nearest airport is 5 km (3 mi) away at Qinhuangdao, with frequent flights limited to Shanghai and Shijiazhuang.

BOAT AND FERRY TRAVEL Qinhuangdao is one of the biggest harbors in China. Destinations include Dalian (14 hours), Shanghai (28 hours), Qingdao (12 hours), and Tianjin (18 hours). Contact CITS in Qinhuangdao for prices and schedules.

BUS TRAVEL An excellent minibus service runs between Beidaihe, Qinhuangdao, and Shanhaiguan. Buses leave every 30 minutes, cost Y6, and make frequent stops. The bus station in Beidaihe is at the intersection of Heishi Lu and Haining Lu. Buy tickets on the bus.

TRAIN TRAVEL Trains traveling up the coast from Beijing all pass through Beidaihe, Shanhaiguan, and Qinhuangdao.

SAFETY AND PRECAUTIONS
China is safe for travelers, but be alert and watch your belongings. Street food is generally safe if cooked at a high heat and not left out in the sun. Be especially careful with seafood, and only dine at crowded places where the food cannot sit too long.

TIMING
A half day is sufficient to see what the village has to offer. Most tourists see Baidaihe while on a Great Wall tour. If the weather allows, it can be a great place to bicycle ride and linger for a bit longer.

ESSENTIALS
Air Contact Qinhuangdao Airport (✉ *169 Yingbin Lu, Qinhuangdao* ☎ *0335/306–2579*).

Boat and Ferry Contacts Qinhuangdao CITS (✉ *100 Heping Dajie, Qinhuang-dao* ☎ *0335/323–1117*) **Qinhuangdao Tourism Bureau** (✉ *11 Gangcheng Dajie, Qinhuangdao* ☎ *0335/366–1001*).

Bus Contact Beidaihe Station (✉ *Beining Lu and Haining Lu* ☎ *0335/418–3077*).

Medical Assistance If you are ill in Beidaihe, go to Qinhuangdao—it has superior medical facilities. **Qinhuangdao Hospital** (✉ *281 Hebei Lu, Qinhuangdao* ☎ *0335/404–1695*).

Train Contact Beidaihe Train Station (✉ *Chezhan Lu*).

Visitor and Tour Info The closest tourism center is in Qinhuangdao. **Qinhuangdao CITS** (✉ *100 Heping Dajie, Qinhuangdao* ☎ *0335/323–1117*). **Qinhuangdao Tourism Bureau** (✉ *11 Gangcheng Dajie, Qinhuangdao 066001* ☎ *0335/366–1001*).

EXPLORING
The best way to get around on a sunny day is to rent a bicycle and cruise up and down the seafront.

Lianfeng Hill Park (*Lianfengshan Gongyuan*). North of the middle beach you'll find this lovely park, where quiet paths through a pine forest lead to the **Guanyin Temple** (Guanyin Si). Look for the aviary, known as the Birds Singing Forest. There are also good views of the sea from the top of Lianfeng Hill. ✉ *West side of town 066000* ☎ *0335/404–1591* 🎫 *Y30* 🕐 *Daily 8–5.*

The rugged landscape around Shanhaiguan.

WHERE TO EAT AND STAY

In summer, seafood restaurants line the beach, and you only need to point at the most appetizing thing squirming in red buckets for the waiter to serve up a delicious fresh meal. A plateful of fresh mussels should cost about Y15, fresh crabs a little more. More good seafood restaurants are clustered on Haining Lu near the beach.

¢–$$
ECLECTIC

✕ **Kiesslings.** Opened by Austrians six decades ago, this is the town's only foreign-owned restaurant. It serves both Chinese and Western dishes, but is best known for its tasty baked goods at breakfast. Its decor is a little old-fashioned, but that is part of its charm. The restaurant is usually open from May through September, but call ahead to make sure. ⊠ *Dongjing Lu, behind Beidaihe Guesthouse for Diplomatic Missions* ☎ *0335/404–1043* ▭ *No credit cards.*

$

🏨 **Beidaihe Guesthouse for Diplomatic Missions** *(Beidaihe Waijiao Renyuan Binguan).* Catering to foreign visitors, the guesthouse has several staff members who speak English remarkably well. Reflecting its past as a lodging for Russian diplomats, it has a building reserved for "distinguished guests." The attractive complex, made up of low-slung buildings from the 1960s, is set among cypresses and pines in a peaceful spot overlooking its own private beach. Rates for more expensive rooms include breakfast. **Pros:** the classic Beidaihe experience. **Cons:** some older buildings could use renovation. ⊠ *1 Baosan Lu* ☎ *0335/428–0600* ⇨ *165 rooms* ⌂ *In-hotel: restaurant, bar, tennis court, gym, beachfront, laundry service* ▭ *AE, DC, MC, V* ⊗ *Closed Nov.–Mar.*

¢

🏨 **Jinshan Hotel.** On a quiet stretch of sand, this hotel is made up of five two-story buildings linked by tree-lined paths. The rooms are clean and comfortable, although they are beginning to show their age. One of the town's branches of the China International Travel Service (CITS) is on the premises. Stay here in summer, as few of the facilities are open in low season. **Pros:** on the beach. **Cons:** some rooms are worn. ⊠ *4 Dongsan Lu,* ☎ *0335/404–1338* ☞ *267 rooms* ♿ *In-hotel: 2 restaurants, bar, gym* ☰ *AE, DC, MC, V.*

SHANHAIGUAN

3

1 hr (35 km [22 mi]) by minibus northeast of Beidaihe; 5 hrs (280 km [174 mi]) by minibus east of Beijing; 5 hrs (360 km [223 mi]) southwest of Shenyang.

On the northern tip of the Bohai Coast, Shanhaiguan is the end of the road for the Great Wall. Here the eastern end of the massive structure plunges into the sea. During the Ming Dynasty, Shanhaiguan was fortified to prevent hordes of mounted Manchurian warriors from pushing to the south. Now local tourists swarm the town during the summer. An impressive wall still surrounds the old town, though the warriors on the battlements are now mannequins.

GETTING HERE AND AROUND
Some trains from Beijing to Beidaihe continue on to Shanhaiguan, but they are the slower trains and take around five hours. To save time, catch a train to the nearby town of Qinhuangdao, about three hours from Beijing. From Qinhuangdao, take a bus or a taxi to Shanghaiguan.

AIR TRAVEL The nearest airport is in the industrial city of Qinhuangdao, with very limited destinations.

BUS TRAVEL An excellent minibus service runs from Shanhaiguan to Beidaihe and Qinhuangdao. Buses leave every 30 minutes, cost Y6, and make frequent stops. The bus station in Beidaihe is at the intersection of Heishi Lu and Haining Lu. Buy tickets on the bus.

TAXI TRAVEL The half-hour taxi ride between Beidaihe and Shanhaiguan costs about Y80.

TRAIN TRAVEL Shanhaiguan has the fewest trains, so it's worth booking a ticket to Qinhuangdao and then catching a bus to Shanhaiguan.

TIMING
After several modes of transportation to arrive in this part of the region, you might not want to rush out so quickly. A few days can easily be spent at both. Shanhaiguan and Beidaihe come alive in the summer (many restaurants and tourist facilities completely shut down in late October). If pressed for time, concentrate more on Qingdao in Shandong.

ESSENTIALS
Air Contact Qinhuangdao Airport (⊠ *169 Yingbin Lu, Qinhuangdao* ☎ *0335/306–2579*).

Boat and Ferry Contacts Qinhuangdao CITS (⊠ *100 Heping Dajie, Qinhuangdao* ☎ *0335/323–1117*). **Qinhuangdao Tourism Bureau** (⊠ *11 Gangcheng Dajie, Qinhuangdao* ☎ *0335/366–1001*).

Bus Contact Shanhaiguan Station (⊠ *Xinkai Xi Lu* ☎ *0335/502–3879*).

Medical Assistance **Qinhuangdao Hospital** (✉ *281 Hebei Lu, Qinhuangdao* ☎ *0335/404–1695*)

Train Contact **Shanhaiguan Train Station** (✉ *Off Nanguan Da Jie*).

EXPLORING
TOP ATTRACTIONS

The **First Gate Under Heaven** *(Tianxiadiyiguan)* is the city's eastern portal. Walking along the top (you have to pay an extra Y2, but it's worth it), you can gaze down at the fortifications and imagine how intimidating they must have been to potential invaders. Not that it worked forever: the Manchus overran the city in 1644. Through binoculars you can see remaining sections of the Great Wall snaking up nearby mountains. ✉ *East side of the city* ☎ *0335/5051106* ☎ *Y40, includes admission to Great Wall Museum* ☉ *Daily 8:30–8.*

The **Great Wall Museum** *(Changcheng Bowuguan)*, housed in a Qing Dynasty–style building past the First Gate Under Heaven, has a diverting collection of historic photographs and cases full of military artifacts, including the fierce-looking weaponry used by attackers and defenders. There are some English captions, but they are not everywhere. ✉ *South of First Gate Under Heaven* ☎ *Y40, includes admission to First Gate Under Heaven* ☉ *Daily 7–4.*

One way to leave behind the crowds at Old Dragon Head is to climb the wall as it climbs **Jiao Mountain** *(Jiao Shan)*, about 4 km (2½ mi) from the city. The beginning of the section has been retrofitted with handrails and ladders up the sides of watchtowers, but you can keep climbing until you reach the "real" wall. On a clear day the view makes it worth the effort. There is no public transportation, but Jiao Shan is only a 10-minute taxi ride from Shanhaiguan. ☎ *Y30 for cable car* ☉ *Daily 8–5.*

Legend has it that the Great Wall once extended into the Bohai Sea, ending with a giant carved dragon head. The structure that today is called **Old Dragon Head** *(Lao Long Tou)* has been totally rebuilt. It's still a dramatic sight, with the Great Wall jutting out into the sea with waves smashing at its base. On the beach there are motorboats that will take you out to snap a few photos. Some Ming Dynasty naval barracks have also been re-created, and you can dress up in imperial costumes and pretend you're a naval officer. ☎ *Y50* ☉ *Daily 8–5.*

WORTH NOTING

About 8 km (5 mi) down the coast from Old Dragon Head is **Mengji-angnu Miao**, a shrine commemorating a local legend. As the story goes, a woman's husband died while building the Great Wall. She wept as she searched for his body, and in sympathy the Wall split open before her, revealing the bones of her husband and others buried within. Overcome with grief, she threw herself into the sea. The temple has statues of the woman, a symbol of wifely dedication. The shrine is a 10-minute taxi ride northeast of town. ☎ *Y30* ☉ *Daily 7–4.*

WHERE TO EAT AND STAY

¢–$ ✕ **Wang Yan Lou.** Probably the most upmarket option in town, Wang
CHINESE Yan Lou serves excellent local seafood. Don't be put off by the bland exterior or the plastic tablecloths—the food is better than appearances

Extreme Climbs on the Great Wall

If you want to walk around the Great Wall but avoid the hordes of tourists, persistent postcard sellers, and Kentucky Fried Chicken outlets, then Huanghua is your best bet.

Huanghua is a rugged, unrestored part of the wall about 37 mi (60 km) from Beijing. Here the wall lies in two sections, almost 7 mi (11 km) long. A reservoir divides the two parts, and local fishermen are always at work among the parapets and beacon towers.

In summer the whole area is buried in swathes of yellow flowers (*huang hua*). In winter the sections can be icy and too dangerous to climb.

A SENSE OF HISTORY

According to legend, the Ming Dynasty general who oversaw construction spared no expense. He ended up being beheaded for going over budget. But thanks to his thoroughness, you feel as if you're walking through the past as you huff up those steep inclines. There is almost no rebuilt brickwork here (aside from an initial walkway that allows you to safely ascend the wall). Be aware that the natural weathering of the bricks makes the climb a little precarious. This reason alone keeps the tour buses away, so it's a worthwhile trade-off.

THE COST

Not long ago, the main danger at Huanghua wasn't the crumbling bricks or sheer drops, but locals keen to extort an entrance fee from visitors. They sometimes carried pitchforks and other sharp implements for added incentive. The government stamped out that practice, and now everyone must pay a flat rate of Y25.

GETTING THERE

Despite being only 37 mi (60 km) from Beijing, there are no direct public transportation options. However, it does not take much effort to reach Huanghua. From Beijing's Dongzhimen long-distance bus station, catch Bus 916 to Huairou, which leaves every 20 minutes from 5:30 am to 6:30 pm. If the traffic is awful, this can take up to three hours; at the minimum, it takes about 70 minutes. When you arrive at the transit station, taxi drivers will find you before you even get off the bus, all keen to take you on the remaining 30-minute journey to the wall. If you are an avid bargainer, you can hire a taxi for Y40 per car.

Another option is to hire a car for the day to take you to Huanghua from Beijing: expect to pay at least Y400. You can approach any taxi driver or ask your hotel to help arrange this.

would suggest. The menu is only in Chinese. ⊠ *Guancheng Xi Lu* 🖾 *No phone* ▭ *No credit cards*.

¢ 🏯 **First Pass Hotel.** Built to resemble a mansion from the time of the Qing Dynasty, this hotel is one of the best in Shanhaiguan. The owners have put a great deal of effort into the common areas, with ornate woodwork on the balconies and colorful lanterns lighting the corridors at night, but the guest rooms are basic. The restaurant, in one of the many courtyards, serves standard northern Chinese cuisine, so expect dumplings for breakfast and noodles for lunch. **Pros:** the best option in a town without many options. **Cons:** rooms not as nice as lobby.

⊠ *1 Dong Da Jie* ☎ *0335/513–2188* ☞ *120 rooms* ⚿ *In-room: no TV. In-hotel: restaurant, laundry service* ⊟ *No credit cards.*

¢ 🔟 **North Street Hotel.** Inside the city wall, this family-run lodging is a great deal as long as you don't expect too many comforts. Clean but shabby rooms are clustered around a pretty courtyard. The place may be a little noisy if the hotel is full. Still, the hotel has a lot more atmosphere than many nearby establishments. **Pros:** inexpensive. **Cons:** worn rooms and fixtures. ⊠ *2 Mujia Hutong* ☎ *0335/505–1680* ☞ *64 rooms* ⚿ *In-room: no phone, no TV* ⊟ *No credit cards.*

SHANDONG

More than 93 million people call Shandong home, and an annual influx of domestic tourists considerably adds to that number. Most flock to this region for Qingdao, China's most attractive coastal city and best known for its beer (known in the West as Tsingdao) and Bavarian architecture, the well-preserved town of Qufu, home of the philosopher Confucius, and Mount Tai, the most revered of all China's sacred mountains.

JI'NAN

3 hours (500 km [220 mi]) by express train south of Beijing; 2½ hours (395 km [245 mi]) by express train west of Qingdao.

It may be Shandong's provincial capital, but Ji'nan is overshadowed in almost every way by its coastal rival, Qingdao. However, this modern and easygoing place is an enjoyable transit point to other destinations. A good place to stay if you are going to visit the nearby Qufu, Taishan, or Qingdao, Ji'nan can be enjoyed in its own right, particularly for its many springs, which have earned the city the nickname "Spring City."

In 1901 Ji'nan was hauled into the 20th century by the construction of a railway line linking it to Qingdao. German, English, and Japanese companies found Ji'nan to be a convenient place to do business. A few buildings they had built are still in the downtown area (although they are increasingly overshadowed by new shopping centers and hotels).

Ji'nan's three main sights are Thousand Buddha Mountain, Big Bright Lake, and Gushing from the Ground Spring. These and a handful of other attractions easily occupy visitors for a day or so.

GETTING HERE AND AROUND

Your best option for traveling from Beijing is to catch one of the four daily D-coded express trains, the first of which leaves the Beijing South Train Station at 8:20 am and the last of which departs at 7:25 pm. The trip takes slightly over three hours. There are buses, but the journey can take more than seven hours.

AIR TRAVEL Regular flights link Ji'nan Yaoqiang Airport with Beijing, Shanghai, Hong Kong, and other major Chinese cities. The airport is 40 km (25 mi) northeast of downtown Ji'nan. The journey takes 45 minutes in a taxi and costs around Y100.

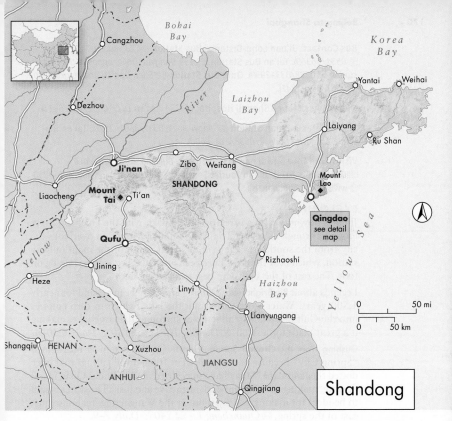

BUS TRAVEL Regular buses link Ji'nan with Mount Tai's nearest city, Tai'an (one hour), and Qufu (three hours). Buses ply the route between Ji'nan and Qingdao every 20 minutes, taking four to five hours.

TRAIN TRAVEL Ji'nan is on the Beijing–Shanghai line and the Beijing–Qingdao line, so there is no shortage of trains. On an express train, the journey from the capital takes between three and 4½ hours. Tai'an, the city nearest Mount Tai, is also on the Beijing–Shanghai rail line.

SAFETY AND PRECAUTIONS

Constant construction often leaves the pavement broken. Always watch where you are going, not just when crossing streets. If you have any breathing problems, you may want to consider wearing a face mask due to high levels of dust and pollution.

TIMING

Jinan's sights are relatively close together, making one day enough time to comfortably visit them as well as walk around the city.

TOURS
ESSENTIALS

Air Contact Ji'nan Yaoqiang Airport (✉ *Near Yaoqiang Village* ☎ *0531/96888*).

Bus Contacts Ji'nan Long-Distance Bus Station (✉ *23 Jiluo Lu*
☎ *0531/96369*). **Tai'an Bus Station** (✉ *139 Dongyue Dajie, opposite the train
station* ☎ *0538/833–2938*). **Qufu Bus Station** (✉ *Shen Dao Lu and Jingxuan Lu*
☎ *0537/441–1241*).

Medical Assistance Shengli Hospital (✉ *324 Jingwu Lu* ☎ *0531/793–8911*).

Train Contacts Ji'nan Station (✉ *Jingyi Jie* ☎ *0531/8601–2520*). **Tai'an Station** (✉ *Yingzhe Dajie* ☎ *0538/210–8600*).

Visitor and Tour Info Ji'nan CITS (✉ *6th fl., Building 30, 1 Jiefang Lu*
☎ *0531/8292–7071*). **Ji'nan Tourist Service** (✉ *86 Jingshi Lu* ☎ *800/420–8858*
⊕ *www.travelshandong.us*).

EXPLORING

Ji'nan's downtown area is relatively compact, with the Hucheng River
looping through its center. Thousand Buddha Mountain overlooks the
city from the southeast. The grid of streets south of the main railway
station, which bear the most European influence, are worth walking on
foot. The rest of the sights are best reached via taxi.

Legends about **Big Bright Lake** *(Daming Hu)* have been around for nearly
1,500 years. Water from springs fill the lake, which in turn empties
into the Gulf of Bohai. Small temples surround the large lake, making
it a great place for a stroll. ✉ *Daming Hu Lu* ☜ *Y30* ☉ *Daily 6:30–6.*

Gushing from the Ground Spring *(Baotu Quan).* Ji'nan is nicknamed
"Spring City" because of the more than 100 natural springs that once
dotted the landscape. Many have since dried up, but Baotu Quan is still
flowing, making the adjacent park attractive and lush. The water is said
to be ideal for making tea; try it out at the Wangheting Teahouse, just
east of the spring. ✉ *Quancheng Lu* ☜ *Y40* ☉ *Daily 7–9.*

One interesting architectural legacy of the foreign occupation is an
imposing redbrick **Protestant Church**, with its landmark twin towers.
Built in 1927, it is still in use. ✉ *425 Jing Si Lu.*

**NEED A
BREAK?**

Shandong Elite Teahouse (✉ *9 Qianfoshan Lu*) makes for a lovely break
after climbing nearby Qianfoshan. The exquisite traditional Chinese
teahouse is decorated with lattice wooden paneling, vases, and musical
instruments and serves many varieties of tea. The entire menu is beautifully written in Chinese, but the non-English-speaking staff are friendly and
do their best to help.

On the southern outskirts of the city is **Thousand Buddha Mountain** *(Qianfoshan),* one of the country's most sacred religious sites. It was called
Mt. Li in ancient times. In the early days of Sui Dynasty many statues
were chiseled into the rock, and it became known as Thousand Buddha Mountain. It is still the focus of religious festivals, although most
of the statues have been lost to the ravages of time and the Cultural
Revolution. If visiting in March or September, look out for the park's
temple fairs. Getting to the top of the mountain requires a 30-minute
climb or a ride on the cable car (Y25 round-trip). Either way you'll be
rewarded with a good view of Ji'nan—air quality permitting. For your

Burning joss sticks at the Thousand Buddha Mountain.

child, there's an excellent slide to whiz you back to the bottom. ⊠ *18 Jing Shiyi Lu, off Qianfoshan Lu* ⊡ *Y30* ⊙ *Daily 6 am–6 pm.*

WHERE TO EAT

¢–$
VEGETARIAN
★

✕ **Foshan Yuan.** This well-known restaurant is always packed and has a foreign-friendly English menu (with pictures). Everything is freshly prepared, and the space is pleasant (and very clean). The spicy carrot dumplings come highly recommended. The restaurant closes early, at 9 pm, so that the staff can prepare food for the homeless. It's a bit difficult to find, because it sits on a nameless street; show the name of the restaurant in Chinese to anyone in the area to help point you in the right direction. ⊠ *off of Foshan Jie, just north of Wen Hua Xi Lu* ☏ *0531/8602–7566* ▭ *No credit cards.*

¢–$
WESTERN

✕ **Jenny's Cafe.** Centrally located and easily recognized by its inviting blue awning, Jenny's is a favorite among Ji'nan's small expat community. The only true Western restaurant in town, the space is cute, but the kitchen only manages to churn out mediocre renditions of American, Italian, and Mexican classics. That said, it's a nice place to sit outside and enjoy a bottomless cup of Joe and a slice of cheesecake. They also have a fully stocked bar if you need something stronger. ⊠ *2 Wen Hua Xi Lu* ☏ *0531/8260–0214* ▭ *No credit cards.*

¢–$
SHANGHAINESE

✕ **Jiu Wan Ban.** On a street filled with 24-hour joints, this cheerful place is the one locals rate as the best. You choose from pre-plated platters of fresh local fish, which are then cooked as you watch. Try the seafood version *xiaolongbao*, the little dumplings that are a specialty of Shanghai. ⊠ *18 Chaoshan Jie* ☏ *0531/8612–7228* ▭ *No credit cards.*

WHERE TO STAY

¢–$ 🏠 **C.Sohoh.** Smack dab in the center of the city, this business hotel is a welcome relief from the large chains. It is small, quaint, and inexpensive, and the staff will go to all lengths to simplify your stay and direct you to the city's attractions. Business rooms all have computers with free Internet access and new stone showers. The well-maintained rooms have Chinese tea

sets and various other touches to personalize them. The hotel sign reads, C.Sohoh, but the hotel also goes by the name Shunhe on some booking sites. Don't let this be confusing, and use the address as a guide (it's directly across the street from the Sofitel). **Pros:** personalized service, great location. **Cons:** staff speak spotty English, small rooms. ⊠ *53 Luoyang Lu* ☎ *0531/8613–8888* ↪ *125 rooms* ⚭ *In-hotel: restaurant, room service* ▭ *AE, DC, MC, V.*

$ 🏠 **Sheraton Ji'nan.** The city's newest and most luxurious hotel offers a
★   superior level of service and luxury. Located in the East New Town, Ji'nan's central business district, this massive, rectangular structure has lovely views of the surrounding mountains or of the Olympic Sports Centre—a massive, lotus-shaped sports venue built specifically to host the 11th Chinese National Games and worth a visit for the distinctive architecture. Spacious guest rooms include a range of fabulous amenities, including Egyptian cotton sheets and rain-forest showerheads. Pamper yourself at their world-class Shina Spa, work up a sweat in the well-equipped fitness center and steam room, or simply dip your toes in either the indoor or outdoor pool. It's a true oasis in a gritty, concrete jungle. **Pros:** excellent facilities, great Japanese restaurant. **Cons:** isolated location away from the city center. ⊠ *8 Long Ao North Road.* ☎ *0531/8602–9999* ↪ *410 rooms* ⚭ *In-room: refrigerator, Wi-Fi. In-hotel: 3 restaurants, bar, room service, pool, gym, laundry service, no-smoking rooms* ▭ *AE, DC, MC, V.*

$$–$$$$ 🏠 **Sofitel Silver Plaza Ji'nan.** This 49-story cylinder in the center of town looks like a tube of lipstick. The lobby incorporates classical design elements with massive marble columns and chandeliers. The sleek guest rooms are spacious and have recently been renovated. Imported salami and Parma ham are expertly plated by the Italian head chef at Biscotti, the signature restaurant. The hotel is well managed, with an international team. Check the Web site for frequent promotions. **Pros:** excellent location, good Western food. **Cons:** small bathrooms. ⊠ *66 Luoyuan Dajie* ☎ *0531/8606–8888* ⊕ *www.sofitel.com/asia* ↪ *426 rooms* ⚭ *In-room: safe, refrigerator, Wi-fi. In-hotel: 3 restaurants, room service, bar, pool, gym, laundry service, no smoking rooms* ▭ *AE, DC, MC, V.*

NIGHTLIFE

Banjo (⊠ *54 Foshan Jie*) is a funky, eclectic bar that has become a fixture for local expats. It's set among a row of Chinese, Japanese, and Korean restaurants that are very lively at night.

Full Speed Ahead!

Bullet trains are rapidly changing the country's landscape, making life easier for everyone, including tourists. What took days now takes hours. A prime example is the Guangzhou–Wuhan high-speed railway, which only a few years ago took 10 hours, now travels over 600 miles in three hours (reaching top operational speeds of 350 km/h or 217 mph). Reliable, comfortable, and clean, these sleek and efficient trains are a convenient way to quickly jump between major cities and avoid taking domestic flights or long bus rides. And thanks to generous government funding, which is fueling a construction boom, the entire high-speed network is expected to reach 10,000 miles by 2020.

Most five-star hotels have business centers or travel desks that can help you book tickets for a small fee (Y30–60/ticket). With a country of 1.3 billion upwardly-mobile people, remember to book in advance—up to 10 days is recommended for long distances, but short distances such as Ji'nan to Qingdao or Hangzhou to Shanghai have frequent daily departures and can be booked the day before. At the station, look for the D-coded trains and the letters CRH, which signify high-speed rail. Just remember, this is still China; there's plenty of pushing and shoving to get to an assigned seat.

SHOPPING
Shandong Curio's City (✉ *283 Quancheng Lu*) is a cluster of small antiques shops huddled around an attractive courtyard. Jade, jewelry, and local antiques are beautifully displayed.

SIDE TRIP TO MOUNT TAI

Reaching 5,067 feet above sea level, **Mount Tai** *(Taishan)* is the most venerated of the five sacred mountains of China. A destination for pilgrims for 3,000 years, the mountain was named a UNESCO World Heritage Site in 1987. Confucius is said to have climbed the mountain and said as he scanned the horizon: "The world is very small." Much later, the Marxist Mao Zedong reached the top and even more famously said: "The East is red." If you are keen to reach a ripe old age, legend has it that climbing Mount Tai means you'll live to 100. It is possible to climb the cut-stone steps to the summit in a day, but many people prefer to stay overnight on the mountain. The classic photo—sunrise over the cloud-hugged mountainside—is actually a rare sight because of the mist. Human sacrifices were made on the summit, but today you will only encounter large crowds throughout the year.

GETTING HERE AND AROUND
Mount Tai is near the town of Tai'an, a major stop on the Shanghai–Beijing railway. Dozens of trains travel through Tai'an daily. Buses from Ji'nan to Tai'an leave the bus terminal opposite the main train station every 25 minutes between 5 am and 6 pm. From any spot in Tai'an, a taxi to Taishan takes less than 15 minutes and costs about

The Confucius Temple on top of the beautiful Mt. Tai.

Y10. ⊠ *About 50 km (30 mi) south of Ji'nan* 🗓 *Dec. 1–Jan. 31, Y100; Feb. 1–Nov. 30, Y125.*

WHERE TO STAY

¢–$ 🏨 **Shenqi Hotel.** It's the only real hotel on the summit, but it's overpriced considering the barely adequate rooms. Still, there are unusual extras, such as a bell that rings when it's time to get up for sunrise. **Pros:** perfect place to watch the sunrise on Mount Tai. **Cons:** overpriced, very basic rooms. ⊠ *Summit of Mount Tai, 10 Tianjie* ☎ *0538/822–3866* 🛏 *62 rooms* 🍴 *In-hotel: restaurant, bar, laundry facilities* 🖃 *AE, DC, MC, V.*

SIDE TRIP TO QUFU

Qufu is the birthplace of the country's most famous philosopher, Confucius, and so it's of massive significance to the Chinese people. Confucius's impact was immense in China, and his code of conduct was to dominate daily life until it fell out of favor during the Cultural Revolution. His teachings—that son must respect father, wife must respect husband, ordinary citizens must respect officials—were swept away by Mao Zedong because of their associations with the past. Qufu suffered greatly during the Cultural Revolution, with the Red Guards smashing statues and burning buildings. But the pendulum has swung back, and Confucius's teachings are back in favor. It's a lovely place, with timbered houses surrounded by the town walls.

GETTING THERE AND AROUND

Regular buses run trips from Ji'nan to Qufu. The Qufu bus station is south of the town center at the intersection of Shen Dao and Jingxuan Lu.

EXPLORING QUFU

Within the city walls, the **Confucius Temple** is a cluster of temples that occupy about a fifth of the city center. The 466 buildings cover more than 50 acres, making this one of the largest architectural complexes left from ancient China, comparable to Beijing's Forbidden City or Chengde's Summer Resort. The Hall of Great Achievements is one of the most ornate of the temples; don't miss its 28 stone pillars carved with dragons. The courtyards are full of gnarled trees, and the many memorial halls have fine calligraphy, stone columns, and old furnishings on display. ⊠ *Banbi Jie*

🎟 *Feb. 16–Nov. 14, Y110; Nov. 15–Feb. 15, Y90* ⊙ *Daily 8–5.*

Adjacent to the Confucius Temple is the **Confucius Family Mansion.** Although not as big as the Confucius Temple, the private home consists of around 450 rooms. It dates from the 16th century and illustrates the power and glory enjoyed by Confucius's descendants. ⊠ *Banbi Jie* 🎟 *Feb. 16–Nov. 14, Y75; Nov. 15–Feb. 15, Y60* ⊙ *Daily 8–5.*

Confucius and his descendants have been buried in this tree-shaded cemetery for the past 2,000 years. Surrounded by a 10-km (6-mi) wall, **Confucian Forest** has more than 100,000 pine and cypress trees. It's one of the only places in the city where you can escape the crowds. ⊠ *Lindao Lu* 🎟 *Feb. 16–Nov. 14, Y50; Nov. 15–Feb. 15, Y40* ⊙ *Daily 8–5.*

WHERE TO STAY

¢ 🏨 **Queli Hotel.** In a small town lacking options, this budget hotel is a decent choice. A short walk from the Confucius Temple and Confucius Family Mansion, the property's traditional exterior blends perfectly with the town's architecture. The public areas can get noisy, so be sure to request a room backing the courtyard and fountain to ensure a peaceful night's sleep. **Pros:** prime location for attractions. **Cons:** very simple accommodations, hard beds. ⊠ *1 Queli Lu* ☎ *0537/486–6818* 🛏 *150 rooms* ⚒ *In-hotel: restaurant, laundry service* ═ *AE, MC, V.*

QINGDAO

5½ hrs (540 km [335 mi]) by train southeast of Beijing; 2½ hrs by train (390 km [242 mi]) east of Ji'nan.

Qingdao has had a turbulent century, but it's emerged as one of China's most charming cities. It was a sleepy fishing village until the end of the 19th century, when Germany, using the killing of two German missionaries as a pretext, set up another European concession to take advantage of Qingdao's coastal position. The German presence lasted only until 1914, but locals continued to build German-style houses, and large parts of the Old Town make visitors feel as if they have stumbled into a town in the Black Forest. Unlike many cities that had foreign concessions, Qingdao has recognized the historical value of these buildings and is now enthusiastic about preserving them. With its seafront promenades, winding colonial streets, and pretty parks, Qingdao is probably China's best city for strolling.

WISEMAN PASS

If you want to soak up as much Confucianism as possible during your visit to Qufu, get a ticket that grants access to all three sites. During high season, that's Y185 for a ticket that covers the Confucius Temple, Confucius Family Mansion, and the Confucian Forest. The low-season price is Y160.

Home to the country's best-known beer, Tsingtao, Qingdao is very accommodating when it comes to alcohol consumption. (Look for beer being sold on the streets in plastic bags.) But wine drinkers should take heart, as the region is also developing a much-talked-about wine industry.

The city is a destination for golfers, having many of the country's best courses. But Qingdao added a new sport of note when it hosted the sailing events of the 2008 Olympics in the new Qingdao Sailing Center. Beijing invested a whopping $370 million for its world-class International Sailing Center.

GETTING HERE AND AROUND

A comfortable way to get to Qingdao is aboard one of the several daily D-coded express trains that link Qingdao to Beijing (six hours). It's best to buy tickets from travel agents or through your hotel, as lines are long and there are few English speakers at the station.

The long-distance bus terminal is opposite the train station. Taxis are a cheap way to get around. Getting anywhere in town will generally cost less than Y30.

AIR TRAVEL   Qingdao Liuting Airport is 30 km (19 mi) north of the city. In a taxi, the journey takes 40 minutes and costs around Y80. Some hotels have airport shuttles. Direct flights link Qingdao with Osaka and Seoul, as well as Hong Kong and other major Chinese cities.

BUS TRAVEL   Buses travel between Ji'nan and Qingdao every 20 minutes; the trip is four to five hours.

TRAIN TRAVEL   Direct trains link Qingdao with Ji'nan (three hours), Beijing (six hours), and Shanghai (10 hours).

TIMING

Qingdao is a very pleasant seaside city. Two full days is enough to see the sights, as they are grouped together on opposite sides of the city. The city has enough attractions and nightlife to keep you happily occupied for a few nights.

ESSENTIALS

Air Contact Qingdao Liuting Airport (✉ *Near Liuting Village* ☎ *0532/8471–5777*).

Boat and Ferry Contact Qingdao Ferry Terminal (✉ *6 Xinjiang Lu, 1 mi (2 km) north of the train station* ☎ *0532/8282–5001*).

Bus Contact Qingdao Long-Distance Bus Station (✉ *2 Wenzhou Lu* ☎ *0532/8371–8060*).

Medical Assistance International Clinic of Qingdao Municipal Hospital (✉ *5 DongHai Zhong Lu* ☎ *0532/8593–7690*).

Train Contact Qingdao Station (✉ *2 Tai'an Lu* ☎ *0532/8297–5423*).

Visitor and Tour Info Qingdao CITS (✉ *6F, A Yuyuan Dasha Office Building, 73 Xianggang Zhong Lu* ☎ *0532/8386–3960*). **Qingdao Tourism Administration** (✉ *7 Minjiang Lu* ☎ *0532/8591–2029*).

EXPLORING
TOP ATTRACTIONS
St. Michael's Cathedral *(Tianzhu Jiaotang)* is a Qingdao landmark, with its towering 200-foot twin steeples and red-tile roof. The classic neo-Gothic structure was built by the Germans in 1934, and was badly damaged during the Cultural Revolution. The surrounding area is a great place to explore, with distinctive old German buildings contrasting with uninspired, modern Chinese block architecture. Muslim vendors hawk fragrant lamb kebabs on the cobbled streets leading to the church. Masses are still held here. ✉ *15 Zhejiang Lu* 💳 *Y8* 🕒 *Mon.–Sat. 8–5, Sun. 10–5.*

The striking former **German Governor's Residence** *(Qingdao Ying Bin-guan)* was transformed into a museum in 1996. Built in 1906 as the official residence of the governor-general of the then-German concession, it is set on a hill overlooking the Old City. The interior resembles a Bavarian hunting lodge, with wood paneling and a wide staircase leading from the foyer up to the bedrooms. Among the famous leaders who have stayed here is a Who's Who of names from recent Chinese history: Mao Zedong, Zhou Enlai, and Deng Xiaoping. ✉ *26 Longshan Lu, below Xinhao Hill Park* 💳 *Y15* 🕒 *Daily 8:30–4:30.*

After the German Governor's Residence, the **Granite Mansion** (Huashi Lou), built in 1903, is Qingdao's second most famous example of traditional German architecture. This mini-castle was built as a villa for a Russian aristocrat, but soon became a retreat for the governor. ✉ *18 Huanghai Lu* 💳 *Y6.5* 🕒 *Daily 8–5:30.*

Qingdao's **Protestant Church** *(Jidu Jiaotang)* is easy to spot: look for the large green spire resembling those topping medieval castles. It was built in 1910 at the southwest entrance of Xinhao Hill Park. If you climb up to the bell tower, you are rewarded with an excellent view. ✉ *15 Jiangsu Lu* 💳 *Mon.–Sat. Y8; free on Sun.* 🕒 *Daily 8:30–4:30.*

The largest of the city's parks, **Sun Yat-sen Park** *(Zhongshan Gongyuan)*, is inland from Hui-quan Bay and has a number of

> **WORD OF MOUTH**
>
> "Drinking beer out of a plastic bag thru a straw in front of a Gothic church in Qingdao, China, had to be one of the most hysterical moments on my two week tour."
>
> —jilly

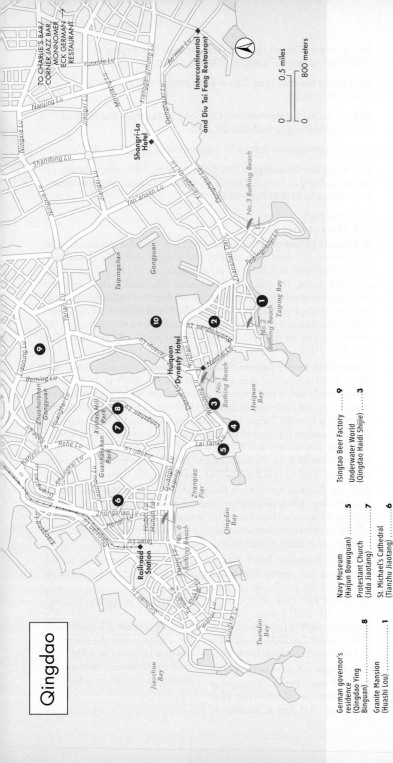

Qingdao

TO CHARLIE'S BAR,
CORNER JAZZ BAR,
MONNOMER
ECK GERMAN
RESTAURANT →

Intercontinental
and Diu Tai Feng Restaurant

Shangri-La
Hotel

0   0.5 miles
0   800 meters

No. 3 Bathing Beach

Taipingshan

Gongyuan

No. 2
Bathing Beach

Taiping Bay

Huiquan
Dynasty Hotel

No. 1
Bathing Beach

Huiquan
Bay

Zhushuishan
Gongyuan

Xinhao Hill
Park

Guanhaishan
Park

Lai Yang

Zhanqiao
Pier

Zhongshan Lu

Qingdao
Bay

Railroad
Station

Bathing
Beach

No. 6
Bathing Beach

Tuandao Bay

Jiaozhou Bay

German governor's
residence
(Qingdao Ying
Binguan) 8

Granite Mansion
(Huashi Lou) 1

Lu Xun Park
(Lu Xun Gongyuan) 4

Navy Museum
(Haijun Bowuguan) 5

Protestant Church
(Jida Jiaotang) 7

St. Michael's Cathedral
(Tianzhu Jiaotang) 6

Sun Yat-sen Park
(Zhongshan Gongyuan) ..10

Tsingtao Beer Factory ..9

Underwater World
(Qingdao Haidi Shijie) ..3

attractions, including a small zoo, a botanical garden, and the Zhan-shan Buddhist Temple. Qingdao's TV tower, a city landmark, offers visitors striking views from its observation deck. Originally planted by the Japanese in 1915 while under their occupation, the park contains some 20,000 cherry trees (which blossom annually only for a two-week period), and holds the annual Cherry Blossom Festival at the end of May. ✉ *28 Wendeng Lu* ☎ *0532/8287–0564* 🎟 *Y12* ⊙ *Daily 5 am–9 pm.*

Beer fans should make a pilgrimage to the **Tsingtao Beer Factory** *(Tsingdao Pijiu Chang).* A guide walks you through the facility, then gives you a multitude of freshly made beer samples. There is also an excellent museum on the history of the brewery, built in 1903 by—who else?—the Germans. ✉ *56 Dengzhou Lu* ☎ *0532/383–3437* 🎟 *Y50* ⊙ *Daily 8:30–4:30.*

WORTH NOTING

Built in 1929, **Lu Xun Park** *(Lu Xun Gongyuan), named for the distin-guished Chinese writer and revolutionist,* faces the rocky coastline of Huiquan Bay. As you pass through the traditional Chinese archway, walk along narrow stone paths, relax in the pavilions, and watch the waves crash. Small pine trees combined with rugged reefs make for very attractive vistas of the sea ✉ *West end of No. 1 Beach* 🎟 *Y5* ⊙ *Daily 7:30–6:30.*

The **Eight Passes** (Badaguan), named after the Great Wall's eight strategic passes, is a scenic area that lies in between Taiping and Huiquan Cape (around No. 2 Beach). It's far away from the city noise and pollution, so it makes for a lovely escape. The grounds of more than 200 European-style villas are landscaped with peach trees, pine trees, and ginkgoes. It's often referred to as "Little Switzerland."

NEED A BREAK?

In a German-style building dating from the 1930s, Café Roland (✉ **9 Taip-ing Jiao Er Lu** ☎ **0532/8387–5734**) has a lovely wooden interior and a view of No. 3 Beach. After walking around the Eight Passes, try the excellent, homemade rum-raisin ice cream.

In the upper yard of the **Navy Museum** *(Haijun Bowuguan)* you'll find an indoor exhibition documenting the history of the Chinese Navy. Outside are the big guns, including Russian-made fighter planes, fixed-turret and antiaircraft naval guns, rockets, tanks, ground artillery, naval vessels (including three moored in the adjacent harbor), and even an old biplane. The displays are dusty, so this museum is for hard-core naval fans only. ✉ *8 Lai Yang Lu* ☎ *0532/286–6784* 🎟 *Y50* ⊙ *Daily 8:30–5.*

☺ **Underwater World** *(Qingdao Haidi Shijie).* Located near No. 1 Beach, this family-friendly attraction features a moving platform that offers 360-degree views of the surrounding marine life. Four underground levels, interactive video displays, and tacky marine shows will enter-tain the kids for hours. ✉ *1 Laiyang Lu* ☎ *0532/8289–2187* 🎟 *Y90* ⊙ *Daily 8–5:30.*

WHERE TO EAT

It's no surprise that Qingdao's specialty is seafood. Locals flock to Minjiang Lu, where the time between choosing a fish from tanks and having it arrive steaming on your plate is about three minutes.

When choosing a restaurant, look for displays of Qingdao's new sanitation rating "smiley face" logos. A green smiling logo means the restaurant has high sanitation standards; a yellow neutral face means there are a few problems; a red frown face indicates very poor sanitation. Establishments that have received yellow and red face icons are given a period of time in which to improve, but you may want to avoid those as long as you see anything less than a smile!

> ### GANBEI!
>
> The **International Beer Festival**, China's biggest beer festival, has been held annually since 1991. It begins in mid-August, lasts for two weeks, and causes hotel prices to skyrocket. Hundreds of beers from all over the world are available for tasting. As a foreigner, be prepared for a lot of attention and drinking challenges by easy-going, young Chinese. As opposed to "Ganbei" which directly translates to "dry glass," say "*sui yi,*" meaning drink at a comfortable pace. You won't see any lederhosen, but it's still great fun.

$-$$
SEAFOOD

✕ **Cui Zhu Yuan.** Don't be offended when you're brought a bib and plastic gloves when you walk into this brightly lighted restaurant. You'll need them for the signature dish: tiny lobsters served in a rich, spicy sauce. There might be some work getting to the fleshy bits, but that's half the fun. Other Qingdao specialties, like spicy clams, are excellent. ⊠ *129 Minjiang Lu* ☎ *0532/8576–5286* 🚫 *No credit cards.*

$-$$
CANTONESE
Fodor'sChoice
★

✕ **Din Tai Fung.** The newest branch of this chain with outlets stretching from L.A. to Jakarta is located next to the Qingdao Olympic Sailing Center, facing the giant Olympic rings with great sea views. Inside the posh Marina City Mall, Din Tai Fung offers the freshest and arguably the best steamed pork dumplings (*xiao long bao*) in the city. Each dumpling is stuffed with delicate fillings, and lovingly "pleated" precisely 18 times. There is an English picture menu with a lot of vegetarian-friendly selections. Recommended are the vegetable dumplings (*jiaozi*) and the cold Shaoxing sesame and chili chicken. Cleanliness and efficiency make up for the uninspired modern decor. ⊠ *Bai Li Guang Chang, Marina City Mall, 86 Ao'men Lu* ⊕ *www.dintaifungusa. com* 🚫 *AE, DC, MC, V.*

$$-$$$
GERMAN

✕ **Monomer Eck German Restaurant and Bar.** This spacious restaurant offers a wide range of cuisines, but a full page is dedicated to German favorites. The Nuremburg sausages served with traditional Bavarian sauerkraut and spiced-up mashed potatoes are excellent. Despite the slow service and American '90s music, this is a charming place to linger over a range of German draft beers. It's also on a lively bar street, so a nightcap is easy. ⊠ *173 Jiangxi Lu,* ☎ *0532/8592–1096* 🚫 *No credit cards.*

$$-$$$
SEAFOOD

✕ **Qingdao Restaurant** (*Qingdao Caiguan*). At this popular restaurant you wander around displays of uncooked dishes laid out on ice and tanks filled with mussels and crabs, all ready to be whisked away to the

Qingdao has lovely seafront promenades, winding colonial streets, and pretty parks.

kitchen and cooked to order. The decor isn't exciting, but the food is excellent and the service is doting. ✉ *17 Aomen Lu* ☎ *0532/8388–0098* ⊟ *DC, MC, V.*

WHERE TO STAY

¢ 🏨 **Badaguan Hotel.** If your priority is peace and quiet, this hotel in the scenic Badaguan neighborhood is a good choice. Set in established gardens, it feels miles away from the hustle and bustle of the city. The guest rooms look a little dusty, but are otherwise adequate. The location near No. 2 Beach makes up for any deficiencies. **Pros:** a bargain for beautiful ocean views in an out-of-the-way location. **Cons:** outside of city center. ✉ *19 Zhengyangguan Lu* ☎ *0532/8203–8666* ⟿ *300 rooms* ♿ *In-room: Internet. In-hotel: restaurant, tennis courts, gym, laundry service* ⊟ *AE, DC, MC, V.*

$–$$ 🏨 **Huiquan Dynasty Hotel.** Opposite the city's most popular beach, this well-established hotel revels in its enviable location. Diners at the 25th-floor revolving restaurant enjoy great views of the ocean. It's worth paying for a room overlooking the ocean, as the rooms in the rear overlook a busy road. There is a branch of the CITS travel agency on the premises. **Pros:** great ocean views from some rooms; very convenient beach access. **Cons:** a musty odor pervades some rooms; old machines in fitness room. ✉ *6 Nanhai Lu* ☎ *0532/8287–1122* ⟿ *405 rooms* ♿ *In-room: Internet. In-hotel: 2 restaurants, room service, bar, pool, gym, laundry service* ⊟ *AE, DC, MC, V.*

$$–$$$$ 🏨 **InterContinental Qingdao.** Possibly the most luxurious property in Qingdao, this ultramodern international hotel is the city's newest lodging addition. Contemporary rooms have dark wood paneling, a built-in

mood lighting system, stand-alone bath tubs, DVD players, and coast-line or skyline views. If price is no object, splurge for one of two Aqua Suites, which include private Jacuzzis and outdoor terraces with dazzling marina views. It's adjacent to the Olympic Sailing Venue and a short walk from the upmarket Marina City shopping complex. **Pros:** location next to marina waterfront promenade. **Cons:** inconsistent service for a five-star; pricey Internet connection. ☒ *98 Ao Men Lu* ☎ *0532/665–6666* ⊕ *www.intercontinental.com* ☜ *422 rooms* △ *In-room: safe, refrigerator, Wi-fi. In-hotel: 3 restaurants, bar, pool, gym, laundry service* ☰ *AE, DC, MC, V.*

$$–$$$
Fodor's Choice
★

🏨 **Shangri-La.** Only a block from the scenic coastline, the Shangri-La is also close to some of the best shopping and eating in town. Legions of bellboys wait to take you and your luggage up to your well-appointed room. Q Bar, popular with local expats, is a stylish place for a pre-dinner drink. Upgrade to the new Valley Wing for well-appointed rooms and excellent personalized service. **Pros:** convenient to beach. **Cons:** restaurants and shops a little far from the hotel on foot. ☒ *9 Xiang Gang Zhong Lu* ☎ *0532/8388–3838* ⊕ *www.shangri-la.com* ☜ *696 rooms* △ *In-room: safe, refrigerator, Internet. In-hotel: 3 restaurants, room service, bar, tennis court, pool, gym* ☰ *AE, DC, MC, V.*

NIGHTLIFE AND THE ARTS

Most of the action takes place in the eastern part of the city. Jiangxi Lu and Minjiang Lu are two lively streets east of Zhongshan Park with a smattering of decent nightlife options.

Charlie's Bar (☒ *167 Jiangxi Lu* ☎ *532/8575–8560*) is a cozy, laid-back bar with a sports-pub atmosphere, a long wooden bar, and Guinness on draft. In the same neighborhood is the **Corner Jazz Club** (☒ *153 Minjiang Lu* ☎ *532/8589–7919*), a popular place with both Chinese and foreigners, despite the lack of jazz. Here you'll find locals playing dice games, foreigners playing foosball, and everyone drinking, dancing, and having a good time. At the **Tsingdao Brewery Bar** (☒ *56 Dengzhou Lu* ☎ *0532/8383–3437*) you can drink from the source. The bar does get rowdy since prices are kept low, but if cost is more of a consideration than ambience, this can be an excellent night out.

SPORTS AND THE OUTDOORS

Chinese visitors come to Qingdao by the tens of thousands for the beaches. Each of the seven sandy beaches that run along the coast for more than 6 mi (10 km) has a variety of facilities ranging from changing rooms to kiosks renting inflatable toys. Sometimes the water quality isn't the greatest, so it's worth inquiring at your hotel.

BEACHES

No. 1 Beach is the busiest, and in summer it can be difficult to find a place for your towel. If your goal is peace and quiet, head to **No. 2 Beach,** as fewer Chinese tourists venture out that way. In the summer, watch out for the armies of brides and bridegrooms using the beaches for their wedding photos.

GOLF

The 18-hole **Qingdao International Golf Club** (✉ *Songling Lu* ☎ *0532/8896–0001*) is 20 minutes from downtown. It has driving ranges, a pro, and a fine-dining restaurant. Booking ahead, especially on weekends, is recommended.

WATER SPORTS

With the sailing center for the 2008 Olympics, the Qingdao waterfront is completely transformed. Besides the athletic facilities, there are a conference center, a luxury hotel, a cruise-ship terminal, a yacht club, and a marina. Several other places will also help you get on or in the water.

Near No. 1 Beach, **Qingdao Qinhai Scuba Diving Club** (✉ *5 Huiquan Lu* ☎ *0532/8387–7977*) is the only government-certified diving club in northern China. All equipment is provided, and you can get your diving certificate in 12 classes.

One of the country's largest yacht clubs, **Yinhai International Yacht Club** (✉ *30 Donghai Zhong Lu* ☎ *0532/8588–6666* 🌐 *www.yinhai.com.cn*) has more than 30 yachts for rent, and offers lessons to beginners and more experienced sailors. The club is in the east of town, near the Olympic Sailing Center.

SHOPPING

The north end of Zhongshan Lu has a cluster of antiques and cultural artifacts shops. The largest antiques shop is the **Qingdao Arts and Crafts Store** (✉ *212 Zhongshan Lu* ☎ *0532/8281–7948*), with four floors of porcelain, scroll paintings, silk, gold, jade, and other stones. The **Cultural Relics Store** (✉ *40 Zhongshan Lu* ☎ *0532/8285–4435*) is also worth a look.

Very near the Catholic church is **Michael's** (✉ *15 Zhejiang Lu* ☎ *0532/8286–6790*), a gallery specializing in calligraphy.

SIDE TRIPS FROM QINGDAO

Rising to a height of more than 3,280 feet, **Mount Lao** *(Laoshan)* is nearly as famous as the province's other famous mountain, Mount Tai. A place of pilgrimage for centuries, Laoshan once had nine palaces, eight temples, and 72 convents. Many of these places have been lost over the years, but a number of the temples remaining are worth a look for their elegant architecture and their excellent views out to sea. With sheer cliffs and cascading waterfalls, the beautiful mountain is widely recognized in China as a source of the country's best-known mineral water (a vital ingredient in the local brew, Tsingtao). It's possible to see the mountain's sights in less than a day. Tourist buses to Laoshan leave from the main pier in Qingdao. ✉ *40 km (25 mi) east of Qingdao* 🎫 *Apr. 1–Oct. 31, Y70; Nov. 1–Mar. 31, Y50* 🕒 *Daily 7–5.*

Near Laoshan is **Huadong Winery,** Shandong's best winery. Although not as famous as the province's brewery, it's nevertheless already won a string of prizes. The vines were imported from France in the 1980s. Both the grapes and wines are available for tasting. The beautiful scenery alone makes this a worthwhile side trip from Qingdao. Visit the winery's **Qingdao Office** (✉ *15 Donghai Xi Lu* ☎ *0532/8387–4778*) to book a tour. ✉ *Nanlong Kou* ☎ *0532/8881–7878.*

JIANGSU

Coastal Jiangsu is defined by water. This eastern province is crossed by one of the world's great rivers, the mystical Yangtze, and has a coastline stretching hundreds of miles along the Yellow Sea. Jiangsu is also home to the Grand Canal, an ancient feat of engineering. This massive waterway, the longest ancient canal in the world, with some parts dating from the 5th century BC, allowed merchants to ship the province's plentiful rice, vegetables, and tea to the north. Within the cities, daily life was historically tied to the water, and many old neighborhoods are still crisscrossed by countless small canals.

As a result of its trading position, Jiangsu has long been an economic and political center of China. The founder of the Ming Dynasty established the capital in Nanjing, and it remained there until his son moved it back north to Beijing. Even after the move, Nanjing and Jiangsu retained their nationwide importance. After the 1911 revolution, the province once again hosted the nation's capital in Nanjing.

Planning a trip in the province is remarkably easy. The cities are close together and connected by many buses and trains. Autumn tends to be warm and dry, with ideal walking temperatures. Spring can be rainy and windy, but the hills burst with blooms. Summers are infamously oppressive, hot, and humid. The winter is mild, but January and February are often rainy.

REGIONAL TOURS

Jiangsu Huate International Travel Service has a number of guides who speak English. Jinling Business International Travel Service offers a range of options for travelers. The company has its own fleet of comfortable cars with knowledgeable drivers. It can arrange trips throughout the region.

Tour Contacts Jiangsu Huate International Travel Service (✉ *33 Jinxiang He Lu, Nanjing* ☎ *025/8337–8695* ⊕ *english.hitravels.com*). **Jinling Business International Travel Service** (✉ *Jinling Hotel, 2 Hanzhong Lu, Nanjing* ☎ *025/8473–0501*).

NANJING

2–2½ hrs (309 km [192 mi]) by express train west of Shanghai.

The name *Nanjing* means Southern Capital, and for six dynastic periods, as well as during the country's tenure as the Republic of China, the city was China's administrative capital. It was never as successful a capital as Beijing, and the locals chalk up the failures of several dynasties

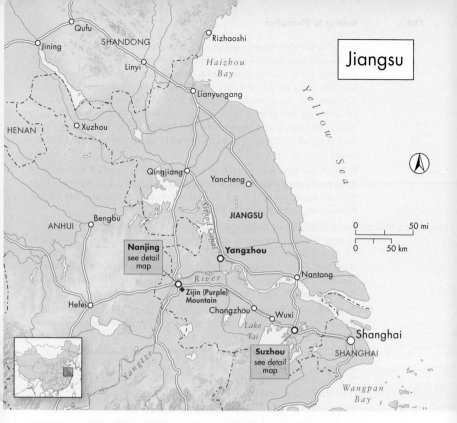

here to bad timing, but it could be that the laid-back atmosphere of the Yangtze Delta just isn't as suited to political intrigue as the north.

Nanjing offers travelers significantly more sites of historical importance than Shanghai. Among the most impressive are the massive Ming Dynasty sections of the city wall, built to surround and protect the city in the 14th century. There are also a number of traditional monuments, tombs, and gates that reflect the glory of Nanjing's capital days.

The city lies on the Yangtze, and the colossal Second Bridge or the more subdued park at Swallow Rock are great places for viewing the river. The sheer amount of activity on the river is testimony to its continued importance as a corridor for shipping and trade. Downtown, the streets are choked with traffic, but the chaotic scene is easily avoided with a visit to any of the large parks. You can also take a short taxi ride to Ziin (Purple) Mountain, where quiet trails lead between Ming Tombs and the grand mausoleum of Sun Yat-sen.

GETTING HERE AND AROUND
Regular daily flights connect Nanjing with all other major Chinese cities. The airport is located just 36 km (22 mi) from the city center.

Bus travel in this area of China is considerably more comfortable than elsewhere, thanks to a network of highways linking the cities and a fleet of luxury buses with comfortable seats and air-conditioning. Train travel is another good option, and there are frequent departures to many destinations in Jiangsu. Getting around Nanjing by taxi is both fast and inexpensive, though taxi drivers generally cannot speak any English, so be prepared with the address of your destination written in Chinese. For the more adventurous, bicycles can be rented from some small hotels and tourist agencies; the city is very bicycle-friendly, with mostly flat roads and many dedicated bicycle lanes. The Nanjing subway is quick, comfortable, and extremely inexpensive, with distance-based fares starting at Y2.

■TIP➜ The best way to explore some of Nanjing's tourist destinations, once you're on Purple Mountain, is aboard the tourist bus that runs from the train station to Ming Tomb, Sun Yat-sen Botanical Gardens, Sun Yat-sen Mausoleum, and Spirit Valley Pagoda. Fare is Y3.

AIR TRAVEL Most flights from Europe or North America go through Shanghai or Beijing before continuing on to Nanjing's Lukou Airport, but there are direct flights from Asian hubs like Seoul, Singapore, Nagoya, and Bangkok. From Nanjing several flights leave daily for Shanghai, Beijing, Guangzhou, Xiamen, Wuhan, and Hong Kong; flights leave daily for Xi'an, Chengdu, and Zhengzhou.

Taxis from Nanjing Lukou Airport, 36 km (22 mi) southwest of the city, should take between 20 and 30 minutes. The fare should be between Y90 and Y120.

BUS TRAVEL Buses departing from or going to other Jiangsu destinations, such as Shanghai, Suzhou, and Yangzhou, are both frequent and comfortable. Nanjing's main long-distance bus station lies west of the railway station at Zhongyang Men.

The trip to Shanghai takes between three and four hours, and the trip to Suzhou can take as little as two hours; buses to both cities depart from the Zhongshan Nan Road Bus Station. Buses bound for Yangzhou leave frequently from the main long-distance bus station and take an hour.

TRAIN TRAVEL Trains can be a convenient way to get to Nanjing, but be mindful of what kind of ticket you buy—all trains are not created equal. The K- or T-coded tickets are for faster trains; local trains can take two or three times longer to reach a destination. High-speed D-coded trains are the fastest, usually serving two major destinations with few stops in between. Trains depart for Shanghai about every half hour, and take between two and four hours.

SAFETY AND PRECAUTIONS

Nanjing is a large, crowded city, but is safe to explore day or night. Use common sense in crowded places such as the metro and train stations, where petty theft is frequent. Drink only bottled water, and wash your hands frequently. Locals, as in most Chinese cities outside of Shanghai and Beijing, have a tendency to stare. Don't be offended, just smile, and you will almost always receive a smile in return.

TIMING

Considering the massive size of the city and the sheer number of attractions, try to devote at least two to three full days exploring.

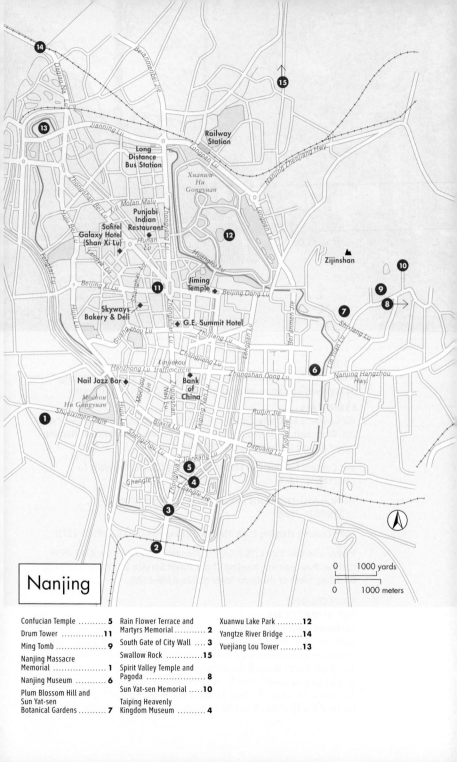

Nanjing

A happy visitor at the Ming Tombs.

TOURS

Major hotels will often arrange a tour guide for a group. Nanjing China Travel Service can arrange almost any type of tour of the city.

ESSENTIALS

Air Contacts Air China (☎ 025/8449–9378 ⊕ www.airchina.com.cn/en/index. jsp). **Dragonair** (☎ 025/8331–1999 Ext. 810 ⊕ www.dragonair.com). **Nanjing Lukou Airport** (✉ Jiangning Qu ☎ 025/248–0063).

Bus Contact Nanjing Bus Station (✉ Jianing Lu and Zhongyang Lu ☎ 025/8550–4973).

Medical Assistance First Aid Station (✉ 231 Zhongshan Lu ☎ 025/8663–3858).

Train Contact Nanjing Train Station (✉ Long Pan Lu ☎ 025/8582–2222).

Visitor and Tour Info CITS (✉ 202/1 Zhongshan Bei Lu ☎ 025/8342–8999 ⊕ www.citsnjview.com). **Nanjing China Travel Service** (✉ 12 Baixin Building, Baizi Ting, south of the Drum Tower ☎ 025/8336–6582).

EXPLORING

TOP ATTRACTIONS

Confucian Temple *(Fuzimiao)*. The traditional-style temple overlooks the Qinhuai, a tributary of the Yangtze. Lit with neon at night, the surrounding area is the city's busiest shopping and entertainment district The back alleys behind the temple, once home to China's most famous district of courtesans, now house a toy market and excellent curio shops. This area also has the best bazaars for souvenirs and crafts. Evening tours of the Qinhuai River leave from in front of the temple. The cost is

Y40 per person. ⊠ *Zhongshan Lu and Jiankang Lu, on the Qinhuai River* ☎ *Y15* ⊕ *www.njfzm.com* ⊙ *Daily 9–10 pm.*

Fodor's Choice
★
Ming Tomb (*Ming Xiaoling*). The ancient tomb of the founder of the Ming Dynasty, called Tomb of Filial Piety, is one of the largest burial mounds in China. The emperor Hong Wu, who chose Nanjing for the Ming Dynasty capital, was born a peasant and orphaned early on. He became a monk and eventually led the army that overthrew the Yuan Dynasty. Visitors approach the tomb through a grand entrance of stone animals. The lions, elephants, camels, and mythical creatures kneel in tribute to the emperor and stand as guardians to the tomb. Winding paths behind them make the Ming Tomb area a rewarding place to explore, but as in all Chinese tombs, the entrance is hidden to foil looters. For a detailed history, buy a book at the entrance shop; English signage is sparse. ⊠ *Mingling Lu, on Purple Mountain* ☎ *Y70 (includes Plum Blossom Hill and Sun Yat-sen Botanical Park)* ⊙ *Daily 6:30–6.*

> **GOING UNDERGROUND**
>
> Getting around a city the size of Nanjing can be a daunting task, but the city's easy-to-use subway system has made navigating safer and easier. Line 1 has 32 stations and basically runs north–south for almost 29 miles. Line 2 runs mainly east to west for more than 25 miles, and has 26 stations. Fares are inexpensive, only Y2 to Y4 depending on how many stations you travel.

3

Nanjing Massacre Memorial (*Datusha Jinianguan*). In the winter of 1937, Japanese forces occupied Nanjing. In the space of a few days, thousands of Chinese were killed in the chaos, which became known as the "Rape of Nanjing." This monument commemorates the victims, many of whom were buried in mass graves. Be advised, this is not for the squeamish. Skeletons have been exhumed from the "Grave of Ten Thousand" and are displayed with gruesomely detailed explanations as to how each lost his or her life. The memorial also displays artifacts from the Sino-Japanese reconciliation after World War II, which ended the conflict between the two countries on a less strident, more hopeful note. To get here, take Bus 7 or 37 from Xinjiekou. ⊠ *418 Shui Ximen Da Jie, west of Mouchou Lake Park* ☎ *025/8661–2230* ⊕ *www.nj1937. org* ☎ *Free* ⊙ *Tues.–Sun. 8:30–4:30.*

Nanjing Museum (*Nanjing Bowuguan*). With one of the largest and most impressive collections in China, the Nanjing Museum has excellent displays that set objects in historical context. For instance, beside the shelves of ancient pottery there is a re-created kiln to illustrate how traditional objects were formed. The permanent collection is contained in 11 exhibition halls, and includes excellent works in jade, silk, and bronze. There's also a treasure room with some eye-popping displays. ⊠ *Zhongshan Dong Lu, inside Zhongshan Gate, east of the city center* ☎ *025/8480–2119* ☎ *Y20* ⊙ *Daily 9–4:30.*

☿ **South Gate of City Wall** (*Zhonghua Men*). Built as the linchpin of the city's defenses, this is less a gate than a complete fortress, with multiple courtyards and tunnels where several thousand soldiers could withstand a siege. It was rarely attacked; armies wisely avoided it in favor of the less heavily fortified areas to the north. Today bonsai enthusiasts have displays in several of the courtyards. ⊠ *Southern end of Zhonghua Lu, south side of city wall* ⊠ *Y20* ⊙ *Daily 8–6.*

Taiping Heavenly Kingdom Museum *(Taiping Tianguo Lishi Bowuguan).* Commemorating a particularly fascinating period of Chinese history, this museum follows the life of Hong Xiuquan, a Christian who led a peasant revolt in 1859. He ultimately captured Nanjing and ruled for 11 years. Hong, who set himself up as emperor, claimed to be the younger brother of Jesus. On display are artifacts from the period. After browsing the museum, you can walk around the grounds of the Ming Dynasty garden compound that houses the museum. During the day it is the calmest spot in Nanjing. In the evening from 6 to 11 there are performances of opera and storytelling. Reasonably priced English-speaking guides make up for the lack of English signage. ⊠ *128 Zhanyuan Lu, beside the Confucian Temple* ☎ *025/8662–3024* ⊠ *Museum only, Y30; including performance, Y70* ⊙ *Daily 8:30–5.*

Xuanwu Lake Park *(Xuanwu Hu Gongyuan).* More lake than park, this pleasant garden is bounded by one of the longer sections of the monumental city wall, which you can climb for a good view of the water. Purple Mountain rises in the east, and the glittering skyscrapers of modern Nanjing are reflected on the calm water. Causeways lined with trees and benches connect several large islands in the lake. Small pedal boats cost Y15/hour. ⊠ *Off Hunan Lu, in the northeast corner of the city, outside the city wall* ⊠ *Y30* ⊙ *Daily 9–9.*

WORTH NOTING

Drum Tower *(Gulou).* The traditional center of ancient Chinese cities, the 1382 Drum Tower housed the drums used to signal important events, from the changing of the guard to an enemy attack or a fire. Today it holds only one drum. A tearoom at the top offers city views. ⊠ *1 Dafang Xiang, beside Gulou People's Square* ☎ *025/8663–1059* ⊠ *Y5* ⊙ *Daily 8:30 am–5:30 pm.*

> **CAUTION**
>
> Be careful when crossing the street—look both ways, look again, and keep looking as you cross. Nanjing has seen an explosion of private auto ownership in the past decade, and no comparable program of driver education. Pedestrians may have the green walk light, but they are generally not given the right of way when cars make right turns, and running red lights is not uncommon. Motorbikes and bicycles ignore all lights and signage as a rule, and even take over the sidewalks.

NEED A MAS-SAGE?
Shou Jia Massage *(⊠ 136 Chang Jiang Lu [a very short walk from the 1912 entertainment area] ☎ 025/8470-2129)* is a health center that's serious about all things TCM (traditional Chinese medicine). The center trains and employs the visually impaired for back rubs, and the friendly staff bring you endless cups of medicinal tea.

Spirit Valley Temple and Pagoda (*Linggu Si and Linggu Ta*). The temple commemorates Xuan Zang, the monk who brought Buddhist scriptures back from India. Farther up the hill is a nine-story granite pagoda with a staircase that spirals up the central pillar. The top is dizzyingly high. This pagoda was built as a solemn memorial to those killed by the Nationalists in 1929; today vendors sell plastic balloons to throw off the top balcony. Also on the grounds is the brick Beamless Hall, which was constructed without any wood or beams to support it. The magnificent 14th-century architecture is now given over to propagandistic "historical" reenactments. Although the temple and pagoda aren't worth a special trip, they are close to Ming Tomb and other attractions around Purple Mountain. ⊠ *Ta Lu, southeast of Sun Yat-sen Memorial* ☎ *025/8444–6443* 🎫 *Y80 (includes everything)* ⏱ *Sept.–May, daily 8:30–5, June–Aug., daily 6:30–6:30.*

Plum Blossom Hill and Sun Yat-sen Botanical Gardens (*Meihuashan and Zhongshan Zhiwuyuan*). This hillside explodes with plum blossoms in early spring. The garden is nice for a picnic, but is only worth a special trip when the flowers are in bloom. The exhibits at the botanical gardens, on the other hand, are a rewarding experience for anyone interested in the flora of China. ⊠ *1 Shixiang Lu, northeast of Nanjing Museum* 🎫 *Y70 (includes Ming Tomb)* ⏱ *Daily 6:30–6:30.*

Rain Flower Terrace and Martyrs Memorial (*Yuhua Tai Lieshi Lingyuan*). The terrace gets its name from the legend of Yunzhang, a 15th-century Buddhist monk who supposedly pleased the gods so much with his recitation of a sutra that they showered flowers on this spot. The site was used for a more grim purpose in the 1930s, when the Nationalists used it to execute their left-wing political enemies. The site was transformed into a memorial park with massive statues of heroic martyrs, soaring obelisks, flower arrangements of the hammer and sickle, and a moving museum that uses personal objects to convey the lives of some of those executed here. ⊠ *215 Yuhua Lu, outside Zhonghua Gate* ⊕ *www.cnbg.net/default_en.asp* 🎫 *Free* ⏱ *Daily 8–5.*

Swallow Rock (*Yanzi Ji*). North of the city, this small park overlooking the Yangtze is worth the trip. Paths wind up the hill to several lookout points for what may be Nanjing's best view of this great river. The park's name comes from the massive boulder over the water. The rock is well known because the famous Chinese poet Li Bai was once inspired to write a poem here; the poem is now etched into the rock. To get here, take Bus 8 to the last stop. ⊠ *Northeast of Mount Mufu, on the Yangtze* 🎫 *Y10* ⏱ *Daily 7:30–6.*

PEDESTRIAN STREETS

In the **Confucius Temple Area** (*Fuzimiao*) are souvenir and shopping streets around the Qinhuai River. ⊠ *By the intersection of Zhongshan Lu and Jiankang Lu.*

Hunan Road is a section of streets filled with snacks, shops, and restaurants. ⊠ *Hunan Lu, west of Zhongshan North Rd. and east of Zhongyang Lu.*

In the **Xinjiekou City Center**, around the big malls and shopping centers are several bustling walking streets. ⊠ *Xinjiekou between Huaihai Lu and Zhongshan Lu.*

Sun Yat-sen Memorial *(Zhongshan Ling).* Acknowledged by the Nationalist and Communist governments alike, the father of modern China lies buried in a delicately carved marble sarcophagus. His resting place is the center of a solemn and imposing monument to the ideas that overthrew the imperial system. On the mountain are steep trails up the pine-covered slopes that feel worlds away from the bustle of Nanjing. A popular destination for Chinese tourists, the mausoleum gets crowded on weekends. ☒ *Lingyuan Lu, east of the Ming Tomb* ☎ *Y80 (includes Spirit Valley Temple and Pagoda)* ☉ *Sept.–May, daily 8:30–5, June–Aug., daily 6 am–6:30 pm.*

Yangtze River Bridge *(Changjiang Daqiao).* Completed in 1968 at the height of the Cultural Revolution, the bridge is decorated in stirring Socialist-Realist style. Huge stylized flags made of red glass rise from the bridge's piers, and groups of giant-size peasants, workers, and soldiers stride forward heroically. The Great Bridge Park lies on the south side. From here you can take an elevator up to a small museum. ☒ *End of Daqiao Nan, northwest section of the city* ☎ *Free* ☉ *Daily 9–5.*

Yuejiang Lou Tower. This massive tower complex, built in the new millennium in Ming Dynasty style, looks out over a broad sweep of the Yangtze River. The founding emperor of the Ming Dynasty wrote a poem describing his plans to have a tower built here where he could view the river. Other imperial business got in the way, and for several centuries the building remained on paper. The grand tower and its surrounding buildings were built in 2001 in a historically accurate style, but it somehow seems too sterile. ☒ *202 Jianning Lu, northwest corner of the city* ☎ *025/5880–3977* ☎ *Y40* ☉ *Daily 7–5.*

WHERE TO EAT

For more information on bars and restaurants in Nanjing, pick up a copy of the local bilingual *Map Magazine* at your hotel. Printed monthly, it has the latest listings and reviews of many popular spots in the city, as well as upcoming cultural events.

$$–$$$
CHINESE
★

✕ **Dingshan Meishi Cheng.** One of Nanjing's finest restaurants and a popular choice among locals, Dingshan Meishi Cheng serves local cuisine in a traditional setting. The food here is not as hot as that from Sichuan, nor as sweet as that from Shanghai. There's a set-price menu that includes four cold dishes, four hot dishes, and a whopping 18 small dessert dishes, all for Y60. ☒ *5 Zhanyuan Lu, near Confucian Temple* ☎ *025/5220–9217* ▭ *AE, MC, V.*

$$–$$$
CHINESE

✕ **Hong Ni Restaurant.** It's hard to miss the Hong Ni—its facade lights up the neighborhood with a three-story neon extravaganza. Although the exterior is pure Las Vegas, the cuisine is excellent Yangzi Delta food from neighboring Zhejiang Province. Prices are reasonable, and everything is served in a sleek dining room. The seafood dish is highly recommended. It's downtown, near the Xinjiekou traffic circle, and many members of the staff speak English. ☒ *23 Hongwu Lu* ☎ *025/8689–9777* ▭ *No credit cards.*

$–$$
CHINESE
VEGETARIAN

✕ **Jimingsi Vegetarian Restaurant.** Inside the Jiming Temple, this establishment cooks up Chinese fare with absolutely no meat. Although the menu lists pork, fish, chicken, and goose dishes, the food is all vegetarian. The chefs use tofu, wheat gluten, and vegetables to create tasty interpretations of meat. An English menu features a limited selection of the best dishes. Tofu threads and the Sichuan "fish" are recommended. This restaurant is noteworthy more for its view of the temple grounds than its food, but overall it's worth a visit. ⊠ *Jiming Temple, off Beijing Dong Lu, south of Xuanwu Lake Park* ☎ *025/8771–3690* ▭ *No credit cards* ⊗ *No dinner.*

$$–$$$ ✕ **Punjabi.** Indian chefs slap naan dough to the sides of clay barrels and
INDIAN proudly watch guests enjoy the food through the glass kitchen. Popular northern Indian fare (butter chicken, mutter aloo) covers a majority of the menu, with biryani's and dosas toward the back. All dishes have been authentically prepared at this Nanjing location for more than 10 years. Look for the large red and blue sign halfway down Hunan Pedestrian Street pointing you down the alley. ⊠ *Western Food Street King Lion Palace, Lion Bridge Hu Nan Rd.* ☎ *025/832–45421* ▭ *No credit cards.*

$$ ✕ **Shizi Lou.** Anchoring the strip of restaurants of Shizi Qiao, near the
CHINESE Shanzi Road Market, Shizi Lou is a great introduction to Huaiyang
★ fare. Resembling an indoor market, you can walk between stands and point to the dishes you want to sample. The "stinky tofu" is very good, and not as malodorous as it's billed to be. The place is famous for local meatballs, with a dozen types from which to choose. ⊠ *29 Hunan Lu, near Shizi Bridge* ☎ *025/8360–7888* ▭ *No credit cards.*

¢ ✕ **Skyways Deli.** Popular with local expats, especially the foreign stu-
CAFÉ dents studying at Nanjing University, Skyway is the perfect antidote to oily Chinese food. Clean and sterile, this user-friendly deli offers a sandwich checklist allowing you to choose, check, and chow in a matter of minutes. Delicious homemade breads are complimented with a range of imported meats and cheeses. Most impressive are the bakery items, especially the chocolate-dipped coconut macaroons and the Swedish Napoleon cookies. Consistent and satisfying. ⊠ *160 Shanghai Lu* ☎ *025/ 8331–7103* ▭ *No credit cards.*

WHERE TO STAY

$ 🏨 **Central Hotel.** Steps aways from Xinjiekou, the heart of the city, this odd hotel has an offbeat charm. The lobby is ridiculously bright, with its retro Vegas decor. Thankfully, the rooms do not match the lobby, and are stylish and reasonably priced. The helpful 24-hour travel desk can arrange day tours in and around Nanjing or set up farther-flung excursions. **Pros:** good value; convenient location. **Cons:** standard rooms noticeably lower quality than executive rooms. ⊠ *75 Zhongshan Lu* ☎ *025/8473–3888* 🛏 *354 rooms* ♨ *In-hotel: 2 restaurants, bar, pool, gym* ▭ *AE, MC, V.*

$$ 🏨 **G.E. Summit.** Centrally located on the metro Line 1 and connected to
★ an upscale shopping mall, the Summit's services and facilities are much better that most other five-star domestically owned hotels. Rooms are well laid out and decorated in soothing earth tones. High-quality mattresses are especially welcome after a day of exploring. The gym is well equipped, with brand-new Lifetime Fitness machines. Booking through the company Web site is good for weekend packages and complimentary breakfast buffets. **Pros:** good location; bang for your buck. **Cons:**

staff speak spotty English. ✉ *1 Zhujiang Lu* ☎ *025/8321–8888* ⊕ *www. gesummithotel.com* ⇌ *rooms* ⚲ *In-hotel: 2 restaurants, bar, pool, gym, laundry, no-smoking rooms* ▭ *AE, DC, MC, V.*

$–$$ 🏨 **Grand Hotel.** This elliptical building in the center of town is a good base for seeing the sights. It overlooks the busy shopping centers and office buildings in the commercial center of the city. Along with standard amenities, it has a good Western restaurant. **Pros:** family-friendly (babysitting services available); helpful staff. **Cons:** some rooms and facilities need renovations. ✉ *208 Guangzhou Lu* ☎ *025/8331–1999* ⊕ *www.njgrandhotel.com* ⇌ *305 rooms, 11 suites* ⚲ *In-hotel: 5 restaurants, bar, tennis court, pool, gym* ▭ *AE, DC, MC, V.*

$$$–$$$$ 🏨 **Jinling Hotel.** Nanjing's best-known hotel has a great location in the center of the city. It's a huge modern building connected to a shopping center. The travel agency on the first floor provides friendly and efficient service. On the second floor is the most authentic Japanese food in town. The guest rooms have every comfort, including high-speed Internet, an in-room safe, and 24-hour room service. **Pros:** luxurious accommodations; attentive service; wide array of shopping and other facilities. **Cons:** expensive. ✉ *2 Xinjiekou* ☎ *025/8471–1888 or 025/8472–2888* ⊕ *www.jinlinghotel.com/en* ⇌ *592 rooms, 33 suites* ⚲ *In-hotel: 9 restaurants, bar, pool, gym* ▭ *AE, MC, V.*

¢–$ 🏨 **Lakeview Xuanwu Hotel.** This modern hotel's guest rooms have excellent views of Xuanwu Lake. If you don't feel like venturing far for dinner, the 20th-floor revolving restaurant serves an all-you-can-eat buffet with Western and Chinese cuisine. The hotel can also help you arrange day trips around the city. **Pros:** great views; good value. **Cons:** service can be slow; some outdated facilities. ✉ *193 Zhongyang Lu* ☎ *025/8335–8888* ⊕ *www.xuanwu.com.cn* ⇌ *258 rooms, 47 suites* ⚲ *In-hotel: 6 restaurants, bar, gym* ▭ *AE, DC, MC, V.*

$–$$ 🏨 **Mandarin Garden Hotel.** Although many hotels of its caliber seem impersonal, this well-appointed establishment is inviting and friendly. Its setting on the north side of the Confucian Temple keeps you far from the noise of the city. The excellent rooftop bar affords a good view of the skyline. The Galaxy Restaurant on the second floor serves Cantonese food. Guests are treated to an excellent breakfast buffet. **Pros:** excellent location; friendly staff. **Cons:** furnishings getting old; some amenities not quite deluxe. ✉ *9 Zhuang Yuan Jing* ☎ *0255/220–2555 or 0255/220–2988* ⇌ *477 rooms, 24 suites* ⚲ *In-hotel: 12 restaurants, bar, pool, gym, no-smoking rooms* ▭ *AE, MC, V.*

¢ 🏨 **Nanjing Hotel.** Built in 1936, the old-fashioned hotel surrounded by lawns and trees seems pleasantly out of place in such a busy area of town. The staff are well trained and pleasant. A separate section has simpler, less attractive rooms but for half the standard rate. Rooms have different amenities, so ask to see a few before you decide. **Pros:** inexpensive; all basic amenities. **Cons:** some advertised amenities not available in certain rooms. ✉ *259 Zhongshan Bei Lu* ☎ *025/8682–6666* ⇌ *310 rooms, 14 suites* ⚲ *In-hotel: 3 restaurants, gym* ▭ *AE, MC, V.*

$–$$ 🏨 **Sofitel Galaxy Hotel.** Top-rate facilities make this centrally located

Fodor's Choice hotel one of the city's best. The well-appointed rooms are what you

★ would expect of any Sofitel, equipped with elegant furniture, plasma

TVs, and complimentary in-room Internet access. Weather and smog permitting (Nanjing is infamous for smog), views from the upper floors of this 48-story tower showcase Nanjing's skyline. Check out the Web site for special offers and packages. **Pros:** premium facilities; great location **Cons:** smells like cigarette smoke in public area ⊠ *9 Shanxi Lu* ☎ *025/8371–8888* 🛏 *278 rooms* ⚭ *In-hotel: 3 restaurants, bars, pool, gym, no-smoking rooms* ▤ *AE, MC, V.*

NIGHTLIFE

Nanjing's nightlife centers around the 1912 neighborhood, named for the year the Republic of China was founded. A few dozen restaurants, bars, and cafes are packed into several blocks at the intersection of Taiping Lu and Changjiang Lu, a 15-minute walk northeast of the city center. Locals start with dinner, relax over drinks, charge up with coffee at the Starbucks or Costa Coffee, hit the dance floor at a trendy club, stagger out to a late-night tea shop, and catch a cab back home—all without ever having to cross a lane of traffic. All the bars get going by about 10 pm, and close at 2 am.

In 1912, the **Blue Marlin** (⊠ *Off Taiping Lu* ☎ *no phone*) is a good place to start the night, with a large selection of imported beers and decently poured drinks. Live music after 8 pm on weekends. If brave, enter one of the many constantly changing clubs next door. Each club tries to outdo the other with the sobering number of chandeliers and blaring music.

★ **Nail Jazz Bar.** A cut above the rest, this smartly decorated jazz bar includes a tiny stage offering live weekend jazz. Caricatures of world leaders adorn the funky walls while an artsy crowd lounges in cozy, long wooden tables. The drink list is extensive, offering a very eclectic, Belgium dominated, imported beer selection. Music is played at an appropriate level, making this central bar a great place to linger. (⊠ *10 Luolang Xiang (200 m south of the Sheraton Hotel)* ☎ *025/8653–2244*).

Walking out of the noisy, chaotic Nanjing streets and into **Finnegan's Wake** (⊠ *South Zhongshan Road, No. 6 Cinnalane* ☎ *025/8653–2244*) will give you a sense of calm and encourage you to stay awhile. The extensive (and pricey) menu offers good Irish fare—the blue cheese burger and shepherd's pie are recommended. The friendly Scottish owner may well be the one to pour your Kilkenny on draft, while his Irish buddy belts out Celtic music.

SHOPPING

The best place to buy traditional crafts, art, and souvenirs is the warren of small shops in the center of the city. The lavish embroidered robes once worn by the emperors were traditionally produced in Nanjing, and the **Brocade Research Institute** (⊠ *240 Chating Dong Jie, behind Nanjing Massacre Memorial* ☎ *025/8651–8580*) has a fascinating museum and workshop where the brocades are still produced using massive traditional looms. Their gift shop sells beautiful examples of traditional brocade.

Nanjing is a convenient place to pick up many of the traditional crafts of Jiangsu—purple sand teapots, flowing silks, interesting carvings, and folk paper cuttings. The **Nanjing Arts & Crafts Company** (✉ *31 Beijing Dong Lu* ☎ *025/5771–1189*) has a range of items, from jade and lacquerware to tapestries. Prices are high but so is quality.

In the courtyard of the Confucian Temple, the **Chaotian Gong Antique Market** (✉ *Zhongshan Lu and Jiankang Lu* ☎ *No phone*) has an array of curios, from genuine antiques to fakes of varying quality. Vendors' opening prices can border on the ludicrous, especially with foreign customers, but some good-natured bargaining can yield good buys. The market is open every day, but is liveliest on weekend mornings.

The **Shanxi Lu Night Market** (✉ *Hunan Lu and Matai Jie* ☎ *No phone*) has all sorts of odd items and some good finds waiting to be unearthed by savvy shoppers.

Northwest of the Drum Tower, the **Fabric Market** (✉ *215 Zhongshan Bei Lu* ☎ *No phone*) sells silks, linen, and traditional cotton fabrics. Bargaining is necessary, but the prices are reasonable. A good basic ballpark to pay is Y40 to Y60 per meter of silk. The vendors can also arrange tailoring.

YANGZHOU

1 hr (106 km [66 mi]) northeast of Nanjing, 3½ hrs (300 km [185 mi]) from Shanghai.

Yangzhou has quietly transformed itself into one of the most pleasant cities in Eastern China. With a population of half a million—minuscule by Chinese standards—the town has a laid-back feel. Yangzhou is small enough to be seen in one day, but is charming enough to make you want to linger for a few days.

Because it's on the Grand Canal, Yangzhou flourished in the Tang Dynasty. Drawing on thousands of years as a trade center for salt and silk, Yangzhou maintains a cosmopolitan feel. Indeed, some of the most interesting sites in Yangzhou demonstrate a blending of cultures: Japanese relations are evidenced in the monument to Jian Zhen, a monk who helped spread Buddhist teachings to Japan. European influence is seen in the Sino-Victorian gardens of He Yuan, and Persian contact is preserved in the tomb of Puddahidin, a 13th-century trader and descendant of Mohammed.

GETTING HERE AND AROUND

The best way to get to or from Yangzhou is by bus. It lies on the Beijing–Shanghai and Nanjing–Nantong highways. Huaihai Road Bus Station has departures from 6:30 in the morning until 6:30 in the evening. Suzhou is 230 km (143 mi) south, about two hours away. Shanghai, about 300 km (186 mi) away, takes 3½ hours. Trains to Yangzhou are not as convenient as the bus.

AIR TRAVEL Currently, there is no airport in Yangzhou, but there are rumors of plans to build one. Check with a travel agent before you go.

The Wang Residence was spared during the Cultural Revolution because it had been converted into a factory.

BUS TRAVEL Frequent bus service runs between Yangzhou and Nanjing and Suzhou, and on to Shanghai. Most routes have air-conditioned buses. The Yangzhou bus station is about 6 km (4 mi) west of the city.

TRAIN TRAVEL There is a train station in Yangzhou, but only the slower trains stop here. If you are coming from nearby Nanjing or Zhenjiang, a train is a good option.

TOURS

Hotels are the chief source of tourist information in Yangzhou. Not only for the young, China Youth Travel in Yangzhou can put together any kind of trip, from morning boat rides around Slender West Lake to evening cruises down the Great Canal. The staff speak English, and has the most experience working with foreign travelers.

TIMING

Many travelers are tempted to explore Yangzhou as a day trip from Nanjing, but we recommend spending the night. After dark, multicolored lights illuminate the city's canals.

ESSENTIALS

Bus Contact Yangzhou Bus Station (✉ *Jiangyang Zhong Lu* ☎ *0514/8786–1812*).

Medical Assistance Yangzhou No. 1 People's Hospital (✉ *45 Taizhou Lu* ☎ *0514/8790–7353*).

Train Contact Yangzhou Train Station (✉ *Wenhe Xi Lu* ☎ *0514/8268–6282*).

Visitor and Tour Info Yangzhou China Youth Travel Agency (✉ *6 Siwangting Lu* ☎ *0514/8793–3876*).

EXPLORING
TOP ATTRACTIONS

The **Da Ming Temple** *(Daming Si)* is one of the more interesting Buddhist shrines in Eastern China. Maybe the most arresting detail is the mural behind the main laughing Buddha image, where the gender-bending god Guanyin stands on a turtle's head. Another highlight on the temple grounds is the Fifth Spring Under Heaven. Most of the ancient Tang Dynasty springs are no longer usable, but this one still flows. The high mineral content of the water makes it especially suited for tea, which you can sip in a small teahouse overlooking the temple gardens. Also on the grounds is a Tang-style monument to a Chinese missionary who traveled to Japan, Jian Zhen. ⊠ *8 Pingshan Tang Lu, next to Slender West Lake* ☎ *0514/8734–0720* ✉ *Mar.–June and Sept.–Nov., Y45; Dec.–Feb. and July–Aug., Y30* ☉ *Daily 7:45–5.*

Rather than flowers, **Ge Garden** *(Ge Yuan)* is planted with more than 60 varieties of bamboo, and is a virtual rainbow of greens. There are yellow stalks, striped stalks, huge treelike stands, and dwarf bamboo with delicate leaves. The emerald stalks stand out against whitewashed walls and black undulating rooflines. Note the loose bricks in the path, arranged to clack as you walk. Catch your breath with a cup of tea in the tea hall. ⊠ *10 Yangfu Dong Lu, east of Yangzhou Hotel* ☎ *0514/8793–5233* ⊕ *www.ge-garden.net/english/* ✉ *Mar.–May and Sept.–Nov., Y40; June–Aug. and Dec.–Feb., Y30* ☉ *Daily 7:15–6.*

Originally part of a river, **Slender West Lake** *(Shou Xi Hu)* was created during the Qing Dynasty by rich salt merchants hoping to impress the emperor on his visit to Yangzhou. The park is planted in willows, bamboo, and flowers, and can be enjoyed briskly in 45 minutes or savored for a full afternoon. Pavilions, tearooms, and bowed bridges are all about the grounds. The **fishing terrace** is where the emperor decided he'd try his hand at angling. The merchants reportedly had their servants wade into the lake and hook a fish on each line he cast. Another mark left by the emperor is in the form of the **White Pagoda**, actually a *dagoba*, a Buddhist monument shaped like a bottle. The emperor casually remarked that Slender West Lake only lacked a dagoba like the one in Beijing. By the time the sun shone through the morning mist, there was the emperor's dagoba—more or less. The permanent structure was completed much later. Apparently all the flattery had the desired effect, because Yangzhou prospered up until the 20th century as a center of trade in China. ⊠ *28 Da Hongqiao Lu, in the northern part of the city* ☎ *0514/8733–0189* ⊕ *www.shouxihu.com/sxhen/index.php* ✉ *Mar.–May and Sept.–Nov., Y90; June–Aug. and Dec.–Feb., Y60* ☉ *Daily 7–6.*

Fodor's Choice
★

Unremarkable when it was built, **Wang's Residence** *(Wangshi Xiaoyuan)* is now one of Yangzhou's highlights. This courtyard house was one of many large private homes owned by Yangzhou's prosperous merchant class. It alone was spared the wrath of the Cultural Revolution because it had been converted into a factory. The highlight is the detailed carvings, chief among them the crisscrossing bamboo design carved in layers out of *nanmu*, a glimmering wood now extinct in this area of China. There's even a bomb shelter in the small inner garden—a reminder of the Japanese invasion. English translations are few, but a few guides can lead in English. ⊠ *14 Di Gong Di, between Taizhou Lu and Guoqing Lu* ☎ *0514/8732–8869* ⬚ *Y25* ⊙ *Daily 8–5:30.*

WORTH NOTING

The **Garden Tomb of Puhaddin** *(Puhading Mu)* faces the Grand Canal, from where you climb a stairway to a graveyard of marble-slab headstones. In the back is a garden with a charming pavilion that is a combination of Persian and Chinese traditional design. Largely ignored by local tourists, a visit to the garden tomb is reminder of the past Arab influence. ⊠ *Laopai Lu at Quanfu Lu, near Jiefang Bridge* ⬚ *Y10* ⊙ *Daily 7:30–4:30.*

Dating from the 1880s, the Victorian-influenced **He Garden** *(He Yuan)* is notable for its melding of European and Chinese architecture. While Ge Garden flows in traditional style, He Garden has a more rigid design. However, the attention to detail and perspective subtly brings together design values of East and West, making the garden more than a mere imitation of European design. ⊠ *66 Xuning Men Dalu, southeast corner of the city* ☎ *0514/8723–2360* ⬚ *Y40* ⊙ *Daily 7:30–5:30.*

WHERE TO EAT

$–$$
CHINESE
✕ **Fu Chun Teahouse.** With a history going back more than a century, Fu Chun serves traditional local food. It's best known for its desserts; try the sweet rice buns, layer cakes, or any of their other bite-size snacks. Wash it all down with flavorful green tea. ⊠ *35 Desheng Qiao Lu* ☎ *0514/8723–3326* ▭ *No credit cards.*

$$$
AMERICAN
✕ **Old Brewery.** Owned by a pleasant, and often present, Chinese-American, this large brewery/restaurant has the only truly "Western" food offered in the city. The entrance is lined with large, stainless-steel tanks containing proudly crafted home brews. The menu offers everything from USDA beef tenderloin (at ridiculous prices) to lasagna. The thin-crusted pizzas are heaped with cheese and other fresh ingredients. Its canal-side location makes it ideal for after dinner strolls. ⊠ *128 Nantong Donglu, Guangling district* ☎ *0514/ 8721–5225* ▭ *No credit cards.*

WHERE TO STAY

$–$$
🛏 **Metropark Hotel.** This modern hotel is conveniently located in the city center. Past the grand lobby are guest rooms with Asian-inspired decor. The helpful staff can arrange a car and driver if you want to explore the area. **Pros:** friendly staff; great location; clean and comfortable rooms. **Cons:** more geared toward business travelers. ⊠ *559 Wenchang Quanfu Lu* ☎ *0514/8732–2888* ⊕ *www. metroparkhotels.com* ⤴ *242 rooms, 25 suites* ⚭ *In-room: safe, Internet. In-hotel: 4 restaurants, bar, gym* ▭ *AE, MC, V.*

¢–$
🛏 **Ramada Yangzhou Casa.** Located along the Grand Canal in an enviable city-center location and within striking distance of the Slender West Lake and Ge Garden, the

> ### REPLANTING GARDENS
>
> Many of the country's historic gardens have been recently pieced back together. Most were ravaged during the Cultural Revolution, when for years Red Guard troops were encouraged to smash China's heritage to pieces. To this day, China is still replanting gardens, repairing temples, and restoring historic architecture.

Adopting in China

For some, the gardens, the architecture, the history, and the scenery are all secondary reasons to visit Yangzhou. Theirs is a more personal and momentous trip. On the outskirts of town there is a white-tiled compound called the Yangzhou Social Welfare Institute. This is where American parents and Chinese children come together to form families. Since Chinese law began promoting foreign adoption in 1991, there has been a huge surge in the number of families adopting from China. More than 50,000 children have been brought to the United States from China over the past 15 years.

More than 95% of children in orphanages are female. There persists a strong preference for boys, especially in rural areas. This is largely due to a combination of bias and traditional social structures whereby girls marry out and males help provide for the family. An unintended consequence of the One Child Policy exacerbates prejudices against women. Some Chinese parents, desperate to have a male child, take drastic measures like gender-selective abortion and even abandon their girls on the steps of orphanages.

The first wave of American-adopted Chinese girls are already teens. As they come of age, their transracial families face unique challenges as they grapple with questions of racial and cultural identity. Support groups, social organizations, and even specialized heritage tour groups address these questions and assist children in learning more about their places of birth.

Casa is one of the city's newest hotels. Modern guest rooms are available at discounted online rates, making it a wonderful bargain. The heated indoor pool is the best in town, and all guest rooms include a complimentary, though limited, breakfast buffet. **Pros:** great location; modern rooms and facilities. **Cons:** new staff; lengthy check-in/check-out times. ⊠ *318 Wen Chang Zhong Lu* ☎ *0514/8780–0000* ✆ *142 rooms* ⚜ *In-hotel: 2 restaurants, bar, fitness room, pool* ▭ *AE, MC, V.*

¢–$ 🏨 **XiYuan Hotel.** Rooms at this hotel border on drab and are quite small, but the location, near Slender West Lake and many restaurants and stores, is convenient. Staff are friendly and helpful, but speak limited English. **Pros:** a bargain compared to other upscale hotels in Yangzhou; convenient central location. **Cons:** language barrier with staff; rooms are drab and cramped. ⊠ *1 Feng Le Shang Jie* ☎ *0514/8780–7888* ⊕ *www.xiyuan-hotel.com* ✆ *270 rooms, 12 suites* ⚜ *In-hotel: 4 restaurants, gym, no-smoking rooms* ▭ *AE, MC, V.*

NIGHTLIFE

Similar to the 1912 area in Nanjing and opposite the Old Brewery, Yangzhou's 1912 area is a collection of extravagant Chinese restaurants, bars, and karaoke dives. The area expats tend to gather at the Old Brewery.

SUZHOU

Approximately 90 minutes (217 km [135 mi]) by express train southeast of Nanjing, or 1 hr (84 km [52 mi]) by express train west of Shanghai. Approximately 3½ hrs (225 km [140 mi]) by train on Nanjing–Shanghai rail line southeast of Nanjing, or 1 hr (84 km [52 mi]) by train west of Shanghai.

Suzhou has long been known as a place of culture, beauty, and sophistication. It produced scores of artists, writers, and politicians over the centuries, and it developed a local culture based on refinement and taste. Famous around the world for its carefully designed classical gardens, Suzhou's elegance extends even to its local dialect—Chinese often say that two people arguing in the Suzhou dialect sound more pleasant than lovers talking in standard Chinese.

Unlike in other cities in Eastern China, glass-and-steel office parks have been barred from the Old City center here, and this preservation makes Suzhou a pleasant place to explore. There is excellent English signage on the roads, and the local tourism board has even set up a convenient information center to get you on the right track.

Only an hour outside of Shanghai, the tourist trail here is well worn, and during the high season you will find yourself sharing these gardens with packs of foreign and domestic tour groups. It's worth getting up early to hit the most popular places before the crowds descend.

GETTING HERE AND AROUND

Buses bound for Nanjing (two hours) and Yangzhou (three hours) depart from the North Bus Station. Frequent trains to Nanjing take two to three hours. It's a popular route, so be sure to buy tickets in advance. Trains to Yangzhou take 3½ hours.

Buses to Shanghai take about an hour. Trains, which depart about every 20 minutes, take anywhere from 40 minutes to 1½ hours.

AIR TRAVEL   Suzhou is served by Shanghai's international airports, Hongqiao and Pudong. Hongqiao Airport is about 86 km (53 mi) from Suzhou, and shuttle buses run throughout the day. The trip takes less than two hours. If you are coming into Pudong, buses that make the 120-km (65-mi) trip from the airport leave about once an hour.

BUS TRAVEL   Bus service between Suzhou and Nanjing is frequent. The Suzhou bus station is just outside the Pingmen Gate.

TRAIN TRAVEL   Nanjing and Suzhou are on the same rail line, which continues on to Shanghai. Tickets can be purchased through your hotel. At the stations, the lines are long and vendors curt with non-Chinese speakers.

TIMING

Suzhou has more than enough attractions to merit two full days. Gardens are spread throughout the city so traveling to and fro takes a bit of time.

ESSENTIALS

Air Contacts China Eastern Airlines (✉ *192 Renmin Lu* ☎ *0512/6522–2788* ⊕ *www.ce-air.com*). **China Southern Airlines** (✉ *943 Renmin Lu* ☎ *0512/6524–3437* ⊕ *www.cs-air.com/en*).

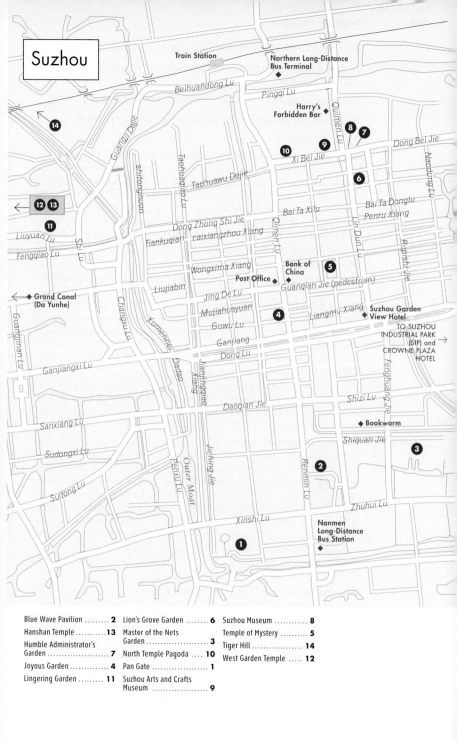

Suzhou

Train Station

Northern Long-Distance Bus Terminal

Beihuandong Lu

Pingqi Lu

Harry's Forbidden Bar

Quimen Lu

Dong Bei Jie

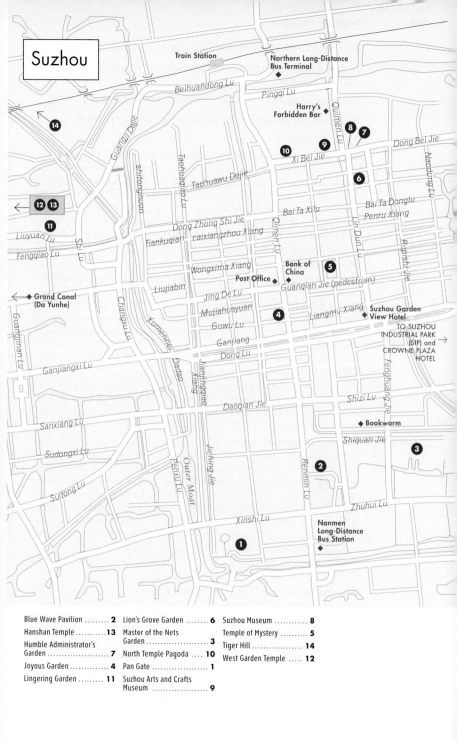

Xi Bei Jie

Guangji Dajie

Shitongnuon

Taohelaqi Lu

Taohuawu Dajie

Bai Ta Xilu

Bai Ta Donglu

Penru Xiang

Maodung Lu

Lin Dun Lu

Rupishi Jie

Dong Zhong Shi Jie

Tiankuqian caixiangzhou Xiang

Wongxima Xiang

Liujiabin

Qimen Lu

Bank of China

Post Office

Guanqian Jie (pedestrian)

Liuyuan Lu

Fengqiao Lu

Shi Lu

Jing De Lu

Mujiahuayuan

Guwu Lu

Ganjiang

Dong Lu

Liangmu Xiang

Suzhou Garden View Hotel

TO SUZHOU INDUSTRIAL PARK (SIP) and CROWNE PLAZA HOTEL

Grand Canal (Da Yunhe)

Guangjinan Lu

Changxu Lu

Xumenni

Jianjingqiao Xiang

Dadao

Ganjiangxi Lu

Daoqian Jie

Shizi Lu

Fenghuang Jie

Sanxiang Lu

Sudongxi Lu

Bookworm

Shiquan Jie

Sudong Lu

Outer Moat

Penxu Lu

Jiehng Jie

Renmin Lu

Zhuhui Lu

Xinshi Lu

Nanmen Long-Distance Bus Station

Blue Wave Pavilion **2**	Lion's Grove Garden **6**	Suzhou Museum **8**
Hanshan Temple **13**	Master of the Nets Garden **3**	Temple of Mystery **5**
Humble Administrator's Garden **7**	North Temple Pagoda ... **10**	Tiger Hill **14**
Joyous Garden **4**	Pan Gate **1**	West Garden Temple **12**
Lingering Garden **11**	Suzhou Arts and Crafts Museum **9**	

Bus Contact Suzhou Bus Station (✉ *29 Xihui Lu* ☎ *0512/6753–0686*).

Medical Assistance Suzhou People's Hospital No. 2 (✉ *26 Daoqian Jie* ☎ *0512/6522–3691.*

Train Contact Suzhou Train Station (✉ *Beihuan Xi Lu* ☎ *0512/6753–2831*).

Visitor and Tour Info CITS (✉ *18 Da Jing Xiang* ☎ *0512/6511–7505*).

EXPLORING

Suzhou is threaded by a network of narrow waterways. The canals that now seem quaint were once choked with countless small boats ferrying goods between the city's merchants. All of these small channels lead eventually to imperial China's main conduit of trade and travel, the **Grand Canal** *(Da Yunhe)*, which passes through the outskirts of town. The **Precious Belt Bridge** (Baodai Qiao) is an ancient bridge of 53 arches that bound over Tantai Lake where it meets the Grand Canal. ✉ *Beyond Pingmen Gate, north on Renmin Lu.*

TOP ATTRACTIONS

Blue Wave Pavilion *(Canglang Ting)*. The Blue Wave Pavilion is the oldest existing garden in Suzhou, dating back more than 900 years to the Song Dynasty. With a simple design, the garden grounds feel a little wilder than the relative newcomers. The central pond is an expansive stretch of water that reflects the upturned eaves of the surrounding buildings. More than 100 different lattice designs shading the windows provide visual variety as you saunter the long corridor over the water. A rocky hill rises in the center of the pond, atop which stands the square Blue Wave Pavilion. The **Pure Fragrance Pavilion** showcases Qing Dynasty furniture at its most extreme; the entire suite is created from gnarled banyan root. ✉ *East of Renmin Lu, between Shiquan Jie and Xinshi Lu* 🌊 *Apr. 16–Oct. 30, Y20; Oct. 31–Apr. 15, Y15* ⊙ *Daily 7:30–5:30.*

Fodor's Choice ★ **Humble Administrator's Garden** *(Zhuo Zheng Yuan)*. More than half of Suzhou's largest garden is occupied by ponds and lakes. The garden was built in 1509 by Wang Xianjun, an official dismissed from the imperial court. He chose the garden's name from a Tang Dynasty line of poetry reading "humble people govern," perhaps a bit of sarcasm considering the grand scale of his private residence. In the summer the pond is filled with fragrant lotuses. Check out their well-maintained Web site for information on spring and summer flower and bonsai exhibitions. ✉ *178 Dongbei Jie, 1 block east of Lindun Lu* ☎ *0512/6751–0286* ⊕ *www.szzzy.cn* 🌊 *Apr. 16–Oct. 30, Y70; Oct. 31–Apr. 15, Y50* ⊙ *Daily 7:30–5:30.*

Lingering Garden *(Liu Yuan)*. Windows frame other windows, undulating rooflines recall waves, and a closed corridor transforms into a room open to the pond at this interesting garden. The compound provides an endless array of architectural surprises: in a corner an unexpected skylight illuminates a planted nook; windows are placed to frame bamboos as perfectly as

The Humble Administrator's Garden is the largest garden in Suzhou.

if they were painted. The **Mandarin Duck Hall** is particularly impressive, with a lovely moon gate engraved with vines and flowers. In the back of the garden stands a 70-foot-tall rock moved here from Lake Taihu. Ongoing solo musical performances on erhu and zither enliven the halls. ⊠ *338 Liuyuan Lu, west of the moat* ☎ *0512/6557–9466* ⊕ *www.gardenly.com* ✉ *Apr. 16–Oct. 30, Y40; Oct. 31–Apr. 15, Y30* ⊙ *Daily 7:30–5.*

★ **Lion's Grove Garden** *(Shizi Lin).* This garden uses countless gnarled formations from nearby Lake Taihu to create a surreal moonscape. A labyrinth of man-made caves surrounds a small lake. There's a popular local saying that if you talk to rocks, you won't need a psychologist, making this garden a good place to spend a 50-minute hour. A tearoom on the second floor of the main pavilion overlooks the lake. ⊠ *23 Yuanlin Lu, 3 blocks south of the Humble Administrator's Garden* ☎ *0512/6727–8316* ⊕ *www.szszl.com* ✉ *Y30* ⊙ *Daily 8:15–5:30.*

★ **Master of the Nets Garden** *(Wangshi Yuan).* All elements of Suzhou style are here in precise balance: rock hills, layered planting, and charming pavilions overlooking a central pond. The garden is a favorite spot on tour-group itineraries. To avoid the crowds, visit in the evening, when you can saunter from room to room enjoying traditional opera, flute, and dulcimer performances—as the master himself might have enjoyed. Performances are held from mid-March to mid-November. ⊠ *11 Kuo Jia Tou Gang, west of Shiquan Lu* ☎ *0512/6529–3190* ⊕ *www.szwsy. com* ✉ *Apr. 16–Oct. 30, Y30; Oct. 31–Apr. 15, Y20* ⊙ *Daily 7:30–5 (last ticket sold at 4:30).*

Temple of Mystery *(Xuanmiao Guan)*. One of the best-preserved Taoist compounds, the Temple of Mystery backs a large square that is now a lively market. Founded in the 3rd century, the temple is a rare example of a wooden structure that has lasted centuries, with parts from the 12th century. Fortunately, it suffered little damage in the Cul-

tural Revolution, and retains a splendid ceiling of carefully arranged beams and braces painted in their original colors. ⊠ *Guanqian Jie* ☎ *0512/6777–5479* ⊠ *Y10* ⊙ *Daily 8:30–5.*

Tiger Hill *(Huqiu)*. This hill is the burial place of the king of the State of Wu, who founded the city in 514 BC. At the top of the approach is a huge sheet of stone called **Thousand Man Rock,** where legend has it that the workers who built the tomb were thanked for their work with an elaborate banquet. The wine, alas, was drugged, so they died to keep the secret of the tomb's entrance. Modern archaeologists think they have discovered it hidden under the artificial lake. The secret may be out, but the king's wish to rest in peace is ensured by the fact that excavating the tomb would bring down the fragile Song Dynasty pagoda that stands above. The **Leaning Pagoda** is one of the most impressive monuments in Suzhou, with Persian influence evident in the arches and other architectural elements. A helpful audio guide explains many of the park's legends. ⊠ *Huqiu Lu, northwest of the city* ☎ *0512/6532–3488* ⊠ *Apr. 16–Oct. 30, Y60; Oct. 31–Apr. 15, Y40* ⊙ *Daily 7:30–5.*

WORTH NOTING

Hanshan Temple *(Hanshan Si)*. Best known as a subject of one of the Tang Dynasty's most famous poems, which described the sound of its massive bell at midnight, this large, pristinely painted temple may leave those unfamiliar with the ancient poetry feeling a little underwhelmed. The place has the frenetic feel of a tourist attraction rather than the serenity of a temple. Literary pilgrims can line up to ring the temple bell themselves for an extra charge. ⊠ *24 Hanshan Si Nong* ☎ *0512/6533–6634* ⊠ *Apr. 16–Oct. 30, Y20; Oct. 31–Apr. 15, Y15* ⊙ *Daily 8–5.*

Joyous Garden *(Yi Yuan)*. The youngest garden in Suzhou, Joyous Garden was built in 1874. It borrows elements from Suzhou's other famous gardens: rooms from the Humble Administrator's, a pond from the Master of the Nets. The most unusual feature in the garden is an oversize mirror, inspired by the founder of Zen Buddhism, who stared at a wall for years to find enlightenment. The garden's designer hung the mirror opposite a pavilion, to let the building contemplate its own reflection. From April to October the garden doubles as a popular teahouse in the evening. ⊠ *343 Renmin Lu, 1 block south of the Temple of Mystery* ☎ *0512/6524–9317* ⊠ *Y15* ⊙ *Daily 7:30 am–midnight.*

North Temple Pagoda *(Beisi Ta)*. One of the symbols of ancient Suzhou, this temple towers over the Old City. This complex has a 1,700-year history, dating to the Three Kingdoms Period. The wooden pagoda has nine levels; you can climb as high as the eighth level for what might be the best view of Suzhou. Within the grounds are the Copper Buddha Hall and Plum Garden, which, built in 1985, lacks the history and the complexity of Suzhou's other gardens. ✉ *Xibei Jie and Renmin Lu, 2 blocks west of Humble Administrator's Garden* ☎ *0512/6753–1197* 🔁 *Y25* ⊙ *Mar.–Oct., daily 7:45–6.*

Pan Gate *(Pan Men).* Traffic into Old Suzhou came both by road and canals, so the city's gates were designed to control access by both land and water. This gate—more of a small fortress—is the only one that remains. In addition to the imposing wooden gates on land, a double sluice gate can be used to seal off the canal and prevent boats from entering. A park is filled with colorful flowers, in contrast to the subdued traditional gardens elsewhere in the city. A small platform extends over a pond, where voracious carp turn the water into a thrashing sheet of orange and yellow as they compete for food that tourists throw down. You can climb the **Ruiguang Pagoda,** a tall, slender spire originally built more than 1,000 years ago. ✉ *1 Dong Dajie, southwest corner of the Old City* ☎ *0512/6526–0004* 🔁 *Panmen Gate Y40; Ruigang Pagoda Y6* ⊙ *Daily 8–4:45.*

Suzhou Arts and Crafts Museum. The highlight here is watching artists in action. They carve jade, cut latticework fans from thin sheets of sandalwood, and fashion traditional calligraphy brushes. Perhaps most amazing is the careful attention to detail of the women embroidering silk. The attached shop is a good place to pick up quality crafts. ✉ *58 Xibei Jie, between Humble Administrator's Garden and the North Pagoda* ☎ *0512/6753–4874* 🔁 *Y15* ⊙ *Daily 9–5.*

Suzhou Museum. This is the most modern building to emerge amid a neighborhood of traditional architecture. The museum is the valedictory work for 90-year-old modernist master I.M. Pei. A controversy erupted over whether to allow Pei to construct the glass-and-steel structure in historical Suzhou. Like his crystal pyramid in the courtyard of the Louvre, this building thrives on juxtapositions of old and new. The museum houses historical objects from Suzhou's ancient past and an impressive collection of Ming and Qing Dynasty paintings and calligraphy. ✉ *204 Dongbei Jie, next to Humble Administrator's Garden* ☎ *0512/6757–5666* ⊕ *www.szmuseum.com* 🔁 *Free; English language docent tours Y100* ⊙ *Tues.–Sun. 9–5. Closed Monday.*

West Garden Temple *(Xi Yuan Si).* This temple is most notable for the **Hall of 500 Arhats** *(Wubai Luohan Tang),* which houses 500 goldpainted statues of these Buddhist guides. They are humorous carvings: one struggling with dragons, another cradling a cat. ✉ *8 Xiwan Lu, across from Lingering Garden* 🔁 *Y25* ⊙ *Daily 7–5.*

WHERE TO EAT

Shiquan Jie is quickly becoming one of the city's restaurant hubs, with both Suzhou-style restaurants and Chinese regional cuisine from Xinjiang to Yunnan. Many offer English menus.

$

CHINESE

✕ **Chamate.** Originally from Taiwan, this contemporary teahouse–restaurant opened its first mainland branch in 2002 in Shanghai's ultraposh Xin Tian Di neighborhood, and has been going gangbusters

Exploring the Water Villages

Centuries-old villages, preserved almost in their original state, are scattered around Suzhou. Bowed bridges span narrow canals, as traditional oared boats paddle by, creating an almost perfect picture of a way of life long past. A trip to one of these villages will probably be a highlight of your trip to Eastern China.

Be careful which village you choose, though. The tourist dollars that flow in may have saved these villages from the wrecking ball, but they have also changed their character to differing degrees. Those closest to the larger cities can be the most swamped by tour groups. Trekking to an out-of-the-way destination can pay off by letting you find a village that you will have all to yourself.

The most famous of the water villages is undoubtedly **Zhouzhuang**. Its fame is partly due to its proximity from Suzhou and Shanghai, just 45 minutes and an hour away, respectively. As a result, more than 2.5 million visitors head to the water village of Zhouzhuang each year to catch a glimpse of Old China. Its charm is reduced by the sheer number of tourists who elbow their way through the streets. Next to the "ancient memorial archway," which isn't ancient at all, is a ticket window. The steep entrance fee of Y100 gets you into the water-village-turned-gift shop.

Crowds aside, Zhouzhuang is fun for families. Several residences, some 500 years old, let you see what life was like in the Ming and Qing dynasties. There are several storefronts where you can see brick making, bamboo carving, and basket weaving—traditional crafts that up until recently were in widespread use throughout

the countryside. The food is typical country fare, making it a nice break from the fancier cuisine of Suzhou and Shanghai. The most famous dish, a fatty cut of pork leg, is too oily for most Western palates. But there are also pickled vegetables and wild greens to sample. For crafts, skip the snuff bottles and teapots, which are of low quality. Opt for something you probably won't find elsewhere: homemade rice wine, rough-hewn ox-horn combs, and bamboo rice baskets.

Buses to Zhouzhuang leave from Suzhou's North Bus Station every 20 minutes between 7 am and 5 pm. The 1½-hour trip costs Y25.

The pick of the water villages is **Tongli**, 30 minutes from Zhouzhuang and 1½ hours from Suzhou. There's a slightly more reasonable entrance fee of Y80. A number of locals still live and work here, making this village seem more authentic than Zhouzhuang. The streets are cobbled, and the complete absence of cars makes Tongli feel like it's from a different era. You can still find yourself wandering on quaint side streets or creeping down impossibly narrow alleyways that open onto canals and bridges. Tongli is the largest of the water villages, imminently photographable, and a pleasure to explore. Near the entrance gate are several private homes offering beds, and throughout the village are tea shops and small tables set out in front of the canals. Hiring a boat (Y60 for up to six people) to float down the canals gives you a different perspective on the town.

A favorite spot in Tongli is Tuisi Garden, a slightly smaller version of the private courtyard parks found in

3

The canals of Tongli.

Suzhou. Tongli is also home to the **Ancient Chinese Sexual Culture Museum,** housed in a former girl's school. The controversial exhibition of ancient erotic toys and art is the project of a retired university professor. ✉ *Entrance to town* ☎ *0512/6332–2973* 🖃 *Y20.*

Buses to Tongli leave from the square in front of Suzhou Train Station every 30 minutes between 7 am and 5 pm. The journey costs Y8.

Even farther off the beaten path is **Luzhi,** about a half hour from Suzhou and Zhouzhuang. It is a popular tourist destination, but it is still relatively untouched by large tour groups, and is a more peaceful water-town experience. It has been described as a "museum of bridges." There are more than 40 here, in all different shapes and sizes. Many of the older women in the village preserve traditional customs, wearing traditional headdresses and skirts. Luzhi is also notable for the spectacular **Baosheng Temple**

(✉ *Luzhi* ☎ *0512/6501–0011*), a yellow-walled compound built in 503 that is famous for its breathtaking collection of Buddhist arhats. Arranged on a wall of stone, these clay sculptures are the work of Yang Huizhi, a famous Tang Dynasty sculptor. They depict Buddhist disciples who have gained enlightenment; these works, made more than 1,000 years ago, impart the character and artistry of their creator. The temple also features a well-preserved bell from the end of the Ming Dynasty. Luzhi-bound buses leave from the square in front of Suzhou Train Station every 30 minutes between 6:30 am and 6:30 pm. The 40-minute ride costs Y10.

since—they have properties in Beijing, Hangzhou, Ningbo, Suzhou, and Qingdao. This one is located in the city center, just off the main pedestrian drag. The clean, cozy atmosphere and user-friendly picture menu with English captions make this the perfect place to relax. We recommend a steaming pot of red kumquat tea. Healthy soups, dim sum, and gooey Taiwanese deserts are also available. ⊠ *Off Guanqian Jie, 62 Gongxiang* ☎ *0512/6581–0360* ▭ *No credit cards.*

$$–$$$ ✕ **Deyuelou.** This restaurant has served Suzhou-style food for more
CHINESE   than 400 years. The menu boasts a wide array of fish dishes and a
★   particularly tasty *deyue tongji* (braised chicken). It also specializes in the ancient art of "garden foods"—an assortment of small dishes arranged to resemble various sorts of gardens, with foods portraying flowers, trees, and rocks. You can also try the local-style dim sum. ⊠ *27 Taijian Nong and 8 Taijian Nong, south of the Temple of Mystery* ☎ *0512/6523–8940* ▭ *AE, MC, V.*

$$–$$$ ✕ **Pine and Crane** (*Songhelou*). The food is the type once served on riv-
CHINESE   erboats during banquet cruises—hence the popular designation "boat
★   food." A particularly good dish is the *songshu guiyu,* or "squirrel-shaped Mandarin fish." (Don't let the English translation turn you off: it's a sweet-and-sour boneless fried river fish.) The other fish dishes are just as delicious. ⊠ *72 Taijian Nong, south of the Temple of Mystery* ☎ *0512/6770–0688* ▭ *AE, MC, V.*

WHERE TO STAY

$$ 🏨 **Crowne Plaza Hotel Suzhou.** Located in the Suzhou Industrial Park and set against the beautiful Jinji Lake, this nautical-themed property is designed in the shape of a giant cruise ship. The Czech architect successfully imbued a sense of maritime luxury in the elegant and spacious rooms, where the flick of a switch automatically opens the carmel-colored curtains for expansive lake views. The atrium lobby bar has an enormous, world-map carpet. It's fun to unwind over a drink and test your knowledge of geography. **Pros:** infinity-edge outdoor swimming pool; state-of-the-art fitness center. **Cons:** pricey in-room Internet access; outside the city center. ⊠ *68 Xinggang Lu, Suzhou Industrial Park* ☎ *512/6761–6688* ⊕ *www.crowneplaza.com* ⤳ *344 rooms* ⌂ *In-room: safe, refrigerator, Wi-Fi. In-hotel: 2 restaurants, room service, bar, tennis courts, pool, gym, laundry service, Internet terminal, no-smoking rooms* ▭ *AE, DC, MC, V.*

¢–$ 🏨 **Gloria Plaza Hotel Suzhou.** This prime piece of real estate faces the historic Ping Jiang Lu and sits alongside one of the canals that lead to the Humble Administrator's Garden. Though the rooms are large and comfortable enough, they're bland and in need of renovation. But for the price and location, the Gloria Plaza is worth mentioning. **Pros:** great breakfast; convenient location. **Cons:** carpets and furnishings are worn. ⊠ *535 Ganjiang Dong Lu* ☎ *0512/6521–8855* ⊕ *www.gphsuzhou.com* ⤳ *294 rooms* ⌂ *In-room: safe, Internet. In-hotel: 2 restaurants, room service, bar, gym, laundry service, no-smoking rooms* ▭ *AE, DC, MC, V.*

$ 🏨 **Nanyuan Guest House.** After a day of exploring Suzhou's gardens, return to a garden of your own. The 10 acres surrounding the Nanyuan Guest House are pleasantly planted with bamboo, and rocks and ponds are sprinkled throughout its courtyards. The selling point, however, is the location two blocks from the Master of the Nets Garden. The apricot-and-mauve rooms are spread among six buildings. **Pros:** beautiful grounds. **Cons:** inadequate facilities for business travelers. ⊠ *249 Shiquan Jie,* ☎ *0512/6778–6778* ➱ *104 rooms* ⌂ *In-room: refrigerator. In-hotel: 2 restaurants, room service, bar, laundry service, Internet* ▤ *AE, DC, MC, V.*

\$\$ **Fodor's Choice** **★** ▥ **Pan Pacific Suzhou.** Formerly the Sheraton Hotel and Towers, the Pan Pacific Suzhou is still the city's most luxurious and unique five-star hotel. A two-story stone entrance topped by a pagoda lobby is modeled after the Pan Gate. Here musicians welcome guests by playing the erhu (Chinese violin) and singing traditional ballads in the Suzhou Pingtan dialect. The new Pacific Club rooms are pricier, but the extra cost buys access to a two-hour happy hour, all-day snacks, afternoon tea in the club lounge, and use of the business center. All guests can use the fitness center, and the striking outdoor Roman-style pool is fun. Try to get a courtyard-facing room, as views of the garden are stunning. The pagoda lounge bar overlooks Suzhou's gardens, canals, peach trees, and the Ruiguang Pagoda in nearby Pan Gate. **Pros:** beautiful architecture and gardens. **Cons:** in an older part of town. ⊠ *259 Xinshi Lu* ☎ *0512/6510–3388* ⊕ *www. www.panpacific.com* ➱ *481 rooms* ⌂ *In-hotel: 3 restaurants, room service, bar, pool, gym, laundry service, Wi-Fi, no-smoking rooms* ▤ *AE, DC, MC, V.*

\$ ▥ **Suzhou Garden View Hotel.** Set back from the main road by a canal, this peaceful hotel is convenient to most of the city's sights—a whole day can be spent wandering the grounds around the hotel. Pleasant rooms are laid out around a large courtyard and garden, which is centered by a welcoming teahouse. Each of the 188 rooms is decorated differently, so even if you pre-booked, be sure to ask to see a few in different categories before settling in. Adjustments can be made with some polite assertiveness. **Pros:** great value; distinctive touches. **Cons:** congested area; difficult to find taxi, small bathrooms, poor amenities. ⊠ *66 Luo Guaqia, Lindun Lu* ☎ *0512/6777–8888* ⊕ *www.szrj-h.com* ➱ *188 rooms* ⌂ *In-room: refrigerator, Internet. In-hotel: 3 restaurants, bar, gym, laundry* ▤ *AE, MC, V.*

NIGHTLIFE AND THE ARTS

At night Perfect Ten Street, the stretch of Shiquan Jie between Renmin Lu and Hengfeng Lu, is home to a thriving cluster of Irish pubs, small hole-in-the wall Chinese bars, and karoke clubs. Storefronts change quickly, but you are guaranteed to find something lively and fun. Midnight is when the scene heats up.

★ **The Bookworm.** Housed in a freestanding, terraced, canal-side town house, this is the perfect (and only) place in Suzhou to peruse thousands

3

of English language books and magazines while sipping on imported wines and beer. This café/restaurant/bar/library plays host to a diverse range of international and local authors, scholars, and journalists. Check out the well-maintained Web site for a calendar of current events, author talks, book signings, and monthly specials. Travel guidebooks, international magazines, and some select books also available for sale. The space fills up at night and becomes more of a bar. ⊠ *77 Gunxi Fang, off of Shi Quan Jie on Ping Qiao Zhi Jie Bridge* ☎ *0512/6581–6752* ▭ *MC, V.*

★ **Harry's Forbidden Bar.** Set in a magnificent 200-year-old wooden house and featuring traditional six-sided red lanterns, and an intricately carved, dark-wood mezzanine, this romantic venue hosts nightly local bands and serves pints of Guinness on tap. The dimly lit interior illuminates dozens of private rooms separated by patterned screens. Local Chinese bands play at 9 nightly. ⊠ *118 Qimen Lu* ☎ *0512/6521–9319* ▭ *No credit cards.*

OFF THE BEATEN PATH

Pingjiang Lu is an ancient, well-preserved street in the city center. Dating back 800 years, this north-to-south canal features bygone scenes of daily life. Quaint whitewashed canal-side houses with overhanging balconies and black-tiled roofs cluster under weeping willows and jasmine trees. Arched bridges reflected in the canals are picture-perfect. Although the area is gradually becoming trendy, with coffee shops, bars, hostels, and art galleries, it's still possible to duck into one of the alleyways and experience a way of life unchanged for hundreds of years.

Le Pont des Arts. This French-owned contemporary art and photography studio has constantly rotating exhibits of both Chinese and foreign artists. Their mission is to develop "a dialogue between old and modern [China]." ⊠ *112–115 Ping Jiang Lu* ☎ *0512/6581–3330* ▭ *MC, V.*

SHOPPING

Districts around the gardens and temples teem with silk shops and outdoor markets. The city's long history of wealth and culture has encouraged a tradition of elegant and finely worked craft objects. One of the best-known crafts is double-sided embroidery, where two separate designs are carefully stitched on both sides of a sheet of silk. The city is also famous for its finely latticed sandalwood fans. Both are available at the Suzhou Arts and Crafts Museum. The area outside the gate of the Master of the Nets Garden has dozens of small stalls selling curios and inexpensive but interesting souvenirs.

The **Friendship Store** (⊠ *504 Renmin Lu* ☎ *0512/6523–6165*) has a selection of local products in silk, wood, and jade. Quality is good, but better deals can be had elsewhere. Since 1956 the **Suzhou Cultural Relics Store** (⊠ *1208 Renmin Lu* ☎ *0512/6523–3851*) has been selling antiques, calligraphy, jades, and other items. You can get jewelry and carvings at the **Suzhou Jade Carving Factory** (⊠ *33 Baita Xi Lu* ☎ *0512/6727–1224*).

Near the North Pagoda, the **Suzhou Silk Museum Shop** (⊠ *661 Renmin Lu* ☎ *0512/6753–4941*) is really the reason to come to the Silk Museum.

ANHUI

Eastern China's most rural province, Anhui has a rugged terrain that forces families to fight their hardscrabble farmland for every acre of harvest. Today it remains significantly poorer than its neighbors, with an average income half of that in neighboring Zhejiang. But what Anhui lacks in material wealth it makes up for in splendid natural landscape. Travelers here enjoy countryside largely untouched by the last century. Near Huangshan (Yellow Mountain), towering granite peaks loom over green fields, and round-shouldered water buffalo plow the flooded rice paddies.

The foothills of Huangshan have a remarkable wealth of historical architecture. Tiny communities dot the landscape in Shexian and Yixian counties. Many of these villages were far enough out of the way that even the zealous Red Guards of the Cultural Revolution left them alone. Today there are whole villages that remain exactly as they have been for 200 years.

Anhui boasts significant contributions to Chinese civilization. Of the treasures of classical Chinese education, Anhui produces the most famous paper and ink. Hui opera, an ancient musical form developed in the province, was a major influence on Beijing Opera. Hui cuisine is considered one of the country's finest culinary traditions, making use of mountain vegetables and simple, bold flavors.

Most of the province's attractions for tourists lie in the south, accessible from Shanghai, Hangzhou, and Nanjing.

REGIONAL TOURS

Nearby Nanjing is a good place in which to make arrangements for your travels in Anhui, particularly around Huangshan. For organized tours and other arrangements, contact **Jiangsu Huate International Travel Service** (⊠ *33 Jinxiang He Lu, Nanjing* ☎ *025/8337–8695* ⊕ *www.english.hitravels.com*).

HUANGSHAN (YELLOW MOUNTAIN)

5½ hrs (250 km [155 mi]) by train west of Nanjing; 3½ hrs by long-distance bus.

Fodor's Choice ★ Eastern China's most impressive natural landscape, Huangshan has peaks that rise like islands through roiling seas of clouds. A favorite retreat of emperors and poets of old, its peaks have inspired some of China's most outstanding artworks and literary endeavors. They were so beguiling that years of labor went into their paths, which are actual stone steps rising up—sometimes gradually into the forest, sometimes sharply through a stone tunnel and into the mist above. Since 1990 the area has been a UNESCO World Heritage Site.

The common English translation—Yellow Mountain—is misleading. Huangshan is not a single mountain but rather a series of peaks that stretch across four counties. To complicate matters, the name is not a reference to color. The region was originally called the "Black Mountains," but a Tang Dynasty emperor renamed it to honor Huangdi, the

Yellow Emperor. And according to legend, it was from these slopes that he rode off to heaven on the back of a dragon.

The mountain is renowned for its gnarled stone formations, crooked pines, and seas of mists. Most of these trees and rocks have names; some are obvious, whereas others require dedicated squinting and a leap of the imagination. Generations of Chinese poets and travelers have humanized these peaks and forests through this practice, and left their indelible mark on the area.

Be forewarned, though: Huangshan has its own weather. More than 200 days a year, precipitation obscures the famous views. It can be sunny below, but up in the mountains it's raining. But even on the foggiest of days the wind is likely to part the mist long enough to make out mysterious peaks. 🚉 *Mar. 1–Nov. 30, Y230; Dec. 1–Feb. 28, Y150.*

GETTING HERE AND AROUND

Most long-distance transportation, including trains and airplanes, arrives in Tunxi, the largest city near Yellow Mountain. Be aware, however, that Tunxi is still 1 to 1½ hours away from Yellow Mountain. Minibuses to Tangkou and other destinations around the base of the mountain leave from the plaza in front of Tunxi's train station. The cost should be Y15 to Y30. There are also plenty of taxi drivers who are happy to offer their services, usually for around Y70 per carload.

Some buses from Nanjing, Hangzhou, and Shanghai go directly to Tangkou, the entrance at the base of the mountain. The airport is close to Tunxi, about a Y15 to Y20 cab ride from the mountain.

AIR TRAVEL   If you plan to fly to Yellow Mountain, you'll land at the Huangshan City Airport near Tunxi, about 1 to 1½ hours away. There are direct flights to Beijing, Guangzhou, Shanghai, and Ji'nan.

TAXI AND MINIBUS TRAVEL   In Tunxi, minibuses and taxis that congregate around the train station will take you to Yellow Mountain. For about Y20 they will drop you at the main gate at the bottom of the mountain or at the beginning of the climbing section.

TRAIN TRAVEL   Trains travel to Tunxi, where you can catch a minivan or taxi to Yellow Mountain. The ride takes about an hour.

SAFETY AND PRECAUTIONS

The roads leading to Huangshan can be very dangerous in heavy rain or the winter months. Check the local weather forecast, as good weather is essential. Minibuses and taxis drive too fast in sometimes questionable vehicles.

TIMING

Treks range from two days and one night to five days and four nights. Most people opt for somewhere in between. Thanks to the cable cars along the way, you can take in a lot of scenery in one full day.

TOURS

Tours up the mountain are unnecessary. A better bet is to buy a good map from one of the local vendors and chart the path you want to take. Some Tunxi companies offer trips that include accommodations for little more than the cost of the admission price to the park. And there's

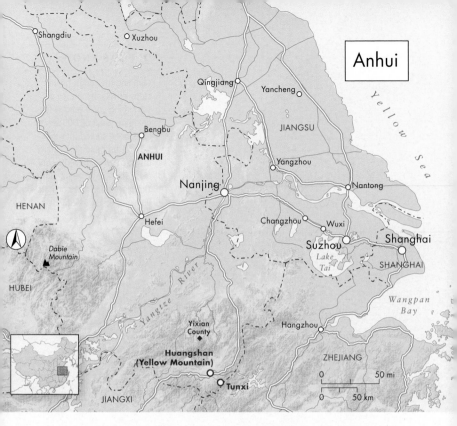

no need to spend the day with strangers—you can hike on your own, joining the rest of the group in time to catch the bus back.

The Tunxi branches of China Travel Service (CTS) can arrange transportation and book a place to stay on the mountain. It also has info on getting out and exploring the surrounding countryside. You can also get info from China International Travel Service, or CITS.

ESSENTIALS

Nearly all services are 1½ hours away in Tunxi.

Medical Assistance Beihai Medical Center (⊠ Across from Beihai Hotel, Huangshan ☎ 0559/558–2555). **Jade Screen Tower First-Aid Station** (⊠ Jade Screen Tower Hotel ☎ 0559/558–2288).

Visitor and Tour Info CTS (⊠ 12 Qianyuan Bei Lu, Tunxi ☎ 130/1312–1152 ⊠ 1Binjiang Xi Lu, Tunxi ☎ 0559/231–8319 ⊕ www.chinatravelservice.com). **Huangshan Travel Net** (⊠ 27 Xin'an North Rd., Tunxi District, Huangshan ☎ 0559/251–2155 or 0559/251–2133 ⊕ www.uhuangshan.com).

EXPLORING

There are two primary hiking routes up the mountain. The Eastern Steps, a straightforward path through forests, is both the shortest and the easiest. The Southern Steps (some guidebooks call these the Western Steps, which causes confusion with another set of steps used primarily

by porters) require more effort, but they pay off with remarkable scenery. The steep, winding path reveals sheer peaks and precipitous lookouts over mist-enshrouded valleys.

Climbing up is physically taxing, but climbing down is mentally exhausting, requiring far more concentration. If you have the time and the leg muscles, it's nice to ascend the South Steps, where the scenery stretches before you. The views are a good excuse to stop and catch your breath.

EASTERN STEPS

The Eastern Steps begin at the **Cloud Valley Temple Cable Car Station.** The cable car takes eight minutes to traverse what takes hikers three or more hours. Large windows provide an aerial view of the mountain and bamboo forests below. This area was once home to several monasteries, nunneries, and temples. By the beginning of the 20th century they had been abandoned, but the name Cloud Valley Temple Area remains. ✉ *Y80* ◷ *Weekdays 6:30–4:30, weekends 6:30–5.*

The Eastern Steps are quicker than the Southern Steps, but the scenery isn't as rewarding and there are fewer scenic side routes. Along the way is a **Fascinating Pavilion,** most notable as a rest stop along the way. There's a short half-hour side hike to **Pipeng,** with a good view out over a number of the smaller eastern peaks. By the time you reach **Cloud Valley,** the landscape that makes Huangshan famous begins to come into view. **Beginning to Believe Peak** is the start of the awe-inspiring landscape, and the first true majestic vista on this path.

SOUTHERN STEPS

The steep Southern Steps are by far the tougher path. However, the climb pays off with great views. There are also some beautiful side trails. Although the Eastern Steps feel like a walk through the woods, the Southern Steps truly feel like an ascent into the clouds. The steps begin around the Hot Springs, at the **Mercy Light Temple** area. **Midway Mountain Temple** has facilities to rest, eat, and even stay overnight, but no temple. It's here that the splendor of Huangshan comes into full view. At the **Three Islands at Penglai,** a trio of peaks poke out from a sea of mist. If you're feeling energetic, a side tour of **Heavenly Capital Peak** affords spectacular views out over the rest of the range. The effort is worth a try even if it looks cloudy, because the mist can sometimes clear by the time you get to the top. This may not be the highest peak in the range, but it is one of the steepest.

The **Jade Screen Cable Car** runs parallel to the Southern Steps, leaving riders close to the Welcoming Guests Pine. It can close unexpectedly in inclement weather. ✉ *Y80* ◷ *Weekdays 6:30–4:30, weekends 6:30–5.*

HUANGSHAN TRAVEL NET

The best place for current information about the region is the English-language Huangshan Travel Net, run in conjunction with the local CTS. The site is the brainchild of CTS's Victor Zhang, one of the area's most knowledgeable guides. He has arranged tea tours, bike tours, and architecture tours. The site allows users to plan their own trip to the mountain. Resources and bookings for Tunxi are also available.

THE SUMMIT

The entrance to the summit area is announced by the **Welcoming Guest Pine,** a lone pine clinging to the edge of a cliff, one branch outstretched. Behind it a sheer stone slope rises out of the clouds. Continuing up, you can climb **Lotus Peak,** the tallest in the province. A walk through **Turtle Cave,** an arched pathway straight through the hillside, brings the weary traveler to **Bright Top Peak,** slightly lower than Lotus, and an easier climb.

The newly opened **Xihai Grand Canyon** loop starts at the Cloud Dispelling Pavilion and ends at the Haixin Ting Pavilion. Rock formations called "Upside Down Boot" and "Lady Playing Piano" may be clumsily named, but they are stunning. The farther along you walk, the fewer travelers you'll come across. At the southern end of the loop, near Haixin, the trail reaches the **Immortal's Walk Bridge,** a dizzying arch over the misty abyss that leads to a terrace on one of the mountain's spires. A huge landscape spreads out beneath, without a single tour group in sight.

A highlight of any trip is sunrise, visible from several places on the mountain. Most hikers arrive well after dawn, but you'll be rewarded with the spectacle of Huangshan materializing from the shadows if you arrive just before first light. A popular spot near the Beihai Hotel is the **Dawn Pavilion.** There are several less crowded peaks with equally good views a little farther from the hotels. **Refreshing Terrace, Lion Peak,** and **Red Cloud Peak** all provide unobstructed views of the rising sun.

Compared to the ascent, the summit area is relatively level, but there is still a good amount of stair climbing. It takes about three to four hours to walk the full summit circle, and considerably more if you take side trails.

WHERE TO EAT

Five areas of Huangshan offer lodging. Tangkou, a village that has sprung up to serve mountain climbers, has the most for travelers, including hotels, restaurants, grocery stores, and shops to gear up for the long climb ahead. Tangkou sits near the front gate of the park, and buses run regularly to the trailheads for both the Southern and Eastern steps. If you want to take the shorter route up the Eastern Steps, the Cloud Valley Temple Area is a convenient option. The Hot Springs area has been reopened after renovation, and is a much more pleasant option than Tangkou.

Several small, basic huts are along the Southern Steps, but it would be better to push to the end of the path to the hotels in the Summit Area. *Although these lodgings are more expensive than those below, they are your only option if you want to*

BE PREPARED

Most paths are well maintained with good steps and sturdy handrails, but Huangshan still has sheer drop-offs and steep, uneven, rain-slicked steps. A walking stick (sturdy wooden dragon-head staffs are on sale around the mountain) will help steady your ascent. It can get very cold on the peaks, and rain can come unexpectedly. Dress in layers, and consider bringing a hooded sweatshirt to stay warm.

catch the sunrise. As a bonus, you'll have the dew-drenched forests to yourself for a few hours before the latecomers arrive. Reservations are strongly recommended, especially for weekends; this is a popular destination for Chinese travelers, as well as tourists from Japan and Korea.

$$–$$$
CHINESE
✕ **Celebrity's Banquet.** The best restaurant on the summit, Celebrity's Banquet celebrates local culture with a range of traditional Hui dishes. Soups of dried vegetables, jellied tofu, braised pork, and a delicately flavored pumpkin soup shouldn't be missed. ⊠ *Xihai Hotel, Grand Canyon Loop, Summit Area* ☎ *0559/558–8888* ▤ *AE, MC, V.*

$$–$$$
CHINESE
✕ **Tangzhen Hotel Restaurant.** This budget hotel is nothing to write home about, but the food is especially good. Locals come from all around the area to dine here. Specialties include cured mandarin fish, pork with bamboo, and mountain stone frogs. ⊠ *At the main entrance to Huangshan, Tangkou* ☎ *0559/556–2665* ▤ *No credit cards.*

WHERE TO STAY

$$–$$$
🏨 **Baiyun Hotel.** This hotel offers comfortable rooms and a good location on the summit—a short walk away from Bright Top Peak. An excellent restaurant downstairs serves great river fish, as well as mountain vegetables and mushroom dishes. **Pros:** good location; great restaurant. **Cons:** few amenities. ⊠ *Tianhai Area, Summit Area* ☎ *0559/558–2708* ⇆ *80 rooms, 1 suite* ⚴ *In-hotel: restaurant, bar* ▤ *AE, MC, V.*

$$
🏨 **Beihai Hotel.** This is one of the nicest places to stay on the mountain. A few extras like the sauna are a welcome end to a day of hiking. The rooms are set among rhododendrons and azaleas on the hillside. Ask for the front-facing rooms, which have better views—and rent for the same price as the rooms in the back. **Pros:** location. **Cons:** some rooms have unpleasant views. ⊠ *Huangshan Scenic Area, Summit Area* ☎ *0559/556–2555* 🖶 *0559/556–2996* ⇆ *137 rooms, 2 suites* ⚴ *In-room: refrigerator, Internet. In-hotel: restaurant, bar* ▤ *AE, MC, V.*

¢–$$
🏨 **Huangshan Xingang Hotel.** Because practically every guest is coming up or down the mountain, the staff here is a great repository of knowledge of what to see, how to climb, and the best routes to take. Like most hotels in the area, this place has rooms that are somewhat small but are clean and get lots of sun. They are good places to rest up for the climb ahead. **Pros:** great for a comfortable stop before your climb. **Cons:** basic amenities. ⊠ *At the main entrance to Huangshan, Tangkou* ☎ *0559/556–1048* ⇆ *115 rooms, 2 suites* ⚴ *In-hotel: restaurant, bar* ▤ *AE, MC, V.*

$$–$$$$
🏨 **Jade Screen Tower.** The views from this hotel are unmatched, though as at most of the hotels on the summit the rooms are small. Nonetheless the location is good: at the top of the Southern Steps near the cable car station. It's the first proper hotel you'll reach after a long climb. **Pros:** great place to catch the sunrise. **Cons:** limited facilities. ⊠ *Past Welcoming Guest Pine, Summit Area* ☎ *0559/558–2288* ⇆ *29 rooms, 1 suite* ⚴ *In-hotel: 2 restaurants* ▤ *AE, MC, V.*

¢
🏨 **Peach Blossom Hotel.** A winding road takes you over a bridge and past a double waterfall to this resort between the main gate of the mountain park and the beginning of the Southern Steps. The no-frills rooms are clean and comfortable. The Peach Blossom also has great Chinese and Western food, with specialties like bamboo chicken. **Pros:** convenient

to hot springs. **Cons:** not good for watching the sunrise. ✉ *Huangshan Scenic Area, Hot Springs* ☎ *0559/558–5666* ↩ *141 rooms, 4 suites* ⚲ *In-hotel: restaurant, bar* ▭ *AE, MC, V.*

$$ 🏨 **Yungu Hotel.** Tucked in among the trees, these traditional-style buildings blend well in the forest landscape. Cheaper than staying on the summit, the guest rooms here are also larger and better outfitted. **Pros:** charming surroundings. **Cons:** language barrier with some staff; hotel restaurant is not the best. ✉ *Next to the cable-car station, Cloud Valley Temple Area* ☎ *0559/558–6444* ↩ *100 rooms* ⚲ *In-hotel: 2 restaurants, bar, gym* ▭ *AE, DC, MC, V.*

TUNXI

5½ hrs (250 km [155 mi]) by train west of Nanjing; 3½ hrs by long-distance bus.

Tunxi, also called Huangshan City, is the gateway to the Yellow Mountain area. Apart from being a transportation hub, Tunxi also has a charming strip of shops and restaurants and is a convenient place from which to take trips to Shexian and Yixian counties, famous for their historical architecture.

GETTING HERE AND AROUND

Unless you arrive on a long-distance bus bound for Tangkou, or have joined a chartered excursion to Yellow Mountain, your bus or train is probably bound for Tunxi, around 40 mi (65 km) from the mountain.

AIR TRAVEL   From Huangshan City Airport near Tunxi, flights travel daily to Beijing and Guangzhou, twice daily to Shanghai, and twice a week to Hong Kong. Taxies to the airport from Tunxi cost about Y15 to Y20.

BUS TRAVEL   Buses are a convenient way of getting to Tunxi from Zhejiang, Jiangsu, and even Shanghai. Buses that run hourly from Hangzhou take 3½ hours and cost Y65. The route takes you through some gorgeous scenery. Buses from Nanjing take around five hours and cost Y80. From Shanghai, buses take eight to nine hours and cost Y120.

TRAIN TRAVEL   Several trains depart daily for Nanjing, and there are two trains each day for Shanghai (12–13 hours, Y160).

TIMING

Tunxi is a transit hub. Travelers might spend a night while waiting to start the Huangshan trek. It can also be a good place to arrange tours and meet other climbers.

TOURS

Guides are a good idea if you are exploring the countryside around Huangshan. CTS has private village tours in Yixian county and architecture tours in Shexian counties.

ESSENTIALS

Air Contacts Air China (✉ *23 Huashan Lu* ☎ *0559/953–4111* ✉ *49 Huashan Donglu* ☎ *0559/254–1222* ⊕ *www.airchina.com.cn/en/index.jsp*). **Huangshan City Airport** (✉ *West of Tunxi on Yingbin Dadao* ☎ *0559/293–4111*).

Bus Contact Tunxi Bus Station (✉ *95 Huangshan Dong Lu* ☎ *0559/235–3952*).

Medical Assistance **People's Hospital of Huangshan City** (✉ *4 Liyuan Lu, Huangshan* ☎ *0559/251–7036*).

Train Contact **Huangshan Train Station** (✉ *Northern end of Qianyuan Beilu* ☎ *0559/211–6222*).

Visitor and Tour Info **CITS** (✉ *2 Binjiang Xi Lu* ☎ *0559/254–2110* ⊕ *www. huangshantour.com/english*). **CTS** (✉ *12 Qianyuan Bei Lu* ☎ *130/1312–1152 (English-speaking hotline)* ✉ *1Binjiang Xi Lu* ☎ *0559/231–8319* ⊕ *www. chinatravelservice.com*).

EXPLORING

In Tunxi, the best place to pick up souvenirs is along **Old Street** *(Lao Jie)*. The street is quiet in the daytime but comes alive in the early evening. Shops stay open until about 10 or 11. There's a lot of junk, but you may find some treasures.

WHERE TO EAT AND STAY

$–$$

CHINESE

Fodor's Choice

★

✕ **Diyilou.** All sorts of small dishes are sold at this lively shop. Diners order by pointing to sample dishes, so the lack of an English menu is no problem. With hundreds of dishes on rotation, there's something for everyone. Local specialties include tender bamboo shoots, four-mushroom soup, red-braised tofu, and a white mushroom-wrapped meatball that is not to be missed. ✉ *247 Tunxi Lao Jie, at Lao Jie* ☎ *0559/253–9797* ▭ *AE, MC, V.*

¢–$$

🛏 **Huashan Hotel.** This large hotel sits at a perfect location in Tunxi, just a block away from the shopping district of Old Street. The lobby is enormous, as are the guest rooms. Some are a bit musty; ask to see a few before you decide. The hotel restaurant is inexpensive and acceptable, but for a nicer meal venture out into the charming surroundings of Old Street. The service is thorough, if a little confused at times. **Pros:** great access to Old Street. **Cons:** staff's limited English; musty rooms. ✉ *3 Yanan Lu, 1 block north of Old St.* ☎ *0559/232–2888* ⤶ *186 rooms, 14 suites* ⚐ *In-room: refrigerator, Internet. In-hotel: 2 restaurants, tennis court, pool, gym* ▭ *AE, MC, V.*

SHOPPING

When shopping along Lao Jie, the best offerings are traditional calligraphy ink and paper. The best ink stones are sold at **Sanbai Yanzhai** (✉ *173 Lao Jie* ☎ *0559/253–5538*).

Another traditional craft is bamboo carving. The **Stone and Bamboo Shop** (✉ *122 Lao Jie* ☎ *0559/751–5042*) sells exquisite examples.

SIDE TRIP TO SHEXIAN COUNTY

Shexian County has been called a living architectural art museum because of its natural beauty and array of historic buildings. Over the centuries, it has inspired philosophers, poets, and painters. Today, there is no lack of tourists but it's a pleasant day trip from Tunxi.

GETTING HERE AND AROUND

Buses run throughout the day from the Tunxi long-distance bus station. The trip should take about 45 minutes and costs approximately Y10. Once you get to Shexian Bus Station in Huizhou Old City, you can board a minibus or take a taxi to outlying scenic spots. However,

The shops and restaurants on Old Street in Tunxi.

if you are traveling with several people, it will be well worth hiring a car and driver for the day. Many of these places are remote, and you may find the bulk of your day wasted waiting for minibuses or trying to find a taxi.

EXPLORING SHEXIAN COUNTY

Huizhou Old Town (⊠ *Shexian County Center* ☎ *0559/653–1586* ✆ *Y80* ☉ *Daily 7:30–6:30*) boasts a centuries-old city wall and a magnificent four-sided memorial gate guarded by sculptures of frolicking lions.

The **Huashan Mysterious Grottoes** (⊠ *Between Xiongcun and Tunxi* ☎ *0559/235–9888* ✆ *Y70* ☉ *Daily 7:30–6:30*) are a combination of natural caves and rooms carved into the rock. No one is quite certain when or why they were built, but they are impressive, and newly illuminated with colored lights.

The most famous series of **Memorial Arches** (⊠ *3 mi [5 km] west of Huizhou Old Town* ☎ *No phone* ✆ *Y80* ☉ *Daily 8–5:30*) are in Tangyue Village. Dating from the Ming and Qing dynasties, these archways represent traditional values like morality, piety, and *female* chastity.

Near Huizhou Old Town, **Yuliang Village** overlooks a Tang Dynasty dam with water gurgling over its sloped sides. Fishermen in wooden skiffs still make their living here. A narrow street parallel to the river is nice for a stroll. Most families leave their doors open, allowing a peak into homes where pages from magazines are used as wallpaper and aluminum foil is a common decoration. Inexpensive pedicabs travel from the Shexian bus station to Yuliang Village, or you can catch Bus 1 from the train station. ☎ *No phone* ✆ *Y30* ☉ *Daily 7:30–6:30.*

SIDE TRIP TO YIXIAN COUNTY

A pleasant day trip from Tunxi, Yixian County is the site of some beautiful ancient architecture set in peaceful surroundings. Don't expect a quiet day with the village to yourself; Yixian County receives nearly 2.5 million visits per year. But don't let that deter you: the UNESCO World Heritage sites in the area offer a rare glimpse of what ancient Anhui may have been like and are stunningly photogenic.

GETTING HERE AND AROUND

To get to Yixian County destinations, take the buses that leave from in front of Tunxi's train station. They cost about Y10 and depart every 20 minutes. Because of a nearby military base, a police-issued travel permit costing Y50 is required for travel in Yixian County. The ticket offices at the gates of Xidi Village and Hongcun Village can take care of this for you. A passport is necessary to register for the permits.

EXPLORING YIXIAN COUNTY

An arched bridge leads to **Hongcun Village** (✉ *Eastern Yixian County* ☎ *0559/251–7464* ✇ *Y80* ⊙ *Daily 6:30–6:30*). From above, the village is said to resemble a buffalo. Two 600-year-old trees mark its horns, a lake its belly, and even irrigation streams are its intestines. In recent years a number of films have been partially shot here, including Ang Lee's *Crouching Tiger, Hidden Dragon*. Several large halls and old houses are open to tour. The Salt Merchants House is especially well preserved, with intricate decorations and carvings that were unharmed during the Cultural Revolution.

A UNESCO World Heritage Site, **Xidi Village** (✉ *Yixian Xidi Village* ☎ *0559/515–4030* ✇ *Y80* ⊙ *Daily 6:30–6:30*) is known for its exquisite memorial gate. There were once a dozen gates, but they were destroyed during the Cultural Revolution. The existing gate was left standing as a "bad example" to be criticized. There are several houses with excellent examples of brick carving and an impressive Clan Temple with massive ginkgo columns and beams.

ENGLISH	PINYIN	CHINESE CHARACTERS
HEBEI	**HÉBĚI**	河北
Chengde	Chéngdé	承德
Bifeng Hotel	Bìfēng jiǔdiàn	碧峰酒店
Chengde Chinese-Western Hospital	Chéngdé zhōngxī jiéhé yīyuàn	承德中西结合医院
China International Tourist Service (CITS)	Zhōngguó guójì lüxíngshè	中国国际旅行社
Club Rock	Bàngchuí fēng	棒槌峰
Da Qinghua Dumbling	Dàqīnghuà jiaózī	大清花饺子
Eight Outer Monasteries	Wàibā miào	外八庙
Hong Men Internet Bar	Hóngmén wāngbā	鸿门网吧
Mongolian Yurts Holiday Inn	Ménggùbāo dùjiàcūn	蒙古包度假村
Mountain Resort	bìshǔ shānzhuāng	避暑山庄
Shenghua Hotel	Shènghuá dà jiǔdiàn	盛华大酒店
Temple of the Potaraka Doctrine	Pùtuózōngchéng sì	普陀宗乘寺
Temple of Universal Happiness	Pùlè sì	普乐寺
Temple of Universal Peace	Pùníng sì	普宁寺
Beidaihe	Béidàihé	北戴河
Beidaihe Waijiao Renyuan Binguan	Béidàihé wàijiāo rényuán bīnguǎn	北戴河外交人员宾馆
Emperor Qin Shi Huang's Palace	Qínhuáng gōng	秦皇宫
Guanyin Temple	Guānyīn sì	观音寺
Guesthouse for Diplomatic Missions	Běi dài hé Bīnguǎn	北戴河宾馆
Jinshan Hotel	Jīnshān Dà JiùDiàn	金山大酒店
Kiesslings	Qīshìlín cāntīng	起士林餐厅
Lianfeng Hill Park	Líanfēngshān gōngyuán	联峰山公园
Shanhaiguan	Shānhǎiguān	山海关
cable car	lǎn chē	缆车
First Gate Under Heaven	Tīanxià dìyīguān	天下第一关
Great Wall Museum	Chángchéng bówùguǎn	长城博物馆
Jiao Mountain	Jī shān	角山
Jingshan Hotel	Jīngshān bīnguǎn	京山宾馆
Long Distance Bus Station	chángtú qìchēzhàn	长途汽车站
Longevity Mountain	Chángshòu shān	长寿山
Mengjiangnu Miao	Mèngjiāngnǚ miào	孟姜女庙

ENGLISH	PINYIN	CHINESE CHARACTERS
North Street Hotel	Běijīe zhāodàisùo	北街招待所
Old Dragon Head	Lǎolóngtóu	老龙头
Qinhuangdao Airport	Qínhuángdǎo jīcháng	秦皇岛机场
Wang Yan Lou	Wǎngyān lóu	王严楼
Yangsai Hu	Yángsāihú	羊腮胡
SHANDONG	**SHĀNDŌNG**	**山东**
Ji'nan	Jǐnán	济南
Big Bright Lake	Dàmínghú	大明湖
Confucian Forest	Kǒnglín	孔林
Confucius Family Mansion	Kǒngfǔ	孔府
Confucius Temple	Kǒngmiào	孔庙
C.Sohoh	Shún hé Jiǔ diàn	舜和酒店
Foshan Jie	Fóshānjī	佛山街
Gushing from the Ground Spring	Bàotūquán	趵突泉
Jenny's Cafe	Xī cài cān tíng Měi shí	西餐 (美食)
Long Distance Bus Station	chángtú qìchē zǒngzhàn	长途汽车总站
Mount Tai	Tàishān	泰山
Protestant Church	Jīdū jiàotáng	基督教堂
Qufu	Qūfù	曲阜
Sheraton Ji'nan	Jǐ nán xǐ lái déng jiǔ diàn	济南喜来登酒店
Sofitel Silver Plaza	Sū fēi té yín zuò dǎ jiǔ diàn	索菲特银座大酒店
Tai'an	Tài'ān	泰安
Tai'an Bus Station	Tài'ān qìchēzhàn	泰安汽车站
Thousand Buddha Mountain	Qiānfóshān	千佛山
Train Station	Huǒchēzhàn	火车站
Yaoqiang Airport	Yáoqiáng jīchāng	遥墙机场
Qingdao	Qīngdǎo	青岛
Catholic Church	Tiānzhǔ jiàotáng	天主教堂
Charlie's Bar	Chá lǐ sī jiǔ diàn	查理斯酒吧
Corner Jazz Club	Jiē yú jué shì ba	街角爵士吧
Din Tai Feng	Dín Tāi Fēng	鼎泰丰
Ferry Terminal	Qīngdǎo gǎngkèyùnzhàn	青岛港客运站
German Governor's Residence	Qīngdǎo yíngbīnguǎn	青岛迎宾馆
Granite Mansion	Huāshílóu	花石楼

ENGLISH	PINYIN	CHINESE CHARACTERS
Guanhaishan Park	Guānhǎishān gōngyuán	观海山公园
Huadong Winery	Huádōng Bǎilì jiǔzhuāng	华东百利酒庄
Intercontinental Hotel	Hǎi ér ōu zhōu jí jiǔ diàn	青岛海尔洲际酒店
Liuting Airport	Liútíng jīchǎng	流亭机场
Long Distance Bus Station	chángtú qìchēzhàn	长途汽车站
Lu Xun Park	Lǔxùn gōngyuán	鲁迅公园
Minjiang Lu	Mǐnjiāng lù	闽江路
Monomer Eck German Restaurant	Dé guó cān tīng	德国餐厅
Mount Lao	Láoshān	崂山
Navy Museum	hǎijūn bówùguǎn	海军博物馆
No. 1 Beach	dìyī hǎishuǐyùchǎng	第一海水浴场
No. 2 Beach	dì'èr hǎishuǐyùchǎng	第二 海水浴场
Protestant Church	Jīdū jiàotáng	基督教堂
Shangri-La Hotel	Xiāng gé lǐ lá jiǔ diàn	香格里拉酒店
Sun Yat-sen Park	Zhōngshān gōngyuán	中山公园
Train Station	Huǒchēzhàn	火车站
Tsingdao Beer Factory	Qīngdǎo píjiǔchǎng	青岛啤酒厂
Underwater World	Qīngdǎo hǎidǐ shìjiè	青岛海底世界
Zhongshan Lu	Zhōngshān lù	中山路
JAINGSU	**JĪANGSU**	**江苏**
Nanjing	Nánjīng	南京
Blue Marlin	Lán yú	蓝枪鱼
Central Hotel	Nān jíng zhōng xīn dǎ jiǔ diàn	南京中心大酒店
China Travel Service	Zhōngguó lǚxíngshè	中国旅行社
Confucian Temple	Fūzǐmiào	夫子庙
Dingshan Meishi Cheng	Díng shān měi shì	丁山 美食
Drum Tower	Gǔlóu	鼓楼
Finnegan's Wake Irish Barb	Oū zhōu héng rěn	欧洲烹饪
Grand Hotel	Gǔ nán dū fàn diàn	南京古南都饭店
G.E. Summit	Jīn yīng guó jì jiǔ diàn	金鹰国际酒店
Hong Ni Restaurant	Hóng Nī	红泥饭店
Hunan Road	Húnán lù	湖南路
Jingmingsi Vegetarian Restaurant	Jì mǐng sì sǔ shì fàn diànn	鸡鸣寺素食'

ENGLISH	PINYIN	CHINESE CHARACTERS
Jinling Hotel	Jīn líng fàn diàn	南京金陵饭店
Lakeview Xuanwu Hotel	Xuán wǔ fàn diàn	南京玄武饭店
Lukou Airport	Lùkǒu jīchǎng	禄口机场
Mandarin Garden Hotel	Zhuàn yuán lóu jiǔ diàn	状元楼酒店
Ming Tomb	Míngxiàolíng	明孝陵
Nail Jazz Bar	Dīng zi ba	钉子吧
Nanjing Hotel	Nanjing jiudian	南京酒店
Nanjing Massacre Memorial	dàtúshā jìniànguǎn	大屠杀纪念馆
Nanjing Museum	Nánjīng bówùguǎn	南京博物馆
Plum Blossom Hill	Méihuā shān	梅花山
Punjabi Indian Restaurant	Běn jié bǐ ìn dù cán tīng	本杰比印度餐厅
Rain Flower Terrace and Martyrs Memorial	Yùhuātái lièshìlíngyuán	雨花台烈士陵园
Skyways Deli	Yún zhōng shì pǐn diàn	云中食品店
Shizi Lou Restaurant	Shī zi lóu	狮子楼
Shou Jia Massage	Shǒu jiā án mò	手佳按摩
South Gate of City Wall	Zhōnghuá mén	中华门
Sofitel Galaxy Hotel	Sū fēi té yín hé dà jiǔ diàn	索菲特银河大酒店
Spirit Valley Temple and Pagoda	Línggǔsì, Línggǔtǎ	灵谷寺，灵谷塔
Sun Yat-sen Botanical Gardens	Zhōngshān zhíwùyuán	中山植物园
Sun Yat-sen Memorial	Zhōngshānlíng	中山陵
Swallow Rock	Yànzǐjī	燕子矶
Taiping Heavenly Kingdom Museum	Tàipíngtiānguó lìshǐ bówùguǎn	太平天国历史博物馆
Train Station	Huǒchēzhàn	火车站
Xinjiekou	Xīnjiēkǒu	新街口
Xuanwu Lake Park	Xuánwǔhú gōngyuán	玄武湖公园
Yangtze River Bridge	Chángjiāng dàqiáo	长江大桥
Yuejiang Lou Tower	Yuèjiāng lóu	阅江楼
Zhongshan Nan Road Bus Station	Zhōngshān nán lù qìchēzhàn	中山南路汽车站
Zhongyangmen Bus Station	Zhōngyāng mén qìchēzhàn	中央门汽车站
Yangzhou	Yángzhōu	扬州
China Youth Travel Agency	Zhōngqīnglǚ	中青旅
Daming Temple	Dàmíngsì	大明寺

ENGLISH	PINYIN	CHINESE CHARACTERS
Garden Tomb of Puhaddin	Pǔhādīngmù	普哈丁墓
Ge Garden	Gèyuán	个园
He Garden	Héyuán	何园
Long Distance Bus Station	chángtú qìchēzhàn	长途汽车站
Old Brewery	Lǎo pái jiǔ guǎng	老啤酒厂
Metropark Hotel	Yuán yáng zhòu jìng huà dà jiǔ diàn	原扬州京华大酒店
Yangzhou Ramada Casa Hotel	Yáng zhōu huà měi dá kǎi shā jiǔ diàn	扬州华美达凯莎酒店
Slender West Lake	Shòu Xīhú	瘦西湖
Train Station	Huǒchēzhàn	火车站
Wang's Residence	Wāngshì xiǎoyuàn	汪氏小苑
Xiyuan Hotel	Xī yuán dá jiǔ diàn	西园大酒店
Suzhou	Sūzhōu	苏州
Ancient Chinese Sexual Culture Museum	gǔdài xìngwénhuà zhǎnshì	古代性文化展示
Baosheng Temple	Bǎoshèngsì	保圣寺
Blue Wave Pavilion	Cānglàngtíng	沧浪亭
Bookworm	Lǎo shū chóng	老书虫
Chamate	Yī Chá Yī Zuò	一茶一坐
Crowne Plaza Hotel	Sú zhōu zhōng yín xīng guān jià rì jiǔ diàn	苏州中茵皇冠假日酒店
Deyue lou Restaurant	Dé yuè lóu fàn diàn	得月楼饭店
Gloria Plaza Hotel	Kǎi cài dá jiǔ diàn	凯莱大酒店
Grand Canal	Dàyùnhé	大运河
Hanshan Temple	Hánshānsì	寒山寺
Henry's Forbidden Bar	Héng lǐ jiǔ ba	亨利酒吧
Humble Administrator's Garden	Zhuōzhèngyuán	拙政园
Joyous Garden	Yíyuán	怡园
Lingering Garden	Líuyuán	留园
Lion's Grove Garden	Shīzilín	狮子林
Long Distance Bus Station	chángtú qìchēzhàn	长途汽车站
Luzhi	Lùzhí	直
Master of the Nets Garden	Wǎngshīyuán	网师园
North Temple Pagoda	Běisìtǎ	北寺塔
Pan Gate	Pánmén	盘门

ENGLISH	PINYIN	CHINESE CHARACTERS
Shiquanjie Street	Shíquánjiē	十全街
Pine and Crane Restaurant	Sòng hè lóu fān diàn	松鹤楼
Suzhou Arts & Crafts Museum	Sūzhōu gōngyìměishù bówùguǎn	苏州工艺美术博物馆
Suzhou Garden View Hotel	Sú zhōu rěn jià dá jiǔ diàn	苏州人家大酒店
Suzhou Museum	Sūzhōu bówùguǎn	苏州博物馆
Suzhou Pan Pacific	Sú zhōu wú gōng tái pǐng yáng dá jiǔ diàn	苏州吴宫泛太平洋大酒店
Temple of Mystery	Xuánmiàoguān	玄妙观
Tiger Hill	Hǔqiū	虎丘
Tongli	Tónglǐ	同里
Train Station	Huǒchēzhàn	火车站
Water Villages	Shuǐxiāng	水乡
West Garden Temple	Xīyuánsì	西园寺
Zhouzhuang	Zhōuzhuāng	周庄
ANHUI	**ĀNHUĪ)**	**安徽**
Huangshan	Huángshān	黄山
Baiyun Hotel	Bái yún bìn guǎn	白云宾馆
Beihai Hotel	Běi hǎi bìn guǎn	北海宾馆
Cloud Valley scenic area	Yúngǔ jǐngqū	云谷景区
Cloud Valley Temple Cable Car	Yúngǔsì suǒdào	云谷寺索道
Hot Springs scenic area	wēnquán jǐngqū	温泉景区
Jade Screen Cable Car	Yùpíng suǒdào	玉屏索道
North Sea scenic area	Běihǎi jǐngqū	北海景区
Tangkou	Tāngkǒu	汤口
Tianhai scenic area	Tiānhǎi jǐngqū	天海景区
Tunxi	Túnxī	屯溪
Huangshan Xingang Hotel	Huáng shān xīn gǎng jiǔ diàn	黄山新港大酒店
Bus Station	chángtú qìchēzhàn	长途汽车站
Huangshan City Airport	Huángshān shì jīchǎng	黄山市机场
Train Station	Huǒchēzhàn	火车站
Tunxi (Huangshan City)	Túnxī (Huángshān shì)	屯溪 （黄山市）
Tunxi Old Street	Túnxī lǎojiē	屯溪老街
Shexian	Shè xiàn	歙县
Hongcun Village	Hóng cūn	宏村

3

ENGLISH	PINYIN	CHINESE CHARACTERS
Huashan Mysterious Grottoes	Huàshān míkū	华山谜窟
Huizhou Old Town	Huīzhōu lǎochéng	徽州老城
Long Distance Bus Station	chángtú qìchēzhàn	长途汽车站
Tang Yue Memorial Arches	Tángyuè páilouqún	堂樾牌楼群
Train Station	Huǒchēzhàn	火车站
Xidi Village	Xī dī	西堤
Yixian County	Yī xiàn	黟县
Yuliang Village	Yúliáng gǔzhèn	渔梁古镇

Shanghai

WORD OF MOUTH

"I loved Shanghai as much the second time as the first. I found the people very welcoming and the city has an electric energy that delights me. I think it is interesting about the energy—I find that some cities have it and some don't (just like people, I guess!) Shanghai has it, Beijing does not."

—ekscrunchy

WELCOME TO SHANGHAI

TOP REASONS TO GO

★ **Skyline Views.** Head to the top of the *Jetsons*-esque Pearl Tower or the pagoda-inspired Jin Mao and count the cranes restructuring the city's skyline.

★ **Shanghai Museum.** The Bund and the glamorous Plaza 66 are the up-and-coming designer areas. If you want something more "Chinese," the boutiques in and around Xintiandi offer very stylish fusion pieces.

★ **Shopping Overload.** The Hong Kong Heritage Museum chronicles the city's history. On a Lantau Island hill, the 242-ton Tian Tan Buddha statue sits in the lotus position beside the Po Lin Buddhist Monastery.

★ **Yu Garden.** When not too crowded, the garden offers peace and beauty amid the clamor of the city, with rocks, trees, and walls curved to resemble dragons, bridges, and pavilions.

1 The Bund. Shanghai's famous waterfront boulevard is lined with art-deco buildings and souvenir stands. It's great for people-watching, being watched yourself, shopping for increasingly chic clothes, and sampling some of Shanghai's most famous restaurants. It's also where you'll get that postcard view of the futuristic skyline in Pudong.

2 Xintiandi. Shopping, bars, restaurants, and museums mix together in restored traditional *shikumen* (stone gate) houses. Xintiandi is a popular location for hanging out and people-watching, and there are a few great boutiques. The small museums have interesting exhibits related to Shanghai's and the Communist Party's history.

3 Former French Concession. Whether you're an architecture fanatic, a photographer, a romantic, or just plain curious, a wander through these streets is always a wonderful way to pass an afternoon. Fuxing Lu is a good long walk, and the streets around Sinan Lu and Fuxing Park have some real architectural treats. Take your time, and allow for breaks at cafés or in small boutiques.

Check Out Receipt

BPL- North End Branch Library
617-227-8135
http://www.bpl.org/branches/north.htm

Wednesday, June 28, 2017 7:09:02 PM

Item: 39999070484991
Title: The risk agent
Material: Book
Due: 07/19/2017

Item: 39999060211081
Title: Fodor's ... Hong Kong.
Material: Book
Due: 07/19/2017

Item: 39999069670196
Title: Fodor's China.
Material: Book
Due: 07/19/2017

Total items: 3

Thank You!

GETTING ORIENTED

Shanghai is fast and tough, so bring good shoes and a lot of patience. Don't expect the grandeur of ancient sights, but rather relish the small details like exquisitely designed art-deco buildings or laid-back cafés. Shanghai hides her gems well, so it's important to be observant and look up and around. The crowds of people and the constant change can make travelers weary, so take advantage of the wide range of eateries and convenient benches.

4 Nanjing Lu. People come from all over China to shop on what was once China's premier shopping street—and it sometimes feels as though they're all here at the same time. Although it's still a little tawdry, like a phoenix rising from the ashes, pedestrian-only Nanjing Dong Lu is undergoing a massive face-lift, and trendy designer boutiques are beginning to emerge alongside pre-1960s department stores and old-fashioned silk shops.

Updated
by Sophie
Friedman

Shanghai, or "City Above the Sea," lies on the Yangzi River delta, and until 1842 it was a small fishing village. After the first Opium War the village was carved up into autonomous concessions administered concurrently by the British, French, and Americans. As the most Westernized city in China after Hong Kong, Shanghai is at the forefront of China's modernization. Almost a quarter of the world's construction cranes stand in this city. Still, architectural remnants of a colonial past survive along the winding, bustling streets.

In its heyday, Shanghai had the best art, the greatest architecture, and the strongest business in Asia. With dance halls, brothels, glitzy restaurants, international clubs, and a racetrack, it catered to the rich. The Paris of the East was known as a place of vice and indulgence. Amid this glamour and degradation the Communist Party held its first meeting in 1921.

In the 1930s and '40s the city suffered raids, invasions, and occupation by the Japanese. After the war's end, Nationalists and Communists fought a three-year civil war for control of China. The Communists declared victory in 1949 and established the People's Republic of China. Between 1950 and 1980 Shanghai's industries soldiered on through periods of extreme famine and drought, reform, and suppression. Politically, the city was central to the Cultural Revolution and the Gang of Four's base. The January Storm of 1967 purged many of Shanghai's leaders, and Red Guards set out to destroy the "Four Olds": old ways of ideas, living, traditions, and thought.

In 1972, with the Cultural Revolution still going, Shanghai hosted the historic meeting between Premier Zhou Enlai and U.S. president Richard Nixon. In 1990 China's leader, Deng Xiaoping, chose Shanghai as the center of the country's commercial renaissance, and it has again become one of China's most open cities ideologically, socially, culturally, and economically.

■TIP→ Shanghai is a sprawling city with large districts. We have created a series of smaller neighborhoods centered on the main attractions. You still need to know the official districts when dealing with hotels, taxis, and tourist resources, so those are listed with each address.

PLANNING

WHEN TO GO

The best time to visit Shanghai is early fall, when the weather is good and crowds diminish. Although temperatures are scorching and the humidity can be unbearable, summer is the peak tourist season, and hotels and transportation can get very crowded.

Avoid the two main national holidays, Chinese New Year (which ranges from mid-January to mid-February) and the National Day holiday (during the first week of October), when 1.3 billion people are on the move.

GETTING HERE AND AROUND
TO AND FROM THE AIRPORT

Shanghai has two major airports: most international flights go through the newer Pudong International Airport (PVG), which is 45 km (30 mi) east of the city, whereas many domestic routes operate out of the older Hongqiao International Airport (SHA), 15 km (9 mi) west of the city center.

Taking a taxi is the most comfortable way into town from Pudong International Airport. Expect to pay around Y160 to Y180 for the hour-long or so trip to Puxi; getting to the closer Pudong area takes 40 minutes, and should cost no more than Y100. At rush hour, journey times can easily double. Speed demons may wish to catch the Maglev train, which tops out at 431 km/h (268 mph) and connects at Longyang Road metro station in Pudong to Lines 2 and 7, which can get you downtown in about 25 minutes. It costs Y50 for a single trip, Y80 per round-trip and Y40 if you present your boarding pass or ticket from a same-day flight. For a mere Y5 you can hop on Line 2 at Pudong International Airport, cross the platform at Guanlan Road Station, and be downtown in just under an hour. Note that the Maglev runs 6:30 am–9:30 pm and the metro 9:30 am–9:15 pm.

From Hongqiao a taxi to Puxi will cost you Y30–Y60 and takes 30 to 40 minutes; expect an hour for the costlier trip to Pudong hotels. A taxi from one airport to the other takes about an hour and costs Y200 to Y240. You can take metro Line 2 from Hongqiao for Y5, though note that you'll have to hop a shuttle bus from one terminal to another. Line 2 now runs from Hongqiao Airport to Pudong Airport, making runs between the two significantly cheaper.

Many hotels offer free airport transfers to their guests. Otherwise, shuttle buses link Pudong Airport with a number of hotels (routes starting with a letter) and transport hubs (routes starting with a number) in the city center. Most services run every 10 to 20 minutes between roughly 7 am and the last flight arrival (usually around midnight). Trips to Puxi take about 1½ hours and cost between Y19 and Y30. From Hongqiao,

Bus 925 runs to People's Square, but there's little room for luggage. It costs Y4.

AIR TRAVEL

Shanghai's two major airports make it easy to get here from the rest of the world. Continental Airlines runs daily direct flights from Newark to Pudong; Delta goes direct from Pudong to Tokyo and Detroit, and Virgin to Heathrow. Loads of budget airlines also service both Puding and Hongqiao, so you can hop Air Asia to Kuala Lumpur, China Southern to Seoul, or Thai Airways to Bangkok.

BIKE TRAVEL

Few hotels rent bikes, but you can inquire at bike shops or even corner stores, where the rate is around Y30 a day, plus a refundable deposit. Note that for about Y200 you can buy your own basic bike. Shanghai's frenzied traffic is not for the faint of heart, though most secondary streets have wide, well-defined bike lanes.

BUS TRAVEL

Taking buses is not a nightmare, but as they are often crowded, slow, and difficult to negotiate without speaking Chinese, it is easier to stick to the metro.

FERRY TRAVEL

Ferries run around the clock every 10 minutes between the Bund and Pudong's terminal just south of the Riverside Promenade. The per-person fare is Y2 each way.

SUBWAY TRAVEL

Shanghai's quick and efficient subway system—called the Shanghai metro—is an excellent way to get around town, and the network grows exponentially every year. English maps and exit signs abound, and the single-ticket machines have an English option, too. In-car announcements for each station are given in both Chinese and English. Keep your ticket handy: you'll need to insert it into a second turnstile as you exit at your destination.

■ TIP→ Transport cards that cost a refundable Y30 are available from metro stations. Top them up with as much money as you like, and use them to pay for taxi, metro, and bus rides. They aren't discounted, but they'll save you time you would have spent joining queues and fumbling for cash. To purchase say, "Wo yao yi ka" (我想一卡), which means "I want a card."

TAXI TRAVEL

Taxis are plentiful, cheap, and easy to spot. Your hotel concierge can call for one by phone or you can hail one on the street. The available ones have a small lit-up sign on the passenger side. If you're choosing a cab from a line, peek at the driver's license on the dashboard. The lower the license number, the more experienced the driver. Drivers with a number below 200,000 can usually get you where you're going. Most cab drivers don't speak English, so it's best to give them a piece of paper with your destination written in Chinese. (Keep a card with the name of your hotel on it handy for the return trip.) Taxis start at Y12 for the first 2.40 km; after 11 pm this jumps to Y16.

HEALTH AND SAFETY

Tap water in Shanghai is safe for brushing teeth. However, it contains a high concentration of metals, so you should buy bottled water to drink. It is available at every corner store—look for FamilyMart, Kedi, AllDays, and Watsons—and will cost you between Y1 and Y3. Make sure that food has been thoroughly cooked and is served to you fresh and hot; avoid vegetables and fruits that you haven't washed (in bottled or purified water) or peeled yourself. Shanghai's polluted air can bring on, or aggravate, respiratory problems. If you're a sufferer, take the cue from locals, who wear surgical masks or a scarf or bandana as protection.

The most reliable places to buy prescription medication is at the 24-hour pharmacy at the World Link Medical Center or the Shanghai United Family Health Center (⇨ *Medical Services, below*). During the day, the Watson's chain is good for over-the-counter medication, but has limited selection and poor service; it has dozens of branches around over town. Chinese pharmacies offer a fuller range of imported over-the-counter drugs and are usually open 24-hours; look for the green cross on a white sign. Pantomiming works well for things like band-aids, ace bandages, and cough medicine, so do not feel embarrassed to use hand gestures.

There is almost no violent crime against tourists in China, partly because the penalties are severe for those who are caught—China's yearly death-sentence tolls run into the thousands. Single women can move about Shanghai with little to no hassle, though as in all major cities, handbag-snatching and pickpocketing do happen in markets and on crowded buses or trains.

Shanghai is full of people looking to make a quick buck. The most common scam involves people persuading you to go with them for a tea ceremony, which is often so pleasant that you don't smell a rat until several hundred dollars appear on your credit-card bill. "Art students" who pressure you into buying work is another common scam. Avoiding such scams is as easy as refusing *all* unsolicited services—be it from taxi or pedicab drivers, tour guides, or potential "friends." Simply put: if someone is offering you something, you don't want it. It is not considered rude to ignore them; do so.

Shanghai traffic is as manic as it looks, and survival of the fittest (or the biggest) is the main rule. Do not be afraid to cross when the light is red, as you may not have a chance once it's green. Beware of buses, which make wide turns and regularly ignore pedestrians' rights.

HOURS OF OPERATION

Almost all businesses close for Chinese New Year and other major holidays.

Shops: Stores are generally open daily 10 to 7; some stores stay open as late as 10 pm, especially in summer.

Temples and Museums: Most temples and parks are open daily 8 to 5. Museums and most other sights are generally open 9 to 4, six days a week, with Monday being the most common closed day.

Banks and Offices: Government offices are open weekdays 9 to 5, but some close for lunch (between noon and 2). Most banks are open seven

Tips to Unlocking the City

NAVIGATING THE STREETS
Shanghai is divided into east and west sides by the Huangpu River. The metro area is huge, but the city center is a relatively small district in Puxi (west of the river). On the east side lies the district that has undergone massive urbanization in the past decade, with a housing boom, the construction of towering office buildings, and even plans to open a Shanghai Disneyland in 2015—Pudong (east of the river). The city is loosely laid out on a grid, and most neighborhoods are easily explored on foot. Massive construction makes pavements uneven and the air dusty, but if you can put up with this, walking is the best way to really get a feel for the city and its people. Taxis are readily available and good for traveling longer distances, and the subway network covers almost all of downtown.

Major east–west roads are named for Chinese cities and divide the city into *dong* (east), *zhong* (middle), and *xi* (west) sections. North–south roads divide the city into *bei* (north) and *xi* (west) segments. The heart of the city is found on its chief east–west streets—Nanjing Lu, Huaihai Lu, and Yan'an Lu.

■**TIP→** Street signs in Shanghai are written in Chinese characters and in English, not in pinyin, the transliteration of Chinese. However, when asking for directions or speaking to taxi drivers, pinyin will guide your pronunciation; for this reason we have written all our street names as Nanjing Xi Lu or Shiji Dadao, not West Nanjing Road or Century Avenue. Note that our maps are still in English to help you better acquaint yourself.

NAVIGATING VOCABULARY
Below are some terms you'll see on maps and street signs and in the names of most places you'll go:

Dong is east, **xi** is west, **nan** is south, **bei** is north, and **zhong** means middle. **Jie** and **lu** mean street and road, respectively, **da dao** means avenue, **da** means big, and **xiao** means small.

Qiao, or bridge, is part of the place name at just about every entrance and exit on the ring roads.

Men, meaning door or gate, indicates a street that passed through an entrance in the fortification wall that surrounded the city hundreds of years ago. The entrances to parks and some other places are also referred to as *men.* For example, Xizhimen literally means Western Straight Gate.

---

days a week from 9 to 6. Bank branches and CITS tour desks in hotels offer 24 hour ATMs. Many hotel currency-exchange desks stay open 24 hours.

VISITOR INFORMATION
The best thing to hit Shanghai since an extended metro system is the Shanghai Call Centre (☎ 962288), where a host of English-speaking operators answer any question you have, help you communicate with taxi drivers, and provide restaurant, bar, and shopping recommendations. There are also a number of French-, German-, and Spanish-speaking operators. Though you'll see what appear to be information

DID YOU KNOW?

Nanjing Road (Nánjīng Lù) is the main shopping street in Shanghai and has been so for more than a century. At the start of the 20th century, the street was home to a number of franchised stores, eight big department stores, and at least one casino. Today, a long swath of Nanjing Road is pedestrian only.

BEST CITY TOURS

These day tours are a nice way to unwind post-flight, and can help you get your bearings on that stressful first afternoon.

BOAT TOURS

Huangpu River boat tours afford a great view of Pudong and the Bund, but after that it's mostly ports and cranes.

Huangpu River Cruises launches several small boats for one-hour daytime or nighttime cruises. The company also runs a 3½-hour trip up and down the Huangpu River between the Bund and Wusong, where the Huangpu meets the Yangzi River. You'll see barges, bridges, and factories, but not much scenery. All tours depart from the Bund at 239 Zhongshan Dong Lu. Purchase all tickets at the dock or through CITS; prices range Y50 to Y150. ⊠ *153 Zhongshan Dong Er Lu (the Bund), Huangpu* ☎ *021/6374–4461.*

Shanghai Oriental Leisure Company runs 40-minute boat tours along the Bund from the Pearl Tower's cruise dock in Pudong. Prices range from Y50 to Y70, and tickets can be purchased at the gate to the Pearl Tower. Follow the brown signs from the Pearl Tower to the dock. ⊠ *Oriental Pearl Cruise Dock, 1 Shiji Dadao (Century Avenue), Pudong* ☎ *021/5879–1888.*

Shanghai Scenery Co., Ltd. This company owns three boats that run one-hour tours along the Huangpu River starting from Yangzijiang Dock. Day tours cost Y50 and night tours, Y88–Y98. ⊠ *108 Huangpu Lu, Huangpu* ☎ *021/6356–1932* ⊕ *www.shanghaiscenery.com.*

BUS TOURS

Grayline Tours has escorted half- and full-day coach tours of Shanghai as well as one-day trips to Suzhou, Hangzhou, and other nearby waterside towns. Prices range from around Y250 to Y1,000. ⊠ *A19, 2F Youth Centre Plaza, 1888 Hanzhong Lu, Putuo 200070* ☎ *021/6150–8061* ⊕ *www.graylineshanghai.com.*

Jinjiang Tours runs a full-day bus tour of Shanghai that includes the French Concession, People's Square, Jade Buddha Temple, Yu Garden, the Bund, and Xintiandi. Tickets cost Y2,500, lunch included. ⊠ *161 Chang Le Lu, Luwan* ☎ *021/6415–1188* ⊕ *www.jjtravel.com.*

HERITAGE TOURS

Shanghai Jews, a half-day tour, is available daily in Hebrew or English and takes visitors to the sites of Shanghai's Jewish history. The cost is Y400 per person. ☎ *1300/214–6702* ⊕ *www.shanghai-jews.com.*

kiosks on the street, bypass these; they're manned by semi well-meaning college students but rarely offer any valuable information.

ESSENTIALS

Airport Information Hongqiao International Airport (☎ *021/6268–8918* ⊕ *www.shanghaiairport.com*). **Pudong International Airport** (☎ *021/9608–1388* ⊕ *www.shanghaiairport.com*).

Bike Rental Bohdi Bikes (☎ *021/5266–9013 or 139/1875–3119* ⊕ *www.bohdi.com.cn*).

Bus Contact Shanghai Long Distance Bus Station (✉ *North Square, Shanghai Railway Station, 1662 Zhongxing Lu, Zhabei* ☎ *021/6605–0000*).

Consulate United States Consulate (✉ *1469 Huaihai Zhong Lu, Xuhui* ☎ *021/6433–6880, 021/6433–3936 after-hours emergencies* ✉ *Citizen Services Section, Westgate Mall, 8th fl., 1038 Nanjing Xi Lu, Jing'an* ☎ *021/3217–4650* ⊕ *www.shanghai.usconsulate.gov*).

Emergency Contacts Fire (☎ *119*). **International SOS Medical Services 24-hour Alarm Center** (☎ *021/6295–0099*). **Police** (☎ *110, 021/6357–6666 [English]*). **Shanghai Ambulance Service** (☎ *120*).

Ferry Contacts China-Japan International Ferry Company (✉ *908 Dongdaming Lu, Hongkou* ☎ *021/6595–7988*). **China International Travel Service** (*CITS* ☎ *021/6289–8899* ⊕ *www.cits.com.cn*). **Pudong–Puxi ferry** (✉ *Puxi dock, the Bund at Jinling Lu, Huangpu* ✉ *Pudong dock, 1 Dongchang Lu, south of Binjiang Dadao, Pudong*). **Shanghai Ferry Company** (☎ *021/6537–5111 or 021/5393–1185* ⊕ *www.shanghai-ferry.co.jp*).

Medical Services Huadong Hospital (✉ *Foreigners' Clinic, 2F, 221 Yanan Xi Lu, Jing'an* ☎ *021/6248–3180 Ext. 30106*). **Huashan Hospital** (✉ *Foreigners' Clinic, 15F, 12 Wulumuqi Zhong Lu, Jing'an* ☎ *021/6248–9999 Ext. 2531 for 24-hour hotline*). **Shanghai East International Medical Center** (✉ *551 Pudong Nan Lu, Pudong* ☎ *021/5879–9999* ⊕ *www.seimc.com.cn*). **Shanghai United Family Health Center** (*private* ✉ *1139 Xian Xia Lu, Changning* ☎ *021/5133–1900, 021/5133–1999 emergencies* ⊕ *www.unitedfamilyhospitals.com*). **SOS International Shanghai Office** (✉ *Sun Tong Infoport Plaza, 22nd fl., Unit D-G, 55 Huaihai Xi Lu, Xuhui* ☎ *021/6295–0099 emergencies* ⊕ *www.internationalsos.com*). **World Link Medical Center** (✉ *Room 203, West Tower, Shanghai Center, 1376 Nanjing Xi Lu, Jing'an Hongqiao Clinic* ✉ *Mandarine City, 1F, Unit 30, 788 Hongxu Lu, Minhang, Jian Qiao Clinic* ✉ *51 Hongfeng Lu, Jian Qao, Pudong* ☎ *021/6445–5999*).

Postal Services Post Office (✉ *276 Suzhou Bei Lu, Hongkou* ✉ *Shanghai Center, 1376 Nanjing Xi Lu, Jing'an* ✉ *133 Huaihai Lu, Xuhui* ☎ *021/6393–6666 Ext. 00*). ✉ *105 Tianping Lu*).

Subway Contacts Maglev Train (☎ *021/2890–7777* ⊕ *www.smtdc.com*). **Shanghai Metro Passenger Information** (☎ *021/6318–9000* ⊕ *www.shmetro.com*).

Train Contacts Shanghai Railway Station (✉ *303 Moling Lu, Zhabei* ☎ *021/6317–9090*). **Shanghai South Railway Station** (✉ *Between Liuzhou Lu and Humin Lu, Zhabei* ☎ *021/5435–3535*).

Visitor Info China International Travel Service (CITS) (✉ *1277 Beijing Xi Lu, Jing'an* ☎ *021/6289–4510* ⊕ *www.cits.net*). **Shanghai Tourist Information Services** (✉ *Yu Garden, 149 Jiujiaochang Lu, Huangpu* ☎ *021/6355–5032* ✉ *Hongqiao International Airport* ☎ *021/6268–8899*).

EXPLORING SHANGHAI

Today beauty and charm coexist with kitsch and commercialism. From the colonial architecture of the Former French Concession to the forest of cranes and the neon-lit high-rises of Pudong, Shanghai is a city of paradox and change.

OLD CITY

Tucked away in the east of Puxi are the remnants of Shanghai's Old City. Once encircled by a thick wall, a fragment of which still remains, the Old City has a sense of history among its fast disappearing old *shikumen* (stone gatehouses), temples, and markets. Delve into narrow alleyways where residents still hang their washing out on bamboo poles and chamber pots are still in use. Burn incense with the locals in small temples, sip tea in a teahouse, or get a taste of Chinese snacks and street food. This is the place to get a feeling for Shanghai's past, but you'd better get there soon, as the wrecker's ball knows no mercy.

GETTING AROUND

This area could take a very long afternoon or morning, as it's a good one to do on foot. Browsing the shops in and around the Yu Garden might add a couple of hours. At press time, Shanghai's ever expanding metro system had not quite yet reached Old City. However, it's a short walk east from Nanjing Dong Lu station on Line 2, and a slightly longer walk south from Huangpi Nan Lu on Line 1. If you get off the metro at Nanjing Dong Lu, walk slightly east and you will be able to pick up a taxi outside of rush hour. During rush hour, we do not recommend going here. If you are exiting Huangpi Nan Lu station, you will have an easier time hailing a cab and do not need to walk in a specific direction. Again, it is difficult during rush hour for anyone to get a cab, so be forewarned. ■TIP→ Taxis are nearly impossible to find in this area when you want to leave.

EXPLORING

Chen Xiangge Temple. If you find yourself passing by this tiny temple on your exploration of the Old City, you can make an offering to Buddha with the free incense sticks that accompany your admission. Built in 1600 by the same man who built Yu Garden, it was destroyed during the Cultural Revolution and rebuilt in the 1990s. The temple is now a nunnery, and you can often hear the women's chants rising from the halls beyond the main courtyard. ⊠ *29 Chenxiangge Lu, Huangpu* ☎ *021/6320–0400* ✈ *Y5* ☺ *Daily 7–4.*

Old City Wall. The Old City used to be completely surrounded by a wall, built in 1553 as a defense against Japanese pirates. Most of it was torn down in 1912, except for one 50-yard-long (40-meter-long) piece that still stands at Dajing Lu and Renmin Lu. You can walk through the remnants and check out the rather simple museum nearby, which is dedicated to the history of the Old City (the legends are in Chinese). Stroll through the tiny neighboring alley of Dajing Lu for a lively panorama of crowded market life in the Old City. ⊠ *269 Dajing Lu, at Renmin Lu, Huangpu* ☎ *021/6326–6171* ✈ *Y5* ☺ *Daily 9–4:30.*

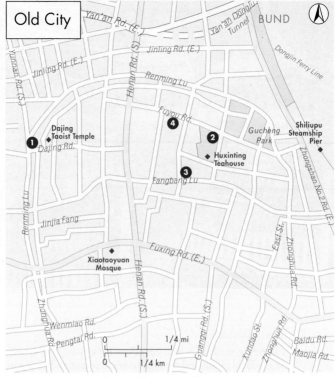

Temple of the City God. At the southeast end of the Yu Gardens bazaar, this Taoist Temple of the City God was built during the early part of the Ming Dynasty, and was destroyed by fire in 1924. The main hall was rebuilt in 1926, and has been renovated many times over the years. Inside are gleaming gold figures, and atop the roof you'll see statues of crusading warriors—flags raised, arrows drawn. ✉ *Xi Dajie Lu, Huangpu* ☏ *021/6386–8649* 🎫 *Y10* ⏱ *Daily 8:30–4:30.*

Fodor'sChoice
★
Yu Garden. Since the 18th century, this complex, with its traditional red walls and upturned tile roofs, has been a marketplace and social center where local residents gather, shop, and practice *qi gong* in the evening. Although a bit overrun by tourists and not as impressive as the ancient palace gardens of Beijing, Yu Garden is a piece of Shanghai's past, and one of the few old sights left in the city.

To get to the garden itself, you must wind your way through the Yu Gardens bazaar. The garden was commissioned by the Ming Dynasty official Pan Yunduan in 1559 and built by the renowned architect Zhang Nanyang over 19 years. When it was finally finished it won international praise as "the best garden in southeastern China." In the mid-1800s the Society of Small Swords used the garden as a gathering place for meetings. It was here that they planned their uprising with the Taiping rebels against the French colonists. The French destroyed

A view of a teahouse in the Yu Garden at night.

the garden during the first Opium War, but the area was later rebuilt and renovated.

Winding walkways and corridors bring you over stone bridges and carp-filled ponds and through bamboo stands and rock gardens. Within the park are an **old opera stage,** a **museum** dedicated to the Society of Small Swords rebellion, and an **exhibition hall,** opened in 2003, of Chinese calligraphy and paintings. One caveat: the park is almost always thronged with Chinese tour groups, especially on weekends. As with most sights in Shanghai, don't expect a tranquil time alone. ⊠ *218 Anren Lu, bordered by Fuyou Lu, Jiujiaochang Lu, Fangbang Lu, and Anren Lu, Huangpu* ☎ *021/6326–0830 or 021/6328–3251* ⊕ *www. yugarden.com.cn* 🎫 *Y40* ☙ *Gardens, daily 8:30–5.*

XINTIANDI AND CITY CENTER

Xintiandi is Shanghai's showpiece restoration project. Reproduction *shikumen,* or stone gatehouses, contain expensive bars, restaurants, and chic boutiques. It's at its most magical on a warm night, when locals, expats, and visitors alike pull up a chair at one of the outside seating areas and watch the world go by.

Another good people-watching spot is the area around People's Square, which has some magnificent examples of modern and historical architecture and a smattering of some of Shanghai's best museums. The adjoining People's Park is a pleasant green space where it's possible to escape the clamor of the city for a while.

GETTING AROUND

People's Square metro station is the point of convergence for Shanghai's metro Lines 1, 2, and 8. The underground passageways can be confusing and often packed, so it's best to take the first exit and then find your way aboveground. Xintiandi can be reached by taking Line 10 to the Xintiandi stop or Line 1 to the Huangpi Nan Lu station, which is a block or two north of Xintiandi.

The sights in this area are divided

> **DRAGON BOAT DAY**
>
> Two thousand years ago, a poet named Qu Yuan threw himself into the river in protest against the emperor. To commemorate him, people now race dragon boats and eat *zongzi* (sticky rice dumplings). The date of the Dragon Boat Festival varies, but is often in late May or early June.

into two neat clusters—those around People's Square and those around Xintiandi. You can easily walk between the two in 20 minutes. Visiting all the museums in the People's Square area could take a good half day. Xintiandi's sights don't take very long at all, so you could go before dinner, check out the museums, and then settle down for a pre-dinner drink.

TOP ATTRACTIONS

Fodor's Choice
★

Dongtai Lu Antiques Market. A few blocks east of Xintiandi, antiques dealers' stalls line the street. You'll find porcelain, Victrolas, jade, and anything else worth hawking or buying. The same bowls and vases pop up in multiple stalls, so if your first bargaining attempt isn't successful, you'll likely have another opportunity a few stores down. Prices have shot up over the years, and fakes abound, so be careful what you buy. ⊠ *Dontgai Lu, off Xizang Lu, Huangpu* ☉ *Daily 10–6.*

Fodor's Choice
★

People's Square. Once the southern half of the city's racetrack, Shanghai's main square has become a social and cultural center. The **Shanghai Museum** is inside it, and the Municipal Offices, Grand Theater, and Shanghai Urban Planning Center surround it. During the day, visitors and residents stroll, fly kites, and take their children to feed the pigeons. In the evening kids roller-skate, ballroom dancers hold group lessons, and families relax together. Weekends here are especially busy. ⊠ *Best place to enter is at Xizang Lu/Renmin Dadao (People's Avenue) Huangpu.*

Fodor's Choice
★

Shanghai Museum. One of Shanghai's treasures, this museum has the country's premier collection of relics and artifacts. Eleven galleries exhibit Chinese artistry in all its forms: paintings, bronzes, sculpture, ceramics, calligraphy, jade, Ming and Qing dynasties furniture, coins, seals, and art by indigenous populations. Its bronze collection is one of the best in the world, and its dress and costume gallery showcases intricate handiwork from several of China's 52 minority groups. If you opt not to rent the excellent audio guide, information is well presented in English. You can relax in the museum's pleasant tearoom or buy postcards, crafts, and reproductions of the artwork in the bookshop. ⊠ *201 Renmin Dadao (People's Avenue), Huangpu* ☎ *021/6372–3500* ⊕ *www.shanghaimuseum.net* ⊠ *Free, Y20 for Chinese audio guide, Y40 for foreign-language audio guide* ☉ *Daily 9–5.*

Fodor's Choice
★

Xintiandi. By WWII around 70 percent of Shanghai's residents lived in shikumen, or stone gatehouses. Over the last two decades most have been razed in the name of progress, but this 8-acre collection of stone gatehouses was renovated

into an upscale shopping and dining complex and renamed Xintiandi, or New Heaven on Earth. The restaurants are busy from lunchtime until past midnight, especially those with patios for watching the passing parade of shoppers. Just off the main thoroughfare are the visitor center and the **Shikumen Museum** (⊠ *House 25, North Block, 123 Xingye Lu, Luwan* ☎ *021/3307–0337*), a shikumen restored to 1920s style and filled with furniture and artifacts collected from nearby houses. Exhibits explain the European influence on shikumen design, the history of the Xintiandi renovation, as well as future plans for the entire 128-acre project. ⊠ *181 Taicang Lu, Luwan* ⊹ *Bordered by Taicang Lu, Madang Lu, Zizhong Lu, and Huangpi Nan Lu* ☎ *021/6311–2288* ⊕ *www.xintiandi.com* 🖃 *Museum Y20* ☉ *Museum, daily 11–11.*

WORTH NOTING

Grand Theater. The spectacular front wall of glass shines as brightly as the star power in this magnificent theater. Its three stages host the best domestic and international performances. The dramatic curved roof atop a square base is meant to invoke the Chinese traditional saying, "the earth is square and the sky is round." ■TIP➔ See it at night. ⊠ *300 Renmin Dadao (People's Avenue), Huangpu* ☎ *021/6386–8686* ⊕ *www.shgtheatre.com.*

Park Hotel. This art-deco structure overlooking People's Park was originally the tallest hotel in Shanghai. Completed in 1934, it had luxury rooms, a nightclub, and chic restaurants. Today it's more subdued, and the lobby is the most vivid reminder of its glorious past. It was also apparently an early inspiration for famous architect I. M. Pei (creator of the glass pyramids at the Louvre). ⊠ *170 Nanjing Xi Lu, Huangpu* ☎ *021/6327–5225* ⊕ *www.parkhotel.com.cn.*

People's Park. In colonial days this park was the northern half of the city's racetrack. Today the 30 acres of flower beds, lotus ponds, and trees are crisscrossed by a large number of paved paths. There's also an art gallery, the **Museum of Contemporary Art,** and a bar and restaurant, **Barbarossa,** inside. ⊠ *231 Nanjing Xi Lu, Huangpu* ☎ *021/6327–1333* 🖃 *Free* ☉ *Daily 6–6 in winter and 5–7 in summer.*

Shanghai Art Museum. At the northwest corner of People's Park, the former site of the Shanghai Library was once a clubhouse for old Shanghai's sports groups, including the Shanghai Race Club. The building is now the home of the state-run Shanghai Art Museum. Its permanent collection includes paintings, calligraphy, and sculpture, but its rotating exhibitions have favored modern artwork. There's a museum store, café, and a rooftop restaurant. ⊠ *325 Nanjing Xi Lu, at Huangpi Bei Lu,*

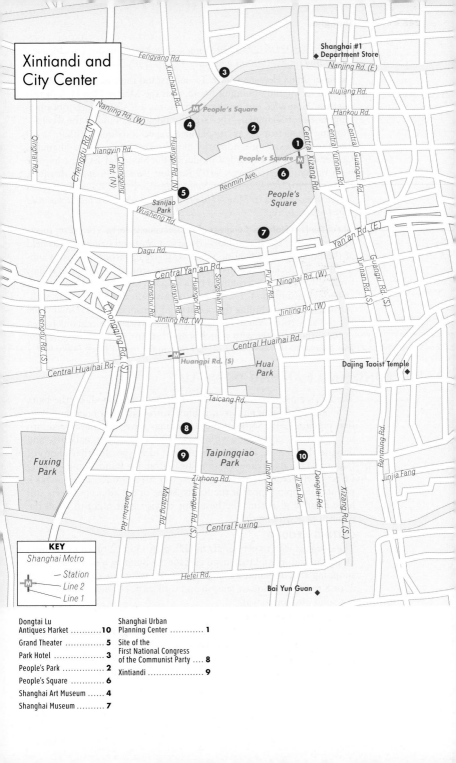

Xintiandi and City Center

Fengyang Rd.

Shanghai #1 Department Store

Nanjing Rd. (E)

Jiujiang Rd.

Hankou Rd.

3

People's Square

Nanjing Rd. (W)

4

2

Jiangyin Rd.

1

People's Square

6

Renmin Ave.

5

Sanijao Park

Wusheng Rd.

People's Square

7

Yan'an Rd. (E)

Dagu Rd.

Central Yan'an Rd.

Ninghai Rd. (W)

Jinling Rd. (W)

Jinling Rd. (W)

Central Huaihai Rd.

Huangpi Rd. (S)

Huai Park

Dajing Taoist Temple

Central Huaihai Rd. (S)

Taicang Rd.

8

9

Taipingqiao Park

10

Fuxing Park

Zizhong Rd.

Jinjia Fang

Central Fuxing

Hefei Rd.

Bai Yun Guan

Huangpu ☎ 021/6327–2829 ⊕ www.sh-artmuseum.org.cn ☞ Varies, depending on exhibition; generally Y20 ☼ Daily 9–5.

Shanghai Urban Planning Center. To understand the true scale of Shanghai and its ongoing building boom, visit the Master Plan Hall of this museum. Sprawled out on the third floor is a 6,400-square-foot planning model of Shanghai—the largest model of its kind in the world—showing the metropolis as city planners expect it to look in 2020. You'll find familiar existing landmarks like the Pearl Tower and Shanghai Center as well as a detailed model of the Shanghai Expo, complete with miniature pavilions. ⊠ *100 Renmin Dadao (People's Avenue), Huangpu ☎ 021/6372–2077 ⊕ www.supec.org ☞ Y30 unless there is a special exhibition ☼ Mon.–Thurs. 9–5, Fri.–Sun. 9–6, last ticket sold 1 hr before closing.*

Site of the First National Congress of the Communist Party. The secret meeting on July 31, 1921, that marked the first National Congress was held at the Bo Wen Girls' School, where 13 delegates from Marxist, Communist, and Socialist groups gathered from around the country. Today, ironically, the site is surrounded by Xintiandi, Shanghai's center of conspicuous consumption. The upstairs of this restored shikumen is a well-curated museum detailing the rise of communism in China. Downstairs lies the very room where the first delegates worked. It remains frozen in time, the table set with matches and teacups. ⊠ *374 Huangpi Nan Lu, Luwan ☎ 021/5383–2171 ☞ Free, audio tour Y10 ☼ Daily 9–4.*

THE BUND AND NANJING DONG LU

The city's most recognizable sightseeing spot, the Bund, on the bank of Shanghai's Huangpu River, is lined with massive foreign buildings that predate 1949. Some of these buildings have been developed into hip "lifestyle" complexes with spas, restaurants, bars, galleries, and designer boutiques. The Bund is also an ideal spot for that photo of Pudong's famous skyline. Leading away from the Bund, Nanjing Dong Lu is slowly returning to being the stylish street it once was, and it's a popular shopping spot for the locals. Some of the adjacent streets still have a faded glamour. The best time to visit is at night to stroll the neon-lit pedestrian road.

GETTING AROUND

The simplest way to get here is to take metro Line 2 or 10 to Nanjing Dong Lu station, and then head east for the Bund or west for the main shopping area of Nanjing Dong Lu. Alternatively, you can take Line 1, 2, or 8 to People's Square station and walk east, but be aware that this is a solid 30-minute walk.

SAFETY AND PRECAUTIONS

As in any tourist area, there are pickpockets. Not so much a safety issue as an annoyance are the "art students," who invite you to see paintings; avoid this, as not only will you be subject to the hard sell, but the paintings are also overpriced and usually of poor quality.

One of the many cafés on the Bund overlooking the Pudong.

EXPLORING

Bank of China. Here old Shanghai's Western architecture (British art deco in this case) mixes with Chinese elements. In 1937 it was designed to be the highest building in the city and surpassed the neighboring Cathay Hotel (now the Peace Hotel) by a hair, except for the green tower on the Cathay's roof. ✉ *23 The Bund, Zhongshan Dong Yi Lu, Huangpu* ☎ *021/6329–1979.*

Fodor's Choice
★

The Bund. Shanghai's waterfront boulevard best shows both the city's pre-1949 past and its focus on the future. Today the municipal government has renovated the old buildings of this most foreign face of the city, highlighting them as tourist attractions, and even tried for a while to sell them back to the very owners it forced out after 1949. Currently the area is undergoing a massive transformation, including the closure of half the lanes of traffic along the waterfront and a revamp of the northern area near Suzhou Creek. One of the warehouses has been turned into a haunted house called Shanghai Nightmare, so if you're visiting in August, September, or October, be sure to look it up online.

On the riverfront side of the Bund, Shanghai's street life is in full force. The city rebuilt the promenade, making it an ideal gathering place for both tourists and residents. In the morning, just after dawn, the Bund is full of people ballroom dancing, doing aerobics, and practicing kung fu, qi gong, and tai chi. The rest of the day people walk the embankment, snapping photos of the Oriental Pearl Tower, the Huangpu River, and each other. Be prepared for the aggressive souvenir hawkers; while you can't completely avoid them, try ignoring them or telling them *"bu yao,"* which means "Don't want." In the evening

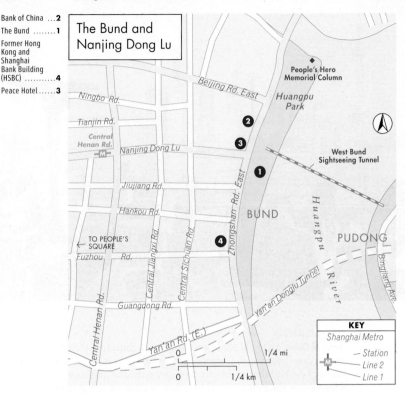

The Bund and
Nanjing Dong Lu

lovers come out for romantic walks between the floodlit buildings and tower. ✉ *5 blocks of Zhongshan Dong Yi Lu between Jinling Lu and Suzhou Creek, Huangpu.*

Former Hong Kong and Shanghai Bank Building (HSBC). One of the Bund's most impressive buildings, this domed structure was built by the British in 1921–23, when it was the second-largest bank building in the world. After 1949 the building was turned into Communist Party offices and City Hall; now it is used by the Pudong Development Bank. In 1997 the bank made the news when it uncovered a beautiful 1920s Italian-tile mosaic in the building's dome. In the 1950s the mosaic was deemed too extravagant for a Communist government office, so it was covered by white paint, which protected it from being found by the Red Guards during the Cultural Revolution. It was then forgotten until the Pudong Development Bank renovated the building. If you walk in and look up, you'll see the circular mosaic in the dome—an outer circle painted with scenes of the cities where HSBC had branches at the time: London, Paris, New York, Bangkok, Tokyo, Calcutta, Hong Kong, and Shanghai; a middle circle made up of the 12 signs of the zodiac; and the center painted with a large sun and Ceres, the Roman goddess of abundance. ✉ *12 The Bund, Zhongshan Dong Yi Lu, Huangpu* ☎ *021/6161–6188* 🎟 *Free* ⊙ *Weekdays 9–5:30, weekends 9–5.*

A BRIEF HISTORY

The district's name is derived from the Anglo-Indian, and literally means "muddy embankment." In the early 1920s the Bund became the city's foreign street: Americans, British, Japanese, French, Russians, Germans, and other Europeans built banks, trading houses, clubs, consulates, and hotels in styles from neoclassical to art deco.

As Shanghai grew to be a bustling trading center in the Yangtze Delta, the Bund's warehouses and ports became the heart of the action. With the Communist victory, the foreigners left Shanghai, and the Chinese government moved its own banks and offices here.

★ **Peace Hotel.** This hotel at the corner of the Bund and Nanjing Dong Lu is among Shanghai's most treasured old buildings. If any establishment will give you a sense of Shanghai's past, it's this one. Its high ceilings, ornate woodwork, and art-deco fixtures are still intact. Following a renovation in 2010, the jazz bar, tea lounge, Dragon Phoenix Restaurant, original lobby and shopping arcade, and ballroom have all been restored to their original glory, evoking old Shanghai cabarets and gala parties.

The south building was formerly the Palace Hotel. Built in 1906, it is one of the oldest buildings on the Bund. The north building, formerly the Cathay Hotel, built in 1929, is more famous historically. It was known as the private playroom of its owner, Victor Sassoon, a wealthy landowner who invested in the opium trade. The Cathay was actually part of a complete office and hotel structure collectively called Sassoon House. Victor Sassoon himself lived and entertained his guests in the green penthouse. The hotel was rated on a par with the likes of Raffles in Singapore and the Peninsula in Hong Kong. It was *the* place to stay in old Shanghai; Noël Coward wrote *Private Lives* here. Now it's a swank five-star hotel with unbeatable history and a near-Bund address. ⊠ *20 Nanjing Dong Lu, Huangpu.*

FORMER FRENCH CONCESSION

With its tree-lined streets and crumbling old villas, the Former French Concession is possibly Shanghai's most visitor-friendly area, with ample shade and sidewalks meant to be pounded. It's a wonderful place to go wandering and make serendipitous discoveries of stately architecture, groovy boutiques and galleries, or cozy cafés. Here much of Shanghai's past beauty remains, although many of the old buildings are in desperate state of disrepair. One of the major roads through this area, Huaihai Lu, is a popular shopping location, with shops selling international and local brands. Julu Lu, Fumin Lu, Fuxing Xi Lu, and Yongfu Lu are where many of Shanghai's restaurants, bars, and clubs are located, so if you are looking for an evening out, head to this area.

DID YOU KNOW?

One short stretch of the famous Bund contains 52 buildings in dramatically different architectural styles, including Romanesque, Gothic, Renaissance, Baroque, Neo-classical, Beaux-Arts, and, of course, Art Deco. In fact, Shanghai has some of the finest Art Deco architecture in the world.

GETTING AROUND

This is a lovely area to walk around, so it might be best to leave cabs behind and go on foot. The only site that is at a distance is Soong Qingling's Former Residence, which is a bit farther down Huaihai Lu. Access it via metro Line 1 at Hengshan Lu if you don't want to walk. Any of the four Line 1 metro stops (Huangpi Nan Lu, Shaanxi Nan Lu, Changshu Lu, or Hengshan Lu) will land you somewhere in the French Concession area. Line 7 also connects at Changshu Lu.

EXPLORING

Cathay Theare. Once part of millionaire Victor Sassoon's holdings, the art deco Cathay Cinema was one of the first movie theaters in Shanghai. The building still serves as a theater, showing a mix of Chinese and Western films. ⊠ *870 Huaihai Zhonglu, at Maoming Nan Lu, Luwan* ☎ *021/5404–0415* ⊕ *www.guotaifilm.com.*

Former Residence of Dr. Sun Yat-sen. Dr. Sun Yat-sen, the father of the Chinese republic, lived in this two-story house for five years, from 1919 to 1924. His wife, Soong Qingling, continued to live here after his death until 1937. Today it's been turned into a museum, and tours are conducted in Chinese and English. ⊠ *7 Xiangshan Lu, Luwan* ☎ *021/6437– 2954* ⊠ *Y8* ⊙ *Daily 9–4:30.*

Fuxing Park. The grounds of this European-style park—known as French Park before 1949—provide a bit of greenery in crowded Shanghai. Here you'll find people practicing tai chi and lovers strolling hand in hand. ⊠ *105 Fuxing Zhong Lu, Luwan* ☎ *021/5386–1069* ⊠ *Free* ⊙ *Daily 6–6.*

Lyceum Theatre. In the days of Old Shanghai, the Lyceum was the home of the British Amateur Drama Club. The old stage got a face-lift in 2003 and is still in use as a concert hall. ⊠ *57 Maoming Nan Lu, Luwan* ☎ *021/6217–8530.*

Soong Qingling's Former Residence. While she first came to national attention as the wife of Dr. Sun Yat-sen, Soong Qingling became revered in her own right for her dedication to the Communist Party. Indeed, many mainland Chinese regard her as the "Mother of China." (On the other hand, Soong's sister, Meiling, married Chiang Kai-shek, who was the head of the Nationalist government from 1927 to 1949, at which point the couple fled to Taiwan.) This three-story house, built in 1920 by a German ship owner, was Soong's primary residence from 1948 to 1963. It has been preserved as it was during her lifetime, and includes her 4,000 books in the study and furniture in the bedroom that her parents gave as her dowry. The small museum next door has some nice displays from Soong Qingling and Sun Yat-sen's life, including pictures from their 1915 wedding in Tokyo. ⊠ *1843 Huaihai Zhong Lu, Xuhui* ☎ *021/6437–6268* ⊕ *www.shsoong-chingling.com* ⊠ *Y20* ⊙ *Daily 9–4:30.*

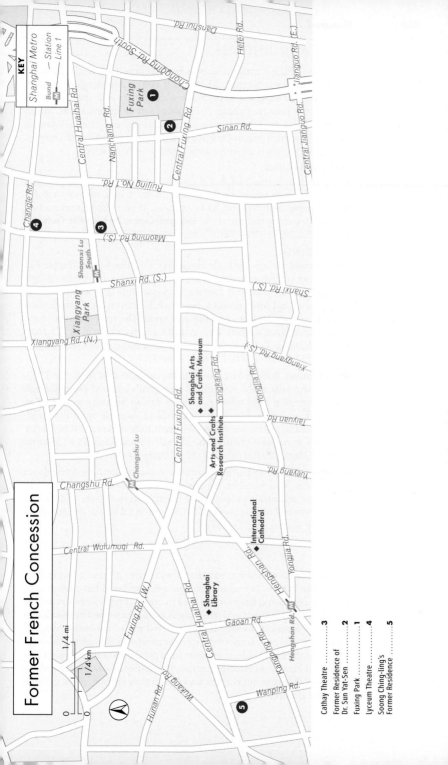

Former French Concession

KEY

Shanghai Metro

■━ Bund

Ⓜ — Station

— Line 1

Fuxing Park ① ②

Sinan Rd.

Central Huaihai Rd.

Nanchang Rd.

Central Fuxing Rd.

Chongqing Rd. South

Danshui Rd.

Hefei Rd.

Jianguo Rd. (E.)

Ruijing No.1 Rd.

Maoming Rd. (S.)

Changle Rd. ④

Shaanxi Lu South ③

Central Jianguo Rd.

Shanxi Rd. (S.)

Xiangyang Park

Xiangyang Rd. (N.)

Shanxi Rd. (S.)

Xiangyang Rd. (S.)

Shanghai Arts and Crafts Museum ♦

Arts and Crafts Research Institute ♦

Yongkang Rd.

Yongjia Rd.

Taiyuan Rd.

Central Fuxing Rd.

Changshu Lu

Changshu Rd. Ⓜ

Yueyang Rd.

Central Wulumuqi Rd.

International Cathedral ♦

Fuxing Rd. (W.)

Central Huaihai Rd.

Wukang Rd.

Shanghai Library ♦

Gaoan Rd.

Hengshan Rd.

Yongjia Rd.

Kangping Rd.

Hengshan Rd. Ⓜ

Wanping Rd. ⑤

Hunan Rd.

1/4 mi
1/4 km
0

NANJING XI LU AND JING'AN

Shanghai's glitziest malls and some five-star hotels are along the main street in this area, Nanjing Xi Lu. So if you're into designer threads, luxury spas, or expensive brunches, you can satisfy your spending urges and max out your credit here. For those of a more spiritual bent, Jingan Temple, whose reconstruction is ongoing, is one of Shanghai's largest temples. The small Jingan Park across the street is popular with couples. Behind the temple is an interesting network of back streets.

GETTING AROUND

Sights are thin in this area, but if you like international designer labels, this is where you can work the plastic. Metro Line 2 takes you to **Jin-gan Si (Temple)** and Nanjing Xi Lu stations. If you want to take a taxi afterward, joining the line at the **Shanghai Centre/Portman Ritz-Carlton** is a good idea, especially when it's raining.

EXPLORING

Jingan Temple. Originally built about AD 300, the Jingan Temple has been rebuilt and renovated numerous times. The temple's Southern-style halls, which face a central courtyard, gleam with new wood carvings of elephants and lotus flowers, but the hall interiors have stark, new concrete walls, and feel generally antiseptic. The temple's main draw is its copper Hongwu bell, cast in 1183 and weighing in at 3.5 tons. ✉ *1686 Nanjing Xi Lu, next to the Jing'an Si subway entrance, Jing'an* ☏ *021/6256–6366* ✉ *Y10* ⊙ *Daily 7:30–5.*

Moller Mansion. Built by Swedish shipping magnate Eric Moller in 1936, this massive villa is the epitome of Shanghai's colonial-era buildings. It is a surprising sight when you climb Yan'an highway from Jing'an into the French Concession. It's a complete anomaly from the buildings around it, which are either '70s high-rises or squat Chinese-style buildings. It currently houses the Shanghai Race Club. ✉ *30 Shaanxi Nan Lu, Jing'an* ☏ *021/6247–8881* ⊙ *Daily 10–4.*

Paramount. Built in 1933, the Paramount was considered the finest dance hall in Asia. Now at night, the domed roof of this art-deco dance hall glows blue and inside people dance the afternoon and the night away. ✉ *218 Yuyuan Lu, Jing'an* ☏ *021/6249–8866* ✉ *Varies depending on the dance session time* ⊙ *Daily.*

PUDONG

Shanghai residents used to say that it was better to have a bed in Puxi than an apartment in Pudong, but the neighborhood has come a long way in recent years, from a rural area to one that represents a futuristic city of wide boulevards and towering skyscrapers topped by the Shanghai World Financial Center, fondly referred to as "the bottle-opener." Apartments here are some of the most expensive in Shanghai. Although a little on the bland side, it is home to expat compounds designed in a medley of bizarre architectural styles, international schools, and malls. However, there are quite a few sites here worth visiting, particularly if you have children.

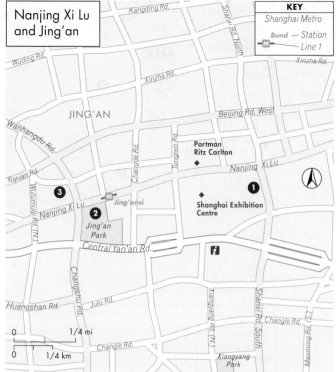

GETTING AROUND

The Bund Tourist Tunnel is a strange and rather garish way of making the journey under the Huangpu River to Pudong. You might get a few laughs from the light displays. Otherwise, you can take the metro on Line 2 to Lujiazui, or catch the ferry from the Bund.

Outside of the Lujiazui metro stop, Pudong is not a walking-friendly area, as there are large, rather featureless distances between the sights. You can either take the metro to get around or jump in a cab. If you visit all the sights, you could easily spend a day out here.

TOP ATTRACTIONS

★ **Jinmao Tower.** This gorgeous 88-floor (eight being the Chinese number implying wealth and prosperity) industrial art-deco pagoda houses one of the highest hotels in the world—the Grand Hyatt Shanghai takes up the 53rd to 87th floors. The 88th-floor observation deck, reached in 45 seconds by two high-speed elevators, offers a 360-degree view of the city. The Jinmao combines the classic 13-tier Buddhist pagoda design with postmodern steel and glass. Check out the Hyatt's dramatic 33-story atrium or the Cloud Nine bar on the 87th floor. ⊠ *88 Shiji Dadao, Pudong* ☎ *021/5047–0088* ⊡ *Observation deck Y70* ☉ *Daily 8 am–10 pm.*

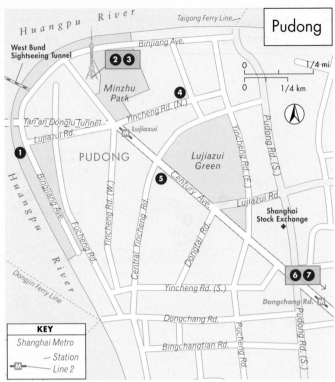

★ **Oriental Pearl Tower.** This quirky tower (1,535 feet or 468 meters) has become the pride and joy of the city, a symbol of the brashness and glitz of today's Shanghai. This UFO-like structure is especially kitschy at night, when it flashes with colored lights against the classic beauty of the Bund. Its three spheres are supposed to represent pearls (as in "Shanghai, Pearl of the Orient"). An elevator takes you to observation decks in the tower's three spheres. Go to the top sphere for a 360-degree bird's-eye view of the city, or grab a bite in the Tower's revolving restaurant. On the bottom floor is the Shanghai History Museum. ⊠ *1 Shiji Dadao (Century Avenue), Pudong* ☏ *021/5879–1888* ✆ *Y150 including the museum* ⊙ *Daily 8 am–9:30 pm.*

☾ **Shanghai History Museum.** This impressive museum in the base of the
★ Pearl Tower recalls Shanghai's pre-1949 history. Inside, you can stroll down a re-created Shanghai street circa 1900 or check out a street-car that used to operate in the concessions. Dioramas depict battle scenes from the Opium Wars, shops found in a typical turn-of-the-20th-century Shanghai neighborhood, and grand Former French Concession buildings of yesteryear. ⊠ *1 Shiji Dadao, Pudong* ☏ *021/5879–1888* ✆ *Y35* ⊙ *Daily 8 am–9:30 pm.*

WORTH NOTING

Century Park. This giant swathe of green in Pudong is a great place to take children, as it has a variety of vehicles for hire, good flat paths for rollerblading, and pleasure boats. On a fine day, pack a picnic and a kite and head to designated picnic areas as well as woods to explore and grass to play on. ⊠ *1001 Jinxiu Lu, Pudong* ☎ *021/3876–0588* ⊕ *www. centurypark.com.cn* ◻ *Y10* ⊙ *Daily 7 am–6 pm.*

Riverside Promenade. Although the park that runs 2,750 yards (2,514 meters) along the Huangpu River is sugary-sterile in its experimental suburbia, it still offers the most beautiful views of the Bund. You can stroll on the grass and concrete and view a perspective of Puxi unavailable from the west side. If you're here in the summer, you can "Enjoy Wading," as a sign indicates, in the chocolate-brown Huangpu River from the park's wave platform. ⊠ *Bingjiang Dadao, Pudong* ◻ *Free.*

4

☺ **Shanghai Ocean Aquarium.** As you stroll through the aquarium's 12,000-foot-long (3,658-meter-long) clear sightseeing tunnel, you may feel like you're walking your way through the seven seas—or at least five of them. The aquarium's 10,000 fish represent 300 species, five oceans, and four continents. You'll also find penguins and species representing all 12 of the Chinese zodiacal animals, such as the tiger barb, sea dragon, and seahorse. ⊠ *1388 Lujiazui Ring Road, Pudong* ☎ *021/5877–9988* ⊕ *www.sh-aquarium.com* ◻ *Y120 adults, Y80 children* ⊙ *Daily 9–6;* ⊙ *9–9.*

☺ **Shanghai Science and Technology Museum.** This museum, a favorite attraction for kids in Shanghai, has more than 100 hands-on exhibits in its six main galleries. Earth Exploration takes you through fossil layers to the earth's core for a lesson in plate tectonics. Spectrum of Life introduces you to the animal and plant kingdoms within its simulated rain forest. Light of Wisdom explains basic principles of light and sound through interactive exhibits, and simulators in AV Paradise put you in a plane cockpit and on television. Children's Technoland has a voice-activated fountain and miniature construction site. In Cradle of Designers, you can record a CD or assemble a souvenir. Two IMAX theaters and an IWERKS 4D theater show larger-than-life movies, but mostly in Chinese. All signs are in English; the best times to visit are weekday afternoons. ⊠ *2000 Shiji Dadao, Pudong* ☎ *021/6854–2000* ⊕ *www.sstm. org.cn* ◻ *Y60; there are separate prices for the IMAX and IWERKS* ⊙ *Tues.–Sun. 9–5:15.*

NORTH SHANGHAI

Although often neglected in favor of their more glamorous neighboring areas, the northern Shanghai districts of Putuo, Hongkou, and Zhabei still offer some interesting sights. Hongkou District, particularly, is still relatively undeveloped and unchanged, and buildings from the past are still visible behind cheap clothing stores. An area with an interesting history, it has the most sights worth seeing, as well as the lush green sweep of Lu Xun Park. The old buildings and warehouses around Suzhou Creek, which feeds into the Huangpu, are slowly being turned into a hip and happening arty area, particularly the M50 development. Also in Putuo District is another one of Shanghai's main temples, the Jade Buddha Temple.

GETTING AROUND

North Shanghai's sights are in three distinct areas. The galleries at M50 open later in the morning, so it may be best to head to some other sites first. Many of them are closed on Mondays. Qipu Lu also gets very busy as the day goes on, and is unbearable on weekends.

For the Jade Buddha Temple and M50, you can hop off the metro Line 3 or 4 at Zhongtan Lu, and then it's a short walk to M50 and a longer one to Jade Buddha. You can take the Pearl Line to East Baoxing Lu and Hongkou Stadium for Lu Xun Park and Duolun Lu. The easiest way to get around is by taxi.

EXPLORING

Duolun Lu. Designated Shanghai's "Cultural Street," Duolun Road takes you back in time to the 1930s, when the 1-km-long (½-mi-long) lane was a favorite haunt of writer Lu Xun and fellow social activists. Bronze statues of those literary luminaries dot the lawns between the well-preserved villas and row houses, whose first floors are now home to antiques shops, cafés, and art galleries. As the street takes a 90-degree turn, its architecture shifts 180 degrees with the seven-story stark gray **Shanghai Doland Museum of Modern Art.** ⊠ *Off Sichuan Bei Lu, Hongkou.*

★ **Jade Buddha Temple.** Completed in 1918, this temple is fairly new by Chinese standards. During the Cultural Revolution, in order to save the temple when the Red Guards came to destroy it, the monks pasted portraits of Mao Zedong on the outside walls so the Guards couldn't tear them down without destroying Mao's face as well. The temple is built in the style of the Song Dynasty, with symmetrical halls and courtyards, upturned eaves, and bright yellow walls. The temple's great treasure is its 6½-foot-tall (2-meter-tall) seated Buddha made of white jade with a robe of precious gems, originally brought to Shanghai from Burma. Other Buddhas, statues, and frightening guardian gods of the temple populate the halls, as well as a collection of Buddhist scriptures and paintings. The monks who live and work here can sometimes be seen worshipping. It's madness at festival times. ⊠ *170 Anyuan Lu, Putuo* ☎ *021/6266–3668* ⊕ *www.yufotemple.com* 🎫 *Y30* ☉ *Daily 8–4:30.*

M50 is a cluster of art galleries and artists' studios by Suzhou Creek. This is home to some of Shanghai's hottest galleries, where you will see works from China's best artists mixed with new and not so well-known ones. There are also a couple of shops selling music and art supplies and a couple coffee shops. Don't be shy about nosing around—there are galleries on many floors of these old factories and warehouses, and sometimes artists will be around for a chat. ⊠ *50 Moganshan Lu, Putuo* 🎫 *Free* ☉ *Daily, although most galleries are closed on Mon. Opening times vary depending on the gallery.*

Ohel Moishe Synagogue and Huoshan Park. Currently called the Jewish Refugee Memorial Hall of Shanghai, the Ohel Moishe Synagogue served as the spiritual heart of Shanghai's Jewish ghetto in the 1930s and '40s. In this sanctuary-turned-museum, whose restoration was completed in

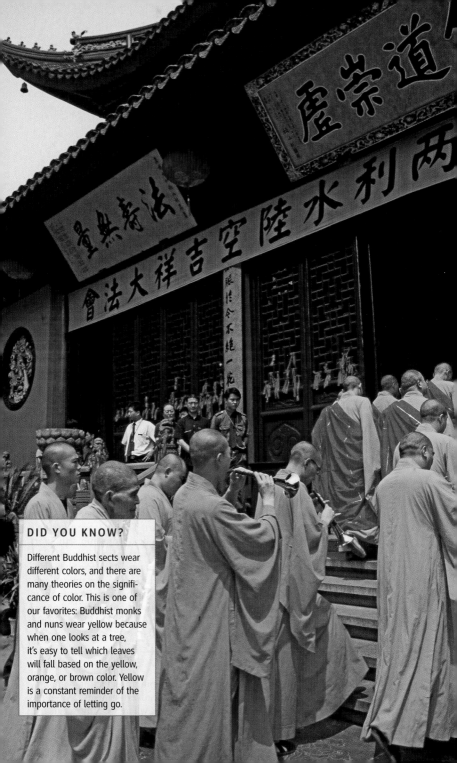

DID YOU KNOW?

Different Buddhist sects wear different colors, and there are many theories on the significance of color. This is one of our favorites: Buddhist monks and nuns wear yellow because when one looks at a tree, it's easy to tell which leaves will fall based on the yellow, orange, or brown color. Yellow is a constant reminder of the importance of letting go.

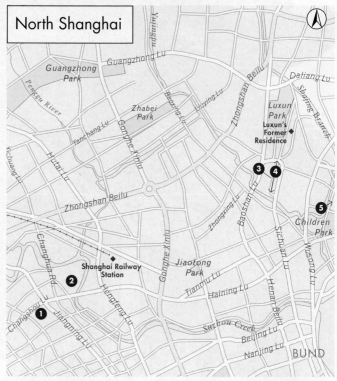

North Shanghai

2008, visitors can see a reconstruction of the main room of the synagogue and see artworks inspired by the story of Jews in Shanghai. An outside building has photos, newspaper clippings, and a film (narrated in Chinese). Around the corner, down a lane just as well preserved, Huoshan Park bears a memorial tablet in the immigrants' honor. ✉ *62 Changyang Lu, Hongkou* ☎ *021/6541–5008* 💲 *Y50* ⊘ *Mon.–Sat. 9–4.*

Shanghai Doland Museum of Modern Art. Opened in December 2003, this is Shanghai's first official venue for modern art. The six-story museum's 14,400 square feet of exhibition space include a tiny shop selling art books and a metal spiral staircase that's a work of art in itself. The exhibitions, which change frequently, are cutting-edge for Shanghai. They've showcased electronic art from American artists, examined gender issues among Chinese, and featured musical performances ranging from Chinese electronica to the *dombra*, a traditional Kazak stringed instrument. ✉ *27 Duolun Lu, Hongkou* ☎ *021/6587–2530* 💲 *Varies according to the exhibition* ⊘ *Daily 10–5:30.*

XUJIAHUI AND SOUTH, HONGQIAO AND GUBEI

Buyers throng the large malls in the shopping precinct at Xujiahui, which shines with neon and giant billboard advertisements. Down the road are the districts of Hongqiao and Gubei, where wealthy expats live

TEE OFF

Some 20 clubs dot the country-side within two hours of downtown Shanghai. Some clubs run buses, so call to inquire; some are on metro lines, and others suggest that you take a taxi. All clubs run on a membership basis, but most allow non-members to play when accompanied by a member.

Grand Shanghai International Golf and Country Club. This club has a Ronald Fream–designed 18-hole championship course and driving range. ⊠ *18 Yangcheng Zhonglu, Yangcheng Lake Holiday Zone, Kunshan City, Jiangsu Province* ☎ *0512/5789–1999* ⊕ *www. grandshanghaigolf.com.cn.*

Shanghai Binhai Golf Club. Peter Thomson designed the Scottish links–style, 27-hole course at this club in Pudong. Another 27 holes are on the books. ⊠ *Binhai Resort, Baiyulan Dadao, Nanhui County* ☎ *021/3800–1888 (reservation hotline)* ⊕ *www.binhaigolf.com.*

Shanghai International Golf and Country Club. This 18-hole course designed by Robert Trent Jones Jr. is Shanghai's most difficult. There are water hazards at almost every hole. ⊠ *961 Yin Zhu Lu, Zhu Jia Jiao, Qingpu District* ☎ *021/5972–8111.*

Shanghai Links Golf and Country Club. This Jack Nicklaus–designed 18-hole course is about a 45-minute ride east of downtown. It's open to the public on Tuesday for Ladies' Day. ⊠ *1600 Lingbai Lu, Tianxu Township, Pudong* ☎ *021/5897–3068* ⊕ *www.shanghailinks.com.cn.*

Shanghai Riviera Golf Resort. The late Bobby J. Martin designed this 18-hole course and driving range. ⊠ *277 Yangtze Lu, Nanxiang Town, Jiading District* ☎ *021/5912–6888* ⊕ *www.srgr.cn.*

Shanghai Silport Golf Club. This club hosts the Volvo China Open. Its 27-hole course on Dianshan Lake was designed by Bobby J. Martin; nine holes designed by Roger Packard opened in 2004. ⊠ *1 Xubao Lu, Dianshan Lake Town, Kunshan City, Jiangsu Province* ☎ *0512/5748–1111* ⊕ *www.silport.com.cn.*

Shanghai Sun Island International Club. You'll find a 27-hole course designed by Nelson & Haworth plus an excellent driving range at this club. ⊠ *2588 Shantai Lu, Zhu Jia Jiao, Qingpu District* ☎ *021/6983–3001* ⊕ *www.sunislandclub.com.*

Tianma Country Club. Tianma is the most accessible course to the public. Its 18 holes have views of Sheshan Mountain. ⊠ *3958 Zhaokun Lu, Tianma Town, Songjiang District* ☎ *021/5766–1666* ⊕ *www.tianmacc. com.*

in high-walled compounds and drive huge SUVs. You're likely to find a larger concentration of Western-style restaurants and supermarkets here if you are feeling homesick.

GETTING AROUND

Metro Line 1 takes you right into the depths of the Grand Gateway Mall at Xujiahui. The other sights are fairly far-flung, so it's a good idea to jump into a taxi. If you are going to places like the Shanghai Botanical Gardens from the center of town, be prepared for a large taxi bill. Otherwise, you can get off at Shanghai South Railway Station.

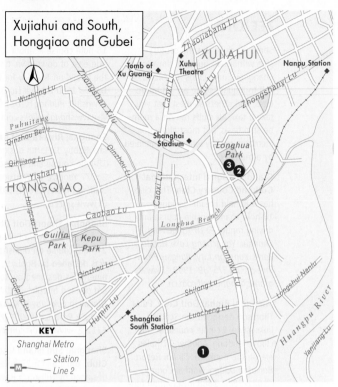

EXPLORING

Longhua Martyrs Cemetery may seem a tranquil now, but it has had a bloody history. It has been the execution site of many Communists, particularly during the Guomingdang crackdown in 1927. Nowadays, it's full of large Soviet-style sculpture and immaculate lawns. The most chilling is the small, unkempt, grassy execution area accessed by a tunnel where the remains of murdered Communists were found with leg irons still on in the 1950s. ✉ *180 Longhua Lu, Xuhui* ☎ *021/6468–5995* ⊕ *www.slmmm.cn* ✉ *Y1* ☼ *Daily 6–5, Museum 9–4.*

★ **Longhua Temple** *(Longhua Si).* Shanghai's largest and most active temple has as its centerpiece a seven-story, eight-sided pagoda. While the temple is thought to have been built in the 3rd century, the pagoda dates from the 10th century; it's not open to visitors. Near the front entrance of the temple stands a three-story bell tower, where a 3.3-ton bronze bell is rung at midnight every New Year's Eve. Along the side corridors of the temple you'll find the Longhua Hotel, a vegetarian restaurant, and a room filled seven rows deep with small golden statues. The third hall is the most impressive. Its three giant Buddhas sit beneath a swirled red and gold dome. ✉ *2853 Longhua Lu, Xuhui* ☎ *021/6456–6085 or 021/6457–6327* ✉ *Y10 with free incense* ☼ *Daily 7–4:30.*

Shanghai Botanical Gardens. Spread over 200 acres, the garden has areas for peonies and roses, azaleas, osmanthus, bamboo and orchids, and medicinal plants. Its Penjing Garden is among the world's best. *Penjing* translates as "pot scenery," and describes the Chinese art of creating a miniature landscape in a container. More than 2,000 bonsai trees line the Penjing Garden's courtyards and corridors. The Chinese Cymbidium Garden has more than 300 varieties. Within the Grand Conservatory are towering palms and more than 3,500 varieties of tropical plants. ⊠ *1111 Longwu Lu, Xuhui* ☎ *021/5436–3369* ⊕ *www.shbg.org* 🎫 *Y15 for entrance through main gate only* ☉ *Daily 7–5.*

WHERE TO EAT

4

You'll notice that most Chinese restaurants in Shanghai have large, round tables. The reason becomes clear the first time you eat a late dinner at a local restaurant and are surrounded by jovial, laughing groups of people toasting and topping off from communal bottles of beer, sharing cigarettes, and spinning the lazy Susan loaded with food. Whether feting guests or demonstrating their growing wealth, hosts will order massive, showy spreads.

Shanghai's standing as China's most international city is reflected in its dining scene. You can enjoy *jiaozi* (dumplings) for breakfast, foie gras for lunch, and Kobe beef for dinner. It's traditional to order several dishes, plus rice, to share among your party. Tipping is not expected, but sophistication comes at a price. Although you can eat at Chinese restaurants for less than Y20 per person, most simple Western meals cost a more Western price.

Most restaurants in Shanghai offer set lunches—multicourse feasts—at a fraction of the usual price. Also, check out the "Restaurant Events" section of City Weekend, *That's Shanghai,* or *Smartshanghai.com,* all of which list dining discounts and promotions around town.

Use the coordinate (✛ B2) at the end of each listing to locate a site on the Where to Eat in Shanghai map.

ON THE MENU

Shanghainese food is fairly typical Chinese, with dark, sweet, and oily dishes served in great abundance. The dish sizes can be quite small—it's not unusual for two diners to polish off six dishes plus rice. The drink of choice is *huangjiu,* or yellow wine. It's a mild-tasting sweetish rice wine, which pairs well with the local cuisine.

Shanghai is full of fine restaurants from around the world, but sometimes the finest dining experience in the city can be had with a steamer tray of *xiaolongbao*—Shanghai's signature dumplings, which are small, steamed buns filled with pork and crab meat in broth. They're best eaten by poking a hole in the top with a chopstick or your finger—but watch out, they're hot!—and sucking out the innards. Match dumplings with a cold beer. River fish is often the highlight (and most expensive part) of the meal, and hairy crab is a seasonal delicacy.

MEAL TIMES

Dinner hours in restaurants begin at around 5 pm, but often carry on late into the night. Many of the classic, local restaurants popular with the Shanghainese only close after the last diners have left, which sometimes keeps them open until the wee hours of the morning. Generally, though, dinner is eaten between 6 and 11 pm.

PRICES

Even in the fanciest restaurants, main courses are unlikely to cost more than US$45. However, famous restaurants charge as much as the international market will bear—prices that often don't reflect the quality of the dining experience. If you're looking for an excellent meal and you don't care about the restaurateur's name, then exceptional dining experiences can be had for half the price.

Great local food can be found for supremely cheap prices (10 cents to $5 per dish), even in fairly nice restaurants. The experience of eating at a small, unknown restaurant is pure China.

WHAT IT COSTS IN YUAN					
	¢	$	$$	$$$	$$$$
For Two People	under Y40	Y40–Y80	Y81–Y150	Y151–Y300	over Y300

Prices are for a main course at dinner.

OLD CITY

Narrow and crowded, the Old City is all that's left of Old China in Shanghai. The area is home to the spectacular Yuyuan Gardens, and is a good location to find traditional-style food in an authentic environment. We recommend that the adventurous go out into the side streets around Fangbang Lu in search of authentic Chinese snacks. ■ TIP➜ When dining in these small local restaurants always ask the price first—with no English menu, many sellers in this area aren't above raising the price after your first bite. To do so, say "duo shao tien?" Note, however, that if you are clearly foreign and do not speak Chinese, you will be paying the foreigner price.

$$ ✕ **Lv Bo Lang.** A popular stop for visiting dignitaries, Lv Bo Lang (pro-
CHINESE   nounced "Lü Bo Lang") is a perfect photo op of a restaurant. The traditional three-story Chinese pavilion with upturned eaves sits next to the Bridge of Nine Turnings in the Yu Garden complex. The food is good but not great, with many expensive fish choices on the menu. Among the best dishes are the crab meat with bean curd, the braised eggplant with chili sauce, and the sweet *osmanthus* cake, made with the sweetly fragrant flower of the same name. ⊠ *115 Yuyuan Lu, Huangpu* ☎ *021/6328–0602* ⌲ *Reservations essential* ▤ *AE, DC, MC, V* ✛ *F3*.

XINTIANDI AND CITY CENTER

The center of the gastronomic city, the City Center and Xintiandi contain some of the finest restaurants in the city, like T8 and the trendy Barbarossa.

Cheap snacks can be found on the streets around the Old City.

$$
MIDDLE EASTERN

✕ **Barbarossa.** Modern Middle Eastern food in a setting taken from the *Arabian Nights*, Barbarossa is a popular evening destination. The interior is amazing, albeit possibly flammable, with billowing draperies swathing the space, and the food and service are reasonable. At around 10 pm, Barbarossa becomes a club, so don't aim for a late dinner unless you like mingling with the party people. ⊠ *People's Square, 231 Nanjing Xi Rd., next to the Shanghai Art Museum, Luwan* ☎ *021/6318–0220* ▭ *AE, DC, MC, V* ♻ *D2.*

$–$$
AMERICAN

✕ **Kabb.** Serving burgers, salads, and other standards of American food, this café in Xintiandi is distinguished for its superb location. The food is good but without distinction, though the portions are massive. Service is slightly indifferent, and the pricing is rather high for such pedestrian fare. However, it does fill the bill for a quick lunch on the sidewalk tables. ⊠ *Xintiandi, 181 Taicang Lu, 5 Xintiandi Bei Li, Luwan* ☎ *021/3307–0798* ▭ *AE, DC, MC, V* ♻ *D3.*

$$$
INTERNATIONAL
Fodor's Choice
★

✕ **T8.** A veteran of the Shanghai fine dining scene, T8 has garnered its share of headlines for its stunning interior and inspired contemporary cuisine. The restaurant occupies a traditional shikumen house within Xintiandi and has modernized the space with raw stone floors, carved-wood screens, and imaginative lighting that transforms shelves full of glasses into a modern-art sculpture. The show kitchen turns out exciting fusion dishes from fresh seasonal ingredients. Like the clientele, the wine list is exclusive, with many labels unavailable elsewhere in Shanghai. ⊠ *Number 8, North Block, Xintiandi, Lane 181 Taicang Lu, Luwan* ☎ *021/6355–8999* ⌖ *Reservations essential* ▭ *AE, DC, MC, V* ⊗ *No lunch Monday* ♻ *D4.*

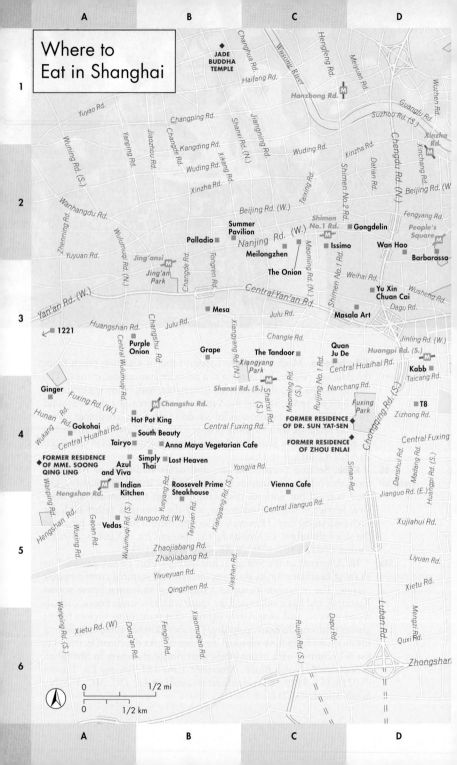

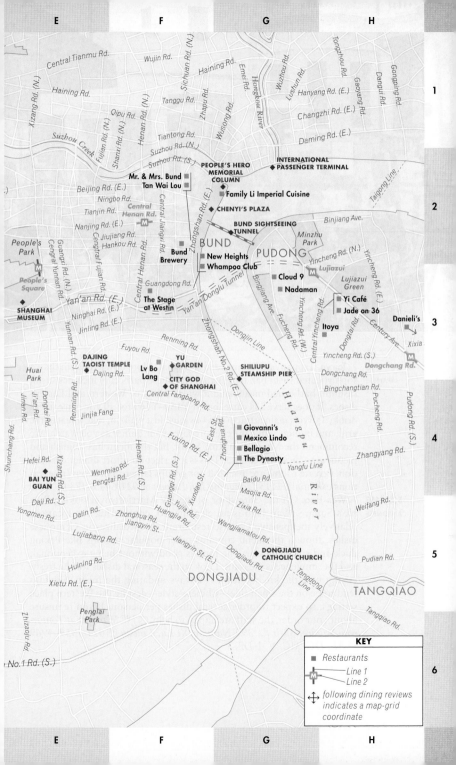

Xintiandi is a great place to hang out and watch the crowds pass by.

$$
JAPANESE

✕ **Tairyo.** Teppanyaki has invaded Shanghai. More down to earth than a sophisticated sushi bar, teppanyaki (Japanese barbecue) includes sushi, sashimi, barbecued meats, and a wide variety of Western and Eastern dishes. It does serve à la carte, but at Y150–Y160 for all you can eat and drink, Tairyo's main attraction is obvious. Just walk in, take a seat at the grill, and indulge while the chef prepares your dinner as you watch. We recommend the Mongolian King Steak, but the menu has English and pictures, so pick and choose. This is a perfect no-effort dinner destination. Private rooms are available for groups larger than seven (reservations essential). ⊠ *15 Dongping Lu, Luwan* ☎ *021/6445–4734* ✣ *A4.*

$$$–$$$$
CANTONESE

✕ **Wan Hao.** On the 38th floor of the JW Marriott overlooking People's Square, Wan Hao is an elegant and, considering the location, relatively inexpensive Chinese restaurant. It specializes in Cantonese dishes, though the menu contains other popular options like Peking duck and spicy chicken. The food is good without being exceptional, and the ambience is pleasant. Look to the seasonal dishes for the freshest options; the kitchen team is always updating the menu. Servings tend to be on the small side—Chinese-style—despite the Western place settings, so expect to order several dishes per person. If you're unsure about your order, the staff are happy to help. ⊠ *JW Marriott at Tomorrow Square, 38th fl., 399 Nanjing Xi Lu, Luwan* ☎ *021/5359–4969* ▭ *AE, DC, MC, V* ✣ *D2.*

NANJING DONG LU AND THE BUND

The Bund is the heart of modern Shanghai, with the colonial history of Puxi facing the towering steel and glass of Pudong. The stellar view of the river and Pudong has attracted some of the finest restaurant development in town. However, many visitors complain that the Bund restaurants are more style than substance. We find that it's well worth your effort to experience what this area has to offer.

$$ AMERICAN ★

✕ **Bund Brewery.** Ostensibly a brew pub, the Bund Brewery is more popular as an off-Bund dinner alternative. The food is modern, well-portioned pub fare, and the service reasonably attentive. It's a good choice for an unpretentious meal after a day's Bund sightseeing, or before heading out the clubs for the evening. The calamari comes highly recommended. ⊠ *11 Hankou Lu, Huangpu* ☎ *021/6321–8447* ▤ *AE, DC, MC, V* ✛ *F2.*

$$$$ MANDARIN

✕ **Family Li Imperial Cuisine.** This spectacular restaurant, a newer branch of the famous Beijing Imperial restaurant, deserves a visit despite high prices (set menus begin at Y600). Using family recipes smuggled from the Forbidden City a century ago, Family Li gives the closest thing to a taste of imperial food. There are only nine rooms, and only set menus are served. Reservations more than 24 hours in advance are a must. ⊠ *Huangpu Park, 500 East Zhongshan Yi Rd., Huangpu* ☎ *021/5308–1919* ⌕ *Reservations essential* ▤ *AE, DC, MC, V* ✛ *G2.*

$$$$ FRENCH

✕ **Mr & Mrs Bund.** Shanghai-famous French chef Paul Pairet's Bund-side eatery serves food until 4 am Tuesday through Saturday. With 32 wines by the glass and inventive dishes like foie-gras crumble, a giant French fry, and lip-smacking lemon tart, you'll leave here more than satisfied. ⊠ *Bund 18, 1 Zhongshan Dong Yi Rd., 6th fl., Huangpu* ☎ *021/6323–9898* ▤ *AE, DC, MC, V* ✛ *F2.*

$$$ AMERICAN ★

✕ **New Heights.** Perched atop prestigious Three on the Bund, New Heights is a surprisingly unpretentious restaurant. With a gorgeous terrace overlooking the river and a solid menu of generally North American standard fare, this is an excellent destination for the weary Bund tourist. We recommend it for a late lunch basking in the afternoon sun on the terrace. Try the hamburger with a cold beer. ⊠ *Three on the Bund, 7th fl., 3 Zhong Shan Dong Yi Rd., Huangpu* ☎ *021/6321–0909* ▤ *AE, DC, MC, V* ✛ *F3.*

$$–$$$ ECLECTIC ★

✕ **The Stage at Westin.** Although The Stage is usually a fairly standard five-star buffet, it is also home to Shanghai's most popular Sunday champagne brunch. Costing almost Y500 and booked two to three weeks in advance, the brunch at the Westin has become an institution. Check it out if you feel the need for some decadent indulgence, as you'll feast on crab legs, pasta, soup, and loads of champagne. It runs from 11:30 to 2:30. ⊠ *Level 1, The Westin Shanghai Bund Center, 88 Henan Zhong Rd., Huangpu* ☎ *021/6335–0577* ⌕ *Reservations essential* ▤ *AE, DC, MC, V* ✛ *F3.*

$$ CHINESE FUSION

✕ **Tan Wai Lou.** Bund18's Chinese restaurant, Tan Wai Lou, serves up nouveau Cantonese cuisine in a refined setting. The food is good and well presented, though the non-Chinese service can be a little jarring for a diner expecting a classic Chinese meal. Still, the seafood is very fresh and the view of the Huangpu spectacular. ⊠ *Bund18, 5th fl., 18*

4

Zhongshan Dong Yi Rd., Huangpu ☎ *021/6339–1188* ✍ *Reservations essential* ▤ *AE, DC, MC, V* ✜ *F2.*

$$$
CHINESE FUSION

✕ **Whampoa Club.** A popular member of the Bund scene, Whampoa Club is nouveau Chinese at its best. With a focus on fresh seafood and interesting interpretations of Shanghai classics, this is a destination worth checking out. As befits a celebrity venue, prices are steep, but generally worth the expense. ⊠ *Three on the Bund, 4th fl., 17 Guangdong Lu, 4th fl., Huangpu* ☎ *021/6321–3737* ✍ *Reservations essential* ▤ *AE, DC, MC, V* ✜ *F3.*

$$
SICHUAN

✕ **Yu Xin Chuan Cai.** Yu Xin offers fantastic Sichuan food and is extremely popular with the locals. Each of the two locations seats hundreds and is always full. Book ahead, or be prepared to wait around 30 to 60 minutes for a table. Try the tea-smoked duck. ⊠ *3F, 333 Chengdu Bei Lu Huangpu* ☎ *021/5298–0438, 021/5298–0439* ✍ *Reservations essential* ▤ *Local only* ✜ *D3.*

FORMER FRENCH CONCESSION

$$
INTERNATIONAL
Fodor's Choice
★

✕ **Azul and Viva.** In creating his continent-hopping New World cuisine, owner Eduardo Vargas drew upon his globe-trotting childhood and seven years as a restaurant consultant in Asia. As a result, the menus in Azul, the tapas bar downstairs, and Viva, the restaurant upstairs, feature a delicious, delicate balance of flavors that should please any palate. Classics like beef carpaccio contrast with cutting-edge dishes like coffee-glazed pork. Lunch and weekend brunch specials are lower-priced. The relaxed, romantic interior—dim lighting, plush pillows, and splashes of color against muted backdrops—invites you to take your time on your culinary world tour. ⊠ *18 Dongping Lu, Xuhui* ☎ *021/6433–1172* ▤ *AE, DC, MC, V* ✜ *A4.*

$–$$
CAFÉ

✕ **Ginger.** Tucked away in the avenues of the French Concession, Ginger is a European-flavored café. Small and intimate, Ginger is a place for conversations over lunch or a relaxing afternoon coffee. We recommend having your drinks in the tiny enclosed terrace for a rare tranquil Shanghai moment. ⊠ *299 Fuxing Xi Lu, near Huashan Lu, Xuhui* ☎ *021/6433–9437* ▤ *AE, DC, MC, V* ✜ *A4.*

$–$$
JAPANESE

✕ **Gokohai.** Possibly the best shabu-shabu restaurant in Shanghai, Gokohai is a hidden gem. Shabu-shabu is Japanese hotpot—each diner gets a pot and chooses a selection of meats (served in enormous, sombrero-shaped piles) and vegetables to cook in the broth. You'll need to ask for the all-you-can-eat deal for Y88 (drinks not included), because it is not mentioned on the menu. ⊠ *1720 Huaihai Lu, near Wuxing Lu, Xuihui* ☎ *021/6471–7657* ✍ *Reservations recommended* ▤ *Local only* ✜ *A4.*

> **WORD OF MOUTH**
>
> "One small shop had two vats of boiling broth whereby each person takes a basket and fills it with whatever food they want to eat.... I picked some pork meat, two types of mushrooms, cabbage and thin noodles. The cook finished off the soup with some hot sauce and other spices." —monicapileggi

¢–$
CHINESE
★

✕ **Grape.** Entry-level Chinese food at inexpensive prices has been Grape's calling card since the mid-1980s. This cheerful two-story restaurant remains a favorite among expatriates and travelers wandering the Former French Concession. The English menu, with photos, includes such recognizable fare as sweet-and-sour pork and lemon chicken, as well as delicious dishes like garlic shrimp and *jiachang doufu* (home-style bean curd), all of which are served with a smile. ⊠ *55 Xinle Lu, Luwan* ☎ *021/5404–0486* ▤ *No credit cards* ⊹ *B3.*

¢–$ ✕**Hot Pot King.** *Huo guo*, or hotpot, is a popular Chinese ritual of at-
CHINESE the-table cooking, in which you simmer fresh ingredients in a broth. Hot Pot King reigns over the hotpot scene in Shanghai because of its extensive menu as well as its refined setting. The most popular of the 17 broths is the yin-yang, half spicy red, half basic white pork-bone broth. Add in a mixture of veggies, seafood, meat, and dumplings for a well-rounded pot, then dip each morsel in the sauces mixed tableside by your waiter. The minimalist white and gray interior has glass-enclosed booths and well-spaced tables, a nice change from the usual crowded, noisy, hotpot joints. ⊠ *1416 Huaihai Rd., 2nd fl., Xuhui* ☎ *021/6473–6380* ⊠ *3F, 222 Huaihai Lu, People's Square* ☎ *021/5396–5572* ▤ *AE, DC, MC, V* ⊹ *A4.*

¢–$ ✕**Indian Kitchen.** The Indian chefs working their magic in the show
INDIAN kitchen provide the entertainment while you wait for a table at this tremendously popular restaurant. Delicious butter chicken marsala and tandoor-cooked chicken tikka taste as good as they look in the picture menu, which is packed with classic Indian dishes. The many bread selections include taste-bud tingling spring onion *parotas* (fried flat bread). ⊠ *572 Yongjia Lu, Xuhui* ☎ *021/6473–1517* ⊠ *480 Minsheng Lu., Pudong* ☎ *021/5821–9875* ⌲ *Reservations essential* ▤ *AE, DC, MC, V* ⊹ *A4.*

$–$$ ✕**Lost Heaven.** Lost Heaven serves Yunnan cuisine—Southern Chinese
YUNNAN from the borders of Myanmar and Cambodia. The food is reminiscent
★ of Thai cuisine, and well-prepared, while the dining room evokes Yunnan architecture despite its location in the middle of the French Concession. Service is acceptable without being polished. ⊠ *38 Gaoyou Lu</str>, Luwan* ☎ *021/6433–5126* ⊠ *17 Yan'an Dong Lu, The Bund* ☎ *21/6330–0967* ▤ *AE, DC, MC, V* ⊹ *B4.*

$$–$$$ ✕**Mesa.** Nestled on the quiet residential street Julu Lu, Mesa is a little
INTERNATIONAL hard to find. The unassuming facade is backed with a stark minimalist
☾ decor, which belies the sophistication of the seasonal menu. The cuisine is contemporary, meaning the chef has been allowed to experiment, and the results are impeccable. The wine list is comprehensive, with an excellent by-the-glass selection, and not overpriced. ⊠ *748 Julu Lu, Luwan* ☎ *021/6289–9108* ☉ *Brunch Sat. and Sun. 9:30–4. Babysitting available for brunch* ▤ *AE, DC, MC, V* ⊹ *B3.*

$$ ✕**The Purple Onion.** Prolific Shanghai restaurateur David Laris has
INTERNATIONAL done it again. He's serving Mediterranean-ish fare—toothsome piz-
Fodor'sChoice zas, caprese salad, and chicken-liver mouse—in a dining room whose
★ style is part goth, part aubergine. The outdoor patio is enormous and lovely. Space here fills up fast. ⊠ *16, La. 351, Huashan Lu, Xuhui* ☎ *021/6248–8020* ▤ *AE, DC, MC, V* ⊹ *A3.*

$–$$ ✕**Quan Ju De.** The original Beijing branch of this restaurant has been
MANDARIN *the* place to get Peking duck since 1864. This Shanghai branch opened

in 1998, but the Peking duck is just as popular here. Few dishes are more definitively Chinese than Peking duck, the succulent, slow-roasted bird that is never quite properly prepared overseas. The ambience here is "old Chinese" to the point of absurdity, complete with hostesses dressed in traditional imperial outfits including platform tasseled shoes and flashy headpieces, and with lattice screens scattered throughout the dining room. The menu has both pictures and English text to explain the different types of duck available. One minor drawback is the size of the portions. There are no half-ducks on the menu, and a full duck is rather a lot for two people. ⊠ *786 Huaihai Zhong Lu, 4th fl., Luwan* ☎ *021/5404–5799* ⌘ *Reservations essential* ▭ *AE, DC, MC, V* ✛ *C3.*

$$$–$$$$ ✕ **Roosevelt Prime Steakhouse.** Located in the historic Marshall Mansions
AMERICAN   of the French Concession, Roosevelt offers the best steak in the city
Fodor's Choice   (and quite possibly the country) in a relaxed steak-house ambience.
★   The meat is USDA Prime, cooked to your specification in an imported stone oven. These steaks are not cheap, ranging in price from Y300 to Y1,200 for the Porterhouse, though regular mains are considerably more reasonable. Try the mac and cheese with black truffle, and the excellent Caesar salad. ⊠ *160 Taiyuan Lu, Xuhui* ☎ *021/6433–8240* ⊕ *www.rooseveltsteakhouse.com* ▭ *AE, DC, MC, V* ✛ *B5.*

$–$$ ✕ **Simply Thai.** Unpretentious Thai fare at moderate prices has earned
THAI   this restaurant a loyal expat clientele. Customers flock to the tree-
Fodor's Choice   shaded patio to savor such favorites as green and red curries (on the
★   spicy side) and stir-fried rice noodles with chicken (on the tame side). The appetizers are all first-rate, especially the crispy spring rolls and samosas. The wine list includes a half-dozen bottles under Y200, a rarity in Shanghai. The branch in Xintiandi is a bit noisier, but features the same great food and prices. ⊠ *5C Dongping Rd., Xuhui* ☎ *021/6445–9551* ⌘ *Reservations essential* ▭ *AE, DC, MC, V* ✛ *B4.*

$–$$ ✕ **South Beauty.** As the sliding-glass front door opens—revealing a walk-
SICHUAN   way between two cascading walls of water—it splits the restaurant's
★   trademark red Chinese-opera mask in two. Likewise, the menu is split down the middle between cooler Cantonese cuisine and sizzling hot Sichuan fare. Don't be fooled: even dishes with a one-pepper rating, like sautéed baby lobster, will singe your sinuses. ⊠ *28 Taojiang Lu, Xuhui* ☎ *021/6445–2581* ⌘ *Reservations essential* ▭ *AE, DC, MC, V* ✛ *A4.*

$$–$$$ ✕ **The Tandoor.** Don't miss the unbelievable *murgh malei kebab* (tandoori
INDIAN   chicken marinated in cheese and yogurt mixture), or try some vegetable curries—*palak aloo* (spinach with peas) or *dal makhani* (lentil). Outfitted with mirrors, Indian artwork, and Chinese characters dangling from the ceiling, the restaurant is ingeniously designed to show the route of Buddhism from India to China. The management and staff, all from India, remain close at hand throughout the meal to answer questions and attend to your needs. ⊠ *Jinjiang Hotel, South Building, 59 Maoming Nan Lu, Luwan* ☎ *021/6472–5494* ⌘ *Reservations essential* ▭ *AE, DC, MC, V* ✛ *C3.*

$ ✕ **Vedas.** In the heart of the Former French Concession, Vedas is a
INDIAN   popular destination for quality Indian food at affordable prices. Decor
★   is dark and comfortable. The menu focuses on northern Indian cuisine, and the hand-pulled naan bread, thick and succulent curries, fiery

Hot pot can be found in almost every city in China.

vindaloos, and house-made chutneys are excellent. Vedas is extremely popular, and always bustling. Don't expect an intimate, tranquil dining experience, but do expect spectacular food and great service. ✉ *550 Jianguo Xi Lu, Xuhui* ☎ *021/6445–8100* ✍ *Reservations essential* ▭ *AE, DC, MC, V* ✚ *A5.*

$–$$ ✕ **Vienna Café.** Coffee, cakes, and excellent breakfasts, Vienna is a
CAFÉ Shanghai institution, for those in the know. This is not a trendy café,
Fodor's Choice nor is it trying to be anything other than an Austrian coffeehouse. With
★ a wood-paneled main room and a tiny solarium, this is perfect setting for a Sunday breakfast. Try an Einspanner with the Sachertorte, and never mind the effects on your waistline. ✉ *25 Shaoxing Lu, near Ruijin Er Lu, Xuhui* ☎ *021/6445–2131* ▭ *No credit cards* ✚ *C4.*

NANJING XI LU AND JING'AN

$–$$ ✕ **1221.** This stylish but casual eatery is a favorite of hip Chinese and
SHANGHAINESE expatriate regulars. The dining room is streamlined chic, its crisp white
★ tablecloths contrasting with the warm golden walls. Shanghainese food is the mainstay, with a few Sichuan dishes. From the extensive 26-page menu (in English, pinyin, and Chinese), you can order dishes like sliced *you tiao* (fried bread sticks) with shredded beef, a whole chicken in a green-onion soy sauce, and *shaguo shizi tou* (pork meatballs). ✉ *1221 Yanan Xi Lu, Changning* ☎ *021/6213–6585 or 021/6213–2441* ✍ *Reservations essential* ▭ *AE, DC, MC, V* ✚ *A3.*

$ ✕ **Anna Maya Vegetarian Cafe.** This quaint café tucked away in the French
VEGETARIAN Concession has comfy furniture and Wi-Fi, making it a good place to kick back. Snack on fresh-squeeze juices, quiche, salads, soups, or a

great veggie burger. The vegan chocolate tofu cheesecake will satisfy even the most die-hard carnivore. ⊠ *3 Taojiang Lu, Luwan* ☎ *21/6433–4602* ✛ *B4.*

¢–$
VEGETARIAN
Fodor'sChoice
★

✕ **Gongdelin.** A two-story gold engraving of the Buddha pays tribute to the origins of the inventive vegetarian dishes this restaurant has served for 80 years. Chefs transform tofu into such surprising and tasty creations as mock duck, eel, and pork. The interior is just as inspired, with Ming-style wood-and-marble tables, metal latticework, and a soothing fountain. Tables fill up quickly after 6 pm, so either arrive early or buy some goodies to go at the take-out counter. ⊠ *445 Nanjing Xi Lu, Huangpu* ☎ *021/6327–0218* ▤ *AE, DC, MC, V* ✛ *D2.*

$$$–$$$$
ITALIAN
★

✕ **Issimo.** Located in the JIA hotel and run by Salvatore Cuomo, Issimo is a great (albeit upmarket) Italian restaurant. The food is well prepared and plentiful (all pastas are for two), and the ambience is as exquisite as a designer boutique venue should be. The menu is small and focused on seasonal offerings, and the wine list excellent. Reservations are recommended. ⊠ *JIA Shanghai, 2nd fl., 931 West Nanjing Lu, entrance on Taixing Lu, Jingan* ☎ *021/6287–9009* ▤ *AE, DC, MC, V* ✛ *C2.*

$
INDIAN

✕ **Masala Art.** A star of the Indian dining scene, Masala Art is a little hard to find but worth the effort. Serving excellent breads and sublime curries in an understated dining area, Masala Art wins praise for fine food at very reasonable prices. ⊠ *397 Dagu Lu, Jing'an* ☎ *021/6327–3571* ◬ *Reservations essential* ▤ *AE, DC, MC, V* ✛ *D3.*

$$$
SHANGHAINESE
Fodor'sChoice
★

✕ **Meilongzhen.** Probably Shanghai's most famous restaurant, Meilongzhen is one of the oldest dining establishments in town, dating from 1938. The building served as the Communist Party headquarters in the 1930s, and the traditional Chinese dining rooms still have their intricate woodwork and mahogany and marble furniture. The exhaustive menu has more than 80 seafood options, including such traditional Shanghainese fare as Mandarin fish, and dishes with a more Sichuan flair, like shredded spicy eel and prawns in chili sauce. Since this is a stop for most tour buses, expect a wait if you haven't booked ahead. ⊠ *No. 22, 1081 Nanjing Xi Lu, Jing'an* ☎ *021/6253–5353* ◬ *Reservations essential* ▤ *AE, DC, MC, V* ✛ *C2.*

$–$$
CANTONESE

✕ **The Onion.** On the high-traffic sector of Nanjing Xi Lu, Onion is a simple-concept Cantonese restaurant serving quality Cantonese dishes at reasonable prices. The decor is light and airy, with well-spaced tables and efficient service. The menu is extensive and bilingual, with lunch specials and dim sum. This is a very low-stress restaurant, and a great destination for a simple and satisfying meal. ⊠ *881 Nanjing Xi Lu, 3rd fl., Jing'an* ☎ *021/6267–5477* ▤ *No credit cards* ✛ *C2.*

$$–$$$
ITALIAN

✕ **Palladio.** As befits the showcase Italian restaurant at the Ritz, the award-winning Palladio is simply excellent. With a seasonal menu and positively obsequious service, this restaurant will always satisfy your senses—though it might also deplete your wallet. Set lunches begin at Y200, and dinners soar into the heady heights. ⊠ *Portman Ritz-Carlton, 1376 Nanjing Xi Lu, Jing'an* ☎ *021/6279–7188* ◬ *Reservations essential* ▤ *AE, DC, MC, V* ✛ *B2.*

$$$–$$$$
CANTONESE

✕ **Summer Pavilion.** Helmed by Ho Wing, the former chef of Hong Kong's famed Jockey Club, Summer Pavilion serves delicious Cantonese specialties ranging from simple dim sum to delicacies such as bird's-nest soup and abalone. As befits the Portman Ritz-Carlton, the restaurant's dining room is elegant, with black and gold accents and a raised platform that makes you feel as though you're center stage—a sense heightened by the attentive servers, who stand close at hand, but not too close, anticipating your needs. ⊠ *Portman Ritz-Carlton, 2nd fl., 1376 Nanjing Xi Lu, Jing'an* ☎ *021/6279–8888* ⌂ *Reservations essential* ▭ *AE, DC, MC, V* ✛ *B2.*

PUDONG

$$–$$$
CONTEMPORARY

✗ **Cloud 9.** Pudong can be an intimidating concrete jungle, with little respite in sight. If you're looking for refreshment on your Pudong safari, try Cloud 9 on the 87th floor of the Hyatt. Be aware, this is not a cheap lounge—there is a dress code, but the view is spectacular. Kick back and drink in the city laid out beneath you, while nibbling at their tasty Asian-inspired tapas and snacks. ⊠ *Grand Hyatt, 87th fl., 88 Shiji Dadao (Century Avenue), Pudong* ☎ *021/5049–1234* ⌂ *Reservations essential* ▭ *AE, DC, MC, V* ✛ *G2.*

$$–$$$
ITALIAN
★

✗ **Danieli's.** One of the finest Italian restaurants in the city, Danieli's is worth the commute to Pudong. The intimate dining area is spacious without being overwhelming, and the staff are very well trained. Their business lunch is famed for its speed and quality, but it is at dinner that Danieli's really shines. The menu is well balanced with seasonal dishes, and boasts an excellent five-course set menu. Prices can be expensive, especially for wine, but it is worth the money. ⊠ *St. Regis, 889 Dongfang Lu, Pudong* ☎ *021/5050–4567* ⌂ *Reservations essential.* ▭ *AE, DC, MC, V* ✛ *H3.*

$–$$
JAPANESE

✗ **Itoya.** The waitstaff's precision teamwork makes dining at Itoya a pleasure. Servers pause to greet all guests in unison. You're handed a hot towel upon sitting down and instantly after finishing your meal. The menu sticks to traditional Japanese fare: tempura, sushi, sashimi. In line with its location directly across from the Grand Hyatt's entrance, the restaurant also has several budget-busting items such as Kobe beef and lobster sashimi. ⊠ *178 Huayuan Shiqiao Lu, Pudong* ☎ *021/5882–9679* ▭ *AE, DC, MC, V* ✛ *H3.*

$$$$
INTERNATIONAL
Fodor'sChoice
★

✗ **Jade on 36.** This is a restaurant that must be experienced to be believed. Perched on the 36th floor of the Shangri-La tower, the Jade lounge/restaurant is simply beautiful, and offers great views of Pudong. There is no à la carte menu; instead, diners choose from a selection of set menus named simply by colors and sizes. The cuisine is innovative and extremely fresh, the service impeccable, and the view pleasant. Menus vary from five to eight courses, with an emphasis on fresh seafood and tender meats. The jumbo shrimp in a jar is especially enjoyable, as is the signature lemon tart. It's an expensive indulgence, but worth every penny. ⊠ *Pudong Shangri-La, 36th fl., 33 Fu Cheng Lu, Pudong* ☎ *021/6882–8888* ▭ *AE, DC, MC, V* ✛ *G3.*

$$$–$$$$
JAPANESE

✗ **Nadaman.** Sleekly elegant and stylized, Nadaman is modern Japanese dining taken to its extreme. The accents of raw granite merged into a formalized designer interior reflect the restaurant's origins in modern Tokyo, looking almost overdesigned. With a focus on freshness and

4

presentation, Nadaman gives diners superb cuisine at a price tag to match. The sushi is some of the finest in the city. ⊠ *Pudong Shangri-La, 2nd fl., 33 Fu Cheng Lu, Pudong* ☎ *021/6882–8888* ⚇ *Reservations essential* ▭ *AE, DC, MC, V* ✛ *G2.*

$$$

ECLECTIC

✕ **Yi Café.** Popular and busy, the Yi Café at the Shangri-La is an open-kitchen that serves a world of cuisines. The Yi Café is very popular with the Lujiazui business set, as well as local diners, for the quality and variety of the food. It's a great place to people-watch over a selection of the finest dishes Asia has to offer. This experience doesn't come cheap, at Y268 per person, but it's worth it. The restaurant slightly under-represents Western cuisine, focusing more on Asian dishes. ⊠ *Pudong Shangri-La, 2nd fl., 33 Fu Cheng Lu, Pudong* ☎ *021/6882–8888* ▭ *AE, DC, MC, V* ✛ *H3.*

HONGQIAO AND GUBEI

¢–$

TAIWANESE

✕ **Bellagio.** Taiwanese expatriates pack the bright, sunlit dining room of Bellagio for an authentic taste of home. Red fabric–covered chairs and black streamlined tables contrast with the white walls and decorative moldings. Waiters, chic in black sweaters, move efficiently between the closely spaced tables. The menu includes such traditional entrées as three-cup chicken, as well as 25 noodle dishes spanning all of Southeast Asia. Save room for dessert: shaved-ice snacks are obligatory Taiwanese treats, and come in 14 varieties. ⊠ *778 Huangjin Cheng Dao, by Gubei Lu, Changning* ☎ *021/6278–0722* ⚇ *Reservations not accepted* ▭ *AE, DC, MC, V* ✛ *G4.*

$–$$

CANTONESE

✕ **The Dynasty.** Although its cuisine is mostly Cantonese, Dynasty does serve some other regional fare, such as first-rate Peking duck and Sichuan-influenced hot-and-sour soup. The Cantonese seafood dishes, especially the prawns and lobster, are particularly good, and the shrimp *jiaozi* (dumplings) are delicious. Keyhole cutouts in the subdued pewter walls showcase Chinese vases and artifacts. Thick carpets mute any hotel noise, but the prices quickly remind you that this is indeed a hotel restaurant. ⊠ *Renaissance Yangtze, 2099 Yanan Xi Lu, Changning* ☎ *021/6275–0000* ⚇ *Reservations essential* ▭ *AE, DC, MC, V* ✛ *G4.*

$$–$$$

ITALIAN

★

✕ **Giovanni's.** Its Italian courtyard with a penthouse view provides a wonderful backdrop for Giovanni's traditional Italian fare. The antipasta and calamari are delicious, and the pastas are served perfectly al dente. Seasonal promotions keep the menu fresh. ⊠ *Sheraton Shanghai Hongqiao Hotel, 27th fl., 5 Zunyi Nan Lu, Changning* ☎ *021/6275–8888* ⚇ *Reservations essential* ▭ *AE, DC, MC, V* ✛ *G4.*

$–$$

MEXICAN

✕ **Mexico Lindo.** Fiery fare in a south-of-the-border setting has made Mexico Lindo Cantina & Grill the best entry on Shanghai's limited Mexican-dining scene. This Spanish-style casa is hidden off Hongmei Lu, down a tiny alley that's evolved into a well-respected restaurant row. In addition to tacos, fajitas, and quesadillas, the menu includes spicy prawns—rated three peppers—and a tasty one-pepper carnita pork burrito. A stairway mural depicts farm workers as well as fiesta revelers, whose ranks you can join with the eight margaritas and eight tequilas on the drink menu. ⊠ *Villa 1, 3911 Hongmei Lu, Changning* ☎ *021/6262–2797* ⚇ *Reservations essential* ▭ *AE, DC, MC, V* ✛ *G4.*

WHERE TO STAY

Shanghai's stature as China's business capital means that its hotels cater primarily to business clientele, though there are some boutique hotels that focus on leisure travelers. Business hotels can be divided into two categories: modern Western-style hotels that are elegant and nicely appointed and hotels built during the city's glory days, which became state-run after 1949. The latter may lack great service, modern fixtures, and convenient facilities, but they often make up for it in charm, tradition, history, and value.

Judging by the number of five-star and Western chain hotels now in Shanghai, the city has proven just how grandly it has opened to the outside world. The Grand Hyatt, JW Marriott, Westin, Portman and Pudong Ritz-Carltons, and St. Regis aren't merely hotels; they're landmarks on the Shanghai skyline. Even the historic properties that make up the other half of Shanghai's hotel market feel the pressure to update their rooms and facilities.

Use the coordinate (✣ B2) at the end of each listing to locate a site on the Where to Stay in Shanghai map.

RESERVATIONS AND RATES

Increasing competition means there are bargains to be had, especially during the low season from November through March. Avoid traveling during the three national holidays—Chinese New Year (mid-January to mid-February), Labor Day (May 1), and National Day (October 1)—when rooms and prices will be at a premium.

Rates are generally quoted for the room alone; breakfast, whether continental or full, is usually extra. All hotel prices listed here are based on high-season rates.

WHAT IT COSTS IN YUAN					
	¢	$	$$	$$$	$$$$
For Two People	under Y700	Y700–Y1,100	Y1,101–Y1,400	Y1,401–Y1,800	over Y1,800

Prices are for two people in a standard double room in high season, excluding 10%–15% service charge.

OLD CITY

$$$$ 🏨 **The Westin Shanghai.** With its distinctive room layouts, glittering glass staircase, and 90-plus works of art on display, the Westin Shanghai is a masterpiece near the majestic Bund. Crowne Deluxe rooms are miniature suites; sliding doors divide the sitting area, bathroom, and bedroom (the only problem is that all these divisions make the rooms feel on the small side). Luxurious amenities include rain-forest showers, extra deep tubs, and Westin's trademark Heavenly Beds. Pampering continues at the Banyan Tree spa, and the Sunday champagne brunch at the Stage restaurant is considered the best in town by Shanghai's glitterati. **Pros:** very attentive service. **Cons:** expensive for what you get; far from most shopping. ✉ *Bund Center, 88 Henan Zhonglu, Huangpu* ☎ *021/6335–1888 or*

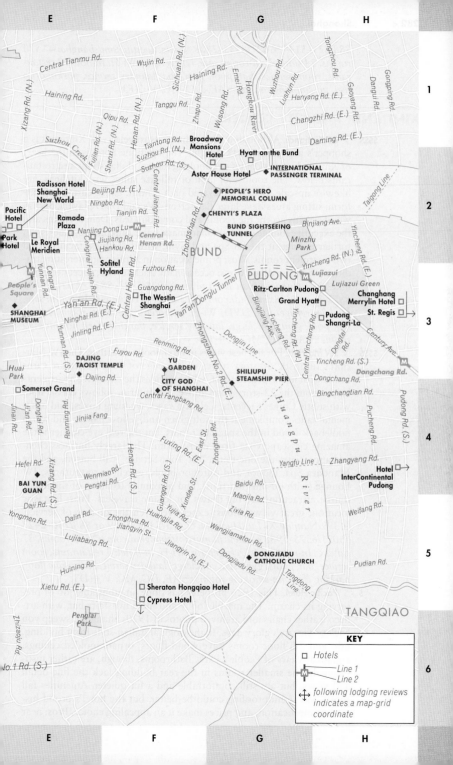

888/625–5144 🖷 *021/6335–2888* ⊕ *www.westin.com/shanghai* ⟲ *570 rooms, 24 suites* ☖ *In-room: safe, refrigerator, Wi-Fi. In-hotel: 3 restaurants, room service, bar, pool, gym, spa, laundry service, parking (no fee), no-smoking rooms* ⊟ *AE, DC, MC, V* ⊕ *F3.*

XINTIANDI AND CITY CENTER

$$$$ 🏙 **88 Xintiandi.** Although it targets business travelers, 88 Xintiandi is a shopper's and gourmand's delight. The boutique hotel is in the heart of Xintiandi, its balconies overlooking the top-dollar shops and restaurants below. The rooms, all mini or full-size suites with kitchens, are likewise upscale. Beds are elevated on a central, gauze-curtained platform; sitting areas have large flat-screen TVs and DVD players. Stylish wood screens accent the rooms and common areas. Deluxe rooms and the executive lounge overlook man-made Lake Taipingqiao. Guests can further indulge at the 88 Spa and Gym, with full fitness facilities and two treatment rooms. **Pros:** prime location in Xintiandi; interesting traditional Chinese decor. **Cons:** occasionally slack service; street noise gets in. ✉ *380 Huangpi Nan Lu, Luwan* ☎ *021/5383–8833* 🖷 *021/5353–8877* ⊕ *www.88xintiandi.com* ⟲ *12 suites, 41 rooms* ☖ *In-room: safe, kitchen, refrigerator, DVD, Wi-Fi. In-hotel: restaurant, room service, bar, pool, gym, concierge, laundry service, parking (fee), no-smoking rooms* ⊟ *AE, DC, MC, V* ⊕ *D4.*

$$$$ 🏙 **JW Marriott.** For the best views in Puxi, look no further. The JW Marriott's futuristic 60-story tower on the edge of People's Square turns heads with its 45-degree twist, which divides the executive apartments below from the 22-story hotel above. The interior follows classic lines with subtle Chinese accents. Celadon vases, wedding boxes, and ornamental jades complement the soft green-and-yellow palette and warm fiddleback wood in the spacious rooms, but the real eye-catcher is the amazing cityscape vista from every room. The largely business clientele appreciates the one-touch "At Your Service" call button, and the Mandara Spa, indoor and outdoor pools, excellent restaurants, JW Lounge (with 60-plus martinis), and proximity to many of the major tourist attractions are big draws for leisure travelers. **Pros:** fantastic location; great views. **Cons:** expensive given the quality of service. ✉ *399 Nanjing Xi Lu, Huangpu* ☎ *021/5359–4969 or 888/236–2427* 🖷 *021/6375–5988* ⊕ *www.jwmarriottshanghai.com* ⟲ *305 rooms, 37 suites* ☖ *In-room: safe, refrigerator, Wi-Fi. In-hotel: 3 restaurants, room service, bar, pools, gym, spa, concierge, laundry service, executive floor, parking (fee), no-smoking rooms* ⊟ *AE, DC, MC, V* ⊕ *D3.*

$ 🏙 **Pacific Hotel.** This 1926 property has done an admirable job of preserving its charm. The marble lobby and the downstairs bar, with art-deco leather chairs and archived photos of 1920s Shanghai, sweep you back to the city's glory days. In the original Italian-style front building, 6th- and 7th-floor rooms have wood floors, ornate molded ceilings, and great views of People's Park. Bathrooms, though, are rather institutional. The smaller rooms in the rear building lack the fine detail and views, but are still comfortable and a bit quieter. Amenities fall short, and soundproofing could be better, but the hotel's proud history, prime location, and prices make it an appealing choice. **Pros:** near

WHICH NEIGHBORHOOD?

Shanghai may have an excellent subway system and cheap, plentiful taxis, but if you want to take full advantage of Shanghai's popular tourist sights, restaurants, and nightlife, opt to stay in downtown **Puxi,** incorporating the quiet, leafy green Former French Concession, the historic promenade of the Bund, and the bustling shopping street of Nanjing Dong Lu. From these neighborhoods you'll have easy access to all of Shanghai's dynamic neighborhoods.

FORMER FRENCH CONCESSION
Sneak away from the city's frenetic energy in one of the historic hotels lining the Former French Concession's tree-lined streets. Excellent restaurants and shopping abound, and the neighborhood's relaxing atmosphere can be a nice break after a hectic day of sightseeing. A short cab or metro ride takes you straight to any of the city's sights on the Bund and Nanjing Dong Lu.

HONGQIAO DEVELOPMENT ZONE
Hongqiao is not a destination for leisure travelers. A combination of residential complexes and business offices, Hongqiao lacks many sights or restaurants. Unless business

brings you here or you have an early flight from the Hongqiao airport, there aren't many reasons to stay so far from the action.

THE BUND AND NANJING DONG LU
Breathtaking views of the Pudong skyline, skyscrapers juxtaposed with Victorian architecture, and easy access to great shopping and some of the city's best restaurants are just a few reasons to stay here. Best of all, most major sites, from the Bund to the Shanghai Museum, are all within comfortable walking distance. If you want to see modern Shanghai, this is the place to be.

PUDONG
Although Pudong—with its shiny new skyscrapers and wide boulevards—can feel impersonal, and it's too far from downtown Puxi for some, it has some of the city's best hotels, all close to Pudong International Airport. Phenomenal views of the Bund are a major bonus. But if you stay here, be prepared to spend at least 30 minutes shuttling back and forth to Puxi (and it could take even longer during rush hour, as millions of locals compete to flag down taxis or squeeze into subway cars).

People's Park. **Cons:** erratic service; aging property. ⊠ *108 Nanjing Xi Lu, Huangpu* ☎ *021/6327–6226* 🖹 *021/6372–3634* ☞ *177 rooms, 5 suites* ⚃ *In-room: safe (some), refrigerator, Internet. In-hotel: restaurant, room service, bars, spa, laundry service, parking (fee).* ▭ *AE, DC, MC, V* ✛ *E2.*

\$\$ 🍴 **Park Hotel** *(Guoji Fandian).* Once Shanghai's tallest building, the 20-story Park Hotel is now dwarfed on the Puxi skyline and eclipsed by other hotels whose glory days are present instead of past. Recently named a China Cultural Heritage Site, this 1934 art-deco structure overlooking People's Park still has great views and a musty charm, particularly in its restored marble lobby. Rooms are clean and bright, with prints of historic buildings from around the world. But bathrooms are tiny, and the hotel's limited English service and facilities have definitely slipped to second-rate. **Pros:** central location; heritage property. **Cons:** aging rooms; inadequate service. ⊠*170 Nanjing Xi Lu, Huangpu* ☎*021/6327–5225* ☐*021/6327–6958* ⊷*225 rooms, 25 suites* ⚴ *In-room: safe, refrigerator, Wi-Fi. In-hotel: 3 restaurants, bars, gym, concierge, laundry service, parking (no fee), no-smoking rooms* ⊟*AE, DC, MC, V* ✛*E2.*

$$$$ ⊡ **Radisson Hotel Shanghai New World.** A prominent figure not only on People's Square, but also on the Shanghai skyline, the flying-saucer dome-topped Radisson New World is best known for its revolving restaurant, Epicure on 45. Rooms are divided between the lower Park Tower and the higher City Tower. Park Tower rooms are more expensive but have the best views, facing People's Square. Though the hotel caters primarily to business travelers, suites—each with a huge living room, kitchen/dining room, and spacious bath—are convenient for families. In addition, most rooms have flat-screen TVs. Many travelers still prefer the tranquil garden setting of the Radisson's Xingguo hotel in the French Concession, but it cannot compete with the New World's central location and city views. ■TIP➔ Ask about special weekend packages. **Pros:** prime location. **Cons:** dark decor; taxis not readily available. ⊠*88 Nanjing Xi Lu, Huangpu* ☎*021/6359–9999* ☐*021/6358–9705* ⊕*www.radisson.com/shanghaicn_newworld* ⊷*429 rooms, 91 suites* ⚴ *In-room: safe, refrigerator, Internet. In-hotel: 3 restaurants, room service, bar, pool, gym, spa, concierge, laundry service, parking (fee), no-smoking rooms* ⊟*AE, DC, MC, V* ✛*E2.*

$$$ ⊡ **Somerset Grand.** Designed as serviced apartments for expats, the Somerset Grand's suites are great for families wanting extra space plus the usual hotel amenities. The twin 34-story towers have 334 one- to three-bedroom suites, ranging from 82 to 232 square meters (890 to 2,500 square feet). (One-bedroom suites have only one king-size bed.) The units feel homey, with blue-and-pink floral comforters and rugs and a small kitchen. Kids can burn off steam at the pool and in the playroom. There's a great French restaurant and coffee shop on the grounds; the hotel is two blocks from the restaurants and shops at Xintiandi and 10 minutes from the subway. **Pros:** suites; good for kids. **Cons:** institutional decor. ⊠*8 Jinan Lu, Luwan* ☎*021/6385–6888* ☐*021/6384–8988* ⊕*www.the-ascott.com* ⊷*334 suites* ⚴ *In-room: safe, kitchen, refrigerator, Internet. In-hotel: tennis courts, pool, gym, concierge, laundry facilities, laundry service, parking (fee), no-smoking rooms* ⊟*AE, DC, MC, V* ✛*E4.*

THE BUND AND NANJING DONG LU

$$$$ ⊡ **Hyatt on the Bund.** At the North End of the Bund near the banks of the ★ Suzhou River, the Hyatt on the Bund offers beautifully appointed rooms in an airy and modern building. This location will only improve as the government continues its modernization of the Bund, but for now it is a little awkward on its own. However, the main Bund is just a short walk across the bridge, and the Hyatt on the Bund is reasonably accessible to most of the city. **Pros:** beautiful facilities; excellent restaurant. **Cons:** rather bland neighborhood; can be difficult to get taxis. ✉ *199 Huangpu Lu, near Wuchang Lu and the Bund, Bund* ☎ *021/6393–1234* 🖷 *021/6393–1313* ⊕ *www.shanghai.bund.hyatt.com* 🛏 *600 rooms, 31 suites* ⚬ *In-room: safe, refrigerator, Internet. In-hotel: 4 restaurants, room service, bars, pool, gym, spa, laundry service, executive floor, airport shuttle, no-smoking rooms* ▭ *AE, DC, MC, V* ✛ *G2.*

$$$$
Fodor'sChoice
★

🏨 **Le Royal Meridien.** Dominating the foot of the Nanjing Pedestrian Street, the Meridien has changed the face of Puxi hospitality. High ceilings, massive rooms, excellent amenities, and attentive staff make this a premium destination. Ask for a park view—the "Bund" view overlooks four blocks of run-down Shanghai, but the view over People's Park is simply wonderful. However, the large banks of small elevators can make navigating the hotel's many levels a little frustrating. **Pros:** location; excellent facilities. **Cons:** service hiccups; annoying elevator system. ✉ *505 Nanjing Dong Lu, Huangpu* ☎ *021/3318–9999* ⊕ *www. lemeridien.com.cn* 🛏 *646 rooms, 115 suites* ⚬ *In-room: safe, refrigerator, Internet. In-hotel: 4 restaurants, room service, bars, pool, gym, spa, laundry service, executive floor, airport shuttle, parking (fee), no-smoking rooms* ▭ *AE, DC, MC, V* ✛ *E2.*

$$$–$$$$
Fodor'sChoice
★

🏨 **Ramada Plaza.** With its ornate lobby resembling a European opera house, the Ramada Plaza Shanghai brings a touch of grandeur to the Nanjing Road pedestrian walkway. Statues of Greek gods reign from atop intricate inlaid tables. Soaring marble columns direct the eye skyward to a stained-glass skylight. Although the fair-sized rooms lack great views, they do face in toward a dramatic atrium, topped by yet another and the executive lounge. An indoor swimming pool, one of the largest in Shanghai, is housed inside an addition reminiscent of an ancient Chinese palace. **Pros:** location; you can usually get a room for less than the rack rate if you inquire while reserving. **Cons:** no views. ✉ *719 Nanjing Dong Lu, Huangpu* ☎ *021/6350–0000 or 800/854–7854* 🖷 *021/6350–6666* ⊕ *www.ramadainternational.com* 🛏 *376 rooms, 36 suites* ⚬ *In-room: safe, Wi-Fi. In-hotel: 4 restaurants, room service, bar, pool, gym, spa, concierge, laundry service, executive floor, parking (no fee), no-smoking rooms, Internet* ▭ *AE, DC, MC, V* ✛ *E2.*

$$$

🏨 **Sofitel Hyland.** Directly on the Nanjing Road pedestrian mall, the Sofitel Hyland is a convenient base for shopping and exploring the city center and the Bund. The rooms in this 30-story French-managed hotel are somewhat small, but have been spruced up with prints of Chinese emperors and small replicas of terra-cotta warrior statues. The top-floor Sky Lounge serves Sunday brunch with views of the Bund and downtown, and Le Pub 505 brews up its own beer. **Pros:** location. **Cons:** small rooms and poor frontage. ✉ *505 Nanjing Dong Lu, Huangpu* ☎ *021/6351–5888*

> **DRINK AND A VIEW**
>
> Check out the spectacular Vue bar at the Hyatt on the Bund and enjoy expansive vistas and rooftop hot tub.

Le Royal Meridien

JIA Shanghai

🕾 *021/6351–4088* ⊕ *www.accorhotels-asia.com* 🛏 *299 rooms, 73 suites* ⚿ *In-room: safe, refrigerator, Internet. In-hotel: 3 restaurants, room service, bars, pool, gym, spa, laundry service, executive floor, airport shuttle, parking (fee), no-smoking rooms* ☰ *AE, DC, MC, V* ✢ *E2.*

FORMER FRENCH CONCESSION

$$ 🏨 **Anting Villa Hotel.** Two blocks from the metro and the Hengshan Road nightlife district, the Anting Villa Hotel is a convenient and surprisingly quiet retreat tucked away down a small side street. Superior rooms in the 10-story hotel tower have been refurbished in a "Spanish style" with garishly bright red pillowcases and leather-covered furniture; some rooms now come with flat-screen TVs. It's worth it to pay a little extra for a garden-view room with vistas of the cedar-shaded grounds and namesake 1932 Spanish-style villa. Although English service is limited, the hotel's staff are eager and friendly. **Pros:** central location; eager-to-please service. **Cons:** a little faded; can be hard to communicate. ✉ *46 Anting Lu, Xuhui* 🕾 *021/6433–1188* 🖷 *021/6433–9726* ⊕ *antingvilla. sinohotel.com* 🛏 *135 rooms, 11 suites* ⚿ *In-room: safe, refrigerator, Wi-Fi. In-hotel: restaurant, room service, gym, laundry service, parking (no fee), no-smoking rooms* ☰ *AE, DC, MC, V* ✢ *A5.*

$$$$ 🏨 **Crowne Plaza.** This hotel on the far western side of the Former French Concession makes up for its out-of-the-way location with service. The staff here are among the friendliest in town, and makes guests, mostly business travelers, feel at home. Though the hotel's rooms are not as elegant as those of its competitors, it does have the biggest club lounge in Shanghai, with a mezzanine floor and a sleek black marble-topped bar. **Pros:** good service; amenity-packed. **Cons:** you'll need taxis to get to and from the hotel. ✉ *400 Panyu Lu, Xuhui* 🕾 *021/6280–8888 or 800/227–6963* ⊕ *www.shanghai.crowneplaza.com* 🛏 *488 rooms, 12 suites* ⚿ *In-room: safe, kitchen (some), refrigerator, Internet. In-hotel: 4 restaurants, room service, bars, pool, gym, executive floor, parking (no fee), no-smoking rooms* ☰ *AE, DC, MC, V* ✢ *A4.*

$$$ 🏨 **Donghu Hotel.** Just off the frenzied shopping street of Huaihai Road, the Donghu Hotel remains one of Shanghai's best-preserved hotels from the city's 1920s heyday. The hotel's seven buildings have a surprising array of restaurants—Korean barbecue and Japanese in addition to the standard Chinese and Western fare—an indoor pool, and a wide variety of room options. "Superior" rooms in Building 7 don't quite live up to their title, and are simply furnished with twin beds and rather mismatched yellow wallpaper and red carpet. We suggest the Donghu deluxe rooms across the street at Building 1; with their traditional Chinese furniture and dark-wood paneling, these spacious rooms make you feel as if you've stepped back in time. **Pros:** traditional and elegant; numerous dining options. **Cons:** poor service and upkeep. ✉ *70 Donghu Lu, Xuhui* 🕾 *021/6415–8158* ⊕ *www.donghuhotel.com* 🛏 *240 rooms, 30 suites* ⚿ *In-room: safe (some), Wi-Fi. In-hotel: 6 restaurants, room service, pool, gym, concierge, laundry service, parking (fee), Internet* ☰ *AE, DC, MC, V* ✢ *B4.*

$$$–$$$$ 🏨 **Jing An Hotel.** The weekly chamber-music concert in its lobby is just one example of how the Jing An Hotel has retained its elegance

and charm after 70 years. In a 1½-acre garden, the Spanish-style main building's lobby has beautiful stained-glass windows. The ornate upstairs dining rooms often host prominent city officials. Although facilities are lacking compared to the newer hotels in town, and the rooms in the Jing An New Building should be avoided at all costs (bathrooms are barely the size of

> ### SIZE MATTERS
>
> Elaborately carved wooden door frames and lintels (at Jing An Hotel) direct the eye upward toward the 10-foot (3-meter) ceilings that make for some of the most spacious hotel rooms in Shanghai.

a closet), the hotel's proximity to the subway line and its lush Former French Concession setting make this hotel a lovely respite from Shanghai's crowded sidewalks. **Pros:** near public transportation; beautiful surroundings. **Cons:** poorly maintained facilities; inconsistent service. ⊠ *370 Huashan Lu, Xuhui* ☎ *021/6248–0088* 🖷 *021/6249–6100* ⊕ *www.jinganhotel.net* ⤳ *210 rooms, 17 suites* ⚷ *In-room: safe, refrigerator, Internet. In-hotel: 2 restaurants, room service, bars, gym, concierge, laundry service, airport shuttle, parking (fee), no-smoking rooms* ▭ *AE, DC, MC, V* ✛ *A3.*

$$$$ 🏨 **Okura Garden Hotel.** Its parklike setting in the heart of the French Concession makes this 33-story Garden Hotel a favorite Shanghai retreat, especially for Japanese travelers familiar with the Okura Group name. The first three floors, which were once old Shanghai's French Club, have been restored, with cascading chandeliers, frescoes, and art-deco details at every turn. Average-size standard rooms are simply furnished with silk wallpaper and European-style furniture, and, unlike deluxe rooms and suites, lack flat-screen TVs. The romantic third-floor terrace bar overlooks the two-acre garden, and the Japanese and French restaurants serve excellent but high-priced food. For those who want to stay connected, cell phones are available for rent at the concierge desk. **Pros:** gorgeous surroundings; near French Concession and Nanjing Xi Lu. **Cons:** you'll pay a hefty fee for all the beauty. ⊠ *58 Maoming Nan Lu, Luwan* ☎ *021/6415–1111* ⊕ *www.gardenhotelshanghai. com* ⤳ *478 rooms, 22 suites* ⚷ *In-room: safe, refrigerator, Internet. In-hotel: 5 restaurants, room service, bars, tennis courts, pool, gym, concierge, laundry service, executive floor, airport shuttle, parking (no fee), no-smoking rooms* ▭ *AE, DC, MC, V* ✛ *C3.*

$ 🏨 **Old House Inn.** Hidden down a small lane, Old House Inn is one of
Fodor's Choice   Shanghai's few boutique hotels, and a must if you're looking for a
★   personalized experience that the larger hotels just can't offer. What this tiny gem lacks in amenities (there's no elevator, gym, concierge, or business facilities), it makes up for with its authentic Chinese style and charm. All rooms are decorated with antique dark-wood furniture and traditional porcelains, and the friendly staff are so eager to please that they'll even run down to the end of the lane and find you a taxi. Adjacent to the hotel is the swanky Purple Onion restaurant, popular with both expats and trendy locals for its fantastic patio. ■TIP➔ **Book well in advance to snag one of the moderately priced king-size rooms. Pros:** quaint and quiet; extremely helpful staff. **Cons:** small; limited services.

✉ *No. 16, Lane 351, Huashan Lu, Xuhui* ☎ *021/6248–6118* ⊕ *www. oldhouse.cn* 🛏 *12 rooms* ⚒ *In-room: safe, refrigerator, Internet. In-hotel: no elevator, restaurant, bar, laundry service, parking (no fee)* ▭ *AE, DC, MC, V* ✛ *A3.*

$$$$ 🏨 **Regal International East Asia Hotel.** Its exclusive Shanghai International Tennis Center is the Regal's trump card among five-star hotels. The center has 10 tournament courts as well as one of the city's best health clubs (it's not only huge, but all cardio machines come with personal TVs). The spacious rooms were renovated in 2005 and have flat-screen TVs. Club rooms have a curvilinear desk and ergonomic chair and a funky chaise longue; deluxe rooms have compact bathrooms with marble sinks and huge mirrors. The Hengshan Road metro station and the bar and restaurant district are just a block away, but there's plenty of entertainment downstairs at the hotel's 12-lane bowling alley and gorgeous Fragrance Chinese restaurant. **Pros:** easy access to public transportation and entertainment; lots of activities for nights you want to stay in. **Cons:** on a high-traffic bar street. ✉ *516 Hengshan Lu, Xuhui* ☎ *021/6415–5588* ⊕ *www.regal-eastasia.com* 🛏 *278 rooms, 22 suites* ⚒ *In-room: safe, DVD (some), Internet. In-hotel: 3 restaurants, room service, bar, tennis courts, pool, gym, concierge, executive floor, parking (no fee), no-smoking rooms, Wi-Fi* ▭ *AE, DC, MC, V* ✛ *A5.*

$$$–$$$$ 🏨 **Ruijin Guest House.** Formerly the Morriss Estate, the Ruijin show-
★ cases how opulently *taipans* (expatriate millionaire businessmen) lived in Shanghai's heyday of the 1930s. Rooms within the two preserved villas—No. 1 and Old No. 3—are rich with detail: high ceilings, ornate plaster moldings, bamboo-etched glass. The two other buildings are significantly shorter on charm but still overlook the verdant grounds, which are shared with several top-notch restaurants (as well as the once-hip Face bar) and provide direct access to the bars on Maoming Road. New No. 3 may lack the historic cachet of the other buildings, but its standard rooms, which come with a king-size bed and hot tub, are definitely a steal. **Pros:** location. **Cons:** inconsistent facilities and service. ✉ *118 Ruijin Er Lu, Luwan* ☎ *021/6472–5222* 🖷 *021/6473–2277* ⊕ *www.shedi.net.cn/outedi/ruijin* 🛏 *62 rooms, 20 suites* ⚒ *In-room: safe, refrigerator, Internet. In-hotel: restaurant, room service, bars, laundry service, parking (no fee), no-smoking rooms* ▭ *AE, DC, MC, V* ✛ *C4.*

NANJING XI LU AND JING'AN

$$$$ 🏨 **The Four Seasons.** With palm trees, fountains, and golden-hued marble as warm as sunshine, the lobby of the Four Seasons establishes the hotel's theme as an elegant oasis in bustling downtown Puxi. Opened in 2002, this 37-story luxury hotel caters to its largely business clientele. It has impeccable service, a 24-hour business center, a gym, and butler service. The spacious rooms—just 12 to 15 per floor—include DVD/CD players, flat-screen TVs, safes big enough for a laptop, and

marble showers and tubs (one of each). Nanjing Road and the Shanghai Museum are within a 10-minute walk, but there are convincing reasons to stay in: the Jazz 37 club, the exceptional Si Ji Xuan Cantonese restaurant, and the relaxing ground-floor lounge that's perfect for people watching. ■TIP→ you don't want to miss one of the spa's indulgent Balinese treatments. **Pros:** beautiful building; amenity- and entertainment-heavy. **Cons:** amenities may discourage you from getting out of the hotel. ⊠ *500 Weihai Lu, Jing'an* ☎ *021/6256–8888 or 800/819–5053* 🖷 *021/6256–5678* ⊕ *www.fourseasons.com* 🛏 *360 rooms, 79 suites* ⌂ *In-room: safe, refrigerator, DVD, Internet, Wi-Fi. In-hotel: 4 restaurants, room service, bar, pool, gym, spa, concierge, laundry service, executive floor, parking (fee), no-smoking rooms, Wi-Fi* ⊟ *AE, DC, MC, V* ✛ *C3.*

$$$$ **JIA Shanghai.** Discreetly housed in a vintage ar- deco building on Nanjing Xi Lu, JIA's unprepossessing exterior masks its elegant and styled interior. The 55 rooms and suites are thoughtfully designed and just a touch over the top, making a stay in JIA an experience in itself. Every room is equipped with a kitchenette or kitchen for a pleasant, homey experience. Service is very good for China, though not quite world-class yet. Generally, the experience is smooth and unobtrusive, welcoming guests without destroying the sense of comfortable privacy. Issimo, the in-house restaurant, is genuinely extraordinary, with impeccable interiors and superb food. The service is impeccable and the menu small but very well thought out. **Pros:** exquisite design and unique setting; kitchenettes; privacy. **Cons:** no pool; no business center. ⊠ *931 West Nan Jing Lu, near Tai Xing Lu (entrance on Tai Xing Lu), Jing'an* ☎ *021/6217–9000* 🛏 *55 rooms* ⌂ *In-room: kitchenette, refrigerator, DVD, Internet, Wi-Fi. In-hotel: restaurant, room service, bar, gym, laundry facilities, laundry service, public Wi-Fi, airport limo, no parking* ⊟ *AE, D, DC, MC, V* ✛ *C2.*

Fodor's Choice ★

$$$$ 🔲 **The Portman Ritz-Carlton.** Outstanding facilities and a prime location in the Shanghai Center have made the Portman Ritz-Carlton one of the city's top attractions since its opening in 1998. The 50-story hotel devotes three floors solely to its fitness center and another four to its executive club rooms. The two-story lobby—a popular networking spot and the location of the best afternoon tea in town—exudes cool refinement with its ebony, marble, and chrome touches. In addition to the Shanghai Center's surrounding shops, banks, airline offices, and restaurants, the hotel has its own deli and four top-notch restaurants. **Pros:** renovated in 2008 with plasma TVs, DVD players, and improved decor; superb location. **Cons:** very expensive; uneven service. ⊠ *1376 Nanjing Xi Lu, Jing'an* ☎ *021/6279–8888 or 800/241–3333* 🖷 *021/6279–8887* ⊕ *www.ritzcarlton.com* 🛏 *510 rooms, 68 suites* ⌂ *In-room: safe, refrigerator, Internet. In-hotel: 4 restaurants, room service, bars, tennis court, pool, gym, concierge, laundry service, executive floor, parking (fee), no-smoking rooms* ⊟ *AE, DC, MC, V* ✛ *B2.*

$$$$ **URBN.** Innovatively designed and environmentally friendly, URBN is Shanghai's first carbon-neutral hotel. Made with environmentally sensitive technology and recycled materials, URBN is a truly unique place to stay. The staff is attentive and well trained, making guests feel at home

Fodor's Choice ★

from the moment they step into the hotel's tree-shaded courtyard. The design is superb, with a leather-encased reception desk, slate decor, and a quiet, private bar on the top floor. URBN provides a wide variety of alternative entertainments, including Chinese cookery, calligraphy and tai chi classes, bike tours, and yoga lessons. **Pros:** eco-friendly; luxe setting, some of the best cocktails in town; elegant design. **Cons:** not terribly suitable for mobility-impaired guests. ⊠ *183 Jiaozhou Lu, near Beijing Xi Lu, Jing'an* ☎ *021/5153–4600* 🖶 *021/5153–4610* ⊕ *www.urbnhotels.com* 🛏 *24 rooms, 2 suites* ♿ *In-room: safe, refrigerator, DVD, Internet. In-hotel: 1 restaurant, room service, bar, laundry service, executive floor, no-smoking rooms, Wi-Fi* ⊟ *AE, DC, MC, V* ✛ *B2.*

PUDONG

4

¢–$ 🏨 **Changhang Merrylin Hotel.** The Merrylin Corporation is better known throughout China for its restaurants than its hotels, and Changhang Merrylin Hotel's exceptional Chinese restaurant overshadows its fair-size inexpensive rooms. Decor aspires to European grandeur, but comes off as amusingly tacky. Reliefs and golden statues of frolicking nymphs dominate the lobby, and rooms are decked out in gold-flecked wallpaper and crackled white-painted fixtures. Service can be brusque, but the hotel is within three blocks of the 10-story Next Age Department Store and metro Line 2 to Puxi. **Pros:** inexpensive; convenient to shopping and public transportation; delicious food in the restaurant. **Cons:** poor service. ⊠ *818 Zhangyang Lu, Pudong* ☎ *021/5835–5555* 🖶 *021/5835–7799* 🛏 *192 rooms, 32 suites* ♿ *In-room: refrigerator, Internet (some). In-hotel: 3 restaurants, room service, bar, concierge, laundry service, airport shuttle, parking (fee)* ⊟ *AE, DC, MC, V* ✛ *H3.*

$$$$ 🏨 **Grand Hyatt.** Views, views, views are what this hotel is all about—
★ occupying floors 53 through 87 of the spectacular Jin Mao Tower, the Grand Hyatt's interior is defined by art-deco lines juxtaposed with Space Age grillwork and sleek furnishings and textures. The 33-story central atrium is a marvel in itself—a seemingly endless cylinder with an outer-space aura. Room amenities are space age as well: CAT 5 optical lines for laptop use; Internet connections on the flat-screen TV through a cordless keyboard; and three high-pressure shower heads in the bathroom. Views from the rooms are spectacular; corner rooms have two walls of pure glass for endless panoramas of the Oriental Pearl Tower, the majesty of the Bund, and the expanse of the city below. ■ TIP➔ But watch out—being that high up puts you literally in the clouds and at the mercy of Shanghai's foggy weather. **Pros:** beautiful rooms; hi-tech amenities make you feel like you're already in the future; fantastic city views. **Cons:** extremely pricey; no guarantee of clear views. ⊠ *Jin Mao Dasha, 88 Shiji Dadao (Century Avenue), Pudong* ☎ *021/5049–1234 or 800/233–1234* ⊕ *www.shanghai.grand.hyatt.com* 🛏 *510 rooms, 45 suites* ♿ *In-room: safe, refrigerator, Internet, Wi-Fi. In-hotel: 5 restaurants, room service, bars, pool, gym, spa, concierge, laundry service, executive floor, parking (fee), parking (no fee)* ⊟ *AE, DC, MC, V* ✛ *H3.*

$$$$ 🏨 **Hotel InterContinental Pudong.** The pièce de résistance of the 24-story InterContinental is a nearly 200-foot-high Italian Renaissance–inspired atrium, decorated with red Chinese lanterns, that shines natural light

onto the 19 guest floors, six of which are executive floors. A vivid coat of red livens up the hallways and spacious guest rooms, which all have separate tub and shower. The restaurants cater to a wide range of tastes: Japanese, Cantonese, Shanghainese, Chaozhou, and continental. The open kitchen of Level One restaurant turns out a great lunch buffet with samples of all those cuisines. **Pros:** well priced for its amenities. **Cons:** not the best location for exploration on foot. ⊠ *777 Zhangyang Lu, Pudong* ☎ *021/5831–8888 or 800/327–0200* 🖷 *021/5831–7777* ⊕ *www.shanghai.intercontinental.com* ↝ *317 rooms, 78 suites* ⚒ *In-room: safe, refrigerator, Internet. In-hotel: 4 restaurants, room service, bar, pool, gym, concierge, laundry service, executive floor, parking (fee), no-smoking rooms* ▤ *AE, DC, MC, V* ✛ *H4.*

$$$$
Fodor's Choice
★

▣ **Pudong Shangri-La.** The Shangri-La occupies one of the most prized spots in Shanghai: overlooking the Huangpu River, opposite the Bund, near the Pearl Tower in Lujiazui. The hotel's breathtaking water's-edge views, white-glove service, and spacious rooms attract a mix of business and leisure travelers. The Shangri-La's two towers comprise the largest luxury hotel in Shanghai, with almost 1,000 guest rooms and 10 dining choices. Although rooms in Tower 2, behind the original hotel, come with 32-inch plasma TVs, DVD players, and fax machines, many return guests still prefer the rooms in Tower 1 for their gloriously unobstructed views of the Bund. **Pros:** fantastic property; good restaurants. **Cons:** expensive; not ideal for nonbusiness travelers. ⊠ *33 Fucheng Lu, Pudong* ☎ *021/6882–8888 or 800/942–5050* 🖷 *021/6882–6688* ⊕ *www.shangri-la.com* ↝ *916 rooms, 65 suites* ⚒ *In-room: safe, refrigerator, Internet. In-hotel: 8 restaurants, room service, bars, tennis court, pools, gym, spa, concierge, laundry service, executive floor, parking (fee), no-smoking rooms* ▤ *AE, DC, MC, V* ✛ *H3.*

$$$$

▣ **Ritz-Carlton Pudong.** The Ritz boasts a 55th-floor spa with staggering views of the Huangpu River and the entire Puxi skyline, an Italian restaurant called SCENA, and a rooftop bar called Flair that's such a good lookout point you may never want to leave the hotel. Service is impeccable, with prices to match. It's located next to the shiny, new ifc mall, which houses city'super, a high-end Hong Kong grocery chain in its basement. **Pros:** located above the Lujiazui Line 2 metro station and next to ifc mall; easy access to financial center; great views. **Cons:** though only one metro stop from downtown, still feels far away. ⊠ *8 Shiji Dadao (Century Avenue), Lujiazui* ☎ *021/2020–1888* ⊕ *www. ritzcarlton.com* ↝ *285 rooms* ⚒ *In-room: a/c, phone, safe, kitchen (some), refrigerator (some), DVD, Internet, Wi-Fi. In-hotel: 3 restaurants, room service, bar, pool, gym, spa, laundry facilities, laundry service, Internet terminal, Wi-Fi hotspot, parking (paid), some pets allowed* ▤ *MC, V, DC, AE* ✛ *H3.*

$$$$
Fodor's Choice
★

▣ **St. Regis.** Every guest is a VIP at the St. Regis. The amphitheater-like lobby sets the stage for the most indulgent hotel experience in Shanghai. The 318 rooms in this 40-story red-granite tower—its design lauded by *Architectural Digest*—spare no expense, with Bose wave radios, Herman Miller Aeron chairs, and rain-forest showers that give you the feeling of being under a waterfall. At 500 square feet (46 square meters), standard rooms compare to other hotels' suites. The two women-only

URBN

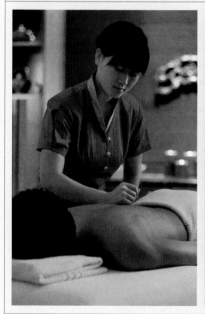

Pudong Shangri-La

St. Regis

Spa Treatments

Around Shanghai are hundreds of blind massage parlors, inexpensive no-frills salons whose blind masseurs are closely attuned to the body's soft and sore spots. Be careful you haven't wandered into a brothel, though! At the other end of the spectrum lie the hotel spas, luxurious retreats where pampering is at a premium. Here are just a few of the massage outlets in Shanghai that can attend to your needs.

The **Banyan Tree Spa** (✉ *Westin Shanghai, 88 Henan Zhong Lu, 3rd fl., Huangpu* ☎ *021/6335–1888* ⊕ *www. banyantreespa.com*), the first China outpost of this ultraluxurious spa chain, occupies the third floor of the Westin Shanghai. The spa's 13 chambers as well as its treatments are designed to reflect *wu sing,* the five elemental energies of Chinese philosophy: earth, gold, water, wood, and fire. Relax and enjoy one of five different massages (Y850 plus service charge), facials, body scrubs, or indulgent packages that combine all three.

With instructions clearly spelled out in English, **Double Rainbow Massage House** (✉ *47 Yongjia Lu, Luwan* ☎ *021/6473–4000*) provides a cheap (Y45–Y80), nonthreatening introduction to traditional Chinese massage. Choose a masseur, state your preference for soft, medium, or hard massage, then keep your clothes on for a 45- to 90-minute massage. There's no ambience, just a clean room with nine massage tables.

Dragonfly (✉ *20 Donghu Lu, Xuhui* ☎ *021/5405–0008* ⊕ *www. dragonfly.com.cn*) is one in a chain of therapeutic retreat centers that has claimed the middle ground between expensive hotel spas and workmanlike blind-man massage parlors. Don the suede-soft treatment robes for traditional Chinese massage (Y155) or take them off for an aromatic oil massage (Y252).

The Three on the Bund complex includes the first **Evian Spa** (✉ *Three on the Bund, Zhongshan Dong Yi Lu, Huangpu* ☎ *021/6321–6622* ⊕ *www. threeonthebund.com*) outside of France. Its 14 theme rooms offer treatments from head to toe, and nine different massages and a detox package (Y1,300) will ease the effects of pollution and late-night Shanghai partying.

With its exposed wood beams, unpolished bricks, and soothing fountains, the **Mandara Spa** (✉ *399 Nanjing Xi Lu, Huangpu 200003* ☎ *021/5359– 4969* ⊕ *www.mandaraspa.com*) in the JW Marriott resembles a traditional Chinese water town. Face, beauty, and body treatments include the spa's signature Mandara massage, a 75-minute treatment in which two therapists administer a blend of five massage styles: Shiatsu, Thai, Lomi Lomi, Swedish, and Balinese.

Ming Massage (✉ *298 Wulumuqi Nan Lu, Xuhui* ☎ *021/5465–2501*) is a Japanese-style salon that caters to women, who receive a 20% discount daily from 11 to 4. Cross over the footbridge to one of five small treatment rooms for a foot, body, or combination "Ming" massage (Y178).

floors are unique in Shanghai. Butlers address all your needs 24/7 (you can even contact them by e-mail), from in-room check-in to room service, and as part of a new program they can arrange to escort guests personally to visit local artists' studios. The hotel's location—15 minutes from the riverfront—is a drawback, but the fitness center and 24-hour gym, along with the remarkable Danieli's Italian restaurant, add to this pampering property's appeal. **Pros:** beautiful; service will make you feel like visiting royalty. **Cons:** far away from downtown. ⊠ *889 Dongfang Lu, Pudong* ☎ *021/5050–4567 or 800/325–3589* 📠 *021/6875–6789* ⊕ *www.stregis.com/shanghai* ⤵ *274 rooms, 44 suites* ⚘ *In-room: safe, refrigerator, Internet, Wi-Fi. In-hotel: 3 restaurants, room service, bars, tennis court, pool, gym, spa, concierge, laundry service, parking (fee), no-smoking rooms* ⊟ *AE, DC, MC, V* ⊹ *H3.*

4

NORTH SHANGHAI

$$ 🏨 **Astor House Hotel.** The oldest hotel in China, the Astor House does an admirable job of capturing the ambience of Victorian Shanghai. The lobby's dark-wood columns and vaulted ceilings are accented by potted orchids and photos of famous visitors from the hotel's illustrious past (including Charlie Chaplin, Ulysses Grant, and Albert Einstein). The hotel has maintained its popularity with both budget and business travelers with its spacious, high-ceilinged rooms, often decorated with historical memorabilia, that more than compensate for the hotel's lack of views. We especially like Executive Room A, with its hardwood floors, oriental carpet, and rain-forest shower. ∎**TIP➜** Skip the renovated modern penthouse rooms—they lack the historic charm of the lower floors. **Pros:** gorgeous building; good price. **Cons:** confused service; spartan furnishings. ⊠ *15 Huangpu Lu, Hongkou* ☎ *021/6324–6388* ⊕ *www.pujianghotel.com/index.htm* ⤵ *127 rooms, 3 suites* ⚘ *In-room: safe (some), DVD (some), Internet. In-hotel: 2 restaurants, room service, bar, gym, concierge, laundry service, parking (no fee), no-smoking rooms* ⊟ *AE, DC, MC, V* ⊹ *G2.*

$ 🏨 **Broadway Mansions Hotel.** One of Shanghai's revered old buildings, the Broadway Mansions has anchored the north end of the Bund since 1934. The worn wood furniture, industrial bathrooms, and steam radiators betray their age. In contrast, business rooms are strikingly modern, with cool gray-and-tan decor, glass-topped desks and nightstands, and separate marble showers and tubs. River-view rooms cost Y100 extra; request a higher floor to reduce the street noise. **Pros:** location; a sense of Shanghai history. **Cons:** service irregular; rooms worn. ⊠ *20 Suzhou Bei Lu, Hongkou* ☎ *021/6324–6260 Ext. 2326* ⊕ *www.broadwaymansions.com* ⤵ *161 rooms, 72 suites* ⚘ *In-room: safe (some), Internet. In-hotel: 2 restaurants, room service, bars, gym, laundry service, executive floor, airport shuttle, parking (no fee)* ⊟ *AE, DC, MC, V* ⊹ *G2.*

HONGQIAO AND GUBEI

$$–$$$ 🏨 **Cypress Hotel.** Once part of tycoon Victor Sassoon's estate, the Cypress Hotel's shaded, stream-laced grounds remain a tranquil retreat in noisy Shanghai. From all of the hotel's rooms you can look out over the garden and actually hear birdsong rather than car horns. The extensive health club boasts a swimming pool and outdoor tennis courts, which help to compensate for the hotel's limited English-speaking staff and location far from downtown Puxi. **Pros:** luxuriously quiet; beautiful environment. **Cons:** very far from downtown. ⊠ *2419 Hongqiao Lu, Hongqiao* ☎ *021/6268–8868* 🖷 *021/6268–1878* ⤺ *141 rooms, 8 suites* ⌂ *In-room: safe, refrigerator, Wi-Fi. In-hotel: 2 restaurants, room service, bar, tennis courts, pool, gym, laundry service, airport shuttle, parking (fee), no-smoking rooms* ▭ *AE, DC, MC, V* ✛ *F5.*

$$$$ 🏨 **Sheraton Shanghai Hongqiao Hotel.** Even after 16 years, the Sheraton
Fodor'sChoice   Grand is still the go-to hotel for savvy business travelers staying in Hong-
★   qiao. Formerly the Westin, this Japanese-managed property has four club floors, one-touch service by phone, and golf privileges at Shanghai International Golf Club. Oriental rugs, antique pottery, folding Chinese screens, and wooden masks and statues, all chosen by the hotel's general manager on his travels, add personal touches that cannot be found at any other hotel in town. Spacious standard rooms include large desks and ergonomic chairs, and the plush grand rooms have oriental carpets and overstuffed chairs in the separate bed and sitting rooms. A grand staircase sweeps you from the formal lobby up to the second floor and the exceptional Bauernstube deli. Giovanni's serves Italian food as impressive as its views from atop the 27th floor. **Pros:** beautifully decorated. **Cons:** far from downtown. ⊠ *5 Zunyi Nan Lu, Hongqiao* ☎ *021/6275–8888 or 888/625–5144* 🖷 *021/6275–5420* ⊕ *www. sheratongrand-shanghai.com* ⤺ *474 rooms, 22 suites* ⌂ *In-room: safe, DVD, refrigerator, Internet. In-hotel: 5 restaurants, room service, bars, tennis court, pool, gym, concierge, laundry service, executive floor, Wi-Fi, parking (fee), no-smoking rooms* ▭ *AE, DC, MC, V* ✛ *F5.*

ARTS AND NIGHTLIFE

Fueled equally by expatriates and an increasingly adventurous population of locals, Shanghai boasts an active and diverse nightlife. Shanghai lacks the sort of performing-arts scene one would expect from a city its size, but it's getting there. Things like acrobatics are solely of interest to tourists; however, traditional forms of Chinese opera remain popular with older citizens and are even enjoying a resurgence among young people.

THE ARTS

For modern culture more in tune with Shanghai's vibe, head to the Shanghai Dramatic Arts Center. Despite being a state-owned institution, it manages to offset sumptuous historical epics with small, provocative plays that examine burning social issues like infidelity, divorce, finances, and AIDS. The center also does projects in conjunction with the city's handful of struggling but plucky modern-dance pioneers, who also perform at private venues like Zhijiang Dream Factory and Downstream Warehouse and, occasionally, on larger stages.

ACROBATICS

Shanghai Acrobatics Troupe. The Shanghai Acrobatics Troupe performs remarkable gravity-defying stunts at both the Shanghai Center Theater and Shanghai Circus World, a glittering gold and green dome located in the center of Jing'an that seats more than 1,600 people. ⊠ *Shanghai Center Theater, 1376 Nanjing Xi Lu, Jing'an* ☎ *021/6279–8945* ⊠ *Shanghai Circus World, 2266 Gong He Xin Lu, Zhabei* ☎ *021/6652–7750* ⊙ *Shows daily at 7:30 pm* ⊠ *Y100–Y200.*

CHINESE OPERA

Kunju Opera Troupe. Kun opera, or Kunju, originated in Jiangsu Province more than 400 years ago. Because of the profound influence it exerted on other Chinese opera styles, it's often called the mother of Chinese opera. Its troupe and theater are located in the lower part of the Former French Concession. ⊠ *9 Shaoxing Lu, Luwan* ☎ *021/6437–1012* ⊠ *Y30–Y280* ⊙ *Performances Sat. at 7:15.*

Yifu Theatre. Not only Beijing Opera but also China's other regional operas, such as Huju, Kunju, and Yueju, are performed regularly at this theater in the heart of the city center. Considered the marquee theater for opera in Shanghai, it's just a block off People's Square. Call the box office for schedule and ticket information. ⊠ *701 Fuzhou Lu, Huangpu* ☎ *021/6351–4668.*

DANCE AND CLASSICAL MUSIC

★ **Downstream Garage.** Experimental-dance troupe Niao and other avant-garde dance and theater performers use this small, underground space for rehearsals and occasional performances. ⊠ *Longcao Lu, La. 200, No. 100, 3rd fl., Xujiahui* ☎ *021/5448–3368.*

Jing An Hotel. Every Sunday, the Shanghai Symphony Orchestra performs chamber music in the lobby of the Jing An Hotel. Past concerts have included pieces by Bach, Ravel, and Chinese composer Huang Yongxi. ⊠ *San Diego Hall, Jing An Hotel, 370 Huashan Lu, Jing'an* ☎ *021/6248–1888 Ext. 687* ⊠ *Y20.*

Shanghai Center Theater. This stage serves as a home to tourist favorites the **Shanghai Acrobatic Troupe** and has hosted performers such as the Israel Contemporary Dance Group and Wynton Marsalis. The building's distinct bowed front was designed to resemble the Marriott Marquis Theater in New York's Times Square. ⊠ *Shanghai Center, 1376 Nanjing Xi Lu, Jing'an* ☎ *021/6279–8663.*

Shanghai Concert Hall. City officials spent $6 million in 2003 to move this 73-year-old hall two blocks to avoid the rumble from the nearby highway. Only then did they discover that they had moved it to sit over an even more rumbling subway line. Oops. It's the home of the Shanghai Symphony Orchestra, and also hosts top-level classical musicians from around China and the world. ⊠ *523 Yanan Dong Lu, Jing'an* ☎ *021/6386–9153.*

TMSK Bar in Xintiandi is a designers dream.

THEATER

Lyceum Theatre. Although the renovation of Shanghai's oldest theater sadly replaced the dark wood with glaring marble and glass, the design of the space makes for an intimate theater experience. The Lyceum regularly hosts drama and music from around China as well as smaller local plays and Chinese opera performances. ⊠ *57 Maoming Nan Lu, Luwan* ☎ *021/6217–8539.*

★ **Majestic Theatre.** Once Asia's largest movie theater, this elegantly restored, beautiful 1930s art-deco gem regularly presents top-ticket theater from China's major troupes, as well as novelty acts and some Western performances. The venue does not have an affiliated drama troupe, so the space is open to all sundry comers. ⊠ *66 Jiangning Lu, Jing'an* ☎ *021/6217–4409.*

Fodor's Choice
★ **Shanghai Dramatic Arts Center.** Shanghai's premier theater venue and troupe, with several busy stages, the Dramatic Arts Center presents an award-winning lineup of its own original pieces, plus those of other cutting-edge groups around China. It also stages Chinese-language adaptations, sometimes very inventive, of Western works, such as a festival of Samuel Beckett works reinterpreted through Chinese opera. It also invites a steady lineup of renowned international performers, such as the Royal Shakespeare Company. Despite being a state-owned institution, the Shanghai Dramatic Arts Center manages to offset sumptuous historical epics with small, provocative plays that examine burning social issues like infidelity, divorce, finances, and AIDS. ⊠ *288 Anfu Lu, Xuhui* ☎ *021/6473–4567* ⊕ *www.china-drama.com.*

Zhijiang Dream Factory. A small private commercial theater in the trendy Tonglefang New Factories, Zhijiang stages a mixture of its own, visiting international, and collaborative theater and dance productions, as well as frequent rock concerts. It primarily targets young, white-collar Shanghainese. ⊠ *28B Yuyao Lu, New Factories Building 10, 4F, Jing'an* ☎ *021/6255–4062.*

NIGHTLIFE

BARS

XINTIANDI AND CITY CENTER

Barbarossa. Above the lily pond in People's Park and next to the MoCA, this beautiful Moroccan restaurant switches into a bar at night. Usually quiet and classy, it switches to hot, hip, and hopping on weekend nights, especially in summertime. ⊠ *231 Nanjing Xi Lu, Huangpu* ☎ *021/6318–0220.*

TMSK. Short for Tou Ming Si Kao, this exquisitely designed little bar is an aesthete's dream. Glisteningly modern, TMSK is stunning—as are the prices of its drinks. ⊠ *Xintiandi North Block, Unit 2, House 11, 181 Taicang Lu, Luwan* ☎ *021/6326–2227.*

THE BUND AND NANJING DONG LU

Bar Rouge. In the trendy, upscale Bund 18 complex, Bar Rouge is the destination du jour of Shanghai's beautiful people. It has retained that distinction for a surprisingly long time. Pouting models and visiting celebrities are among the regular clientele. ⊠ *Bund 18 7F, 18 Zhongshan Dong Lu, Huangpu* ☎ *021/6339–1199.*

Number Five. One of the few unpretentious bars on the Bund, Five wears its position in the basement of the Glamour Bar with pride. Affordable drinks, generously proportioned pub food, Wednesday swing-dancing nights, and sports broadcasts attract a crowd of dedicated regulars. ⊠ *20 Guangdong Lu, BF, the Bund, Huangpu* ☎ *021/6289–9108.*

★ **Three on the Bund.** The sophisticated Three complex, suitably enough, encloses three different bars: the swanky **Nougatine** on the fourth floor; the sleek white **Laris** on the sixth floor; and the more casual **New Heights/Third Degree** on the seventh floor. ⊠ *3 Zhongshan Dong Lu, Huangpu* ☎ *021/6321–0909.*

FORMER FRENCH CONCESSION

★ **Arch Bar and Café.** For an artsy expatriate circle, head to Arch. Its location in Shanghai's copy of the Flatiron Building and in a popular residential district attracts architects and design professionals. Try the cheesecake. ⊠ *439 Wukang Lu, Xuhui* ☎ *021/6466–0807.*

Fodor's Choice **Cotton's.** This friendly, laid-back favorite moved many times before set-
★ tling into the current old garden house. Busy without being loud, Cotton's is a rare place where you can have a conversation with friends—or make some new ones. ⊠ *132 Anting Lu, Xuhui* ☎ *021/6433–7995.*

Face. Once the see-and-be-seen place in Shanghai, Face's hipster clientele has mostly moved to Manifesto with former owner Charlie, leaving it a tourist destination. But it's still beautiful: candlelit tables outside and a four-poster bed inside are the most vied-for spots in this colonial villa

LOCAL BREWS

Northern Chinese swear by their Baijiu, a strong, usually sweet, clear liquor, but Shanghainese opt for milder poison. Most beloved is Huangjiu, a brown brew from Shaoxing with a mild taste that resembles whiskey, which may explain why the latter is the most popular foreign liquor among locals. Huangjiu's quality is determined by whether it was brewed 2, 5, or 10 years ago. It is usually served warm, sometimes with ginger or dried plum added for kick.

Beer is also widely consumed; although there is a Shanghai beer brand, it is cheap, very bitter, and mostly found in the suburbs. More common are Suntory, or Sandeli, a local brewery opened by the Japanese brand, and Reeb (yes, it's meant to be "beer" spelled backward), or Li Bo. Most bars, however, serve Tsingtao and imports like Tiger, Heineken, and Budweiser, which are more expensive. More premium imported beers can also be had, but the markup is steep.

with Indonesian furnishings. ⊠ *Bldg. 4, Ruijin Hotel, 118 Ruijin Er Lu, Luwan* ☎ *021/6466–4328.*

O'Malley's. The most family-friendly of Shanghai's Irish pubs, O'Malley's has the requisite Guinness on tap and live Irish music. Its outdoor beer garden packs in crowds—both singles and families—in the summer and during broadcasts of European soccer and rugby matches. ⊠ *42 Taojiang Lu, Xuhui* ☎ *021/6474.*

★ **Time Passage.** Shanghai has always been a place more inclined toward slick nightclubs and posh wine bars than mellow conversation dives, but Time Passage has always been the exception. Cheap beers, friendly service, and a cool, if grungy, atmosphere makes it the best way to start—or end—a night on the town. ⊠ *Huashan Lu, La. 1038, No. 183, Xuhui,* ☎ *021/6240–2588* ✛ *by Fuxing Lu.*

NANJING XI LU AND JING'AN

★ **Manifesto.** The mastermind behind Face opened this coolly minimalist yet warmly welcoming space and took most of his clientele with him. Popular with foreigners and local white-collars alike, it serves up standard cocktails plus excellent tapas from its sister restaurant Mesa. Enjoy the patio during the warmer months. ⊠ *748 Julu Lu, Jing'an* ☎ *021/6289–9108.*

PUDONG

B.A.T.S. *(Bar at the Shangri-La).* Tucked away in the basement of the Shangri-La, B.A.T.S.'s crowd ebbs and flows depending on the quality of the band. The cavelike, brick-walled space has diner-style booths arranged around a large central bar. ⊠ *Pudong Shangri-La, 33 Fucheng Lu, Pudong* ☎ *021/6882–8888.*

★ **Cloud 9.** Perched on the 87th floor of the Grand Hyatt, Cloud 9 is the highest bar in the world. It has unparalleled views of Shanghai from among—and often above—the clouds. The sky-high views come with sky-high prices: ■TIP➔ There's a Y120 minimum in the evening, so go in the late afternoon to avoid this. The class is offset with kitsch, as

Chinese fortune-tellers and various artisans ply their skills to customers. ⊠ *Grand Hyatt, 88 Shiji Dadao, Pudong* ☎ *021/5049–1234.*

★ **Jade on 36.** This gorgeous, swanky spot in the new tower of the Pudong Shangri-La has swish drinks in a swish setting. Exquisite design and corresponding views (when Shanghai's pollution levels cooperate) have made Jade popular with the *in* set. ⊠ *Pudong Shangri-La, Tower 2, 36F 33 Fucheng, Pudong* ☎ *021/6882–3636.*

HONGQIAO AND GUBEI

Fodor's Choice
★ **The Door.** The stunningly extravagant interior of the Door distracts from the bar's overpriced drinks. Take in the soaring wood-beam ceilings, sliding doors, and a museum's worth of antiques as you listen to the eclectic house band, which plays modern, funky riffs on Chinese music on the *erhu, pipa,* and other traditional instruments. ⊠ *4F, 1468 Hongqiao Lu, Changning* ☎ *021/6295–3737.*

DANCE CLUBS

XIANTIANDI AND CITY CENTER

Rojam. A three-level techno behemoth, Rojam is like a never-ending rave that bulges with boogiers and underground lounge lizards from the under-30 set. ⊠ *4/F, Hong Kong Plaza, 283 Huaihai Zhong Lu, Luwan* ☎ *021/6390–7181.*

FORMER FRENCH CONCESSION

The Apartment. Located above The Shelter, this loft-style lounge has a sometimes-singer on the piano, midcentury furniture, and pricy drinks. The roof deck, though, is the best part. It's got ample seating, its own bar and bathroom, and a lovely view, and is the ideal spot to enjoy this bar's small plates menu. ⊠ *3F, 47 Yongfu Lu, by Fuxing Lu, Luwan* ☎ *021/6437–9478.*

The Shelter. Opened by a collective of Shanghai's leading DJs, the former bomb-shelter basement is not for the claustrophobic but is a favorite of Shanghai scenesters, with cheap drinks and low cover. ⊠ *47 Yongfu Lu, by Fuxing Lu, Luwan* ☎ *021/6437–0400.*

NANJING XI LU AND JING'AN

Judy's. A veteran on the club scene, Judy's is infamous for its hard-partying, meat-market crowd. The den of iniquity was memorialized in Wei Hui's racy novel *Shanghai Baby.* ⊠ *78–80 Tongren Lu, Jing'an* ☎ *021/6289–3715.*

Fodor's Choice
★ **Muse.** This is the first and founding member of the Muse group, which now has three spots—Muse, M2, and Muse at Park 97. All play hip-hop, house, and electro and throw themed parties. It's loud, it's crowded, it's where people end up after hitting a few other drinking establishments. ⊠ *Muse, 68 Yuyao Lu, New Factories, Jing'an* ☎ *021/6218–8166* ⊠ *M2, 283 Huaihai Zhong Lu, People's Square* ☎ *021/6288–6222* ⊠ *Muse at Park 97, 2A Gaolan Lu, French Concession* ☎ *021/5383-2328.*

Wooden Box Cafe. On a quiet lane off busy Nanjing Xi Lu, this café and bar mimics the inside of a tree house, with high ceilings and wood paneling on the rounded walls. The performers here play a variety of jazz and acoustic-style music, which you can listen to while tucking

NIGHTLIFE LOWDOWN

Offerings range from world-class swank to dark and dingy dens or from young Shanghainese kids screaming experimental punk to Filipino cover bands singing "Hotel California" in a hotel basement. Prices, scenes, crowds, and ambience can range just as wildly.

Maoming Nan Lu has long been Shanghai's nightlife hub, with the slightly seedy offerings of the main drag contrasting with the classy, upscale venues—most notably, **Face**—in the adjacent Ruijin Guest House, a hotel complex that takes up an entire city block. It has mostly closed down, with the action migrating to **Da Tong Mill**, which is underground and houses more than 40 bars and clubs, including D10 Ultra Lounge, a bar shaped like a plane.

Tongren Lu, formerly Jing'an's seedy street, does have some good clubs for those who like their nightlife on the wild side. **Julu Lu**, lined with bars, is still going strong, with upscale offerings like Dr. Wine, Velvet Lounge, and People Seven. Note that on both Da Tong Mill and Tongren Lu, there are "fishing girls," who ask gents to give them money to buy drinks in exchange for their company (or something more)—and then they either pocket the money or take a cut from the bar.

Those looking for less blatant sexual commerce should head to the bar, restaurant, and shopping complex of **Xintiandi**, an old Shanghai pastiche and tourist favorite with an array of clean and pleasant but pricey bars. **The Bund** is also a center for upscale dining and drinking, and every year sees new, swank destinations debuting in its historic halls. **Hengshan Lu** and **Fuxing Xi Lu** also offer concentrations of bars and clubs, including The Shelter, mentioned above.

into small bites and putting away red and white wines and beer. ⊠ 9 *Qinghai Lu, Jing'an* ☎ *021/5213–2965.*

GAY–LESBIAN BARS AND CLUBS

Eddy's. Flamboyant, occasional drag queen Eddy has had to move his male-friendly bar all over the city over the years, but has found an apparently permanent home on this quiet stretch of Huaihai. ⊠ *1877 Huaihai Zhong Lu, Luwan* ☎ *021/6282–0521.*

Pink Home. Pretty boys are always welcome at this happening home of the men's pick-up scene. ⊠ *18 Gaolan Lu, Xuhui* ☎ *021/5383–2208.*

Vogue in Kevin's. At the heart of Shanghai's "alternative"—that is, gay—scene, Vogue in Kevin's is a popular party and pick-up spot. The circular bar is a good perch for people-watching and serves a small selection of Thai food. ⊠ *House 4, 946 Changle Lu, Xuhui* ☎ *021/6248–8985.*

KARAOKE

Karaoke is ubiquitous in Shanghai; most nights the private rooms at KTV (Karaoke TV) establishments are packed with Shanghainese crooning away with their friends. Many KTV bars employ "KTV girls" who sing along with (male) guests and serve cognac and expensive snacks. (At most establishments, KTV girls are also prostitutes.)

Hang out with the beautiful people at Rouge Bar on the Bund.

Haoledi. Crowded at all hours with locals of all ages crooning pop favorites, the popular Haoledi chain has branches virtually everywhere. These listed are just a few of the outlets downtown. ✉ *1111 Zhaojiabang Lu, Xuhui* ☎ *021/6311–5858* ✉ *180 Xizang Zhong Lu, Luwan* ☎ *021/6311–5858* ✉ *438 Huaihai Zhong Lu, Luwan* ☎ *021/6311–5858.*

Party World. This giant establishment is one of Shanghai's most popular KTV bars, and among the few that are dedicated to the KTV instead of the KTV girls. ✉ *459 Wulumuqi Bei Lu, Jing'an* ☎ *021/6374–1111* ✉ *109 Yandan Lu, inside Fuxing Park, Luwan* ☎ *021/5306–3888* ✉ *68 Zhejiang, Huangpu* ☎ *021/6374–1111.*

LIVE MUSIC

XINTIANDI AND CITY CENTER
CJW. The acronym says it all: cigars, jazz, and wine are what this swank lounge is all about. Its second location atop the Bund Center has a breathtaking view of the river and the glittering Pudong skyline. ✉ *Xintiandi, House 2, 123 Xingye Lu, Luwan* ☎ *021/6385–6677* ✉ *Bund Center 50F, 222 Yanan Dong Lu, Huangpu* ☎ *021/6329–9932.*

FORMER FRENCH CONCESSION
★ **JZ Club.** JZ continues its role as the king of Shanghai's jazz offerings. Various house bands and stellar guest performers mix it up nightly. Look for plush seating and drink prices to match. ✉ *46 Fuxing Xi Lu, Xuhui* ☎ *021/6431–0269.*

Cotton Club. A dark and smoky jazz and blues club, the Cotton Club is an institution in Shanghai, and still one of the best places to catch live jazz. It's in a great neighborhood for bar hopping, so head here for the 9 pm set and get your night rolling with a nice tune in your step. ⊠ 8 *Fuxing Xi Lu, Xuhui* ☏ 021/6437–7110.

★ **House of Blues and Jazz.** Decked out in memorabilia from Shanghai's jazz era of the 1930s, Blues and Jazz would be a great bar even without the music, but the several nightly sets make it a must-visit, and their Bund-side location has dark-wood paneling and low lighting. Be forewarned that there is smoking here. ⊠ 60 *Fuzhou Lu, Huangpu* ☏ 021/6437–5280.

NANJING XI LU AND JING'AN

★ **Jazz 37.** The Four Seasons' jazz bar matches its penthouse view with a stylish interior. Grab a canary-yellow leather chair by the white grand piano for some top-quality live jazz. ⊠ *The Four Seasons, 37F, 500 Weihai Lu, Jing'an* ☏ 021/6256–8888.

NORTH SHANGHAI

Bandu Music. An unpretentious café and bar in the M50 art compound, Bandu sells hard-to-find CDs and holds concerts of traditional Chinese folk music every Saturday night. ⊠ 50 *Moganshan Lu, Unit 11, 1F, Zhabei* ☏ 021/6431–0269.

XUJIAHUI AND SOUTH SHANGHAI

★ **288/The Melting Pot.** With live music of varying styles nightly, and up-and-coming rockers on weekend, this laid-back bar is a favorite with a range of rockers and office fodder, Chinese and foreigners alike. ⊠ 288 *Taikang Lu, Xuhui* ☏ 021/ 6467–9900.

Fodor's Choice **Yuyintang.** No one has done as much to bring Shanghai rock out from
★   the underground and into the open as has the Yuyintang collective. Headed by sound engineer and former musician Zhang Haisheng, the group started organizing regular concerts around town and eventually opened their own space. Regular concerts, usually on Friday and Saturday nights or Sunday afternoons, spotlight the best and latest in Chinese music. ⊠ 1731 *Yanan Xi Lu, but entered on Kaixuan Lu, Little White Building in Tianshan Park, Xuhui* ☏ 021/5237–8662 ⊕ *www. yuyintang.org.*

SHOPPING

Shanghai gets up late, and opening hours really vary. Local supermarkets open early, but malls don't usually open until 10 and boutiques at 11. The upside is that stores tend to stay open later, with many closing at 10 pm. Markets generally start earlier, at around 7:30 or 8:30, and close at around 6. Most stores are open seven days a week. ■TIP➔ Shopping here is a voyage of discovery that is best done on foot so as to uncover the little surprises, especially in areas like the Former French Concession.

XINTIANDI AND CITY CENTER

ANTIQUES

★ **Dong Tai Antique Shop.** Friendly owner Mr. Liu sells a range of lamps, gramophones, fans, and other electrical equipment salvaged from Shanghai's glorious past. Some of his stock has been bought by chic restaurants like M on the Bund, and most are in some kind of working order. A small glass lamp base will set you back about Y150 if you stand your ground. ✉ *11 Dongtai Lu, Luwan* ☎ *021/6385–8793.*

BOOKS AND ART SUPPLIES

Chaterhouse Books. An oasis for the starved reader, this bookstore stocks a good range of magazines in English and other languages and English books, including children's books and a comprehensive selection of travel guides. ✉ *Shop B1-K Shanghai Times Square, 99 Huaihai Zhong Lu, Luwan* ☎ *021/6391–8237* ⊕ *www.chaterhouse.com.cn* ✉ *Shop 68, 6F Super Brand Mall, 168 Lujiazui Xi Lu, Pudong* ☎ *021/5049–0668* ✉ *Shop 202B, 2F Shanghai Centre, 1376 Nanjing Xi Lu, Huangpu* ☎ *021/6279–7633* ✉ *Shop 68, 6F Super Brand Mall, 168 Lujiazui Xi Lu, Pudong* ☎ *021/5049–0668* ✉ *Shop 19, LG1 Shanghai ifc Mall, 8 Shiji Dadao (Century Avenue), Huangpu* ☎ *021/3897–0509.*

GIFTS

Fodor's Choice **Shanghai Museum Shop.** The selection of books on China and Chinese
★ culture at the main store is impressive, and there are some children's books. Expensive reproduction ceramics are available as well as smaller gift items such as magnets, scarves, and notebooks. Cool purchases like a Chinese architecture–ink stamp (Y90) make great gifts. A delicate bracelet with Chinese charms costs Y150. ✉ *Shanghai Museum, 201 Renmin Dadao (People's Avenue), Huangpu* ☎ *021/6372–3500* ✉ *123 Taicang Lu, Luwan* ☎ *021/6384–7900.*

NANJING DONG LU AND THE BUND

ANTIQUES

Shanghai Antique and Curio Store. A pleasant departure from the touristy shops in the area, this government-owned store is an excellent place to gauge whether you are being taken for a ride elsewhere. Goods start with small pieces of embroidery, and range from ceramics to wedding baskets (traditionally used to hold part of the bride's dowry). Some of the pieces may not be taken out of the country, as a sign in the ceramics store warns. ✉ *192–246 Guangdong Lu, Huangpu* ☎ *021/6321–5868.*

ART

★ **Studio Rouge.** A small but well-chosen collection of mainly photography and paintings by emerging and established artists crowds this simple space. Look for Studio Rouge M50 in Moganshan Lu; it houses the works of more international artists. ✉ *Building 7, 50 Moganshan Lu, Putuo* ☎ *1380/174–1782 (mobile).*

4

BOOKS AND ART SUPPLIES

Yangzhenhua Bizhuang. Calligraphy supplies at excellent prices—fine brushes start at just Y2—can be purchased at this long-established shop. It still has the original glass counters and dark-wood shelves and a staff that relaxes at the back with tea and pumpkin seeds. ⊠ *290 Fuzhou Lu, Huangpu* ☎ *021/6322–3117.*

CERAMICS

Blue Shanghai White. The eponymous colored ceramics here are designed and hand-painted by the owner, and are made in Jingdezhen, once home to China's imperial kilns. Some larger pieces are made with wood salvaged from demolition sites around Shanghai. Prices start at Y60 for a cup to Y30,000 for a screen with ceramic panels. ⊠ *17 Fuzhou Lu, Room 103, Huangpu* ☎ *021/6323–0856* ⊕ *www.blueshanghaiwhite.com.*

CLOTHING AND SHOES

Bund 18. The glamorous collection of shops here sells high-end designer clothing and accessories such as Marni, Ermenegildo Zegna, Cartier, and Giorgio Armani. The boutique **Younik** stands out by specializing in Shanghai-based designers, including Lu Kun. ⊠ *18 Zhongshan Dong Yi Lu, Huangpu* ☎ *021/6323–7066* ⊕ *www.bund18.com.*

★ **Suzhou Cobblers.** Beautifully embroidered handmade shoes and slippers with quirky designs such as cabbages are sold alongside funky bags made from rice sacks. Children's shoes are also available. Also sold here are sweet knitted toys and children's sweaters. ⊠ *17 Fuzhou Lu, Room 101, Huangpu* ☎ *021/6321–7087* ⊕ *www.suzhou-cobblers.com.*

PEARLS AND JEWELRY

Ling Ling Pearls and Jewelry. Traditional pearl necklaces and inexpensive fashion jewelry that is hipper than the competition's stand out here. Pearl and stone combinations are priced high, but large discounts are often given sans haggling. The shop is in **Pearl City,** among the other pearl and jewelry sellers. ⊠ *2F, Pearl City, 558 Nanjing Dong Lu, 2nd fl., Huangpu* ☎ *021/6322–9299.*

★ **Amy Lin's Pearls and Jewelry.** Friendly owner Amy Lin has sold pearls to European first ladies and American presidents, but treats all her customers like royalty. Her shop among the fake bags at Fenshine Plaza has inexpensive trinket bracelets, strings of seed pearls, and stunning Australian seawater pearl necklaces. ⊠ *Shop 30, 3F, Fenshine Fashion and Accessories Plaza, 580 Nanjing Xi Lu, Huangpu* ☎ *021/5228–2372 or* ⊕ *www.amy-pearl.com.*

FORMER FRENCH CONCESSION

ANTIQUES

Brocade Country. The English-speaking owner, Liu Xiao Lan, has a Miao mother and a broad knowledge of her pieces. The Miao sew their history into the cloth, and she knows the meaning behind each one. Many pieces are antique-collector's items, and Ms. Liu has also started designing more wearable items. Antique embroidery can cost an arm and a leg, but smaller embroidery pieces are affordable and flat and easy to slip into a suitcase. ⊠ *616 Julu Lu, Jing'an* ☎ *021/6279–2677.*

TOP SHOPPING STOPS

Duolun Lu is a pedestrian street in Shanghai's historic Hongkou. Not only is it lined with examples of old architecture and home to a modern-art gallery, but its stalls and curio stores are ripe for browsing.

Moganshan Lu, a complex near Aomen Lu, once housed poor artists. It is now being developed and repackaged as M50, a hot new art destination with galleries, cafés, and stores moving in to make this a happening place to shop and hang out.

Taikang Lu is a former factory district that's now home to artists and designers. It has a hip and laid-back vibe, particularly on weekdays, and is fast becoming Shanghai's SoHo. You won't find Andy Warhols at the International Artists Factory, but there is definitely some worthwhile shopping.

In **Xintiandi** exclusive and expensive stores are housed in reproduction traditional Shikumen buildings. Get ready to work that plastic.

Xujiahui, where six major shopping malls and giant electronics complexes in Puxi converge, looks like it's straight out of Tokyo. Shop 'til you drop, or play with the gadgets and compare prices at the electronics shops.

Yu Garden, a major tourist haunt in the Old Town area of Shanghai, can be overwhelming, but hard bargaining brings rewards. The amount and variety of goods for sale here are phenomenal. It is continually expanding as vendors move out of old buildings in the surrounding areas.

Also check out these streets that specialize in specific traditional products: **Fenyang Lu** and **Jinling Lu** for musical instruments; **Changle Lu** and **Maoming Lu** for *qipao* (Chinese-style dresses); and **Fuzhou Lu** for books and art supplies, including calligraphy supplies.

★ **Madame Mao's Dowry.** This covetable collection of mostly revolutionary-propaganda items from the '50s, '60s, and '70s is sourced from the countryside and areas in Sichuan Province and around Beijing and Tianjin. Mixed in are hip designs from local and international designers. Although this could be your one-stop shopping experience, remember this is communism at capitalist prices: expect to pay Y800 for a small Revolution-era teapot and around Y1,800 for a Revolution-era mirror. ✉ *207 Fumin Lu, Luwan* ☎ *021/65403–3551* ⊕ *www.madame-maos-dowry.com* ✉ *Gallery: 50 Moganshan Lu, Building 6, 5th fl., Putuo* ☎ *021/6276–9932.*

CARPETS

Torana House. Two stories here are filled with carpets handmade by Tibetan artisans in rural areas using top-quality wool and featuring auspicious symbols. This is also a good place to pick up an antique piece from Tibet or Xinjiang. ✉ *164 Anfu Lu, Xuhui* ☎ *021/5404–4886* ⊕ *www.toranahouse.com.*

CLOTHING AND SHOES

Boutique Cashmere Lover. The small collection of wickedly soft cashmere and blends is contemporary in design; some have Chinese details. ✉ *248 Taikang Lu, No. 31, Luwan* ☎ *021/6473–7829.*

Feel. The qipao may be a traditional Chinese dress, but Feel makes it a style for modern times as well with daring cut-outs and thigh skimming designs. ✉ *La. 210, No. 3, Room 110, Taikang Lu, Luwan* ☎ *021/5465–4519 or 021/6466–8065* ✉ *Shop 305, The Loft, 508 Jiashan Lu, Luwan* ☎ *021/5465–9319.*

insh and Helen Li *(In Shanghai).* A local designer sells cheeky clothes that are not for the fainthearted at these two locations. Skirts barely cover bottoms, but there are cute takes on traditional qipao, as well as a more lifestyle-oriented range in the streetside store. It's a good place for T-shirts featuring stylish Chinese-inspired designs. ✉ *200 Taikang Lu, Luwan* ☎ *021/6466–5249* ⊕ *www.insh.com.cn* ✉ *11A, Lane 210, Taikang Lu* ☎ *021/6415–7877.*

L'Atelier Mandarine. Clothing and accessories focus on children and lounging. The French designer uses natural fabrics such as silk, cotton, and cashmere for her own designs, as well as stocking other local labels. The simple and chic designs let the quality of the fabric speak for itself. ✉ *Studio No. 318, No. 3, La. 210, Taikang Lu, Luwan* ☎ *021/6473–5381.*

★ **Shanghai Tang.** This is one of China's leading fashion brands, with distinctive acid-bright silks, soft-as-a-baby's-bottom cashmere, and funky housewares. Sigh at the beautiful fabrics and designs and gasp at the inflated prices. ✉ *Xintiandi 15, North Block 181, Taicang Lu, Luwan* ☎ *021/6384–1601* ✉ *JinJiang Hotel, Shop E, 59 Maoming Nan Lu, Luwan* ☎ *021/5466–3006* ✉ *Shangri-La Hotel, Lobby Level, 33 Fucheng Lu, Pudong* ☎ *021/5877–6632* ⊕ *www.shanghaitang.com.*

★ **Shanghai Trio.** Chinese fabrics mixed with French flair, irresistible children's clothes in bright colors and sweet little kimonos, great utilitarian satchels that scream urban chic, and crafty necklaces are the stars of this range. The shop has expanded recently to accommodate a housewares collection, with items such as blankets at Y800. ✉ *Xintiandi, 181 Taicang Lu, Luwan* ☎ *021/6355–2974* ⊕ *www.shanghaitrio.com.cn.*

GIFTS AND HOUSEWARES

Harvest Studio. Drop in to watch the Miao women with their distinctive hair knots embroidering, and sometimes singing. This studio sells Miao-embroidered pillows, purses, and clothing, as well as the silver jewelry that traditionally adorns the Miao ceremonial costume. They also have

Shanghai is known for high-end shopping.

a funky range of contemporary cotton and jersey pieces. ✉ *3 La. 210, Room 118, Taikang Lu, Luwan* ☎ *021/6473–4566.*

Jooi. This Danish-owned design studio focuses on bags and accessories in fabrics ranging from industrial felt to shiny patent. Now, it also incorporates Nest, devoted to eco-friendly products. ✉ *Studio 201, International Artist Factory, La. 210, Taikang Lu, Luwan* ☎ *021/6473–6193* ⊕ *www.jooi.com.*

TEA

Shanghai Huangshan Tea Company. The nine Shanghai locations of this teashop sell traditional Yixing teapots as well as a huge selection of China's best teas by weight. The higher the price, the better the tea. ✉ *605 Huaihai Zhonglu, Luwan* ☎ *021/5306–2974.*

PUDONG

MALLS

Super Brand Mall. At 10 stories, this is one of Asia's largest malls. It has a massive Lotus supermarket, along with a mind-boggling array of international shops and food stops and a movie complex. It can be overwhelming if you don't love to shop. ✉ *168 Lujiazui Lu, Pudong* ☎ *021/6887–7888* ⊕ *www.superbrandmall.com.*

Xinmei Union Square. Smaller, newer, and funkier than Pudong's other malls, Xinmei focuses on hip foreign brands such as Miss Sixty, G-Star Raw, Fornarina, and Swatch. ✉ *999 Pudong Nan Lu, Pudong* ☎ *021/5134–1888.*

NORTH SHANGHAI

ANTIQUES

Henry Antique Warehouse. This company is the antique Chinese–furniture research, teaching, and training institute for Tongji University. Part of the showroom sometimes serves as an exhibition hall for the modern designs created jointly by students and the warehouse's 50 craftsmen. Wandering through the pieces on display is a trek through Chinese history; from intricately carved traditional altar tables to 1920s art-deco furniture. ✉ *796 Suining Lu, Changning* ☎ *021/5219–4871* ⊕ *www. antique-designer.com.*

ART

1918 Artspace. Excellent up-and-coming artists such as Jin Shan are showcased at this independent gallery's warehouse space. ✉ *78 Changping Lu, Putuo* ☎ *021/5228–6776* ⊕ *www.1918artspace.com.*

★ **M50.** This complex on Moganshan Lu is one of the hippest places in Shanghai. Get down to these old warehouses and hang out with the crowds. It's a great place to spend time wandering around the smaller galleries, chatting to the artists and dealers, and seeing China's more established artists' work as well. ✉ *50 Moganshan Lu, Putuo* ☎ *021/6266–0963* ⊕ *www.m50.com.cn.*

ShanghART. The city's first modern-art gallery, ShanghART is *the* place to check out the work of art-world movers and shakers such as Ding Yi, Xue Song, and Shen Fan. Here you can familiarize yourself with Shanghai's young contemporary avant-garde artists. The gallery represents around 30 local artists, as well as putting on great shows and openings in its adjacent H Space. They sell some catalogs of artists they represent and of past shows. ✉ *50 Moganshan Lu, Putuo* ☎ *021/6359–3923* ⊕ *www.shanghartgallery.com* ✉ *F-Space 315–317, 800 Guoshu Dong Lu, Yangpu* ☎ *021/5506–5989.*

TEA

Tianshan Tea City. This place stocks all the tea in China and then some. More than 300 vendors occupy the three floors. You can buy such famous teas as West Lake dragon well tea and Wuyi red-robe tea, and the tea set to serve it in. ✉ *520 Zhongshan Xi Lu, Changning* ☎ *021/6259–9999* ⊕ *www.dabutong.com.*

XUJIAHUI AND SOUTH SHANGHAI

ANTIQUES

★ **Hu & Hu Antiques.** Co-owner Marybelle Hu worked at Taipei's National Palace Museum as well as Sotheby's in Los Angeles before opening this shop with sister-in-law Lin in 1998. Their bright, airy showroom contains Tibetan chests and other rich furniture as well as a large selection of accessories, from lanterns to mooncake molds. Their prices are a bit higher than their competitors, but so is their standard of service. ✉ *Alley 1885, 8 Caobao Lu, Minhang* ☎ *021/3431–1212* ⊕ *www.hu-hu.com.*

ENGLISH	PINYIN	CHINESE
EXPLORING		
Bank of China	Zhōngguó yínháng	中国银行
Bund	Wàitanān	外滩
Cathay Cinema	guótài diànyǐngyuàn	泰影院
Century Park	shìjì gōngyuán	世公
Chen Xiangge Temple	chén xiāng gé	Xiangge寺
Dongtai Road Antiques Street	Dōngtái lù	东台路
Duolun Road	Duōlún lù	多伦路
Former Hong Kong and Shanghai Bank Building	Pǔdōng fāzhǎn yūnhöng	浦东发展银行
Fuxing Park	Fùxīng gōngyuán	复兴公园复兴公园
Grand Theater	Shànghǎi dàjùyuàn	上海大剧院
Grayline Tours	huīxiàn lǚyóu	灰线旅游
Huangpu River Cruises	Pǔjiang yóulan	浦江游览
Jade Buddha Temple	Yùfósì	玉佛寺
Jinjiang Tours	Jīnjiāng lǚyóu	锦江旅游
Jinmao Tower	jinmào dàshà	金茂大厦金茂大
Longhua Temple	lónghuá sì	寺
Longhua Martyrs Cemetery	lónghuá lièshì língyuán	烈士陵
Lyceum Theatre	Lánxīn dàxìyuàn	兰馨大戏院
M50	Chūnmíng yìshù chanyĚyuan	春明艺术产业园
Nanjing Road	Nánjīng ling Lu	南京路
Nanjing Dong (East) Road	Nánjīng dōng lù	南京东路
Nanjing Xi Lu (Nanjing West Road)	Nánjīng xī lù	南京西路
Old City Wall	dàjìng gé	老城
Oriental Pearl Tower	dōngfāng míngzhū diànshìtǎ	方明珠塔
Paramount	bǎilĚmÈn	派拉蒙
Park Hotel	Guójì fàndiàn	国际饭店
Peace Hotel	Hépíng fàndiàn	和平饭店
People's Park	rénmín guǎngchǎng	人民公
People's Square	rénmín góngyuán	人民广场
Shanghai Art Museum	Shŕnghǎi bǔwǔguǎn	上海美
Shanghai Botanical Gardens	Shŕnghǎi zhíwuyuán	上海植物
Shanghai Jews	ShàngàiyoÛtàirÈn	上海犹太人
Shanghai Museum	Shŕnghǎi bów¨gu„n	上海博物

ENGLISH	PINYIN	CHINESE
Shanghai Ocean Aquarium	Shǐnghǎi hǎiyáng shuǐzúguǎn	上海海洋水族
Shanghai Oriental Leisure Company	Shàngài mǐngzhū shuǐshàng yúlè fāzhǎn yǒuxiàn gōngsī	上海明珠水上娱乐发展有限公司
Shanghai Scenery Co.	Shàngàifēngcǎi	上海风采
Shanghai Science and Technology Museum	Shàngàikējìguǎn	上海科技
Shanghai Sightseeing Bus Centre	Shàngàilǚyóu jísàn zhōngxīn	上海旅游集散中心
Shanghai Urban Planning Center	Shǐnghǎi chéngshí guīhuà zhǎnlǎnguǎn	上海城市中心
Xintiandi	Xīntiāndì	新天地
Yu Gardens	Yùyuān	豫园
WHERE TO EAT		
1221	Yīèrèryī cāntīng	1221餐厅
Barbarossa	Bābālùshā	芭芭露莎
Bellagio	Bǎilègōng	百乐宫
Cloud 9	Jiǔchòngtiān	九重天
The Dynasty	Mǎnfúlóu	满福楼
Family Li Imperial Cuisine	Lìjiā cài	历家菜
Ginger Café	Jīngé kā fēi	金格咖啡
Giovanni's	Jífànnísī	吉范尼斯
Gokohai	Yùxiānghǎi	钰香海
Gongdelin	Gōngdélín	功德林
Grape	Pútáoyuán	葡萄园
Hot Pot King	Láifúlóu	来福楼
Indian Kitchen	Yìndù xiǎochú	印度小厨
Itoya	Yīténgjiā	伊藤家
Jade on 36	Fěicuìsānshíliù	翡翠36
Kabb	Kǎibóxī	凯博西
Lost Heaven	Huāmǎtiāntáng	花马天堂
Masala Art	Xiāngliàoyìshù	香料艺术
Meilongzhen	Méilóngzhèn	梅龙镇
Mesa	Méisà cāntīng	梅萨餐厅
Mexico Lindo Restaurant	Língdé Mòxīgē cāntīng	灵得墨西哥餐厅
Mr and Mrs Bund	YXiānshēng hé xiǎojiě wàitándé	先生和小姐外滩雅德
New Heights	Xīnshìjiǎo Cāntīng jiǔláng	新视角餐厅酒廊
The Onion	Yángcōng cāntīng	洋葱餐厅

ENGLISH	PINYIN	CHINESE
Palladio	Pàlánduǒ	帕兰朵
The Purple Onion	XīntiāndZǐ yángcōng	紫洋葱新天地
Quan Ju De	Quánjùdé	全聚德
Roosevelt Prime Steakhouse	Luósīfú dǐngjí niúpáiguǎn	罗斯福顶级牛排馆
Simply Thai	Tiāntài cāntīng	天泰餐厅
South Beauty	Qiàojiāngnán	俏江南
The Stage At Westin Restaurant	Wǔtái cān tīng	舞台餐厅
Summer Pavilion	Xiàyuàn	夏苑
T8	T bā	T 8
Tairyo	Tailáng	太郎
The Tandoor	Tiāndōulǐ Yìndù cāntīng	天都里印度餐厅
Vienna Café	Weíyěnà kā fēi	维也纳咖啡
Wan Hao	Wànháo	万豪
Whampoa Club	Huángpǔhuì	黄埔会
Yi Café	Yí kāfēi	怡咖啡
Yu Xin Chuan Restaurant	Yúxìn chuāncài	渝信川菜

WHERE TO STAY		
88 Xintiandi	88 xīntiāndì jiǔdiàn	88 新天地酒店
Anting Villa Hotel	Antíng biéshù huāyuán jiǔdiàn	安亭别墅花园酒店
Astor House Hotel	Pǔjiāng fàndiàn	浦江饭店
Broadway Mansions	Shāngài dàshà	上海大厦
Crowne Plaza	Yínxīng Huángguān Jiàrì Jiǔdiàn	银星皇冠假日酒店
Cypress Hotel	Longbài fàndiàn	龙柏饭店
Donghu Hotel	Dōnghú Bīnguǎn	湖
Four Seasons Hotel	Sìjì jiǔdiàn	四季酒店
Grand Hyatt	Shāngài jīnmào jūnyuè dàjiǔdiàn	上海金茂君悦大酒店
Hotel InterContinental	Jīnjiāngtāngchén zhōujì dàjiǔdiàn	锦江汤臣洲际大酒店
JIA	Shāngài jiā jiǔdiàn	上海家酒店
Jinjiang Hotel	Jǐnjiāng fàndiàn	锦江饭店
JW Marriott	J.W.wànháo jiǔdiàn	JW 万豪酒店
Le Royal Meridien	Shāngài Shìmàohuángjiāàiměi jiǔdiàn	上海世茂皇家艾美酒店
Okura Garden Hotel	Huāyuán fàndiàn	花园饭店
Old House Inn	Lǎoshīguāng jiǔdiàn	老时光酒店

ENGLISH	PINYIN	CHINESE
Pacific Hotel	Jīnmén dàjiǔdiàn	金门大酒店
Park Hotel	Guójì fàndiàn	国际饭店
The Portman Ritz-Carlton	Bōtèmàn Lìjiā jiǔdiàn	波特曼丽嘉酒店
The Pudong Ritz-Carlton	Shànghǎi pǔdōng lì sī kǎěr dùn	上海浦东丽思卡尔顿上海世茂皇家艾美酒店
Pudong Shangri-La	Pǔdōng Xiānggélǐlā jiǔdiàn	浦东香格里拉酒店
Radisson Hotel Shanghai New World	Xīnshìjiè Lìshēng dàjiǔdiàn	新世界丽笙大酒店
Ramada Plaza	Nánxīn Yǎhuáměidá dàjiǔdiàn	南新雅华美达大酒店
Regal International East Asia	Fùháo Huánqiúdōngyà jiǔdiàn	富豪环球东亚酒店
Ruijin Guest House	Ruìjīn bīnguǎn	瑞金宾馆
Sheraton Hongqiao Hotel	Hóng qiáo xǐ lái dēng dà fàn diàn	虹桥喜 来登 大饭店
Somerset Grand	Shèngjiè gāojí fúwù gōngyù	盛捷高级服务公寓
The St. Regis	ShǎngàiRuìjí Hóngtǎ dàjiǔdiàn	上海瑞吉红塔大酒店
URBN	YàyuÈ jiǔdiàn	雅悦酒店
The Westin Shanghai	Wēisītīng dàfàndiàn	威斯汀大饭店
ARTS AND NIGHTLIFE		
The Apartment		汉俱
Arch Bar and Cafe	Jiǔjiān jiǔbā	玖间酒吧
Bandu Music	Bàndù yīnyuè	半度音乐
Barbarossa	Bābālùshā jiǔbā	巴巴路莎酒吧
B.A.T.S. (in Pudon Shangri-La)	Biānfú jiǔbā (Pǔdōng Xiānggélǐlā Diàn ⊠	蝙蝠酒吧（浦东香格里拉店）
Club JZ	Chúncuì juéshìyuè jiǔbā	纯粹爵士乐酒吧
Cotton Club	Miánhuā jùlèbù	棉花俱乐部
Cotton's	Miánhuā jiǔbā	棉花酒吧
The Door	Qiánmén jiǔbā	乾门酒吧
Downstream Warehouse	Xiàhémǐcāng	下河米仓
Haoledi	Hǎolèdī KTV	好乐迪KTV
House of Blues and Jazz	Bùlǔsī yǔ juéshì zhīwū	布鲁斯与爵士之屋
Jade on 36 (in Pudon Shangri-La)	Fěicuì 36 jiǔbā (Pǔdōng Xiānggélǐlā diàn)	翡翠36酒吧（浦东香格里拉店）
Jazz 37 (in Four Seasons)	Juéshì 37 jiǔbā (sìjì jiǔdiàn nèi)	爵士37酒吧四季酒店内）
Jing An Hotel	Jìng'ān bīnguǎn	静安宾馆
Kunju Opera Troupe	Shànghǎi kūnjùtuán	上海昆剧团
The Lab	Shíyànshì	实验室

ENGLISH	PINYIN	CHINESE
Live Bar	Xiànchǎng jiǔbā	现场酒吧
Lyceum Theatre	Lánxīn dàxìyuàn	兰馨大戏院
Majestic Theatre	Měiqí dàxìyuàn	美琪大戏院
Number Five	Waitān wǔhào jiǔbā	外滩五号酒吧
O'Malley's	Oumǎlì jiǔbā	欧玛莉酒吧
Party World	Qiánguì KTV	钱柜KTV
Rojam	Luójié jiǔbā	罗杰酒吧
Shanghai Acrobatics Troupe	Shànghǎi aájìtuán	上海杂技团
Shanghai Center Theater	Shànghǎi shāngchéng jùyuàn	上海商城剧院
Shanghai Concert Hall	Shànghǎi yīnyuètīng	上海音乐厅
Shanghai Dramatic Arts Center	Shànghǎi huàjù yìshù zhōngxīn	上海话剧艺术中心
Three on the Bund	Wàitān sānhào	外滩三号
Time Passage	Zuotianjintianmingtian jiǔbā	昨天今天明天酒吧
TMSK (short for Tou Ming Si Kao)	Tòumíngsīkǎo jiǔbā	透明思考酒吧
Yifu Theatre	Yīfū wǔtái	逸夫舞台
Yuyintang	Yùyīntáng	育音堂

SHOPPING

1918 Artspace	Yījiǔyībā yìshù kōngjiān	一九一八 艺术空间
Amy Lin's Pearls and Jewelry	ìmǐnlínshì zhūbǎo	艾敏林氏珠宝
Blue Shanghai White	Hǎishàngqīnghuā	海上青花
Brocade Country	Jǐnxiùfǎng	锦绣纺
Bund 18	Wàitān shíbā hào	外滩十八号
Chaterhouse Books	Sānlián shūdiàn	三联书店
Dongtai Antique Shop	Dōngtái gǔwándiàn	东台古玩店
Double Rainbow Massage House	Shuāngchǎihong ànmúo	双彩虹按摩
Dragonfly	Yōuting bǎojiàn huìsuǒ	悠亭保健会所
Evian Spa	Yīyún shuǐliáo	依云水疗
Feel	Jīnfěnshìjiā	金粉世家
Henry Antique Warehouse	Hànruì gǔdiǎn jiājù	汉瑞古典家俱
Hu & Hu Antiques	ǔyuè jiājù	古悦家俱
insh	Yīngshàng gōngmào	莺裳工贸
Jooi	Ruìyì	瑞逸
Ling Ling Pearls & Jewelry	ínglíng zhūbǎo	玲玲珠宝
M50	Chūnmíng yìshù chanyĚyuan	春明艺术产业园
Madame Mao's Dowry	LMáotaì shèjì	毛太设计

ENGLISH	PINYIN	CHINESE
Mandara Spa	Màndámèng shuǐliáo	蔓达梦水疗
Ming Massage	Míngyī ànmó	明一按摩
Shanghai Antique and Curio Store	ShǎngàiwÈnwˇ shāngdiàn	上海文物商店
ShanghArt	Xiánggénà huàláng	香格纳画廊
Shanghai Huangshan Tea Company	Shǎngàihuángshān cháyè yǒuxiàn gōngsī	上海黄山茶叶有限公司
Shanghai Museum Shop	ShǎngàibÛowˇuguǎn shāngdiàn	上海博物馆商店
Shanghai Tang	Sh‡nghǎitān	上海滩
Shanghai Trio	Shǎngàizǔhé	上海组合
Studio Rouge	Hóngzhài dāngdài yìshù huàláng	红寨当代艺术画廊
Super Brand Mall	Zhèngdà guǎngchǎng	正大广场
Tianshan Tea City	Dàbùtóng Tiānshān chāchéng	大不同天山茶城
Torana House	Túlánnà	图兰纳
Xinmei Union Square	xīnméi lišnhǐ guǎngchǎng	新梅合

Eastern China

ZHEJIANG AND FUJIAN

WORD OF MOUTH

"Having traveled all over the world, I have to say Hangzhou's West Lake is unusually wonderful. The combination of traditional architecture and soaring pagodas with an international flair on the East side made me linger longer than planned"

—johnya

WELCOME TO EASTERN CHINA

TOP REASONS TO GO

★ **Hangzhou Teatime.** Sip sublime Longjing tea and buy silk in the footsteps of Marco Polo at Hangzhou's romantic West Lake.

★ **Qiantian Tidal Bore.** Marvel at one of nature's most enthralling spectacles: the mighty tidal bore at the mouth of Zhejiang's Qiantian River.

★ **Gulangyu.** Wander through narrow alleyways filled with a fascinating blend of Chinese and European architecture, and recharge in seaside garden pavilions without dodging traffic on this historic, car-free island.

★ **Shaoxing Wine.** Dramatized by one of China's most famous writers, Lu Xun, Shaoxing wine is celebrated throughout the region. Potent for sure, Shaoxing wine is de rigueur for local dining.

★ **Hakka Roundhouses.** The founder of modern China, Dr. Sun Yat-sen, came from China's proud Hakka minority people, whose ancient tradition of rounded-home architecture is now treasured.

1 Hangzhou. Described by Marco Polo as the finest and noblest city in the world, Hangzhou is famous for the beautiful West Lake. In recent years Hangzhou has also emerged as one of China's most vibrant cities. Outside the city, visit the plantations that produce the area's famous Longjing tea, or stroll in forested hills to take in the views of the surrounding area.

2 Shaoxing. Shaoxing is famed for its historic homes and many traditional bridges. This small, well-preserved town is perhaps the best place to experience the historic atmosphere of a traditional Yangze Delta town. Visit the stunning Figure 8 Bridge, which is indeed shaped like a figure eight and was erected more than 800 years ago.

3 Ningbo. A perfect blend of old and new, this bustling seaside metropolis is the ideal place to comfortably veer off the standard tourist trail. Climb the ancient Tianfeng Pagoda to survey the busy masses, and as night falls, head over to Laowaitan, the city's entertainment district complete with a centuries-old Portuguese church and dozens of international bars and restaurants.

4 Xiamen. With a bird's-eye view of the Taiwan Straight, Xiamen is poised to profit from the windfall of increased economic activity between Taiwan and the mainland. Famous for its party atmosphere and popular with young expats, Xiamen's trendy clubs and upscale restaurants are becoming as popular as the city's famous beaches and botanical gardens.

JIANGXI

Wuyi Mountain Natural Reserve

Shaowu

Sanming

Changting

Longyan

Hakka Settlements of Yongding

GUANGDONG

JIANGSU

SHANGHAI

Huzhou

Jiaxing

Wangpan Bay

ANHUI

Hangzhou

1

Shaoxing

2

3 Ningbo

Fuyang

Sheng Xian

Yiwu

Jinhua

ZHEJIANG

Linhai

Jiaojing

Quzhou

Huangyan

Lishui

Wenzhou

Rui'an

Fuan

Tongshan

Xiapu

Ningde

Nanping

Fuzhou

Meizhou

FUJIAN

Fuqing

HAITAN ISLAND

NANRI ISLAND

Putian

Nan'an

Quanzhou

Quanzhou

4 Xiamen

KINMEN ISLAND

Zhangzhou

0   75 mi

0   75 km

5

GETTING ORIENTED

With thousands of miles of coastline, the provinces of Zhejiang and Fujian are the rounded belly section of China's east coast. Indeed, their shores front the East China Sea and the South China Sea. Zhejiang Province's primary ports of call are the cities of Ningbo and Hangzhou, both of which are within two hours of Shanghai by bus. Hangzhou is also famous as the southernmost city of the Grand Canal. Directly south of Zhejiang is the lush and mountainous province of Fujian. With its proximity to the Taiwan Straight, the wealthy coastal cities of Fujian are convenient to each other, but the province's mountainous interior make them a long train trip away from the rest of the region.

Updated by
Daniel Garber

A microcosm of the forces at play in contemporary China is presented in the provinces on the country's eastern coast. The past's rich legacy and the challenges and aspirations for China's future combine in a present that is dizzying in its variety and speed of transformation.

Zhejiang and Fujian, often overlooked on the standard Beijing–Shanghai–Hong Kong tourist trail, offer some of the country's most verdant scenery and a plethora of diversions, like hiking through ancient Hakka villages, bicycling along lush tea fields, and lounging or windsurfing on lively beaches.

Zhejiang has always been a hub of culture, learning, and commerce. The cities, with their elegant gardens, elaborate temples, and fine crafts, evoke the sophisticated and refined world of classical China's literati. Since the Southern Song Dynasty (1127–79), large numbers of Fujianese have emigrated around Southeast Asia. As a result, Fujian Province has strong ties to overseas Chinese. In 1979 Fujian was allowed to form the first Special Economic Zone (SEZ)—a testing ground for capitalist market economy—at Xiamen. Today, although Xiamen is a wealthy place with a vibrant economy, the city has managed to retain its Old World charm.

PLANNING

WHEN TO GO

Fall and spring are the ideal times to visit the region. Spring, especially April and May, has very comfortable temperatures, and the trees and flowers are in full bloom. Hangzhou's spectacular cherry blossoms bloom in spring, dotting the gardens surrounding the West Lake. Summers are hot and muggy, and winters are short (the temperature rarely dips below zero) but miserably wet, windy, and chilly. Typhoons can strike any time from late summer through autumn. The region has a long and very pleasant fall season—moderate weather and clear skies lasting into early December. Chinese tourists flood in during the two "Golden Week" holidays at the start of May and October and during the Lunar New Year (late January-early February), so avoid traveling during these times.

GETTING HERE AND AROUND

Shanghai is generally the best place to begin exploring Eastern China. It has good amenities, and with two airports and train stations it offers myriad connections across the country. Do not travel by bus unless it's absolutely necessary: even the smaller cities can be reached by rail. Most major travel agents in Shanghai speak English. If you want to make Hangzhou your base, many cheap flights are available, although choice of destinations is more limited.

AIR TRAVEL

Air travel in Eastern China is very straightforward and simple. Hangzhou's Xiaoshan airport is modern and well connected, and domestic flights are abundant. Hangzhou is increasingly adding more international routes, already including Amsterdam (KLM), Kuala Lumpur (Air Asia), Tokyo (Air China), and Paris (Lufthansa). Ningbo recently added direct flights to Taipei (Hainan Air), and Xiamen is well connected to Jakarta (Air China), Singapore (Silk Air), and Manila (Philippine Airlines).

BUS TRAVEL

Traveling by bus in Eastern China is a great way to get around, as even tiny cities and villages will have a station. Large cities such as Hangzhou will have several bus stations, so make sure to confirm where exactly you are departing from. Buses in Eastern China will usually be relatively new, air-conditioned vehicles, and almost always leave on time. The biggest headache you'll likely encounter is trying to navigate through the masses at the stations to buy your tickets. Ask your hotel to purchase tickets in advance, as line etiquette in China is nonexistent and can be frustrating, especially for non-Mandarin speakers. If traveling between major cities, such as between Hangzhou and Ningbo, buses leave frequently, so just show up and get on the next available departure.

CAR TRAVEL

Hiring a driver in China is possible, but unreasonably expensive. Considering that taxis are cheap and abundant, and most cities have (or are in the process of building) user-friendly subways, navigating Chinese cities is fairly easy. Always remember to carry the Chinese address written down in advance. If you insist on hiring a car, plan on paying at least $150 for an eight-hour day. Hangzhou Car Service operates an impressive fleet of Japanese, German, and American vehicles, and can arrange city tours, intercity transport, and airport pickup.

Contact Info Hangzhou Car Service (✉ *based out of Shenzhen* ☎ 075/2594–1385 ⊕ *www.hangzhoucarservice.com*).

TRAIN TRAVEL

Bullet trains are the easiest, quickest, and most comfortable option. Look for D-coded trains, or the letters CHR (China High-Speed Rail). Shanghai to Hangzhou, for example, takes approximately one hour and 40 minutes (with 20 departures daily each way), compared to almost three hours by bus. On the contrary, slow trains are uncomfortable for long distances and best avoided.

HEALTH AND SAFETY

Many big cities have foreign doctors and clinics catering to the expatriate community. These clinics charge exponentially more than Chinese hospitals, but hygiene standards are comparable to those of North America and Western Europe. Chinese hospitals, crowded and grimy, should be used as a last resort.

Petty crime is common, especially in crowded places such as train and bus stations. Travelers should use common sense and keep an eye on valuables at all times. Violent crime targeting foreigners in China is practically nonexistent, and most foreigners should feel comfortable walking around any time of day.

China maintains very lax personal safety standards, so always keep an eye on your children. Things to look out for are missing railings on stairs, protruding electrical wires, concealed potholes, poor footing, unprotected cooking implements, and hazardous traffic.

MONEY MATTERS

Prices are negotiable everywhere except supermarkets. Do not accept prices quoted in foreign currency, and never pay more than you think the article is really worth. Tourist markups can hit 1,000% in major attractions. Don't be afraid to shout "*Tai gui le!*" ("too expensive"), laugh at the seller, and walk away. He or she will probably call you back with a better price.

China is not a tipping country; however, tips constitute the majority of a tour guide's income.

RESTAURANTS

Zhejiang cuisine is often steamed or roasted, and has a subtler, salty flavor; specialties include yellow croaker with Chinese cabbage, sea eel, drunken chicken, and stewed chicken. In Shaoxing locals traditionally start the day by downing a bowl or two of *huang jiu* (rice wine), the true breakfast of champions. Shaoxing's most famous dish is its deep-fried *chou dofu*, or stinky tofu. Try it with a touch of the local chili sauce.

The cuisine of Fujian has its own characteristics. Spareribs are a specialty, as are soups and stews using a soy and rice-wine stock. The coastal cities of Fujian offer a wonderful range of seafood, including river eel with leeks, fried jumbo prawns, and steamed crab.

HOTELS

Hotels in this region cater to all budgets, from dingy hostels to luxurious five-star resorts and international chains offering every amenity. Expect cheaper options to have hard beds, unreliable air-conditioning, non-English-speaking staff, and to be unable to except foreign credit cards. High-end international chains, such as the Shangri-la, Sheraton, and Sofitel are consistently lavish. Unlike many other Southeast Asian countries, boutique-style hotels and family-run guesthouses are few. One exception is a domestic chain called the Orange Hotel, with dozens of locations in Hangzhou, Ningbo, and Nanjing, where comfortable and imaginative rooms are available from US$30 to $65 a night.

WHAT IT COSTS IN YUAN					
	¢	$	$$	$$$	$$$$
Restaurants	under Y25	Y25–Y49	Y50–Y99	Y100–Y165	over Y165
Hotels	under Y700	Y700–Y1,099	Y1,100–Y1,399	Y1,400–Y1,800	over Y1,800

Restaurant prices are for a main course, excluding tax and tips. Hotel prices are for a standard double room, including taxes.

VISITOR INFORMATION

Tourist kiosks are ubiquitous in major cities and tourist destinations, but cater to domestic tourists. The lack of professionalism and English can be frustrating. The best sources for visitor information are the English-language city magazines that offer articles of local interest, special-event calendars, advice, transportation timetables, and colorful maps. Copies of *More Hangzhou* (⊕ *www.morehangzhou.com*), Nanjing's *Map Magazine* (⊕ *www.maiqiu.cn*), and *Xiamen Wave* (⊕ *www.xiamenwave.com*) can all be found at international hotels and foreign restaurants, including Starbucks.

TOURS

Countless pricey tour operators serve Eastern China, and travelers who want to avoid the stress of getting around may opt to join one. However, considering that China is remarkably safe and taxis are cheap and plentiful, it is not always advised. Taking the subway or a long walk to only one attraction can be more fascinating than a whole day's worth of attractions with a large group of strangers.

If you do opt to join a tour, focus on a special-interest tour. Tea lovers should consider **Seven Cups** (*www.sevencups.com*), which offers serious tea enthusiasts 13 to 15 day visits to Chinese tea gardens and hands-on experience with harvest and production methods of China's finest teas. Based in Arizona, you can contact them directly (☎ 520/628–2952).

Experience the Tu Lou Hakka Roundhouse with **Discover Fujian** (*1118 Xianhe Lu, 10th floor* ☎ *592/398–9901* ⊕ *www.discoverfujian.com*) They lead day trips, as well as four to five day trips, to the ancient, circular structures along with local village excursions at reasonable prices.

ZHEJIANG

The province of Zhejiang showcases the region's agricultural prowess and dedication to nature, even as it is one of China's most populous urban regions. The capital city of Hangzhou is famous for its West Lake, which is visited by millions of tourists annually. A center of culture and trade, Zhejiang is also one of China's wealthiest provinces. Hangzhou served as one of the country's eight ancient capital cities, after the Song Dynasty rulers fled Jurchen invaders. Throughout history, the city also benefited from its position as the last stop on the Grand Canal, the conduit for supplying goods to the imperial north.

Shaoxing showcases another aspect of Zhejiang life. The small-town flavor of this city-on-canals survives, despite a growing population.

Several high-profile figures helped put Shaoxing on the map, including former Premier Zhou Enlai and novelist Lu Xun.

Geographically, the river basin's plains in the north near Shanghai give way to mountains in the south of the province. Besides grain, the province also is recognized in China for its tea, crafts, silk production, and long tradition of sculpture and carving.

HANGZHOU

Approximately 1 hr and 40 mins (180 km 112 mi) southwest of Shanghai by express train.

Residents of Hangzhou are immensely proud of their city, and will often point to a classical saying that identifies it as an "earthly paradise." Indeed, Hangzhou is one of the country's most enjoyable cities. The green spaces and hilly landscape that surround the city make Hangzhou unique in Eastern China. Add to the experience a thriving arts scene, sophisticated restaurants, and vibrant nightlife, and Hangzhou vies with nearby Shanghai as the hippest city in the East.

GETTING HERE AND AROUND

Hangzhou is best accessed by train; the tourist express takes around an hour from Shanghai. Buses will get you to Shanghai in two hours or to Suzhou in 2½ hours. Hangzhou has several bus stations spread around the city serving different destinations—buses to Shanghai use the East Bus Station, whereas those to Suzhou use the North Bus Station.

AIR TRAVEL Hangzhou Xiaoshan International Airport, about 27 km (17 mi) southeast of the city, has frequent flights to Hong Kong, Guangzhou, and Beijing, which are all about two hours away. There are also flights to other major cities around the region.

Major hotels offer limousine service to the airport. Taxis to the airport cost around Y120. A bus (Y15 per person) leaves from the CAAC office on Tiyuchang Lu every 30 minutes between 5:30 am and 8:30 pm.

BOAT AND FERRY TRAVEL You can travel overnight by ferry between Hangzhou and Suzhou on the Grand Canal. Tickets are available through CITS or at the dock. It's a slow trip, and it's at night.

Many boats ply the waters of West Lake. Ferries charge Y35 for trips to the main islands. They depart when there are enough passengers, usually every 20 minutes. Small private boats charge Y80 for up to four people, but you can choose your own route. You can head out on your own boat for Y20, but you can't dock at the islands. Prices are fixed, but boat operators often try to overcharge you.

BUS TRAVEL Hangzhou is the bus hub for the province and has four stations. The West Bus Station (Xi Zhan) has several buses daily to the Yellow Mountain, as well as to Nanjing. The East Bus Station (Dong Zhan) is the town's biggest, with several hundred departures per day to destinations like Shaoxing (one hour), Suzhou (2½ hours), and Shanghai (two hours). About 9 km (5 mi) north of the city is the North Bus Station (Bei Zhan), where there are buses to Nanjing (4 to 4½ hours).

Within Hangzhou, in addition to regular city buses, a series of modern, air-conditioned buses connect most major tourist sights. Bus Y1 connects Baidi Causeway, Solitary Hill Island, Yue Fei Mausoleum, the Temple of the Soul's Retreat, and Orioles Singing in the Willow Waves. Bus Y3 runs to Precious Stone Hill, the China National Silk Museum, and the China Tea Museum.

TAXI TRAVEL Hangzhou's clean, reliable taxi fleet makes it easy to get from West Lake to far-flung sights like the Temple of the Soul's Retreat and the China Tea Museum (Y30–Y45).

■TIP➜ Avoid looking for a taxi between 4 and 5 pm, as ALL drivers are finishing their shifts and refuse to pick up anyone. This is true all over China.

TRAIN TRAVEL Travel between Shanghai and Hangzhou is very efficient. Fast trains take about an hour, while local trains take two or more. The train station can be chaotic, but hotel travel desks can often book advance tickets for a small fee. Trains also run to Suzhou (three hours), Nanjing (5½ hours), and most cities in Fujian.

SAFETY AND PRECAUTIONS

Hangzhou is a very safe city. Travelers should feel comfortable walking around anytime, day or night. As in most Chinese cities, however, crowded streets and senseless, unpredictable drivers mean that crossing the street can be dangerous. Be cautious in crowded places, such as the train station, and keep a close eye on valuables. Drink only bottled water and only take licensed taxis with working meters.

RENT A BIKE

Shaded by willow trees, West Lake is one of the country's most pleasant places for bicycling. This path, away from car traffic, is also a quick way to move between the area's major sights. Numerous bike-rental shops are around Orioles Singing in the Willow Waves Park. The rental rate is about Y10 per hour. A deposit and some form of identification are required.

TIMING

Give yourself at least two full days to properly explore the city. The West Lake and the pagodas and gardens that dot its periphery will occupy at least a full day. Hefang Pedestrian Street, Lingyin Temple, and a variety of museums will fill another day. Hangzhou, more than any other city in China, shouldn't be rushed. It's easy to spend four to five days exploring the tea fields and surrounding villages.

TOURS

Hotels can set up tours of the city's sights. You can also hire a car, driver, and translator through CITS, which has an office east of West Lake in the building of the Zhejiang Tourism Board. It's relatively inexpensive, and you'll be given discounts you wouldn't be able to negotiate for yourself. Smaller travel services tend to be less reliable and less experienced with the needs of foreign travelers.

Taxi drivers at the train station or in front of hotels will often offer tours. Although these can be as good as official ones, your driver's knowledge of English is often minimal.

ESSENTIALS

Air Contacts CAAC (⊠ 390 Tiyuchang Lu ☎ 0571/8515–4259). **Dragonair** (⊠ Radisson Plaza Hotel Hangzhou, 5th floor, 333 Ti Yu Chang Lu ☎ 0571/8506–8388). **Hangzhou Xiaoshan International Airport** (⊠ Hangzhou Xiaoshan District ☎ 0571/8666–1234).

Bank Bank of China (⊠ 140 Yan An Lu ☎ 0571/8501–8888).

Boat and Ferry Contact CITS (⊠ Huancheng Bei Lu ☎ 0571/8515–3360).

Bus Contacts East Bus Station (⊠ 71 Genshan Xi Lu310012 ☎ 0571/8694–8252; 0571/8696–4011 for tickets). **North Bus Station** (⊠ 766 Moganshan Lu ☎ 0571/8809-7761;. **West Bus Station** (⊠ 357 Tianmushan Lu ☎ 0571/8522–2237).

Medical Assistance (⊠ **International Service Clinic of Sir Run Run Shaw Hospital** (⊠ 3 East Qingchun Lu, 5th floor, Tower 3 ☎ 0571/8600–6118).

Train Information Hangzhou Train Station (⊠ 1 Huan Cheng Dong Lu, near intersection of Jiang Cheng Lu and Xihu Da Dao ☎ 0571/8782–9418).

A picture-perfect sunset over West Lake.

Visitor and Tour Info **Hangzhou Travel and Tourism Bureau** (✉ *484 Yanan Lu* ☎ *0571/8515–2645*). **Zhejiang CITS** (✉ *1 Shihan Lu, next to the Hangzhou Tourism Bureau* ☎ *0571/8516–0877*). **Zhejiang Comfort Travel** (✉ *Shangri-La Hotel Hangzhou, 78 Beishan Lu* ☎ *0571/8796–5005*).

EXPLORING HANGZHOU

WEST LAKE ATTRACTIONS

West Lake *(Xihu)*. With arched bridges stretching over the water, West Lake is the heart of leisure in Hangzhou. Originally a bay, the whole area was built up gradually throughout the years, a combination of natural changes and human shaping of the land. The shores are idyllic and imminently photographable, enhanced by meandering paths, artificial islands, and countless pavilions with upturned roofs. Two pedestrian causeways cross the lake: **Baidi** in the north and **Sudi** in the west. They are named for two poet–governors from different eras who invested in landscaping and developing the lake. Ideal for strolling or biking, both walkways are lined with willow and peach trees, crossed by bridges, and dotted with benches where you can pause to admire the views. ✉ *East of the city, along Nanshan Lu.*

The Bai Causeway ends at the largest island on West Lake, **Solitary Hill Island** *(Gushan)*. A palace for the exclusive use of the emperor during his visits to Hangzhou once stood here. On its southern side is a small, carefully composed park around several pavilions and a pond. A path leads up the hill to the **Seal Engraver's Society** *(Xiling Yinshe* ☎ *0571/8781–5910* 🎫 *Y5* 🕙 *Daily 9–5)*. Professional carvers will design and create seals. The society's garden has one of the best views of the lake.

WEST LAKE IS THE BEST

A famous poem that says, "Of all the lakes, north, south, east and west, the one at West Lake is the best." Start exploring where Pinghai Road meets Harbin Road in the northeastern part of the lake. There's a fabulous boardwalk with weeping willows, restaurants, and a lakeside teahouse.

Wending north, you can cross the street to ascend a small hill capped with the Baochu Pagoda. Here the views of West Lake are some of the best in the city. Once you climb down, you can venture to the Baidi and Sudi causeways through the middle of the lake. Don't miss the classical Lingyin Temple, nestled in the nearby hills.

Take a guided boat from the southern shore by night, when the Three Pools Mirroring the Moon pagoda is alight. This stone pagoda has six incised circles. When candles are set inside them, the light appears as romantic moons.

Solitary Hill Island is home to the **Zhejiang Provincial Museum** (*Zhejiang Bowuguan* ☎0571/8797–1177 ⊕ *www.zhejiangmuseum.com* 🎫 *Free* ☉ *Weekdays 8:30–4:30*). The museum has a good collection of archaeological finds, as well as bronzes and paintings. ⊠ *West Lake (on northern West Lake, southern foot of Gushan Mountain)* 🎫 *Free* ☉ *Daily 8–dusk*.

NEED A BREAK?

Reward yourself with a heavenly and inexpensive foot or full-body massage at **Cathay View Foot Massage** (⊠ 7 Qingbo Jie ☎ 0571/8768–0118). We recommend the 90-minute (Y98) foot massage, which includes a foot bath, a 30-minute shoulder and back rub, and endless tea, fruit, and snacks in a cozy, dimly lit private room (up to four people). They might try to up-sell with a "special" potion added to the foot bath water; be firm and insist on the "zui putong" (most common) massage and sit back and relax. Located just off Nanshan Lu, down a small street near the Crystal Orange Hotel.

Fodor's Choice ★

On the southeastern shore of West Lake is the **Evening Sunlight at Thunder Peak Pagoda** (*Leifeng Xizhao*). Local legend says that the original Thunder Peak Pagoda was constructed to imprison a snake-turned-human who lost her mortal love on West Lake. The pagoda collapsed in 1924, perhaps finally freeing the White Snake. A new tower, completed in 2002, sits beside the remains of its predecessor. There's a sculpture on each level, including a carving that depicts the tragic story of the White Snake. The foundation dates to AD 976 and is an active archaeological site, where scientists uncovered a miniature silver pagoda containing what is said to be a lock of the Buddha's hair; it's on display in a separate hall. The view of the lake is breathtaking, particularly at sunset. ⊠ *15 Nanshan Lu* ☎ *0571/8796–4515* ⊕ *www.leifengta.com. cn* 🎫 *Y80* ☉ *Mar. 16–Nov. 15, daily 8 am–9 pm; Nov. 16–Mar. 15, daily 7:30–5:30*.

On the southern side of the lake is the man-made island of **Three Pools Reflecting the Moon** (*Santan YinGyue*). Here you'll find walkways surrounding several large ponds, all connected by zigzagging bridges. Off the island's southern shore are three stone Ming Dynasty pagodas. During the Mid-Autumn Moon Festival, held in the middle of September, lanterns are lit in the pagodas, creating the three golden disks that give the island its name. Boats costing between Y35 and Y45 run between here and Solitary Hill Island. ⊠ *West Lake* 🚢 *Y45 (includes boat ride)* ⊙ *Daily 7–5:30.*

WORD OF MOUTH

"About touring Hangzhou—this last time I finally succumbed to paying for a ride in those open, golf-cart-like vehicles. It was wonderful. I wish I had done this on my very first trip to Hangzhou. The motorized carts—with a fringe on the top—circle completely around West Lake. One entire circle costs 40 Yuan (slightly less than $5) per person." —easytraveler

The slender spire of Protecting Chu Pagoda rises atop **Precious Stone Hill** (*Baoshi Shan*). The brick and stone pagoda is visible from about anywhere on the lake. From the hilltop, you can see around West Lake and across to Hangzhou City. Numerous paths from the lakeside lead up the hill, which is dotted with Buddhist and Taoist shrines. Several caves provide shade from the hot summer sun. ⊠ *North of West Lake.*

Along the eastern bank of the lake is **Orioles Singing in the Willow Waves** (*Liulang Wenying*), a nice place to watch boats on the lake. This park comes alive during the Lantern Festival, held in the winter. Paper lanterns are set to float on the river, under the willow bows. ⊠ *Near the intersection of Hefang Jie and Nanshan Lu.*

OTHER TOP ATTRACTIONS

From worm to weave, the **China National Silk Museum** (*Zhongguo Sichou Bowuguan*) explores traditional silk production, illustrating every step of the process. By the end, you'll comprehend the cost of this fine fiber made from cocoons of mulberry-munching larvae. On display are looms, brocades, and a rotating exhibit of historic robes from different Chinese dynasties. The first-floor shop has the city's largest selection of silk, and sells it by the meter. The museum is south of West Lake, on the road to Jade Emperor Hill. ⊠ *73–1 Yuhuangshan Lu* ☎ *0571/8703–7173* ⊕ *www.chinasilkmuseum.com* 🖃 *Free* ⊙ *Daily 8:30–4:30.*

★ The fascinating **China Tea Museum** (*Zhongguo Chaye Bowuguan*) explores all facets of China's tea culture, such as the utensils used in the traditional ceremony. Galleries contain fascinating information about the varieties and quality of leaves, brewing techniques, and gathering methods, all with good English explanations. A shop also offers a range of tea for sale, without the bargaining you'll encounter at Dragon Well Tea Park. ⊠ *Off Longjing Lu, north of Dragon Well Tea Park* ⊕ *www. teamuseum.cn* 🖃 *Free* ⊙ *Daily 8:30–4:30.*

Equally celebrated as West Lake, and a short ride southwest of the lake, is **Dragon Well Tea Park** (*Longjing Wencha*), set amid rolling tea plantations. This park is named for an ancient well whose water is considered ideal for brewing the famous local Longjing tea. Distinguishing

Buddha sculptures on the face of the Peak That Flew from Afar.

between varieties and grades of tea can be confusing for novices, especially under the high pressure of the eager hawkers. It is worth a preliminary trip to the nearby tea museum to bone up first. The highest quality varieties are very expensive, but once you take a sip you will taste the difference. Opening prices are intentionally high, so be sure to bargain. ■TIP➔ Continue walking south on Longjing Lu from the tea museum for stunning scenery uphill toward the park. The tea park has minimal rates posted (Y2/3), but it's likely that someone will let you in for free. ✉ *Longjing Lu, next to Dragon Well Temple.*

Fodor's Choice One of the major Zen Buddhist shrines in China, the **Temple of the Soul's**
★ **Retreat** *(Lingyin Si)* was founded in AD 326 by Hui Li, a Buddhist monk from India. He looked at the surrounding mountains and exclaimed, "This is the place where the souls of immortals retreat," hence the name. This site is especially notable for religious carvings on the nearby **Peak That Flew from Afar** (Feilai Feng). From the 10th to the 14th century, monks and artists sculpted more than 300 images on the mountain's face and inside caves. Over the centuries this shrine has changed due to wars and revolution. The main temple was restored in 1974 following the end of the Cultural Revolution. The temple and carvings are among the most popular spots in Hangzhou. To avoid the crowds, try to visit during the week. The temple is about 3 km (2 mi) southwest of West Lake. ✉ *End of Lingyin Lu* ☎ *0571/8796–9691* ✎ *Park Y35, temple Y30* ⊙ *Park daily 5:30 am–6 pm, temple daily 7–5.*

WORTH NOTING

Atop **Moon Mountain** (Yuelin Shan) stands the impressive **Pagoda of Six Harmonies** *(Liuhe Ta)*. Those who climb to the top of the seven-story pagoda are rewarded with great views across the Qiantang River. Originally lanterns were lighted in its windows, and the pagoda served as a lighthouse for ships navigating the river. On the 18th day of the eighth lunar month, the pagoda is packed with people wanting the best seat for Qiantang Reversal. On this day the flow of the river reverses itself, creating large waves that for centuries have delighted observers. Behind the pagoda in an extensive park is an exhibit of 100 or so miniature pagodas, representing every Chinese style. The pagoda is 2½ km (1½ mi) south of West Lake. ⊠ *Fuxing Jie, on the Qiantang River* ✉ *Y20* ☉ *Daily 6 am–6:30 pm.*

> **FOR THE KIDS**
>
> One of our favorite child-friendly places is the garden behind the **Pagoda of Six Harmonies** in Hangzhou. Climb the stairs of the seven-story Pagoda, visit the garden, and play among the miniature re-creations of China's most famous pagodas and temples. This park is an ideal place to picnic. The pagoda is 2½ km (1½ mi) south of West Lake. (⊠ *Fuxing Jie, on the Qiantang River310011* ✉ *Y20* ☉ *Daily 6 am–6:30 pm.*

In the hills southwest of the lake is **Running Tiger Spring** *(Hupao Quan)*. According to legend, a traveling monk decided this setting would be perfect for a temple, but was disappointed to discover that there was no source of water. That night he dreamed of two tigers that ripped up the earth around him. When he awoke he was lying next to a spring. On the grounds is an intriguing "dripping wall" cut out of the mountain. Locals line up with jugs to collect the water that pours from its surface, believing that the water has special qualities—and it does. Ask someone in the temple's souvenir shop to float a coin on the surface of the water to prove it. ⊠ *Hupao Lu, near the Pagoda of Six Harmonies* ✉ *Y15* ☉ *Daily 6 am–6 pm.*

At the foot of Qixia Hill is **Yellow Dragon Cave** *(Huanglong Dong)*, famous for a never-ending stream of water spurting from the head of a yellow dragon. Nearby are a garden and a stage for traditional Yue opera performances that are given daily. In a nearby grove you'll see examples of rare "square bamboo." ⊠ *Shuguang Lu* ☎ *0571/8798–5860* ✉ *Y15* ☉ *Daily 7:30–6.*

Near Solitary Hill Island stands the **Yue Fei Mausoleum** *(Yue Fei Mu)*, a shrine to honor General Yue Fei (1103–42), who led Song armies against foreign invaders. When he was a young man, his mother tattooed his back with the commandment to "Repay the nation with loyalty." This made Yue Fei a hero of both patriotic loyalty and filial piety. At the height of his success, a jealous rival convinced the emperor to have Yue Fei executed. A subsequent leader pardoned the warrior and enshrined him as a national hero. Statues of Yue Fei's accusers kneel in shame nearby. Traditionally, visitors would spit on statues of the traitors, but a recent sign near the statue asks them to glare instead. ⊠ *Beishan Lu, west of Solitary Hill Island* ✉ *Y25* ☉ *Daily 7:30–6.*

WHERE TO EAT

For traditional Hangzhou food, check out Gaoyin Jie. It's a lively strip of restaurants, snack stalls, and teahouses. Expect touts, English menus, and blazing neon signs.

$–$$

MIDDLE EASTERN

✕**Dong Yi Shun.** Lines form all day at the take-out window for the sesame-coated naan breads and plump, well-seasoned lamb skewers. Sit inside for a large picture menu of Western Chinese and Middle Eastern dishes. The lamb and cheese pancake with a side order of Arabic yogurt comes highly recommended. It's a great alternative to oily Chinese dishes. Walk off the calories afterwards on neon-lit Gaoyin Street. ✉ *99 Gaoyin Jie* ☎ *0571/8780–5163* 🖃 *No credit cards.*

$$

INDIAN

✕**Haveli.** A sign of the city's cosmopolitan atmosphere, Nanshan Lu is home to several good international restaurants. The best of these is this authentic Indian restaurant, with a solid menu of dishes ranging from lamb vindaloo to chicken tandoor cooked in a traditional oven. End your meal with a fantastic mango-flavored yogurt drink. Choose either the dining room with a high peaked ceiling and exposed wood beams or the large patio. A belly dancer performs nightly. ✉ *77 Nanshan Lu, south of Orioles Singing in the Willow Waves* ☎ *0571/8702–9177* 🖃 *AE, DC, MC, V.*

$

CAFÉ

Honey Moon Desserts. Originated in Hong Kong, this popular, Asian-inspired dessert spot is rapidly expanding all over the mainland. Occupying a prime piece of real estate along the main commercial drag of the West Lake, this bright place is sleek and spotless. Trendy Hangzhou locals pack this place at all hours for the inventive and exotic creations. The mango or durian pancake filled with fresh whipped cream is yummy, and the almond and walnut soup is creamy and refreshing. An English picture menu will help guide you. ✉ *98 You Dian Road* ☎ *0571/8796–9691* 🖃 *No credit cards.*

$–$$

VEGETARIAN

✕**Lingyin Si Vegetarian Restaurant.** Inside the Temple of the Soul's Retreat, this restaurant has turned the Buddhist restriction against eating meat into an opportunity to invent a range of delicious vegetarian dishes. Soy replaces chicken and beef, meaning your meal is as benevolent to your health as to the animal world. ✉ *End of Lingyin Si Lu, western shore of West Lake* ☎ *0571/8796–9691* 🖃 *No credit cards* ⊘ *No dinner.*

$$–$$$

CHINESE FUSION

Fodor's Choice

★

✕**Louwailou Restaurant.** Back in 1848, this place opened as a fish shack on West Lake. Business boomed and it became the most famous restaurant in the province. Specializing in Zhejiang cuisine, Louwailou makes special use of lake perch, which is steamed and served with vinegar sauce. Another highlight is the classic *su dongpo,* pork slow cooked in yellow-rice wine and tender enough to cut with chopsticks. Hangzhou's most famous dish, Beggar's Chicken, is wrapped in lotus leaves and baked in a clay shell. It's as good as it sounds. ✉ *30 Gushan Lu, southern tip of Solitary Hill Island* ☎ *0571/8796–9682* 🖃 *AE, MC, V.*

> **WORD OF MOUTH**
>
> "If just relaxing is the aim, then Hangzhou is a better choice than Shanghai, I'd say, but three nights would almost certainly be enough." —PeterN_H

The Qiantang Tidal Bore

During the autumnal equinox, when the moon's gravitational pull is at its peak, huge waves crash up the Qiantang River. Every year at this time, crowds gather at a safe distance to watch what begins as a distant line of white waves approaching. As it nears, it becomes a towering, thundering wall of water.

The phenomenon, known as a tidal bore, occurs when strong tides surge against the current of the river. The Qiantang Tidal Bore is the largest in the world, with speeds recorded up to 25 mi an hour and heights of 30 feet. The Qiantang has the best conditions in the world to produce these tidal waves. Incoming tides are funneled into the shallow riverbed from the Gulf of Hangzhou. The bell shape narrows and concentrates the wave. People have been swept away in the past, so police now enforce a strict viewing distance.

5

WHERE TO STAY

¢–$ ⬛ **Crystal Orange Hotel.** Both domestic and foreign visitors love this ★ quirky boutique hotel so much that branches are now popping up in several other Chinese cities. All locations provide a similar room style and level of service, but the Hangzhou property is a step up from the rest (notice the Crystal prefix). The airy lobby is artfully decorated with Andy Warhol's Marilyn Monroe pop art, and the glass elevator gives a fun, bird's eye view. Rooms are clean and quiet, but be sure to request one facing outward for better views. Each room has a pet goldfish to keep solo travelers company. Book ahead, since this place fills up weeks in advance. **Pros:** excellent location near West Lake; bicycle rental. **Cons:** bad breakfast; limited amenities. ⊠ *122 Qingbo Jie* ☎ *0571/2887–8988* ⤴ ⚘ *In-room: safe, Internet. In-hotel: bicycles, laundry service, no-smoking rooms* ▭ *MC, V.*

$$ ⬛ **Dragon Hotel.** Within walking distance of Precious Stone Hill and the Yellow Dragon Cave, this hotel stands in relatively quiet and attractive surroundings. It's a massive place, but feels much smaller because its buildings are spread around peaceful courtyards with ponds, a waterfall, and a gazebo. Two towers house the medium-size guest rooms, which are decorated in pale greens and blues. Although it has plenty of facilities, the hotel lacks the polish of its Western competitors. **Pros:** good location; newly renovated. **Cons:** indifferent service; little English is spoken. ⊠ *120 Shuguang Lu, at Hangda Lu* ☎ *0571/8799–8833* ⊕ *www.dragon-hotel.com* ⤴ *499 rooms, 29 suites* ⚘ *In-room: safe, refrigerator, Internet. In-hotel: 4 restaurants, room service, bar, pool, gym, bicycles, laundry service, no-smoking rooms* ▭ *AE, DC, MC, V.*

$$$–$$$$ ⬛ **Hyatt Regency Hangzhou.** Hangzhou's most recognizable and centrally
Fodor's Choice located hotel, the Hyatt Regency combines careful service, comfort-
★ able rooms, and a great location. Rooms are sleekly furnished, and the beds are ultrasoft; be sure to ask for a room on an upper floor for unobstructed views. A large pool overlooks West Lake. Inside there's a day spa, as well as excellent Chinese and Western restaurants. About two blocks north is Hubin Yi Park Boat Dock, where you can catch

boats that ply the lake. **Pros:** gorgeous view; good service; excellent pool. **Cons:** long check-in time; beginning to show its age. ⊠ *28 Hu Bin Lu* ☎ *0571/8779–1234* ⊕ *www.hyatt.com* ⤳ *390 rooms, 23 suites* ⌂ *In-room: safe, refrigerator, Internet. In-hotel: 3 restaurants, room service, bar, pool, gym, spa laundry service, no-smoking rooms* ⊟ *AE, DC, MC, V.*

$$$–$$$$ ⊞ **Shangri-La Hotel Hangzhou.** Set on the site of an ancient temple, the
Fodor's Choice Shangri-La is a scenic and historic landmark. The hotel's 40 hillside
★ acres of camphor and bamboo trees merge seamlessly into the nearby gardens and walkways surrounding West Lake. Spread through two wings, the large rooms have a formal feel, with high ceilings and heavy damask fabrics. Request a room overlooking the lake. The gym and restaurants are all top caliber. A first-floor garden bar is an elegant spot to relax with a drink. **Pros:** excellent location; staff speak fluent English. **Cons:** poor customer service; long check-in times. ⊠ *78 Beishan Lu* ☎ *0571/8797–7951* ⊕ *www.shangri-la.com* ⤳ *355 rooms, 37 suites* ⌂ *In-room: safe, refrigerator, Internet. In-hotel: 3 restaurants, room service, bar, tennis court, pool, gym, bicycles, laundry service, no-smoking rooms* ⊟ *AE, DC, MC, V.*

$$–$$$ ⊞ **Sofitel Westlake Hangzhou.** A stone's throw from West Lake, this high-end hotel is in a lively neighborhood of restaurants, bars, and shops. Gauzy curtains and etched-glass and -wood columns divide the distinctive lobby, distinguished by a gold-and-black mural of the city's landmarks. The rooms—most of which have lake views—are thoughtfully designed, with sleek oval desks, fabric-covered headboards, and a glass privacy screen in the bathroom. A Roman-style pool overcomes its drab basement location. The hotel is a block north of Orioles Singing in the Willow Waves. **Pros:** good location; helpful staff. **Cons:** small rooms; many rooms with poor views. ⊠ *333 Xihu Dadao* ☎ *0571/8707–5858* ⊕ *www.accor.com* ⤳ *186 rooms, 15 suites* ⌂ *In-room: safe, refrigerator, Internet, Wi-Fi. In-hotel: 4 restaurants, room service, bar, pool, gym, spa, laundry service, no-smoking rooms* ⊟ *AE, DC, MC, V.*

$ ⊞ **Wyndham Grand Plaza Royale West Lake Hangzhou.** With the timeless and picturesque West Lake only a few steps away, this space-ship-shaped international hotel combines excellent customer service with flawless mountain, lake, and garden views. Spacious and romantic rooms feature dark purples and gold-framed mirrors. At night the exterior is illuminated with tiny white dots, as if a UFO has landed on the eastern shores of the West Lake. Don't hesitate to ask the hotel's army of foreign-guest-service "ambassadors" questions; they know the city and can give good insider recommendations. The authentic Thai restaurant is hands-down the best in town. **Pros:** great location, great customer service **Cons:** locker rooms need renovation ⊠ *555 Fengqi Lu* ☎ *0571/8761–6888* ⊕ *www.wyndham.com* ⤳ *283 rooms* ⌂ *In-room: safe, refrigerator, Internet. In-hotel: 3 restaurants, room service, bar, pool, gym, laundry service, no-smoking rooms* ⊟ *AE, DC, MC, V.*

NIGHTLIFE AND THE ARTS

Maya Bar (⊠ *79 Shuguang Lu* ☎ *0571/8999–7628*) is known for its generous pours and a consistent Tex-Mex menu, and occasional live music has made this place popular with expats and locals for more

After dark on Hefangjie Street.

than eight years. For a more refined night out, head to the southeastern edge of the West Lake and visit **JZ Club** (✉ *6 Liuying Rd., at the intersection of Nanshan Lu* ☎ *0571/8702–8298* ⊕ *www.jzclub.cc)*, a well-established jazz club that attracts a cultured clientele. **Eudora Station** (✉ *101–7 Nanshan Lu* ☎ *0571/8791–4760)>*is the newest addition to Nanshan Road's ever-expanding foreign bar and restaurant scene. It fills up on the weekend thanks to live music and cheap drink specials. If you're craving something familiar, the pizzas and salads are decent.

SHOPPING

The best souvenirs to buy in Hangzhou are green tea and silk, but all sorts of wooden crafts, silk fans and umbrellas, and antiques are sold in small shops sprinkled around town. For the best Longjing tea, head to Dragon Well Tea Park or the China Tea Museum.

Fodor's Choice ★ Hefang Street is a lively, crowded pedestrian street and not to be missed on a visit to Hangzhou. Restored old buildings are beautifully illuminated at night and house tea shops, ancient traditional Chinese apothecaries, clothing boutiques selling *qipaos* (traditional silk Chinese dresses), scrolls, calligraphy and wooden fans. Artists draw caricatures, candymakers sculpt sugar into art, blind masseurs alleviate tension, and storytellers re-create ancient Chinese legends. Start at Wushan Square and walk west. At night the glowing Chenghuang Pavilion, perched on a mountain top next to the square, is enchanting.

China Silk City (*Zhongguo Sichou Cheng* ✉ *217 Xinhua Lu, between Fengqi Lu and Tiyuchang Lu* ☎ *0571/8510–0192)* sells silk ties, pajamas, and shirts, plus silk straight off the bolt. About three blocks

north of the China Tea Museum, the **Xihu Longjing Tea Company** (✉ *108 Longjing Lu* ☎ *0571/8796–2219*) has a nice selection of Longjing tea.

The **Night Market** (✉ *Renhe Lu, east of Huansha Lu*) has Hangzhou's best late-night snacks, and you'll find accessories of every kind—ties, scarves, pillow covers—as well as knockoff designer goods and fake antiques. It's open nightly 6–10:30.

SHAOXING

68 km (42 mi) east of Hangzhou.

★ Shaoxing is alive in the Chinese imagination thanks to the famous writer Lu Xun, who set many of his classic works in this sleepy southern town. A literary revolutionary, Lu Xun broke tradition by writing in the vernacular of everyday Chinese, instead of the stiff, scholarly prose previously held as the only appropriate language for literature.

Today much of the city's charm is in exploring its narrow cobbled streets. The older sections of the city are made up of low stone houses connected by canals crisscrossed by arched bridges. East Lake is no match for the grandeur of Hangzhou's West Lake, but its bizarre rock formations and caves make for interesting tours. Shaoxing is also famous for its celebrated yellow-rice wine, used by cooks everywhere.

GETTING HERE AND AROUND
The most reliable and comfortable way to travel to Shaoxing is by train. Regular train and luxury bus services run to Shaoxing from Hangzhou and Shanghai a few times a day.

BUS TRAVEL Hangzhou's East Bus Station has dozens of buses each day to Shaoxing. In Shaoxing, buses to Hangzhou leave from the main bus station in the north of town, at the intersection of Jiefang Bei Lu and Huan Cheng Bei Lu. Luxury buses take about an hour.

TAXI TRAVEL Although Shaoxing is small enough that walking is the best way to get between many sights, the city's small red taxis are relatively inexpensive. Most trips are Y15.

TRAIN TRAVEL Trains between Hangzhou and Shaoxing take about an hour, but do not leave as frequently as buses. The Shaoxing train station is 2½ km (1½ mi) north of the city, near the main bus station.

TIMING
Shaoxing's major attractions can be seen in a day trip from Hangzhou.

ESSENTIALS
Bank Bank of China (✉ *568 Zhongxing Bei Lu* ☎ *0575/8514–3571*).

Bus Contact Shaoxing North Bus Station (✉ *2 Jiefang Bei lu* ☎ *0575/8513–0794*).

Medical Assistance Shaoxing People's Hospital (✉ *61 Shaoxing Dongjie* ☎ *0575/8822–8888*).

Train Contact Shaoxing Train Station (✉ *Shaoxing Chezhan Lu* ☎ *0575/8802–2584*).

EXPLORING SHAOXING
TOP ATTRACTIONS

The city's quiet northern neighbor-hoods are amenable to wandering, with several historic homes and temples that are now preserved as museums. The largest is the **Cai Yuanpei's House** (✉ *13 Bifei Alley, Xiaoshan Lu* ☎ *0575/8511–0652* 🎟 *Y8* ◷ *Daily 8–5*). The owner was a famous educator during the republic, and his family's large compound is decorated with period furniture.

WORD OF MOUTH

"It's a little further afield but look up information on Shaoxing, which is larger, but both laced with canals and with large areas of ancient housing, ancient bridges (particularly the Ba Zi Qiao-Bridge in the Shape of an Eight), and other historical sites." —PeterN_H

In a city of bridges, **Figure 8 Bridge** *(Bazi Qiao Bridge)* is the city's fin-est and best known. Its long, sloping sides rise to a flat crest that looks like the character for eight, an auspicious number. The bridge is over 800 years old, and is draped with a thick beard of ivy and vines. It sits in a quiet area of old stone houses with canal-side terraces where people wash clothes and chat with neighbors. ✉ *Bazi Qiao Zhi Jie, off Renmin Zhong Lu.*

The **Lu Xun Family Home** *(Lu Xun Gu Ju)* was once the stomping ground of literary giant and social critic Lu Xun. The extended Lu family lived around a series of courtyards. Nearby is the local school where Lu honed his writing skills. Explore a traditional Shaoxing home and see some beautiful antique furniture. This is a popular destination, so it's wise to book a tour in high season. Consult your concierge for details. ✉ *398 Lu Xun Zhong Lu, 1 block east of Xianhen Hotel* ☎ *0575/8513– 2080* 🎟 *Free with ID or passport* ◷ *Daily 8:30–5.*

WORTH NOTING

Near the Figure 8 Bridge is the bright pink **Catholic Church of St. Joseph**, dating from the turn of the 20th century. A hybrid of styles, the Italian-inspired interior is decorated with passages from the Bible in Chinese calligraphy. ✉ *Bazi Qiao Zhi Jie, off Renmin Zhong Lu.*

The narrow **East Lake** *(Dong Hu)* runs along the base of a rocky bluff rising up from the rice paddies of Zhejiang. The crazily shaped cliffs were used as a rock quarry over the centuries, and today their sheer gray faces jut out in sheets of rock. You can hire a local boatman to take you along the base of the cliffs in a traditional black awning boat for Y40. ✉ *Yundong Lu, 3 km (2 mi) east of the city center* 🎟 *Y25* ◷ *Daily 7:30–5:30.*

The **Zhou Enlai Family Home** (✉ *369 Laodong Lu* ☎ *0575/8513–3368* 🎟 *Y18* ◷ *Daily 8–5*) belonged to the first premier of Communist China, who came from a family of prosperous Shaoxing merchants. Zhou is credited with saving some of China's most important historic monu-ments from destruction at the hands of the Red Guards during the Cultural Revolution. The compound, a showcase of traditional archi-tecture, has been preserved and houses exhibits on Zhou's life, ranging from his high-school essays to vacation snapshots with his wife.

What's Cooking

Shaoxing secured its place in the Chinese culinary pantheon with Shaoxing wine, the best yellow-rice wine in the country. Although cooks around the world know the nutty-flavored wine as a marinade and seasoning, in Shaoxing the fermented brew of glutinous rice is put to a variety of uses, from drinking straight up (as early as breakfast) to sipping as a medicine (infused with traditional herbs and remedies). Like grape wines, Shaoxing mellows and improves with age, as its color deepens to a reddish brown. It is local custom to bury a cask when

a daughter is born and serve it when she marries.

The wine is an excellent accompaniment to Shaoxing snacks such as pickled greens and the city's most popular street food, *chou doufu,* which means "stinky tofu." The golden-fried squares of tender tofu taste great, if you can get past the pungent odor. Also, look for dishes made with another Shaoxing product, fermented bean curd. With a flavor not unlike an aged cheese, it's rarely eaten by itself, but complements fish and sharpens the flavor of meat dishes.

WHERE TO EAT

¢–$

CHINESE FUSION

✕**Sanwei Jiulou.** This restaurant serves up local specialties, including warm rice wine served in Shaoxing's distinctive tin kettles. Relaxed and distinctive, it's in an old restored building and appointed with traditional wood furniture. The second story looks out over the street below. ⊠ *2 Lu Xun Lu* ☎ *0575/8893–5578* ☐ *No credit cards.*

¢

CHINESE

✕**Xianheng Winehouse** *(Xianheng Jiudian).* Shaoxing's most famous fictional character, the small-town scholar Kong Yiji, would sit on a bench here, dining on wine and boiled beans. Forgo the beans, but the fermented bean curd is good, especially with a bowl of local wine. ⊠ *179 Lu Xun Zhong Lu, 1 block east of the Sanwei Jiulou* ☎ *0575/8511– 6666* ☐ *No credit cards.*

WHERE TO STAY

$

🏨 **New Century Grand Hotel Shaoxing.** This Chinese hotel chain is the newest and most modern lodging option in Shoaxing. Rooms are decorated in muted colors and light wood paneling. Comfy beds have quilted headrests, and sleek bathrooms are fitted with water-saving fixtures. Opt for a deluxe room if you want one large bed. A pleasant walk directly west of the hotel past the Shen Family Garden will lead to the Lu Xun Memorial (about one mile). **Pros:** Everything is brand-new; good location. **Cons:** indifferent service; limited English ability. ⊠ *278 Remin East Road* ☎ *0575/8809–8888* ⬎ *365 rooms* ♨ *In-room: safe, refrigerator, Internet. In-hotel: 2 restaurants, pool, gym* ☐ *AE, DC, MC, V.*

$–$$

🏨 **Shaoxing Xianheng Hotel.** Conveniently located near many of the city's restaurants and a quick walk north to Lu Xun Memorial, the Shaoxing Xianheng claims to be the only eco-hotel in the province (though the lack of third-party oversight in China makes this difficult to prove). Regardless, rooms are comfortable, and most have been recently remodeled. However, always ask to see a room before accepting it, since there's a lot of inconsistency in quality. They also have a decent Italian restaurant if you're hankering for some Western food. **Pros:** centrally located; good value. **Cons:** inconsistent English; some rooms need updating. ⊠ *680 Jiefang Nan Lu* ☎ *0575/8806–8688* ⤴ *207 rooms* ⚄ *In-hotel: 2 restaurants, bar, gym* ▭ *AE, MC, V.*</R>

SHOPPING

On the shopping street called **Lu Xun Zhong Lu**, in addition to calligraphy brushes, and fans, scrolls, and other items decorated with calligraphy, look for shops selling the local tin wine pots. In the traditional way of serving yellow-rice wine, the pots are placed on the stove to heat up wine for a cold winter night. Also popular are traditional boatmen's hats, made of thick waterproof black felt.

NINGBO

139 km (86 mi) southeast of Hangzhou, 150 km (93 mi) south of Shanghai.

The country's fifth biggest port, Ningbo is one of China's most prosperous cities, and an easy place to explore on foot. Rivers and canals flow through a city that is generously sprinkled with tranquil gardens and parks. Colonial architecture and centuries-old pagodas and temples are mixed (rather unfortunately) with featureless, communist-style apartment blocks and hideous glass and steel towers. Unlike Shanghai, Hangzhou, and Suzhou, Ningbo is not set up for tourism. This makes it a relaxing and authentic place to explore. Join the locals for bottomless cups of tea and mah-jongg in one of the many parks, or burn through some cash in the city's lively markets, ritzy shopping malls, and trendy nightclubs.

Ningbo, translated as "tranquil waves," sits at the confluence of three rivers (the Yuyao, Fenghua, and Yongjiang) that eventually snake their way to the nearby sea. Ningbo's history stretches back thousands of years. In the 7th century, the Tang Dynasty developed a complicated system of canals, and trade with Japan and Korea boomed. The Portuguese, with their keen eye for location, settled in as early as the 16th century, and left behind a fair number of churches that are still in use today. More recently, during the Second World War the Japanese bombed the city with fleas carrying the bubonic plague.

GETTING HERE AND AROUND

It's best to travel here by bus, though the express train does connect it with both Hangzhou and Shanghai. The South Bus Station (across the street from the Asia Garden Hotel) has a steady stream of buses leaving every 10–15 minutes from 6 am to 8 pm for Hangzhou and Shanghai, as well as other destinations.

AIR TRAVEL   Ningbo's Lishe International Airport is about 20 minutes from downtown (7 mi). There are connections to all major Chinese cities, as well as Hong Kong and Seoul. Major hotels offer free airport shuttle buses, and some have free luxury buses to Shanghai. Ask upon check-in, as you must book in advance. A bus (Y10) leaves from the CAAC office every hour from 7:20 am to 6:20 pm.

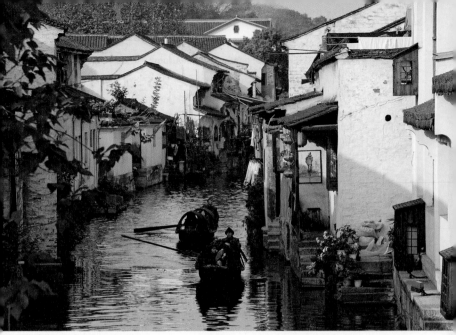
One of Shaoxing's famous Waterways.

BUS TRAVEL Ningbo has five long-distance bus stations. The Ningbo Passenger Transportation Center (NPTC) and the South Bus Station are the most useful for travelers. The NPTC serves Nanjing, Suzhou, and Yangzhou, as well as Fujian and Anhui provinces. The South Bus Station serves Hangzhou, Shanghai, and Wenzhou. The North Bus Station serves counties around Ningbo, Jiangbei District, and Putuo Mountain. Buses from the West Bus Station head to many scenic areas in and around Ningbo.

TAXI TRAVEL Taxis are cheap and plentiful. Areas of interest are not far apart and should cost no more than Y15, with about Y40 to the airport.

TRAIN TRAVEL Currently, Ningbo has one passenger train station (the South Rail Station) with express trains. Talks of closing it for renovation and using the East Rail Station (Y30 taxi ride from city center) are in the works, so inquire at your hotel. Taking the bus to Hangzhou and Suzhou is more convenient. There is a five-hour express train to Xiamen.

TIMING
Ningbo has enough to occupy you for two full days, but the major attractions can be seen in one day. The city center is compact, and can be explored on foot.

TOURS
The centrally located Ningbo Tourist Board is an excellent place to grab city maps, find the free English magazine called *Ningbo Guide,* and get advice on attractions outside the city. The magazine is a must for foreigners, and has a perfect map clearly labeling all the hot spots.

ESSENTIALS

Air Contact Ningbo Lishe International Airport (✉ *Yinzhou District* ☎ *0574/8742–7888*).

Bank Bank of China (✉ *139 Yao Hang Street* ☎ *0574/8719–8889*).

Bus Contacts South Bus Station (✉ *6 Nanshan Lu* ☎ *0574/8713–1834*). **East Bus Station** (✉ *707 Ningchuan Lu* ☎ *0574/8792–4570*). **Ningbo Passenger Transportation Center** (✉ *181 Tongda Lu* ☎ *0574/8709–1212*).

Medical Assistance Yinzhou No. 2 Hospital (✉ *1 Qianhe Lu* ☎ *0571/8303–9999*.

Train Information South Train Station (✉ *19 Nanzhan Dong Lu* ☎ *0574/5616–2224*.

Visitor and Tour Info Ningbo Tourist Board (✉ *90 Dashani Jie* ☎ *0574/8727–6116*). **CAAC** (✉ *91 Xingning Road 315192* ☎ *0574/8742–7888*).

EXPLORING

Moon Lake is a lovely park that surrounds a 1,400-year-old lake; it's dotted with teahouses, pavilions with up-turned eaves, and a generous amount of landscaped greenery. Weeping willows line crooked paths that wrap around bamboo groves. In addition to being a peaceful place for a leisurely stroll, the park is centrally located in the city center and a useful point of reference. ✉ *Liuting Lu* ☎ *No phone.*

Fodor's Choice **Tian Yi Ge.** Down a peaceful alley off Changchun Road, just west of
★ Moon Lake, the Tian Yi Pavilion is the oldest private library in China. Built in 1596 and founded by Fan Qin, this spiritual place features gold-plated, wood-paneled buildings, bamboo groves, pools, and a rockery. The scholarly setting, worth a visit for the architecture alone, preserves an atmosphere of seclusion and contemplation. ✉ *5 Tianyi Lu* ☎ *0574/8729–4832* 🚍 *Y30* ◷ *Daily 8–5.*

Tianfeng Pagoda. Seven stories high, this ancient hexagonal structure was first built in AD 695, destroyed, and rebuilt several times over. The current building was completed in the 14th century and is surrounded by a tiny garden complete with gigantic rocks and several inviting stone benches. For a great view of the pagoda, walk directly across the street from the main entrance, enter the market, and walk up to the second floor. For a great view of the entire city, continue climbing to the top for only Y5. ✉ *Near intersection of Jiefang Nanlu and Kaiming Jie* 🚍 *Y5 to climb* ◷ *Daily 8–4.*

Drum Tower. Located just off Zhongshan Lu in the city center, this huge yellow pavilion, complete with a medieval clock tower, was built in AD 821. Climb to the top for a birds'-eye view of the entire city. The tower marks the entrance to an interesting pedestrian street lined with restored, Ming Dynasty–style buildings. Here you'll find tiny shops, makeshift stalls, and every kind of local snack imaginable. It's an ideal spot for people-watching. ✉ *Gongyuan Lu and Zhongshan Xi Lu* 🚍 *Free* ◷ *Daily 8–4.*

ZhongShan Park. In one of Ningbo's most delightful parks you'll find winding stone-lined paths that snake over arched bridges and slender canals flowing past pavilions and teahouses. During the humid summer months the city's seniors fan themselves with oversized paper fans, crack sunflower seeds, gossip, and drink tea. Impromptu groups of musicians huddle together; old men play traditional Chinese instruments as women belt out ear-piercing renditions of Chinese opera. A perfect antidote to the overwhelming commercialism of the Drum Tower Pedestrian Street and a wonderful place to relax and soak up the atmosphere. ⊠ *Gongyuan Lu, at the end of the Drum Tower pedestrian shopping street* ☎ *Free* ☉ *Daily sunrise–sunset.*

> **SWEET DUMPLINGS**
>
> Be sure to try the city's famous *tangyuan*, sweet little sugar dumplings served in a bowl of cloudy-colored syrup and eaten like soup. There's no better a place to sample this specialty than **Gang Ya Gou** (缸鸭狗). It's a bit difficult to find, but most locals can point you in the right direction (⊠ *Kaiming Jie, near Tianyi Square* ☎ *0571/8732–0228*).

Jiangbei Catholic Church. Home to China's highest percentage of Christians, Ningbo is also home to several active churches. Marking the beginning of the Laowaitan district, this church was built by the Portuguese in 1872 and is considered to be the best preserved in Zhejiang Province. On any given day Chinese couples can be found taking their wedding photos. ⊠ *2 Zhong Ma Lu, Laowaitan* ☎ *0574/8735–5903* ☎ *Free* ☉ *Irregular masses in Chinese, check the outside of the church for current postings.*

WHERE TO EAT

¢–$ ✕ **Lebanese Restaurant.** On the eastern edge of Moon Lake, this Lebanese-

MIDDLE EASTERN owned halal restaurant has consistently excellent food. One bite of the

★ olive-oil-and-pine-nut drizzled hummus and you'll immediately forgive the rather bland interior. A long-standing favorite with the city's Islamic community, the restaurant serves a variety of lamb kebabs, eggplant-based dips, and fresh mint yogurt that are all delicious. An English-language picture menu will help guide you. ⊠ *320 Zhenming Lu* ☎ *0574/8731–5861* ▭ *No credit cards.*

$$ ✕ **Nancy's Thai Fusion.** A Ningbo landmark, this authentic Thai restau-

THAI rant was an instant hit when it first opened in 2003. A mix of Thai-Chinese architecture and an enormous neon pink sign make it easy to spot. The first level is a well-stocked bar with a decent selection of foreign wines that are reasonably priced by the bottle. The second floor contains the romantic dining section, where private rooms are available. Recommended dishes include the *tom kha gai* (a coconut and chicken soup), fresh papaya salad, and expertly seasoned curries. ⊠ *103 Zhenming Lu* ☎ *0574/8731–8266* ▭ *D, DC, MC, V.*

¢ ✕ **Vegetarian Life Style.** This Ningbo branch of one of Shanghai's most

VEGETARIAN famous vegetarian restaurants serves all of its dishes sans egg, meat, and alcohol. The restaurant also promises to enforce a no-smoking policy, which is highly unusual in China. Veggie creations are easy to order, thanks to an English-language picture menu. The nourishing and delicious spinach dumplings, fresh juices, and mock-meat dishes are consistently delicious. ⊠ *16 Liuting Jie* ☎ *0574/8730–1333* ▭ *No credit cards.*

5

$$$$ ✕ **Zhuangyuanlou Restaurant.** This local chain serves up traditional
CHINESE   Ningbo cuisine in an opulent setting, and has a stellar reputation for
quality and freshness. The restaurant is located in the city's most exclusive mall, the He Yi Center, and has gigantic, red and gold doors and
intricately carved antique furniture. Hostesses are decked out in red
qipaos (elaborate silk dresses). If you're feeling bold, try the exotic and
expensive local specialties. The steamed turtle, fried yellow-fish with
fresh blueberries, and the kungfu pork rib are highly recommended
Ningbo delicacies. ⊠ *He Yi Shopping Center, off He Yi Lu and on Yu
Yao River* ☏ *0574/2796–6667* ⊟ *No credit cards.*

WHERE TO STAY

¢   ⌸ **Asia Garden Hotel.** With a convenient location next to the South Bus
Station, this large three-star hotel is a short walk from Ningbo's main
attractions. The rooms are clean and functional, but don't expect much
luxury for the price. It is popular with domestic travelers and often
quite busy, and the city-center location makes up for the aging rooms.
This was the first hotel in town to serve foreigners before the major
chains arrived. **Pros:** near all the main sights; CNN in rooms. **Cons:**
rooms in need of renovation; staff speak limited English. ⊠ *271 Mayuan*
☏ *0574/8711–6888* ↻ *172 rooms* ⌂ *In-room: Internet, safe, refrigerator. In-hotel: 2 restaurants, laundry service* ⊟ *No credit cards.*

$$ ⌸ **Shangri-La Ningbo.** Overlooking the confluence of the city's three riv-
ers, Ningbo's most opulent international hotel offers personalized ser-
vice, first-rate facilities, and panoramic, cityscape views. Splurge for one
of the Horizon Club Rooms, and you'll be immediately escorted to the
club lounge upon check-in and treated like royalty. All rooms feature
floor-to-ceiling windows revealing the vast sprawl of this city of 6 mil-
lion, along with free broadband Internet access, elegant furniture, and
the Shangri-la's signature toiletries and plush bathrobes. The cozy, dimly
lit Lobster Bar and Grill will prepare your imported Wagyu beef to per-
fection, offers a decent wine selection, and has live music that will make
you want to linger. **Pros:** sleek indoor lap pool; outdoor tennis courts,
a heavenly spa. **Cons:** mandatory swimming cap to use the pool. ⊠ *88
Yuyuan Lu315040* ☏ *0574/8799–8888* ⊕ *www.shangri-la.com* ↻ *563
rooms* ⌂ *In-room: safe, refrigerator, Internet. In-hotel: 3 restaurants,
room service, 2 bars, pool, gym, spa, laundry service* ⊟ *AE, DC, MC, V.*

$$ ⌸ **Sheraton Ningbo.** Excellent customer service and a convenient location
make this an ideal base from which to explore the city. A massive marble
lobby features an unusual, spiky glass chandelier, and spiral staircases
lead onto an atrium-style floor with guest rooms. The more expensive
club rooms are worth the price, which includes super-fast check-in, all
day coffee and tea, and a cocktail hour (actually three hours) in the
club lounge. A rejuvenating 15-minute back rub is also on the happy
hour menu. Connected to the Portman Plaza Starbucks and across the
street from several lively bars, this top-notch hotel offers great weekend
specials on its Web site. **Pros:** location; staff speak good English. **Cons:**
very busy lobby. ⊠ *50 Caihong Lu* ☏ *0574/8768–8688* ↻ *380 rooms*
⌂ *In-room: safe, refrigerator, Internet. In-hotel: 3 restaurants, room
service, 2 bars, pool, gym, spa, laundry service* ⊟ *AE, DC, MC, V.*

NIGHTLIFE

If you're looking for a fun night out, head over to Laowaitan, the city's premier entertainment district and Ningbo's answer to Shanghai's Bund. It's designed to look like a mini European city, complete with cobblestone streets. The atmosphere here is so exotic for the Chinese that hundreds of local couples come here to take their wedding photos.

For something a little more low-key, there is a cluster of bars on a small side street directly opposite the Sheraton. The most popular is the **Londoner** (✉ *46 Portman Jie* ☎ *0574/8193–6777)*, which has Guinness on tap and a good mix of locals and expats. Inquire ahead for live music.

SHOPPING

At the **Antiques Market Curio Bazaar** (✉ *100 Zhongshan Xi Lu),* you'll find small clusters of galleries and stalls that sell a variety of jade and antique bric-a-brac of varying levels of authenticity. We like the beautiful Chinese scrolls with traditional watercolor paintings and calligraphy and the kitschy Mao-era memorabilia. Bargain hard, offer a fraction of the asking price, and walk away disinterested, as prices are inflated for tourists. Head east down Zhongshan Xi Lu toward **Gu Lou** (✉ *Fujiao Jie),* where restored traditional buildings are stuffed to capacity with every cheaply made Chinese product. It is car free, a great place to wander and soak up modern Chinese culture.

Just east of the Tianfeng Pagoda is **Tianyi Square** (✉ *88 Zhongshan Dong Lu),* Ningbo's most famous shopping and entertainment complex. Look for the enormous Gothic Yaohang Street Catholic Church just outside the square if you need to sit for a break.

A major and and somewhat newer shopping area is **He Yi Avenue** (✉ *66 He Yi Lu).* Riverfront shopping, dining, and nightlife are combined with high-end luxury retail outlets, including Gucci and several Swarovski's. This is where Ningbo's créme de la créme comes to spend money on Japanese *mochi* balls, wood-fired pizza, and *macchiatos.*

OFF THE BEATEN PATH

Mount Putuo. On this tiny island, only 12.5 square km (8 miles), you'll find Putuoshan, one of China's four sacred Buddhist mountains. Legend has it that a ninth century Japanese monk got caught in a storm, and Guanyin, the Buddhist goddess of mercy, miraculously appeared and guided him safely to the mountain. In thanks, he erected Puji Si, the area's most famous temple. The island can easily be explored on foot and completely circumnavigated in a day. Take time to lounge on Thousand Step Beach, photograph the enormous 108-feet-high bronze Guanyin Statue, eat fresh seafood, and climb Mount Putuo (or take the cable car) for fabulous island vistas. The population is only 3,000, 1,000 of whom are monks and nuns. Getting to the island is fairly easy, with frequent boats leaving from Ningbo's wharf. Ask your hotel for advice, as points of departures do change. From Shanghai, there is a 12-hour overnight ferry leaving at 8 pm from the Wusong Passenger Transport Center. There is also a daily speedboat taking about 3½ hours from Shanghai leaving at 8 am. Entrance fees are comparatively steep and constantly changing. The island can get crowded, so it's best to avoid weekends and Chinese holidays. There is plenty of accommodation on the island, but prices are higher in the summer and on weekends.

FUJIAN

One of China's most beautiful provinces, Fujian has escaped the notice of most visitors. This is because the region, though not too far off the beaten path, is usually passed over in favor of more glamorous destinations like Hong Kong or Shanghai. The city of Xiamen is clean and beautiful, and the surrounding area has some of the best beaches north of Hainan. And Gulangyu is a rarity in modern China: a tree-filled island with undisturbed colonial architecture and absolutely no cars.

XIAMEN

200 km (124 mi) southwest of Fuzhou; 500 km (310 mi) northeast of Hong Kong.

By Chinese standards, Xiamen is a new city: it dates back only to the late 12th century. Xiamen was a stronghold for Ming loyalist Zheng Chenggong (better known as Koxinga), who later fled to Taiwan after China was overrun by the Qing. Xiamen's place as a dynasty-straddling city continues to this day due to its proximity to Taiwan. Some see Xiamen as a natural meeting point between the two sides in the decades-long separation. Only a few miles out to sea are islands that still technically belong to the Republic of China, as Taiwan is still officially known.

Xiamen is today one of the most prosperous cities in China, with beautiful parks, amazing temples, and waterfront promenades that neatly complement the port city's historic architecture.

GETTING HERE AND AROUND

The best way to reach Xiamen is by plane. The city is also accessible by long-distance train or sleeper bus, but these types of transportation entail much longer travel times.

AIR TRAVEL Xiamen Airport, one of the largest and busiest in China, lies about 12 km (7 mi) northeast of the city. A taxi from downtown should cost no more than Y60. Most carriers service Xiamen, which has connections to many cities in China, as well as international destinations like Jakarta, Manila, Penang, and Singapore.

BUS TRAVEL Xiamen has luxury bus service to all the main cities along the coast as far as Guangzhou and Shanghai. The long-distance bus station is on Hubin Nan Lu, just south of Yuandang Lake.

TAXI TRAVEL In Xiamen taxis can be found around hotels or on the streets; they're a convenient way to visit the sights on the edge of town. Most taxi drivers do not speak English, so make sure that all your addresses are written in Chinese. Any hotel representative will do this for you.

■ TIP➜ Make sure the name of your destination (not only the address) is written. Numbers do not always make sense in Chinese cities, and it is too crowded to cruise slowly searching for hidden address signs.

TRAIN TRAVEL Rail travel to and from Xiamen isn't as convenient as in many other cities. Many journeys involve changing trains at least once. The railway station is about 3 km (2 mi) northeast of the port; bus service between the station and port is frequent.

TIMING

Xiamen is a very pleasant city, well worth a few days of exploring and hiking. Much cleaner than other Chinese cities, it's a great place to recharge and take in some fresh air.

ESSENTIALS

Air Contacts Dragonair (✉ *Seaside Bldg., Jiang Dao Lu, Xiamen* ☎ *0592/202–5433*). **Philippine Airlines** (✉ *Xiamen Airport* ☎ *0592/239–4729* ⊕ *www.philippineairlines.com*). **Xiamen Airlines** (✉ *22 Dailiao Lu, Xiamen* ☎ *0592/602–2961* ⊕ *www.xiamenair.com.cn*). **Xiamen Airport** (☎ *0592/602–0017*).

Banks Bank of China (✉ *10 Zhongshan Lu* ☎ *0592/506–6466*). HSBC (✉ *189 Xiahe Lu* ☎ *0592/239–7799*).

Bus Contact Long-Distance Bus Station (✉ *56 Hubin Nan Lu* ☎ *0592/203–1246*).

Internet Javaromas (✉ *31–13 Jianye Lu* ☎ *0592/514–5677*).

Medical Assistance **Xiamen Changgung Hospital** (✉ *123 Zhenfei Lu, Xinjang Industrial Area Xiamen* ☎ *0592/620–3456*).

Train Contact **Xiamen Train Station** (✉ *Xiahe Lu* ☎ *0592/203–8888*).

Visitor and Tour Info CTS (✉ *2 Zhongshan Lu* ☎ *0592/212–6917*.

Continued on page 354

348

DID YOU KNOW

In China, there are three
major schools of Buddhism:
the Chinese school, embraced
mainly by Han Chinese; the
Tibetan school (or Lamaism)
as practiced by Tibetans and
Mongolians; and Theravada,
practiced by the Dai and other
ethnic minority groups in the
southwest of the country.

SPIRITUALITY IN CHINA

Even though it's officially an atheist nation, China has a vibrant religious life. What are the differences between China's big three faiths of Buddhism, Taoism, and Confucianism? Like much else in the Middle Kingdom, the lines are often blurred.

Walking around the streets of any city in China in the early 21st century, it's hard to believe that only three decades ago the bulk of the Middle Kingdom's centuries-old religious culture was destroyed by revolutionary zealots, and that the few temples, mosques, monasteries, and churches that escaped outright destruction were desecrated and turned into warehouses and factories, or put to other ignoble uses. Those days are long over, and religion in China has sprung back to life. Even though the official line of the Chinese Communist Party is that the nation is atheist, China is rife with religious diversity.

Perhaps the faith most commonly associated with China is Confucianism, an ethical and philosophical system developed from the teachings of the sage Confucius. Confucianism stresses the importance of relationships in society and of maintaining proper etiquette. These aspects of Confucian thought are associated not merely with China (where its modern-day influence is dubious at best, especially in a crowded subway car), but also with East Asian culture as a whole. Confucianism also places great emphasis on filial piety, the respect that a child should show an elder (or subjects to their ruler). This may account for Confucianism's status as the most officially tolerated of modern China's faiths.

Taoism is based on the teachings of the *Tao Te Ching*, a treatise written in the 6th century BC, and blends an emphasis on spiritual harmony with that of the individual's duty to society. Taoism and Confucianism are complementary, though to the outsider, the former might seem more steeped in ritual and mysticism. Think of it this way: Taoism is to Confucianism as Catholicism is to Protestantism. Taoism's mystic quality may be why so many westerners come to China to study "the way," as Taoism is sometimes called.

Buddhism came to China from India in the first century AD and quickly became a major force in the Middle Kingdom. The faith is so ingrained here that many Chinese openly scoff at the idea that the Buddha wasn't Chinese.

Buddhism teaches that the best way to alleviate suffering is to purify one's mind.

TEMPLE FAUX PAS

The Wenshu Monastery is a top sight in Chengdu.

■ Chinese worshippers are easygoing. Even at the smallest temple or shrine, they understand that some people will be visitors and not devotees. Temples in China have relaxed dress codes, but you should follow certain rules of decorum.

■ You're welcome to burn incense, but it's not required. If you do decide to burn a few joss sticks, take them from the communal pile and be sure to make a small donation. This usually goes to temple upkeep or local charities.

■ When burning incense, two sticks signify marriage, and four signify death.

■ Respect signs reading no photo in front of altars and statues. Taoist temples seem particularly sensitive about photo taking. When in doubt, ask.

■ Avoid stepping in front of a worshipper at an altar or censer (where incense is burned).

■ Speak quietly and silence mobile phones inside of temple grounds.

■ Don't touch Buddhist monks of the opposite sex.

■ Avoid entering a temple during a ceremony.

TEMPLE OBJECTS

For many, temple visits are among the most culturally edifying parts of a China trip. Large or small, Chinese temples incorporate a variety of objects significant to religious practice.

INCENSE

Incense is the most common item in any Chinese temple. In antiquity, Chinese people burned sacrifices both as an offering and as a way of communicating with spirits through the smoke. This later evolved into a way of showing respect for one's ancestors by burning fragrances that the dearly departed might find particularly pleasing.

CENSER

Every Chinese temple will have a censer in which to place joss sticks, either inside the hall or out front. Larger temples often have a number of them. These large stone or bronze bowls are filled with incense ash from hundreds of joss sticks placed by worshippers. Some censers are ornate, with sculpted bronze rising above the bowls.

BAGUA

Taoist temples will have a bagua: an octagonal diagram pointing toward the eight cardinal directions, each representing different points on the compass, elements in nature, family members, and more esoteric meanings. The bagua is often used in conjunction with a compass to make placement decisions in architectural design and in fortune telling.

STATUES

Chinese temples are known for being flexible, and statues of various deities and mythical figures. Confucius is usually rendered as a wizened man with a long beard, and Taoist temples have an array of demon deities.

PRAYER WHEEL

Used primarily by Tibetan Buddhists, the prayer wheel is a beautifully embossed hollow metal cylinder mounted on a wooden handle. Inside the cylinder is a tightly wound scroll printed with a mantra. Devotees believe that the spinning of a prayer wheel is a form of prayer that's just as effective as reciting the sacred texts aloud.

"GHOST MONEY"

Sometimes the spirits need more than sweet-smelling smoke, and this is why many Taoists burn "ghost money" (also known as "hell money"), a scented paper resembling cash. Though once more popular in Taiwan and Hong Kong (and looked upon as a particularly capitalist superstition on the mainland), the burning of ghost money is now gaining ground throughout the country.

CHINESE ASTROLOGY

According to legend, the King of Jade invited 12 animals to visit him in heaven. As the animals rushed to be the first to arrive, the rat snuck a ride on the ox's back. Just as the ox was about to cross the threshold, the rat jumped past him and arrived first. This is why the rat was given first place in the astrological chart. Find the year you were born to determine what your astrological animal is.

RAT

1936 · 1948 · 1960 · 1972 · 1984 · 1996 · 2008 · 2020

Charming and hardworking, Rats are goal setters and perfectionists. Rats are quick to anger, ambitious, and lovers of gossip.

OX

1937 · 1949 · 1961 · 1973 · 1985 · 1997 · 2009 · 2021

Patient and soft-spoken, Oxen inspire confidence in others. Generally easygoing, they can be remarkably stubborn, and they hate to fail or be opposed.

TIGER

1938 · 1950 · 1962 · 1974 · 1986 · 1998 · 2010 · 2022

Sensitive, and thoughtful, Tigers are capable of great sympathy. Tigers can be short-tempered, and are prone to conflict and indecisiveness.

RABBIT

1939 · 1951 · 1963 · 1975 · 1987 · 1999 · 2011 · 2023

Talented and articulate, Rabbits are virtuous, reserved, and have excellent taste. Though fond of gossip, Rabbits tend to be generally kind and even-tempered.

DRAGON

1940 · 1952 · 1964 · 1976 · 1988 · 2000 · 2012 · 2024

Energetic and excitable, short-tempered and stubborn, Dragons are known for their honesty, bravery, and ability to inspire confidence and trust.

SNAKE

1941 · 1953 · 1965 · 1977 · 1989 · 2001 · 2013 · 2025

Snakes are deep, possessing great wisdom and saying little. Snakes are considered the most beautiful and philosiphical of all the signs.

HORSE

1942 · 1954 · 1966 · 1978 · 1990 · 2002 · 2014 · 2026

Horses are thought to be cheerful and perceptive, impatient and hot-blooded. Horses are independent and rarely listen to advice.

GOAT

1943 · 1955 · 1967 · 1979 · 1991 · 2003 · 2015 · 2027

Wise, gentle, and compassionate, Goats are elegant and highly accomplished in the arts. Goats can also be shy and pessimistic, and often tend toward timidity.

MONKEY

1944 · 1956 · 1968 · 1980 · 1992 · 2004 · 2016 · 2028

Clever, skillful, and flexible, Monkeys are thought to be erratic geniuses, able to solve problems with ease. Monkeys are also thought of as impatient and easily discouraged.

ROOSTER

1945 · 1957 · 1969 · 1981 · 1993 · 2005 · 2017 · 2029

Roosters are capable and talented, and tend to like to keep busy. Roosters are known as overachievers, and are frequently loners.

DOG

1946 · 1958 · 1970 · 1982 · 1994 · 2006 · 2018 · 2030

Dogs are loyal and honest and know how to keep secrets. They can also be selfish and stubborn.

PIG

1947 · 1959 · 1971 · 1983 · 1995 · 2007 · 2031

Gallant and energetic, Pigs have a tendency to be single-minded and determined. Pigs have great fortitude and honesty, and tend to make friends for life.

EXPLORING XIAMEN
TOP ATTRACTIONS
The rather hilly **Hong Shan Park** *(Hong Shan Gong Yuan)* has a small Buddhist temple, a lovely waterfall, and beautiful views of the city and the harbor. There's also a lovely teashop serving Iron Buddha tea, a Fujian specialty. ⌧ *Siming Nan Lu, near Nanputuo Temple* ✉ *Free.*

Nanputuo Temple *(Nanputuo Si)* dates from the Tang Dynasty. It has been restored many times, most recently in the 1980s, following the Cultural Revolution. Built in the exuberant style that visitors to Taiwan will find familiar, it has roofs that are decorated with brightly painted flourishes of clustered flowers, sinewy serpents, and mythical beasts. Pavilions on either side of the main hall contain tablets commemorating the suppression of secret societies by the Qing emperors. As the most important of Xiamen's temples, it is nearly always the center of a great deal of activity as monks and worshippers mix with tour groups. Attached to the temple complex is an excellent vegetarian restaurant. To get here, take Bus 1 or 2 from the port. ⌧ *Siming Nan Lu, next to Xiamen University* ✉ *Y3* ☉ *Daily 7:30–6:30.*

NEED A BREAK?

Coffee Map (⌧ *Siming, Laohu Cheng Dian, off Siming Nan Lu* ☎ *No phone* ☉ *Daily 8 am–10 pm*) is an unassuming Taiwanese-owned tea and coffee stand. Their huge menu offers lots of delicious caffeinated drinks and the tiny, air-conditioned seating area is an oasis out of Xiamen's oppressive summer humidity. It's down a small alley just opposite Xiamen University's main gate and near Nanputuo Temple.

Housed in a fascinating mix of traditional and colonial buildings close to Nanputuo Temple is **Xiamen University** *(Xiamen Daxue)*. It was founded in the 1920s with the help of Chinese people living abroad. The **Museum of Anthropology** *(Renlei Bowuguan)*, dedicated to the study of the Neolithic era, is one of the most popular destinations. It has a very good collection of fossils, ceramics, paintings, and ornaments. It's open daily 8:30 to 11 and 3 to 5. ⌧ *End of Siming Nan Lu.*

Surrounding a pretty lake, the **10,000 Rock Botanical Garden** *(Wanshi Zhiwuyuan)* has a fine collection of more than 4,000 species of tropical and subtropical flora, ranging from eucalyptus and bamboo trees to orchids and ferns. There are several pavilions, of which the most interesting are those forming the **Temple of the Kingdom of Heaven** *(Tianjie Si)*. ⌧ *Huyuan Lu, off Wenyuan Lu* ✉ *Y40* ☉ *Daily 8–6.*

WORTH NOTING
In the southern part of the city, the **Overseas Chinese Museum** *(Huaqiao Bowuguan)* was founded by the wealthy industrialist Tan Kah-kee. Three halls exhibit, with the help of pictures and documents, personal items, and relics associated with the great waves of emigration from southeastern China during the 19th century. ⌧ *493 Siming Nan Lu* ☎ *0592/208–5345* ✉ *Free* ☉ *Tues.–Sun. 9:30–4.*

Commemorating Dr. Sun Yat-sen, **Zhong Shan Park** *(Zhong Shan Gong Yuan)* is centered around a statue to the great man. It has a small zoo, lakes, and canals you can explore by paddleboat. The annual Lantern

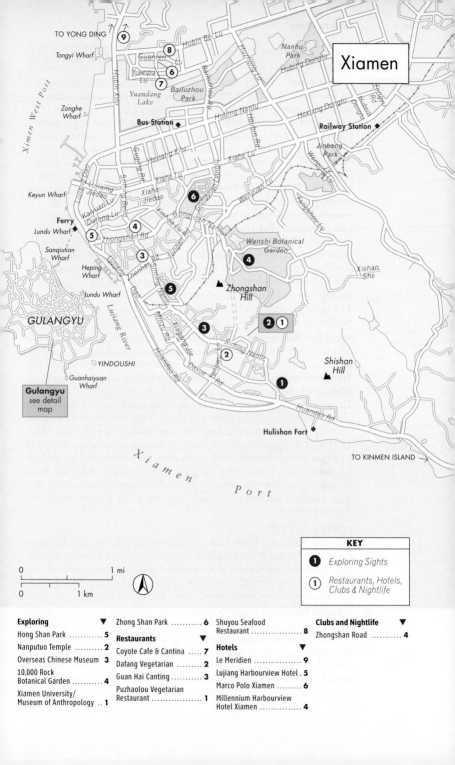

Xiamen

TO YONG DING

Tongyi Wharf

Guanren Lu

Yuanpu Lu

Hubin Beilu

Nanhu Park

Hubing Donglu

Bailuzhou Park

Yuandang Lake

Xiamen West Port

Zonghe Wharf

Bus Station

Railway Station

Jinbang Park

Hexiang Xilu

Xiahe Lu

Xiahe Lu

Keyun Wharf

Lujiang Jiedao

Kaiyuan Lu

Wenyuan Lu

Ferry

Lundu Wharf

Sanqiutian Wharf

Zhongshan Rd

Wanshi Botanical Garden

Heping Wharf

Zhenhai

Xishan She

Lundu Wharf

Zhongshan Hill

GULANGYU

Lujiang River

YINDOUSHI

Siming Nanlu

Shishan Hill

Guanhaiyuan Wharf

Gulangyu see detail map

Huandao Rd

Hulishan Fort

Xiamen Port

TO KINMEN ISLAND

0 ——— 1 mi
0 ——— 1 km

Festival is held here. ☒ *Zhong Shan Lu and Zhenhai Lu* ☑ *Free.*

Kinmen Island. History buffs will be fascinated by a trip to this remnant of China's bitter civil war. The island is coined "the island Chairman Mao couldn't capture." Though barely a stone's throw from mainland China, this little chunk of land is still controlled by Taiwan, and Taiwanese guards patrol its shores. It has only recently been opened to tourists; a visit is possible, but you'll need to do some planning. At this writing, there were still no English guides, but that's sure to change. Apple Tours (⊕ *www.appletravel.cn*) can arrange the boat to the island for Y180, but the return ticket must be bought once on Kinmen.

WIRED ON THE BEACH

Xiamen has at least a dozen laid-back cafés with wireless networks. Recently China's largest wine importer, ASC Wines, began pouring a steady stream of fine vino into the island of old Amoy. Yet Xiamen's main attraction is still its subdued beach scene. One of the best places for an endless Xiamen summer is Siming, just east of downtown. Framed by mountains and defined by clean beaches, its sunsets are timeless. The beaches of Gulangyu Island are another favorite, since cars have been banned from the isle.

Hakka Roundhouses *(Yong Ding Tu Lou).* Legend has it that when these four-story-tall structures were first spotted by the American military, fear spread that they were silos for some unknown gigantic missile. They were created centuries before by the Hakka, or Guest People, an offshoot of the Han Chinese who settled all over southeastern China. These earthen homes are made of raw earth, glutinous rice, and brown sugar, reinforced with bamboo and wood. They are the most beautiful example of Hakka architecture. The roundhouses are in Yong Ding, 210 km (130 mi) northwest of Xiamen. Joining a tour group or hiring a private car for around Y800 (with some bargaining and not including ticket price) is your best option for getting there. Ask your hotel to help arrange the trip. You can also join a domestic tour group on a large bus for a fraction of the price, but you won't have as much freedom to explore.

WHERE TO EAT

Although Xiamen is known for its excellent seafood, the city's Buddhist population means it has excellent vegetarian cuisine. Xiamen is probably the best place outside of Taiwan to experience Taiwanese cuisine, and many restaurants advertise their *Taiwan Wei Kou* and *Taiwan Xiao Chi,* meaning "Taiwanese flavor" and "Taiwanese snacks."

$$ ✕**Coyote Café and Cantina.** Xiamen's only Mexican restaurant serves
MEXICAN   solid favorites in a friendly environment. It's a tiny restaurant with a tiny sign, but a generous happy hour; steak fajitas and lakeside views will make the jaunt worthwhile. Don't expect generous sides of sour cream or guacamole, but after a few well-poured margaritas it won't matter. The service is a bit slow, but the staff can speak some English. ☒ *58–2 Yuandang Lu* ☎ *0592/504–6623* ⊟ *No credit cards.*

The Hakka Roundhouses were added to the UNESCO World Heritage List in 2008.

¢–$ ✕ **Dafang Vegetarian Restaurant.** Across from Nanputuo Temple, this rea-
VEGETARIAN sonably priced restaurant is popular with students. But don't just come
for the low prices—it also has excellent food. Try the sweet-and-sour
soup or the mock duck. English menus are available. ✉ *3 Nanhua Lu*
☎ *0592/209-3236* ▭ *No credit cards.*

$–$$ ✕ **Guan Hai Canting.** On the rooftop of the waterfront Lujiang Hotel, this
SEAFOOD terrace restaurant has beautiful views over the bay. The Cantonese chef
prepares delicious seafood dishes and dim-sum specialties like sweet
pork buns and shrimp dumplings. ✉ *54 Lujiang Lu, across from ferry
terminal* ☎ *0592/266-2398* ▭ *AE, MC, V.*

$–$$ ✕ **Puzhaolou Vegetarian Restaurant.** The comings and goings of monks
VEGETARIAN add to the atmosphere at this restaurant next to the Nanputuo Temple.
Popular dishes include black-fungus soup with tofu and stewed yams
with seaweed. You won't find any English menus, so ask for one of the
picture menus. ✉ *Nanputuo Temple, 515 Siming Nan Lu* ☎ *0592/208-
5908* ▭ *No credit cards.*

$$–$$$ ✕ **Shuyou Seafood Restaurant.** Shuyou means "close friend," and that's
SEAFOOD how you're treated at this upscale establishment. Considered one of the
★ best seafood restaurants in China (and certainly in Xiamen), Shuyou
serves fresh seafood in an opulent setting. Downstairs, the tanks are
filled with lobster, prawns, and crabs, and upstairs diners feast on seafood dishes cooked in Cantonese and Fujian styles. If you're in the mood
for other fare, the restaurant is also known for its excellent Peking duck
and goose liver. ✉ *Hubin Bei Lu, between Marco Polo and Sofitel hotels*
☎ *0592/509-8888* ▭ *AE, MC, V.*

WHERE TO STAY

$$
Fodor's Choice
★

Le Meridien. Tucked away in Xianyue Hill and with sweeping views of Xiamen Bay, this stunning property feels more like a high-end Southeast-Asian resort than a crowded Chinese metropolitan lodging. From the jasmine-scented aroma when you walk through the door to the tasteful elevator music, every detail is carefully planned and executed. Sleek guest rooms are decorated with furnishings reminiscent of mid-century modern design (think Barcelona chairs), and come equipped with iPod decks and DVD players. Guests are spoiled for choice when it comes to physical activities. Choose from trekking through the area's lush hills, bicycling on nearby trails, or a couple games tennis. **Pros:** tropical setting; very reasonable prices. **Cons:** outside the city center. ✉ *7 Guanjun Road* ☎ *0592/770–9999* ⊕ *www.lemeridien.com* ↘ *348 rooms* ⚬ *In-room: safe, refrigerator, Wi-fi. In-hotel: 3 restaurants, bar, pool, gym, tennis courts, laundry, no-smoking rooms* ▤ *AE, DC, MC, V.*

> **WORD OF MOUTH**
>
> "Xiamen was the highlight of my trip. I wish I could have stayed longer. The tiny alleys off Zhongshan Lu Pedestrian Street gave a taste of China 500 years ago. Stopping to bargain for oolong tea from an elderly lady made me feel like a local."—ruddles

$–$$
Lujiang Harbourview Hotel. In a refurbished colonial building, this hotel has an ideal location opposite the ferry pier and the waterfront boulevard. The rooms are about what you'd expect for the price, but many have ocean views. A rooftop-terrace restaurant looks over the straits. **Pros:** phenomenal location; good prices. **Cons:** limited English is spoken; rooms are small. ✉ *54 Lujiang Lu* ☎ *0592/202–2922* ▤ *0592/202–4644* ↘ *153 rooms, 18 suites* ⚬ *In-room: safe, Internet. In-hotel: 4 restaurants, bar* ▤ *AE, MC, V.*

$$$
Marco Polo Xiamen. Standing between the historic sights and the commercial district, the Marco Polo has an excellent location. The hotel's glass-roof atrium makes the lobby bar a nice place to relax after a day's sightseeing. Nightly entertainment includes a dance band from the Philippines. The guest rooms are comfortable if a bit bland. **Pros:** good location; helpful staff. **Cons:** noise; poor reservation service. ✉ *8 Jianye Lu* ☎ *0592/509–1888* ⊕ *www.marcopolohotels.com* ↘ *246 rooms, 38 suites* ⚬ *In-room: safe, Internet. In-hotel: 3 restaurants, bar, pool, gym, no-smoking rooms* ▤ *AE, MC, V.*

$$
★

Millenium Harbourview Hotel Xiamen. With an excellent location overlooking the harbor, this hotel is among the best in the city. Rooms are spacious and comfortable, and the staff are friendly and attentive. The hotel's restaurants are particularly good, and the first-floor coffee shop is the only place in Xiamen to get a good New York–style deli sandwich. Golfers will like the first-floor bar, which has a small putting green. **Pros:** excellent service; travel agents on staff. **Cons:** noise; some rooms very dark. ✉ *12-8 Zhenhai Lu* ☎ *0592/202–3333* ⊕ *www.millenniumhotels.com/cn/millenniumxiamen/index.html* ↘ *334 rooms, 7 suites* ⚬ *In-room: safe, Internet. In-hotel: 4 restaurants, bar, pool, gym, no-smoking rooms* ▤ *AE, MC, V.*

NIGHTLIFE AND THE ARTS

The Zhongshan Lu pedestrian street near the ferry pier is charming in the evening, when the colonial-style buildings are lighted with gentle neon. This waterfront promenade is a popular spot for young couples walking arm in arm.

SPORTS AND THE OUTDOORS

Xiamen offers some excellent hiking opportunities. Most notable of these are the hills behind the Nanputuo Temple, where winding paths and stone steps carved into the sheer rock face make for a fairly strenuous climb. For a real challenge, hike from Nanputuo Temple to 10,000 Rock Garden. If you're still in the mood for a climb after spending a few hours enjoying the garden's beautiful landscape, another more serpentine trail (a relic of the Japanese occupation) leads to Xiamen University. The hike takes the better part of an afternoon.

The area around Xiamen has fine public beaches. Sunbathers abound nearly anywhere along Huandao Lu, the road that circles the island.

5

GULANGYU

5 minutes by boat from Xiamen.

The best way to experience Gulangyu's charm is to explore its meandering streets, stumbling across a particularly distinctive old mansion or the weathered graves of missionaries and merchants. These quiet back alleys are fascinating to wander in, with the atmosphere of a quiet Mediterranean city punctuated by touches of calligraphy or the click of mah-jongg tiles to remind you where you really are. And unlike most Chinese communities, Gulangyu does not permit cars, so you won't take your life in your hands when crossing the street. This island is easy to reach by ferry from Xiamen.

GETTING HERE AND AROUND

Boats to the island run from early in the morning until midnight, and depart from the ferry terminal across from the Lujiang. Electric buses are available on the island.

BOAT AND FERRY TRAVEL Ferry service from the Xiamen Ferry dock starts at 5:45 am, with departures every 10 to 15 minutes. The trip there is free, but it costs Y8 to return to Xiamen. The ferry does not run after midnight, so check the last departure time before you leave Xiamen to avoid getting stranded.

TIMING

Gulangyu is small enough to be explored on a day trip from Xiamen, but a night here would be well spent.

TOURS

The best—and really, the only—way to see Gulangyu is on foot. Take a morning or afternoon to climb up the narrow, winding streets to see the hundreds of colonial-era mansions (ranging from restored to ramshackle) that are the heart of this fabulous trove of late-19th- and early-20th-century architecture.

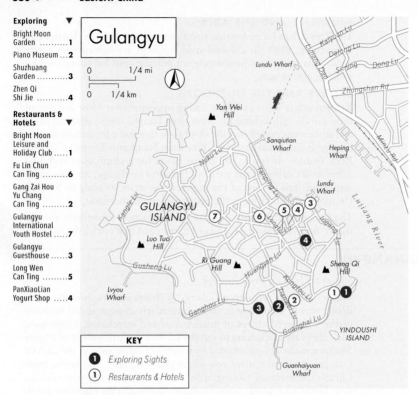

ESSENTIALS

Many sights on Gulangyu charge admission fees, but a tour aboard the island's electric bus includes admission to all sites included on the tour. Island ATMs are available near major tourist sites, but it is best to do your banking before heading out.

EXPLORING GULANGYU

Piano Museum. Gulangyu holds a special place in the country's musical history, thanks to the large number of Christian missionaries who called the island home in the late 19th and early 20th centuries. Gulangyu has more pianos per capita than anyplace else in China, with one home in five having one. "Chopsticks" to Chopin—and everything in between—can be heard being played by the next generation's prodigies. The Piano Museum *(Island of Drumming Waves)* is a must for any music lover. ⊠ *45 Huangyan Lu* ☎ *0592/206–0238* ⊒ *Y30* ⊘ *Daily 8:15–5:15.*

Bright Moon Garden. The garden is a fitting seaside memorial to Koxinga, a famous Ming general. A massive stone statue of him stares eastward from a perch hanging over the sea. From the ferry terminal, turn left and follow oceanfront Tianwei Lu until you come to Bright Moon Garden *(Haoyue Yuan).* ⊠ *Tianwei Lu* ☎ *No phone* ⊒ *Y15* ⊘ *Daily 8–7.*

Shuzhuang Garden *(Shuzhuang Huayuan).* This lovely garden is immaculately kept and dotted with pavilions and bridges, some extending out to rocks just offshore. To walk here, just continue along Tianwei Lu. ⊠ *Tianwei Lu* ☎ *No phone* 🎫 *Y40* ⊘ *Daily 8–7.*

Zhen Qi Shi Jie. Skillfully mixing history and oddities, Zhen Qi Shi Jie is one of the country's odder museums. Part of the museum displays the usual historical information about Fujian and Taiwan. The other part is a veritable museum of oddities, offering pickled genetic mutations like two-headed snakes, conjoined twin sheep, and a few live exhibits like gigantic tortoises. The room of ancient Chinese sex toys will please some and mystify others. ⊠ *38 Huangyan Lu and 4 Donghua Lu* ☎ *0592/206–9933* 🎫 *Y50* ⊘ *Daily 8–6.*

WHERE TO EAT

¢–$ ✕ **Fu Lin Chun Can Ting.** Serving home-style seafood cooked to order, this closet-size restaurant is almost always packed with locals during peak hours. If it comes from the sea, you'll find it here, with steamed crab, deep-fried shrimp, and whole fish served in a variety of tantalizing styles. ⊠ *109 Long Tou Lu* ☎ *0592/206–2847* 🖃 *No credit cards.*

SEAFOOD

$ ✕ **Gang Zai Hou Yu Chang Can Ting.** The name of this restaurant means Behind Gang Zai Beach, which suggests the short distance seafood travels from the ocean to the plate. Gang Zai Hou serves excellent oyster soup, steamed crabs, and just about anything else that swims. ⊠ *14 Gang Hou Lu* ☎ *0592/206–3719* 🖃 *No credit cards.*

SEAFOOD

$ ✕ **Long Wen Can Ting.** Serving fresh seafood dishes, this large restaurant near the ferry terminal is popular with tourists from Taiwan. The chef unabashedly admits to being an enthusiastic consumer of his own cuisine—never a bad sign. Specialties include whole steamed fish, oyster soup, and a wide variety of seafood dishes. The decor is traditional Chinese. ⊠ *21 Long Tou Lu* ☎ *0592/206–6369* 🖃 *No credit cards.*

SEAFOOD

¢ ✕ **PanXiaoLian Yogurt Shop.** A lovely little shop that's easy to spot thanks to its large orange awning and conspicuous, Thai-inspired exterior. They're reputed to serve the best yogurt in Xiamen. A small English menu offers a few choices, including plain homemade yogurt or yogurt topped with fresh, sweet mangoes. Walls in soothing shades of green and yellow serve as a canvas for massive jungle paintings. Grab a seat by the window, enjoy the world music soundtrack, and watch the domestic tourists go by. ⊠ *8 Long Tou Lu* ☎ *No Phone* 🖃 *No credit cards.*

CAFÉ

WHERE TO STAY

$ 🏨 **Bright Moon Leisure and Holiday Club.** Located in Bright Moon Garden, this lovely little hotel consists of nine wooden houses perched on seaside cliffs. The rooms are simple and bare-bones, but what it lacks in amenities it more than makes up for with amazing views. **Pros:** quiet; fantastic views. **Cons:** few amenities; limited English. ⊠ *3 Zhangzhou Lu* ☎ *0592/206–9730* 🖷 *0592/206–3401* ⤵ *15 rooms* ♨ *In-hotel: beachfront, laundry service* 🖃 *AE, MC, V.*

¢ 🏨 **Guanlangyu Guesthouse.** This friendly guesthouse is a wonderful deal for the money. It's set back in a semi-tropical garden and has seaside views, and the staff are careful and attentive. You can't miss the big, warped tree that partially hides the white, low-rise guesthouse from view. Rooms are spotless, if somewhat blandly decorated, but have large windows that allow for lots of sunlight. **Pros:** beautiful setting;

No cars are allowed on Gulangyu Island.

quiet rooms; attentive staff. **Cons:** staff speak limited English. ⊠ *25 Huangyuan Lu* ☎ *0592/206–3856* ⤶ *15 rooms* ⚘ *In-hotel: restaurant, laundry service* ▭ *No credit cards.*

¢ 🏨 **Gulangyu International Youth Hostel.** If you're looking to save a few dollars, you'd be hard-pressed to find cheaper accommodations. In the former German Embassy, this place retains a Bavarian feel. High-ceiling rooms have beds, desks, and antique lighting fixtures. In addition to dorm rooms with four and eight beds, it's possible to book private rooms for up to two people. Be sure to specify en suite if you want a private bathroom. **Pros:** extremely inexpensive. **Cons:** simple accommodations; no air-conditioning. ⊠ *18 Lu Jiao Lu* ☎ *0592/206–6066* 🖶 *0592/206–6022* ⤶ *6 rooms* ⚘ *In-room: no a/c (some). In-hotel: laundry facilities, Internet terminal* ▭ *No credit cards.*

ENGLISH	PIN YIN	CHINESE CHARACTERS
ZHEJIANG	**ZHÉJIĀNG**	浙江
Hangzhou	Hángzhōu	杭州
Baidi	Báidī	白堤
China National Silk Museum	Zhōngguósīchóubówùguǎn	中国丝绸博物馆
China Silk City	Zhōngguósīchóuchéng	中国丝绸城
China Tea Museum	Zhōngguócháyébówùguǎn	中国茶叶博物馆
Crystal Orange Hotel	Juzi shuipin jiudian	桔子水晶酒店
Dragon Hotel	Huánglóngfàndiàn	黄龙饭店
Dragon Well Tea Park	Lóngjǐngwénchá	龙井闻茶
Dong Yi Shun	Dong yi shun	东伊顺
Eudora Station	Yi Duo Rui Zhan	亿多瑞站
Evening Sunlight at Thunder Peak Pagoda	Léifēngxīzhào	雷锋夕照
Gao Yin Street	Gao Yin Jie	高银街
Gushan Island	Gūshāndǎo	孤山岛
Hangzhou Aquarium	Hángzhōuhǎidǐshíjié	杭州海底世界
Hefang Jie	Hefang Jie	河坊街
Hyatt Regency Hangzhou	Hángzhōukǎiyuéjiǔdiàn	杭州凯悦酒店
JZ (Jazz) Club	Huang lou	黄楼
Lingyin Si Vegetarian Restaurant	Língyǐnsísùzhāi	灵隐寺素斋
Liulang Wenying Park	Liǔlàngwényínggōngyuán	柳浪闻莺公园
Louwailou Restaurant	Lóuwàilóu	楼外楼
Maya Bar	Ma Ya Jiu Ba	玛雅酒吧
Moon Mountain	Yùelúnshān	月轮山
night market	Yéshì	夜市
Orioles Singing in the Willow Waves	Liǔlàngwényíng	柳浪闻莺
Pagoda of Six Harmonies	Liùhétǎ	六和塔
Peak That Flew from Afar	Fēiláifēng	飞来峰
Precious Stone Hill	Bǎoshíshān	宝石山
Protecting Chu Pagoda	Bǎoshūtǎ	宝塔
Redstar Hotel	Hángzhōuhóngxīngwénhuàdàshà	杭州红星文化大厦
Running Tiger Dream Spring	Hǔpǎomèngquán	虎跑梦泉
Seal Engraver's Society	Xīlíngyínshè	西泠印社
Shangri-La Hotel Hangzhou	Hángzhōuxiānggélǐlāfàndiàn	杭州香格里拉饭店
Sofitel Westlake Hangzhou	Hángzhōusuǒfēitéxīhúdàjiǔdiàn	杭州索菲特西湖大酒店

ENGLISH	PIN YIN	CHINESE CHARACTERS
Sudi	Sūdī	苏堤
Temple of the Soul's Retreat	Língyǐnsí	灵隐寺
Three Pools Reflecting the Moon	Sāntányínyuè	三潭印月
Wushan Square	Wu Shan Guang Chang	吴山广场
Wyndham Grand Plaza Royale	Wen de mu da jiu dian	温德姆大酒店
Xihu	Xīhú	西湖
Xihu Longjing Tea Company	Xīhúlóngjǐngcháyègōngsī	西湖龙井茶叶公司
Yellow Dragon Cave	Huánglóngdòng	黄龙洞
Yue Fei Mausoleum	Yuéfēimù	岳飞墓
Zhejiang Provincial Museum	Zhèjiāngshěngbówùguǎn	浙江省博物馆
Zhongshan Gongyuan	Zhōngshāngōngyuán	中山公园
Shaoxing	Shāoxíng	
Bazi Qiao Bridge	Bāzíqiáo	八字桥
Cai Yuanpei's House	Càiyuánpéigùjūn	蔡元培故居
Catholic Church of St. Joseph	Tiānzhǔjiàotáng	天主教堂
Dragonair	Gǎnglónghángkōnggōngsī	港龙航空公司
East Bus Station	Hángzhōuqìchēdōngzhàn	杭州汽车东站
East Lake	Dōnghú	东湖
Hangzhou International Airport	Hángzhōuxiāoshānguójíjīchǎng	杭州萧山国际机场
Hangzhou Red Cross Hospital	Hángzhōuhóngshízìhuíyǐyuàn	杭州红十字会医院
Hangzhou Travel and Tourism Bureau	Hángzhōushìlǚyóujúrǎn	杭州市旅游局
Lu Xun Family Home	Lǔxùngùjūn	鲁迅故居
Minhang Ticket Office	Mínhángshòupiàochù	民航售票处
North Bus Station	Hángzhōuqìchēběizhàn	杭州汽车北站
Sanwei Jiulou	Sānwéijiǔlóu	三味酒楼
Shaoxing People's Hospital	Shàoxīngrénmínyǐyuàn	绍兴人民医院
Shaoxing International Hotel	Shàoxíngguójídàjiǔdiàn	绍兴国际大酒店
Shaoxing Xianheng Hotel	Shàoxíngxúnhēngdàjiǔdiàn	绍兴咸亨大酒店
West Bus Station	Hángzhōuqìchēxīzhàn	杭州汽车西站
Xianheng Winehouse	Xánhēngjiǔdiàn	咸亨酒店
Zhejiang Medical University Affiliated Hospital No. 1	Zhèjiāngyīkēdàxuédíyīfùshǔyǐyuàn	浙江医科大学第一附属医院
Zhejiang Women's International Travel Service	Zhèjiāngfùnǚguójílǚxíngshé	浙江妇女国际旅行社
Zhou Enlai Family Home	Zhōuēnláigùjūn	周恩来故居

ENGLISH	PIN YIN	CHINESE CHARACTERS
Ningbo	Ningbo	
Asia Garden Hotel	Ya zhou hua yuan bin guan	亚洲华园宾馆
Curio Bazaar	Fanzhai guwan ji shi	宁波市范宅古玩集市
Drum Tower	Gu lou	鼓楼
Gang Ya Gou	Gang Ya Gou	缸鸭狗
He Yi Center	Heyi da dao gouwu zhongxin	和义大道 购物中心
Jiangbei Catholic Church	Jiangbei sheng jiao tang	江北基督教圣教堂
Laowaitan	Laowaitan	老外滩
Lebanese Restaurant	Li ba nan can ting	黎巴嫩餐厅
Moon Lake	Hu Yue	月湖
Nancy's Thai Fusion	Nan xi tai cai guan	南茜泰菜馆.
Ningbo Tourist Board	Ningbo Luyou fuwu zhongxin	旅游服务中心
Mount Putuo	Putuoshan	普陀山
Shangri-La Hotel	Xiang ge li la jiu dian	香格里拉酒店
Sheraton Hotel	Xi aid eng jiu dian	喜来登酒店
South Bus Station	Nanzhan qiche zhan	南站汽车站
South Rail Station	Nanzhan huoche zhan	南站火车站
Tianfeng Pagoda	Tian Feng Ta	天封塔
Tian Yi Pavilion	Tian Yi Ge	天一阁
Tian Yi Square	Tian Yi Guang Chang	天一广场
Vegetarian Lifestyle	Zao zi shu jing su can ting	枣子树净素餐厅
Zhongshan Park	Zhongshan gong yuan	中山公园
Zhuangyuanlou Restaurant	Zhuangyuanloujiudian	状元楼酒店
FUJIAN	**FÚ JIÀN**	
Xiamen City	xià mén shí	
10,000 Rock Botanical Garden	wàn shí zhí wù yuán	万石植物园
Coyote Café and Cantina	Moxige canting	墨西哥餐厅
Dafang Vegetarian	dà fāng sˇ shí guǎn	大方素食馆
Guan Hai Canting	guān hǎi cān tīng	观海餐厅
Hakka Roundhouses	ké jiā tǔ lóu	客家土楼
Hong Shan Park	huáng shān gōng yuán	黄山公园
Kinmen/Jinmen	jīn mén	金门
Le Meridian	Ai mei jiudian	艾美酒店
Lujiang Hotel	lù jiāng bīn guǎn	鹭江宾馆
Nanputuo Temple	nán pǔ tuó sí	南普陀寺

5

ENGLISH	PIN YIN	CHINESE CHARACTERS
Overseas Chinese Museum	huá qiáo bó wˇ guǎn	华侨博物馆
Panxiaolian Yogurt Shop	panxiaolian	潘小莲
Puzhaolou Vegetarian Restaurant	pǔ zhào lóu sù cài guǎn	普照楼素菜馆
Shuyou Seafood Restaurant	shū yǒu hǎi xiān dà jiǔ lóu	舒友海鲜大酒楼
Xiamen University	xià mén dà xué	厦门大学
Zhong Shan Park	zhōng shān gōng yuán	中山公园
Gulangyu	gǔ làng yǔ	
Bright Moon Garden	hǎo yuè yu·n	皓月园
Bright Moon Leisure and Holiday Club	hǎo yuè xiū xián dù jià jū lé bù	皓月休闲度假俱乐部
Fu Lin Chun Can Ting	fú lín chūn cān tīng	福林春餐厅
Gang Zai Hou Yu Chang Can Ting	gǎng zǎi hòu yù chǎng cān tīng	港仔后浴场餐厅
Gulangyu Guesthouse	Gulangyu bin guan	鼓浪屿宾馆
Gulangyu International Youth Hostel	gǔ làng yǔ guó jí qīng nián lv3 shé	鼓浪屿国际青年旅舍
Holiday Inn Crowne Plaza Harbourview	hǎi jǐng huáng guān jià rì jiǔ diàn	海景皇冠假日酒店
Long Hai White Beach Ancient Crater	lǔng hǎi bái tán huǒ shān kǒu	龙海白滩火山口
Long Wen Can Ting	lóng wén cān tīng	龙文餐厅
Long distance bus station	cháng tú qì chē zhàn	长途汽车站
Marco Polo Xiamen	mǎ kě bō luó dà jiǔ diàn	马可波罗大酒店
Museum of Anthropology	rén lèi bó wù guǎn	人类博物馆
Piano Museum	gāng qín bó wù guǎn	钢琴博物馆
Quanzhou	quán zhōu	泉州
Shuzhuang Garden	shū zhuāng huā yuán	菽庄花园
Temple of the Kingdom of Heaven	tiān jié sí	天届寺
Tourist Complaint Hotline	lǔ yóu tóu sù ré xiàn	旅游投诉热线
Wanshi Botanical Garden	wàn shí zhí wù yuán	万石植物园
Zhen Qi Shi Jie	zhēn qí shí jié	珍奇世界
Zhongshan Lu	zhōng shān lù	中山路

Hong Kong

WORD OF MOUTH

"You can spend hours in Hong Kong Park—watching or joining the morning crowd doing their Tai Chi, having a great run, and being struck by the contrasting harmonies of the non-stop frenzy of HK side-by-side with the serenity of the park."

—rizzuto

WELCOME TO HONG KONG

TOP REASONS TO GO

★ **Harbor Views.** The skyline that launched a thousand postcards . . . See it on a stroll along the Tsim Sha Tsui waterfront, from a Star Ferry crossing the harbor, or from the top of Victoria Peak.

★ **Dim Sum.** As you bite into a moist *siu mai* it dawns on you why everyone says you haven't done dim sum until you've done it in Hong Kong.

★ **Cultural Immersion.** The Hong Kong Heritage Museum chronicles the city's history. On a Lantau Island hill, see the 242-ton Tian Tan Buddha statue sits in the lotus position beside the Po Lin Buddhist Monastery.

★ **Shopping as Religion.** At Kowloon's street markets, clothes, electronics, and souvenirs compete for space with food carts. Antiques fill windows along Hollywood Road.

★ **Horsing Around.** Every year, Hong Kongers gamble more than US$10 billion, and the Happy Valley Racetrack is one of their favorite places to do it.

1 Hong Kong Island. It's only 78 square km (30 square mi), but it's where the action is, from high finance to nightlife to luxury shopping. The commercial districts—Western, Central, and Wan Chai—are on the north coast. Southside is home to small towns, quiet coves, and reserve areas. A 20-minute taxi ride from Central can have you breathing fresh air and seeing only greenery.

2 Kowloon. This peninsula on the Chinese mainland is just across from Central and bounded in the north by the string of mountains that give it its poetic name: *gau lung,* "nine dragons" (there are eight mountains, the ninth dragon was the emperor who named them).

3 New Territories. The expanse between Kowloon and the Chinese border feels far removed from urban congestion and rigor. Nature reserves (many with great trails), temples, and traditional Hakka villages fill its 200 square mi. Conversely public housing projects have led to the creation of new towns like Sha Tin and Tsuen Mun, some of which are now home to a half million people.

4 Outer Islands. Off the west coast of Hong Kong Island lie Lamma, Cheung Chau, and Lantau islands. Lantau, which is home to the Tian Tau Buddha, is connected by ferries to Hong Kong Island and by a suspension bridge to west Kowloon.

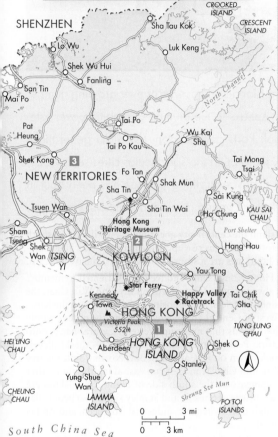

SHENZHEN

Lo Wu

Sha Tau Kok

CROOKED
ISLAND

CRESCENT
ISLAND

Luk Keng

Shek Wu Hui

Fanling

San Tin

Mai Po

Tai Po

Pat
Heung

Tai Po Kau

Wu Kai
Sha

Shek Kong

Fo Tan

Tai Mong
Tsai

NEW TERRITORIES

Sha Tin

Shak Mun

Tsuen Wan

Sha Tin Wai

Sai Kung

Ho Chung

KAU SAI
CHAU

Sham
Tseng

**Hong Kong
Heritage Museum**

Port Shelter

Shek
Wan

TSING
YI

KOWLOON

Hang Hau

Yau Tong

Star Ferry

Kennedy
Town

**Happy Valley
Racetrack**

Tai Chik
Sha

HONG KONG

Victoria Peak
552m

TUNG LUNG
CHAU

HEI LING
CHAU

**HONG KONG
ISLAND**

Shek O

Aberdeen

Stanley

Yung Shue
Wan

CHEUNG
CHAU

**LAMMA
ISLAND**

Sheung Sze Mun

PO TOI
ISLANDS

0   3 mi

0   3 km

South China Sea

GETTING
ORIENTED

Hong Kong Island and
the Kowloon Peninsula
are divided by Victoria
Harbour. On Hong Kong
Island, the central city
stretches only a few kilometers south before mountains
rise up. But the city really
also continues several
more kilometers north
into Kowloon. In the main
districts, luxury boutiques
are a stone's throw from
old hawker stalls, and a
modern, high-tech horse-
racing track isn't far from
a temple housing more
than 10,000 buddhas.

6

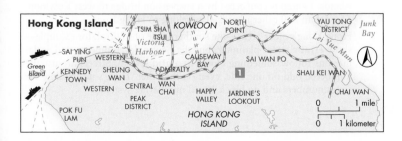

Hong Kong Island

TSIM SHA
TSUI

KOWLOON

NORTH
POINT

YAU TONG
DISTRICT

Junk
Bay

Victoria
Harbour

Lei Yue Mun

SAI YING
PUN

WESTERN

Green
Island

KENNEDY
TOWN

SHEUNG
WAN

ADMIRALTY

CAUSEWAY
BAY

SAI WAN PO

SHAU KEI WAN

WESTERN

CENTRAL

WAN
CHAI

HAPPY
VALLEY

JARDINE'S
LOOKOUT

CHAI WAN

PEAK
DISTRICT

POK FU
LAM

**HONG KONG
ISLAND**

0   1 mile

0   1 kilometer

By Victoria
Patience and
Eva Chui
Loiterton
Updated by
Cherise Fong
and Doretta
Lau

The Hong Kong Island skyline, with its ever growing number of skyscrapers, speaks to the triumph of ambition over fate. Whereas it took Paris and London 10 to 20 generations and New York six to build the spectacular cities seen today, in Hong Kong almost everything you see has been built in the time since today's young investment bankers were born.

On Hong Kong Island the central city goes only a few kilometers south into the island before mountains rise up. In the main districts and neighborhoods luxury boutiques are a stone's throw from old hawker stalls.

When you're on Hong Kong Island and feeling disoriented, remember that the water is always north. Central, Admiralty, and Wan Chai, the island's main business districts, are opposite Tsim Sha Tsui on the Kowloon Peninsula. West of Central are Sheung Wan and the other (mainly residential) neighborhoods that make up Western. Central backs onto the slopes of Victoria Peak, so the districts south of it—the Midlevels and the Peak—look down on it. Causeway Bay, North Point, Quarry Bay, Shau Kei Wan, and Chai Wan East run east along the shore after Wan Chai. Developments on the south side of Hong Kong Island are scattered: the beach towns of Shek O and Stanley sit on two peninsulas on the southeast; high-tech Cyberport, industrial Aberdeen, and Ap Lei Chau are to the west.

West of Hong Kong Island lie Lamma, Cheung Chau, and Lantau islands. Lantau is connected by a suspension bridge to west Kowloon. More than 200 other islands also belong to Hong Kong.

Hong Kong's older areas—the southern side of Central, for example—show erratic street planning, but the newer developments and reclamations follow something closer to a grid system. Streets are usually numbered odd on one side, even on the other. There's no baseline for street numbers and no block-based numbering system.

PLANNING

WHEN TO GO

Hong Kong's high season, from September through late December, sees sunny, dry days and cool, comfortable nights. January and February are mostly cool and dank, with long periods of overcast skies. March and April are fairly pleasant, and by May the temperature is consistently warm and comfortable.

June through August are the cheapest months for one reason: they coincide with the hot, sticky, and very rainy typhoon (hurricane) season. Hong Kong is prepared for blustery assaults; if a big storm approaches, the airwaves crackle with information, and your hotel will post the appropriate signals (a No. 10 signal indicates the worst winds, and a black warning means a rainstorm is brewing). This is serious business—bamboo scaffolding and metal signs can come hurtling through the streets like spears, trees can break or fall, and large areas of the territory can flood. Museums, shops, restaurants, and transport shut down at signal No. 8, but 7-Elevens and cinemas typically stay open.

GETTING HERE AND AROUND

Air Travel. The sleek **Hong Kong International Airport (HKG)** (☎ *852/2181–8888* ⊕ *www.hkairport.com*) is universally referred to as Chek Lap Kok, which is where it's located. **Cathay Pacific** (☎ *800/233–2742 in U.S., 2747–1888 in Hong Kong* ⊕ *www.cathay-usa.com*) is Hong Kong's flagship carrier. Cathay has nonstop flights from Los Angeles and San Francisco on the west coast and from New York–JFK on the east. **Singapore Airlines** (☎ *800/742–3333 in U.S., 852/2520–2233 in Hong Kong* ⊕ *www.singaporeair.com*) offers direct flights to San Francisco and Newark. **Continental** (☎ *800/231–0856 in U.S., 852/3198–5777 in Hong Kong* ⊕ *www.continental.com*) also has a nonstop flight to Hong Kong from Newark.

Ground Transportation. The **Airport Express** train service (☎ *2881–8888 for MTR hotline* ⊕ *www.mtr.com.hk*) is the quickest way to and from the airport. High-speed trains whisk you to Kowloon in 19 minutes and Central in 24 minutes. **Citybus** (☎ *2873–0818* ⊕ *www.nwstbus.com.hk*) runs five buses ("A" precedes the bus number) from Chek Lap Kok to popular destinations. Taxis from the airport cost around HK$340 for Hong Kong Island destinations and HK$270 for Kowloon destinations, plus HK$5 per piece of luggage stored in the trunk. Two limo services in the arrivals hall, **Parklane** (☎ *2261–0303* ⊕ *www.hongkonglimo.com*) and **Intercontinental** (☎ *2261–2155* ⊕ *www.trans-island.com.hk*), range from HK$500 to HK$600.

Bus Travel. A network of double-decker buses covers most of Hong Kong. When determining bus direction, buses ending with the letter "L" eventually connect to the Kowloon–Canton Railway; buses ending with the letter "M" connect to an MTR station; "A" enders go to the airport; and buses ending with the letter "X" are express.

Bus Information Citybus (☎ *2873–0818* ⊕ *www.citybus.com.hk*); Hong Kong Island, cross-harbor and airport routes. **Kowloon Motor Bus** (KMB ☎ *2745–4466* ⊕ *www.kmb.com.hk*) mainly serves Kowloon and New Territories. **Long Win Bus**

THE OCTOPUS

Public transportation options are many and varied—all are good, too. An "Octopus" stored-value card is by far the most convenient way to get around Hong Kong. It's used on all forms of public transport: you just swipe it over the ticket-gate sensor to deduct your fare, which will be cheaper than a regular one. You can buy an Octopus card (☎ 2266–2222 ⊕ www.octopuscards.com) in any MTR, KCR, or Airport Express Station. They cost HK$150, of which HK$50 is a refundable deposit, and the other HK$100 is for you to use. (If you return them in less than a month, you forfeit HK$7 of your deposit as a processing fee.) You can refill the cards at any ticket counter, at speedy machines in stations, or at a 7-Eleven or Wellcome supermarket, where you can also use them to pay for purchases.

Company (☎ 2261–2791 ⊕ www.kmb.com.hk) serves north Lantau, including Tung Chung. **New World First Bus** (☎ 2136–8888 ⊕ www.nwfb.com.hk) runs services on Hong Kong Island and in New Kowloon.

Car Travel. Frankly, you'd be mad to rent a car on Hong Kong Island or Kowloon. Maniac drivers, driving on the left, and traffic jams make driving here severely stress-inducing.

Heavy daytime traffic in Central and Tsim Sha Tsui means taxis aren't the best option. Outside these areas, or after dark, they're much more useful. Many drivers don't speak English so have your destination written in Chinese.

Information Hawk Rent-a-Car (☎ 2516–9822 ⊕ www.hawkrentacar.com.hk). **Parklane Limousine** (☎ 2730–0662 ⊕ www.hongkonglimo.com) rents Mercedes with drivers.

Ferry Travel. The **Star Ferry** (☎ 2367–7065 ⊕ www.starferry.com.hk) is a Hong Kong icon that's sailed across the harbor since 1888. Double-bowed, green-and-white vessels connect Central and Wan Chai with Kowloon in seven minutes, daily from 6:30 am to 11:30 pm; the ride costs HK$2.20.

New World First Ferry (NWFF) (☎ 2131–8181 ⊕ www.nwff.com.hk) runs nine routes from Central to the islands of Lantau and Cheung Chau.

Subway and Train Travel. By far the best way to get around Hong Kong is on the Mass Transit Railway, or MTR, which now provides all subway and train services in Hong Kong. Subways run every two to five minutes between 6 am and 1 am daily. Station entrances are marked with a dark red circle symbol containing the outline of a person with arms and legs outstretched in white.

You buy tickets from ticket machines or from English-speaking workers at the counters. Fares range from HK$3.60 to HK$23.50. A special Tourist MTR One-Day Pass (HK$50) allows you unlimited rides in a day.

The train network connects Kowloon to the eastern and western New Territories. Trains run every 5 to 8 minutes. Fares range from HK$3.70

to HK$47.50; you can pay by Octopus card or buy tickets from sales counters or ticket machines.

Information MTR (☎ *2881–8888* ⊕ *www.mtr.com.hk*).

Tram Travel. The **Peak Tram** (☎ *2849–6754* ⊕ *www.thepeak.com.hk*) is actually a funicular railway. Since 1888 it's been rattling up the 1,207 feet the hill from Central to Victoria Peak tram terminus. A steep ascent, on a clear day it offers fabulous panoramas. Both residents and tourists use it; most passengers board at the lower terminus between Garden Road and Cotton Tree Drive. (The tram has five stations.) The fare is HK$22 one way, HK$33 round-trip, and it runs every 15 minutes from 7 am to midnight daily. A shuttle bus runs between the lower terminus and the Star Ferry.

Hong Kong Tramways (☎ *2548–7102* ⊕ *www.hktramways.com*) runs old-fashioned double-decker trams along the north shore of Hong Kong Island. Routes start in Kennedy Town (in the west), and go all the way through Central, Wan Chai, Causeway Bay, North Point, and Quarry Bay to Shau Kei Wan. A branch line turns off in Wan Chai toward Happy Valley, where horse races are held in season.

Destinations are marked on the front of each tram; board at the back and get off at the front, paying HK$2 regardless of distance (by Octopus or with exact change) as you leave. Although trams move slowly, for short hops between Central and Western or Admiralty they can be quicker than the MTR.

6

NAVIGATING

Hong Kong's streets may seem utterly chaotic, but its public transport system is not. On the northern side of Hong Kong Island, look for the tracks or listen for the "ding-ding" of the tram, which runs straight across the island west to east. This is the same route that the MTR (underground railway) follows, so you should be able to walk to an MTR station from any tram stop between Sheung Wan and Shau Kei Wan. In Kowloon, orient yourself in relation to Nathan Road: Most buses running southbound down Nathan Road terminate at the Star Ferry Concourse in Tsim Sha Tsui, unless they're crossing over to Hong Kong Island.

The MTR, which links most of the areas you'll want to visit, is quick, safe, clean, and user-friendly. Signs and announcements are in both Chinese and English, and exits often lead directly into shopping malls.

Pay with a rechargeable Octopus card. You can use it on the MTR, buses, trams, the Star Ferry, the Peak Tram, and even at vending machines, convenience stores, fast-food restaurants, public swimming pools, and the racetrack.

It's often not worth taking the MTR for one stop, as stations are close, so walk or take the tram. The MTR paid areas also include underground pedestrian passageways between nearby stops such as Tsim Sha Tsui and East Tsim Sha Tsui or Central and Hong Kong Station.

Most MTR stations have multiple exits, so consult the detailed station maps to determine which exit lets you out closest to your destination.

If you're crossing Central, use the covered walkways that link its main buildings, thus avoiding stoplights, exhaust fumes, and weather conditions (but not crowds). The same can apply to the pedestrian overpasses in Mong Kok. Note that signs marked "subway" refer to a subterranean passageway, not to the MTR.

On Hong Kong Island, Queen's Road changes its suffix every so often, resulting in Queen's Road East, Queen's Road Central, and Queen's Road West. However, these suffixes don't exactly correspond with the districts, so part of Queen's Road Central is actually in Western. As street numbers start again with each new section, be sure you know which part you're headed for, or better still, the intersecting street. The same goes for Des Voeux Road.

VISITOR INFORMATION

Swing by the Hong Kong Tourist Board (HKTB) visitor center before even leaving the airport. It publishes stacks of helpful free exploring booklets and maps, offers free classes and workshops on local culture, runs a plethora of tours, and operates a multilingual helpline. Its detailed, comprehensive Web site is a fabulous resource. If you're planning on visiting several museums in a week, pick up a Museum Weekly Pass, which gets you into seven museums for HK$30. Buy it at participating museums or at the HKTB visitor center at the Tsim Sha Tsui Star Ferry Concourse.

Hong Kong Tourist Board (*HKTB*✉ *Hong Kong International Airport, Arrivals Level, Terminal 1, Lantau* ⊙ *Daily 7 am–11 pm*✉ *The Peak Piazza, Victoria Peak Central* ⊙ *Daily 9–9*✉ *Star Ferry Concourse, Tsim Sha Tsui, Kowloon* ⊙ *Daily 8–8* ☎ *2508–1234 [hotline daily 9–6]* ⊕ *www.discoverhongkong.com*).

PASSPORTS AND VISAS

Citizens of the United States need only a valid passport to enter Hong Kong for stays up to three months. You need at least six months' validity on your passport before traveling to Asia. Upon arrival, officials at passport control will give you a Hong Kong entry slip. Keep this slip safe; you must present it with your passport for your return trip home. If you're planning to pop over the border into mainland China, you must first get a visa.

SAFETY

Hong Kong is an incredibly safe place—day and night. The police maintain law and order, but a few pickpockets are still about, especially in Tsim Sha Tsui. So avoid carrying large amounts of cash or valuables with you, and you should have no problems.

Nearly all consumer dissatisfaction in Hong Kong stems from the electronics retailers in Tsim Sha Tsui. Get some reference prices online before buying, and always check the contents of boxed items before you leave the shop.

ESSENTIALS

Consulate U.S. Consulate General (✉ *26 Garden Rd., Central* ☎ *2523–9011* ⊕ *www.usconsulate.org.hk*).

Emergency Contacts Police, fire, and ambulance (☎ *999*). **Hong Kong Police and Taxi Complaint Hotline** (☎ *2527-7177*).

Hospitals and Clinics Caritas Medical Centre (public) (✉ *111 Wing Hong St., Sham Shui Po, Kowloon* ☎ *3408–7911* ⊕ *www.ha.org.hk*). **Hong Kong Adventist Hospital** (private) (✉ *40 Stubbs Rd., Midlevels, Western* ☎ *2574–6211* ⊕ *www. hkah.org.hk*). **Hong Kong Central Hospital** (private) (✉ *1 Lower Albert Rd., Central* ☎ *2522–3141* ⊕ *www.hkch.org*). **Prince of Wales Hospital** (public) (✉ *30–32 Ngan Shing St., Sha Tin, New Territories* ☎ *2632–2211* ⊕ *www.ha.org. hk/pwh*). **Queen Elizabeth Hospital** (public) (✉ *30 Gascoigne Rd., Yau Ma Tei, Kowloon* ☎ *2958–8888*). **Queen Mary Hospital** (public) (✉ *102 Pok Fu Lam Rd., Pok Fu Lam, Western* ☎ *2855–3838* ⊕ *www.ha.org.hk/qmh*).

Pharmacy Watsons (☎ *2868–4388*).

Postal Services General Post Office (✉ *2 Connaught Rd., Central* ☎ *2921–2222* ⊕ *www.hongkongpost.com*). **Kowloon Central Post Office** (✉ *405 Nathan Rd., Tsim Tsa Shui*). **DHL** (☎ *2400–3388* ⊕ *www.dhl.com.hk*). **Federal Express** (☎ *2730–3333* ⊕ *www.fedex.com/hk_english*). **UPS** (☎ *2735–3535* ⊕ *www.ups.com*).

EXPLORING HONG KONG

WESTERN

6

Western has been called Hong Kong's Chinatown, and though it's a strange-sounding epithet, there's a reason for it. The area is light-years from the dazzle of Central, despite being just down the road. And although developers are making short work of the traditional architecture, Western's colonial buildings, rattling trams, Old World medicine shops, and lively markets still recall bygone times.

THE TERRITORY

The Midlevels Escalator forms a handy boundary between Western and Central. Several main thoroughfares run parallel to the shore, each farther up the slope: Des Voeux Road (where the trams run), Queen's Road, Hollywood Road (where SoHo starts), and Caine Road (where the Midlevels begin).

As to how far west Western goes, it technically reaches all the way to Kennedy Town, where the tram lines end, but there isn't much worth noting beyond Sheung Wan.

GETTING AROUND

The most scenic way to Sheung Wan is on a tram along Des Voeux Road. From Central or Admiralty it's probably the quickest, too: no traffic, no subway lines, or endless underground walks. There are stops every two or three blocks. The Sheung Wan MTR station brings you within spitting distance of Western Market.

The Macau Ferry Terminal is behind the MTR (use Exit D). **Turbojet** (☎ *2859–3333* ⊕ *www.turbojet.com.hk*) vessels run every 15 minutes with a reduced schedule from midnight to 7 am. You can usually buy tickets on the spot (from HK$134), but reservations are recommended on weekends. ■ TIP➔ You need your passport to go to Macau.

The Midlevels Escalator is fun up as far as SoHo. Buses 3B, 40, and 40M run between the university and Jardine House in Central, as does

Shopping at the Western Market.

green Minibus 8. Both pass the top of Ladder Street. Expect a taxi from Central to the Midlevels to cost HK$20.

TOP ATTRACTIONS

Fodor'sChoice **University Museum and Art Gallery, The University of Hong Kong.** Chinese
★ harp music and a faint smell of incense float through its peaceful rooms.
The small but excellent collection of Chinese antiquities includes ceramics and bronzes, some dating from 3000 BC; fine paintings; lacquerware; and carvings in jade, stone, and wood. There are some superb
ancient pieces: ritual vessels, decorative mirrors, and painted pottery.
The museum has the world's largest collection of Nestorian crosses, dating from the Mongol Period (1280–1368). These belonged to a hereti-
cal Christian sect who came to China from the Middle East during the
Tang Dynasty (618–907).

There are usually two or three well-curated temporary exhibitions
on: contemporary artists who work in traditional mediums are often
featured. ■TIP➔ Don't miss part of the museum: the collection is spread
between the T. T. Tsui Building and the Fung Ping Shan Building, which
you access via a first-floor footbridge. The museum is out of the way—
20 minutes from Central via Buses 3A, 23, 40, 40 M, or 103, or a
15-minute uphill walk from Sheung Wan MTR—but it's a must for the
true Chinese art lover. ⊠ *94 Bonham Rd., Pokfulam, Western* ☎ *2241-
5500* ⊕ *www.hku.hk/hkumag* ☒ *Free* ☉ *Mon.–Sat. 9:30–6, Sun. 1–6*
Ⓜ *Sheung Wan.*

WORTH NOTING

Hong Kong Museum of Medical Sciences. You can find out all about medical episodes at this private museum, which is housed in a redbrick building at the top of Ladder Street that references Edwardian style architecture. The 11 exhibition galleries cover 10,000 square feet, and present information on both Western and Chinese medical practices. ⊠ *2 Caine La., Midlevels, Western* ☎ *2549–5123* ⊕ *www.hkmms.org.hk* 🖃 *$5–$10* ⊙ *Tues.–Sat. 10–5, Sun. and holidays 1–5* Ⓜ *Sheung Wan, Exit A2.*

Man Mo Temple. It's believed to be Hong Kong Island's oldest temple, though no one knows exactly when it was built—the consensus is sometime around the arrival of the British in 1841. It's dedicated to the Taoist gods of literature and of war: Man, who wears green, and Mo, dressed in red. The temple bell, cast in Canton in 1847, and the drum next to it are sounded to attract the gods' attention when a prayer is being offered—give it a ring to make sure yours are heard. ■TIP➜ **To check your fortune, stand in front of the altar, ask a question, select a small bamboo cylinder, and shake it until a stick falls out. The number on the stick corresponds to a written fortune. Then go next door, where an English-speaking fortune-teller can tell you what it means for HK$20.** ⊠ *Hollywood Rd. at Ladder St., Sheung Wan, Western* ⊙ *Daily 8–6* Ⓜ *Sheung Wan, Exit A2.*

Western Market. The Sheung Wan district's iconic market, a hulking brown-and-white colonial structure, is a good place to get your bearings. Built in 1906, it functioned as a produce market for 83 years. Today it's a shopping center selling trinkets and fabrics—the architecture is what's worth the visit. Nearby is the Chinese herbal medicine on Ko Shing Street and Queen's Road West, dried seafood on Wing Lok Street and Des Voeux Road West, and ginseng and bird's nest on Bonham Strand West. ⊠ *323 Des Voeux St. Central, Sheung Wan, Western* ⊙ *Daily 10 am–midnight* Ⓜ *Sheung Wan, Exit B or C.*

CENTRAL

Shopping, eating, drinking—Central lives up to its name when it comes to all of these. But it's also Hong Kong's historical heart, packed with architectural reminders of the early colonial days. They're in stark contrast to the soaring masterpieces of modern architecture that the city is famous for. Somehow the mishmash works. With the harbor on one side and Victoria Peak on the other, Central's views—once you get high enough to see them—are unrivaled. It's a hot spot for both locals and expatriates, packed with people, sights, and life.

THE TERRITORY

The Midlevels Escalator forms the boundary of Central with Western. Streets between Queen's Road Central and the harbor are laid out more or less geometrically. On the south side of Queen's Road, however, is a confusion of steep lanes. Overhead walkways connect Central's major buildings, an all-weather alternative to the chaotic streets below.

GETTING AROUND

Central MTR station is a mammoth underground warren with a host of far-flung exits. A series of travelators join it with Hong Kong Station, under the IFC Mall, where Tung Chung Line and Airport Express trains

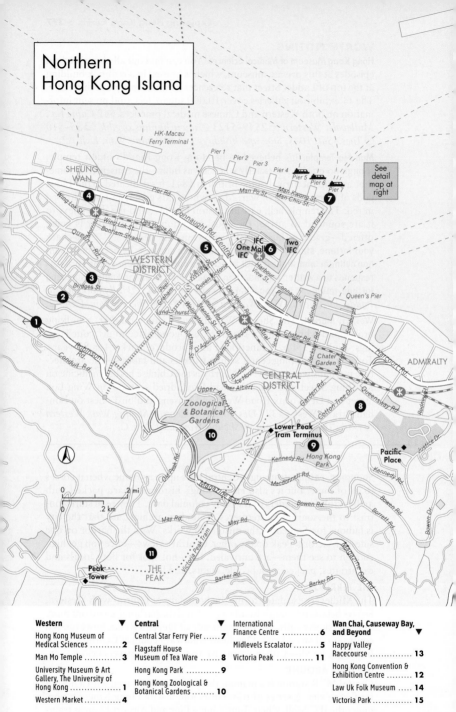

Northern Hong Kong Island

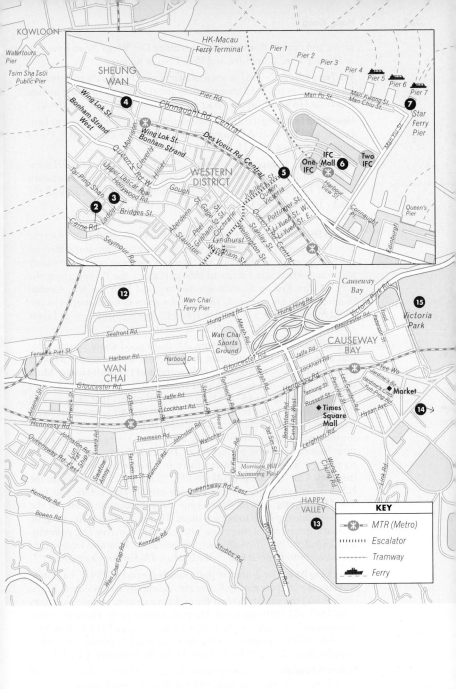

arrive and depart. Rattling old trams along Des Voeux Road have you at Sheung Wan, Admiralty, and Wan Chai in minutes.

Star Ferry (☎ 2367–7065 ⊕ *www.starferry.com.hk*) vessels to Kowloon leave Pier 7 every 6–12 minutes 6:30 *am*–11:30 *pm*; the nine-minute trip costs HK$2.50 (upper deck) on weekdays, HK$3 on weekends.

New World First Ferry (☎ 2131–8181 ⊕ *www.nwff.com.hk*) goes to Lantau (from Pier 6) and Cheung Chau (Pier 5). Crossings take 35–55 minutes and cost HK$11.50–HK$32.20.

Discovery Bay Transportation Service (☎ 2987–7351 ⊕ *www.hkri.com/ icms2/template?series=88*) has high-speed boats for the northeastern coast of Lantau Island every 20–30 minutes from Pier 3 around the clock. Trips take 25–30 minutes and cost HK$27.

TOP ATTRACTIONS

Central Star Ferry Pier. Take in the view of the Kowloon skyline from the pier. For arguably the best panorama of Central's architecture, start on the Kowloon side at the Tsim Sha Tsui pier and take one of the sturdy green-and-white Star Ferries to this pier; enjoy the skyline along the way. ⊠ *Man Kwong St. between Rumsey and Man Yiu Sts., Central* ☎ *2367–7065 for ferries, 2118–6201 for tours* ⊕ *www.starferry.com. hk* 🖾 *round-trip HK$55 (day) or HK$110 (night); Symphony of Lights Harbour Cruise HK$150* Ⓜ *Hong Kong Station, Exit.*

Fodor'sChoice
★

Flagstaff House Museum of Tea Ware. All that's good about British colonial architecture is exemplified in the simple white facade, wooden monsoon shutters, and colonnaded verandas of Flagstaff House. More than 600 pieces of delicate antique teaware from the Tang (618–907) through the Qing (1644–1911) dynasties fill rooms that once housed the commander of the British forces. ■TIP→ Skip the lengthy, confusing tea-ceremony descriptions; concentrate on the porcelain itself. Look out for the unadorned brownish-purple clay of the Yixing pots: unglazed, their beauty hinges on perfect form. There's a carved wooden booth on the first floor where you can listen to Chinese tea songs. Head to the **Lock Cha Tea Shop** (☎ *2801–7177* ⊕ *www.lockcha.com*), in the K.S. Lo Gallery annex, where you can sample teas before you buy. The Hong Kong Tourist Board runs tea appreciation classes at the shop—phone the shop to book a place. Try the Tie Guan Yin, a highly aromatic green tea. ⊠ *Hong Kong Park, 10 Cotton Tree Dr., Admirality, Central* ☎ *2869–0690* ⊕ *www.lcsd.gov.hk/ce/Museum/Arts/english/ tea/intro/eintro.html* 🖾 *Free* ☉ *Wed.–Mon. 10–5* Ⓜ *Admiralty, Exit C1.*

Ⓒ
Fodor'sChoice
★

Hong Kong Park. The 8-hectare park, which opened in 1991, is a respite from the skyscrapers that spill over into Admiralty from Central. Previously it was the site of Victoria Barracks, a garrison, and the buildings from 1842 and 1910 still stand. The park is home to the Flagstaff House Museum of Tea Ware and the Edward Youde Aviary. ⊠ *19 Cotton Tree Dr., Admirality, Central* ☎ *2521–5041* ⊕ *www.lcsd.gov.hk/parks/hkp/ en/index.php* 🖾 *Free* ☉ *Daily 6 am–11 pm* Ⓜ *Admiralty, Exit C1.*

Midlevels Escalator. The unimaginatively named Midlevels is midway up the hill between Victoria Peak and the Western and Central districts. Running through it is the escalator, which connects the now-defunct Central Market (at the border of Central and Western) with several

A clear day on Victoria Peak.

main residential roads. Free of charge and protected from the elements, this series of moving walkways makes the uphill journey a cinch. Before 10 am they move only downward, carrying yuppies bearing coffee to work. ⊠ *Next to 100 Queen's Rd. Central, Central* ⊗ *6–midnight* Ⓜ *Central, Exit D1.*

Fodor's Choice **Victoria Peak.** Soaring 1,805 feet above sea level, the peak looks over
★   Central and beyond. Residents here take special pride in the positions to which they have, quite literally, risen; theirs is the island's most exclusive address. The steep tracks up to it start at the **Peak Tram Terminus,** near St. John's Cathedral on Garden Road. ⊠ *Tram between Garden Rd. and Cotton Tree Dr., Central* ☎ *2522–0922* ⊕ *www.thepeak.com. hk* ✉ *HK$25 one-way, HK$36 round-trip* ⊗ *7 am–midnight.*

WORTH NOTING

Hong Kong Zoological & Botanical Gardens. Farther uphill on Central's eastern edge is this welcoming green breathing space. It includes a children's playground and numerous gardens, but the real attractions are the dozens of mammals, birds, and reptiles housed in zoological exhibits. Buses 3B, 12, and 13 run from Central; the walk from the Central MTR stop is quite a distance and uphill. ⊠ *Albany Rd. between Robinson and Upper Albert Rds., Central* ☎ *2530–0154* ⊕ *www.lcsd.gov.hk/parks/ hkzbg/en/* ✉ *Free* ⊗ *Daily 6 am–10 pm* Ⓜ *Central.*

International Finance Centre. One building towers above the rest of Central's skyline: Two IFC, or the second tower of the International Finance Centre. The tall, tapering structure has been compared to at least one—unprintable—thing and is topped with a clawlike structure straight out of Thundercats. Designed by Argentine architect Cesar Pelli (of

London's Canary Wharf fame), its 88 floors measure a whopping 1,362 feet. Opposite stands its dinky little brother, the 38-floor One IFC. The massive IFC Mall stretches between the two, and Hong Kong Station is underneath. If you wish to see the breathtaking views from Two IFC, you can visit the Hong Kong Monetary Authority (⊠ *55/F, Two IFC* ☎ *2878–1111* ⊕ *www.info.gov.hk/hkma*). Upon arrival, you may need to register your passport with the concierge. ⊠ *8 Finance St., Central* ⊕ *www.ifc.com.hk* ✉ *Free* ⊗ *Hong Kong Monetary Authority weekdays 10–6, Sat. 10–1* Ⓜ *Hong Kong Station, Exit A2.*

WAN CHAI, CAUSEWAY BAY, AND BEYOND

The Happy Valley horse races are a vital part of Hong Kong life, so it's only fitting that they're in one of the city's most vital areas. A few blocks back from Wan Chai's new office blocks are crowded alleys where you might stumble across a wet market, a tiny furniture-maker's shop, or an age-old temple. Farther east, Causeway Bay pulses with Hong Kong's best shopping streets and hundreds of restaurants. At night the whole area comes alive with bars, restaurants, and discos, as well as establishments offering some of Wan Chai's more traditional services (think red lights and photos of seminaked women outside).

THE TERRITORY

Wan Chai's trams run mostly along Hennessy Road, with a detour along Johnston Road at the neighborhood's western end. Queen's Road East runs parallel to these two streets to the south, and a maze of lanes connect it with Hennessy.

The thoroughfares north of Hennessy—Lockhart, Jaffe, and Gloucester, which is a freeway—are laid out in a grid. Causeway Bay's diagonal roads make it hard to navigate, but it's small; wander around, and before long you'll hit something familiar.

GETTING AROUND

Both Wan Chai and Causeway Bay have their own MTR stops, but a pleasant way to arrive from Central is on the tram along Hennessy Road. All the lines go through Wan Chai, but check the sign at the front if you're going beyond. Some continue to North Point and Shau Kei Wan, via Causeway Bay, while others go south to Happy Valley.

The underground stations are small labyrinths, so read the signs carefully to find the best exit. Traffic begins to take its toll on journey times farther east—the MTR is a better option for Shau Kei Wan and Chai Wan.

The Star Ferry runs between Tsim Sha Tsui and Wan Chai every 8–20 minutes. Boats leave from the ferry pier just east of the convention center.

Like all of Hong Kong, Wan Chai isn't really dangerous at night, but single women strolling the streets in the wee hours might get unwanted attention from groups of drunk expats. Taxis are a good idea late at night.

TOP ATTRACTIONS

Happy Valley Racecourse. The biggest attraction east of Causeway Bay for locals and visitors alike is this local legend, where millions of Hong Kong dollars make their way each year. The races make great Wednesday nights out on the town. Aside from the excitement of the races, there are restaurants, bars, and even a racing museum to keep you amused. The easiest way to reach the racecourse is to take the tram to Happy Valley. ⊠ *Sports Rd. at Wong Nai Chung Rd., Happy Valley, Causeway Bay* ⊕ *www.racecourses.hkjc.com/english/come_racing/racecourses/happy_valley* ⊠ *$10* ⊘ *Wed. 5:15 or 5:30 during racing season* Ⓜ *Causeway Bay, Exit A.*

Victoria Park. Hong Kong Island's largest park is a welcome breathing space on the edge of Causeway Bay and bounded by Hing Fat, Gloucester, and Causeway roads. It's beautifully landscaped and has recreational facilities for swimming, lawn bowling, tennis, and rollerskating. At dawn every morning hundreds practice tai chi chuan here. It's also the site of midautumn's Lantern Carnival, with the trees a mass of colorful lights. Just before Chinese New Year (late January to early February), the park hosts a huge flower market. On the eve of Chinese New Year, after a traditional family dinner at home, much of Hong Kong happily gathers here to shop and wander until the early hours of the new year. ⊠ *Causeway Rd. between Hing Fat St. and Gloucester Rd., Causeway Bay* ☎ *2890–5824* ⊕ *www.lcsd.gov.hk/parks/vp/en/index.php* ⊠ *Free* ⊘ *24 hours* Ⓜ *Tin Hau, Exit A2.*

WORTH NOTING

Hong Kong Convention & Exhibition Centre. Land is so scarce that developers usually only build skyward, but the HKCEC is an exception. It sits on a spit of reclaimed land jutting into the harbor. Its curved-glass walls and swooping roof make it look like a tortoise lumbering into the sea or a gull taking flight, depending on whom you ask. Of all the international trade fairs, regional conferences, and other events held here, by far the most famous was the 1997 Handover ceremony. An obelisk commemorates it on the waterfront promenade, which also affords great views of Kowloon.

Outside the center stands the *Golden Bauhinia*. This gleaming sculpture of the Bauhinia flower, Hong Kong's symbol, was a gift from China celebrating the establishment of the Hong Kong SAR in 1997. The police hoist the SAR flag daily at 7:50 am. ⊠ *1 Expo Dr., Wan Chai* ☎ *2582–8888* ⊕ *www.hkcec.com.hk* Ⓜ *Wan Chai, Exit A.*

Law Uk Folk Museum. This restored Hakka house was once the home of the Law family, who arrived here from Guangdong in the mid-18th century. It's the perfect example of a triple-*jian*, double-*lang* residence. Jian are enclosed rooms—here, the bedroom, living room, and workroom at the back. The front storeroom and kitchen are the *lang*, where the walls don't reach up to the roof, and thus allow air in. Although the museum is small, informative texts outside and displays of rural furniture and farm implements inside give a powerful idea of what rural Hong Kong was like. It's definitely worth a trip to bustling industrial Chai Wan, at the eastern end of the MTR, to see it. Photos show what the area looked like in the 1930s—these days a leafy square is the only reminder of the woodlands and fields that once surrounded this buttermilk-color dwelling. ⊠ *14 Kut Shing St., Chai Wan, Eastern* ☎ *2896–7006* ⊕ *www.lcsd.gov.hk/CE/Museum/History/en/luf.php* ⊠ *Free* ⊘ *Mon.–Wed., Fri. and Sat. 10–6, Sun., holidays 1–6* Ⓜ *Chai Wan, Exit B.*

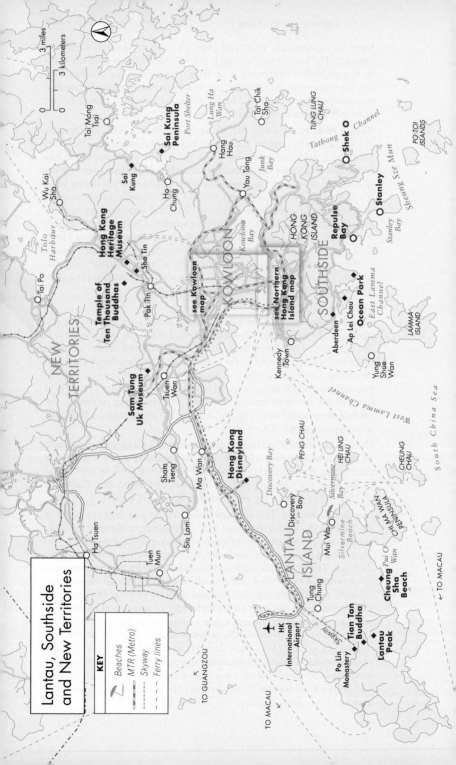

SOUTHSIDE

For all the unrelenting urbanity of Hong Kong Island's north coast, its south side consists largely of green hills and a few residential areas around picturesque bays. With beautiful sea views, real estate is at a premium; some of Hong Kong's wealthiest residents live in beautiful houses and luxurious apartments here. Southside is a breath of fresh air—literally and figuratively. The people are more relaxed, the pace is slower, and there are lots of sea breezes.

TRANSPORTATION FROM CENTRAL TO . . .

Aberdeen: 30 minutes via Bus 70 or 91. (Ap Lei Chau is 15 minutes from Aberdeen on Bus 90B or 91; 10 minutes by sampan.)

Deep Water Bay: 20 minutes via Bus 6, 64, 260, or 6A.

Ocean Park: 30 minutes via Central Pier #7 and Bus 629.

Repulse Bay: 30 minutes via Bus 6, 6A, 6X, 66, 64, or 260.

Shek O: 50 minutes via MTR to Shau Kei Wan and then Bus 9 to the last stop.

Stanley: 40 minutes via Bus 6, 6A, 6X, 66, 64, or 260.

Note that express buses skip Aberdeen and Deep Water Bay, heading directly to Repulse Bay and Stanley. Buses run less frequently in the evening, so it's more convenient to grab a taxi (they're everywhere).

TOP ATTRACTIONS

Ocean Park. Most Hong Kongers have fond childhood memories of this aquatic theme park. It was built by the omnipresent Hong Kong Jockey Club on 170 hilly acres overlooking the sea just east of Aberdeen. Highlights include the four resident giant pandas; Marine Land's enormous aquarium; Ocean Theatre, where dolphins and seals perform; and such thrill rides as the gravity-defying Abyss Turbo. The park is accessible by a number of buses including the 72, 72A, 260, and M590; get off at the stop after the Aberdeen tunnel. ⊠ *Ocean Park Rd., Aberdeen, Southside* ☎ *3923–2323* ⊕ *www.oceanpark.com.hk* ☑ *HK$250 adults; HK$125 kids* ⊙ *Daily 10–7.*

Stanley. This peninsula town lies south of Deep Water and Repulse bays. There's great shopping in the renowned Stanley Market, whether you want casual clothes, sneakers, cheap souvenirs, cheerful bric-a-brac— even snow gear. Stanley's popular beach is the site of the Dragon Boat Races held every June. ⊠ *Stanley, Southside.*

WORTH NOTING

Repulse Bay. The tranquil area is home to a landmark apartment building with a hole in it. Following the principles of feng shui, the opening was incorporated into the design so the dragon that lives in the mountains behind can readily drink from the bay. The popular Repulse Bay Verandah Restaurant and Bamboo Bar (⇨ *Quick Bites*) is a great place for a meal with majestic bay views. The beach is large and wide, but be warned: it's the first stop for most visitors. At the beach's east end, huge statues of Tin Hau—Goddess of the Sea and Goddess of Mercy—border on gaudy. In the 1970s, when worshippers were planning to erect just one statue, they worried she'd be lonely, so an additional statue

was created to keep her company. ✉ *Beach Rd. at Seaview Promenade, Repulse Bay, Southside* ☎ *2812–2483.*

Shek O. The seaside locale is Southside's easternmost village. Weekend beachgoers and hikers crowd the Thai restaurant on the left as you enter town. Every shop here sells the same inflatable beach toys—the bigger the better, it seems. Cut through town to a windy road that takes you to the "island" of Tai Tau Chau, really a large rock with a lookout over the South China Sea. Little more than a century ago, this open water was ruled by pirates. You can hike through nearby Shek O Country Park, where the bird-watching is great, in less than two hours. ✉ *Southside.*

LANTAU ISLAND

A decade of manic development has seen Lantau become more than just "the place where the Buddha is." There's a mini-theme park at Ngong Ping to keep the Buddha company. Not to be outdone, Disney has opened a park and resort on the northeast coast. And, of course, there's the airport, built on a massive north coast reclamation. At 55 square mi, Lantau is almost twice the size of Hong Kong Island, so there's room for all this development and the laid-back attractions—beaches, fishing villages, and hiking trails—that make the island a great getaway.

6

THE TERRITORY

Most Lantau roads lead to Tung Chung, the north shore new town, close to Hong Kong International Airport. It's connected to Kowloon by the lengthy Tsing Ma Bridge, which starts near Hong Kong Disneyland, on Lantau's northeast tip.

The Tung Chung Road winds through mountains and connects north Lantau with the southern coast. Here, the South Lantau Road stretches from the town of Mui Wo in the east to Tai O in the west, passing Cheung Sha Beach, and Ngong Ping.

GETTING AROUND

The speediest way to Lantau from Central is the MTR's Tung Chung line (HK$18), which takes about half an hour. A trip by ferry is a 35-minute crossing from Central with great views.

New World First Ferry (☎ *2131–8181* ⊕ *www.nwff.com.hk*) vessels to Mui Wo leave every 30–40 minutes from Central's Pier 6 (HK$13–HK$25.50).

Bus routes are winding, and rides can be heart-stopping. There's service every half hour from Tung Chung and Mui Wo to Ngong Ping, more frequently to Tai O.

The most direct (and daring) way to Ngong Ping is the 25-minute trip on the **Ngong Ping 360 Skyrail** (☎ *2109–9898* ⊕ *www.np360.com. hk* ✂ *HK$74 one-way; HK$107 round-trip* ☉ *Weekdays 10–6, Sat. 10–6:30, Sun. 9–6:30).*

You can reach Tung Chung by a red taxi from Kowloon or Central, but the long, toll-ridden trip will cost around HK$340 from Central. Blue taxis travel Lantau (but can't leave it)—and hairpin bends make costs add up.

TOP ATTRACTIONS

☺ **Hong Kong Disneyland.** Though Hong Kong's home to Mickey Mouse is tame compared to other Magic Kingdoms, it's fast bringing Mai Kei Lo Su—as the world's most famous mouse is known locally—to a mainland audience. ⊠ *Fantasy Rd., Lantau Island* ⊕ *www.park. hongkongdisneyland.com* ⊡ *HK$350 adults, HK$250 kids* ⊙ *Daily 10–8 or 9* Ⓜ *Disneyland Resort.*

Fodor'sChoice **Tian Tan Buddha.** Hong Kongers love superlatives, even if making them
★ true requires strings of qualifiers. So the Tian Tan Buddha is the world's largest Buddha—that's seated, located outdoors, and made of bronze. Just know its vast silhouette is impressive. Steep stairs lead to the lower podium, essentially forcing you to stare up at all 202 tons of Buddha as you ascend. At the top, cool breezes and fantastic views over Lantau Island await.

It's hard to believe today, but from its foundation in 1927 through the early '90s, **Po Lin Monastery** was virtually inaccessible by road. These days, it's at the heart of Lantau's biggest attraction. The monastery proper has a gaudy, commercial, orange temple complex. Still, it's the Buddha people come for.

The peaceful **Wisdom Path** runs beside 38 halved tree trunks arranged in an infinity shape on a hillside. Each is carved with Chinese characters that make up the Heart Sutra, a 5th-century Buddhist prayer that expresses the doctrine of emptiness. The idea is to walk around the path—which takes five minutes—and reflect. Follow the signposted trail to the left of the Buddha.

People were fussing about **Ngong Ping Village** before its first stone was laid. Ngong Ping Village is a moneymaking add-on to the Tian Tan Buddha. Walking With Buddha is intended to be an educational stroll through the life of Siddhartha Gautama, the first Buddha, but it's more of a multimedia extravaganza that shuns good taste with such kitsch as a self-illuminating Bodhi tree and piped-in incense. No cost has been spared in the dioramas that fill the seven galleries—ironic, given that each represents a stage of the Buddha's path to enlightenment and the eschewing of material wealth. ⊠ *Ngong Ping, Lantau Island* ☎ *2109–9898 Ngong Ping hotline* ⊕ *www.plm.org.hk/eng/home.php* ⊡ *Monastery and path free. Walking with Buddha: HK$35* ⊙ *Buddha daily 10–5:30. Monastery and path daily 8–6* Ⓜ *Tung Chung.*

WORTH NOTING

Cheung Sha Beach. Two miles of golden sand 5 mi southwest of Mui Wo make this Hong Kong's longest. It gets breezy here, but that's why windsurfers love it; it rarely gets too crowded. Upper Cheung Sha Beach is equipped for barbecues, and there is also a refreshment stand. ⊠ *South Lantau Rd., Lantau Island* ☎ *2852–3220.*

Lantau Peak. The most glorious views of Lantau—and beyond—are from atop Fung Wong Shan, or Lantau Peak, but at 3,064 feet it's not for the faint-hearted. It's a strenuous 7½ mi walk west from Mui Wo, or you can begin at the Po Lin Monastery—still a demanding two hours. You can also elect to take a bus to a trail that is closer to the summit, and climb from stage three of the Lantau Trail. ⊠ *Lantau Island.*

DID YOU KNOW?

The Tian Tan Buddha is surrounded by six smaller bronze statues known as "The Offering of the Six Devas." These offerings of flowers, incense, lamp, ointment, fruit, and music symbolize charity, morality, patience, zeal, meditation, and wisdom—all necessary traits if one wishes to reach Nirvana.

KOWLOON

There's much more to the Kowloon than rock-bottom prices and goods of dubious provenance. Just across the harbor from Central, this piece of Chinese mainland takes its name from the string of mountains that bound it in the north: *gau lung,* "nine dragons" (there are actually eight mountains, the ninth represented the emperor who named them). Although less sophisticated and wilder than its island-side counterpart, Kowloon's dense, gritty urban fabric is the backdrop for Hong Kong's best museums and most interesting spiritual sights. And there's street upon street of hard-core consumerism in every imaginable guise.

THE TERRITORY

Kowloon's southernmost district is Tsim Sha Tsui (TST), home to the Star Ferry Pier. The waterfront extends a few miles to TST East. Shops and hotels line Nathan Road, which runs north from the waterfront through the market districts of Jordan, Yau Ma Tei, and Mong Kok.

New Kowloon is the unofficial name for the sprawl beyond Boundary Street. The district just north is Kowloon Tong. Two spiritual sights—Wong Tai Sin and Lok Fu—are a little farther east. The tongue sticking out into the sea to the south was the runway of the old Kai Tak Airport. Kowloon City is a stone's throw west.

GETTING AROUND

The most romantic way from Hong Kong Island to southern Tsim Sha Tsui (TST) is by Star Ferry. There are crossings from Central every 6–12 minutes and a little less often from Wan Chai.

TST is also accessible by MTR. Underground walkways connect the station with the Tsim Sha Tsui East station on the East Rail Line, where trains depart every 10–15 minutes for the eastern New Territories. The Kowloon Airport Express station is amid a construction wasteland west of TST, connecting with Austin station on the West Rail; for now hotel shuttles link it to the rest of Kowloon.

The MTR is your best bet for Jordan, Yau Ma Tei, Mong Kok, Kowloon Tong, Lok Fu, and Wong Tai Sin. But you'll need a bus or cab to reach Kowloon City from Wong Tai Sin or TST East.

TSIM SHA TSUI

One of the best things to see in Tsim Sha Tsui (TST) is, well, Central. There are fabulous cross-harbor views from the **Star Ferry Pier** as well as from the ferries themselves. The sweeping pink-tile **Hong Kong Cultural Centre** and the Former KCR (Kowloon–Canton Railway) Clock Tower are a stone's throw away, the first stop along the breezy pedestrian **TST East Promenade,** which starts at the Avenue of Stars and stretches a couple of miles east. ■TIP➔ Try to visit the promenade once in the daytime and once at 8 pm for the Symphony of Lights, a nightly show in which 44 skyscrapers light up on cue as a commentator introduces them in time to a musical accompaniment.

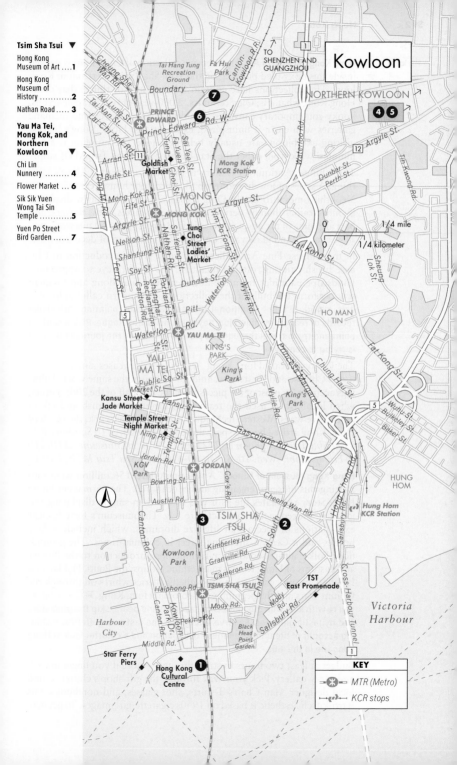

Kowloon

NORTHERN KOWLOON

TO SHENZHEN AND
GUANGZHOU

Tai Hang Tung
Recreation
Ground
Boundary

Fa Hui
Park

PRINCE
EDWARD

Prince Edward Rd. W.

Goldfish
Market

Mong Kok
KCR Station

MONG
KOK

MONG KOK

Tung
Choi
Street
Ladies'
Market

Dundas St.

YAU MA TEI

YAU
MA
TEI

KING'S
PARK

King's
Park

Kansu Street
Jade Market

Temple Street
Night Market

King's
Park

HO MAN
TIN

Gascoigne Rd.

KGV
Park

JORDAN

HUNG
HOM

TSIM SHA
TSUI

Hung Hom
KCR Station

Kowloon
Park

TST
East Promenade

Tsim Sha Tsui

Victoria
Harbour

Harbour
City

Star Ferry
Piers

Hong Kong
Cultural
Centre

Black
Head
Point
Garden

1/4 mile

1/4 kilometer

KEY

MTR (Metro)

KCR stops

TOP ATTRACTIONS

Hong Kong Museum of Art. An extensive collection of Chinese art is packed inside this boxy tiled building on the Tsim Sha Tsui waterfront in Kowloon. The collections here contain a heady mix of things that make Hong Kong what it is: Qing ceramics, 2,000-year-old calligraphic scrolls, kooky contemporary canvases. Thankfully it's organized into thematic galleries with clear, if uninspired, explanations. Hong Kong's biggest visiting exhibitions are usually held here too. The museum is a few minutes' walk from either the Star Ferry or Tsim Sha Tsui MTR stop.

The Chinese Antiquities Gallery is the place to head if Ming's your thing. A series of low-lit rooms on the third floor houses ceramics from Neolithic times through the Qing Dynasty. Unusually, they're displayed by motif rather than by period: dragons, phoenixes, lotus flowers, and bats are some of the auspicious designs. Bronzes, jade, lacquerware, textiles, enamel, and glassware complete this collection of decorative art.

In the Chinese Fine Art Gallery you get a great introduction to Chinese brush painting, often difficult for the Western eye to appreciate. Landscape paintings from the 20th-century Guangdong and Lingnan schools form the bulk of the collection, and modern calligraphy also gets a nod. ■TIP➔ Traditional Chinese landscape paintings are visual records of real or imagined journeys—a kind of travelogue. Pick a starting point and try to travel through the picture, imagining the journey the artist is trying to convey.

The Contemporary Hong Kong Art Gallery showcases a mix of traditional Chinese and Western techniques—often in the same work. Paintings account for most of the pieces from the first half of the 20th century, when local artists used the traditional mediums of brush and ink in innovative ways. Western techniques dominate later work, the result of Hong Kong artists' having spent more time abroad. ✉ *10 Salisbury Rd., Tsim Sha Tsui, Kowloon* ☎ *2721–0116* ⊕ *hk.art.museum* 🎫 *HK$10* 🕐 *Fri. and Sun.–Wed. 10–6, Sat. 10–8* Ⓜ *Tsim Sha Tsui MTR, Exit E.*

Hong Kong Museum of History. A whopping HK$156 million went into making this museum engaging and educational. The permanent Hong Kong Story re-creates life as it was rather than simply displaying relics of it: indeed, actual artifacts are few. The museum's forte is clear explanations of spectacular life-size dioramas, which include village houses and a Central shopping street in colonial times. The ground-floor Folk Culture section is a Technicolor introduction to the history and customs of Hong Kong's main ethnic groups: the Punti, Hakka, and Hoklo. Upstairs, gracious stone-walled galleries whirl you through the Opium Wars and the beginnings of colonial Hong Kong. ■TIP➔ Unless you're with kids who dig models of cavemen and bears, skip the prehistory and dynastic galleries. Reserve energy for the last two galleries: a chilling account of life under Japanese occupation and a colorful look at Hong Kong life in the '60s.

Budget at least two hours to stroll through—more if you linger in each and every gallery. Pick your way through the gift shop's clutter to find local designer Alan Chan's T-shirts, shot glasses, and notebooks. His retro-kitsch aesthetic is based on 1940s cigarette-girl images. To get here from the Tsim Sha Tsui MTR, walk along Cameron Road, then left for a block along Chatham Road South. A signposted overpass takes you to the museum. ⊠ *100 Chatham Rd. S, Tsim Sha Tsui, Kowloon* ☎ *2724– 9042* ⊕ *www.hk.history.museum* ☞ *HK$10; free Wed.* ⊗ *Mon. and Wed.–Sat. 10–6, Sun. and holidays 10–7* Ⓜ *Tsim Sha Tsui, Exit B2.*

WORTH NOTING

Nathan Road. The famous Kowloon road runs several miles north from Salisbury Road in TST. It's filled with hotels, restaurants, and shops— indeed, retail space is so costly that the southern end is dubbed the Golden Mile. The mile's most famous tower block is ramshackle Chung-king Mansions, packed with cheap hotels and Indian restaurants. It was the setting for arty local director Wong Kar-Wai's film *Chungking Express*. To the left and right are mazes of narrow streets with even more shops selling jewelry, electronics, clothes, souvenirs, and cosmetics. Skulking individuals chanting "copy watch" and "copy suit" are on every street corner—at least they're honest about the "Rolexes" they sell. ⊠ *Nathan Rd. between Salisbury Rd. and Boundary St., Tsim Sha Tsui and Mong Kok, Kowloon* Ⓜ *Tsim Sha Tsui, Jordan, Yau Ma Tei, Mong Kok, Prince Edward.*

YAU MA TEI, MONG KOK, AND NORTHERN KOWLOON

TOP ATTRACTIONS

Fodor's Choice
★

Chi Lin Nunnery. Not a single nail was used to build this nunnery, which dates from 1934. Instead, traditional Tang Dynasty architectural techniques involving wooden dowels and bracket work hold its 228,000 pieces of timber together. Most of the 15 cedar halls house altars to bodhisattvas (those who have reached enlightenment)—bronze plaques explain each one.

Feng shui principles governed construction. The buildings face south toward the sea, to bring abundance; their backs are to the mountain, provider of strength and good energy. The temple's clean lines are a vast departure from most of Hong Kong's colorful religious buildings—here polished wood and gleaming Buddha statues are the only adornments.

The Main Hall is the most imposing—and inspiring—part of the monastery. Overlooking the smaller second courtyard, it honors the first Buddha, known as Sakyamuni. The soaring ceilings are held up by 28 cedar columns, measuring 18 feet each. They also support the roof—no mean feat, given that its traditionally made clay tiles make it weigh 176 tons.

Courtyards and gardens, where frangipani flowers scent the air, run beside the nunnery. The gardens are filled with bonsai trees and artful rockeries. Nature is also present inside: the various halls and galleries all look onto two courtyards filled with geometric lotus ponds and manicured bushes. ■TIP→ Combine Chi Lin Nunnery with a visit to Sik Sik Yuen Wong Tai Sin Temple, only one MTR stop or a short taxi ride away. ⊠ *5 Chi Lin Dr., Diamond Hill, Kowloon* ☎ *2354–1789* ☞ *Free* ⊗ *Nunnery daily 9–4:30, lotus-pond garden daily 7–7* Ⓜ *Diamond Hill, Exit C2.*

Fodor's Choice
★

Sik Sik Yuen Wong Tai Sin Temple. There's a practical approach to prayer at one of Hong Kong's most exuberant places of worship. Here the

The Chi Lin Nunnery is located at the foot of Diamond Hill in north Kowloon.

territory's three major religions—Taoism, Confucianism, and Buddhism—are all celebrated under the same roof. You'd think that highly ornamental religious buildings would look strange, with highly visible vending machines and LCD displays in front of them, but Wong Tai Sin pulls it off in cacophonous style. The temple was established in the early 20th century, on a different site, when two Taoist masters arrived from Guangzhou with the portrait of Wong Tai Sin—a famous monk who was born around AD 328—that still graces the main altar. In the '30s the temple was moved here; continuous renovations make it impossible to distinguish old from new.

Start at the incense-wreathed main courtyard, where the noise of many people shaking out *chim* (sticks with fortunes written on them) forms a constant rhythmic background. After wandering the halls, take time out in the Good Wish Garden—a peaceful riot of rockery—at the back of the complex. At the base of the complex is a small arcade where soothsayers and palm readers are happy to interpret Wong Tai Sin's predictions for a small fee. At the base of the ramp to the Confucian Hall, look up behind the temple for a view of Lion Rock, a mountain in the shape of a sleeping lion. ■ TIP→ If you feel like acquiring a household altar of your own, head for Shanghai Street in Yau Ma Tei, the Kowloon district north of Tsim Sha Tsui, where religious shops abound. ⊠ *Wong Tai Sin Rd., Wong Tai Sin, Kowloon* ☎ *2327–8141* ⊡ *Donations expected. Good Wish Garden: HK$2* ⊗ *Daily 7–5:30* Ⓜ *Wong Tai Sin, Exit B2 or B3.*

WORTH NOTING

Flower Market. Stalls containing local and imported fresh flowers, potted plants, and even artificial blossoms cover Flower Market Road, as well as parts of Yuen Po Street, Yuen Ngai Street, Prince Edward Road West, and Playground Field Road. ⊠ *Flower Market Rd. between Yuen Ngai St. and Yuen Po St., Mong Kok, Kowloon* ⊡ *Free* ⊙ *7–7* Ⓜ *Mong Kok East, Exit C; Prince Edward, Exit B1.*

⚲ **Yuen Po Street Bird Garden.** Next to the Flower Market, more than 70 stalls sell different types of twittering, fluttering birds of numerous colors, shapes and sizes. Birdcages and food, from seeds to live grasshoppers, are also for sale. ⊠ *Yuen Po St. between Boundary St. and Prince Edward Rd. West, Mong Kok, Kowloon* ⊙ *7 am–8 pm* Ⓜ *Mong Kok East, Exit C; Prince Edward, Exit B1.*

THE NEW TERRITORIES

Rustic villages, incense-filled temples, green hiking trails, pristine beaches—the New Territories have a lot to offer. Until a generation ago the region was mostly farmland with the occasional walled village. Today, thanks to a government housing program that created "new towns" like Sha Tin and Tuen Mun with up to 500,000 residents, parts of the region are more like the rest of Hong Kong. Within its expansive 518 square km (200 square mi), however, you'll still feel far removed from urban congestion. Here you can visit the area's lushest parks and glimpses traditional rural life in the restored walled villages and ancestral clan halls.

THE TERRITORY

The New Territories borders mainland China to the north and Sai Kung Peninsula to the east. Places worth visiting are a fair distance from each other, so day trips here take some planning—and some patience. Note that fewer people speak English away from the city center.

It's best to choose two or three sights to visit in a day, allowing 15–30 minutes of travel time between each, depending on whether you're going by bus or taxi.

GETTING AROUND

Between the bus and MTR, you can get close to many sights. Set off on the MTR from Central to Tsuen Wan; from there, taxis, buses, and minibuses will take you to places such as the Yuen Yuen Institute and Tai Mo Shan. For Sha Tin and other spots in the east, take the MTR to Kowloon Tong; transfer to the East Rail line to Sha Tin station. To reach the Sai Kung Peninsula, take the MTR from Central to Choi Hung, then the green Minibus 1A to Sai Kung Town.

To tour at your own pace, consider hiring a car and driver.

Ace Hire Car (☎ *2893–0541*) charges HK$220 per hour (three-hour minimum), exclusive of tunnel tolls.

For a HK$5 call charge, you can hire a cab from the **Hong Kong Kowloon Taxi Knowledge Association** (☎ *2574–7311*) to pick you up and take you anywhere in Hong Kong.

TOP ATTRACTIONS

Hong Kong Heritage Museum. This fabulous museum is Hong Kong's largest, yet it still seems a well-kept secret: chances are you'll have most of its 10 massive galleries to yourself. They ring an inner courtyard, which pours light into the lofty entrance hall.

The New Territories Heritage Hall is packed with local history—6,000 years of it. See life as it was in beautiful dioramas of traditional villages—one on land, the other on water (with houses on stilts). The last gallery documents the rise of massive urban New Towns. There's even a computer game where you can design your own.

In the T. T. Tsui Gallery of Chinese Art, exquisite antique Chinese glass, ceramics, and bronzes fill nine hushed second-floor rooms. The curators have gone for quality over quantity. Look for the 4-foot-tall terra-cotta *Horse and Rider*, a beautiful example of the figures enclosed in tombs in the Han Dynasty (206 BC–AD 220). The Tibetan religious statues and *thankga* paintings are unique in Hong Kong.

The Cantonese Opera Hall is all singing, all dancing, and utterly hands-on. The symbolic costumes, tradition-bound stories, and stylized acting of Cantonese opera can be impenetrable: the museum provides simple explanations and stacks of artifacts, including century-old sequined costumes that put Vegas to shame. ■TIP➔ Don't miss the opera hall's virtual makeup display, where you get your on-screen face painted like an opera character's.

Kids love the Children's Discovery Gallery, where hands-on activities for 4- to 10-year-olds include putting a broken "archaeological find" together. The Hong Kong Toy Story charts more than a century of local toys. ⊠ *1 Man Lam Rd., Sha Tin, New Territories* ☎ *2180–8188* ⊕ *www.hk.heritage.museum* ⊡ *HK$10; free on Wed.* ⊙ *Mon. and Wed.–Sat. 10–6, Sun. and holidays 10–7* Ⓜ *Che Kung or Sha Tin.*

Temple of Ten Thousand Buddhas. You climb some 400 steps to reach this temple: but look on the bright side, for each step you get about 32 Buddhas. The uphill path through dense vegetation is lined with life-size golden Buddhas in all kinds of positions. If you're dragging bored kids along, get them to play "Spot the Celebrity Lookalike" on the way. ■TIP➔ In summer bring water and insect repellent. Prepare to be dazzled inside the main temple: its walls are stacked with gilded ceramic statuettes. There are actually nearly 13,000 Buddhas here, a few more than the name suggests. They were made by Shanghai craftsmen, and have been donated by worshippers since the temple was built in the 1950s. Kwun Yum, goddess of mercy, is one of several deities honored in the crimson-walled courtyard.

Look southwest on a clear day and you can see nearby **Amah Rock,** which resembles a woman with a child on her back. Legend has it that this formation was once a faithful fisherman's wife who climbed the mountain every day to wait for her husband's return, not knowing he'd been drowned. Tin Hau, goddess of the sea, took pity on her and turned her to stone.

The temple is in the foothills of Sha Tin, in the central New Territories. Take Exit B out of Sha Tin station, walk down the pedestrian ramp, and take the first left onto Pai Tau Street. Keep to the right-hand side of the road and follow it around to the gate where the signposted path starts. ■ TIP➔ Don't be confused by the big white buildings on the left of Pai Tau Road. They are ancestral halls, not the temple. ✉ *Off Pai Tau St., Sha Tin, New Territories* 🎫 *Free* ☉ *Daily 9–5:30* Ⓜ *Sha Tin, Exit B.*

WORTH NOTING

Sam Tung Uk Museum. A walled Hakka village from 1786 was saved from demolition to create this museum. It's in the middle of industrial Tsuen Wan, in the western New Territories, so its quiet whitewashed court-yards and small interlocking chambers contrast greatly with the nearby residential towers. Hakka villages were built with security in mind, and this one looks more like a single large house than a village. Indeed, most Hakka village names end in *uk,* which literally means "house"—Sam Tung Uk translates as "Three Beam House." Rigid symmetry dictated the village's construction: the ancestral hall and two common chambers form the central axis, which is flanked by the more private areas. The front door is angled to face west–southwest, in keeping with feng shui principles of alignment between mountain and water. Traditional furniture and farm tools are displayed in each room. ■ TIP➔ Head through the courtyards and start your visit in the exhibition hall at the back, where a display gives helpful background on Hakka culture and pre-industrial Tsuen Wan—explanations are sparse elsewhere. You can also try on a Hakka hat. ✉ *2 Kwu Uk La., Tsuen Wan, New Territories* 🎫 *2411–2001* 🌐 *www. heritagemuseum.gov.hk/english/branch_sel_stu.htm* 🎫 *Free* ☉ *Wed.– Mon. 9–5* Ⓜ *Tsuen Wan, Exit B3.*

Sai Kung Peninsula. To the east of Sha Tin, this landmass has a few small towns and Hong Kong's most beloved nature preserve. The hikes through the hills surrounding **High Island Reservoir** are spectacular, and the beaches are among the territory's cleanest. Seafood restaurants dot the waterfront at Sai Kung Town as well as the tiny fishing village of Po Toi O in Clear Water Bay. Take the MTR to Choi Hung and then Bus 92 or 96R, or Minibus 1 to Sai Kung Town. Instead of taking the bus, you can also catch a taxi along Clearwater Bay Road, which will take you into forested areas and land that's only partially developed with Spanish-style villas overlooking the sea. At Sai Kung Town you can rent a sampan that will take you to one of the many islands in the area for a day at the beach. Sai Kung Country Park has several hiking trails that wind through majestic hills overlooking the water. This excursion will take a full day, and you should go only if it's sunny. ✉ *Sai Kung Peninsula, Kowloon.*

6

WHERE TO EAT

Updated by
Dorothy So

No other city in the world boasts quite as eclectic a dining scene as the one in Hong Kong. Luxurious fine-dining restaurants opened by celebrity chefs, such as Gray Kunz and Joël Robuchon, are just a stone's throw away from humble local eateries doling out thin noodles served with some of the best wonton shrimp dumplings, or delicious slices of tender barbecued meat piled atop bowls of fragrant jasmine rice.

Never judge a book by its cover—the most unassuming eateries are often the ones that provide the most memorable meals. At noodle-centric restaurants, fishball soup with ramen noodles is an excellent choice, and the goose, suckling pig, honeyed pork, and soy-sauce chicken are good bets at the roast-meat shops. A combination plate, with a sampling of meats and some greens on a bed of white rice, is a foolproof way to go. Street foods are another must-try; for just a couple of bucks, sample curry fishballs, skewered meats, stinky tofu, and all sorts of other delicious tidbits. If you have the chance, visit a *dai pai dong* (outdoor food stall) and try the local specialties.

For fine dining with a unique Hong Kong twist, you can always hit up places like the exclusive and extravagant Krug Room or try Alvin Leung's one-of-a-kind "X-treme Chinese" fare at Bo Innovation.

Finally, remember that Hong Kong is the world's epicenter of dim sum. While you're here you must have at least one dim sum breakfast or lunch in a teahouse. Those steaming bamboo baskets you see conceal delicious dumplings, buns, and pastries—all as comforting and delicious as they are exotic.

MEAL TIMES

Locals eat lunch between noon and 1:30 pm; dinner is around 8. Dim sum begins as early as 10 am. Reservations aren't usually necessary except during Chinese holidays or at of-the-moment or high-end hotel restaurants like Alain Ducasse's SPOON or the Caprice. There are certain classic Hong Kong preparations (e.g., beggar's chicken, whose preparation in a clay pot takes hours) that require reserving not just a table, but the dish itself. Do so at least 24 hours ahead.

You'll also need reservations for a meal at one of the so-called private kitchens—unlicensed culinary speakeasies, which are often the city's hottest tickets. Book several days ahead, and if possible, join forces with other people. Some private kitchens only take reservations for parties of four, six, or eight.

PRICES

The ranges in our chart reflect actual prices of main courses on dinner menus (unless dinner isn't served). That said, the custom of sharing dishes affects the ultimate cost of your dinner. Further, we exclude outrageously expensive dishes—abalone, bird's-nest soup, shark's-fin soup.

Don't be shocked that you've been charged for everything, including tea, rice, and those side dishes placed automatically on your table. At upmarket and Western-style restaurants, tips are appreciated (10% is generous); the service charge on your bill doesn't go to the waitstaff.

WHAT IT COSTS IN HK$				
	¢	$	$$	$$$	$$$$
At dinner	under HK$50	HK$50–HK$100	HK$100–HK$200	HK$200–HK$300	over HK$300

Prices are per person for a main course at dinner and exclude the customary 10% service charge.

HONG KONG ISLAND

Reviews listed alphabetically within neighborhoods. Use the coordinate (⌖ B2) at the end of each listing to locate a site on the Where to Eat and Stay in Hong Kong map.

WESTERN

$$–$$$
CANTONESE
Fodor's Choice
★

✕ **Tim's Kitchen.** Most of the home-spun dishes at this award-winning restaurant require at least a day's advanced ordering. But the little extra fuss is worth it. One signature dish pairs a meaty crab claw with winter melon—a clean and simple combo that allows the freshness of the ingredients to shine. The fist-size "glassy" king prawn looks unassuming, paired with nothing but a slice of Yunnan ham on a plain, ungarnished plate. Take a bite, though, and you'll be amazed at how succulent and delectably creamy it is. Word of warning—some of the more intricate dishes can get pretty pricy. But simpler (and cheaper) options are also available, such as pomelo skin sprinkled with shrimp roe, and stir-fried flat rice noodles with beef. ⌖ *84–90 Bonham Strand E, Sheung Wan, Western* ☎ *2543–5919* ⊕ *www.timskitchen.com.hk* ⌖ *Reservations essential* ☰ *MC, V* ⊘ *Closed Sun.* Ⓜ *Wan Chai* ⌖ *A3.*

6

CENTRAL

$$$$
FRENCH

✕ **Amber.** When the Landmark Mandarin Oriental hotel opened in 2005, its aim was to be seen as the preeminent hotel on Hong Kong Island. It made sense that it would contain a flagship power-lunch restaurant that aspires to a similar level of impeccable, modern style. Chef Richard Ekkebus's menu includes creative dishes such as line-caught amadai with orange and fennel confit, and *bottarga* grated potatoes bouillabaisse, as well as sea urchin in lobster gelatin with cauliflower, caviar, and seaweed waffle. ⌖ *Landmark Mandarin Oriental Hotel, 15 Queen's Rd., Central* ☎ *2132–0066* ⊕ *www.amberhongkong.com* ☰ *AE, DC, MC, V* Ⓜ *Central* ⌖ *B3.*

$$
ECLECTIC

✕ **Café Deco Bar & Grill.** As is often the case where there's a captive audience, dining up at the Peak Galleria mall is a crapshoot. This huge eatery is no exception: you come for the views, not the food. The best strategy might be to come here in time for sunset, hit Café Deco just for drinks and appetizers, and enjoy the vistas; then head down to the city for dinner. Dishes on the overly ambitious menu traverse five or six continents, and are dramatically prepared by chefs in open kitchens (which will, at least, amuse the kids). Oysters are good, and the pizzas and pastas are okay, but you should avoid the insipid Southeast Asian fare and overpriced steaks. When you book (and you must), be sure to request a table with a view, as many tables in the place have none, which defeats the purpose of coming. ⌖ *1st fl., Peak Galleria, 118 Peak Rd., The Peak, Central* ☎ *2849–5111* ⊕ *www.cafedecogroup.com* ⌖ *Reservations essential* ☰ *AE, DC, MC, V* ⌖ *A6.*

$$$
ITALIAN
✗ **DiVino.** This ultracool wine bar serves small plates for casual snacking, and mixed platters ideal for sharing. Not surprisingly, it's popular with the drinks-after-work crowd—and you get complimentary savory treats with any drink from 6 to 8 pm. But don't underestimate the cuisine: the tailor-made cold-cut platters, for starters, are superb. The cheese board is served with crusty, oven-warm bread. Pasta main courses include Gorgonzola and black-truffle penne, and lobster linguine with fresh tomatoes. The place also stays open for revelry late into the evening. ⊠ *Shop 1, 73 Wyndham St., Central* ☎ *2167–8883* ⊕ *www.divino. hk* ☐ *AE, DC, MC, V* ☺ *No lunch Sun.* Ⓜ *Central* ✛ *A3.*

$$$
ECLECTIC
✗ **Jimmy's Kitchen.** One of the oldest restaurants in Hong Kong, Jimmy's opened in 1928 and serves comfort food from around the world to a loyal clientele in a private-club atmosphere. The restaurant underwent a major renovation in 2006, adding a full British bar to complement their new look. Its handy location just off Queen's Road in Central and a menu that offers a wide selection of both Western and Asian dishes including steak, borscht, goulash, bangers and mash, curry, and burgers have made Jimmy's a favorite with both Chinese locals and tourists looking for a taste of home. It's not cheap, but it's a good choice for a night out with friends, especially if your group's cravings are pulling you in different directions. ⊠ *Ground fl., South China Bldg., 1–3 Wyndham St., Central* ☎ *2526–5293* ☐ *AE, DC, MC, V* Ⓜ *Central* ✛ *A3.*

$$$
CANTONESE
✗ **Lung King Heen.** It's made a serious case for being the best Cantonese restaurant in Hong Kong. Where other contenders tend to get too caught up in prestige dishes and name-brand chefs, Lung King Heen focuses completely on taste. When you try a little lobster-and-scallop dumpling, or a dish of house-made XO sauce that is this divine, you will be forced to reevaluate your entire notion of Chinese cuisine. ⊠ *Podium 4, Four Seasons Hotel, 8 Finance St., Central* ☎ *3196–8880* ⊕ *www.fourseasons. com* ⚲ *Reservations essential* ☐ *AE, DC, MC, V* Ⓜ *Central* ✛ *B2.*

¢
CANTONESE
✗ **Mak's Noodles Limited.** Mak's looks like any other Hong Kong noodle shop, but it's one of the best-known in town, with a reputation that belies its humble decor. The staff are attentive, and the menu includes some particularly inventive dishes, such as tasty pork-chutney noodles. The real test of a good noodle shop, however, is its wontons, and here they're fresh, delicate, and filled with whole shrimp. And don't miss the *sui kau,* filled with minced chicken and shrimp. ⊠ *77 Wellington St., Central* ☎ *2854–3810* ☐ *No credit cards* Ⓜ *Central* ✛ *A3.*

$$$$
FRENCH
✗ **Restaurant Pétrus.** Commanding breathtaking views atop the Island Shangri-La, Restaurant Pétrus scales the upper Hong Kong heights of prestige, formality, and price. This is one of the city's few flagship hotel restaurants that have not attempted to reinvent themselves as fusion; sometimes traditional French haute cuisine is the way to go. Likewise, the design of the place is in the old-school restaurant-as-ballroom mode. The kitchen has a particularly good way with foie gras, and the wine list is memorable, with verticals of Chateau Pétrus among the roughly 1,500 celebrated vintages. The dress here is business casual—no jeans or sneakers. ⊠ *56th fl., Island Shangri-La, Pacific Place, Supreme Court Rd., Admiralty, Central* ☎ *2820–8590* ⊕ *www.shangri-la.com* ⚲ *Reservations essential* ☐ *AE, DC, MC, V* Ⓜ *Admiralty* ✛ *C4.*

$$–$$$
CANTONESE

✕**Yung Kee.** Close to Hong Kong's famous bar and dining district of Lan Kwai Fong, Yung Kee has turned into a local institution since it first opened shop as a street-food stall in 1942. It serves authentic Cantonese cuisine amid riotous decor and writhing gold dragons. Locals come here for roast goose with beautifully crisp skin and tender meat, as well as dim sum. Other award-winning dishes include the "cloudy tea" smoked pork, which needs to be reserved a day in advance, and deep-fried prawns with mini crab roe. More adventurous palates may wish to check out the thousand-year-old preserved eggs. ✉ *32–40 Wellington St, Lan Kwai Fong, Central* ☎ *2522–1624* ⊕ *www.yungkee. com.hk* ▤ *AE, DC, MC, V* Ⓜ *Central* ✛ *A3.*

WAN CHAI, CAUSEWAY BAY, AND BEYOND
WAN CHAI

$$$$
CONTEMPORARY
Fodor's Choice
★

✕**Bo Innovation.** The mastermind behind this deservedly renowned and upscale "private kitchen" is Alvin Leung, who dubbed himself the "demon chef" and had that moniker tattooed on his arm. Leung entered the dining scene back in 2003 with a private kitchen named Bo InnoSeki in Central. From there, he set up Bo Innovation, which serves what he calls "X-treme Chinese" cuisine, applying molecular gastronomy, French, and Japanese cooking techniques to traditional Cantonese dishes. The restaurant has moved to a bigger spot in Wan Chai with outdoor seating, but Leung's cooking remains quirky and hard to define. The Australian Wagyu strip loin with black-truffle *cheung fun,* or rice roll, is a winner, as well as the signature molecular *xiao long bao* (soup dumpling). At dinner, choose between the eight-course tasting menu (HK$680) or the 12-course chef's menu (HK$1,080); à la carte dining is not available. Tables are often full on Friday and Saturday, so book in advance. ✉ *Shop No. 13, 2nd fl., J Residence, 60 Johnston Rd., Wan Chai* ☎ *2850–8371* ⊕ *www.boinnovation.com* ⚱ *Reservations essential* ▤ *AE, DC, MC, V* ☉ *Closed Sun. No lunch Sat.* Ⓜ *Wan Chai* ✛ *A4.*

$–$$
CANTONESE

✕**Che's Cantonese Restaurant.** Smartly dressed locals in the know head for this casually elegant dim sum specialist, which is in the middle of the downtown bustle yet well concealed on the fourth floor of an office building. From the elevator, you'll step into a classy Cantonese world. It's hard to find a single better dim sum dish than Che's crispy pork buns, whose sugary baked pastry conceals the brilliant saltiness of stewed pork within. Other dim sum to try include panfried turnip cake; rich, tender braised duck web (foot) in abalone sauce; and a refreshing dessert of cold pomelo and sago with mango juice for a calming end to an exciting meal. ✉ *4th fl., The Broadway, 54–62 Lockhart Rd., Wan Chai* ☎ *2528–1123* ▤ *AE, DC, MC, V* Ⓜ *Wan Chai* ✛ *E4.*

$$$
ITALIAN

✕**Cinecittà.** Come here for fine Roman cuisine in this foodie enclave just around the corner from Pacific Place. As the name suggests, the theme is Italian cinema, centered on Fellini and his works. The interior is mostly white and glass, the atmosphere trendy and elegant, and the food always top-notch. Order from the menu or ask the chef to compose a tasting selection for you. Pastas are homemade and excellent. ✉ *9 Star St., Wan Chai* ☎ *2529–0199* ⊕ *www.elite-concepts.com* ▤ *AE, DC, MC, V* Ⓜ *Wan Chai* ✛ *D4.*

6

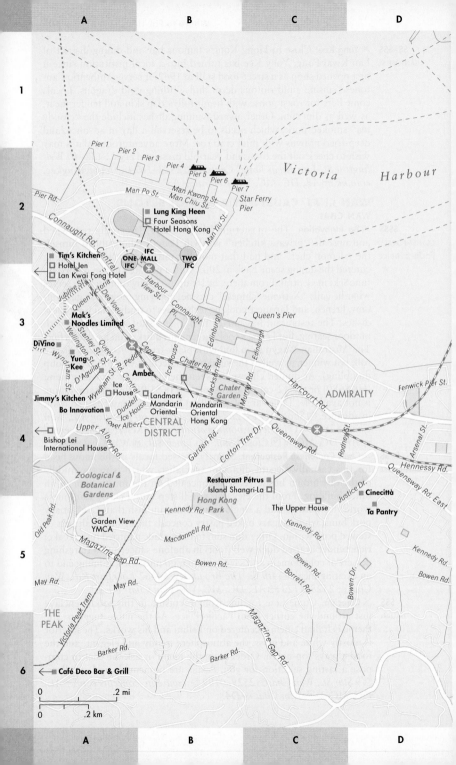

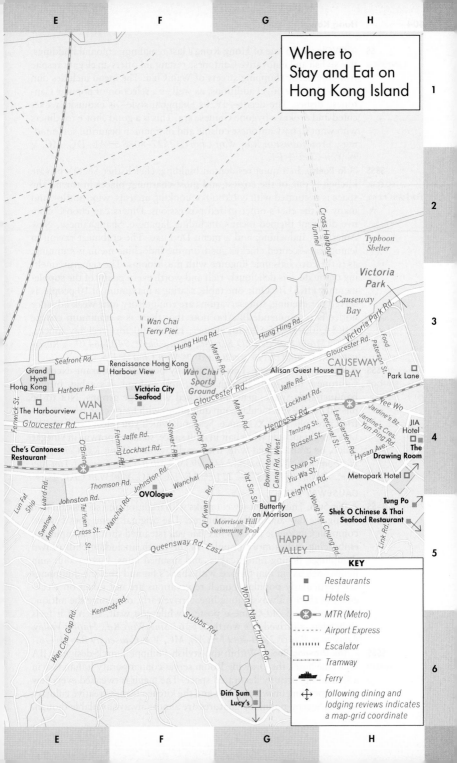

$$ CANTONESE ✕ **OVOlogue.** In one of Hong Kong's last remaining colonial buildings, this stylish and innovative Cantonese restaurant offers an elegant respite from the hectic shopping streets of Wan Chai. The menu includes dim sum with a few novel additions, as well as a selection of popular Cantonese dishes. The decor—1920s Shanghai style—is exquisitely executed and evokes a bygone Chinese era. This is a good choice for diners who want to try Cantonese cuisine and dim sum in beautiful surroundings. ⊠ *66 Johnston Rd., Wan Chai* 🕾 *2527–6088* 🖃 *AE, DC, MC, V* Ⓜ *Wan Chai* ✛ *F4.*

$$$$ ECLECTIC Fodor's Choice ★ ✕ **Ta Pantry.** In a quiet residential building, chef Esther Sham's private kitchen is one of the coziest and most charming places in town. The space is decorated with cookbooks, cooking utensils, wine bottles, and many of the chef's other prized possessions. Diners can choose from five different themed menus, including Japanese, Shanghainese, New American, Indochine, and a menu De Luxe. The crabmeat ravioli in lemongrass-scented chicken jus from the Indochine menu is stunning, as is the coco balsamic linguine with mushrooms. The signature melting onion duck is deliciously rich and worth every penny of the supplementary HK$150. Only one table, seating a maximum of 10 people, is served per evening, so reservations are compulsory (one week advance notice is recommended). Also note that there is a minimum charge (HK$4,400–HK$5,500 for dinner; HK$2,200 for weekday lunch). ⊠ *1C, Moon Star Ct., 2D Star St., Wan Chai* 🕾 *9403–6430* ◈ *Reservations essential* 🖃 *No credit cards* Ⓜ *Wan Chai* ✛ *D5.*

$$$ SEAFOOD ✕ **Victoria City Seafood.** This perennially popular restaurant excels at Cantonese dim sum, Shanghainese, and seafood. It's a big, bright, banquet-style space, generally packed with large groups. Not to be missed are the spectacular soup dumplings with hairy-crab roe and stir-fried rice rolls with XO sauce. Seafood, which you select live from the tank, might include whitebait in chili sauce, steamed prawns in vinegar sauce, or crab cooked with fried garlic. ⊠ *Sun Hung Kai Center, 30 Harbour Rd., Wan Chai* 🕾 *2827–9938* ⊠ *5th fl. Citic Tower, 1 Tim Mei Ave., Admiralty* 🕾 *2877–2211* 🖃 *AE, DC, MC, V* Ⓜ *Wan Chai* ✛ *F4.*

CAUSEWAY BAY

$–$$ CANTONESE ✕ **Dim Sum.** This elegant jewel breaks with tradition and serves dim sum during the day and in the nighttime. The original menu goes beyond common Cantonese morsels like *har gau* (steamed shrimp dumplings), embracing dishes more popular in the north, including chili prawn dumplings, Beijing onion cakes, and steamed buns. Luxury dim sum items, such as siu mai topped with shark's fin and abalone dumplings are particularly popular. Lunch reservations are not taken on weekends, so there's always a long line. Arrive early, or admire the antique telephones and old Chinese posters while you wait. Even if it feels somewhat contrived, it's worth it. ⊠ *63 Sing Woo Rd., Happy Valley, Causeway Bay* 🕾 *2834–8893* 🖃 *AE, MC, V* Ⓜ *Causeway Bay* ✛ *G6.*

$$$$ ITALIAN Fodor's Choice ★ ✕ **The Drawing Room.** Within the stylish Philippe Starck-designed JIA boutique hotel, the Drawing Room serves contemporary Italian fare in a slicked up, artfully decorated space. The menu is tweaked every few days depending on what's fresh and the kitchen team's creative culinary whims. Several popular signatures are almost always available though,

Street food in Hong Kong is cheap and delicious.

such as the panfried quail and foie gras, and the inspiring trio of Wagyu short rib, Wagyu beef tenderloin, and ox tongue. Two different tasting menu options are offered every night, but the dishes are also available for à la carte ordering. The place is a dining hot spot, so reservations are a definite must. ⊠ *1st fl., JIA Boutique Hotel,1–5 Irving St., Causeway Bay* ☎ *2915–6628* ⊕ *www.thedrawingroom.com.hk* ⚜ *Reservations essential* ▭ *AE, MC, V* ☼ *Closed Sun.* Ⓜ *Central* ✛ *H4.*

EASTERN

$ ✕ **Tung Po.** Arguably Hong Kong's most famous—if not most perpetu-

CANTONESE   ally packed—indoor *dai pai dong*. Tung Po takes over five stall spaces

Fodor's Choice   in Java Road market's cooked food center, boasting tables large enough

★   to fit 18 guests and with walls scribbled with their ever-growing list of specials. The food is Hong Kong cuisine with a few fusion innovations. Try the spaghetti with chewy rounds of cuttlefish, which is flavored and dyed with aromatic jet-black fresh squid ink and sprinkled with chopped herbs. The seafood dishes and stir-fries are all satisfying, but it's really the atmosphere that makes Tung Po a must-visit spot. Owner Robby Cheung is one of the friendliest and most delightful characters in the Hong Kong food and beverage industry. Later in the evening, he'll blast the latest pop songs from the sound system. And if you're lucky, you might just catch him in one of his moonwalking moods. ⊠ *2nd fl., Java Road Cooked Food Centre, 99 Java Rd., North Point, Eastern* ☎ *2880–9399* ▭ *No credit cards* Ⓜ *North Point* ✛ *H5.*

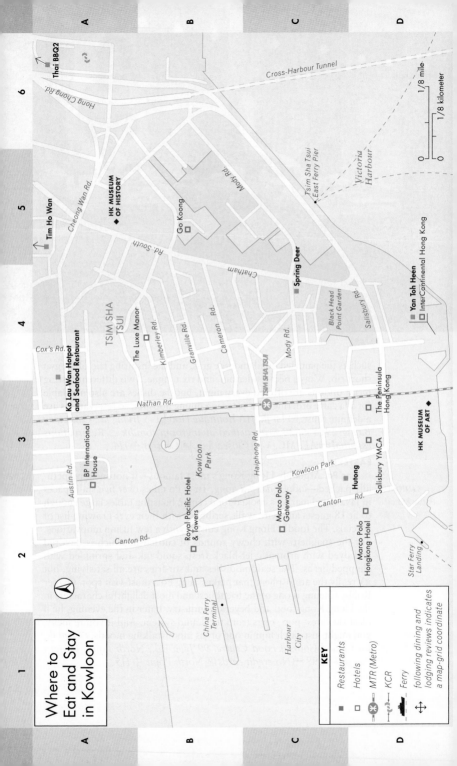

Where to Eat and Stay in Kowloon

TSIM SHA TSUI

Thai BBQ2

Tim Ho Wan

HK MUSEUM OF HISTORY ♦

Go Koong

Spring Deer

Ko Lau Wan Hotpot and Seafood Restaurant

Cox's Rd.

The Luxe Manor

BP International House

Austin Rd.

Kowloon Park

Royal Pacific Hotel & Towers

Marco Polo Gateway

Marco Polo Hongkong Hotel

China Ferry Terminal

Harbour City

Hutong

Salisbury YMCA

The Peninsula Hong Kong

HK MUSEUM OF ART ♦

Star Ferry Landing

Yan Toh Heen

InterContinental Hong Kong

Black Head Point Garden

Tsim Sha Tsui East Ferry Pier

Victoria Harbour

Cross-Harbour Tunnel

Hong Chong Rd.

Cheong Wan Rd.

Mody Rd.

Chatham Rd. South

Kimberley Rd.

Granville Rd.

Cameron Rd.

Nathan Rd.

Haiphong Rd.

Canton Rd.

Kowloon Park

Canton Rd.

Salisbury Rd.

Mody Rd.

TSIM SHA TSUI

1/8 mile

1/8 kilometer

0

KEY

- ■ Restaurants
- □ Hotels
- Ⓜ MTR (Metro)
- KCR
- Ferry
- ↔ following dining and lodging reviews indicates a map-grid coordinate

SOUTHSIDE

$$$
MEDITERRANEAN

✗ **Lucy's.** Turn left after Delifrance to find this warm, intimate eatery hidden inside the famous Stanley Market and rarely uncovered by tourists. You may feel like you've walked into someone's house when you enter the small, shabby-chic dining room, but Lucy's is a professionally run restaurant offering excellent, home-cooked food. The daily specials are a very safe bet, and often include risottos and grilled or roasted meat; there are also plenty of fresh fruits and veggies on the menu. Desserts, especially the pecan pudding with toffee cream sauce, are not to be missed. More upscale than most of the beachside restaurants here and with oodles more character, Lucy's is a perfect end to a relaxed day browsing in the market, and easily your best bet in Stanley. ⊠ *Ground fl., 64 Stanley Main St., Stanley, Southside* ☎ *2813–9055* ▭ *AE, MC, V* ✛ *G6.*

$
ASIAN

✗ **Shek O Chinese & Thai Seafood Restaurant.** The seaside village of Shek O lies past Stanley, and is worth a trip for the large sandy beach and fresh local seafood. For the quality and variety of food, this casual eatery is an all-time favorite. Come here for simple seaside dining at its best—the menu is extensive, and everything's good and fresh—but prepare for plastic tables and toilets that are best approached with caution. This is a great spot for relaxing and dining with friends or family for a very reasonable price. ⊠ *303 Shek O Village, main intersection, next to bus stop, Shek O, Southside* ☎ *2809–4426 or 2809–2202* ▭ *AE, DC, MC, V* ✛ *H5.*

KOWLOON PENINSULA

Use the coordinate (✛ B2) at the end of each listing to locate a site on the Where to Eat and Stay in Kowloon map.

TSIM SHA TSUI

$$
KOREAN
Fodor's Choice
★

✗ **Go Koong.** Go Koong is one of the best Korean restaurants in town. The menu covers extensive ground, from raw meats and seafood sizzling on the tabletop barbecue grill to hearty kimchi stews and thick egg-based pancakes studded with shrimp, squid, and scallions. The complimentary *banchans* (Korean appetizers) are a feast in themselves, with more than 10 different items available every day. Order the smoked duck-breast salad to start before moving on to more substantial fare, such as the tender beef ribs steamed in whole pumpkin. Korean classics, including *japchae* glassy noodles and *bibimbap* stonepot rice are all awesome, so prepare to be spoiled for choice. If you still have room at the end of the meal, remember to try the pat *bingsoo*—a giant bowl of crunchy shaved ice laced with sweetened red beans and fresh fruit. ⊠ *Shop 202, Toyomall, 9 Granville Rd., Tsim Sha Tsui East, Kowloon* ☎ *2311–0901* ▭ *AE, V* Ⓜ *Tsim Sha Tsui* ✛ *B5.*

$$$–$$$$
NORTHERN
CHINESE

✗ **Hutong.** It's not hard to see why Hutong is one of the hottest tables in Hong Kong: it has some of the most imaginative food in town, yet it's completely Chinese. Meanwhile, its spot at the top of the dramatic One Peking Road tower overlooks the entire festival of lights that is the Island skyline. Best among a sensational selection of northern Chinese creations are crispy, deboned lamb ribs, whose crackling skin conceals a deep, tender gaminess within. More subtle are Chinese spinach in a

6

well-developed herbal ginseng broth, and delicate scallops with fresh pomelo. Hutong is a good choice for a memorable meal in Hong Kong. Make sure to reserve well in advance. ⊠ *28th fl., 1 Peking Rd., Tsim Sha Tsui, Kowloon* 🕾 *3428–8342* ⊕ *www.aqua.com.hk* ⚑ *Reservations essential* ⊟ *AE, DC, MC, V* Ⓜ *Tsim Sha Tsui* ⊕ *C3.*

$$
MANDARIN
✕ **Spring Deer.** With shades of pastel blue and green in a somber interior and waiters in bland uniforms, this Peking duck specialist looks like something out of 1950s communist Beijing. The crowd, too, is hilariously old-school, which only adds to your duck experience. You'll see locals with noodle dishes, stir-fried wok meat dishes, and so forth, but the Peking duck is the showstopper—it might be the best in town. Even the peanuts for snacking, which are boiled to a delectable softness, go above and beyond the call of duty. ⊠ *1st fl., 42 Mody Rd., Tsim Sha Tsui, Kowloon* 🕾 *2366–4012 or 2366–5839 or 2723-3673* ⊟ *AE, DC, MC, V* ⚑ *Reservations essential* Ⓜ *Tsim Tsa Shui* ⊕ *C4.*

$$$$
CANTONESE
✕ **Yan Toh Heen.** This Cantonese restaurant in the InterContinental Hong Kong sets formal elegance against expansive harbor views, and its food is at the top of its class in town. Exquisite is hardly the word for the place settings, all handcrafted with green jade. Equally successful are dim sum, sautéed Wagyu beef with mushrooms and shishito pepper (a mild green chili pepper), and exemplary braised whole abalone in oyster sauce. The vast selection of seafood transcends the usual tank to offer a selection of shellfish like red coral crab, cherrystone clam, and sea whelk. There is also a selection of "health" dishes, showcasing the hotel's innovative preventative health concept with delicious and nutritious dishes created by Chef Lau Yiu Fai. Shorts are not allowed. ⊠ *Lower level, Hotel InterContinental Hong Kong, 18 Salisbury Rd., Tsim Sha Tsui, Kowloon* 🕾 *2313–2323* ⊕ *www.hongkong-ic.intercontinental.com* ⚑ *Reservations essential* ⊟ *AE, DC, MC, V* Ⓜ *Tsim Sha Tsui* ⊕ *D4.*

YAU MA TEI, MONG KOK, AND NORTHERN KOWLOON

$$
CANTONESE
✕ **Ko Lau Wan Hotpot and Seafood Restaurant.** Those seeking authentic Cantonese hotpot need look no further. Locals flock here for the tender beef and a wide selection of seafood, served in thin slices that you cook at your table in a piping-hot soup (the soup selection is quite extensive, but the satay broth and the fish stock with crab are particularly tasty.) The owner runs his own fish farm in the seaside district of Sai Kung—no wonder the cuttlefish or shrimp balls and the sea urchin, amberjack, and abalone sashimi are all so tantalizingly fresh. The adventurous should try the geoduck, a giant clam, popular among Hong Kongers, which can be eaten raw with soy sauce and wasabi or slightly cooked in a soup. ⊠ *1st fl., 21–23 Hillwood Rd., Jordan Kowloon* 🕾 *3520–3800* ⊕ *www.hotpotexpress.com* ⊟ *MC, V* ☾ *No lunch; open from 6 pm to 3 am daily* Ⓜ *Jordan* ⊕ *A4.*

¢–$
THAI
Fodor's Choice
★
✕ **Thai BBQ 2.** This might not be the prettiest of places to have your meal, but the Thai food here is truly awesome, and about as authentic you can get in Hong Kong. This is literally a point-and-order place, since some of the best items are the ones that aren't on the menu. One of these is the moo kata; various raw meats and offal are cooked on a raised, dome-shape charcoal powered grill, which is surrounded by a mote of boiling broth. The meat juices trickle down from the grill to

flavor the broth, which can also be used to cook the meats or accompanying greens, mushrooms, and vermicelli. The moo kata is designed to share, especially over a few rounds of cold Singha beer. ⊠ *17 Nam Kok Rd., Mong Kok, Kowloon* ☎ *2718–6219* ▭ *No credit cards* Ⓜ *Mong Kok* ⬦ *A6.*

¢ ✕**Tim Ho Wan.** Don't let the undiscerning storefront fool you—Tim Ho Wan is an award-winning eatery that serves up some of the city's best dim sum. Opened by a former Four Seasons Hotel chef, this humble Mong Kok eatery makes all of its shrimp dumplings, roast pork–filled rice rolls, siu mai pork dumplings, and such, fresh to order. It's top-quality food at dirt-cheap prices. But be warned—the shop is small, and its popularity is immense. So go at off hours between 2:30 pm and 5 pm, or you might find yourself waiting up to half an hour for a seat. ⊠ *2–8 Kwong Wah St., Mong Kok, Kowloon* ☎ *2332–2896* ▭ *No credit cards* Ⓜ *Mong Kok* ⬦ *A5.*

DIM SUM

Fodor's Choice
★

6

WHERE TO STAY

Updated by
Cherise Fong

Whether you're a business traveler or a casual tourist, you'll inevitably be caught up with the manic pace of life here. Luckily, Hong Kong's hotels are constantly increasing their efforts to make you feel at home, so you can enjoy wonderful views of either city life or the world-famous harbor, free from stress.

From the standard budget stays to the centrifugal views emanating from the luxurious upper-level suites of the Peninsula's flagship hotel over Victoria Harbour, you're sure to find a style and site to fit your fancy. Prices tend to reflect quality of service and amenities more than location, so it's worth choosing neighborhood over notoriety. Business-oriented hotels may tout more in-room tech gadgets and eco-friendly options, but better upgrade to executive club privileges if you appreciate free Wi-Fi and complimentary buffets in the VIP lounge.

The rock stars of Hong Kong's hotel industry are perfectly situated around Victoria Harbour, where unobstructed harbor views, sumptuous spas, and reputable service all compete for the patronage of business-suited jet-setters, status-sensitive mainland tourists, and any visitor willing to splurge on uncompromised, premium service and accommodations. Farther up the hills, on both Kowloon and Hong Kong Island sides, tony boutique hotels have opened over the past five years seducing travelers who simply want a safe and cozy place to crash in a trendy locale. And as hip new shopping malls and arcades of all shapes and sizes continue their conquest of Hong Kong's dense real estate, brand-name hotels are coming along. While most big hotels are already attached to a mall, watch for the resurrected Ritz-Carlton on the 102nd to 118th floors of West Kowloon's International Commerce Centre. And with innovations in hospitality on the horizon, look out for

Hotel ICON in Tsim Sha Tsui East, unconventionally associated with Polytechnic University's School of Hotel and Tourism Management.

RESERVATIONS AND RATES

Hong Kong's high season ranges from October through April, covering both family holidays and business conventions. Most hotels have reliable online booking systems, but phone reservations are also accepted, and receptionists speak English.

Specify arrival and departure dates, number of guests; room type (standard, deluxe, suite), and any specific preferences. Make sure to find out what is, and what is not, included in the room rate, such as breakfast, in-room Wi-Fi, and local calls. A credit-card deposit is generally required to secure reservations.

Flights from the United States often arrive in the evening, so it's a good idea to inform the hotel when you plan to arrive. Some hotels will not otherwise hold a booking after 6 pm.

Unless stated otherwise in the review, hotels are equipped with elevators, and all guest rooms have air-conditioning, TV, telephone, and private bathroom. Note that bathrooms with showers but no bathtubs are common in smaller hotels, so be sure to check if this is a concern. Almost all hotels have designated no-smoking rooms or floors, or even premises. Many also have designated "special access" rooms for guests in wheelchairs.

WHAT IT COSTS IN HK$					
	¢	$	$$	$$$	$$$$
For two people	under HK$700	HK$700– HK$1,100	HK$1,100– HK$2,100	HK$2,100– HK$3,000	over HK$3,000

Prices are for two people in a standard double room in high season, excluding 10% service charge and a 3% government tax.

HONG KONG ISLAND

Reviews listed alphabetically within neighborhood. Use the coordinate (⊕ B2) at the end of each listing to locate a site on the Where to Eat and Stay in Hong Kong map.

WESTERN

$$ 🏨 **Hotel Jen.** This business hotel, which opened in early 2008, has a sleek, Zen-like atmosphere, with lots of white and other calming neutral colors, beige wood, glass-walled bathrooms, and plenty of natural light. Rooms have daybeds in front of their large windows, which are perfect for reading or enjoying the view—be it harbor, city, or mountain—while long desks accommodate those with work to get done. The bright and uncluttered Sky Lounge, reserved exclusively for hotel guests, is generally not crowded, and makes a nice place to relax. The 52-foot outdoor rooftop pool, with its expansive views of the bay, is another soothing destination. The hotel's immediate vicinity shuts down after dark, but in the morning it's only a short walk to the galleries and antique shops around Hollywood Road. **Pros:** secluded residential location; relaxing atmosphere; free Wi-Fi. **Cons:** an approximate 20-minute walk to the

WHERE SHOULD I STAY?

	NEIGHBORHOOD VIBE	PROS	CONS
Western	A sprawling neighborhood with hidden alleyways, antique shops, Chinese medicine markets and temples.	Western is akin to the residential extension of Central, with less traffic and similarly spectacular views. Most accessible on foot, and a leisurely tram ride during off-peak hours.	May require steep footwork if your destination is not near the main road, where the trams and MTR run. Even taxis have difficulty navigating many narrow, one-way streets.
Central	A dense international finance center full of banks, shopping malls, and footbridges above traffic. High up the escalators, Midlevels is an exclusive residential getaway.	Home to major luxury brands' flagship stores, as well as grand hotels, fine restaurants, and famous nightlife area Lan Kwai Fong. Midlevels offers quiet views from above the fray.	Congested streets by day, crowded bars by night. Midlevels escalators only run uphill after morning rush hour.
Wan Chai, Causeway Bay, and Beyond	Wan Chai hosts a strip of street-level bars in addition to the designer Star Street area. Causeway Bay is the haven of hip young locals who come to eat, shop, and hang out in upstairs cafes.	Wan Chai has stylish restaurants, the convention center, and some performing-arts venues. Causeway Bay, home to Victoria Park, is conveniently situated with hotels in all price ranges.	The Wan Chai bar strip can get seedy, while Causeway Bay is extremely crowded on weekends. Eastern is mostly for business or residents.
Southside	Lower building density means more space and fewer people, with a fishing-village atmosphere around Aberdeen.	Proximity to great beaches right on Hong Kong Island, as well as to Stanley Market and Cyberport.	Be prepared for a lot of car and bus rides along winding roads, often in slow traffic.
Lantau Island	Hong Kong's largest island hosts disparate attractions: an international airport, an outlet shopping mall, natural scenery, Hong Kong Disneyland, and AsiaWorld-Expo.	MTR end-of-the-line town Tung Chung is the point of access to the Ngong Ping scenic cable-car ride and Citygate outlet shopping. Some may prefer a more resortlike setting inside Disneyland.	Inconvenient for exploring the rest of Hong Kong, as even Tung Chung is a half-hour MTR ride out from Central.
Kowloon	The "wild" side of Hong Kong, culminating in the commercial centers of Mong Kok and Tsim Sha Tsui—if not the air-conditioned mall in West Kowloon.	Shopping paradise indeed, for both malls and markets. The TST promenade, including the touristy Avenue of Stars, offers postcard views of the Hong Kong skyline.	Kowloon is not everyone's idea of a holiday—outside residential areas the streets (even pedestrian) are generally noisy, crowded and congested.

6

closest MTR stop; no nearby nightlife. ⊠ *508 Queen's Rd. W, Western* ☎ *2974–1234* ⊕ *www.hoteljen.com* ⟳ *280 rooms* ⚲ *In-room: safe, DVD (some), Internet, Wi-Fi. In-hotel: 3 restaurants, room service, bar, pool, gym, laundry service, Wi-Fi hotspot, parking (paid)* ⊟ *AE, DC, MC, V* Ⓜ *Sheung Wan* ✛ *A3.*

CENTRAL

$ 🏠 **Bishop Lei International House.** Owned and operated by the Catho-
Fodor's Choice   lic diocese of Hong Kong, this deluxe guesthouse is off the Midlevels
★   Escalator (exit left on Mosque Street). If you've ever dreamed of living a life of privilege in Midlevels, this is your chance to do it in style, complete with red-clad concierge standing in front of world city clocks. Many of the rooms were renovated in 2008 but remain small, so best book one of the 120-numbered rooms and suites with harbor views. Although the hotel is economically priced in a residential area, it has a fully equipped business center, workout room with view, pleasant outdoor pool, and restaurant serving Chinese and Western meals, in addition to buffet breakfast. **Pros:** unique perch near escalators; good value. **Cons:** lots of walking down steps after morning rush hour, if not you'll have to take a taxi, bus or shuttle. ⊠ *4 Robinson Rd., Midlevels, Central* ☎ *2868–0828* ⊕ *www.bishopleihtl.com.hk* ⟳ *227 rooms* ⚲ *In-room: safe, refrigerator, Internet, Wi-Fi. In-hotel: restaurant, pool, gym, laundry service, Wi-Fi hotspot* ⊟ *AE, DC, MC, V* Ⓜ *Central* ✛ *A4.*

$$$$ 🏠 **Four Seasons Hotel Hong Kong.** The opening of the Four Seasons Hotel Hong Kong in September 2005 brought an air of civilized class to the International Finance Centre complex, proving that top-quality customer service could soften the glare of commercial luxury-brand shops and faceless investment banks. Home to two award-winning restaurants and a lavish spa, the hotel's most attractive feature may be its outdoor infinity pool, heated in winter, which lets you swim right up to the horizon to contemplate the harbor from above. While the pool terrace is a destination in itself, be sure to enjoy the pool's complimentary mini-spa amenities, exclusive to guests. All rooms are comfortably spacious and elegantly decorated with TV over the bathtub, no luxury is overlooked. **Pros:** spacious rooms; great views; attention to detail. **Cons:** hot breakfast not included; views are of the less exciting side of Victoria Harbour. ⊠ *International Finance Centre, 8 Finance Rd., Central* ☎ *3196–8888* ⊕ *www.fourseasons/hongkong* ⟳ *399 rooms* ⚲ *In-room: safe, refrigerator, DVD, Internet, Wi-Fi. In-hotel: 5 restaurants, room service, bar, pools, gym, spa, laundry service, Wi-Fi hotspot* ⊟ *AE, DC, MC, V* Ⓜ *Hong Kong* ✛ *B2.*

$$ 🏠 **The Garden View–YWCA.** This attractive cylindrical guesthouse on a hill overlooks the Hong Kong Zoological and Botanical Gardens and beyond. Its clean, well-designed rooms make excellent use of small irregular shapes and emphasize each room's picture windows. If you want to do your own cooking, ask for a suite, which comes with a kitchenette; if not, the coffee shop serves European and Asian food. You can also use the outdoor pool and gym in the adjacent YWCA. The Garden View is a five-minute drive, or an uphill 20-minute walk, from Central. **Pros:** zoo and aviary views; within walking distance of Central. **Cons:** traffic can get bad during rush hours due to a nearby school. ⊠ *1*

MacDonnell Rd., Midlevels, Central ☎ *2877–3737* ⊕ *www.hotel.ywca. org.hk* ⤵ *141 rooms* ♿ *In-room: kitchen (some), Internet. In-hotel: restaurant, pool, gym, laundry service* ▤ *AE, MC, V* Ⓜ *Central* ✛ *A5.*

$$$$ ⊡ **Island Shangri-La.** This trademark elliptical building has become an icon of Hong Kong, as has *The Great Motherland of China,* the world's largest Chinese silk painting, which is housed in its glass atrium. The painting, which spans 16 stories, can be viewed from elevators soaring up and down through the atrium, carrying guests to their rooms. The lobby of this deluxe hotel sparkles with 771 Austrian crystal chandeliers hanging from high ceilings and huge, sun-drenched windows. Take the elevator up from the 39th floor and see the mainland's misty mountains drift by. Rooms are some of the largest on Hong Kong Island, and have magnificent views of the harbor, city, or Peak; all boast opulent furniture and tasteful design, a chandelier, as well as all-in-one bedside control panels. For upscale dining there's the scenic, formal French restaurant Pétrus on the top floor. **Pros:** dazzling lobby; quality service; free Wi-Fi. **Cons:** no real spa. ✉ *Two Pacific Place, Supreme Court Rd., Admiralty, Central* ☎ *2877–3838* ⊕ *www.shangri-la.com/island* ⤵ *565 rooms* ♿ *In-room: safe, DVD, Internet, Wi-Fi. In-hotel: 7 restaurants, room service, bar, pool, gym, laundry service, Wi-Fi hotspot, parking (paid)* ▤ *AE, DC, MC, V* Ⓜ *Admiralty* ✛ *C4.*

$$ ⊡ **Lan Kwai Fong Hotel.** Opened west of the famous nightlife district in
Fodor's Choice 2006, this oriental-themed boutique hotel is popular with Westerners
★ who appreciate its Chinese decor and more friendly SoHo location. Inspired by the cozy feel of an old Hong Kong apartment building, the relatively small rooms are enlarged by bay windows with plunging views of both the harbor and surrounding cityscape, while tiny bathrooms are gracefully outfitted with wooden ladder towel racks and faux antique Chinese doors. Inner walls may be thin, but the outdoor Breeze lounge is a pleasant place to relax in a neighborhood already crawling with art galleries, cafés, and design shops. Look for the live turtles on either side of the modest entranceway. **Pros:** hotel and neighborhood have lots of character. **Cons:** narrow roads surrounding the hotel are often congested. ✉ *3 Kau U Fong, Soho, Central* ☎ *3650– 0000* ⊕ *www.lankwaifonghotel.com.hk* ⤵ *163 rooms* ♿ *In-room: safe, kitchen (some), Internet, Wi-Fi. In-hotel: 2 restaurants, room service, bar, gym, laundry service* ▤ *AE, DC, MC, V* Ⓜ *Sheung Wan* ✛ *A3.*

$$$$ ⊡ **The Landmark Mandarin Oriental.** The interior design of this boutique-size hotel is dazzling, with spacious rooms featuring seven-foot round spa bathtubs placed in the center of giant bathrooms with city views. Everything from iPod docks to surround-sound speakers is controlled through your TV remote. Upstairs, the 25,000-square-foot holistic spa includes vitality pools, aromatherapy steam rooms, and Roman, Turkish, and Moroccan baths; the MO Bar offers all-day fine dining, cocktails, and live music till late. And all of this is implausibly concealed within the financial mitochondrion of the city, inside Hong Kong's most exclusive shopping arcade. **Pros:** you can't get more central in Central. **Cons:** no harbor views, not even from the spa. ✉ *15 Queen's Rd., Central* ☎ *2132–0188* ⊕ *www.mandarinoriental.com/landmark* ⤵ *113 rooms* ♿ *In-room: refrigerator, DVD, Internet, Wi-Fi. In-hotel:*

6

3 restaurants, room service, bar, pool, gym, spa, laundry service, Wi-Fi hotspot ⊟ *AE, DC, MC, V* Ⓜ *Central* ⊹ *B4.*

$$$$ 🎬 **Mandarin Oriental Hong Kong.** In September 2006, the legendary Man-
☕ darin, which has served the international elite since 1963, completed a
top-to-bottom renovation that included the installation of one of the city's
most elaborate spas. The hotel is such a symbol of Hong Kong's colonial
and financial history that rumors of the renovations sparked fierce debate
among the business set. However, the Mandarin has not lost its charac-
teristic charm in the face of modernization; sumptuous materials and
furnishings, including silky cognac drapes, honey leather armchairs, and
Black Forest Chinese marble bathrooms, are the norm in guest rooms,
but now so are flat-screen TVs and iPod docks. The Mandarin can even
provide children's slippers and bathrobes, while adults can choose from
a pillow menu. On the 25th floor, rising high above the Central skyline, Michelin-starred French restaurant Pierre and the panoramic M
bar continue to sparkle at night, while the downstairs Clipper Lounge is
a long-standing venue for traditional high tea. Exploring the spa area is
a delight in itself, as every corridor, alleyway, and room feels like a classic Oriental boudoir, concealing hidden delights. **Pros:** every room feels
luxuriously spacious and exquisite; Statue Square views. **Cons:** in-room
Wi-Fi isn't free. ✉ *5 Connaught Rd., Central* 📞 *2522–0111* ⊕ *www.*
mandarinoriental.com/hongkong 🛏 *501 rooms* ᐊ *In-room: safe, DVD,*
Wi-Fi. In-hotel: 9 restaurants, room service, bars, pool, gym, spa, laundry
service, Wi-Fi hotspot ⊟ *AE, DC, MC, V* Ⓜ *Central* ⊹ *B3.*

$$$ 🎬 **The Upper House.** The hotel's vertically inclined architecture invites
Fodor'sChoice guests to journey upward to the House, where an elevator opens at the
★ 42nd-floor Sky Lounge lobby. But the real breakthrough experience
takes place inside each and every spacious guest room, equipped with
both 42- and 19-inch TVs, surround sound and video-on-demand, not
to mention splendid bay-window harbor and city views. Paperless mini-
malism is embodied in a single iPod Touch, which serves as reception
check-in and -out, hotel directory, and information concierge. Addi-
tional services are personalized rather than centralized (also available
by phone). Meanwhile, the House does its best to make you feel at
home by offering in-room complimentary cookies, candies, beer, juice,
and a full espresso machine. **Pros:** relaxing space in eco-friendly envi-
ronment; great views. **Cons:** "uphill" access to a location with limited
pedestrian appeal. ✉ *Pacific Place,88 Queensway, Admiralty, Central*
📞 *2918–1838* ⊕ *www.upperhouse.com* 🛏 *117 rooms* ᐊ *In-room: safe,*
refrigerator, Internet, Wi-Fi. In-hotel: restaurant, room service, bar,
gym, laundry service, Wi-Fi hotspot, parking (paid) ⊟ *AE, DC, MC,*
V Ⓜ *Admiralty* ⊹ *C5.*

WAN CHAI, CAUSEWAY BAY, AND BEYOND
WAN CHAI

$$$$ 🎬 **Grand Hyatt Hong Kong.** A ceiling painted by Italian artist Paola
Dindo tops the Hyatt's art-deco-style lobby, and black-and-white
photographs of classic Chinese scenes hang on the walls. Elegant
guest rooms have sweeping harbor views above the convention cen-
ter, accented by curving wooden desks and black-marble bathroom
counters. The One Harbour Road Cantonese restaurant is notable, but

JIA

The Upper House

the breakfast and dessert buffets at Tiffin are decadent, where a pianist and live trio play throughout the day. The Plateau spa establishes a Zen-like calm, with soothing views across the harbor, while outdoor sports facilities include a curvaceous swimming pool, tennis and squash courts, and a driving range. The hotel is especially convenient if you're spending time at the Hong Kong Convention & Exhibition Centre, which is connected to the building. **Pros:** sports facilities; nice spa. **Cons:** quiet outside the hotel at night. ✉ *1 Harbour Rd., Wan Chai* ☎ *2588–1234* ⊕ *www.hongkong.grand.hyatt.com* ⬎ *553 rooms* ⌂ *In-room: safe, Internet, Wi-Fi. In-hotel: 9 restaurants, room service, bars, tennis courts, pool, gym, spa, laundry service, Wi-Fi hotspot, parking (paid)* ⊟ *AE, DC, MC, V* Ⓜ *Wan Chai* ⊕ *E3.*

WORD OF MOUTH

"There are also hotels in Causeway Bay, the far eastern section of Wan Chai. I am not a huge fan of this area for a first-time tourist, as there are no major tourist sights in the area, so you will spend time getting to sights (and then back to your hotel to collect luggage, etc). If you are here *exclusively* for clothes shopping, then Causeway Bay is a good location." —Cicerone

$$ 🛏 **The Harbourview.** This waterfront YMCA property has small but relatively inexpensive rooms near the Wan Chai Star Ferry pier. Rooms are pleasantly decorated and offer enviable harbor views. The hotel is well placed if you want to attend cultural events in the evening: both the Arts Centre and the Academy for Performing Arts are next door. It's also opposite the Hong Kong Convention & Exhibition Centre. The pedestrian overpass will get you across Wan Chai or to the Star Ferry quickly without stepping down into the traffic, that is, until you get to Hennessy Road. For a small fee, you can also use the Salisbury YMCA's excellent indoor sports facilities just across the harbor. **Pros:** use of Salisbury YMCA facilities; affordable rates for reliable service and decent rooms. **Cons:** not right next to the MTR. ✉ *4 Harbour Rd., Wan Chai* ☎ *2802–0111* ⊕ *www.theharbourview.com.hk* ⬎ *320 rooms* ⌂ *In-room: safe, refrigerator, Wi-Fi. In-hotel: 2 restaurants, room service, laundry service, Wi-Fi hotspot* ⊟ *AE, DC, MC, V* Ⓜ *Wan Chai* ⊕ *E4.*

$$$$ 🛏 **Renaissance Hong Kong Harbour View.** Sharing the Hong Kong Convention & Exhibition Centre complex with the Grand Hyatt is this more modest but attractive hotel. Guest rooms are medium in size with plenty of mirrors that reflect the modern decor. Many rooms have harbor views, but others overlook the hotel's 11,000-square-foot recreational area, featuring a voluptuously sprawling outdoor pool, driving range, jogging trails, and playground, which should also keep the kids busy. The wonderfully scenic, soaring lobby lounge hosts a live jazz band in the evening and is a popular rendezvous spot for locals and visiting businesspeople. **Pros:** harborside recreational garden. **Cons:** a little walk away from the MTR, but the Star Ferry is accessible via pedestrian overpass. ✉ *1 Harbour Rd., Wan Chai* ☎ *2802–8888* ⊕ *www.renaissancehotels.com/hkghv* ⬎ *862 rooms, 53 suites* ⌂ *In-room: safe, refrigerator, Internet, Wi-Fi. In-hotel: 4 restaurants, room service, tennis courts, pool, gym, laundry service, Wi-Fi hotspot, parking (paid)* ⊟ *AE, DC, MC, V* Ⓜ *Wan Chai* ⊕ *E3.*

CAUSEWAY BAY

¢ **Alisan Guest House.** There are many upstairs guest houses with tiny
Fodor's Choice rooms nestled in the old apartment buildings of Causeway Bay, but
★ Alisan is one of the few that prioritize cleanliness, safety, and friendly
hospitality, all for a budget price. The no-frills rooms are furnished
with single, double, or triple beds, and some of these have views of the
yachts just across Gloucester Road. It's almost like staying in a real
Hong Kong apartment, with the convenience of an en-suite washroom
and shower. Book early and opt to pay in cash or via PayPal, as there
is a 5% service charge for credit cards. Look for the entrance to Hoi To
Court on Cannon Street, and take the elevator to the fifth-floor reception. **Pros:** friendly staff; good location; free Wi-Fi. **Cons:** small rooms
and windows; surcharge to pay with credit card. ⊠ *Flat A, 5/F, Hoi
To Court, 275 Gloucester Rd., Causeway Bay* ☎ *2838–0762* ⊕ *home.
hkstar.com/~alisangh* ⟿ *30 rooms* ♿ *In-room: Wi-Fi. In-hotel: Internet
terminal, Wi-Fi hotspot* ⊟ *MC, V* Ⓜ *Causeway Bay* ✣ *H3.*

$ **Butterfly on Morrison.** Opened in 2009 and tucked away behind Times
Fodor's Choice Square, this second Butterfly hotel, in between Wan Chai and Causeway
★ Bay, offers pleasing views of Happy Valley and surroundings from its
ultramodern rooms with wall-to-wall windows. Standard rooms run
small and there is no restaurant on the premises, not even a gym, but
every room has a refrigerator and electric kettle, and the hotel's Internet lounge offers free coffee and tea. Besides, the hotel is not far from
Causeway Bay's own low-profile bar scene. It is a good choice for independent travelers who aren't fussy about facilities but love a great view.
Pros: new, modern rooms with good views of the neighborhood. **Cons:**
no in-hotel facilities. ⊠ *39 Morrison Hill Rd., Wan Chai* ☎ *3962–8333*
⊕ *www.butterflyhk.com/butterfly-on-morrison* ⟿ *93 rooms* ♿ *In-room:
safe, refrigerator, DVD, Internet. In-hotel: laundry service, Internet
terminal* ⊟ *AE, DC, MC, V* Ⓜ *Causeway Bay* ✣ *G5.*

$$ **JIA.** The first boutique hotel designed by Philippe Starck in Asia
Fodor's Choice is a destination in itself, beginning with the dark lobby and its sur-
★ real silver, antiquelike sculptural furniture. This is also where guests
can enjoy complimentary afternoon tea and cakes, evening wine, and
soft drinks. Accommodations consist of studios or one-bedroom suites,
plus two-bedroom duplex penthouses. All rooms are decorated in airy
white, with sheer-curtain separations and marble-finish bathrooms and
kitchenettes equipped with dining tables and cookware. Hot breakfast
is served downstairs in the all-wood decor of Madera tapas and wine
bar, while the award-winning Drawing Room restaurant offers con-
temporary Italian cuisine in an art gallery setting. Guests receive free
access to the California Fitness gym around the corner, as well as an
exclusive Insider Access Card, which gives membership privileges at
several nightlife venues, not to mention evening harbor tours on the
famous Aqua Luna junk. **Pros:** designer rooms at a reasonable price,
which includes free Wi-Fi, breakfast, and selected drinks in the lobby.
Cons: no views; trendy lobby and surrounding venues feel more like
a nightclub. ⊠ *1–5 Irving St., Causeway Bay* ☎ *3196–9000* ⊕ *www.
jiahongkong.com* ⟿ *54 rooms* ♿ *In-room: safe, kitchen, refrigera-
tor, DVD, Internet, Wi-Fi. In-hotel: 2 restaurants, room service, bars,*

6

laundry facilities, laundry service, Wi-Fi hotspot ▭ *AE, DC, MC, V* Ⓜ *Causeway Bay* ✛ *H4.*

$$ 🏨 **Metropark Hotel Causeway Bay.** This contemporary hotel offers simple but effectively designed rooms, which have extensive views of the park, the harbor, or the hills. The tiny lobby leads into Vic's bar; the Café du Parc serves French-Japanese fusion cuisine. The rooftop pool may be small, but offers a spectacular view of Victoria Park and beyond. Besides, this hotel is situated on the quieter side of Victoria Park, near the public swimming pool and Tin Hau's street food of Electric Road. **Pros:** spectacular views for less. **Cons:** limited hotel facilities. ⊠ *148 Tung Lo Wan Rd., Causeway Bay* ☎ *2600–1000* ⊕ *www.metroparkhotel.com* ⤏ *266 rooms* ⚬ *In-room: safe, refrigerator, Internet, Wi-Fi (some). In-hotel: restaurant, room service, bar, pool, gym, spa, laundry service, Wi-Fi hotspot* ▭ *AE, DC, MC, V* Ⓜ *Tin Hau* ✛ *H4.*

$$ 🏨 **Park Lane.** This elegant hotel overlooks Victoria Park from the Causeway Bay side, backing into Hong Kong Island's busiest pedestrian streets for shopping and entertainment, especially on weekends. Rooms have smart glass-top tables, a glass-walled bathroom, sitting area, and marvelous views of the harbor, Victoria Park, or the city, looking east. The rooftop restaurant offers an even more panoramic view, serving international cuisine with a touch of Asian flavor. **Pros:** eastward Victoria Park views. **Cons:** often crowded; no pool. ⊠ *310 Gloucester Rd., Causeway Bay* ☎ *2293–8888* ⊕ *www.parklane.com.hk* ⤏ *810 rooms* ⚬ *In-room: safe, Internet. In-hotel: 4 restaurants, room service, bar, gym, laundry service, Wi-Fi hotspot, parking (paid)* ▭ *AE, DC, MC, V* Ⓜ *Causeway Bay* ✛ *H4.*

LANTAU ISLAND

$$ 🏨 **Disney's Hollywood Hotel.** Like its sister, the Disneyland Hotel, Disney's Hollywood Hotel could theoretically be viewed simply as one of Asia's best airport hotels. But that would hardly do justice to the creativity and attention to detail that so brightly color every aspect of your stay here. The theme is the golden age of Hollywood, and you may smile at its loving display of Americana, from the New York–theme restaurant to the art-deco frontage of the cocktail lounge. Of course, this is Disneyland, and there are the Chef Mickey restaurants, too. There's a playroom, Malibu Toy Shop, as well as a number of activities for kids. Rooms are on the smaller side, and a bit more "Goofy" than they are at the Disneyland Hotel, with perhaps even greater appeal for the children. **Pros:** great value. **Cons:** cut off from other Hong Kong attractions. ⊠ *Hong Kong Disneyland Resort, Lantau Island* ☎ *3510–5000* ⊕ *www. hongkongdisneyland.com* ⤏ *600 rooms* ⚬ *In-room: safe, refrigerator, Internet. In-hotel: 3 restaurants, room service, bars, tennis court, pool, gym, spa, children's programs (ages 2–12), laundry service* ▭ *AE, DC, MC, V* Ⓜ *Disneyland.*

$$ 🏨 **Hong Kong Disneyland Hotel.** Modeled in Victorian style after the Grand Floridian in Florida's Walt Disney World Resort, this top-flight hotel is beautifully executed on every level, from the spacious rooms with balconies overlooking the sea to the topiary of Mickey's Maze, and grand, imposing ballrooms that wouldn't be out of place in a fairy-tale castle. There's a daily schedule of activities, many for children, although

adults may enjoy the horticulture tours; downstairs, Disney characters meet and greet guests during the enormous buffet breakfast. Don't overlook Disneyland as a place to stay before or after your early-morning or late-night flight—it's minutes from the airport. **Pros:** great for kids. **Cons:** cut off from the rest of Hong Kong. ✉ *Hong Kong Disneyland Resort, Lantau Island* ☎ *3510–6000* ⊕ *www.hongkongdisneyland.com* ⤶ *400 rooms* ♨ *In-room: safe, refrigerator, Internet. In-hotel: 3 restaurants, room service, bars, tennis court, pool, gym, spa, children's programs (ages 2–12), laundry service, parking (free)* ▭ *AE, DC, MC, V* Ⓜ *Disneyland.*

$$$ 🏨 **Regal Airport Hotel.** Ideal for passengers in transit, this is one of the largest airport hotels in the world. The Airport Express can deliver you to Hong Kong Island in about 25 minutes, and a free shuttle bus can take you to Tsim Sha Tsui in a little more time depending on traffic. It's also connected directly to the passenger terminal by an air-conditioned, moving walkway. Consistently voted one of the best airport hotels in the world, it has a Thai-themed spa with an impressive range of treatments. Some rooms have terrific views of planes landing from afar; those with balconies overlook the hotel's two swimming pools and make you feel like you're staying in a resort. **Pros:** direct access to the airport on foot; refreshing pool and spa facilities. **Cons:** far removed from Hong Kong sights. ✉ *9 Cheong Tat Rd., Hong Kong International Airport, Lantau Island* ☎ *2286–8888* ⊕ *www.regalhotel.com* ⤶ *1,171 rooms* ♨ *In-room: safe, refrigerator, Wi-Fi. In-hotel: 6 restaurants, room service, bars, pool, gym, spa, laundry service, parking (paid)* ▭ *AE, DC, MC, V* Ⓜ *Airport.*

KOWLOON

TSIM SHA TSUI

$$ 🏨 **BP International House.** Built by the Boy Scouts Association, this grand hotel on the northern side of Kowloon Park offers excellent value. A portrait of association founder Baron Robert Baden-Powell, hangs in the spacious, modern lobby. The rooms are small and spartan but not uncomfortable, and all have standard hotel amenities. Some rooms are bigger than others, so be sure to inquire before you're assigned a room. A multipurpose hall hosts exhibitions, conventions, and concerts. Another attraction for budget travelers is the self-service coin laundry. **Pros:** affordable panoramic harbor views from the Kowloon side. **Cons:** can get crowded with business and tour groups. ✉ *8 Austin Rd., Tsim Sha Tsui, Kowloon* ☎ *2376–1111* ⊕ *www.bpih.com.hk* ⤶ *529 rooms* ♨ *In-room: safe, refrigerator, Internet, Wi-Fi. In-hotel: 3 restaurants, bar, laundry facilities, laundry service, Internet terminal, Wi-Fi hotspot, parking (paid)* ▭ *AE, DC, MC, V* Ⓜ *Austin or Jordan* ✛ *A3.*

$$$$ 🏨 **InterContinental Hong Kong.** Given its exceptional location at the protruding tip of the Kowloon peninsula, the InterContinental is often listed as one of the most desirable hotels in Asia, as it affords a truly panoramic front-row view of the entire coast of Hong Kong Island from its palatial yet ultramodern five-star environment. The restaurant line-up features Spoon by Alain Ducasse and Nobu, while the lower-level lobby lounge tea sets and Harbourside buffets keep passersby

Fodor's Choice
★

6

Intercontinental

The Peninsula

The Luxe Manor

drooling as they ogle the property from the Avenue of Stars. Contemporary rooms designed with Asian accents include deep-sunken tubs in the marbled bathrooms, while corner suites enjoy spacious outdoor terraces with their own Jacuzzi. **Pros:** exceptional views; modern design; extravagant spa. **Cons:** exclusive location offers little retreat from the touristy Avenue of Stars. ⊠ *18 Salisbury Rd., Tsim Sha Tsui, Kowloon* ☎ *2721–1211* ⊕ *www.hongkong-ic.intercontinental.com* ⟲ *495 rooms* △ *In-room: safe, refrigerator, DVD, Internet, Wi-Fi. In-hotel: 6 restaurants, room service, bar, pool, gym, spa, laundry service, parking (paid)* ⊟ *AE, DC, MC, V* Ⓜ *Tsim Sha Tsui* ✛ *D4.*

$$

Fodor's Choice

★

🏨 **The Luxe Manor.** This midrange manor, which opened in late 2006, adds a fresh dose of fantasy to the Knutsford Terrace neighborhood with its chic surrealist flair. The elusive lobby sets the tone with white line drawings of penny farthings, compasses, and clocks against dark magentas, purples, gold, and black, all centered around a bright red armchair. Rooms are predominantly white, with empty picture frames painted on the wall above the bed, a funky faux-drawer cupboard and gold-framed flat-screen TV, all of which help to compensate for the total lack of views. Six theme suites offer six different interior experiences, but the most fun is the Mirage suite, with its four door handles, tilted nightstand, and fake-silhouette closets. Upstairs, the lush Dada bar and lounge hosts stand-up comedy, art exhibits, and a resident jazz band that plays Thursday through Saturday nights. On the first floor the white-walled Aspasia restaurant features very fine Italian cuisine. **Pros:** price includes buffet breakfast; free Wi-Fi; attentive service. **Cons:** no views. ⊠ *39 Kimberley Rd., Tsim Sha Tsui, Kowloon* ☎ *3763–8880* ⊕ *www.theluxemanor.com* ⟲ *159 rooms* △ *In-room: safe, Internet, Wi-Fi. In-hotel: 2 restaurants, room service, bars, gym, laundry service, Wi-Fi hotspot* ⊟ *AE, DC, MC, V* Ⓜ *Tsim Sha Tsui* ✛ *B4.*

$$$

🏨 **Marco Polo Hongkong Hotel.** This is the largest of three Marco Polo hotels situated along Canton Road within the wharf-side Harbour City shopping complex, which share pool, gym, and spa facilities. The hotel's location on the western edge of Tsim Sha Tsui means that most rooms have sweeping views of Hong Kong Island, the sea, and West Kowloon, although windows aren't exactly floor to ceiling. The Marco Polo Hongkong enjoys a long-standing reputation among European and American travelers, and is the official hotel for the Hong Kong Sevens rugby players. The largest Oktoberfest in town also takes place here, with more than 1,000 beer-swilling participants, so be sure to check out the hotel's Guinness World Record-setting collection of rum in the Lobby Lounge before they get there. **Pros:** westward views; Harbour City convenience. **Cons:** full in late March during the Hong Kong Sevens tournament; boisterous crowds during Oktoberfest. ⊠ *Harbour City, Canton Rd., Tsim Sha Tsui, Kowloon* ☎ *2113–0088* ⊕ *www.marcopolohotels.com* ⟲ *664 rooms* △ *In-room: safe, refrigerator, Internet, Wi-Fi. In-hotel: 3 restaurants, room service, bar, pool, laundry service, parking (paid)* ⊟ *AE, DC, MC, V* Ⓜ *Tsim Sha Tsui* ✛ *D2.*

$$$$

Fodor's Choice

★

🏨 **The Peninsula Hong Kong.** Established in 1928, The Peninsula is an oasis of Old World glamour amid the chaos of Tsim Sha Tsui. Anyone who has savored classic high tea with live chamber music in the lobby, or sipped

6

cocktails at the bar of the Philippe Starck–designed Felix restaurant with its panoramic views of the territory, can attest to this. When staying here, guests have a choice of accommodations in the original building, with its high-ceiling apartmentlike suites, or in the newer upper wing, where Kowloon and harbor views from suites equipped with iron telescopes make you feel like you own Hong Kong. All rooms are furnished to reflect the territory's colonial heritage, complete with marbled bathrooms, but also include modern audio-visual systems, outside weather indicators, mood lighting, and remote-controlled curtains. In celebration of its 81st anniversary, the Peninsula added two MINI Clubman cars to its already famous fleet of Rolls-Royce Phantoms, so grab the included iPhone with GPS and go for a complimentary scenic ride far away from the crowds. **Pros:** Old World glamour; impeccable service; unrivalled views from upper-level rooms; free Wi-Fi; helicopter rides. **Cons:** not for those on a budget. ⊠ *Salisbury Rd., Tsim Sha Tsui, Kowloon* ☎ *2920–8888* ⊕ *www. peninsula.com* ⤳ *354 rooms* ⬧ *In-room: safe, DVD, Internet, Wi-Fi. In-hotel: 9 restaurants, room service, bars, pool, gym, spa, laundry service, parking (free)* ═ *AE, DC, MC, V* Ⓜ *Tsim Sha Tsui* ✛ *D3.*

$$ ⊡ **Royal Pacific Hotel & Towers.** As part of the China Hong Kong City complex, which includes a terminal for ferries to mainland China and Macau, the Royal Pacific sits literally on the western edge of Tsim Sha Tsui. Guest rooms are arranged in two blocks: hotel and tower wings. Tower-wing rooms, renovated in mid-2010, have large harbor views and are luxuriously furnished, while the smaller hotel-wing rooms have Kowloon Park and city views. The small lobby already seems far removed from the Harbour City crowds, as it opens out to restaurants on long and peaceful rooftop decks facing West Kowloon. In the other direction, a footbridge connects the hotel directly to Kowloon Park, which has a giant outdoor swimming-pool complex. **Pros:** both Kowloon Park and quiet westward sea views; footbridge to the park. **Cons:** no outdoor rooftop pool. ⊠ *China Hong Kong City, Canton Rd., Tsim Sha Tsui, Kowloon* ☎ *2736–1188* ⊕ *www.royalpacific.com.hk* ⤳ *673 rooms* ⬧ *In-room: safe, kitchen (some), refrigerator (some), Internet, Wi-Fi (some). In-hotel: 4 restaurants, room service, bar, gym, laundry service, Wi-Fi hotspot, parking (paid)* ═ *AE, DC, MC, V* Ⓜ *Tsim Sha Tsui* ✛ *B2.*

$$ ⊡ **Salisbury YMCA.** This upscale YMCA is Hong Kong's most popu-
ⓒ lar and is a great value for your money. Across the street from the Peninsula and opposite the Cultural Centre, Space Museum, and Museum of Art, it's ideally situated for theater, art, and concert crawls. Most rooms, decorated in a chirpy yellow, have at least partial harbor views of the ferry pier, but it's worth the small upgrade to full harbor view, or even to suites with wider views through bigger windows. Alternatively, you could also crash in one of seven four-bed dorm

WORD OF MOUTH

"The Salisbury YMCA admittedly has no charm but the view from the harbor view rooms really is spectacular and the location is very convenient for just about anything. If you need a bit of posh, you just go next door to the Peninsula or diagonally across the way to the InterContinental for drinks or a meal or a stroll."
—marya_

rooms. The Y premises also consist of a rooftop garden, chapel, hair salon, bookshop, and excellent health and fitness facilities, including a large indoor pool, squash courts, and climbing walls. **Pros:** prime views at modest prices; indoor activities to occupy the whole family. **Cons:** busy lobby reflects the Y's recreational roots. ✉ *41 Salisbury Rd., Tsim Sha Tsui, Kowloon* ☎ *2368–7888* ⊕ *www.ymcahk.org.hk* ⤳ *363 rooms* ⚸ *In-room: safe, refrigerator, Internet, Wi-Fi. In-hotel: 2 restaurants, room service, pool, gym, laundry facilities, laundry service, Internet terminal, Wi-Fi hotspot* ⊟ *AE, DC, MC, V* Ⓜ *Tsim Sha Tsui* ✛ *D3.*

AFTER DARK

By Eva Chui Loiterton
Updated by Samantha Leese

A riot of neon, heralding frenetic after-hours action, announces Hong Kong's nightlife districts. Clubs and bars fill to capacity, evening markets pack in shoppers looking for bargains, restaurants welcome diners, cinemas pop corn as fast as they can, and theaters and concert halls prepare for full houses.

The neighborhoods of Wan Chai, Lan Kwai Fong, and SoHo are packed with bars, pubs, and nightclubs that cater to everyone from the hippest trendsetters to bankers ready to spend their bonuses, and more laid-back crowds out for a pint. Partying in Hong Kong is a way of life; it starts at the beginning of the week with a drink or two after work, progressing to serious barhopping and clubbing on the weekends. Wednesday is a big night out here—so much so that the staff at one famous club sport "Thursday Sucks" T-shirts on the quiet day after. Work hard, play harder is the motto in Hong Kong, and people follow it seriously.

Because each district has so much to offer, and since they're all quite close to each other, it's perfectly normal to pop into two or three bars before heading to a nightclub. At the other end of the spectrum, the city's arts and culture scene is equally lively, with innovative music, dance, and theater. Small independent productions as well as large-scale concerts take to the stage across the territory every weekend. You simply cannot go home without a Hong Kong nightlife story to tell!

HONG KONG ISLAND

WESTERN

BARS

Club 71. This bohemian diamond-in-the-rough was named in tribute to July 1, 2003, when half a million Hong Kongers successfully rallied against looming threats to their freedom of speech. Tucked away on a terrace down a market side street, the quirky, unpretentious bar is a mainstay of artists, journalists, and left-wing politicians. The outdoor area closes around midnight. ✉ *B/F, 67 Hollywood Rd., Sheung Wan, Western* ☎ *2858–7071* ☉ *Closes 2 am* Ⓜ *Central.*

GAY AND LESBIAN SPOTS

Volume. Down a leafy residential staircase where Hollywood Road meets Aberdeen Street, Volume feels a little like the backstage of a small-town cabaret with faux tiger-fur seats, red-velvet curtain, dancer's pole, and mirror ball dominating the decor. The club hosts a friendly,

HONG KONG'S TOP FIVE NIGHTLIFE SPOTS

dragon-i: The door's clipboard-wielding glamazons will not make entry easy, but this is easily the kingpin of the big Central clubs, and second home to the city's extravagant elite.

Felix: Aqua Spirit may be trendier, but Phillipe Starck–designed Felix is an institution. The best view of the skyline is marketing currency in Kowloon, and this penthouse bar really matches its claim.

The Pawn: Modern panache and history's charm combine to make this one of the most unique establishments in town. Order a bottle of wine and settle onto one of the vintage couches in the ever-popular "living room."

Solas: Unofficial epicenter of Wyndham Street's seismic after-dark action, Solas is difficult to beat if you're looking for somewhere loud and lively to meet new people over well-mixed drinks.

Volume: A fun, friendly, and diverse crowd distinguishes Volume from many of the city's more aloof gay establishments. The Wednesday evening happy hour is the best mixer on the scene.

mixed crowd of gays, lesbians, and their friends, thanks to free entry and an open-door policy. New Arrivals Wednesdays are a staple of the scene, welcoming tourists and newbies, and attracting locals with free vodka between 7 and 9:30 pm. Weekends are reliably hyper, with dance anthems filling the floor till the wee hours. The entrance is just below street level, around the corner from the main road. ⊠ *83–85 Hollywood Rd., Sheung Wan, Western* ☎ *2857–7683* ⊗ *Closes late* Ⓜ *Sheung Wan.*

CENTRAL

On weekends the streets of Lan Kwai Fong are liberated from traffic, and the swilling hordes from both sides of the street merge into one heaving organism. A five-minute walk uphill is SoHo. Back in the '90s it took local businesses some effort to convince district councillors that the sometimes vice-associated moniker (which in this case stands for South of Hollywood Road) was a good idea, but Hong Kong is now proud of this très chic area, a warren of streets stuffed with commensurately priced restaurants, bars, and late-night boutiques. Midway between Lan Kwai Fong's madness and SoHo's bohemian glamour is Wyndham Street, home to an array of sophisticated bars, nightclubs, and restaurants and strict domain of the over 25s.

BARS

Barco. Had enough of the crowds and looking for a quiet drink and conversation that you can actually hear? Barco is the place. It's cozy, with a small lounge area and an even smaller courtyard in the back, and an assortment of board games if you're feeling playful. ⊠ *42 Staunton St., SoHo, Central* ☎ *2857–4478* ⊗ *Closes 1 am* Ⓜ *Central.*

F.I.N.D.S. The name of this supercool restaurant and bar is an acronym of Finland, Iceland, Norway, Denmark, and Sweden. Inspired by Scandinavian winters, the striking decor is pale blue and white, with sparkling granite walls. There's a large outdoor terrace with comfortable seating.

About 30 premium vodkas are served. You can also try a cocktail from the adventurous molecular mixology menu. ⊠ *2nd fl., LKF Tower, 33 Wyndham St., Central* ☎ *2522–9318* ⊙ *Closes 3 am* Ⓜ *Central.*

Le Jardin. For an otherworldly, cosmopolitan vibe, check out this casual bar with a lovely outdoor terrace overlooking the gregarious alfresco dining lane known locally as Rat Alley. Walk through the dining area and up a flight of steps. It's a little tricky to find, but the leafy, fairy-lit setting is worth it. ⊠ *1st fl., 10 Wing Wah La., Central* ☎ *2877–1100* ⊙ *Closes 4 am* Ⓜ *Central.*

Lei Dou. Meaning simply "here" in Cantonese, this boudoir-styled spot, hidden away in the heart of the action, is where those in the know (and those seeking discretion) come to wind down in style. Lei Dou's fans love it for its decadent, low-lit decor, down-tempo jazz, and comfortable seating. ⊠ *Ground fl., 20–22 D'Aguilar St., Central* ☎ *2525–6628* ⊙ *Closes 3 am* Ⓜ *Central.*

Lux. The well-heeled drink martinis and designer beers at this swanky corner spot. It has a prime location in Lan Kwai Fong and is a great bar for people-watching; it also serves excellent food in booths at the back. ⊠ *California Tower, 30–32 D'Aguilar St., Lan Kwai Fong, Central* ☎ *2868–9538* ⊙ *Closes 4 am.*

MO Bar. This plush bar in the Landmark Mandarin Oriental is where the banking set goes to relax. You'll pay top dollar for the martinis (up to HK$150), but the striking interior makes it worthwhile. A huge, red-light circle dominates an entire wall, the "O" being a Chinese symbol of shared experience. ⊠ *The Landmark Mandarin Oriental, 15 Queen's Rd. Central, The Landmark, Central* ☎ *2132–0077* ⊙ *Closes 2 am* Ⓜ *Central.*

RED Bar. Although its shopping mall location, outdoor terrace self-service policy, and incongruous affiliation with the next-door gym may not seem appealing, once you arrive, you'll throw all your preconceived notions into the harbor. On the roof of IFC Mall, RED has breathtaking views of the city, making it a great place to grab an early dinner and relax with a cocktail while watching the sunset. ⊠ *Level 4, Two IFC, 8 Finance St., Central* ☎ *8129–8882* ⊙ *Closes 2 am* Ⓜ *Hong Kong.*

Fodor's Choice ★ **Solas.** Positioned a floor below super-club dragon-i, this red-lit, always crowded bar is Wyndham Street's party central. Expect a mostly expat crowd of twenty- and thirtysomethings, who come straight from work on weekdays. To avoid the excited crush on Wednesday's ladies' night and on weekends, head for the booths along the walls and leave before the DJ starts to spin at around 11 pm. ⊠ *60 Wyndham St., SoHo, Central* ☎ *3162–3710* ⊙ *Closes 4 am* Ⓜ *Central.*

Staunton's Wine Bar & Cafe. Adjacent to Hong Kong's famous outdoor escalator is this popular bistro-style café and bar. Partly alfresco, it's the perfect place to people-watch, whether from the balcony or from the steps, where you can hang out on foam picnic mats. You can come for a drink at night or for coffee or a meal during the day. It's also a Sunday-morning favorite for nursing hangovers over brunch. ⊠ *10–12 Staunton St., SoHo, Central* ☎ *2973–6611* ⊙ *Closes 3 am* Ⓜ *Central.*

Art Spaces

Fringe Club. The pioneer of Hong Kong's alternative arts scene has been staging excellent independent theater, music, and art productions since opening in 1983. The distinctive brown-and-white-stripe colonial structure was built as a cold-storage warehouse in 1892. It was derelict when the Fringe moved in; and the painstaking renovation has earned awards. Light pours through huge windows into the street-level Economist Gallery, with its small, well-curated exhibitions.

The übercool Fotogalerie, upstairs, is Hong Kong's only photography gallery. Downstairs, meat and cheese were once sold in the space that now houses the Fringe Theatre. The lighting box of the smaller Studio Theatre was once a refrigeration unit, built to preserve not food but winter clothes from summer mildew. Fringe productions are sometimes in Cantonese, so check the program carefully. ⊠ *2 Lower Albert Rd., Central* ☎ *2521-7251 general inquiries, 3128-8288 box office* ⊕ *www.hkfringe.com.hk* ☜ *Galleries free* ⊙ *Art galleries and box office: Mon.–Sat. noon–10. Fotogalerie: Mon.–Thurs. noon–midnight, Fri. and Sat. 10:30 am–3 am. Fringe Gallery Bar: Mon.–Thurs. 4 pm–midnight, Fri. and Sat. 4 pm–3 am* Ⓜ *Central, Exit D2.*

Hong Kong Arts Centre. A hodge-podge of activities takes place in this deceptively bleak concrete tower, financed with horse-racing profits donated by the Hong Kong Jockey Club. Intriguing contemporary art exhibitions are held in the 14th-floor Goethe Gallery, a white-cube space. Thematic cycles of art-house flicks run in the basement Agnès b. CINEMA! Community theater groups are behind much of the fare at the Shouson Theatre and smaller McAulay Studio, though international drama and dance troupes sometimes appear. Quality is hit and miss, so check newspaper reviews for advice. From Wan Chai MTR, cross the footbridge to Immigration Tower, then dogleg left through the open plaza until you hit Harbour Road: the center is on the left. ⊠ *2 Harbour Rd., Wan Chai* ☎ *2582-0200, 2802-0088 Goethe Gallery* ⊕ *www.hkac.org.hk* ☜ *Free* ⊙ *Center: daily 10–8. Goethe Gallery: weekdays 10–8, Sat. 2–6* Ⓜ *Wan Chai, Exit C.*

Ma Tau Kok Cattle Depot. A former slaughterhouse in industrial To Kwa Wan has become a happening hub of independent art. It's divvied up into spaces run by different groups. In July 1997—as Hong Kong was handed back to China—a group of young local artists formed the Artists' Commune (⊠ *Unit 12* ☎ *2104-3322* ⊕ *www.artist-commune.com* ☜ *Free* ⊙ *Tues.–Sun. 2–8*), whose massive loftlike premises showcase offbeat works. Expect funky, well-curated pickings at 1aspace (⊠ *Unit 14* ☎ *2529-0087* ⊕ *www.oneaspace.org.hk* ☜ *Free* ⊙ *Tues.–Sun. 2–8*), a cool, sleek gallery. The easiest way to get here is by taxi from Tsim Sha Tsui (around HK$50) or from Lok Fu MTR (around HK$35). ⊠ *63 Ma Tau Kok Rd., To Kwa Wan, Kowloon.*

—Victoria Patience

Lan Kwai Fong is Hong Kong's famous bar and dining district.

DISCOS AND NIGHTCLUBS

Azure. Head skyward to this cosmopolitan, bi-level club at the top of the 30-story Hotel LKF. The downstairs lounge is a sophisticated space with pool tables, couches, and a soundtrack of ambient tunes. Upstairs, take in a 270-degree panorama of the harbor from the smoker's terrace, or dance to funky house music inside. ⊠ *29th fl., Hotel LKF, 33 Wyndham St., Central* ☎ *3518–9330* ⊙ *Closes 2 am* Ⓜ *Central.*

Fodor'sChoice
★
dragon-i. The entrance is marked by an enormous birdcage (filled with real budgies and canaries) made entirely of bamboo poles. Have a drink on the busy alfresco deck by the doorway or step inside the rich, red playroom, which doubles as a restaurant at lunchtime and in the early evening. The club's notorious Model's Night takes place on Wednesdays, and is a playground for the city's young and beautiful. ⊠ *The Centrium, 60 Wyndham St., Central* ☎ *3110–1222* ⊙ *Closes 5 am* Ⓜ *Central.*

Drop. This pint-size gem is where celebrities party—usually until sunrise—when they're in town. Hidden down an alley beside a late-night food stand, its location only adds an air of exclusivity to the speakeasy feel. Excellent fresh-fruit martinis are its forte. Drop has two incarnations: after-dinner cocktail lounge before midnight and impenetrable fortress later on, so arrive early to avoid disappointment. ⊠ *Basement, On Lok Mansion, 39–43 Hollywood Rd., entrance off Cochrane St., Central* ☎ *2543–8856* ⊙ *Closes 6 am* Ⓜ *Central.*

Yumla. This tiny, alternative club is the den of local DJ talent, and the only noncommercial music space in Central (you won't hear this music on the radio). As such, it has garnered a band of fiercely loyal regulars, which can make the casual visitor feel out of place. Even with a cover charge of HK$100 on weekends, the place can get mercilessly packed. But if you're there for the music, it's worth it. Check the Web site for schedules and promotions. ⊠ *Lower basement, 79 Wyndham St., Central* ☎ *2147–2382* ⊕ *www.yumla.com* ⊗ *Closes late* Ⓜ *Central.*

GAY AND LESBIAN SPOTS

Propaganda. Off a quaint but steep cobblestone street is one of *the* most popular gay clubs in Hong Kong. Propaganda holds a near-monopoly on the late-night scene. The art-deco bar area hosts quite the flirt-fest, while the sunken dance floor has poles on either side for go-go boys to flaunt their wares. It's pretty empty during the week, despite the free-entry happy hour

Tuesday through Thursday nights; the crowds arrive well after midnight on weekends. The entrance is in an alleyway, Ezra Lane, which runs parallel to Hollywood Road and is best accessed from Pottinger Street. ⊠ *1 Hollywood Rd., Central* ☎ *2868–1316* ⊗ *Closes 5:30 am* Ⓜ *Central.*

MUSIC CLUBS

The Cavern. This large bar at the top of Lan Kwai Fong is a laid-back space where locals and out-of-towners alike come to drink beer, eat peanuts, tap their feet to the lively cover bands, and watch the swelling streets from the pavement tables. ⊠ *Shop 1, ground fl., LKF Tower, 33 Wyndham St., entrance on D'Aguilar St., Central* ☎ *2121–8969* ⊗ *Closes 4 am* Ⓜ *Central.*

Fodor'sChoice

★ **Fringe Club.** The arts-minded mingle in this historic redbrick building that also houses the members-only Foreign Correspondents' Club, next door. The Fringe is the headquarters for Hong Kong's alternative arts scene, and normally stages live music twice a week. The outdoor roof bar, with its potted plants and fairy lights, is laid-back and serves reasonably priced drinks. If the weather is unfriendly, go to the ground-floor gallery bar to rub shoulders with regulars, from students to the city's who's who in arts and film. ⊠ *2 Lower Albert Rd., Central* ☎ *2521–7251* ⊗ *Closes 3 am.*

WAN CHAI

Wan Chai is the pungent night flower of the nocturnal scene, where the way of life served as inspiration for the novel *The World of Suzie Wong.* It now shares the streets with hip wine bars, salsa nights, old men's pubs, and after-parties that continue past sunrise. The seedy "hostess bars" in this neighborhood are easy to spot and avoid, with curtained entrances guarded by old ladies on stools and suggestive names in neon.

But some things never change: the busiest nights are still when there's a navy ship in the harbor on an R&R stopover. Wednesday's ladies' night, with half-price drinks, is also a big draw.

BARS

1/5 nuevo. Once one of Hong Kong's slickest nightspots, 1/5 moved down to street level in 2007 and morphed into a tapas lounge and cocktail bar, hence the addition of "nuevo" to its name. High-flyers, financiers, and expats populate this dark, sophisticated Star Street hangout. ⊠ *9 Star St., Wan Chai* ☎ *2529–2300* ⊗ *Closes 2 am* Ⓜ *Wan Chai.*

Mes Amis. In the heart of Wan Chai, on the corner of Lockhart and Luard roads, Mes Amis is a friendly, high-ceilinged bar that also serves food. Its corner setting and open bi-fold doors mean that none of the action outside is missed, and vice versa—the perpetual crowd inside is on display to those on the street. ⊠ *83 Lockhart Rd., Wan Chai* ☎ *2527–6680* ⊗ *Closes 5 am* Ⓜ *Wan Chai.*

Fodor's Choice
★ **The Pawn.** In a district plagued by controversial redevelopment, this attractive historic building, a former pawnshop, has been preserved with minimal fuss. The stylish interior is outfitted with retro furniture, while carefully selected vestiges from its less salubrious days give the space a decadent, vintage feel. The long balcony overlooking the iconic Hong Kong tramway is a great place for spying on bustling everyday life below. Upstairs is the restaurant, serving quality gastro-pub fare. Above that is the pretty, wood-accented roof garden—a favorite of the art and journalist crowds. ⊠ *62 Johnston Rd., Wan Chai* ☎ *2866–3444* ⊗ *Closes 2 am* Ⓜ *Wan Chai.*

DISCOS AND NIGHTCLUBS

Joe Bananas. This disco and bar has a reputation for all-night partying and general good times. People dressed too casually are strictly excluded: no shorts, sneakers, or T-shirts (the only exception is the Rugby Sevens weekend, when even Joe can't turn away the thirsty swarm). Arrive before 11 pm to avoid the line. ⊠ *23 Luard Rd., Wan Chai* ☎ *2529–1811* ⊗ *Closes 5 am* Ⓜ *Wan Chai.*

PUBS

Carnegie's. Named after the Scotsman and steel baron Andrew Carnegie, whose family sailed to America in the late 1800s, this rock-and-roll bar lives up to its name. Although Carnegie himself probably didn't imagine bar-top dancing to classic rock tunes at an establishment bearing his name, the Scottish owners feel that the spirit of his love of music lives on regardless. ⊠ *53–55 Lockhart Rd., Wan Chai* ☎ *2866–6289* ⊗ *Closes 3 am* Ⓜ *Wan Chai.*

KOWLOON

Central and Wan Chai are undoubtedly the king and queen of nightlife in Hong Kong. If you're staying in a hotel, however, or having dinner across the water in Kowloon, Ashley Road and Knutsford Terrace still make for a fun night out.

BARS

FodorsChoice ★ **Aqua Spirit.** Inside One Peking, an impressive curvaceous skyscraper, this very cool bar is on the mezzanine level of the top floor. The high ceilings and raking glass walls offer up unrivaled views of Hong Kong Island and the harbor filled with ferries and ships. ⊠ *29th fl. and 30th fl., One Peking, 1 Peking Rd., Tsim Sha Tsui, Kowloon* ☎ *3427–2288* ⊙ *Closes 2 am* Ⓜ *Tsim Sha Tsui.*

Bahama Mama's. You'll find tropical rhythms at the Caribbean-inspired bar, where world music plays and the kitsch props include a surfboard over the bar and the silhouette of a curvaceous woman showering behind a screen over the restroom entrance. ⊠ *4–5 Knutsford Terr., Tsim Sha Tsui, Kowloon* ☎ *2638–2121* ⊙ *Closes 4 am* Ⓜ *Tsim Sha Tsui.*

FodorsChoice ★ **Felix.** High up in the Peninsula Hotel, this bar is immensely popular with visitors; it not only has a brilliant view of the island, but the interior was designed by the visionary Philippe Starck. Don't forget to check out the padded mini-disco room. Another memorable feature is the male urinals, situated right by glass windows overlooking the city. ⊠ *28th fl., Peninsula Hong Kong, Salisbury Rd., Tsim Sha Tsui, Kowloon* ☎ *2920–2888* ⊙ *Closes 2 am* Ⓜ *Tsim Sha Tsui.*

HOSTESS CLUBS

FodorsChoice ★ **Club BBoss.** It's hard to fathom the size of a club that can accommodate 3,000 people, but with more than 60,000 square feet of space, more than 1,000 staff, a rotating stage, and three nightly cabaret shows to entertain a crowd of moneyed execs, Club BBoss is hostess paradise. Women are welcome, provided they are accompanying male customers. ⊠ *Mandarin Plaza, Tsim Sha Tsui East, Kowloon* ☎ *2369–2883* ⊙ *Closes 4 am* Ⓜ *Tsim Sha Tsui East.*

PUBS

Delaney's. Both branches of Hong Kong's pioneer Irish pub have interiors that were shipped here from the Emerald Isle, and the mood is as authentic as the furnishings. Guinness and Delaney's ale (a specialty microbrew) are on tap, and there are corner snugs (small private rooms) and an Irish menu. The crowd includes some genuine Irish regulars; get ready for spontaneous outbursts of fiddling and other Celtic traditions. Happy hour runs from 5 to 9 pm daily. ⊠ *Basement fl., 71–77 Peking Rd., Tsim Sha Tsui, Kowloon* ☎ *2301–3980* Ⓜ *Tsim Sha Tsui* ⊠ *Ground fl., One Capital Place, 18 Luard Rd., Wan Chai* ☎ *2804–2880* ⊙ *Closes 3 am* Ⓜ *Wan Chai.*

SHOPPING

By Victoria Patience and Sofia Suárez Updated by Jo Baker

They say the only way to get to know a place is to do what the locals do. When in Rome, scoot around on a Vespa and drink espresso. When in Hong Kong, shop. For most people in this city, shopping is a leisure activity, whether that means picking out a four-figure party dress, rifling through bins at an outlet, upgrading a cell phone, or choosing the freshest fish for dinner.

Shopping is so sacred that sales periods are calendar events, and most stores close on just three days a year—Christmas Day and the first two days of Chinese New Year. Imagine that: 362 days of unbridled purchasing. Opening hours are equally conducive to whiling your life away browsing the racks: all shops are open until 7 or 8 pm; many don't close their doors until midnight.

It's true that the days when everything in Hong Kong was mind-bogglingly cheap are over. It *is* still a tax-free port, so you can get some good deals. But it isn't just about the savings. Sharp contrasts and the sheer variety of experiences available make shopping here very different from back home.

You might find a bargain or two elbowing your way through a chaotic open-air market filled with haggling vendors selling designer knockoffs, the air reeking of the *chou tofu* ("stinky" tofu) bubbling at a nearby food stand. But then you could find a designer number going for half the usual price in a hushed marble-floor mall, the air scented by designer fragrances worn by fellow shoppers. What's more, in Hong Kong the two extremes are often within spitting distance of each other.

Needless to say, thanks to travelers like you running out of space in their suitcases, Hong Kong does a roaring trade in luggage. No need to feel guilty, though—shopping here is practically cultural research. All you're doing is seeing what local life is really like.

6

WESTERN

DEPARTMENT STORES

Wing On. Great values on household appliances, kitchenware, and crockery have made Wing On a favorite with locals on a budget since it opened in 1907. It also stocks clothes, cosmetics, and sportswear, but don't expect to find big brands (or even brands you know). You *can* count on rock-bottom prices and an off-the-tourist-trail experience, though. ⊠ *211 Des Voeux Rd., Central, Sheung Wan, Western* ☎ *2852–1888* ⊕ *www.wingonet.com* Ⓜ *Sheung Wan, Exit E3*⊠ *Cityplaza, 18 Tai Koo Shing Rd., Tai Koo, Eastern* Ⓜ *Tai Koo, Exit D2*⊠ *Wing On Kowloon Centre, 345 Nathan Rd., Jordan, Kowloon* Ⓜ *Jordan, Exit A.*

MARKETS

Western Market. This redbrick Victorian in the Sheung Wan district is the oldest existing market building in Hong Kong; when built in 1906 it was used as a produce market. These days the first floor has a few unmemorable shops selling crafts, toys, jewelry, and collectibles; second-floor shops sell a remarkable selection of fabric. A more surreal experience is lunch, dinner, or high tea in the Grand Stage Chinese restaurant and ballroom on the top floor. After a great Chinese meal you can while away the afternoon with the old-timers trotting around the room to a live band belting out the cha-cha and tango. ⊠ *Des Voeux Rd., Western* ⊕ *www.westernmarket.com.hk* Ⓜ *Sheung Wan.*

WHY PAY RETAIL?

As Central becomes Sheung Wan, a little lane called Wing Kut Street (between Queen's Road Central and Des Voeux Road) is home to costume-jewelry showrooms and wholesalers, many of whom accept retail customers and offer bargain-basement prices.

CLOTHING

Sin Sin Atelier. Sin Sin's conceptual, minimalist clothes, jewelry, and accessories retain a Hong Kong character, while drawing from other influences—especially Japanese. She also has an art space directly across the road and a fine art gallery up the hill in SoHo. ⊠ *Ground fl., 52 Sai St., off Hollywood Rd. at Cat St. end, Western* ☎ *2521–0308* ⊕ *www.sinsin.com.hk.*

CENTRAL

DEPARTMENT STORES

Fodor's Choice
★

City'super. Wherever you're from and whatever you're missing, whether it's fresh oysters from France or Japanese cosmetics, this gourmet supermarket and international variety store is the place to begin your search. Locals and tourists looking for gadgets, inexpensive jewelry and accessories, and quirky products like bottled water for pets often find what they're looking for here, and this store will never bore you. The Times Square location often has international-theme food festivals. Be sure to check out the Japanese imported sweets like Royce Chocolate's unusual chocolate chips. ⊠ *IFC Mall, 8 Finance St., Central* ☎ *2234–7128* ⊕ *www.citysuper.com.hk* Ⓜ *Hong Kong, Exit A1*⊠ *Times Square, 1 Matheson St., Causeway Bay* Ⓜ *Causeway Bay, Exit A*⊠ *Harbour City, 3 Canton Rd., Tsim Sha Tsui, Kowloon* Ⓜ *Tsim Sha Tsui, Exit A1.*

Sincere. Hong Kong's most eclectic department store stocks everything from frying pans to jelly beans. Run by the same family for more than a century, Sincere has several local claims to fame: it was the first store in Hong Kong to give paid days off to employees, the first to hire women in sales positions—beginning with the founder's wife and sister-in-law—and the first to establish a fixed-price policy backed up by the regionally novel idea of issuing receipts. Although you probably won't have heard of its clothes or cosmetic brands, you might come across a bargain. ⊠ *173 Des Voeux Rd., Central* ☎ *2544–2688* ⊕ *www.sincere. com.hk* Ⓜ *Sheung Wan, Exit E3.*

MALLS AND CENTERS

Fodor's Choice
★

IFC Mall. The people at the International Finance Centre love superlatives: having made Hong Kong's tallest skyscraper (Two IFC), they built the city's poshest mall under it. A quick glance at the directory—Tiffany, Kate Spade, Prada, Gieves & Hawkes—lets you know that the IFC isn't for the faint of pocket. Designer department store Lane Crawford has its flagship store here, and agnès b.'s whimsical multi-boutique fashion and lifestyle flagship sits under a large skylight styled after the shop owner's summer house in the south of France. Even the mall's cinema multiplex is special: the deluxe theaters have super-comfy seats with extra legroom and blankets for those chilled by the air conditioning. If you finish your spending spree at sunset, go for a cocktail at RED or Isola, two rooftop bars with fabulous harbor views. The Hong Kong Airport Express station (with in-town check-in service) is under the mall, and the Four Seasons Hotel connects to it. Avoid the mall between 12:30 and 2, when it's flooded with lunching office workers from the two IFC towers. ⊠ *8 Finance St., Central* ⊕ *www.ifc.com.hk* Ⓜ *Hong Kong, Exit A1.*

SPECIALTY SHOPS
ANTIQUES DEALERS

Altfield Gallery. If only your entire home could be outfitted by Altfield. Established in 1980, the elegant gallery carries exquisite antique Chinese furniture, Asia-related maps and topographical prints, Southeast Asian sculpture, and decorative arts

> **LAW ON YOUR SIDE**
>
> Although mainland law forbids that any item more than 120 years old leave China, the SAR isn't held to this rule. It's perfectly legal to ship your antique treasures home.

from around Asia, including silver artifacts and rugs. Altfield Home, on the same floor, features a selection of larger furniture pieces and china. ✉ *2nd fl., Prince's Bldg., 10 Chater Rd., Central* ☎ *2537–6370* ⊕ *www.altfield.com.hk* Ⓜ *Central.*

Chine Gallery. Dealing in antique furniture and rugs from China and furniture from Japan, this dark, stylish gallery accommodates international clients by coordinating its major exhibitions with the spring and fall auction schedules of Christie's and Sotheby's. ✉ *42A Hollywood Rd., Central* ☎ *2543–0023* ⊕ *www.chinegallery.com* Ⓜ *Central.*

Teresa Coleman Fine Arts Ltd. You can't miss the spectacular textiles hanging in the window of this busy corner shop. Specialist Teresa Coleman sells embroidered costumes from the Imperial Court, antique textiles, painted and carved fans, jewelry, lacquered boxes, and engravings and prints. ✉ *79 Wyndham St., Central* ☎ *2526–2450* ⊕ *www.teresacoleman.com* Ⓜ *Central.*

Yue Po Chai Antique Co. One of Hollywood Road's oldest shops is at the Cat Street end, next to Man Mo Temple. Its vast and varied stock includes porcelain, stone carvings, and ceramics. ✉ *Ground fl., 132–136 Hollywood Rd., Central* ☎ *2540–4374* Ⓜ *Central.*

ART GALLERIES

Alisan Fine Arts. This authority on contemporary Chinese artists sits in a quiet corner of the sleek Prince's Building shopping arcade. Styles range from traditional to abstract, and media include oil, acrylic, and Chinese ink. Founded in 1981 by Alice King, this was one of the first galleries in Hong Kong to promote the genre. ✉ *3rd fl., Prince's Bldg., 10 Chater Rd., Central* ☎ *2526–1091* ⊕ *www.alisan.com.hk.*

Grotto Fine Art. Director and chief curator Henry Au-yeung writes, curates, and gives lectures on 20th-century Chinese art. His hidden gallery (hence the "grotto" in the name) focuses exclusively on local Chinese artists, with an interest in the newest and most avant-garde works. Look for paintings, sculptures, prints, photography, mixed-media pieces, and conceptual installations. ✉ *2nd fl., 31C–D Wyndham St., Central* ☎ *2121–2270* ⊕ *www.grottofineart.com* Ⓜ *Central.*

Hanart TZ Gallery. This is a rare opportunity to compare and contrast cutting-edge and experimental art from mainland China, Taiwan, and Hong Kong selected by one of the field's most respected authorities. Unassuming curatorial director Johnson Chang Tsong-zung also cofounded the Asia Art Archive, and has curated exhibitions at the São Paolo and Venice biennials. ✉ *2nd fl., Henley Bldg., 5 Queen's Rd., Central* ☎ *2526–9019* ⊕ *www.hanart.com* Ⓜ *Central.*

6

It's easy to spend money in Hong Kong.

Schoeni Art Gallery. Known for promoting Chinese art on a global scale, this gallery, founded by Manfred Schoeni in 1992, has represented and supported various artists from mainland China with styles ranging from neorealism to postmodernism. Manfred's daughter Nicole now pinpoints exciting new artists for her prominent clientele. Past exhibition catalogs are placed atop Chinese antiques, which are also presented in this huge space. You're likely to pass the Hollywood Road branch first, but the Old Baily Street gallery, up the hill, is the bigger and better of the two. ✉ *Upper ground fl., 21–31 Old Bailey St., Central* ☎ *2869–8802* ⊕ *www.schoeniartgallery.com* Ⓜ *Central.*

CLOTHING

HONG KONG COUTURE

Barney Cheng. One of Hong Kong's best-known, locally based designers, Barney Cheng creates haute-couture designs and prêt-à-porter collections, infusing his glam, often sequined, pieces with wit. When the Kennedy Center in Washington, D.C., hosted an exhibition titled "The New China Chic," Cheng was invited to display his works alongside those by the likes of Vera Wang and Anna Sui. It's pretty much only open during office hours though, so call ahead for a weekend appointment. ✉ *12th fl., World Wide Commercial Bldg., 34 Wyndham St., Central* ☎ *2530–2829* ⊕ *www.barneycheng.com* Ⓜ *Central.*

Lu Lu Cheung. A fixture on the Hong Kong fashion scene for more than a decade, Lu Lu Cheung creates designs that ooze comfort and warmth. In both daytime and evening wear, natural fabrics and forms are represented in practical yet imaginative ways. ✉ *The Landmark, 15 Queen's Rd. Central, Central* ☎ *2537–7515* ⊕ *www.lulucheung.com.hk* Ⓜ *Central* ✉ *Shop B, G/F, 50 Wellington St., Central* Ⓜ *Central.*

Ranee K. Designer Ranee Kok Chui-Wah's showrooms are scarlet dens cluttered with her one-off dresses and eclectic women's wear that bring new meanings to "East meets West." Known for her quirky cheongsams and dresses, she has also collaborated with brands such as Furla and Shanghai Tang. Special clients and local celebrities enjoy her custom tailoring, too. ⊠ *Ground fl., 16 Gough St., Central* ☎ *2108–4068* ⊕ *www. raneek.com* Ⓜ *Central.*

Fodor's Choice
★

Shanghai Tang. In addition to the brilliantly hued—and expensive— displays of silk and cashmere clothing, you'll find custom-made suits starting at around HK$18,000, including fabric from a large selection of Chinese silks. You can also have a cheongsam (a sexy slit-skirt silk dress with a Mandarin collar) made for around HK$8,000, including fabric. Ready-to-wear Mandarin suits are in the HK$5,000–HK$6,000 range. Among the Chinese souvenirs are novelty watches with mahjongg tiles or dim sum instead of numbers. You can find outlets scattered across Hong Kong, including the airport's Terminal One. ⊠ *12 Pedder St., Central* ☎ *2525–7333* ⊕ *www.shanghaitang.com* Ⓜ *Central* ⊠ *1881 Heritage Bldg., 2A Canton Rd., Tsim Sha Tsui, Kowloon* Ⓜ *Tsim Sha Tsui.*

JEWELRY

Chocolate Rain. The collections—dreamed up by a Hong Kong fine arts graduate—consist of pieces handcrafted of recycled materials, jade, crystals, precious stones, and mother-of-pearl. The showroom also displays works by the designer's friends, and it doubles as a classroom for jewelry-making courses. ⊠ *Ground fl., 67a Peel St., SoHo, Central* ☎ *2975–8318* ⊕ *www.chocolaterain.com* Ⓜ *Central.*

Qeelin. With ancient Chinese culture for inspiration and *In The Mood for Love* actress Maggie Cheung as the muse, something extraordinary was bound to come from Qeelin. Its name was cleverly derived from the Chinese characters for male ("qi") and female ("lin"), and symbolizes harmony, balance, and peace. The restrained beauty and meaningful creations of designer Dennis Chan are exemplified in two main collections: Wulu, a minimalist form representing the mythical gourd as well as the lucky number eight; and Tien Di, literally "Heaven and Earth," symbolizing everlasting love. Classic gold, platinum, and diamonds mix with colored jades, black diamonds, and unusual materials for a truly unique effect. A sweeter addendum to the collection was added recently in the form of Bo Bo, the panda bear. ⊠ *IFC Mall, 8 Finance St., Central* ☎ *2389–8863* ⊕ *www.qeelin.com* Ⓜ *Central* ⊠ *Peninsula Shopping Arcade, Salisbury Rd., Tsim Sha Tsui, Kowloon* Ⓜ *Tsim Sha Tsui* ⊠ *Ocean Terminal, Harbour City, 3 Canton Rd., Tsim Sha Tsui, Kowloon* Ⓜ *Tsim Sha Tsui.*

Tayma Fine Jewellery. Unusual colored "connoisseur" gemstones are set by hand in custom designs by Hong Kong–based jeweler Tayma Page Allies. The collection is designed to bring out the personality of the individual wearer, and includes oversize cocktail rings, distinctive bracelets, pretty earrings, and more. ⊠ *Prince's Bldg., 10 Chater Rd., Central* ☎ *2525–5280* ⊕ *www.taymajewellery.com* Ⓜ *Central.*

6

DIAMONDS

Ronald Abram Jewellers. Looking at the rocks in these windows can feel like a visit to a natural history museum. Large white- and rare-color diamonds sourced from all over the world are a specialty here, but the shop also deals in emeralds, sapphires, and rubies. With years of expertise, Abrams dispenses advice on both the aesthetic merits and the investment potential of each stone or piece of jewelry. ⊠ *Mezzanine, Mandarin Oriental, 5 Connaught Rd., Central* ☎ *2810–7677* ⊕ *www.ronaldabram.com* Ⓜ *Central*⊠ *Mezzanine, Shop 10, Peninsula Shopping Arcade Salisbury Rd., Tsim Sha Tsui, Kowloon* Ⓜ *Tsim Sha Tsui.*

JADE

Edward Chiu. Everything about Edward Chiu is *fabulous*, from the flamboyant way he dresses to his high-end jade jewelry. The minimalist, geometric pieces use the entire jade spectrum, from deep greens to surprising lavenders. He's also famous for contrasting black-and-white jade, setting it in precious metals and adding diamond or pearl touches. ⊠ *IFC Mall, 8 Finance St., Central* ☎ *2525–2618* ⊕ *www.edwardchiu.com* Ⓜ *Central.*

PEARLS

Super Star Jewellery. Discreetly tucked in a corner of Central, Super Star looks like any other small Hong Kong jewelry shop—with walls lined by display cases filled with the usual classic designs (old-fashioned to some) in predominantly gold and precious stones. What makes them stand out are the good prices and personalized service. The cultured pearls and mixed strands of colored freshwater pearls are not all shown, so ask Lily or one of her colleagues to bring them out. ⊠ *The Galleria, 9 Queen's Rd. Central, Central* ☎ *2521–0507* Ⓜ *Central.*

WATCHES

Eldorado Watch Co Ltd. At this deep emporium of watch brands, seek the advice of one of the older staffers who look like they've been there since the British landed. Brands include Rolex, Patek Philippe, Girard-Perregaux, among others. ⊠ *Ground fl., Peter Bldg., 60 Queen's Rd., Central* ☎ *2522–7155* Ⓜ *Central.*

TAILOR-MADE CLOTHING

Blanc de Chine. Blanc de Chine has catered to high society and celebrities, such as actor Jackie Chan, for years. That's easy when you're housed on the second floor of an old colonial building (just upstairs from Shanghai Tang) and you rely on word of mouth. The small, refined tailoring shop neatly displays exquisite fabrics. Next door is the Blanc de Chine boutique filled with lovely ready-made women's wear, menswear, and home accessories. With newer stores in New York and Beijing, it appears the word is getting out. Items here are extravagances, but they're worth every penny. You'll also find another branch just opposite on the second floor of the Landmark mall. ⊠ *Pedder Bldg., 12 Pedder St., Central* ☎ *2104–7934* ⊕ *www.blancdechine.com* Ⓜ *Central.*

Linva Tailors. It's one of the best of the old-fashioned cheongsam tailors, in operation since the 1960s. Master tailor Mr. Leung takes clients through the entire process and reveals a surprising number of variations in style. Prices are affordable but vary according to fabric, which ranges from basics to special brocades and beautifully embroidered silks. ⊠ *38 Cochrane St., Central* ☎ *2544–2456* Ⓜ *Central.*

Fodor's Choice **Shanghai Tang—Imperial Tailors.** Upscale Chinese lifestyle brand Shanghai
★ Tang has the Imperial Tailors service in select stores, including the Central flagship. A fabulous interior evokes the charm of 1930s Shanghai, and gives an indication of what to expect in terms of craftsmanship and price. From silk to velvet, brocade to voile, fabrics are displayed on the side walls, along with examples of fine tailoring. The expert tailors here can make conservative or contemporary versions of the cheongsam. Men can also have a Chinese *tang* suit made to order. Expect to pay from between HK$6,000 to HK$20,000 ⊠ *Ground fl., 12 Pedder St., Central* ☎ *2525–7333* ⊕ *www.shanghaitang.com* Ⓜ *Central* ⊠ *1881 Heritage Bldg., 2A Canton Rd., Tsim Sha Tsui, Kowloon* Ⓜ *Tsim Sha Tsui.*

MEN'S TAILORS

A-Man Hing Cheong Co., Ltd. People often gasp at the very mention of A-Man Hing Cheong in the Mandarin Oriental Hotel. For some it symbolizes the ultimate in fine tailoring, with a reputation that extends back to its founding in 1898. For others it's the lofty prices that elicit a reaction. Regardless, this is a trustworthy source of European-cut suits, custom shirts, and excellent service. ⊠ *Mezzanine, Mandarin Oriental, 5 Connaught Rd., Central* ☎ *2522–3336* Ⓜ *Central.*

Ascot Chang. This self-titled "gentleman's shirtmaker" makes it easy to find the perfect shirt, even if you could get a better deal in a less prominent shop. Ascot Chang has upheld exacting Shanghainese tailoring traditions in Hong Kong since 1955, and now has stores in New York, Beverly Hills, Manila, and Shanghai, in addition to offering online ordering and regular American tours. The focus here is on the fit and details, from 22 stitches per inch to collar linings crafted to maintain their shape. Among the countless fabrics, Swiss 200s two-ply Egyptian cotton by Alumo is one of the most coveted and expensive. Like many shirtmakers, Ascot Chang does pajamas, robes, boxer shorts, and women's blouses, too. It also has developed ready-made lines of shirts, T-shirts, neckties, and other accessories. ⊠ *Prince's Bldg., 10 Chater Rd., Central* ☎ *2523–3663* ⊕ *www.ascotchang.com* Ⓜ *Central* ⊠ *IFC Mall, 8 Finance St., Central* Ⓜ *Central* ⊠ *Peninsula Hong Kong, Salisbury Rd., Tsim Sha Tsui, Kowloon* Ⓜ *Tsim Sha Tsui* ⊠ *New World Centre, InterContinental Hong Kong, 18–24 Salisbury Rd., Tsim Sha Tsui, Kowloon* Ⓜ *Tsim Sha Tsui.*

Jantzen Tailor. Catering to expatriate bankers since 1972, this reputable yet reasonable tailor specializes in classic shirts; it also makes suits and women's garments. The comprehensive Web site displays its commitment to quality, such as hand-sewn button shanks, Gygil interlining, and Coats brand thread. ⊠ *5th fl., 25 Des Voeux Rd., Central* ☎ *2570–5901 or 2810–8080* ⊕ *www.jantzentailor.com* Ⓜ *Central.*

Yuen's Tailor. Need a kilt? This is where the Hong Kong Highlanders Reel Club comes for custom-made kilts. The Yuen repertoire, however, extends to well-made suits and shirts. The tiny shop is on an unimpressive gray walkway and is filled from floor to ceiling with sumptuous European fabrics. It's a good place to have clothes copied; prices are competitive. ⊠ *2nd fl., Escalator Link Alley, 80 Des Voeux Rd., Central* ☎ *2815–5388* Ⓜ *Central.*

ADMIRALTY

CLOTHING

HONG KONG COUTURE

Vivienne Tam. You know it when you walk into a Vivienne Tam boutique—the strong Chinese-motif prints and modern updates of traditional women's clothing are truly distinct. Don't let the bold, ready-to-wear collections distract you from the very pretty accessories, which include footwear with Asian embellishments such as jade. Tam is one of the best-known Hong Kong designers and, even though she's now based outside the SAR, the city still claims her as its own. ⊠ *Pacific Place, 88 Queensway, Admiralty, Central* ☎ *2918–0238* ⊕ *www. viviennetam.com* Ⓜ *Admiralty* ⊠ *Harbour City, Canton Rd., Tsim Sha Tsui, Kowloon* Ⓜ *Tsim Sha Tsui* ⊠ *Festival Walk, 80 Tat Chee Ave., Kowloon Tong, Kowloon* Ⓜ *Central.*

DEPARTMENT STORES

Fodor'sChoice ★

Chinese Arts & Crafts. Head to this long-established mainland company to blitz through that tiresome list of presents in one fell swoop. It stocks a huge variety of well-priced brocades, silk clothing, carpets, and cheap porcelain. In direct contrast to the thrill of digging through dusty piles at the open-air Jade Market, it provides a clean, air-conditioned environment in which to shop for classic jade jewelry—the prices aren't too outrageous. Incongruously scattered throughout the shops are specialty items like large globes with lapis oceans and landmasses inlaid with semiprecious stones for a mere HK$70,000. Other more accessible—and more packable—gifts include appliqué tablecloths and cushion covers or silk dressing gowns. ⊠ *Pacific Place, Admiralty, Central* ☎ *2827–6667* ⊕ *www.cacgift.com* Ⓜ *Admiralty, Exit F* ⊠ *Asia Standard Tower, 59 Queen's Rd., Central* Ⓜ *Central, Exit D2* ⊠ *China Resources Bldg., 26 Harbour Rd., Wan Chai* Ⓜ *Wan Chai, Exit A5* ⊠ *Star House, 3 Salisbury Rd., Tsim Sha Tsui, Kowloon* Ⓜ *Tsim Sha Tsui, Exit F.*

Fodor'sChoice ★

Lane Crawford. This prestigious Western-style department store has been the favorite of local label-lovers for years—not bad for a brand that started out as a makeshift provisions shop back in 1850. The massive flagship store in the IFC Mall feels like a monument to fashion's biggest names, with exquisitely designed acres divided up into small gallerylike spaces for each designer. The phenomenal brand list includes everything from haute couture through designer denim to Agent Provocateur lingerie. Sales here are more like fashionista wrestling matches, with everyone pushing and shoving to find bargains. ⊠ *Podium 3, IFC Mall, 8 Finance St., Central* ☎ *2118–3388; 2118–7777 Lane Crawford concierge* ⊕ *www. lanecrawford.com* Ⓜ *Hong Kong, Exit A1* ⊠ *Pacific Place, 88 Queensway, Admiralty, Central* Ⓜ *Admiralty, Exit F* ⊠ *Gateway Mall, 3 Canton Rd., Tsim Sha Tsui, Kowloon* Ⓜ *Tsim Sha Tsui, Exit E* ⊠ *Times Square, 1 Matheson St., Causeway Bay* Ⓜ *Causeway Bay, Exit A.*

WAN CHAI, CAUSEWAY BAY, AND BEYOND

CLOTHING

HONG KONG CASUAL

Giordano. Hong Kong's version of the Gap is the most ubiquitous local source of basic T-shirts, jeans, and casual wear. Like its U.S. counterpart, the brand now has a bit more fashion sense and slick ad campaigns, but still offers reasonable prices. A few of its hundreds of stores are listed here, but you'll have no problem finding one on almost every major street. A new line, **Giordano Concepts,** offers more stylish (and pricier) urban wear in neutral colors. Customer service is generally good, even if the young, energetic staff screech "hello" then "bye-bye" at every customer in a particularly jarring way. ⊠ *Ground fl., Capitol Centre, 5–19 Jardine's Crescent, Causeway Bay* ☎ *2921–2955* ⊕ *www. giordano.com.hk* Ⓜ *Causeway Bay* ⊠ *Ground fl., 43–45 Queen's Rd Central., Central* Ⓜ *Central* ⊠ *Ground fl., 74–76 Nathan Rd., Tsim Sha Tsui, Kowloon* Ⓜ *Tsim Sha Tsui.*

HONG KONG CASUAL

Giordano Ladies. If Giordano is the Gap, Giordano Ladies is the Banana Republic, albeit with a more Zen approach. Find clean-line modern classics in neutral black, gray, white, and beige; each collection is brightened by a single highlight color, red one season, blue the next, and so on. Everything is elegant enough for the office and comfortable enough for the plane. ⊠ *1st fl., Capitol Centre, 5–19 Jardine's Crescent, Causeway Bay* ☎ *2923–7118* ⊕ *www.giordanoladies.com* Ⓜ *Causeway Bay* ⊠ *1st fl., Manson House, 74–78 Nathan Rd., Tsim Sha Tsui, Kowloon* Ⓜ *Tsim Sha Tsui.*

HONG KONG COUTURE

Olivia Couture. The surroundings are functional, but the gowns, wedding dresses, and cheongsams by local designer Olivia Yip are lavish. With a growing clientele, including socialites looking to stand out, Yip is quietly making a name for herself and her Parisian-influenced pieces. ⊠ *Ground fl., Bartlock Centre, 3 Yiu Wah St., Causeway Bay* ☎ *2838– 6636* ⊕ *www.oliviacouture.com* Ⓜ *Causeway Bay.*

HONG KONG COUTURE

Spy Henry Lau. Local bad boy Henry Lau brings an edgy attitude to his fashion for men and women. Bold and often dark, with a touch of bling, his clothing and accessories lines are not for the fainthearted. ⊠ *1st fl., Cleveland Mansion, 5 Cleveland St., Causeway Bay* ☎ *2317–6928* ⊕ *www.spyhenrylau.com* Ⓜ *Causeway Bay* ⊠ *Shop C, ground fl., 11 Sharp St., Causeway Bay* Ⓜ *Causeway Bay* ⊠ *21 Staunton St., SoHo, Central* Ⓜ *Central.*

GIZMOS, GADGETS, AND ACCESSORIES

Broadway. Like its more famous competitor, Fortress, Broadway is a large electronic-goods chain. It caters primarily to the local market, so some staff members speak better English than others. Look for familiar name-brand cameras, computers, sound systems, home appliances, and mobile phones. Just a few of the many shops are listed here. ⊠ *7th fl., Times Square, 1 Matheson St., Causeway Bay* ☎ *2506–0228* ⊕ *www. ibroadway.com.hk* Ⓜ *Causeway Bay* ⊠ *3rd fl., Ocean Centre, Harbour City, Canton Rd., Tsim Sha Tsui, Kowloon* Ⓜ *Tsim Sha Tsui* ⊠ *Ground fl., 78 Sai Yeung Choi St. S, Mong Kok, Kowloon* Ⓜ *Mong Kok.*

Fodor's Choice ★

Fortress. Part of billionaire Li Ka-shing's empire, this extensive chain of shops sells electronics with warranties—a safety precaution that draws

Shopping for bargains at Stanley Village Market.

the crowds. It also has good deals on printers and accessories, although selection varies by shop. You can spot a Fortress by looking for the big orange sign. For the full list of shops, visit the Web site. ⊠ *Times Square, 7th fl., 1 Matheson St., Causeway Bay* ☎ *2506–0031* ⊕ *www. fortress.com.hk* Ⓜ *Causeway Bay* ⊠ *3rd fl., Ocean Centre, Harbour City, Canton Rd., Tsim Sha Tsui, Kowloon* Ⓜ *Tsim Sha Tsui* ⊠ *Chung Kiu Commercial Bldg., 47–51 Shan Tung St., Mong Kok, Kowloon* Ⓜ *Mong Kok* ⊠ *Lower ground fl., Melbourne Plaza, 33 Queen's Rd. Central, Central* Ⓜ *Central.*

COMPUTERS **DG Lifestyle Store.** An appointed Apple Center, DG carries Mac and iPod products. High-design gadgets, accessories, and software by other brands are add-ons that meld with the sleek Apple design philosophy. ⊠ *Times Square, 1 Matheson St., Causeway Bay* ☎ *2506–1338* ⊕ *www.dg-lifestyle.com* Ⓜ *Causeway Bay* ⊠ *IFC Mall, 8 Finance St., Central* Ⓜ *Central* ⊠ *Mega Box, Kowloon Bay, Kowloon* Ⓜ *Kowloon Bay.*

Fodor'sChoice **Wanchai Computer Centre.** You'll
★ find honest-to-goodness bargains
COMPUTERS on computer goods and accessories in the labyrinth of shops here. And you can negotiate prices. Your

computer can be put together by a computer technician in less than a day if you're rushed; otherwise, two days is normal. The starting price is HK$6,000 depending on the hardware, processor, and peripherals you choose. This is a great resource, whether you're a techno-buff who's interested in assembling your own computer (a popular pastime with locals), or a technophobe looking for discounted earphones. ⊠ *130 Hennessy Rd., Wan Chai* ☎ *No phone* Ⓜ *Wan Chai.*

SOUTHSIDE

MARKETS

Fodor'sChoice

★

Stanley Village Market. This was once Hong Kong's most famed bargain trove for visitors, but its ever-growing popularity means that Stanley Village Market no longer has the best prices around. Still, you can pick up some good buys in sportswear and casual clothing if you comb through the stalls. Good-value linens—especially appliqué tablecloths—also abound. Dozens and dozens of shops line a main street so narrow that awnings from each side meet in the middle, and on busy days your elbows will come in handy. Weekdays are a little more relaxed. One of the best things about Stanley Market is getting here: the winding bus ride from Central (routes 6, 6X, 6A, or 260) or Tsim Sha Tsui (route 973) takes you over the top of Hong Kong Island, with fabulous views on the way. ⊠ *Stanley Village, Southside* ☉ *Daily 11–6.*

6

KOWLOON PENINSULA

MALLS AND CENTERS

Fodor'sChoice

★

Harbour City. The four interconnected complexes that make up Harbour City contain almost 700 shops between them—if you can't find it here, it probably doesn't exist. Pick up a map on your way in, as it's easy to get lost. **Ocean Terminal,** the largest section, runs along the harbor and is divided thematically, with kids' wear and toys on the ground floor and sports and cosmetics on the first. The top floor is home to white-hot street-wear store LCX *(⇨ above).* Near the Star Ferry pier, the **Marco Polo Hong Kong Hotel Arcade** has branches of the department store Lane Crawford. Louis Vuitton, Prada, and Burberry are some of the posher boutiques that fill the **Ocean Centre** and **Gateway Arcade,** parallel to Canton Road. Most of the complex's restaurants are here, too. A cinema and three hotels round up Harbour City's offerings. Free Wi-Fi is available. ⊠ *Canton Rd., Tsim Sha Tsui, Kowloon* ⊕ *www.harbourcity.com.hk* Ⓜ *Tsim Sha Tsui, Exit E.*

CLOTHING

CASHMERE

Fodor'sChoice

★

Pearls & Cashmere. Warehouse prices in chic shopping arcades? It's true. This old Hong Kong favorite is elegantly housed in hotels on both sides of the harbor. In addition to quality men's and women's cashmere sweaters in classic designs and in every color under the sun, they also sell reasonably priced pashminas, gloves, and socks, which make great gifts. In recent years the brand has developed the more fashion-focused line BYPAC. ⊠ *Mezzanine, Peninsula Hotel Shopping Arcade, Salisbury*

The Choice Is Joyce

Local socialites and couture addicts still thank Joyce Ma, the fairy godmother of luxury retail in Hong Kong, for bringing must-have labels to the city. Others may be catching up, but her Joyce boutiques are still ultrachic havens outfitted with a *Vogue*-worthy wish list of designers and beauty brands.

Joyce Beauty. Love finding unique beauty products from around the world? Then this is the place for you, with cult perfumes, luxurious skin solutions, and new discoveries to be made. Bring your credit card—"bargain" isn't in the vocabulary here. ⊠ *Ground fl., New World Tower, 16–18 Queen's Rd. Central, Central* ☎ *2367-0860* Ⓜ *Central*⊠ *The Gateway, 3–27 Canton Rd., Tsim Sha Tsui, Kowloon* Ⓜ *Tsim Sha Tsui*⊠ *Festival Walk, 80 Tat Chee Ave., Kowloon Tong, Kowloon* Ⓜ *Kowloon Tong.*

Joyce Boutique. Not so much a shop as a fashion institution, Joyce Boutique's hushed interior houses the worship-worthy creations of fashion's greatest gods and goddesses. McCartney, Galliano, Dolce

& Gabbana, Prada, Miyake: the stock list is practically a mantra. Joyce sells unique household items, too, so your home can live up to your wardrobe. ⊠ *New World Tower, 16 Queen's Rd., Central* ☎ *2810-1120* ⊕ *www.joyce. com* Ⓜ *Central, Exit G* ⊠ *Pacific Place, 88 Queensway, Admiralty, Central* Ⓜ *Admiralty, Exit F* ⊠ *Harbour City, Tsim Sha Tsui, Kowloon* Ⓜ *Tsim Sha Tsui, Exit F.*

Joyce Warehouse. Fashionistas who've fallen on hard times can breathe a sigh of relief. Joyce's outlet on Ap Lei Chau, the island offshore from Aberdeen in Southside, stocks last season's duds from the likes of Jil Sander, Armani, Ann Demeulemeester, Costume National, and Missoni. Prices for each garment are reduced by about 10% each month, so the longer the piece stays on the rack, the less it costs. Bus 90B gets you from Exchange Square to Ap Lei Chau in 25 minutes; then hop a taxi for the four-minute taxi ride to Horizon Plaza. ⊠ *21st fl., Horizon Plaza, 2 Lee Wing St., Southside* ☎ *2814-8313* ⊗ *Mon.–Sun. 10–7.*

Rd., Tsim Sha Tsui, Kowloon ☎ *2723–8698* Ⓜ *Tsim Sha Tsui* ⊠ *Mezzanine, Mandarin Oriental, 5 Connaught Rd., Central* Ⓜ *Central.*

JEWELRY

WATCHES **Artland Watch Co Ltd.** Elegant but uncomplicated, the interior of this established watch retailer is like its service. The informed staff will guide you through the countless luxury brands on show and in the catalogs from which you can also order. Prices here aren't the best in Hong Kong, but they're still lower than at home. ⊠ *Ground fl., Mirador Mansion, 54–64B Nathan Rd., Tsim Sha Tsui, Kowloon* ☎ *2366–1074* Ⓜ *Tsim Sha Tsui* ⊠ *Ground fl., New Henry House, 10 Ice House St., Central* Ⓜ *Central.*

DIAMONDS **TSL Jewellery.** One of the big Hong Kong chains, TSL (Tse Sui Luen), specializes in diamond jewelry, and manufactures, retails, and exports its designs. Its range of 100-facet stones includes the Estrella cut, which reflects nine symmetrical hearts and comes with international certification. Although its contemporary designs use platinum settings, TSL also sells pure, bright, yellow-gold items targeted at Chinese customers. ⊠ *G9–10, Park Lane Shopper's Blvd., Nathan Rd., Tsim Sha Tsui, Kowloon* ☎ *2332–4618* ⊕ *www.tsljewellery.com* Ⓜ *Tsim Sha Tsui* ⊠ *Ground fl., 1 Yee Woo St., Causeway Bay* Ⓜ *Causeway Bay.*

TAILOR-MADE CLOTHING
MEN'S TAILORS

David's Shirts Ltd. Customers have been enjoying the personalized service of David Chu since 1961. All the work is done in-house by Shanghai-nese tailors with at least 20 years' experience each. There are more than 6,000 imported European fabrics to choose from, each prewashed. Examples of shirts, suits, and accessories—including 30 collar styles, 12 cuff styles, and 10 pocket styles—help you choose. Single-needle tailoring, French seams, 22 stitches per inch, handpicked, double-stitched shell buttons, German interlining—it's all here. Your details, down to on which side you wear your wristwatch, are kept on file should you wish to use its mail-order service in the future. ⊠ *Ground fl., Wing Lee Bldg., 33 Kimberley Rd., Tsim Sha Tsui, Kowloon* ☎ *2367–9556* ⊕ *www.davidsshirts.com* ⊠ *Mezzanine, Mandarin Oriental, 5 Connaught Rd., Central* Ⓜ *Central.*

Maxwell's Clothiers Ltd. After you've found a handful of reputable, high-quality tailors, one way to choose between them is price. Maxwell's is known for its competitive rates. It's also a wonderful place to have favorite shirts and suits copied and for straightforward, structured women's shirts and suits. It was founded by third-generation tailor Ken Maxwell in 1961 and follows Shanghai tailoring traditions, while also providing the fabled 24-hour suit upon request. The showroom and workshop are in Kowloon, but son Andy and his team take appointments in the United States, Canada, and Europe twice annually. The motto of this family business is "Simply let the garment do the talking." ⊠ *7th fl., Han Hing Mansion, 38–40 Hankow Rd., Tsim Sha Tsui, Kowloon* ☎ *2366–6705* ⊕ *www.maxwellsclothiers.com* Ⓜ *Tsim Sha Tsui.*

Fodor's Choice ★ **Sam's Tailor.** Unlike many famous Hong Kong tailors, you won't find the legendary Sam's in a chic hotel or sleek mall. But don't be fooled. These digs in humble Burlington House, a tailoring hub, have hosted everyone from U.S. presidents (back as far as Richard Nixon) to performers such as the Black Eyed Peas, Kylie Minogue, and Blondie. This former uniform tailor to the British troops once even made a suit for Prince Charles in a record one hour and 52 minutes. The men's and women's tailor does accept 24-hour suit or shirt orders, but will take about two days if you're not in a hurry. Founded by Naraindas Melwani in the 1950s, "Sam" is now his son, Manu Melwani, who runs the show with the help of his own son, Roshan, and about 55 tailors behind the scenes. In 2004 Sam's introduced a computerized bodysuit that takes measurements without a tape measure. (It uses both methods, however.) These tailors also make annual trips to Europe and North America. (Schedule updates are listed on the Web site). ⊠ *Burlington House, 90–94 Nathan Rd., Tsim Sha Tsui, Kowloon* ☎ *2367–9423* ⊕ *www.samstailor.com* Ⓜ *Tsim Sha Tsui.*

6

W. W. Chan & Sons Tailors Ltd. Chan is known for excellent-quality suits and shirts, classic cuts, and has an array of fine European fabrics. It's comforting to know that you'll be measured and fitted by the same master tailor from start to finish. The Kowloon headquarters features a mirrored, hexagonal changing room so you can check every angle. Tailors from here travel to the United States several times a year to fill orders for its customers; if you have a suit made here and leave your address, they'll let you know when they plan to visit. ⊠ *2nd fl., Burlington House, 92–94 Nathan Rd., Tsim Sha Tsui, Kowloon* 🕾 *2366–9738 or 2366–2634* ⊕ *www.wwchan.com* Ⓜ *Tsim Sha Tsui.*

WOMEN'S TAILORS

Mode Elegante. Don't be deterred by the somewhat dated mannequins in the windows. Mode Elegante is a favorite source for custom-made suits among women and men in the know. Tailors here specialize in European cuts. You'll have your choice of fabrics from the United Kingdom, Italy, and elsewhere. Your records are put on file so you can place orders from abroad. It'll even ship the completed garment to you almost anywhere on the planet. Alternatively, you can make an appointment with director Gary Zee, one of Hong Kong's traveling tailors who make regular visits to North America, Europe, and Japan. ⊠ *11th fl., Star House, 3 Salisbury Rd., Tsim Sha Tsui, Kowloon* 🕾 *2366–8153* ⊕ *www.modeelegante.com* Ⓜ *Tsim Sha Tsui.*

DEPARTMENT STORES

Fodor'sChoice ★ **Yue Hwa Chinese Products Emporium.** Five floors contain Chinese goods, ranging from clothing and housewares through tea and traditional medicine. The logic behind the store's layout is hard to fathom, so go with time to rifle around. As well as the predictable tablecloths, silk pajamas, and chopstick sets, there are cheap and colorful porcelain sets and offbeat local favorites like mini-massage chairs. The top floor is entirely given over to tea—you can pick up a HK$50 packet of leaves or an antique Yixing teapot stretching into the thousands. ⊠ *301–309 Nathan Rd., Jordan, Kowloon* 🕾 *3511–2222* ⊕ *www.yuehwa.com* Ⓜ *Jordan, Exit A* ⊠ *55 Des Voeux Rd., Central* Ⓜ *Central, Exit B* ⊠ *1 Kowloon Park Dr., Tsim Sha Tsui, Kowloon* Ⓜ *Tsim Sha Tsui, Exit E.*

MALLS AND CENTERS

Fodor'sChoice ★ **Festival Walk.** Don't be put off by Festival Walk's location in residential Kowloon Tong—it's 20 minutes from Central on the MTR. Make the effort to get here: Festival Walk has everything from Giordano (Hong Kong's answer to the Gap) to Vivienne Tam. By day the six floors sparkle with sunlight, which filters through the glass roof. Marks & Spencer and Esprit serve as anchors; Armani Exchange and Calvin Klein draw the elite crowds; while Camper and agnès b. keep the trend spotters happy. Hong Kong's best bookstore, Page One, has a big branch downstairs. The mall also has one of the city's largest ice

> ### WORD OF MOUTH
>
> "Go to the bird market and flower market early in the morning, with a stop at the Jade Market and then a visit to the Wong Tai Sin temple to get your fortune told, and that is a morning in Kowloon."
> —Cicerone

rinks, as well as a multiplex cinema, perfect if you're shopping with kids who want a respite from the sometimes scorching-hot weather. ⊠ *80 Tat Chee Ave., Kowloon Tong, Kowloon* ⊕ *www.festivalwalk.com.hk* Ⓜ *Kowloon Tong, Exit C2.*

MARKETS

Flower Market. Huge bucketfuls of roses and gerbera spill out onto the sidewalk along Flower Market Road, a collection of street stalls selling cut flowers and potted plants. Delicate orchids and vivid birds of paradise are some of the more exotic blooms. During Chinese New Year there's a roaring trade in narcissi, poinsettias, and bright yellow chrysanthemums, all auspicious flowers. ⊠ *Flower Market Rd., off Prince Edward Rd. W, Mong Kok, Kowloon* ☉ *Daily 7 am–7:30 pm* Ⓜ *Prince Edward, Exit B1.*

Ⓒ **Goldfish Market.** Goldfish are considered auspicious in Hong Kong (though aquariums must be positioned in the right place to bring good luck to the family), and this small collection of shops is a favorite local source. Shop fronts are decorated with bags of glistening, pop-eyed creatures waiting for someone to take them home. Some of the fishes inside shops are rarities and fetch unbelievable prices. ⊠ *Tung Choi St., Mong Kok, Kowloon* ☉ *Daily 10–6* Ⓜ *Mong Kok, Exit B2.*

Kansu Street Jade Market. Jade in every shade of green, from the milkiest apple tone to the richest emerald, fills the stalls of this market. If you know your stuff and haggle insistently, you can get fabulous bargains. Otherwise, stick to cheap trinkets. Some of the so-called "jade" sold here is actually aventurine, bowenite, soapstone, serpentine, and Australian jade—all inferior to the real thing. ⊠ *Kansu St. off Nathan Rd., Yau Ma Tei, Kowloon* ☉ *Daily 10–4* Ⓜ *Yau Ma Tei, Exit C.*

Ladies' Market. Block upon block of tightly packed stalls overflow with clothes, bags, and knickknacks along Tung Choi Street in Mong Kok. Despite the name, there are clothes for women, men, and children here. Most offerings are imitations or no-name brands; rifle around enough and you can often pick up some cheap and cheerful basics. Haggling is the rule here: a poker face and a little insistence can get you dramatic discounts. At the corner of each block and behind the market are stands and shops selling the street snacks Hong Kongers can't live without. Pick a place where locals are munching and point at whatever takes your fancy. Parallel **Fa Yuen Street** is Mong Kok's unofficial sportswear market. ⊠ *Tung Choi St., Mong Kok, Kowloon* ☉ *Daily noon–11 pm* Ⓜ *Mong Kok, Exit E.*

Fodor's Choice ★ **Temple Street Night Market.** Each night, as it gets dark, the lamps strung between the stalls of this Yau Ma Tei street market slowly light up, and the air fills with the smells wafting from myriad food carts. Hawkers try to catch your eye by flinging clothes up from their stalls. Cantonese opera competes with pop music, and vendors' cries and shoppers' haggling fills the air. Adding to the color here are the fortune-tellers and the odd magician or acrobat who has set up shop in the street. Granted, neither the clothes nor cheap gadgets on sale here are much to get excited about, but it's the atmosphere people come for—any purchases are a bonus. The market stretches for almost a mile, and is one of Hong Kong's liveliest nighttime shopping experiences. ⊠ *Temple St., Mong Kok, Kowloon* ⊙ *Daily 5 pm–midnight; best after 8 pm* Ⓜ *Jordan, Exit A.*

CLOTHING

HONG KONG CASUAL

F.C.K. (Fashion Community Kitterick). One of the trendiest local chains sells several brands including Kitterick, indu homme, K-2, a.y.k., and the Lab. These are clothes that Hong Kong's brand-conscious youth are happy to wear. ⊠ *6th fl, Langham Place Mall, 8 Argyle St., Mong Kong, Kowloon* ☎ *2721–0836* ⊕ *www.kitterick.com.hk* Ⓜ *Mong Kok* ⊠ *Silvercord 30 Canton Rd., Tsim Sha Tsui, Kowloon* Ⓜ *Tsim Sha Tsui.*

JEWELRY

PEARLS **Sandra Pearls.** You might be wary of the lustrous pearls hanging at this little Jade Market stall. The charming owner, Sandra, does, in fact, sell genuine and reasonably priced cultured and freshwater pearl necklaces and earrings. Some pieces are made from shell, which Sandra is always quick to point out, and could pass muster among the snobbiest collectors. ⊠ *Stalls 381 and 447, Jade Market, Kansu St., Yau Ma Tei, Kowloon* ☎ *9485–2895* Ⓜ *Yau Ma Tei.*

> ### ITS GOOD TO BE JADED
>
> The Chinese believe that jade brings luck, and it's still worn as a charm in amulets or bracelets. A jade bangle is often presented to newborns, and homes are often adorned with jade statues or other carved decorative items.

SIDE TRIP TO MACAU

By Hiram Chu
Updated by
Doretta Lau

Enter the desperate, smoky atmosphere of a Chinese casino, where frumpy players bet an average of five times more than the typical Vegas gambler. Sit down next to grandmothers who smoke like chimneys while playing baccarat—the local game of choice—with visiting high rollers. Then step out of the climate-controlled chill and into tropical air that embraces you like a warm, balmy hug. Welcome to Macau.

The many contrasts in this tiny enclave of 559,000 people serve as reminders of how very different cultures have embraced one another's traditions for hundreds of years. Though Macau's population is 95% ethnic Chinese, there are still vibrant pockets of Portuguese and Filipino expats. And some of the thousands of Eurasians—who consider themselves neither Portuguese nor Chinese, but something in between—can trace the intermarriage of their ancestors back a century or two.

Macau's old town, while dominated by the buildings, squares, and cobblestone alleyways of colonial Portugal, is tinged with eastern influences as well, as in the Buddhist temple at the intersection of the Travessa de Dom Quixote and Travessa de Sancho Panca. In Macau you can spend an afternoon strolling the black sands of Hác-Sá Beach before feasting on a dinner of *bacalhau com natas* (dried codfish with a cream sauce), grilled African chicken (spicy chicken in a coconut-peanut broth—a classic Macanese dish), Chinese lobster with scallions, or fiery prawns infused with Indian and Malaysian flavors. Wash everything down with *vinho verde*, the crisp young wine from northern Portugal, and top it all off with a traditional Portuguese *pastel de nata* (egg-custard tart) and dark, thick espresso.

EXPLORING MACAU

Macau is a small place, where on a good day you could drive from one end to the other in 30 minutes. This makes walking and bicycling ideal ways to explore winding city streets, nature trails, and long stretches of beach. Most of Macau's population lives on the peninsula attached to mainland China. The region's most famous sights are here—Senado Square, the Ruins of St. Paul's, A-Ma Temple—as are most of the luxury hotels and casinos. As in the older sections of Hong Kong, cramped older buildings stand comfortably next to gleaming new structures.

TOURS

Depending on your mind-set, tours of Macau can either be spontaneously joined or meticulously made-to-order. If you're just debarking for the day at the main ferry terminal, find the **New Sintra Tours** (✉ *Macau Ferry Terminal, Av. da Amizade P853/2872–8050*) counter, where you can book tours for the day.

For a tour of the islands, **Cotai Travel** (✉ *Shop 1028, Venetian Macao-Resort-Hotel* ☎ *853/8118–2930 or 853/8118–2833*) hosts daily tours from 9 to 1 that include the Taipa Houses Museum and the A-Ma Cultural Village on Coloane for MOP$270 per person.

Book at least one day in advance from one of many travel agents in Hong Kong. Browse your options at the travel counters of the main ferry terminals in either Macau or Hong Kong, or check ⊕ *www.macautourism.gov.mo* for a list of authorized travel agencies in Macau; some offer tours in multiple languages.

Estoril Tours (✉ *Shop 3711, 3rd fl., Shun Tak Centre, 200 Connaught Rd., Central, Hong Kong* ☎ *2559–1028* ⊕ *www.estoril.com.mo*) will customize a private group tour, from bungee-jumping off the Macau Tower to wandering through Coloane Village or a day visiting museums.

GETTING HERE AND AROUND

AIR TRAVEL International flights (from Asia) come into Macau, but there are no planes from Hong Kong. Fifteen-minute helicopter flights fly between Hong Kong's Shun Tak Centre and the Macau Ferry Terminal on Sky Shuttle; they leave every 30 minutes from 9 am to 11 pm daily. Prices are HK$2,600 Monday to Thursday with a HK$200 surcharge on Friday, Saturday, Sunday, and holidays. Reservations are essential.

Sky Shuttle (☎ *853/2872–7288 Macau Terminal; 2108–9898 Shun Tak Centre* ⊕ *www.skyshuttlehk.com*).

Macau International Airport (☎ *853/2886–1111* ⊕ *www.macau-airport.gov.mo*).

FERRY TRAVEL Ferries run every 15 minutes with a reduced schedule from midnight to 7 am. Prices for economy/ordinary and super/deluxe run HK$134–HK$275. VIP cabins begin at HK$944 (four seats) to HK$1,416 (six seats). Weekday traffic is usually light, so you can buy tickets right before departure. Weekend tickets often sell out, so make reservations. You can book tickets up to 90 days in advance with China Travel

THE BASICS

The Macau Government Tourist Office (MGTO) is well managed. **Macau Government Tourist Office** (*MGTO ⊠ Macau Ferry Terminal, Macau ☎ 853/2833–3000 ⊕ www. macautourism.gov.mo ⊠ Shun Tak Centre, 200 Connaught Rd., Central, Hong Kong ☎ 2857–2287*).

To enter Macau, Americans, Canadians, and EU citizens need only a valid passport for stays of up to 90 days.

The Macanese pataca (MOP) has a fixed exchange rate of MOP$1.032 to HK$1 and roughly MOP$7 to US$1. Patacas come in 10, 20, 50, 100, 500, and 1,000 MOP banknotes plus 1, 5, and 10 MOP coins. A pataca is divided into 100 avos, which come in 10-, 20-, and 50-avo coins. Hong Kong dollars are accepted in Macau on a 1:1 basis.

Language: Chinese and Portuguese are Macau's official languages. Cantonese and Mandarin are widely spoken. English is unreliable outside tourist areas. It's best to print your destination in Chinese characters for taxi drivers.

Service (⊕ *www.ctshk.com*) agencies or directly with CotaiJet or TurboJET by phone or online. Booking by phone requires a Visa card. You must pick up tickets at the terminal at least a half hour before departure.

Most ferries leave from Hong Kong's Shun Tak Centre Sheung Wan MTR station in Central, though limited service is available from First Ferry at Kowloon's Tsim Sha Tsui terminal. In Macau most ferries disembark from the main Macau Ferry Terminal, but CotaiJet services the terminal on Taipa Island. The trip takes one hour one way. Buses, taxis, and free shuttles to most casinos and hotels await on the Macau side.

CotaiJet (☎ *853/2885–0595 in Macau, 2359–9990 in Hong Kong ⊕ www.cotaijet.com.mo*). **First Ferry** (☎ *2131–8181 ⊕ www.nwff.com. hk*). **TurboJET** (☎ *2859–3333 information, 2921–6688 reservations ⊕ www.turbojet.com.hk*).

BUS TRAVEL Public buses are clean and affordable; trips to anywhere in the Macau Peninsula cost MOP$3.20. Service to Taipa Island is MOP$4.20, service to Coloane is MOP$5, and the trip to Hác Sá is MOP$6.40. Buses run 6:30–midnight and require exact change upon boarding. But you can get downtown for free, via casino shuttles, from the official Border Gate crossing just outside mainland China, from the airport, and from the Macau Ferry Terminal.

CAR TRAVEL As in Hong Kong, Macau motorists drive on the left-hand side of the road. Road signs are in Chinese and Portuguese only. Rental cars with Avis are available at the Grand Lapa Hotel. Regular cars start at MOP$499 on weekdays and MOP$599 on weekends. Book three to four days in advance for weekend rentals.

Avis (☎ *853/2833–6789 in Macau, 2926–1126 in Hong Kong ⊕ www. avis.com*).

BY TAXI Taxis are inexpensive but not plentiful in Macau. The best places to catch a cab are the major casinos—the Wynn, Sands, and Venetian. Carry a bilingual map or ask the concierge at your hotel to write the

Pedestrian-only Largo do Senado preserves the Portuguese influence that shaped Macau for centuries.

name of your destination in Chinese. All taxis are metered, air-conditioned, and reasonably comfortable. The base charge is MOP$13 for the first 1.6 km (1 mi) and MOP$1.50 per additional 230 m. Trips between Coloane and either the Macau Peninsula or Taipa incur respective surcharges of MOP$5 or MOP$2. Drivers don't expect a tip.

DOWNTOWN MACAU

Chances are you'll arrive at the Macau Ferry Terminal after sailing from Hong Kong. There's not much to see around the terminal itself, so hop into one of the many waiting casino or hotel shuttles and head straight downtown, less than 10 minutes away. From there it's a short walk to the city's historic center, along the short stretch of road named Avenida Almeida Ribeiro, more commonly known as San Ma Lo, which is Macau's commercial and cultural heart.

TOP ATTRACTIONS

Fodor'sChoice ★ **Fortaleza da Guia.** The Guia Fortress, built between 1622 and 1638 on Macau's highest hill, was key to protecting the Portuguese from invaders. You can walk the steep, winding road up to the fortress or take a five-minute cable-car ride from the entrance of Flora Garden on Avenida Sidónio Pais. Once inside the fort, notice the gleaming white Guia Lighthouse (you can't go inside, but you can get a good look at the exterior) that's lit every night. Next to it is the Guia Chapel, built by Clarist nuns to provide soldiers with religious services. The chapel is no longer used for services, but restoration work in 1998 uncovered elaborate frescoes mixing Western and Chinese themes. They're best seen when the morning or afternoon sun floods the chapel. ⊠ *Guia Hill, Downtown* ☎ *853/8399–6699* ⊠ *Free* ☺ *Daily 9–5:30.*

Fodor's Choice
★

Largo do Senado. The charming Senado Square, Macau's hub for centuries, is lined with neoclassical-style colonial buildings painted bright pastels. Only pedestrians are allowed on its shiny black-and-white tiles, and the alleys off it are packed with restaurants and shops. Take your time wandering. There are plenty of benches on which to rest after shopping and sightseeing. Come back at night, when locals of all ages gather to chat and the square is beautifully lit.

The magnificent yellow **Igreja de São Domingos** (*St. Dominic's Church* ✉ *Largo de São Domingos, Downtown* ☎ *No phone* ⏱ *Daily 8–6*) beckons you to take a closer look. After a restoration in 1997, it's again among Macau's most beautiful churches, with a cream-and-white interior that takes on a heavenly golden glow when illuminated for services. The church was originally a convent founded by Spanish Dominican friars in 1587. In 1822 China's first Portuguese newspaper, *The China Bee*, was published here. The church became a repository for sacred art in 1834 when convents were banned in Portugal.

It's hard to ignore the imposing white facade of **Santa Casa da Misericordia** (✉ *2 Travessa da Misericordia* ☎ *853/2857–3938 or 853/8399–6699* 🎟 *MOP$5* ⏱ *Mon.–Sat. 10–1 and 2–5:30*). Founded in 1569 by Dom Belchior, Macau's first bishop, the Holy House of Mercy is the China coast's oldest Christian charity, and it continues to take care of the poor with soup kitchens and health clinics, as well as providing housing for the elderly. The exterior is neoclassical, but the interior is done in a contrasting opulent, modern style. A reception room on the second floor contains paintings of benefactress Marta Merop.

The neoclassical **Edificio do Leal Senado** (*Senate Bldg.* ✉ *163 Av. de Almeida Ribeiro, Downtown* ☎ *853/2833–7676* 🎟 *Free* ⏱ *Tues.–Sun. 9–9*) was built in 1784 as a municipal chamber and continues to be used by the government today. An elegant meeting room on the first floor opens onto a magnificent library based on one in the Mafra Convent in Portugal, with books neatly stacked on two levels of shelves reaching to the ceiling. Art and historical exhibitions are frequently hosted in the beautiful foyer and garden. ✉ *Downtown*.

Macau Canidrome. The greyhound track looks run-down and quaint compared to the bigger Jockey Club and glitzy casinos, but it offers a true taste of Macau in a more popular neighborhood near the China border crossing. The Canidrome opened in 1932; it tends to attract a steady crowd of older gamblers several times a week for the slower-pace, lower-stakes gambling rush of betting on fast dogs chasing an electronic rabbit. Check out the parade of race dogs before each race. You can sit on benches in the open-air stadium, at tables in the air-conditioned restaurant, or in an upstairs box seat. ✉ *Av. do Artur Tamagnini Barbosa at Av. General Castelo Branco, Downtown* ☎ *853/2833–3399, 853/2826–1188 to place bets* ⊕ *www.macauyydog.com* 🎟 *Public stands MOP$10, private boxes MOP$120* ⏱ *Mon., Thurs., and weekends 6 pm–11 pm; first race at 7:30.*

Fodor's Choice
★

Macau Tower Convention & Entertainment Centre. Rising 1,000 feet above the peaceful San Van Lake, the world's 10th-largest freestanding tower recalls Sky Tower, a similar structure in Auckland, New Zealand. And it should, as both were designed by New Zealand architect Gordon Moller. The Macau Tower offers a variety of thrills, including the Mast Climb, which challenges the daring and strong of heart and body with a two-hour climb on steel rungs 344 feet up the tower's mast for incomparable views of Macau and China. Other thrills include the Skywalk, an open-air stroll around the tower's exterior—without handrails; the SkyJump, an assisted, decelerated 765-foot descent; and the classic bungee jump. More subdued attractions inside the tower are a mainstream movie theater and a revolving lunch and dinner buffet at the 360 Café. ⊠ *Largo da Torre de Macau, Downtown* ☎ *853/2893–3339* ⊕ *www.macautower.com.mo* ✉ *MOP$588 for the Skywalk to MOP$1; 888 for the Mast Climb; photos extra* ⊙ *Observation deck: weekdays 10–8:45, weekends and holidays 9–8:45.*

> **WORLD HERITAGE**
>
> In 2005 "The Historic Centre of Macau" was listed as China's 31st UNESCO World Heritage Site. The term "center" is misleading, as the site is really a collection of churches, buildings, and neighborhoods that colorfully illustrate Macau's 400-year history. Included in it are China's oldest examples of Western architecture and the region's most extensive concentration of missionary churches.

Fodor's Choice **Ruínas de São Paulo** *(Ruins of St. Paul's Church).* Only the magnificent, ★ towering facade, with its intricate carvings and bronze statues, remains from the original Church of Mater Dei, built between 1602 and 1640 and destroyed by fire in 1835. The church, an adjacent college, and Mount Fortress, all Jesuit constructions, once formed East Asia's first Western-style university. Now the widely adopted symbol of Macau, the ruins are a primary tourist attraction, with snack bars and antiques and other shops at the foot of the site.

Behind the facade of São Paulo is the **Museum of Sacred Art and Crypt** (☎ *No phone* ✉ *Free* ⊙ *Daily 9–6*), which holds statues, crucifixes, and the bones of Japanese and Vietnamese martyrs. There are also some intriguing Asian interpretations of Christian images, including samurai angels and a Chinese Virgin and Child.

The **Templo de Na Tcha** is a small Chinese temple built in 1888, during the Macauan plague. The hope was that Na Tcha Temple would appeal to a mythical Chinese character who granted wishes and could save lives. The **Troco das Antigas Muralhas de Defesa** (Section of the Old City Walls) is all that remains of Macau's original defensive barrier, and borders the left side of the Na Tcha Temple. These crumbling yellow walls were built in 1569 and illustrate the durability of *chunambo*, a local material made from compacted layers of clay, soil, sand, straw, crushed rocks, and oyster shells. ⊠ *Top end of Rua de São Paulo, Downtown* ☎ *853/8399–6699* ⊙ *Daily 8–5.*

Fodor's Choice **Templo de A-Ma** *(A-Ma Temple).* Thought to be Macau's oldest building, ★ this temple, properly Ma Kok Temple but known to locals as simply A-Ma, is also one of Macau's most picturesque. The structure had its origins in the Ming Dynasty (1368–1644), and was influenced by Confucianism, Taoism, and Buddhism, as well as local religions. Vivid red calligraphy on large boulders tells the story of the goddess A-Ma (also known as Tin Hau), the patron of fishermen. A small gate opens onto prayer halls, pavilions, and caves carved directly into the hillside. ⊠ *Rua de São Tiago da Barra, Largo da Barra, Downtown* ⊙ *Daily 7–6.*

WORTH NOTING

⟳ **Macau Fisherman's Wharf.** More of a distraction than an amusement park, this developing complex of minor attractions nonetheless has an Old World decadence. Its centerpiece is the Roman Amphitheatre, which hosts outdoor performances, but its main draws are the lively themed restaurants on the west side, such as AfriKana B.B.Q and Camões. Across from the toylike Babylon Casino, the Rocks Hotel heralds a series of themed accommodations to come. Children's rides and games, on the east end, include a role-playing war game and an underground video-game arcade. Come for the food and stay after dark, as Fisherman's Wharf is even more active at night. ⊠ *Av. da Amizade, at Av. Dr. Sun Yat Sen, Downtown* ☎ *853/8299–3300* ⊕ *www.fishermanswharf.com.mo* ☜ *Admission free, rides and games MOP$20–MOP$200* ⊙ *Open 24 hours.*

Quartel dos Mouros. The elegant yellow-and-white building with Moorish architectural influences built onto a slope of Barra Hill is the Moorish Barracks. It now houses the Macau Maritime Administration, but was originally constructed in 1874 for Indian police regiments brought into the region, a reminder of Macau's historic relationship with the Indian city of Goa. The barracks are not open to the public but visitors can tour the ornamented veranda. ⊠ *Barra Hill, Inner Harbour* ☎ *853/8399–6699* ☜ *Free* ⊙ *Veranda open 24 hours.*

TAIPA ISLAND

The island directly south of peninsular Macau was once two small islands that were, over time, joined by deposits from the Pearl River Delta. It's connected to peninsular Macau by three long bridges. The region's two universities, horse-racing track, scenic hiking trails, and its international airport are all here.

Like downtown Macau, Taipa has been greatly developed in the past few years, yet it retains a visual balance between old Macau charm and modern sleekness. Try to visit on a weekend, so you can shop for clothing and crafts in the traditional flea market that's held every Sunday from morning to evening in Taipa Village.

Macau Jockey Club. After Dr. Stanley Ho bought the Macau Jockey Club (MJC) in 1991, he transformed what was a quiet trotting track into a lucrative high-stakes racing facility. However horse racing is now a more retro gambling option in Asia's rising casino hotspot of Macau, and the local MJC pales in comparison to the truly world-class Hong Kong Jockey Club. Nonetheless the MJC continues to operate year-round, hosting an average of 100 races and entertaining a majority of local middle-aged men, as well as some younger, more curious spectators who come to see the horses close up in between races (every 30 minutes). If you're game, you can place bets at a number of stations throughout Macau and Hong Kong, as well as by phone and on the Internet. ⊠ *Estrada Governador Albano de Oliveira, Taipa* ☎ *853/2882–0868* ⊕ *www.macauhorse.com* ☜ *Grandstand seating MOP$20.*

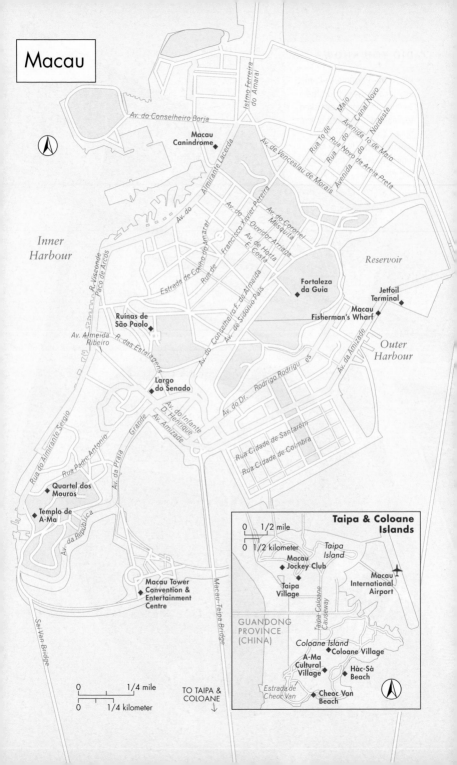

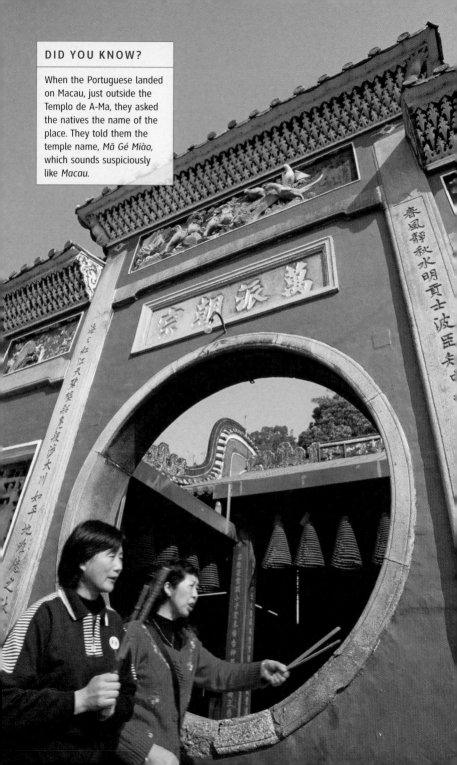

FodorśChoice
★
Taipa Village. Its winding streets are packed with restaurants, bakeries, shops, temples, and other buildings with traditional South Chinese and Portuguese design elements. The aptly named Rua do Cunha (Food Street) has many great Chinese, Macanese, Portuguese, and Thai restaurants. Several shops sell homemade Macanese snacks, including steamed milk pudding, almond cakes, beef jerky, and coconut candy.

Atop a small hill overlooking Taipa Village, the beautiful **Carmel Garden** (⊠ *Av. de Carlos da Maia, Taipa* ✆ *Free* ☉ *Daily 24 hours*) has a number of palm trees that provide great shade. Within the garden stands the brilliant white-and-yellow Nossa Senhora do Carmo (Church of Our Lady of Carmel), built in 1885 and featuring a hand-some single-belfry tower. Paths lead down from the Carmel Garden to the **Taipa Houses-Museum** (⊠ *Av. da Praia, Carmo Zone, Taipa* ☎ *853/2882–7103* ✆ *MOP$5; free Sun.* ☉ *Tues.–Sun. 10–6*). These five sea-green houses were originally residences of wealthy local merchants, and were converted into small museums and exhibition spaces. They were all fully restored shortly before the Macau handover, and are interesting examples of Porto-Chinese architecture. Official receptions are often held here, as are changing art exhibitions. The Venetian Casino and the Cotai complex construction block a once marvelous view of Coloane and the South China Sea.

> **WORD OF MOUTH**
>
> "I do enjoy the old town parts of Macau city, and also find that Taipa and Coloane (especially Coloane), have much less of a city feel, offer some nice beaches and parks, and are mostly devoid of the hordes of tourists you can find in the old town in Macau. The little town near Hác Sá is cute and the village of Coloane itself has a Tin Hau temple and very good egg tarts at the Lord Stow Bakery. In Macau city itself, once you get out of the main historic core around the cathedral and the steps of St Paul's, it can be very quiet indeed and much less crowded."
> —Cicerone

COLOANE ISLAND

Centuries ago, Coloane was a wild place, where pirates hid in rocky caves and coves, awaiting their chance to strike at cargo ships on the Pearl River. Early in the 20th century the local government sponsored a huge planting program to transform Coloane from a barren place to a green one. The results were spectacular—and enduring. Today this island is idyllic, with green hills and clean sandy beaches.

Once connected to Taipa Island by a thin isthmus, Coloane is now almost completely fused with Taipa via the huge Cotai reclaimed land project, where the "Strip" was completed in 2010. Regardless of the recent development boom, Coloane remains the destination of choice for anyone seeking natural beauty and tranquility.

TOP ATTRACTIONS

☉
FodorśChoice
★
A-Ma Cultural Village. A path just south of Seac Pai Van Park leads to A-Ma Cultural Village, a huge complex built in a traditional Qing Dynasty style. It pays homage to Macau's namesake, the goddess of the

sea. The vibrancy and color of the details in the bell and drum towers, the tiled roofs, and the carved marble altars are truly awe-inspiring. It's as if you've been transported back to the height of the Qing Empire and can now see temples in their true state of greatness. Other remarkable details include the striking rows of stairs leading to Tian Hou Palace at the entrance. Each row features painstakingly detailed marble and stone carvings of auspicious Chinese symbols: a roaring tiger, double lions, five cranes, the double phoenix, and a splendid imperial dragon. The grounds here also have a recreational fishing zone and an arboretum with more than 100 species of local and exotic flora.

Behind A-Ma Cultural Village is the 560-foot-tall **Coloane Hill,** crowned by a gleaming white-marble statue of A-Ma (commemorating the year of Macau's handover), soaring 65 feet and visible from miles away. You can make the short hike up to the top or take one of the shuttle buses that leave from the foot of the hill every 30 minutes. ⊠ *Off Estrada de Seac Pai Van Coloane Island South* ⊗ *Daily 8–6.*

Fodor's Choice **Coloane Village.** Quiet, relaxed Coloane Village is home to traditional
★ Mediterranean-style houses painted in pastels, as well as the baroque-style Chapel of St. Francis Xavier and the Taoist Tam Kung Temple. The surrounding narrow alleys have surprises at every turn; among many things you may encounter are fishermen repairing their junks or a local baptism at the chapel.

The village's heart is a small square around a fountain with a bronze Cupid. The surrounding Macanese and Chinese open-air restaurants are among the region's best; some are the unheralded favorites of chefs visiting from Hong Kong and elsewhere in Asia.

WORTH NOTING

Cheoc Van Beach. Perfect for romantic walks, this beach is in a sheltered cove, with a nice seafood restaurant to one side, the Marine Club with kayak rentals on the other side, and a charming pousada (historic inn) overlooking the ocean. Be warned that there are lots of stray, though generally friendly, dogs on this beach. ⊠ *Off Estrada de Cheoc Van, Coloane Island South* ⊗ *Open 24 hours.*

Ⓒ **Hác-Sá.** Translated from the Chinese, hác-sá means "black sand," although the sands of the area's biggest beach are actually a deep gray. Playgrounds, picnic areas, and restaurants are all within walking distance. Even if you don't stay at the resident five-star Westin Resort, you can use the public sports complex, which is equipped with an Olympic-size swimming pool, tennis courts, and other sports facilities, for a fee. Also nearby is the Hác-Sá Reservoir BBQ park with picnic and barbecue facilities, boat rentals, and water-sports outfitters. ⊠ *Off Estrada de Hác Sá, Coloane Island South* ⊗ *Open 24 hours.*

WHERE TO EAT

WHAT IT COSTS IN MOP$					
	¢	$	$$	$$$	$$$$
At Dinner	under $50	$51–$100	$101–$200	$201–$300	over $300

Restaurant prices are per person for a main course at dinner and exclude the customary 10% service charge.

DOWNTOWN MACAU

$$

PORTUGUESE

Fodor's Choice

★

✕ **Dom Galo.** "Quirky" springs to mind when describing the colorful decor of Dom Galo, from plastic monkey puppets to funky chicken toys hanging from the ceilings. Located near the MGM Grand, it draws a wide clientele, from graphic designers to gambling-compliance lawyers to 10-year-old Cantonese kids celebrating birthdays. The waitstaff are from the Philippines and the owner is Portuguese—which means service is usually spot-on. And the food is good: *insalada de polvo* (octopus salad), king prawns, and steak fries served with a tangy mushroom sauce. Pitchers of sangria are essential with any meal here. So, too, are reservations, as this place becomes increasingly popular with tourists. ✉ *Av. Sir Andars Ljung Stedt, Downtown* ☎ *853/2875–1383* ⌕ *Reservations essential* ▭ *MC, V.*

$$

CANTONESE

Fodor's Choice

★

✕ **Fat Siu Lau.** Well known to both locals and Hong Kong visitors, Fat Siu Lau has kept its customers coming back since 1903 with delicious Macanese favorites and modern creations. For best results, try ordering whatever you see the chatty Cantonese stuffing themselves with at the surrounding tables, and you won't be disappointed. It will probably be whole curry crab, grilled prawns in a butter garlic sauce, and the famous roasted pigeon marinated in a secret marinade. The newer Fat Siu Lau 2 is on Macau Lan Kwai Fong Street and offers the same great food. ✉ *64 Rua da Felicidade, Downtown* ☎ *853/2857–3580* ⌕ *Reservations essential* ▭ *MC, V.*

$$–$$$

SHANGHAINESE

✕ **Portas do Sol.** Originally a Portuguese restaurant, Portas do Sol has been transformed into a destination for exquisite dim sum and Chinese cuisine. Tiny, sweet Shanghainese pork buns, turnip cakes, steamed rice-flour crepes, and soup dumplings are some of the traditional fare, and there are some innovative new creations that look like miniature jewels on the plate. For dessert you can choose from a wide variety of Chinese sweets, including coconut-milk sago pudding, double-boiled papaya with snow fungus (a tasteless mushroom that becomes gelatinous when cooked), and sweet red-bean porridge with ice cream. Evening diners may or may not appreciate the cabaret show and ballroom dancing. Reservations are a good idea on weekends, as this place fills up with Hong Kong and mainland visitors. ✉ *Hotel Lisboa, Av. da Amizade, Downtown* ☎ *853/8803–3100* ▭ *AE, MC, V.*

MACAU OUTER HARBOUR

$$$$

STEAK

Fodor's Choice

★

✕ **Copa Steakhouse.** The first traditional American steak house in Macau, the Copa has a selection of premium quality steaks and seafood, along with a range of cigars and cocktails in an interior that looks like 1960s Las Vegas. Sip a cocktail at the bar near the grand piano, and get ready for huge slabs of American and Australian beef, grilled to juicy perfection before your eyes in the open kitchen. The Japanese Kagoshima beef tops the list at MOP$2,188. Other dishes include sautéed sea scallops and fresh oysters when in season. For dessert, try the sinfully rich crème brûlée. ⊠ *Sands Casino, 203 Largo de Monte Carlo, Outer Harbour* ☎ *853/8983–8222* ▤ *AE, MC, V* ☉ *Closed Sun. No lunch.*

MACAU INNER HARBOUR

$$$
PORTUGUESE
Fodor's Choice
★

✕ **A Lorcha.** Vastly popular A Lorcha (the name means "wooden ship") celebrates the heritage of Macau as an important port with a maritime theme for the menu. Don't miss the signature dish, Clams Lorcha Style, with tomato, beer, and garlic. Other classics include *feijoada* (Brazilian pork-and-bean stew), steamed crab, and perfectly smoky and juicy fire-roasted chicken. Excellent desserts include thick mango pudding and sinfully dense serradura. Watch for racers during the Grand Prix, as the Macanese owner Adriano is a fervent Formula fan. ⊠ *289 Rua do Almirante Sérgio, Inner Harbour* ☎ *853/2831–3193* ⌕ *Reservations essential* ▤ *AE, MC, V* ☉ *Closed Tues.*

$$$
MACANESE

✕ **Litoral.** One of the most popular local restaurants, Litoral serves authentic Macanese dishes that are simple, straightforward, and deliciously satisfying. It is tastefully decorated with whitewashed walls and dark-wood beams. Must-try dishes include the tamarind pork with shrimp paste, as well as codfish baked with potato and garlic, and a Portuguese vegetable cream soup. For dessert, try the *bebinca de leite,* a coconut-milk custard, or the traditional egg pudding, *pudim abade de priscos.* Variously priced set menus are also available, and reservations are recommended on weekends. ⊠ *261 Rua do Almirante Sergio, Inner Harbour* ☎ *853/2896–7878* ▤ *AE, MC, V.*

COLOANE

$$
PORTUGUESE
Fodor's Choice
★

✕ **Fernando's.** Everyone in Hong Kong and Macau knows about Fernando's, but the vine-covered entrance close to Hác-Sá Beach is difficult to spot. The open-air dining pavilion and bar have attracted beachgoers for years now, and the enterprising Fernando has built a legendary reputation for his tiny Portuguese restaurant. The menu focuses on seafood paired with homegrown vegetables, and diners choose from among the bottles of Portuguese reds on display rather than from a wine list. The informal nature of the restaurant fits in with the satisfying, home-style food such as grilled fish, baked chicken, and huge bowlfuls of spicy clams, all eaten with your fingers and washed down with crisp vinho verde. ⊠ *Hác-Sá Beach 9, Coloane Island South* ☎ *853/2888–2531* ⌕ *Reservations not accepted* ▤ *No credit cards.*

WHERE TO STAY

WHAT IT COSTS IN MOP$					
	¢	$	$$	$$$	$$$$
For two people	under MOP$700	$701–$1,100	$1,101–$2,100	$2,101–$3,000	over $3,000

Hotel prices are for two people in a standard double room in high season, excluding 10% service charge and 3% government tax.

DOWNTOWN MACAU

$$ ▨ **Hotel Lisboa.** Macau's infamous landmark, with its distinctive, labyrinthine interior architecture, rumored connections to organized crime, open prostitution, and no-limit VIP rooms, now stands in the shadow of its Grand Lisboa sister. The two are connected by a bridge and share facilities, such as the Grand's modern pool, gym, and spa. The advantages to staying in the older structure are nostalgic value and lower price. And though the Grand Lisboa opened in early 2007, the Hotel Lisboa was renovated one year later, so the rooms are just as luxurious, with hardwood floors and Jacuzzi baths. Take your time to wander through the hotel's corridors displaying jade and artworks from Dr. Stanley Ho's private collection, before running into an ostentatiously gilded staircase. Many people come to the Lisboa expressly for its restaurants: Robuchon a Galera and Portas do Sol (⇨ *Where to Eat*). **Pros:** historical interior; central location; superior restaurants; linked to the Grand Lisboa. **Cons:** old building; low ceilings; smoky casino. ⊠ *2–4 Av. de Lisboa, Downtown* ☏ *853/2888–3888, 800/969–130 in Hong Kong* ⊕ *www.hotelisboa.com* ⋧ *1,000 rooms, 28 suites* ⌂ *In-room: safe, DVD, Internet. In-hotel: 5 restaurants, room service, pool, gym, spa, laundry service, no-smoking rooms* ☰ *AE, DC, MC, V.*

$ ▨ **Hotel Sintra.** Minutes away from Senado Square and right down the street from the New Yaohan department store, the Sintra is a good three-star antechamber to the Lisboan kingdom, with its own built-in Mocha mini-casino accessible through the lobby. Its cozy, carpeted rooms are decorated in soothing brown-and-cream color schemes, while the staff are smartly dressed and helpful. Breakfast is an extra MOP$99 for an American buffet. **Pros:** in the heart of downtown; simple but tasteful decor. **Cons:** small rooms; small casino. ⊠ *Av. De Dom João IV, Downtown* ☏ *853/2871–0111, 800/969–145 in Hong Kong* ⊕ *www. hotelsintra.com* ⋧ *240 rooms, 11 suites* ⌂ *In-room: safe, refrigerator, Internet. In-hotel: restaurant, room service, Wi-Fi hotspot, no-smoking rooms* ☰ *AE, DC, MC, V.*

$$$ ▨ **MGM Grand.** In Macau, the golden lion statue stands guard on the peninsula's southern coast, as guests penetrate into the MGM's spectacular Grande Praça (Grand Square), an 82-foot-tall floor-to-glass-ceiling space modeled after a Portuguese town square that serves as an inner courtyard and has fine dining under the stars. A few million Hong Kong dollars were invested in the permanent chandelier sculpture and original drawings by Dale Chihuly decorating the hotel lobby and reception. Chihuly's glassworks line the hall linking the art gallery to the patisserie, giving it a warm pink glow, while the M Bar plays soft jazz and lounge music. The rooms are everything you'd expect in the way of comfort and elegance from a luxury accommodation, with the decor adhering to a muted cream, brown, and beige color palette, but it's the classy world around them, outside the casino, that distinguishes this hotel from the rest. **Pros:** tasteful architecture; Chihuly artwork; refined dining and lounge options. **Cons:** inseparable from the casino, which can get smoky and loud; high-traffic location. ⊠ *Av. Dr. Sun Yat Sen, Downtown* ☏ *853/8802–8888* ⊕ *www.mgmgrandmacau.com* ⋧ *494 rooms, 99 suites* ⌂ *In-room: safe, refrigerator (some), DVD (some),*

Fodor's Choice
★

6

Wi-Fi. In-hotel: 8 restaurants, room service, bars, pool, spa, laundry service, Wi-Fi hotspot, parking (paid), no-smoking rooms ▭ *AE, MC, V.*

MACAU OUTER HARBOUR

$$$ ⚇ **Grand Lapa Hotel.** The hotel, formerly the Mandarin Oriental, is ele-
☾ gant, with an understated opulence. The rooms feature bright Portuguese decor, with views of the city or of the resort itself. The Grand Lapa is also widely known for deluxe treatments in the enormous spa complex next to the gorgeous, tropical swimming pool on the landscaped grounds. You'll feel like you're in a lush rain forest as you look out from the traditional Mediterranean architecture of the hotel. The hotel's renowned restaurants include the Café Bela Vista for its endless buffet, and Naam, the exquisite Thai restaurant popular with locals and visitors alike. **Pros:** classic luxury facilities; on-site rock climbing; kid's club. **Cons:** old casino; high-traffic location. ✉ *956–1110 Av. da Amizade, Outer Harbour* ☎ *853/8793–3261, 2881–1288 in Hong Kong, 800/526–6567 in U.S.* ⊕ *www.mandarinoriental.com/grandlapa* ⤳ *388 rooms, 28 suites* ⟁ *In-room: safe, refrigerator, Internet, Wi-Fi. In-hotel: 4 restaurants, room service, bar, tennis courts, pools, gym, spa, water sports, children's programs (ages 3–12), laundry service, Wi-Fi hotspot, no-smoking rooms* ▭ *AE, DC, MC, V.*

$$ ⚇ **Rocks Hotel.** The posh-yet-quaint Rocks Hotel is modeled after the charm of 18th-century Victorian England. Each room and suite is individually decorated, with a novelty old-fashioned bathtub in addition to a modern shower stall. Balconies offer low sea views on all sides. The extensive Asian and American breakfast buffet will keep you fueled during your day's adventures. The foyer is impressive, with its grand staircase under sparkling chandeliers, although some real birds in the giant gilded cage would liven up the lobby. **Pros:** distinctive decor; low-key fine dining. **Cons:** no pool or spa; inside an amusement park. ✉ *Macau Fisherman's Wharf, Outer Harbour* ☎ *853/2878–2782, 800/962–863 in Hong Kong* ⊕ *www.rockshotel.com.mo* ⤳ *66 rooms, 6 suites* ⟁ *In-room: safe, Internet. In-hotel: restaurant, room service, bar, gym, laundry service, parking (free), no-smoking rooms* ▭ *AE, DC, MC, V.*

$$$ ⚇ **Sands Macao.** Las Vegas casino tycoon Sheldon Anderson's first venture in Macau, the Sands is nothing if not luxurious. Spacious rooms have deep, soft carpets, large beds, and huge marble bathrooms with Jacuzzis. If you opt to become a high-rolling member, you can stay in one of the 51 deluxe or executive suites, ranging in size from 650 to 1,300 square feet, with all-in-one remote-control plasma TV, karaoke, curtains, and lighting, plus personal butler service on request. VIP members also have privileges such as high-limit gaming rooms at both the Sands and Venetian casinos. But all guests can enjoy the outdoor heated pool on the 6th floor, as well as the exclusive sauna, spa, and salon. **Pros:** heated outdoor pool; across the street from Fisherman's Wharf. **Cons:** not as new as the Venetian; near lots of vehicle traffic. ✉ *203 Largo de Monte Carlo, Outer Harbour* ☎ *853/2888–3388* ⊕ *www. sands.com.mo* ⤳ *258 rooms, 51 VIP suites* ⟁ *In-room: safe, DVD. In-hotel: 6 restaurants, room service, bar, pool, spa, laundry service, parking (paid)* ▭ *AE, MC, V.*

MACAU INNER HARBOUR

$$$$
Fodor's Choice
★

Pousada de São Tiago. The spirit of the structure's past life as a 17th-century fortress permeates every part of this romantic and intimate lodging, making it ideal for a honeymoon or wedding. Even the front entrance is impressive: an ascending stone tunnel carved into the mountainside with water seeping through in quiet trickles. The pousada reopened in mid-2007 after a major renovation that consolidated accommodations into 12 modern luxury suites, each with Jacuzzi bathrooms and large balconies for room-service breakfast. Stop for high tea in the mirrored lounge, or sip a cocktail on the terrace under 100-year-old trees. **Pros:** all the modern comfort of a luxury hotel inside a 17th-century fortress; intimate, sunset views of the Inner Harbour. **Cons:** small pool; limited facilities; you'll need to call a taxi to go out. ✉ *Fortaleza de São Tiago da Barra, Av. da República, Inner Harbour* ☎ *853/2837–8111, 800/969–153 in Hong Kong* ⊕ *www.saotiago.com. mo* ⊃ *12 suites* ☐ *In-room: Internet, Wi-Fi. In-hotel: restaurant, room service, bar, pool, laundry service, Wi-Fi hotspot, parking (free), no-smoking rooms* ▭ *AE, MC, V.*

$$
Fodor's Choice
★

Sofitel Macau at Ponte 16. Ever since its February 2008 opening, Ponte 16 has pioneered the revamp of Macau's retro Western port into an emerging casino and commercial pole. The neighborhood may not be there yet, but Sofitel is Ponte 16's jewel in the crown, with lush, sleek suites and a giant, curvaceous pool, complete with cocktail and juice bar, just outside the indoor buffet lounge. Adventurous and up-and-coming, it has all the edgy perks—grab it while it's hot. **Pros:** giant outdoor pool with bar serving everything from fresh fruit to fine wine; some rooms have unique views of the Inner Harbour. **Cons:** in a still-developing neighborhood; heavy traffic outside. ✉ *Rua do Visconde Paço de Arcos, Inner Harbour* ☎ *853/8861–0016* ⊕ *www.sofitel.com* ⊃ *389 rooms, 19 suites* ☐ *In-room: safe, DVD, Internet. In-hotel: restaurants, room service, bar, pool, gym, spa, laundry service, parking (free), no-smoking rooms* ▭ *AE, DC, MC, V.*

TAIPA

$$$$
Fodor's Choice
★

Altira. Towering over northern Taipa, the Altira offers stunning sea views of the Macau Peninsula from every room, suite, and villa. Even standard rooms are like suites, with a dedicated lounge, walk-in wardrobe, and circular stone bath. There's a panoramic-view swimming pool, a two-level spa with 12 treatment rooms, Aurora's Sunday buffet brunch, VIP gaming rooms, and the 24-hour Crystal Club, which provides starlight seating on the rooftop for cool cocktails in a romantic setting. The vertically designed Altira reaches high to set a standard of chic above all the mushrooming kitsch. **Pros:** glowing sea views from every room; panoramic-view pool; open-air rooftop bar. **Cons:** may sometimes be noisy from nearby construction; still a taxi (or shuttle) ride from the peninsula. ✉ *Av. de Kwong Tung, Taipa* ☎ *853/2886–8888* ⊕ *www.crown-macau.com* ⊃ *184 rooms, 24 suites, 8 villas* ☐ *In-room: safe, refrigerator (some), DVD (some), Internet, Wi-Fi. In-hotel: 6 restaurants, room service, bar, pool, gym, spa, laundry service, parking (paid), no-smoking rooms* ▭ *AE, MC, V.*

6

Rickshaws await the gamblers leaving the Casino Lisboa, the gambling den that started it all.

COLOANE

$ 🏨 **Pousada de Coloane.** At Cheoc-Van Beach at the southernmost tip of Coloane Island, Pousada de Coloane offers a quiet, natural setting, nestled in the lush hills and mountains of Macau's south. There are ample opportunities for kayaking, hiking, and swimming. A winding path paved with Portuguese azulejo tiles leads you to the spacious terrace overlooking the beach, ideal for outdoor wedding receptions and other celebrations. The open terrace garden and restaurant offers traditional Portuguese, Macanese, and Chinese favorites cooked in a heavy, home-style tradition, but there are also other seafood restaurants down on the beach. All 30 rooms have private hot tubs, cable TV, and balconies overlooking the beach, with the mountains of mainland China in the distance. **Pros:** intimate coastal location; sea-view balconies. **Cons:** limited facilities; no in-room Internet. ✉ *Cheoc Van Beach, Coloane Island South* ☎ *853/2888–2143* ⊕ *www.hotelpcoloane.com.mo* ⇆ *30 rooms* ⚷ *In-room: safe (some), Internet. In-hotel: restaurant, room service, bar, pool, laundry service, Wi-Fi hotspot, parking (free)* ▤ *MC, V.*

$$ 🏨 **Westin Resort.** Built into the side of a cliff, the Westin is surrounded by
ⓒ the black sands of Hác-Sá Beach and lapping waves of the South China
Fodor's Choice Sea. This is where you truly get away from it all. Every room faces the
★ ocean; the place glows as much from the sunny tropical color scheme as from the sunshine. The vast private terraces are ideal for alfresco dining and afternoon naps. Guests also receive access to the renowned PGA-standard, 18-hole Macau Golf and Country Club, which was built on the rocky cliffs and plateaus above the hotel. There are half-day and full-day programs for kids that include arts and crafts, games, sports, and treasure hunts. **Pros:** green surroundings; golf-club access;

fun for kids. **Cons:** isolated location; limited access. ⊠ *1918 Estrada de Hác Sá, Coloane Island South* ☎ *853/2887–1111, 800/228–3000 in Hong Kong* ⊕ *www.starwoodhotels.com/westin* ⤴ *208 rooms, 20 suites* ♿ *In-room: safe, Internet. In-hotel: 3 restaurants, room service, bars, golf course, tennis courts, pools, gym, spa, beachfront, bicycles, children's programs (ages 3–12), laundry service, parking (free), no-smoking rooms* ▭ *AE, DC, MC, V.*

AFTER DARK

Old movies, countless novels, and gossip through the years have portrayed Macau's nightlife as a combustible mix of drugs, wild gambling, violent crime, and ladies of the night. Up until the 1999 handover back to mainland China, this image of Macau was mostly accurate, and worked to drive away tourists.

Outside of the casinos and a few restaurants, today's Macau shuts down after 11 pm. You can slip into any dark, elegant lounge bar inside the larger hotels and enjoy live music and expensive cocktails, but don't expect much energy or big crowds. And most late-night saunas are glorified brothels, with "workers" from China, Vietnam, Thailand, and Russia. Because casino-hotel lounges often double as coffee shops in the morning or around midday, some "nightlife" hot spots may open as early as 7 am.

CASINOS

In February 2006 Macau surpassed Las Vegas in gambling revenue. By June 2008 Macau's casinos were turning over 2.6 times the revenue of their Vegas Strip counterparts. Small wonder that international casino groups have swarmed the region, and they continue to drive Macau's explosive double-digit growth.

From the late 1960s until 2001, Macau native Dr. Stanley Ho owned all the casinos, helping him to become one of the world's wealthiest people. One of the first steps the Chinese government took after the 1999 handover was to break up Dr. Ho's monopoly and award casino licenses to several consortiums from Las Vegas. The grand plan to transform Macau from a quiet town that offered gambling into one of the world's top gaming destinations has become a reality.

THE SCENE

Gambling is lightly regulated, so there are only a few things to remember. No one under age 18 is allowed into casinos. Most casinos use Hong Kong dollars in their gaming and not Macau patacas, but you can easily exchange currencies at cashiers. High- and no-limit VIP rooms are available on request, where minimum bets range from HK$50,000 to HK$100,000 per hand. You can get cash from credit cards and ATMs 24 hours a day, and every casino has a program to extend additional credit to frequent visitors. Most casinos don't have strict dress codes outside of their VIP rooms, but men are better off not wearing shorts or sleeveless shirts. Minimum bets for most tables are higher than those in Las Vegas, but there are lower limits for slots and video gambling.

The players here may not look sophisticated, but don't be fooled. Many of Macau's gamblers are truly hard-core. Average bets are in the hundreds per hand, and many people gamble until they're completely exhausted or completely broke, usually the latter.

Macau is also famous for gambling's sister industries of pawn shops, loan sharks, seedy saunas, and prostitution. This underbelly is hidden, though. You won't encounter such things unless you seek them out.

DOWNTOWN

Casino Lisboa. Welcome to the casino that started it all. First opened in 1965 by Dr. Stanley Ho, this iconic Macau gaming den is replete with ancient jade ships in the halls, gilded staircases, and more baccarat tables than you can shake a craps stick at. It's great for a few rounds of HK$50 dai-siu—dice bets over cups of iced green tea. Most of the gamblers are from neighboring Guangdong Province, and Cantonese is the lingua franca. Other popular pastimes at this storied casino revolve around international fine-dining venues and colorful coffee shops, if you care to wander around a maze of marbled floors and low ceilings. Make the Old Lisboa your first casino stop in Macau to get a perspective on how far this city has come since 2004, when the Sands Macao jump-started "Asia's Las Vegas." ⊠ *Av. de Lisboa, Downtown* ☎ *853/2837–5111* ⊕ *www.hotelisboa.com.*

Galaxy StarWorld. As you enter the StarWorld empire you're greeted by tall girls in high heels, while a mariachi band serenades you from across the lobby. Up the escalator, locals typically lay it all down for baccarat, but the upstairs stud poker tables are also picking up momentum. The gaming floors are small and have a couple of Chinese-style diners if you get peckish, but the cool Whisky Bar (⇨ *After Dark*) on the 16th floor of the adjacent hotel is an atmospheric place to either begin or wind down your evening. The neon-blue building is just across from the Wynn and down the block from the MGM Grand. Its live lobby entertainment and local holiday attractions add a kitschy, friendly feel. ⊠ *Av. da Amizade, Downtown* ☎ *853/2838–3838* ⊕ *www.galaxyentertainment.com.*

Grand Lisboa. Meet the veteran Casino Lisboa's younger, more spectacular sister. Opened by Dr. Stanley Ho, this casino has taken Macau by storm with its giant disco ball–like orb, the "precious pearl" at the base of a spouting lotus tower of glitz. With more than 300 tables and about 500 slot machines, the Grand Lisboa's main gaming floor is anchored with a glowing egg statue and a leggy Paris cabaret show every 15 minutes. For more serious spectators, the one-hour, HK$380 "Tokyo Nights" show entertains six times a day in a separate theater. The second floor features craps and sports betting, and has a great bar. True to Lisboa tradition, the Grand also has a variety of dining choices, from the baroque Don Alfonso Macau 1890 to the Round the Clock Coffee Shop and a deli between the first and second gaming floors. ⊠ *2–4 Av. de Lisboa, Downtown* ☎ *853/2838–5111* ⊕ *www.grandlisboa.com.*

MGM Grand. Opened in December 2007, the MGM Grand is a stylish addition to Macau's gambling scene. The lavish lounges, Dale Chihuly glass sculptures, Portuguese-inspired architecture, and fine dining of the 1,088-square-meter Grande Praça arcade add to the gaming ambience.

The gambling floor itself is popular with high rollers from Hong Kong, including business tycoons who are just in for a few days. One of the main owners, Pansy Ho (like her brother Lawrence Ho), is often cast as the product of her father, the "gambling godfather," Dr. Stanley Ho, but is a high-octane business professional in her own right. The glitz-and-glam energy and high-society appeal are evidence that this is the only casino in Macau with a woman's classy touch. ✉ *Av. Dr. Sun Yat Sen, Downtown* 📞 *853/8802–8888* ⊕ *www.mgmgrandmacau.com.*

Fodor's Choice **Sands Macao.** Thanks to Paul Steelman's design, the Sands Macao has
★ one of the largest parking entrances on earth. And until its sibling, the Venetian, stole the spotlight, this casino was the largest on earth. It's the first casino you'll see on the peninsula even before debarking from the ferry. Past the sparkling 50-ton chandelier entrance, its grand gaming floor is anchored with a live cabaret stage above an open bar and under a giant screen. Several tiers are tastefully linked with escalators leading to the high-stakes tables upstairs, just outside the 888 Buffet and food court. Its relatively friendly atmosphere and location, just across from Fisherman's Wharf and near the bar street in NAPE, is well suited as a warm-up to your night out. ✉ *203 Largo de Monte Carlo, Downtown* 📞 *853/2888–3333* ⊕ *www.sands.com.mo.*

Fodor's Choice **Wynn Macau.** Listen for theme songs such as "Diamonds are Forever,"
★ "Luck Be a Lady," or "Money, Money" as you watch the Wynn's outdoor Performance Lake dazzle you with flames and fountain jets of whipping water, which entrance gamblers and tourists every 15 minutes from 11 am to midnight. Inside the "open hand" structure of Steve Wynn's Macau resort, the indoor Rotunda Tree of Prosperity also wows guests with feng shui glitz. Opened in several stages beginning in 2006, the Wynn's expansive, brightly lit gaming floor, fine dining, buffet meals, luxury shops, deluxe spa, and trendy suites make it one of the more family-friendly resorts to visit. ✉ *Rua Cidade de Sintra, Downtown* 📞 *853/2888–9966* ⊕ *www.wynnmacau.com.*

TAIPA

Fodor's Choice **Altira Macau.** Touting itself as Macau's first "six-star" integrated resort,
★ the Altira is indeed stellar. Previously known as Crown Macau, its five swank, '70s-style gaming floors are decked out in browns and taupes with mod-style chandeliers. Opened in May 2007, this is the only classy casino on the island of Taipa. Facing the glow of casinos to the north on the peninsula, the strength of the Altira casino rests in its abundant selection of game play, from baccarat to straight-up slots to posh VIP gaming rooms. Its VIP resort suites and fine-dining components Aurora and Kira, not to mention the elegantly discreet 38 Lounge on the roof, with outdoor seating open 24 hours, add to the overall ambience. It is equidistant from the peninsula and Cotai. ✉ *Av. de Kwong Tung, Taipa* 📞 *853/2886–8888* ⊕ *www.altiramacau.com/.*

Fodor's Choice **Venetian Macao-Resort-Hotel.** With 10.5 million square feet of space for
★ gambling, shopping, eating, and sleeping, the Venetian is twice the size of its sister property in Las Vegas. The faux-Renaissance decoration, built-in canals plied by crooning gondoliers, live carnival acts, and upscale luxury brands are sheer spectacle, with more than a touch of

6

pretension. The 550,000-square-foot gaming floor has some 3,000 slot machines and more than 750 tables of casino favorites. The sprawling property also includes 3,000 suites, a 15,000-seat arena, and Cirque du Soleil's ZAIA Theater. So it's no wonder the Venetian is the must-see megacomplex that everyone's talking about. ⊠ *Estrada da Baía de N. Senhora da Esperança, Cotai* ☎ *853/2882–8888* ⊕ *www. venetianmacao.com.*

SHOPPING

Macau, like Hong Kong, is a free port for most items, which leads to lower prices for electronics, jewelry, and clothing than other international cities. But the experience is completely different, with a low-key atmosphere, small crowds, and compact areas. It is a hub for traditional Chinese arts, crafts, and even some antiques (but be aware that there are many high-quality reproductions in the mix, too). Macau's major shopping district is along its main street in the downtown area, Avenida Almeida Ribeiro, more commonly known by its Chinese name, **San Ma Lo**; there are also shops downtown on **Rua Dos Mercadores** and its side streets; in **Cinco de Outubro**; and on the **Rua do Campo**.

Most of Macau's shops operate year-round with a short break in late January for Chinese New Year and are open from 10 am to 8 pm and later on weekends. While most shops accept all major credit cards, specialty discount shops usually ask for cash, and street vendors accept only cash. For most street vendors and some smaller stores, some friendly bargaining is expected; ask for the "best price," which ideally produces instant discounts of 10%–20%. The shopping mantra here is "bargain hard, bargain often."

Pearl River Delta

GUANGZHOU AND SHENZHEN

WORD OF MOUTH

"The whole city of Shenzhen was built up during the last 25 years. There was basically nothing before that, so you won't find any historical sites. But that doesn't mean there's nothing to see."

—rkkwan

WELCOME TO PEARL RIVER DELTA

TOP REASONS TO GO

★ **Feel the Buzz!:** This region is the undisputed engine driving China's economic boom, and whether you're in older Guangzhou or the "instant city" of Shenzhen, you're sure to feel the buzz of a communist nation on a capitalist joyride.

★ **Explore the Ancient:** Though thoroughly modern, the Pearl River Delta has not lost touch with its ancient roots. From the temples of Guangzhou to the Ming Dynasty walled city of Dapeng in Shenzhen, a journey through the PRD is a journey through the centuries.

★ **Soak Up Some Colonial Splendor:** Guangzhou's well-preserved examples of architecture date back to the 19th century, when European merchants amassed fortunes in the opium trade, and the buildings from which they once plied their trade still stand on Shamian Island.

★ **Shopping! Shopping! Shopping!:** Need we say more? Guangzhou is one of the best places to buy inexpensive clothes in China.

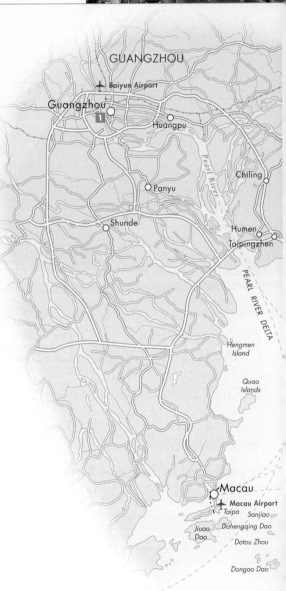

1 **Guangzhou.** After you've recovered from the initial confusion produced by the crowds, heavy traffic, and pollution, turn to the city's unique cuisine, sights, culture, and history, such as Colonial Shamian and the nearby Baiyun Mountain.

2 **Shenzhen.** Come to Shenzhen for excellent shopping and dining at affordable prices. Or head to Overseas Chinese Town to take in some art and culture. If you enjoy a round or two of golf, the city's Mission Hills Golf Club promises to blow your mind.

GETTING ORIENTED

The Pearl River Delta is a massive triangle. Guangzhou is at the top, Shenzhen on the east corner, and Zhuhai on the west. The area as a whole is just a bit too spread out for any one corner to make a good base of operations from which to explore the others. We recommend beginning at one corner and making your way around. Guangzhou is fairly dense, so leave yourself three days in which to soak it all in before heading down to Shenzhen. From Shenzhen's Shekou Harbor it's a one-hour ferry ride to Zhuhai, which takes less than a day to explore before either returning to Guangzhou or heading into nearby Macau or Hong Kong.

7

Updated
by Michael
Standaert

The Pearl River Delta is China's workshop, its fastest-growing, ever-changing, and most affluent region. The province of Guangdong's annual GDP outranks that of Saudi Arabia. It's been the industrial engine powering China's meteoric economic rise. You will find some of the greatest shopping, a flourishing nightlife, and a culinary scene that most regions can only dream of.

The Pearl River Delta is also among China's most polluted regions, and this is saying a lot. From the southern suburbs of Guangzhou city to the northern edge of Shenzhen, industry stretches in all directions. Tens of thousands of factories churn out the lion's share of the world's consumer products. This hyper-industry has polluted the entire area's soil, water, and air so badly that in Hong Kong (on the region's southern tip) pollution is an overriding public concern. On a bad day the air quality in Guangzhou can actually be described as *abusive*. On top of all of this, much of the region is noisy and chaotic.

But things are getting better. Air quality is slowly improving, some manufacturing is being shuttered or moving inland, and with Guangzhou hosting the Asian Games in late 2010, the city has undergone a dramatic face-lift. Most of the facades of buildings along the main roads have been cleaned and repainted, and the subway system has been expanded. In Shenzhen the subway system, at this writing, will have doubled its length by the end of 2011, and there are plans to extend it even further.

So why would the pleasure traveler even visit Pearl River Delta? History enthusiasts head to Guangzhou, Guangdong Province's ancient capital and the historic center of Cantonese culture and the revolution that overthrew the last dynasty. Gourmands flock to both Guangzhou and Shenzhen to indulge in some of the best examples of Chinese cuisine. (However, while much of the food at higher-end restaurants is sourced from outside the Pearl River Delta, local dives are mostly using vegetables and other produce grown locally, so best not to frequent them for three meals a day.) Culture vultures visit the many temples, shrines, and museums scattered throughout the region. And shopaholics? A visit to the Pearl River Delta will quickly dismiss any lingering notions that China is still a nation bound by the tenets of Marx and Mao.

PLANNING

WHEN TO GO

The best time to go is spring and autumn, when temperatures and humidity are much lower than in summer, but this is complicated by a few factors. Unless you have friends in the hotel industry, don't even think about visiting Guangzhou during the annual spring trade fair, when hotel prices double or triple. Don't travel anywhere in China during the Golden Week holiday, which takes place annually from October 1 through 7. So what do we recommend? September, October (excluding Golden Week), and early to mid-November.

GETTING HERE AND AROUND

The best way to get around the Pearl River Delta is by train and bus, though trains are decidedly less confusing than the bus systems. With a little assistance from your hotel, you should be able to manage.

AIR TRAVEL

With Hong Kong, Macau, Shenzhen, and Zhuhai all in such close proximity, the Pearl River Delta airspace is one of the most heavily trafficked in the world. This will give you plenty of options, depending on where you are flying in from and where you want to go. Flying from another mainland city to Shenzhen or Zhuhai is usually cheaper than flying to Hong Kong or Macau. Cathay Pacific out of Hong Kong is one of the best airlines going, and can get you around the Southeast Asia region or further abroad, while Shenzhen Air and China Southern are quality mainland airlines linking Shenzhen and Zhuhai with many other cities throughout China. The major airports are the Baiyun International Airport north of Guangzhou, and Bao'an International Airport northwest of Shenzhen.

BUS TRAVEL

Bus travel through the area can often be the best way to go, though it is complicated for the uninitiated. At the Guangzhou main railway station where metro Lines 2 and 5 cross, you can go to the "Guangdong Automobile Station" (really the long-distance bus station, confusingly translated) and catch buses to most other cities in the Pearl River Delta. There is an English-speaking ticket window for foreigners, and all the bus waiting areas have the names of the destinations in pinyin. Your hotel might be able to help you by writing a detailed note about where you want to go.

CAR TRAVEL

You can't legally drive yourself in China, but you could hire a driver for around Y500–Y600 per day and up, depending on whether the driver speaks English and what kind of car you want.

TRAIN TRAVEL

It is quick and easy to get from Guangzhou to Shenzhen by train, though from Guangzhou to Zhuhai it's better to take a bus. By around 2015 there will be a high-speed rail train that burrows under Hong Kong's

Kowloon district, cuts through Shenzhen, and terminates in Guangzhou that should cut travel times between the two major hubs considerably.

HEALTH AND SAFETY

Take the usual precautions against appearing conspicuously wealthy, and carry with you only the amount of cash you need. Crowded places, such as stations and clubs, often harbor pickpockets, so keep your eyes on your bags and your wallet in your front pocket. If you see a local wearing a backpack on the front of his or her body, it's probably a good idea to do the same.

MONEY MATTERS

ATMs abound in the more developed areas of Guangzhou and Shenzhen, and most take foreign cards, so getting cash is relatively simple.

RESTAURANTS

Most Cantonese dishes are stir-fried or steamed, although roasted meats such as barbecued chicken and pork are also popular. A Cantonese mid-morning favorite is dim sum, or small dishes such as dumplings and pastries. Filled with meat and vegetables, they are a perfect way to start the day, though many traditional dim sum places stop serving by mid-afternoon. When you go out to eat, go with as many people as you can find so that you can try as many different dishes as possible.

While Guangzhou is more of a Cantonese-food capital, you can find many other types of food in Shenzhen. Since the city has basically only 30 years of history, most of the people there are from elsewhere in China—so Hunan, Sichuan, and Fujian-style dishes can be found easily. Also, more specific styles of food such as Chaozhou, with its seafood porridges and fish-ball soups, and Hakka, with its more home-style healthy medicinal soups and excellent tofu dishes, are plentiful.

HOTELS

Hotels in Guangzhou and Shenzhen tend to be better than in most places in China, especially on the high-end, since they've had to cater more to visitors from Hong Kong or businesspeople coming from abroad. English is usually spoken at these. On the mid-range or lower end, you'll find reasonably priced budget hotels, sometimes quite clean, other times not so, but usually conveniently located. Finding an English-speaking desk person at these can be hit and miss. Best to avoid those too close to glowing neon "spas" or karaoke clubs, unless you're into the kinds of services sometimes provided in these venues.

WHAT IT COSTS IN YUAN				
	¢	$	$$	$$$	$$$$
Restaurants	under Y25	Y25–Y49	Y50–Y99	Y100–Y165	over Y165
Hotels	under Y700	Y700–Y1,099	Y1,100–Y1,399	Y1,400–Y1,800	over Y1,800

Restaurant prices are for a main course, excluding tax and tips. Hotel prices are for a standard double room, including taxes.

VISITOR INFORMATION

While China is a large tourist destination, visitor information facilities are not widely available. The best place to check for information is online at China-specific travel Web sites or on places like the Fodor's Web site for the latest information.

TOURS

Splendid Tours (*Lobby, 2nd Level, Sheraton Hong Hong Hotel & Towers* ✉ *20 Nathan Road, Tsim Sha Tsui, Kowloon Hong Kong* ☎ *852/2316— 2151* ⊕ *www.splendid.hk*) runs good Shenzhen and Guangzhou tour services out of Hong Kong, though these are sometimes temporarily halted because of changes in group tourist visa restrictions on the mainland. Check the Web site for current details.

China Travel Service Limited (☎ *852/2853-3533* ⊕ *www.ctshk.com/ english/index.htm*) has 40 offices in Hong Kong, Kowloon, and the New Territories, and can arrange just about any type of travel experience that might interest you in the Pearl River Delta. CTS can assist with visas and booking discount hotel rooms. They are open weekdays 9 am to 7 pm, Saturday 9 am to 5 pm, and Sunday and holidays 9:30 to 12:30 and 2 to 5.

GUANGZHOU

120 km (74½ mi; 1½ hrs) north of Hong Kong.

Guangzhou (also known as Canton), the capital of Guangdong Province, is both a modern boomtown and an ancient port city. This metropolis of more than 7 million people has all the expected accoutrements of a competitive, modern Chinese city: skyscrapers, heavy traffic, efficient metro, and serious crowds. Guangzhou is an old city with a long history. Exploring its riverfront, parks, temples, and markets, one is constantly reminded of the impact its irrepressible culture, language, and cuisine has made on the world.

In the early 20th century Guangzhou was a hotbed of revolutionary zeal, first as the birthplace of the movement to overthrow the last dynasty (culminating in the 1911 Revolution), and then as a battleground between Nationalists and Communists in the years leading to the 1949 Communist Revolution. Following the open-door policy of Deng Xiaoping in 1979, the port city was able to resume its role as a commercial gateway to China.

Though known for its polluted air, as most major Chinese cities can be, Guangzhou is starting to get a little cleaner. The Asian Games in 2010 spurred the city to extend the subway system, clean up ramshackle parts of the city, and institute air-pollution controls. In Guangzhou's parks, temples, winding old-quarter backstreets, restaurants, river islets, and museums, the Old City and a more refined way of life are never far away.

GETTING HERE AND AROUND

Most travelers enter Guangzhou either by train or plane. Long-distance trains pull in at the Guangzhou East Station. This station is also on the metro line. One-way tickets to or from Hong Kong cost between

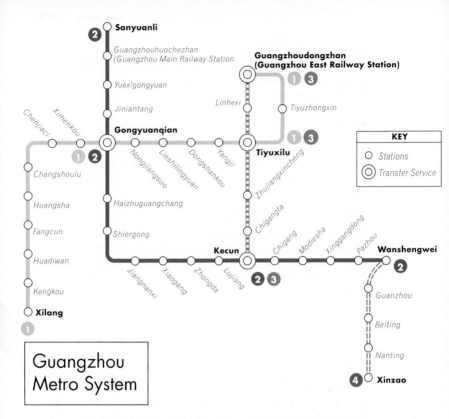

Guangzhou Metro System

Y100 and Y170. To get to Shenzhen, take the Hong Kong metro to the border, go through customs, and then enter the train station if you're heading to Guangzhou or hop onto the Shenzhen metro if you're staying within the city.

Guangzhou is connected to Shenzhen (approximately 100 km [62 mi] to the south) by the aptly named Guangzhou–Shenzhen expressway. Buses from Guangzhou to Hong Kong leave from the Guangzhou East Station and from major hotels such as the China and the Garden hotels, and cost about Y75.

AIR TRAVEL Guangzhou's Baiyun Airport currently offers five flights per day to Hong Kong and around 10 to Beijing between 9 am and 9 pm. It has direct flights to Paris, Los Angeles, Singapore, Bangkok, Sydney, Jakarta, and Phnom Penh, and a number of cities in North America.

BUS TRAVEL Guangzhou Provincial Passenger Bus Station is the largest bus station in Guangdong Province. Buses depart from here daily to the neighboring Guangxi, Hunan, Fujian, and Jiangxi provinces. There are also deluxe buses to Shenzhen, Hong Kong, and Macau. The easiest way from Guangzhou to Hong Kong is by the deluxe bus. Buses also depart from the Guangzhou Main Train Station for many areas throughout Guangdong and elsewhere in China.

Guangzhou by Underground

Guangzhou's subway system is cheap, clean, and (unlike Beijing's) reasonably efficient. Divided into six lines that span both sides of the Pearl River, most of the areas of interest to casual visitors are found on Lines 1 or 2 (the red and yellow lines on the maps).

The terminus of Line 1 is Guangzhoudongzhan, or Guangzhou East Train Station, which is where trains leave for Hong Kong. This area is also the heart of the Tianhe, Guangzhou's financial district. Gongyuanqian is the interchange for Lines 1 and 2. The most interesting temples and shrines are within walking distance of stations along Line 1, with signs in English pointing the way.

Ask your hotel concierge to give you an English subway map. *See subway map in this chapter.* For walking-tour-friendly neighborhoods, we recommend Dongshankou Station. This is a lovely little area with plenty of shopping opportunities. Tree-lined streets just off the avenue are filled with enclosed gardens and old houses with traditional architecture. The area surrounding the Linhex Station is the most modern part of the city. This is a good neighborhood to walk in with your head tilted skyward.

Of course, if you really want to continue on an anti-car trip, get off at Gongyuanqian Station (where Lines 1 and 2 intersect) and walk to the Beijing Road Pedestrian Mall: the hip, trendy, and car-free heart of young consumerism in Guangzhou.

7

SUBWAY TRAVEL Guangzhou's clean and efficient underground metro currently has six lines connecting 98 stations, including the new East and old Central railway stations. Tickets range from Y2 for short trips to Y14 for the longest leg.

TAXI TRAVEL Although taxis in Guangzhou are cheap and plentiful, traffic can sometimes be a nightmare, as it is in most major Chinese cities. Bring a book or some tunes, sit back, and "enjoy" the ride.

TRAIN TRAVEL Five express trains (Y234 first class, Y190 second class) depart daily for Guangzhou East Railway Station from Hong Kong's Kowloon Station. The trip takes about 1¾ hours. The last train back to Hong Kong leaves at 5:25 pm. Trains between Shenzhen's Luohu Railway Station and Guangzhou East Railway Station run every hour and cost between Y80 and Y100.

SAFETY AND PRECAUTIONS
Most cities in China are quite safe; guns are not an issue in the way they are in other cities, particularly in the United States. There are spots in Shenzhen and Guangzhou that can be seedy though, and bag-snatchers and pickpockets aren't unheard of. Foreigners who overimbibe at clubs and bars can be the target of opportunists trying to separate you from your wallet, so watch how much you drink or stay with the group.

TIMING
Two or three days in Guangzhou and two days in Shenzhen are probably enough to get a good taste of each city. Zhuhai can be a day excursion out of Macau.

REGIONAL TOURS

A popular tour company in Guangzhou is **GZL International Travel Service** (☎ 86020/8633–8680 ⊕ *www.myorientours.com* ✉ *service@myorientours.com*).

ESSENTIALS

Air Contacts China Southern Airlines (✉ 181 Huanshi Lu, on left as you exit Guangzhou railway station [Guangzhou Main Station metro]) ☎ 020/95539 24-hr hotline ⊕ www.csair.com/en/).

Baiyun International Airport (✉ Airport International Office Building, South Area of Guangzhou Baiyun International Airport, ☎ 020/3606–6999). **Zhuhai International Airport** (☎ 0756/889–5494).

Banks HSBC (✉ G2, G/F, Garden Hotel, No. 368 Huan Shi Dong Lu, Guangzhou ☎ 020/8313–1888; 800/830–2880 from within China ⊕ www.hsbc.com.cn). **Bank of China** (✉ 197 Dongfeng Xilu ☎ 020/8333–8080; 95566 hotline inside China ⊕ www.boc.cn).

Bus Contacts Citybus (☎ 852/2873–0818). **Guangdong Provincial Bus Station** (✉ 145 Huanshi Xi Lu ☎ 020/8666–1297). **Guangzhou Bus Station** (✉ 158 Huanshi Xi Lu ☎ 020/8668–4259). **Tianhe Bus Station** (✉ 633 Yanling Lu, Tianhe District ☎ 020/3708–5070).

Medical Assistance Shenzhen People's Hospital (✉ 1017 Dongmen Bei Lu N, Shenzhen ☎ 0755/2553–3018 Ext. 2553; 1387 [Outpatient Dept.]).

Subway Contact Guangzhou Metro (☎ 020/8328–9033 ⊕ www.gzmtr.com/en).

Train Contacts Guangzhou East Railway Station (✉ 1 Dongzhan Lu Tianhe District ☎ 020/6134–6222). **Guangzhou Railway Station** (✉ Huanshixi Lu ☎ 020/6135–7222).

EXPLORING

Guangzhou is a massive, sprawling metropolis divided into several districts and many more neighborhoods. Roughly speaking, the city is divided in half by the Pearl River, which runs from east to west and separates the Haizhu District (a large island) from the districts in the north. Most of the explorations we're recommending will keep you north of the Pearl River, since this is where the majority of the more culturally edifying parts of Guangzhou lie.

CULTURAL ATTRACTIONS

TOP ATTRACTIONS

The Qingping Market has undergone a few changes over the past few years; the sprawling cluster of stalls was once infamous for its wet market, a hotbed of animal slaughter. It always had a good selection of knickknacks, as well as a large section of medicinal goods (ginseng, fungi, and herbs, as well as more cruelly obtained items like bear bile and essence of tiger prostate), but the wet market scared all but the

A nighttime Zhujiang River cruise.

heartiest visitors away. Following SARS, the government decided to close the bloodier, less hygienic stalls. A large section of the old market was been cleared away to make room for a shiny new mall-like structure with stalls dedicated to traditional medicines. The funkier and older outdoor section of the market still exists off to one side, but for the most part items on sale are of the flora and not the fauna variety.

Shamian Island. More than a century ago the Mandarins of Guangzhou designated a 44-acre sandbank outside the city walls in the Pearl River as an enclave for foreign merchants. The foreigners had previously lived and done business in a row of houses known as the Thirteen Factories, near the present Shamian, but local resentment after the Opium Wars—sometimes leading to murderous attacks—made it prudent to confine them to a protected area, which was linked to the city by two bridges that were closed at 10 every night.

The island soon became a bustling township, as trading companies from Britain, the United States, France, Holland, Italy, Germany, Portugal, and Japan built stone mansions along the waterfront. With spacious gardens and private wharves, these served as homes, offices, and warehouses. There were churches for Catholics and Protestants, banks, a yacht club, football grounds, a cricket field, and the Victory hotel.

Shamian was attacked in the 1920s but survived until the 1949 Revolution, when its mansions became government offices or apartment houses and the churches were turned into factories. In recent years, however, the island has resumed much of its old character. Many colonial buildings have been restored, and both churches have been beautifully renovated and reopened to worshippers. Worth visiting is **Our Lady of**

Guangzhou

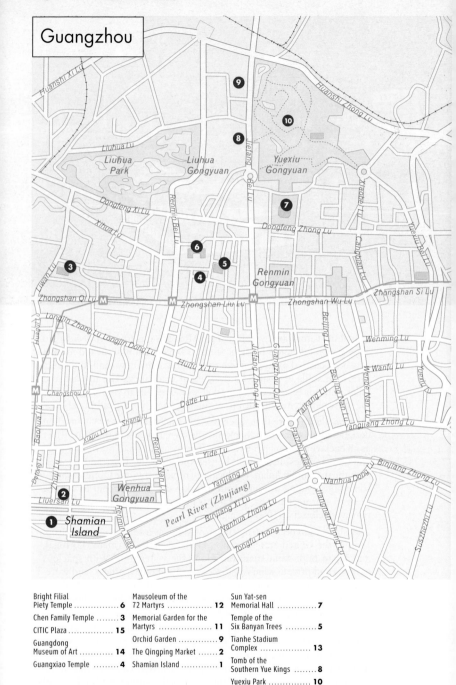

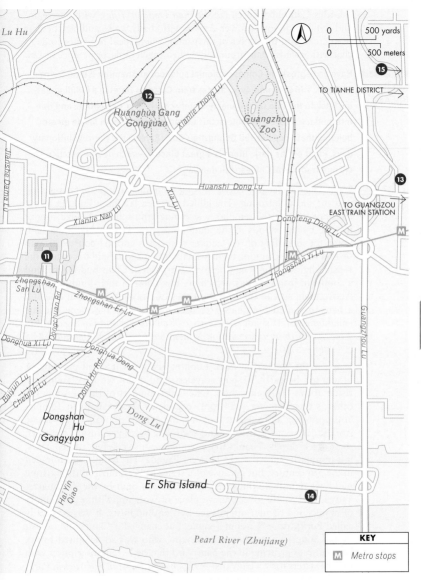

Lu Hu

0   500 yards

0   500 meters

15

TO TIANHE DISTRICT

12

Huanghua Gang Gongyuan

Guangzhou Zoo

Xianlie Zhong Lu

Jianshe Dama Lu

Huanshi Dong Lu

13

Xia Lu

TO GUANGZOU EAST TRAIN STATION

Xianlie Nan Lu

Dongfeng Dong Lu

M

11

Zhongshan San Lu

Dongyuan Rd.

Zhongshan Er Lu

M

Zhongshan Yi Lu

M

M

Guangzhou Lu

7

Donghua Xi Lu

Donghua Dong

Baiyun Lu

Chebian Lu

Dong Hu Rd.

Dongshan Hu Gongyuan

Dong Lu

Hai Yin Qiao

Er Sha Island

14

Pearl River (Zhujiang)

KEY
M   *Metro stops*

Lourdes Catholic Church (⊠ *Shamian Dajie at Yijie*), with its cream-and-white neo-Gothic tower. A park with shady walks and benches has been created in the center of the island, where local residents come to chat with friends, walk around with their caged birds, or practice tai chi.

NEED A BREAK?

Have an espresso in Chinese colonial splendor at Shamian Island Blenz Coffee (⊠ *46 Shamian Ave.*), across from Customs Hotel in a building dating back to the late Qing Dynasty. Comfy couches, strong coffee, and free Internet access are available in this Canadian coffee chain inside an old building that once housed Guangzhou's U.S. Bank in the pre-revolutionary days. Right on the park, Blenz is a great place to watch people practice tai chi and traditional Chinese fan dancing.

Bright Filial Piety Temple. This is the oldest Buddhist temple in Guangzhou and the most charming. The gilded wooden laughing Buddha at the entrance heralds the temple's welcoming atmosphere. A huge bronze incense burner stands in the main courtyard. Beyond the main hall, noted for its ceiling of red-lacquer timbers, is another courtyard with several treasures, among them a small brick pagoda said to contain the tonsure hair of Hui-neng (the sixth patriarch of Chan Buddhism), and a couple of iron pagodas, which are the oldest of their kind in China. Above them spread the leafy branches of a myrobalan plum tree and a banyan, called Buddha's Tree because it is said Hui-neng became enlightened in its shade. ⊠ *Corner of Renmin Bei and Guangxiao Lu, 2 blocks north of metro station Ximenkou, Liwan* Ⓜ *Ximenkou* 🚇 *Y5* ⊙ *Daily 6–5:30.*

Temple of the Six Banyan Trees. Look at any ancient scroll painting or lithograph by early Western travelers, and you'll see two landmarks rising above old Guangzhou. One is the minaret of the mosque; the other is the 56-meter (184-foot) pagoda of the Six Banyan Temple. Still providing an excellent lookout, the pagoda appears to have nine stories, each with doorways and encircling balconies. Inside, however, there are 17 levels. Thanks to its arrangement of colored, carved roofs, it is popularly known as the Flowery Pagoda. The temple was founded in the 5th century, but because of a series of fires, most of the existing buildings date from the 11th century. It was built by the Zen master Tanyu, and is still a very active place of worship, with a community of monks and regular attendance by Zen Buddhists. It was originally called Purificatory Wisdom Temple, but changed its name after a visit by the Song Dynasty poet Su Dongpo, who was so delighted by six banyan trees growing in the courtyard that he left an inscription with the characters for six banyans. ⊠ *Haizhu Bei Lu, south of Yuexiu Park, Liwan* 🚇 *Y5–10* ⊙ *Daily 8:30–5.*

WORTH NOTING

Chen Family Temple. The Chen family is one of the Pearl River Delta's oldest clans. In the late 19th century local members, who had become rich merchants, decided to build a memorial temple. They invited contributions from the Chens—and kindred Chans—who had emigrated overseas. Money flowed in from 72 countries, and no expense was spared.

One of the temple's highlights is a huge ridgepole frieze. It stretches 90 feet along the main roof and depicts scenes from the epic *Romance of Three Kingdoms*, with thousands of figures against a backdrop of ornate houses, monumental gates, and lush scenery. Elsewhere in the huge compound of pavilions and courtyards are friezes of delicately carved stone and wood, as well as fine iron castings and a dazzling altar covered with gold leaf. The temple also houses a folk-arts museum and shop. ⊠ *7 Zhongshan Qi Lu, Liwan* ☎ *Y15* ⊗ *Daily 8:30–5:20* Ⓜ *Chengjia Ci.*

Guangxiao Temple. This impressively restored temple and city-gate complex, also known as the Five Celestials Shrine, was once the front gate for the wall that surrounded the city. The shrine and remaining sections of the wall in Yuexiu Park are the only standing remains of old Guangzhou's fortifications. There's also an impressive model of how the city looked when the air was clean, the roads were filled with horse-drawn carts, and foreigners were confined on pain of death to one small section of the city. ⊠ *Renmin Bei Lu, 3 blocks north of the Ximenkou metro, Liwan* Ⓜ *Ximenkou* ☎ *10* ⊗ *Daily 8–5.*

PARKS AND MUSEUMS
TOP ATTRACTIONS

★ **Orchid Garden.** This garden offers a wonderfully convenient retreat from the noise and crowds of the city. It's spread over 20 acres, with paths that wind through groves of bamboo and tropical trees to a series of classic teahouses. Here you can sit and enjoy a wide variety of Chinese teas brewed the traditional way. There are tables inside and on terraces that overlook the ponds. As for the orchids, there are 10,000 pots with more than 2,000 species of the flower, which present a magical sight when they bloom (peak time is May and June). ⊠ *Jiefang Bei Lu, Liwan* ☎ *Y8* ⊗ *Daily 8–5.*

★ **Tomb of the Southern Yue Kings.** In 1983 bulldozers clearing ground for the China Hotel uncovered the intact tomb of Emperor Wen Di, who ruled Nan Yue (southern China) from 137 to 122 BC. The tomb was restored and its treasures placed in the adjoining **Nan Yue Museum.** The tomb contained the skeletons of the king and 15 courtiers—guards, cooks, concubines, and a musician—who were buried alive to attend him in death. Also buried were several thousand funerary objects, clearly designed to show off the accomplishments of the southern empire. The tomb—built of stone slabs—is behind the museum and is remarkably compact. ⊠ *867 Jiefang Bei Lu, around the corner from the China Hotel, Liwan* ☎ *Y12* ⊗ *Daily 9–5:30.*

Guangdong Museum of Art is a major cultural establishment of the "new Canton," and regularly hosts the works of painters, sculptors, and other artists from around China and the world. An excellent sculpture garden surrounds the large complex. It's on Ersha Island; the Web site has a map to help you find your way—so print it out before you go. ⊠ *38 Yanyu Lu, Er Sha Island, Yuexiu* ☎ *020/8735–1468* ⊕ *www.gdmoa. org* ☎ *Y15* ⊗ *Tues.–Sun. 9–5.*

Zhenhai Tower, in Yuexiu Park, was built in 1380 and later incorporated into the city wall.

WORTH NOTING

★ **Yuexiu Park.** To get away from the bustle, retreat into Yuexiu Park in the heart of town. The park covers 247 rolling acres and includes landscaped gardens, man-made lakes, recreational areas, and playgrounds. Visit the famous **Five Rams Statue** (Wuyang Suxiang), which celebrates the legend of the five celestials who came to Guangzhou riding on goats to bring grains to the people. Guangzhou families like to take each other's photo in front of the statue before setting off to enjoy the park. ✉ *Jiefang Bei Lu, across from China Hotel, Liwan* ☎ *020/8666–1950* ⊕ *www.yuexiupark-gz.com* ✉ *Free* ⊗ *Daily 6 am–11 pm.*

REVOLUTIONARY MEMORIALS

In the center of the city are memorials to people who changed Chinese history during the 20th century, using Guangzhou as a base of operations. The most famous were local boy Dr. Sun Yat-sen, who led the overthrow of the Qing Dynasty, and Communist Party founders Mao Zedong and Zhou Enlai.

Mausoleum of the 72 Martyrs. In a prelude to the successful revolution of 1911, a group of 88 revolutionaries staged the Guangzhou armed uprising, only to be defeated and executed by the authorities. Of those killed, 72 were buried here. Their memorial, built in 1918, incorporates a mixture of international symbols of freedom and democracy, including replicas of the Statue of Liberty. ✉ *Xianlie Zhong Lu, Yuexiu* ✉ *Y10* ⊗ *Daily 6 am–8:30 pm.*

Memorial Garden for the Martyrs. Built in 1957, this garden has been planted around a tumulus that contains the remains of 5,000 revolutionaries killed in the 1927 destruction of the Guangzhou Commune by the Nationalists. This was the execution site of many victims. On the grounds is the **Revolutionary Museum,** which displays pictures and memorabilia of Guangdong's 20th-century rebellions. ⊠ *Zhongshan San Lu, Yuexiu* ⊠ *Y3* ☼ *Daily 8–7.*

Sun Yat-sen Memorial Hall. Dr. Sun's Memorial Hall is a handsome pavilion that stands in a garden behind a bronze statue of the leader. Built in 1929–31 with funds mostly from overseas Chinese, the building is a classic octagon, with sweeping roofs of blue tiles over carved wooden eaves and verandas of red-lacquer columns. Inside is an auditorium with seating for 5,000 and a stage for plays, concerts, and ceremonial occasions. ⊠ *Dongfeng Zhong Lu, Liwan* ⊠ *Y5–10* ☼ *Daily 8–6.*

TIANHE-DISTRICT SIGHTS

The Tianhe District is Guangzhou's newly designated business and upmarket residential area. Among the buildings is the 80-story **CITIC Plaza,** which soars 396 meters (1,300 feet) and is China's second-tallest building. The **Guangzhou East Railway Station** (⊠ *Linhe Lu, Tianhe*), with its vast entrance hall, is worth a peak, even if you don't have a train to catch. A hub for most of Guangzhou's sporting events, the **Tianhe Stadium Complex** (⊠ *Huanshi Dong Lu, East Guangzhou, Tianhe*) has two indoor and two outdoor arenas that are equipped for international soccer matches, track-and-field competitions, as well as pop concerts and large-scale ceremonies. The complex is surrounded by a pleasantly landscaped park with outdoor cafés and tree-shaded benches. The park includes a bowling center with 38 lanes and lots of video games.

7

WHERE TO EAT

Guangzhou has numerous Indian, Italian, Thai, and Vietnamese restaurants, and owing to the recent influx of Middle Eastern traders, in some parts of town it's easier to find a falafel than a shrimp dumpling. Of course this isn't to say that Guangzhou's traditional delicacies have been usurped. Amazing seafood dishes and braised and barbecued meats are still available in delicious variety, and succulent dim sum still rules the roost as the city's hometown favorite.

Use the coordinate (✛ B2) at the end of each listing to locate a site on the Where to Eat and Stay in Guangzhou map.

$–$$$
CHINESE

✕**Banxi Restaurant.** On the edge of Liwan Lake, this restaurant has a series of teahouse rooms and landscaped gardens interconnected by zigzag paths and bridges that have the feel of a Taoist temple. One room is built on a floating houseboat. The food is as tasty as it looks, with dishes such as scallop and crab soup, and quail eggs cooked with shrimp roe on a bed of green vegetables. ⊠ *151 Longjin Xi Lu, Liwan Park* ☏ *020/8172-1328* ▭ *AE, MC, V* ✛ *A4.*

$$$$
CONTINENTAL

✕**Connoisseur.** This premier restaurant feels like Regency France, with its arched columns, gilded capitals, gold-framed mirrors, lustrous drapes, and immaculate table settings. The French chef specializes in lamb and steak dishes, though the menu has become decidedly more European as of late, with non-French items such as Irish stew now included. The menu changes every six months or so. ⊠ *Garden Hotel,*

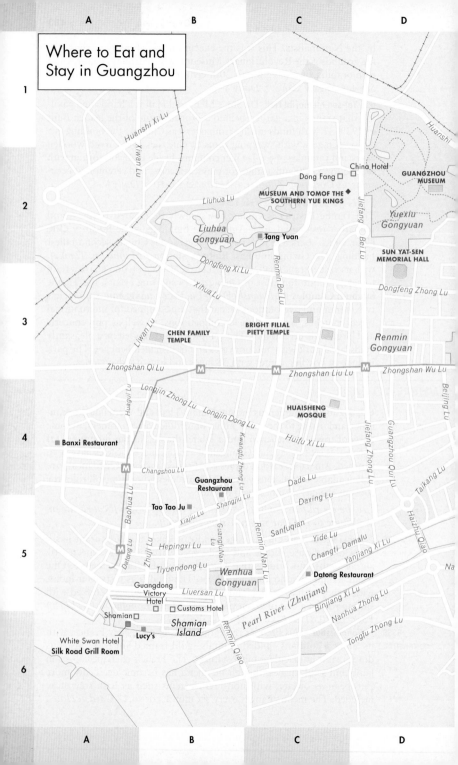

Where to Eat and Stay in Guangzhou

A   **B**   **C**   **D**

Huanshi Xi Lu

Xiwan Lu

Liuhua Lu

Dong Fang

China Hotel

GUANGZHOU MUSEUM

MUSEUM AND TOM OF THE SOUTHERN YUE KINGS

Yuexiu Gongyuan

Liuhua Gongyuan

Tang Yuan

SUN YAT-SEN MEMORIAL HALL

Dongfeng Xi Lu

Xihua Lu

Renmin Bei Lu

Jiefang Bei Lu

Dongfeng Zhong Lu

CHEN FAMILY TEMPLE

BRIGHT FILIAL PIETY TEMPLE

Renmin Gongyuan

Liwan Lu

Zhongshan Qi Lu

Ⓜ

Ⓜ Zhongshan Liu Lu

Ⓜ Zhongshan Wu Lu

Huagui Lu

Longjin Zhong Lu

Longjin Dong Lu

HUAISHENG MOSQUE

Beijing Lu

Kwangfu Zhong Lu

Huifu Xi Lu

Jiefang Zhong Lu

Guangzhou Qui Lu

■ Banxi Restaurant

Ⓜ

Changshou Lu

Guangzhou Restaurant

Dade Lu

Taikang Lu

Baohua Lu

Tao Tao Ju ■

Shangjiu Lu

Daxing Lu

Xiajiu Lu

Sanfuqian

Hazhu Qiao

Datong Lu

Zhuji Lu

Hepingxi Lu

Guanghan Lu

Renmin Nan Lu

Yide Lu

Changti Damalu

Yanjiang Xi Lu

Na

Tiyuendong Lu

Wenhua Gongyuan

■ Datong Restaurant

Ⓜ

Guangdong Victory Hotel

Liuersan Lu

Customs Hotel

Shamian Island

Pearl River (Zhujiang)

Binjiang Xi Lu

Nanhua Zhong Lu

Shamian □

Lucy's

Renmin Qiao

Tongfu Zhong Lu

White Swan Hotel

Silk Road Grill Room

A   **B**   **C**   **D**

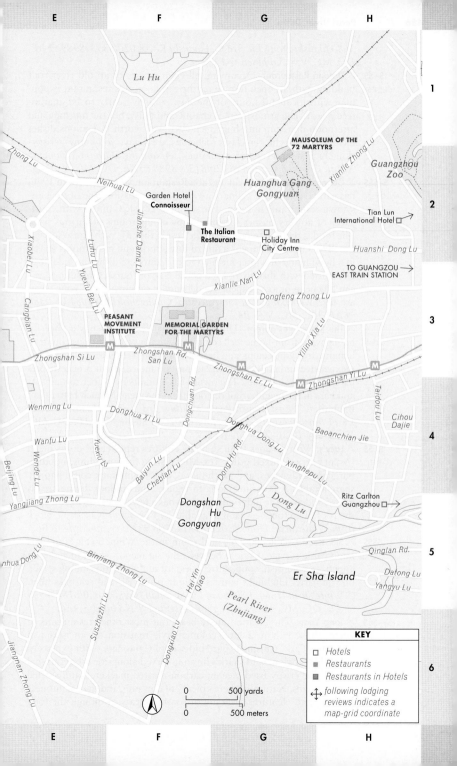

368 Huanshi Dong Lu, 3rd fl., Huanshi Rd. ☎ *020/8333–8989* ▭ *AE, DC, MC, V* ⊘ *No lunch* ✛ *F2.*

$–$$ ✕ **Datong Restaurant.** Occupying all eight stories of an old riverfront
CHINESE building with an open terrace on the top floor, this restaurant is popular with locals all hours of the day, so arrive early to be guaranteed a seat. The atmosphere is chaotic and noisy, but the morning and
afternoon dim sum and huge menu are well worth it. Famous dishes
include stewed chicken claws (delicious, we'll have you know), crispy-
skin chicken, and roasted *Xishi* duck. ⊠ *Nanfang Dasha, 63 Yanjiang
Xi Lu, Colonial Canton* ☎ *020/8188–8988* ▭ *AE, DC, MC, V* ✛ *C5.*

$–$$$ ✕ **Guangzhou Restaurant.** Guangzhou Restaurant, which opened in 1936,
CANTONESE has earned a string of culinary awards, and is possibly one of the best-
known restaurants in town. The setting is classic Canton, with court-
yards of flowery bushes surrounded by dining rooms of various sizes.
The food is reputed to be among the best in the city, with house special-
ties like "Eight Treasures," a mix of fowl, pork, and mushrooms served
in a bowl made of winter melon. Other Cantonese dishes include duck
feet stuffed with shrimp, roasted goose, and of course, dim sum. Meals
can be cheap or very expensive, depending on how exotic your tastes
are. ⊠ *2 Wenchang Nan Lu, Ancestral Guangzhou* ☎ *020/8138–0388*
▭ *AE, DC, MC, V* ✛ *B4.*

$ ✕ **The Italian Restaurant.** This aptly named restaurant has a cheerful
ITALIAN home-away-from-home feel, complete with flags from various countries
hanging from the ceiling and beers from around the world. The food is
inexpensive and good, with pizzas, pastas, and excellent brochette pre-
pared by an Italian chef. The owner has a number of other restaurants
and bars in the neighborhood. Food from the menu is much better than
the buffet. ⊠ *East Tower, Pearl Building, 3rd fl., 360 Huanshi Zhong
Lu., 1 block west of Garden Hotel* ☎ *020/8386–3840* ▭ *AE, DC, MC,
V* ⊘ *Daily 10:30–2, 6–11* ✛ *F2.*

$–$$ ✕ **Lucy's.** With cuisines from so many cultures represented on its menu
ECLECTIC (Asian curries, mixed grills, Tex-Mex dishes, fish-and-chips, noodles,
burgers, sandwiches, and much more), a UN think tank could happily
share a table. A favorite among foreigners, the outdoor dining area is
lovely, and even the indoor dining area has a few trees growing through
the roof. Take-out service is available. ⊠ *3 Shamian Nan Jie, 1 block
from White Swan Hotel* ☎ *020/8121–5106* ▭ *No credit cards* ✛ *B6.*

$$$$ ✕ **Silk Road Grill Room.** This grill room in the White Swan Hotel has
ECLECTIC impeccable service. Choose between the set menu, which includes an
appetizer, cold dish, soup, entrée, dessert, and drink (excluding wine),
or à la carte. Highlight entrées include prime rib and sea-bass fillet.
⊠ *White Swan Hotel, 1 Shamian Lu, Shamian Island* ☎ *020/8188–6968*
▭ *AE, DC, MC, V* ⌃ *Reservations essential* ⊘ *No lunch* ✛ *A6.*

$$–$$$ ✕ **Tang Yuan.** The location alone beats out most other restaurants in
CANTONESE Guangzhou. It is in a faux colonial-style mansion on an island in
Liuhuahu Park. Cuisine is pure old-school Cantonese, with expensive
dishes like abalone and shark's fin soup served alongside more rational
staples like crispy fried pigeon, carbon-roasted mackerel, and stuffed
garlic prawns. Naturally, there's plenty of dim sum, and the "Cantonese
combo plate" features a variety of roasted meats. Although the food

CLOSE UP

To Your Health!

Good-bye Starbucks, hello Wong Chun Loong! For decades the Loong beverage franchise has dominated the Guangzhou scene, and for good reason. They serve drinks that are thirst-quenching, healthy, and taste good (sometimes). The most popular drinks are *huomaren,* a beverage made from crushed hemp seeds (it's the brown beverage displayed on the counter) and *yezi,* or coconut milk. A cup of either costs only Y5.

Wong Chun Loong also brews Chinese medicinal teas—some of the bitterest stuff you're ever likely to taste. If you'd like to try some, point to your throat and say *"wo gan mao"*—"I have a cold." If you're nice, they may give you a free piece of candy to cut the aftertaste.

There are about 800 branches in the city, so you're bound to stumble on one of them.

at Tang Yuan is excellent, most people come here for the opulence as well. Admission fee for the park is waived for guests of the restaurant, and a golf cart waits at the park's entrance on Liuhua Road to whisk diners to the restaurant's palatial front door. ⊠ *Lihuahu Park, Dongfeng Xi Lu and Renmin Bei Lu, 2 blocks west of Yuexiu Gongyuan metro station* ☎ *020/3623–6993* ▤ *AE, DC, MC, V* ✣ *C2.*

$$$$
CANTONESE
✕ **Tao Tao Ju.** Prepare yourself for garish decor, shouted conversations of fellow diners, and a menu full of weird animal parts. Tao Tao Ju (which, roughly translated, means "house of happiness") is one of the most revered traditional Cantonese restaurants in the city. Soups are a favorite, and the menu (available in English) has many that you're unlikely to find elsewhere. The kudzu and snakehead soup is delicious, and they have more than 200 varieties of dim sum. They're also open from 7:00 am to midnight. ⊠ *20 Dishipu Lu, Shangxiajiu* ☎ *020/8139–6111* ▤ *AE, DC, MC, V* ✣ *B5.*

WHERE TO STAY

Use the coordinate (✣ B2) at the end of each listing to locate a site on the Where to Eat and Stay in Guangzhou map.

$$$
▦ **China Hotel.** Managed by Marriott, this hotel is part of a multicomplex that includes office and apartment blocks, a shopping mall big enough to get lost in, and a range of restaurants to satisfy any appetite. The hotel is favored by business travelers because it's connected to the metro and close to the Trade Fair Exhibition Hall. The business center has 16 meeting rooms, and the piano bar in the lobby offers champagne brunches. **Pros:** close to metro, newly renovated rooms. **Cons:** very much a businessperson's hotel. ⊠ *Liuhua Lu Liwan* ☎ *020/8666–6888* ⊕ *www.marriott.com* ⇨ *724 rooms, 126 suites* ♿ *In-room: Internet. In-hotel: 4 restaurants, bars, tennis court, pool, gym* ▤ *AE, DC, MC, V* Ⓜ *Yuexu Gongyuan* ✣ *D2.*

¢
▦ **The Customs Hotel.** This four-story establishment has an attractive colonial facade that blends well with the surrounding area. The bright

interior surrounds an inner courtyard. Standard rooms are tastefully decorated with Republic-era furniture made of dark wood, though the suites seem more cluttered. If possible, get a room facing Shamian Avenue, the quiet, tree-lined street that runs the length of the island. There is a karaoke bar and a lovely backyard garden. (If the Customs Hotel is full, the owners have also just opened the Shamian Clubhouse in a 100-year-old building down the street, with 14 standard rooms, 2 suites, a restaurant, a bar, and a mah-jongg room.) **Pros:** quiet neighborhood, inexpensive. **Cons:** some prefer characterless hotels. ⊠ *No. 35 Shamian Ave., Shamian Island, Colonial Guangzhou* ☎ *20/8110–2388, www. gzzchotel.com* ✍ *customshotel@126.com* ☞ *49 rooms, 7 suites* ⚐ *In-room: Internet. In-hotel: 2 restaurants, bar* ☐ *AE, DC, MC, V* ✛ *B5.*

$$–$$$ 🏨 **Dong Fang.** Across from Liuhua Park and the trade-fair headquarters, this complex is built around a 22½-acre garden with pavilions, carp-filled pools, and rock gardens. The lobby is done up in a Renaissance motif, complete with pillars and gold-and-white floor tiling. The shopping concourse has Chinese antiques and carpets. The hotel recently added an 86,000-square-foot convention center. Discounts up to 30% for rooms in the off-season are not unheard of. **Pros:** spacious gardens, choice of restaurants. **Cons:** not for those who are averse to gigantic. ⊠ *120 Liuhua Lu* ☎ *020/8666–9900; 852/2528–0555 in Hong Kong* ⊕ *www.hoteldongfang.com* ☞ *699 rooms, 101 suites* ⚐ *In-room: Internet. In-hotel: 2 restaurants, gym* ☐ *AE, DC, MC, V* ✛ *C2.*

¢–$ 🏨 **Garden Hotel.** In the northern business suburbs, this huge, aging hotel is famous for its spectacular garden that includes an artificial hill, a waterfall, and pavilions. The cavernous lobby, decorated with enormous murals, has a bar–lounge set around an ornamental pool. Though long considered the standard of luxury in Guangzhou, the Garden is now being given a run for its money by other hotels. **Pros:** spacious premises and gardens, pleasant staff. **Cons:** Some standard rooms in need of renovation. ⊠ *368 Huanshi Dong Lu, Huanshi Road* ☎ *020/8333–8989* ⊕ *www.thegardenhotel.com.cn* ☞ *828 rooms, 42 suites* ⚐ *In-room: Internet. In-hotel: 7 restaurants, bar, tennis courts, pool, gym* ☐ *AE, DC, MC, V* ✛ *F2.*

$$–$$$ 🏨 **Guangdong Victory Hotel.** Over the past few years this Shamian Island
Fodor's Choice hotel has undergone upgrades that have bumped it up from budget
★ class. The two wings, both originally colonial guesthouses, have been beautifully renovated. The main building has a pink-and-white facade, an imposing portico, and twin domes on the roof, where you'll find a pool and an excellent sauna facility. Standard rooms are more than adequate, and the hotel still retains a fairly inexpensive dining room on the first floor. **Pros:** historic, elegant building; peaceful area; great view of the city from the rooftop pool. **Cons:** shabby fitness center. ⊠ *53 Shamian Bei Lu, Shamian Island* ☎ *020/8121–6688* ⊕ *www.vhotel.com* ☞ *328 rooms, 15 suites* ⚐ *In-room: Internet. In-hotel: 2 restaurants, bar, pool, gym* ☐ *AE, DC, MC, V* ✛ *B5.*

$$$ 🏨 **Holiday Inn City Centre.** This 20-year-old, centrally situated hotel has large tasteful rooms that are arranged according to Chinese feng shui principles. The top three executive floors have suites and a lounge–restaurant area with stellar views of smog-shrouded Guangzhou. In

Qingping Market is not for the squeamish.

addition to all its lovely facilities, the hotel also has enough meeting rooms to host a Tony Robbins seminar. **Pros:** good-sized rooms; central location. **Cons:** not what you'd call quaint. ⊠ *28 Guangming Rd., Overseas Chinese Village, Huanshi Dong* ☎ *020/6128–6868* ⊕ *www. guangzhou.holiday-inn.com* ⤳ *430 rooms, 38 suites* ☖ *In-room: Internet. In-hotel: restaurant, bar, pool, gym* ☰ *AE, DC, MC, V* ⊹ *G2.*

$$$ 🏨 **Ritz-Carlton Guangzhou.** Bringing five-star luxury to Guangzhou's emerging Pearl River New City, the Ritz-Carlton Guangzhou features posh rooms with marble baths, a smattering of international restaurants and bars, and a swank spa. In addition to its hundreds of standard guest rooms, the Ritz offers 35 suites and 58 club-level rooms—all of which feature featherbeds draped with gentle Egyptian cotton linens. After a day of exploring the city, rest your tender soles at the spa, which pampers guests with treatments such as aquatherapy beds and a wet lounge with a sauna. **Pros:** in-house Terra restaurant offers unique cuisine; Churchill Bar offers fine cognacs and cigars. **Cons:** during the seasonal Canton Fairs during April and October, booking early is paramount. ⊠ *3 Xing An Lu, Pearl River New City, Guangzhou, China* ☎ *20/3813–6888* 🖷 *20/3813–6666* ⊕ *www.ritzcarlton.com* ⤳ *351 rooms, 35 suites* ☖ *In-room: safe, refrigerator, DVD, Wi-Fi. In-hotel: 4 restaurants, room service, bars, pool, gym, spa, Wi-Fi hotspot* ☰ *AE, DC, MC, V* ⊹ *H5.*

¢ 🏨 **Shamian.** This is a great hotel for visitors on a budget. Its rooms are a little spartan and the lobby cramped, but it is clean and friendly, and the location—right in the middle of Shamian Island—is second to none. **Pros:** great location. **Cons:** no restaurant in hotel. ⊠ *52 Shamian Nan Jie, Shamian Island* ☎ *020/8121–8288* ⊕ *www.gdshamianhotel.com*

🛏️ *48 rooms, 10 suites* ▭ *AE, DC, MC, V* ⚓ *A6.*

$$-$$$ 🏨 **Tian Lun International Hotel.** A new, upscale boutique hotel next to Guangzhou East Railway Station offers large luxury rooms with a sleek edge. The colors are kept to soft blacks, grays, and beige. The buffet in the second-floor café is beautifully arranged around a centerpiece of coral, and the high ceilings lend an air of sophistication.

Pros: near metro and train stations; clean and comfortable rooms. **Cons:** lack of English TV channels. ✉️ *172 Linhe Lu Central, Tianhe District* ⚓ *next to Guangzhou East Railway Station* ☎️ *020/8393–6388* 🌐 *www.tianlun-hotel.com* 🛏️ *403 rooms, 23 suites* ⚓ *In-room: Internet. In-hotel: 3 restaurants, pool, gym* ▭ *AE, DC, MC, V* ⚓ *H2.*

$$ 🏨 **White Swan Hotel.** Occupying a marvelous site on Shamian Island, beside the Pearl River, this huge luxury complex—at 27 years old, one of the most established modern hotels in Guangzhou—has landscaped gardens, two pools, a jogging track, and a separate gym and spa. Its presidential suite is just that; reserved for heads of state, it has been occupied by such "luminaries" as Richard Nixon and Kim Jong-Il. Its restaurants are second to none; the windows of the elegant lobby bar and coffee shop frame the panorama of river traffic. **Pros:** quiet neighborhood; good view of Pearl River. **Cons:** Rooms have not been renovated for several years. ✉️ *Yi Shamian Lu, Shamian Island, Colonial Canton* ☎️ *020/8188–6968; 852/2524–0192 in Hong Kong* 🌐 *www. whiteswanhotel.com* 🛏️ *843 rooms, 92 suites* ⚓ *In-room: Internet. In-hotel: 9 restaurants, bar, pools, gym* ▭ *AE, DC, MC, V* ⚓ *A6.*

NIGHTLIFE AND THE ARTS

PUBS AND BARS

Bingjiang Xilu (✉️ *South of Shamian Island, across the Pearl River*) is *the* street for bar-hopping. Very popular with a younger crowd, it has great views, and if you get bored with looking north across the river you can always cross the bridge to **Yanjiang Xilu** and drink at some of the bars on that side.

Huanshi Dong Lu. Yuexiu and the area behind the Garden Hotel are popular with locals and expats (short- and long-term). Two favorites are **Gypsy** and **Cave,** located on opposite ends of the Zhujiang Building. Cave has a distinct meat-market vibe and features nightly performances by a scantily clad woman whose specialty is dancing with snakes. Gypsy reeks of hashish and is much mellower.

The Paddy Field (✉️ *38 Huale Lu, behind Garden Hotel* ☎️ *020/8360–1379*) makes you long for Ireland. There are darts, pints of Guinness and Kilkenny, and football matches on a massive screen.

1920 Restaurant (✉ *183 Yanjiang Zhong Lu* ☎ *020/8333–6156*) serves up Bavarian food and imported wheat beers on a lovely outdoor patio. Entrées start at Y60, beers at Y30.

The **Café Lounge** (✉ *China Hotel, lobby* ☎ *020/8666–6888*) has a mellow vibe, big comfortable bar stools, quiet tables for two, live music on weekends, and a fine selection of cigars.

The big attraction of the **Hare and Moon** (✉ *White Swan Hotel, Yi Shamian Lu, Shamian Island* ☎ *020/8188–6968*) is the panorama of the Pearl River as it flows past the picture windows.

IN THE NEWS

Some good publications to check out for regularly updated info on ongoing cultural happenings are *City Weekend* and *That's PRD*.

DANCE CLUBS

Deep Anger Music Power House (✉ *183 Yanjiang Lu* ☎ *020/8317–7158* ☞ *Free* ☉ *Daily 8 pm–2 am*) is a cool dance club located in a building that was a theater back in the days of Sun Yat-sen. Lounge lizards and history buffs will enjoy sipping a beer here.

Soho Bar (✉ *87 Changdi Dama Lu* ☎ *020/8319–5095* ☞ *Y50–Y100 depending on night* ☉ *8 pm–3 am*) is the biggest and hippest dance club in Guangzhou. Get your jive on to house and electronica inside, or chill in the outdoor area if you've lost your hearing.

ART AND CULTURE

If you think Guangzhou's high culture begins and ends with Cantonese opera, think again, pilgrim—the art and performance scene here is vibrant, and getting more so every day. The city is undergoing a cultural broadening, as evidenced by the opening of small art spaces, more eclectic forms of theater, and more national attention focused on the city's major museums. Of course, purists need not panic; the Cantonese opera has hardly disappeared.

Xinghai Concert Hall (✉ *33 Qingbo Lu, Er Sha Island* ☎ *020/8735–2222 Ext. 312 for English*) is the home of the Guangzhou Symphony Orchestra, and puts on an amazing array of concerts featuring national and international performers. The concert hall is surrounded by a fantastic sculpture garden, and is next door to the Guangzhou Museum of Art, making the two an excellent mid-afternoon to evening trip.

☉ **Guangzhou Puppet Art Center** (✉ *51 Hongde Lu* ☎ *020/8431–0227*) hosts live puppet shows every Saturday and Sunday at 10:30 am and 3 pm.

Guangdong Modern Dance Company (✉ *13 Shuiyinhenglu, Shaheding* ☎ *020/8704–9512* ⊕ *www.gdmdc.com*) is mainland China's first professional modern-dance company, and the troupe is regularly praised by publications such as the *New York Times* and the *Toronto Sun*. This theater is their home base. Their English-language Web site has a full performance schedule.

GALLERIES AND PERFORMANCE SPACES

If eclectic art is your thing, then **Vitamin Creative Space** (✉ *29 Hengyi Jie, inside of Xinggang Cheng, Haizhu District* ☎ *020/8429–6760* ⊕ *www. vitamincreativespace.com* ☉ *Mon.–Sat. 10 am–6 pm*) might be worth

Shop 'til you drop in Guangzhou.

the trip. But be warned, it's located in the back of a semi-enclosed vegetable market and not easy to find even if you speak Chinese. Call first (the curator speaks English), and someone will escort you from in front of the market. Hours are somewhat erratic, but the art can be as wonderfully weird as anything you're likely to find in China.

SHOPPING

MALLS AND MARKETS

Shangxiajiu (✉ *Follow signs from Changshou Lu metro*) is a massive warren of old buildings and shops and considered the user-friendly heart of Old Guangzhou. The half-mile main street is a pedestrian mall boasting nearly 250 shops and department stores. The buildings in Shangxiajiu are old, but the stores are the same ones as in "modern Guangzhou." Even though the overall decibel level hovers around deafening, the area isn't without its charms. Our favorite shops are the small storefronts offering dried-fruit samples, which are very addictive. The area draws a big, younger crowd, but there are a few quiet back alleys that keep it from feeling too overwhelming. There's also a wide variety of street stalls selling a large selection of delicious edibles.

Beijing Road Pedestrian Mall (✉ *Follow signs from Gongyuanqian metro*) offers an interesting contrast to Shangxiajiu. Shangxiajiu offers new stores in old buildings, whereas Beijing Road makes no pretense at being anything other than a fully modern, neon-draped pedestrian mall, similar to Beijing's Wangfujing Street or Shanghai's Nanjing Street. Pedestrianized and open from around 10 am until 10 pm, this is where city teenagers buy sensible, midrange Hong Kong–style clothes and increasingly garish local brands. Noisy and fun, the street is lined with cheap food stalls, cafés, and fast-food chains.

Haizhu Plaza (✉ *Haizhu Sq., north of Haizhu Bridge, Haizhu* Ⓜ *Guang-chang* ⊗ *Daily 10–6*) is a massive, two-story flea and souvenir market where casual shoppers and wholesale buyers alike bargain for kitsch—think toys, faux antiques, and Cultural Revolution–themed knick-knacks. Merchants keep calculators at hand for entering figures in the heat of negotiation, and vendors sell a variety of snacks from carts located by the exits.

La Perle (✉ *367 Huanshi Dong Lu, across from the Garden Hotel* ⊗ *Daily 10–10*) has genuine designer clothes at expensive prices, with shops such as Versace, Louis Vuitton, Polo, and Prada.

Zhanxi Market. At this wholesale and retail market you can get bargains on jeans, suits, and many other kinds of clothing. Be prepared to bargain, though sellers are not as aggressive as in some places like Beijing. (✉ *Zhan Xi Rd.,* ✛ *near to the Guangzhou railway station and the provincial bus station* ⊗ *9–late*).

ANTIQUES AND TRADITIONAL CRAFTS

On Shamian Island the area between the White Swan and Victory hotels has a number of small family-owned shops that sell paintings, carvings, pottery, knickknacks, and antiques.

Guangzhou Arts Centre (✉ *698 Renmin Bei Lu* ☎ *020/8667–9898*) has a fine selection of painted scrolls. The Arts Centre is located inside the Friendship Theatre.

BOOKSTORES

Guangzhou Books Center (✉ *123 Tianhe Lu* ☎ *020/3886–4208 Chinese only*) is a chain with seven floors of books on every subject, including some bargain-priced art books in English.

SIDE TRIP TO BAIYUN MOUNTAIN

17 km (10½ mi) north of central Guangzhou.

Baiyun Mountain (Baiyun Shan). Also known as White Cloud Mountain, this peak gets its name from the halo of clouds that, in the days before heavy pollution, appeared around the peak following a rainstorm. The mountain is part of a 28-square-km (17-square-mi) resort area, and consists of six parks, 30 peaks, and myriad gullies. **Santailing Park** is home to the enormous Yuntai Garden, of interest to anybody with a thing for botany. **Fei'eling Park** has a nice sculpture garden, and **Luhu Park** is home to Jinye Pond, as pure and azure a body of water as you're likely to find within 100 mi. All in all, a trip to Baiyun Mountain is a good way to get out of the city center—maybe for a day of hiking—without traveling too far. Couples climbing to the top of the mountain may wish to bring a small lock with them to show their commitment to each other and add it to the thousands of other locks that lovers have clipped to chains at the top. ⊕ *www.baiyunshan.com.cn* ✉ *Y5 for Baiyun Mountain; small additional fees for other parks.* ⊗ *Daily 9–5.*

GETTING HERE AND AROUND

Bus 24 leaves from Dongfeng Zhonglu, just north of Renmin Gongyuan, and travels to the cable car (Y25) at the bottom of the hill near Luhu Park. The 15-km (9-mi) trip takes between half an hour and one hour, depending on traffic. A taxi shouldn't set you back more than Y100.

SHENZHEN

112 km (70 mi; 1 hr by express train, 2½ hrs by express bus) from Guangzhou. Walk across border from Hong Kong's Luohu KCR (Kowloon–Canton Railway) train station.

Shenzhen may be China's youngest city, but this is one metropolis that's definitely come of age. A small farming town until 1980, Shenzhen was chosen by Deng Xiaoping as an incubator in which the seeds of China's economic reform were to be nurtured. The results are the stuff of legend; a quarter century later Shenzhen is now China's richest, and, according to some, its most vibrant city.

Until recently, most visitors thought of China's youngest city as a place to pass through on the way from Hong Kong to Guangzhou. But over the last several years this has changed as more expats choose to call Shenzhen home, and more travelers discover that the city is a unique destination in itself.

GETTING HERE AND AROUND

Tens of thousands of people cross from Hong Kong into Shenzhen (and back) daily, usually over the Luohu border crossing. Over the weekends, numbers can triple. Most visitors take the metro from Kowloon to the crossing and walk into Shenzhen. A more expensive—but infinitely more pleasant—way is to take the ferry from Hong Kong's Central ferry pier to Shekou Harbor. Here immigration lines are a fraction of what they can be in Luohu.

AIR TRAVEL Shenzhen's Bao'an International Airport is very busy, with flights to 50 cities. There is commuter service by bus between the airport and Hong Kong, as well as a ferry link between the Shenzhen and Hong Kong airports. Bus service links the Shenzhen Railway Station, via Huaren Dasha, direct to Shenzhen Airport for Y25 (one way).

BOAT AND The Web site *www.shenzhenparty.com* maintains an updated schedule
FERRY TRAVEL for trains and ferries. The Turbojet Company runs regular ferries connecting Hong Kong, Shenzhen, Macau, and Zhuhai. Check their Web site for schedules and prices. One-way from Hong Kong to Shenzhen is around Y70.

BUS TRAVEL Air-conditioned express buses crisscross most of the Pearl River Delta region several times a day. Buses for Shenzhen leave from a number of places, including the China Travel Service branches in Central and Wan Chai.

SUBWAY Shenzhen's metro has two lines, and tickets range between Y2 and Y8.
TRAVEL At this writing, Line 1 is being extended and is expected to connect with the Bao'an International Airport by the end of 2011. This should cut travel time to downtown Shenzhen and also to Shekou (where you can catch a ferry to Hong Kong). The north-south Line 4 is also being

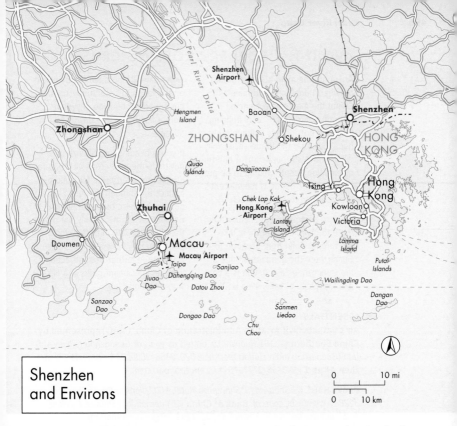

Shenzhen and Environs

| 0 | | 10 mi |
| 0 | | 10 km |

extended, and three new lines are being built that are slated to be finished sometime in 2011.

TRAIN TRAVEL Shenzhen can easily be reached from Hong Kong by taking the metro from Hong Kong's Kowloon Tong station to Luohu Railway Station and then crossing over to Shenzhen on foot. Metro trains depart from Luohu to Hong Kong every five minutes. Trains between Guangzhou East Railway Station and Shenzhen's Luohu Railway Station depart every hour and cost between Y80 and Y100.

SAFETY AND PRECAUTIONS
Shenzhen is safe for the most part, but keep an eye on your bags and watch how much you drink around the expat bar areas; prostitutes and pickpockets have been known to prey on drunken foreigners.

TIMING
Shenzhen can be an interesting city to live in, but it's not that exciting as a tourist destination. A day or two is probably sufficient.

TOURS
⇨ *See specific tours listed in Guangzhou and Hong Kong.*

AVOID THE BORDER-CROSSING CRUSH

At Luohu (the main border crossing between Hong Kong and mainland China) the masses are funneled through a large three-story building. From the outside this building looks huge, but from the inside—especially when you're surrounded by a quarter of a million people waiting to be processed—the crossing is reminiscent of a scene from *Soylent Green*.

If you're going through Shenzhen en route to or from Guangzhou, take the through train from Kowloon to Guangzhou. The immigration line at the Guangzhou East Station is a comparative piece of cake, even on the worst days. It's possible to buy tickets on the fly on this commuter train, but we advise booking anywhere from a few hours to a day or two in advance.

If you're heading into Shenzhen, why not trade the mad crush of Luohu for an hour-long ferry ride followed by a quick trip through the much less popular border crossing at Shekou Harbor? Ferries are usually not more than half full. Although this won't bring you into downtown Shenzhen, you'll be no farther from attractions like the amusement parks and Mission Hills Golf Club.

ESSENTIALS

Air Contacts Civil Aviation Administration of China, CAAC represented by China Southern (✉ *181 Huanshi Lu, on left as you exit Guangzhou railway station [Guangzhou main station metro]* ☎ *020/8668–2000; 24-hr hotline*). **Shenzhen Airport** (☎ *0755/2777–7821* ⊕ *eng.szairport.com*).

Banks HSBC (✉ *Shop No. 9, Shangri-la Hotel, 1002 Jianshe Rd.* ☎ *755/8266–3228* ⊕ *www.hsbc.com.cn*). **Bank of China** (✉ *International Finance Building, 2022 Jianshe Rd., Luohu District* ☎ *755/2233–8888* ⊕ *www.boc.cn*).

Boat and Ferry Contacts Hong Kong-Macau Ferry Terminal (✉ *Shun Tak Centre, Connaught Rd., Central* ☎ *853/2546–3528*). **Shenzhen Party** (⊕ *www.shenzhenparty.com/travel*). **The Turbojet Company** (☎ *852/2859–3333*) ⊕ *www.turbojet.com.hk*).

Bus Contact Shenzhen Luohu Bus Station (✉ *1st–2nd fls., East Plaza, Luohu District* ☎ *755/8232–1670*).

Medical Assistance Shenzhen People's Hospital (✉ *Dongmen Bei Lu N* ☎ *0755/2553–3018 Ext. 2553; 1387 [Outpatient Dept.]*).

Subway Contact Shenzhen Metro (☎ *020/8310–6622 for information in English; 020/8310–6666*).

Train Contacts The Mass Transit Rail (MTR) (☎ *852/2881–8888* ⊕ *www.mtr.com.hk*). **Shenzhen Railway Station** (✉ *Luohu District* ☎ *020/8232–8647*).

EXPLORING SHENZHEN

Sprawling Shenzhen is composed of several districts. Luohu and Futian are the "downtown" districts, with most of the major shopping areas, financial districts, and hundreds of hotels. Reputable and not-so-reputable spas and massage parlors abound near the railway station in

Luohu, mainly catering to Hong Kongers over for the day. Look for the famous Queen's Spa in Louhu—open 24 hours and with five floors, you could almost use it as a hotel.

A foray outside the sprawl of Shenzhen proper is worth the trip if you have the time; Yantian and Longgang are great destinations for beaches and atmospheric historical buildings, respectively.

LUOHU, FUTIAN, NANSHAN, AND SHEKOU

Futian, Shenzhen's trading hub, is also where Shenzhen's gourmands go for a night of gastronomic pleasure. The Zhenhua Road restaurant district in Futian is where scores of excellent restaurants compete for the patronage of Shenzhen's very discriminating diners. CoCo Park in the Futian district is probably the city's most hopping nightspot.

The Shekou neighborhood in the Nanshan district is also a popular area for its many bars and restaurants, though a bit more laid-back than the club scene in the east. Shekou was the first Special Economic Zone, marking the earliest baby step of modern China's transformation from state-planned to market economy, and one of China's oldest modern expat areas. Nowadays the neighborhood is best known for Sea World Plaza, a pedestrian mall featuring restaurants, bars, and a completely landlocked oceangoing vessel (now transformed into a bar, hotel, and nightclub complex), and the Shekou bar street.

Nanshan's Overseas Chinese Town, or Huaqiao Cheng, is Shenzhen's arts and theme-park district. Here you will find the **OCT Park**, an urban expanse of greenery and sculptures. There are two excellent museums, the **Hexiangning Museum of Contemporary Chinese Art** and the more underground-feeling **OCAT** (Overseas Chinese Art Terminal). The OCT also has three popular theme parks.

TOP ATTRACTIONS

Window of the World gives a miniature makeover to 130 of the world's most famous landmarks, and is China's biggest and busiest homegrown theme park. Divided into eight geographical areas interconnected by winding paths and a full-size monorail, it includes—randomly scaled—the Taj Mahal, Mount Rushmore, Sydney Harbor Opera House, and a 100-meter-high (328-foot-high) Eiffel Tower that can be seen from miles away. There is also a fireworks show at 9 pm on weekends and holidays, which, for adults, is best viewed from across the street at the Crowne Plaza's rooftop V-Bar. ⊠ *OCT, Nanshan District, Shenzhen* ☎ *0755/2660–8000* ⊕ *www.szwwco.com* ✉ *Y120* ☾ *Daily 9 am–10:30 pm* Ⓜ *Window of the World.*

WORTH NOTING

In addition to its statue-filled Overseas Chinese Town Park, the OCT neighborhood is packed with other museums.

SHENZHEN VIA UNDERGROUND

Shenzhen's metro Line 1 runs from the terminus at Luohu Station to the Shenzhen University stop, though at this writing it will extend all the way to Bao'an International Airport by the end of 2011. What's more, many stations have sculptures, murals, and other objets d'art. The metro is cheap, easy to use, and has announcements in Chinese and English.

The **Hexiangning Art Museum** is free on Friday and features contemporary and classical art from all over China. ✉ *Shenzhen shi Huaqiaocheng Shennan Dadao hao, OCT, Nanshan District* 📞 *0755/2660–4540* ⊕ *www.hxnart.com* ⊗ *Tues.–Sun. 10–6* Ⓜ *Huaqiaocheng.*

The **OCT Contemporary Art Terminal.** Shenzhen shi Huaqiaocheng Enping Lu is where you'll find works from the hippest artists from Beijing and beyond. ✉ *OCT, Nanshan District* 📞 *0755/2691–6199* ⊕ *www.ocat. com.cn* 🎫 *Free* ⊗ *Tues.–Sun. 10–5:30* Ⓜ *Huaqiaocheng.*

> **PLAY TIME**
>
> The theme parks in OCT could all be visited in a single day, but for the sake of sanity, we recommend visiting only two for the day. They are connected by an elevated monorail that costs Y20.

OUTER SHENZHEN

Just east of Luohu, Yantian is Shenzhen's beach district. **Dameisha** and **Xiaomeisha** are two beaches adjacent to one another, which offer sun, surf, and strange statues of colorful winged men doing what appears to be beachfront tai chi. Dameisha is a public beach, whereas Xiaomeisha has a Y20 admission price. Both are about 40 minutes from Luohu by taxi. These beaches can tend to be overcrowded in the summer, though Xichong Beach, another 30 minutes by taxi to the east, is larger and much more secluded than its neighbors close to town. The water quality is also better, and some surfing can be found here.

Like the rapidly disappearing hutong neighborhoods of Beijing, **Dapeng Fortress** in the Longgang district is a living museum. The Old Town contains homes, temples, shops, and courtyards that look pretty much the way they did when they were built over the course of the Ming (1368–1644) and Qing (1644–1911) dynasties. For the most part, the residences are occupied, the shops are doing business, and the temples are active houses of worship. Dapeng's ancient city is surrounded by an old stone wall, and entered through a series of gates.

The **Hakka Folk Customs Museum and Enclosures** is another walled town. This one was built (and formerly occupied) by the Hakka, or Kejia as they are known in Mandarin—Han Chinese who are said to have migrated from north to south ages ago, bringing with them their own cuisine, traditions, and intriguingly peculiar building design.

Both of these slices of ancient China are about an hour away from the modern heart of Luohu by taxi.

TOP ATTRACTIONS

Minsk World. This is Shenzhen's most popular—and perhaps strangest—tourist attraction. It's pretty cheesy but young kids might get a kick out of it. Essentially, it's a decommissioned Soviet-era aircraft carrier that a group of businessmen bought in the late 1990s. Parked in perpetuity on the top deck of the ship (which is as long as three football fields placed end to end, and gets wickedly hot in the summer) are several Soviet fighter planes and helicopters. Every hour on the hour comely young ladies in military costumes perform a dance routine combining sensuality with martial flair and twirling rifles. ✉ *Shatoujiao, Dapeng*

Don't miss the floor show at Minsk World.

Bay, Yantian District, Shenzhen ☎ 0755/2535–5333 ⊕ www.szminsk. com (Chinese only) 🎟 Y110 ⊗ Daily 9:30–7:30.

Dapeng Fortress was built more than 600 years ago, and is an excellent example of a Ming Dynasty military encampment (1368–1644). The fortress was originally built to resist Japanese pirates harassing the southern coastal areas of Guangdong. However, the fortress is best known as the site of the British Naval attack of September 4, 1839, in which British forces attacked China in what is widely considered the beginning of the Opium Wars. ✉ Pengcheng Village, Dapeng Town, Longgang District, Shenzhen ☎ 0755/8431–9269 🎟 Y20 ⊗ Daily 10–9.

Hakka Folk Customs Museum and Enclosures is a large series of concentric circular homes built inside an exterior wall that basically turns the whole place into a large fort. Inside the enclosure are a large number of old Hakka residences, some of which are still filled with tools and furniture left over from the Qing Dynasty. While some restoration projects elsewhere might pretty things up to the point of making the site look unreal, the opposite is true here. ✉ Luoruihe Village, Longgang Township, Longgang District, Shenzhen ☎ 0755/8429–6258 🎟 Y20 ⊗ Daily 10–6.

WORTH NOTING

If you're interested in watching art in the making, spend an afternoon at the **Dafen Oil Painting Village**, a small town 20 minutes by taxi from Luohu, which employs thousands of artists painting everything from originals to copies of classics. Where do all those oil paintings you find in motels come from? Visit Dafen and you'll know. Be aware that opening hours are sporadic. ⊠ *Shen Hui Rd., Bu Ji St., Longgang District* ☏ *0755/8473–2633* ⊙ *Daily 10–6:30.*

WHERE TO EAT

From the heavy mutton stews of Xinjiang to the succulent seafood dishes of Fujian, Shenzhen is home to thousands of restaurants existing not to please the fickle palates of visitors but to alleviate the homesickness of people pining for native provinces left behind.

$$–$$$$
ECLECTIC
Fodor's Choice
★

✕ **360.** One of the brighter stars on the Shenzhen haute-cuisine scene, 360 takes up the top two floors of the Shangri-la Hotel and offers sumptuous dishes like homemade pasta with eggplant, zucchini, and pesto sauce and ginger-crusted-salmon fillet with couscous and lemon-celery sauce. The ambience is chic, and the view from any table in the house is breathtaking. For food, decor, and view we can't recommend this place highly enough. ⊠ *31st fl., Shangri-la Hotel, 1002 Jianshe Rd., Luohu* ☏ *0755/8396–1380* ▭ *AE, DC, MC, V* Ⓜ *Luohu.*

$$$–$$$$
ITALIAN
★

✕ **Blue.** Arguably one of the finest Italian restaurants in China, the decor, as the name suggests, is blue—blue walls, ceilings, and mellow indigo lighting. The food is expensive, but worth every penny. If you're really in the mood for decadence, try the dessert tray—chocolates, pastries, and eight different types of mousse surround a caramelized sugar statue of David. ⊠ *Crowne Plaza Hotel, 3rd fl., 9026 Shen Nan Rd., OCT/ Nanshan District* ☏ *0755/2693–6888 Ext. 8022, 8023, or 8106* ▭ *AE, DC, MC, V.*

$$$$
CONTEMPORARY

✕ **Greenland Lounge.** This favorite is known for its international-style buffet and truly unique selection of Chinese teas. The glass-domed roof and smart-casual ambience make this a popular spot for Shenzhen's movers and shakers. ⊠ *Lobby, Pavilion hotel, 4002 Huaqiang Rd. N, Futian District* ☏ *0755/8207–8888 Ext. 8213* ▭ *AE, DC, MC, V.*

$$$
INDIAN

✕ **Little India.** This is definitely more than your average curry house. The Nepalese chef offers cuisine from both northern India and Nepal. The restaurant is especially known for its tandoori dishes and for its selection of baked *nan* breads. Little India is also the only restaurant in the Sea World Plaza that offers hookahs, though they'll gently ask you to smoke on the outdoor pavilion during peak hours. ⊠ *Shop 73–74, Sea World Plaza, Shekou District* ☏ *0755/2685–2688* ▭ *MC, V.*

$$–$$$$
CHINESE FUSION

✕ **Sunday Chiu Chow King.** The dim sum and other Cantonese dishes are good, but what really sets this place apart is the excellent Chaozhou (or Chiu Chow) cuisine. Well known on both sides of the border,

ADVENTUROUS EATING

The Futian District's Zhenhua Road, just two blocks north of the Hua Qiang metro station, is one of the few food streets that has not succumbed to the franchise blight of McDonald's and KFC. There are very few English menus and even less Western food, so be prepared to be adventurous. Two good choices are the North Sea Fishing Village Restaurant, whose waitstaff speak a bit of English, and has live seafood in tanks out front allowing diners to point and choose, and Lao Yuan Zi, a restaurant with a definite *Crouching Tiger Hidden Dragon* vibe.

this restaurant is usually packed on weekends with noisy diners from Hong Kong. Try the crispy fried tofu and steamed seafood balls, or the yin-yang soup (it's the soup that looks like a yin-and-yang symbol, made up of rice congee on one side and creamed spinach on the other—just point to the picture on the menu). All of these are Chaozhou specialty dishes. ⊠ *Jenshe Lu, 9th–10th fls., Sandao CenterLuohu ⊹ 2 blocks north of Shangri-La Hotel* ☎ *0755/8231–0222* ▭ *V* Ⓜ *Luohu.*

¢ ✕ **Yokohama.** Enjoy excellent sushi and amazing views of the fishing
JAPANESE boats and ferries of Shekou Harbor to the east and Nanshan Moun-
★ tain to the north. This is a good place to stop before taking the ferry to Hong Kong or Macau. Sashimi is the freshest around, and other dishes are the real deal. The clientele is mostly Japanese, which is always a good sign. Try a side dish of *oshinko* (traditional Japanese pickles)—unlike many lesser Japanese restaurants in China, Yokohama takes no shortcuts with its oshinko, and offers eight different types. ⊠ *Shekou Harbor, Nanhai Hotel, 10th fl., Shekou District* ☎ *0755/2669–2888 Ext. 393* ▭ *AE, DC, MC, V.*

WHERE TO STAY

$$$$ 🏨 **Crowne Plaza.** This hotel holds its own among the best hotels in Asia.
Fodor's Choice The theme is pure Italian Renaissance, right down to the Venetian gon-
★ dolier uniforms worn by the staff, and the wide spiral staircases and long hallways give the place an M. C. Escher aura. The Crowne's swimming pool is the largest in Shenzhen, and extends from an indoor pool under a domed roof to a connected outdoor pool with a swim-up bar. One regular patron told us that she comes back "because anywhere you look in this hotel there's something interesting." The Crowne also has a number of excellent restaurants. **Pros:** near metro; stylish decor; good restaurants. **Cons:** you may not have been thinking Italy when you came to China. ⊠ *Shenan Rd., OCT/Nanshan District ⊹ Across from Windows of the World metro station* ☎ *0755/2693–6888* ⊕ *www. crowneplaza.com* ⤳ *368 rooms, 47 suites* ⌂ *In-hotel: 4 restaurants, bars, pool, gym* ▭ *AE, DC, MC, V.*

¢–$ 🏨 **Nan Hai.** This hotel's retro Space Age exterior, featuring rounded balconies that look as if they might detach from the mother ship at any moment, is the first sight greeting visitors on coming over on the ferry from Hong Kong. Although one of Shenzhen's older luxury hotels, the Nan Hai still holds its own in the moderate-luxury class, offering a lobby piano bar, attractive rooms with balconies and sea views, and a number of excellent restaurants. **Pros:** near pier for ferries to Hong Kong Island and to Hong Kong International Airport. **Cons:** dated decor. ⊠ *1 Gongye Yilu, Shekou/ Nanshan District* ☎ *0755/2669– 2888* ⊕ *www.nanhai-hotel.com*

OUT IN SHENZHEN

One of the byproducts of China's rapid modernization has been the shedding of old taboos. Although it's an overstatement to say that being gay is no longer taboo, it is safe to say that the closet door has been opened in a big way. And nowhere is this truer than in Shenzhen, which has always prided itself on being ahead of the curve.

↗ *396 rooms and suites* ⛄ *In-hotel: 3 restaurants, bar, tennis courts, pool, gym* ⊟ *AE, DC, MC, V.*

$$–$$$ ▦ **The Pavilion.** With a great location in the heart of the Futian business district and a gorgeous interior (check out the domed-glass roof over a central piano bar–teahouse), the Pavilion is one of the top international-class hotels in Shenzhen. Service is good, especially for a locally managed hotel, and most staff members speak English. The meeting rooms have everything an international traveler could need. **Pros:** good location and service. **Cons:** rooms don't have much character. ⊠ *4002 Huaqiang Bei Lu, Futian District* ☎ *0755/8207–8888* ⊕ *www. pavilionhotel.com* ↗ *297 rooms and suites* ⛄ *In-hotel: 3 restaurants, bar, pool, gym* ⊟ *AE, DC, MC, V.*

¢–$ ▦ **Seaview O-City Hotel Shenzhen.** Staying in the OCT District but can't afford the Crowne Plaza? The nearby Seaview O-City Hotel is a good bet, albeit far less luxurious. Though rack prices are steep, discounts of up to 40% are usually available. The Seaview is clean, comfortable, has a water view, and, as it's across the street from the Hexiangning Art Museum, is popular with visiting artists. The second-floor restaurant serves excellent Western food, and the third-floor Cantonese restaurant is good for dim sum. **Pros:** affordable, water views. **Cons:** pretty standard. ⊠ *Nos. 3–5 Guangqiao St., OCT, Nanshan District, Shenzhen* ⊹ *Directly in front of Huaqiao Cheng metro* ☎ *0755/2660–2222* ⊕ *www.octhotels.com* ↗ *437 rooms, 17 suites* ⛄ *In-hotel: 2 restaurants, bar, gym* ⊟ *AE, DC, MC, V.*

$$$$ ▦ **Shangri-La Shenzhen.** The location (practically straddling the border with Hong Kong) has made it a popular meeting place and a city landmark. Rooms are first-class, hospitality is excellent, and the hotel features in-house wireless Internet and top-notch spa facilities. What really makes Shangri-La worth a visit is the 360 Lounge and Restaurant, which takes up the top two floors of the hotel and offers a view of Shenzhen. The Shangri-La also has a number of other excellent restaurants, making it a good choice for visitors who might not want to come into contact with the neighborhood's rougher edges. **Pros:** near Lowu shopping malls. **Cons:** noisy and crowded neighborhood. ⊠ *1002 Jianshe Lu, Luohu District, Shenzhen* ⊹ *Luohu, east side of train station* ☎ *0755/8233–0888* ⊕ *www.shangri-la.com* ↗ *552 rooms, 30 suites* ⛄ *In-hotel: 5 restaurants, 3 bars, pool, gym* ⊟ *AE, DC, MC, V.*

NIGHTLIFE AND THE ARTS

Shenzhen's nightlife is so happening that it's not unusual to run into people—expats and Chinese—who have come in from Hong Kong and Guangzhou just to party. The two major nightlife centers are the Coco Park in the Futian District and Shekou in the Nanshan District (Coco Park tends to be flashier and Shekou a bit more laid-back), but a couple of cool spots are in the OCT District as well.

Club Viva! (⊠ *140 Coco Park Shopping Park Futian District* ☎ *137/ 9825–6176*) is the current hot spot in Coco Park. From salsa music to hip-hop, you can dance the night away at the indoor club or enjoy

A pedestrian walkway in the center of Shenzhen City.

a mojito in the comfy seats of the outdoor patio while you mingle with Shenzhen's young professional crowd.

True Color (✉ *3/4F Dongyuan Mansion, 1 Dongyuan Lu, Luohu District* ☎ *0755/8227–4834*) has one of the coolest party scenes in Shenzhen, and attracts top-name international DJs. Musical tastes range from trance to house, and the party usually doesn't break up until dawn.

V-Bar (✉ *Crowne Plaza Hotel, rooftop OCT District* ☎ *0755/2693–6888*) is without a doubt the hottest nightspot in the OCT, featuring a live band, a holographic globe hovering over a circular bar, and a fireworks show on weekends at 9 pm, courtesy of the Windows of the World theme park across the street. The V-Bar is the only bar in town with an attached swimming pool.

The Terrace (✉ *Sea World Square, Shekou District* ☎ *0755/2682–9105*) is the place in Shekou to dance, drink, and party. The Filipino house band rocks the joint almost every night, but you can also find blues, reggae, and other music here any night of the week. If you need a rest from dancing, slip out to the outdoor balcony for a cocktail and a view over the Shekou area. There's also good Thai and American food served here.

SHOPPING

Dongmen Shopping Plaza (✉ *Laojie Metro Station, Exit A Luohu District, Shenzhen* ☎ *No phone*) is Shenzhen's oldest shopping area. It's a sprawling pedestrian plaza with both large shopping centers for name-brand watches, shoes, bags, cosmetics, and clothes, and plenty of smaller outdoor shops. If you're into people-watching, grab a glass of bubble

Wu Xiangbin, the head of Mission Hills Golf Academy, gives a student some pointers.

tea and soak up the sights—the plaza is like a low-rent version of the fashionista youth culture in Tokyo's Ginza.

CITIC City Plaza (⊠ *1093 Shennan Rd., Shenzhen* ☎ *0755/2594–1502* ⊗ *Daily 10:30 –10* Ⓜ *Kexueguan*) offers upscale shopping for the time-conscious business traveler. Shops include Japanese department stores **Seibu** and **Jusco** and **Louis Vuitton, Polo,** and **Tommy Hilfiger.** There's also a food court on the lower level that's not a bad place to take a break over some coffee or a bowl of noodle soup.

Luohu Commercial City (⊠ *Adjacent to the Hong Kong Border Crossing/Luohu metro station, Shenzhen* ☎ *No phone* ⊗ *Daily 10–10*) is a stalwart of Shenzhen mixed-bag shopping. On one hand its location (straddling the Hong Kong–Shenzhen border) makes it a good place to do last-minute shopping for pirate DVDs, shoddy electronics, and knockoffs of just about any name brand you can think of, and stalls selling semiprecious stones and feng shui knickknacks on the second floor are pretty cool. On the other hand, Luohu Commercial City has some of the most aggressive touts you're likely to find in Shenzhen. If having "DVD? Rolex watch?" shouted every 20 seconds doesn't bother you, this place might be worth the trip.

San Dao Plaza (⊠ *Jenshe Lu, Luohu, Shenzhen* ⊗ *9–8* Ⓜ *Luohu*) This four-story extravaganza is the area's best market for medicinal herbs, tea, and tea-related products. The top two floors contain a series of stalls where merchants sell

FORE!

Although manufacturing is undoubtedly the Pearl River Delta's raison d'être, golfing may well come in as a close second with more than 30 courses.

a wide range of Chinese teas. Visitors are generally invited to *lai, he cha,* or come drink tea. Don't worry, it isn't considered rude to have a cup without buying anything, but you'll find it hard to leave empty-handed. Downstairs there is also a large vegetable market, and small shops selling traditional Chinese herbal medicines, incense, and religious items.

GOLF

The **Guangzhou Luhu Golf and Country Club** (✉ *Lujing Rd.* ☎ *020/8350–7777*) has 18 holes spread over 180 acres of Luhu Park, 20 minutes from the Guangzhou Railway Station and 30 minutes from Baiyun Airport. The 6,820-yard, par-72 course was designed by renowned architect Dave Thomas. The club has a 75-bay driving range and a clubhouse with restaurants, pro

shop, tennis courts, pool, and gym. Members' guests and those from affiliated clubs pay Y637 in greens fees on weekdays, Y1,274 on weekends. Nonmembers pay Y849 and Y1,486, respectively. These prices include a caddie. Clubs can be rented for Y265. The club is a member of the International Associate Club network.

The **Lakewood Golf Club** (✉ *Da'nan Mountain, Jinding District* ☎ *0756/338–3666*) is about 20 minutes from the Zhuhai Ferry Terminal, and is the most popular of the city's five golf clubs. Both its Mountain Course and its Lake Course are 18 holes, and are said to be challenging. Visitor packages, including greens fees and a caddy, are Y420 weekdays and Y820 weekends. Golf carts cost Y200.

The **Sand River Golf Club** (✉ *1 Shahe Donglu, Nanshan District Shenzhen* ☎ *0755/2690–0111* ☉ *Daily 7 am–9 pm*) is another popular club, though not nearly as large as Mission Hills. Sand River offers two courses, one of which was designed by Gary Player and is floodlighted for night playing. Other facilities include a large driving range, a lake, and various resort amenities. Greens fees: 9 holes Y515 weekdays and Y930 weekends; 18 holes Y1,030 weekdays and Y1,860 weekends; caddies Y160 to Y180.

Mission Hills Golf Club (✉ *Nan Shan, Da Wei, Sha He, Bao'an District, Shenzhen* ☎ *0755/2690–9999; 852/2826–0238 in Hong Kong* ⊕ *www.missionhillschina.com*) has 10 18-hole courses (two of which offer nighttime playing), as well as a spectacular clubhouse, a tennis court, two restaurants, and an outdoor pool. There's also a five-star hotel on the premises for golfers serious about trying every course. Mission Hills offers a shuttle bus service from Hong Kong and Shenzhen (call Shenzhen: 0755/2802–0888 or Hong Kong: 852/2973–0303 for schedule). Greens fees: Y600 weekdays and Y1,000 weekends; caddies Y150.

SIDE TRIPS TO ZHONGSHAN AND ZHUHAI

Two other cities worth visiting in the Pearl River Delta are Zhongshan and Zhuhai. Though some casual visitors might chose to spend more than one day in this region, both are small enough to be seen in an afternoon.

Zhongshan is 78 km (48 mi) from Guangzhou and 61 km (38 mi) north-west of Macau. Until recently it was a picturesque port, where a cantilever bridge over the Qi River was raised twice a day to allow small freighters to pass. Today the Old Town has been all but obliterated by modern high-rises, and the surrounding farms are now factories. However, there are still a few spots of historical note worth seeing.

Zhongshan was the birthplace of Sun Yat-sen and is home to the **Sun Yat-sen Memorial Hall** (⊠ *Sunwen Zhong Lu* 🔄 *Y20* ⊙ *Daily 9–5*). Considered the father of the Chinese revolution that overthrew the corrupt Qing Dynasty, he is one of the few political figures respected on both sides of the Taiwan Straits. The **Xishan Temple** (⊠ *Xishan Park* 🔄 *Y5* ⊙ *Daily 9–5*) is a beautifully restored temple that's also worth a visit. Probably the most popular spot in town is **Sunwen Xilu,** a pedestrian mall lined with dozens of restored buildings. At the end of the street is the lovely **Zhongshan Park,** home of the seven-story Fufeng Pagoda and the world's largest statue of . . . you guessed it, Sun Yat-sen.

Bordering Macau, and a little over an hour away by ferry from Hong Kong and Shenzhen, most people don't see **Zhuhai** as a major destination. The city does, however, have a nice long coastline and many small offshore islands. Lover's Road, a 20-km (12½-mi) stretch of road hugging the shoreline, is Zhuhai's signature attraction, as beachside drives are rare in China. The road leads to the **Macau Crossing,** and has enough bars and restaurants to draw a steady crowd of Macau party-goers. Near the Macau border, across from the bus station, is **Yingbin Street,** a popular shopping area. Cheap seafood restaurants stay open well after midnight and, thanks to a variety of hawkers, street musicians, and food stalls, it makes for a fascinating evening stroll.

GETTING HERE AND AROUND

Regular bus service to Zhongshan and Zhuhai runs from Guangzhou's three long-distance bus stations: Liuhua bus station, Guangdong long-distance bus station, and Haizhu Passenger Station.

Bus Contacts Zhuhai Gongbei Bus Station (⊠ *No. 1 Lianhua Rd., Gongbei District* ☎ *756/888–8554*). **Zhongshan Bus Station** (⊠ *Fuhua Rd., Shiqiben West District* ☎ *760/863–3825*).

ENGLISH	PINYIN	CHINESE CHARACTERS
GUANGZHOU	**GUĂNGZHŌU**	**广州**
1920 Restaurant	1920 Cāntīng	1920餐厅
Baiyun International Airport	Báiyún Guójì Jīchǎng	白云国际机场
Baiyun Mountain	Bàiyùnshān	白云山
Banxi Restaurant	Bànxī Jiǔjiā	泮溪酒家
Beijing Road Pedestrian Mall	Běijīng Lù Bùxíngjiē	北京路步行街
Bingjiang West Road	Bīnjiāng Xī Lù	滨江西路
Bright Filial Piety Temple	Guāngxiào Sì	光孝寺
Chen Family Temple	Cheìnjiā Cì	陈家祠
China Hotel	Zhōngguó Dàjiǔdiàn	中国大酒店
Citybus Hong Kong Office	Xiānggǎng Chéngbā Bàngōngshì	香港城巴办公室
Civil Aviation Administration of China	Zhōngguoì Mínhàng Zǒngjù	中国民航总局
Connoisseur	Míng Shì Gé	名仕阁
Datong Restaurant	Dàtoìng Jiǔdiàn	大同酒店
Deep Anger Music Power House	Pàoxiào	咆哮
Dong Fang	Dōngfāng Bīnguǎn	东方宾馆
Five Rams Statue	Wǔyàng Sùxiàng	五羊塑像
Friendship Theatre	Yǒuyí Jùyuàn	友谊剧院
Garden Hotel	Huāyuán Jiǔdiàn	花园酒店
GITIC Plaza	Zhōngxìn Guǎngchǎng	中信广场
Guangdong Modern Dance Company	Guǎngdōng Xiàndàiwǔ Tuán	广东现代舞团
Guangdong Museum of Art	Guǎngdōng Měishù Guǎn	广东美术馆
Guangdong Victory Hotel	Guǎngdōng Shènglì Bīnguǎn	广东胜利宾馆
Guangxiao Temple	Guāngxiào Sì	光孝寺
Guangzhou Arts Centre	Guǎngzhōu Yìshù Zhōngxīn	广州艺术中心
Guangzhou Books Center	Guǎngzhōu Goǔshū Zhōngxīn	广州购书中心
Guangzhou Luhu Golf & Country Club	Guǎngzhōu Lùhù Gāoěrfūqiù Xiāngcūn Jùleìbù	广州麓湖高尔夫球乡村俱乐部
Guangzhou Puppet Art Center	Guǎngdōng Mùǒu Yìshù Zhōngxīn	广东木偶艺术中心
Guangzhou Restaurant	Guǎngzhōu Jiǔjiā	广州酒家
Haizhu Plaza	Hǎizhū Guǎngchǎng	海珠广场
Hare and Moon	Yuètù Jiǔbā	月兔酒吧

ENGLISH	PINYIN	CHINESE CHARACTERS
Holiday Inn City Centre	Wénhuà Jiàrì Jiǔdiàn	文化假日酒店
Huanshi Dong Lu	Huànshì Dōng Lù	环市东路
La Perle	Lìbǎi Guǎngchǎng	丽柏广场
Lucy's	Lùsī Jiǔbā	露丝酒吧
Mausoleum of the 72 Martyrs	Huánghuā Gǎng Qīshí'eìr Lièìshì Lìngyuàn	黄花岗七十二烈士陵园
Memorial Garden for the Martyrs	Lièìshì Lìngyuàn	烈士陵园
Orchid Garden	Lànpǔ Gōngyuàn	兰圃公园
Our Lady of Lourdes Catholic Church	Shāmiàn Táng	沙面堂
Qingping Market	Qīngpìng Shìchǎng	清平市场
Ritz-Carlton Guangzhou	Lìzīkǎi'erdūn Jiǔdìan Guǎngzhōu	n/a
Shamian	Shāmiàn Bīnguǎn	沙面宾馆
Shamian Island	Shāmiàn Dǎo	沙 面 岛
Shangxiajiu	Shàngxiajiǔ	上下九
Shangxiajiu Street	Shàng Xià Jiǔ	上下九
Shenzhen People's Hospital	Shēnzhèn Rénmín Yīyuàn	深圳人命医院
Silk Road Grill Room	Sīchoìu Zhīlù	"丝绸之路" 扒房
Sun Yat-sen Memorial Hall	Sūn Zhōngshān Jìnìàn Tàng	孙中山纪念堂
Tang Yuan	Tàng Yuàn	唐苑
Tao Tao Ju	Tàotào Jū	陶陶居
Taxis	chūzū chē	出租车
Teem Plaza	Tiānhé Chéng	天河城
Temple of the Six Banyan Trees	Liùroìng Si	六榕寺
The Café Lounge	n/a	n/a
The Customs Hotel	Hǎiguān Bīnguǎn	海关宾馆
The Italian Restaurant	Xiǎojiē Fēngqíng	小街风情
The Paddy Field	Àiěrlàn Cānbā	爱尔兰餐吧
Tian Lun International Hotel	Tiānlún Wànyí Jiǔdiàn	天伦万怡酒店
Tianhe District	Tiānhé Qū	天河区
Tianhe Stadium Complex	Tiānhé Tǐyù Zhōngxīn	天河体育中心
Tomb of the Southern Yue Kings	Nànyuè Wàng Mù	南岳王墓
Tower Controlling the Sea	Zheìnhǎi Loìu	镇海楼
Vitamin Creative Space	Wéitāmìng Yìshù Kōngjiān	维他命艺术空间
White Swan Hotel	Báitiáné Jiǔdiàn	白天鹅酒店

ENGLISH	PINYIN	CHINESE CHARACTERS
White Swan Hotel Golf Practice Center	Báitiān Eì Gāoěrfū Liànxìchǎng	白天鹅酒店高尔夫练习场
Xinghai Concert Hall	Xīnghǎi Yīnyuètīng	星海音乐厅
Yan Yang Tian Agency	Yàn Yàng Tiān Lǚxíngshè	广州艳阳天旅行社
Yuexiu Park	Yuèlxiù Gōngyuàn	越秀公园
Zhanxi Market	Zhànxī Shìchǎng	站西
Zhuhai International Airport	Zhūhǎi Guójì Jīchǎng	珠海国际机场
SHENZHEN	**SHENZHÈN**	深圳
Huaqiaocheng station	Huànqiàochéng Zhàn	华侨城站
OCT district	HuàQiào Chéng	华侨城
360	Sānbǎi Liùshí Dù Jiǔbā	360度酒吧
Blue	Yìdàlì Cāntīng	意大利餐厅
Boao Scenic Zone	Boìào fēngjǐng Qu	博鳌风景区
Chiu Chow Cuisine	Chàozhōu Cài	潮洲菜
CITIC City Plaza	Shēnzhèn Zhōngxìn Dàshà	深圳中信大厦
Crowne Plaza	Wēinísī Huàngguān Jiàrì Jiǔdiàn	威尼斯皇冠假日酒店
Dafen Oil Painting Village	Dàfēn Yoìuhuà Shìjiè	大芬油画世界
Dapeng Fortress	Dàpéng Gǔchéng	大鹏古城
Dongmen Shopping Plaza	Dōngmén Lǎojiē	东门老街
Foshan	Foìshān	佛山
Futian	Fùtiàn	福田
Futian district Shenzhen	Shēnzhèn Fùtiàn	深圳福田
Greenland Lounge	Lǜjiànlàng Dàtàngbā	绿涧廊大堂吧
Guangzhou Luhu Golf and Country Club	Guǎngzhōu Lùhú Gāo'erfū Xiāngcūn Jùlèbù	广州麓湖高尔夫球乡村俱乐部
Haikou	Hǎikǒu	海口
Hainan Island	Hǎinàn Dǎo	海南岛
Hakka Folk Customs Museum and Enclosures	Kèjiā Mínsú Bówùguǎn Hé Wéiwū	客家民俗博物馆和围屋
Hexiangning Art Museum	Héxiāngníng Měishùguǎn	何香凝美术馆
Huaqiao Cheng Metro	Huàqiàochéng Dìtiězhàn	华侨城地铁站
Lakewood Golf Club	Zhūhǎi Cùhù Gāoěrfù Qiùhù	珠海翠湖高尔夫球会
Little India	Xiǎo Yìndù Cāntīng	小印度餐厅
Lo Wu Commercial City	Luoìhù Shāngyè Chéng	罗湖商业城
Longgang	Loìnggǎng	龙岗
Luohu Commercial City	Luoìhù	罗湖

ENGLISH	PINYIN	CHINESE CHARACTERS
Macau Ferry Terminal	Àomén Mǎtoìu	澳门码头
Minsk World	Míngsīkè Hàngmǔ	明思克航母世界
Mission Hills Golf Club	Guānlàn Gāoěrfū	观澜高尔夫
Nan Hai	Nànhǎi	南海
Nanshan	Nànshān	南山
OCT Contemporary Art Terminal	OCT Dāngdài Yìshù Zhōngxīn	OCT当代艺术中心
Outer Shenzhen	Shēnzhèn zhōubiān,	深圳周边
Overseas Chinese Town	Huàqiáo Chéng	华侨城
San Dao Plaza	Sāndǎo Zhōngxīn	三中心
Sand River Golf Club	Shāhé agāoěrfū Qiùhù	沙河高尔夫球会
Seaview O-City Hotel Shenzhen	Shēnzhèn Hǎijǐng àosītīng Jiǔdiàn	深圳海景奥斯汀酒店
Shangri-La Shenzhen	Shēnzhèn Xiānggélǐlā Jiǔdiàn	深圳香格里拉酒店
Shekou	Shékǒu	蛇口
Shenzhen Airport	Shēnzhèn Jīchǎng	深圳机场
Shenzhen Longgang Tourist Bureau	Shēnzhènshì Loìnggǎng Lǚyoìujù	深圳市龙岗区旅游局
Sun Yat-sen Memorial Hall	Zhōngshān Jìniàntàng	中山纪念堂
Sunday Chiu Chow King	Sāndǎo Chàohuàng Yuècài Jiǔloìu	三岛潮皇粤菜酒楼
Sunwen Xilu	Sūnwén Xīlù	孙文西路
The Pavilion	Shèngtíngyuàn Jiǔdiàn	圣廷苑酒店
The Terrace	n/a	n/a
True Color	Běnsè Yīnyuè	本色音乐
V-Bar	Ǖī Bā	V 吧
Window of the World	Shìjiè Zhīchuāng	世界之窗
Xishan Temple	Xīshān Miào	西山庙
Yantian	Yàntiàn	盐田
Yingbin Street	Yínbīn Dàdào	迎宾大道
Yokohama	Héngbīn Rìběn Liàolǐ	滨日本料理
Zhongshan City	Zhōngshān Shì	中山市
Zhuhai	Zhūhǎi	珠海

The Southwest

GUANGXI, GUIZHOU, AND YUNNAN

WORD OF MOUTH

"The karsts around the Li river are the most spectacular of their kind. I've seen similar around Phanga, Tam Coc, Halong, etc., but they pale in comparison to this area."

— Hanuman

WELCOME TO THE SOUTHWEST

TOP REASONS TO GO

★ **Lose Yourself in Lijiang:** Treasured by the Chinese and home to a UNESCO World Heritage Site, the winding cobblestone lanes of Lijiang beckon to all.

★ **Lush Xishuangbanna Rain Forests:** Hugging the borders of Laos and Myanmar, this small city in Yunnan is home to the legendary Dai minority people, who make you feel far from the rest of China.

★ **Trek Tiger Leaping Gorge:** Explore the deepest gorge in the world, and one of the most scenic spots in all of Yunnan, and possibly China.

★ **Guizhou's Eye-Popping Huangguoshu Falls:** Travel to the Baishui River in Guizhou, where the largest waterfall in China plummets 230 feet.

★ **Cycling around Yangshuo:** Snake your way through this strange lunarlike landscape of limestone karsts.

1 Guangxi. Having inspired countless paintings and poems in the past, the spectacular karst scenery of Guilin and Yangshuo today inspires travelers who are in search of an unforgettable Chinese experience. Capital city Nanning is being groomed as China's gateway to Vietnam. Guangxi is officially Guangxi Zhuang Autonomous Region, not a province.

2 Guizhou. Off the beaten path, this fascinating province is known for its undulating mountains, terraced fields, traditional villages, frequent festivals, and China's largest waterfall, Huangguoshu. More than a third of the population is made up of Dong, Hui, Yao, Zhuang, and Miao (known in the West as the Hmong) peoples.

GETTING ORIENTED

Southwest China can be summed up in one word: diversity. The regions of Guangxi, Guizhou, and Yunnan offer some of China's most singular travel experiences. Guilin and Yangshuo in Guangxi are surrounded by other-worldly karst mountains and idyllic rivers. Qianling Park in Guizhou's capital, Guiyang, has a beautiful Buddhist temple, hundreds of monkeys, and amazing city views. Stretching between Tibet and Vietnam, Yunnan Province's geographic, biological, and ethnic diversity is unparalleled anywhere else in China. This part of the world must be seen to be believed.

8

3 Yunnan. The sleepy towns of Lijiang and Dali offer glimpses into the centuries-old traditions of the Naxi and Bai ethnic groups. For a more rugged experience, hike through the breathtaking Tiger Leaping Gorge. If a slow boat on the Mekong appeals, head south to Jinghong and chill out in the tropics.

Updated by
Chris Horton
and Daniel
Siekman

The southwestern provinces are the most alluring destinations in the country. This region lays claim to some of the most breathtaking scenery in all of China—from the moonscape limestone karsts and river scenery of Yangshuo, to China's mightiest waterfall in Guizhou, to Yunnan's tropical rain forests and spectacular Tiger Leaping Gorge.

Rich in ethnic diversity and culture, Yunnan is home to almost a third of China's ethnic minorities. In 1958 Guangxi became an autonomous region in an attempt to quell the friction between the Zhuang minority and the ethnic Han majority. Yunnan, Guangxi, and Guizhou represent the complex tapestry of China's ethnic diversity.

In Kunming, Dali, and villages around Yunnan, the Yi and Bai peoples hold their Torch Festivals on the 24th day of the sixth lunar month. They throw handfuls of pine resin into bonfires, lighting the night sky with clouds of sparks. The Dai Water Splashing Festival in the rainforests of Xishuangbanna on the 22nd day of the third lunar month is liquid pandemonium. Its purpose is to wash away the sorrow of the old year and refresh you for the new.

Dali has two festivals of note: the Third Moon Fair (middle of third lunar month) during which people from all around Yunnan come to Dali to sell their wares; and the Three Temples Festival (usually May). The Sister's Meal Festival, celebrated in the middle of the third lunar month by Miao people throughout Guizhou, is dedicated to unmarried women. During the great rice harvest, special brightly colored dishes are made, and at nightfall there's much ado about courtship, dancing, and old-fashioned flirting. The Zhuang Singing Festival turns Guangxi's countryside into an ocean of song. On the third day of the third lunar month, the Zhuang gather and sing to honor Liu Sanjie ("Third Sister Liu"), the goddess of song. Singing "battles" ensue between groups who sing—often improvising—at each other until one group concedes.

PLANNING

WHEN TO GO

When you are packing for travel in Southwest China, think of the region as three distinct zones separated by altitude. Steamy tropical lowlands spread across the southern halves of Yunnan and Guangxi. The mountainous highlands of central and northwest Yunnan are characterized by intense, high-UV sun, long rainy seasons, and cold winters. Somewhere in between are the cloudy mountain scenes found throughout Guizhou and northern Guangxi. Each zone requires a different packing strategy.

In summer the monsoon rains can be heavy. Keep abreast of weather reports on the Internet at any of the numerous cafés, hostels, and hotels. Temperatures don't get as hot as the tropics or as cold as the highlands, but summers can be quite hot in Guilin and Yangshuo, and winters in Guiyang can be cold enough for snow. The best time of year is spring, in April or early May. Winter months can be surprisingly cold (except in southern Guangxi and Yunnan), and the summertime heat is stifling. Mid-September can also be a comfortable time to travel. The falls at Huangguoshu are at their best in the rainy season from May through October.

GETTING HERE AND AROUND

With new roads, faster trains, and more airports every year, traveling around Southwest China is becoming increasingly convenient. If you're short on time, flying within the region is the best option, with most flights taking around an hour or less. If you're not in a hurry, trains and buses are a cheap and scenic option.

AIR TRAVEL

Southwest China's air network is constantly expanding, with most popular travel destinations served by their own airports. China Eastern Airlines is the dominant carrier in the region. Kunming, Guilin, Nanning, and Guiyang all have international airports, and cities such as Lijiang, Jinghong and Dali are also reachable by air.

BUS TRAVEL

Traveling around Southwest China by bus is a good way to cover the shorter distances in your travels. The regional bus network is efficient and is primarily served by luxury coaches. Keep in mind that in general there is no English spoken on buses here.

CAR TRAVEL

There are no legal car services (for either personal rental or for hiring personal drivers), only buses and taxis.

HEALTH AND SAFETY

Malaria was once a problem in southern Yunnan and Guangxi, but luckily today it is not an issue when traveling around Southwest China. Gastrointestinal problems are the main health concern in this part of the country—make sure that food you consume is cooked thoroughly in a hygienic environment. Altitude sickness can be a problem if you're flying into northwest Yunnan; make sure to take it easy for the first day or two after arriving.

MONEY MATTERS

Money can be changed in the major hotels or at the Bank of China. The Guilin and Nanning airports have branches and ATMs, and all Bank of China ATMs take international cards. The Kunming airport has a foreign exchange counter just outside the international arrivals gate.

Foreign bank cards on the Cirrus or Plus systems can be used at ATMs displaying their respective logos. Bank of China and ICBC are your best bets. When traveling to remote parts of the region, have cash on hand, as ATMs accepting foreign cards are rare.

RESTAURANTS

In addition to great Chinese food, usually on the spicier side of the spectrum, Southwest China is home to a rainbow of ethnic cuisines, with Dai, Bai, and Tibetan being some of the most notable. Yunnan has the most diverse culinary offerings, which even include some breads and cheeses. Wild mushrooms are available every May through September.

HOTELS

Locally run hotels in Southwest China's larger cities offer adequate service and amenities for a reasonable price, but tend to lack English-speaking staff. There is a growing number of international five-stars in Kunming, Guiyang, and Nanning that offer a higher degree of service as well as better in-hotel dining. Cities like Dali, Lijiang, and Yangshuo have plenty of comfortable and cheap small hotels and guesthouses. The guesthouses are often good places to get home-cooked local meals.

WHAT IT COSTS IN YUAN					
	¢	$	$$	$$$	$$$$
Restaurants	under Y25	Y25–Y49	Y50–Y99	Y100–Y165	over Y165
Hotels	under Y700	Y700–Y1,099	Y1,100–Y1,399	Y1,400–Y1,800	over Y1,800

Restaurant prices are for a main course, excluding tip (there is no sales/retail tax in China). Hotel prices are for a standard double room, including taxes.

VISITOR INFORMATION

This part of China has virtually nothing in the way of useful English-language tourist info, but there is a smattering of locally run English-language Web sites with travel information and forums. Western-style cafes and guesthouses are usually good places to ask around as well.

TOURS

Although they are generally cheaper, Chinese package tours are best avoided, as they tend to be big, loud, and aimed at getting you to buy junk. In Southwest China's larger cities, hotels are often the most convenient places to make transportation arrangements. In travel hot spots such as Yangshuo, Lijiang, and Dali there are plenty of English-speaking local travel agents.

China Minority Travel (✉ 63 Bo'ai Lu, Dali ☎ 0872/267–7824 ⊕ www. china-travel.nl) is one of the oldest travel agencies in Southwest China. Run by a Dutch and Tibetan couple since the 1990s, China Minority Travel has tours exploring virtually every corner of Southwest China.

Watching a Dragon Boat race at the Water Splashing Festival in Xishuangbanna.

Wild China (✉ *Room 801, Oriental Place, 9 Dongfang Dong Lu, Chaoyang, Beijing* ☎ *010/6465–6602* ⊕ *www.wildchina.com*) specializes in unique itineraries in Yunnan, Guizhou, and Guangxi and can create journeys tailored to specific interests.

GUANGXI

Known throughout China for its fairy-tale scenery, Guangxi's rivers, valleys, and stone peaks have inspired painters and poets for centuries. From the distinctive terraced rice fields of Longsheng, which resemble a dragon's spine, to the karst rock formations that surround Guilin and Yangshuo and rise from the coastal plain in the south, Guangxi is quite possibly the most picturesque of China's regions.

A significant portion of Guangxi's population consists of ethnic minorities: the Dong, Gelao, Hui, Jing, Miao, Shui, Yao, Yi, and, in particular, the Zhuang people, who constitute about a third of the province's population. Guangxi has often seen conflict between these indigenous peoples and the Han, who established their rule only in the 19th century. Today it is one of five autonomous regions, which, in theory, have an element of self-government.

The climate is subtropical and affected by seasonal monsoons, with long, hot, humid, and frequently wet summers and mild winters. Guangxi is one of the most popular travel destinations in China.

GUILIN

500 km (310 mi; 13 hrs by train) northwest of Hong Kong; 1,675 km (1,039 mi; 22 hrs by train) southwest of Beijing.

Guilin has the good fortune of being situated in the middle of some of the world's most beautiful landscapes. This region of limestone karst hills and mountains, rising almost vertically from the earth, has a dreamy, hypnotic quality. They were formed 200 million years ago, when the area was under the sea. As the land beneath began to push upward, the sea receded, and the effects of the ensuing erosion over thousands of years produced this sublime scenery.

Architecturally, the city lacks charm, having been heavily bombed during the Sino-Japanese War and rebuilt in the utilitarian style popular in the 1950s. Still, the river city is replete with beautiful parks and bridges, and has a number of historic sites that make it worthy of exploration. It's also a good base from which to explore northern Guangxi.

GETTING HERE AND AROUND

AIR TRAVEL About 28 km (17 mi) southwest of the city center, Guilin Liangjiang International Airport has flights to cities throughout China as well as throughout Asia. An airport shuttle bus, which operates daily from 6:30 am to 8 pm, runs between the airport and the Aviation Building located at 18 Shanghai Lu, across the street from the main bus station. The cost is Y20 per person.

BUS TRAVEL The main bus station in Guilin is just north of the train station on Zhongshan Nan Lu. Short- and long-distance buses connect Guilin to nearby cities, including Yangshuo, Longsheng, Liuzhou, and Nanning. Long-distance sleeper coaches travel to cities throughout the Pearl River Delta.

TRAIN TRAVEL Guilin is linked by daily rail service with most major cities in China. Most long-distance trains arrive at Guilin's South Railway Station.

SAFETY AND PRECAUTIONS

Like most cities in Southwest China, Guilin is generally safe, but one should be careful when crossing the street, as pedestrians don't get much respect from drivers.

TIMING

Although it is increasingly overshadowed by nearby Yangshuo, Guilin is a pleasant city that's well worth a stop. Most of the sights can be taken in within a couple of days.

ESSENTIALS

Air Contact Guilin Liangjiang International Airport (☎ 0773/284–5359).

Banks Bank of China (✉ 5 Shanhu Bei Lu ☎ 0773/280–2867 ✉ Guilin Liangjiang International Airport ☎ 0773/284–4020).

Bus Contact Guilin Bus Station (✉ Off Zhongshan Nan Lu ☎ 0773/382–2153).

Medical Assistance Guilin People's Hospital (✉ 12 Wenming Lu ☎ 0773/282–8712).

Public Security Bureau PSB Guilin (✉ 16 Shi Jia Yuan Rd. ☎ 0773/282–3334).

Train Contact Guilin Railway Station (✉ Off Zhongshan Nan Lu ☎ 0773/216–4842).

Visitor and Tour Info China International Travel Service (CITS) (✉ 11 Binjiang Lu ☎ 0773/288–0319). **China Travel Service (CTS)** (✉ 11 Binjiang Lu ☎ 0773/283–3986 ⊕ en.guilincits.com).

EXPLORING

TOP ATTRACTIONS

The 492-foot **Peak of Solitary Beauty** *(Duxiu Feng),* with carved stone stairs leading to the top, offers an unparalleled view of Guilin—and a short but intense workout for your legs. It's one of the attractions of the **Prince City Solitary Beauty Park (Jing Jiang Wang Cheng).** Surrounded by an ancient wall, outside of which vendors hawk their wares, sits the heart of Old Guilin. Inside are the decaying remains of an ancient Ming Dynasty palace built in 1393 and Guilin's Confucius temple. Sun Yat-sen lived here for a few months in the winter of 1921 (a fact duly noted on the wall by the outside gate). Cixi, the former empress dowager of China, inscribed the character for "longevity" on a rock within these walls. ✉ *Heart of Old Guilin, in center of city, 2 blocks north of Zhengyang Lu Pedestrian Mall* ☎ *No phone* 🎫 *Y70* ⊙ *Daily 7:30–6:30.*

Guilin

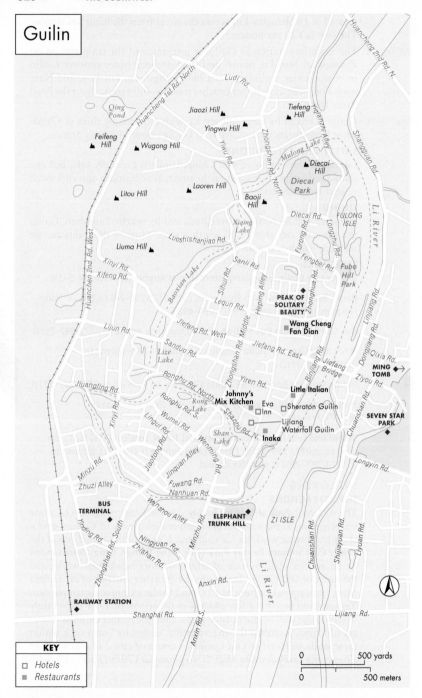

Qing Pond

Ludi Rd.

Huancheng 1st Rd. North

Jiaozi Hill ▲

Tiefeng Hill ▲

Yingwu Hill ▲

Hejianzhi Alley

Mulong Lake

Shangguan Rd.

Huancheng 2nd Rd. N.

Feifeng Hill ▲

Wugong Hill ▲

Zhongshan Rd. North

Ywu Rd.

Diecai Hill ▲

Diecai Park

Li River

Laoren Hill ▲

Litou Hill ▲

Baoji Hill ▲

Diecai Rd.

FULONG ISLE

Xiqing Lake

Furong Rd.

Longzhu Rd.

Liuma Hill ▲

Luoshishanjiao Rd.

Fengbei Rd.

Fubo Hill Park

Banxian Lake

Sanli Rd.

Xinyi Rd.

Xifeng Rd.

Sihui Rd.

Heping Alley

Zhonghua Rd.

Huanchen 2nd Rd. West

Lequn Rd.

PEAK OF SOLITARY BEAUTY ◆

Lijun Rd.

Jiefang Rd. West

Zhongshan Rd. Middle

Wang Cheng Fan Dian ■

Sanduo Rd.

Lize Lake

Jiefang Rd. East

Linjiang Rd.

Jiuangling Rd.

Ronghu Rd. North

Yiren Rd.

Binjiang Rd.

Jiefang Bridge

Dongjiang Rd.

Qixia Rd.

MING TOMB ◆

Xinyi Rd.

Rong Lake

Ronghu Rd. S.

Shanhu Rd. N.

Johnny's Mix Kitchen ■

Eva Inn □

Little Italian ■

Ziyou Rd.

Chuanshan Rd.

SEVEN STAR PARK ◆

Lingui Rd.

Wumei Rd.

Shan Lake

□ Sheraton Guilin

Lijiang Waterfall Guilin □

Inaka ■

Jiaotong Rd.

Jinquan Alley

Wenming Rd.

Longyin Rd.

Minzu Rd.

Zhuzi Alley

Fuwang Rd.

Nanhuan Rd.

Wanshou Alley

BUS TERMINAL ◆

Minzhu Rd.

ELEPHANT TRUNK HILL ◆

ZI ISLE

Chuanshan Rd.

Shijiayuan Rd.

Liyuan Rd.

Yinding Rd. South

Zhongshan Rd. South

Ningyuan Rd.

Zhishan Rd.

Anxin Rd.

Li River

RAILWAY STATION ◆

Shanghai Rd.

Anxin Rd. S.

Lijiang Rd.

| 0 | 500 yards |
| 0 | 500 meters |

KEY

□ Hotels
■ Restaurants

Seven Star Park *(Qixing Gongyuan)* gets its name from the arrangement of its hills, said to resemble the Big Dipper. At the center of this huge park on the east side of the Li River is **Putuo Mountain** (Putuoshan), atop which sits a lovely pavilion housing a number of famous examples of Tang calligraphy. Indeed, calligraphy abounds on the side of this hill, mostly the work of Ming Dynasty Taoist philosopher Pan Changjing. Nearby is **Seven Star Cliff** (Qixing Dong), with several large caves open for exploration. The largest contains rock formations that are thought to resemble a lion with a ball, an elephant, and other figures. An inscription in the cave dates from AD 590. Seven Star Park also contains the Guilin City Zoo, which is only worth a stop if you have kids in tow. It costs an additional Y30. ⊠ *1 km (½ mi) east of downtown Guilin* ☎ *No phone* 💲 *Y35* ☉ *Daily 6–9:30.*

Elephant Trunk Hill *(Xiangbi Shan)* once appeared on Chinese currency bills. On the bank of the river in the southern part of the city, it takes its name from a rock formation arching into the river like the trunk of an elephant. Nearby is a grotto covered in poetic inscriptions inspired by the beauty of the place, some by the greatest poets of the Song Dynasty. ⊠ *Binjiang Lu, across from Golden Elephant Hotel* ☎ *0773/258–6602* 💲 *Y40* ☉ *Daily 7 am–9:30 pm.*

WORTH NOTING

East of the town is the **Ming Tomb** *(Zhu Shouqian Ling),* the tomb of Zhu Shouqian, the nephew of the first Ming emperor, who founded a principality here. It makes a pleasant excursion by bicycle and its gates combine with the surrounding hills for good photo opportunities. To get here, take Jiefang Dong Lu east about 9 km (5 mi). ⊠ *Jiefang Dong Lu* ☎ *773/589–3921* 💲 *Y20* ☉ *Daily 8:30–4:30.*

WHERE TO EAT

Guilin's notable local dishes are limited to horse meat and rice noodles. Freshwater fish is popular with locals, but eat it only if you dare. The Zhengyang Lu pedestrian street has the best variety of dining spots.

$$–$$$
JAPANESE
✕ **Inaka.** Resembling a Japanese home, this excellent restaurant sits at the southern end of the Zhengyang Lu Pedestrian Mall. The interior, which recalls that of a temple, has a low-key vibe. The sashimi and sushi—not easy to find in cities away from the coast—are fresh and excellent. The best deals are the four-course lunch specials, which begin with miso soup and end with a dessert made from sweetened bean curd. ⊠ *1 Zhengyang Lu* ☎ *0773/280–2888* 🖃 *MC, V.*

$–$$
WESTERN,
CHINESE
✕ **Johnny's Mix Kitchen.** This pleasant new restaurant is popular with locals for its selection of Asian dishes including curries, stir-fries, and dumplings, as well as its American breakfasts, pizzas, steaks, and salmon. Staff are friendly, and there is free Wi-Fi for before or after your meal. ⊠ *66 Binjiang Lu, Guilin* ☎ *0773/285–8666* 🖃 *No credit cards.*

$–$$
ITALIAN
★
✕ **Little Italian.** Formerly known as The Here, this little restaurant may have the best Western food in Guilin. The menu is straightforward: pizza, pasta, and sandwiches made fresh when you order. The cozy urban decor creates an ideal environment for reading a book, checking your e-mail on the free Wi-Fi, or planning the next step in your trip.

8

The Zhuang and the Miao

The famous Miao hair pieces.

The Zhuang are China's largest minority population, totaling more than 16 million. Most Zhuang are in Guangxi Zhuang Autonomous Region (where they constitute more than 85% of the population), Guizhou, Yunnan, and Guangdong provinces. The Zhuang language is part of the Tai-Kadai family, related to Thai and fellow Chinese minority the Dai. Historically, the Zhuang have had almost constant friction with China's Han majority, but that's improved since the Guangxi Zhuang Autonomous region was established in 1958. In many ways the Zhuang are becoming assimilated into the dominant Han Chinese culture, but they have still preserved their strong culture and its music and dance traditions. Clothing varies from region to region, but mostly consists of collarless embroidered jackets buttoned to the left, loose wide trousers or pleated skirts, embroidered belts, and black square headbands.

The Miao are also a large minority group spread across much of southern China. Throughout their history, the Miao have had to deal with Han China's southward expansion, which drove them into marginal, chiefly mountainous areas in southern China and northern areas of Myanmar, Thailand, Laos, and Vietnam. Living in such isolated regions, the Miao group developed into several subsets, including Black, Red, Green, and Big Flowery Miao. Most of China's nearly 10 million Miao are in Guizhou Province, where local markets feature their intricate and expert craftsmanship, especially jewelry, embroidery, and batik. The Miao are also renowned for their festivals, particularly the Lusheng festival, which occurs from the 11th to the 18th of the first lunar month. Named after a Miao reed instrument, Lusheng is a week of lively music, dancing, horse races, and bullfights. The Guizhou city of Kaili is the center of Miao festivals, hosting more than 120 each year.

Most of the young, friendly staff speak English. ✉ *1–4, 18 Binjiang Lu* 📷 *0773/311–1068* ⊟ *No credit cards.*

¢–$ ✕ **Wang Cheng Fan Dian.** This restaurant south of the Peak of Solitary
CHINESE Beauty is extremely popular with students from the nearby college.
It serves a wide variety of dishes, including many made with horse,
including noodles stir-fried with horse and a spicy hotpot with horse
and vegetables. ✉ *56 Zhengyang Lu, 1 block north of pedestrian mall*
📷 *0773/282–2284* ⊟ *No credit cards.*

WHERE TO STAY

¢ 🏨 **Eva Inn.** The best economy hotel in Guilin at this writing, Eva Inn
★ offers clean, modern rooms at very reasonable rates. The hotel's east
side and rooftop café offer great views of the Li river and Elephant
Trunk Hill—to the west is plenty of shopping and dining at the Zhengyang Pedestrian Mall. Rooms are not luxurious, but all the necessities
are there. Some staff speak good English. **Pros:** great location; good
value. **Cons:** rooms could be a bit bigger. ✉ *66 Binjiang Lu, on west
bank of Li River* 📷 *0773/283–0666* 🛏 *113 rooms* ♿ *In-room: a/c,
refrigerator, Internet. In-hotel: restaurant, laundry service, Internet terminal.* ⊟ *AE, MC, V.*

$$$–$$$$ 🏨 **Lijiang Waterfall Guilin** (*Lijiang Da Pubu Jiudian*). Overlooking the
river, this luxury hotel also has breathtaking views of Elephant Trunk
Hill and Seven Star Park. Rooms are clean, spacious, and—as the hotel
is one of the city's newest—extremely modern. Five excellent restaurants
offer Asian and Western cuisine. Every night at 8:30 the hotel hosts a
15-minute water show that turns the back of the building into a mas-
sive waterfall. **Pros:** reasonable rooms for reasonable rates. **Cons:** occa-
sionally chaotic due to conferences; staff doesn't speak much English.
✉ *1 Shanhu Bei Lu* ✛ *South end of Zhengyang Lu Pedestrian Street*
📷 *0773/282–2881* ⊕ *www.waterfallguilin.com* 🛏 *430 rooms, 23 suites*
♿ *In-room: safe, refrigerator, Internet. In-hotel: 5 restaurants, bar, pool,
gym, laundry service, no-smoking rooms* ⊟ *AE, MC, V.*

$$$ 🏨 **Sheraton Guilin** (*Guilin Xilaideng Fandian*). This recently renovated
★ Sheraton is easily the nicest hotel in town. The lobby is very chic, with
its sunny atrium and glass elevators that whisk you up to your room.
Rooms are clean and spacious, and the club lounge on the top floor
offers rooftop seating with river and mountain views. The Chinese
restaurant on the first floor offers a delicious culinary tour of Sichuan
and Guangdong, while the Western restaurant on the second floor offers
tasty Western standards as well as some interesting fusion dishes. **Pros:**
professional management; English-speaking staff. **Cons:** slightly overpriced; in-room Internet access is not free. ✉ *15 Binjiang Lu, on west
bank of Li River* 📷 *0773/282–5588* ⊕ *www.sheraton.com/guilin* 🛏 *411
rooms, 19 suites* ♿ *In-room: safe, refrigerator, Internet. In-hotel: 3 restaurants, room service, bar, Internet terminal* ⊟ *AE, MC, V.*

NIGHTLIFE AND THE ARTS

Enjoy cold beer and street-side seating at **Paulaner** (✉ *2 Zhengyang Lu*
📷 *0773/286–8698*), which has a good selection of mostly German and
Chinese beers plus pizza, pasta, and sandwiches.

8

DID YOU KNOW?

Most of the magnificent Longji terraced fields were built about 500 years ago, during the Ming Dynasty. They're called Dragon's Backbone because the peaks of the mountain range resemble the backbone of the dragon, and the water-filled terraces shimmer like a dragon's scales. If you stand at the summit, you can see the dragon's backbone curving off to the horizon.

Guangxi's Silver-Toothed Touts

Aggressive touts are a fact of life for Western travelers in hyper-capitalist China. Guangxi Province is known for the tenacity of its touts—mostly older tribal women with silver teeth (as is the local custom). To these wandering merchants a Western traveler is a coin purse with legs.

It's not uncommon for half a dozen of these women to surround you at any given site, shouting "water" and "postcard." They'll follow you around until you buy something from each of them.

It's hard for travelers to maintain equilibrium when confronted with a gaggle of old women who seem doggedly intent on turning a hiking trip around, say, the Longsheng Rice Terraces into a no-win trinket-buying binge. Polite

"no, thank you's" can soon escalate into expletive-laden tirades, inevitably leading to remorse for cursing a poverty-stricken old woman.

What's worse, cursing accomplishes nothing. No sooner will the last bitter word leave your lips than Granny will thrust a pack of commemorative postcards at you and shout "10 yuan!"

Consider the purchasing of minor souvenirs or unwanted sodas as part of the experience; keep a few yuan handy for just that, and deal with it smilingly. Failing that, you can always run. But remember, these old women know all the shortcuts, and you'll tire out and need to buy a beverage anyway. And maybe some postcards as well.

Just around the corner from Paulaner, **Back Garden Irish Pub** (✉ *Zhengyang Pedestrian Street, at bottom of Mingcheng Hotel, Guilin* ☎ *773/280-3869*) offers standard bar grub with a well-stocked bar and friendly owner. The pub has occasional live music performances. Guinness is available only in bottles, there's none on tap—yet.

LONGSHENG LONGJI RICE TERRACES

120 km (74 mi; 3 hrs by bus) northwest of Guilin.

A mesmerizing pattern of undulating fields has been cut into the hills up to a height of 2,625 feet at the **Longsheng Longji Rice Terraces**. These terraces, known as the "Dragon's Backbone," are amazing in both their scale and their beauty. They are worked, and have been for generations, by rice farmers from the local Yao, Dong, Zhuang, and Miao communities, who build their houses in villages on the terraced hills. 🎫 *Y50.*

GETTING HERE AND AROUND

Buses are the best way to get to Longsheng. The only alternative to a bus is to pay a premium to retain a taxi's services for the day, which will set you back at least Y500.

Buses heading to Longsheng from Guilin's bus station leave every 15 minutes and take about 4 hours (Y15). The express bus back to Guilin takes 3 hours and departs from Longsheng every two hours (Y20).

SAFETY AND PRECAUTIONS

If hiring a cab to take you to Longsheng, it is best to avoid making the trip at night, as the road is full of sharp corners and is not well lit. Make sure your shoes have plenty of ankle support if you plan on hiking in the rice terraces; you'll avoid a twist or sprain.

TIMING

The Longji Rice Terraces make for a fulfilling day trip from Guilin, but shutterbugs may want to catch the terraces at sunrise and sunset over the course of two or three days to maximize the chance of getting that perfect shot.

TOURS

Longsheng is not home to any local tour companies. Travel plans in Longsheng are best arranged through Guilin travel agencies, and the stretch of Binjiang Lu south of the Sheraton has several English-speaking travel agencies.

WHERE TO EAT AND STAY

¢–$ ✕ **Li Qing Restaurant.** This extremely popular restaurant, in addition to
CHINESE   more well-known Chinese dishes, serves a number of traditional dishes like bamboo stuffed with sticky rice, and stir-fried mixed vegetables. ✉ *Ji Lu, Ping'an* ☎ *0773/758–3048* ▭ *No credit cards.*

¢   ⊡ **Li Qing Guesthouse.** In the nearby village of Ping'an, the Li Qing Guesthouse is run by sisters Liao Yan Li and Liao Yan Qing. The guesthouse is two houses; the older one has dorm-style rooms, and the newer one has single and double rooms with private baths. **Pros:** friendly staff cater well to Western guests. **Cons:** can be noisy on weekends. ✉ *Ji Lu, Ping'an* ☎ *0773/758–3048* ↩ *12 rooms* ⅙ *In-hotel: restaurant, Internet terminal* ▭ *No credit cards.*

YANGSHUO

70 km (43 mi; 90 min by bus) south of Guilin.

Yangshuo has taken center stage as Guangxi's top tourist destination. At the heart of the city is West Street, a pedestrian mall extending to the Li River. Many visitors are content to spend a few days wandering up and down the main drag, eating, drinking, and gazing over the low-slung traditional structures facing toward the fang-shaped peaks that surround the town. Yangshuo is fast becoming a destination for adventure travel, and the countryside is filled with opportunities for biking, hiking, rock climbing, and caving.

GETTING HERE AND AROUND

Arriving via train or airplane means traveling through Guilin. You can also get from Guilin to Yangshuo by bus or minibus, or via a costly but pleasant boat trip.

AIR TRAVEL   Guilin Liangjiang International Airport is the gateway to Yangshuo. Taxis from Guilin Airport to Yangshuo cost around Y250.

BOAT TRAVEL   The boat that traverses the Li River from Guilin to Yangshuo takes approximately four hours. At Y380 for a round-trip ticket, it's costlier than other modes of travel, but the trip is pleasant and scenic. Tickets are available from any of the countless travel agents in Guilin or Yangshuo.

BUS TRAVEL   Departing from the Guilin Train Station, express luxury buses travel between Guilin and Yangshuo every half hour between 7 am and 8 pm. The trip takes a little over an hour in these air-conditioned and smoke-free buses that cost Y20.

SAFETY AND PRECAUTIONS

The town of Yangshuo is quite safe, but it is worth being extra careful if cycling outside of town, where cars tend to be faster and not always willing to yield much road space.

TIMING

Two or three days is enough time to take in Yangshuo's town and surrounding areas. If you're in need of a break from traveling, a week or two can slip by quickly here.

> ### BACKPACKERS' PARADISE
>
> Yangshuo is bliss for hipster backpackers. Its 20,000 surrounding karst limestone mountains are part and parcel of the Southeast Asia backpacker circuit that was forged in the 1970s and remains well trodden to this day. Today Yangshuo's main strip known as "Xijie" or "West Street" throbs with the commingling cacophony of Hong Kong canto-pop, reggae, hip-hop, and classic rock. You can order everything from lasagna to enchiladas to pad thai noodles. It's also the ideal place to get the lowdown on the best deals from English-speaking waitstaff or fellow travelers.

TOURS

If getting wet and muddy underground is your idea of a good time, look no farther than Water Cave, the deepest and largest underground grotto in the area. Accessible only by flat-bottom boat, Water Cave has hikes between stalactites, a mud bath, and a number of crystal-clear pools perfect for washing off all that mud. Tours can be arranged through any of the many travel agencies in the Xi Jie area. Charm Yangshuo Tour is recommended.

ESSENTIALS

Bank Bank of China (✉ 93 Pantao Lu ☎ 0773/882–0260).

Bus Contact Yangshuo Bus Station (✉ Pantao Lu, across from Yangshuo Park ☎ 0773/882–2188).

Public Security Bureau PSB Yangshuo (✉ Pan Tao Lu ☎ 0773/882–2178).

Visitor and Tour Info China International Travel Service (CITS) (✉ Xi Jie, near Pantao Lu ☎ 0773/882–7102). **Charm Yangshuo Tour** (✉ Pantao Lu ☎ 0773/881–4355).

EXPLORING

Probably the most popular destination in Yangshuo, **Moon Hill** *(Yueliang Shan)* is named after the large hole through the center of this karst peak. Amazing vistas await at the top of the several trails that snake up the hill's side. ✉ *Yangshuo–Gaotian Lu* ☎ *No phone* 🎟 *Y15* ☉ *Daily 6 am–7:30 pm.*

In the center of town, **Yangshuo Park** *(Yangshuo Gongyuan)* is where older people come to play chess while children scamper about in small playgrounds. The park has a number of statues and ponds worth seeing,

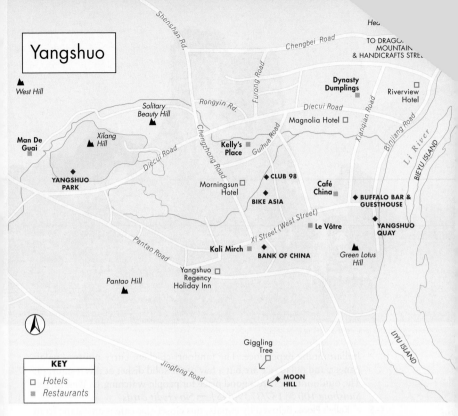

and Yangshuo Park Peak has a small pagoda offering excellent views of the surrounding town. For a more intense climb with even better views, ascend the television tower, across the street from the park's entrance. ⊠ *Diecui Lu, at Pantao Lu, across from Yangshuo Bus Station* 🎫 *Free* 🕙 *Daily.*

WHERE TO EAT

¢–$$
ECLECTIC
✕ **Café China.** In addition to shepherd's pie and baguette sandwiches, Café China serves an addictive rotisserie chicken that is made from a highly guarded local recipe. The kitchen roasts between 12 and 18 chickens each night, so diners in the know call the chef's mobile number (☎ 1380-783–0498) at least an hour in advance. One chicken will set you back Y50. ⊠ *34 Xi Jie* ☎ *1380/783–0498* 🖃 *No credit cards.*

¢–$$
NORTHERN
CHINESE
★
✕ **Dynasty Dumplings.** This local favorite serves some of the best northern-style dumplings in the area. Don't leave without trying them, either steamed or fried. You'll also find excellent local specialties like *pi jiu yu* (beer fish) and *tian luo niang* (stuffed river snails). English menus are available, and the Beijing couple who own this place is very friendly. ⊠ *21 Xianqian Jie, across from Magnolia Hotel* ☎ *0773/890–2058* 🖃 *No credit cards.*

$–$$
INDIAN
✕ **Kali Mirch Indian Cuisine.** A delicious option if you're looking to take a break from Chinese food and approximations of Western food, Kali Mirch's spices and chefs come directly from India, offering an authentic

Li river and the limestone karsts of Yangshuo.

Indian dining experience. The tandoori chicken, curry mutton, palak paneer, and pulao rice are but a few of the solid dishes at this restaurant. The outdoor tables are a good place for people-watching. ✉ *West Street, Sunshine 100* 🕿 *137/3739-6451* 🖃 *No credit cards.*

¢–$ ╳ **Kelly's Place.** Beloved by expats, this closet-size café is an escape from
ECLECTIC   the hustle and bustle of West Street. On any given night, English teachers can be found drinking beer in the cobblestone pavilion. There are tasty Chinese-style dumpling soups. ✉ *43 Guihua Lu, 1 block north of Xi Jie* 🕿 *0773/881–3233* 🖃 *No credit cards.*

$–$$ ╳ **Le Vôtre.** A restored building dating from the Qing Dynasty is the
FRENCH   setting for this French restaurant. The dining room looks more like a museum than a restaurant. The restaurant serves excellent Western-style specialties like grilled lamb chops and pasta primavera, as well as fine pizza. ✉ *79 Xi Jie* 🕿 *0773/882–8040* 🖃 *No credit cards.*

¢–$ ╳ **Man De Guai.** At this family-owned restaurant popular with locals
CHINESE   but almost unknown to travelers, you'll find an amazing array of local dishes. There are no English menus, but the owners will bring you into the kitchen and let you pick out what you want. This place is hard to find: look for it on the small street two blocks north of the bus station, next to the large statue of Guanyin, the Buddha of Compassion. ✉ *41 Yangshuo Xie Bilian Dong* 🕿 *0773/691–0959* 🖃 *No credit cards.*

WHERE TO STAY

¢   🏠 **The Giggling Tree.** Nestled among the karst mountains outside of
Yangshuo, the Giggling Tree is one of China's coolest guesthouses. These
Fodor's Choice   renovated traditional farmhouses two miles outside of the noisy town
★   offer amazing views, good Chinese and Western food, bicycle rental, and

relaxing terraces in a very chilled-out countryside setting. Owned by a Dutch couple with children, much of the guesthouse has been designed with families in mind. Rooms are clean, spacious, and nicely designed. **Pros:** beautiful views; quiet countryside; good food. **Cons:** not always easy to get a taxi when you need one. ✉ *Aishanmen Village* ☎ *136/6786-6154* ⊕ *www.gigglingtree.com* ⤳ *22 rooms* ⚿ *In-room: a/c, no phone (some), refrigerator (some), DVD (some), Wi-Fi. In-hotel: restaurant, room service, bar, bicycles, laundry service* ▭ *No credit cards.*

¢ 🏨 **Magnolia Hotel** *(Baiyulan Jiudian).* Built around a traditional courtyard, the Magnolia has a glass-roofed lobby overlooking a lovely carp pond. Rooms have big windows, most with amazing views of the mountains, the river, or both. The family suite is particularly nice: two adjoining rooms that give parents and children a little privacy. **Pros:** comfortable rooms; off the beaten path. **Cons:** uninspiring decor. ✉ *7 Diecui Lu* ☎ *0773/881–9288* ✉ *magnoliahotel@hotmail.com* ⤳ *26 rooms, 1 suite* ⚿ *In-room: Internet. In-hotel: laundry service, Wi-Fi hotspot, no-smoking rooms* ▭ *AE, MC, V.*

¢ 🏨 **Morningsun Hotel** *(Chenguang Jiudian).* With a lovely enclosed courtyard, the Morningsun Hotel has the look of a Ming Dynasty guesthouse. The guest rooms also carry on the traditional style (except for the brass and glass bathrooms). The staff at this family-run establishment are extremely friendly. Reserve ahead, as the hotel tends to fill up on weekends and holidays. **Pros:** friendly staff; near Xi Jie. **Cons:** rooms feel a bit "cold." ✉ *4 Chengzhong Lu* ☎ *0773/881–3899* ⊕ *www. morningsunhotel.com* ⤳ *23 rooms* ⚿ *In-hotel: restaurant, laundry service, Internet terminal, no-smoking rooms* ▭ *AE, MC, V.*

Fodor's Choice
★

¢ 🏨 **Riverview Hotel** *(Wangjianglou Kezhan).* With its curvaceous tile roof and balconies with stunning views of the Li River, the Riverview is one of the town's nicest budget hotels. The guest rooms are tastefully appointed with dark-wood furniture. The first-floor restaurant, with alfresco seating and a great river view, is a lovely place to get breakfast or a coffee even if you're staying somewhere else. **Pros:** comfortable restaurant seating; river view. **Cons:** slightly isolated from the rest of town. ✉ *11 Binjiang Lu* ☎ *0773/882–2688* ⊕ *www.riverview.com.cn* ⤳ *38 rooms* ⚿ *In-hotel: restaurant, bar, laundry service, Internet terminal* ▭ *AE, MC, V.*

8

¢ 🏨 **Yangshuo Regency Holiday Hotel.** At the entrance to the tourist district, this hotel has clean rooms with soft beds and nice views of the surrounding mountains. Its location makes it a good base for exploring the area. It faces the main road through town, so some rooms are noisy. **Pros:** central location; nice scenery. **Cons:** noisy area; touts offering everything from taxis to sex wait outside at night. ✉ *117 Xi Jie* ☎ *0773/881–7198* ⊕ *www. ys-holidayhotel.com* ⤳ *52 rooms*

WORD OF MOUTH

"I rented a mountain bike for 20 yuan (less than $3) for the day—a regular bike was half that. Armed with a little map I rode through town and out to a spot. where I had prepaid and arranged a bamboo raft. It was a great trip through beautiful scenery. My bicycle was strapped to the raft and at the end I hopped on and rode back into town—a couple of kilometers." —NeoPatrick

♿ *In-room: Internet. In-hotel: 2 restaurants, laundry service, Internet terminal, no-smoking rooms, refrigerator* ⊟ *AE, MC, V.*

NIGHTLIFE

With a good selection of imported and local beers, **Buffalo Bar** (⊠ *50 Xianqian Jie* ☎ *0773/881–3644*) is very popular with expats. You can meet a few around the pool table. **Club 98** (⊠ *42 Guihua Jie* ☎ *0773/ 881–4605*) serves mixed drinks and imported beers in a pleasant atmosphere, and has a pool table.

SPORTS AND THE OUTDOORS

BIKING

Cheaply made mountain bikes are available for rent all over Yangshuo at a cost of about Y10 per day. However, if you want a better-quality mountain bike, **Bike Asia** (⊠ *42 Guihua Lu, 2nd floor* ☎ *0773/882–6521* ⊕ *www.bikeasia.com*) rents them for Y30 per day. The company leads short trips to the villages along the Li River.

BOATING

Starting as a humble spring at the top of Mao'er Mountain, the majestic Li River snakes through Guangxi, connecting Yangshuo to many other towns along the way. One of the country's most scenic—and less polluted—rivers, its banks are lined with stone embankments where people practice tai chi. The best spots for swimming can be found north of the city, where the stone walls give way to sand. Several local companies offer rides on bamboo rafts along the Li River and on the Yulong River, a smaller tributary. You can bargain with them at the stone quay at the end of West Street.

ROCK CLIMBING

Yangshuo is the undisputed rock-climbing capital of China. The oldest and most trusted climbing club in Yangshuo is **Chinaclimb** (⊠ *45 Xianqian Jie* ☎ *0773/888–1033* ⊕ *www.chinaclimb.com*). Led by a mostly Australian staff, climbs are perfect for novices and experts alike. Half-day treks cost between Y200 and Y300, including equipment and transportation.

SHOPPING

West Street is filled with shops selling everything from tourist junk to high-quality minority handicrafts. Also explore Dragon Head Mountain Pier Handicrafts Street (*Longtou Shan Matou Gongyi Jie*), a cobblestone street running along the river. You can bargain merchants down to half the original asking price or even less.

Johnny Lu's Café and Books (⊠ *7 Chengzhong Jie* ☎ *1323/783–1208*) is Yangshuo's best place to find secondhand books (with some new books too); it has a full selection of travel books.

SIDE TRIPS FROM YANGSHUO

Yangshuo is an exceptional base from which to explore the villages along the Li River, many of which date back hundreds of years. About 8 km (5 mi) southeast of Yangshuo sits **Fuli**, a Ming Dynasty town built on the river's northern bank. Fuli has narrow, winding cobblestone streets and a number of ancient temples worth exploring. Fuli is where you'll find the **Peng Family Painted Scroll Factory** (⊠ *55 Fuling Bei Jie* ☎ *0773/894–2416*), a family-run shop that's been producing handmade scrolls and painted fans for generations. You'll find these for sale in Yangshuo for two or three times the price you can get them for here. From Fuli you can travel up the river to other villages such as Xinzhai, Degongzha, and Puyi, which has a large weekend market. Many of the people living in these villages still dress in traditional clothing.

NANNING

350 km (217 mi; 5 hrs by train) southwest of Guilin; 440 km (273 mi; 24 hrs by train) southeast of Guiyang; 600 km (372 mi; 16 hrs by train) west of Hong Kong.

Built along the banks of the Yong River, Nanning is the capital of Guangxi Zhuang Autonomous Region. The city isn't a major tourist draw, but it is a pleasant place to stop for a day or two. Many travelers come here for a visa before continuing into Vietnam.

GETTING HERE AND AROUND

Nanning is most accessible by bus from elsewhere in Guangxi. For anything beyond, it's a flight or an overnight train.

AIR TRAVEL Nanning Wuxu International Airport is 31 km (19 mi) southwest of Nanning and has flights throughout China, including to Guilin, though not to Yangshuo.

BUS TRAVEL There are frequent buses between Nanning and Guilin (four-plus hours). There is no direct service between Nanning and Yangshuo, meaning a change of buses or a taxi in Guilin.

TRAIN TRAVEL Nanning's train station is at the northwestern edge of town, and offers frequent service to Guilin. The fastest of these takes four hours.

SAFETY AND PRECAUTIONS

Nanning is a quiet and safe city, but some areas can be poorly lit at night—make sure you watch where you're going after sundown.

TIMING

Nanning doesn't have much going on tourism-wise, but is an otherwise pleasant city with nice parks. Two or three days is enough to get a feel for the city.

ESSENTIALS

Air Contact Nanning Wuxu International Airport (☎ *0771/209–5160*).

Banks Bank of China (⊠ *39 Gu Cheng Lu* ☎ *0771/281–1267* ⊠ *Nanning Wuxu International Airport* ☎ *0771/482–4538*).

Bus Contact Nanning Bus Station (⊠ *65 Huadong Lu* ☎ *0771/242–4529*).

Medical Assistance Nanning First Municipal People's Hospital (✉ *89 Qixing Lu* ☏ *0771/267–7885*).

Public Security Bureau PSB Nanning (✉ *5 Ke Yuan East Rd, Xi Xiang Tang* ☏ *110 or 0771/289–1302*).

Train Contact Nanning Station (✉ *North end of Chaoyang Lu* ☏ *0771/243–2468*).

Visitor and Tour Info China International Travel Service (CITS) (✉ *40 Xinmin Lu* ☏ *0771/532–0165*).

EXPLORING

Surrounding White Dragon Lake, **People's Park** *(Renmin Gongyuan)* has some 200 species of rare trees and flowers. Here you'll find the remains of fortifications built by a warlord in the early part of the 20th century. ✉ *1 Renmin Dong Lu* ☑ *Free* ☉ *Daily 8:30–6.*

The **Guangxi Zhuang Autonomous Region Museum** *(Guangxi Zhuang Zizhiqu Bowuguan)* focuses on Guangxi's numerous ethnic minorities. In the back are magnificent full-size reconstructions of ethnic minority houses, pagodas, and drum towers set among attractive pools and bridges. A collection of more than 300 bronze drums made by local people is also on display. ✉ *34 Minzu Dadao* ☑ *Free* ☉ *Daily 8:30–11:30 and 2:30–5.*

In the southeastern part of the city, **South Lake** *(Nan Hu)* covers more than 200 acres. A bonsai exhibition and an orchid garden are in the surrounding park. The park is encircled by a wide path that's ideal for strolling or jogging. There are a few bars along the lake's north side. ✉ *Gucheng Lu* ☑ *Free* ☉ *Daily.*

WHERE TO EAT

$–$$
CHINESE

×**Beifang Renjia.** Tired of eating the local rice noodles? This is where many of Nanning's transplants from northeastern China come to dine on traditional *dongbei cai*. A large dumpling menu is complemented by a full range of northeastern favorites such as *disanxian* (potato, eggplant, and green pepper in brown sauce), moo shu pork, plus a long list of unique breads and noodle dishes. Wash it all down with a cold Harbin beer. Staff are friendly but can't speak English; the menu has photos and English text. ✉ *86 Taoyuan Lu* ☏ *0771/530–4263* ▭ *No credit cards.*

$–$$
ITALIAN
☕
Fodor's Choice
★

×**The Here.** Homemade breads and pastas, delicious salads, pizzas, sandwiches, and main courses, a great beer selection, and the best coffee in Guangxi—The Here is the best Western food you'll find for hundreds of miles in any direction. Once one of Nanning's hardest-to-find restaurants, The Here has relocated to a new three-story building all its own behind the Admiral City Mall on Minzu Dadao, a short stroll from the Marriott. In addition to the amazing food and drinks, the staff are friendly, speak English, and seem to genuinely enjoy themselves. The decor is plush and comfortable, and the music is chilled out. A true oasis. ✉ *131 Minzu Dadao, B10, North Square (Central) Admiral City Mall* ☏ *0771/588–7183* ▭ *No credit cards.*

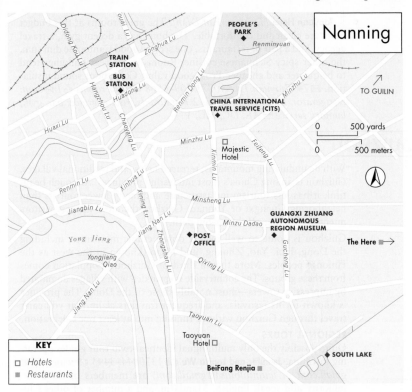

Nanning

PEOPLE'S PARK
Renminyuan

TRAIN STATION
BUS STATION

CHINA INTERNATIONAL TRAVEL SERVICE (CITS)

TO GUILIN

0   500 yards
0   500 meters

Lidong Kou Lu
ouai Lu
Zonghua Lu
Renmin Dong Lu
Minzhu Lu
Feifeng Lu

Hangzhou Lu
Huadong Lu
Chaoyang Lu

Huaxi Lu

Majestic Hotel

Minzhu Lu
Xinmin Lu

Renmin Lu
Xinhua Lu
Xining Lu

Jiangbin Lu
Jiang Nan Lu
Zhongshan Lu

Minsheng Lu

Minzu Dadao

GUANGXI ZHUANG AUTONOMOUS REGION MUSEUM

Gucheng Lu

The Here

Yong Jiang
Yongjiang Qiao

POST OFFICE

Qixing Lu

Jiang Nan Lu

Taoyuan Lu

Taoyuan Hotel

KEY
□ Hotels
■ Restaurants

BeiFang Renjia

SOUTH LAKE

8

WHERE TO STAY

$–$$ ★ **Majestic Hotel** *(Mingyuan Xindu Jiudian)*. This older luxury hotel, close to the main square, has been refurbished reasonably well and is efficiently run. Its low price, excellent location, and fine gym make it a top choice in Nanning. **Pros:** one of Nanning's nicest swimming pools; professional staff/management. **Cons:** one of the tougher places in town to catch a cab; not much of interest in the immediate vicinity. ⊠ *38 Xinmin Lu* ☎ *0771/283–0808* ⇱ *298 rooms* ⌂ *In-room: safe, refrigerator, Internet. In-hotel: 2 restaurants, bar, pool, gym, laundry service* ☐ *AE, DC, MC, V.*

$ **Nanning Marriott.** The first real five-star in Nanning, the Marriott is located in the city's northeast, near the China-ASEAN Expo Center, where a new Southeast Asia-focused central business district for Nanning is starting to spring up. Rooms feel new, clean, and comfortable, with plenty of space and modern bathrooms. The hotel's Western restaurant has the city's best buffet and a nice bistro feel. The Cantonese restaurant is good, but the decor is a bit dark. The bar is one of Nanning's classiest, serving up a wide variety of quality wines and cocktails. **Pros:** good service **Cons:** far from the city center. ⊠ *131 Minzu Dadao* ☎ *771/536–6688* ⊕ *www.nanningmarriott.com* ⇱ *334 rooms* ⌂ *In-room: a/c, safe, refrigerator, Internet. In-hotel: 2 restaurants, room service, bar, pool, gym, spa, laundry service* ☐ *AE, DC, MC, V.*

ċ ☑ **Taoyuan Hotel** *(Taoyuan Fan Dian)*. The guest rooms at this budget hotel are clean and comfortable. The hotel has a decent gym, a travel agency, and a pair of restaurants, one serving good Cantonese dim sum, the other spicy Sichuanese cuisine. Rooms in the rear buildings tend to be quieter and cheaper. **Pros:** good value. **Cons:** poor sound insulation. ✉ *74 Taoyuan Lu* ☎ *0771/209–6868* → *400 rooms* ⚙ *In-room: refrigerator, Internet. In-hotel: 2 restaurants, room service, bar, gym, laundry service* ≡ *AE, DC, MC, V.*

GUIZHOU

With its undulating mountains, terraced fields, and traditional villages, Guizhou is among China's most interesting provinces. Although beautiful, it has less tourism infrastructure and many fewer tourists than neighboring Guangxi or Yunnan. Guizhou therefore attracts visitors intent on heading off the beaten path.

Guizhou is home to well over a dozen ethnic minorities, including the Dong, Hui, Yao, Zhuang, and Miao (known in the west as the Hmong) peoples. More than a third of Guizhou's population comes from these groups. The countryside is sprinkled with villages dominated by impressive towers—most notably those of the Dong. The province is known for its festivals, and frequent travelers claim that you can't travel through Guizhou without running into at least one celebration.

REGIONAL TOURS

Quite possibly the only multilingual identical-twin tour guides operating in China, **Jennifer and Louisa Wu** (☎ *1370844–3445* ✉ *wujennife@gmail.com or wuminlouisa@gmail.com*) are members of the Miao minority and speak English, Mandarin, and a number of other Chinese languages fluently. They are both highly familiar with Guizhou and Yunnan, and divide their time leading short and longer tours around these provinces. Rates for a group are negotiable, but generally average around Y250 per day.

Founded by a native of neighboring Yunnan Province who then went on to receive a Harvard MBA, **WildChina Travel** (☎ *888/902–8808 [US]; 106/465–6602 (China)* ✉ *info@wildchina.com* ⊕ *www.wildchina.com*) runs several high-end tours that either pass through Guizhou or are entirely dedicated to the province. Most focus on the province's incredible minority cultures and include village homestays. A one-week tour of Guizhou is $1,760, including food and lodging but not international airfare.

GUIYANG

350 km (217 mi; 12 hrs by fastest train) northwest of Guilin; 425 km (264 mi; 12 hrs by train) northwest of Nanning; 850 km (527 mi; 20½ hrs by train) northwest of Hong Kong; 1,650 km (1,023 mi; 21 hrs by train) southwest of Beijing.

The capital Guiyang is a pleasant place to begin an exploration of the province. Like most cities in China, it is fast losing its older quarters, but even in the heart of downtown enough remain to make a short stay

Continued on page 544

FOR ALL THE TEA IN CHINA

Legend has it that the first cup dates from 2737 BC, when Camellia sinensis leaves fell into water being boiled for Emperor Shenong. He loved the result, tea was born, and so were many traditions.

Historically, when a girl accepted a marriage proposal she drank tea, a gesture symbolizing fidelity. Betrothal gifts were known as "tea gifts," engagements as "accepting tea," and marriages as "eating tea." Today the bride and groom kneel before their parents, offering cups of tea in thanks.

Serving tea is a sign of respect. Young people proffer it to their parents or grandparents; subordinates do the same for their bosses. Pouring tea also signifies submission, so it's a way to say you're sorry. When you're served tea, show your thanks by tapping the table with your index and middle fingers.

And forget about adding milk or sugar. Not only is most Chinese tea best without it, but why dilute and sweeten a beverage long known by herbalists to be good for you? Even modern medicine acknowledges that tea's powerful antioxidants reduce the risk of cancer and heart disease. It's also thought to be such a good source of fluoride that Mao Zedong eschewed toothpaste for a green-tea rinse. Smiles, everyone.

In China, tea was first discovered by the Emporer Shennong.

HISTORICAL BREW

Tea preparation is a careful affair.

THE RISE AND FALL OF EMPIRES

Tea has a long and tumultuous history, making and breaking empires in both the East and the West. Bricks of tea were used as currency, and Chinese statesmen kept rebellious northern nomads in check by refusing to sell it to them.

Rumor has it that tea caused the downfall of the Song Empire. Apparently, tea-whisking was Emperor Huizong's favorite pastime: he was so obsessed with court tea culture that he forgot all about trivial little matters like defense. The country became vulnerable to invasion and fell to the Mongols in 1279.

Genghis preferred airag (fermented mare's milk), but after the Mongol's defeat, the drink of kings returned with a vengeance to the court of the Ming Dynasty (1368–1644). Tea as we know it today dates to this period: the first Ming emperor, Hongwu, set the trend of using loose-leaf tea by refusing to accept tea tribute gifts in any other form.

TEA GOES INTERNATIONAL

The first Europeans to encounter the beverage were navigators and missionaries who visited China in the mid-16th century. In 1610, Dutch traders began importing tea from China into Europe, with the Portuguese hot on their heels. It was initially marketed as a health drink and took a while to catch on. By the 1640s, tea had become popular among both the Dutch and Portuguese aristocracy, initially the only ones who could afford it.

Although we think of tea as a quintessentially British drink, it actually arrived in America two years before it appeared in Britain. When the British acquired New Amsterdam (later New York) in 1664, the colony consumed more tea than all the British isles put together.

Tea was available in Britain from about 1554 onward, but Brits were wary of the stuff at first. What tipped the scales in tea's favor was nothing less than celebrity product endorsement. King

All types of tea come from one plant.

Charles II married the Portuguese princess Catherine of Braganza in 1662. She arrived in England with tea and fine porcelain tea ware in her dowry and a healthy addiction to the stuff. Members of the royalty were the 16th century's trendsetters: tea became the thing to drink at court; pretty soon the general public was hooked, too.

STORMS IN A TEACUP

Tea quickly became a very important—and troublemaking—commodity. Religious leaders thought the drink sinful and doctors declared it a health risk. In Britain, ale-brewers were losing profits and pressure groups successfully persuaded the government to tax tea at 119%. On top of all this, the immensely powerful British East India Company held the monopoly on tea importation.

Tea's value skyrocketed: by 1706, the retail price of green tea in London was equivalent to $300 for 100 g (3.5 oz), far beyond the reach of normal people. Tea smuggling quickly became a massive—and often cut-throat—business. To make sought-after tea supplies stretch even further, they were routinely mixed with twigs, leaves, animal dung, and even poisonous chemicals.

Back in the New World, Americans were fed up with paying taxes that went straight back to Britain. Things came to a head when a group of patriots dressed as Native Americans peacefully boarded British ships in Boston harbor and emptied 342 chests of tea into the water. The act came to be known as the Boston Tea Party and was a vital catalyst in starting the American Revolution.

The War of Independence wasn't the only war sparked by tea. In Britain, taxes were axed and, as tea was suddenly affordable for everyone, demand grew exponentially. But China remained the world's only supplier, so that by the mid-19th century, tea was causing a massive trade deficit. The British started exporting opium into China in exchange for tea, provoking two Opium Wars. In the 1880s, attempts to grow tea in India were finally successful and Indian tea began to overtake Chinese tea on the market.

These days, over 3.2 million metric tons of tea are produced annually worldwide. After water, tea is the world's favorite drink. Though Britain and Ireland now consume far more tea per capita than China, tea is still a regular presence at the Chinese table and is inextricably bound to Chinese culture.

ANCIENT TRADE ROUTES

The Ancient Tea and Horse Caravan Road, also known as the Southern Silk Road, is a trade corridor dating back to the Tang Dynasty (618–907). The 4,000-km route emerged more than 1,200 years ago and was actually still in use until recently.

Back in the heyday of the Caravan Road, Xishuangbanna, Dali, Lijiang, and many other parts of Yunnan were important outposts on the route. Tea, horses, salt, medicinal herbs, and Indian spices all featured prominently in this massive network.

During World War II, the route was used to smuggle supplies from India into the interior of Japanese-occupied China.

DRINKING IN THE CULTURE

The way tea was prepared historically bears little resemblance to the steep-a-teabag method many westerners employ today. Tea originally came in bricks of compressed leaves bound with sheep's blood or manure. Chunks were broken, ground into a powder, and whisked into hot water. In the first tea manual, *Cha Jing (The Way of Tea)*, Tang-dynasty writer Lu Yu describes preparing powdered tea using 28 pieces of teaware, including big brewing pans and shallow drinking bowls.

The potters of Yixing (near Shanghai) gradually transformed wine vessels into small pots for steeping tea. Yixing pottery is ideal for brewing: its fine unglazed clay is highly porous, and if you always use the same kind of tea, the pot will take on its flavor.

Today the most elaborate Chinese tea service—which requires only two pots and enough cups for all involved—is called *gong fu cha* (skilled tea method). Although you can experience it at many teahouses, most people consider it too involved for every day. They simply brew their leaf tea in three-piece lidded cups, called *gaiwan*, tilting the lid as they drink so that it acts as a strainer.

Green Tea leaves in a Chinese gaiwan

THE CEREMONY

1 Rinse teapot with hot water.

2 Fill with black or oolong to one third of its height.

3 Half-fill teapot with hot water and empty immediately to rinse leaves.

4 Fill pot with hot water, let leaves steep for a minute; no bubbles should form.

5 Pour tea into small cups, moving the spout continuously over each, so all have the same strength of tea.

6 Pour the excess into a second teapot.

7 Using the same leaves, repeat the process up to five times, extending the steeping time slightly.

TEA TIMELINE

Japanese tea ceremony

350 AD	"Tea" appears in Chinese dictionary.
618–1644	Tea falls into and out of favor at Chinese court.
7th c.	Tea introduced to Japan.
1610–1650	Dutch and Portuguese traders bring tea to Europe.
1662	British King Charles II marries Portugal's Catherine of Braganza, a tea addict. Tea craze sweeps the court.
1689	Tea taxation starts in Britain; peaks at 119%.

HOW TEA IS MADE

Chinese tea is grown on large plantations and nearly always picked by hand. Pluckers remove only the top two leaves. A skilled plucker can collect up to 35 kg (77 lbs) of leaves in a day; that's 9 kg (almost 20 lbs) of tea, or 3,500 cups. After a week, new top leaves will have grown, and bushes can be plucked again. Climate and soil play an important role on a tea plantation, much as they do in a vineyard. But what really differentiates black, green, and oolong teas is the way leaves are processed.

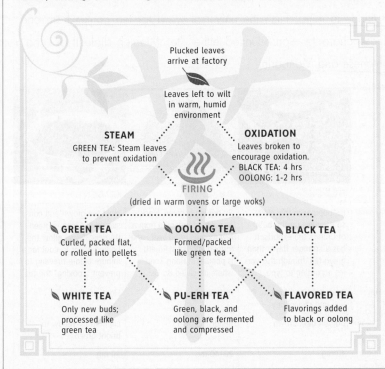

Plucked leaves
arrive at factory

Leaves left to wilt
in warm, humid
environment

STEAM
GREEN TEA: Steam leaves
to prevent oxidation

OXIDATION
Leaves broken to
encourage oxidation.
BLACK TEA: 4 hrs
OOLONG: 1-2 hrs

FIRING
(dried in warm ovens or large woks)

GREEN TEA
Curled, packed flat,
or rolled into pellets

OOLONG TEA
Formed/packed
like green tea

BLACK TEA

WHITE TEA
Only new buds;
processed like
green tea

PU-ERH TEA
Green, black, and
oolong are fermented
and compressed

FLAVORED TEA
Flavorings added
to black or oolong

8

IN FOCUS FOR ALL THE TEA IN CHINA

Boston Tea Party

1773	Boston Tea Party: Americans dump 342 chests of tea into Boston Harbor, protesting British taxes.
1784	British tea taxes slashed; consumption soars.
1835	Tea cultivation starts in Assam, India.
1880s	India and Ceylon produce more tea than China.
1904	Englishman Richard Blechynden creates iced tea at St. Louis World's Fair.
1908	New York importer Thomas Sullivan sends clients samples in silk bags—the first tea bags.
2004	Chinese tea exports overtake India's for the first time since the 1880s.

TYPES OF TEA

Some teas are simply named for the region that produces them (Yunnan or Assam); others are evocatively named to reflect a particular blend. Some are transliterated (like Keemun); others translated (Iron Goddess of Mercy). Confused? Keep two things in mind. First, the universal word for tea comes from one Chinese character—pronounced either "te" (Xiamen dialect) or "cha" (Cantonese and Mandarin).

	BLACK	PU-ERH	GREEN
Overview	It's popular in the West so it makes up the bulk of China's tea exports. It has a stronger flavor than green tea, though this varies according to type.	Pu-erh tea is green, black, or oolong fermented from a few months to 50 years and formed into balls. Pu-erh is popular in Hong Kong, where it's called Bo Le.	Most tea grown and consumed in China is green. It's delicate, so allow the boiling water to cool for a minute before brewing to prevent "cooking" the tea.
Flavor	From light and fresh to rich and chocolatey	Rich, earthy	Light, aromatic
Color	Golden dark brown	Reddish brown	Light straw-yellow to bright green
Caffeine per Serving	40 mg	20–40 mg	20 mg
Ideal Water Temperature	203°F	203°F	160°F
Steeping Time	3–5 mins.	3–5 mins.	1–2 mins.
Examples	Dian Hong (chocolatey aftertaste; unlike other Chinese teas, can take milk). Keemun (Qi Men; mild, smoky; once used in English breakfast blends). Lapsang Souchong (dried over smoking pine; strong flavor). Yunnan Golden (full bodied, malty).	Buying Pu-erh is like buying wine: there are different producers and different vintages, and prices vary greatly.	Bi Luo Chun (Green Snail Spring; rich, fragrant). Chun Mee (Eyebrow; pale yellow; floral). Hou Kui (Monkey Tea; nutty, sweet; floral aftertaste). Long Ding (Dragon Mountain; sweet, minty). Long Jing (Dragon's Well; bright green; nutty).

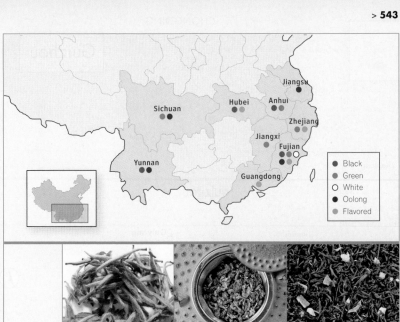

	WHITE	OOLONG	FLAVORED
Overview	The rare white tea is made from the newest buds, picked unopened at day-break and processed like green tea. Small batches mean high prices. It's a tea for refined palates.	Halfway between green and black tea, this tea is more popular in China than elsewhere. The gong fu cha ceremony best re-veals its complexities.	Petals, bark, and other natural ingredients are added to black or green tea to create these brews. Earl Grey is black tea scented with bergamot (a recipe supposedly given to the tea's 18th-century namesake by a Mandarin). Jasmine tea is green tea dried with jasmine petals. Others include lychee congou and rose congou: black tea dried with lychee juice or rose petals. Flavor, color, caffeine content, and ideal preparation depend on the tea component of the blend. Don't con-fuse flavored teas with the caffeine-free herbal teas made from herbs, roots, and blossoms (e.g., chamomile, peppermint, rosehips, licorice, ginger).
Flavor	Very subtle	Aromatic, lighter than black tea	
Color	Very pale yellow	Pale green to pale brown	
Caffeine per Serving	15 mg	30 mg	
Ideal Water Temperature	185°F	203°F	
Steeping Time	4–15 mins	1–9 mins.	
Examples	Bai Hao Yin Zhen (Silver Needle; finest white tea; sweet and very delicate, anti-toxin qualities). Bai Mu Dan (White Peony; smooth and refreshing).	Da Hong Pao (Scarlet Robe; comes from only 4 bushes; full bodied, floral). Tie Guan Yin (Iron Goddess of Mercy; legend has it a farmer repaired statue of the god-dess, who rewarded him with the tea bush shoot; golden yellow; floral).	

Map legend:
- ● Black
- ● Green
- ○ White
- ● Oolong
- ● Flavored

Provinces shown: Jiangsu, Hubei, Anhui, Sichuan, Zhejiang, Jiangxi, Fujian, Yunnan, Guangdong

8

IN FOCUS FOR ALL THE TEA IN CHINA

here worthwhile. The main streets of the sprawling city are Zunyi Lu, Ruijin Lu, Zhonghua Lu, and Yan'an Lu.

GETTING HERE AND AROUND

AIR TRAVEL Guiyang Airport lies 9 mi (15 km) to the southeast of the city. There are direct flights between Guiyang and most of China's main cities.

BUS TRAVEL Guiyang's main long-distance bus station has been temporarily relocated to a new urban district being constructed north of the city, and will eventually move again to an as yet undetermined location. Luckily, the smaller bus station on Jiefang Lu just north of Guiyang's train station still has regular bus service to Anshun (2 hrs), Kaili (2 hrs), and other destinations around Guizhou and the rest of China. Day tours can also be booked to Huangguoshu Falls (Y298–Y358 including entrance fees) and Huaxi Park and environs (Y198) at a kiosk just outside the train station.

TRAIN TRAVEL Direct trains link Guiyang with Chongqing (9 hrs), Guilin (12 hrs), Kunming (10 hrs), Liuzhou (8 hrs), Nanning (12 hrs), and Shanghai (26 hrs). The train station is at the southwest edge of the city at the southern end of Zunyi Lu.

SAFETY AND PRECAUTIONS

As in most other Chinese cities, unprovoked violent crime against tourists is exceedingly rare. The largest threat to personal safety in Guiyang is probably the frenetic traffic. Use the city's numerous pedestrian tunnels whenever possible, and never expect car or electric scooter drivers to follow traffic rules or exercise sound judgment. As when traveling anywhere, be careful with your valuables and stay vigilant for pickpockets and bag snatchers.

TIMING

Not including side trips, a day or two is enough time to visit most of the sights and sample some local delicacies.

ESSENTIALS

Air Contact Guiyang Airport (✉ *Southeast of the city* ☎ *0851/549–8908*).

Bank Bank of China (✉ *30 Dusi Lu* ☎ *0851/582–0925*).

Bus Contact Guizhou Stadium Bus Station (✉ *Jiefang Lu, one block north of the train station* ☎ *0851/579–3381*).

Public Security Bureau PSB Guiyang (✉ *Administrative Service Hall of Guiyang, Yingbin Dadao, Jinyang New Area* ☎ *0851/798–7284*).

Train Contact Guiyang Railway Station (✉ *Zunyi Lu* ☎ *0851/818–1222*).

Visitor and Tour Info China International Travel Service (CITS), Guizhou (✉ *1 Hequn Lu* ☎ *0851/690–1506*). **WildChina Travel** ✉ ☎ *888/902–8808 (U.S.); (86)106/465–6602 [China]* ✍ *info@wildchina.com* ⊕ *www.wildchina.com*).

EXPLORING

TOP ATTRACTIONS

ⓒ Just outside the city, **Qianling Park** *(Qianling Gongyuan)* covers 740
★ acres. It has a bit of everything, including thousands of plants and a collection of birds and monkeys (many of which roam wild through the park). Dominating the park is a 4,265-foot-high mountain that has fine views of the town from its western peak. The **Unicorn Cave** *(Qilin Dong),* discovered in 1531, was used as a prison for the two Nationalist generals, Yang Hucheng and Chang Xueliang, who were accused by the Guomindang of collaborating with the Communists when Chiang Kai-shek was captured at Xi'an in 1937. ✉ *187 Zaoshan Lu 2½ km (1 mi) northwest of city* ☒ *Free* ⊙ *Daily 6:30 am–10 pm.*

Underground Gardens *(Dixia Gongyuan)* is the poetic name for a cave about 25 km (15 mi) south of the city. In the cave, at a depth of 1,925 feet, a path weaves its way past the various rock formations, which are illuminated to emphasize their similarity with animals, fruits, and other living things. ✉ *25 km (15 mi) south of Guiyang* ☎ *0851/511–4014* ☒ *Y5* ⊙ *Daily 9 am–5 pm.*

WORTH NOTING

ⓒ With bamboo groves, **Hebin Park** *(Hebin Gongyuan),* sits on the banks of the Nanming River. In many ways it is the stereotypical Chinese public park experience, with senior citizens practicing dance and tai chi in the park's pavilions, young couples strolling hand in hand, and the omnipresent sound of music and public announcements playing from

Huangguoshu Falls, the largest of a series of nine waterfalls.

loudspeakers. For the children, there is a Ferris wheel and other rides. ⊠ *Ruijin Nan Lu* ⬚ *Free* ⊘ *Daily 5 am–midnight.*

Filled with ornamental gardens, **Huaxi Park** *(Huaxi Gongyuan)* sits on the banks of the Huaxi, known as the River of Flowers. The Huaxi Waterfall is nearby, as is a recently developed restaurant and nightlife street. ⊠ *18 km (11 mi) south of Guiyang* ⬚ *Y6* ⊘ *Daily 8–6.*

WHERE TO EAT

Every province has a number of dishes that locals are fiercely proud of. In Guizhou this is unquestionably *suan tang yu*, or sour fish soup. It combines a mouth-numbing number of herbs, spices, and local vegetables to make a dish that is at once spicy and savory. Another wonderfully named dish is *lian ai doufu guo*, or "the bean curd in love." It's a strip of vegetable- or meat-stuffed tofu toasted to a golden brown and sprinkled with sesame oil. It's a popular dish with couples.

$–$$
INTERNATIONAL

✕ **Highlands Coffee** (Gaoyuan Kafei). Understated modern decor, comfy seating, and high-quality imported coffee brewed by skilled baristas are the highlights here. There are also tasty panini on homemade bread and other seasonal dishes, as well as a wide selection of teas, smoothies, and desserts. Owner Chris—an affable American expatriate—is often present, and always tries to make visitors feel at home in Guiyang. The smoking area is ventilated to the outside and completely separated from the rest of the dining area. ⊠ *1 Liudong Jie, Bo'ai Lu* ☎ *0851/582-6222* ⊕ *www.highlands-coffee.com* ⬚ *No credit cards.*

$$
SEAFOOD
★

✕ **Old Kaili Sour Fish Restaurant** *(Lao Kaili Suan Tang Yu).* Sour fish soup, Guiyang's signature dish, is the specialty at this venerated local joint. The soup—an import from the city of Kaili—is cooked at your table, so you are able to add just the right amount of seasoning. Should yours be too spicy, remember that a bit of white rice—*not* water—is the best method for dousing culinary flames. ✉ *55 Shengfu Lu* ☎ *0851/584–3665* ▭ *No credit cards.*

WHERE TO STAY

¢–$ 🏨 **Guizhou Park Hotel** *(Guizhou Fandian).* Located in Guiyang's north near Qianling Park, and at one time the most luxurious hotel in town, this glass tower is showing its age somewhat. But its well-appointed rooms nevertheless remain a good value for the price. **Pros:** comfortable rooms; staff can speak some English. **Cons:** somewhat isolated. ✉ *66 Beijing Lu* ☎ *0851/682–3888* ⟿ *358 rooms* ⚬ *In-room: safe, refrigerator. In-hotel: 2 restaurants* ▭ *AE, DC, MC, V.*

¢–$ 🏨 **Nenghui Jiudian.** A central location and great accommodations and facilities at reasonable prices mean that this handsome modern hotel offers lot of bang for the yuan. Guest rooms are large and bright, with high ceilings, big firm beds, modern furniture, and clean bathrooms. **Pros:** central location for not much money. **Cons:** noisy part of town; little English spoken by staff. ✉ *38 Ruijin Nan Lu* ☎ *0851/589–8888* ⟿ *117 rooms* ⚬ *In-room: safe, refrigerator, Internet. In-hotel: restaurant, laundry service* ▭ *AE, DC, MC, V.*

$$$–$$$$ 🏨 **Sheraton Guiyang Hotel.** One of the best five-star hotels in Guiyang, the
★   Sheraton Guiyang has everything a high-end traveler needs: a bar with amazing city views, a full-service spa, the best international dining in town, and an attentive English-speaking staff. Rooms are very comfortable, with excellent views of the city and the surrounding mountains from rooms located on the 20th floor or up. **Pros:** by a small park; excellent city views. **Cons:** not for B&B lovers. ✉ *49 Zhonghua Nan Lu* ☎ *0851/588–8888* ⊕ *www.sheraton.com/guiyang* ⟿ *305 rooms, 41 suites* ⚬ *In-room: safe, refrigerator, Internet. In-hotel: 3 restaurants, bar, gym, spa, laundry service* ▭ *AE, DC, MC, V.*

SIDE TRIP TO HUANGGUOSHU FALLS

Fodor's Choice The Baishui River streams over nine sets of rocks, creating nine water-
★   falls over a course of 2 km (1 mi). At the highest point, **Huangguoshu Falls** *(literally, Yellow Fruit Trees Falls)* drops an eye-popping 230 feet. The largest in China, these falls are set in lush countryside where you'll find numerous villages. You can enjoy them from afar or by wading across the **Rhinoceros Pool** *(Xiniu Jian)* to the **Water Curtain Cave** *(Shuilian Dong)* hidden behind the main falls. Seven kilometers (4½ mi) downstream is the **Star Bridge Falls** *(Xingqiao Pu).* The falls are at their best from May through October. To avoid switching buses en route at the city of Anshu, book a seat on a tour bus. Any of the travel agents at local hotels or around the bus and train stations can help you with arrangements. ✉ *160 km (99 mi) southwest of Guiyang* ☎ *400/683–3333* ▱ *Y180* ☽ *Daily dawn–dusk.*

KAILI

200 km (124 mi; 3 hrs by train) east of Guiyang.

Capital of the Qian Dongnan Miao and Dong Autonomous Region, Kaili serves as the starting point for a journey to the Miao and Dong

8

Festivals of Guizhou

Since the province is comprised of various ethnic groups—including the Dong, Hui, Yao, Zhuang, and Miao peoples—Guizhuo is a gallery of traditional customs. Festivals are held throughout the year in Guiyang and elsewhere in the province. Many of these festivals are named after the dates on which they're held. These dates are according to a lunar calendar, so the festival called Eighth Day of the Fourth Month is not on April 8, but on the eighth day of the fourth lunar month (usually sometime in May).

Siyueba, which translates as Eighth Day of the Fourth Month, is when the Miao, Buyi, Dong, Yao, Zhuang, Yi, and other peoples of the province celebrate spring. Similar to Mardi Gras (but without the drinking or bawdy behavior), the festival is a major holiday in the region. Guiyang is a great place to check out the festival. The area around the fountain in the city center erupts with music, dancing, and general merrymaking.

An important traditional festival of Guiyang's Buyi population is **Liuyue-liu**, or Sixth Day of the Sixth Month. Held in midsummer, as the name implies, this festival sees thousands of Buyi people from the region gathering on the banks of the Huaxi River. As the story goes, a beautiful Buyi maiden embroidered an image of mountains and rivers of immense beauty. It was so inspiring that a miscreant plotted to steal it, and on the sixth day of the sixth lunar month he sent his minions to take it by force. The maiden cast her embroidery into the air, where it was transformed into the beautiful mountains and rivers seen here today.

Among the Miao people who live in and around Kaili a bullfight is a contest between the bulls themselves. The **Miao Bullfight Festival** traditionally takes place between the planting of rice seedlings and their harvest a few months later, usually between the sixth and eighth lunar months. Owners of bulls meet beforehand to size up the competition prior to agreeing to the fight. The atmosphere on fight day is lively, with drinking, music, and exchanging of gifts. Fireworks entice the bulls into combat until one falls down or runs away.

An important fertility festival among the Miao people is the **Sister's Meal Festival**, when unmarried women harvest rice from the terraced fields and prepare a special dish of sticky rice colored blue, pink, and yellow. Men arrive to serenade the women, and the women offer gifts of rice wine and small packets of rice wrapped in cloth. In the evening, women dress up for a night of dancing.

villages that dominate eastern Guizhou. More than two-thirds of the population is Miao, and their villages are along the eastern and northeastern outskirts of Kaili. The Dong communities are to the southeast. To get a real flavor for these peoples, attend festivities at one of the more than 100 annual festivals.

GETTING HERE AND AROUND

The fastest way to get from Guiyang to Kaili is often by bus, which can take as little as two hours. If you hear there is construction on the highway, however, the three-hour train ride may be a better option, as roadwork can stretch the bus ride closer to four hours.

BUS TRAVEL   The long-distance bus station just north of the Guiyang train station has Kaili-bound buses every 20 minutes or so. Buses usually don't leave until they're full. Tickets are about Y60.

TRAIN TRAVEL   Kaili's small train station is three hours from Guiyang. Trains passing through Kaili connect to Guilin, Kunming, Beijing, Shanghai, and much of the rest of China.

SAFETY AND PRECAUTIONS

Like other Chinese cities, Kaili is a safe place for foreign visitors, and violent crime directed at tourists is rare. Nevertheless, it is worth bearing in mind that Kaili remains relatively poor and off the beaten path: take special care, especially if out alone at night. Also keep an eye on the city's taxi drivers, who frequently refuse to start their meters and try to charge highly inflated rates for short rides.

TIMING

Though the sites in Kaili could conceivably occupy a day's time, the city is better viewed as a stepping-off point for multiday tours of the surrounding countryside and its scenic ethnic villages.

TOURS

Tour operator WildChina offers trips that take travelers from Guiyang to Kaili via several minority villages. Accommodation during the trips ranges from five-star hotels to a homestay in a Miao village. Guizhou can sometimes be difficult for tourists to navigate, particularly non-Chinese speakers: this tour offers a hassle-free and off-the-beaten-path look at Guizhou minority culture with English-speaking guides.

ESSENTIALS

Bank Bank of China (⊠ *Beijing Dong Lu near the city's main roundabout*).

Bus Contact Kaili Bus Station (⊠ *Wenhua Bei Lu* ☏ *No phone*).

Train Contact Kaili Train Station (⊠ *Qingjiang Lu* ☏ *No phone*).

EXPLORING

In Jinquanhu Park the **Drum Tower** *(Gu Lou)* is the Dong people's gathering place for celebrations.

The **Minorities Museum** (*Zhou Minzu Bowuguan* ⊠ *5 Guangchang Lu* ☏ *Free* ☾ *Mon.–Sat. 9–5*) displays arts, crafts, and relics of the local indigenous peoples.

Outside town the local villages are of great interest. To the north is the Wuyang River, which passes by many mountains, caves, and Miao villages. At **Shibing** you can take boat rides through spectacular limestone gorges and arrange stops at these towns. South of Kaili are the Dong villages of **Leishan, Rongjiang,** and **Zhaoxing.** The latter village, set in a beautiful landscape, is known for its five drum towers.

WHERE TO EAT AND STAY

¢ 🏨 **Guotai Dajiudian.** Largely on the basis of its downtown location and clean—if slightly shabby—guest rooms, the Guotai continues to compare favorably with flashier, more expensive options that have appeared on the outskirts of town. The staff—mostly made up of members of the Miao minority group—are very friendly. The restaurant serves a variety of traditional Miao dishes alongside other Chinese fare. **Pros:** good rooms and location. **Cons:** restaurant service can be less than responsive; little English spoken by staff. ✉ *6 Beijing Dong Lu* 📞 *0855/826–9888* 🛏 *73 rooms* ⚲ *In-room: Internet. In-hotel: restaurant, room service, laundry service* 🖃 *No credit cards.*

YUNNAN

Hidden deep in southwestern China, Yunnan is one of the country's most fascinating provinces. Its rugged and varied terrain contains some of China's most beautiful natural scenery, as well as the headwaters of three of Asia's most important rivers: the Yangtze, Mekong, and Salween. Stunning mountains, picturesque highland meadows, and steamy tropical jungles are inhabited by Bai, Dai, Naxi, Hani, and dozens of other ethnic groups, many of which can only be found in Yunnan.

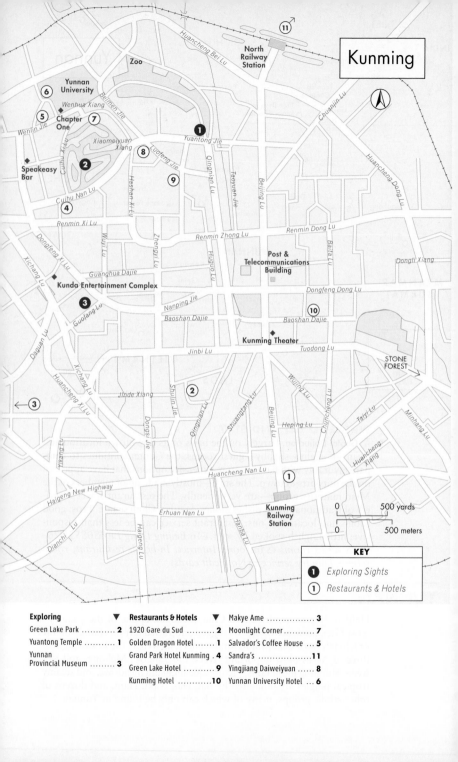

Kunming

Zoo

Yunnan University

North Railway Station ⑪

Wenhua Xiang

Chapter One ⑤ ⑥ ⑦

Speakeasy Bar

Xiaomeiyuan Xiang

❶ Yuantong Jie

❷

⑧ Luofeng Jie

⑨

Cuihu Nan Lu

④

Renmin Xi Lu

Renmin Zhong Lu

Renmin Dong Lu

Dongtu Xiang

Guanghua Dajie

Post & Telecommunications Building

Kunda Entertainment Complex

Dongfeng Dong Lu

❸

Nanping Jie

Baoshan Dajie

Baoshan Dajie

⑩

Kunming Theater

Jinbi Lu

Tuodong Lu

STONE FOREST

❸

Jinde Xiang

❷

Heping Lu

Huancheng Nan Lu

① Kunming Railway Station

Erhuan Nan Lu

0 ___ 500 yards
0 ___ 500 meters

KEY

❶ Exploring Sights

① Restaurants & Hotels

Exploring ▼

Green Lake Park **2**

Yuantong Temple **1**

Yunnan Provincial Museum ... **3**

Restaurants & Hotels ▼

1920 Gare du Sud **2**

Golden Dragon Hotel **1**

Grand Park Hotel Kunming . **4**

Green Lake Hotel **9**

Kunming Hotel **10**

Makye Ame **3**

Moonlight Corner **7**

Salvador's Coffee House ... **5**

Sandra's **11**

Yingjiang Daiweiyuan **8**

Yunnan University Hotel ... **6**

Yunnan sits atop the Yunnan-Guizhou Plateau, with the Himalayas to the northwest and Myanmar, Laos, and Vietnam to the south. Yunnan was central to the Ancient Tea and Horse Caravan Route, an important trade route that connected China with the rest of Southeast Asia for thousands of years. Today Yunnan is one of the top travel destinations in China, with Lijiang, Dali, and Jinghong getting most of the attention. Countless lesser-known but equally amazing places are scattered throughout the province.

Roughly the size of California, Yunnan is becoming increasingly accessible to the outside world. More convenient air travel makes it possible to have breakfast by the Mekong in Jinghong and dinner overlooking the old mountain town of Lijiang the same day. Yunnan still has plenty of places that are off the beaten path.

REGIONAL TOURS

China Minority Travel (✉ *63 Bo'ai LuDali* ☎ *0872/267–9549* ⊕ *www. china-travel.nl*) offers multiple-destination tours of Yunnan with visits to the province's lesser-known gems, including Yuanyang, Lugu Lake, and Zhongdian (Shangri-la). The agency, which is based in Dali, has been organizing Yunnan tours for more than a decade. Multiple-day treks, family-oriented tours, and custom itineraries are all available.

KUNMING

400 km (248 mi; 10½ hrs by train) southwest of Guiyang; 650 km (403 mi; 18½ hrs by train) southwest of Chengdu; 1,200 km (744 mi; 18 hrs by train) west of Hong Kong.

With its cool mountain air and laid-back locals, Kunming is one of China's most comfortable big cities, and is an ideal base for Yunnan travels. It's one of the few cities in the country that regularly has blue skies, and is nicknamed the "Spring City." Despite this moniker, weather can be gray and soggy during the summer monsoon season and gray and cold around January and February.

Kunming is changing rapidly as the city is transforming into China's gateway to Southeast Asia. But despite the disappearance of the Old City and increasingly congested traffic, Kunming retains its unique character as a relaxed and somewhat idiosyncratic metropolis.

GETTING HERE AND AROUND

AIR TRAVEL Kunming is a busy air hub, with flight links all over China as well as direct routes to Southeast Asia, Nepal, India, and the United Arab Emirates, among others. The airport is at the southern end of Chuncheng Lu, in the city's southeast, about 20 minutes by taxi from the center of town. Taxi fare is Y20 to Y30.

Kunming also has daily flights to Lhasa, Tibet, via a brief stopover in Shangri-la. Travelers to Tibet will need to have Tibet travel permits in hand to board the Lhasa flight.

Starting in late 2011 or early 2012, all flights will be shifted to a massive new international airport about 30 km (19 mi) northeast of downtown that is expected to vastly expand the scope of Kunming's direct international flights.

8

The Yuantong Temple is the largest temple in Kunming.

BUS TRAVEL Kunming has five long-distance bus stations: the north, east, south, west and northwest Bus Transit stations. All buses bound for Dali, Lijiang and Shangri-la depart from the west station; buses to Laos depart from the south station; and buses to Guangxi Province and the Yunnan-Vietnam border crossing at Hekou depart from the east station.

CAR TRAVEL If you need a car and driver while you're in Kunming, you can make arrangements through your hotel. Expect to pay at least Y500 for a car to the Stone Forest. Alternatively, if you speak a little Chinese or you luck into one of the few English-speaking cabbies in Kunming, you can haggle for a taxi that should be cheaper than the hotel's option.

TRAIN TRAVEL The main station is at the southern terminus of Beijing Lu. There are day and overnight trains to both Dali (six to eight hours) and Lijiang (7½ to 10 hours), as well as other Southwest China destinations.

SAFETY AND PRECAUTIONS

Kunming is generally safe, and violent crime against tourists is rare. Watch out for pickpockets, especially on crowded city buses. When riding overnight on long-distance buses be exceedingly careful with your valuables, as many thieves ride those buses to steal money and electronics from sleeping passengers. Negotiate Kunming's frenetic traffic carefully, and watch out for noiseless electric scooters, which often illegally travel in the wrong direction. Finally, Kunming drivers frequently ignore pedestrian right-of-way laws.

TIMING

A day or two in Kunming should suffice for most travelers. Yunnan has a multitude of spectacular sights, and sticking around in the city for too long means a lot of missed opportunities elsewhere.

TOURS

No group tours of Kunming are recommended, especially because most agencies in the city have little to no fluency in English and spend more time in shops than at attractions.

ESSENTIALS

Air Contact Kunming Airport (✉ *Chuncheng Lu* ☎ *0871/711–6114*).

Bank Bank of China (✉ *515 Beijing Lu* ☎ *0871/319–2910*).

Bus Contact West Bus Transit Station (*Chunyu Lu at Yining Lu* ☎ *0871/532–7326*).

Medical Assistance Kunming First People's Hospital (✉ *504 Qingnian Lu* ☎ *0871/318–8200*).

Public Security Bureau PSB Kunming (✉ *411 Beijing Lu* ☎ *110*).

Train Contact Kunming Train Station (✉ *Beijing Lu* ☎ *0871/534–9414 or 0871/351–1534*).

Visitor and Tour Info Kunming Tourism Authority (*17 Dongfeng Dong Lu 8th floor* ☎ *0871/314–9748* ⊕ *www.kmta.gov.cn*). **GoKunming** (⊕ *www.gokunming.com* ✉ *team@gokunming.com*).

> ### BIKING KUNMING
>
> Kunming is one of the best cities in China for biking. Small brown signs point toward historical and cultural sights. The signs are in Chinese, but just follow the arrows. Start at Green Lake Park, and explore the winding lanes shooting off in every direction. Heading south, you'll find the few remaining pockets of Old Kunming. Continuing south, there are several small parks, temples, and pagodas.
>
> Group tours leave Saturday morning at 9 from **Xiong Brothers Bike Shop** (✉ *Unit 5, 51 Beimen Jie* ☎ *0871/519–1520*).

EXPLORING

Fodor'sChoice
★

In the north-central part of the city, **Green Lake Park** (*Cuihu Gongyuan*) is filled with willow- and bamboo-covered islands connected by stone bridges. Green Lake itself was once part of Dianchi Lake, but it was severed from that larger body of water in the late 1970s. The park is a favorite gathering place for Kunming's older residents, who begin to congregate in the park for singing and dancing in the late morning and stay until the gates close at 11 pm. In summer the lake is filled with pink and white lotus blossoms. In winter the park fills with migrating seagulls from Siberia. ✉ *Cuihu Nan Lu* 🎫 *Free* ⊙ *Daily 7–11.*

★ **Yuantong Temple** (*Yuantong Si*), the largest temple in the city, dates back some 1,200 years to the Tang Dynasty. The compound consists of a series of gates leading to the inner temple, which is surrounded by a pond brimming with fish and turtles. The chanting of worshippers in the serene environment makes it hard to believe you're in the middle of a big city. In the back of the compound a temple houses a statue of Sakyamuni, a gift from the king of Thailand. ✉ *30 Yuantong Jie* 🎫 *Y6* ⊙ *Daily 8–6.*

The **Yunnan Provincial Museum** (*Yunnansheng Bowuguan*) is a window into Yunnan's history. The museum focuses primarily on the Dian Kingdom, which ruled much of Yunnan from 1000 BC to 1 BC. Most of

Ethnic Minorities of the Southwest

The future leaders of the Naxi people.

With 26 of the country's 56 ethnic minorities living within its borders, Yunnan is like no other place in China. Many of the groups in this region have long resisted Han influence.

DAI

Related to Thais and speakers of languages belonging to the Tai-Kadai family, the Dai seem much more Southeast Asian than Chinese. In China they are primarily located in the Xishuangbanna, Dehong, and Jingpo regions of southern Yunnan, but can also be found in Myanmar, Laos, and Thailand. They practice Theravada Buddhism, the dominant form of Buddhism in Southeast Asia. The linguistic, cultural, and religious connections with Southeast Asia give Dai-inhabited regions a decidedly un-Chinese feel. Within China, they are most famous for their spicy and flavorful food and their Water Splashing Festival (water is used to wash away demons and sins of the past and bless the future). Many grow rice and produce such crops as pineapples, so villages are concentrated near the Mekong (Lancang) and Red (Honghe) rivers. The Dai population here has ebbed

and flowed with China's political tide, and many are now returning after the turmoil of the 1960s and '70s.

NAXI

Living primarily in the area around Lijiang and neighboring Sichuan, the Naxi culture is unique, even when compared with other minority groups in China. The society is traditionally matriarchal, with women dominating relationships, keeping custody of children, and essentially running the show. Some Naxis practice Buddhism or Taoism, but it is the shamanistic culture of the Dongba and Samba that set their spiritualism apart from other groups. The Dongba (male shamans) and Samba (female shamans) serve their communities as mediators, entering trancelike states and communicating with the spirit world in order to solve problems on earth. Naxi script, like Chinese script, is made up of ideograms. These pictographs are vivid representations of body parts, animals, and geography used to express concrete and abstract concepts. Despite numbering fewer than 300,000, the Naxi are one of the better-known ethnic groups in China.

BAI

The Bai, also known as the Minjia, are one of the more prominent minorities in Yunnan, although they are also found in Guizhou and Hunan provinces. Primarily centered around Dali prefecture, the Bai are known for their agricultural skills and unique architecture style. The Bai also have some of the most colorful costumes, particularly the rainbow-colored hats worn by women. The Bai, along with the Yi people, were part of the Nanzhao Kingdom, which briefly rose to regional dominance in Southwest China and Southeast Asia during the Tang Dynasty, before giving way to the Kingdom of Dali. The Dali region and the Bai have essentially been a part of the Chinese sphere of influence since the Yuan Dynasty, during which the Yuan's Mongolian armies conquered the area in the 13th century. The Bais' highly productive rice paddies were seen as an asset by the Yuan, who let them operate under relative autonomy. Today the Bai and their festivals, including the Third Moon Festival and Torch Festival, are major attractions for domestic and international tourists.

YI

Descendants of the Qiang people of northwestern China, the Yi (aka Sani) are scattered across southwestern China in Yunnan, Sichuan, and Guizhou provinces as well as Guangxi Zhuang Autonomous Region. The largest concentration of the more than 6.5 million Qiang descendants are in Sichuan's Liangshan region. They live in isolated, mountainous regions and are known for being fierce warriors. Notable traits include their syllabic writing system, ancient literature, and traditional medicine—all of which are still being used today. The Yi also sport extravagant costumes that vary according to geographical region. Massive black mortarboard-style hats, blue turbans, ornate red headdresses, and other headwear complement brilliantly colored vests and pants. Their language is part of the Tibeto-Burman language family and similar to Burmese. Some Yi also live in Vietnam, where they are called the Lolo.

8

A group of Bai women.

CLOSE UP

Yunnan Cuisine

Dian cuisine is the term for Han Chinese cuisine found in Yunnan, especially around Kunming. Dian-style dishes are similar to Sichuan dishes and tend to favor spicy and sour flavors. Rice is a staple here, as is a type of rice noodle called *mixian*. A favorite dish is *guoqiao mixian*, a boiling, oily broth served with raw pork and vegetables that you cook yourself. *Qiguo ji* (steampot chicken), another trademark Dian-style dish, uses a special earthenware pot to steam chicken and vegetables into a savory soup.

One thing that sets Dian cuisine apart from that of the rest of China is the dairy products. *Rubing* is made from goat's milk, and is typically fried

and served with dried chili peppers or sugar. It is a little drier and less pungent than regular goat cheese. *Rushan*, or "milk fan," is a long strip of a cheese that is spread with a salty or sweet sauce. Wrapped around a chopstick, it makes a handy snack.

Street barbecue is a major part of the Yunnan culinary experience. Every kind of meat and vegetable is on offer, as well as quail eggs, *chou doufu* (stinky tofu), and *erkuai* (rice pancakes with sweet or savory fillings). Most restaurants in Yunnan close early, but barbecue stands stay open until the wee hours, making them a good place for a late-night snack.

---

what you'll see here is more than 2,000 years old. Exhibits have good English captions. ⊠ *118 Wuyi Lu* ☎ *0871/617–9656* ⊕ *www.ynbwg.cn* ✉ *ynbwg@yahoo.com.cn* 🎟 *Free* 🕙 *Daily 9:30–4:30.*

WHERE TO EAT

$$
YUNNAN
✗ **1910 La Gare du Sud** (Huoche Nan Zhan). Located in a historic renovated railroad station, 1910's great ambience and ample outdoor seating are of equal appeal to the menu full of tasty Yunnan cuisine. The structure was built in the early 20th century by French colonists, and was once a final stop on the 535-mile French railroad linking Hanoi to Kunming. Try fried rubing cheese, a spicy salad of Garland chrysanthemum greens, grilled tilapia, or a dish made with Yunnan's prized cured ham. The menu is in English, with photos of most of the dishes. ⊠ *8 Houxin Jie* ☎ *0871/316-9486* 🚫 *No credit cards.*

$–$$$$
TIBETAN
✗ **Makye Ame.** As much a cultural experience as a gastronomical adventure, Makye Ame is known for its Tibetan and Indian song-and-dance performances. The shows are enjoyable, but loud. For a quieter meal, ask for one of the rooms in the back or the cozy teahouse upstairs. Foodwise, Makye Ame serves a large variety of Tibetan dishes, including stone-cooked yak, *malai kafta* (large potato and cashew balls in a curried yogurt sauce), and an incomparable *xianggu* (shiitake-mushroom) platter. A cold Lhasa beer or some homemade yogurt wine rounds out one of the city's more memorable meals. ⊠ *Jinhuapu Lu, next to Yimen Hotel* ☎ *0871/833–6300* 🚫 *No credit cards.*

$$$–$$$$
THAI
✗ **Moonlight Corner.** With Thai owners, Thai chefs, and fresh imported Thai ingredients, Moonlight Corner is arguably the best Thai restaurant in China. Its original location in north Kunming was already quite popular, but this new location on the north side of Green Lake Park has

been booming with locals and foreigners since it opened in late 2008. Try favorites such as Thai barbecued chicken, tom yam gong, pineapple fried rice, green papaya salad, or grilled fish, or go for lesser-known gems such as lemongrass salad or the Thai-style iced tea. If the sun is out, sit out front and enjoy one of the best park views in the area. ⊠ *16 Cuihu Dong Lu* ☎ *0871/513–8088* ▭ *No credit cards.*

$–$$ ✕ **Salvador's Coffee House.** Regularly packed to capacity and brewing
AMERICAN some of Kunming's best coffee out of a custom blend of Yunnan beans,
ⓒ Salvador's also has an extensive food menu and is in the vanguard of
Fodor'sChoice China's burgeoning organic food movement. About half of its ingre-
★ dients are organic, and more are being added regularly, with the goal of becoming one of the few entirely organic eateries in China. Popular main dishes include burritos, quesadillas, and falafel. Salvador's has comfy sofas for lounging and outdoor seating ideal for people-watching on bustling Wenhua Xiang. ⊠ *76 Wenhua Xiang* ☎ *0871/536–3525* ▭ *No credit cards.*

$$–$$$ ✕ **Sandra's.** Upon first tasting a dish from Sandra's eclectic mix of Euro-
PAN-EUROPEAN pean cuisine, many customers cannot believe they are in remote western China—the food is on par with many of the finest restaurants back home. Owner Sandra, a gregarious German expatriate, whips up dishes such as handmade ravioli, Viennese schnitzel, and barbecued kanga-roo fillets, while always finding time to stop for a friendly chat with customers. Sandra's world-class food and wide range of reasonably priced imported wines make for the best Western dining experience in Kunming. Sandra and her assistant Xiao Hua run the entire restaurant themselves, and seating is limited: make your reservation early. ⊠ *D-7 Beichen Garden Walkway, Beichen Zhong Lu* ☎ *1582/526–7010* ▭ *No credit cards* ✉ *sandrasinkunming@gmail.com*

¢–$ ✕ **Yingjiang Daiweiyuan.** This may be the best place in Kunming to enjoy
DAI Dai cuisine, which is known for intense flavors and chili peppers. If you want to go straight for the spice, try the *gui ji* or "ghost chicken," a cold chicken salad that is slightly sour and extremely spicy. Tamer options include pineapple rice, fennel omelets, dried beef, wild mushrooms, fried fish, and tapioca with cookies in coconut milk. Dai cuisine features many dishes and ingredients that are foreign even to coastal Chinese. ⊠ *67 Luofeng Jie* ☎ *0871/512–2251* ▭ *No credit cards.*

WHERE TO STAY

$–$$ ▦ **Golden Dragon Hotel** *(Jinlong Fandian).* Although a bit on the drab side, this locally owned hotel offers moderately priced rooms and a reasonable standard of service. **Pros:** close to train and bus stations. **Cons:** far from the city center. ⊠ *575 Beijing Lu* ☎ *0871/313–3015* ⓦ*www.gdhotel.com.cn* ⇴ *150 rooms* ⚷ *In-room: Internet. In-hotel: 2 restaurants, bar, pool* ▭ *AE, DC, MC, V.*

$–$$ ▦ **Grand Park Hotel Kunming.** A stone's throw from Cuihu Park, the Grand Park's hotel buffet and its Western and Cantonese restaurants are solid dining options, but there are plenty of food and drink choices just a short stroll away. Rooms are clean and modern with higher floors offering good views of Kunming and Cuihu Park. The bland decor isn't up to snuff for the prices you're paying. **Pros:** clean and comfort-able rooms; central location. **Cons:** not Kunming's best value. ⊠ *20*

Kunming's Flying Tigers

Despite being in the hinterland of Southwest China, Kunming played a crucial role in World War II by preventing Japanese forces from taking control of all of China. At the center of this role was the American Volunteer Group, best known by its local nickname *feihu*, or the Flying Tigers, because of the shark faces painted on their fuselages.

The group of around 300 American servicemen was led by the mysterious Claire L. Chennault. A retired captain in the U.S. Air Force, Chennault first came to Kunming in 1938, when Madame Chiang Kai-shek, wife of the country's leader, asked him to organize a Chinese air force to counter the

relentless attacks from the Japanese, who were busily bombing much of China with little opposition.

Supply routes to China's capital were being taken out one after another, leaving just one road. Chennault argued that a group of American pilots could defend this crucial supply artery, as well as push the Japanese out of the region.

The Flying Tigers were tenacious fighters. They swept through much of China to combat the constant bombing by Japanese forces. Their record was second to none in World War II. They had more than 50 enemy encounters and were never defeated.

Honghuaqiao ☎ *0871/538–6688* ⊕ *www.parkhotelgroup.com/gpkm/* ⟿ *315 rooms, 14 suites* ☊ *In-room: safe, Internet. In-hotel: 2 restaurants, bar, pool, gym* ⊟ *AE, DC, MC, V.*

\$\$–\$\$\$ **Green Lake Hotel** *(Cuihu Binguan).* Adjacent to Cuihu (Green Lake) Park, this hotel is one of Kunming's nicest; recent renovations mean that now is a great time to visit. The Western restaurant is located on the first floor, and the Cantonese restaurant across the lobby is a favorite of local businessmen and officials. The grand marble-and-wood lobby is filled with plush chairs and sofas, and the coffee shop has excellent coffee drinks and homemade ice cream. The guest rooms are Kunming's cleanest and most comfortable. The restaurant hosts regular performances of traditional music. **Pros:** great location; good service; comfortable rooms. **Cons:** many staff members speak little or no English. ⊠ *6 Cuihu Nan Lu* ☎ *0871/515–8888* ⊕ *www.greenlakehotel. com.cn* ⟿ *301 rooms, 6 suites* ☊ *In-room: safe, Internet. In-hotel: 2 restaurants, bar, pool, gym* ⊟ *AE, DC, MC, V.*

¢–\$ **Kunming Hotel.** The oldest of the luxury hotels in town is centrally located and has reasonably comfortable rooms, although they have not been renovated for some years. There is a pool and a practice range for golfers on the premises. **Pros:** central location. **Cons:** feels a little dated. ⊠ *52 Dongfeng Dong Lu* ☎ *0871/316–2063* ⊕ *www.kmhotel. com.cn* ⟿ *267 rooms, 53 suites* ☊ *In-hotel: 3 restaurants, bars, pool, gym* ⊟ *AE, DC, MC, V.*

¢   **Yunnan University Hotel.** In the heart of the university area, Yunnan University Hotel is one of the city's best bargains. Standard rooms all have clean bathrooms. On the west side of Yunnan University, the hotel has backdoor access to one of China's most beautiful college

The Stone Forest in Yunnan is a UNESCO World Heritage Site.

campuses. **Pros:** close to Wenlin Jie and Cuihu Park. **Cons:** minimal facilities and services; location is chaotic during rush hour. ⊠ *Yieryi Dajie* ☎ *0871/503–4190* ⤏ *84 rooms* ⚷ *In-room: no phone, no TV. In-hotel: restaurant, laundry facilities* ▭ *V* ⭐ ⦿*BP.*

NIGHTLIFE AND THE ARTS

ARTS

Kunming's nascent art scene can be taken in at **Chuangku** (⊠ *101 Xiba Lu* ☎ *No phone*). A group of warehouses that have been converted into galleries, Chuangku is also home to a smattering of cafés and restaurants. **Yunart Gallery** (⊠ *16 Cuihu Dong Lu* ☎ *No phone* ⊕ *www. yunartgallery.cn*) occupies the central area of the high-end Gingko Elité compound at the north end of Cuihu Park. The gallery highlights up-and-coming local artists.

Chinese dance legend Yang Liping may have retired after breaking her leg during her last tour in 2005, but the Yunnan native's award-winning dance and musical production **Dynamic Yunnan** (⊠ *Kunming Theater, 427 Beijing Lu* ☎ *0871/313–0033*) still plays to full-capacity crowds when not touring around Asia. It's an impressive fusion of the storytelling, songs, and dances of indigenous groups.

NIGHTLIFE

When evening falls, Kunming's growing expat population tends to congregate at the bars, cafés, and restaurants of Wenlin Jie and Wenhua Xiang (literally Culture Forest Street and Culture Alley). **Chapter One** (⊠ *146 Wenlin Jie* ☎ *0871/536–5635*) is a favorite bar for expats. **Dune Café** ☎ *0871/534–7236*) is an expat bar with an impressive selection of Belgian ales.

SHOPPING

If you're looking for a good deal on tea, look no farther than the wholesale tea market at the southeast corner of Beijing Lu and Wujing Lu. Within the market you'll find an amazing variety of green teas, black teas, flower teas, and herbal teas. It's a wholesale market, but all vendors will sell you small quantities.

Qianju Jie is one of the more popular shopping streets in the city, near the intersection of Wenlin Jie and Wenhua Xiang. On Wenhua Xiang is **Mandarin Books** (⊠ *52 Wenhua Xiang 9–10* ☎ *0871/551–6579* ⊕ *www. mandarinbooks.cn*), one of the best foreign-language bookstores in all of China.

SIDE TRIP TO THE STONE FOREST

Fodor's Choice
★

One of the most interesting sites near Kunming is a geological phenomenon known as the **Stone Forest** *(Shilin)*. This cluster of dark gray-limestone karst formations has been twisted into unusual shapes since being formed beneath the sea 270 million years ago. Many have been given names to describe their resemblance to real or mythological animals (phoenixes, elephants, and turtles).

You can take walks through the park, which is dotted with small lakes and pools. Here you'll find plenty of Sani women eager to act as guides and sell you their handicrafts. The area where most tourists venture has, inevitably, become rather commercialized, but there are plenty of similar formations in other parts of the park if you wander off the main trail. The journey here takes you through the hilly countryside dotted with timber-frame architecture typical of the area. ⊠ *Lu'nan* ☑ *Y175* ⊘ *24 hrs.*

GETTING HERE AND AROUND

The Stone Forest is 125 km (78 mi) southeast of Kunming. There are several ways to get here, the best being a car and driver. One can be arranged through your hotel and should cost between Y500 and Y600. Another option is the cheap bus tours (Y20 round-trip) that leave each morning from the area around the train station. Reservations aren't necessary. This trip takes at least four hours, as the driver makes numerous stops at souvenir stands and junk stores along the way.

DALI

250 km (155 mi; 4 hrs by bus) northwest of Kunming; 140 km (87 mi; 3 hrs by bus) south of Lijiang.

Dali is one of those rare places that feel completely cut off from the rest of the world yet has high-speed Internet access. The rustic town is perched at the foot of the towering Cangshan Mountains and overlooks lovely Erhai Lake. Its typically sunny weather, sleepy atmosphere, and gorgeous sunsets have made it one of Yunnan's most popular destinations.

> ## WORD OF MOUTH
>
> "In Dali you'll see many minorities dressed in their own dress & many natural areas of great beauty. The people appear to be much more Tibetan than Chinese." —merckxxx

Home to the Bai people, Dali has been inhabited for more than 4,000 years, serving as a major rice-production base for the region. Today tourism is rejuvenating the town. The upside of this building boom is a greater variety of restaurants and hotels; the downside is that the Old Town is constantly being demolished and reconstructed. A planned high-speed rail link with Kunming means now is the time to see Dali before it changes even more.

GETTING HERE AND AROUND

AIR TRAVEL There are multiple daily flights from Kunming to Dali. Dali's airport is at the southern tip of Erhai Lake. Taxis between the airport and the Old Town cost Y90. The trip takes just under an hour.

BUS TRAVEL Buses from Kunming to Dali take four hours. Bus tickets are available at Kunming's West Bus Station. Most buses drop you off in "New Dali," the nondescript city of Xiaguan. A 25-minute cab ride gets you from there to the Old Town. It should cost Y35 to Y40, depending on your haggling skills.

TRAIN TRAVEL Train service between Kunming and Dali costs about the same as a bus (both are around Y120), but the train trip takes seven hours, which is three hours longer than a bus trip.

SAFETY AND PRECAUTIONS

Several hikers have died in the mountains above Dali in recent years; all of them were hiking alone. It is strongly advised that if you do any hiking around the mountains—other than the path connecting the cable cars—you do so with at least one other person.

TIMING

Most of the major sites in and around Dali can be enjoyed within two or three days. Many travelers find themselves arriving in Dali with ambitious itineraries, but end up staying a week or more doing little more than relaxing and enjoying the town's lazy vibe.

TOURS

China Minority Travel lets you explore the villages surrounding Erhai Lake. The first stop on the day-trip is nearby Xizhou, a village that resembles Dali before the tourism boom. Afterward, enjoy lunch on the ferry across Erhai Lake before arriving at Wase to explore the village's market. The trip is Y2,000 for up to four people, including a guide, transportation, and lunch. Prices may be higher during Chinese holidays.

ESSENTIALS

Air Contact Dali Airport (☎ 0872/242-8909).

THE TORCH FESTIVAL

One of the more exciting festivals in Southwest China is the Torch Festival, which is celebrated by both the Yi and Bai minorities on the 24th day of the sixth lunar month (in June or July). Dali's Old Town is one of the best (and worst) places to catch the festival. The chaotic celebration is rivaled only by Chinese New Year. However, many local children like to frighten travelers with the flames, especially on Foreigner Street. Anyone who wants to see the festival without worrying about getting singed by pyromaniac children might want to go to Xizhou—the first town north of Dali.

8

CLOSE UP

Dali and the Nanzhao Kingdom

The idyllic scenery belies Dali's importance as the center of power for the Nanzhao Kingdom. The easily defensible area around Erhai Lake was the kingdom's birthplace, which began as the Bai- and Yi-dominated Damengguo in 649. Almost a century later, Damengguo was expanded to include the six surrounding kingdoms ruled by powerful Bai families. This expansion was supported by the ruling Chinese Tang Dynasty, and the kingdom was renamed Nanzhao.

The primarily Buddhist Nanzhao Kingdom was essentially a vassal state of the Tang Dynasty until AD 750, when it rebelled. Tang armies were sent in 751 and 754 to suppress the insurgents, but they suffered humiliating defeats. Emboldened by their victories, Nanzhao troops helped the kingdom acquire a significant amount of territory. Before reaching its high point with the capture of Chengdu and Sichuan in 829, the Nanzhao Kingdom had expanded to include all of present-day Yunnan, as well as parts of present-day Burma, Laos, and Thailand.

Although the capture of Chengdu was a major victory for Nanzhao, it appears to have led directly to its decline. The Tang Dynasty couldn't stand for such an incursion and sent large numbers of troops to the area. They eventually evicted Nanzhao forces from Sichuan by 873. About 30 years later the Nanzhao leaders were finally overthrown, ending the story of their meteoric rise and fall.

Medical Assistance Dali First Municipal People's Hospital (⊠ *217 Tai'an Lu, Dali* ☏ *0872/212–4462*).

Banks Bank of China (⊠ *Fuxing Lu i*). **ICBC** (⊠ *Huguo Lu*).

Public Security Bureau PSB Dali (⊠ *Huguo Lu* ☏ *110*).

Train Contact Xiaguan Train Station (⊠ *Dianyuan Lu, Xiaguan*).

Visitor and Tour Info China Minority Travel (⊠ *63 Bo'ai Lu* ☏ *0872/267–9549* ⊕ *www.china-travel.nl*).

EXPLORING

Dali's Old Town, called Dali Gucheng, is surrounded by attractive reconstructions of the old city wall and gates. Go to the wall's southwest corner and take the stairs to the top for a great view of the city and the surrounding mountains. Outside the bustling center of the Old Town are countless little alleys lined with old Bai-style homes.

Dali has two popular pedestrian streets, Huguo Lu and Renmin Lu, both of which run east–west, or uphill–downhill. Huguo Lu, better known as Foreigner Street, is lined with the cafés that made Dali famous in the 1990s, but the street has begun to lose its luster. High rents and cutthroat competition have taken a toll on quality and service.

The most famous landmark in Dali, the **Three Pagodas** *(Santa Si)*, appears on just about every calendar of Chinese scenery. The largest, 215 feet high, dates from AD 836 and is decorated on each of its 16 stories with Buddhas carved from local marble. The other two pagodas, also richly

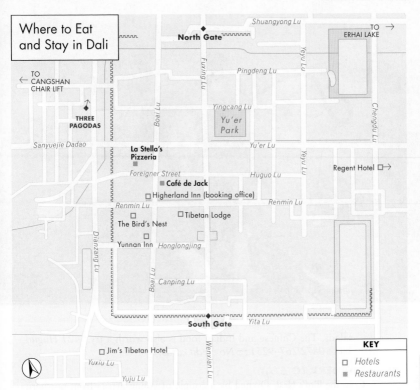

Where to Eat
and Stay in Dali

Shuangyong Lu

North Gate

TO
ERHAI LAKE

TO
CANGSHAN
CHAIR LIFT

Pingdeng Lu

Yingcang Lu

THREE
PAGODAS

Yu'er
Park

Sanyuejie Dadao

Yu'er Lu

La Stella's
Pizzeria

Regent Hotel

Foreigner Street

Huguo Lu

■ Café de Jack

□ Higherland Inn (booking office)

Renmin Lu

Renmin Lu

□ Tibetan Lodge

The Bird's Nest

□

□

Yunnan Inn

Honglongjing

Canping Lu

South Gate

Yita Lu

□ Jim's Tibetan Hotel

Yuxiu Lu

Yuju Lu

KEY

□ *Hotels*

■ *Restaurants*

8

decorated, are more elegant in style. When the water is still, you can ponder their reflection in a nearby pool. A massive new Chan (Zen) Buddhist Temple has been built behind the pagodas. The pagodas are a 20-minute walk from the Old Town. ✉ *1 km (½ mi) north of Dali Gucheng* 💴 *Y121* ⊙ *Daily 7 am–8 pm.*

WHERE TO EAT

For a taste of authentic local Bai dishes like *paojiao zhurou* (pork with pickled peppers) or *chao rubing* (fried goat cheese), try any of the local restaurants on Renmin Lu just east of the intersection with Fuxing Lu. None of these restaurants have English menus or service, but they generally have their ingredients on display.

¢–$$ ✕ **Café de Jack.** In business since 1989, Café de Jack still offers good break-
ECLECTIC fasts and friendly service. Get the strongest cup of Yunnan coffee in Dali and catch up with the rest of the world via the Wi-Fi or in-house Net bar. All three floors are a bit different: the first floor feels like a bar, the second floor is more like a restaurant, and the rooftop is a perfect place to kick back with a beer. ✉ *82 Bo'ai Lu* ☎ *0872/267–1572* 💳 *No credit cards.*

¢–$$ ✕ **La Stella's Pizzeria.** Located at the top of Foreigner Street, Stella's is
PIZZA one of the best all-around restaurants in town. The pizzas, cooked in a
Fodor'sChoice wood-fired oven, feature traditional toppings, as well as Chinese favor-
★ ites such as corn. Other highlights include lasagna, nachos, and Greek

A cormorant fisherman on the Li river.

salads. The Chinese and Indian food is also worth a try. ⊠ *21 Huguo Lu* ☎ *0872/267–9251* ▭ *No credit cards.*

WHERE TO STAY

¢ ⚏ **The Bird's Nest.** Owned by a couple of young artists from northern China, the Bird's Nest is centered around a tranquil courtyard just behind the popular Bird Bar. The hotel offers comfortable rooms and friendly service at a reasonable price. An added bonus if you're traveling in a group or just want to live it up is the hotel's free-standing villa with courtyard across the street for Y800 a day. **Pros:** comfortable rooms; chilled-out courtyard. **Cons:** The adjacent Bird Bar can be noisy. ⊠ *22 Renmin Lu* ☎ *0872/266–1843* ⊕ *www.birdbardali.com* ⇱ *11 rooms, 1 villa* △ *In-hotel: restaurant, laundry service, Wi-Fi hotspot* ▭ *No credit cards.*

¢–$$ ⚏ **Higherland Inn.** Up in the verdant mountains behind the Old Town sits the Higherland Inn. At 8,500 feet, it's the perfect place to start a hike or enjoy the view. The walls are a little thin, so it's not the best place for light sleepers. Meals are similar to those you'd find in town, and feature both Chinese and Western dishes. There is a booking office in Dali at 67 Bo'ai Lu, near Renmin Lu; reserve ahead to get a discount on the Y30 fee to ascend the mountains. **Pros:** beautiful scenery; clean air; quiet at night. **Cons:** not easy to get to. ⊠ *Cangshan Daorendong* ☎ *0872/266–1599* ⇱ *8 rooms* △ *In-hotel: restaurant* ▭ *No credit cards.*

¢ ⚏ **Jim's Tibetan Hotel.** Outside the south gate, this is one of the city's
Ⓢ newest lodgings. It's in the quiet Yulu Xiaoqu neighborhood, making it ideal for those wanting to avoid the hubbub of the Old Town. Decorated in traditional Tibetan and Bai styles, the hotel is run by a Tibetan

and Dutch couple who speak English. It's the only place in Dali with a playground. Ask about booking tours of Dali and beyond. **Pros:** kid-friendly; clean. **Cons:** feels a little isolated from the Old Town. ✉ *13 Yuxiu Lu* ☎ *0872/267–7824* ⊕ *www.china-travel.nl* ⤳ *13 rooms* ⚷ *In-room: Wi-Fi. In-hotel: restaurant, bar* ▭ *No credit cards.*

¢–$$ 🏨 **Regent Hotel.** Dali's only five-star hotel, the Regent seems unnecessary when compared to the highly affordable options in the Old Town. If you have to stay in a five-star, this is the one. **Pros:** good quality and service. **Cons:** feels isolated from the Old Town. ✉ *Yu'er Lu* ☎ *0872/266–6666* ⊕ *www.regenthotel.cn* ⤳ *501 rooms* ⚷ *In-room: Internet. In-hotel: restaurant, bar, pool, laundry facilities* ▭ *AE, DC, MC, V.*

¢ 🏨 **Tibetan Lodge.** Near the top of Renmin Lu, Tibetan Lodge puts you in the middle of a long stretch of bars and restaurants. The guest rooms are clean and well equipped. Tibetan Lodge has bicycles for rent, plus a variety of tour options. **Pros:** solid value; good location. **Cons:** can seem too "backpacky" at times. ✉ *58 Renmin Lu* ☎ *0872/266–4177* ⤳ *20 rooms* ⚷ *In-hotel: restaurant, bar, bicycles, Internet terminal* ▭ *No credit cards.*

¢ 🏨 **Yunnan Inn.** Owned by acclaimed Chinese artist Fang Lijun, this guest-
★ house is in a class by itself. Eschewing traditional architecture for a more modern style, Fang has created one of the city's most pleasant places to stay. Great rooftop views and the chance to visit Fang's studio set this guesthouse apart. Even better, standard rooms start at just Y80. **Pros:** unique style; quiet at night. **Cons:** often booked; staff don't speak much English. ✉ *3 Honglongjing* ☎ *0872/266–3741* ⤳ *10 rooms* ⚷ *In-hotel: restaurant, bar, Internet terminal* ▭ *No credit cards.*

NIGHTLIFE

Bad Monkey (✉ *74-76 Renmin Lu,* ☎ *No phone*) Owned by foreigners, the Bad Monkey is Dali's most popular watering hole. In addition to a very extensive bar, the Monkey has recently started brewing its own beer, with every batch selling out quickly. Drinks aside, the kitchen stays open until early morning and does decent fish-and-chips and good pizza.

Café de Jack (✉ *82 Bo'ai Lu* ☎ *0872/267–1572*) often has live music in the evening.

SHOPPING

Foreigner Street is lined with Bai women who have been selling the same jewelry, fabrics, and Communist kitsch for nearly two decades. Don't be afraid to walk away when bargaining; vendors will often drop their prices at the last minute.

Bo'ai Lu and Renmin Lu are peppered with a variety of shops featuring outdoor clothing and equipment; handicrafts from India, Nepal, and

> ## CAFÉ SOCIETY
>
> Dali has some of the best coffee shops in China, particularly on Renmin Lu. Coffee drinks made with Yunnan-grown beans are at **Tea Utopia** (✉ *59 Renmin Lu* ☎ *0872/267–3777*). For Dali's best coffee and tea, head to **Guiqu Laixi** (✉ *258 Renmin Lu* ☎ *0872/267–6737*), whose owner is a Chinese-antiques collector.

8

Southeast Asia; as well as Chinese antiques. Fuxing Lu, aimed primarily at Chinese tourists, is where you'll find local teas, specialty foods, and, most prominently, jade. Much of it is of low quality, so buy only if you know something about jade.

SIDE TRIPS FROM DALI

★ With a peak that rises to more than 14,765 feet, **Cangshan** *(Green Mountain)* can be seen from just about any place in Dali. A 16 km (10 mi) path carved into the side of the mountain halfway between the summit and the Old Town offers spectacular views of Dali and the surrounding villages. There are also several temples, grottoes, and waterfalls just off the main trail. If you don't want to climb several thousand feet to get to the path, there is a cable car (more like a ski lift) that will take you up and back for Y60. To get to the cable car, follow Yu'er Lu to the foot of the mountain. The cost of taking the cable car up the mountain is Y90 and footing it is Y30.

Almost any street off Fuxing Lu will bring you to the shore of **Erhai Lake** *(Erhai Hu)*. You may catch a glimpse of fishermen with their teams of cormorants tied to their boats. In good weather, ferries are a wonderful way to see the lake and the surrounding mountains. The ferries cost between Y30 and Y70 (depending on your ability to bargain). More interesting perhaps—and cheaper—would be to hire one of the local fishermen to paddle wherever you want to go. Boats depart from the village of Zhoucheng.

DID YOU KNOW?

The cormorants used by fishermen on Erhai Lake have a collar around their necks that prevents them from swallowing the fish they have caught.

Among the prettiest towns in the area is **Xizhou**, about 20 km (12 mi) north of Dali. It has managed to preserve a fair amount of its Bai architecture. The daily morning market and occasional festivals of traditional music attract a fair number of tourists from neighboring Dali. Buses to Xizhou leave from Dali's west gate and cost Y4.

There are a handful of towns with markets known for local crafts, household goods, and antiques (beware of fakes!). **Shaping** has the most popular market in the area, taking place every Monday morning. The town sits on the lake's northern shore, and can be most easily reached by boat or by hiring a car and driver. **Wase** is a popular area market featuring Bai clothing. The town is on the opposite side of the lake from Dali and can be reached by car or boat.

LIJIANG

150 km (93 mi; 3 hrs by bus) north of Dali; 320 km (198 mi; 7 hrs by bus) northwest of Kunming; 550 km (341 mi; 20 hrs by bus) southwest of Chengdu.

Lijiang is probably the most famous travel destination in Yunnan, as its Old Town was named a UNESCO World Heritage Site. At the base of majestic Jade Dragon Snow Mountain, Lijiang is home to the Naxi people, who are related to Tibetans but have their own language and culture.

The old town in Lijiang at dusk.

Lijiang's Old Town is a labyrinth of winding alleys, fish-filled streams, and old Naxi houses with tile rooftops. Traditional Naxi singing and dancing are on display nightly at Sifang Jie, the square in Old Town's center.

GETTING HERE AND AROUND

AIR TRAVEL There are multiple daily flights between Lijiang and Kunming. The airport is 30 mi (a half-hour) south of Lijiang. A Y20 bus from the airport terminates on the edge of the Old Town. A taxi to the Old Town will run you Y80.

TRAIN TRAVEL There are day and night trains from Kunming to Lijiang. The ride takes seven hours.

BUS TRAVEL Lijiang's main bus stations are on Xin Dajie and the south side of Xiangelila Dadao. Bus trips from Kunming to Lijiang take seven hours.

SAFETY AND PRECAUTIONS

Lijiang gets a lot of foot traffic, which has made the cobbled paths in the Old Town quite slippery. Also, if taking a taxi, make sure they use the meter, as some drivers may try to pull a fast one.

TIMING

Lijiang is good for two or three days of taking in the Old Town and surrounding areas. If you're feeling active, it may be worth cutting your time in the Old Town short and heading for Tiger Leaping Gorge for a day or two.

TOURS

Vistiors don't tend to use tour guides in this area. Lijiang has plenty of English signs in the Old Town and on Jade Dragon Snow Mountain/ Black Dragon Pool; tour guides aren't needed in Tiger Leaping Gorge.

ESSENTIALS

Air Contact Lijiang Airport (☎ *0888/517–3088*).

Bank Bank of China (✉ *Dong Dajie*).

Bus Contact Xianggelila Bus Station (✉ *Xiangelila Dadao*).

Medical Assistance Lijiang People's Hospital (✉ *Fuhui Lu* ☎ *0888/512–2393*).

Public Security Bureau PSB Lijiang (✉ *Fuhui Lu* ☎ *110*).

Visitor and Tour Info China International Travel Service (CITS) (✉ *Xin Dajie* ☎ *0888/512–3508*).

EXPLORING

With so many shops and markets, much of Lijiang's Old Town feels more like a Special Economic Zone than a UNESCO-protected site. However, it's still possible to get away for an interesting stroll. Helpful English maps around town help you navigate the maze.

The **Visitor Center for Nature and Culture in Northwest Yunnan** is a small but fascinating museum of the region's cultural and biological diversity. Exhibits include one in which area villagers were given cameras to document their daily lives. One exhibit compares photos taken in the 1920s with those taken more recently. The museum is funded by the Nature Conservancy. ✉ *42 Xianwen Xiang, at Guangyi Jie* ☎ *0888/511–5969* 💲 *Free* ⊙ *Daily 9–6.*

If you can find it, the **Pujian Temple** (*Pujian Si*) is a tranquil place to get away from the crowds. You can refuel with some local snacks from the temple's vegetarian snack restaurant. Try fried Naxi potatoes (they're purple) or *jidoufen,* a bean concoction that can be eaten hot as a porridge or cold and cut up like noodles. The ubiquitous Naxi *baba* bread is also quite good. Wash it all down with a pot of Tibetan yak butter tea. ✉ *Qi Yi Jie* 💲 *Free* ⊙ *Daily 8–6.*

Outside the old town, the **Black Dragon Pool Park** (*Heilongtan Gongyuan*) has a tranquil pavilion where locals come to play cards and drink tea. It is also one of the most popular places to photograph nearby Jade Dragon Snow Mountain. The park is home to the **Dongba Research Institute Museum** (*Dongba Yanjiu Suo*), a museum devoted to Naxi Dongba culture. ✉ *Xinde Lu* 💲 *Y80* ⊙ *Daily 6:30 am–8 pm.*

WHERE TO EAT

¢–$ ✕ **Lamu's House of Tibet.** One of the most consistent restaurants in the
ECLECTIC Old Town, Lamu's serves Tibetan, Chinese, and Naxi cuisine, as well as familiar dishes like lasagna and french fries. The pleasant atmosphere, traditional Tibetan decor, and helpful staff make Lamu's one of Lijiang's better dining options. ✉ *56 Jishan Xiang, Xinyi Jie* ☎ *0888/511–5776* ⊟ *No credit cards.*

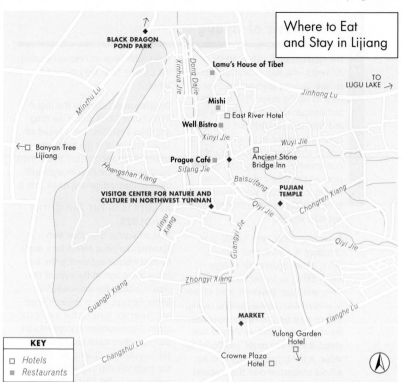

BLACK DRAGON
POND PARK

Lamu's House of Tibet

Mishi

East River Hotel

Well Bistro

Xinyi Jie

Banyan Tree
Lijiang

Prague Café

Ancient Stone
Bridge Inn

Sifang Jie

Baisuifang

PUJIAN
TEMPLE

VISITOR CENTER FOR NATURE AND
CULTURE IN NORTHWEST YUNNAN

TO
LUGU LAKE →

Jinhong Lu

Wuyi Jie

Minzhu Lu

Xinhua Jie

Dong Dajie

Hoangshan Xiang

Jinyu Xiang

Guangyi Jie

Qiyi Jie

Chongren Xiang

Qiyi Jie

Zhongyi Xiang

Guangbi Xiang

Changshui Lu

MARKET

Yulong Garden
Hotel

Crowne Plaza
Hotel

Xianghe Lu

8

KEY

□ *Hotels*
■ *Restaurants*

$$–$$$$
ECLECTIC
Fodor'sChoice
★
✕ **Mishi.** Easily the best restaurant in the Old Town, Swedish-owned Mishi serves the perfect balance of local and international cuisine. The relaxing environment combines Scandinavian design with traditional Naxi sensibilities. Standout dishes include sizzling yak meat on a roof tile, panfried salmon with lemon butter, and fried spareribs. In a town full of bars, Mishi has one of the best selections of liquor and beer, which go perfectly with the plush seating inside or the relaxing interior courtyard. ⊠ *52 Mishi Xiang, off Xinyi Jie* ☎ *0888/518–7605* ▭ *No credit cards.*

¢–$
CAFÉ
✕ **Prague Café.** The town's top choice for good coffee and fresh juices, Prague Café also serves good food, especially American-style breakfast and pizza. Favorite meals include Japanese-style *katsudon*, pork cutlets in a savory sauce. Prague is also a nice place to hang out and chat with tea or a beer at night. It has a good book collection and free Internet access. ⊠ *80 Mishi Xiang, at Xinyi Jie* ☎ *0888/512–3757* ▭ *No credit cards.*

¢–$
CAFÉ
✕ **Well Bistro.** Near the Old Well, this small eatery serves a nice variety of international food at reasonable prices in a pretty setting away from the town square. Its coffee is very good, and it's a top choice for breakfast. This is one of the best places in town to hunker down with a hot drink and a good book on a cold or rainy day. ⊠ *32 Mishi Xiang, at Xinyi Jie* ☎ *0888/518–6431* ▭ *No credit cards.*

Naxi Music of Lijiang

The Naxi culture is rich in artistic elements—the Naxi pictographs, architecture, Dongba shamans, and, not least of all, the music. It is a complex and intricate musical blending of Han and Naxi musical traditions that has commonly served as entertainment, as well as a measuring stick for Confucian social relationships. Naxi musicians and members of social clubs related to the music were considered to be of a higher status than the average Naxi villager.

Today Naxi music, with its 500 years of history, is a sonic time capsule, giving us the opportunity to hear songs dating as far back as the Tang, Song, and Yuan Dynasties. Most of the Naxi-inhabited counties around Lijiang feature their own orchestras specializing in the two extant versions of Naxi music: Baisha fine music and Dongjing music. A third type, Huangjing music, fell out of practice over the centuries and has since been lost.

THE ROOTS OF RHYTHM

Legend has it that Baisha fine music developed as a result of Kublai Khan's gratitude for Naxi assistance during his conquest of Yunnan during the Yuan Dynasty. The Khan is believed to have left a group of his best musicians and their musical canon with the Naxi in Lijiang. Baisha fine music is one of the grander Chinese musical styles, with large orchestras including the Chinese flute, the lute, and the zither.

Dongjing music came to this region from central China during the Ming and Qing dynasties, and is based on Taoist classics. It is the better preserved of the two musical styles, most likely because the Naxi incorporated more of their indigenous music into it.

BEAUTY IS IN THE EAR OF THE BEHOLDER

Naxi orchestras have their own standards for what makes for a quality Naxi musical experience, the key factor being age. In the eyes of the Naxi, the older the musicians, the better. Perhaps this is because fewer and fewer are learning the traditional styles. The musicians' instruments are also old, often much older than the septuagenarians playing the music—the craftsmanship 100 years ago was better than today. Naxi orchestras refuse to play any modern music. They only jam to centuries-old tunes.

For many travelers, Naxi music is an aural step back in time. Others find it screechy and grating. You can catch a show at a number of venues in Lijiang's Old Town and the new city. The most famous groups are the Baihua and Dayan orchestras. Tickets can typically be purchased starting at Y100 at most hotels and guesthouses.

WHERE TO STAY

¢ 🖺 **Ancient Stone Bridge Inn.** Two of the rooms in this guesthouse look directly out over a brook, a small pedestrian street, and pair of bridges. It's a bit more expensive than the average guesthouse, but the perfect setting may justify the extra few yuan. The front door is locked at midnight. **Pros:** good location; inexpensive. **Cons:** in slight need of a renovation. ⊠ *71 Wuyi Jie Xingrenxia* ☎ *0888/518–4001 or 139/8882–5829* 🛏 *10 rooms* ⚘ *In-hotel: laundry service* ▭ *No credit cards.*

$$$$ **Banyan Tree Lijiang.** The only luxury resort near Lijiang (for now), Banyan Tree is made up of villas designed to resemble Naxi courtyard homes. Each self-contained accommodation features its own hot tub or swimming pool. Located in the old Naxi capital of Baisha at the foot of mist-covered Jade Dragon Snow Mountain, the hotel has spectacular unobstructed views. It has all the amenities you would expect in a world-class resort, from Thai massage in the spa to fine dining in the Bai Yun restaurant. **Pros:** nearly perfect service and accommodations; breathtaking scenery. **Cons:** very expensive. ⊠ *Yuerong Lu,* ☏ *0888/533–1111* ⊕ *www.banyantree.com* ⇝ *55 villas* ⚴ *In-room: safe, Internet. In-hotel: 2 restaurants, room service, bar, gym, spa, laundry service* ▭ *DC, MC, V.*

¢–$ **Crowne Plaza Hotel.** Filling the gap between the small hotels and guesthouses in the Old Town and the ultraluxurious Banyan Tree, Crowne Plaza is the beginning of what is likely to be a wave of international five-stars moving into Lijiang in the coming years. Rooms are comfortable and spacious, staff speak good English, and kids eat free at the Chinese or Brazilian restaurants. The gym and pool are both clean and modern, and there are babysitting services should you want to leave the kids behind for a night on the town. **Pros:** comfortable; high level of service. **Cons:** a bit removed from the Old Town. ⊠ *276 Xianghe Lu, Lijiang* ☏ *888/558–8888* ⊕ *www.ichotelsgroup.com* ⇝ *270 rooms* ⚴ *In-room: a/c, safe, refrigerator, Internet. In-hotel: 2 restaurants, room service, bar, pool, gym, children's programs, laundry service.* ▭ *DC, MC, V.*

¢ **East River Hotel** *(Dong He Ju).* Around the corner from Mishi, East
★ River Hotel offers some of the most comfortable rooms—and bathrooms—in the Old Town. Outside the modern comfort of the guest rooms a traditional courtyard with a clear stream running through it beckons. Although a little more expensive than most of its competition, East River Hotel is worth it. Complimentary breakfast comes with the room. **Pros:** quiet; idyllic courtyard. **Cons:** hard to find. ⊠ *68 Mishi Xiang, off Xinyi Jie* ☏ *0888/515–1668* ⇝ *40 rooms* ⚴ *In-hotel: restaurant, Internet terminal* ▭ *No credit cards.*

¢ **Yulong Garden Hotel.** This hotel offers a pleasant combination of traditional architecture and modern convenience. It's a good option for visitors who want the amenities of a hotel, like an on-site restaurant and bar. It may not be special, but it is very clean and well maintained, and the hot water is reliable. **Pros:** more amenities than most guesthouses. **Cons:** staff can be hard to find when you need them. ⊠ *Dinghong Lu* ☏ *0888/518–2888* ⇝ *150 rooms* ⚴ *In-hotel: restaurant, bar, laundry service* ▭ *AE, MC, V.*

NIGHTLIFE AND THE ARTS

Traditional Naxi music and dancing can be found in the town square at Sifang Jie beginning in the afternoon and lasting into the evening. There is also a variety of cultural performances held daily around Lijiang.

Black Dragon Pool Park with Jade Dragon Snow Mountain in the distance.

The most impressive cultural event is **Lijiang Impression** (✉ *Ganhai Scenic District* ☎ *0888/888–8888*), produced by director Zhang Yimou (2008 Beijing Olympics opening ceremony, *Red Sorghum, Raise the Red Lantern*). Zhang takes Lijiang's Dongba culture and beautiful surroundings as his muse. Set at the base of Jade Dragon Snow Mountain and using the mountain as an integral part of the scenery, this music and dance performance makes full use of its spectacular location. The show takes place daily at 1:20 pm, and costs Y190–Y260, depending on how close to the front you want to be.

At the Meeting Hall of Lijiang, the **Mountain Spirit Show** (✉ *Minzu Lu* ☎ *No phone*) offers fire eating and other extraordinary feats by the Yi shaman. The performance, daily at 8 pm, costs Y120.

SIDE TRIPS FROM LIJIANG

Towering majestically over Lijiang, the 18,360-foot **Jade Dragon Snow Mountain** *(Yulong Xue Shan)* is one of non-Tibetan China's most spectacular peaks. The mountain's jagged, snow-covered face is one of the defining sights of a trip to Lijiang. The well-maintained road to the scenic area is a nice drive, passing numerous villages and offering fine valley and mountain views. The park entrance is about a 30-minute drive from Old Town. Taxis should cost around Y40 one way, and Y100 or more if you want the driver to wait for you. Most hotels and guesthouses can book trips to the mountain. ☞ *Y80* ⊘ *Daily 7–5.*

ⓒ ▦ **Wenhai Ecolodge.** Accessible only by foot or on horseback, Wenhai Ecolodge is one of the country's first "green" resorts. It's located in the mountain valley that is home to Lake Wenhai, a seasonal lake that appears between July and March. When the basin is filled, the lake is home to black-necked cranes, black storks, and several varieties of ducks. There is excellent hiking in the valley, and the chance to come across some of the area's endangered plants and animals such as the giant laughing thrush and the winter wren. The 12-room lodge is designed to minimize environmental impact, and has excellent views of nearby Jade Dragon Snow Mountain. It's highly recommended for nature lovers and conservation-minded travelers. Room price includes three meals per day. **Pros:** fascinating for nature lovers. **Cons:** remote; rougher than some travelers can handle. ⊠ *Lake Wenhai* ☎ *1390/888– 1817* ⊕ *www.northwestyunnan.com/wenhai_ecolodge.htm* ⤳ *12 rooms* ⌂ *In-hotel: restaurant* ▭ *No credit cards* ⦿ *FAP.*

★ A 2½-hour drive from Lijiang, **Tiger Leaping Gorge** *(Hutiao Xia)* is home to some of China's most breathtaking mountain scenery. Lucky for travelers who have not yet seen this spectacular scenery, plans to dam the gorge were scrapped by the government in late 2007. By water, the gorge winds about 16 km (10 mi); following it by land on the upper trail is a 40-km (25-mi) hike, which can be leisurely hiked in two days or done in one day if you're fit enough. The upper trail and a paved road below connect the towns of Qiaotou in the west and Daju in the east, and there is a ferry across the river near Daju that stops service at 5 pm. The easiest way to tackle the trek from Lijiang is to take the 8:30 am or 9 am bus on Xin Dajie to Qiaotou and hike toward Daju.

There are several guesthouses in the gorge, scattered at distances to accommodate hikers at any stage of their trek. All offer food, hot showers, and beds for Y20 to Y40. Many of the guesthouses have expanded and upgraded accommodations in the past couple of years, so there is more selection and even some higher-end rooms for Y150. The guesthouses have put up signs and arrows to let hikers know how much farther until the next lodging. If you don't mind not hiking the whole gorge, stop in Walnut Garden, where you can take one of the regular buses back to Lijiang. If you continue to Daju, there are only two buses a day to Lijiang, at 8:30 am and 1 pm.

Nuisances along the trail include fake "toll collectors," who will attempt to take your money, and aggressive local dogs. The former require patience and politeness to deal with, the latter the ability to stand one's ground—and it's useful to have a large stick.

JINGHONG AND THE XISHUANGBANNA REGION

390 km (243 mi; 12 hrs by bus) southwest of Kunming; 400 km (250 mi; 12 hrs by bus) south of Dali.

Jinghong is the capital of southern Yunnan's Xishuangbanna Dai Autonomous Region, which borders Laos and Myanmar. Xishuangbanna is home to the Dai, a people related to Thais and Laotians, who, like their cousins to the south, love very spicy food.

Jinghong sits on the banks of the muddy Mekong, although this stretch of the legendary river is known locally as the Lancang. This is where China meets Southeast Asia; it feels more and more like Laos or Thailand the farther you travel from Jinghong. Even inside the city the architecture, the clothing, and even the barbecue seem much more like what you'd find in Vientiane or Chiang Mai.

Jinghong has experienced a small tourist boom; it now has its own airport, with flights to Kunming and other cities. But despite the increase in economic activity, Jinghong still moves at about the same speed as the Mekong.

GETTING HERE AND AROUND

AIR TRAVEL Jinghong's international airport has service to Kunming and Chengdu, as well as destinations in Thailand, Cambodia, and Laos. It's about 15 minutes west of the city center. From the airport, take the Number 1 bus into town for Y2, or opt for a taxi for Y30.

BUS TRAVEL Jinghong's two main bus stations are Jinghong Bus Station, north of Zhuanghong Lu on Mengle Lu, and Banna Bus Station, just north of the intersection of Mengle Dadao and Xuanwei Lu. Both bus stations have services to Kunming and Dali. For shorter routes, head to Banna Bus Station.

SAFETY AND PRECAUTIONS

Be sure to drink plenty of water—Jinghong gets hot, and dehydration is a risk as you explore town.

TIMING

Spend a day exploring downtown Jinghong, and add an extra day if you plan to tour out to the surrounding countryside.

TOURS

Tours organized by Forest Café are your best bet for a tailored English-language tour of Xishuangbanna.

ESSENTIALS

Air Contact Jinghong Airport (☎ 0691/212–3003).

Bus Contacts Jinghong Bus Station (✉ Mengle Dadao ☎ 0691/212–2487).
Banna Bus Station (✉ Minhang Lu ☎ 0691/212–4427).

Medical Assistance Xishuangbanna People's Hospital (✉ 4 Galan Zhong Lu ☎ 0691/212–3221).

Bank Bank of China (✉ 96 Galan Zhong Lu).

Public Security Bureau PSB Jinghong (✉ Xuanwei Dadao ☎ 110).

Visitor and Tour Info China International Travel Service (CITS) (✉ Galan Zhong Lu ☎ 0691/213–1165). **Forest Cafe** (✉ 23 Mengla Lu ☎ 0691/898–5122).

EXPLORING

Even a short walk around Jinghong reveals its colorful mix of Dai, Chinese, Thai, and Burmese influences. It's a small enough town that you can cover most of it on foot in a day. Bordered by the Lancang River to the east, the city quickly begins to thin out as you head west.

The **Lancang River** *(Lancang Jiang)* is the name of the Mekong River in China, where it originates before flowing into Southeast Asia. It is easiest to access the river from Jinghong at the Xishuangbanna Bridge—there is a path there that follows alongside the river and is ideal for strolling or biking.

On the southeastern edge of Jinghong is **Manting Park** *(Manting Gongyuan),* a pleasant park where you can have a closer look at some of the area's indigenous plants. Also worth exploring is the large peacock aviary. The park is especially lively around mid-April, when people gather here to celebrate the Water Splashing Festival. ✉ *35 Manting Lu* ☎ *0691/216–0296* *Y40* *Daily 7:30 am–7:30 pm.*

★ **Xishuangbanna Tropical Flower and Plant Garden** *(Xishuangbanna Redai Huahuiyuan)* is an interesting place to spend several hours walking among fragrant frangipani, massive lily pads, drooping jackfruit, and thousands of other colorful and peculiar plants. This is one of China's finest gardens, featuring a well-designed layout arranged into themed sections including tropical fruits, palms, and rubber trees. Don't walk through too fast, or you'll miss out on some of the more unique plants such as *tiaowu cao,* or "dancing grass," which actually stands up if you sing at it. Each plant's placard features English and Latin names. ✉ *99 Xuanwei Dadao* *Y40* *Daily 7:30–6.*

THE WATER SPLASHING FESTIVAL

The Dai Water Splashing Festival is held in Dai-inhabited areas of southern Yunnan, including the cities of Jinghong and Ruili.

Originally, water was poured gently upon the backs of family members to wash away the sins of the past year and provide blessings for the coming year. Today it has become a water war, replete with squirt guns, buckets of ice water, and other weapons. It is quite a bit of fun, and a great way to cool off. Just remember to leave any cameras, watches, or cell phones back in your room.

WHERE TO EAT

$–$$ CHINESE ✕ **Foguang Yuan**. Tucked away behind a school and a police station, Foguang Yuan is a hidden gem. The restaurant is actually several dining areas built around a patch of jungle. The Dai architecture and beautiful tropical setting alone merit a visit, but the restaurant also serves an excellent array of Dai and Chinese classics. There are no English menus, so venture into the kitchen and point to what looks good. ✉ *2 Jiaotong Xiang, near Yiwu Lu* ☎ *0691/213–8608* *No credit cards.*

¢–$ CHINESE ✕ **Forest Café**. Run by the brother-sister team of Sara and Stone Chen, both of whom are fluent in English, this café serves the best Western-style breakfasts in town. The kitchen makes its own whole-wheat bread and uses only organic mountain rice in its dishes. The staff can also arrange trips to a variety of local villages. The café publishes a useful bilingual map of Jinghong ✉ *23 Mengla Lu* ☎ *0691/898–5122* *No credit cards.*

¢–$$ CHINESE ✕ **Meimei Café**. Meimei's is a good place to compare notes with other travelers, as many people come here to buy tickets or book tours. One of the few places in Jinghong with English-speaking staff, Meimei Café serves Western, Chinese, and Dai food, as well as good coffee and juice drinks. ✉ *Menglong Lu* ☎ *0691/216–1221* *No credit cards.*

WHERE TO STAY

¢–$ 🏨 **Crown Hotel.** In the heart of Jinghong, this hotel has several low-slung buildings in a parklike setting with a large swimming pool. Standard rooms start at Y480, but if you haggle a bit you can likely get a better rate. There is also a good night market outside the hotel. **Pros:** near night market; pool open to nonresidents, Y10 at entrance on Meng-peng Lu. **Cons:** almost no English-speaking staff. ⊠ *70 Mengle Dadao* ☎ *0691/219–9888* ⤴ *88 rooms* ♨ *In-hotel: restaurant, laundry service* 🚫 *No credit cards.*

¢ 🏨 **Golden Banna Hotel.** Across the street from the Crown Hotel, Golden Banna is a decent, no-frills accommodation option in Jinghong. The standard rooms are clean and have private bathrooms. Don't expect much in the way of service or amenities, however. **Pros:** good value. **Cons:** drab decor. ⊠ *55 Mengle Dadao* ☎ *0691/213–6666* ⤴ *100 rooms* ♨ *In-hotel: restaurant* 🚫 *AE, MC, V.*

SHOPPING

Zhuanghong Lu, in the northern part of town, is filled with Burmese jade and goods from Thailand. There is a small but vibrant night market on Mengla Lu outside the Crown Hotel.

SIDE TRIPS FROM JINGHONG

One of China's first serious attempts at ecotourism, the 900-acre **Sanchahe Nature Reserve** is home to wild elephants. Two hours north of Jinghong, the park also features a butterfly farm and a cable car that offers breathtaking views. Lodging is in "tree houses" about 25 feet above ground—a unique place to spend a night. It is best to avoid visiting during the summer, when the weather can be rainy. Arrange transportation through your hotel.

One of the more scenic areas of Xishuangbanna is **Ganlan Basin** *(Ganlanba)*, 37 km (23 mi) from Jinghong. Minority peoples still live in bamboo huts here in the beautiful rain forest. The area is famous in Yunnan for its tropical flowers and the millions of butterflies that inhabit this valley. If you want to spend a few days hiking and investigating the basin, you can stay at one of the many village guesthouses, most of which accept foreigners.

ENGLISH	PINYIN	CHINESE
GUANGXI	**GUǍNGXĪ**	**广西**
Guilin	Guìlín	桂林
Back Garden Irish Pub	Hòu yuán Ài'ěrlán jiǔbā	后园爱尔兰酒吧
China International Travel Service (CITS)	Zhōngguó guójì lǚxíngshè	中国国际旅行社
China Travel Service (CTS)	Zhōngguó lǚxíngshè	中国旅行社
Elephant Trunk Hill	Xiàngbíshān	象鼻山
Eva Inn	Sìjì chūntiān jiǔdiàn	四季春天酒店
Guilin Bus Station	Guìlín kèyùnzhàn	桂林客运站
Guilin People's Hospital	Guìlín rénmín yīyuàn	桂林人民医院
Guilin Railway Station	Guìlín huǒchēzhàn	桂林火车站
Inaka	Tángjiànlì	唐剑利
Johnny's Mix Kitchen	Sìjì xiāng	四季香
Lijiang Waterfall Guilin	Líjiāng dàpòbù fàndiàn	漓江大瀑布饭店
Little Italian	zhè lǐ	这里
Ming Tomb	Jìngjiāngwáng líng	靖江王陵
Paulaner	Bólóng	柏龙
Peak of Solitary Beauty	Dúxiùfēng	独秀峰
Prince City Solitary Beauty Park	Jìngjiāngwáng chéng	靖江王城
Putuo Mountain	Pǔtuóshān	普陀山
Seven Star Cliff	Qīxīngyán	七星岩
Seven Star Park	Qīxíng gōngyuán	七星公园
Sheraton Guilin	Guìlín Dàyǔ dàfàndiàn	桂林大宇大饭店
Wang Cheng Fan Dian	Wángchéng fàndiàn	王城饭店
Yangshuo	Yángshuò	阳朔
Buffalo Bar	Niútóu bā cāntīng	牛头吧餐厅
Café China	Yuánshǐrén	原始人
Charm Yangshuo Tour	n/a	n/a
Club 98	jiǔbā jùlèbù	98俱乐部
Dynasty Dumplings	Yīpǐnjū	一品居
Fuli	fúlì	福利
The Giggling Tree	Gēgēshù fàndiàn	格格树饭店
Kali Mirch Indian Cuisine	Hēi hújiāo cāntīng	黑胡椒餐厅
Kelly's Place	Dēnglóngfēngwèi guǎn	灯笼风味馆
Le Vôtre	Lèdéfǎshì cāntīng	乐得法试餐厅
Li Quing Guesthouse	Lìqíng bīnguǎn	丽晴宾馆

8

ENGLISH	PINYIN	CHINESE
Li Quing Restaurant	Lìqíng fànguǎn	丽晴饭馆
Longsheng Longji Rice Terraces	Lóngshènglóngjī tītián	龙胜龙脊梯田
Magnolia Hotel	Báiyùlán jiǔdiàn	白玉兰酒店
Man De Guai	Mǎndéguǎi	满得拐
Moon Hill	Yuèliàng shān	月亮山
Morningsun Hotel	Chénguāng jiǔdiàn	晨光酒店
Peng Family Painted Scroll Factory	Péngshì shànhuà gōngyìchǎng	彭氏扇画工艺厂
PSB Yangshuo	Yángshuò gōng'ānjú	阳朔公安局
Riverview Hotel	Wàngjiāng lóu	望江楼
Yangshuo Bus Station	Yángshuò kèyùnzhàn	阳朔客运站
Yangshuo Park	Yángshuò gōngyuán	阳朔公园
Yangshuo Regency Holiday Hotel	Lìjǐng jiàrì bīngguǎn	丽景假日宾馆
Nanning	Nánníng	南宁
Bank of China	Zhōngguó yínháng	中国银行
Beifang Renjia	Běifāngrénjiā	北方人家
Guangxi Zhuang Autonomous Region Museum	Guǎngxī Zhuàngzú zìzhìqū bówùguǎn	广西壮族自治区博物馆
The Here	zhè lǐ	这里
Majestic Hotel	Míngyuánxīndū dàjiǔdiàn	明园新都大酒店
Nanning Bus Station	Nánníng kèyùnzhàn	南宁客运站
Nanning First Municipal People's Hospital	Nánníng dìyī rénmín yīyuàn	南宁市第一人民医院
Nanning Marriott	Nánníng Jīnwěiwànháo jiǔdiàn	南宁金伟万豪酒店
Nanning Wuxu International Airport	Nánníng Wúxū guójì jīchǎng	南宁吴圩国际机场
People's Park	Báilóng gōngyuán	白龙公园
PSB Nanning	Nánníng gōng'ānjú	南宁公安局
South Lake	Nánhú	南湖
Taoyuan Hotel	Táoyuán dàjiǔdiàn	桃源大酒店
GUIZHOU	GUÌZHŌU	贵州
Guiyang	Guìyáng	贵阳
Guiyang Longdongbao Airport	Guìyáng Lóngdòngbǎo jīchǎng	贵阳龙洞堡机场
Guiyang Railway Station	Guìyáng huǒchēzhàn	贵阳火车站
Guiyang Stadium Bus Station	Guìzhōu tǐyùguǎn chángtú qìchē kèyùn zhàn	贵州体育馆长途汽车客运站
Guizhou Park Hotel	Guìzhōu fàndiàn	贵州饭店

ENGLISH	PINYIN	CHINESE
Hebin Park	Hébīn gōngyuán	河滨公园
Highlands Coffee	Gāoyuán kāfēi	高原咖啡
Huangguoshu Falls	Huángguǒshù pùbù	黄果树瀑布
Huaxi Park	Huāxī gōngyuán	花溪公园
Nenghui Jiudian	Nénghuī jiǔdiàn	能辉酒店
Old Kaili Sour Fish Restaurant	Lǎokǎilǐ suāntāngyú	老凯里酸汤鱼
PSB Guiyang	Guìyáng gōng'ānjú	贵阳公安局
Qianling Park	Qiánlíng gōngyuán	黔灵公园
Sheraton Guiyang Hotel	Guìyáng Xǐláidēng jiǔdiàn	贵阳喜来登酒店
Underground Gardens	Guìyáng dìxià gōngyuán	贵阳地下公园
Unicorn Cave	Qílín dòng	麒麟洞
WildChina Travel	Bìshān lǚyóu gōngsī	碧山旅游公司
Kaili	Kǎilǐ	凯里
Bank of China	Zhōngguó yínháng	中国银行
Drum Tower	Gǔlóu	鼓
Guotai Dajiudian	Guótài dàjiǔdiàn	国泰大酒店
Jinquanhu Park	Jīnquán hú	金泉湖
Kaili Bus Station	Kǎilǐ kèyùnzhàn	凯里客运站
Kaili Train Station	Kaǐlǐ huǒchēzhàn	凯里火车站
Minorities Museum	zhōu mínzú bówùguǎn	州民族博物馆
YUNNAN	**YÚNNÁN**	**云南**
Kunming	Kūnmíng	昆明
1910 La Gare du Sud	Huǒchē nánzhà	火车南站
Bank of China	Zhōngguó yínháng	中国银行
Chapter One	n/a	n/a
China Minority Travel	n/a	n/a
Chuangku	Chuàngkù	创库
Dune Café	Shāqiū kāfēi	沙丘咖啡
Dynamic Yunnan	Yúnnán yìngxiàng	云南映象
GoKunming	n/a	n/a
Golden Dragon Hotel	Jīnlóng fàndiàn	金龙饭店
Grand Park Hotel Kunming	Kūnmíng Jūnlè jiǔdiàn (qián Hǎiyì jiǔdiandiàn)	昆明君乐酒店 (前海逸酒店)
Green Lake Hotel	Cuìhú bīnguǎn	翠湖宾馆
Green Lake Park	Chuìhū gōngyuán	翠湖公园
Kunming Airport	Kūnmíng jīchǎng	昆明机场

8

ENGLISH	PINYIN	CHINESE
Kunming First People's Hospital	Kūnmíng dìyī rénmín yīyuàn	昆明第一人民医院
Kunming Hotel	Kūnmíng fàndiàn	昆明饭店
Kunming Train Station	Kūnmíng huǒchēzhàn	昆明火车站
Kunming Tourism Authority	Kūnmíng shì lǚyóu jú	昆明市旅游局
Makye Ame	Mǎjíāmǐ	玛吉阿米
Moonlight Corner	n/a	n/a
PSB Kunming	n/a	n/a
Salvador's Coffee House	Sàěrwǎduō	萨尔瓦多
Sandra's		no Chinese name
Stone Forest	Shílín	石林
West Bus Transit Station	n/a	n/a
Xiong Brothers Bike Shop	Xióngshìxiōngdì zìxíngchē	熊氏兄弟自行车
Xizhan Bus Station	xīzhàn kèyùnzhàn	西站客运站
Yingjiang Daiweiyuan	Yíngjiāng Dǎiwèiyuán	
Yuantong Temple	Yuántōngsì	圆通寺
Yunart Gallery	Yunart huàláng	Yunart 画廊
Yunnan Provincial Museum	Yúnnán shěng bówùguǎn	云南省博物馆
Yunnan University Hotel	Yúndà bìnguǎn	云大宾馆
Dali	Dàlǐ	大理
Bad Monkey	n/a	n/a
The Bird's Nest	Niǎowō	鸟窝
Cafe de Jack	Yīnghuāyuán xīcāntīng	樱花园西餐厅
Cangshan	Cāngshān	苍山
China Minority Travel	Zhōngguó shǎoshùmínzú lǚyóu gōngsī	中国少数民族旅游公司
Dali Airport	Dàlǐ jīchǎng	大理机场
Dali First Municipal People's Hospital	Dàlǐ shì dìyī rénmín yīyuàn	大理市第一人民医院
Erhai Lake	Erhǎi	洱海
Guiqu Laixi	Guīqùláixī	归去来兮
Higherland Inn	Gāodì	高地
ICBC	Gōngshāng yínháng	工商银行
Jim's Tibetan Hotel	Jímǔ zhàngshì jiǔdiàn	吉姆藏式酒店
La Stella's Pizzeria	Xīnxīng bǐsà fáng	新星比萨房
PSB Dali	n/a	n/a
Regent Hotel	Fēnghuāxuěyuè dàjiǔdiàn	风花雪月大酒店

ENGLISH	PINYIN	CHINESE
Shaping	n/a	n/a
Three Pagodas	Sāntǎ sì	三塔寺
Tibetan Lodge	Qīngnián lǚguǎn	青年旅馆
Wase	n/a	n/a
Xiaguan Train Station	Xiàguān huǒchēzhàn	下关火车站
Xizhou	n/a	n/a
Yunnan Inn	Fēngyuèshānshuǐ kèzhàn	风月山水客栈
Lijiang	Lìjiāng	丽江
Ancient Stone Bridge Inn	Dàshíqiáo kèzhàn	大石桥客栈
Banyan Tree Lijiang	Lìjiāng Yuèróng zhuāng	丽江悦榕庄
Black Dragon Pool Park	Hēilóngtán gōngyuán	黑龙潭公园
Crowne Plaza Hotel	n/a	n/a
Dongba Research Institute Museum	n/a	n/a
East River Hotel	Dōnghéjū	东河居
Jade Dragon Snow Mountain	Yùlóng xuěshān	玉龙雪山
Lamu's House of Tibet	Xīzàngwū xīcānguǎn	西藏屋西餐馆
Lijiang Airport	Lìjiāng jīchǎng	丽江机场
Lijiang Impression	n/a	n/a
Lijiang People's Hospital	Lìjiāng rénmín yīyuàn	丽江人民医院
Mishi	Mǐsīxiāng	米思香
Prague Cafe	Bùlāgé kāfēiguǎn	布拉格咖啡馆
PSB Lijiang	n/a	n/a
Pujian Temple	Pǔxiánsì	普贤寺
Tiger Leaping Gorge	Hǔtiàoxiá	虎跳峡
Visitor Center for Nature and Culture in Northwest Yunnan	Diānxīběi zìrán yǔ wēnhuà zhī chuāng jiē lùsè lǚyóu tuīguǎng zhōngxīn	滇西北自然与文化之窗暨绿色旅游推广中心
Well Bistro	Jǐngzuó cānguǎn	井卓餐馆
Wenhai Ecolodge	Wénhǎi shēngtài lǚguǎn	文海生态旅馆
Xianggelila Bus Station	Xiānggélǐlā kèyùnzhàn	香格里拉客运站
Yulong Garden Hotel	Yùlóng huāyuán jiǔdiàn	玉龙花园酒店
Jinghong	Jǐnghóng	景洪
Banna Bus Station	Bǎnnàkèyùnzhàn	版纳客运站
Crown Hotel	Huángguān dàjiǔdiàn	皇冠大酒店
Foguang Yuan	Fóguāng yuán	佛光园
Forest Café	Sēnlín kāfēiwū	森林咖啡屋

8

ENGLISH	PINYIN	CHINESE
Ganlan Basin	Gǎnlǎn bà	橄榄坝
Golden Banna Hotel	Jīnbǎnnà jiǔdiàn	金版纳酒店
Jinghong Airport	Jǐnghóng jīchǎng	景洪机场
Jinghong Bus Station	Jǐnghóng kèyùnzhàn	景洪客运站
Lancang River	Láncāng jiāng	澜沧江
Manting Park	Màntīng gōngyuán	曼听公园
Meimei Café	Měiměi kāfēitīng	美美咖啡厅
PSB Jinghong	n/a	n/a
Sanchahe Nature Reserve	Sānchàhé zìrán bǎohùqū	三岔河自然保护区
Xishuangbanna	Xīshuāngbǎnnà	西双版纳
Xishuangbanna People's Hospital	Xīshuāngbǎnnàzhōu rénmín yīyuàn	西双版纳州人民医院
Xishuangbanna Tropical Flower & Plant Garden	Xīshuāngbǎnnà rèdài huāhuìyuán	西双版纳热带花卉园

Sichuan and Chongqing

WORD OF MOUTH

"After dinner . . . we took photos of a little boy. He was so cute sitting in his little chair. The parents tried to get him to say hello but he just stared at us. I showed the parents the photos I took and they smiled. We really enjoyed our encounters with the Chinese during our trip and they seemed to enjoy us too."

—monicapileggi

WELCOME TO SICHUAN AND CHONGQING

TOP REASONS TO GO

★ **Emeishan:** Hike 10,000 feet to the top of one of China's holy mountains and a UNESCO World Heritage Site.

★ **Giant Panda Breeding Research Base:** Stroll through the bamboo groves, bone up on the latest in genetic biology and ecological preservation, and check out cute baby pandas.

★ **Horseback riding in Songpan:** Marvel at the raw beauty of northern Sichuan's pristine mountain forests and emerald-green lakes from the back of these gentle beasts.

★ **Liquid Fire:** Savor some of the spiciest food on the planet in Chongqing's many hotpot restaurants.

★ **An engineering miracle or madness:** Enjoy a lazy riverboat ride through the surreal Three Gorges, and stand in awe of one of China's latest engineering feats, the mighty Three Gorges Dam.

QINGHAI

Jiuzhaigou **3**
Natural Preserve ◆

Songpan ○

TIBET

DAXUE SHAN

SHALUI SHAN

Jinsha Jiang (Yangzi)

Dujiangyan **1**

Chengdu ○

Kangding ○

Litang ○

Ya'an ○

Emeishan **2**

Gongga Shan ▲

Leshan ○

SICHUAN

YUNNAN

Jinsha Jiang (Yangzi)

1 **Chengdu.** Sichuan's capital and culinary hub is also one of the last bastions of the art of tea drinking. While bent on modernizing, the capital city still retains its laid-back character. Kick back and enjoy!

2 **Emeishan.** One of China's holy mountains, it has almost 50 km (31 mi) of paths leading to the summit. Take time out to enjoy the lush mountains around Emeishan, which also produce some of the world's best tea.

GETTING ORIENTED

If you're after a China experience where the cuisine is fiery and pandas can be found in the forests gnawing on bamboo, Sichuan Province in southwestern China is a good bet. Sichuan's capital of Chengdu is smack-dab in the middle of the province, and the logical point to begin your sojourn. Chengdu's flat, gridlike layout is ideal for strolls and biking. It's also acclaimed for its many outdoor gear shops that can equip one for any of Sichuan's local and neighboring natural wonders. For those interested in witnessing the mighty Three Gorges Dam, the city of Chongqing, 150 mi southeast of Chengdu, is where the best Yangtze tour boats begin their journey downriver, through the Gorges and to the dam.

3 Juizhaigou Natural Preserve. Nestled between the snowcapped peaks of the Aba Autonomous Prefecture in northern Sichuan lies the Jiuzhaigou Reserve, a wonderland of turquoise.

4 Chongqing. Formerly part of Sichuan proper, Chongqing is its own exploding municipality with more than 15 million residents. Chongqing's meandering alleys will appeal to those who love getting lost in Venice-like twisting streets. This is also the jumping-off point for the Three Gorges river ride.

Updated by
Chris Horton,
Patrick Scally,
Dan Siekman

Renowned for spicy cuisine, giant pandas, beautiful women and fiery tempers, Sichuan is one of China's most interesting and influential provinces. Chongqing is known as China's "mountain city." All those hills are the reason why its women are famous for their shapely legs. Vast and modern, while still retaining many of its old buildings—for now—Chongqing features a nice balance of modern Chinese dynamism and Sichuan spice.

With a population of more than 100 million, Sichuan is known for its people's proud, independent spirits. One of the most famous Sichuanese ever, former paramount leader of China Deng Xiaoping, was purged from the Communist Party twice before taking control and launching the reforms that have converted the country from economic pariah to the second-largest economy in the world.

Sichuan's resilience met what may have been its biggest test ever with the 2008 Wenzhou earthquake that claimed nearly 90,000 lives. Most of the important cultural sites that were damaged in the earthquake have since been repaired, and the province is now moving forward again.

Often referred to as Szechuan cooking in the West, Sichuan's cuisine is famous in China for its liberal use of the chili pepper as well as the curious, numbing flavor of the *huajiao*, also known as the Sichuan pepper. Dishes such as mapo tofu, eggplant in fish sauce, kungpao chicken, and the ubiquitous hotpot are popular dishes that originated in this part of the country.

The variety of ingredients found in Sichuan cooking are a reflection of the province's diverse topography. The eastern half of Sichuan is dominated by the Sichuan Basin, an area of high agricultural output that in dynastic times was fought over by rival kingdoms. Heading westward, the basin gives way to mountains that become increasingly awe-inspiring as Han Sichuan yields to the province's Tibetan regions.

Sichuan's capital of Chengdu is currently one of China's most happening cities. During the day, leisure-loving residents sip on tea while chatting or playing mah-jongg. When the sun goes down, there is plenty of amazing food to sample from around China and the world, with one of China's best live music scenes waiting afterward.

Once the capital of Sichuan—and China—the megacity of Chongqing sits to the east of the province and now answers directly to Beijing. With the completion of the Three Gorges Dam, which allows seagoing barges to make it all the way to Chongqing, the city is now changing faster than ever in its new role as Western China's seaport.

PLANNING

WHEN TO GO

Chengdu and eastern Sichuan are hot and humid, with temperatures around 35° to 50°F in winter and 75° to 85°F in summer. Chongqing is known for its broiling summer temperatures—sometimes over 100°F. The western plateau is cold but intensely sunny (bring sunscreen and sunglasses). In winter temperatures drop to -15°F. Summers are around 65°F.

GETTING HERE AND AROUND

Traveling in and out of Sichuan and Chongqing has never been more convenient. The rapid modernization of the two cities and their surrounding rural areas has changed what was once a difficult area for traveling into a corridor of connectivity within and without the region.

AIR TRAVEL

Chengdu and Chongqing are both modern cities with international airports serving regional, domestic, and international destinations. Since the launch of their new high-speed rail link, the two cities are no longer connected by flights. Sichuan Airlines is the largest local airline and serves smaller destinations throughout the province, including Jiuzhaigou.

BUS TRAVEL

Taking buses around Sichuan is a convenient and economical option for short-distance travel. It is worth keeping abreast of the weather situation in western Sichuan, as heavy rains in the area can cause large—occasionally fatal—landslides that can close roads for days.

TRAIN TRAVEL

Chengdu and Chongqing are both major hubs in China's national rail network. Chengdu is one of the only Chinese cities with a rail link to Lhasa. The 44-hour train ride passes through Qinghai Province before entering Tibet.

MONEY MATTERS

Banks and ATMs are plentiful in cities and tourist destinations throughout this region, but it is worth keeping in mind that sometimes ATMs can break down. It is advisable to secure sufficient cash before going into remote areas, just in case. Foreign bank cards are sometimes not accepted by ATMs in smaller banks—stick with Bank of China for cash withdrawals.

RESTAURANTS

Eating out in Sichuan and Chongqing can be a boisterous affair, with the tables surrounding you filled with loud, animated diners. Almost anything in these parts comes with some serious spice, so if you can't take the heat it's worthwhile to learn the phrase "Bu lade" (boo-lah-duh, "not spicy") to make sure the staff know to take it easy on the chilies. In addition to great Sichuan cuisine, Chengdu and Chongqing also have a growing number of quality international restaurants.

HOTELS

Chinese-run hotels in Sichuan and Chongqing offer adequate service and amenities for a reasonable price, but English isn't usually spoken by many staff. There are more and more international five-star hotels in Chengdu and Chongqing, which offer international levels of service and high-end dining. In destinations such as Jiuzhaigou and Ciqikou, guesthouses are also an option.

WHAT IT COSTS IN YUAN					
	¢	$	$$	$$$	$$$$
Restaurants	under Y25	Y25–Y49	Y50–Y99	Y100–Y165	over Y165
Hotels	under Y700	Y700–Y1,099	Y1,100–Y1,399	Y1,400–Y1,800	over Y1,800

Restaurant prices are for a main course, excluding tips (there is no sales/retail tax in China). Hotel prices are for a standard double room, including taxes.

VISITOR INFORMATION

Chengdu and Chongqing don't offer much useful English-language visitor information, but hotels, cafés, and guesthouses are good places to ask around. Major parks such as Jiuzhaigou often have English-language materials and maps at their entrances, plus signposting in English, even if park staff speak only Chinese.

TOURS

Western Sichuan Tours (✉ *13 Yulin Nan Lu, 6-3-15, Chengdu* ☎ *139/8003–5421* ⊕ *www.wstourix.com* is a travel agency offering tours focused on Sichuan's mountainous and rugged west.

Intowestchina (✉ *71 Qinglong Ji, Chengdu* ☎ *028/8558–2963* ⊕ *www.intowestchina.com* offers tours of Chengdu, western Sichuan and destinations beyond including Shangri-La and Tibet.

SICHUAN

Throughout history, Sichuan has been known as the "Storehouse of Heaven," due not only to its abundance of flora and fauna, but also to its varied cuisine, culture, and customs.

Geographically, it's dominated by the Sichuan Basin, which covers much of the eastern part of the province. The Sichuan Basin—also known as the Red Basin because of the reddish sandstone that predominates in the region—accounts for almost half its area. On all sides the province is surrounded by mountains: the Dabashan in the northeast, the Wushan

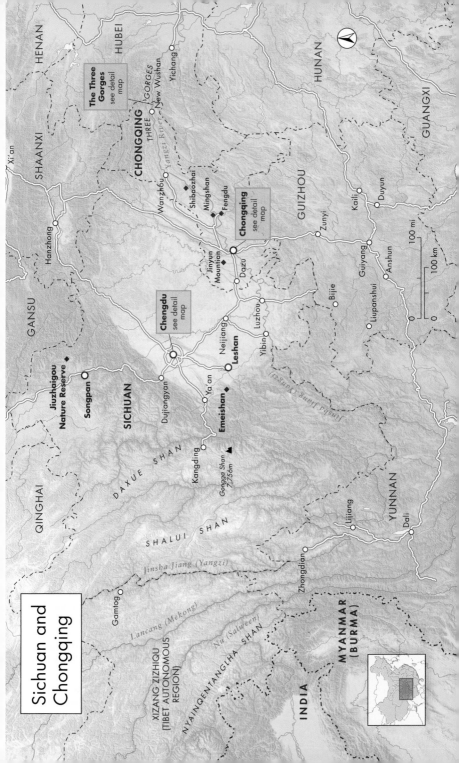

in the east, the Qinghai Massif in the west, and the Yunnan and Guizhou plateaus in the south.

Sichuan's relative isolation made communication with the outside world difficult and fostered the development of valley, plains, and mountain cultures with distinct characteristics. The Tibetans living deep in the foothills of the Himalayas share space with Qiang, Hui, and Han settlers. In the mountains to the south toward Yunnan, there are dozens of peoples living side by side, such as the Yi, Naxi, Mosu, Miao, and Bai. These cultures all have their own religions and philosophies, with Buddhism and Taoism the dominant religions in the area.

The mountain of Emeishan is a pilgrimage site for millions of Buddhists, as is the Great Buddha in nearby Leshan. Its distance from the epicenter spared the area from any major quake damage. In Songpan, north of the capital city of Chengdu, Muslims, Buddhists, Christians, and Taoists live alongside each other in harmony. One of China's most famous national parks is in Jiuzhaigou, far to the north in Aba Prefecture. The natural springs, dense forests, dramatic cliffs, and sprawling waterfalls make Jiuzhaigou Nature Reserve one of the country's most popular tourist destinations. And if you need more urban comforts, Chengdu is an increasingly international city with food from all over the world, top-notch hotels, dizzying nightlife, and what must be more teahouses per square inch than any other city in the world.

REGIONAL TOURS
The China Culture Center in Beijing offers excellent custom tour options for Sichuan with English-speaking guides, including trips to the panda reserves. Visit ⊕ *www.chinaculturecenter.org.*

CHENGDU

240 km (149 mi; 2 hrs by train) northwest of Chongqing; 1,450 km (900 mi; 25 hrs by train) southwest of Beijing; 1,300 km (806 mi; 27 hrs by train) northwest of Hong Kong.

Don't go to Chengdu when you're young—is what rural Sichuanese parents advise children who might be corrupted by this modern, energetic city. But despite the warnings, Chengdu is what you want it to be: while some visitors seek out the pulsating nightlife, others are happy to while away the days strolling in the city's many parks or sipping tea and cracking sunflower seeds in one of its multitude of tea gardens.

The city is changing at a dizzying pace. Much of the Old City has been razed to make room for modern high-rises. But there is still much to see in terms of history and culture. Temples and memorials demonstrate Chengdu's position as the cosmopolitan capital of Western China. The city is also a great center for Sichuan cooking, which many believe is the best in China. The Sichuanese cuisine is famous for its spicy peppers and strong flavors. Chengdu has too many good restaurants to list, and the hole-in-the-wall around the corner may serve the tastiest Sichuan dishes you'll eat.

All roads into Southwest China lead through Chengdu. As the gateway to Tibet, this city is the place to secure the permits and supplies needed

Plight of the Panda

Mysterious, endangered, and cuddly are a few of the monikers typically associated with China's best-known symbol. Dwindling in population would be another. Given China's recent economic reforms, pandas face a mixed future. On the one hand, economic growth and overpopulation are increasingly affecting their habitat. On the other hand, more state and international resources are pouring into special research institutes like Sichuan's Panda Breeding Research Base. What will be the ultimate fate

of these stoic creatures? It's hard to say. One thing is certain though: those who visit ecological panda preserves are part of the solution.

for your trip there. Journeys south to Yunnan or north to Xi'an pass through here as well. Lying in the middle of Sichuan Province, Chengdu is also a good base for excursions to the scenic spots dotting Sichuan.

⚠ Like many big cities in China, Chengdu is very polluted. Bring eyedrops, anti-bacterial wipes, and possibly even a face mask.

GETTING HERE AND AROUND

Chengdu is the transportation hub of Western China. Bus, train, and plane connections are as convenient as they get in China. ■TIP→ The Chengdu Tourism Bureau has a shuttle bus between the city's three major sights: Du Fu's Cottage, the Memorial of the Marquis of Wu, and the Tomb of Emperor Wang Jian. With your ticket stub, you can hop aboard the bus free of charge. The bus leaves every 20 minutes.

Chengdu is built along a main north–south artery and surrounded by three ring roads. Bikes are a great way to get around. If you are on foot, many of the city's sights are within walking distance of Tian Fu Plaza. Snag a cab or brave the buses if you are going farther afield.

AIR TRAVEL Chengdu Shuangliu International Airport is about 16 km (10 mi) southwest of the city. From here you can fly to Beijing (2½ hours), Guangzhou (two hours), Kunming (1 hour), Shanghai (2½ hours), or many other domestic destinations. There are a few international connections, but these may be canceled without notice.

Bus service links the airport terminal and downtown Chengdu, with Bus 303 traveling to the center of town. Taxis should cost about Y55.

BUS TRAVEL There are three main bus stations in Chengdu. The Xinnanmen Bus Station, in the city center, has buses to almost every town in Sichuan. The Wuguiqiao Bus Station, east of the city, is used mainly for travelers to Chongqing or Yibin. The Chadianzi Bus Station, in the northwestern part of the city, has buses to destinations in the mountains to the north and west (including Jiuzhaigou and Songpan).

9

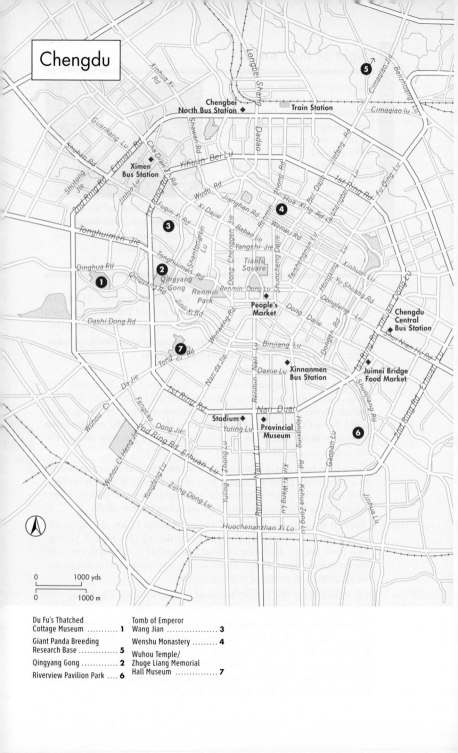

Chengdu

Chengbei
North Bus Station ◆

Train Station

Xinhua Xi Rd

Longbei Shang

Guankang Lu

Shuhan Rd

Ermun Rd

Cha Dian Zi Rd

Shawan Rd

Dadao

Cimaqiao Jie

Baizhang Jie

Cimaqiao lu

Shytong Jie

2nd Ring Rd

Jinlu Lu

Fuqin Rd

Qinhua Rd

Tonghuimen Jie

Ximen
Bus Station ◆

Yihuan Bei Lu

Wudu Rd

Jianghan Rd

Xi Dajie

Zhong Rd

Renmin

Hua Xing Rd

Bei Dajie

Jiefang Rd

1st Ring Rd

Fu Qing Li

❸

Fuqin Xi Rd

Shantongren

Tonghuimen Rd

Dong Chenggen Jie

Babao Jie

Yangshi Jie

Tianfu
Square

Wenwu Rd

Lisheng'an Rd

❹

Qinghua Rd

❶

Qingyang Rd

❷

Qingyang
Gong

Jinli Xi Rd

Renmin
Park

Renmin Dong Lu

Shuncheng Dajie

Taishengnan Lu

Xinhua Lu

Yu Shuang Rd

Hongxing

Dashi Dong Rd

People's
Market

Dong Dajie

Dongfeng Lu

Chengdu
Central
Bus Station ◆

Wenweng Rd

Binjiang Lu

Dengan Rd

Anr Nan He Rd

❼

Tong Ci Rd

Nan da Jie

Daxue Lu

Xinnanmen
Bus Station ◆

Renmin

Juimei Bridge
Food Market

Shuijiang Rd

1st Ring Rd

Da Jie

Fangcao
Dong Jie

Stadium ◆

Yuling Lu

Nan Duan

Provincial
Museum ◆

Hongxing Rd

❻

Wuhou Ci

2nd Ring Rd Erhuan Lu

Wuhou Ci Heng Jie

Zijing Lu

Yongfang Lu

Zijing Dong Lu

Zhong Lu

Renmin

Xin Xi Wang Lu

Kehua Zong Lu

Gaopan Lu

Jinhua Lu

Ermun Rd

2nd Ring Rd

Huochenanzhan Xi Lu

0   1000 yds
0   1000 m

TRAIN TRAVEL Chengdu sits on the Kunming–Beijing railway line, therefore connections are reliable. The Chengdu Railway Station is in the northern part of the city. It's a Y20 cab ride from Tianfu Plaza.

SAFETY AND PRECAUTIONS

As in most areas across China, foreign travelers are generally not targets of violent crime. The biggest threats to personal safety are from traffic accidents and vehicle collisions with pedestrians. Stay alert for vehicles on both streets and sidewalks, and do not assume that drivers will follow traffic laws. Pickpockets, bag-snatchers, and other thieves can also be a problem. Stay alert on the street and while riding trains and buses, and don't leave valuables unsecured in hotel rooms.

TIMING

Chengdu deserves at least a few days, but travelers coming from remote areas of China may wish to stay longer to take a break in the city's increasingly cosmopolitan atmosphere.

TOURS

A good resource for package and individual tours in Chengdu and throughout Sichuan is the tour agency Intowestchina.

ESSENTIALS

Air Contact Chengdu Shuangliu International Airport (☎ 028/8520–5555 ⊕ www.cdairport.com).

Bank Bank of China (✉ Renmin Nan Lu).

Bus Contacts Chadianzi Bus Station (✉ Sanhuan Lu). **Wuguiqiao Bus Station** (✉ Dongguicun Sanzhu). **Xinanmen Bus Station** (✉ 57 Linjiang Lu).

Consulate U.S. Consulate (✉ 4 Lingshiguan Lu, Chengdu ☎ 028/8558–3992 ⊕ http://chengdu.usembassy-china.org.cn/).

Medical Assistance For emergency medical assistance (✉ PSB; Foreigner's Police, Wenwu Lu, part of Xinhua Dong Lu; 40 Wenmiaohou Jie ☎ 110 or 028/8674–4683) anywhere in China, dial 120; for all other emergencies call 110. **International Medical Center and Foreigners Clinic** (✉ 37 Guo Xue Lu, Chengdu ☎ 028/8542–2408).

Train Contact Chengdu Train Station (Erhuan Lu ☎ 028/8370–9580).

Visitor and Tour Info China International Travel Service (CITS✉ 65 Renmin Nan Lu, at Er Duan ☎ 028/6648–8000 or 028/6648–8333). **Intowestchina** (✉ 71 ☎ 028/8558–2963 ⊕ www.intowestchina.com).

EXPLORING CHENGDU

TOP ATTRACTIONS

Du Fu's Thatched Cottage Museum *(Du Fu Caotang)* is named for the famous poet Du Fu (712–770) of the Tang Dynasty, whose poetry continues to be read today. A Manchurian, he came to Chengdu from Xi'an and built a small hut overlooking the bamboo and plum tree–lined Huanhua River. During the four years he spent here he wrote more than 240 poems. After his death the area became a garden; a temple was then added during the Northern Song Dynasty (960–1126). A replica of his cottage now stands among several other structures, all built during the Qing Dynasty. Some of Du Fu's calligraphy and poems are on display

The Wenshu Monastery in Chengdu.

here. English-speaking guides are available, as are English translations of his poems. ✉ *37 Qinghua Lu* ☎ *028/8731–9258* ⊕ *www.dfmuseum. org.cn* 🎫 *Y60* ⏱ *May–Oct., daily 7:30–7; Nov.–Apr., daily 8–6:00.*

☾ The **Giant Panda Breeding Research Base** *(Daxiongmao Bowuguan)* is
★ worth the 45-minute drive to walk the peaceful bamboo groves, snap pictures of the lolling pandas, and catch a glimpse of the tiny baby pandas that are born with startling regularity. After all, who doesn't love pandas? For those interested in efforts to save these creatures, the research center is excellent. Crews of scientists help pandas breed and care for the young in a safe, controlled environment. Guests can also briefly hold a baby or juvenile giant panda for a donation to the center of Y1,000. Visitors who have done it report that handlers are very conscientious about the health and safety of the animals while they are being held, and if they don't deem the pandas ready to be held money is refunded and visitors must come back for another try. ■TIP➔ **Visit early in the morning, when the pandas are most active.** To get here, book a tour through your hotel for about Y70 per person or take Chengdu Tourism Bus Line 902 for just Y1 from Linjiang Lu, a few meters west of the Xinnanmen Bus Station. ✉ *26 Panda Rd. (Jiefang Lu)* ☎ *028/8351–0033* ⊕ *www.panda.org.cn* ✉pandabase@tom.com 🎫 *Y60* ⏱ *Daily 7–6:30.*

Built during the Tang Dynasty, **Qingyang Gong** is the oldest Taoist temple in the city, and one of the most famous in China. Six courtyards open out onto each other before arriving at the sculptures of two goats, which represent one of the earthly incarnations of Lao Tzu (the legendary founder of Taoism). If you arrive midmorning, you can watch the day's first worshippers before the stampede of afternoon pilgrims. The temple grounds are filled with nuns and monks training at the Two Immortals Monastery, the only such facility in Southwest China. A small teahouse is on the premises. ⊠ *9 Yihuan Lu at Xi Erduan* ☎ *028/8776–6584* ⊕ *www.qingyanggong.com* ✉ *Y10* ⊗ *Daily 8–6:30.*

★ Named after Manjusri, the bodhisattva of transcendent wisdom, **Wenshu Monastery** (*Wenshu Yuan*) is one of the most important Zen Buddhist monasteries in China,

and has been around almost as long as the religion itself. It was originally constructed during the Sui Dynasty (617 bc–605 bc), around the same time of Zen Buddhism's emergence in China. The monastery and accompanying temples have since been destroyed several times, most notably during the Ming Dynasty, after which the monks are said to have continued sitting among the ruins chanting sutras. It is notable for hundreds of antique statues crafted from a variety of materials that have survived upheavals of times past better than the actual buildings. The attractive 11-tiered Thousand Buddha Peace Pagoda is actually a rather late addition—it was built in 1988 based off an original Sui Dynasty pagoda. The on-site tea garden is a great place to relax in the afternoon. ⊠ *15 Wenshu Yuan Jie, off Renmin Zhong Lu* ✉ *Y5* ⊗ *Daily 8–6.*

The **Wuhou Temple** (*Wuhou Ci*) complex houses the **Zhuge Liang Memorial Hall Museum**, a shrine to the heroes that made the Shu Kingdom legendary during the Three Kingdoms Period. The temple here was constructed in 221 to entomb the earthly remains of Shu Emperor Liu Bei. During the Ming Dynasty, Liu Bei's subjects were also housed here, most notably Zhuge Liang. Liu Bei's most trusted adviser during the Three Kingdoms Period, Zhuge Liang is a legendary figure in Sichuan, and in some respects more honored than his master. The temple burned during the wars that toppled the Ming Dynasty and was rebuilt in 1671–72 during the Qing Dynasty. The main shrine, Zhaolie Temple, is dedicated to Liu Bei; the rear shrine, Wu Hou Temple, to Zhuge Liang. There is also the Sworn Brotherhood Shrine, which commemorates Liu Bei, Zhang Fei, and Guan Yu's "Oath in the Peach Garden." English guides are available for Y80 for groups up to 10 people.

The Sichuan Opera performs here nightly from 7:30 to 10. The Y180 ticket is expensive, but the face-changing, fire-breathing, lyre-playing ensemble might make you forget that. If that doesn't work, get a free massage from one of the elegantly dressed masseuses touring the audience area. ⊠ *231 Wuhou Ci Da Jie* ☎ *028/8555–2397* ⊕ *www.wuhouci.net.cn* ✉ *Y60* ⊗ *Daily 8–9.*

9

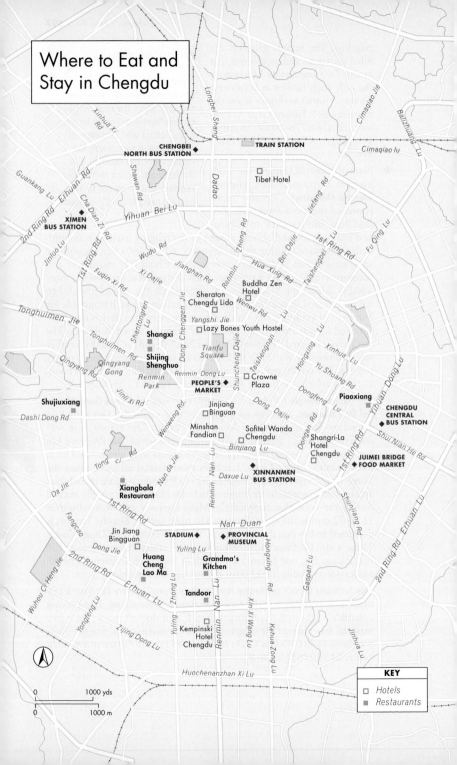

Where to Eat and Stay in Chengdu

CHENGBEI NORTH BUS STATION ◆
TRAIN STATION
Tibet Hotel □

Longbei Shang
Cimaqiao Jie
Balizhuang Lu
Cimaqiao Lu

Xinhua Xi Rd
Guankang Lu
2nd Ring Rd · Erhuan Rd
Shawan Rd
Dadao
Jiefang Rd
1st Ring Rd.
Fu Qing Lu

XIMEN BUS STATION ◆
Cha Dian Zi Rd
Yihuan Bei Lu
Wudu Rd
Zhong Rd
Renmin
Hua Xing Rd
Bei Dajie
Taishengbei Lu

Jinluo Lu
1st Ring Rd
Fuqin Xi Rd
Xi Dajie
Jianghan Rd
Buddha Zen Hotel □
Wenwu Rd
Taishengnan

Tonghuimen Jie
Shantongren Lu
Dong Chengen Jie
Sheraton Chengdu Lido □
Yangshi Jie
Lazy Bones Youth Hostel □

Shangxi ■
Shijing Shenghuo ■
Tianfu Square
Shuncheng Dajie
Hongxing Lu
Xinhua Lu
Yihuan Dong Lu

Qingyang Rd
Qingyang Gong
Renmin Park
Renmin Dong Lu
Crowne Plaza □
Dong Dajie
Piaoxiang ■
CHENGDU CENTRAL BUS STATION ◆

Shujiuxiang ■
Dashi Dong Rd
Jinli Xi Rd
Wenweng Rd
Jinjiang Binguan □
Dongfeng Lu
Dongan Rd
Shui Nian He Lu

Tong ci Rd
Da Jie
Minshan Fandian □
Sofitel Wanda Chengdu □
Binjiang Lu
Shangri-La Hotel Chengdu □
Shunjiang Rd
JUIMEI BRIDGE FOOD MARKET ◆

Xiangbala Restaurant ■
Nan da Jie
Renmin Nan Lu
Daxue Lu
XINNANMEN BUS STATION ◆
1st Ring Rd · Erhuan Lu

Fangcao
1st Ring Rd
Nan Duan
Hongxing Lu
Gaopan Lu

Jin Jiang Bingguan □
STADIUM ◆
Yuling Lu
PROVINCIAL MUSEUM ◆

Wuhou Ci Heng Jie
2nd Ring Rd
Erhuan Lu
Dong Jie
Huang Cheng Lao Ma ■
Grandma's Kitchen ■
Xin Xi Wang Lu
Kehua Zong Lu
Jinhua Lu

Yongfeng Lu
Zijing Dong Lu
Zhong Lu
Yuling
Tandoor ■
Renmin Nan Lu

Kempinski Hotel Chengdu □

Huochenanzhan Xi Lu

KEY
□ Hotels
■ Restaurants

0   1000 yds
0   1000 m

WORTH NOTING

The four-story wooden pavilion in **Riverview Pavilion Park** *(Wangjiang Lou Gongyuan)*, dating from the Qing Dynasty, offers splendid views of the Fu River and the surrounding countryside. The poet Xue Tao, who lived in Chengdu during the Tang Dynasty, was said to have spent time near the river, from which she apparently drew water to make paper for her poems. The pavilion stands amid more than 150 species of bamboo, a plant revered by the poet. ⊠ *30 Wangjiang Lu* ☎ *028/8522–3389* ⊕ *www.wangjianglou.com* 🎫 *Y20* ⊘ *Daily 8–6.*

NEED A BREAK?

Not many people know that some of the best green tea comes from the mountains of western Sichuan. In Chengdu, *hua cha* (flower tea) is the most popular. Hua cha has such a potent aroma because it has been doctored up with jasmine or chrysanthemum. If you want to sample some good tea, head to People's Park, Wenshu Temple, or the recently redeveloped *kuan xiangzi* and *zhai xiangzi* (wide and narrow alley) area.

In the northwest section of Chengdu stands the 49-foot-high, 262-ft-diameter **Tomb of Emperor Wang Jian** *(Wang Jian Mu)*, which honors the ruler of the Kingdom of Shu from ad 847 to 918. Made of red sandstone, it is distinguished by the male figures that support the platform for the coffin and the carvings of musicians, thought to be the best surviving record of a Tang Dynasty musical troupe. There are a lovely park and teahouse on the grounds, both quite popular among locals. ⊠ *Off Fuqin Dong Lu* 🎫 *Y30* ⊘ *Daily 8–4:50.*

WHERE TO EAT

In Chengdu, hotpot is easy to find. A walk down just about any street will turn up at least one restaurant serving this local specialty: a boiling vat of chili oil, red peppers, and mouth-numbing spices into which you dip duck intestines, beef tripe, chicken livers, or (for the less adventurous) bamboo shoots and mushrooms. Hotpot restaurants tend to be open-air affairs, often spilling out onto the sidewalk.

$-$$
AMERICAN

✕ **Grandma's Kitchen.** If you're sick of hotpot, this is the place to go. Hamburgers and other American foods are served up at decent prices. It's an excellent choice for breakfast, but also a good standby any time of day. The Renmin Nan Lu branch is cozy (perhaps too cozy), but most people are too busy enjoying their food to notice. ⊠ *143 Kehua Bei Lu* ☎ *028/8524–2835* ⊠ *22 Renmin Nan Lu, at Si Duan* ☎ *028/8555–3856* 🗖 *AE, MC, V.*

$$$-$$$$
SICHUAN
★

✕ **Huang Cheng Lao Ma.** Built and run by artists, this amazing restaurant on Second Ring Road South is a must for visitors to Chengdu. Huang Cheng Lao Ma is a massive brick-and-stone building with sculpted pillars rising up either side with a stone facade depicting scenes from old Chengdu. The hotpot here comes in traditional spicy varieties and also wild mushroom, seafood, and "soft/clear soup" styles (soft soup—*qing tang*—means no spices!). Not only will you get an idea of the creativity in architecture and cuisine in modern China, but there are often photo exhibitions from local artists. The top floor is a high-end teahouse and performance area. ⊠ *20 Erhuan Lu, Nan San Duan* ☎ *028/8513–9999* ⊕ *www.hclm.net* 🗖 *AE, DC, MC, V.*

$$–$$$
SICHUAN

✕ **Piaoxiang.** This restaurant is renowned for its efforts to update Sichuanese dishes, transforming traditional into something wonderful. Simple fare like *dou hua* (soft tofu) and *hue guo rou* (twice-cooked pork) is fresh and tasty, and includes much less oil than your average spot. The menu is mostly ribs, tofu, and chili sauce, but more refined than the typical street stall. ⊠ *60 Yihuan Lu, Dong San Duan* ☎ *028/8437–9999* ☰ *No credit cards.*

$$$
CHINESE FUSION

★

✕ **Shangxi.** Pan-Asian ingredients imbued with Sichuanese flavors and presented in the style of European haute cuisine are Shangxi's specialty: it's a pricey but worthwhile splurge. Housed in a building on the recently redeveloped historic Zhai Xiangzi (Narrow Alley), dining areas are ranged around a beautiful stone courtyard with trees and a koi pond. Try crispy shredded rabbit, "fish fragrance" lobster balls, or a wild-greens salad. The menu is in English with photos. ⊠ *38 Zhai Xiangzi* ☎ *028/8669–9115* ☰ *MC, V* ☉ *10–8.*

$
SICHUAN

✕ **Shijing Shenghuo.** Steer clear of this Sichuanese eatery if your palette can't take a little fire—most dishes have liberal amounts of hot pepper. Shijing Shenghuo's name translates literally as "life in the marketplace," and it's located on Jing Xiangzi parallel to the Zhai Xiangzi dining and shopping street. Dishes include Sichuan favorites like kungpao chicken, "pockmarked granny's tofu," and "lion's head" pork meatballs. If the culinary heat becomes too great, it can be doused with some rice or a sip of one of a wide variety of local clear grain alcohols. ⊠ *8 Jing Xiangzi, Zhai Xiangzi/Kuan Xiangzi* ☎ *028/8663–3618* ☰ *No credit cards* ☉ *10–9.*

$$$$
SICHUAN

★

✕ **Shujiuxiang.** Private rooms, tasteful decoration, and unusual ingredients set one of Chengdu's most upscale hotpot restaurants apart from the numerous other joints that crowd the city. Diners order boiling pots of clear broth or fiery spicy-numb broth in which to cook exotic ingredients such as asparagus (seasonal), wild Yunnan mushrooms, and—for the adventurous—goose intestines. Of course, the usual hotpot goodies are also available, including shaved beef and mutton and a range of veggies and tofus. Waiters are attentive, but don't speak much English. Room fees range from Y100 for a room that accommodates up to five people to Y300 for a room that fits more than 20. ⊠ *5 Baihua Xi Lu, Qingyang DistrictChengdu* ☎ *028/8703–2499* ☰ *No credit cards.*

$$–$$$
INDIAN

✕ **Tandoor.** Just a couple of blocks southwest from the American Consulate, this northern Indian restaurant serves Chengdu's best Indian fare. The decor, a sophisticated combination of wood and mirrors, makes a meal here seem like a special occasion. Tandoor is named after the traditional clay oven used in India, so it's no surprise that the devoted Punjabi chef serves up delicious tandoori chicken and freshly baked flatbreads. ⊠ *Behind the Sunjoy Inn, 34 Renmin Nan Lu, Si Duan* ☎ *028/8555–1958* ☰ *AE, DC, MC, V.*

¢–$
TIBETAN

✕ **Xiangbala Restaurant.** For a taste of Tibet, come here. Groups of Tibetan cowboys crowd around tables shooting the breeze as solitary monks eat quietly in the corner. Everything is traditional—the kitchen makes its own yogurt and uses yak meat from the grasslands. The tea, which arrives in a big pot, is delicious. The Tibetan- and Chinese-language menus have pictures, which smooths the ordering process somewhat. Some bread, yak noodles, and a few dumplings will satisfy almost anyone. The restaurant sits on a street of Tibetan establishments near Wuhou Temple. ⊠ *Wuhou Ci Dong Jie Xin 3, Fu 3* ☎ *028/8558–6009 or 138/8181–1045* ▭ *No credit cards.*

WHERE TO STAY

¢ ▣ **Buddha Zen Hotel.** Drawing inspiration from the nearby Wenshu Zen Buddhist monastery, this reasonably priced boutique hotel has carefully designed antique wooden decorations, a peaceful courtyard, wonderful staff, and good food. Located on the Wenshu Fang walking street, it is very popular and often fully booked in advance: reserve early and try to get a room facing the inner courtyard rather than the street for the most Zen-like experience. The Chinese restaurant is attractive and serves good food; staff members do an excellent job of giving recommendations and directions to places around the city. **Pros:** good location and service. **Cons:** street outside can be noisy; restaurant is not vegetarian. ⊠ *B6-6 Wenshu Fang, near Wenshu Temple* ☎ *028/8692–9898* ⊕ *www.buddhazenhotel.com* ☝ *35 rooms* ♨ *In-room: a/c, safe, Internet. In-hotel: restaurant, laundry service* ▭ *AE, MC, V.*

$–$$ ▣ **Crowne Plaza.** In the heart of Chengdu, this luxury hotel owned by the U.K.-based Intercontinental Hotel group is convenient for strolls around downtown, including the central Tianfu Square. The hotel underwent a light renovation in 2010, so decor is bright and new, if a little staid. The restaurants are not as snazzy as those at the other top-notch hotels, with the exception of the attractive Japanese restaurant. **Pros:** clean and new; near shopping. **Cons:** lacks character; staff's English could be better. ⊠ *31 Zong Fu Jie* ☎ *028/8678–6666; 800/830–2628 toll-free (in U.S.)* ⊕ *www.crowneplaza.com* ☝ *402 rooms, 80 suites* ♨ *In-room: Internet, satellite TV. In-hotel: 4 restaurants, bars, gym, pool, business center, laundry service* ▭ *AE, DC, MC, V.*

$$ ▣ **Jinjiang Binguan.** For years this was the city's best hotel—foreign dignitaries and bigwigs from Beijing could always be found milling around the lobby. Now, with five-star hotels all over the city, the Jinjiang has lost a little of its luster. But it has nice in-hotel shopping, one of the finest Chinese restaurants in the city, and a dance club that is surprisingly popular. Although a bit dated, the guest rooms have cable TV, Internet, and spacious bathrooms. **Pros:** great riverside location; large rooms. **Cons:** basic; not very exciting. ⊠ *80 Renmin Nan Lu, Er Duan* ☎ *028/8550–6666* ⊕ *www.jjhotel.com* ☝ *456 rooms* ♨ *In-room: Internet. In-hotel: 3 restaurants, bar, laundry service, Internet terminal* ▭ *AE, MC, V.*

$$ ▣ **Kempinski Hotel Chengdu.** Although it's generally geared toward business travelers, leisure explorers can grab great deals at the Kempinski, especially on last-minute bookings. The rooms are large, modern, and clean, with polished marble bathrooms. Staff members work hard to be helpful. The breakfast buffet has good variety, and the Harmony Chinese Restaurant and German deli are eminently serviceable—an added bonus is the Munich-style Paulaner brewhouse and restaurant with nightly band performances. **Pros:** good value; near the airport **Cons:** far from some tourist sites; no pool. ⊠ *42 Renmin Nan Lu, Si Duan,* ☎ *028/8526–9999* ⊕ *www.kempinski.com* ☝ *471 rooms* ♨ *In-room:*

a/c, safe, Internet, satellite TV. In-hotel: 4 restaurants, bar, gym, spa, day care, laundry service = *AE, MC, V.*

¢   **Lazy Bones Hostel.** The exceedingly helpful staff members here speak better English than those at most of Chengdu's five-star hotels, which might make the basic private rooms and occasionally frat house–like atmosphere a passable choice for Western travelers. Lazy Bones is a standard backpacker hostel with an attached café/bar, pool, and Ping Pong tables, but it is generally well managed and pleasant, with a vibrant atmosphere. The location in the central business district is convenient, and the private rooms are clean if no-frills. **Pros:** good value; helpful English-speaking staff. **Cons:** small rooms; lacks many amenities. ⊠ *16 Yangshi Jie, Renmin Zhong Lu* ☎ *028/6537–7889* ⊕ *www. chengduhostel.com* ⊅ *20 private rooms* ⌂ *In-room: a/c. In-hotel: restaurant, bar, laundry facilities, laundry service, Wi-Fi* = *No credit cards.*

$ **Minshan Fandian.** The Minshan leapt from four to five stars after a major renovation in 2010, and seems out to prove a point: a locally owned hotel can match and even exceed the quality and value of international chains. Decorations manage to be luxurious but restrained, with relaxing earth tones created out of marble and wood and embellished with touches of glass and copper. The comfortable guest rooms have large beds and look out either on the Fu River or toward downtown, as well as featuring nice touches like espresso machines and separate showers and bathtubs. Staff members generally communicate well in English, and there are good Chinese and French restaurants. **Pros:** great value; excellent service. **Cons:** noisy streets outside. ⊠ *55 Renmin Nan Lu, Er Duan* ☎ *028/8558–3333* ⊕ *www.minshan.com.cn* ⊅ *383 rooms* ⌂ *In-room: safe, Internet. In-hotel: 3 restaurants, bar, pool, gym, laundry service, Wi-Fi* = *AE, DC, MC, V.*

$$$ **Shangri-La Hotel, Chengdu.** Luxury and exceptional service are hallmarks of the Singapore-based Shangri-La chain, and the Chengdu property delivers both. From the moment one walks into the expansive marble lobby there is always a cheerful employee nearby to offer assistance. On the first floor are the international fusion restaurant Café Z, which serves great breakfast, and Mooney's Irish Pub, a popular nighttime gathering spot for Chengdu expatriates. The guest rooms are larger than most in China and decorated in soothing dark tones. **Pros:** great service; good restaurants and bar. **Cons:** slightly inconvenient location. ⊠ *9 Binjiang Dong Lu* ☎ *028/8888–9999* ⊕ *www.shangri-la. com* ⊅ *593 rooms* ⌂ *In-room: safe, coffeemaker, Internet, satellite TV. In-hotel: 3 restaurants, room service, 2 bars, pool, gym, spa, laundry service, Wi-Fi* = *AE, MC, V.*

$$ **Sheraton Chengdu Lido.** In the central business district, the Sheraton Chengdu Lido was one of the city's first luxury hotels. It's still among the best. The rooms are immaculate and very comfortable, and the service is conscientious. Amenities, such as the glass-roofed swimming pool, are world-class. The somewhat northward location puts you closer to many popular attractions than other hotels clustered around the river, including the Giant Panda Breeding Research Base. **Pros:** helpful staff; comfortable, large rooms. **Cons:** room decor is boring. ⊠ *15 Renmin Zhong Lu, Yi Duan* ☎ *028/8676–8999; 800/810–3088 toll-free*

(in U.S.) ⊕ *www.sheraton.com/chengdu* ⇲ *413 rooms* ♿ *In-hotel: 2 restaurants, bar, pool, gym, laundry service, Internet terminals* ▭ *AE, DC, MC, V.*

$$ ⛨ **Sofitel Wanda Chengdu.** A modern glass tower situated along the Fu River, the Sofitel Wanda seems to thrive on the consistency of a major international brand without standing out in most areas, especially customer service. But the restaurants are a bright spot—as might be expected from a European-based hotelier—so expect to be taken on a culinary journey from China to Japan to France. The guest rooms are well appointed, including flat-screen satellite TV, and have comfortable beds and bright, clean bathrooms, but the decorations are a somewhat unappealing jumble of styles. **Pros:** clean and modern; good location. **Cons:** staff sometimes rude; expensive food; noise from street. ⊠ *15 Binjiang Zhong Lu* ☎ *028/6666–9999; 800/830–2688 toll free (in U.S.)* ⊕ *www.sofitel.com* ⇲ *262 rooms, 100 suites* ♿ *In-room: safe, Internet. In-hotel: 3 restaurants, bars, pool, gym* ▭ *AE, MC, V.*

¢–$ ⛨ **Tibet Hotel.** Near the train station and built by the Tibet Autonomous Region government, this hotel is a good option for those planning trips to Tibet. A tourist office in the hotel lobby specializes in travel to Tibet. The Tibetan restaurant, however, suffers from a surprising lack of Tibetan food. The guest rooms are clean and comfortable, and decorated with fabric printed with traditional Tibetan designs. **Pros:** good value; convenient for Tibet trips. **Cons:** far from airport and many dining and nightlife areas. ⊠ *10 Renmin Bei Lu* ☎ *028/8318–3388 or 800/886–5333* ⊕ *www.tibet-hotel.com* ⇲ *260 rooms* ♿ *In-room: Internet. In-hotel: 3 restaurants, Wi-Fi hotspot* ▭ *AE, DC, MC, V.*

NIGHTLIFE AND THE ARTS

The redeveloped old **Zhai Xiangzi**, or Narrow Alley, is a walking street packed with restaurants, bars, shops, and one of the city's many Starbucks outlets—all built in a traditional Chinese style. Flanked by the parallel Kuan Xiangzi and Jing Ziangzi (Wide Alley and Well Alley), it is popular among tourists and locals alike. Chengdu has an increasingly chic and sophisticated bar scene, with more Western-style establishments serving high-quality beer, wine, and mixed drinks. Newcomer **Jellyfish** (⊠ *143 Kehua Bei Lu* ☎ *028/8525–1789*), east of the American Consulate and near Sichuan University, has generated buzz for its innovative, inexpensive, and strong cocktails. **8 trees wine bar** (⊠ *1 Binjiang Lu, storefront 21* ☎ *028/8669–9060*), along the Fu River near downtown, has a large selection of international wines—with an emphasis on French—paired with a medley of tasty international snacks. Near Sichuan University, **The Leg and Whistle** ⊠ *19 Kehua Jie* ☎ *028/8546-1958* has beers from around the world. For a more local experience, visit the massive cluster of bars running along the river on Wangjiang Lu roughly across from the Shangri-La Hotel. Beers are purchased warm the dozen and mixed with ice cubes. Young businessmen wheel and deal and occasionally slip into a local karaoke joint for some tipsy crooning.

■**TIP→** For goings-on, check out the monthly English-language magazine Chengdoo Citylife, available at many bars.

For the classic pub feel, the **Shamrock Irish Bar** (⊠ *15 Renmin Nan Lu, Si Duan* ☎ *028/8523–6158*) is an old standby around the corner from the U.S. Consulate. On weekends this pub is filled with expats, students, and a smattering of travelers to listen to live music or a DJ. Guinness on tap is a bit steep at Y60 but nevertheless refreshing; other beers range from Y20 to Y40. South of the U.S. Consulate is the **Bookworm** (⊠ *Yu-jie East Road 2–7, 28 Renmin Nan Lu* ☎ *028/8552–0117*), a relaxed spot with good coffee, clinking glasses, comfy chairs, and 1,000 books.

SHOPPING

The main shopping street is **Chunxi Lu**, east of Tianfu Square. A good place to shop for souvenirs is **Song Xian Qiao Antique City** (⊠ *22 Huan Hua Bei Lu*), the country's second-largest antiques market, with more than 500 separate stalls selling everything from Mao-era currency to fake Buddha statues to wonderful watercolor paintings. It's near Du Fu's Cottage and Wu Hou Temple. Wenshu Fang near Wenshu Monastery is another of the city's redeveloped pedestrian areas built with traditional architecture. It has a lot of shops for buying souvenirs like tea and local handicrafts, as well restaurants and hotels.

EMEISHAN

★ *100 km (62 mi; 3 hrs by train) southwest of Chengdu.*

The 10,000-foot-high Emeishan (literally, Lofty Eyebrow Mountain) in southern Sichuan is one of China's holiest Buddhist pilgrimage sites. The temples here survived the Cultural Revolution better than most others in China, due in part to courageous monks. Still, of the hundreds of temples that once were found here, only 20 remain. Today it is one of the better-known tourist attractions in the country.

■ **TIP→** When coming to Emeishan, bring enough cash to last your whole visit. There are several ATMs in the area that accept foreign cards, but they can be unreliable, and most are difficult to find or require a long taxi ride to get to.

GETTING HERE AND AROUND

To get here, most people take a shuttle bus from Chengdu or Leshan, but you can also take the train. The trip from Chengdu takes about two to three hours by bus or three hours by train. If you arrive by train, you'll have to catch a bus to visit the area's sites. Inexpensive public buses travel between destinations, but schedules vary and stops are often unmarked.

BUS TRAVEL   There are departures from Chengdu's Xinnanmen station every half hour and from Leshan every hour on the hour between 7 am and 6 pm. One-way tickets on shuttle buses cost between Y35 and Y45, and the trip takes about two hours. Also departing from Leshan are buses that travel directly to Emeishan's Baoguo Si. They depart every half hour between 9 and 5 for about Y10.

TRAIN TRAVEL   A train from the Chengdu North Railway Station bound for Kunming passes through Emei Town; it takes two to three hours and costs about Y22.

The Wannian monastery at Emeishan.

SAFETY AND PRECAUTIONS

The biggest threats here are the unpredictable weather on top of the mountain and the Tibetan macaques that inhabit its slopes. Bring warm clothes and enough money to seek shelter at the mountaintop hotel, and don't approach the monkeys too closely or let them gather around you in groups. Also, be careful of falls or twisted ankles on the slippery stone staircases that run up the mountain.

TIMING

Climbing the mountain from base to peak and back again can take anywhere from three to six days depending on fitness levels. A day of relaxation and recovery for tender joints and muscles will likely be in order afterward. Seeing the mountain by shuttle bus up the paved roads that run most of the way to the top and the chairlift that goes the rest of the way can be accomplished in as little as a day.

TOURS

Good shuttle bus and trail infrastructure and relatively clear English signage mostly render organized tours of Emeishan unnecessary, but guides can be booked through hotels in Emeishan Town, the cluster of hotels and restaurants at the base of the mountain.

ESSENTIALS

Bank Agricultural Bank of China (⊠ *Near Baoguo Monastery* ☎ *083/3559–3397*).

Medical Assistance Emeishan Renmin Hospital (⊠ *94 Santaishan Jie* ☎ *083/3553–4524 or 083/3552–2725*).

Train Contact Emeishan Station (☎ *083/3516–8609*).

Visitor and Tour Info Emeishan Travel Agency (✉ *94 Ningshan Lu at Zhong-duan, Emeishan* ☎ *083/3552–4244*).

EXPLORING EMEISHAN

You can hike the 25 miles of stone staircase to the Golden Summit of Emeishan in two to three days. It's a difficult climb—the stairs up the mountain somehow make it seem more arduous. On the first day, hike until a bit before nightfall and walk into one of the temples along the way to sleep for Y20 to Y40 per person. Most hikers can reach the summit by nightfall of the second day or sometime on the third day. Stay a night near the top of the mountain and rise early: the clouds that often obscure views during the day are bathed in a breathtaking amber color at sunrise. It's a wonderful journey. You will find the natural surroundings as enchanting as the temples.

> **MONKEY BUSINESS**
>
> The mountain is known for its wily golden monkeys, who have been known to steal items (such as cameras) and hang them in trees. They will try to surround you, screaming, pointing, and jumping in an intimidating manner. A sound strategy is to walk quickly through the band before they can increase in number.

The most common route to the top is past Long Life Monastery. This route takes you past the Elephant Bathing Pool, the crossroads for tourists and pilgrims headed up or down the mountain. The pool was once used by Bodhisattva Puxian to wash the grime off his white elephant. This place is usually crowded, but once you ascend from here you will be mostly free of the madding crowd.

A recommended route down is the long shoulder of the mountain past Magic Peak Monastery, another highlight of the climb. The monks here personify the compassion and simplicity of Buddhism, and the scenery is beyond compare. After a hard climb down, sharing a simple meal in the courtyard and then staying the night in the monastery is magical.

The best times to climb are in the spring or fall. The summer can be uncomfortably hot at the lower altitudes, but once you ascend to the mountain's upper reaches you might want to stay a few extra days to avoid the stifling summer heat below. The true beauty of Emeishan appears after the halfway point, when most of the tourists are below you. Bring a change of clothes for the sweaty part of the journey and a warm jacket for the summit. Water and food are available on the mountain, carried by pipe-puffing porters to the stalls along the way.

DID YOU KNOW?

The mountain is part of a range that stretches from Ya'an in the north to Xichang in the south. These mountains produce some of the world's best green tea. Emei's local tea is called Zhu Ye Qing (Jade Bamboo Leaf), and there are several types and grades. It's possible to buy organic Zhu Ye Qing around the mountain and in Emei Town. Look for the Long Dong Organic Brand.

For an easier pilgrimage, use the Y40 minibus service from the Mount Emei Tourist Transportation Center below Declare Nation Temple *(Baoguo Si)* up to **The Leidong Terraces**, from where the climb to the top will take about two hours. To avoid climbing altogether, ride the cable car (Y40 up, Y30 down) to the summit from Jieyin Dian (although there are often long lines).

Direct bus service (two hours) links Chengdu with Baoguo Si via the tourist transportation center at the foot of the mountain. Trains to and from Chengdu stop in the town of Emei, about 6 km (4 mi) from the mountain.

WHERE TO EAT AND STAY

$-$$ ✕ **Emei Kaoyu.** Located among several other decent restaurants on "Good Eats Street" (*Haochi Jie*), Emei Kaoyu lays out a variety of fresh vegetable ingredients every day. After diners have selected their veggies, the restaurant turns them into delicious stir-fries. Try fiddle-head ferns fried with local bacon. The street is located just up the hill from the bus station at the base of the mountain. ⊠ *Haochi Jie, Emei* ☎ *138/0813–5338.* ▭ *No credit cards.*

¢ ⊡ **Baoguo Monastery.** This monastery at the foot of the mountain is one of the many accommodations available to those journeying to the Golden Summit. Few people stay here, because it sits near the start of the path up the mountain, but if you are arriving late this quiet, if slightly damp, hotel is a good option. The monks have even added some higher-end rooms in recent years with air conditioning and TV. **Pros:** quiet, a monastic experience. **Cons:** pretty basic. ⊠ *Baoguo Si,* ☎ *No phone* ⋞ *30 rooms* ⚋ *In-hotel: restaurant* ▭ *No credit cards.*

¢–$ ⊡ **Emeishan Grand Hotel** (*Emeishan Dajiudian*). This hotel sits at the foot of the mountain, offering good access for those going on early hikes. The rooms are comfortable, and have clean bathrooms. **Pros:** nice rooms, good location. **Cons:** staff could be more helpful. ⊠ *Baoguo Si* ☎ *0833/552–6888* ⊕ *www.emshotel.com.cn* ⋞ *465 rooms* ⚋ *In-hotel: 3 restaurants, bar* ▭ *AE, MC, V.*

¢ ✕ **Teddy Bear Hotel.** Arriving at the Emei Bus Station, you will likely be
★ approached by touts offering to take you to the Teddy Bear Café. It's a good idea to go with them. Despite its odd name and spartan decor, the Teddy Bear is one of the few hotels in town with an English-speaking staff. Owner Andy and his wife are friendly and will help you in any way they can, doing everything from loaning walking sticks to arranging guides. The guest rooms are not the best bargain in the area, but they are clean, comfortable, and carry the pleasant scent of the soft-wood paneling from which the inside of the hotel is constructed. ⊠ *43 Baoguosi Lu, Emei* ☎ *0833/559–0135* ⊕ *www.teddybear.com.cn* ⚋ *In-room: a/c. In-hotel: restaurants, bar, laundry service* ▭ *No credit cards.*

LESHAN

★ *165 km (102 mi; 3 hrs by bus) south of Chengdu.*

Leshan is famous for the Great Buddha, carved into the mountainside at the confluence of the Dadu, Qingyi, and Min rivers. The Great Buddha—a UNESCO World Heritage Site—was initiated by the monk Haitong in 713, but he didn't live to see its completion in 803. The statue, blissfully reclining, has overlooked the swirling, choppy waters

for 1,200 years. The city's new museum, up the Dadu River from the Great Buddha, is worth a stop.

GETTING HERE AND AROUND

BUS TRAVEL   Buses to Leshan leave from Chengdu's Xinnanmen station every 30 minutes between 7:30 am and 7:30 pm. Buses from Chongqing to Leshan leave every hour from 6:30 to 6:30. From Leshan's Xiao Ba Bus Station, take public bus Line 13 directly to the Great Buddha's main gate.

TRAIN TRAVEL   The train trip between Chengdu and Leshan takes between 1½ and 2½ hours and costs Y8 to Y109.

SAFETY AND PRECAUTIONS

Leshan is generally safe. Watch out for slippery paths, and make sure you're well hydrated for long walks in the steamy forested park that surrounds the Great Buddha.

TIMING

One day is sufficient to see the Buddha and surrounding park and Buddhist pavilions.

TOURS

Boats at a dock about 1,500 feet up the river from the main gate will take you for a bumpy ride to within camera distance of the Giant Budda. The 40-minute trip is Y40 per person. From the boat you will be able to see two heavily eroded guardians that flank the main statue.

ESSENTIALS

Bank Bank of China (⊠ *35 Huangjiashan* ☎ *0833/212–5246*).

Medical Assistance Leshan Renmin Hospital (⊠ *76 Baita Jie* ☎ *0833/211–9304*).

Visitor and Tour Info Leshan Information Office (⊠ *Huahuwan, Luzi Jie* ☎ *0833/230—2131*).

EXPLORING LESHAN

At 233 feet, the **Giant Buddha** *(Da Fo)* is the tallest stone Buddha and among the tallest sculptures in the world. The big toes are each 28 feet in length. The construction of the Giant Budda was started in ad 713 by a monk who wished to placate the rivers that habitually took local fishermen's lives. Although the project took more than 90 years to complete, it had no noticeable effect on the waters. It's possible to clamber down, by means of a cliff-hewn stairway, from the head to the platform where the feet rest. You can also take a boat ride (about Y40) to see the statue in all its grandeur from the river. ☎ *0833/230–2121* 🎫 *Y90 (includes Wu You Temple)* ⊙ *Daily 8–5:30.*

There are also several temples or pagodas in the park that houses the Giant Budda, including **Wu You Temple** *(Wuyou Si)*, a Ming Dynasty temple with a commanding view of the city. You might find yourself staring at the lifelike figures and wonder about the people they were modeled after. 🎫 *Y90 (includes Giant Budhda)* ⊙ *Daily 8–5:30.*

WHERE TO EAT AND STAY

¢–$ ✕ **Sanjiang Fandian.** This Chinese restaurant run by a husband and wife
CHINESE   serves up some great fish dishes. The buffets are guaranteed to please; the food is primarily fish from the waters around the feet of the Giant

9

Budda with local specialties like *dou hua* (soft tofu) and bamboo shoots. The restaurant is one of several facing the water, so there's a nice view. ⊠ *North of the main gate to the Giant Budda, Bizi Jie* ☎ *130/0642–2361* ⊟ *No credit cards.*

¢–$ 🏨 **Jiazhou Hotel.** This "Hotel California" is on the opposite side of the river from the Giant Budda and has comfortable accommodations and clean bathrooms. A café across the parking lot serves passable Western food. **Pros:** clean; good location. **Cons:** food could be better. ⊠ *19 Baitu Lu* ☎ *083/3213–9888* 🖷 *083/3213–3233* ⇗ *190 rooms* ⌂ *In-hotel: restaurant* ⊟ *No credit cards.*

JIUZHAIGOU NATURAL PRESERVE

★ *350 km (217 mi; 8–10 hrs by bus) north of Leshan; 225 km (140 mi; 4–6 hrs by bus) northwest of Chengdu.*

High among the snowcapped peaks of the Aba Autonomous Prefecture of northern Sichuan lies the **Jiuzhaigou Reserve** *(Jiuzhaigou Ziran Bao Hu Qu)*, a spectacular national park filled with lush valleys, jagged peaks, a dozen large waterfalls, and most famously, a collection of iridescent lakes and pools. Jiuzhaigou has become one of the country's most popular tourist destinations, with more than 1½ million people visiting every year.

The preserve's cerulean and aqua pools are among the most beautiful in the world, and the park's raw natural beauty has been compared to Yellowstone National Park. Also similar to Yellowstone are the crowds—throngs of Chinese tourists descend daily on this 800-km (497-mi) stretch of lush forests, piercing peaks, languid lakes, and clear pools. UNESCO has awarded the park heritage status for its "Man and Biosphere" program.

Jiuzhaigou is a natural reserve and a collection of villages, mostly of Tibetan and Qinang origin. (The name Jiuzhaigou translates as Nine Villages.) The dramatic increase in tourism has had a great impact upon the locals, many of whom have been removed from their homes in order to "protect" the park.

Management of Jiuzhaigou Nature Reserve has been turned over to a private company, so admission is much more expensive than in previous years, but there are also more services available, such as the introduction of an environment-friendly transportation route through the park—plied by so-called green buses that have reduced emissions. For those who want to avoid tour buses and local guides, walkways and signs direct travelers along the way. There are now many hotels around the park, including a five-star resort tucked in the wilderness.

This region is spectacular, with limestone and karst formations, temperate rain forests, and dozens of bright turquoise, orange, and emerald-green pools. The park shelters 76 mammal species, including pandas, black bears, and deer. The climate is wet in the spring and fall, very snowy and cold in the winter, and bright and warm in the summer. 🎫 *Y310* ☎ *0837/773–9753* ⊕ *www.jiuzhai.com* ☉ *Apr. 1–Nov. 15, daily 7–6; Nov. 16–Mar. 31, daily 8:00–5:30.*

GETTING HERE AND AROUND

AIR TRAVEL You can fly to Jiuhuang Airport, one hour south of Jiuzhaigou in Huanglong. There are aggressive cabbies waiting to take you to Songpan for Y100 (one hour). Tour buses run to the Jiuzhai Valley (two hours). Your hotel should arrange a transfer; otherwise a shuttle bus will cost Y45.

BUS TRAVEL Several buses a day shuttle passengers from Chengdu's Xinnanmen Bus Station or Chadianzi Bus Station.

SAFETY AND PRECAUTIONS

When hiring a car to go between Songpan and Jiuzhaigou, do not switch cars midway through the journey, as both drivers will try to claim your agreed-upon fare.

TIMING

The park can be seen in one day, although it is a hectic day. If you want to go camping and explore sites outside the national park, three days should suffice.

TOURS

If you want to experience Jiuzhaigou as the Chinese do, sign up with any of the numerous package tours in Chengdu and Chongqing. A word to the wise: be prepared to be herded along by a guide armed with a flag and a bullhorn. General information on tours from Chengdu and Chongqing is available from China Travel Service.

ESSENTIALS

Air Contact Jiuzhaigou Huanglong Airport (☎ 0837/724–3700 ⊕ www. jzairport.com).

Bank Agricultural Bank of China (☎ 0837/773—9717).

Visitor and Tour Info China Travel Service (☎ 028/6866–3866, 028/6866–3138, or 028/6655–1188). **Jiuzhaiguo Park Office** (☎ 0837/773–9753) ⊕ www. jiuzhai.com.

EXPLORING JIUZHAIGOU

Exploring the park is made easier by frequent ranger stations and signs in English. As you explore the Y-shaped Jiuzhaigou Nature Reserve, your first stop will undoubtedly be the Zaru Valley, on your left. You'll find the Zaru Temple and the Hejiao Stockade farther up the Zaru Valley. Deeper in the valley you'll pass the stunning Shunzheng Terrace Waterfall before you reach Mirror Lake and Nuorilang Falls. On the right side of this path you'll find the fabled Nine Villages, where it is possible to have a meal with the locals. These sights alone are worth the trip, and many tourists head back after marveling at Mirror Lake.

From Mirror Lake, veer left to the Zechawa Village, an impossibly beautiful small Tibetan community. From the village, the path travels through a temperate rain forest interspersed with dozens of turquoise-colored pools. At the far end of the left branch of the Y is Long Lake, a beautiful and peaceful place that carries barely a trace of the modernization happening all around. Down the right branch of the Y is a series of amazing small lakes, including Five Flower Lake and Arrow Bamboo Lake, crisscrossed by wooden walkways.

WHERE TO EAT AND STAY

Did someone say yak? Near the main gate of Jiuzhaigou Reserve you'll find restaurants selling dried yak, cured yak, pickled yak, smoked yak, yak hotpot, fried yak, and—well, you get the point. Sample the *sampas* (barley-and-yak-butter tea cakes).

$$$ 🏨 **Intercontinental Resort Jiuzhai Paradise.** Tucked away in a valley 20 km (12.5 mi) from the Jiuzhaigou Nature Reserve, this is the region's most luxurious lodging. The sprawling complex was designed around a Qiang-style village that sits under a glass dome. The foyer is truly one of a kind, covered by a glass-and-metal dome that lets in sunlight during the day and allows glimpses of the moon at night. The rooms are extravagantly decorated, and there's a nightly performance by Tibetan dancers. A daily bus takes you to the national park's main gate. **Pros:** pretty location; nice rooms. **Cons:** less than stellar food and service. ⊠ *Near Jiuzhaigou Nature Preserve* ☎ *0837/778–9999* B*0837/778–8988* ⊕ *www.intercontinental.com* ➳ *1,020 rooms, 131 suites* ♿ *In-hotel: 5 restaurants, room service, bar, pool, gym, spa, Wi-Fi* ⊟ *AE, MC, V.*

$$$ 🏨 **Sheraton Jiuzhaigou Resort.** This was the region's first luxury hotel, located about 1,000 feet from the mouth of the Jiuzhai Valley. With dozens of peaked roofs, the resort vaguely resembles an ancient castle. Surrounded by the mountains, the hotel has incredible views from its nicely decorated guest rooms. **Pros:** good service and location. **Cons:** dated rooms. ⊠ *Jiuzhaigou Scenic Spot, Jiuzhaigou* ☎ *800/810–3088* 🖷 *0837/773–9688* ⊕ *www.sheraton.com/jiuzhaigou* ➳ *482 rooms, 20 suites* ♿ *In-hotel: 3 restaurants, room service, bar, pool, gym, spa, laundry service, wireless Internet* ⊟ *AE, MC, V.*

¢ 🏨 **YouU Hostel.** All things considered, this may be the best value in the area. The hostel is a 15-minute cab ride south of the Jiu Zhai Valley. It sits on a quiet pedestrian street with several restaurants and places to shop. The rooms, which run the gamut from dorm-style to suites, are spotless, cozy, and comfortable. **Pros:** helpful staff. **Cons:** sporadic hot water. ⊠ *Building 4, Khampa Lingka Plaza* ☎ *0837/776–3111* 🖷 *0837/776–3111* ➳ *60 rooms, 6 suites* ♿ *In-hotel: restaurant, café, laundry facilities, Internet* ⊟ *No credit cards.*

SONGPAN

350 km (217 mi; 8–10 hrs by bus) northwest of Chengdu.

Songpan has experienced quite a construction boom over the past five years. The village with a couple of dirt roads and no accommodations has become a small, ever-growing town with several hotels and even Western-style restaurants. The locals have spruced up the streets and built nice new wooden signs, often with English translations. The old

A bridge in Songpan.

town is not that old any longer, but the mosque by the river is a beautiful sight in the morning when the sunlight reflects off of the minaret.

Most people visit Songpan for the horses, and they do not leave disappointed. These horseback-riding treks through the surrounding countryside go on and on, the longest being 10 days.

GETTING HERE AND AROUND

AIR TRAVEL Don't be fooled by the name of Songpan's Jiuzhaigou Huanglong Airport—it's about 88 km (55 mi) from Jiuzhaigou. There are no buses from the airport to Songpan, and cabs charge Y100.

BUS TRAVEL Buses from Chengdu's Xinnanmen and Chadianzi bus stations shuttle passengers daily, with several buses departing between 6:30 am and 9:30 am. Tickets cost Y123.

HORSE TREKS

Shun Jiang Horse Treks (☎ *0837/880–9118*) offers horseback tours into the mountains and past Tibetan villages that haven't changed for centuries. If you don't have camping gear, they can provide everything you may need. The trips cost Y200 per person, per day. Prices, destinations, and duration of trips are all negotiable. All meals provided are vegetarian.

WHERE TO EAT AND STAY

¢–$ ✕ **Emma's Kitchen.** Located on the main drag just down the street from the bus station, Emma's has both Western and Chinese fare. Prices are reasonable, and the staff speak English. ✦ *Near the Songpan bus station* ☎ *0837/723–1088* ▭ *No credit cards.*

¢ ⊡ **Old House Hotel**. Located next to the bus station, this guesthouse has a café with good coffee and wireless Internet. The owner is an incredibly helpful woman, and her son speaks very good English. **Pros:** convenient location, helpful staff. **Cons:** small rooms. ⊠ *Long Distance Bus Station* ☎ *0837/723–1368* 🖉 *Dongshan_6666@sina.com* 🛏 *15 rooms* ⧖ *In-hotel: café, Internet terminal* ▭ *No credit cards.*

CHONGQING AND THE YANGTZE RIVER

After decades of lobbying for special economic status, in 1997 Beijing finally allowed Chongqing to formally separate from Sichuan. This maneuver facilitated Chongqing's rise from a stunted onetime capital to the region's industrial powerhouse, and allowed for the long-planned Three Gorges Dam Project to move forward.

Called the Mountain City (also the name of the local beer), Chongqing has features unlike any other Chinese city. Instead of the ubiquitous bicycle, Chongqing has the Stickman Army. Stickmen are peasants for hire who wander the streets of Chongqing carrying stuff up and down the hills. The city is also riddled with tunnels, many of which were dug during the sieges of WWII. Built on the side of a mountain, the city has an upper and a lower level, so it's not unusual for buildings to have two or more "ground floors."

The city is the major jumping-off point for the Three Gorges cruise down the Yangtze River. The classic novel *The Three Kingdoms* takes place along this stretch of the river, and the cliffs are lined with caves and tombs dating back to the Yellow Emperor. The Three Gorges Dam is now complete, and the water level is steadily rising—millions of people have been displaced, entire villages swamped, and countless historical artifacts lost forever—but China needs energy, and the western regions need a reliable inland port with deepwater capacity, therefore the dam stays.

DID YOU KNOW?

Chongqing is the heart of the BaYu Culture—vibrant, colorful, and proud—with its own version of Sichuan Opera, its own cuisine, and a history of rebelliousness. Chongqingese are known for their directness and fiery tempers.

REGIONAL TOURS

Tour Contact Chongqing Dongfang Travel Service (⊠ *5 Chaoqiang Lu, Chongqing* ☎ *0236/371–0326*).

CHONGQING

240 km (149 mi; 4 hrs by bus) southeast of Chengdu; 1,800 km (1,116 mi; 3 hrs by plane) southwest of Beijing; 1,025 km (636 mi; 34 hrs by train) northwest of Hong Kong.

With a layout reminiscent of Hong Kong and a distinct Sichuanese vibe, Chongqing is one of the most interesting and dynamic cities in Western China. The "Mountain City," as it is known, is much more three-dimensional than your average Chinese metropolis, so prepare for plenty of hills and stairs. It is also one of China's hottest cities in the summer, but the plentiful trees and growing numbers of skyscrapers offer plenty of shade in the afternoon.

The central peninsula area of Yuzhong district, between the Jialing River to the north and the Yangtze River to the south, is the most interesting and dynamic area of Chongqing. Within Yuzhong, most of the action is centered around the Jiefang Bei (Liberation Monument) area, where you will find the bulk of Chongqing's top hotels, restaurants, bars, and clubs.

WORD OF MOUTH

"Some of my relatives just came back from China, and suffered from some mild to moderate altitude sickness at Huanglong National Park in Sichuan Province…If you're planning a trip to Jiuzhaigou and Huanglong, and flying directly from Chengdu, please give yourself a lot of time to acclimate before going to Huanglong." —rkkwan

There's plenty to do outside of the city center, however, with scenic mountains in the south, the old Ming town of Ciqikou to the northwest, and the fantastic Buddhist caves at Dazu, farther afield.

And of course, Chongqing is the launch point for most Yangtze River cruises. Currently in a period of rapid change, this city is definitely worth staying in for a few days before heading downriver.

GETTING HERE AND AROUND

Chongqing is smack-dab in the middle of China, connected by rail, bus, and plane to every major city in the country. The Chongqing airport is well connected, with daily flights to all major cities in China. For travel between the east coast and Chongqing, flying is your most comfortable option. For trips to Chengdu, the high-speed rail link is the best bet.

Chongqing's light-rail line from the city center to the zoo in the south is worth the Y10 round-trip ticket price. The two stations in the city center (Jiao Chang Kou and Lin Jiang Men) are easily accessible from Jiefang Bei. The line curves north to the Jialing River—above ground—and goes through six riverside stations before it heads south to the terminal station at the zoo.

AIR TRAVEL Traffic permitting, Chongqing's Jiangbei International Airport is a 40-minute drive north by taxi from the city center. The airport has flights to every major domestic, and some international hubs, mostly within Asia. Book tickets at any hotel or the travel agencies around Liberation Monument.

BOAT AND FERRY TRAVEL Boats go on the Yangtze from Chongqing all the way to Shanghai (seven days), but the most popular route is the cruise downstream from Chongqing to Yichang or Wuhan (three to four days) or upstream from Wuhan to Chongqing. Most major sights, including the Three Gorges and Three Little Gorges, lie between Chongqing and Yichang. Tourist boats offer air-conditioned cabins with a television and private bath; the ordinary passenger steamers used by most Chinese offer minimal comforts. Tickets can be arranged through CITS or your travel agent.

BUS TRAVEL   The shared train and bus station may be the most inconvenient, crowded, and annoying station in the world. Once your taxi has maneuvered through the corrugated tin walls and piles of baggage, finding buses or trains is not hard, however.

From Chongqing to Chengdu is a well-trodden path. The bus departs every hour, takes five to six hours, and costs Y120. Buses are viable as far as Yibin or within the municipality itself (Dazu and Beibei), but trains are recommended for all other destinations.

CAR TRAVEL   Traveling around the city by taxi is often the most convenient way to navigate the winding roads and long distances here. Meters start at Y5, and even long cab rides tend to be much cheaper than they would be elsewhere in China. There is a Y3 fuel surcharge added to every fare, so don't be surprised when your driver asks for three more than what the meter is displaying.

TRAIN TRAVEL   The train and bus station share a location. Trains leave Chongqing every minute for every conceivable city in China. If you're going to Chengdu, the ultra-modern high-speed rail link has cut the travel time from four hours to just two hours. A hard seat on the train is Y98 and a soft seat is Y117. Trains leave every day from Chongqing North Station at 9:59 am, 10:50 am, 12:57 pm, 3:18 pm, 4:28 pm, 6:52 pm, 9:05 pm, and 10:55 pm.

SAFETY AND PRECAUTIONS

Despite its size, Chongqing is a very safe city in terms of crime. But with all the construction and demolition taking place above street level, it is worth being careful where you walk when on the sidewalk for falling debris. Also, during the hotter times of the year make sure to drink plenty of water when hiking around.

TIMING

One could easily stay in Chongqing for a week without seeing everything, but most of the sights of interest in and around the city can be visited within three or four days.

TOURS

At night the high-rises that ring the hills around the city give off a glow that reflects off the rushing rivers below. A night boat cruise is a romantic way to appreciate the charms of the Mountain City. Tickets can be bought at any hotel, or at the **Chongqian Huanyu Travel Agency**. Cruises can be booked with or without dinner. ⊠ *18 Xinyi St., across from the port* ☎ *023/6380–3350* ✉ *Y38–Y550* ☉ *24 hours.*

ESSENTIALS

Bank Bank of China (⊠ *Minzu Lu*).

Bus Contact Chongqing Long Distance Bus Group (☎ *023/6888–1939 or 023/8908–8458*).

Train Contact Cai Yuan Ba Train Station (⊠ *Off of Nan Qu Lu* ☎ *023/6168–1114*).

Internet Most hotels in the city center are wired, and there are Internet cafés in the smaller streets that radiate from the Liberation Monument.

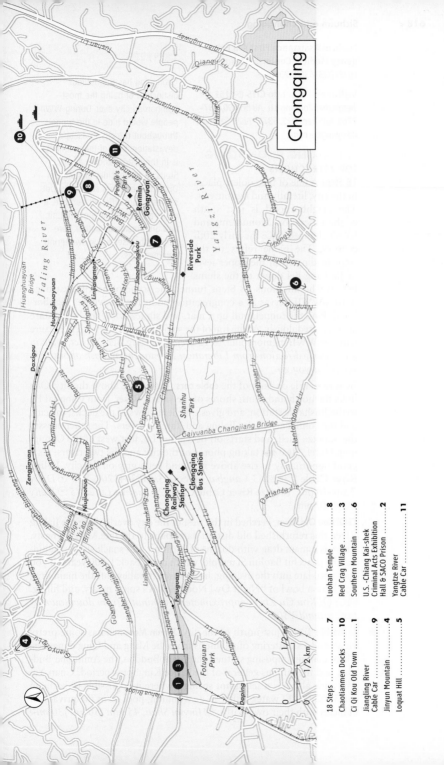

Chongqing

Medical Assistance First Aid Emergency Medical Center (✉ 1 Jiankang Lu ☎ 023/6369–2008).

Visitor and Tour Info CITS (✉ 151 Jiefangbei Zourong Lu, A8 ☎ 400/887–7761 toll free; 023/6372–7120 ⊕ www.hikeyangtze.com).

EXPLORING CHONGQING

TOP ATTRACTIONS

18 Steps is one of the coolest places in the city, literally and figuratively. The neighborhood is just south of the Liberation Monument, and hasn't changed since the early 20th century. The name refers to the steps leading from the upper level of Jie Fang Bei down to the slums

> ### 18 STEPS
>
> Chongqing has the dubious distinction of being the most-bombarded city ever. During WWII people would hide in the tunnels throughout the city to escape devastation. One of these tunnels is in the district known as 18 Steps, in present-day Jiefang Bei District. The tunnel still exists, but serves a very different purpose. It emits a constant flow of cool air, and area residents gather here to cool themselves on sweltering summer days.

below. The infamous 18 Steps tunnel, the scene of horrible carnage during WWII, serves as a congregation point for the whole neighborhood. Find the tunnel, pull up a mat, and sip tea while the locals stare at you incredulously. At the top of the steps is a teahouse with a treasure trove of WWII memorabilia. ✉ *18 Steps, Jie Fang Bei District, walk in a southerly direction from Liberation Monument and ask about "Shi Ba Ti" as you go.*

Be sure to ride on both of the **cable cars** that dangle above the city. One links the north and south shores of the Jialing River, from Cangbai Lu to the Jinsha Jie station, and gives excellent views of the docks, the city, and the confluence of the Jialing and Yangtze rivers. The other crosses the Yangtze itself, and starts off of Xinhua Lu, just west of the Chongqing Hotel. Ideal for taking photos of the city and the two rivers, it's a good opportunity to rise above it all and get a grip on the city. **Jialing River Cable Car** ✉ 63 Cangbai Lu ☎ 023/6383–4320 🎫 Y5 ⊙ Daily 7 am–10 pm. **Yangtze River Cable Car** ✉ 24 Xinhua Lu 🎫 Y5 ⊙ Daily 7 am–10 pm.

Ci Qi Kou Old Town. Perched in the west of the city overlooking the Jialing River, this refurbished old district dates back to the late Ming Dynasty. There is a main drag with dozens of souvenir and snack shops, including the peaceful Baolun Si temple, which dates back 1,500 years. If you stay until late into the evening, head down the alleys off the main drag and have a bowl of "Night Owl Noodles." It's spicy, meaty, and filling. ✉ *Ci Qi Kou Gu Zhen, approximately 30 minutes from downtown by taxi, around Y30.*

★ In Beibie Town, just north of the city, **Jinyun Mountain** has some pretty views and a smattering of pavilions from the Ming and Qing dynasties. Three contain imposing statues: the Giant Buddha, the Amitabha Buddha, and the famous general of the Three Kingdoms period, Guan Yu. The park also has a set of **hot springs,** where it is possible to bathe in the 30°C (86°F) water, either in a swimming pool or in the privacy of cubicles with their own baths. ✉ *Jinyun Shan, 45 min (50 km [30 mi])*

Continued on page 625

A CULINARY TOUR OF CHINA

For centuries the collective culinary fragrances of China have drifted far beyond its borders and tantalized the entire world. Now with China's arms open to the world, a vast variety of Chinese flavors—from the North, South, East, and West—are more accessible than ever.

Four corners of the Middle Kingdom

In dynasties gone by, a visitor to China might have to undertake a journey of a thousand li just to feel the burn of an authentic Sichuanese hotpot, and another to savor the crispy skin and juicy flesh of a genuine Beijing roast duck. Luckily for us, the vast majority of regional Chinese cuisines have made successful internal migrations. As a result, Sichuanese cuisine can be found in Guangzhou, Cantonese dim sum in Urumuqi, and the cumin-spiced lamb-on-a-stick, for which the Uigher people of Xinjiang are famous, is now grilled all over China.

Before you begin your journey, remember, a true scholar of Middle Kingdom cuisine should first eliminate the very term "Chinese food" from their vocabulary. It hardly encompasses the variety of provincial cuisines and regional dishes that China has to offer, from succulent Shanghainese dumplings to fiery Sichuanese hotpots.

To guide you on your gastronomic journey, we've divided the country's gourmet map along the points of the compass—North, South, East, and West. Bon voyage and bon appétit!

Following the revolution, it was hard to find authentic Chinese cuisine.

NORTH

THE BASICS

Cuisine from China's Northeast is called dongbei cai, and it's more wheat than rice based. Vegetables like kale, cabbage, and potatoes are combined with robust, thick soy sauces, garlic (often raw), and scallions.

Even though many Han Chinese from southern climates find mutton too gamey, up north it's a regular staple. In many northern cities, you can't walk more than a block without coming across a small sidewalk grill with yang rou chua'r, or lamb-on-a-stick.

NOT TO BE MISSED

The most famous of all the northern dishes is Peking duck, and if you've ever had it well prepared, you'll know why Beijingers are proud of the dish named for their city.

The fowl is cleaned, stuffed with burning millet stalks and other aromatic combustibles, and then slow-cooked in an oven heated by a fire made of fragrant wood. Properly cooked, Peking duck should have crispy skin, juicy meat, and none of the grease. Peking duck is served with pancakes, scallions,

Peking duck sliced table-side.

and a delicious soy-based sauce with just a hint of sweetness.

LEGEND HAS IT

Looking for the best roast duck in Beijing? You won't find it in a luxury hotel. But if you happen to find yourself wandering through the Qianmendong hutong just south of Tiananmen Square, you may stumble upon a little courtyard home with a sign in English reading LI QUN ROAST DUCK. This small and unassuming restaurant is widely considered as having the best Peking roast duck in the capital. Rumor has it that the late leader Deng Xiaoping used to send his driver out to bring him back Li Qun's amazing ducks.

THE CAPITAL CITY'S NAMESAKE DISH

A perfectly prepared duck

Scallions

Soy based hoisin sauce

Pancakes

SOUTH

(left) Preparing for the feast. (top right) Dim sum as art. (bottom right) Place your order.

IN FOCUS A CULINARY TOUR OF CHINA

9

THE BASICS

The dish most associated with Southern Chinese cuisine is dim sum, which is found in great variety and abundance in Guangdong province, as well as Hong Kong and Macau. Bite-size dim sum is usually eaten early in the day. Any good dim sum place should have dozens of varieties. Some of the most popular dishes are *har gao*, a shrimp dumpling with a rice-flour skin, *siu maai*, a pork dumpling with a wrapping made of wheat flour, and *chaa-habao*, a steamed or baked bun filled with sweetened pork and onions. Adventerous eaters should order the chicken claws. Trust us, they taste better than they look.

> The Cantonese saying *"fei qin zou shou"* roughly translates to "if it flies, swims or runs, it's food."

For our money, the best southern food comes from Chaozhou (Chiuchow), a coastal city only a few hours' drive north of its larger neighbors. Unlike dim sum, Chaozuo cuisine is extremely light and understated. Deep-fried bean curd is also a remarkably fresh Chaozuo dish.

NOT TO BE MISSED

One Chaozuo dish that appeals equally to the eye and the palate is the plain-sounding mashed vegetable with minced chicken soup. The dish is served in a large bowl, and resembles a green-and-white yin-yang. As befitting a dish resembling a Buddhist symbol, a vegetarian version substituting rice gruel for chicken broth is usually offered.

SOUTHWEST AND FAR WEST

Southwest

THE BASICS

When a person from the Southwest asks you if you like spicy food, consider your answer well. Natives of Sichuan and Hunan take the use of chilies, wild pepper, and garlic to blistering new heights. These two areas have been competing for the "spiciest province in China" title for centuries. The penchant for fiery food is likely due to the weather—hot and humid in the summer and harshly cold in the winter. But no matter what the temperature, if you're eating Sichuan or Hunan dishes, be prepared to sweat.

Southwest China shares some culinary traits with both Southeast Asia and India. This is likely due to the influences of travelers from both regions in centuries past. Traditional Chinese medicine also makes itself felt in the regional cuisine. Theory has it that sweating expels toxins and equalizes body temperature.

As Chairman Mao's province, Hunan has a number of dishes with revolutionary names. The most popular are red-cooked Hunan fish *(hongshao wuchangyu)* and red-cooked pork *(hongshao rou)*, which was said to have been a personal favorite of the Great Helmsman.

Sichuan pepper creates a tingly numbness.

NOT TO BE MISSED

One dish you won't want to miss out on in Sichuan is *mala zigi*, or "peppery and hot chicken." It's one part chicken meat and three parts fried chilies and a Sichuanese wild pepper called *huajiao* that's so spicy it effectively numbs the tongue. At first it feels like eating Tiger Balm, but the hot-cool-numb sensation produced by crunching on the pepper is oddly addictive.

KUNG PAO CHICKEN

One of the most famous Chinese dishes, Kung Pao chicken (or gongbao jiding), enjoys a legend of its own.

Though shrouded in myth, its origin exemplifies the improvisational skills found in any good Chinese chef. The story of Kung Pao chicken has to do with a certain Qing Dynasty era (1644–1911) provincial governor named Ding Baozhen, who arrived home unexpectedly one day with a group of friends in tow. His cook, caught in between

shopping trips, had only the chicken breast and a few vegetables he was planning to cook for his own dinner. The crafty chef diced the chicken into tiny bits and fried it up with everything he could find in the cupboard—some peanuts, sugar, onion, garlic, bits of ginger, and a few handfuls of dried red peppers—and hoped for the best.

(top left) Tibetan dumplings. (center left) Uyghur-style pilaf. (bottom left) Monk stirring tsampa barley. (right) Juggling hot noodles in the Xinjiang province.

Far West

THE BASICS

Religion is the primary shaper of culinary tradition in China's Far West. Being a primarily Muslim province, chefs in Xinjiang don't use pork products of any kind. Instead, meals are likely to be heavy on spiced lamb. Baked flat breads coated in sesame seeds are a specialty. Whole lamb roasted on a spit, fine spicy tomato salads, and lightly spiced mutton and vegetable soups are also favorites.

NOT TO BE MISSED

In Tibet, climate is the major factor dictating cuisine. High and dry, the Tibetan plateau is hardly suited for rice cultivation. Whereas a Han meal might include rice, Tibetan cuisine tends to include tsampa, a ground barley usually cooked into a porridge. Another staple that's definitely an acquired taste is yak butter tea. Dumplings, known as *momo*, are wholesome and filling. Of course, if you want to go all out, order the yak penis with caterpillar fungus.

EAST

(top left) Cold tofu with pork and thousand-year-old eggs. (top right) Meaty dumplings. (bottom right) Letting off the steam of Shanghai: soup dumplings. (bottom left) Steamed Shanghai hairy crabs.

THE BASICS

The rice, seafood, and fresh vegetable-based cooking of the southern coastal provinces of Zhejiang and Jiangsu are known collectively as huiyang cai. As the area's biggest city, Shanghai has become a major center of the culinary arts. Some popular dishes in Shanghai are stir-fried freshwater eels and finely ground white pepper, and red-stewed fish—a boiled carp in sweet and sour sauce. Another Shanghai favorite are xiaolong bao, or little steamer dumplings. Similar to Cantonese dim sum, xiaolong bao tend to be more moist. The perfect steamed dumpling is meant to explode in your mouth in a juicy burst of meat.

NOT TO BE MISSED

Drunken anything! Shanghai chefs are known for their love of cooking with wine. Dishes like drunken chicken, drunken pigeon, and drunken crab are all delectable meals cooked with prodigious amounts of Shaoxing wine. People with an aversion to alcohol should definitely avoid these. Another meal not to be missed is hairy freshwater crabs, which only come into season in October. One enthusiast of the dish was 15th-century poet and essayist Li Yu, who wrote of the dish in near-erotic terms. "Meat as white as jade, golden roe . . . to use seasoning to improve its taste is like holding up a torch to brighten the sunshine."

by bus north of the city ✉ *Y15 for admission to the park, Y30–Y200 for use of the hot springs* ☉ *Daily 8:30–6.*

Originally built about 1,000 years ago (Song Dynasty), and rebuilt in 1752 and again in 1945, the **Luohan Temple** is a popular place of worship, and a small community of monks is still active here. One of the main attractions is the 500 lifelike painted clay arhats—Buddhist disciples who have succeeded in freeing themselves from the earthly chains of delusion and material greed. At the back of the temple you can order tea, get a massage, and eat a vegetarian meal every day at 11 am for Y2. ✉ *7 Luohan Si, across from Carrefour* ✉ *Y10* ☉ *Daily 8 am–5 pm.*

Southern Mountain is the highest point in the city, and at 935 feet it's the most popular place from which to view Chongqing. For a thousand years Nan Shan has been the route over which travelers and traders of medicine, tea, spices, and silk entered the city and headed on to Sichuan. Besides spectacular views, the following sites are also on the mountaintop: **The Chongqing Anti-Japanese War Ruins Museum** (✉ *Y20* ☉ *Daily 8:30–5:30*) is a collection of new houses built where the Nationalist Army had its headquarters during WWII. There are a few pictures and maps here, but we found the price too steep for what was offered. For the highest view of Chongqing City, check out the **Viewing Pavilion** (✉ *Y20* ☉ *Daily 8 am–6 pm*), a half-moon pavilion facing north across the Yangtze River. The **Luo Jun Cave Taoist Temple** (✉ *Y6* ☉ *Daily 7:30 am–4:30 pm*) is a 1,700-year-old temple that has been completely renovated but still sees very little traffic. The main temple entrance is accessible from the far side of the mountain, but we recommend slipping through the back door, which is a nice walk up the mountain's main road. The main temple sits on top of five caves that were used by Taoist monks centuries ago for meditation and contemplation. ✉ *Nanping District* ☉ *Daily 7 am–11 pm.*

Red Crag Village is where Zhou Enlai, among other luminaries of the Chinese Communist Party, lived between 1938 and 1945, and where the Chongqing office of the Chinese Eighth Route Army was situated. The **Revolutionary History Museum** (Geming Bowuguan) has been completely rebuilt, and now houses a small wax museum of Communist heroes, a few old reels depicting Japanese bombing missions, and several Communist-style oil murals. However, there are no English guides or translations. ✉ *Hongyan Bus Terminus* ✉ *Free* ☉ *Daily 8:30–5.*

9

DID YOU KNOW?

There are dozens of hole-in-the-wall restaurants all along the stone steps that serve the cheapest, tastiest food in town.

WORTH NOTING

Perhaps not as busy and bustling as once upon a time, **Chaotianmen Docks** still offer an opportunity to get a glimpse of China at work and see the various boats departing for the Three Gorges river cruise. It's also a nice place to witness the merging of the muddy-brown Yangtze River and the blue-green Jialing River. ✉ *Shaanxi Lu.*

The 804-foot **Loquat Hill** has great views of the bustle on the river below. At night, enjoy the city lights. There's also a small park with no entrance fee. ✉ *Zhongshan Er Lu* ☉ *Daily 8–7.*

U.S.–Chiang Kai-shek Criminal Acts Exhibition Hall and SACO Prison. SACO stands for the Sino-American Cooperation Organization, a collaboration between Chiang Kai-shek and the U.S. government and dedicated to the training and supervision of agents for the Nationalist Party gov-

ernment that fought the Communists before retreating to Taiwan. It was jointly run by the Chinese and the Americans, who built prisons outside Chongqing where sympathizers of the Communist Party were imprisoned and tortured. The exhibition hall houses a few photographs and examples of the restraining devices used on the prisoners but has nothing in English. The prisons are a considerable walk from the exhibition hall. The SACO museum is a complex of four separate sites in the Sha Ping Ba suburb in northwest Chongqing, at the foot of and atop Gele Mountain. There is also the option of hiring a car and a guide with passable English for Y140. The prisons are not worth the price, but Gele Mountain is worth the climb; it is peaceful and often misty, and has several small pavilions, a playground, and a monument to the martyrs at the summit. ⊠ *Foot of Gele Mountain, Sha Ping Ba District* ⊡ *Free* ⊙ *Daily 8:30–5.*

WHERE TO EAT

$$–$$$　✕ **La Paella.** One of the newest Western fine-dining experiences in
SPANISH　Chongqing, this restaurant was started by three Chinese friends who spent more than 20 years each on the Iberian Peninsula. True to its name, the restaurant serves a variety of authentic Spanish paellas, plus tapas, salads, steak, seafood, and pizza. The bar mixes good margaritas and tequila sunrises, and also has tasty sangria. Be warned: La Paella can get very busy on weekends and doesn't take reservations. ⊠ *89 SML Plaza, south of Jiefang Bei, Chongqing* ☎ *811/6326–4697* ▤ *No credit cards.*

$　✕ **Paradise Café.** This is the only real Western-style café in the Yuzhong
CAFÉ　District that isn't a Starbucks. The baristas at this locally owned establishment know what they're doing when it comes to espresso drinks—one of the reasons why it's popular with Chongqing expats. Spacious, relaxed, and decorated in warm tones, it's a good place to catch up on e-mails via the free Wi-Fi or chat over cappuccinos. It's located south of the Jiefang Bei at SML Plaza, which makes it a good jumping-off point for an evening out. ⊠ *A-2, SML Plaza, south of Jiefang Bei, Chongqing* ☎ *No phone* ▤ *No credit cards.*

$$　✕ **Qiqi Shanyu Hot Pot.** If you ask a local to name the best example of
HOT POT　classic Chongqing-style hotpot—the city's signature dish—you might be steered to this clean, bright restaurant. Sure enough, it serves up a highly authentic version of the famous bright-red spicy and numbing broth that is the dish's hallmark. The big pot of broth is served hot, and soon comes to a boil over a burner in the center of the table. Diners choose from a range of kinds of tofu, vegetables, and raw shaved beef and mutton and cook these ingredients at their table by placing them in the broth. Qiqi Shanyu has all the classic ingredients, but also has a few tricks up its sleeve, such as compartmentalized pots for cooking

different ingredients with different cooking times. Unusual but highly recommended ingredients include duck and eel. ✉ *69 Linjiang Lu, room 29, 2nd floor, building B, Zourong Plaza, Chongqing* ☎ *023/6379–9369* ▭ *No credit cards.*

$$–$$$ ╳ **Xiaotian'e Sichuan Restaurant.**
SICHUAN Some of the best authentic Sichuanese dishes in Chongqing are served in this restaurant on the bank of the Yangtze. An after-dinner stroll along the banks of the river surrounded by the lights of the city is a great cap to the meal. A house specialty is water-boiled fish slices: the water actually has liberal amounts of oil, dried chilies, whole numbing Sichuan peppercorns, and other spices that create an explosion of flavor. Other good choices are cold rice noodles, tofu-stuffed dumplings, and spicy fried chicken. If you want a seat overlooking the river, try to beat the dinner rush and arrive around 6 o'clock. ✉ *88 Jiabin Lu, 11th Floor, Hongyadong, Chongqing* ☎ *023/6303–9958* ▭ *No credit cards.*

> **CHONGQING NOODLES**
>
> Southern China was not always known for its noodles, as such fare was traditionally the domain of northerners. But during the mass migrations south and west over the past century, noodle culture has been introduced to the Mountain City. Now Chongqing has some of the tastiest bowls anywhere in the nation. Chongqing noodles come in all varieties, and there are too many noodle stands to count.

WHERE TO STAY

$–$$ 🏨 **Hilton Chongqing.** The Hilton is in a leafy, quiet neighborhood near Lianglukou Stadium and the Cultural Palace. Plush rooms have the firmest beds in town and fabulous bathrooms to boot. Rooms on the hotel's western side are quieter and offer leafy sunset views. The rooftop pool is the perfect place to unwind. There are often discounted rooms on weekends. **Pros:** modern and clean; helpful staff. **Cons:** could be closer to shopping. ✉ *139 Zhongshan San Lu* ☎ *023/8903–9999* ⊕ *www.hilton.com.cn* ⇅ *435 rooms and suites* ⚭ *In-room: Internet. In-hotel: 4 restaurants, pool, spa* ▭ *AE, MC, V.*

$ 🏨 **Howard Johnson ITC Plaza Chongqing.** At the moment, HoJo is the top five-star hotel in Chongqing. All rooms feel brand-new, have soft carpet, flat-screen TVs, and the nicest bathrooms in town. The Sixth Sense Western restaurant on the 8th floor is one of the best places in Chongqing for Western food. The Impression Chinese restaurant blends Sichuan haute cuisine with French-Chinese fusion dishes for a unique dining experience. There always seems to be an English-speaking staff member ready to help when you need it. **Pros:** good value; great location. **Cons:** frequently full of large tour groups. ✉ *66 Qingnian Lu, Chongqing* ☎ *023/6366–6666* ⊕ *www.hojo.com* ⇅ *445 rooms* ⚭ *In-room: a/c, safe, refrigerator, Internet. In-hotel: 2 restaurants, room service, bar, pool, gym, laundry service* ▭ *AE, MC, V.*

$$ 🏨 **InterContinental Chongqing.** One of Chongqing's newer luxury hotels, the InterContinental has one of the city's top breakfast buffets, a luxurious spa, and a newly renovated swimming pool and gym. Its rooms are on a par with Chongqing's other top hotels in terms of comfort, but it lacks good river views. The convenient location in the center of

Yuzhong's central business district means good access to nearby food and drink options, as well as several cultural sites. **Pros:** convenient downtown location **Cons:** upper-level views tend to be obscured. ✉ *101 Minzu Lu, Chongqing* ☎ *023/8906–6888* ⊕ *www.intercontinental.com* ⤶ *338 rooms* ☐ *In-room: a/c, safe, refrigerator, Internet. In-hotel: 2 restaurants, room service, bar, pool, gym, spa, laundry service* ▭ *AE, MC, V.*

$$ ⌕ **JW Marriott.** The Marriot is just off the city's main drag within short walking distance of virtually any site near Liberation Monument. Although it is no longer the newest five-star in town, it still maintains high levels of service and cleanliness. The shopping arcade on the ground floor is a nice place to spend an hour or two, and if you're in the mood for steak and excellent views, visit the restaurant on the top floor. **Pros:** variety of food; good pool. **Cons:** bugs; air-conditioning problems. ✉ *77 Qing Nian Lu, Yu Zhong District* ☎ *023/6388–8888* ⊕ *www.marriotthotels.com* ⤶ *460 rooms and suites* ☐ *In-hotel: 5 restaurants, pool, gym, spa* ▭ *AE, DC, MC, V.*

¢ ⌕ **Number 9 Business Hotel.** This no-frills business hotel is located between the Chaotianmen port and the Yuzhong central business district, and is one of the top hotel values in the city. Only a few years old, it's recently renovated rooms are clean and comfortable, but not very spacious. **Pros:** inexpensive, clean rooms. **Cons:** not much in the way of in-hotel facilities. ✉ *29 Xinyi Jie* ☎ *023/8806–0909* ⤶ *180 rooms* ☐ *In-room: a/c, safe, refrigerator, Internet In-hotel: laundry service.* ▭ *No credit cards.*

¢ ⌕ **Yu Du Da Jiu Dian.** A fine option if the foreign hotels are out of your price range but you still want to stay in the Jiefang Bei area. The hotel's great location makes up for its fading decor. The entire street down from the Liberation Monument is filled with food stands during the afternoon and evening hours, so you won't starve. Next door, on the third floor is the Newcastle Arms, an English-style pub with Y20 beers and Y300 bottles of booze. **Pros:** location. **Cons:** starting to feel a little old; noise from outside. ✉ *168 Bayi Lu* ☎ *023/6382–8888* 🖷 *023/6381–8168* ⤶ *160 rooms* ☐ *In-room: Internet. In-hotel: 3 restaurants* ▭ *AE, MC, V.*

NIGHTLIFE AND THE ARTS

Hong Ya Cave (*Hong Ya Dong* ✉ *56 Cangbai Lu, south bank of the Jialing River, Yuzhong District*) is a recently built complex that fuses Ba Yu cultural performances with traditional Chinese architecture and elements of the American mall. It overlooks the Jialing River and has a brightly lit waterfall and paved streets built right into the mountainside. The main attraction is the Ba Yu dance performance, a dancing primer for Chongqing customs and folklore. At times it's racy, and the historical aspects of Ba Yu culture have been dumbed down, but the costumes, choreography, and the bit on the Devil Town of Fengdu make it an evening well spent. For the **Ba Yu Theatre** (☎ *023/6303–9968; 023/6303–9969 ticket reservations* 🎟 *Y180–Y580* ⊙ *Show schedule changes often, so it's best to call or stop by in advance*).

De Yi World (*De Yi Shi Jie* ✉ *Ci Qi Lu, Yu Zhong District, near Jie Fang Bei, around the corner from the Marriott Hotel*) is a large complex of bars, karaoke rooms, and dance clubs. If you want to party with the locals, we recommend **Falling** (⊠ *Basement of De Yi World Complex* ☎ *No phone* 🖼 *Free* ⊘ *6 pm–sunrise*), a cramped club with a little dance floor that is packed on weekends. The music is good for Chinese club standards.

SHOPPING

Carrefour (*Jialefu* ⊠ *Cangbai Lu* ⊘ *9 am–11 pm*), near Chaotianmen Port, is the largest foreign-owned department store chain in China. The France-based giant sells everything from congee to caviar, plus there's a decent import section with all the goodies one misses from home. Carrefour is the best place in Chongqing to stock up on Western food and drink before a Yangtze cruise.

SIDE TRIP TO DAZU

★ *3 hrs (160 km [99 mi]) by bus northwest of Chongqing.*

The Buddhist caves outside of this sprawling city were recently named a UNESCO site. They rival those at Datong, Dunhuang, and Luoyang. The sculptures, ranging from teeny-tiny to gigantic, contain unusual domestic detail, as well as purely religious works. There are two major sites at Dazu—Bei Shan and Baoding Shan. Work at the caves began in the 9th century (during the Song and Tang Dynasties) and continued for more than 250 years.

Baoding Shan is the more impressive of the two sites, where the carvings were completed according to a plan. Here you will find visions of hell reminiscent of similar scenes from medieval Europe; the Wheel of Life; a magnificent 100-foot reclining Buddha; and a gold, 1,000-armed statue of the goddess of mercy.

The best way to reach Dazu is to book a tour through your hotel or a travel agency. Every agency gives the Dazu tour for between Y220 and Y250, which includes transportation, lunch, and the entrance fee. If you would like to go it alone, there are minibuses by the Liberation Monument that can take you there for about Y180 to Y230 round-trip. Leave early, as seats sell out. 🖼 *Y85* ⊘ *Daily 8–5.*

WHERE TO STAY

¢ 🔲 **Dazu Binguan.** Most foreign guests end up staying in this serviceable but unimaginative hotel. The on-site travel agency can help you buy bus or train tickets. **Pros:** prime location. **Cons:** uncomfortable beds, dirty carpet. ⊠ *350 Longgang Zhonglu* ☎ *023/4372–1888* 🖷 *023/4372–2907* 🛏 *132 rooms* ⚲ *In-room: Internet. In-hotel: 2 restaurants, bar* ⊟ *AE, DC, MC, V.*

THE THREE GORGES

The third-longest river in the world after the Amazon and the Nile, the Yangtze cuts across 6,380 km (3,956 mi) and seven provinces before flowing out into the East China Sea. After descending from the

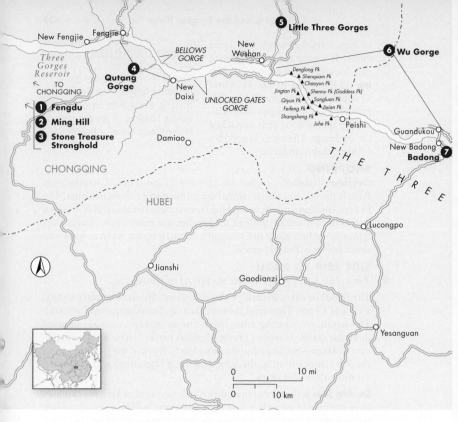

mountain ranges of Qinghai and Tibet, the Yangtze crosses through Yunnan to Sichuan, winding its way through the lush countryside between Sichuan and Hubei before flowing northward toward Anhui and Jiangsu. Before the 20th century, many lost their lives trying to pass through the fearsome stretch of water running through what is known as the Three Gorges—the complicated system of narrow cliffs between Fengjie, in Sichuan, and Yichang, in Hubei.

The spectacular scenery of the Three Gorges—Qutang, Wu, and Xiling—has survived the rising waters of the newly dammed Yangtze River. A trip through the Three Gorges offers a glimpse of the new China moving full steam ahead. Almost all of the cities and towns in the area are in the middle of a construction and tourism boom. The Yangtze itself has endless streams of passenger and cargo boats moving up and downstream.

While there is no doubt that much of the Three Gorges' charm has been diminished by the flooding of the area, what's done is done, and the Gorges are still scenic and fascinating. Sitting on deck and taking in the moon and stars on a clear night while heading downstream is a great way to escape the hustle and bustle of Chinese cities.

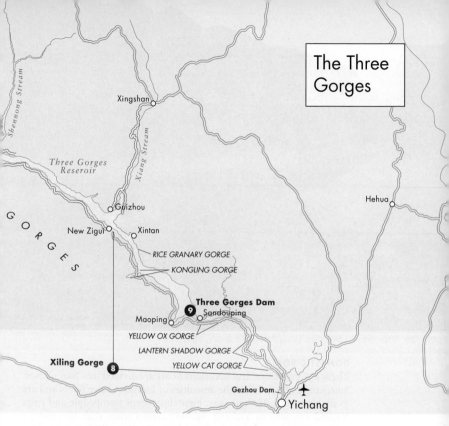

The Three Gorges

BOAT TOURS

Riverboat options depend on how much money you want to spend and how comfortably you want to travel. Riverboat rides essentially come in two forms: luxury and domestic. Domestic cruises are much cheaper and have fewer amenities. No matter which option you choose, book ahead, as berths are limited.

LUXURY CRUISE BOATS

The foreign-owned ships, such as the Victoria Series boats, are big, quadruple-decker liners and by far the most comfortable option. In addition to spacious decks from which to soak up the breathtaking views, many boats are equipped with a gym, a ballroom, a business center with Internet connection, and bars and restaurants. There are also a few shops in case you run out of film or other necessities.

The ticket price includes the admission cost for most of the sites along the way, except the Little Three Gorges. A one-way package tour ranges from Y3,793 to Y4,583, and the boats themselves are divided into three-, four-, and five-star service. Prices fluctuate, so be sure to check ahead.

One of the Victoria cruise ships sailing through the Qutang Gorge.

DOMESTIC BOATS

These less expensive, less luxurious boats are divided into four classes. Suites offer almost all of the amenities of Luxury Cruise Boats and are available for Y2,084 one way. First class sleeps two people and costs Y1,042 one way to Yichang. Spartan rooms come with two beds, a private bathroom, TV, and air-conditioning. Second class sleeps four people and costs Y503 for a one-way ticket. Third class sleeps six to eight people and costs Y347 one way. Both second and third classes have bunk beds, shared bathrooms that aren't always kept clean, and views from lower decks are sometimes limited. Unlike those of the luxury cruise lines, these prices do not include the price of entry to sites along the way. The domestic boats usually serve good Chinese food, depending on the class you choose. Avoid any Western dishes that are on the menu. Sometimes there is no shop on board, so stock up beforehand. If you go in winter, bring an extra blanket and dress warmly.

The tour operators have been consolidated into one company, and most tours get booked through them. Offices can be found throughout the Chaotianmen District.

Contact Chongqing Port International Travel Service (✉ *18 Xinyi St., Chaotianmen, Yu Zhong District, Chongqing* ☎ *023/6310–0595* ⊕ *www.cqpits.com*). Prices range from Y476 for the least expensive tour to Y4,600 for the costliest.

HYDROFOIL

This option is used by those returning from Yichang to Chongqing, who don't want to do the whole trip over again in reverse. Prices may vary, but currently it is Y280 from Yichang to Chongqing and takes about six hours. You have to get off at Wanxian and take a bus back

CLOSE UP

Dam the Yangtze

Nearly a century ago, Chinese leader Sun Yat-sen first proposed damming the Three Gorges area of the Yangtze River, a project that subsequently appealed to Chiang Kai-shek and even the invading Japanese, both of whom prepared plans for the project.

It wasn't until the 1990s under the Communist government that China began building the world's largest power generator, the Three Gorges Dam. In addition to power generation, the dam's locks are big enough to handle containerized sea barges, allowing Chongqing to be the world's farthest inland seaport.

Construction of the main body of the Three Gorges Dam was finished in 2006, and the 26th generator was installed in late 2008. The planned addition of eight more generators by 2011 will bring total power generation capacity to an unmatched 22.5 gigawatts.

Even in China, the sheer scale of this project is staggering. The $26 billion dam is more than 600 feet high and a mile wide. By 2010 it had an installed capacity of 18.2 gigawatts and was able to generate 80,000 gigawatt-hours of power annually.

As with any infrastructure project of its scope, the dam has been controversial from the beginning, with critics focusing on its massive social, cultural, and environmental costs.

The reservoir created by the flooding of the Three Gorges area was preceded by the forced relocation of more than 1.2 million people. Many of these people are now migrant workers in nearby cities.

The rising river levels also resulted in the submerging of many significant and valuable relics and buildings dating back to the beginning of Chinese civilization. Although some artifacts and buildings were moved uphill, it is widely acknowledged that the flooding of the gorges incurred major cultural losses.

It is the environmental impact of the dam project that has attracted the most negative publicity, with serious potential ramifications both upstream and downstream from the dam.

Behind the dam, millions of acres of forest were drowned, and landslides have become a bigger problem than before. The reduced ability of the Yangtze to flush itself clean of wastewater and other pollution has led to the reservoir's containing higher levels of pollution than the river did before damming.

Downstream, it is the lack of sediment that threatens riverbanks, which could become more prone to flooding. The economic dynamo of Shanghai, which is built on the river's floodplain, could also become more vulnerable to inundation after being deprived of normal silt deposits.

While disaster has been averted so far, the heavy rains of the first half of 2010 provided a jittery first major test for the dam, which almost filled to capacity. There are also concerns about cracks already appearing in the dam and its seismological impact.

9

into Chongqing. This costs Y120 and takes another 3½ hours. If you're pressed for time, an airport in Yichang has daily flights to Chongqing.

SIGHTS EN ROUTE

On the banks of the Yangtze, **Fengdu**, also known as Guicheng or the "city of devils," is filled with temples, buildings, and statues depicting demons and devils. During the Tang Dynasty, the names of two local princely families, Yin (meaning "hell") and Wang (meaning "king"), were linked through marriage, making them known as Yinwang, or the "king of hell." Part of the old city has been submerged in the Three Gorges Dam project. You can take a series of staircases or a cable car to the top of the mountain. 🎫 *Y80* ☯ *Daily 6–6*.

The bamboo-covered **Ming Hill** *(Mingshan)* has a Buddhist temple, a pavilion, and pagodas with brightly painted dragons and swans emanating from the eaves. The hill has a nice view of the Yangtze River.

Stone Treasure Stronghold *(Shibaozhai)* is actually a rectangular rock with sheer cliffs, into which is built an impressive 12-story pagoda, constructed by Emperor Qianlong (1736–96) during the Qing Dynasty. Wall carvings and historical inscriptions describing the construction of the building can be seen along the circuitous stairway that leads from the center of the pagoda to the top. The pagoda was damaged by the earthquake, but has been renovated since. 🎫 *Y50* ☯ *Daily 8–7*.

Three Gorges (San Xia). The Three Gorges lie in the heart of China, along the fault lines of what once were flourishing kingdoms. Those great kingdoms vanished into history and became, collectively, China.

The westernmost gorge, **Qutang Gorge** *(Qutang Xia)* is the shortest, at 8 km (5 mi). The currents here are quite strong due to the natural gate formed by the two mountains, Chijia and Baiyan. There are cliff inscriptions along the way, so be sure to have your guide point them out and explain their significance. Several are from the Warring States period over 1,000 years ago. Warriors' coffins from that period were discovered in the caves on these mountains, and some still remain.

Next, a short turn leads to Wushan, at the entrance to Wu Gorge. Here you can change to a smaller boat navigated by local boatmen to the **Little Three Gorges** *(Xiao San Xia* 🎫 *Y240)*. The Little Three Gorges (Dragon Gate Gorge, Misty Gorge, and Emerald Gorge) are spectacular and not to be missed. They are striking and silent, rising dramatically out of the river. If you have time, take a trip to the old town of Dachang near the end of the Little Three.

The impressive **Wu Gorge** *(Wu Xia)* is 33 km (20 mi) long. Its cliffs are so sheer and narrow that they seem to be closing in upon you as you approach in the boat. Some of the cliff formations are noted for their resemblances to people and animals. Most notable is the Goddess Peak, a beautiful pillar of white stone.

At the city of **Badong**, in Hubei, just outside the eastern end of Wu Gorge, boats leave for Shennongjia on the Shennong River, offering passengers an opportunity to take in the costumes and traditions of Tujia and Miao ethnic minorities.

Xiling Gorge *(Xiling Xia)*, 66 km (41 mi) long, is the longest and deepest of all the gorges, with cliffs that rise up to 4,000 feet. There are no stops along here, and it is undoubtedly the most peaceful and contemplative leg of the journey.

Xiling Gorge ends at the **Three Gorges Dam** *(San Xia Da Ba)*. Nothing that you've seen or read about this project can possibly prepare you for its massive scale. Sit back in awe as the boat approaches this great dam and then slowly slips down the locks into the lower reaches of the river. ✉ *Y180.*

9

ENGLISH	PINYIN	CHINESE CHARACTERS
SICHUAN	**SÌCHUĀN**	
Chengdu	Chéngdū	成都
Anlan Cable Bridge	Ānlán suòqiáo	安澜索桥
Chen Mapo Doufu	Chénmápó dòufù	陈麻婆豆腐
Chengdu Chaoshou Canting	Chéngdūlóngchāoshǒu cāntīng	成都龙抄手餐厅
Chengdu Grand Hotel	Chéngdū dàfàndiàn	成都大饭店
Chengdu Zoo	Chéhngdū dòngwùyuán	成都动物园
Chunxi Lu	Chūnxī lù	春熙路
Du Fu's Cottage	Dùfǔ cǎotáng	杜甫草堂
Du River Canal Irrigation System	Dūjiāngyàn shuǐlì gōngchéng	都江堰水利工程
Dujiangyan	Dūjiāngyàn	都江堰
Giant Panda Breeding Research Base	dàxióngmāo bówùguǎn	大熊猫博物馆
Grandma's Kitchen	Zhǔmú de chúfáng	祖母的厨房
Half Dozen Pub	Dàndāpíjiǔ	半打啤酒馆
Jiaotong Hotel	Jiāotōngfàndiàn	交通饭店
Jinjiang Binguan	Jǐnjiāng bīngguǎn	锦江宾馆
Jinjiang Theater	Jǐnjiāng jùyuàn	锦江剧场
Memorial of the Marquis of Wu Zhuge Liang Memorial Hall	Wǔhóu sì	武侯祠
Minshan Fandian	Min Shan Fan Dian	岷山饭店
Old House	Lǎofángzǐ	老房子
Piaoxiang	Piāoxiāng	飘香
Qingyang Palace	Qīngyáng gōng	青羊宫
Renmin Park	rénmín gōngyuán	人民公园
Repeat Qingaong Palace	Qīngyánggōng	青羊宫
Riverview Pavilion Park	Wàngjiānglóu gōngyuán	望江楼公园
Shizi Lou Dajiudian	Shīzǐlóu dàjiǔdiàn	n/a
Sim's Cozy Guest House	Guānhuá qīngnián lǚguǎn	观华青年旅馆
Tibet Hotel	Xīzàng fàndiàn	西藏饭店
Tomb of Emperor Wang Jian	Wángjiàn mù	王建墓
Two Princes Temple	Erwáng miào	二王庙
Wenshu Monastery	Wénshūyuàn	文殊院
Xiangbala Restaurant	Xiāngbālā cānguǎng	n/a
Zhaojue Temple	Zhāojué sì	昭觉寺
Ziyunxuan	Zhǐyúnxuān	紫云轩

ENGLISH	PINYIN	CHINESE CHARACTERS
Emeishan	Éméi shān	n/a
Baoguo Monastery	Bàoguó sì	报国寺
Emeishan Hotel	Éméi dàfàndiàn	峨嵋山大酒店
Golden Summit Temple	Jīndǐng sì	金顶寺
Jieyin Dian	Jiēyīndiàn	接引殿
Teddy Bear Cafe	Xiǎoxióng kāfēi	小熊咖啡
Leshan	Lèshān	乐山
Giant Budda	Lèshān dàfó	乐山大佛
Jiuzhaigou	Jiǔzhàigōu	九寨沟
Lingyun Temple	Língyún sì	n/a
Wuyou Temple	Wūyóu sì	乌尤寺
Songpan	Sōngfān	松潘
Hailougou Glacier	Hǎiluógōu bīngchuán	海螺沟冰川
Kangding	Kàngdìng	康定
Chongqing	Chóngqìng	重庆
Badong	Bādōng	巴东
Baoding Shan	Bǎodìng shān	保定山
cable cars	diàn dǎn chē	电缆车
Chaotianmen Docks	Cháotiānmén mǎtóu	朝天门码头
Check Great Changjiang Bridge	Chóngqìng dàqiáo	重庆大桥
Chengdu Train Station	Chéngdū huǒchézhàn	成都火车站
Chongqing	Chóngqìng	重庆
Chongqing Fandian	Zhóngqìng fàndiàn	重庆饭店
Chongqing Train Station	Chóngqìng huǒchē zhàn	重庆火车站
Dazu	Dàzú	大足
Dazu Binguan	Dàzú bīngguǎn	n/a
Fengdu	Fēngdū	丰都
Gezhou Dam	Gēzhōubà	葛洲坝
Great Changjiang Bridge	Chángjiāng dàqiáo	长江大桥
Holiday Inn Yangtze Chongqing	Yángzhǐjiāng jiǎrì fàndiàn	扬子江假日饭店
hot springs	wēnquán	温泉
Jinyun Mountain	Jìnyún shān	缙云山
Jinyun Mountain	Jìnyún shān	缙云山
Lao Sichuan	Lǎosìchuān	老四川
Little Three Gorges	xiǎo Sānxiá	小三峡
Loquat Hill	Pípá shān	枇杷山

9

ENGLISH	PINYIN	CHINESE CHARACTERS
Luohan Temple	Luóhàn sì	罗汉寺
Min Hill	Mín shān	岷山
Painters Village	Huànjiā zhīcūn	画家之村
Qutang Gorge	Qútángxiá	瞿塘峡
Red Crag Village	Hóngyáncūn	红岩村
Renmin Binguan	Rénmín bīnguǎn	人民宾馆
Shibaozhai	Shíbǎozhài	石宝寨
Three Gorges	Sānxiá	三峡
Tibet Tourism Office	Xīzàng lǚyóu bànshìchù	西藏旅游办事处
U.S. Consulate	Měiguó lǐngshìguǎn	美国领事馆
U.S.-Chiang Kai-shek Criminal Acts Exhibition Hall & SACO Prison	zhōngměi hézuòsuǒ	中美合作所
Wu Gorge	Wūxiá	巫峡
Wushan	Wūshān	巫山
Xiling Gorge	Xīlíngxiá	西岭峡
Yangzi River	Chángjiāng	长江
Yizhishi Fandian	Yìzhīshí fàndiàn	颐之时饭店

The Silk Road

SHAANXI, GANSU, QUINGHAI, AND XINJIANG

WORD OF MOUTH

"Walking through Old Kashgar and visiting the Sunday market were highlights of our trip. I remember there were many families living in Old Kashgar and we have some fabulous photos of the children."

—Kwoo

WELCOME TO THE SILK ROAD

TOP REASONS TO GO

★ **Terracotta Warriors:** Visit one of the nation's most haunting and memorable sites—the vast life-size army of soldiers, built to outlast death.

★ **Discover Dunhuang:** Satisfy your inner archaeologist at the magnificent Mogao caves and scale the shifting slopes of Singing Sand Mountain.

★ **Seek Solace at Kumbum Monastery:** Visit one of the six great monasteries of the Tibetan Buddhist sect known as Yellow Hat, reputedly the birthplace of the sect's founder, Tsong Khapa.

★ **Tour Turpan:** Discover the ruins of the ancient city-states Jiaohe and Gaochang, destroyed by Genghis Khan and his unstoppable Mongol hordes.

★ **Kashgar and the Karakorum Highway:** Explore Central Asia's largest and liveliest bazaar before heading south to the snow-capped Pamir Mountains and crystal-clear Karakul Lake.

TIBET

1 Shaanxi. Visit the tomb of China's first emperor and its army of thousands of terra-cotta warriors in Xian. Shaanxi is the starting point of the fabled Silk Road that brought silks and spices from China to Rome more than two millennia ago.

2 Gansu. Arid and mountainous, Gansu has served as a corridor to the West for thousands of years. Heralded sites include the Mogao Grottoes, Singing Sand Mountain, and the remote Labrang Monastery.

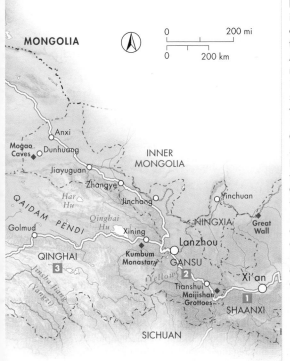

GETTING
ORIENTED

There was no single "Silk Road," but scores of trading posts that formed an overland trade network that linked China, Central Asia, and Europe. The current "Silk Road" received its moniker from German scholar Baron Ferdinand von Richtofen in the mid-19th century, when the Chinese section of the route stretched to Xian in Shaanxi Province. After passing through the famed Jade Gate, which divided China from the outside world, it webbed out in three directions to several key cities in Xinjiang: Ürümqi in the north, Korla in the center, Hotan in the south, and Kashgar in the west.

10

3 Qinghai. Away from the industrialized cities, on the vast open plains, semi nomadic herders, clad in brown robes slashed with fluorescent pink sashes, still roam the grasslands.

4 Xinjiang. Chinese in name only, Xinjiang is a land of vast deserts and ancient Silk Road settlements, including legendary Kashgar. The region is populated by Uyghurs, China's largest minority group.

SHAANXI

By Michael
Manning
Updated by
Helena Iveson

Shaanxi has more often than not been the axis around which the Chinese universe revolved. It was here more than 6,000 years ago that Neolithic tribes established the earliest permanent settlements in China. In 221 bc the territories of the Middle Kingdom were unified here under the Qin Dynasty (from which the name "China" is derived). Propitiously located at the eastern terminus of the famed Silk Road, Shaanxi later gave birth to one of the ancient world's greatest capitals, Changan, a city enriched financially and culturally by the influence of foreign trade.

But nothing lasts forever: as the Silk Road fell into disuse and China isolated itself from the outside world, Shaanxi's fortunes declined. Flood, drought, and political unrest among the province's large Muslim population made Shaanxi a very difficult place to live for most of the past 1,000 years. It's only since the founding of the People's Republic in 1949 that the area has regained some of its former prominence, both as a center of industry and as a travel destination.

PLANNING

WHEN TO GO

The best time to visit is from early May to late October, when it's warm and the land is in bloom with grasses and flowers. It's also high tourist season, when many festivals take place.

In spring, wildflowers make a colorful, riotous appearance on the mountain meadows, rolling grasslands, and lush valleys.

Dry, sunny summers provide blue skies and long days, optimal for exploring and photographing the region. Lunchtime, however, can be insufferably hot, and most tourists follow the locals' lead in taking a midday siesta. Clear skies last usually through October, while winter brings sub-freezing temperatures and a dearth of travelers. Although solitude may have its charms, a few sights close for the off-season.

GETTING HERE AND AROUND

The regional capital Ürümqi is the main travel hub: here it's possible to get flights across the province as well as train and bus services to every corner of the region. To avoid long and back-breaking journeys by bus, it's worth flying at least occasionally, and with tickets often heavily discounted there's not always a huge price differential. The train is also more comfortable than buses and extremely efficient—and with the great scenery, time passes quickly.

AIR TRAVEL

Air China, China Southern, and Hainan Airlines are the main airlines that fly into Ürümqi, Xian, and Lanzhou from major cities in China. From Ürümqi there are daily flights to Kashgar, Hami, Korla, and Hotan, saving you a day-long bus or train ride. Tickets are easy to come by and regularly heavily discounted; check online English-language travel agencies such as ⊕ *www.elong.net.*

BUS TRAVEL

Spectacular scenery and time for contemplation are the rewards for taking bus journeys. The negatives include long hours, regular breakdowns, and often, smoking on board. In Xinjiang, long-distance bus routes crisscross the province, and from Ürümqi there are sleeper buses for the 24-hour journey to Kashgar, but flying is often a similar price. There are, however, tourist buses from Ürümqi to Heavenly Lake, and from Xian to the Terracotta Warriors; these are well run and worth making use of. Sometimes buses or hiring a car can be the only options, for example if you want to travel from Kashgar to Karakul Lake and onto Pakistan.

CAR TRAVEL

It's simple to hire a driver in major tourist destinations such as Xian, Ürümqi, Kashgar, and Turpan; ask your hotel or contact a local tourist agency. It's very unlikely that your driver will speak English, so make sure that he/she knows your destination beforehand and whether tolls and other sundry costs are included in the price. Expect to pay around Y800 a day for a modern, comfortable car.

10

TRAIN TRAVEL

Shaanxi and Gansu provinces are well connected to major cities in the rest of China, with direct trains from Beijing and Shanghai to Xian, Lanzhou, and Dunhuang. Xinjiang and Qinghai are more isolated, though there are trains from all the above cities to Xining and Ürümqi. From Xining (and Lanzhou) it's possible to catch a daily service to Lhasa in Tibet, which takes around 24 hours, though all foreign tourists will need to get a Tibet Travel Permit and book a tour before boarding. From Ürümqi there are regular services to Kashgar, Korla, Hotan, Turpan, and Hami, and Almaty in Kazakstan. ■TIP➔ For all train tickets, save yourself the hassle and ask your hotel or travel agency to book for you—it's not worth the stress!

HEALTH AND SAFETY

In an emergency, your first stop should be a good hotel. Even if you are not a guest, or if you don't speak Chinese or have a Chinese friend to call on, get a hotel involved to arrange treatment and provide translation. If you call them directly, you will find that the emergency services do not speak any English.

TRAVELING IN THE DESERT

Things change quickly from uncomfortable to painful to dangerous in the intense heat of northwest China's expansive deserts. Temperatures in the summer reach 100°F (40°C), with some areas—the depression around Turpan in particular—soaring to 120°F (50°C). Many of the sites you'll be visiting are remote and lack even the most basic facilities.

In conditions like these, it's unwise to travel without abundant water, as well as strong sunscreen, sunglasses, hand sanitizer, a good hat, toilet paper, and some heat-resistant snacks (dried fruit and nuts). If you're a fan of cold water, buy frozen plastic bottles in the morning and they'll stay cool until lunchtime.

> ### WOMEN'S WEAR
>
> Many places along the Silk Road have large Muslim communities, and it's courteous to dress appropriately when there. Women will feel less conspicuous in Xinjiang if they dress as most locals do and wear long trousers and cover their shoulders. Scarves aren't necessary, but they can be good protection against dust.

MONEY MATTERS

It is now possible to use foreign bank cards in all major cities in the region, including Xian, Ürümqi, and Lanzhou. But the farther away you get from industrialized places, the less likely it is that your card will work in a local ATM. Be sure to have a supply of cash to avoid getting stranded. Traveler's checks can be cashed and foreign currency converted at Bank of China branches and major hotels. Tipping is completely unnecessary in restaurants and hotels: some more expensive hotels will add a service charge, but there is no need to add anything extra.

RESTAURANTS

Restaurants vary from street-side stalls to modern indoor restaurants with air-con and English menus, though don't expect cutting-edge style and ambience in any of the eateries in this part of the world.

The cuisine in Shaanxi revolves around noodles and *jiaozi* (dumplings) rather than rice, and lamb is the meat of choice. A Xian Muslim specialty is *yangroù paomo*, a spicy lamb soup poured over broken pieces of flat bread. Other popular Muslim street foods are *heletiao* (buckwheat noodles marinated in soy sauce and garlic) and *roùjiamo* (pita bread filled with beef or pork and topped with cumin and green peppers).

Gansu and Qinghai don't offer many culinary surprises, but in Xinjiang, where temperatures can reach scorching levels, you'll find a variety of local ices, ice cream, and *durap* (a refreshing mix of yogurt, honey, and crushed ice). ⚠ Buyer beware. While delicious, ices might not be as pure or hygienic as you'd like. Traditional Uyghur dishes like *bamian* (lamb and vegetables served over noodles) and *kevap* (spicy lamb kebabs) are ubiquitous, and often washed down with fresh pomegranate juice. Grapes from Turpan and melons from the oasis town of Hami are famous throughout China.

HOTELS

Cities that see a regular influx of tourists, such as Xian and Ürümqi, offer the full spectrum of lodging options. The more remote the area, the fewer the choices, and standards are lower than you might be used to; also, don't expect your credit cards to be accepted. There are almost no boutique options in the region, though in Kashgar there are some dusty hotels that have historic interest, remnants from when the city was a center for trade between the east and west.

WHAT IT COSTS IN YUAN					
	¢	$	$$	$$$	$$$$
Restaurants	under Y25	Y25–Y49	Y50–Y99	Y100–Y165	over Y165
Hotels	under Y700	Y700–Y1,099	Y1,100–Y1,399	Y1,400–Y1,800	over Y1,800

Restaurant prices are for a first course, second course, and dessert. Hotel prices are for two people in a standard double room in high season, including tax and service.

VISITOR INFORMATION

Travelers should use guidebooks, online forums, and travel agencies for information; unfortunately, as in the rest of China, official tourist information is hard to come by.

TOURS

Sino NZ Tourism Group. This well-run travel agency, run out of Xian Apartment Guesthouse, offers Xian City and Terracotta Warrior tours. Their walking tour around Xian is highly recommended; prices depend on the size of your group, and they have basic or with-frills options: for city tours, expect to pay upwards of Y100. ⊠ *Hong Cheng Guoji Gong Yu Xi Hua Men* ☎ *131/4925–0037* ⊕ *www.xianapartmentshq.com.*

CITS. The Xian branch of China's state-run travel service gets much better reports than many other branches, thanks to the friendliness of its young, well-trained staff. CITS will cater tours to your requirements, and although they might be more expensive than options offered at youth hostels, they offer nicer cars and smaller groups. They lead groups to key Silk Road destinations. ⊠ *48 Changan Bei Lu* ☎ *029/8539–9999* ⊕ *www.chinabravo.com.*

XIAN

1½ hrs by plane or 12 hrs by train southwest of Beijing; 15 hrs by train west of Shanghai.

Many first-time visitors to Xian are seeking the massive terra-cotta army standing guard over the tomb of China's first emperor.

Shaanxi

Xian was known in ancient times as Changan (meaning Long Peace), and was one of the largest and most cultured cities in the world. During the Tang Dynasty—considered by many Chinese to be the nation's cultural pinnacle—the city became an important center for the arts. Not surprisingly, this creative explosion coincided with the height of trade on the Silk Road, bringing Turkish fashions to court and foreigners from as far away as Persia and Rome. Although the caravan drivers of yesteryear have long since turned to dust, their memory lives on in the variety of faces seen in Xian.

GETTING HERE AND AROUND

AIR TRAVEL Although Xian's Xianyang Airport is an inconvenient 50 km (30 mi) northwest of the city center in neighboring Xianyang, it has daily flights to and from Beijing, Shanghai, Hong Kong, Guangzhou, Chengdu, Kunming, Dunhuang, and Ürümqi. International destinations include Japan, South Korea, Singapore, and Thailand. At the time of this writing the airport was in the middle of a major expansion.

If your hotel doesn't arrange transportation, taxis will try to squeeze every last yuan out of your wallet; head to the official taxi rank and know that a decent price is around Y120. Buses are a far more economical option, costing Y25 and running every 20 minutes. There are six routes to choose from, with Route 1 to the Bell Tower and 2 to the train station the most useful—make sure you have the name in Chinese.

BUS TRAVEL Just about every bus in Xian passes through the traffic circle around the Bell Tower. If your Chinese is shaky, it's best to stick to taxis.

The long-distance bus station, on Jiefang Lu across the street and just west of the train station, has buses to Lanzhou, Xining, and other destinations throughout Shaanxi and Henan. Tourist destinations like the Terracotta Warriors Museum are served from the parking lot between the train station and the Jiefang Hotel.

CAR TRAVEL Because so many of the sights lie outside the city proper, hiring a taxi or a car and driver gives you the freedom to depart when you like instead of waiting for the rest of the tour. Prices start at about Y800 per day, but vary widely based on the type of vehicle and whether you need an English-speaking guide. Every major hotel can arrange car services.

TRAIN TRAVEL The train station lies on the same rail line as Lanzhou. Those arriving in Xian by train disembark north of the old city walls. The train station is close to most hotels; a taxi should cost less than Y10. The foreigners' ticket window, on the second floor above the main ticket office, is open daily 8:30 to 11:30 and 2:30 to 5:30. It sometimes closes without explanation. For a small booking fee, hotels and travel agencies can get tickets.

SAFETY AND PRECAUTIONS

All normal precautions here apply, especially when it comes to pickpocket prevention at tourist destinations.

TIMING

If you're in a rush, you can see the main city sights plus a day trip to the Warriors in two days; however, Xian is one of China's more appealing cities, and is a rewarding place to stay for longer periods of time. Stay a few days longer, and enjoy the unique ambience of the city's Muslim quarter and great food.

TOURS

Every hotel offers its own guided tours of the area, usually dividing them into eastern area, western area, and city tours. Most tour operators have special English-language tour guides.

Bargaining may get you a much better deal. And check more than one company to make sure you are being charged the going rate. One of the best places to comparison shop is on the second floor of the Bell

---

TREASURES OF SHAANXI

Shaanxi gave birth to 13 major Chinese dynasties, including the Zhou, Qin, Han, and Tang states. The Tang is considered China's Golden Age. Consider first hitting the Shaanxi History Museum. Once you've steeped yourself in its chronology, local "must-see" destinations like Xian's Drum Towers, Muslim Quarter, and Great Goose Pagodas will make much more sense. So, too, will the awe-inspiring army of terra-cotta warriors at the tomb of China's first emperor. True fans of history can even make the trip to China's own "Valley of the Kings" near Xianyang.

10

The Bell Tower in Xian.

Tower Hotel, where several tour companies vie for your business. Try Golden Bridge first, but there are other good options.

EASTERN TOUR By far the most popular option from Xian, tours that head east of the city usually visit the Tomb of the First Qin Emperor, the Terracotta Warriors Museum, and the Huaqing Hot Springs, all in the town of Lintong. Many tours also stop at the Banpo Matriarchal Clan Village in eastern Xian. The China International Travel Service (CITS) offers this tour for Y350, which includes all admission tickets and an English-speaking guide. The journey takes most of the day; plan on leaving after breakfast and returning in time for dinner.

If you don't want a guide, you're better off taking Bus 306, which leaves constantly from the parking lot between the Xian train station and the Jiefang Hotel. The 60-minute journey costs Y7. The Terracotta Warriors are the last stop. To travel between any of the sites in Lintong, a taxi should cost between Y5 and Y10 (although drivers ask foreigners for Y15). To get back to Xian, simply wait along the road for a bus headed to the city.

WESTERN TOUR Less popular than the eastern tour, this excursion varies wildly from operator to operator. Find out what you're getting for the money. Amateur archaeologists and would-be tomb raiders will hardly be able to tear themselves away from the sites in what's been called China's own Valley of the Kings; others will appreciate some of the relics, but may tire of what appear to be mounds of dirt or holes in the ground. Know there is no English-language signage.

Of the 18 imperial tombs on the plains west of Xian, a list of the best should include the Qian Tomb, resting place of Tang Dynasty Empress

Wu Zetian, China's only female sovereign. A number of her relatives—many sentenced to death by her own decree—are entombed in the surrounding area. The tomb of Prince Yi De contains some beautifully restored frescoes. Other stops on the western tour might include the Xianyang City Museum in Xianyang and the Famen Temple in Famen. Sino NZ Tourism Group offers a customizable western tour for between Y400 and Y800, depending on the number of people. Plan on spending the whole day visiting these sites.

ESSENTIALS

Air Contact Xian Xianyang Airport (☏ *029/8879–8450*).

Bank Bank of China (✉ *396 Dong Da Jie* ✉ *157 Jiefang Lu* ✉ *21 Xianning Xi Lu.*

Bus Contact Xian Bus Station (✉ *Jiefang Lu* ☏ *029/8462–9427*).

Internet Hai An Xian Internet Bar (✉ *323 Jiefang Lu* ☏ *029/8741–0555* 💴 *Y1 per hour* ⊙ *8 am–midnight*). Bring your passport.

Medical Assistance In case of an emergency, contact your hotel manager for assistance. If you speak Chinese (or are traveling with someone who does), you can also call emergency numbers. For an ambulance, call 120. **People's Hospital** (✉ *214 Youyi Lu* ☏ *029/8525–1331*).

Police (☏ *110*).

Train Contacts You can also purchase train tickets at the main CITS tourism office (48 Changan Bei Lu). **Xian Huochezhan** (✉ *Huancheng Bei Lu and Jiefang Lu* ☏ *029/8213–0402*).

Visitor and Tour Info CITS (✉ *48 Changan Bei Lu* ☏ *029/8522–3170* ⊕ *www.chinabravo.com* ✉ *Bell Tower Hotel, 110 Nan Da Jie* ☏ *029/8760–0227*). **Golden Bridge Travel** (✉ *Bell Tower Hotel, 110 Nan Da Jie* ☏ *029/8760–0219*). **Sino NZ Tourism Group** (✉ *Hong Cheng Guoji Gong Yu, Xi Hua Men* ☏ *13149250037* ⊕ *www.xianapartmentshq.com*).

EXPLORING

TOP ATTRACTIONS

Bell Tower. Xian's most recognizable structure, the Bell Tower was built in the late 14th century in what was then the center of the city. It's still good a reference point. The tower marks the point where Xi Da Jie (West Main Street) becomes Dong Da Jie (East Main Street) and Bei Da Jie (North Main Street) becomes Nan Da Jie (South Main Street). To reach the tower, which stands isolated in the middle of a traffic circle, use any of eight entrances to the underground passageway. Once inside the building, you'll see Ming Dynasty bells on display. Concerts are given six times daily (9, 10:30, 11:30, 2:30, 4, and 5:30). For Y5 you can make your own music by ringing a copy of the large iron bell that gives the tower its name. Don't miss the panoramic views of the city from the third-floor balcony. ✉ *Junction of Dong Da Jie, Xi Da Jie, Bei Da Jie, and Nan Da Jie* ☏ *No phone* 💴 *Y40 includes admission to Drum Tower* ⊙ *Apr.–Oct., daily 8:30 am–9:30 pm; Nov.–Mar., daily 8:30–6*.

Big Wild Goose Pagoda. This impressively tall pagoda lies 4 km (2½ mi) southeast of South Gate, on the grounds of the still-active Temple of

Thanksgiving (Da Ci'en Si). The pagoda was constructed adjacent to the Tang palace in the 7th century ad to house scriptures brought back from India by monk Xuan Zang. It's been rebuilt numerous times since then, most recently during the Qing Dynasty, in Ming style. A park and huge plaza surround the temple, and locals gather here after work to fly kites, stroll hand in hand, and practice calligraphy. In the evening there is a popular water-fountain show synchronized to music at 9 pm. The main entrance gate to the temple is on the plaza's southern edge. ⊠ *Yanta Lu* ☎ *029/8525–5141* ☒ *Y25; additional Y25 to climb the pagoda* ⊙ *Daily 8–6.*

Drum Tower. Originally built in 1380, this 111-foot-high Ming Dynasty building—which used to hold the alarm drums for the imperial city—marks the southern end of Xian's Muslim Quarter. Various ancient drums are on display inside the building, and concerts are given daily at 9, 10:30, 11:30, 2:30, 4, and 5:30. After passing through the tower's massive base, turn left down a small side street called Hua Jue Xiang to find everything from shadow puppets to Mao memorabilia—truly a souvenir heaven. After clearing that gauntlet, you'll find yourself deep inside the Muslim Quarter at the entrance to the Great Mosque. ⊠ *Bei Yuan Men, 1 block west of the Bell Tower* ☎ *No phone* ☒ *Y40 includes admission to Bell Tower* ⊙ *Apr.–Oct., daily 8:30 am–10 pm; Nov.–Mar., daily 8:30–5:30.*

Great Mosque. This lushly landscaped mosque with four graceful court-yards may have been established as early as ad 742, during the Tang Dynasty, but the remaining buildings date mostly from the 18th century. Amazingly, it was left standing during the Cultural Revolution. Stone tablets mark the various pavilions, often bearing inscriptions in both Chinese and Arabic. Look above the doors and gates: there are some remarkable designs, including three-dimensional Arabic script that makes the stone look as malleable as cake frosting. Non-Muslims are not allowed in the prayer hall, as the mosque is still an active place of worship. The place is a bit hard to find. After passing through the Drum Tower, follow a small curving market street called Hua Jue Xiang on the left. (You'll see an English sign posted on a brick wall next to the street's entrance reading "Great Mosque.") When you reach a small intersection, the mosque's entrance is on the left. The bustling **Muslim Quarter** surrounding the mosque is the center of the city's Hui (Chinese Muslim) community. It's a great place to wander, and you'll find endless food stalls offering everything from cold sesame noodles to pan-fried dumplings to spicy mutton kebabs. ⊠ *30 Hua Jue Xiang* ☒ *Y25* ⊙ *May–Sept., daily 8–7; Oct.–Apr., daily 8–5.*

Fodor's Choice
★
Shaanxi History Museum. Although museums in China are often under-whelming, this is a notable exception. The works in this imposing two-story structure, built in 1991, range from crude Paleolithic stone tools to gorgeously sculpted ceramics from the Tang Dynasty. Several terra-cotta warriors taken from the tombs outside town are on display. The exhibits, which have English descriptions, leave no doubt that China has long been the world's most advanced culture. The museum is free; a limited number of tickets are handed out in the morning and the afternoon. To secure tickets, visitors must arrive early to wait in line.

✉ *91 Xiaozai Dong Lu* ☎ *029/8525–4727* ⊕ *www.sxhm.com* 🎫 *Free* ⊙ *Tues.–Sun. 8:30–6.*

South Gate. This is the most impressive of the 13 gates leading through Xian's 39-foot-high city walls. This was the original site of Tang Dynasty fortifications; the walls you see today were built at the beginning of the Ming Dynasty, and they include the country's only remaining example of a complete wall dating to this dynasty. Repairs mean you can travel the entire 14 km (9 mi) around the city on the top of the wall. The trip by bike takes about 90 minutes. Rental bikes are Y20 for 100 minutes, and you must put down a Y100 deposit. Open-air electric cars cost Y50. ✉ *Nan Da Jie* ☎ *029/8727–1696* 🎫 *Y20* ⊙ *Daily 8 am–9 pm.*

WORTH NOTING

Banpo Matriarchal Clan Village. About 5 km (3 mi) east of the city are the remains of a 6,000-year-old Yangshao village, including living quarters, a pottery-making center, and a graveyard. The residents of this matriarchal community of 200 to 300 people survived mainly by fishing, hunting, and gathering, although there is ample evidence of attempts at animal domestication and organized agriculture. The small museum contains stone farming and hunting implements, domestic objects, and pottery inscribed with ancient Chinese characters near the entrance. The archaeological site has been under renovation since 2003, with no end in sight, but there are, at last, English captions throughout. Unless you're interested in documenting one of China's great tourist oddities, avoid the awful model village that sits in a state of semi disrepair toward the rear of the property. ✉ *139 Banpo Lu, off Changdong Lu* ☎ *029/8353–2482* 🎫 *Y35* ⊙ *Daily 8–5.*

Culture Street. Just inside the city wall, this lively, but very touristy pedestrian street is lined with houses that have been rebuilt in traditional Ming style. Shops sell a wide variety of wares, including charming calligraphy and watercolors. If you're coming from South Gate, halfway down the first block you'll find Guanzhong Academy, built in 1609. Take a peek through the gates, as entrance is forbidden. Continue east along the city wall to reach the Forest of Stone Tablets. ✉ *1 block north of South Gate.*

10

★ **Forest of Stone Tablets Museum.** As the name suggests, there is no shortage here of historical stone tablets engraved with content ranging from descriptions of administrative projects to artistic renditions of landscape, portraiture, and calligraphy. One of the world's first dictionaries and a number of Tang Dynasty classics are housed here. One tablet, known as the Popular Nestorian Stela, dates from ad 781, and records the interaction between the emperor and a traveling Nestorian priest. After presenting the empire with translated Nestorian Christian texts, the priest was allowed to open a church in Xian. While non-Chinese speakers may feel frustrated that they can't read the tablets, there are some with English translations. ✉ *15 Sanxue Jie, end of Culture St.* ☎ *029/8728–2184* 🎫 *Y30* ⊙ *Mar.–Nov., daily 8:15–6:45; Dec.–Feb., daily 8:15–5:15.*

★ **Small Goose Pagoda.** Once part of the 7th-century ad Jianfu Temple, this 13-tier pagoda was built by Empress Wu Zetian in 707 to honor her

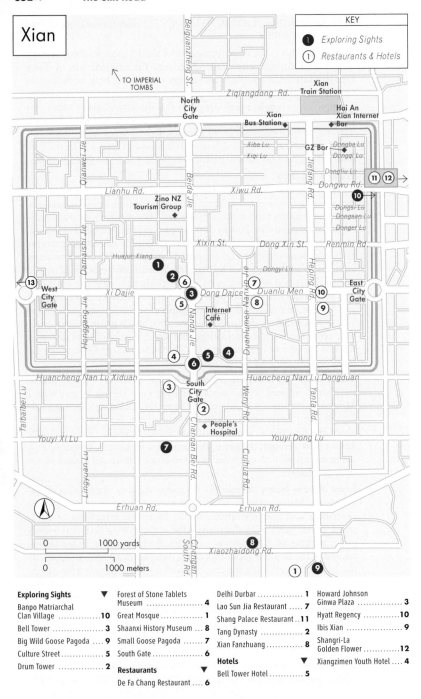

Xian

TO IMPERIAL
TOMBS

KEY

- ❶ *Exploring Sights*
- ① *Restaurants & Hotels*

Beiguanzheng St.

Ziqiangdong Rd.

Xian
Train Station

North
City
Gate

Xian
Bus Station

Hai An
Xian Internet
Bar

Qianwei Jie

Xiba Lu

GZ Bar

Dongba Lu
Dongai Lu

Xiqi Lu

Dongliu Lu

Lianhu Rd.

Beida Jie

Xiwu Rd.

Jiefang Rd.

Dongwu Rd.

⑪ ⑫

Zino NZ
Tourism Group ◆

❿

Damaishi Jie

Dongsi Lu
Dongsan Lu
Donger Lu

Xixin St.

Dong Xin St.

Renmin Rd.

Huajue Xiang

❶

Dongyi Lu

❷ ❻

⑦

Duanlu Men

West
City
Gate

⑬

Xi Dajie

❸

Dong Dajie

East
City
Gate

Hopgang Jie

⑤

Internet
Café ◆

❽

⑩

⑨

Tabaibei Lu

④

⑤ ❹

❻

Nanda Jie

Duanhumen Nan Jie

Heping Rd.

Yanta Rd.

Huancheng Nan Lu Xiduan

Huancheng Nan Lu Dongduan

③

South
City
Gate

②

Wenyi Rd.

People's
Hospital ◆

Youyi Xi Lu

Lingyuan Lu

❼

Changan Bei Rd.

Cuihua Rd.

Youyi Dong Lu

Erhuan Rd.

Erhuan Rd.

0   1000 yards

0   1000 meters

Changan South Rd.

Xiaozhaidong Rd.

❽

① ⑨

predecessor, Emperor Gao Zong. Much less imposing than the Big Goose Pagoda, the smaller pagoda housed Buddhist texts brought back from India by the pilgrim Yiqing in the 8th century. A tremendous earthquake in 1555 lopped off the top two stories of what was originally a 15-story structure; climbing to the top lets you examine the damage. The Xian Museum (entrance Y10) is part of the same

complex, and shows how the ancient capital changed over the centuries. The whole park offers good people-watching opportunities, and is very peaceful compared to other Xian attractions. ⊠ *Youyi Xi Lu, west of Nanguan Zhengjie* ☎ *029/8780–3591* 🎫 *Y25; additional Y20 to climb the pagoda* ☉ *Daily 8–8.*

AROUND XIAN

Famen Temple. Originally built in the 3rd century ad, the temple was the site of an amazing find during renovations in 1981. A sacred crypt housing four of Sakyamani Buddha's finger bones was discovered to hold more than 25,000 coins and 1,000 sacrificial objects of jade, gold, and silver. Many of these objects are now on display in the on-site museum. ⊠ *125 km (80 mi) west of Xian in the town of Famen* ☎ *0917/525–4002* 🎫 *Y90* ☉ *Daily 8–6.*

Hua Shan. A few hours east of Xian lies one of China's five sacred mountains, a traditional watercolor come to life. The 7,218-foot mountain has lovely scenery, including pines reminiscent of a Dr. Seuss creation and sheer granite walls that rise shockingly out of the surrounding plains. The five peaks of Hua Shan reminded ancient visitors of flower petals, hence the name; translated it means "Flower Mountain." Climbing the mountain is not a trip for the fainthearted: unless you're an Olympic athlete, hiking the main trail to the top will take a good seven to nine hours, some of it along narrow passes on sheer cliffs. Thankfully, there's a cable-car ride to North Peak that brings you most of the way up the trail. Don't worry about looking like a wimp; there's plenty of climbing left to do from the cable-car terminal. From Xian you can take a train (three hours, Y12) to Huashan Village, although you'll inconveniently disembark 15 km (9 mi) away in the neighboring town of Mengyuan; frequent minibuses (Y10) link the two places. A better choice is one of the tour buses that leave hourly every morning from the parking lot in front of the Jiefang Hotel, across from the train station. Round-trip bus tickets can be had for Y55. You will be required to provide your passport information when you buy an entrance ticket. 🎫 *Y100 entrance; Y90 one-way/Y150 round-trip cable car; Y40 round-trip minibus from Hua Shan Village to the cable car* ☉ *Cable car operates daily 7–7.*

Huaqing Hot Springs. A pleasure palace during the Tang Dynasty and later, the living quarters of General Chiang Kai-shek during the Chinese Civil War, the destination gets mixed reviews from visitors. Despite the

10

Continued on page 662

THE
TERRACOTTA
SOLDIERS

In 1974, Shaanxi farmers digging a well accidentally unearthed one of the greatest archaeological finds of the 20th century— the Terracotta Soldiers of Qin Shihuang. Armed with real weapons and accompanied by horses and chariots, the more than 8,000 soldiers buried in Qin's tomb were to be his garrison in the afterlife.

(top) Statues depict different military units. (right) Note how the faces differ. Each one is sculpted to be unique.

DID YOU KNOW?

The thousands of life-size soldiers include charioteers, cavalrymen, archers, and infantrymen. They're all arranged according to rank and duty—exactly as they would have been for a real-life battle. Each one has individual facial features, including different mustaches, beards, and hairstyles.

UNCOVERING AN ARMY

WHO WAS QIN SHIHUANG?

After destroying the last of his rivals in 221 BC, Qin Shihuang became the first emperor to rule over a unified China. He established a centralized government headquartered near modern day Xianyang in Shaanxi Province. Unlike the feudal governments of the past under which regional officials developed local bases of power, the new centralized government concentrated all power in the hands of a godlike emperor.

Unfortunately for Qin Shihuang's potential heirs, the emperor's inexhaustible hunger for huge engineering projects created high levels of public unrest. These projects, including a precursor to the Great Wall, his own massive tomb, and numerous roads and canals, required the forced labor of millions of Chinese citizens. In 210 BC, Qin died from mercury poisoning during a failed attempt at making himself immortal. Only four years later, his son was overthrown and killed, bringing an ignominious end to China's first dynasty.

A THANKLESS JOB

The construction of Qin Shihuang's gargantuan tomb complex—which includes the Terracotta Soldiers—was completed by more than 700,000 workers over a period of nearly 40 years. The warriors themselves are believed to have been created in an assembly line process in which sets of legs and torsos were fired separately and later combined with individually sculpted heads. Most workers were unskilled laborers; skilled craftsmen completed more delicate work such as the decoration of the tomb and the molding of heads. The soldiers were then painted with colored lacquer to make them both more durable and realistic. It's believed that all of the workers were buried alive inside the tomb (which hasn't yet been excavated) to keep its location and treasures a secret and protect it from grave robbers.

DISCOVERING THE SOLDIERS

Only five years after the death of Qin Shihuang, looting soldiers set fire to the thick wooden beams supporting the vaults. As wood burned and the structure became unsound, beams and earthen walls came crashing down onto the statues, crushing many soldiers and burying all. In many ways, though, the damage to the vaults was a blessing in disguise. The buried Terracotta Soldiers were forgotten to history, but the lack of oxygen and sunlight preserved the figures for centuries.

Since its rediscovery, only a part of the massive complex has been excavated, and the process of unearthing more warriors and relics continues. No one is sure just how many warriors there are or how far the figures extend beyond the already excavated 700-foot-by-200-foot section. For the time being, most excavation work has stopped while scientists attempt to develop a method of preserving the figures' colored lacquer, which quickly deteriorates when exposed to oxygen.

(top) Warriers were once painted in bright colors.

IN FOCUS THE TERRACOTTA SOLDIERS

10

VISITING THE SOLDIERS

Be sure to walk around to the rear of Vault 1, which contains most of the figures that have already been unearthed. There you can see archaeologists reassembling the smashed sodiers.

Vaults 2 and 3 contain unreconstructed warriors and their weapons and give you an idea of how much work went into presenting Vault 1 as we see it today.

CIRCLE VISION THEATER

Before heading to the vaults, stop by this 360-degree movie theater and learn how the army was constructed, destroyed, forgotten, and then rediscovered. Although the film is cheesy, it's nonetheless entertaining and informative. It gives a sense of what the area may have been like 2,200 years ago.

VAULT 1

Here you'll find about 6,000 warriors, although only 1,000 have been painstakingly pieced together by archaeologists. The warriors stand in their original pits and can only be seen from the walkways erected around the digs. Those in the front ranks are well shaped and fully outfitted except for their weapons, whose wooden handles have decayed over the centuries (the chrome-plated bronze blades were still sharp upon excavation). Walk around to the rear of the vault where you can see terracotta soldiers in various states of reconstruction.

Archaeologists have puzzled together almost 1,000 statues, including warriors, chariots, horses, officials, acrobats, strongmen and musicians. The tallest statues are also the highest in rank; they are the generals.

COLORATION

The colored lacquers that were used not only gave the terracotta soldiers a realistic appearance, but also sealed and protected the clay. Unfortunately, upon exposure to oxygen, these thin layers of color become extremely brittle and flake off or crumble to dust. Chinese scientists are devising excavation methods that will preserve the coloration of warriors unearthed in the future.

Ready on one knee with bow in hand, these archers are poised to rise and fire a deadly salvo at a moment's notice.

Every cavalry rider is accompanied by a life-size terracotta horse.

VISITING THE SOLDIERS

(top) Statues were made in pieces and then assembled. (right) The statue of an officer. (opposite page) The cavalry horses.

VAULT 2

This vault offers a glimpse of unreconstructed figures as they emerge from the ground. It has remained mostly undisturbed since 1999 when archaeologists found the first tricolor figures—look closely and you can still see pink on the soldiers' faces and patches of dark red on their armor. As with ancient Greek sculptures, the warriors were originally painted in lifelike colors and with red armor. Around the sides of the vault, you can take a close-up look at excellent examples of soldiers and their weaponry in glass cases.

VAULT 3

Sixty-eight soldiers and officers in various states of reconstruction stand in what appears to be a military headquarters. Although the condition of the warriors are similar to those in Vault 2, there is one unique figure: a charioteer standing at the ready, though his wooden chariot has been lost to time.

QINYONG MUSEUM

Near Vault 3, an imposing sand-colored pavilion houses two miniature bronze chariots unearthed in the western section of Qin Shihuang's tomb. Found in 1980, these chariots are intricately detailed with ornate gold and silver ornamentation. In the atrium leading to the bronze chariots, look for a massive bronze urn—it's one of the treasures unearthed by archaeologists in their 1999 excavation of an accessory pit near the still-sealed mausoleum. Other artifacts on display including Qin Dynasty tricolor pottery and Qin jade carvings.

GETTING THERE

Practically every hotel and tour company in Xian arranges bus trips to the Terracotta Soldiers as part of an Eastern Tour package. If you aren't interested in having an English-speaking guide for the day, you can save a lot of money by taking one of the cheap buses (Y10 one-way) that leave for the town of Lintong from the parking lot between Xian's train station and the Jiefang Hotel. The ride to the Terracotta Warriors Museum should take between 90 and 120 minutes.

Opening Hours: Mar.–Nov., daily 8:30–5:30; Dec.–Feb., daily 8:30–5.

Admission: Mar.–Nov., Y90 ; Dec.–Feb., Y65. Price includes movie, access to three vaults, and entrance to the Qinyong Museum.

Phone: 029/8139–9001 (main office); 029/8139–9126 (ticket office).

VISITING TIPS

Cameras: You can shoot photographs and videos inside the vaults, a change from previous years when guards brusquely confiscated film upon seeing your camera. You still can't use a flash or tripod, however.

Souvenirs: You can buy postcards and other souvenirs in the shops outside the vaults and the Circle Vision Theater. Alternatively, you can face the fearsome gauntlet of souvenir hawkers outside the main gates; miniature replica terracotta soldiers can be found here for as little as Y1 each. If you're intimidated by the aggressive touts, however, there's nothing available here that you can't get back in Xian. So be strong, don't look them in the eyes, and most important, never stop walking.

Time: You'll likely end up spending two to three hours touring the vaults and exhibits at the Terracotta Warriors Museum. The time spent here will probably be part of a long day-tour visiting a number of sites—the Hauqing Hot Springs and possibly the Banpo Matriachal Clan Village—clustered around the small city of Lintong, east of Xian.

RAIDERS OF THE LOST TOMB

Qin started construction on his enormous, richly endowed tomb, said to be boobytrapped with automatic crossbows, almost as soon as he took the throne. According to ancient records, this underground palace contained 100 rivers of flowing mercury as well as ceilings inlaid with precious stones and pearls representing the stars and planets. Interestingly enough, mercury levels in the area's soil are much higher than

normal, indicating that there may be truth to those records. Though the site of the tomb was rediscovered to the east of Xian in 1974 (soon after the Terracotta Soldiers were unearthed), the government didn't touch it because it lacked the sophisticated machinery needed to excavate safely. Authorities also executed any locals foolish enough to attempt a treasure-seeking foray. In 1999, archaeologists finally began excavations

of the area around the tomb and unearthed some fabulous treasures. They've only scratched the surface, however. Most of the tomb still lies buried. In fact, no one is even certain where its main entrance—reportedly sealed with molten copper— is located. Authorities have delayed further excavations until the tomb can be properly preserved rather than risk damaging what may be China's greatest archaeological site.

IN FOCUS THE TERRACOTTA SOLDIERS

10

name, the hot springs are often out of action, leaving visitors to wander around the garden. You'll probably be happier spending your time on **Li Shan,** the small mountain directly behind Huaqing Hot Springs. It was on these slopes that Chiang was captured, and it has China's first beacon tower and a number of small temples. If you're there in the evening (8.30 pm), catch the light and sound show that uses the mountain as a backdrop. ⊠ *30 km (19 mi) east of Xian in the town of Lintong* ☎ *029/8381–8888* 🖼 *Y70* ⊗ *Daily 8–6.*

Fodor's Choice **Terracotta Warriors Museum.** Discovered in 1974 by farmers digging a
★ well, this archaeological dig, a UNESCO World Heritage site, includes more than 7,000 terra-cotta soldiers standing guard over the tomb of Qin Shihuang, the first emperor of a unified China. The warriors, 1,000 of which have been painstakingly pieced together, come in various forms: archers, infantry, charioteers, and cavalry. Relics are still being found. In 2010, 114 extra warriors were discovered in Pit One. Incredibly, each of the life-size statues is unique, including different mustaches, beards, and hairstyles. An exhibition hall displays artifacts unearthed from distant sections of the tomb, including two magnificently crafted miniature bronze chariots. Allow yourself at least three hours if you want to study the warriors in detail. ⊠ *30 km (19 mi) east of Xian in the town of Lintong* ☎ *029/8139–9170* ⊕ *bj.bmy.com.cn* 🖼 *Mar.–Nov., Y110; Dec.–Feb., Y65* ⊗ *Daily 8:30–5:30.*

Tomb of the First Qin Emperor. The tomb—consisting mainly of a large burial mound—may pale compared to the Terracotta Warriors Museum, but history buffs will enjoy it. According to ancient records, the underground palace took more than 40 years to build, and many historians believe the tomb contains a wealth of priceless treasures, though perhaps we will never know for sure. You can climb to the top of the burial mound for a view of the surrounding countryside, although most visitors hurry off to see the Terracotta Warriors Museum after watching a mildly amusing ceremony honoring the emperor who united China. ⊠ *30 km (19 mi) east of Xian in the town of Lintong* 🖼 *Y40* ⊗ *Apr.–Oct., daily 7–7; Nov.–Mar., daily 8–6.*

WHERE TO EAT

¢–$ ✕ **De Fa Chang Restaurant.** If you think dumplings are just occasional
CHINESE snack food, think again. De Fa Chang, one of Xian's most famous restaurants, is known for its dumpling banquet. Do try the pan-fried *guotie,* stuffed with pork and chives. For the dumpling banquet, head upstairs and choose between the preset menus. Considerably cheaper à la carte dishes can be found downstairs; just grab a plate as a cart passes by your table and be ready to pay on the spot. ⊠ *Xi Da Jie, north side of Bell Tower Sq.* ☎ *029/8721–4060* ▭ *No credit cards.*

$–$$ ✕ **Delhi Darbar.** When you need a change from Chinese food, try this
INDIAN place run by Indian expats for spicy flavors and friendly service. It's near the Big Wild Goose Pagoda. Try the Palak Green Peas Masala with fluffy naan bread. Vegetarians will feel right at home—for once you can rely on waitresses to tell you if there is meat in a dish! ⊠ *3 Huan Ta Xi Lu* ☎ *029/8525–5157* ▭ *No credit cards.*

¢–$
NORTHERN
CHINESE

×**Lao Sun Jia Restaurant.** This traditional, family-run affair has been serving some of the best local Islamic lamb and beef specialties since 1898; it's become so popular that it's grown into a small Xian chain. The decor isn't special, but the food is popular with Xian's large Muslim community. A few famous offerings, such as the roasted leg of lamb or the spicy mutton spareribs, are pricey, but most dishes are inexpensive. Try *pao mo*, the mutton and bread soup. Ask for an English menu. ⊠ *364 Dong Da Jie, near the corner of Duanlu Men* ☏ *029/8721–6929* ⊟ *No credit cards.*

$$$
CANTONESE
★

×**Shang Palace Restaurant.** All of Xian's top hotels have elegant eateries, but Shang Palace deserves special mention for its Cantonese and Sichuan dishes, which are authentic and approachable. On the menu, classics like honey-barbecued pork and stir-fried chicken with chili sit alongside less familiar dishes; note that drinks are pricey. As you dine, musicians pluck away in traditional costumes. Most of the staff speak some English. ⊠ *Shangri-La Golden Flower Hotel, 8 Changle Xi Lu* ☏ *029/8323–2981, Ext. 4386* ⊟ *AE, MC, V.*

$$$
CHINESE
Fodor's Choice
★

×**Tang Dynasty.** Don't confuse the cuisine served in the Tang Dynasty's popular dinner theater with the specialties available at the separate restaurant. While the former serves mediocre, tourist-friendly fare, the latter specializes in Tang Dynasty–imperial cuisine—a taste you're not likely to find back home at your local Chinese restaurant. Locals praise the abalone and other fresh fish dishes as the finest in Xian. You can reserve either for dinner and the show (Y500) or just the show Y220, which starts every night at 8:30 pm. ⊠ *75 Changan Bei Lu Xian* ☏ *029/8782–2222* ⊕ *www.xiantangdynasty.com* ⊟ *AE, MC, V.*

¢–$
CHINESE

×**Xian Fanzhuang.** This restaurant specializes in Shaanxi snacks with a Muslim flavor, as well as "small eats"—street food spruced up for the visitor. Business executives and T-shirt-clad college students alike head to the bustling first-floor dining room for the all-you-can-eat buffet (Y25). An adjacent entrance leads to a second-floor restaurant, where more exotic and expensive dishes—algae flavored with orchid, for example—are prepared. An English menu is available. ⊠ *Xian Hotel, 298 Dong Da Jie* ☏ *029/8727–3185* ⊟ *No credit cards.*

WHERE TO STAY

$–$$
★

Bell Tower Hotel. Relatively inexpensive compared to other hotels in its class, the very popular Bell Tower has spacious, airy rooms with views overlooking downtown Xian. Directly across from the Bell Tower, this hotel puts you within walking distance of many tourist sights. On the second floor, you can compare rates offered by three experienced travel agencies, all competing aggressively for your business. Rooms at the front of the building are more expensive because they have views of the Bell Tower, but some visitors are disturbed by noise from the traffic. **Pros:** excellent location. **Cons:** absence of character; hotel restaurants are mediocre. ⊠ *110 Nan Da Jie* ☏ *029/8760–0000* 🖷 *029/8727–1217* ⊕ *www. belltowehotelxian.cn* ↩ *300 rooms, 11 suites* ⬙ *In-room: safe, refrigerator, Internet. In-hotel: 2 restaurants, bar, laundry service* ⊟ *AE, MC, V.*

$

Howard Johnson Ginwa Plaza. Don't look for the familiar orange roof here. This is a five-star operation rivaling the best in the city, and it's conveniently located just outside the city walls near South Gate. Rooms

10

are outfitted with top-quality European-style furnishings and feature separate workspaces that are much appreciated by travelers. Superior rooms have views of the city wall. **Pros:** attractive lobby; superb variety at mealtimes. **Cons:** nothing individual about this place; language barriers with staff. ⊠ *18 Huancheng Nan Lu* ☎ *029/8818–1111* ⊕ *www. hojochina.com* ⇱ *324 rooms* ⚐ *In-room: safe, Internet. In-hotel: 2 restaurants, bar, spa, laundry service, business center* ⊟ *AE, MC, V.*

\$\$\$–\$\$\$\$ ⚏ **Hyatt Regency.** Although there are newer luxury properties, people return here because of this hotel's friendly staff and location. Near the most popular sights, it's within walking distance of the Bell Tower and the East Gate. The beds are extremely comfortable, and the large windows provide great views of the city. The guest rooms, however, are smaller and drabber than rooms at other comparably priced hotels; chirping birds in the atrium lobby can be annoying when you're trying to fall asleep. **Pros:** walking distance to the city's sights; fun bar; which is an expat hangout; cheerful staff. **Cons:** overpriced breakfast. ⊠ *158 Dong Da Jie* ☎ *029/8723–1234* ⊕ *www.hyatt.com* ⇱ *315 rooms, 22 suites* ⚐ *In-room: safe, Internet. In-hotel: 2 restaurants, bar, tennis court, gym, laundry service, business center* ⊟ *AE, MC, V.*

¢ ⚏ **Ibis Xian.** The best bargain in Xian is part of the French budget hotel chain. It offers excellent rooms and low prices and is run to Western standards, so the beds are comfortable and everything is clean. The hotel is inside the Old City (within walking distance of the Confucius Temple), and a few Chinese bars are up the road. The hotel's travel agent can organize cars and so forth. There's free Wi-Fi in the lobby. **Pros:** great location; friendly service. **Cons:** unappealing breakfast. ⊠ *59 Heping Lu* ☎ *029/8727–5555* ⊕ *www.accorhotels.com* ⇱ *220 rooms* ⚐ *In-room: safe, Internet. In-hotel: restaurant, bar, laundry service, Wi-Fi* ⊟ *AE, MC, V.*

\$\$\$–\$\$\$\$ ⚏ **Shangri-La Golden Flower.** The older of the two Shangri-La's in Xian, this remains one of the city's most luxurious hotels, Still, parts of the hotel could do with a refit, including the fitness center and room bathrooms. The English-speaking staff are very helpful—you'll find yourself wondering how they manage to tidy up your room and turn down your bed during the half hour you spent swimming laps in the indoor pool. The hotel is 15 minutes northeast of the city center. **Pros:** spacious rooms; excellent room service. **Cons:** layout is confusing; rooms are beginning to show their age. ⊠ *8 Changle Xi Lu* ☎ *029/8323–2981; 800/8942–5050 in the U.S.* ⊕ *www.shangri-la.com* ⇱ *416 rooms, 16 suites* ⚐ *In-room: safe, Internet. In-hotel: 2 restaurants, bars, pool, gym* ⊟ *AE, MC, V.*

¢ ⚏ **Xiangzimen Youth Hostel.** The historic building, a converted *siheyuan* house, and its location just steps away from the imposing South Gate, can't be beat. Rooms are hostel-standard—pine furniture and dorm-style bathrooms—but the doubles with private en-suites are more appealing. The common room is lively every night with locals and travelers. The hostel also runs its own inexpensive tours. **Pros:** great staff; great place to meet other travelers. **Cons:** showers in the shared bathrooms leak. ⊠ *16 Xiang Zi Ta Jie* ☎ *029/6286–7888* ⊕ *www.yhaxian. com* ⇱ *40 rooms* ⚐ *In-hotel: restaurant, bar, laundry service, Internet* ⊟ *AE, MC, V.*

NIGHTLIFE AND THE ARTS

Muslim Quarter. One of the busiest parts of town in the evening, this is where crowds converge to shop, stroll, and eat virtually every night of the week. Street-side chefs fire up the stoves and whip up tasty dishes, vendors ply the crowded lanes peddling their wares, and locals and tourists alike jostle in the frenetic pace.

The impressive song and dance performance at **Tang Dynasty** (✉ *75 Changan Bei Lu* ☎ *029/8782–2222* ⊕ *www.xiantangdynasty.com*) is the city's most popular evening of entertainment for foreign visitors. Shows begin at 8:30. **GZ Bar** (✉ *Dong Qi Dao Xiang* ☎ *133/5920–7823*), the only jazz bar of its kind in Xian, is worth seeking out for its nightly live music and cheap beers.

SHOPPING

Predictably, Xian is overloaded with terra-cotta souvenirs. There is more to buy in Xian, however. **Hua Jue Xiang Market** (✉ *Hua Jue Xiang*), the alley leading to the Great Mosque, is one of the best places to find interesting souvenirs. Expect the antique you're eyeing to be fake, no matter how vehemently the vendor insists that your find is "genuine Ming Dynasty." The shops along **Culture Street** (✉ *Wenhua Jie*) are filled with carved jade, calligraphy, and Shaanxi folk paintings. Even if you don't buy anything, it's a nice place for a stroll.

GANSU

Gansu is the long, narrow province linking central China with the desert regions of the northwest. For centuries, as goods were transported through the region, Gansu acted as a conduit between China and the Western world. As merchants made their fortunes from silk and other luxuries, the oasis towns strung along the Silk Road became important trade outposts of the Middle Kingdom. But beyond the massive fortress at Jiayuguan lay the end of the Great Wall, the oasis of Dunhuang, and then perdition. Gansu was the edge of China.

What has long been the poorest province in China is essentially dry, rugged, and barren. The decline of the Silk Road brought terrible suffering and poverty, from which the area has only very recently begun to recover as tourism boosts the local economy. Gansu was in the newspapers in 2008 when Tibetan riots spread from Lhasa. Ethnic Tibetans and monks protested at Labrang Monastery and Xiahe, leading to a harsh crackdown by Chinese police. The area was closed off to foreign tourists for a while, but it is now open and life has returned to normal, though tension remains. But the province was again hit with disaster in 2010, when heavy rain lead to mudslides in Zhouqu, causing 1,500 deaths. The roads between Xiahe and Lanzhou were unaffected.

REGIONAL TOURS

John's Information Cafè. There isn't a lot of choice when it comes to tours in Gansu, but this branch of a small chain of cafés along the Silk Road, owned by the affable John Hu, offers tours to Dunhuang and the Mogao Caves led by English-speaking guides. Prices are negotiable and depend on the number of people traveling, but expect to

pay about Y200 per day excluding admission (which adds up). They can also arrange tours of Lanzhou. ✉ *21 Mingshan Lu, north of the Feitian Hotel, opposite the bus station Dunhuang* ☎ *1399/373–3106* ⊕ *www.johncafe.net.*

LANZHOU

8 hrs by train northwest of Xian; 21 hrs by train southeast of Ürümqi; 2½ hrs by train east of Xining, 18 hours by train from Beijing.

Built on the banks of the Yellow River, the capital of Gansu extends along the base of a narrow gorge whose walls rise to 5,000 feet. A city with a long history, Lanzhou has been nearly ruined by rampant industrialization, and is now one of the world's most polluted urban areas. Though air quality is getting better, in winter the city can be filled with smog. The ethnic mix of the city's population makes the place interesting for a few hours, but plan to stay here only as long as it takes to arrange transportation to somewhere more pleasant, like Xiahe or Dunhuang.

GETTING HERE AND AROUND

The city's Zhongchuan Airport is 70 km (49 mi) north of town. Because of this, most people arrive by train.

AIR TRAVEL   From Lanzhou there are daily flights to Dunhuang, Beijing, Guangzhou, Shanghai, Chengdu, Ürümqi, and Xian. A public bus costing Y30 per person takes more than an hour to reach the airport from the China Northwest Airlines office at 512 Donggang Xi Lu.

BUS TRAVEL   Long-distance buses arrive at the East Station (*Qiche Dongzhan*) on Pingliang Lu, north of the train station. Leaving the city can be a bit more complicated. Buses to major destinations like Xian, Xining, Jiayuguan, and Dunhuang usually leave from East Station, whereas lesser destinations are served by the West Station (*Qiche Xizhan*). Buses to Xiahe depart from South Station (*Qiche Nanzhan*).

Buses originating in Lanzhou often require foreigners to show proof of travel insurance bought from the Chinese company PICC (The People's Insurance Company of China—a monsterously large insurance company) before purchasing tickets. It's unclear why this regulation exists, or why there's usually at least one daily bus to each destination that doesn't require the paperwork. You should be able to purchase insurance with your bus ticket, but this is often not the case. For peace of mind, head straight to the main PICC office on the north side of Qingyang Lu, just east of Jingning Lu. They'll know why you're there. A two-week policy costs Y40. Since the riots of 2008, rules can change at the drop of a hat. At this writing, you were required to show two photocopies of your visa and passport details.

TRAIN TRAVEL   The train station (Lanzhou Huochezhan) is at the southern end of Tianshui Lu, 1 km (½ mi) south of the city's hotels. Because few trains originate here, buying sleeper tickets in Lanzhou can be difficult; your best bet is to buy tickets early or hope for an upgrade onboard.

SAFETY AND PRECAUTIONS
Heavy rain in 2010 led to mudslides that wreaked havoc and caused 1,500 deaths. Because of this, it would pay to check with a tour company such as John's Information cafés before venturing out to the affected areas. Also, there can be friction between ethnic Tibetans and Han Chinese.

TIMING
Lanzhou's appeal is limited; stay only as long as you need to arrange transportation to the province's other worthier attractions.

TOURS
Gansu Western Travel Service offers a day trip to Thousand Buddha Temple and Grottoes that includes all transportation and insurance for around Y400 per person. The company also has tours to Xiahe, including a five-day trip that visits the spectacularly beautiful Tibetan temples at Langmusi on the border with Sichuan. A basic two-day tour from Lanzhou costs between Y600 and Y750 per person, including hotel.

ESSENTIALS
Air Contacts China Northwest Airlines (✉ *512 Donggang Xi Lu* ☎ *0931/882–1964*). **Lanzhou Zhongchuan Airport** (✉ *Zhongchuan* ☎ *0931/896–8160*).

Bank Bank of China (✉ *589 Tianshui Lu* ☎ *0931/888–9942*).

Bus Contacts Lanzhou East Bus Station (✉ *Pingliang Lu* ☎ *0931/841–8411*). **Lanzhou West Bus Station** (✉ *458 Xijin Dong Lu* ☎ *0931/233–3285*). **Lanzhou**

10

South Bus Station (✉ *Lanzhou Nan Gonggongqiche Zhan, Langong Ping Lu,* ☎ *0931/291–4066*).

Train Contact Lanzhou Train Station (✉ *Huoche Zhan Dong Jian, at the southern end of Pingliang Lu and Tianshui Lu* ☎ *0931/882–2142*).

Visitor and Tour Info Gansu Western Travel Service (✉ *Lanzhou Hotel, 486 Donggang Xi Lu* ☎ *0931/885–2929 or 138/9331–8956*).

EXPLORING

Five Springs Mountain Park. In Lanzhou's best park you can sip tea among ancient temples and see impressive views of the city below. The five springs that gave the place its name, unfortunately, have dwindled to a trickle. ✍ *Y6* ⊙ *Daily 8–7.*

Fodor'sChoice
★

Gansu Provincial Museum. The most famous item in the collection of this excellent museum is the elegant bronze "Flying Horse," considered a masterpiece of ancient Chinese art. Other notable objects include a silver plate documenting contact between China and Rome more than 2,200 years ago, and wooden tablets used to send messages along the Silk Road. Exhibits are uniformly subtitled in English. ✉ *3 Xijin Xi Lu, across from the Friendship Hotel* ✍ *Free* ⊙ *Tues.–Sun. 9–5.*

Mountain of the White Pagoda Park. Laid out in 1958, the park covers the slopes on the Yellow River's north bank. It's more of a carnival than a place to relax, but it's a great place for people-watching. ✉ *Entrance at Zhongshan Qiao, the bridge extending over the Yellow River* ✍ *Y7* ⊙ *Daily 7:30–7:30.*

WHERE TO EAT

Many of the best restaurants in Lanzhou are in its upscale hotels; one to try is Zhong Hua Yuan in the Lanzhou Hotel, where an English menu is available. Another place to find a good meal is along Nongmin Xiang Lu, a street that runs behind the Lanzhou Hotel. This is a great place to try the *roujiamo*, a small sandwich filled with onion, chili, and flash-fried lamb or beef.

¢–$
SICHUAN

✕ **Chuanwei Wang.** You can often tell a good restaurant by the lack of empty tables; at mealtimes, this Sichuanese eatery is always packed. There's no English menu, but pictures of almost every dish make ordering simple. If you're stuck, order *gongbao jiding,* a slightly spicy dish of chicken stir-fried with peanuts. ✉ *26 Nongmin Xiang Lu, north of Tianshui Lu* ☎ *0931/887–9879* ▭ *No credit cards.*

$–$$$
CHINESE

✕ **Xinhai Restaurant.** One of Lanzhou's finest eateries, Xinhai is surprisingly affordable. Lanzhou specialties such as braised beef and hand-pulled noodles, as well as Cantonese and Sichuanese dishes, are pictured on the menu; you can also order from the text-only English menu. ✉ *499 Donggang Xi Lu, next to Legend Hotel* ☎ *0931/886–6078* ▭ *No credit cards.*

WHERE TO STAY

¢–$

▦ **Jing Jiang Sun Hotel.** From the marble floors in the lobby to the plush furnishings, this is Lanzhou's top luxury hotel, spread over 25 stories. On the west side of the building, the upper floors have sweeping views of the mountains; if you're trying to stay cool, however, be aware that

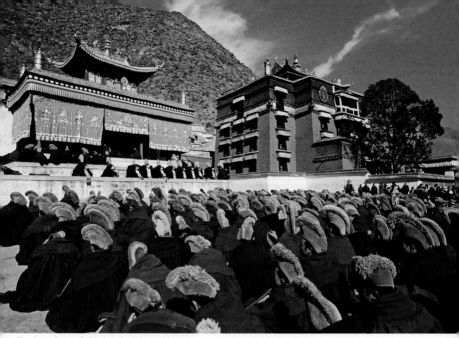

The Great Prayer Festival at the Labrang Monastery.

the sun makes these rooms warmer than those on the east side. **Pros:** excellent value; reception staff speak English. **Cons:** expensive Internet and business-center facilities are sparse; in a commercial part of town ⊠ *481 Donggang Xi Lu* ☎ *0931/880–5511* ⊕ *www.jjsunhotel. com* ⤵ *236 rooms* ⚷ *In-room: safe, Internet. In-hotel: restaurant, gym, laundry service, refrigerator* ▤ *MC, V.*

¢ 🏨 **Lanzhou Hotel**. Built in 1956, this concrete behemoth's Sino-Stalinist exterior hides a modern if drab interior. Pleasant service and clean, standard-size rooms make this hotel a good value; the older east and west wings house shabbier but still decent rooms for half the price. The hotel's renowned Chinese restaurant, Zhong Hua Yuan, cooks up great local cuisine. **Pros:** a local landmark that's easy to find. **Cons:** even the no-smoking rooms can be smoky. ⊠ *486 Donggang Xi Lu, on the corner of Tianshui Lu* ☎ *0931/841–6321* 🖷 *0931/841–8608* ⤵ *476 rooms, 50 suites* ⚷ *In-room: refrigerator. In-hotel: 5 restaurants* ▤ *AE, MC, V.*

SIDE TRIPS FROM LANZHOU

Fodor'sChoice One of the only day trips worth taking from Lanzhou is the **Thousand**
★ **Buddha Temple and Grottoes**. More commonly known by its Chinese name Binglng Si, it's filled with Buddhist paintings and statuary, including an impressive 89-foot-tall Buddha carved into a cliff face. Although the art is disappointing compared to the Mogao Grottoes at Dunhuang, the location, in a 200-foot-high canyon dominated by spectacular cliff formations of porous rock, is stunning. It's best to visit in summer, as access is only by water, and the Yellow River is too low most of the year. If you travel here on your own, you'll need to catch a bus, a ferry, and a jeep. Don't even try it. It's much easier to book a tour. Gansu Western

Travel Service *(⇨ Tours, above)* offers a popular day trip that includes all transportation and insurance for about Y400 per person. You can ask your hotel to make the arrangements. 🚇 *Y50 entrance ⊙ Daily 8–5.*

The canyon is along one side of the Yellow River. The journey through a gorge lined by water-sculpted rocks is spectacular. When the canyon is dry you can travel 2½ km (1½ mi) on foot or by four-wheel-drive vehicle to see the small community of Tibetan lamas at the Upper Temple of Bingling. The temple (Y10) is nothing special, but the twists and turns of the upper gorge are breathtaking, and the monks are friendly.

Fodor'sChoice
★ **Labrang Monastery.** In the remote town of Xiahe, the monastery is a little piece of Tibet along the Gansu-Qinghai border. A world away from Lanzhou, Xiahe has experienced a dizzying rise in the number of travelers over the past decade. Even Tibetan monks clad in traditional fuchsia robes now surf the Internet, play basketball, and listen to pop music. Despite the encroaching modernity, Xiahe is still a wonderful place, attracting large numbers of pilgrims who come to study and to spin the 1,147 prayer wheels of the monastery daily, swathed in their distinctive costume of heavy woolen robes tied with brightly colored sashes. ■**TIP➜ In 2008 foreign tourists were banned from Xiahe after the police crackdown of antigovernment riots in Lhasa and Tibetan areas, including Xiahe. Now travel restrictions are sometimes in place, especially around sensitive anniversaries and dates like the May national holiday. Check on online forums or with your travel agent for up-to-date information.**

The Labrang Monastery is the largest Tibetan lamasery outside Tibet. Founded in 1710, it once had as many as 4,000 monks, a number much depleted due in large part to the Cultural Revolution, when monks were forced to return home and temples were destroyed. Though the monastery reopened in 1980, the government's continued policy of restricted enrollment has kept the number of monks down to about 1,500.

There are two ways to reach Xiahe: by public bus or by private tour. Buses for Xiahe leave from Lanzhou's South Station (Qiche Nanzhan) every hour or two starting at 7:30 am and take five hours. Make sure to purchase tickets in advance, as some departures require travel insurance *(baoxian)*. Also, have two photocopies of your visa and passport information on hand just in case they are required. ✉ *2 km (1 mi) west of long-distance bus station* 🚇 *Y40 including guided tour (10:15 am and 3:15 pm daily) ⊙ Daily sunrise–sunset.*

DUNHUANG

17 hrs by bus northwest of Lanzhou; 6 hrs by bus west of Jiayuguan.

A small oasis town, Dunhuang was for many centuries the most important Buddhist destination on the Silk Road. Just outside of town, beyond the towering dunes of Singing Sand Mountain, you can see the extraordinary caves of the Mogao Grottoes, considered the richest repository of Buddhist art in the world.

Buddhism entered China via the Silk Road, and as Dunhuang was the point of entry to the Chinese world, it was not long before a temple was established here. By ad 366 the first caves were being carved and painted at the Mogao oasis. Work continued until the 10th century, after which they were left undisturbed for nearly 1,000 years.

Adventurers from Europe, North America, and other parts of Asia began plundering the caves at the end of the 19th century, yet most of the statuary and paintings remain. By far the most astounding find was a "library cave" filled with more than 45,000 forgotten sutras and official documents. The contents were mostly sold to Sir Aurel Stein in 1907, and when translated they revealed the extent to which Dunhuang was an ancient melting pot of cultures and religions.

DON'T MISS

A highlight is the daily gathering of monks on a lawn for religious debate in the liveliest fashion. The monks charge at each other in groups, hissing good-naturedly, as older monks supervise with a benevolent air. The debate takes place in the afternoon; ask at the ticket office for times. Another interesting daily event is the gathering of hundreds of chanting monks on the steps of the main prayer hall beginning at 11 am.

Today you'll find a rapidly developing small city that is still, in some ways, a melting pot; tourists from every continent converge upon Dunhuang daily to visit one of the most impressive sites in all of China.

GETTING HERE AND AROUND

AIR TRAVEL The easiest and most expensive way to reach Dunhuang is by air, with regular flights from Beijing, Xian, Lanzhou, and Ürümqi. Dunhuang's airport is 13 km (8 mi) east of town, on the road to the Mogao Grottoes. A taxi ride from the airport costs Y20 to Y30.

BUS TRAVEL Buses from Lanzhou, Turpan, and Jiayuguan depart frequently for Dunhuang, dropping you off at the station in the center of town.

TRAIN TRAVEL Dunhuang's train station is 13 km (8 mi) northeast of the town and serves Lanzhou, Xian, and Jiayuguan. A better-connected station, with services to Beijing and Shanghai, is in the small town of Liuyuan, 120 km (74 mi) away. Taxis from Liuyuan to Dunhuang cost Y120, or you can ride one of the buses that leave hourly for Y15.

SAFETY AND PRECAUTIONS

Taxi drivers often charge extortionate prices to take you out into the desert; never take their opening offer! Dunhuang is an expensive place to visit, as admission costs quickly add up.

TIMING

Aim to spend at least two days in Dunhuang: one day to see the Mogao Caves and Singing Sand Mountain, and the other to spend time in the town itself.

TOURS

If you only have time for one trip out of town, head to the Mogao Grottoes (Y20 for the round-trip bus fare through CITS, admission not included). Don't bother with a tour to Singing Sand Mountain, as it's easy enough to reach on your own by taxi. If you're able to spend

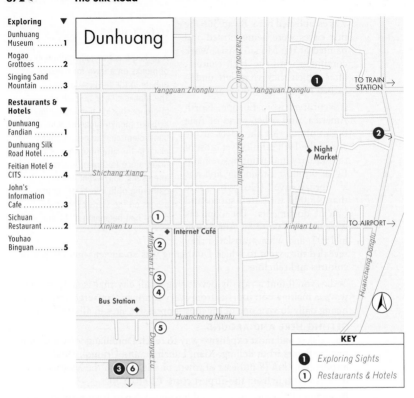

Dunhuang

Yangguan Zhonglu   Yangguan Donglu

TO TRAIN →
STATION

Night
Market

Shichang Xiang

Xinjian Lu   ◆ Internet Café   Xinjian Lu   TO AIRPORT →

Bus Station ◆

Huancheng Nanlu

KEY

❶ *Exploring Sights*

① *Restaurants & Hotels*

an extra day in town, take a tour of sites relating to ancient Dunhuang
(Y130).

ESSENTIALS

Air Contact Dunhuang Airport (✉ *13 km [8 mi] east of town, near the Mogao
Grottoes* ☎ *0937/882–5292*).

Bank Bank of China (✉ *Yangguan Zhong Lu* ☎ *0937/263–0510*).

Bus Contact Dunhuang Bus Station (✉ *Dingzi Lu* ☎ *0937/882–2174*).

Train Contacts Liuyuan Train Station (✉ *Liuyuan Huoche Zhan*
☎ *0937/557–2995*).

Dunhuang Train Station (✉ *Dunhuang Huoche Zhan* ☎ *0937/882–2598*).

Visitor and Tour Info Feitian CITS (✉ *Feitian Hotel, 22 Mingshan Lu*
☎ *0937/883–2714*).

EXPLORING

Dunhuang Museum. The small museum displays objects recovered from
nearby Silk Road fortifications such as reclining Buddhas, sumptuous
wall paintings, and sculptures. If you've visited the Jade Gate or Yangguan Pass, you may enjoy seeing what's been found. ✉ *8 Yangguan
Dong Lu, east of the night market* 🎟 *Free* ☉ *Daily 8–1 and 2–6.*

CLOSE UP

The Silk Road: Then and Now

The history of the Silk Road starts in 138 bc, when Emperor Wudi of the Han Dynasty sent a caravan of 100 men to the west, attempting to forge a political alliance with the Yuezhi people living beyond the Taklamakan Desert. The mission was a failure, and only two men survived the 13-year return journey, but they brought back with them to Chang'an (present-day Xian) tales of previously unknown kingdoms: Samarkand, Ferghana, Parthia, and even Rome. More important, they told stories about the legendary Ferghana horse, a fast and powerful creature said to be bred in heaven. Believing that this horse would give his armies a military advantage over the Huns, Emperor Wudi sent a number of large convoys to Central Asia in order to establish contact with these newly discovered kingdoms—and to bring back as many horses as possible. These envoys of the Han emperor were the first traders on the Silk Road.

The extension of the Silk Road beyond Central Asia to the Middle East and Europe was due to another ill-advised foreign excursion, this time on the part of the Roman Empire. In 55 bc Marcus Licinius Crassus led an army to the east against Parthia, in present-day Syria. The battle was one of

Rome's greatest military defeats, but some of the survivors were able to obtain Chinese silk from the Parthians. Back in Rome, wearing silk became the fashion, and for the first time in history a trade route was established covering the arduous (5,000-mi) journey between East and West.

It might seem odd today, but the two empires knew very little about the origins of their precious cargo. The reason for this common ignorance was the complicated supply chain that transported goods over the Silk Road. No one merchant made the entire journey, but wares were instead brought from kingdom to kingdom, switching hands in the teeming bazaars of wealthy oasis cities along the way.

Over time, the Silk Road became less important due to the opening of sea routes, and was dealt a deathblow by the isolationist tendencies of the Ming Dynasty in the 14th century. Yet today the Silk Road is being resurrected to transport the modern world's most precious commodity: oil. China's rapid development has created an almost insatiable appetite for energy resources. In the last few years pipelines have been completed from Kazakhstan and Xinjiang to Shanghai.

10

Singing Sand Mountain. South of Dunhuang, the oasis gives way to desert. Here you'll find a gorgeous sweep of sand dunes, named for the light rattling sound that the sand makes when wind blows across the surface. At 5,600 feet above sea level, the half-hour climb to the summit is a difficult climb but is worth it for the views, particularly at sunset. Nestled in the sand is **Crescent Moon Lake** *(Yueyaquan)*, a lovely pool that by some freak of the prevailing winds never silts up. Camels, sleds, and various flying contraptions are available at steep prices; try your bargaining skills. ⊠ *Mingshan Lu, 5 km (3 mi) south of town* 🖂 *Y120.*

FodorsChoice **Mogao Grottoes.** The magnificent Buddhist grottoes lie southeast of Dunhuang. At least 40 of the 700 caves—dating from the Northern Wei
★

in the 4th century ad to the Five Dynasties in the 10th century ad—are open to the public. Which caves are open on a given day depends on the whim of local authorities, but you shouldn't worry too much about missing something. Everything here is stunning. You'll almost certainly visit the giant seated Buddhas in caves 96 and 130, the Tang Dynasty sleeping Buddha in cave 148, and the famous "library" in caves 16 and 17, where 45,000 religious and political documents were uncovered at the turn of the 20th century. A flashlight is a useful item for your visit. Note that photographs are not allowed.

This is one site where you should hire an English-speaking guide. At a cost of only Y20 extra, your understanding of the different imagery used in each cave will increase immeasurably. Tours in English take place about three times a day in high season, so you may have to wait to join one. Be sure to verify that the tour is of the same two-hour duration and covers the same number of caves (8–10) as the Chinese tours. After the tour, you'll have time to wander around and revisit any unlocked caves. A fine museum contains reproductions of eight caves not usually visited on the public tour. A smaller museum near the Library Cave details the removal of artifacts by foreign plunderers. If you have a deep interest in the cave art, you may be able to pay Y300 extra to visit other caves that are sealed off to the general public. Ask at the ticket office.

To get here, take a taxi (Y60 to Y80 round-trip) or take the half-hour bus ride that departs from Xinjian Lu, near the corner with Minshan Lu. The bus runs from 8 am to 6 pm, and tickets cost Y8 each way. CITS at the Feitan Hotel also has a daily bus service, leaving Dunhuang at 8 am and returning at noon. A round-trip costs Y20. ⊠ *25 km (17 mi) southeast of town* ☎ *No phone* 🌐 *Y180 for tour; additional Y20 for English-speaking guide* ☉ *Daily 8:30–6.*

WHERE TO EAT

Dunhuang's night market is a 10-minute walk from the most popular hotels. Located between Xinjian Lu and Yangguan Dong Lu, it's worth a visit for cold beer and flavorful lamb kebabs. Small restaurants are clustered together on Mingshan Lu in the center of town.

¢–$
AMERICAN
✕ **John's Information Café.** Cool off after a full day of sightseeing on this trellised patio with an ice-cold beer and plate of noodles. Another option is to come before you start your day for a Western-style breakfast and a cup of joe. The restaurant also arranges overnight camel rides for Y300–Y500 per person,

RENT-A-BIKE

The best way to get around Dunhuang is by bicycle, and you can easily hire one from rental places around town.

depending on group size, and trips to Yadan National Park and elsewhere. ✉ *21 Mingshan Lu, north of the Feitian Hotel* ☎ *1399/373–3106* ⊕ *www.johncafe.net* ⊟ *No credit cards.*

¢–$ | SICHUAN | ✕ **Sichuan Restaurant.** Delicious Sichuanese classics like chicken with peanuts, sweet-and-sour pork, and spicy fried potato strips are available here at very cheap prices. There's an English menu, but prices are much higher than on the Chinese menu. ✉ *75 Mingshan Lu, next to the Dunhuang Trade Union Hotel* ☎ *No phone* ⊟ *No credit cards.*

WHERE TO STAY

¢ ⛫ **Dunhuang Fandian.** If you're looking for something mildly luxurious, this lodging in the center of town

will fit the bill. Rooms are nicer than at the Feitian Hotel, but without an elevator you'll have to climb the stairs to your room. Foreign currency and traveler's checks can no longer be exchanged in the lobby; go to the bank opposite the hotel. **Pros:** central location; excellent value. **Cons:** some noise from a local nightclub if you're on a low floor; Chinese breakfast options only ✉ *16 Mingshan Lu, corner of Xinjiang Lu* ☎ *0937/882–2538* ⊕ *www.dunhuanghotel.com* ⌂ *In-hotel: restaurant, Wi-Fi* ⊟ *No credit cards.*

$–$$ | ★ | ⛫ **Dunhuang Silk Road Hotel.** This cross between a Chinese fortress and an alpine lodge is the most interesting place to stay in Dunhuang, and possibly in the whole of the province. The large, spacious rooms have historical touches like Ming reproduction furniture and traditional wooden shower buckets. The hotel arranges some great tours, including a sunrise camel ride to the sand dunes of Singing Sand Mountain. The fourth-floor café is the perfect spot to appreciate the dunes from a distance. The hotel's only drawback is its location 3 km (2 mi) south of the town center. **Pros:** rooftop terrace; good hotel food. **Cons:** touts approach guests all the time. ✉ *Mingshan Lu* ☎ *0937/888–2088* ⊕ *www.the-silk-road.com/hotel/dunhuanghotel* ⇝ *292 rooms, 8 suites* ⌂ *In-hotel: 2 restaurants, gym, Wi-Fi* ⊟ *AE, MC, V.*

¢ ⛫ **Feitian Hotel.** Dunhuang's most popular budget hotel has a variety of clean, comfortable rooms. For a taste of the high life, you could book yourself a deluxe suite. The hotel is home to the CITS travel office and the departure point for popular tour buses. Best of all, it's in the middle of town. **Pros:** inexpensive basic rooms. **Cons:** large deposits required upon check-in. ✉ *22 Mingshan Lu, ½ block north of the bus station* ☎ *0937/882–2337* 🖷 *0937/882–2337* ⌂ *In-hotel: restaurant, wifi* ⊟ *No credit cards.*

¢ ⛫ **Youhao Binguan.** Across from the bus station, this is Dunhuang's best budget option. The three-bed dorm rooms on the fourth floor are

The dramatic landscape of Qinghai.

acceptable at Y60 per person, but the better options are the doubles with air-conditioning, which start at Y80. Hot water flows from 7:30 pm until midnight. Whatever you do, don't use the sub-par laundry service. **Pros:** decent restaurant; good place to meet backpackers. **Cons:** slow service all around. ⊠ *25 Mingshan Lu* ☎ *0937/882– 2678* ⚄ *In-hotel: laundry service* ▭ *No credit cards.*

QINGHAI

A remote and sparsely populated province on the northeastern border of Tibet, Qinghai's sweeping grasslands locked in by icy mountain ranges are relatively unknown to most Chinese people. They tend to think of the province as their nation's Siberia, a center for prisons and work camps. Yet Qinghai shares much of the majestic scenery of Xinjiang combined with the rich culture of Tibet.

The opening of the railway that links Tibet with the rest of China in 2006 led to an influx of tourists to Qinghai, one of the major stops before the train arrives in Lhasa. Many hoped that tourism would improve Qinghai's economy, which is the smallest in the whole of China. This hasn't quite come to fruition, as the number of foreigners traveling through this stunning region by train came to a dramatic halt in March 2008, when China made the region off-limits after the riots in Lhasa and the Tibetan areas of other provinces. When the area eventually reopened, visitors could not travel independently on the train or on any other mode of transport. For the latest information, check out ⊕ *www.chinatraintickets.net* for timetables and news about permits and costs. An earthquake in April 2010 in the predominately Tibetan area of Yushu in the south of the province killed almost 3,000 people, adding to the province's woes.

Visitors to the region should take in a few of Qinghai's must-see sites. The capital city of Xining is small and receives mixed reports, but it has some charming Tibetan flair. On the northwest edge of the city is the famed North Monastery, a solemn Daoist destination. The Kumbum Monastery is a testament to Tibetan tranquility. For a truly heavenly display, crane your neck skyward at Bird Island on Qinghai Lake several hundred miles to the west of Xining.

REGIONAL TOURS

Tibetan Connections. This locally owned tour company is run out of Xining and offers very interesting off-the-beaten-track hikes, camping trips, and tours through one of the region's most fascinating and beautiful Tibetan areas. ⊠ *International Village, Building 5, Lete Youth Hostel, Xining* ☎ *1370/976–3701* ⊕ *www.tibetanconnections.com.*

China International Travel Service. The main Xining branch of China's state-run travel service is located in the Xining Guesthouse, and offers tours of the city as well as to Bird Island. Despite the services being aimed at international tourists, the office is staffed with people who speak limited English. ⊠ *215 Qiyi Lu, Xining* ☎ *0971/823–8701.*

XINING

4 hrs (225 km [140 mi]) by train or 3 hrs by bus west of Lanzhou; 25 hours (1,900 km [1,200 mi]) by train northeast of Lhasa.

Its name means "peace in the west," so it's no surprise that Xining started out as a military garrison in the 16th century, guarding the empire's western borders. It was also an important center for trade between China and Tibet. A small city by Chinese standards, with a population slightly more than 1.1 million, Xining is no longer cut off from the rest of China. But the city still feels remote; a far-flung metropolis wedged between dramatic sandstone cliffs, Xining is populated largely by Tibetan and Hui peoples.

For travelers, Xining is a convenient base for visits to the important Kumbum Monastery, which sits just outside the city, and the stunning avian sanctuary of Bird Island, 350 km (217 mi) away on the shores of China's largest saltwater lake. Trains linking Tibet to Beijing and Shanghai stop in Xining; this can be a good place to acclimatize to the high altitude before continuing to Tibet.

GETTING HERE AND AROUND

Xining Caojiabao Airport is 30 km (19 mi) east of the city. Shuttle buses costing Y25 per person can get you to or from the airport in about 40 minutes. If you're traveling with someone else, a taxi (Y80–Y100) is a better option. If you arrive by train or bus, you can reach the city's hotels by taking a taxi; a ride should be less than Y10.

If you're planning on traveling to Tibet, use a well-established travel agent to arrange the permits you must secure to visit the area.

10

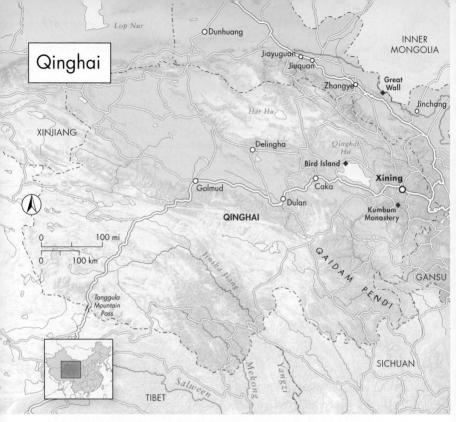

Qinghai

AIR TRAVEL	Daily flights link Xining with Beijing, Shanghai, Chengdu, Guangzhou, Xian, and Shenzhen. There is less frequent service to Lhasa, Ürümqi, Qingdao, and Golmud.
BUS TRAVEL	Tickets for the long, bumpy bus ride to Lhasa can be purchased from any travel agent. Tickets for the journey to Lanzhou (three hours) and Xian (15 hours) are available at the long-distance bus station, a few minutes north of the train station. If your next stop is Dunhuang, but you don't want to backpedal to Lanzhou, take the bus to Jiuquan in Gansu and get a connection farther west; the mountain scenery and small Tibetan villages along the way are spectacular.
TRAIN TRAVEL	The train to Lhasa runs every day, but foreign travelers need to arrange permits and book a tour before they can buy train tickets for the 25-hour journey. You can also travel to Beijing, Shanghai, Lanzhou, Guangzhou, and Chengdu by train.

SAFETY AND PRECAUTIONS

The standard advice for travelers applies here; beware of pickpockets and be on the lookout for taxi drivers with "broken meters."

TIMING

Xining is not a place to linger, as there are other, more appealing cities in the region. Spending a night here to explore and see the city's sights is enough.

TOURS

Xining's more upscale hotels have travel offices that can help you arrange expensive private tours with English-speaking guides to Kumbum Monastery or Bird Island. For less expensive and more innovative tours, head to the Lete Youth Hostel and contact Tibetan Connections. A third option is to hire the services of an enterprising individual like Niu Xiaojun, who speaks good English and has been leading foreigners to off-the-beaten-path destinations for years.

ESSENTIALS

Air Contact Xining Caojiabao Airport (✉ *30 km [20 mi] east of Xining* ☎ *0971/818–8222*).

Bus Contact Xining Main Bus Station (✉ *Jianguo Lu, south of the train station* ☎ *0971/711–2094*).

Medical Assistance Qinghai People's Hospital (✉ *143 Gonghe Lu* ☎ *0971/817–7911*).

Train Contact Xining Railway Station (✉ *Northern end of Jianguo Lu* ☎ *0971/814–9790*).

Visitor and Tour Info Niu Xiaojun (☎ *1319/579–1105*). **Tibetan Connections** (✉ *International Village, Building 5, Lete Youth Hostel, Xining* ☎ *1370/976–3701* ⊕ *www.tibetanconnections.com*).

EXPLORING

Although most travelers don't come to see Xining, there are a few sights in and around the city.

The most important site is the Taoist **North Monastery** *(Beishan Si)*, at the northwest end of town. Construction on this series of mountainside cloisters and pavilions began more than 1,700 years ago during the Northern Wei. Climbing the stairs to the white pagoda at the top gives you a view of the entire city sprawled out beneath you. To get here, take a taxi. ✉ *North end of Chanjiang Lu* 🎫 *Y10* ⏰ *8:30–6.*

Dongguan Mosque. This is one of the largest mosques in all of China and illustrates the ethnic diversity of Xining. Built in the 14th century, its green and white dome and two tall minarets see some 40,000 to 50,000 people for Friday prayers. ✉ *Dongguan Jie* 🎫 *Y10* ⏰ *Daily 8–12 and 2–5. Closed to tourists Fri. 10–12.*

AROUND XINING

★ The magnificent **Kumbum Monastery** *(Ta'Er Si)* lies 25 km (15 mi) southwest of Xining. One of the six great monasteries of the Tibetan Buddhist sect known as Yellow Hat—and reputedly the birthplace of the sect's founder, Tsong Khapa—construction began in 1560. A great reformer who lived in the early 1400s, Tsong Khapa formulated a new doctrine that stressed a return to monastic discipline, strict celibacy, and moral

10

and philosophical thought over magic and mysticism. Tsong's followers have controlled Tibetan politics since the 17th century. Still a magnet for Tibetan pilgrims and, more recently, waves of tourists, Kumbum boasts a dozen prayer halls, an exhibition hall, and monks' quarters (look out for the yak butter sculptures). Unfortunately no photos are allowed. Public buses (Y6) to Huangzhong leave frequently from Zifang Jie Bus Station. Get off at the last stop and walk 2 km (1 mi) uphill, or take a put-put (Y2) to the monastery's gates. Taxis from Xining are Y30. ⊠ *Huangzhong* 🖅 *Y80* 🕙 *8–5.*

WHERE TO EAT

¢ ✕ **Black Tent.** This place serves great Tibetan, Indian, and Nepali food.
INTERNATIONAL All of the workers are Tibetans from Amdo and are very friendly. The atmosphere is great. The menu is in Tibetan and English. Don't miss the momo dumplings. ⊠ *Wen Hua Jie Wen Miao Guang Chang, Wenhua Jie* 🖀 *0971/823–4029* ▤ *No credit cards.*

¢ ✕ **Casa Mia Italian Restaurant.** This restaurant is managed by a local Chi-
ITALIAN nese woman but is financially backed by several European expats who wanted a place to satisfy their cravings for Western food. With free wireless Internet and excellent Italian food, including real espresso coffee, it is very popular among expats. Menus are in English and Chinese, and the staff speak English. ⊠ *10–4 Wu Si Xi Lu* 🖀 *0971/631–1272* ▤ *No credit cards.*

¢–$ ✕ **Jianyin Revolving Restaurant.** Perched atop the 28-story Jianyin Hotel,
ASIAN this slowly revolving restaurant offers mediocre Asian-inspired cuisine. But the food is beside the point. People come here for the spectacular views of the city. There's no minimum, so sipping a cup of tea while enjoying the scenery or playing cards is perfectly acceptable. ⊠ *Jianyin Hotel, 55 Xida Jie, southeast corner of the central square* 🖀 *0971/826–1885* ▤ *No credit cards.*

WHERE TO STAY

¢ 🛏 **Lete Hostel.** This new hostel gets good feedback from guests because it's geared to what budget travelers want: inexpensive rooms, helpful travel information, and a place to meet other backpackers—although the bathrooms could do with an upgrade. The tour agency Tibet Connections is based here. In addition to dorms, there are double rooms with private baths, and small apartments. **Pros:** friendly staff; nice views over the city. **Cons:** dorms can be cold; hard beds even for China. ⊠ *16th floor, International Village Building 5* 🖀 *0971/820–2080* ♨ *In-room: kitchen. In-hotel: Wi-Fi hotspot* ▤ *No credit cards.*

$ 🛏 **Yinlong Hotel.** This ultramodern hotel is considered the finest lodging
Fodor'sChoice between Xian and Ürümqi, but standards seem to have fallen recently.
★ If you can overlook lackadaisical service, rooms are exceptionally comfortable and quiet, with views overlooking Xining's central square. **Pros:** central location; good-quality hotel restaurants; Wi-Fi in rooms. **Cons:** expensive buffet breakfast; small gym; dearth of English speakers. ⊠ *38 Huanghe Lu, north side of the central square, Xining* 🖀 *0971/616–6666* ⊕ *www.ylhotel.net* 🛏 *316 rooms* ♨ *In-room: safe. In-hotel: 5 restaurants, gym, laundry service* ▤ *AE, MC, V.*

Wenshu Hall in the Kumbum Monastery.

SHOPPING

Visitors interested in Tibetan handicrafts will want to stroll through Xining's excellent street markets. The **Jianguo Lu Wholesale Market** (✉ *Jianguo Lu, opposite the main bus station*) sells everything from traditional Tibetan clothing and food to the latest CDs.

SIDE TRIP FROM XINING

★ **Bird Island** *(Niao Dao)* is the main draw at Qinghai Hu, China's largest inland saltwater lake. The name Bird Island is a misnomer: it was an island until the lake receded, connecting it to the shore. The electric-blue lake is surrounded by rolling hills covered with yellow rapeseed flowers. Tibetan shepherds graze their flocks here as wild yaks roam nearby. Beyond the hills are snowcapped mountains. An estimated 100,000 birds breed at Bird Island, including egrets, speckle-headed geese, and black-neck cranes; sadly, the numbers have been much depleted because of the country's efforts to suppress the spread of avian flu. There are two viewing sites: spend as little time as possible at Egg Island in favor of the much better Common Cormorant Island, where you can see birds flying at eye-level from the top of a cliff. The best months to see birds are May and June. If you're taking a tour to Qinghai Hu, make sure that you're headed here and not the much closer tourist trap known as Qinghai Hu 151. To get to Bird Island, either contact a tour agency such as Tibetan Connections, or if you prefer to go under your own steam, catch a tourist bus from Xining Railway Station for Y35 each way. There are a few basic hostels here if you wish to stay overnight. ✉ *350 km (215 mi) northwest of Xining* 🚍 Y78.

10

XINJIANG

The vast Xinjiang Uyghur Autonomous Region, covering more than 1.6 million square km (640,000 square mi), is China's largest province. Even more expansive than Alaska, it borders Mongolia, Russia, Kazakhstan, Kyrgyzstan, Tajikistan, Afghanistan, and Pakistan. Only 40% of Xinjiang's 19.6 million inhabitants are Han Chinese. About 45% are Uyghur (a people of Turkic origin), and the remainder are mostly Kazakhs, Hui, Kyrgyz, Mongols, and Tajiks.

Xinjiang gets very little rainfall except in the northern areas near Russia. It gets very cold in winter and very hot in summer, especially in the Turpan Basin, where temperatures often soar to 120°F. Visitors usually forgive the extreme weather, however, as they're charmed by the locals and awed by the rugged scenery, ranging from the endless sand dunes of the desert to the pastoral grasslands of the north.

Long important as a crossroads for trade with Europe and the Middle East, Xinjiang has nevertheless seldom come completely under Chinese control. For more than 2,000 years the region has been contested and divided by Turkic and Mongol tribes who—after setting up short-lived empires—soon disappeared beneath the shifting sands of time. In the 20th century, Uyghurs continued to resist Chinese rule, seizing power from a warlord governor in 1933 and claiming the land as a separate republic, which they named East Turkestan. China tightened its grip after the 1949 revolution, however, encouraging Han settlers to emigrate to the province to dilute the Uyghur majority, thus increasing ethnic tensions. In the last few years these tensions have blown up into full-scale social unrest. In 2008 and 2009 Uyghurs took to the streets in Ürümqi, Kashgar, and Hotan, protesting that they were not free to practice their religious beliefs. More than 200 people were killed. Chinese authorities say that the vast majority of the dead were Han Chinese, while Uyghur groups claim that a significant proportion of the dead were demonstrators shot by the police. Amnesty International says that hundreds, possibly thousands of Uyghurs are still being detained by police. Ürümqi had a nighttime curfew, and the province's Internet connection was turned off for at least a year, but there were no travel restrictions on tourists, other than the occasional checking of passports. Communications have now been restored.

DID YOU KNOW?

In the 1980s, archaeologists discovered dozens of tombs in various parts of Xinjiang, with bodies that had been buried for about 3,000 years yet remained remarkably preserved thanks to the arid desert climate. Many of the mummies, believed to be forefathers of the Uyghurs, had northern European features, including fair hair and skin.

REGIONAL TOURS
Uyghur Tour & Travel Center. This excellent tour company based in Kashgar organizes tours of the Silk Road, as well as more unusual destinations like traditional Uyghur villages. Tour manager Abdul can also arrange cars to take you along the Karakorum Highway at prices significantly lower than the competition, and the company goes out of its

way to tailor a tour to your requirements. ☒ *Overseas Chinese Hotel 170 Seman Lu* ☎ *0998/220–4012* ⊕ *www.silkroadinn.com.*

CYTS. Based in Ürümqi, Ali, the English-speaking tour guide, offers interesting tailor-made tours to sights across the province, from two-day tours to Heavenly Lake to multistop trips, which can include Turpan and Kashgar. All prices are negotiable. ☒ *Bogda Hotel, 10 Guangming Lu, Ürümqi* ☎ *0991/232–1170.*

ÜRÜMQI

48 hours (2,250 km [1,400 mi]) by train, 4 hrs by plane northwest of Beijing.

Xinjiang's capital and largest city, Ürümqi is at the geographic center of Asia, and has the distinction of being the most landlocked city in the world. It's a new city by Chinese standards, little more than barracks for Qing Dynasty troops when it was built in 1763. Once a sleepy trading post, Ürümqi has grown to a sprawling city with just over 2 million inhabitants. Yet despite this modernization, Ürümqi manages to conjure up the past, especially in the Uyghur-populated area near the International Grand Bazaar.

The Xinjiang Uyghur Autonomous Region.

GETTING HERE AND AROUND

AIR TRAVEL   Many people fly to Ürümqi from Beijing, Shanghai, Hong Kong, or Xian to begin a journey on the Silk Road. The airport is 20 km (12 mi) north of the downtown area, and can be reached by taxi (about Y40) in 30 minutes or via frequent minibuses.

BUS TRAVEL   Long-distance bus travel is often the only way to travel in Xinjiang if you don't want to wait a day or two for the next available train. Every city in the region is served at least daily by buses from Ürümqi. There's even bus service to Almaty, Kazakhstan.

It's usually a straightforward affair buying tickets from the only station in town, but Ürümqi is more complicated. Unless you're going to Hotan or Altai—which have their own separate bus stations—your best bet is to first look for tickets at Nianzigou Station. If you don't like what's available there, or if your destination is Kashgar or Turpan, head to the South Station (Nanjiao Qichezhan).

Buses (Y25 each way after bargaining) leave for Heavenly Lake (Tianchi Hu) at 9:30 am from the north gate of Renmin Park. They usually leave the lake at 6 pm and arrive back in Ürümqi at 7:30 pm. Be careful to get on a regular bus rather than a tour bus that will take you to minor attractions on the way, limiting your time at the lake.

TRAIN TRAVEL   Those arriving by train will find themselves about 2 km (1 mi) southwest of the city center.

MONEY MATTERS

⚠ In China, there's no place more difficult to run out of money than in off-the-beaten-track Xinjiang. But there are ATMS in both Ürümqi and Kashgar, and all the machines accept international credit cards and debit cards. Most banks will also exchange currency and traveler's checks.

SAFETY AND PRECAUTIONS

There is still some tension after the race riots in 2008 and 2009, and there remains a heavy police presence in the city. Foreign tourists may be stopped by security personnel, but there are no travel restrictions. And as always, be sure to secure your valuables when in public places.

TIMING

While there is plenty to see in Ürümqi if you have time, it's fair to say that Xinjiang's best attractions are out of the capital. If the clock is ticking, spend no more than two days enjoying Ürümqi's sights before heading further afield.

> **WHAT TIME IS IT?**
>
> A constant source of confusion for travelers in Xinjiang is figuring out the time. Uyghurs often refer to unofficial Xinjiang time, whereas Han Chinese use standard Beijing time. If in doubt, ask. No matter what time is spoken, you can count on everything in Xinjiang starting two hours later than in Beijing. That is, lunch in Kashgar is usually eaten at 2 pm Beijing time.

TOURS

Ürümqi is a popular place to begin a tour of Xinjiang's vast desert expanses. A private tour probably makes the most sense. Travel agencies are happy to let you pick and choose from a list of destinations. A four-wheel-drive vehicle will cost around Y1,300 per day; a smaller Volkswagen Santana is Y900 per day.

CYTS, in the parking lot of the Bogda Hotel, offers trips lasting from one day to more than three weeks. Seek out English-speaking guide Ali to talk you through the options. A tour of sites around Turpan or a trip to the Heavenly Lake can be accomplished in a single day.

ESSENTIALS

Air Contacts China Southern Airlines (✉ 26 Guangming Lu, Ürümqi ☎ 0991/882-3300 or 0991/950-333). **Ürümqi Airport** (✉ 16 km (10 mi) northwest of the city in Diwopu ☎ 0991/380-1347).

Bank Bank of China (✉ 343 Jiefang Nan Lu, at the corner of Minzhu Lu, behind the Hoi Tak Hotel ☎ 0991/283-4222).

Bus Contacts Ürümqi Nianzigou Station (✉ Western end of Heilongjiang Lu ☎ 0991/587-8898). **Ürümqi South Station** (✉ Yanerwo Lu ☎ 0991/286-6635).

Internet Dragon Netbar (✉ 190 Wuyi Lu ☎ No phone) Y3/hr; open 24 hrs.

Medical Assistance Chinese Medicine Hospital of Ürümqi (✉ 60 Youhao Nan Lu ☎ 0991/242-0963).

Train Contact Ürümqi Train Station (✉ Qiantangjiang Lu ☎ 0991/581-4203).

Visitor and Tour Info CYTS (✉ 10 Guangming Lu, in the parking lot of the Bogda Hotel ☎ 0991/232-1170). **Grassland Travel Service** (✉ 2 Renmin Gongyuan Bei Jie, southwest of the entrance gate to People's Park ☎ 0991/584-1116).

10

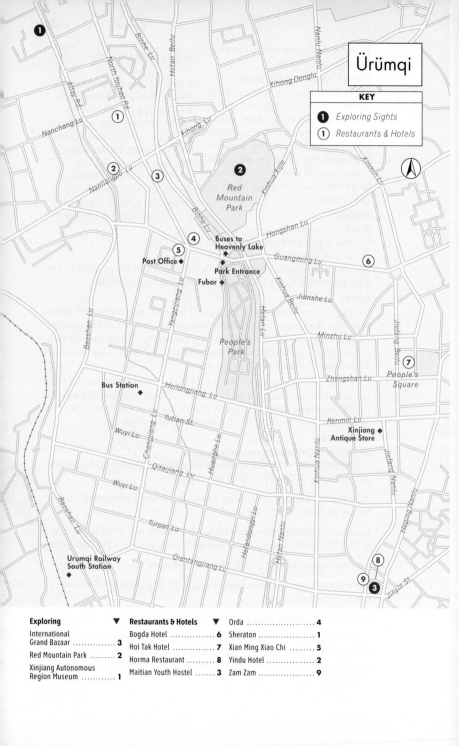

Ürümqi

KEY

① Exploring Sights

① Restaurants & Hotels

①

② Red Mountain Park

Binhe Lu

North Youhao Rd

Altay Rd

Nanchang Lu

Nanliangpo Lu

Hetan Beilu

Xihong Donglu

Nanlu Nanlu

Xihong Lu

Xinhua Xijie

Xinmin Lu

Xinhua Beilu

Hongshan Lu

④ Guangming Lu

⑥

⑤ Buses to Heavenly Lake

Post Office ◆

Fubar ◆ **Park Entrance** ◆

Jianshe Lu

Minzhu Lu

Jiefang Beilu

Baoshan Lu

Yangzijiang Lu

Hetan Lu

People's Park

Zhangshan Lu

⑦ People's Square

Bus Station ◆

Heilongjiang Lu

Yutian St

Changjiang Lu

Renmin Lu

Xinhua Nanlu

Xinjiang Antique Store ◆

Jiefang Nanlu

Wuyi Lu

Qitaijiang Lu

Huanghe Lu

Wuyi Lu

Turpan Lu

Qiantangjiang Lu

Hetan Nanlu

Helandengyi Lu

Urumqi Railway South Station ◆

Baoshan Lu

Hegou Nanlu

⑧

⑨

③ Jinyin St

China's Muslims

UYGHUR

The Muslim Turkic people known as Uyghurs (pronounced "WEE-grs") are one of China's largest—and in the eyes of Beijing, most troublesome—minority groups. Uyghurs mostly live in northwest China's Xinjiang, an "autonomous region" that is one of the most tightly controlled parts of the country after Tibet. Uyghurs are descendants of nomadic Turkic Central Asian tribes. Their language, food, music, dance, clothing, and other customs have little or no relation to those found elsewhere in China. Yet despite a population of nearly 10 million people, most foreigners have never heard of them or their troubled independence movement. Protests and occasional violence in the region during the late 1990s brought a severe crackdown from Beijing; limits were placed on religious education and hundreds of suspected Uyghur separatists were executed. The attacks of September 11, 2001, gave the Chinese government further leverage to oppress Uyghurs in the name of fighting terrorism, and Xinjiang has been relatively quiet since 2009.

HUI

Primarily identifiable by their brimless white caps and headscarves, the Hui are ethnically Chinese Muslims. They are descendants of Middle Eastern traders who came to China via the Silk Road, settling down with a Chinese wives after their conversion to Islam. Over a thousand years' time, the Middle Eastern influence on the Hui appearance became diluted to the point where their facial features are now almost impossible to distinguish from those of Han Chinese. Yet because of cultural differences associated with their Islamic faith, Hui tend to associate with other Hui in largely Muslim neighborhoods. Hui reject eating several kinds of meat that are popular with Han Chinese, including pork, horse, dog, and several types of birds. In what could be seen as a form of respect by the business-savvy Han Chinese, Hui are also generally considered by the Han to be shrewd businesspeople, perhaps a vestige of their history as the descendants of foreign traders.

10

The Jade Road

The residents of Xinjiang are apt to point out that the Silk Road isn't the first road they knew. That honor goes to the "Jade Road," which was established nearly 7,000 years ago. Running from Hotan into today's Qinghai and Gansu provinces, the Jade Road was the artery for Xinjiang's legendary white jade trade. Primarily mined from the Hotan River, Xinjiang jade comes in a number of hues, although small white stones with a reddish-brown exterior are the most highly valued.

Sensuous and smooth to the touch, this "lamb's fat jade" is cloudy with translucent qualities. Chinese emperors have craved it for centuries. Good places to hunt around for all manner of jade in Ürümqi include the swirling International Grand Bazaar and the Xinjiang Antique Store.

Visitors who wish to know more about this region's heady history of jade, silk, and more should visit the Xinjiang Autonomous Region Museum. Here's a quick tip: buy fast. The availability of quality jade has dropped in recent years, and scientists fear the precious stone is being mined to exhaustion.

EXPLORING

International Grand Bazaar. The streets around the bazaar were once full of donkey carts and flocks of sheep. Men in embroidered skullcaps and women in heavy brown wool veils remain, and the whole area maintains the bustling atmosphere of a Central Asian street market. You can bargain for Uyghur crafts here, such as decorated knives, colorful silks, and carved jade. Small shops are tucked into every nook and cranny. The international bazaar itself has been heavily expanded, and now includes a newly built minaret, which you can climb once you've paid the Y20 admission fee. The stalls, while interesting enough, are aimed firmly at tourists; more authentic options are the streets nearby that are filled with traditional ironmongers and Islamic butcher shops. ⊠ *Jiefang Lu, 3 km (2 mi) south of the city center.*

Red Mountain Park. Climbing to the top of the park gives you a picture-perfect view of the snowcapped Heavenly Mountains. An array of incongruously grouped objects—including an eight-story pagoda built by the emperor in 1788 to suppress an evil dragon—are reached via a long set of stairs. Come here in the early evening for the pleasure of seeing the cityscape bathed in the setting sun's golden light. Ignore the cheap carnival rides near the entrance. The park is hard to find, and few tourists venture here, so take a taxi. ⊠ *Off Hongshan Lu* 🖾 *Free* ⊙ *Daily 6 am–1 am.*

Fodor'sChoice ★ **Xinjiang Autonomous Region Museum.** Don't miss the exhibition of perfectly preserved mummies at this superb museum 4 km (2½ mi) northwest of the city center. The mummies—including the 4,000-year-old Beauty of Loulan—were excavated from tombs in various parts of Xinjiang. In addition, the museum has a well-executed exhibition on the region's ethnic minorities. If you are lucky, one of the museum's English-speaking guides will accompany you. There's no extra charge, and it's well worth asking. ⊠ *132 Xibei Lu, 1 block west of the Sheraton Hotel* ☎ *0991/453–4453* 🖃 *Free* ⊗ *Weekdays 10–6.*

WHERE TO EAT

Ürümqi is a good place to have your first taste of Uyghur cuisine. For cheap eats and a great scene, the Wuyi night market is best.

¢ ✕ **Horma Restaurant.** This lunch spot serves classic Uyghur dishes at
NORTHERN incredibly cheap prices. You can go with a standard like rice with lamb
CHINESE and raisins, or look at what other people are eating and point to indicate your selection. The *rounang* (flat bread baked with lamb inside) is especially good. Wash it all down with a can of Muslim-friendly Zam-Zam Cola, Xinjiang's answer to Coke. ⊠ *185 Hanchi Lu, on the northern wall of the International Grand Bazaar* ☎ *No phone* 🖃 *No credit cards.*

¢ ✕ **Orda.** Next door to the Cornfield Youth Hostel, this Kazakh-run no-
NORTHERN frills restaurant offers exotic delicacies like horsemeat and intestines.
CHINESE Ignore those and enjoy a huge plate of tasty pilaf cooked in a stupendously large pot outdoors. There's no English menu. If pilaf runs out, try the *laghman* noodles or chicken stew, *dapanji.* ⊠ *726 Youhao Nan Lu (south of Parksons shopping mall)* ☎ *No phone* 🖃 *No credit cards.*

¢ ✕ **Xian Ming Xiao Chi.** If you need a change from Uyghur fare, this cheap
CHINESE and cheerful fast-food joint, part of a small chain, offers tasty snacks from Xian. Do as the locals do when the temperature rises: try a cooling plateful of cold noodles with cucumber called *liang pi.* Say *bu la* if you don't want your noodles to be spicy. Other specialties include *rou jia mo,* or Chinese-style pork burgers—made from a meat rarely served in this part of the world. ⊠ *33 Yangzi Jiang Lu* ☎ *No phone* 🖃 *No credit cards.*

$ ✕ **Zam Zam.** This smart Uyghur eatery looks as though it should be very
NORTHERN pricey, but the excellent food is the best bargain in town. The ornate
CHINESE room is outfitted with carved wood and Arabic-style arches, and the smartly uniformed staff add to the atmosphere. Few waiters speak Mandarin, let alone English, but there is a picture menu: try the pilaf or the lamb dumplings. No alcohol is served. ⊠ *423 Heping Nan Lu off the International Bazaar* ☎ *0991/843–0555* 🖃 *No credit cards.*

WHERE TO STAY

¢ 🏨 **Bogda Hotel.** A good budget option if you don't want to stay in a dorm, this hotel has rooms that are cleaner and more comfortable than those offered in similarly priced lodgings. Rooms are discounted to Y200 if you ask nicely (in Chinese, because staff don't speak English). Most bathrooms even feature separate shower stalls. **Pros:** good selection of tours available; convenient to banks and restaurants. **Cons:** noisy lobby; little English spoken. ⊠ *10 Guangming Lu* ☎ *0991/886–3910* 🖨 *0991/886–5769* 🛏 *248 rooms* ⌂ *In-hotel: 3 restaurants, gym, laundry service* 🖃 *No credit cards.*

$–$$ 🏨 **Hoi Tak Hotel.** Popular with Chinese tour groups and Hong Kong
★ business travelers, this gleaming white tower offers first-rate views of the snowcapped Tian Shan Mountains. For the best views, request a room on the east side. Though not huge, standard rooms are tastefully appointed and have comfortable beds and ample closet space; Internet access is free. The lobby bar, while straight out of the '70s, makes

10

surprisingly good cocktails. **Pros:** the staff speak English; rooms are good value. **Cons:** not near any attractions or good restaurants. ⊠ *1 Dongfeng Lu, west side of People's Square* ☎ *0991/232–2828* ⊕ *www.hoitakhotel. com* ⟱ *318 rooms, 38 suites* ♿ *In-room: safe, refrigerator, Internet. In-hotel: 7 restaurants, pool, gym, laundry service* ⊟ *AE, MC, V.*

¢ 🏨 **Maitian Youth Hostel.** This hostel near the main Hongshan intersection opened in 2007, and offers basic, clean dorms and simple doubles with private baths. The beds are comfortable enough, but the pine walls that divide rooms are thin, which can make things noisy. Still, the staff are very friendly and helpful, and they offer lots of travel advice. The hotel also makes available a free left-luggage service. **Pros:** staff go out of their way to help. **Cons:** bring your own toilet paper. ⊠ *726 Youhao Nan Lu, next door to Parksons* ☎ *0991/459–1488* ⊕ *www.xjmaitian.com* ⟱ *20 rooms* ♿ *In-hotel: laundry facilities, Wi-Fi* ⊟ *No credit cards.*

$–$$ 🏨 **Sheraton.** The only foreign-run hotel in town (though a Hilton is scheduled to open in 2011), this reliable option opened in 2007, and is very popular with both well-heeled business and leisure travelers. The lobby gleams and rooms are spacious, but the Western-style food in the hotel's restaurants is not up to snuff. The pool is a lovely place to cool off after a day of sightseeing. **Pros:** keen staff; rooms have great bathrooms; great gym. **Cons:** inconvenient for Ürümqi's sights. ⊠ *669 Youhao Bei Lu* ☎ *0991/699–9999* ⊕ *www.starwoodhotels.com* ⟱ *398 rooms, 22 suites* ♿ *In-room: Internet. In-hotel: 5 restaurants, bar, pool, gym, laundry service, business center* ⊟ *AE, MC, V.*

$–$$ 🏨 **Yindu Hotel.** Xinjiang's finest hotel, the Yindu is testament to the influx of cash that has transformed Ürümqi over the past decade. The reception area is inviting, and rooms have great city views and smart decor. The main drawback is that it's a couple of kilometers northwest of the city center. You may also be uneasy with the window between the shower and the bed, which the staff explain is "for your wedding night." **Pros:** comfortable rooms. **Cons:** bad location for exploring the sights. ⊠ *3179 Xihong Xi Lu* ☎ *0991/453–6688* ⊕ *www.yinduhotel. com* ⟱ *308 rooms* ♿ *In-room: safe. In-hotel: 6 restaurants, pool, gym, spa, laundry service AE, MC, V.*

NIGHTLIFE

As with most Chinese cities, every other block in Ürümqi is blighted by high-price karaoke parlors and blaring discos. But there are plenty of places to order a bottle of cold beer, and the best options are on Renmin Gongyuan Bei Jie, where there is also a selection of gay bars.

★ The entertaining song and dance performance at the **International Grand Bazaar Performance Theater** (⊠ *Jiefang Lu, 3 km [2 mi] south of the city center* ☎ *0991/855–5491* 🎫 *Y1888*) is preceded by a ho-hum buffet that unsuccessfully tries to capture the delights of Uyghur cuisine. Never mind the food, as this is your best chance to see Uyghur, Uzbek, Kazakh, Tajik, Tartar, and even Irish dancing all in one spectacular evening. Make reservations through your hotel.

Fubar (⊠ *40 Renmin Gongyuan Bei Jie* ☎ *0991/584–4498* ⊕ *www. fubarchina.com* is the real thing: a tavern serving cold, imported beer and authentic pub grub. The pizza is especially noteworthy, as are the fish-and-chips. This is the best place in Ürümqi to relax after a day exploring the city. The foreign owners are happy to dispense free travel advice, and if you go to Kashgar, look out for their branch there next to the Qinibagh Hotel.

SHOPPING

The **International Grand Bazaar** (⊠ *Jiefang Lu, 3 km [2 mi] south of the city center*) is the best place to go for Uyghur items like embroidered skullcaps, brightly colored carpets, and hand-carved knives. If it's inexpensive gifts you're after, you will find them here.

Xinjiang Antique Store (⊠ *325 Jiefang Nan Lu, south of Renmin Lu* ☎ *0991/282–5161*) has a good selection of genuine antique Chinese bric-a-brac, including jade, jewelry, carpets, and porcelain. As all items come with a state-certified export certificate, you won't have to worry about getting your purchase through customs. There is a smaller branch inside the Xinjiang Autonomous Region Museum.

SIDE TRIPS FROM ÜRÜMQI

Fodor'sChoice
★

Heavenly Lake. About a three-hour ride from Ürümqi is the not-to-be-missed lake, possibly the prettiest lake in China, surrounded by snow-sprinkled mountains. The water is crystal-clear with a sapphire tint. In summer, white flowers dot the hillsides. Unfortunately, tourism has been leaving its ugly footprint. The lake's southern shore is crowded with tour groups posing for snapshots with Mount Bogda in the background. To better appreciate the lake's natural beauty, arrive before the hordes, or stay until after the last bus has departed.

Kazakh families still set up traditional felt tents along the shores of Heavenly Lake from early May to late October, bringing their horses, sheep, and cashmere goats. The Kazakh people have a long history as horse breeders and are known to be skilled riders.

Most foreign visitors stay with the amiable **Rashit** (☎ *1389/964–1550* ⊕ *www.rashityurt.com*), who has been hosting tourists at his family yurt since 1980. For Y50 you get a spot in a cozy yurt and three freshly cooked if basic meals a day. They can also furnish horses and a guide for a day of riding around the lake. The sleeping quarters are communal, and there's no plumbing. However, you'll have a rewarding glimpse into the way your Kazakh hosts live. Rashit or a member of his family meets all buses to escort you to his yurts.

From Ürümqi, day-tour buses (Y25 each way after bargaining plus Y100 entrance fee to the lake) to Heavenly Lake leave at 9:30 in the morning from a small street beside the north gate of People's Park *(Renmin Gongyuan)*. You'll have from about noon to 6 pm to explore the lake, arriving back in the city at 8 pm. Tickets—usually available up until the bus leaves—can be purchased near the buses.

10

TURPAN

2½–3 hrs (184 km [114 mi]) by bus southeast of Ürümqi.

Turpan, which means "the lowest place" in Uyghur, lies in a desert basin at the southern foot of the Heavenly Mountains. Part of the basin lies 505 feet below sea level, the hottest spot in China and the second-lowest point in the world after the Dead Sea. In summer temperatures can soar to more than 50°C (120°F), so come prepared with lots of water and sunscreen.

Turpan's claim to fame is its location between the ruins of two spectacular ancient cities, Jiaohe and Gaochang. Most visitors don't linger in Turpan; the best five sites can easily be visited in a single day. But there are other attractions. Surrounded by some of the richest farmland in Xinjiang, Turpan's vineyards are famous for producing several varieties of candy-sweet raisins popular throughout China.

GETTING HERE AND AROUND

Too close to Ürümqi to have its own airport, Turpan is an inconvenient 60 km (38 mi) south of the nearest train station in Daheyan. A high-speed train link to the town itself is under construction, but no date has been given for its completion. If you arrive by train, take a taxi (Y40) or a public bus (Y7.50) to reach the city. The easiest way to reach Ürümqi from Turpan is by bus (2½ hours). Buses leave every 20 minutes from 7:30 am to 8:30 pm, and cost Y40 one way. The terminal is in the center of town on the north side of Laocheng Lu. Leaving Turpan is more difficult than arriving: one bus daily departs at noon for Kashgar. For any other destination, you'll have to head back to Ürümqi.

SAFETY AND PRECAUTIONS

The harsh, dry climate is probably the most important danger to be aware of; temperatures here have reached 50 °C (120 °F) in the height of summer, and have fallen to –28.9 °C (–20 °F) in winter. Drink plenty of water in hot months, slather on that sunscreen, and stay in the shade.

TIMING

An overnight stay is enough to see the sights that lie on the outskirts of town.

TOURS

You could join an organized group tour around Turpan, but you'll likely spend too much time in annoying tourist traps. With a slightly more expensive taxi tour you can choose your own itinerary and spend hours roaming the ruins of Jiaohe and Gaochang. In the off-season you may be able to secure a taxi for the day for as little as Y150, although prices of Y250 are more common during the summer.

ESSENTIALS

Bus Contact Turpan Bus Station (✉ *27 Laocheng Lu* ☎ *0995/852–2325*).

Train Contact Daheyan Train Station (✉ *Huoche Zhan Lu, Daheyan* ☎ *0995/864–2233*).

Visitor and Tour Info CITS (✉ *Jiaotong Hotel, 125 Laocheng Lu* ☎ *0995/852–1352* ⊕ *www.xinjiangtour.com*).

The Thousand Buddha Caves outside of Turpan.

EXPLORING

Karez Irrigation System. The remarkable 2,000-year-old system allowed the desert cities of the Silk Road to flourish despite an unrelentingly arid environment. In the oasis cities of Turpan and Hami, 1,600 km (990 mi) of underground tunnels brought water—moved only by gravity—from melting snow at the base of the Heavenly Mountains. You can view the tunnels at several sites around the city. Most tour guides take visitors to the largely educational Karez Irrigation Museum. Despite being described as the "underground Great Wall," most visitors are completely underwhelmed by what are essentially narrow dirt tunnels. ⊠ *888 Xincheng Lu, on the city's western outskirts* ⧖ *Y40* ⊙ *Daily 8–7.*

Sugong Mosque and the adjacent **Emin Tower** *(Emin Ta)* form Turpan's most recognizable image, often featured in tourist brochures. Built in 1777, it commemorates a military commander who suppressed a rebellion by a group of aristocrats. The 141-foot conical tower is elegantly spare, with bricks arranged in 15 patterns. The sunbaked roof of the mosque affords a view of the surrounding lush vineyards. You have to pay an extra Y25 if you wish to climb the minaret. This complex lies 4 km (2½ mi) from the city center at the southeast end of town. ⊠ *Go east on Laocheng Lu, turn right on the last paved road before farmland, known as Qiu Nian Zhong Lu* ⧖ *Y50* ⊙ *Daily 8–8.*

AROUND TURPAN

★ **City of Gaochang.** These fascinating city ruins lie in a valley south of the Flaming Mountains. Legend has it that a group of soldiers stopped here in the 1st century bc on their way to Afghanistan, found that water was plentiful, and decided to stay. By the 7th century the city was the capital of the kingdom of Gaochang, which ruled more than 21 other towns, and by the 9th century the Uyghurs had moved into the area from Mongolia, establishing the kingdom of Kharakojam. In the 14th century Mongols conquered and destroyed the kingdom, leaving only the ruins that can still be seen today. Only the city walls and a partially preserved monastery surrounded by muted, almost unrecognizable crumbling buildings remain, an eerie and haunting excursion into the pages of history. Despite repeated plundering of the site, in the early 1900s German archaeologists were able to unearth manuscripts, statues, and frescoes in superb condition. To make the best of your time here, take a donkey cart (time to use your bargaining skills—Y10 is a fair price) to the monastery in the rear right corner; from there you can walk back toward the entrance through the ruins. It's best to go early, as there is little shade. ⊠ *30 km (19 mi) east of Turpan* 🕿 *Y40* 🕙 *Dawn–dusk.*

Fodor'sChoice
★ **City of Jiaohe.** On an island at the confluence of two rivers, these impressive ruins lie in the Yarnaz Valley west of Turpan. The city, established as a garrison during the Han Dynasty, was built on a high plateau, protected by the natural fortification of cliffs rising 100 feet above the rivers. Jiaohe was governed from the 2nd to the 7th century by the kingdom of Gaochang, and occupied later by Tibetans. Despite destruction in the 14th century by Mongol hordes, large fragments of actual streets and buildings remain, including a Buddhist monastery and Buddhist statues, a row of bleached pagodas, a 29-foot observation tower, and a prison. Guards will make sure you stay on the marked paths. Again, try and go early, as there is little shade. ⊠ *8 km (5 mi) west of Turpan* 🕿 *Y40* 🕙 *Dawn–dusk.*

★ **Bezeklik Thousand Buddha Caves.** In a breathtaking valley inside the Flaming Mountains is this ancient temple complex, built between the 5th and 9th century by slaves whose entire lives went into the construction. Many of the fine examples of Buddhist sculpture and wall frescoes were destroyed after Islam came to the region in the 13th century. Other sculptures and frescoes, including several whole murals of Buddhist monks, were removed by 20th-century archaeologists like German Albert von Le Coq, who shipped his finds back to Berlin. Although they remain a feat of early engineering, the caves are in atrocious condition. Go just to see the site itself and the surrounding valley, which is magnificent. The views of the scorched, lunar landscape leading up to the site, which clings to one flank of a steep, scenic valley, make the trip worth the effort. Avoid the nearby Buddha Cave constructed in 1980 by a local artist; it isn't worth an additional Y20. ⊠ *35 km (22 mi) east of Turpan* 🕿 *Y40* 🕙 *Dawn–dusk.*

WHERE TO EAT

Most visitors stick to the restaurants in and around the Turpan Hotel on Qingnian Lu, a pleasant side street shaded by grape vines. The bazaar across from the bus station is a good place to grab lunch for around Y5. A lively night market with rows of kebab and spicy hotpot stands is on Gaochang Lu, a 10-minute walk north from the Turpan Hotel, next to the huge public square and near the China Post building.

¢ ✕**John's Information Café.** Part of a small family-run chain that operates
AMERICAN in destinations along the Silk Road, this popular tourist hangout is far
from authentic, but people flock here for the familiar Western choices
and rock-solid travel advice. Their tours are good, but check carefully
to see what is included. They can also rent bikes and wash laundry.
⊠ *Qingnian Lu, rear of the Turpan Hotel* ☎ *0998/258–1186* ⊕ *www.
johncafe.net* ⊟ *No credit cards.*

¢ ✕**Muslim Restaurant.** Like most hotel restaurants in the region, this one
NORTHERN is poorly lighted and lacks ambience, but it does have a hearty variety
CHINESE of standard Uyghur dishes: lamb, noodles, and vegetables. ⊠ *Turpan
Hotel, 2 Qingnian Nan Lu* ☎ *No phone* ⊟ *No credit cards.*

WHERE TO STAY

¢ 🏨 **Jiaotong Hotel.** This budget option isn't a bad place to stay, despite
noise from the bus station in the rear and the bazaar across the street. It
has recently been renovated, and the rooms are much improved, though
prices have gone up. The on-site travel agency makes arranging tours a
snap, although the staff can be a bit pushy. If you come to Turpan in the
off-season, a deluxe suite with a small balcony overlooking the bazaar
can be had for as little as Y200. **Pros:** bargain twin rooms (Y80); convenient for early buses. **Cons:** bad water pressure; and there can be power
cuts. ⊠ *230 Laocheng Lu, next to the bus station* ☎ *0995/853–1320*
⊠ *67 rooms* ⚬ *In-hotel: restaurant* ⊟ *No credit cards.*

¢ 🏨 **Turpan Hotel.** This study in basic geometry, covered in white tile, has
seen better days, but rooms are relatively clean and large, the Muslim
restaurant is quite good, and the gift shops are handy. Even if you're not
staying here, the indoor swimming pool—open only in the summer—is
a good place to cool off after a day in the desert sun, though the water
looks a little grubby. Admission is Y20 per person. **Pros:** usually offers
good discounts; friendly staff. **Cons:** if you can't get a discount, better
values are available elsewhere; Chinese breakfast options only. ⊠ *2 Qingnian Nan Lu, south of Laocheng Lu* ☎ *0995/856–8888* ⊠ *219 rooms, 5
suites* ⚬ *In-hotel: 3 restaurants, pool, gym, laundry service* ⊟ *V.*

KASHGAR

10

*24 hrs (1,175 km [729 mi]) by train or 1½ hours by plane southwest
of Ürümqi.*

Kashgar, the westernmost city in China, is closer to Baghdad than Beijing. More than 3,400 km (2,100 mi) west of the capital, the city has
been a center of trade between China and the outside world for at least
2,000 years. Today Kashgar is a hub for merchants coming in over the
Khunjerab Pass from Pakistan and the Torugart Pass from Kyrgyzstan.
When these two treacherous mountain passes are open between May 1
and October 30, Kashgar becomes a particularly colorful city, abuzz
not only with curious Western tourists but also with visitors from every
corner of Central Asia.

Despite an increasing Han presence in central Kashgar (symbolized by
one of the largest Mao statues in the country), the city is still overwhelm-
ingly Uyghur. A great deal of modernization has taken place here since
the railway from Ürümqi arrived in 1999. Beijing is showering attention

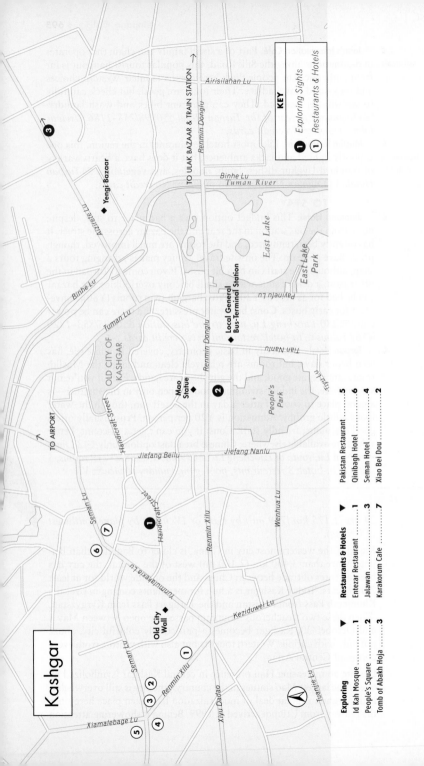

Kashgar

Exploring
- Id Kah Mosque 1
- People's Square 2
- Tomb of Abakh Hoja 3

Restaurants & Hotels ▶
- Entezar Restaurant 1
- Jalawan 3
- Karakorum Cafe 7
- Pakistan Restaurant 5
- Qinibagh Hotel 6
- Seman Hotel 4
- Xiao Bei Dou 2

KEY
- 1 Exploring Sights
- 1 Restaurants & Hotels

TO ULAK BAZAAR & TRAIN STATION

Old City Wall ◆

Mao Statue ◆

Yengi Bazaar ◆

OLD CITY OF KASHGAR

People's Park

East Lake

East Lake Park

Tuman River

Local General Bus-Terminal Station ◆

TO AIRPORT

Airisilahan Lu
Renmin Donglu
Binhe Lu
Tuman River
Binhe Lu
Atizirete Lu
Tuman Lu
Handicraft Street
Renmin Donglu
Tian Nanlu
Payinelu Lu
Jiefang Beilu
Jiefang Nanlu
Handicraft Street
Renmin Xilu
Wenhua Lu
Seman Lu
Yumulayexia Lu
Keziduwei Lu
Tuatie Lu
Seman Lu
Renmin Xilu
Xiamalebage Lu
Xiyu Dadao

and money to boost the local economy and placate Kashgar's Uyghur population. In 2008 local Uyghurs attacked the police and killed 16 officers. This led to a heavy security presence that remains today. Despite protests from Uyghurs and conservationists, in 2009 the government tore down thousands of homes in the Old City. Still, parts of Kashgar remain in a time warp. Only a few blocks from newly built karaoke parlors and car dealerships you can still find blacksmiths, bakers, and cobblers. Much of the city's Uyghur architecture has been demolished, but there are still some traditional houses with ornately painted balconies, as well as large remaining sections of the Old City. Most visitors come to Kashgar for the amazing Sunday Market, the largest bazaar in Central Asia and one of the best photo-ops in all of China.

GETTING HERE AND AROUND
Daunted by the long train journey from Ürümqi, many tourists headed for Kashgar travel by air. The airport is 13 km (8 mi) north of the city center; a taxi to or from your hotel shouldn't cost more than Y30, and minibuses will drop you off at your hotel for Y10. Trains between Ürümqi and Kashgar (24 or 28 hours) depart twice daily; the slow train is half the price of the fast train, but you'll have to do without air-conditioning. The station is 10 km (6 mi) east of town, not far from the livestock market. Taxis from here cost about Y15. Kashgar's long-distance bus station is just east of People's Park in the center of town, although many buses arriving in the city will stop somewhere less convenient to drop you off.

SAFETY AND PRECAUTIONS
Tensions between local Uyghurs and Han Chinese remain, but tourists shouldn't avoid traveling here and are not subject to any travel restrictions.

TIMING
Allow two or three days if possible, and do try and time your stay to include the famous Sunday market.

TOURS
Kashgar is a tourist-friendly city, so you shouldn't have any trouble arranging tours. Uyghur Tour and Travel Center (also known as Abdul's), in the lobby of the Overseas Chinese Hotel, opposite the Seman Hotel, offers a "money-back guarantee." It has received high marks from travelers for the past five years. A day tour of sites within Kashgar will cost about Y400, not including admission tickets. If you're interested in spending a night in the area's only 1,000-star hotel—the Taklamakan Desert—the agency can arrange an all-inclusive overnight camel trek for Y850 per person.

ESSENTIALS
Air Contact Kashgar Airport (⊠ *13 km (8 mi) north of the city center* ☎ *0998/282–3204*).

Bus Contact Kashgar Bus Station (⊠ *Tiannan Lu, on the east side of People's Park* ☎ *0998/282–9673*).

Police Kashgar PSB (⊠ *139 Yumulakexiehai Lu, south of the Qinibagh Hotel* ☎ *0998/282–2814*).

Medical Assistance No. 1 People's Hospital (✉ *Jichang Lu* ☎ *0998/296–2750*).

Train Contact Kashgar Train Station (✉ *Kashi Huoche Zhan* ☎ *0998/256–1298*).

Visitor and Tour Info CITS (✉ *Qinibagh Hotel, 144 Seman Lu* ☎ *0998/298–3156* ⊕ *www.xinjiangtour.com*). **Uyghur Tour and Travel Center** (✉ *Overseas Chinese Hotel, 170 Seman Lu, at Renmin Lu* ☎ *0998/220–4012* ⊕ *www.silkroadinn.com*).

EXPLORING

Id Kah Mosque. Start your tour of the city with a visit to the center of Muslim life in Kashgar. One of the largest mosques in China, the ornate structure of yellow bricks is the result of many extensions and renovations to the original mosque, built in 1442 as a prayer hall for the ruler of Kashgar. The main hall has a ceiling with fine wooden carvings and precisely 100 carved wooden columns. When services aren't being held, you are free to wander the quiet shaded grounds and even to enter the prayer hall. As this is an active site of worship, visitors should dress modestly. ✉ *Ai Teaser Guangchang* ☎ *No Phone* 🎫 *Y20* ⏱ *Dawn–dusk*.

Tomb of Abakh Hoja. About 5 km (3 mi) northeast of the city lies one of the most sacred sites in Xinjiang. The sea-green tiled hall that houses the tomb—actually about two dozen tombs—is part of a massive complex of sacred Islamic structures built around 1640. Uyghurs named the tomb and surrounding complex after Abakh Hoja, an Islamic missionary believed to be a descendant of Mohammed, who ruled Kashgar and outlying regions in the 17th century. Excavations of the glazed-brick tombs indicate that the first occupant was Abakh Hoja's father, who is buried here along with Abakh Hoja and many of their descendants.

The Han, who prefer to emphasize the site's historical connection to their dynastic empire, call it the Tomb of the Fragrant Concubine. When the grandniece of Abakh Hoja was chosen as concubine by the Qing ruler Qianlong in Beijing, Uyghur legend holds that she committed suicide rather than submit to the emperor. In the Han story, she dutifully went to Beijing and spent 30 years in the emperor's palace, then asked to be buried in her homeland. Either way, her alleged tomb was excavated in the 1980s and found to be empty. The tomb is a bit difficult to locate, so take a taxi. ✉ *Off of Aizirete Lu, 2 km (1 mi) east of the Sunday Bazaar* ☎ *No phone* 🎫 *Y30* ⏱ *Daily 9–9*.

People's Square. If you happen to forget which country Kashgar is in, chances are you aren't standing in this square. A statue of Mao Zedong—one of the largest in China—stands with his right arm raised in perpetual salute. The statue is evidence of an unspoken rule in China that directly relates the size of a Mao tribute to its distance from Beijing; the only Mao statue larger than this one is in Tibet. ✉ *Renmin Lu between Lu and Tian Lu* ☎ *No phone*.

WHERE TO EAT

¢–$

NORTHERN

CHINESE

★

✕ **Entezar Restaurant.** Frequented by locals and outfitted with wooden paneling and chandeliers, Entezar is the most formal of Kashgar's Uyghur restaurants. It offers a range of the great cuisine, and the menu is translated into English, including helpful descriptions of each dish.

For those tired of typical Uyghur fare, Muslim-friendly stir-fry dishes are also available. Alcohol is not allowed on the premises. ☒ *320 Renmin Xi Lu, southeast of the Seman Hotel* ☎ *0998/258–3555* ▭ *No credit cards.*

¢–$

NORTHERN
CHINESE

✕ **Jalawan.** It's very easy to join the crowds of locals relaxing at this restaurant, especially underneath the (admittedly) fake trellises of grapes with tables grouped around a fountain. The staff will hand you an English-language menu, though prices are a few yuan higher than on the Chinese-language menu! But when it's all so cheap, you can't complain too much. Try the *lao hu cai*, or tiger salad, an evocatively named dish of cucumber chilies and tomatoes, or the pilaf with a cooling bowl of yogurt. ☒ *Seman Lu, on the roundabout opposite the Seman Hotel* ☎ *0998/258–1001* ▭ *No credit cards.*

¢–$

AMERICAN

✕ **Karakorum Café.** If it's Western food you're craving, head straight to this expat-run café—after weeks of eating noodles, you'll feel it's a veritable breath of fresh air on the Silk Road. The banana smoothies go down well, as does the roast eggplant focaccia. The friendly manager will give you travel advice if asked. ☒ *87 Seman Lu, opposite the Qinibagh Hotel's entrance gate* ☎ *0998/258–2345* ⊕ *www.crowninntashkorgan.com* ▭ *No credit cards.*

¢

MIDDLE EASTERN

✕ **Pakistan Restaurant.** Foreign restaurants are rare in Kashgar, so this dirt-cheap curry joint is a welcome addition. This is where the city's Pakistani residents while away their evenings playing cards and sipping tea. There's an English menu, but its function seems to be primarily illustrative—we visited twice and got the wrong dishes both times; still, in both cases they were delicious! Particularly good were the chickpea and beef and potato curries. There are no chopsticks here, as everything is scooped-up using delicious *roti* flat bread. Hot chai tea served with milk is the best way to wash down your meal. This restaurant's sign is covered by a large tree, so look for the tree instead. ☒ *Seman Lu, opposite the Seman Hotel's rear gate* ☎ *No phone* ▭ *No credit cards.*

¢–$$

SICHUAN

✕ **Xiao Bei Dou.** When you've grown tired of mutton, head here for the best Sichuan-style dishes in Kashgar. Classic selections like sweet-and-sour pork (*tangcu liji*), chicken with peanuts (*gongbao jiding*), and scallion pancakes (*conghuabing*) are all well prepared. There's plenty of cold beer in the refrigerator, and the second-floor covered terrace is perfect on a warm summer evening. An English menu is available, but the selection is limited. ☒ *285 Seman Lu, east of the Seman Hotel* ☎ *No phone* ▭ *No credit cards.*

WHERE TO STAY

¢

⌂ **Qinibagh Hotel.** Of Kashgar's two popular hotels, the Qinibagh is looking the worse for wear, and only their dorm rooms are worth recommending. Located on the site of the former British consulate, this hotel has an interesting history. Constructed in 1908, the consulate building—now an attractive Uyghur restaurant—was home to diplomat Sir George McCartney and his wife for 26 years. Don't expect historic rooms, though—the hotel buildings are '60s-style monstrosities. There are branches of CITS and John's Information Café, two travel resources, on the premises. Dorm rooms are a bargain, and are set around a reasonably attractive courtyard. **Pros:** easy to find; good place to meet

10

other foreigners. **Cons:** tatty around the edges. ✉ *93 Seman Lu, north-west of Id Kah Mosque* ☎ *0998/298–2103* 🖷 *0998/298–2299* ♨ *In-room: refrigerator. In-hotel: 4 restaurants, bar, laundry service* ▤ *V.*

¢ 🛏 **Seman Hotel.** Built in 1890 as the Russian consulate, this edifice served as a center of political intrigue for many years. The oldest wing of the hotel is the original consulate, where fans of the "Great Game" can stay in musty suites with luxurious rugs and old furniture. The hotel's newer rooms range from comfortable to dilapidated, so be sure to look at a few before you decide. The worst rooms are adjacent to a large traffic circle; nicer ones surround a pleasant courtyard in the rear. The hotel is very popular with backpackers, who come for the Y20 beds packed into dorm-style rooms. Travel agencies are clustered around the lobby. **Pros:** near some excellent restaurants; competitive prices from the lobby tour agencies. **Cons:** musty bathrooms in the cheaper rooms and dorms. ✉ *170 Seman Lu, at Renmin Lu* ☎ *0998/258–2129* 🖷 *0998/258–2150* ♨ *In-hotel: 3 restaurants, laundry service* ▤ *AE, DC, MC, V*

SHOPPING

Kashgar's famous **Sunday Market** consists of two bazaars with a distance of almost 10 km (6 mi) between them. The **Yengi Bazaar** on Aizilaiti Lu, about 1½ km (1 mi) northeast of the city center, is open every day, but on Sunday the surrounding streets overflow with vendors hawking everything from boiled sheep's heads to trendy sunglasses. In the covered section you can bargain for decorative knives, embroidered fabrics, and all sorts of Uyghur-themed souvenirs. Behind the bazaar, rows of sleepy donkeys nod off in the bright sunlight, their carts lined up neatly beside them. For the best photos, however, you'll need to head over to the **Ulak Bazaar,** a 10-minute taxi ride to the east. Essentially a livestock market, farmers here tug recalcitrant sheep through the streets, scarf-shrouded women preside over heaps of red eggs, and old Uyghur men squat over baskets of chickens, haggling over the virtues and vices of each hapless hen. In the market for a camel? You can buy one here. On the outskirts of the market you can get an Old World–style straight-razor shave from a Uyghur barber or grab a bowl of *laghman* noodles, knowing that it's flavored with meat that is very, very fresh.

Running alongside the Id Kah Mosque is a narrow lane known as **Handicraft Street.** Walking in either direction, you'll find merchants selling everything from bright copper kettles to wedding chests to brass sleigh bells. At the **Uyghur Musical Instruments Workshop** (✉ *272 Kumdar-waza Lu* ☎ *0998/283–5378*) you can watch the owner or his apprentice working on Uyghur string instruments—stretching snakeskin or inlaying tiny bits of shell to make a Uyghur guitar called a *ravap*.

SIDE TRIPS FROM KASHGAR

The **Karakorum Highway,** a spectacular road winding across some of the most dramatic and inhospitable terrain on Earth, traces one of the major ancient silk routes, from Kashgar south for 2,100 km (1,300 mi) through three great mountain ranges over the Khunjerab Pass into Pakistan. The journey can be hair-raising in part because of rock- and mudslides and in part because of daredevil driving.

Fodor'sChoice **Karakul Lake.** Four hours south of Kashgar, having followed the Gez
★ River valley deep into the heart of the Pamir Mountains, the highway
passes alongside this picturesque lake. At an elevation of 3,800 meters
(12,500 feet), this crystal-blue jewel of a lake is dominated on either
side by stunning snowcapped mountains, including the 7,800-meter
(25,600-foot) peak of **Muztagata,** the "Father of the Ice Mountains."
Arriving at the lake, you'll practically be assaulted by would-be hosts
on camelback, horseback, and motorcycle. Avoid the expensive yurts
near the entrance, and head back along the road to the more secluded
yurts, where it is possible to stay with a local family for Y50 including
(basic) food. Standard food will be limited to bread and butter, tea,
and fried rice dishes, but there is an expensive Chinese restaurant. Toilet facilities in this area are some of the worst in China, and there are
no showers, but the area's beauty makes it worthwhile. Tour the lake
via camel, horse, or motorbike, or just walk around, which will take
about three hours. Bring warm clothing even in the summer, as it can be
downright chilly: during our visit in July, we were applying sunscreen
in the morning and battling sleet in the afternoon.

Any travel agent can arrange tours to Karakul Lake, but most people
make the breathtaking journey by public bus. Buses headed for Tashkurgan, two hours south of the lake, leave Kashgar's long-distance bus
station on Xiyu Dadao every morning at 10. You'll have to pay the
full price of Y51 for your ticket, even though you're not traveling the
full distance. Bring your passport, or you'll be turned back at a border checkpoint in Gezcun or at one of the other checkpoints that have
sprung up along the way. Buses reach the lake in about four hours. To
catch the bus back, wait by the side of the highway and flag it down—
the bus returning to Kashgar from Tashkurgan passes the lake between
11 am and 1 pm. A seat should only cost Y40, but enterprising drivers
will demand Y50. Either way, the bus is much cheaper than private
tours, which will set you back about Y600 per day.

10

ENGLISH	PINYIN	CHINESE
SHAANXI	**SHĀNXI**	陕西
Xian	Xī'ān	西安
Banpo Matriarchal Clan Village	Bànpō Bówùguǎn	半坡博物馆
Bell Tower	Zhōnglóu	钟楼
Big Wild Goose Pagoda	Dàyàn Tǎ	大雁塔
Culture Street	Wénhuà Jiē	文化街
Delhi Durbar	Yìndù Fànguǎn	印度饭馆
Drum Tower	Gǔlóu	鼓楼
Famen Temple	Fǎménsì	法门寺
Forest of Stone Tablets Museum	Bēilín Bówùguǎn	碑林博物馆
Great Mosque	Dàqīngzhēn Sì	大清真寺
GZ Bar	GZ Jiǔba	GZ 酒吧
Hai An Xian Internet Bar	Hǎi'àn Xī'ān Wǎngba	海岸西安网吧
Huaqing Hot Springs	Huáqīng Chí	华清池
Ibis Xian	Xī'ān Yíbìsī Jiǔdiàn	西安宜必思酒店
Shaanxi History Museum	Shǎnxī Lìshǐ Bówùguǎn	陕西历史博物馆
Small Goose Pagoda	Xiǎoyàn Tǎ	小雁塔
South Gate	Nánmén	南门
Terracotta Warriors Museum	Bīngmǎyǒng Bówùguǎn	兵马俑博物馆
Tomb of the Qin Emperor	Qínshǐhuánglíng	秦始皇陵
Xiangzimen Youth Hostel	Xiāngzimén Qīngnián Lǚxíngshè	湘子门 青年旅行舍
GANSU	**GĀNSÙ**	甘肃
Lanzhou	Lánzhōu	兰州
Gansu Provincial Museum	Gānsù Shěng Bówùguǎn	甘肃省博物馆
Labrang Monastery	Lābǔléng Sì	拉卜楞寺
Lanzhou East Bus Station	Lánzhōu Dōng Qìchēzhàn	汽车东站
Lanzhou South Bus Station	Lánzhōu Nán Qìchēzhàn	兰州南汽车站
Lanzhou Train Station	Lánzhōu Huǒchēzhàn	兰州火车站
Lanzhou West Bus Station	Lánzhōu Xī Qìchēzhàn	兰州西汽车站
Lanzhou Zhongchuan Airport	Lánzhōu Zhōngchuān Fēijīchǎng	兰州中川飞机场
Mountain of the White Pagoda Park	Báitǎshān Gōngyuán	白塔山公园
Thousand Buddha Temple and Grottoes	Bǐnglíngsì Shíkū	炳灵寺石窟
Dunhuang	Dūnhuáng	敦煌
Dunhuang Airport	Dūnhuáng Fēijīchǎng	敦煌飞机场

ENGLISH	PINYIN	CHINESE
Dunhuang Bus Station	Dūnhuáng Qìchēzhàn	敦煌汽车站
Dunhuang Museum	Dūnhuáng Bówùguǎn	敦煌博物馆
Mogao Grottoes	Mògāo Kū	莫高窟
Singing Sand Mountain	Míngshā Shān	鸣沙山
QINGHAI	**QĪNGHǍI**	**青海**
Xining	Xīníng	西宁
Bird Island	Niǎo Dǎo	鸟岛
Black Tent	Hēise Zhàngpeng	黑色帐篷
Casa Mia Italian restaurant	Yìdàlì Fànguǎn	意大利饭馆
Jianguo Road Wholesale Market	Jiànguó Lù pPīfā Shìchǎng	n/a
Kumbum Monastery	Tǎ'ěrsì	塔尔寺
Lete Hostel	Xīníng Lǐtǐ Qīngnián Lǚshè	西宁理体青年旅舍
North Monastery	Běichán Sì	北禅寺
Qinghai Lake	Qīnghǎi Hú	青海湖
Shuijin Xiang Market	Shuǐjǐn Xiàng Shāngchǎng	水井巷商场
Xining Bus Station	Xīníng Qìchēzhàn	西宁汽车站
Xining Caojiabao Airport	Xīníng Cáojiābǎo	西宁曹家堡飞机场
Xining Train Station	Xīníng Huǒchēzhàn	西宁火车站
XINJIANG	**XĪNJIĀNG**	**新疆**
Ürümqi	Wūlǔmùqí	乌鲁木齐
Karakorum Café	Kǎlākùli Kāfēitīng	卡拉库里咖啡厅
Bell Tower Square	Zhōnglóu Guǎngchǎng	钟楼广场
Bezeklik Thousand Buddha Caves	Bòzīkèlǐkè Qiān Fódòng	柏孜克里克千佛洞
Maitian Youth Hostel	Màitián Qīngnián Lǚxíngshè	麦田青年旅行舍
Heavenly Lake	Tiānchí Hú	天池湖
Id Kah Mosque	Àitígǎ'ěr Qīngzhēn Sì	艾提尕尔清真寺
International Grand Bazaar	Dàbāzā	大巴扎
Jalawan	ābùdūkǎdíěr	n/a
Karakul Lake	Kǎlākùlēi Hú	喀拉库勒湖
Karez Irrigation Museum	Kǎnérjǐng Bówùguǎn	坎儿井博物馆
Kasghar	Kāshí	喀什
Kasghar Train Station	Kāshí Huǒchēzhàn	喀什火车站
Kashgar Airport	Kāshí Fēijīchǎng	喀什飞机场
Nianzigou Bus Station	Niānzǐgōu Qìchēzhàn	碾子沟汽车站
Old City of Gaochang	Gāochāng Gùchéng	高昌故城

10

ENGLISH	PINYIN	CHINESE
Old City of Jiaohe	Jiāohé Gùchéng	交河故城
Orda Restaurant	Ěrdá	n/a
People's Park	Rénmín Gōngyuán	人民公园
People's Square	Rénmín Guǎngchǎng	人民广场
Red Mountain Park	Hóngshān gGōngyuán	红山公园
Shaanxi	Shǎanxī	陕西
Sheraton	Xīláidēng Wūlǔmùqí Jiǔdiàn	喜来登乌鲁木齐酒店
Sugong Mosque & Emin Tower	Émǐn Tǎ	额敏塔
Tomb of Abakh Hoja	Xiāngfēi Mù	香妃墓
Turpan	Tūlǔfān	吐鲁番
Ürümqi Airport	Wūlǔmùqí Fēijīchǎng	乌鲁木齐地窝堡国际机场
Ürümqi South Bus Station	Wūlǔmùqí Nán Qìchēzhàn	乌鲁木齐南汽车站
Ürümqi Train Station	Wūlǔmùqí Huǒchēzhàn	乌鲁木齐火车站
Xinjiang Autonomous Region Museum	Xīnjiāng Zìzhìqū Bówùguǎn	新疆自治区博物馆

Tibet

THE ROOFTOP OF THE WORLD

WORD OF MOUTH

"My advice is to stay on top of the permit situation on a day-to-day basis before you go. If you go in a group, you shouldn't run into any problems as long as you make sure that they are a reputable operator."

—travelguy120

WELCOME TO TIBET

TOP REASONS TO GO

★ **Barkhor:** Tibetan Buddhism's holiest pilgrimage circuit, the Barkhor is both the heart of Old Lhasa and one of the liveliest people-watching spots in all of China.

★ **Potala Palace:** Towering over Lhasa, this impressive palace of the Dalai Lamas was once the world's tallest structure, and is still a world wonder.

★ **Ganden Monastery:** The most remote of the capital's three great monasteries, Ganden offers stunning views of the Lhasa River Valley and surrounding Tibetan farmland from a height of 14,764 feet.

★ **Gyantse Dzong:** The site of fierce fighting between Tibetan and British troops in 1904, this fortress is one of the few remaining symbols of Tibetan military power.

★ **Everest Base Camp:** Stand in awe beneath the world's tallest mountain.

1 Lhasa. Despite the city's rapid modernization, Lhasa is still one of China's must-visit destinations. From the crowded back alleys of the Barkhor to the imposing heights of the Potala Palace, a mix of Westerners, local Tibetans, Nepalese, and Han Chinese give this city an atmosphere unlike any other place in the world.

2 Gyantse. Past the sapphire waters of Yamdrok Tso and endless fields of golden highland barley, this small city is the gateway to southern Tibet and the Himalayas. An abandoned fortress high above town is testament to the area's former military importance, while the unique architecture at Pelkor Chode Monastery speaks to the city's history as a melting pot of religious denominations.

GETTING ORIENTED

The Tibetan plateau is more than twice the size of France, sandwiched between two Himalayan ridges whose peaks reach an altitude of nearly 9 km (5½ mi). With the opening of the world's highest rail line and significantly improved roads, Tibet is more accessible than ever—once you get the required permits, that is. Lhasa is the best base from which to take day trips to the fertile Kyi-chu Valley or longer jaunts into the southwestern highlands of Tsang to visit Gyantse, Shigatse, and the Everest region. Every hotel and tour operator can arrange four-wheel-drive jeeps with a driver and/or a guide. Tibet is currently undergoing massive infrastructure improvements, and many roads that were once as bumpy as the steep mountain passes have been flattened into perfect stretches of blacktop.

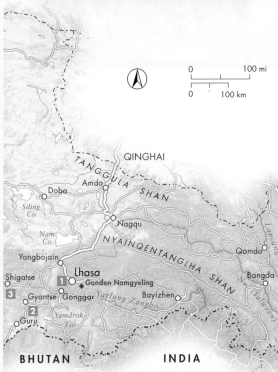

3 Shigatse. Tibet's second-largest city, Shigatse is the traditional capital of the Tsang region and home to the Panchen Lama's seat of power at Tashilhunpo Monastery. The ruined fortress on a hill above town has been rebuilt based on old photographs, but its concrete construction stands as one of the most glaring symbols of the modern world's encroachment on an ancient and sacred land.

4 Everest. You may have trouble breathing when you first see the majestic peaks of the Himalayas, and not only because of the high altitude. The roof of the world is a spectacular place, with roaring snow-melt rivers feeding Tibetan farms and fields of wildflowers below.

By Helena
Iveson

Tibet is all you've heard and everything you've imagined: a land of intense sunshine and towering snowcapped peaks, where crystal-clear rivers and sapphire lakes irrigate terraced fields of golden highland barley. The Tibetan people are extremely religious, viewing their daily toil and the harsh environment surrounding them as challenges along the path to life's single goal, the attainment of spiritual enlightenment. The region's richly decorated monasteries, temples, and palaces—including the Potala Palace—were not constructed by forced labor, but by laborers and artisans who donated their entire lives to the accumulation of good karma.

The death, destruction, and cultural denigration of Tibet that accompanied the Chinese invasion in the early 1950s changed this land forever, as did the Cultural Revolution in the late 1960s. Yet the people remain resilient. Colorfully dressed pilgrims still bring their offerings of yak butter to the temples, and monks work with zeal to repair the damage done to their monasteries. Many young Tibetans, attracted by the wealth and convenience brought by development, have abandoned their ancestors' traditional ways. Coca-Cola, fast food, and pulsing techno music are popular in Lhasa. Yet the changes have not lessened Tibet's allure as a travel destination. Unfortunately, however, tourism has been ever more tightly controlled since violent riots in March 2008 during protests against the central government's influence over religious practice in the region. Tibetans were also protesting years of government policies encouraging migration of majority Han Chinese to Tibet, which has stoked ethnic tensions. As the region's infrastructure is built up, Tibet's GDP is growing at 12% every year, and its small towns are quickly turning into cities; people looking for job opportunities naturally gravitate here. With four packed trains arriving every day in Lhasa, Han Chinese almost certainly outnumber Tibetans in some areas. Still, while The Barkhor in Lhasa and the area around Tashilhunpo Monastery in Shigatse are Tibetan islands in otherwise increasingly Han cities, much of the region remains relatively free of Chinese influence.

PLANNING

WHEN TO GO

Choosing when to visit Tibet is a matter of balancing your tolerance for extreme weather with your tolerance for tourist hordes. The busiest months are July and August, but pleasant weather is common from May through October. However, bear in mind that Tibet can be abruptly closed to non-Chinese travelers during national holidays, such as the May 1st holiday and the October holiday. If you come at the beginning or end of the high season you'll have plenty of breathing space to take in the golden roofs of Tibet's monasteries and the icy peaks of the Himalayas. You may want to schedule your trip to coincide with one of Tibet's colorful celebrations, including the Birth of Buddha Festival (end of May), the Holy Mountain Festival (end of July), the Yogurt Festival (August), and the Bathing Festival (September). If you travel to Tibet in the off-season, many hotels and restaurants may be closed. Whenever you visit, warm clothing, sunglasses, and sunscreen are essentials for the high-altitude climate.

GETTING HERE AND AROUND

Passports and Visas. A visa valid for the People's Republic of China is required. You will also need to get a Tibet Tourism Bureau travel permit, which is arranged by the travel agent who books your tour or transportation to Lhasa. Travel by train or plane without a permit is next to impossible—on Internet forums you may hear of the odd person who claims to manage it, but it's more than likely that you will be refused boarding with no refund. At this writing, no independent travel to Tibet was permitted; only individuals booked on tours to Tibet could travel there. These restrictions change depending on the political situation in Tibet, so it is best to contact travel agents, tour groups, or hotels in the region for information on current policies.

The Chinese government makes it all but impossible for you to travel independently. Groups find it easier to secure a TTB permit as well as permits to visit sites outside of Lhasa. Your TTB permit is based on the tour that you arrange before arriving in Tibet. There are reports of people buying short tours and then trying to buy additional segments in Lhasa but encountering difficulty in doing so because of the dates written on their permits, so it pays to be organized before you get to Tibet and work out exactly what you want to see. A typical package includes flights or the train to Lhasa and a guide, and whereas you used to be able to hang out in Lhasa without a guide, now some sights such as the Potala Palace will not let you in without a guide and a permit. There is no limit, aside from the validity of your Chinese visa, to the length of time you can stay in Tibet, except when the government decides not to allow foreigners in.

AIR TRAVEL

In line with the government's ambitious infrastructure plans for Tibet, there are now four airports, with another two due to open by the end of 2011. One of these, in Nagqu, will be the world's highest airport, at an altitude of 4,436 meters (14,500 ft). Currently, 16 domestic airlines fly into Gongga Airport, about 95 kilometers from Lhasa, connecting Tibet with most major Chinese cities, including Hong Kong. The airport is renowned for having terrible facilities and humorless guards, so don't expect much. Tibet also has smaller airports in Chamdo, Nyingchi, and Ngari prefectures. These have frequent flights to Lhasa and less frequent flights to other nearby Chinese cities. Security on flights bound for Lhasa is much tighter than on other internal flights—expect to be thoroughly searched.

> **WORD OF MOUTH**
>
> "Since the railroad and the railcars are all new, and since the speed was limited on the permafrost at 100km/h (62 mph), the ride was very smooth, and I had no problem getting to sleep at all."
> —rkwan

BUS TRAVEL

There are buses in Tibet, of the rickety, bone-shaking sort, but they tend to cater to locals only. Drivers are often very reluctant to pick up foreign travelers. In Lhasa it's easier, but you will be expected to have your tour guide with you. Most visitors hire a land cruiser to get around once outside of Lhasa.

CAR TRAVEL

As part of the tour you will have to have booked to get into Tibet, a car and driver is usually included. Travel costs are high, because car hire requires both a guide and driver, distances are large, and gas is expensive.

TRAIN TRAVEL

Since 2006 it's been possible to travel on the world's highest railway, complete with oxygen tanks, and arrive in Tibet by train—provided you have your TTB permit. This means that you will need to book a tour that includes your train trip. Now there are direct air-conditioned trains from Beijing, Shanghai, Guangzhou, and Xian to Lhasa several times a week. Everyone has to sign a health waiver saying they're fit to travel. The rail link is not without its controversies—some argue that the train encourages Han migration, and that its construction has had a tremendous environmental impact.

RESTAURANTS

It's fair to say that no one travels to Tibet for its food. Because of its altitude and remoteness, traditional food consists mainly of barley with the odd serving of meat, vegetables, and dairy products. Tsampa is Tibet's staple food, which is barley flour mixed with salted butter tea. Lhasa has Tibet's best dining options, so make the most of the competitive market of hybrid restaurants that serve Chinese, Indian, Nepali, Tibetan, and Western fare. Most have sprung up from backpacker haunts serving perennially favorite dishes, from banana pancakes to yak burgers to chicken masala.

HOTELS

Hotel options in Lhasa have improved significantly in recent years. There are a smattering of boutique hotels and a couple of international-brand properties. Ask, and you may be shown rooms ranging from a depressing 20-person dormitory to a deluxe suite with private bath, balcony, and minibar. Many of the more expensive hotels even equip their rooms with oxygen machines to ease the effects of altitude sickness. Tibetan guesthouses are staffed by locals and are more personable, but some of the shared bathing facilities at the lower-end options can be archaic. It's best to book way in advance during peak season. Outside of Lhasa, standards are much lower, so be prepared to rough it.

WHAT IT COSTS IN YUAN					
	¢	$	$$	$$$	$$$$
Restaurants	under Y25	Y25–Y49	Y50–Y99	Y100–Y150	over Y150
Hotels	under Y200	Y200–Y349	Y350–Y499	Y500–Y999	over Y1,000

Restaurant prices are for a main course. There is no sales tax in China and tipping is not expected. Hotel prices, unless noted, are for a standard double room, including taxes.

VISITOR INFORMATION

Travelers are at the mercy of private travel agents, guidebooks, and online travel forums for the most up-to-date information on Tibet. State-run travel bureaus do exist, but are often downright unhelpful. Because the travel situation is in a constant state of flux, it's difficult to know who to trust, but certain agencies such as Tibet Travel and Snow Lion Tours are very knowledgeable and offer great service, though of course they will want to sell you their services.

TOURS

Foreign travelers are required by law to book a tour when securing a Tibet Travel Bureau permit. Enforcement of this rule has increased in the wake of riots in Lhasa in March 2008, and flexibility has disappeared. The classic six-day trip to Everest Base Camp (Y5,000–Y9,000, depending on group size) is the most popular tour, but others include the two-day trip to Nam Tso Lake (Y1,000–Y1,500), the two-day trip to Samye Monastery (Y800–Y2,500), and the 12-day trip to sacred Mount Kailash (Y7,000–Y14,000). As well as the two companies listed above, another reliable local company is Tibet FIT Travel.

Agents should advise you on the latest changes to travel restrictions and permit requirements. Typically, the cost of an organized tour for a week runs $1,000 to $2,000 per person. When booking a tour, be sure to get confirmation in writing, with details about your hotel and meal arrangements; tours within Lhasa often don't include hotels.

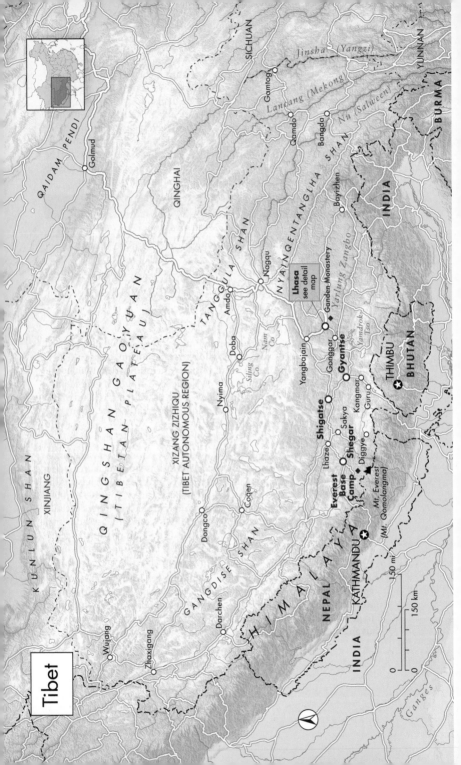

Tibet

QAIDAM PENDI

Golmud

QINGHAI

SICHUAN

Jinsha (Yangzi)

Gamtog

Lancang (Mekong)

Qamdo

Bangda

Nu (Salween)

BURMA

INDIA

Baoyizhen

KUNLUN SHAN

XINJIANG

QINGSHAN GAOYUAN
(TIBETAN PLATEAU)

TANGGULA SHAN

Nagqu

NYAINQENTANGLHA SHAN

Lhasa
see detail
map

Ganden Monastery

Yarlung Zangbo

Amdo

Nam
Co

Siling
Co

Doba

Yangbajain

Gonggar

Gyantse

Yamdrok
Tso

THIMBU

BHUTAN

XIZANG ZIZHIQU
(TIBET AUTONOMOUS REGION)

Nyima

Shigatse

Sakya

Kangmar

Guru

Lhaze

Shegar

Dingye

Everest
Base
Camp

Mt. Everest
(Mt. Qomolangma)

Dongco

Coqen

GANGDISE SHAN

H I M A L A Y A

NEPAL

KATHMANDU

Darchen

Wujiang

Zhaxigang

INDIA

Ganges

50 mi

150 km

0

LHASA

14 hrs by train south of Golmud, 48 hrs by train southwest of Beijing. 2 hrs by plane west of Chengdu, 5 hrs by plane southwest of Beijing.

The capital of Tibet is a treasure trove of monasteries, palaces, and temples. Geographically, the city is divided into a Chinese Quarter to the west and a Tibetan Quarter to the east. The Chinese neighborhood is where you'll find older hotels and Norbulingka Summer Palace. The more colorful Tibetan Quarter is full of small guesthouses, laid-back restaurants, bustling street markets, and Jokhang Temple. There is also a small Muslim Quarter to the southeast of the Barkhor. The old winding lanes in and around the Barkhor are immensely walkable and a great way to rub shoulders with the locals. Don't worry about

getting lost: most of the thoroughfares are circular; if you follow the pilgrims, you'll make it back to the circuit.

GETTING HERE AND AROUND

With the opening of the railroad line in 2006, travelers can now travel easily and cheaply to Tibet from almost anywhere in China. You'll need a Tibet Travel Bureau permit to buy a train ticket, and this should be arranged by your tour group. The gleaming Lhasa Train Station is 15 to 20 minutes southwest of the city center by taxi (Y50).

BY AIR Booking an airline ticket to Lhasa also involves having a Tibet Tourism Bureau permit. Even if you can buy a ticket without the permit, it's highly unlikely that you will be allowed to board.

Air China, Sichuan Airlines, China Southern Airlines, and China Eastern Airlines are some of the 16 airlines with frequent service to Lhasa, with the brand-new Tibet Airlines starting in 2011. The easiest direct route is from Chengdu, which has as many as 10 daily flights during the summer months for about Y1,500 each way. Flights to Lhasa depart from Beijing (five hours), Guangzhou (five hours), Xi'an (3½ hrs), Chongqing (three hours), and Chengdu (two hours). The airport is 53 km (32 mi) southwest of Lhasa, which takes about 45 minutes by taxi (Y180) or more than an hour by shuttle bus (Y25).

If you are coming from Kathmandu, the nonstop flights made four times a week will give you fantastic views of the Himalayas. You must show your permit from the Tibet Tourism Bureau when you check in.

BY BUS Intercity travel by bus is not only long and uncomfortable, it's also not encouraged for foreigners in almost all of Tibet. You can, however,

Lhasa Express

One of history's most audacious engineering projects, the rail line to Lhasa began construction in 2001 after more than 30 years of delays. Chairman Mao first proposed the railroad in the 1960s, along with other infrastructure projects now being realized, like the massive Three Gorges Dam on the Yangtze River. The list of technical challenges confronting the rail line was daunting, as more than 966 km (600 mi) of track needed to be constructed at an altitude of more than 13,000 feet, topping out at Tangula Pass near 17,000 feet. Much of the track rests on semifrozen and constantly shifting permafrost. The line also crosses through six protected environmental reserves, home to endangered species like the Tibetan antelope and the snow leopard.

Swiss engineers, experts on frozen terrain, said the project was impossible, but the Chinese government was having none of it. The first passenger train, carrying President Hu Jintao and a host of other dignitaries, rolled into Lhasa's shiny new station on July 1, 2006. The cultural implications of the railroad to ethnic Tibetans—already a minority in their own land—are obvious. The migration of Han Chinese will continue to expand as the traditional Tibetan way of life in many areas rapidly declines in the face of modernization. Politically, the railroad is another firm sign from Beijing that they have no intention of ever letting Tibet break off into a separate political entity; in fact, plans to extend the railway to Tibet's second-largest city, Shigatse, and over the Himalayas to Kathmandu in Nepal are already being developed.

However, the railway isn't completely negative for the locals. A large number of Tibetans make their livelihood from tourism in the region, which has increased dramatically since the opening of the line. The relatively cheap, quick, and comfortable ride by train has also made it possible for Tibetans working and studying in faraway parts of China to return home and visit their families during holidays, something that was nearly impossible when the only practical way to reach Lhasa was an expensive flight.

take the pilgrim buses that leave every day at 6:30 am from Barkhor Square headed to Ganden Monastery, and to Shigatse from Lhasa Bus station at Jinzhu Lu.

BY CAR Travel by car is the only permitted transportation throughout Tibet for foreigners. When you book a tour, as part of the package you'll get a driver and all the necessary permits. If you're headed to Nepal, make sure you arrange a visa in Lhasa before your departure.

BY TRAIN The train line to Lhasa has rewritten many of the world's records for extreme engineering. It's the world's highest railway, with more than 966 km (600 mi) of track above 13,000 feet, reaching above 16,500 feet in several locations. The line is also home to the world's highest railway station, which at Tangu-la Pass sits at almost 17,000 feet.

The train is comfortable and inexpensive, with free oxygen supplies beneath every seat to combat altitude sickness. Traveling by rail is also

The golden spires of the Jokhang Temple in Lhasa.

the perfect way to see the vast uninhabited expanse of the northern Qinghai-Tibet Plateau, with yaks and antelopes roaming the hills.

SAFETY AND PRECAUTIONS

■ TIP→ Don't openly talk politics with Tibetans. If they speak out against the government they may be charged with treason and receive a 20-year jail term. Public Security Bureau personnel are everywhere, sometimes in uniform, sometimes in civilian clothes or even in monks' robes. The PSB monitors civil unrest, visa extensions, crime, and traffic. Beware of the charming Tibetan who may be a secret policeman trying to entrap you into giving him a photograph of the Dalai Lama. You could be detained and/or deported. PSB offices are in all towns and many of the smaller townships.

TIMING

At a minimum, aim to spend four nights in Lhasa: this allows enough time to acclimatize to the altitude as well as see the main attractions such as Jokhang Temple, Potala Palace, and the Sera and Drepung monasteries.

TOURS

Foreign travelers have already had to purchase tours along with their airline or train tickets, as it is required by Chinese law. Once you're here, you may be able to book other tours if you find there's something else you want to see—the city is overflowing with travel agencies. A good local agency is Tibet FIT Travel.

ESSENTIALS

Air Contact Gongga Airport (*Gongga Feijichang* ⊠ *Airport Rd., Gongga County* ☎ *0891/624–6114 or 0891/624–6009*).

Bank Bank of China (✉ *28 Linkuo Xi Lu* ✉ *20 Beijing Dong Lu* ☎ *0891/682–8547 or 0891/683–5311*).

Medical Assistance TAR People's Hospital (*Xizang Renmin Yiyuan* ✉ *18 Linkuo Bei Lu* ☎ *0891/632–2200*).

Train Contact China Tibet Tourism Bureau (*Zizhiqu Luyouzhu* ✉ *3 Luobulingka Lu* ☎ *0891/683–4315* ⊕ *www.xzta.gov.cn/yww* ⊘ *Daily 8:30–6:30*).

Visitor and Tour Info Access Tibet Tour (✉ *Room 4106, Tibet Hotel, Beijing Zhonglu* ⊕ *www.accesstibettour.com*). **Tibet FIT Travel** (✉ *Inside the Snowlands Hotel, 4 Zangyiyuan Lu, Lhasa* ☎ *0891/634–9239* ⊕ *www.tibetfit.com*). **Snow Lion Tours** (✉ *1 Danjielin Lu, Lhasa* ☎ *13439329243* ⊕ *snowliontours.com*). **Tibet Travel** (⊕ *www.tibettravel.info*). **Tibetan Connections** (⊕ *www.tibetanconnections.com*).

EXPLORING

Your main axis of orientation in Lhasa is Beijing Lu, a street that stretches from the Barkhor in the east to as far as Drepung Monastery in the west, passing right in front of the Potala Palace. The easiest way to get from site to site is by taxi, with journeys between most locations in the city costing no more than Y10. Pedicabs are also available, but agreeing on a price before you hop on is essential; most trips should cost about Y10. Many of the most popular attractions are concentrated in and around the Barkhor area, so walking is always an option.

EXPLORING LHASA

Ani Tsangkung Nunnery. This small colorful convent has a livelier atmosphere than what you'll find at Lhasa's monasteries. Beaming nuns encourage you to wander through the courtyards, listen to their chanting, and watch them make ornamental butter flowers. There's a simple outdoor restaurant—popular at lunchtime—where nuns serve up inexpensive bowls of noodles and *momos* (dumplings). The chief pilgrimage site is the meditation hollow where Songtsen Gampo concentrated his spiritual focus on preventing the flood of the Kyi River in the 7th century. You're free to take photos here without charge—an option not available at many monasteries. ✉ *Waling Lam, southeast of Jokhang Temple* 🎟 *Y30* ⊘ *Daily 9–6*.

Barkhor. Circling the walls of the Jokhang Temple, the Barkhor is not only Tibetan Buddhism's holiest pilgrimage circuit but also the best spot in Lhasa for people-watching. Look for monks sitting before their alms bowls while the faithful constantly spin their prayer wheels. Unless you want to shock the devout with your blatant disregard for tradition, flow with the crowd in a clockwise direction. This wide pedestrian street is also souvenir central, crammed with stalls where vendors sell prayer shawls, silver jewelry, wall hangings, and just about anything that screams "I've been to Tibet!" Don't even think about paying what the vendors ask; many of the items can easily be bargained down to less than a quarter of the original price.

Palha Lupuk Temple. Religious rock paintings dating from as early as the 7th century can be seen at this grotto-style temple. On the third floor

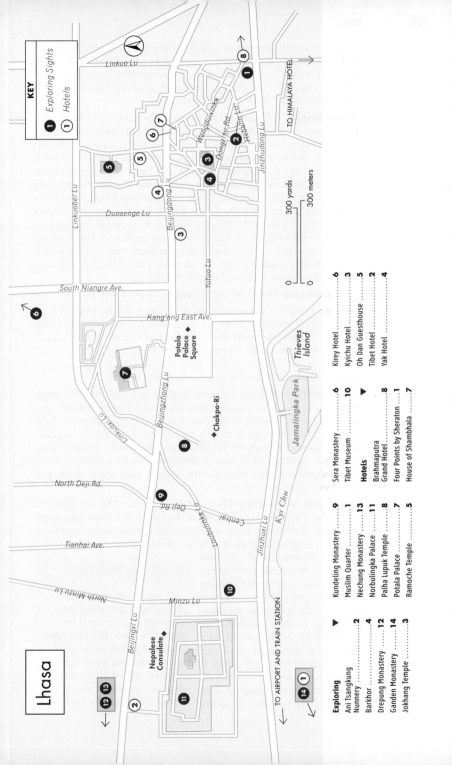

Lhasa

KEY

1 Exploring Sights
① Hotels

Linkuo Lu

Duosenge Lu

South Niangre Ave.

Kang'ang East Ave.

North Deji Rd.

Tianhai Ave.

Minzu Lu

Wangdui Xinlu

Jinzhudong Lu

Yutuo Lu

Beijingdong Lu

Linkuobei Lu

Dongzi su Rd.

Beijingzhong Lu

Linkuo Lu

Kyi Chu

Jinzhuxi Lu

Lombukang Lu

Central Deji Rd.

North Minzu Lu

Beijingxi Lu

Potala Palace Square

◆ Chakpo-Ri

Jamalingka Park

Thieves Island

Nepalese Consulate ◆

TO HIMALAYA HOTEL →

TO AIRPORT AND TRAIN STATION

0   300 yards
0   300 meters

Exploring

Ani Tsangkung Nunnery	9
Barkhor	2
Drepung Monastery	4
Ganden Monastery	12
Jokhang Temple	14
	3

Kundeling Monastery 9
Muslim Quarter 1
Nechung Monastery 13
Norbulingka Palace 11
Palha Lupuk Temple 8
Potala Palace 7
Ramoche Temple 5

Sera Monastery 6
Tibet Museum 10

Hotels ▶

Brahmaputra Grand Hotel 8
Four Points by Sheraton ... 1
House of Shambhala 7

Kirey Hotel 6
Kyichu Hotel 3
Oh Dan Guesthouse 5
Tibet Hotel 2
Yak Hotel 4

you'll find an entrance to a cave with sculptures carved into the granite walls, mostly by Nepalese artists more than a millennium ago. Very few tourists visit, so if you're looking to escape the crowds, head here. ✉ *South face of Iron Mountain, on a small street opposite the western end of the Potala Palace* 🎫 *Y20* ⊙ *Daily 9–8.*

Fodor'sChoice ★ **Jokhang Temple** *(Da Zhao Si)*. This temple is the most sacred building in Tibet. From the gentle flicker of a butter-lamp light dancing off antique murals, statues, tapestries, and *thangkhas* (scroll paintings) to the air thick with incense and anticipation as thousands of Tibetans pay homage day and night, the temple contains a plethora of sensory delights. Most likely built in 647 during Songtsen Gampo's reign, the Jokhang stands in the heart of the Old Town. The site was selected by Queen Wengcheng, a princess from China who became Songtsen Gampo's second wife. His first wife, Princess Bhrikuti from Nepal, financed the building of Jokhang. In her honor, and in recognition of Tibet's strong reliance on Nepal, the Jokhang's main gate faces west, toward Nepal. Among the bits remaining from the 7th century are the four door frames of the inner temple, dedicated to different deities.

⚠ Remember that photos are not allowed inside the buildings.

Over the centuries, renovations have enlarged the Jokhang to keep it the premier temple of Tibet. Its status was threatened in the 1950s when the Chinese Army shelled it and the Red Guards of the Cultural Revolution ransacked it. During this period, the temple was used for various purposes, including as a pigsty. Much of the damage has since been repaired, but a portion of it has been lost forever.

Before entering the Inner Jokhang, you should walk the Nangkhor Inner Circuit in a clockwise direction. It's lined with prayer wheels and murals depicting a series of Buddhist scenes. Continue on to the large Entrance Hall, whose inner chapels have murals depicting the wrathful deities responsible for protecting the temple and the city. Straight ahead is the inner sanctum, the three-story **Kyilkhor Thil,** some of whose many columns probably date from the 7th century, particularly those with short bases and round shafts.

The chapels on the ground floor of the Kyilkhor Thil are the most rewarding. The most revered chapel of the inner hall is **Jowo Sakyamuni Lhakhang,** opposite the entrance. Inside rests a bejeweled statue of Jowo Rinpoche—representing the Buddha at age 12—surrounded by adoring disciples. It was brought to Tibet by Queen Wengcheng and somehow has survived, despite a history of being plastered over and buried in sand. On busy days you may wait in line to enter this shrine, but it's worth it. On the second floor there are a number of small chapels, although many are closed to visitors. Before you leave, climb the stairs next to the main entrance up to the Jokhang's ornately decorated

> ### WORD OF MOUTH
>
> "For anyone with an interest in Tibet, I highly recommend the documentary *Tibet: Cry of the Snow Lion.* You'll learn what really happened in Tibet when the Chinese invaded and what's happening even now. I didn't see it until after we returned but wish I had seen it before going." —PIPERPAT

golden roof. You'll be rewarded with sweeping views of the Barkhor, the Potala Palace, and the snowcapped mountains beyond Lhasa. ✉ *Barkhor* ☎ *0891/632–3129* 💵 *Y85* ⏲ *Daily 8–6:30, but tourists can visit only in the afternoon; mornings are reserved for pilgrims.*

NEED A BREAK?

On the eastern leg of the Barkhor Circuit, Sun Tribe Restaurant (✉ *39 Barkhor Dong Jie* ☎ *0891/634–1990* ▭ *No credit cards*) is a good place to take a break after a visit to the Jokhang Temple. Monks sit around the low tables chatting and sipping tea. Tibetan dishes make up half the menu, the rest being standard Chinese and Western choices —but stick with "the real thing," such as fried yak hooves and momo dumplings.

Kundeling Monastery *(Gongdelin Si)*. This monastery is often overlooked by tourists, so it's less crowded than others around Lhasa. If you arrive in the morning, climb to a second-floor chapel to see monks chanting, beating drums, and playing long bronze prayer trumpets. This temple also contains examples of sand painting, in which millions of colorful grains of sand are arranged in a complex pattern over the course of hours or even days. ✉ *Beijing Zhong Lu and Deji Lu, west of the Potala Palace* ☎ *0891/685–1973* 💵 *Y10* ⏲ *Daily 9–8.*

Muslim Quarter. In perhaps the most Buddhist of cities, the Muslim Quarter—centered on Lhasa's Great Mosque—is a bit of an anomaly. The district was originally intended for immigrants arriving from Kashmir and Ladakh. The Great Mosque (Da Qingzhen Si) with its green minaret was completed in 1716, but very little of the original structure remains. The area is now primarily of interest for its distinct atmosphere, thanks to its Hui Muslim residents and the large concentration of pork-free halal restaurants. ✉ *Lingkor Nan Lu, west of Lingkor Dong Lu.*

Norbulingka Palace. The Seventh Dalai Lama (1708–57), a frail man, chose to build a summer palace on this site because of its medicinal spring, and later had his whole government moved here from the Potala Palace. Successive Dalai Lamas expanded the complex, adding additional palaces, a debating courtyard, a pavilion, a library, and a number of landscaped gardens, which are at their best in summer months. The most recent addition, built by the current Dalai Lama between 1954 and 1956, is an ornate two-story building containing his private quarters. It turned out to be the place from which, disguised as a soldier, he fled to India on March 17, 1959, three days before the Chinese massacred thousands of Tibetans and fired artillery shells into every building in the complex. Only after searching through the corpses did they realize that the Dalai Lama had escaped.

The repair work in the aftermath of the March 1959 uprising is not of high caliber, and much of Norbulingka feels run-down. That said, a collection of the Dalai Lama's carriages and automobiles housed in the **Changsam Palace** are worth a look. More fascinating are the personal effects of the current Dalai Lama housed in the **New Summer Palace,** including his radio and phonograph. You can even peek into the Dalai Lama's bathroom. No photos are allowed inside, unfortunately. There is also a small zoo full of pitiable animals, which is worth avoiding. ✉ *Western end of Luobulingka Lu* 💵 *Y60* ⏲ *Daily 9–12 and 3–4.*

⚠ The legions of Chinese soldiers you will see throughout Lhasa don't take kindly to being photographed. If they spot you taking pictures in their direction, they're likely to approach and want to see your camera.

Fodor's Choice
★

Potala Palace *(Pudala Gong).* The awesome sight that is the Potala Palace is quite rightly considered a wonder of the world. However, virtually nothing remains of the original 11-story Potala Palace, built in 637 by Songtsen Gampo. What you see today is a 17th-century replacement. The Fifth Dalai Lama, anxious to reestablish the importance of Lhasa as the Tibetan capital, employed 7,000 workers and 1,500 artisans to resurrect the Potala Palace on the 7th-century foundation. The portion called the White Palace was completed in 1653. The Red Palace was not completed until 1694, 12 years after the Dalai Lama's death (which was kept secret by the regent in order to prevent interruption of the construction). The Potala Palace has been enlarged since then, and has been continually renovated. Once the headquarters of Tibet's theocracy, the vast complex is now a museum and a UNESCO World Heritage site.

The Potala Palace was the world's tallest building before the advent of modern skyscrapers. Towering above the city from the slopes of Mount Marpori, the structure is 384 feet high; its 1,000 rooms house some 200,000 images. The outer section, the White Palace, was the seat of government and the winter residence of the Dalai Lama until 1951. Inside you can pass through the Dalai Lama's spartan quarters. On either side of the palace are the former offices of the government. The Red Palace, looming above the White Palace, is filled with murals that chronicle Buddhist folklore and ancient Tibetan life. Interspersed among the chapels are eight spectacular tombs covered in nearly five tons of gold. These bejeweled rooms contain the remains of the Fifth through 13th Dalai Lamas.

⚠ Photos are not allowed inside the Palace.

The increasing number of visitors makes it difficult to secure tickets for the Potala Palace, especially in peak season. Have your tour guide arrange tickets ahead of time. Be aware that your guide must accompany you; otherwise your travel agent can be fined. Only 2,300 visitors are allowed in each day. Your ticket allows you up to 90 minutes at the site. ✉ *Beijing Zhong Lu, Gongtian Xian* ☎ *0891/683–4362* 💴 *Y120* ☉ *Low season (Nov.–Apr.), daily 9:30–3; high season (May–Oct.), daily 9–4.*

Ramoche Temple *(Xiao Zhao Si).* This temple was founded by Queen Wengcheng at the same time as the Jokhang Temple. Its three-story structure dates from the 15th century. Despite restorations in the 1980s, it lost much of its former grandeur after the Chinese used it to house the Communist Labor Training Committee during the Cultural Revolution.

GETTING AROUND

Taxis are plentiful in Lhasa. Y10 will get you almost anywhere within the city limits. Getting to Drepung Monastery will cost about Y40. Minibuses ply a fixed route, with fares of about Y2. Bicycle rickshaws are also available for short trips, and normally cost Y3, although they're famous for trying to charge foreigners higher prices.

The Ramoche Temple was intended to house the most revered statue of Jowo Rinpoche. A threat of a Chinese invasion in the 7th century induced Queen Wengcheng to hide the statue in the Jokhang Temple. Some 50 years later it was rediscovered and placed within the Jokhang Temple's main chapel. As a substitute, Jokhang reciprocated with a Nepalese statue of Jowo Mikyo Dorje—representing Buddha as an eight-year-old—richly layered in gold and precious stones. It was

decapitated during the Cultural Revolution and its torso lost in Beijing. Both head and body were found in 1984, put back together again, and placed in a small chapel at the back of the Ramoche Temple's inner sanctum. Be sure to climb to the temple's roof for a spectacular view of the Potala Palace perched high above the rooftops of Lhasa. ⊠ *Xiao Zhao Si Lu, off the north side of Beijing Dong Lu* ☎ *0891/633–6163* 🎫 *Y25* ⏱ *Daily 8–4:30.*

Tibet Museum. For the Chinese interpretation of Tibetan history, politics, and culture, visit this modern museum. The free personal audio guide provides commentary on important pieces from prehistoric times, Chinese dynasties, and traditional Tibetan life. If you are a scholar of history, you may find some of the explanations intriguing. They often have temporary Tibetan art exhibitions. ⊠ *Corner of Luobulingka Lu and Minzu Nan Lu, across from the entrance to Norbulingka Palace* ☎ *0891/681–2210* 🎫 *Y35* ⏱ *10–6.*

DID YOU KNOW?

Underneath the 13-story, 1,000-room fortress of the Potala Palace are the dungeons, inaccessible to tourists. Justice could be harsh—torture and jail time were the punishments for refusing to pay taxes, displaying anger, or insulting a monk. The worst place to be sent was the Cave of Scorpions, where prisoners were the targets of stinging tails.

WHERE TO EAT

$$–$$$
ECLECTIC

✕ **Dunya.** Meaning "The World" in 10 languages, Dunya serves a melting pot of international dishes. The Western food here is disappointing, but the Indian and Nepalese dishes are first-rate; both can be complemented by a bottle of Australian wine or a cup of real coffee—both rarities in Tibet. With its exposed-brick interior and a polite English-speaking staff, Dunya feels like a real restaurant, not another hole-in-the-wall eatery. Upstairs is a well-stocked bar, with a balcony where you'll often find the Dutch, American, and Tibetan friends who run the place chatting with customers. ⊠ *100 Beijing Dong Lu, next to the Yak Hotel* ☎ *0891/633–3374* ▤ *No credit cards* ⏱ *Closed Nov.–Apr.*

¢–$
ECLECTIC

✕ **Makye Ame** *(Ma Ji A Mi).* Ask to be seated by the second-floor windows or on the rooftop terrace for some of the best views of the pilgrims on the Barkhor, which passes right by this legendary corner restaurant. Meat eaters will enjoy the fried yak slices, and vegetarians rave about the spinach-tofu ravioli topped with homemade tomato-basil sauce, as well as the Indian-style bread stuffed with potato and served with curry and yogurt sauces. Ask the staff to explain the legend of Makye Ame, a mysterious woman immortalized in a poem penned by the Sixth Dalai Lama, who spied her in a bar where the café now stands. ⊠ *Southeast corner of Barkhor* ☎ *0891/632–8608* ▭ *No credit cards.*

$$–$$$ ✕ **Shangrila.** Make time in your busy tour schedule for dinner at the
TIBETAN family-run Shangrila. As dancers perform traditional routines, your
★ taste buds will be treated to an 18-course Tibetan buffet—a superb opportunity to try indigenous food such as sautéed yak lung, cold yak tongue, and wild sweet potatoes. The colorful scroll paintings that line the walls, the dark-wood furniture, and the congenial staffers that happily explain the dishes set this place apart from other dinner-and-a-show restaurants. Reservations are necessary—sometimes a day in advance— and you should arrive by 7 pm for the best seats. The performance and buffet are a set price of Y50. ⊠ *122 Beijing Dong Lu, inside the Kirey Hotel* ☎ *0891/636–3880* ▭ *No credit cards.*

¢–$ ✕ **Snowlands** *(Xueyu Canting)* The well-traveled menu at the Snowl-
ECLECTIC ands—covering Chinese, Nepalese, Tibetan, Indian, Italian, and even
Fodor's Choice Mexican cuisine—is your guide to the finest meals in Tibet. Join for-
★ eign aid workers, local business executives, and the small tour groups who flock in droves to this cozy café near the Barkhor. Try the chicken masala with freshly baked *naan* bread, or feast on grilled yak steak in pepper sauce. This place is hugely popular, and the service can be slow, but the food is worth the wait. Fresh cinnamon rolls, apple pie, and croissants are also available. ⊠ *4 Danjielin Lu(north of Barkhor)* ☎ *0891/633–7323* ▭ *No credit cards.*

¢ ✕ **The Summit Cafe.** For the best cup of coffee in town, head to this cute,
CAFÉ peaceful American-owned, European-style café in the center of the Old Town. They use premium Italian espresso machines—perhaps the only ones in the whole of Tibet— and offer great cakes and muffins. There is free Wi-Fi, and a selection of local art decorates the space. ⊠ *1 Danjielin Lu* ☎ *0891/691–3884* ⊠ *Lingkor Bei Lu* ☎ *0891/631–5884* ⊕ *www. thetibetsummitcafe.com* ▭ *No credit cards.*

$$–$$$ ✕ **Tashi 1.** A popular hangout for foreigners, as is Tashi 2 by the Kirey
ECLECTIC Hotel. It's the kind of restaurant where conversations with other diners are inevitable. The most popular dish here is the *bobi*, a kind of tortilla into which sautéed chicken, vegetables, and cream cheese are stuffed. If you're looking to add heft to your meal, try the delicious cauliflower croquettes, which are deep-fried patties of cauliflower, potato, peas, and carrots. The yak burger is also tasty. ⊠ *131 Beijing Dong Lu, at Danjielin Lu* ☎ *0891/633–7305* ▭ *No credit cards.*

WHERE TO STAY

Just as in the rest of China, major Western hotel chains are looking to make their mark in Lhasa. At this writing, the glitzy St. Regis was due to open its 162-room property on Jiangsu Lu (*www.starwoodhotels.*

com), and 2012 will see the opening of a Shangri-la on Lingkor Lu (*www.shangri-la.com*).

$$$$ **Brahmaputra Grand Hotel** *(Yaluzangbu Dajiudian)*. Don't be fooled by the nondescript exterior—once inside the Brahmaputra Grand you'll find every nook and cranny displaying gorgeous, museum-quality Tibetan antiques and artifacts. The only difference here is that everything's for sale. Be careful what you set your heart on—some of the items go for as much as $15,000. From the smartly clad Nepalese bellmen to the gently scented hallways with perfect lighting and dark-wood paneling, you'll be impressed every minute of your stay; the hotel is often ranked one of the best in Lhasa. Even if you're not staying, it's worth visiting the small museum on the second floor. The hotel is 2½ km (1½ mi) east of the Barkhor. **Pros:** spacious rooms; helpful staff. **Cons:** a little far from the center; beds are hard. ⊠ *Gongbutang Lu, Yangcheng Plaza D* ☎ *0891/630–9999* ⊕ *www.tibethotel.cn* ⤳ *186 rooms* ⬡ *In-room: refrigerator, Internet. In-hotel: 2 restaurants, laundry service, Wi-Fi* ⊟ *AE, DC, MC, V.*

$$$$ **Four Points by Sheraton Lhasa.** The first Western-brand property to open in Tibet in a decade, the Four Points provides well-heeled travelers with all they need: comfortably stylish rooms, well trained English-speaking staff, and a good restaurant. Because of Lhasa's high altitude, there's also an on-site doctor who can deal with any altitude sickness. **Pros:** well-appointed rooms. **Cons:** 30-minute walk to the Potala Palace; limited facilities for the price. ⊠ *10 Bo Linkuo Lu, Lhasa* ☎ *0891/634-8888* ⊕ *www.starwoodhotels.com* ⤳ *102 rooms* ⬡ *In-room: a/c, safe, refrigerator, Wi-Fi. In-hotel: restaurant, room service, bar, laundry service, business center* ⊟ *AE, DC, MC, V.*

$$$–$$$$ **House of Shambhala** *(Xiangbala Gong)*. If you want to stay in a tradi-
★ tional Tibetan dwelling, this quiet boutique hotel, part of a small group of heritage hotels in Tibet, is a good choice. The building, which dates back to the 7th century, was once the home of a high-ranking Tibetan general under the 13th Dalai Lama. Suites are decorated with tangerine-colored walls, hardwood floors, sheepskin rugs, and exposed roof beams. The king-size beds are covered with hand-beaded duvets, and the bathrooms are tiled in local slate. The staff are attentive and speak reasonable English. On the rooftop terrace you can lounge on a daybed and order from the downstairs restaurant. This hotel is very small, so reserve far in advance. It's on a small alley next to the Kirey Hotel. **Pros:** friendly staff; less touristy location; nice decor. **Cons:** appliances sometimes don't work. ⊠ *7 Jiri Erxiang* ☎ *0891/632–6533* ⊕ *www.shambhalaserai.com* ⤳ *9 suites* ⬡ *In-room: Internet (free). In-hotel: restaurant, gym, spa, laundry service* ⊟ *AE, MC, V.*

¢ **Kirey Hotel** *(Jiri Binguan)*. A popular budget hotel, the Kirey is filled with everyone from backpackers to bicyclists to tour groups. Rooms here are spotless, but otherwise unremarkable. Something that is special, however, is that the staff here will wash and dry your laundry free of charge. The location, north of Jokhang Temple, can't be beat. Two excellent restaurants are in the courtyard. **Pros:** free laundry service. **Cons:** more of a hostel than a hotel. ⊠ *105 Beijing Dong Lu* ☎ *0891/632–3462* ⤳ *35 rooms* ⬡ *In-hotel: 2 restaurants, bar, bicycles,*

Internet terminal ☰ *No credit cards.*

$ ⊡ **Kyichu Hotel** *(Jiqu Fandian).* This recently refurbished family-run hotel near the city's historic center has a helpful and welcoming staff. In summer the courtyard garden is a lovely place to meet other guests and relax. Rooms are simple, clean, and a good value, but the quality may vary. Try to get one that faces the courtyard. **Pros:** friendly staff; rooms have lots of character **Cons:** big variation in room quality. ⊠ *149 Beijing Dong Lu, Lhasa* ☎ *0891/633-1541* ⊕ *www.hotelkyichu.com* ⬅ *52* ♿ *In-room: a/c, safe, refrigerator, Wi-Fi. In-hotel: restaurant, room service, bar, laundry service* ☰ *AE, DC, MC, V.*

¢–$ ⊡ **Oh Dan Guesthouse** *(Oudan Binguan).* An excellent budget choice, this small hotel sits on a busy pedestrian street between the Jokhang and Ramoche temples, only a few minutes north of the Barkhor. Rooms are simple, but comfortable and clean. Choose from standard rooms with private bathrooms or economy rooms with shared bathrooms. On the rooftop terrace you can sip tea and enjoy an awesome view of Lhasa. Avoid the third or fourth floor, as there is no elevator. **Pros:** great views; well kept. **Cons:** rooms are small. ⊠ *15 Ramoche Lu* ☎ *0891/634-4999* ⬅ *32 rooms* ♿ *In-room: Internet (fee). In-hotel: restaurant, laundry service, business center* ☰ *No credit cards.*

$$$–$$$$ ⊡ **Tibet Hotel** *(Xizang Binguan).* The rooms in this well-maintained hotel feature a touch of Tibetan style, from the vibrant blue carpeting to the golden silk pillows on the crimson sofas. There are several restaurants serving Western and Asian food, but their opening hours are erratic (a problem, as you're a ways from downtown). Many on the staff speak a little English, but their enthusiasm makes it easy to bridge the communication gap. Rooms in the hotel's rear building are bigger, but slightly older. **Pros:** caring staff, great views. **Cons:** lower-level rooms are not as good, hot water supply is erratic, popular with tour groups. ⊠ *64 Beijing Zhong Lu* ☎ *0891/683-4966* ⊕ *www.tibethotel.com.cn* ⬅ *338 rooms* ♿ *In-room: safe, Internet. In-hotel: 5 restaurants, laundry service* ☰ *AE, DC, MC, V.*

$–$$$ ⊡ **Yak Hotel** *(Ya Binguan).* Once the first choice for travelers on a tight budget, the Yak now appeals to travelers of all levels. Regardless of what kind of room you choose, it will be immaculate. Even in the most economical of rooms you will find nice touches like Tibetan chests as bedside tables. If you're sensitive to noise, try to get a room toward the back. Dunya restaurant is to the right of the courtyard. **Pros:** great central location; three-minute walk from Jokhang Temple; outdoor breakfast terrace. **Cons:** some street noise; hot water supply is unreliable. ⊠ *100 Beijing Dong Lu* ☎ *0891/632-3496* ⬅ *120 rooms* ♿ *In-hotel: 2 restaurants, bar, laundry service, Internet terminal* ☰ *No credit cards.*

NIGHTLIFE AND THE ARTS

If you're looking for a bit of excitement, look no farther than **Nee-way Nangma** (⊠ *13 Lingkor Bei Lu*), the city's most popular disco. An hour spent here watching the dance performances set to both pop and traditional folk songs will clear away any ideas you may have about Tibetan culture's being stuck in the past. If you're looking for a quiet spot near the Barkhor to enjoy a drink or a cup of tea after a long day, try **Ganglamedo** (⊠ *127 Beijing Dong Lu*), across from the Yak Hotel. The bar stocks a wide range of liquors.

Tibetan operas are performed by the **Tibet Shol Opera Troupe** (⊠ *6 Lingkor Dong Lu* ☎ *0891/632–1111*) in a theater at the Himalaya Hotel. Tickets cost Y100, and reservations are required.

SHOPPING

ARTS AND CRAFTS

For souvenirs varying from prayer flags to jewel-encrusted horse bridles, stop by one of the hundreds of open-air stalls and small shops that line the roads leading to the Jokhang Temple. Bargain in a tough but friendly manner, and the proprietors may throw in extra items for luck. Many of the goods come from around Tibet and Nepal. On the road between Lhasa and Gongga airport is **The Tanva Carpet Workshop** (*For directions and to arrange a visit, call the factory manager* ☎ *1398/990–8681*). The artisans here use handspun Tibetan highland wool to make both traditional and contemporary carpets using natural dyes. Even if you're not buying, it's interesting to see the whole carpet-making process from start to finish. Tanva makes the carpets that are sold in Torana stores in Beijing and Shanghai.

For quality Tibetan handicrafts, visit **Dropenling** (⊠ *11 Chak Tsal Gang Lu* ☎ *0891/636–0558* ⊕ *www.tibetcraft.com*), down an alley opposite the Muslim Quarter's main mosque. Unlike those at other souvenir shops, all the products here are made by Tibetans, and all profits are returned to the local artisan community.

OUTDOOR EQUIPMENT

West of the Potala Palace, **The Third Pole** (⊠ *6 Luobulingka Lu* ☎ *0891/682–0549*) can outfit you with everything you'll need to enjoy the great outdoors, from good hiking shoes to walking sticks to sunglasses. **Toread** (⊠ *182 Beijing Zhong Lu* ☎ *0891/682–9365*) is a Chinese outdoor clothing brand, and this store features a wide selection of genuine outdoor equipment, as well as warm clothing if you're planning a trip to the mountains.

AROUND LHASA

Many of Lhasa's best sites are clustered around the city center, but three of the most important are more remote. This trio of monasteries are known as the "three pillars of Tibetan Buddhism," having all been founded by religious patriarch Tsongkhapa at the beginning of the 15th century. All three are worth the effort it takes to reach them

The Tibetans

Prayer flags are sold in front of the Jokhang, Tibet's holiest temple.

They live primarily on the Tibet-Qinghai Plateau, but they also make their homes in southern Gansu, western and northern Sichuan, and northwestern Yunnan. Their culture is influenced both by Tibet's extreme geography and their unique interpretation of Buddhism, the line between the two often blurred by a "sacred geography," which deifies many of the region's mountains and lakes. Compared with other forms of Buddhism, Tibetan Buddhism (also known as "Lamaism") places far more emphasis on the physical path to enlightenment. This is why the sight of pilgrims prostrating around the base of a sacred mountain or temple for days or weeks on end is a common one in the region.

When Tibet was annexed by China (or "liberated") in 1959, their supreme spiritual leader the Dalai Lama fled in disguise to India, where he set up a Tibetan government-in-exile in Dharamsala, which became known as "little Lhasa." Since then the Dalai Lama has become an international celebrity and has succeeded in making the struggle for Tibetan independence a focus of global attention, drawing strong condemnation—and brutal crackdowns—from Beijing. Few people realize that the Dalai Lama has actually for many years no longer insisted on independence, but a more moderate form of autonomy like that enjoyed by Hong Kong and Macau. Yet despite international pressure—and perhaps even because of the attention—there seems little hope that Tibet's status will change in the near future.

Meanwhile, Tibet continues to modernize at full speed, with seemingly every road between Lhasa and Mount Everest being upgraded simultaneously. The rail link between Beijing and Lhasa completed in 2006 has promoted "Hanification," or a major increase in the Han Chinese population. It's estimated that 60 to 70 percent of the population in Lhasa is Han Chinese. With only 2.5 million Tibetans living in the Tibet Autonomous Region—and 800 million impoverished Han Chinese nationwide looking for a better way of life—it's only a matter of time before ethnic Tibetans become a small minority in their own homeland.

(especially Ganden Monastery, 90 minutes east of Lhasa) and should be part of any tour of Lhasa.

Fodor's Choice
★ **Ganden Monastery.** If you have time for only one side trip from Lhasa, this rambling monastery with ocher-colored walls is your best bet. It was stablished in 1409 by Tsongkhapa, the founder of the Gelugpa sect, and its abbot is chosen on merit rather than heredity. Of the six great Gelugpa monasteries, Ganden was the most seriously

damaged by Chinese during the Cultural Revolution. Since the early 1980s Tibetans have put tremendous effort into rebuilding the complex; some 300 monks are now in residence. Pilgrims come daily from Lhasa to pay homage to the sacred sites and religious relics.

The monastery comprises eight major buildings. The most impressive structure is the **Gold Tomb of Tsongkhapa** (Serdhung Lhakhang) in the heart of the complex, easily recognized by the recently built white *chorten,* or small shrine, standing before the red building. On the second floor is the chapel of **Yangchen Khang,** with the new golden chorten of Tsongkhapa. The original (1629), made of silver, later gilded, was the most sacred object in the land. In 1959 the Chinese destroyed it, although brave monks saved some of the holy relics of Tsongkhapa, which are now inside the new gold-covered chorten. Be careful walking around this shrine: the buttery wax on the floor is thick and slippery.

A path that circumambulates the monastery starts from the parking lot. From the path, which leads to the spot where Tsongkhapa was cremated in 1419, you'll be treated to breathtaking views of the Lhasa River Valley. You'll need about an hour to complete the circuit. If a visit here is not included in your tour, or if you want to catch public transport with your guide, buses (Y20 round-trip) to Ganden leave from Barkhor Square in front of Jokhang Temple every morning at 6:30, returning to Lhasa at 3 pm. The beautiful 90-minute ride from Lhasa will give you a glimpse of life in rural Tibet. ⊠ *36 km (22 mi) southeast of Lhasa on main Tibet–Sichuan Hwy.* ▧ *Y45* ☉ *Daily 9–4.*

★ **Sera Monastery** *(Sela Si).* This important Gelugpa monastery, founded in 1419, contains numerous temples filled with splendid murals and icons. Originally it was a hermitage for Tsongkhapa and a few of his top students. Within a couple hundred of years it housed more than 5,000 monks.

On the clockwise pilgrimage route, start at the two buildings that will take up most of your visit. **Sera Me Tratsang,** founded in 1419, has a *dukhang* (assembly hall) rebuilt in 1761 with murals depicting Buddha's life. Among the five chapels along the north wall, the one with its exterior adorned with skeletons and skulls is unforgettable. The complex's oldest surviving structure, **Ngagpa Tratsang,** is a three-story

Festivals and Celebrations

Try to time your visit with one of the brilliantly colorful traditional Tibetan festivals. Dancing monks whip up a frenzy to dispel the evil spirits of the previous year at the Year End Festival on the 29th day of the 12th lunar month. The first week of the first lunar month includes Losar (New Year Festival), when Lhasa is filled with Tibetan drama performances, incense offerings, and locals promenading in their finest wardrobe. Grand butter lanterns light up the Barkhor circuit during the Lantern Festival on the 15th of the 1st month. On the seventh day of the fourth month you can join the pilgrims in Lhasa or Ganden to mark the Birth of Sakyamuni (the Buddha), or you may want to wait until the 15th for the celebrations of Saga Dawa (Sakyamuni's enlightenment) and join the pilgrims who climb the Drepung Monastery to burn juniper incense. Picnics at the summer palace of Norbulingka are common during

the Worship of the Buddha in the second week of the fifth month. During Shötun (Yogurt Festival) in the first week of the seventh month, immerse yourself in the operas, masked dances, and picnics from Drepung (6½ km [4 mi] out of Lhasa) to Norbulingka. During the festival, giant thangkas of the Buddha are unveiled in Drepung Monastery, and Tibetan opera troupes perform operas at Norbulingka.

The Tibetan calendar is the same as the lunar calendar, so exact dates as they relate to the Western calendar are only published a year in advance. The approximate dates are as follows: Tibetan New Year (February); the Butter Lantern Festival (late February/ early March); the Birth of Buddha Festival (late May/early June); the Holy Mountain Festival (late July/early August); the one-week Yogurt Festival (August); and the Bathing Festival (September).

---

college for tantric studies. Here you'll find statues of famous lamas and murals depicting paradise.

Continue to the four-story-high **Sera Je Tratsang,** where Manjashuri, the God of Wisdom, listens to monks engaged in philosophical debate in a courtyard just beyond the temple walls. The extremely animated debates—during which emphatic hand movements signify agreement or disagreement—take place daily starting at 3 am. Whatever your feelings are about the excitement of debates, this is one you don't want to miss. ⊠ *At the base of Mt. Phurbuchok, 5 km (3 mi) north of Lhasa* ☎ *0891/638–7453* 🎫 *Y55* ⊘ *Daily 9–4.*

Drepung Monastery. The largest of the Gelugpa monasteries was the residence for lesser lamas. Founded in 1416, it was enlarged in the 16th century by the Second Dalai Lama. By the era of the Fifth Dalai Lama it had become the largest monastic institution in the world, with 10,000 residents. During the Cultural Revolution it suffered only minimally, because the Army used the building as its headquarters and therefore didn't ransack it as much as other temples. The monastery was reopened in 1980, although the number of resident monks has been severely depleted.

The monastery's most important building is the Tshomchen, whose vast assembly hall, the **Dukhang,** is noteworthy for its 183 columns, atrium ceiling, and ceremonial banners. Chapels can be found on all three floors, as well as on the roof. In the two-story **Buddhas of Three Ages Chapel** (*Düsum Sangye Lhakhang*), at the rear of the Dukhang on the ground floor, the Buddhas of past, present, and future are each guarded by two bodhisattvas. A taxi from town will cost between Y40 and Y50. ☎ *0891/686–3149* ✉ *Off Beijing Xi Lu, 8 km (5 mi) west of Lhasa* 🎫 *Y55* ⊙ *Daily 9–6.*

LODGING OPTIONS

In the major towns outside Lhasa you usually have a choice between bland Chinese hotels and rundown guesthouses, about half of which have hot running water.

Nechung Monastery. Many people skip this 12th-century monastery, but that's a big mistake. With a strong focus on beasts, demons, and the afterlife, Nechung is unlike anything else you'll see in Tibet. Murals on the monastery's walls depict everything from humans being dismembered by dogs and vultures to demons wearing long belts of human skulls and engaged in passionate sexual intercourse. Until 1959 this monastery was home to the highly influential Nechung Oracle. Every important decision by a Dalai Lama is made after consulting this oracle, which currently resides in Dharamsala as a member of the government-in-exile. The monastery is 1 km (½ mi) southeast of Drepung Monastery, and it's an easy 40-minute-long ride for hardy cyclists. ✉ *Off Beijing Xi Lu, 8 km (5 mi) west of Lhasa* 🎫 *Y20* ⊙ *Daily 9–4.*

TSANG PROVINCE

The Tibetan province of Tsang includes some of the region's most important historic sites outside of Lhasa, but it's also rich in stunning scenery and dotted with small villages and terraced barley fields filled with brightly decorated yaks. This is your chance to get out of the city and experience rural Tibet, where life seems to have changed little over the past 100 years.

TOURS

If you're trying to find the majestic valleys and towering peaks that Tibet conjures up in the imagination, a journey through Tsang should be part of your itinerary. Typically lasting five days, these tours hit all of the hot spots: the brilliant blue waters of Yamdrok Tso Lake, the Dzong Fortress and Pelkor Chode Monastery in Gyantse, the Tashilhunpo Monastery in Shigatse, and the Base Camp below the world's highest peak at Mount Everest.

Any local travel agency can arrange this tour for you; a good price is in the range of Y1,000 per day, which includes all necessary travel permits. Food, lodging, and admission charges to attractions are often not included.

GYANTSE

6 hrs (180 km [110 mi]) by jeep southwest of Lhasa over the Yong-la Pass. 1½ hrs (90 km [55 mi]) southeast of Shigatse.

With small villages of stone houses beside fields of highland barley, Gyantse feels far removed from Lhasa, although the drive is only about six hours. Home to two of Tsang's most impressive sights—the massive tiered Gyantse Kumbum at Pelkor Chode Monastery and the Gyantse Dzong where British soldiers defeated Tibetans in 1904—Gyantse is an essential stop on the journey toward Everest. Tourist dollars have transformed what was once a small village into a small one bustling with hotels, restaurants, and Internet cafés. However, the sites remain impressive, and the journey to get here over the Yong-la Pass is unforgettable.

GETTING HERE AND AROUND

Coming from Lhasa, don't let your driver take the longer but faster route through Shigatse to reach Gyantse. Insist on being taken via the dirt road over the Yong-la Pass, where the views are absolutely stunning. Few tourists take this route, and the locals will be genuinely surprised to see you. Once in Gyantse, don't feel the need to rush on to Shigatse the same day; you can spend the night and see the sights in the morning without significantly throwing off your touring schedule.

SAFETY AND PRECAUTIONS

At 12,959 feet above sea level, visitors to Gyantse may find the altitude difficult to handle. Take it easy and seek medical assistance if necessary.

TIMING

Most visitors spend a full day and night in Gyantse in preparation for Everest Base Camp and to allow enough time to see the town's attractions.

EXPLORING

Gyantse is easily navigable on foot. Most hotels and restaurants are along Yingxiong Nan Lu, a few minutes south of the unmistakable Dzong Fortress. The Pelkor Chode Monastery is 10 minutes' walking northwest of the fortress; both can easily be visited and toured over the course of about three hours.

Gyantse Dzong. In the 14th and 15th centuries Gyantse rose to political power along with the rise of the Sakyapa monastic order. To get an idea of the amount of construction during this period, make the steep 20-minute climb to the top of this old fortress on the northern edge of town. The building isn't in great shape, but you'll be treated to staggering views of the town and the surrounding Nyang Chu Valley. Signs reading "Jump Off Cliff" aren't making a suggestion, but pointing to the location where Tibetan warriors jumped to their deaths rather than surrender to British troops in 1904. The best way to see everything here is to wind around the fortress clockwise toward the top,

RUSTIC CUISINE

Outside the capital, the variety of food leaves something to be desired, but in areas commonly visited by tourists you should be able to find a simple meal.

Kumbum is one of Tibet's largest stupas.

using the long concrete staircase to descend. Be careful, as there's a slippery bit of concrete at the bottom of the stairs. The **Anti-British Imperialist Museum,** just inside the front gate, is worth a visit for a distorted yet amusing account of the British invasion, sprinkled with obvious propaganda. ⊠ *North end of Yingxiong Lu* ☎ *0892/817–2263* 🖻 *Y30* ⏱ *Daily 9–6:30.*

★ **Pelkor Chode Monastery.** One of the few multidenominational monastic complexes in Tibet—housing Gelugpa, Sakyapa, and Bupa monks— Pelkor Chode is home to the **Gyantse Kumbum.** Built in 1427, this building with its glittering golden dome and four sets of spellbinding eyes rising over uniquely tiered circular architecture is one of the most beautiful in Tibet. Inside there are six floors, each a labyrinth of small chapels adorned with Nepalese-influenced murals and statues. A steep ladder at the rear of the fifth floor provides access to the roof. Impressive in itself, you'll appreciate this complex even more after you've seen it from the heights of Gyantse Dzong. ⊠ *Northwest end of Pelkor Lu* ☎ *0892/817–2680* 🖻 *Y40* ⏱ *Daily 8–7.*

WHERE TO EAT AND STAY

¢–$$ ✕ **Fuqi Sichuan.** If you're getting tired of the same old Western-Tibetan
CHINESE hybrid cuisine, there are lots of well-prepared traditional Chinese dishes here from which you can choose. Best of all, there's an English menu, although the prices on it are nearly double what you'd pay ordering in Chinese. ⊠ *10 Yingxiong Nan Lu, near the Gyantse Hotel* 🖃 *No credit cards.*

¢–$ ✕ **Tashi.** Although it shares the same name and a similar menu with a
ECLECTIC couple of restaurants in Lhasa, this restaurant is unrelated. Still, the

A Once-Mighty Empire

CLOSE UP

The Tibet Autonomous Region (TAR) bears only a passing resemblance to what was once a massive empire that encompassed all of Tibet, Qinghai (except for the area around Xining), western Sichuan, and parts of northern Yunnan. Historically, despite their modern-day reputation for being a peaceful people, Tibetans were known as fierce warriors and feared by their neighbors. They even sacked the Chinese capital of Changan, now Xi'an, in the 8th century.

When the Mongols conquered China in the 13th century and founded the Yuan Dynasty, they also took control of Tibet, adopting Tibetan Buddhism as their official religion. This relationship came back to haunt Tibetans—it was used by China's successive dynasties and governments to legitimize the nation's claim to Tibet. In 1950, with almost 10 years of experience fighting first the Japanese and then the Nationalist government, the People's Liberation Army entered Tibet and quickly crushed all resistance.

Indian, Tibetan, and Western dishes served in the second-floor dining room are well liked by visitors, the yak being highly recommended. ⊠ *North end of Yingxiong Lu, near Pelkor Lu* ▭ *No credit cards.*

$$–$$$$ ⊡ **Gyantse Hotel** *(Jiangzi Fandian).* In business since 1986, this government-run hotel is still the top choice in Gyantse. Rooms here are clean and comfortable, if a bit dark and dreary. Amazingly, televisions here have Bloomberg and the BBC available. Make sure to reserve a room in advance, especially during the busy summer months. If no doubles are available, consider sharing a suite with your traveling companions; each contains two bedrooms with king-size beds and separate bathrooms. **Pros:** TV options; nice interior design; helpful staff. **Cons:** food isn't great; no elevator. ⊠ *2 Shanghai Dong Lu, near Yingxiong Lu* ☎ *0892/817–2222* ♻ *In-hotel: 3 restaurants, bar, laundry service* ▭ *No credit cards.*

$ ⊡ **Jian Zang Hotel** *(Jianzang Fandian).* Less expensive than the Gyantse Hotel, the Jian Zang is where most backpackers spend the night. The rooms here are clean but otherwise unremarkable, and hot water is always available. **Pros:** cheap; decent restaurants nearby. **Cons:** spartan and cramped accommodation. ⊠ *14 Yingxiong Nan Lu* ☎ *0892/817–3720* ♻ *In-hotel: restaurant, laundry service* ▭ *No credit cards.*

SHIGATSE

4½ hrs (280 km [170 mi]) west of Lhasa by jeep. 1½ hrs (90 km [55 mi]) northwest of Gyantse. 6 hrs (240 km [150 mi]) northeast of Shegar.

Tibet's second-largest city, Shigatse, is the traditional capital of Tsang and home to the Tashilhunpo Monastery, Tibet's largest functioning monastic institution. The Tsang kings once ruled over the region from the fortress north of town. Most people only spend a day in Shigatse, visiting the monastery and wandering up and down the city's Walking Street, a tourist-friendly section of Qingdao Lu. The city is divided up into a traditional Tibetan quarter and brand-new Chinese town.

Shigatse is quite pleasant, but you haven't traveled all the way to Tibet to see another unremarkable city.

GETTING HERE AND AROUND

The perfectly smooth road from Lhasa to Shigatse travels alongside the picturesque Tsangpo River beneath the towering walls of Nimo Gorge. Rather than stopping in Shigatse the first time you pass through, consider visiting the city on the way back from Everest Base Camp. Driving from Gyantse all the way to Shegar in a single day will maximize the time you have to spend at the mountain by getting a significant chunk of driving out of the way. Shigatse is the only city outside of Lhasa that foreigners can reliably reach by public transportation. Buses leave starting at 7 am from the Lhasa Bus Station on Jinzhu Lu.

SAFETY AND PRECAUTIONS

Shigaste saw some major rioting during the disturbances in 2008, and there has been a police and army presence here and at Tashilhunpo Monastery ever since.

TIMING

A day is sufficient to walk around the town and see the monastery.

EXPLORING

Everything of interest to foreign visitors, including most hotels and restaurants, is on the stretch of road between the monastery and the fortress, namely Walking Street, which you can recognize by the Chinese-style gates on either end.

Tashilhunpo Monastery. One of the six great Gelugpa institutions, this monastery is the seat of the Panchen Lama and one of the few religious sites in Tibet not destroyed during the Cultural Revolution. The Chapel of Maitreya houses an 85-foot-high statue of the Future Buddha—the largest in the world—covered in more than 600 pounds of gold. More than 1,000 more images are painted on the surrounding walls. You will also be able to visit the Panchen Lama tombs, many of which are lined with photos and sculptures of their later reincarnations. The beautiful stupa of the 10th Panchen Lama, built in 1990 after his death in 1989, is topped with a remarkable likeness of his unmistakable fat, jocular face done in pure gold. As this is the largest functioning monastery in Tibet, the police presence can be a bit heavy at times, especially since the 2008 riots. Refrain from discussing politics or the Dalai Lama. Don't try to take unauthorized photos, as monks here have been known to manhandle those unwilling to pay for a snapshot. Know that camera fees are Y75 per temple. ⊠ *Qingdai Xi Lu* ☎ *0892/882–2114* ⌨ *Y55 basic ticket, Y125 for premier ticket to all areas* ☉ *Daily 9:30–7.*

WHERE TO EAT AND STAY

$

ECLECTIC

✕**Tashi** *(Daxi Canting).* Another in a series of unrelated restaurants with the same name, this Nepali-managed eatery specializes in excellent Indian dishes such as chicken butter masala. There's also Western fare, and they serve a good yak steak. ⊠ *Eastern end of Walking St., near Qingdao Lu* ☎ *0892/883–5969* ⊟ *No credit cards.*

¢–$$

TIBETAN

✕**Yak's Head Tibet** *(Niutou Zangcan).* In the middle of Walking Street, this restaurant has the most extensive Tibetan menu in town (think momo dumplings and yak cheese). Only a few words on the menu have been translated into English, but luckily there's also a photograph of every dish. The few Western dishes are best avoided. Look for the sign with a huge carved yak's head above the entrance. ✉ *14 Walking St.* ☎ *0892/883–7186* 🖃 *No credit cards.*

$–$$ 🏨 **Manasarovar Hotel** *(Shenhu Jiudian)*. This remains the best hotel in town. Unfortunately, it's more than a mile east of the restaurants and shops of Walking Street. Nevertheless, the pleasant rooms have hardwood floors with colorful Tibetan rugs. **Pros:** clean; good Western restaurant. **Cons:** a bit far off; poor service. ✉ *14 Qingdao Lu* ☎ *0892/883–9999* 🛏 *78 rooms* ⚿ *In-hotel: restaurant, laundry service* 🖃 *No credit cards.*

¢–$ 🏨 **Tenzin Hotel.** This is Shigatse's most popular budget hotel, with dorm rooms and some very nice doubles with *en suite* bathrooms and an endless supply of hot water. The hallways and other common areas are decorated with murals depicting various aspects of Tibetan life. There is a half-decent restaurant above the courtyard, and lots of restaurant options are nearby. **Pros:. Cons:** ✉ *8 Bangchelling, across from the Tibetan Market* ☎ *0892/882–2018* ⚿ *In-hotel: restaurant* 🖃 *No credit cards.*

SHEGAR

6 hrs (240 km [150 mi]) southwest of Shigatse. 3½ hrs (110 km [70 mi]) northeast of Rongbuk Monastery and Everest Base Camp.

There isn't much of anything to see in Shegar—which also goes by the name New Tingri—a town so small that its two intersecting streets don't even have names. Nevertheless, it's the best place to spend the night before heading down to Rongbuk Monastery for the hike to Everest Base Camp. Supplies in Shegar are more expensive than in Shigatse, but the gouging here is nothing compared to what you'll find closer to Everest. If the accommodations near Everest sound too rough for you, consider making Base Camp a day trip and spending both nights in the relatively luxurious lodgings in Shegar.

GETTING HERE AND AROUND
The long drive from Shigatse to Shegar is necessary if you want to maximize your time at Everest Base Camp. On the way to Mount Everest, you'll encounter a border area checkpoint about 15 minutes outside of town, so don't forget to bring your passport. About 45 minutes later you'll reach Bang-la Pass on the Friendship Highway, with perhaps the world's best view of the Himalayas. On a clear day you can see four of the world's 10 highest peaks, including Everest, Lhotse, Makalu, and Cho Oyu.

SAFETY AND PRECAUTIONS
The standard advice at being at this altitude applies here; if you feel very ill, you must descend to a lower level immediately.

TIMING
Most visitors here will be very anxious to reach Everest Base Camp as soon as they can, and there is no need to hang out here for more than a night to get acclimatized.

WHERE TO EAT AND STAY

¢–$$ ✕ **Chengyu Friendship Restaurant** (*Chengyu Youyi Canting*). This Sichua-
CHINESE nese restaurant—look out for the English language sign—is overpriced,
but so is almost everything in Shegar. Stick to simple classics like stir-
fried egg with tomato or sweet-and-sour pork, which can be ordered
from an English menu. ✉ *Opposite the gas station* ☎ *0892/894–7121*
🍽 *No credit cards.*

¢ ✕ **Restaurant Number One.** Simple but delicious dishes consisting mainly
of yak meat, eggs, rice, potatoes, and vegetables are served at this rustic
café attached to the Snowland Hotel. These are the only cheap eats in
town. ✉ *Northwest corner of the intersection* ☎ *0892/826–2848* 🍽
No credit cards.

$–$$ 🏨 **Qomolongma Hotel** (*Zhufeng Binguan*). A mediocre government-run
hotel, this is nevertheless the best place to stay anywhere near Mount
Everest. You'll be well rested for your assault on Base Camp the next
day, and the walk to your room down what is perhaps the longest
hallway on earth will help you get used to the altitude. The restaurant
serves both Chinese and Western fare, although we'd recommend sticking with the former. A mountaineering shop can provide you with any
last-minute supplies, although water here is three times as expensive as
you'll pay at the small shops near the town's gas station. **Pros:** best of
a small number of options. **Cons:** limited hot water and a bit grubby.
✉ *From the intersection, go west over a small bridge and turn left into
the entrance* ☎ *0892/826–2775* 🛏 *80 rooms* 🛎 *In-hotel: restaurant, bar,
laundry service, Internet terminal* 🍽 *No credit cards.*

EVEREST BASE CAMP

*14 hrs (670 km [420 mi]) southwest of Lhasa by jeep. 3 hrs (110 km
[70 mi]) southwest of Shegar (New Tingri).*

"Because it's there," mountaineer George Mallory quipped in 1922
when asked why he wanted to climb the tallest mountain on the planet.
The fabled peak is located in the world's highest national park, Qomolangma Nature Reserve, which is a visual delight that alone is worth
the trek from Lhasa. After the monsoon rains in June the hillsides are
covered with a variety of blooming flowers and butterflies. Even from
April to June the light snow blanketing the rugged ground and along
babbling brooks is striking.

GETTING HERE AND AROUND

If you only have eyes for Everest, you can make it here from Lhasa and
back in three days. But you spend about 10 hours driving every day,
skip all the sights along the way, and hang out for only an hour or so at
Everest Base Camp. Most people make this a five-day trip. Not included
in the price of your tour will be the Y180 per person entrance fee for
the national park, plus Y400 per land cruiser or Y600 per van, usually
split among the passengers, and an extra Y180 for the guide's admission. You are not allowed to drive direct to the Base Camp. There is a
car park very close to Rongbuk Monastery, and mini-buses (Y25) take
you from the car park the rest of the way. Have your passport with you.

The scenery is more spectacular than the accommodations at Everest Base Camp.

SAFETY AND PRECAUTIONS
As everywhere in Tibet, altitude sickness is common here, and your body needs time to recover. Roughly one out of every 20 visitors needs to be flown out and back down to lower altitudes. If you become ill, you will want to be evacuated to Lhasa as soon as possible. Also, proper clothing and sunscreen are essential. Bring antibacterial hand wash, since it doesn't require water.

TIMING
Your time at Everest Base Camp is very much dependent on the weather; it can be demoralizing to travel so far and not see the highest mountains in the world because of cloud cover. With this in mind, it's worth planning to stay for at least a couple of days. The best time to enjoy the area is April, May, and June. Avoid traveling here from October to April, as it's cold. July and August is the rainy season, and it's almost impossible to see Mount Everest though the mist.

TOURS
Snowlion Tours (⊕ *www.snowliontours.com*) runs several tours that include a trip to Base Camp and involve trekking along the Ra Chu stream, through small villages, and up to Rongbuk Monastery. All of this company's guides, drivers, and cooks are Tibetan, and accommodations are at Tibetan-run hotels.

You can also visit the world's highest monastery, **Rongbuk Monastery**, on your way to Base Camp. There were once 500 monks living here, but now there are only 20 monks and 10 nuns, who delight in the company of visitors. It is 8 km (5 mi) along a dirt road from the monastery to Base Camp. The 15-minute drive from the monastery is no longer officially allowed, but plenty of jeeps get through with a little cajoling and perhaps a bit of cash. It's more thrilling, however, to make the three-hour walk, even if it is just to say that you trekked the Everest region. Horse-drawn carts are also available for Y30 per person one way, making the trip in about an hour.

WHERE TO EAT AND STAY

Sleeping near Mount Everest is a treat, though the lodgings are underwhelming. The Chinese hotel near Rongbuk Monastery is extremely overpriced, and the monastery's own guesthouse is a rundown flophouse popular with backpackers. If you're tough and up for a once-in-a-lifetime experience, stay in one of the tents at Everest Base Camp. Every tent hotel has a kitchen serving up decent food.

¢ ╳⊞ **Rongbuk Monastery Guesthouse.** This dingy little guesthouse is the most popular lodging near Mount Everest, mainly because it's the only affordable option with four solid walls. Notable is the guesthouse's prison-style lighting system—lights out at 11 pm—and lack of electrical outlets. Still, the restaurant off the courtyard is an excellent place to warm up and chat with fellow adventurers after a long day of trekking. You'll need to bring your own sleeping bag, as the hotel's bedding is not warm. **Pros:** social atmosphere. **Cons:** basic; terrible bathrooms. ✉ *Across from Rongbuk Monastery* ☎ *No phone* ⇗ *25 rooms* ⚓ *In-hotel: restaurant* ⊟ *No credit cards.*

$ ╳⊞ **View Station Hotel.** This pink box not far from Rongbuk Monastery is the only hotel-like lodging near Everest Base Camp. Still, for the price you'd expect private bathrooms and consistently hot water, neither of which is available. If you're insistent on staying in a hotel near Mount Everest, this place will have to do, but you'd probably be happier heading back to Shegar. **Pros:** it's actually a hotel. **Cons:** nothing to brag about and overpriced. ✉ *North of Rongbuk Monastery* ☎ *No phone* ⇗ *40 rooms* ⚓ *In-hotel: restaurant* ⊟ *No credit cards.*

ENGLISH	PINYIN	CHINESE
TIBET	**XĪZÀNG**	**西藏**
Lhasa	Lāsà	拉萨
Ani Tsangkung Nunnery	Āní cāngkōng nǚgū ān	美洲黑杜鹃女修道院
Barkhor	bākuò	八廓
Brahmaputra Grand Hotel	Yǎlǔzàngbù dàjiǔdiàn	雅鲁藏布大酒店
Drepung Monastery	Zhébàng sì	哲蚌寺
Four Points by Sheraton Lhasa	Lāsà Fúpéng Xǐláidēng Jiǔdiàn	拉萨福朋喜来登酒店
Ganden Monastery	Gāndān sì	甘丹寺
Himalaya Hotel	Xǐmǎlāyǎ jiǔdiàn	喜玛拉雅酒店
House of Shambhala	Xiānbālā dàjiǔdiàn	院的香巴拉
Jokhang Temple	Dàzhāo sì	大昭寺
Kirey Hotel	Jírì Lǚguǎn	基列伊酒店
Kundeling Monastery	Kūndélín sì	修道院
Kyichu Hotel	Jīqū Fàndiàn	基区饭店
Lhasa Gongga Airport	Gònggá fēijīchǎng	贡嘎飞机场
Lhasa Hotel	Lāsà fàndiàn	拉萨饭店
Lhasa Train Station	Lāsà huǒchēzhàn	拉萨火车站
Muslim Quarter	Mùsīlín xiǎoqū	穆斯林小区
Nechung Monastery	Nǎiqióng sì	修道院
Norbulingka Palace	Luóbùlínkǎ gōng	罗布林卡宫
Oh Dan Guesthouse	Ōudān bīnguǎn	欧丹宾馆
Palha Lupuk Temple	Pàlālǔfù Shíkū Miao	寺
Potala Palace	Bùdálā Gōng	布达拉宫
Ramoche Temple	Xiǎozhāo sì	小昭寺
Sera Monastery	Sèlā sì	色拉寺
Shangrila	Xiāng Gé Lǐ Lā	香格里拉
Summit Café	Gāofēng kāfēitīng	高峰咖啡厅
TAR People's Hospital	Rénmín Yīyuàn	人民医院
Tashi 1	Zāxī	扎西
Tibet Hotel	Xīzàng bīnguǎn	西藏宾馆
Tibet Museum	Xīzàng bówùguǎn	西藏博物馆
Yak Hotel	Yà Lǔ Guǎn	牦牛旅
Tsang Province	Hōu Zàng Dì Qū	曾省
Gyantse	Jiāngzī	江孜
Gyantse Dzong	Jiāngzī Xiàn	江孜镇
Gyantse Hotel	Jiāngzī fàndiàn	江孜饭店

ENGLISH	PINYIN	CHINESE
Pelkor Chode Monastery	Bái Jū Sí	修道院
Tashi	Zāxī	扎西
Tashilhunpo Monastery.	Zhāshílúnbù Sì	扎什布寺
Shigatse	Rìkāzé	日喀则
Tashi	Zāxī	扎西
Shegar (New Tingri)	Xīn Dìngrì	新定日
Mount Everest (Qomolangma)	Zhūmùlǎngmǎfēng	珠穆朗玛峰
Rongbuk Monastery	Róngbù Sì	修道院

UNDERSTANDING CHINA

China At a Glance

Chinese Vocabulary

CHINA AT A GLANCE

FAST FACTS

- Capital: Beijing
- National anthem: "March of the Volunteers"
- Type of government: Communist
- Administrative divisions: 23 provinces (including Taiwan), 5 autonomous regions, 4 municipalities, 2 special administrative regions (Hong Kong and Macau)
- Independence: October 1, 1949
- Constitution: December 4, 1982
- Legal system: A mix of custom and statute, largely criminal law, with rudimentary civil code
- Suffrage: 18 years of age
- Legislature: Unicameral National People's Congress; 2,985 members elected by municipal, regional, and provincial people's congresses to serve five-year terms; the last elections were in 2008.
- Population: 1.3 billion; the largest in the world
- Population density: 138 people per square km (361 people per square mi)
- Median age: Female 31.7, male 31.2
- Life expectancy: Female 74.3, male 70.3
- Infant mortality rate: 25.3 deaths per 1,000 live births
- Literacy: 86%
- Language: Standard Chinese or Mandarin (official), Yue (Cantonese), Wu (Shanghainese), Minbei (Fuzhou), Minnan (Hokkien-Taiwanese), Xiang, Gan, Hakka dialects
- Ethnic groups: Han Chinese 92%; Zhuang, Uygur, Hui, Yi, Tibetan, Miao, Manchu, Mongol, Buyi, Korean, and other nationalities 8%
- Religion: Officially atheist but Taoism, Buddhism, Christianity, and Islam are practiced.
- Discoveries and Inventions: Decimal system (1400 BC), paper (100 BC), seismograph (AD 100), compass (200), matches (577), gunpowder (700), paper money (800), movable type (1045)

GEOGRAPHY AND ENVIRONMENT

- Land area: 9.3 million square km (3.6 million square mi), the fourth-largest country in the world, and slightly smaller than the United States
- Coastline: 14,500 km (9,010 mi) on the Yellow Sea, the East China Sea, and the South China Sea
- Terrain: Mostly mountains, high plateaus, deserts in west; plains, deltas, and hills in east
- Islands: Hainan, Taiwan, many smaller islands along the coast
- Natural resources: Aluminum, antimony, coal, hydropower, iron ore, lead, magnetite, manganese, mercury, molybdenum, natural gas, petroleum, tin, tungsten, uranium, vanadium, zinc
- Natural hazards: Droughts, earthquakes, floods, land subsidence, tsunamis, typhoons
- Environmental issues: Air pollution (greenhouse gases, sulfur dioxide particulates), especially from China's reliance on coal, which is used to generate 70% of the country's electric power. Acid rain is also a consequence of the burning of China's high-sulfur coal, particularly in the north; deforestation; soil erosion and economic development have destroyed one-fifth of agricultural land since 1949; desertification; trade in endangered species; water pollution from untreated wastes; water shortages

China is an attractive piece of meat coveted by all . . . but very tough, and for years no one has been able to bite into it.

— Zhou Enlai,
Chinese Premier, 1973

ECONOMY

- Currency: Yuan
- Exchange rate: Y6.59 = $1
- GDP: $4.99 trillion
- Inflation: 4.6%
- Per capita income: Y28,240 ($4,283)
- Unemployment: 4.3%
- Workforce: 819.5 million; agriculture 39.5%; industry 27.2%; services 33.2%
- Debt: $149.4 billion
- Major industries: Armaments, automobiles, cement, chemical fertilizers, coal, consumer electronics, food processing, footwear, iron and steel, machine building, petroleum, telecommunications, textiles and apparel, toys Agricultural products: Barley, cotton, fish, millet, oilseed, peanuts, pork, potatoes, rice, sorghum, tea, wheat
- Exports: $1.506 trillion
- Major export products: electrical and other machinery, including data processing equipment, apparel, textiles, iron and steel, optical and medical equipment Export partners: U.S. 21.5%; Hong Kong 18%; Japan 14.9%; South Korea 4.8%
- Imports: $1.307 trillionMajor import products: Chemicals, iron and steel, machinery and equipment, mineral fuels, plastics
- Import partners: Japan 18%; Taiwan 11%; South Korea 10%; U.S. 9%; Germany 6%

POLITICAL CLIMATE

Since the Chinese Communist Party (CCP) took control of the government in 1949, it has shown little tolerance for outside views. Other major political parties are banned and the government is quick to crack down on movements that it doesn't approve of, most recently the Falun Gong. China's size and diversity complicate national politics, with party control weaker in rural areas, where most of the population lives. Successful politicians have sought support from local and regional leaders and must work to keep influential nonparty members from creating a stir. The decade-long struggle for democracy, which ended in the bloody Tiananmen Square protests of 1989, has fragmented and lost much of its power. The party blamed its rise on foreign agitators and reminds the population that political stability is essential for China's economic growth. The poor handling of the SARS outbreak in early 2003 prompted new calls for government reform.

DID YOU KNOW?

- China has nearly 13 million more boys than girls, leading demographers to fear that 40 million Chinese men will remain single in the 21st century.
- The country dropped its Soviet-style centralized economy for a more market-oriented system in 1978. As a result, its GDP had quadrupled by 1998.
- China is the world's largest producer of red meat and rice.
- One out of every three cigarettes in the world is smoked in China.
- The nation consumes more than three times the cigarettes puffed away by U.S. smokers.
- Since the revolution, China has had four constitutions in less than 60 years. The first three couldn't keep up with the rapid pace of change, particularly during the Cultural Revolution.
- China executed more than 17,500 people between 1990 and 1999, more than the rest of the world put together.

CHINESE VOCABULARY

	CHINESE	ENGLISH EQUIVALENT	CHINESE	ENGLISH EQUIVALENT
CONSONANTS				
	b	**b**oat	p	**p**ass
	m	**m**ouse	f	**f**lag
	d	**d**ock	t	**t**ongue
	n	**n**est	l	**l**ife
	g	**g**oat	k	**k**eep
	h	**h**ouse	j	and **y**et
	q	**ch**icken	x	**sh**ort
	zh	ju**dge**	ch	chur**ch**
	sh	**sh**eep	r*	**r**ead
	z	see**ds**	c	do**ts**
	s	**s**eed		
VOWELS				
	ü	**you**	ia	**ya**rd
	üe	**you + e**	ian	**yen**
	a	**fa**ther	iang	**young**
	ai	k**i**te	ie	**ye**t
	ao	n**ow**	o	**a**ll
	e	**ea**rn	ou	**go**
	ei	d**ay**	u	w**oo**d
	er	c**ur**ve	ua	**wa**ft
	i	**yi**eld	uo	**wa**ll
	i (after z, c, s, zh, ch, sh)	**thunder**		

WORD ORDER

The basic Chinese sentence structure is the same as in English, following the pattern of subject-verb-object:

He took my pen.   Tā ná le wǒ de bě.

s   v   o   s   v   o

NOUNS

There are no articles in Chinese, although there are many "counters," which are used when a certain number of a given noun is specified. Various attributes of a noun—such as size, shape, or use—determine which counter is used with that noun. Chinese does not distinguish between singular and plural.

a pen	yìzhī bǐ
a book	yìběn shū

VERBS

Chinese verbs are not conjugated, and they do not have tenses. Instead, a system of word order, word repetition, and the addition of a number of adverbs serves to indicate the tense of a verb, whether the verb is a suggestion or an order, or even whether the verb is part of a question. Tāzaì ná wǒ de bǐ. (He is taking my pen.) Tā ná le wǒ de bǐ. (He took my pen.) Tā you méi you ná wǒ de bǐ? (Did he take my pen?) Tā yào ná wǒ de bǐ. (He will take my pen.)

TONES

In English, intonation patterns can indicate whether a sentence is a statement (He's hungry.), a question (He's hungry?), or an exclamation (He's hungry!). In Chinese, words have a particular tone value, and these tones are important in determining the meaning of a word. Observe the meanings of the following examples, each said with one of the four tones found in standard Chinese: mā (high, steady tone): mother; má (rising tone, like a question): fiber; mā (dipping tone): horse; and mà (dropping tone): swear.

PHRASES

You don't need to master the entire Chinese language to spend a week in China, but taking charge of a few key phrases in the language can aid you in just getting by.

USEFUL TERMS

COMMON GREETINGS	
Hello/Good morning	Nǐ hǎo/Zǎoshàng hǎo
Good evening	Wǎnshàng hǎo
Good-bye	Zàijiàn
Title for a married woman or an older unmarried woman	Tàitai/Fūrén
Title for a young and unmarried woman	Xiǎojiě
Title for a man	Xiēnshēng
How are you?	Nǐ hǎo ma?
Fine, thanks. And you?	Hěn hǎo. Xièxie. Nǐ ne?
What is your name?	Nǐ jiào shénme míngzi?
My name is . . .	Wǐ jiào . . .
Nice to meet you	Hěn gěoxìng rènshì nǐ
I'll see you later.	Huítóu jiàn.

POLITE EXPRESSIONS	
Please	Qǐng.
Thank you	Xièxiè.
Thank you very much.	Fēicháng gǎnxie.

USEFUL TERMS

You're welcome.	Bú yòng xiè.
Yes, thank you.	Shì de, xièxiè.
No, thank you.	Bù, xièxiè.
I beg your pardon.	Qǐng yuánliàng.
I'm sorry.	Hěn baòqiàn.
Pardon me.	Dùibùqǐ.
That's okay.	Méi shénme.
It doesn't matter.	Méi guěnxi.
Do you speak English?	Nǐ shuō Yīngyǔ ma?
Yes.	Shì de.
No.	Bù.
Maybe.	Huòxǔ.
I can speak a little.	Wǐ néng shuō yī diǎnr.
I understand a little.	Wǐ dǐng yì diǎnr.
I don't understand.	Wǐ bù dǐng.
I don't speak Chinese very well.	Wǐ Zhōngwén shuō de bù haǐ.
Would you repeat that, please?	Qǐng zài shuō yíbiàn?
I don't know.	Wǐ bù zhīdaò.
No problem.	Méi wèntí.
It's my pleasure.	Lèyì er wéi.

NEEDS AND QUESTION WORDS

I'd like . . .	Wǐ xiǎng . . .
I need . . .	Wǐ xūyào . . .
What would you like?	Nǐ yaò shénme?
Please bring me . . .	Qǐng gěi wǐ . . .
I'm looking for . . .	Wǐ zài zhǎo . . .
I'm hungry.	Wǐ è le.
I'm thirsty.	Wǐ kǐukě.
It's important.	Hěn zhòngyào.
It's urgent.	Hěn jǐnjí.
How?	Zěnmeyàng?
How much?	Duōshǎo?
How many?	Duōshǎo gè?
Which?	Nǎ yí gè?
What?	Shénme?

USEFUL TERMS

What kind of?	Shénme yàng de?
Who?	Shuí?
Where?	Nǎli?
When?	Shénme shíhòu?
What does this mean?	Zhè shì shénme yìsi?
What does that mean?	Nà shì shénme yìsi?
How do you say . . . in Chinese?	. . . yòng Zhōngwén zěnme shūo?

AT THE AIRPORT

Where is . . .	. . . zài nǎr?
customs?	Hǎigūan
passport control?	Hùzhào jiǎnyàn
the information booth?	Wènxùntái
the ticketing counter?	Shòupiàochù
the baggage claim?	Xínglǐchù
the ground transportation?	Dìmìan jiěotōng
Is there a bus service?	Yǐu qù chéng lǐ de gōnggòng
to the city?	qìchē ma?
Where are . . .	. . . zài nǎr?
the international departures?	Guójì hángbēn chūfē diǎn
the international arrivals?	Guójì hángbēn dàodá diǎn
What is your nationality?	Nǐ shì něi guó rén?
I am an American.	Wǐ shì Měiguó rén.
I am Canadian.	Wǐ shì Jiěnádà rén.

AT THE HOTEL, RESERVING A ROOM

I would like a room . . .	Wǐ yào yí ge fángjiēn.
for one person	děnrén fáng
for two people	shuěngrén fēng
for tonight	jīntīan wǎnshàng
for two nights	liāng gè wǎnshàng
for a week	yí ge xīngqī
Do you have a different room?	Nǐ hái yǐu bié de fángjiēn ma?
with a bath	dài yùshì de fángjiēn
with a shower	dài línyù de fángjiēn
with a toilet	dài cèsuǐ de fángjiēn
with air-conditioning	yǐu kōngtiáo de fángjiēn

USEFUL TERMS

How much is it?	Duōshǎo qián?
My bill, please.	Qǐng jiézhàng.

AT THE RESTAURANT

Where can we find a good restaurant?	Zài nǎr kěyǐ zhǎodào yìjiā hǎo cānguǎn?
We'd like a(n) . . . restaurant.	Wǒmen xiǎng qù yì gè . . . cānguǎn.
elegant	gāo jí
fast-food	kuàicān
inexpensive	piányì de
seafood	hǎixiān
vegetarian	sùshí
Café	Kāfēi diàn
A table for two	Liǎng wèi
Waiter, a menu, please.	Fúwùyuán, qǐng gěi wǒmen càidēn.
The wine list, please.	Qǐng gěi wǒmen jiǔdēn.
Appetizers	Kěiwèi shíwù
Main course	Zhǔ cài
Dessert	Tiándiǎn
What would you like?	Nǐ yào shénme cài?
What would you like to drink?	Nǐ yào hē shénme yǐnliào?
Can you recommend a good wine?	Nǐ néng tūijiàn yí ge hǎo jiǔ ma?
Wine, please.	Qǐng lǎi diǎn jiǔ.
Beer, please.	Qǐng lǎi diǎn píjiǔ.
I didn't order this.	Wǒ méiyǒu diǎn zhè gè.
That's all, thanks.	Jiù zhèxie, xièxiè.
The check, please.	Qǐng jiézhàng.
Cheers!/Bottoms Up!	Gānbēi! Zhù nǐ shēntì
To your health!	jiànkāng.

OUT ON THE TOWN

Where can I find . . .	Nǎr yǒu . . .
an art museum?	yìshù bówùguǎn?
a museum of natural history?	zìránlìshǐ bówùguǎn?
a history museum?	lìshǐ bówùguǎn?
a gallery?	huàláng?
interesting architecture?	yǒuqù de jiànzhùwù?
a church?	jiàotáng?

USEFUL TERMS

the zoo?	dòngwùyuán?
I'd like . . .	Wǐ xiǎng . . .
to see a play.	kàn xì.
to see a movie.	kàn diànyǐng.
to see a concert.	qù yīnyuèhuì.
to see the opera.	kàn gējù.
to go sightseeing.	qù guěnguěng.
to go on a bike ride.	qí děnchē.

SHOPPING

Where is the best place to go shopping for . . .	Mǎi . . . zuì hǎo qù nǎr?
clothes?	yīfu
food?	shíwù
souvenirs?	jìniànpǐn
furniture?	jīajù
fabric?	bùliào
antiques?	gǔdǐng
books?	shūjí
sporting goods?	yùndòng wùpǐn
electronics?	diànqì
computers?	diànnǎo

DIRECTIONS

Excuse me. Where is . . .	Duìbùqǐ . . . zài nǎr?
the bus stop?	Qìchēzhàn
the subway station?	Dìtiězhàn
the restroom?	Xǐshǒujiēn
the taxi stand?	Chūzū chēzhàn
the nearest bank?	Zùijìn de yínháng
the hotel?	Lǚˇguǎn
To the right	Zài yòubiěn.
To the left.	Zài zuǐbiěn.
Straight ahead.	Wǎng qián zhízǐu.
It's near here.	Jiuzài zhè fùjìn.
Go back.	Wǎng húi zǐu.
Next to . . .	Jǐnkào . . .

USEFUL TERMS

TIME

What time is it?	Xiànzài shénme shíjiën?
It is noon.	Zhōngwǔ.
It is midnight.	Bànyè.
It is 9:00 am	Shàngwǔ jǐu diǎn.
It is 1:00 pm	Xiàwǔ yì diǎn.
It is 3 o'clock.	Sēn diǎn (zhōng).
5:15	Wǔ diǎn shíwǔ fēn.
7:30	Qī diǎn sēnshí (bàn).
9:45	Jǐu diǎn sìshíwǔ.
Now	Xiànzài
Later	Wǎn yì diǎnr
Immediately	Mǎshàng
Soon	Hěn kuài

DAYS OF THE WEEK

Monday	Xīngqī yī
Tuesday	Xīngqī èr
Wednesday	Xīngqī sēn
Thursday	Xīngqī sì
Friday	Xīngqī wǔ
Saturday	Xīngqī lìu
Sunday	Xīngqī rì (tiēn)

MODERN CONNECTIONS

Where can I find . . .	Zài nǎr kěyǐ shǐ yòng . . .
a telephone?	diànhuà?
a fax machine?	chuánzhēnjī?
an Internet connection?	guójì wǎnglù?
How do I call the United States?	Gěi Měiguó dǎ diànhuà zěnme dǎ?
I need . . .	Wǐ xūyào . . .
a fax sent.	fě chuánzhēn.
a hookup to the Internet.	yǔ guójì wǎnglù liánjiē.
a computer.	diànnǎo.
a package sent overnight.	liányè bǎ běoguǐ jìchū.
some copies made.	fùyìn yìxiē wénjiàn.
a VCR and monitor.	lùyǐngjī he xiānshiqì.

an overhead projector and markers.	huàndēngjī he biěoshìqì.

EMERGENCIES AND SAFETY

Help!	Jìumìng a!
Fire!	Jìuhuǐ a!
I need a doctor.	Wǐ yào kàn yīshēng.
Call an ambulance!	Mǎshàng jiào jiuhùchē!
What happened?	Fěshēng le shénme shì?
I am/My wife is/My husband is/	Wǐ/Wǐ qīzi/Wǐ Zhàngfu/
My friend is/Someone is . . . very sick.	Wǐ péngyǐu/Yǐu rén . . .
having a heart attack.	bìng de hěn lìhài.
choking.	yēzhù le.
losing consciousness.	yūndǎo le.
about to vomit.	yào ǐutù le.
having a seizure.	yòu fēbìng le.
stuck.	bèi kǎ zhù le.
I can't breathe.	Wǐ bù néng hūxī.
I tripped and fell.	Wǐ bàn dǎo le.
I cut myself.	Wǐ gē shěng le.
I drank too much.	Wǐ jǐu hē de tài duō le.
I don't know.	Wǐ bù zhīdào.
I've injured my . . .	Wǐ de . . . shòushěng le.
head	tóu
neck	bózi
back	Bèi
arm	shǐubèi
leg	tuǐ
foot	jiǎo
eye(s)	yǎnjīng
I've been robbed.	Wǐ bèi qiāng le.

NUMBERS

0	Líng
1	Yī
2	Er
3	Sěn
4	Sì

USEFUL TERMS

5	Wǔ
6	Lìu
7	Qī
8	Bě
9	Jǐu
10	Shí
11	Shíyī
12	Shí'èr
13	Shísěn
14	Shísì
15	Shíwǔ
16	Shílìu
17	Shíqī
18	Shíbě
19	Shíjǐu
20	Ershí
21	Ershíyī
22	Ershí'èr
23	Eshísěn
30	Sěnshí
40	Sìshí
50	Wǔshí
60	Lìushí
70	Qīshí
80	Běshí
90	Jǐushí
100	Yìbǎi
1,000	Yìqiěn
1,100	Yìqiěn yìbǎi
2,000	Liǎngqiěn
10,000	Yíwàn
100,000	Shíwàn
1,000,000	Bǎiwàn

Travel Smart China

WORD OF MOUTH

"There has been some discussion of tipping in China. YES, the tour guides expect tips, and SmarTours gives guidelines for the amounts, stressing that it's purely voluntary based on your satisfaction with the level of service. It added up to about the same amount that cruise ships automatically add to each passenger's bill, $10–13 per day."

—JoyceM

GETTING HERE AND AROUND

Make no mistake: this is one HUGE country. China's efficient train system is a good way of getting around if you're not in a hurry. Note that the fast pace of high-speed rail expansion that will see the total miles in its network double by the end of 2012 is starting to change that. The growing network of domestic flights is a quicker travel option, though for some routes high-speed rail can be cheaper and faster, saving you the two-hour check-in time at most airports.

China's capital, Beijing, is in the northeast. Financial capital Shanghai is halfway down the east coast. The historic city of Nanjing is upriver from Shanghai; head much farther inland and you'll hit the erstwhile capital Xi'an, home to the Terracotta Warriors.

Limestone mountains surround the Guilin area, in southern China. The region's hubs are Guangzhou, capital of Guandong Province, and Shenzhen, an industrial boomtown on the border with Hong Kong. Though part of China, Hong Kong is a Special Autonomous Region, and functions as if it were another country.

Smack bang in the middle of China is Sichuan province. Its capital, Chengdu, is an important financial center, and is a transport hub connecting eastern and western China. Kunming is the capital of the southwestern province of Yunnan. Once the gateway to the Silk Road, it's now a gateway to the bordering countries of Myanmar, Laos, and Vietnam.

Despite ongoing international controversy, Tibet, in the far west of the country, remains a Special Autonomous Region. Its capital, Lhasa, the historic center of Tibetan Buddhism, is a mind-blowing 3,650 meters (11,975 feet) above sea level in the northern Himalayas.

Vast deserts and grassy plains make up much of northwest China. Here the autonomous Xinjiang region is home to a largely Muslim population. Its capital city, Ürümqi, is the world's farthest inland city. Nei Mongolia, or Inner Mongolia, is a great swath of (mostly barren) land that runs across much of northern China.

Maps with street names in Pinyin are available in most Chinese cities, though they're not always up to date. A few crucial words of Chinese can help decode street names. *Lu* means road, *jie* means street, *dalu* is a main road, and *dajie* is a main street. Those endings are often preceded by a compass point: *bei* (north), *dong* (east), *nan* (south), *xi* (west), and *zhong* (middle). These distinguish different sections of long streets. So, if you're looking for Beijing Xi Lu, it's the western end of Beijing Road.

TRAVEL TIMES FROM BEIJING		
To	By Air	By Train
Shanghai	2¼ hours	10–22 hours
Xi'an	2 hours	11–14 hours
Guangzhou	3 hours	20–29 hours
Hong Kong	3¾ hours	24 hours
Guilin	3¼ hours	22–27 hours
Kunming	3¼ hours	38–47 hours
Nanjing	1¾ hours	8–18 hours
Lhasa	6 hours	45 hours
Ürümqi	4 hours	40 hours
Chengdu	3¾ hours	25–31 hours

▌ BY AIR

If you are flying into Asia on a SkyTeam airline (Delta for example), you're eligible to purchase their Asia Pass or a China Pass. The Asia Pass covers more than 15 Chinese cities (including Beijing, Shanghai, Xi'an, and Hong Kong) as well as destinations in 20 other Asian and Australasian countries. The China Pass allows travel to 105 domestic destinations, and prices are based on a zone structure with a minimum purchase of three coupons. The first 1,500 miles cost $300, and a package that covers 10 zones or up to 8,000 miles would cost $1,300. The catch for the China Pass is that you have to fly directly to mainland China on one of the SkyTeam carriers. That means Hong Kong or Macau do not count, though flying directly into Shenzhen or Guangzhou on an international flight would qualify.

Beijing, Xiamen, and Hong Kong are three of the cities included in the One-World Alliance Visit Asia Pass. Cities are grouped into zones, and a flat rate is levied for each flight based on the zone in which the city is located. It doesn't include flights from the United States, however. Inquire through American Airlines, Cathay Pacific, or any other OneWorld member. It won't be the cheapest way to get around, but you'll be flying on some of the world's best airlines.

If you're planning to travel to several different Asian destinations, Cathay Pacific's All Asia Pass is an excellent deal. Starting at $1,599 you get a round-trip ticket from New York (JFK), Los Angeles, or San Francisco to Hong Kong, plus 21 days of unlimited travel to up to two other Asian cities. For $2,199 you get the same package but can travel to up to four cities in Asia. If you just want to combine Hong Kong and one other Cathay destination, though, go for a regular ticket: the airline generally allows a free Hong Kong stopover.

Air Pass Info All Asia Pass (*Cathay Pacific* ☎ *800/233-2742* ⊕ *www.cathaypacific. com*). **Asia Pass** and China Pass (*SkyTeam* ☎ *800/221-1212 Delta* ⊕ *www.skyteam. com*). **Visit Asia Pass** (*OneWorld Alliance* ☎ *800/233-2742 Cathay Pacific* ⊕ *www. oneworld.com*).

Beijing, Shanghai, and Hong Kong are China's three major international hubs. You can catch nonstop or one-stop flights to Beijing from New York (13¾), Chicago (13–14 hours), San Francisco (11½–12½

hours), Los Angeles (11½–13 hours), Sydney (14–16 hours), and London (10½–11½ hours). Though most airlines say that reconfirming your return flight is unnecessary, some local airlines cancel your seat if you don't reconfirm.

Airlines and Airports Airline and Airport Links.com (⊕ *www.airlineandairportlinks.com*) has links to many of the world's airlines and airports.

Airline Security Issues Transportation Security Administration (⊕ *www.tsa.gov*) has answers for almost every question that might come up.

AIRPORTS

Northern China's main hub is the efficient Beijing Capital International Airport (PEK), 20 mi northeast of the Beijing city center. Shanghai has two airports: Pudong International Airport (PVG) is newer and flashier than scruffy Hongqiao International Airport (SHA), but Hongqiao is more efficient and closer to downtown. The main hub in southern China is the fabulous Hong Kong International Airport (HKG), also known as Chek Lap Kok.

There are also international airports at Guangzhou (CAN), Kunming (KMG), Xiamen (XMN), Shenzhen (SZX), Xi'an (XIY), Chengdu (CTU), and Guilin (KWL), among others.

Clearing customs and immigration in China can take a while, especially in the morning, so arrive at least two hours before your scheduled flight time.

While you're wandering in Chinese airports, someone may approach you offering to carry your luggage, or even just give you directions. Be aware that this "helpful" stranger will almost certainly expect payment. Many of the X-ray machines used for large luggage items aren't film-safe, so keep film in your carry-on if you're still using a nondigital camera.

Airport Information Beijing Capital International Airport (☎ *010/6454-1100* ⊕ *www.en.bcia.com.cn*). **Chengdu Shuangliu**

International Airport (☎ 028/8570–2649 ⊕ www.cdairport.com). **Guangzhou Baiyun International Airport** (☎ 020/3606–6999 ⊕ www.guangzhouairportonline.com). **Guilin Liangjiang International Airport** (☎ 0773/284–5114). **Hong Kong International Airport** (☎ 852/2181–8888 ⊕ www.hongkongairport.com). **Kunming Wujiaba Airport** (☎ 0871/711–4300). **Shanghai Hongqiao International Airport** (☎ Info: 86-21-96990 ⊕ www.shanghaiairport.com). **Shanghai Pudong International Airport** (☎ Info: 86-21-96990 ⊕ www.shanghaiairport.com). **Shenzhen Bao'an International Airport** (☎ 0755/2345–6789 ⊕ www.eng.szairport.com). **Xi'an Xianyang International Airport** (☎ 029/0500–2327). **Xiamen Gaoqi International Airport** (☎ 0592/570–6078 ⊕ www.xiagc.com.cn).

FLIGHTS

TO AND FROM CHINA

Air China is China's flagship carrier. It operates nonstop flights from Beijing and Shanghai to various North American and European cities. Although it once had a sketchy safety record, the situation has improved dramatically, and it is now part of Star Alliance (an "alliance" of airlines worldwide that helps facilitate travel between them). Don't confuse it with the similarly named China Airlines, which is operated out of Taiwan.

Air Canada has daily flights to Beijing and Shanghai from Toronto, and daily flights to Hong Kong from Toronto, Calgary, Edmonton, and Vancouver. Cathay Pacific flies to Beijing via Hong Kong. China Eastern and China Southern airlines fly from China to the West Coast of the United States. Japan Airlines and All Nippon fly to Beijing via Tokyo. Northwest and United both have service to Beijing from the United States, and United has a nonstop flight to Shanghai and Beijing from Chicago.

WITHIN CHINA

Air China is the major carrier for domestic routes, flying to more than 160 cities in China. Its main rivals are China Southern

LUCKY NUMBER 8

Sichuan Airlines bought the number 28–8888–8888 for Y2.33 million (US$343,000) during an auction of more than 100 telephone numbers in 2003, making it the most expensive telephone number in the world. The number 8 (*ba* in Chinese) is considered lucky in China, as it is similar to the Cantonese word for "getting rich."

and China Eastern. Smaller Shanghai Airlines has a growing number of national routes, mostly out of Shanghai.

The service on most Chinese airlines is on a par with low-cost American airlines—be prepared for limited legroom, iffy food, and possibly no personal TV. More importantly, always arrive at least two hours before departure, as chronic overbooking means latecomers just don't get on.

You can make reservations and buy tickets for flights within China through airline Web sites or with travel agencies. It's worth contacting a Chinese travel agency like China International Travel Service (CITS) (⇨ *Visitor Information, below*) to compare prices.

Airline Contacts Air China (☎ 800/882–8122 ⊕ www.airchina.com). **China Eastern** (☎ 888/359–5108 ⊕ www.flychinaeastern.us). **China Southern** (☎ 888/338–8988 ⊕ www.flychinasouthern.com).

❚ BY BIKE

For millions of Chinese people bicycles are still the primary form of transport, although the proliferation of cars is making biking less pleasant. Large cities like Beijing, Chengdu, Xi'an, Shanghai, and Guilin have well-defined bike lanes, often separated from other traffic. Travel by bike is extremely popular in the countryside around Guilin, too. Locals don't rate gears much—take your cue from them and just roll along at a leisurely pace. Note that bikes have to give way to motorized vehicles at intersections. If a flat tire or sudden brake failure strikes, seek out the nearest street-side mechanic (they're everywhere), easily identified by their bike parts and pumps.

In major cities some lower-end hotels and hostels rent bikes. Street-side bike rental stations are also proliferating. Otherwise, inquire at bike shops, CITS, or even corner shops. The going rental rate is Y15 to Y30 a day, plus a refundable deposit. Check the seat and wheels carefully.

Most rental bikes come with a lock, but they're usually pretty low quality. Instead, leave your wheels at an attended bike park—peace of mind costs a mere Y0.50. Helmets are just about unheard of in China, though upmarket rental companies catering to foreign tourists usually rent them. They charge much more for their bikes, but they're usually in better condition.

If you're planning a lot of cycling, note that for about Y150 to Y200 you can buy your own basic bike, though expect to pay three or four times that for a mountain bike with all the bells and whistles or for a "Flying Pigeon," the classic heavy-duty model Beijing was once famous for.

The U.S. company Backroads has a China bike tour suitable for families. Bike China Adventures organizes trips of varying length and difficulty all over China. The Adventure Center runs cycling trips along the Great Wall, in Guilin, and out of Hong Kong.

BIKES IN FLIGHT

Most airlines accommodate bikes as luggage, provided they are dismantled and boxed; check with individual airlines about packing requirements. Some airlines sell bike boxes, which are often free at bike shops, for about $20 (bike bags can be considerably more expensive).

Tour Operator The Adventure Center (☎ 800/228–8747 ⊕ www.adventurecenter. com). **Backroads** (☎ 800/462–2848 ⊕ www.

backroads.com). **Bike China Adventures** (☎ 800/818–1778 ⊕ www.bikechina.com).

❚ BY BOAT

Trains and planes are fast replacing China's boat and ferry services. Four- to seven-day cruises along the Yangtze River are the most popular, and thus the most touristy of the domestic boat rides. Both local and international companies run these tours, but shop around, as prices vary drastically.

See chapter 8 for information on Yangtze River cruises. The Shanghai Ferry Company and the China-Japan International Ferry Company both operate weekly services to Osaka, Japan, from Shanghai. You can purchase tickets for both international and domestic services (in Chinese) at local terminals, or through CITS for a small surcharge.

Information China-Japan International Ferry Company (✉ 908 Dongdaming Lu, Shanghai ☎ 021/6325–7642 ⊕ www. shinganjin.com). **Shanghai Ferry Company** (☎ 021/6537–5111 ⊕ www.shanghai-ferry. co.jp).

❚ BY BUS

China now has some fabulous luxury long-distance buses with air-conditioning and movies. Most of these services run out of Beijing and Shanghai. However, buying tickets can be complicated if you don't speak Chinese—you may end up on one of the cramped old-style affairs, much like an old-fashioned school bus (or worse). The conditions on sleeper buses are particularly dire. Taking a train or an internal flight is easier and safer, especially in rural areas where bad road conditions make for dangerous rides.

Big cities often have more than one bus terminal, and luxury services sometimes leave from the private depot of the company operating the service. Services are frequent and usually depart and arrive punctually. You can buy tickets for a small surcharge through CITS.

Bus Information CITS offices are located in every city; see specific city listings for contact information. **Hong Kong Tourist Association** (*HKTA information hotline* ☎ *852/2508–1234* ⊕ *www.discoverhongkong.com*).

▌ BY CAR

Driving oneself is not a possibility when vacationing in mainland China, as the only valid driver's licenses are Chinese ones. However, this restriction should be cause for relief, as city traffic is terrible, drivers manic and maniacal, and getting lost inevitable for first-timers. Conditions in Hong Kong aren't much better, but you can drive there using a U.S. license.

A far better idea is to put yourself in the experienced hands of a local driver and sit back and watch them negotiate the tail-backs. All the same, consider your itinerary carefully before doing so—in big cities taking the subway or walking is often far quicker for central areas. Keep the car for excursions farther afield.

The quickest way to hire a car and driver is to flag down a taxi and hire it for the day—if you're happy with a driver you've used for a trip around town, ask him. After some negotiating, expect to pay between Y350 and Y600, depending on the type of car. Most hotels can make arrangements for you, though they often charge you double that rate.

Another alternative is American car-rental agency Avis, which includes mandatory chauffeurs as part of all rental packages. A car and driver usually cost Y740 to Y850 ($93 to $110) per day. They have offices in Beijing, Nanjing, Suzhou, Hong Kong, Shanghai, Guangzhou, and Shenzhen.

▌ BY TRAIN

China's enormous rail network is one of the world's busiest. Trains are usually safe and run strictly to schedule. There are certain intricacies to buying tickets, which usually have to be purchased in the city of origin. You can buy most tickets 10 days in advance; two to three days ahead is usually enough time, except during the three national holidays—Chinese New Year (two days in mid-January–February), Labor Day (May 1), and National Day (October 1).

The cheapest place for tickets is the train station, where they only accept cash and English is rarely spoken. Most travel agents, including CITS, can book your tickets for a small surcharge (Y20 to Y50). You can also buy tickets through online retailers like China Train Ticket. They deliver the tickets to your hotel, but you often end up paying much more than the station rate.

The train system offers a glimpse of old-fashioned socialist euphemisms. There are four classes, but instead of first class and second class, in China you talk about hard and soft. Hard seats (*yingzuo*) are often rigid benchlike seats guaranteed to numb the buttocks within seconds; soft seats (*ruanzuo*) are more like the seats in long-distance American trains. For overnight journeys, the cheapest option is the hard sleeper (*yingwo*), open bays of six bunks, in two tiers of three. They're cramped, but not uncomfortable; though you take your own bedding and share the toilet with everyone in the wagon. Soft sleepers (*ruanwo*) are more comfortable: their closed compartments have four beds with bedding. Trains between Beijing, Shanghai, Hong Kong, and Xi'an have a deluxe class, with only two berths per compartment and private bathrooms. The nonstop Z-series trains are even more luxurious. Train types are identifiable by the letter preceding the route number: Z is for nonstop, T is for a normal express.

Overpriced dining cars serve meals that are often inedible, so you'd do better to make use of the massive thermoses of boiled water in each compartment and take along your own noodles or instant soup, as locals do. Trains are always crowded, but you are guaranteed your designated seat, though not always the overhead luggage rack. Note that theft on trains is increasing; on overnight trains, sleep with your valuables or else keep them on the inside of the bunk.

You can find out just about everything about Chinese train travel at Seat 61's fabulous Web site. China Highlights has a searchable online timetable for major train routes. The tour operator Travel China Guide has an English-language Web site that can help you figure out train schedules and fares.

Information China Highlights (⊕ www. chinahighlights.com). **Seat 61** (⊕ www.seat61. com/China.htm). **Travel China Guide** (⊕ www. travelchinaguide.com/china-trains/).

SERIOUS TRAINING

The most dramatic Chinese train experience is the six-day trip between Beijing and Moscow, often referred to as the Trans-Siberian railway, though that's actually the service that runs between Moscow and Vladivostok. Two weekly services cover the 8,047 km (5,000 mi) between Moscow and Beijing. The Trans-Manchurian is a Russian train that goes through northeast China, whereas the Trans-Mongolian is a Chinese train that goes through the Great Wall and crosses the Gobi Desert. Both have first-class compartments with four berths (Y2,500) or luxury two-berth compartments (Y3,000). Trains leave from Beijing Station—the cheapest place to buy tickets, though it's easier to get them through CITS.

ESSENTIALS

GREETINGS

Chinese people aren't very touchy-feely with one another, even less so with strangers. Stick to handshakes and low-key greetings when first meeting local people. Always use people's title and surname until they invite you to do otherwise.

SIGHTSEEING

By and large, the Chinese are a rule-abiding bunch. Follow their lead and avoid doing anything signs advise against. Although you won't be banned from entering any sightseeing spots for reason of dress, you'd do well to avoid overly skimpy or casual clothes.

China is a crowded country; pushing, nudging, and line-jumping are commonplace. It may be hard to accept, but it's not considered rude, so avoid reacting (even verbally) if you're accidentally shoved.

OUT ON THE TOWN

It's a great honor to be invited to someone's house, so explain at length if you can't go. Arrive punctually with a small gift for the hosts; remove your shoes outside if you see other guests doing so. Eating lots is the biggest compliment you can pay the food (and the cook).

Smoking is one of China's greatest vices. No-smoking sections in restaurants used to be nonexistent, but they are becoming more common in cities like Beijing and Shanghai.

Holding hands in public is OK, but keep passionate embraces for the hotel room.

DOING BUSINESS

Time is of the essence when doing business in China. Make appointments well in advance and be extremely punctual, as this shows respect. Chinese people have a keen sense of hierarchy in the office: if you're visiting in a group, the senior member should lead proceedings.

Suits are still the norm in China, regardless of the outside temperature. Women should avoid plunging necklines, heavy makeup, overly short skirts, and high heels. Pants are completely acceptable. Women can expect to be treated as equals by local businessmen.

Face is ever-important. Never say anything that will make people look bad, especially in front of superiors. Avoid being pushy or overly buddylike when negotiating: address people as Mr. or Ms. until they invite you to do otherwise, respect silences in conversation, and don't hurry things or interrupt. When entertaining, local businesspeople may insist on paying: after a slight protest, accept, as this lets them gain face.

Business cards are a big deal: not having one is like not having a personality. If possible, have yours printed in English on one side and Chinese on the other (your hotel can usually arrange this in a matter of hours). Proffer your card with both hands and receive the other person's in the same way, then read it carefully and make an admiring comment.

Many gifts, like clocks and cutting implements, are considered unlucky in China. Food—especially presented in a showy basket—is always a good gift choice, as are imported spirits. Avoid giving four of anything, as the number is associated with death. Offer gifts with both hands, and don't expect people to open them in your presence.

LANGUAGE

For language fundamentals, see Language Notes in the back of the book for an explanation of pronunciation and a vocabulary list. Translations of specific place names are located at the end of every chapter. Nearly everyone in mainland China speaks Putonghua (*pǔtōnghuà,* the "common language") another name for Mandarin Chinese. It's written using ideograms, or characters; in 1949 the government also introduced a phonetic writing system that uses the Roman alphabet. Known as Pinyin, it's widely used to label public buildings and station names. Even if you don't speak or read Chinese, you can easily compare Pinyin names with a map.

In Hong Kong the main language spoken is Cantonese, although many people speak English. There are many other local Chinese dialects. Some use the same characters as Putonghua for writing, but the pronunciation is so different as to be unintelligible to a Putonghua speaker. There are several non-Chinese languages (such as Mongolian, Uyghur, and Tibetan) spoken by China's ethnic minorities.

Chinese grammar is simple, but a complex tonal system of pronunciation means it usually takes a long time for foreigners to learn Chinese. Making yourself understood can be tricky; however, the Chinese will appreciate your making the effort to speak a few phrases understood almost everywhere. Try "Hello"—*Ní hǎo* (nee how); "Thank you"—*Xiè xiè* (shee-yeh, shee-yeh); and "Good-bye"— *"Zai jian"* (dzai djan). When pronouncing words written in Pinyin, remember that "q" and "x" are pronounced like "ch" and "sh," respectively; "zh" is pronounced like the "j" in "just"; "c" is pronounced like "ts."

English isn't widely spoken, though the staff in most hotels, travel agencies, and upscale restaurants in major cities is the exception. If you're lost and need help, look first to someone under 30, who may have studied some English in school. In shops, calculators and hand gestures do most of the talking.

A great place to start learning online before your trip is ChinesePod.com, which has free podcasts you can download and listen to any time.

Language Resources *Business Companion: Chinese*, by Tim Dobbins and Paul Westbrook, **Living Language/Random House Inc** (☎ 800/726-0600 ⊕ www.livinglanguage. com). *I Can Read That! A Traveler's Introduction to Chinese Characters*, by Julie Mazel Sussman, **China Books and Periodicals, Inc**

(☎ 415/282-2994 ☏ 415/282-0994 ⊕ www. chinabooks.com). *In the Know in China*, by Jennifer Phillips, **Living Language/Random House Inc** (☎ 800/726-0600 ⊕ www. livinglanguage.com).

ACCOMMODATIONS

The forums on Fodors.com are a great place to start your hotel investigations.

Location is the first thing you should consider. Chinese cities are usually big, and there's no point schlepping halfway across town for one particular hotel when a similar option is available more conveniently.

In major urban centers many four- or five-star hotels belong to familiar international chains, and are usually a safe—if pricey—bet. You can expect swimming pools, a concierge, and business services here. Locally owned hotels with four stars or less have erratic standards both in and out of big cities, as bribery plays a big part in star acquisition. However, air-conditioning, color TV, and private Western-style bathrooms are the norm for three to four stars, and even lone-star hotels have private bathrooms, albeit with a squatter toilet. Extra-firm beds are a trademark of Chinese hotels even in luxury chains.

(⇨ *Restaurant and Hotel price charts appear at the beginning of each chapter.*)

■**TIP**➔ Assume that hotels operate on the European Plan (**EP**, no meals) unless we specify that they use the Breakfast Plan (**BP**, with full breakfast), Continental Plan (**CP**, Continental breakfast), Full American Plan (**FAP**, all meals), or Modified American Plan (**MAP**, breakfast and dinner), or are all-inclusive (AI, all meals and most activities).

APARTMENT AND HOUSE RENTALS

There's an abundance of furnished rental properties for short- and long-term rentals in Beijing, Guangzhou, Hong Kong, Shanghai, and some other cities. Prices vary wildly. At the top end are luxury apartments and villas, usually far from the city center and accessible by (chauffeur-driven) car. Usually described as "serviced apartments" or "villas," these often include gyms and pools, and rents are usually well over $2,000 a month.

There are a lot of well-located mid-range properties in new apartment blocks. They're usually clean, with new furnishings, with rents starting at $500 a month. Finally, for longer, cheaper stays, there are normal local apartments. These are firmly off the tourist circuit and often cost only a third of the price of the mid-range properties. Expect mismatched furniture, erratic amenities, and varying insect populations, although what you get for your money fluctuates, so shop around.

Property sites like Move and Stay, Sublet, and Primacy Relocation have hundreds of apartments in major cities. The online classified pages in local English-language magazines or on expat Web sites are good places to look for cheaper properties.

Contacts Asia Expat (⊕ www.asiaxpat.com). **Move and Stay** (⊕ www.moveandstay.com). **Primacy Relocation** (⊕ www.primacy.com). **Sublet.com** (⊕ www.sublet.com).

HOMESTAYS

Single travelers can arrange homestays (often in combination with language courses) through China Homestay Club. Generally these are in upper-middle-class homes that work out to be at least as expensive as a cheap hotel—prices start from $175 to $235 a week. Nine times out of 10, the family has a small child in need of daily English-conversation classes. ChinaHomestay.org is a different organization that charges a single placement fee of $875 for a stay of three months or less.

Organizations China Homestay Club (⊕ www.homestay.com.cn). **ChinaHomestay. org** (⊕ www.chinahomestay.org).

HOSTELS

Budget accommodation options are improving in China. However, the term "hostel" is still used vaguely—the only thing guaranteed is shared dorm rooms aimed at backpackers; other facilities vary. Backpacking hot spots like Yangshuo have lots of options. Beijing, Shanghai, Hong Kong, and Xi'an all have a few decent hostels, but flea-ridden dumps are also common, so always ask to see your room before paying. New places open all the time, so try to get recommendations from fellow travelers as you go. Note that a private room in a low-end hotel is often just as cheap as so-called hostels; some guesthouses and hotels also have cheaper dorm beds in addition to regular rooms.

China's small but growing Youth Hostelling Association is based in Guangzhou, and has a growing list of affiliates. Backpackers.com is a useful resource for booking budget accommodations online, as is HostelWorld.com. Their prices are sometimes higher than the walk-up rate, but it's good to know you have a bed reserved when you arrive.

Information Backpackers.com (⊕ www. backpackers.com). **Hostelling International—USA** (☎ 301/495–1240 ⊕ www.hiusa. org). **HostelWorld.com** (⊕ www.hostelworld. com). **Youth Hostel Association of China** (☎ 020/8751–3731 ⊕ www.yhachina.com).

HOTELS

All hotels listed have private bath unless otherwise noted. Remember that water is a precious resource in China, and use it accordingly.

When checking into a hotel, you need to show your passport—the desk clerk records the number before you're given a room. Unmarried couples may occasionally have problems staying together in the same room, but simply wearing a band on your left finger is one way to avoid this complication. Friends or couples of the same sex, especially women, shouldn't have a problem getting a room together. There may, however, be regulations about who is allowed in your room, and it's also normal for hotels to post "visitor hours" inside the room.

■ BUSINESS SERVICES AND FACILITIES

Your hotel (or another nearby mid- to top-end one) is the best place to start looking for business services, including translation. Most are very up to speed on businesspeople's needs, and can put you in touch with other companies if necessary. Regus and the Executive Centre are international business-services companies with several office locations in Beijing, Shanghai, and Hong Kong. They provide secretarial services, meeting and conference facilities, and office rentals.

Contacts The Executive Centre (⊕ www. executivecentre.com). **Regus** (☎ 400/120–1205 ⊕ www.regus.cn).

■ COMMUNICATIONS

INTERNET

China's major cities are very Internet-friendly for those bearing laptops. Most mid- to high-end hotels have in-room Internet access; if the hotel doesn't have a server but you have a room phone, you can usually access a government-provided ISP, which only charges you for the phone call. Wi-Fi is growing exponentially—many hotels and even cafés provide it free.

Many hotels also have a computer with Internet access that you can use. Internet cafés are ubiquitous in big cities, and are rapidly spreading to smaller destinations. Known as *wang ba* in Chinese, they're not usually signposted in English, so ask your hotel to recommend one nearby. Prices (and cleanliness) vary considerably, but start at about Y3 to Y10 per hour.

Remember that there is strict government control of the Internet in China. There's usually no problem with Web-based mail, but you may be unable to access news and even blog sites. To get around the restrictions, you can subscribe to a Virtual Private Network or use proxy servers to access certain sites. AnchorFree offers a free VPN called Hotspot Shield, though the service includes annoying pop-up ads. A more reliable service, like those from WiTopia, will cost about $40 a year for safe, fast surfing. If you're going to be in China for a while, investing in a VPN is worth the cost.

PHONES

The country code for China is 86; the city code for Beijing is 10, and the city code for Shanghai is 21. Hong Kong has its own country code: 852. To call China from the United States or Canada, dial the international access code (011), followed by the country code (86), the area or city code without the initial zero, and the eight-digit phone number.

Numbers beginning with 800 within China are toll-free. Note that a call from China to a toll-free number in the United States or Hong Kong is a full-tariff international call. If you need to call home, use your computer and a service like Skype or a Web messenger service with phone access. Beware though and be sure to download the U.S. version of Skype—the Chinese TOM-Skype is constantly monitored by government cyberpolice.

CALLING WITHIN CHINA

The Chinese phone system is cheap and efficient. You can make local and long-distance calls from your hotel or any public phone on the street. Some pay phones accept coins, but it's easier to buy an integrated circuit (IC) calling card, available at convenience stores and newsstands (⇨ *see Calling Cards, below*). Local calls are generally free from landlines, though your hotel might charge a nominal rate. Long-distance rates in China are very low. Calling from your hotel room is a viable option, as hotels can only add a 15% service charge.

Chinese phone numbers have eight digits—you only need to dial these when calling somewhere within the city or area you're in. In general, city codes appear written with a 0 in front of them; if not, you need to add this when calling another city within China.

For directory assistance, dial 114. If you want information for other cities, dial the city code followed by 114 (note that this is considered a long-distance call). For example, if you're in Beijing and need directory assistance for a Shanghai number, dial 021-114. The operators do not speak English, so if you don't speak Chinese you're best off asking your hotel for help.

To make long-distance calls from a public phone you need an IC card (⇨ *Calling Cards)*. To place a long-distance call, dial 0, the city code, and the eight-digit phone number.

CALLING OUTSIDE CHINA

To make an international call from within China, dial 00 (the international access code within China) and then the country code, area code, and phone number.

The United States country code is 1.

IDD (international direct dialing) service is available at all hotels, post offices, major shopping centers, and airports. By international standards, prices aren't unreasonable, but it's vastly cheaper to use a long-distance calling card, known as an IP card *(see Calling Cards, below)*. These cards' rates also beat AT&T, MCI, and Sprint hands-down. If you do need to use these services, dial 108 (the local operator) and the local access codes from China: 11 for AT&T, 12 for MCI, and 13 for Sprint. Dialing instructions in English will follow.

Access Codes AT&T Direct (☏ *800/874–4000 from China: Call 108–11 from southern China; 108–888 from northern China).* **MCI WorldPhone** (☏ *800/444-4444 from*

China: 108–12). **Sprint International Access** (☏ *800/793-1153 from China: 108-13).*

CALLING CARDS

Calling cards are a key part of the Chinese phone system. There are two kinds: the IC card (integrated circuit; *àicei ka*), for local and domestic long-distance calls on pay phones; and the IP card (Internet protocol; *aipi ka)* for international calls from any phone. You can buy both at post offices, convenience stores, and street vendors.

IC cards come in denominations of Y20, Y50, and Y100, and can be used in any pay phone with a card slot—most urban pay phones have them. Local calls using them cost around Y0.30 a minute, and less on weekends and after 6 pm.

To use IP cards, you first dial a local access number. You then enter a card number and PIN, and finally the phone number, complete with international dial codes. When calling from a pay phone, both cards' minutes are deducted at the same time—one for local access (IC card) and one for the long-distance call you placed (IP card). There are countless different card brands; China Mobile, China Unicom, and China Telecom are usually reliable. IP cards come with face values of Y20, Y30, Y50, and Y100. However, the going rate for them is up to half that, so bargain vendors down.

CELL PHONES

If you have a tri-band GSM or a CDMA phone, pick up a local SIM card *(sim ka)* from any branch of China Mobile or China Unicom: there are often branches at international Chinese airports. You'll be presented with a list of possible phone numbers, with varying prices—an "unlucky" phone number (one with lots of 4s) could be as cheap as Y50, whereas an auspicious one (full of 8s) could fetch Y300 or more. You then buy prepaid cards to charge minutes onto your SIM—do this straightaway, as you need credit to receive calls. Local calls to landlines cost Y0.25 a minute, and to cell phones Y0.60, though rates can vary depending on the services you sign up for or add to your SIM. International calls from cell phones are very expensive. Remember to bring an adapter for your phone charger. You can also buy cheap handsets from China Mobile—if you're planning to stay even a couple of days this is probably cheaper than renting a phone.

Contacts Cellular Abroad (☎ 800/287–5072 ⊕ www.cellularabroad.com) rents and sells GMS phones and sells SIM cards that work in many countries. **Mobal** (☎ 888/888–9162 ⊕ www.mobalrental.com) rents cell phones and sells GSM phones (starting at $49) that will operate in 170 countries. Per-call rates vary throughout the world.

▌ CUSTOMS AND DUTIES

Except for the usual prohibitions against narcotics, explosives, plant and animal material, firearms, and ammunition, you can take anything into China that you plan to take away with you. Cameras, video recorders, GPS equipment, laptops, and the like should pose no problems. However, China is very sensitive about printed matter deemed seditious, such as religious, pornographic, and political texts, especially articles, books, and pictures of Tibet. All the same, small amounts of English-language reading matter aren't generally a problem. Customs officials are for the most part easygoing, and visitors are rarely searched. It's not necessary to fill in customs declaration forms, but if you carry in a large amount of cash, say several thousand dollars, you should declare it upon arrival.

You're not allowed to remove any antiquities dating to before 1795. Antiques from between 1795 and 1949 must have an official red seal attached—quality antiques shops know this and arrange it.

U.S. Information U.S. Customs and Border Protection (⊕ www.cbp.gov).

▌ EATING OUT

In China meals are really a communal event, so food in a Chinese home or restaurant is always shared—you usually have a small bowl or plate to transfer food from the center platters into. Although cutlery is available in many restaurants, it won't hurt to brush up on your use of chopsticks, the utensil of choice.

The standard eating procedure is to hold the bowl close to your mouth and shovel in the contents without any qualms. Noisily slurping up soup and noodles is also the norm. Covering the tablecloth in crumbs, drips, and even spat-out bones is a sign you've enjoyed your meal. It's considered bad manners to point or play with your chopsticks, or to place them on top of your rice bowl when you're finished eating (place the chopsticks horizontally on the table or plate). Avoid, too, leaving your chopsticks standing up in a bowl of rice—they look like the two incense sticks burned at funerals.

If you're invited to a formal Chinese meal, be prepared for great ceremony, endless toasts and speeches, and a grand variety of elaborate dishes. Your host will be seated at the "head" of the round table, which is the seat that faces the door. Wait to be instructed where to sit. Don't start eating until the host takes the first bite, and then simply help yourself as the food comes around, but don't take the last piece on a platter. Always let the food touch your plate before bringing it up to your mouth; eating directly from the serving dish is bad form.

For information on food-related health issues, see Health, below.

MEALS AND MEALTIMES

Food is a central part of Chinese culture, and so eating should be a major activity on any trip to China. Breakfast is not usually a big deal—congee, or rice porridge (*zhou*) is the standard dish. Most mid- and upper-end hotels do big buffet spreads, whereas blooming café chains provide lattes and croissants in China's major cities.

Snacks are a food group in themselves. There's no shortage of steaming street stalls selling kebabs, grilled meat or chicken, bowls of noodle soup, and the ubiquituous *baozi* (stuffed dumplings). Many visitors seem to loathe eating from stalls—you'd be missing out on some of the best nibbles around, though. Pick a place where lots of locals are eating to be on the safe side.

The food in hotel restaurants is usually acceptable but vastly overpriced. Restaurants frequented by locals always serve tastier fare at better prices. Don't shy from trying establishments without an English menu—a good phrase book and lots of pointing can usually get you what you want.

If you're craving Western food (or sushi or a curry), rest assured that big cities have plenty of American fast-food chains, and sometimes world-class international restaurants, too. Most higher-end Chinese restaurants have a Western menu, but you're usually safer sticking to the Chinese food.

Meals in China are served early: breakfast until 9 am, lunch between 11 and 2, and dinner from 5 to 9.

Unless otherwise noted, the restaurants listed in this guide are open daily for lunch and dinner.

PAYING

At most restaurants you ask for the bill (mai dan) at the end of the meal, as you do back home. At cheap noodle bars and street stands you often pay up front. Only very upmarket restaurants accept payment by credit card.

RESERVATIONS AND DRESS

Regardless of where you are, it's a good idea to make a reservation if you can. In some places (Hong Kong, for example), it's expected. We only mention them specifically when reservations are essential (there's no other way you'll ever get a table) or when they are not accepted. For popular restaurants, book as far ahead as you can (often 30 days), and reconfirm as soon as you arrive. (Large parties should always call ahead to check the reservations policy.) We mention dress only when men are required to wear a jacket or a jacket and tie.

WINES, BEER, AND SPIRITS

Forget tea, today the people's drink of choice is beer. Massively popular among Chinese men, it's still a bit of a no-no for Chinese women, however. Tsingtao, China's most popular brew, is a 4% lager that comes in liter bottles and is usually cheaper than water. Many regions have their own local breweries, too, and international brands are also available.

When you see "wine" on the menu, it's usually referring to sweet fruit wines or distilled rice wine. The most famous brand of Chinese liquor is Maotai, a distilled liquor ranging in strength from 35% to 53% proof. Like most firewaters, it's an acquired taste.

There are basically no licensing laws in China, so you can drink anywhere, and at any time, provided you can find a place open to serve you.

▌ ELECTRICITY

The electrical current in China is 220 volts, 50 cycles alternating current (AC) so most American appliances can't be used without a transformer. A universal adapter is especially useful in China, as wall outlets come in a bewildering variety of configurations: two- and three-pronged round plugs, as well as two-pronged flat sockets. Although blackouts are uncommon in Chinese cities, villages occasionally lose power for short periods of time.

Consider making a small investment in a universal adapter, which has several types of plugs in one lightweight, compact unit. Most laptops and cell-phone chargers are dual voltage (i.e., they operate equally well on 110 and 220 volts), so require only an adapter. These days the same is true of small appliances such as hair dryers. Always check labels and manufacturer instructions to be sure. Don't use 110-volt outlets marked for shavers only for high-wattage appliances such as hair dryers.

Contacts Steve Kropla's Help for World Travelers (⊕ *www.kropla.com*) has information on electrical and telephone plugs around the world. **Walkabout Travel Gear** (⊕ *www. walkabouttravelgear.com*) has a good coverage of electricity under "adapters."

▌ EMERGENCIES

If you lose your passport, contact your embassy immediately. Embassy officials can also advise you on how to proceed in case of other emergencies. The staff at your hotel may be able to provide an interpreter if you need to report an emergency or crime to doctors or the police. Most police officers and hospital staff members don't speak English, though you may find one or two people who do.

Ambulances generally offer just a means of transport, not medical aid; taking a taxi is quicker, and means you can choose the hospital you want to go to. Where possible, go to a private clinic catering to expats—prices are sky-high, but so are their hygiene and medical standards. Most have reliable 24-hour pharmacies.

U.S. Embassy and Consulate United States Consulate (⊠ *1469 Huaihai Zhong Lu, Xuhui District, Shanghai* ☎ *021/3271–4650; 021/6433–3936 for after-hours emergencies* ⊠ *Citizen Services Section, Westgate Mall, 8th fl., 1038 Nanjing Xi Lu, Jingan District* ☎ *021/3217–4650* ⊕ *www.shanghai. usembassy-china.org.cn).* **United States Embassy** (⊠ *55 Anjialou Lu, Chaoyang District, Beijing* ☎ *010/8531–3000* ⊕ *www.beijing.*

WORD OF MOUTH

Was the service stellar or not up to snuff? Did the food give you shivers of delight or leave you cold? Did the prices and portions make you happy or sad? Rate restaurants and write your own reviews in "Travel Ratings" or start a discussion about your favorite places in "Travel Talk" on www. fodors.com. Your comments might even appear in our books. Yes, you, too, can be a correspondent!

usembassy-china.org.cn). **United States Citizens Services** (⊠ *4 Ling Shi Guan Rd., Chengdu* ☎ *028/8558–3992* ⊕ *www.chengdu. usembassy-china.org.cn* ⊠ *1 South Shamian St., Guangzhou* ☎ *020/8518–7605; 020/8121– 6077 for after-hours emergencies* ⊕ *www. guangzhou.usembassy-china.org.cn).*

General Emergency Contacts Ambulance (☎ *120).* **Fire** (☎ *119).* **Police** (☎ *110).*

▌ HEALTH

The most common types of illnesses are caused by contaminated food and water. Especially in developing countries, drink only bottled, boiled, or purified water and drinks; don't drink from public fountains or use ice. You should even consider using bottled water to brush your teeth. Make sure food has been thoroughly cooked and is served to you fresh and hot; avoid vegetables and fruits that you haven't washed (in bottled or purified water) or peeled yourself. If you have problems, mild cases of traveler's diarrhea may respond to Imodium (known generically as loperamide) or Pepto-Bismol. Be sure to drink plenty of fluids; if you can't keep fluids down, seek medical help immediately. Tap water in major cities like Beijing and Shanghai is safe for brushing teeth, but buy bottled water to drink and check to see that the bottle is sealed.

Infectious diseases can be airborne or passed via mosquitoes and ticks and through direct or indirect physical contact with animals or people. Some, including Norwalk-like viruses that affect your digestive tract, can be passed along through contaminated food. If you are traveling in an area where malaria is prevalent, use a repellant containing DEET and take malaria-prevention medication before, during, and after your trip as directed by your physician. Condoms can help prevent most sexually transmitted diseases, but they aren't absolutely reliable, and their quality varies from country to country. Speak with your physician and/or check the CDC or World Health Organization Web sites for health alerts, particularly if you're pregnant, traveling with children, or have a chronic illness.

SHOTS AND MEDICATIONS

No immunizations are required for entry into China, but it's a good idea to be immunized against typhoid and Hepatitis A and B before traveling, as well as to get routine tetanus-diphtheria and measles boosters. In winter a flu vaccination is also smart, especially if you're infection-prone or are a senior citizen. ■TIP➜ In summer months malaria is a risk in tropical and rural areas, especially Hainan and Yunnan provinces—consult your doctor four to six weeks before your trip, as preventive treatments vary. The risk of contracting malaria in cities is small.

Health Warnings National Centers for Disease Control & Prevention (CDC ☎ 877/394-8747 international travelers' health line ⊕ www.cdc.gov/travel). **World Health Organization** (WHO ⊕ www.who.int).

SPECIFIC ISSUES IN CHINA

Even at China's public hospitals foreigners need to pay fees to register, to see a doctor, and then for all tests and medication. Prices are cheap compared to the fancy foreigner clinics in major cities, where you pay $100 to $150 just for a consultation. However, most doctors at public hospitals don't speak English, and hygiene standards are low—all the more reason to take out medical insurance.

Hong Kong has excellent public and private health care. Foreigners have to pay for both, so insurance is a good idea. Even for lesser complaints, private doctors charge a fortune: head to a public hospital if money is tight. In an emergency you'll always receive treatment first and get the bill afterward—Y570 is the standard ER charge.

The best place to start looking for a suitable doctor is through your hotel concierge, then the local Public Security Bureau. If you become seriously ill or are injured, it is best to fly home, or at least to Hong Kong, as quickly as possible. In Hong Kong, English-speaking doctors are widely available.

Pneumonia and influenza are common among travelers returning from China—talk to your doctor about inoculations before you leave. If you need to buy prescription drugs, try to go to the pharmacies of reputable private hospitals. Do *not* buy them in street-side pharmacies, as the quality control is unreliable.

Avian influenza, commonly known as bird flu, is a form of influenza that affects birds (including poultry) but can be passed to humans. It causes initial flu symptoms, followed by respiratory and organ failure. Although rare, it's often lethal. There have been several outbreaks in Hong Kong and China since 2003. The Hong Kong Government now exercises strict control over poultry farms and markets, and there are signs all over town warning against contact with birds. Things aren't so well controlled on the mainland, however, so be sure that any poultry or eggs you consume are well cooked.

Severe acute respiratory syndrome (SARS), also known as atypical pneumonia, is a respiratory illness caused by a strain of coronavirus that was first reported in parts of Asia—notably Hong Kong—in early 2003. Symptoms include a fever greater than 100.4°F (38°C), shortness of breath, and other flulike symptoms. The disease is thought to spread by close person-to-person contact, particularly respiratory droplets and secretions transmitted through the eyes, nose, or mouth. SARS hasn't returned to Hong Kong or China, but many experts believe that it or other contagious, upper-respiratory viruses will continue to be a seasonal health concern.

OVER-THE-COUNTER REMEDIES

Most pharmacies in big Chinese cities carry over-the-counter Western medicines and traditional Chinese medicines. By and large, you need to ask for the generic name of the drug you're looking for, not a brand name. Acetaminophen—or Tylenol—is often known as paracetomol in Hong Kong. In big cities reputable pharmacies like Watsons are usually a better bet than no-name ones.

▌ HOURS OF OPERATION

Most banks and government offices are open weekdays 9 to 5 or 6, although close for lunch (sometime between noon and 2). Some bank branches and most CTS tour desks in hotels keep longer hours and are open Saturday (and occasionally Sunday) mornings. Many hotel currency-exchange desks stay open 24 hours. Museums open from roughly 9 to 6, six or seven days a week. Everything in China grinds to a halt for the first two or three days of Chinese New Year (sometime in mid-January to February), and opening hours are often reduced for the rest of that season.

Pharmacies are open daily from 8:30 or 9 to 6 or 7. Some large pharmacies stay open until 9 or even later. Shops and department stores are generally open daily 8 to 8; some stores stay open even later in summer, in popular tourist areas, or during peak tourist season.

HOLIDAYS

National holidays in mainland China include New Year's Day (January 1); Spring Festival aka Chinese New Year (late January/early February); Qingming Jie (April 4); International Labor Day (May 1); Dragon Boat Festival (late May/ early June); anniversary of the founding of the Communist Party of China (July 1); anniversary of the founding of the Chinese People's Liberation Army (August 1); and National Day—founding of the People's Republic of China in 1949 (October 1); Chongyang Jie or Double Ninth Festival (ninth day of ninth lunar month). Hong Kong celebrates most of these festivals, and also has public holidays at Easter and for Christmas and Boxing Day (December 25 and 26). (⇨ *Festivals and Seasonal Events in Chapter 1.*)

MAIL

Sending international mail from China is extremely reliable. Airmail letters to any place in the world should take five to 14 days. Express Mail Service (EMS) is available to many international destinations. Letters within any city arrive the next day, and mail to the rest of China takes a day or two longer. Domestic mail can be subject to search, so don't send sensitive materials such as religious or political literature, as you might cause the recipient trouble.

Service is more reliable if you mail letters from post offices rather than mailboxes. Buy envelopes here, too, as there are standardized sizes in China. You need to glue stamps onto envelopes, as they're not self-adhesive. Most post offices are open daily between 8 am and 7 pm; many keep longer hours. Your hotel can usually send letters for you, too.

You can use the Roman alphabet to write an address. Do not use red ink, which has a negative connotation. You must also include a six-digit zip code for mail within China. Sending airmail postcards costs Y4.50 and letters Y5 to Y7.

Long-term guests can receive mail at their hotels. Otherwise, the best place to receive mail is at the American Express office. Most major Chinese cities have American Express offices with client-mail service. Be sure to bring your American Express card, as the staff will not give you the mail without seeing it.

SHIPPING PACKAGES

It's easy to ship packages home from China. Take what you want to send *unpacked* to the post office—everything will be sewn up officially into satisfying linen-bound packages, a service that costs a few yuan. You have to fill in lengthy forms—enclosing a photocopy of receipts for the goods inside isn't a bad idea, as they may be opened by customs along the line. Large antiques stores often offer reliable shipping services that take care of customs in China. Large international couriers operating in China include DHL, Federal Express, and UPS—next-day delivery for a 1-kilogram (2.2-pound) package starts at about Y300. Your hotel can also arrange shipping parcels, but there's usually a hefty markup.

Express Services DHL (☎ *800/810–8000* ⊕ *www.cn.dhl.com*). **FedEx** (☎ *800/988–1888* ⊕ *www.fedex.com*). **UPS** (☎ *800/820–8388* ⊕ *www.ups.com*).

❚ MONEY

China is a cheap destination by most North Americans' standards, but expect your dollar to do more for you in smaller cities than in pricey Shanghai or Beijing. The exception to the rule is Hong Kong, where eating and sleeping prices are on a par with those in the United States.

In mainland China the best places to convert your dollars into yuan are at your hotel's front desk or a branch of a major bank, such as Bank of China, CITIC, or HSBC. All these operate with standardized government rates—anything cheaper is illegal, and thus risky. You need to present your passport to change money.

Prices throughout this guide are given for adults. Substantially reduced fees are almost always available for children, students, and senior citizens.

Although credit cards are gaining ground in China, for day-to-day transactions cash is definitely king.

Currency Conversion Google (⊕ *www. google.com*). **Oanda.com** (⊕ *www.oanda.com*). **XE.com** (⊕ *www.xe.com*).

ITEM	AVERAGE COST
Cup of coffee at Starbucks	Y20–Y25
Glass of local beer	Y10–Y30
Cheapest subway ticket	Y2
2-km (1-mi) taxi ride in Beijing or Shanghai	Y10–Y11
Set lunch in a cheap restaurant	Y20
Hour-long foot massage	Y50
Fake Chloé purse	Y200

ATMS AND BANKS

Your own bank will probably charge a fee for using ATMs abroad; the foreign bank you use may also charge a fee. Nevertheless, you'll usually get a better rate of exchange at an ATM than you will at a currency-exchange office or even when changing money in a bank.

❚ **TIP→** PINs with more than four digits are not recognized at ATMs in many countries. If yours has five or more, remember to change it before you leave.

ATMs are widespread in major Chinese cities. The most reliable ATMs are HSBC's. They also have the highest withdrawal limit, which offsets transaction charges. Of the Chinese banks, your best bet for ATMs is the Bank of China, which accepts most foreign cards. That said, machines frequently refuse to give cash for mysterious reasons—move on and try another. On-screen instructions appear automatically in English.

ATMs are widely available throughout Hong Kong—most carry the sign ETC instead of ATM. Subway stations are a good place to look.

CREDIT CARDS

American Express, MasterCard, and Visa are accepted at most hotels and a growing number of upmarket stores and restaurants. Diners Club is less widely accepted.

Throughout this guide, the following abbreviations are used: **AE**, American Express; **DC**, Diners Club; **MC**, Master-Card; and **V**, Visa.

It's a good idea to inform your credit-card company before you travel. Otherwise, the credit-card company might put a hold on your card owing to unusual activity—not a good thing halfway through your trip. Record all your credit-card numbers—as well as the phone numbers to call if your cards are lost or stolen—in a safe place, so you're prepared should something go wrong. Both MasterCard and Visa have general numbers you can call (collect if you're abroad) if your card is lost, but you're better off calling the number of your issuing bank, since MasterCard and Visa usually just transfer you to your bank; your bank's number is usually printed on your card.

If you plan to use your credit card for cash advances, you'll need to apply for a PIN at least two weeks before your trip. Although it's usually cheaper (and safer) to use a credit card abroad for large purchases (so you can cancel payments or be reimbursed if there's a problem), note that some credit-card companies *and* the banks that issue them add substantial percentages to all foreign transactions, whether they're in a foreign currency or not. Check on these fees before leaving home, so there won't be any surprises when you get the bill.

■ TIP➔ Before you charge something, ask the merchant whether or not he or she plans to do a dynamic currency conversion (DCC). In such a transaction the credit-card processor (shop, restaurant, or hotel, not Visa or MasterCard) converts the currency and charges you in dollars. In most cases you'll pay the merchant a 3% fee for this service in addition to any credit-card company and issuing-bank foreign-transaction surcharges.

Dynamic currency conversion programs are becoming increasingly widespread. Merchants who participate in them are supposed to ask whether you want to be charged in dollars or the local currency, but they don't always do so. And even if they do offer you a choice, they may well avoid mentioning the additional surcharges. The good news is that you *do* have a choice. And if this practice really gets your goat, you can avoid it entirely thanks to American Express; with its cards, DCC simply isn't an option.

Reporting Lost Cards American Express (☎ 800/992–3404 in the U.S.; 336/393–1111 collect from abroad ⊕ www.americanexpress. com). **Diners Club** (☎ 800/234–6377 in the U.S.; 303/799–1504 collect from abroad ⊕ www.dinersclub.com). **MasterCard** (☎ 800/622–7747 in the U.S.; 636/722–7111 collect from abroad; 800/110–7309 in China ⊕ www.mastercard.com). **Visa** (☎ 800/847–2911 in the U.S.; 410/581–9994 collect from abroad; 800/711–2911 in China ⊕ www.visa. com).

CURRENCY AND EXCHANGE

The Chinese currency is officially called the yuan (Y), and is also known as *renminbi* (RMB), or "People's Money." You may also hear it called *kuai,* an informal expression like "buck."

Old and new styles of bills circulate in China, and many denominations have both coins and bills. The Bank of China issues bills in denominations of 1 (burgundy), 2 (green), 5 (brown or purple), 10 (turquoise), 20 (brown), 50 (blue or occasionally yellow), and 100 (red). There are 1 yuan coins, too. The yuan subdivides into 10-cent units called *jiao* or *mao*; these come in bills and coins of 1, 2, and 5. The smallest denomination is the *fen,* which comes in coins (and occasionally tiny notes) of 1, 2, and 5. Counterfeiting is rife in China, and even small stores inspect notes with ultraviolet lamps. Change can be a problem—don't expect much success paying for a Y3 purchase with a Y100 note.

Exchange rates in China are fixed by the government daily, so it's equally good at branches of the Bank of China, at big department stores, or at your hotel's exchange desk. Any lower rates are illegal, so you're exposing yourself to scams. A passport is required. Hold on to your exchange receipt, which you need to convert your extra yuan back into dollars.

In Hong Kong the only currency used is the Hong Kong dollar, divided into 100 cents. Three local banks (HSBC, Standard Chartered, and the Bank of China) all issue bills and each has its own designs. At this writing the Hong Kong dollar was pegged to the U.S. dollar at approximately 7.75 Hong Kong dollars to 1 U.S. dollar. There are no currency restrictions in Hong Kong. You can exchange currency at the airport, in hotels, in banks, and through private money changers scattered through the tourist areas. Banks usually have the best rates, but as they charge a flat HK$50 fee for non-account holders, it's better to change large sums infrequently. Currency-exchange offices have no fees, but they offset that with poor rates. Stick to ATMs whenever you can.

■TIP→ Even if a currency-exchange booth has a sign promising no commission, rest assured that there's some kind of huge, hidden fee. (Oh . . . that's right. The sign didn't say no fee.) And as for rates, you're almost always better off getting foreign currency at an ATM or exchanging money at a bank.

■ PASSPORTS AND VISAS

All U.S. citizens, even infants, need a valid passport with a tourist visa stamped in it to enter China (except for Hong Kong, where you only need a valid passport). It's always best to have at least six months' validity on your passport before traveling to Asia.

Getting a tourist visa to China (known as an "L" visa) in the United States is straightforward. Standard visas are for single-entry stays of up to 30 days, and are valid for 90 days from the day of issue (NOT the day of entry), so don't get your visa too far in advance. The cost for a tourist visa issued to a U.S. citizen is $140;

citizens of other countries can expect to pay between $30 and $90.

Travel agents in Hong Kong can also issue visas to visit mainland China—though this was disrupted during the Olympics, and regulations can change during times of unrest. Note: The visa application will ask your occupation. The Chinese government doesn't look favorably upon those who work in publishing or the media. People in these professions routinely state "teacher" under "occupation." Before you go, contact the embassy or consulate of the People's Republic of China to gauge the current mood.

Hong Kong Travel Agent China Travel Service (*CTS* ☎ *852/2851–1700* ⊕ *www.ctshk. com*) has 36 branches all over Hong Kong.

Children traveling with only one parent do not need a notarized letter of permission to enter China. However, as these kinds of policies can change, being over-prepared isn't a bad idea.

Under no circumstances should you over-stay your visa. To extend your visa, stop by the Entry and Exit Administration Office of the local branch of the Public Security Bureau a week before your visa expires. The office is known as the PSB or the Foreigner's Police; most are open weekdays 9 to 11:30 and 1:30 to 4:30. The process is extremely bureaucratic, but it's usually no problem to get a month's extension on a tourist visa. You need to bring your registration of temporary residency from your hotel and your passport, which you generally need to leave for five to seven days (so do any transactions requiring it beforehand). If you are trying to extend a business visa, you'll need the above items as well as a letter from the business that originally invited you to China saying it would like to extend your stay for work reasons. Rules are always changing, so you will probably need to go to the office at least twice to get all your papers in order.

The Web site ⊕ *www.visatoasia.com/ china.html* provides up-to-date information on visa applications to China.

Chinese Visa Information Chinese Consulate, New York (☏ *212/244–9456* ⊕ *www. nyconsulate.prchina.org*). **Visa Office of Chinese Embassy, Washington** (☏ *202/495– 2266* ⊕ *www.china-embassy.org*). **Visa to Asia** (⊕ *www.visatoasia.com/china.html*).

GENERAL REQUIREMENTS FOR MAINLAND CHINA	
Passport	Must be valid for six months after date of arrival
Visa	Required for U.S. citizens ($140)
Required Vaccinations	None
Recommended Vaccinations	Hepatitis A and B, typhoid, influenza, booster for tetanus-diphtheria
Driving	Chinese driver's license required

▌ PACKING

Most Chinese people dress for comfort, so you can plan to do the same. There's little risk of offending people with your dress: Westerners tend to attract attention regardless of their attire. Fashion capitals Hong Kong and Shanghai are the exceptions to the comfort rule: slop around in flip-flops and worn denims and you WILL feel that there's a neon "tourist" sign over your head. Opt for your smarter jeans or capri pants for sightseeing there.

Sturdy, comfortable walking shoes are a must: go for closed shoes over Tevas, as dust and toe-stomping crowds make them impractical. Northern Chinese summers are dusty and baking hot, so slacks, capris, and sturdy shorts are best. A raincoat, especially a light Goretex one or a fold-up poncho, is useful for an onset of rainy weather, especially in Southern China. During the harsh winters, thermal long johns are a lifesaver—especially in low-star hotel rooms.

That said, in urban centers you can prepare to be unprepared: big Chinese cities are a clothes shopper's paradise. If a bulky jacket's going to put you over the airline limit, buy one in China and leave it behind when you go. All the other woollies—and silkies, the local insulator of choice—you'll need go for a song, as do brand-name jackets. Scarves, gloves, and hats, all musts, are also easy to find.

Most good hotels have reliable overnight laundry services, though costs can rack up on a long trip. Look outside your hotel for cheaper laundries, and bring some concentrated travel detergent for small or delicate items. Note that it's often cheaper to buy things than have your own laundered, so if you're even a little interested in shopping, consider bringing an extra, foldable bag to cart purchases home in.

Keep packets of Kleenex and antibacterial hand wipes in your day pack—paper isn't a feature of many Chinese restrooms, and you often can't buy it in smaller towns. A small flashlight with extra batteries is also useful. The brands in Chinese pharmacies are limited, so take adequate stocks of your potions-n-lotions, feminine-hygiene products (tampons are especially hard to find), and birth control. All of these things are easy to get in Hong Kong.

In your carry-on luggage, pack an extra pair of eyeglasses or contact lenses and enough of any medication you take to last a few days longer than the entire trip.

If you're planning a longer trip or will be using local tour guides, bring a few inexpensive items from your home country as gifts. Popular gifts are candy, T-shirts, and small cosmetic items such as lipstick and nail polish—double-check that none were made in China. Be wary about giving American magazines and books as gifts, as these can be considered propaganda and get your Chinese friends in trouble.

▌ RESTROOMS

Public restrooms abound in mainland China—the street, parks, restaurants, department stores, and major tourist attractions are all likely locations. Most charge a small fee (usually less than Y1), but seldom provide Western-style facilities or private booths. Instead, expect squat toilets, open troughs, and rusty spigots; WC signs at intersections point the way to these facilities. Toilet paper is a rarity, so carry tissues and antibacterial hand wipes in your day pack. The restrooms in the newest shopping plazas, fast-food outlets, and deluxe restaurants catering to foreigners are generally on a par with American restrooms. In post-SARS Hong Kong, public restrooms are well maintained. Alternatively, dip into malls or the lobby of big international hotels to use their loos.

Find a Loo The Bathroom Diaries (⊕ www. thebathroomdiaries.com) is flush with unsanitized info on restrooms the world over—each one located, reviewed, and rated.

▌ SAFETY

There is little violent crime against tourists in China, partly because the penalties are severe for those who are caught—China's yearly death-sentence tolls run into the thousands. Single women can move about without too much hassle. Handbag-snatching and pickpocketing do happen in markets and on crowded buses or trains—keep an eye open and your money safe, and you should have no problems. Use the lockbox in your hotel room to store any valuables, but always carry your passport with you for identification purposes.

China is full of people looking to make a quick buck. The most common scam involves people persuading you to go with them for a tea ceremony, which is often so pleasant that you don't smell a rat until several hundred dollars appear on your credit-card bill. "Art students" who pressure you into buying work is another common scam. The same rules that apply to hostess bars worldwide are also true in China. Avoiding such scams is as easy as refusing *all* unsolicited services—be it from taxi or pedicab drivers, tour guides, or potential "friends."

▌**TIP→ Distribute your cash, credit cards, IDs, and other valuables between a deep front pocket, an inside jacket or vest pocket, and a hidden money pouch. Don't reach for the money pouch once you're in public.**

Chinese traffic is as manic as it looks, and survival of the fittest (or the biggest) is the main rule. Crossing streets can be an extreme sport. Drivers rarely give pedestrians the right-of-way, and don't even look for pedestrians when making a right turn on a red light. Cyclists have less power but are just as aggressive.

The severely polluted air of China's big cities can bring on, or aggravate, respiratory problems. If you're a sufferer, take the cue from locals, who wear surgical masks, or a scarf or bandana as protection.

Contact Transportation Security Administration (*TSA*; ⊕ www.tsa.gov)

▌ TAXES

There is no sales tax in China or Hong Kong. Mainland hotels charge a 5% tax; bigger, joint-venture hotels also add a 10% to 15% service fee. Some restaurants charge a 10% service fee.

▌ TIME

The whole of China is 8 hours ahead of London, 13 hours ahead of New York, 14 hours ahead of Chicago, and 16 hours ahead of Los Angeles. There's no daylight saving time, so subtract an hour in summer.

Time Zones Timeanddate.com (⊕ *www.timeanddate.com/worldclock*) can help you figure out the correct time anywhere in the world.

▌ TIPPING

Tipping is a tricky issue in China. It's officially forbidden by the government, and locals simply don't do it. In general, follow their lead without qualms. Nevertheless, the practice is beginning to catch on, especially among tour guides, who often expect Y10 a day. Official CTS representatives aren't allowed to accept tips, but you can give them candy, T-shirts, and other small gifts. You don't need to tip in restaurants or in taxis.

In Hong Kong, hotels and major restaurants usually add a 10% service charge; in almost all cases, this money does not go to the waiters and waitresses. Add on up to 10% more for good service. Tipping restroom attendants is common, but it is generally not the custom to leave an additional tip in taxis and hair salons.

▌ TOURS

Most guided tours to China take in three or four major cities, often combined with a Yangtze River cruise or a visit to far-flung Tibet. You get a day or two in each place, with the same sights featured in most tours. If you want to explore a given city in any kind of depth, you're better doing it by yourself or getting a private guide.

Shopping stops plague China tours, so inquire before booking as to when, where, and how many to expect. Although you're never obliged to buy anything, they can take up big chunks of your valuable travel time, and the products offered are always ridiculously overpriced. Even on the best tours, you can count on having to sit through at least one or two.

Small groups and excellent guides are what Overseas Adventure Travel takes pride in. The Adventure Center has a huge variety of China packages, including trekking, cycling, and family tours. China Focus Travel has 10 different China tours—they squeeze in a lot for your money. Ritz Tours is a mid-range agency specializing in East Asian tours. R. Crusoe & Son is an offbeat company that organizes small group or tailor-made private tours. For something more mainstream, try Pacific Delight; for serious luxury, head to Artisans of Leisure or Imperial Tours. If you're concerned about responsible tourism, try Wild China, a high-caliber local company with some of the most unusual trips around. For example, one of their cultural trips explores China's little-known Jewish history.

Not all of the companies we list include air travel in their packages. Check this when you're researching your trip.

Recommended Companies Artisans of Leisure (☎ 800/214–8144 ⊕ *www.artisansofleisure.com*). **China Focus Travel** (☎ 800/868–7244 ⊕ *www.chinafocustravel.com*). **Imperial Tours** (☎ 888/888–1970 ⊕ *www.imperialtours.net*). **Overseas Adventure Travel** (☎ 800/493–6824 ⊕ *www.oattravel.com*). **Pacific Delight** (☎ 800/221–7179 ⊕ *www.pacificdelighttours.com*). **R. Crusoe & Son** (☎ 800/585–8555 ⊕ *www.rcrusoe.com*). **Ritz Tours** (☎ 626/289–7777 ⊕ *www.ritztours.com*). **The Adventure Center** (☎ 800/228–8747 ⊕ *www.adventurecenter.com*). **Wild China** (☎ 010/6465–6602 ⊕ *www.wildchina.com*).

SPECIAL-INTEREST TOURS

ART

Ethnic folk art and the Silk Road are two of the focuses of Wild China's art and architecture tours.

Contacts Wild China (☎ 010/6465–6602 ⊕ *www.wildchina.com*).

BIKING

Wild China runs an eight-day bird-watching tour in Yunnan, southwest China.

Contacts **Wild China** (☎ *010/6465–6602* ⊕ *www.wildchina.com*).

CULTURE

Local guides are often creative when it comes to history and culture, so having an expert with you can make a big difference. Learning is the focus of Smithsonian Journeys' small-group tours, which are led by university professors. China experts also lead National Geographic's trips, though all that knowledge doesn't come cheap. Wild China is a local company with some of the most unusual trips around, including visits to ethnic minority groups, Tibet, and little-known Xinjiang province, as well as more conventional historical trips and journeys focusing on traditional festivals.

Contacts **National Geographic Expeditions** (☎ *888/966–8687* ⊕ *www. nationalgeographicexpeditions.com*). **Smithsonian Journeys** (☎ *877/338–8687* ⊕ *www. smithsonianjourneys.org*). **Wild China** (☎ *010/6465–6602* ⊕ *www.wildchina.com*).

CULINARY

Artisans of Leisure's culinary tour takes in Shanghai and Beijing from the cities' choicest establishments, with prices to match. Intrepid Travel is an Australian company specializing in budget, independent travel. Their China Gourmet Traveler tour includes market visits, cooking demonstrations, and lots of eating at down-to-earth restaurants. Imperial Tours Culinary Tour combines sightseeing with cooking lectures and demonstrations, and lots of five-star dining.

Contacts **Artisans of Leisure** (☎ *800/214–8144* ⊕ *www.artisansofleisure.com*). **Imperial Tours** (☎ *888/888–1970* ⊕ *www.imperialtours. net*). **Intrepid Travel** (☎ *203/469–0214 in the U.S.* ⊕ *www.intrepidtravel.com*).

ECOTOURS

Wild China's nature-trekking tours include a weeklong hike through a Sichuan nature reserve, home to the giant panda.

Contacts **Wild China** (☎ *010/6465–6602* ⊕ *www.wildchina.com*).

GOLF

China Highlights organizes short golf packages that combine sightseeing with golfing in Beijing, Shanghai, Kunming, Guangzhou, and Guilin.

Contacts **China Highlights** (☎ *800/268–2918* ⊕ *www.chinahighlights.com*).

HIKING

The Adventure Center's China hikes include an eight-day walk along the Great Wall, a three-week walk along the route of the Communists' 1934 Long March, and a trip that combines mild hikes with Yangtze cruises and sightseeing. Wild China runs ecologically responsible treks in different parts of China, including Tibet.

Contacts **The Adventure Center** (☎ *800/228–8747* ⊕ *www.adventurecenter. com*). **Wild China** (☎ *010/6465–6602* ⊕ *www. wildchina.com*).

▮ VISITOR INFOMATION

For general information before you go, including advice on tours, insurance, and safety, call or visit the Web site of the China National Tourist Office.

The two best-known Chinese travel agencies are the state-run China International Travel Service (CITS) and China Travel Service (CTS), both under the same government ministry. Although they have some tourist information, they are businesses, so don't expect endless resources if you're not buying a tour or flight through them. In theory, CTS offices cater to sightseeing around their area, and CITS arranges packages and tours from overseas; in reality, their services overlap.

The Hong Kong Tourism Board has stacks of online information about events, sightseeing, shopping, and dining in Hong Kong. They also organize tour packages from the United States, and local sightseeing tours.

CONTACTS

China International Travel Service (*CITS* ☎ *626/568–8993* ⊕ *www.citsusa.com*). **China National Tourist Office** (☎ *888/760–8218 New York* ☎ *800/670–2228 Los Angeles* ⊕ *www.cnto.org*). **China Travel Service** (*CTS* ☎ *800/899–8618* ⊕ *www.chinatravelservice. com*). **Hong Kong Tourist Board** (*HKTB* ⊕ *www.discoverhongkong.com*).

ONLINE TRAVEL TOOLS

The Web sites listed in this book are in English. If you come across a Chinese-language site you think might be useful, copy the URL into Google, then click the "Translate this page" link. Translations are literal, but generally work for finding out information like opening hours or prices.

ALL ABOUT CHINA

China Digital Times (⊕ *www. chinadigitaltimes.net*): an excellent Berkeley-run site tracking China-related news and culture in serious depth. **China National Tourism Office** (⊕ *www.cnto.org*): a general overview of traveling in China. **China International Travel Service (CITS)** (⊕ *www.cits.net*): the largest travel agency in China. **China Travel Services (U.S. site)** (*CTS* ⊕ *www.chinatravelservice.com*): the state-run travel agency is a helpful starting place when planning trips.

Chinese Government Portal (⊕ *www.english. gov.cn*). **China Site** (⊕ *www.chinasite.com*): a comprehensive portal with links to thousands of China-related Web sites. **Hong Kong Government** (⊕ *www.info.gov.hk*). **The Oriental List** (⊕ *www.datasinica.com*): a free Internet mailing list giving extremely reliable information about travel in China.

BUSINESS

Business in Hong Kong (⊕ *www.business.gov. hk*): a government-run site packed with advice. **China Business Weekly** (⊕ *www.chinadaily. com.cn/english/bw/bwtop.html*): a weekly magazine from *China Daily* newspaper. **Chinese Government Business Site** (⊕ *english. gov.cn/business.htm*) provides news, links, and information on business-related legal issues from the Chinese government.

CULTURE AND ENTERTAINMENT

Chinese Culture (⊕ *www.chinaculture.org*): detailed, searchable database with information on Chinese art, literature, film, history, and more. The **Leisure and Cultural Services Department** (⊕ *www.lcsd.gov.hk*) has access to Web sites for all of Hong Kong's museums and parks through this government portal.

LOCAL INSIGHT

Asia Expat (⊕ *www.asiaxpat.com*) gives advice and listings from foreigners living in Beijing, Hong Kong, Guangzhou, and Shanghai. **Asia City Magazines** (⊕ *www.asia-city.com*): an online version of quirky weekly rags with the lowdown on everything happening in Shanghai and Hong Kong.

NEWSPAPERS

China Daily (⊕ *www.chinadaily.com.cn*): the leading English-language daily. *People's Daily* (⊕ *www.english.peopledaily.com.cn*): English edition of China's most popular—and most propagandistic—local daily. *South China Morning Post* (⊕ *www.scmp.com*): Hong Kong's leading English-language daily.

GREAT CHINESE READS

Big Name Fiction: Gao Xinjiang's *Soul Mountain*, Ha Jin's *Waiting*, and Dai Sijie's *Mr. Muo's Traveling Couch*. **China 101:** *The China Reader: The Reform Era*, edited by Orville Schell and David Shambaugh; *The Search for Modern China*, by Jonathan Spence; and *A History of Hong Kong*, by Frank Welsh. **How about Mao:** Dr. Li Zhisui's *The Private Life of Chairman Mao*.

INDEX

PHOTO CREDITS

1, Boaz Rottem/age fotostock 2-3, Alvaro Leiva / age fotostock. 5, lu linsheng/iStockphoto. Chapter 1: Experience China. 8-9, José Fuste Raga/age fotostock. 10, Holly Peabody, Fodors.com member. 11 (left), Hong Kong Tourism Board. 11 (right), DK.samco/Shutterstock. 12, Iain Masterton / age fotostock. 13, SEUX Paule / age fotostock. 14, Brian Jeffery Beggerly/Flickr. 15 (left), Hong Kong Tourism Board. 15 (right), Hotel G Beijing. 16 (left), Jarno Gonzalez Zarraonandia/iStockphoto. 16 (top), fotohunter/Shutterstock. 16 (bottom), Jonathan Larsen/Shutterstock. 17 (top left), Hung Chung Chih/Shutterstock. 17 (bottom left), Peter Mukherjee/iStockphoto. 17 (right), loong/Shutterstock. 18 (left), Chunni4691/Shutterstock. 18 (top right), Holger Mette/iStockphoto. 18 (bottom right), George Clerk/iStockphoto. 19 (top left), richliy/Shutterstock. 19 (bottom left), Hung Chung Chih/Shutterstock. 19 (right), Ivan Walsh/Flickr. 20, John Leung/Shutterstock. 21 (left), Eastimages/Shutterstock. 21 (right), gary718/Shutterstock. 22, Marc van Vuren/Shutterstock. 23 (left), Gretchen Winters, Fodors.com member. 23 (right), Steve Slawsky. 24, Sze Kit Poon/iStockphoto. 25 (left), oksana.perkins/Shutterstock. 25 (right), Andrew Kerr/Shutterstock. 32, bbobo, Fodors.com member. 33, qingqing/Shutterstock. 34 (left), Kowloonese/Wikimedia Commons. 34 (top right), Daniel Shichman & Yael Tauger/Wikimedia Commons. 34 (bottom right), Wikimedia Commons. 35 (left), Hung Chung Chih/Shutterstock. 35 (right), rodho/Shutterstock. 36, (left), Chinneeb/Wikimedia Commons. 36 (top right), B_cool/Wikimedia Commons. 36 (bottom right), Imperial Painter/Wikimedia Commons. 37 (left and bottom right), Wikimedia Commons. 37 (top right), Joe Brandt/iStockphoto. 38 (top left, bottom left, and top right), Wikimedia Commons. 38 (bottom right), K.T. Thompson/wikipedia.org. 39 (top left), Wikimedia Commons. 39 (bottom left), ImagineChina. 39 (right), tomislav domes/Flickr. 40, TAO IMAGES/age fotostock. Chapter 2: Beijing. 41, TAO IMAGES/age fotostock. 42, claudio zaccherini/Shutterstock. 43 (left), yxm2008/Shutterstock. 43 (right), Johann 'Jo' Guzman, Fodors.com member. 44, sanglei slei/iStockphoto. 47, TAO IMAGES/age fotostock. 52, lu linsheng/iStockphoto. 53 (top), TAO IMAGES/age fotostock. 53 (bottom), Bob Balestri/iStockphoto. 54, Lance Lee | AsiaPhoto.com/iStockphoto. 55 (left), Jiping Lai/iStockphoto. 55 (right 1), May Wong/Flickr. 55 (right 2), William Perry/iStockphoto. 55 (right 3), bing liu/iStockphoto. 55 (right 4), William Perry/iStockphoto. 56 (bottom left and right), Wikimedia Commons. 56 (top), Helena Lovincic/iStockphoto. 57 (top), rehoboth foto/Shutterstock. 57 (bottom left and right), Wikimedia Commons. 61, P. Narayan/age fotostock. 65, Jose Fuste Raga/age fotostock. 68, Lim Yong Hian/Shutterstock. 77, TAO IMAGES/age fotostock. 78, View Stock/age fotostock. 85, TAO IMAGES/age fotostock. 90, patrick frilet/age fotostock. 98 (top), Red Capital Residence. 98 (bottom left), Hotel G Beijing. 98 (bottom right), Epoque Hotels. 103 (top), Hyatt Hotels. 103 (bottom), Starwood Hotels and Resorts. 109, Werner Bachmeier/age fotostock. 112-13, Sylvain Grandadam/age fotostock. 118, Christian Kober/age fotostock. 123, TAO IMAGES/age fotostock. 130, John W. Warden/age fotostock. 131, Wikimedia Commons. 132-33, Liu Jianmin/age fotostock. 136, Alan Crawford/iStockphoto. 137, Eugenia Kim/iStockphoto. 138, Jarno Gonzalez/iStockphoto. 139, Chris Ronneseth/iStockphoto. 142, JTB Photo/age fotostock. Chapter 3: Beijing to Shanghai. 149, Steve Vidler/age fotostock. 150, Chi King/Flickr. 151 (left), www.seefarseeeast.com/Flickr. 151 (right), Gina Smith/iStockphoto. 152, suecan1/Flickr. 159, richliy/Shutterstock 164, View Stock/age fotostock. 171, David Lyons/age fotostock. 181, sunxuejun/Shutterstock. 188, nozomiiqel/Flickr. 195, Jeff Greenberg/age fotostock. 198, JTB Photo/age fotostock. 205, White Star / Spierenb/age fotostock. 209, suecan1/Flickr. 216, Karl Johaentges/age fotostock. 222, Philippe Michel/age fotostock. Chapter 4: Shanghai. 231, Lucas Vallecillos/age fotostock. 232, bjdlzx/iStockphoto. 233 (left), claudio zaccherini/Shutterstock. 233 (right), Georgio/Wikimedia Commons. 234, Augapfel/Flickr. 239, Tibor Bognar/age fotostock. 244, claudio zaccherini/Shutterstock. 249 and 252-53, José Fuste Raga/age fotostock. 261, SALDARI/age fotostock. 267, Karl Johaentges/age fotostock. 270, JTB Photo/age fotostock. 275, Hippo/age fotostock. 286 (top), Starwood Hotels & Resorts. 286 (bottom), JIA Shanghai. 293 (top), URBN Hotels. 293 (bottom left), Shangri-La Hotels and Resorts. 293 (bottom right), Starwood Hotels & Resorts. 298, 303, and 309, Karl Johaentges/age fotostock. Chapter 5: Eastern China. 317, TAO IMAGES/age fotostock. 318, Jon Mullen/iStockphoto. 319 (left), robert van beets/iStockphoto. 319 (right), hxdbzxy/Shutterstock. 320, China National Tourist Office. 327, SuperStock/age fotostock. 330 and 335, JTB Photo/age fotostock. 336, TAO IMAGES/age fotostock. 341, JTB Photo/age fotostock. 348, SuperStock/age fotostock. 349 (top), TAO IMAGES/age fotostock. 349 (bottom), Mark52/Shutterstock. 350, Shigeki Tanaka/Shutterstock. 351 (left), Yuan yanwu - Imaginechina. 351 (top right), Huiping Zhu/iStockphoto. 351 (bottom right), richliy/Shutterstock. 357, Christian Kober/age fotostock. 362, Shigeki Tanaka/age fotostock. Chapter 6: Hong Kong. 367, Hemis / Alamy. 368, Hong Kong Tourism Board. 369, Ella Hanochi/iStockphoto. 370, Laoshi/iStockphoto. 376, Amanda Hall / age fotostock. 381, Dallas & John Heaton / age fotostock. 386, Ron Yue / Alamy. 389, Raga Jose Fuste / age fotostock. 394, cozyta/Shutterstock. 405, BrokenSphere/wikipedia.org. 415 (top and bottom), Michael Weber. 420 (top), InterContinental Hong Kong/flickr. 420 (bottom left), bryangeek/flickr. 420 (bottom right), The Luxe Manor. 427, Fumio Okada / age fotostock. 434 and 440, Hong Kong Tourism Board. 449, Iain Masterton / Alamy. 454, Steve Vidler / age fotostock. 462, Christian Goupi / age fotostock. Chapter 7: Pearl River Delta. 467, José Fuste Raga/age fotostock. 468, J Aaron Farr/Flickr. 469 (left), Hector Joseph Lumang/iStockphoto. 469 (right), Mission Hills. 470, Rüdiger Meier/Wikimedia Commons. 477, View Stock/age fotostock. 482, Charles Bowman/age fotostock. 489, Steve Vidler/age fotostock. 492, JTB Photo/age fotostock. 499, TAO IMAGES/age fotostock. 503, Robert Francis/age fotostock. 504, Mission Hills. Chapter 8: The Southwest. 511, Philippe Michel/age footstock. 512, Jakrit Jiraratwaro/Shutterstock. 513 (bottom left), Christophe Cerisier/iStockphoto. 513 (top right), Anthon Jackson/Shutterstock. 514, Edwin Lee/Flickr. 517, Christian Kober/age fotostock. 522, Li Xin/age fotostock. 524-25, KingWu/iStockphoto. 530, EcoPrint/Shutterstock. 537 (top), Huang jinguo - Imaginechina. 537 (bottom), discpicture/Shutterstock. 538, Dave Bartruff/age fotostock. 539, YinYang/iStockphoto. 540 (top left), Wikimol/Wikimedia Commons. 540 (bottom), Natallia Yaumenenka/iStockphoto. 540 (top right), Christopher Noble/iStockphoto. 541, Wikimedia Commons. 542 (top), christine gonsalves/iStockphoto. 542 (left), dem10/iStockphoto. 542 (middle), Jason Fasi/Wikimedia Commons. 542 (right), jacus/iStockphoto. 543 (left), Iateasquirrel/Wikimedia Commons. 543 (middle), Juanmonino/iStockphoto. 543 (right), annastock/Shutterstock. 546, JTB Photo/age fotostock. 549, SEUX Paule/age fotostock. 554, CINTRACT Romain/age fotostock. 556, Angelo Cavallii/age fotostock. 557, Dennis Cox/age fotostock. 561, Stefan Auth/age fotostock. 566, Steve Vidler/age fotostock. 569, Andrea Pistolesi/age fotostock. 574, Michele Falzone/age fotostock. Chapter 9: Sichuan and Chongqing. 585, Karl Johaentges/age fotostock. 586 and 587 (top), fenghui/Shutterstock. 587 (bottom), JingAiping/Shutterstock. 588, loong/Shutterstock. 593, Hung Chung Chih/Shutterstock. 596, Jose Fuste Raga/age fotostock. 605, Manfred Bail/age fotostock. 608, José Fuste Raga/age fotostock. 613, Jane Sweeney/age fotostock. 619, FOTOSEARCH RM/age fotostock. 620 (bottom), FotoosVanRobin/Wikimedia Commons. 620 (top), Chubykin Arkady/Shutterstock. 621 (left), ImagineChina. 621 (top right), hywit dimyadi/iStockphoto. 621 (bottom right), Maria Ly/Flickr. 622 (bottom left), Hannamariah/Shutterstock. 622 (top right), zkruger/iStockphoto. 623 (top left), Ritesh Man Tamrakar/Wikimedia Commons. 623 (middle left), Rjanag/Wikimedia Commons. 623 (bottom left), Craig Lovell / Eagle Visions Photography / Alamy. 623 (right), Cephas Picture Library / Alamy. 624 (top left), Eneri LLC/iStockphoto. 624 (bottom left), Man Haan Chung/iStockphoto. 624 (top right), Holger Gogolin/iStockphoto. 624 (bottom right), Eneri LLC/iStockphoto. 632, View Stock/age fotostock. 633, kanate/Shutterstock. Chapter 10: The Silk Road. 639, TORRIONE Stefano/age fotostock. 640 (bottom), Amy Nichole Harris/Shutterstock. 640 (top), Stuart Taylor/Shutterstock. 641 (top), Dada/Flickr. 641 (bottom), Alica Q/Shutterstock. 642, loong/Shutterstock. 648, William Fawcett fotoVoyager.com/iStockphoto. 654 (left), John Goulter/age fotostock. 654-55, Greg Knudsen, Fodors.com member. 656, hanhanpeggy/iStockphoto. 657 (top), Wikimedia Commons. 657 (bottom), André Viegas/Shutterstock. 658 (top), Amy Nichole Harris/Shutterstock. 658 (bottom), zhuda/Shutterstock. 658-59, Martin Puddy/age fotostock. 659 (top inset), Yan Vugenfirer/Shutterstock. 659 (bottom inset), Ke Wang/Shutterstock. 660 (top), Lukas Hlavac/Shutterstock. 660 (bottom), Olaf Schubert /age fotostock. 661, xxapril/iStockphoto. 669, vito arcomano/age fotostock. 676, Aldo Pavan /age fotostock. 681, TAO IMAGES/age fotostock. 684, José Fuste Raga/age footstock. 687, Mark Henley/age fotostock. 693, JTB Photo/age fotostock. 700-01, Philippe Michel/age fotostock. Chapter 11: Tibet. 707, TAO IMAGES/age fotostock. 708 (bottom), Tian Zhan/iStockphoto. 708 (top), Hung Chung Chih/Shutterstock. 709, Terraxplorer/iStockphoto. 710, Helena Lovincic/iStockphoto. 717, Stefan Auth /age fotostock. 722-23, Colin Monteath/age fotostock. 730, McPHOTOs /age fotostock. 733, Angelo Cavalli /age fotostock. 736, Bjorn Svensson/age fotostock. 741, Meiqianbao/Shutterstock.

NOTES

NOTES

NOTES

ABOUT OUR WRITERS

Sophie Friedman is a New Yorker living in Shanghai. She has previously worked at *Time Out New York*, *New York Magazine*, and the *Huffington Post*. Sophie is now a senior editor at Shanghai's biggest English-language magazine, *City Weekend*. She hopes the sometimes-astounding, always-charming sights, restaurants, and bars listed in this book will provide you with as many good memories as they have given her.

Daniel Garber has called China home for nearly five years. After finishing a degree in journalism from New York University, he moved to a small village in Eastern China, bought a tiny pug, and became addicted to Longjing green tea, learning Mandarin and exploring China on an electric motorbike. Daniel updated the Eastern China Chapter.

Dana Kaufman moved to China in 2005 not expecting it to be a life change, and has held a number of jobs ranging from teacher to chef to entrepreneur. In addition to learning Chinese calligraphy, Dana enjoys photographing Asia's most remote and fascinating faces and landscapes. Dana and Daniel met in 2005, fell in love, got engaged, and now own and operate an American restaurant and martini bar in Chengdu. Dana updated the Beijing to Shanghai chapter.

Chris Horton first came to China in 1998 to study Chinese in Beijing. Since then he has worked as a restaurant manager in Dali, a business journalist in Shanghai, and a consultant in sunny Kunming, where he has lived since 2004. This is the third Fodor's China Guide he has updated. This year Chris tackled the Southwest and Sichuan and Chongqing chapters.

Patrick Scally was first wooed by Yunnan Province in 1999, and he fell desperately in love. The intervening 11-year romance has been tempestuous and characterized by angry walk-outs and groveling returns. Although guilty of nearly constant flirtation with other provinces, Patrick's heart will always reside in Southwestern China. Patrick updated the Sichuan chapter this year.

Dan Siekman has been living and working in China since 2006—most recently as a writer and Web marketing consultant in Kunming, the capital of Yunnan province. He has traveled, biked and trekked extensively across western China, from major cities to remote wilderness areas. Dan updated Sichuan and Guiyang.

Helena Iveson moved to Asia from the U.K. in 2003 for a three-month holiday and seven years later she's still there. After six years in Beijing she's recently moved on to Kuala Lumpur, Malaysia. As well as contributing to several guidebooks on China, Australia, Singapore, and Malaysia, she also writes for the *South China Morning Post, the Independent on Sunday, The Australian,* and a host of in-flight magazines. She also is part of a travel company called Bespoke Beijing (*www.bespoke-beijing.com*), which offers personalized advice on visiting the Chinese capital. Helena updated the Beijing shopping and nightlife sections, and the Silk Road and Tibet chapters of this year's guide.

Michael Standaert is a journalist based in Shenzhen, where he reports on environmental policies and infrastructure developments for Bureau of National Affairs, as well as on a variety of other subjects for many other freelance outlets.

Beijing Contributors

Eileen Wen Mooney, a freelance food writer, has been sampling Chinese food throughout Taiwan, Hong Kong, and mainland China for the past 25 years, from street stalls to small hutong eateries to posh contemporary restaurants. She's contributed articles to *Condé Nast Traveler, The Beijinger, Time Out Beijing, Silk Road, City Weekend, The Guardian,* and *Zagat Beijing.* Eileen is the author of *Not Just a Good Food Guide Beijing,* and *Beijing Eats,* the definitive guide to Chinese dining in the capital. Eileen has lived in Beijing since 1994 and continues to explore the city in search of new culinary adventures. This year Eileen updated the Where to Eat and Where to Stay sections.

Paul Mooney, a New York native, is a freelance journalist who has studied and worked in Asia for more than 30 years—the last 16 in Beijing. His articles have appeared in publications such as *Newsweek, The Asian Wall Street Journal, The Far Eastern Economic Review, U.S. News & World Report,* the *South China Morning Post* and the *International Herald Tribune*. Paul is also the author of several travel books on Taiwan and China. For this edition, Paul updated the Exploring and Side Trips sections.

Hong Kong Contributors

Jo Baker writes for *Time* magazine, *Marie Claire, Smart Travel Asia,* and the *South China Morning Post*. She updated the shopping section.

In addition to travel writing, Cherise Fong contributes to CNN.com International and writes copy for the Hong Kong

design studio AllRightsReserved. Cherise updated the Where to Stay section of this chapter.

Doretta Lau is currently a contributor to Artforum.com, where she reports on events and writes exhibition reviews. Doretta updated Hong Kong and Kowloon neighborhoods and the side trip to Macau.

Samantha Leese was born and raised in Hong Kong and is the Hong Kong features editor for *Glass* magazine, and writes on arts and entertainment for the *South China Morning Post, CNN Go,* and *Asia Tatler*. She lives by the beach in Hong Kong. Samantha updated the Nightlife and the Arts section.

Dorothy So studied in Los Angeles, where she developed a passion for exploring different food cultures. Homing in on her interest in food, she moved back to her home city of Hong Kong in 2009 to work as a dining journalist. She updated the Where to Eat section.